TEACHING STUDENTS WHO ARE EXCEPTIONAL, DIVERSE, AND AT RISK IN THE GENERAL EDUCATION CLASSROOM

SHARON R. VAUGHN
University of Texas, Austin
CANDACE S. BOS
Late of University of Texas, Austin
JEANNE SHAY SCHUMM
University of Miami

SEVENTH EDITION

330 Hudson Street, NY NY 10013

Director and Portfolio Manager: *Kevin M. Davis*
Content Producer: *Janelle Rogers*
Senior Development Editor: *Max Effenson Chuck*
Media Project Manager: *Lauren Carlson*
Portfolio Management Assistant: *Anne McAlpine*
Executive Field Marketing Manager: *Krista Clark*
Executive Product Marketing Manager: *Christopher Barry*
Procurement Specialist: *Carol Melville*
Full Service Project Management: *Thistle Hill Publishing Services*
Cover Designer: *Carie Keller*
Cover Image: *Kinzie and Riehm/Offset.com*
Composition: *Cenveo® Publisher Services*
Printer/Binder: *LSC Communications/Owensville*
Cover Printer: *Phoenix Color/Hagerstown*
Text Font: *Adobe Garamond Pro*

Credits and acknowledgments borrowed from other sources and reproduced, with permission, in this textbook appear on the appropriate pages within the text.

Photo Credits: Cindy Charles/PhotoEdit, p. 2; Phovoir/Shutterstock, p. 22; Jaren Wicklund/Fotolia, p. 34; Monkey Business Images/Shutterstock, pp. 42, 64, 140; Paul Vasarhelyi/Shutterstock, p. 76; Pressmaster/Shutterstock, p. 88; Kamira/Shutterstock, p. 103; Christian Schwier/Fotolia, p. 108; AVAVA/Fotolia, p. 127; Jasmin Merdan/Fotolia, p. 145; Bill Aron/PhotoEdit, p. 146; Wavebreakmedia/Shutterstock, p. 168; Will Hart/PhotoEdit, p. 172; Laurent Gluck/BSIP/Alamy Stock Photo, p. 204; Wavebreak Media Ltd/123rf, p. 207; Robin Sachs/PhotoEdit, pp. 223, 280; Syda Productions/Shutterstock, p. 234; Mermet/Photononstop/Glow Images, p. 239; Robin Nelson/ZUMA Press, Inc./Alamy Stock Photo, p. 249; Goodluz/Fotolia, pp. 270, 490; Synchronista/Shutterstock, p. 275; Robin Nelson/PhotoEdit, p. 292; Rawpixel.com/Shutterstock, p. 302; Gregory Bull/AP Images, p. 311; Ted Foxx/Alamy Stock Photo, p. 314; Jim West/Alamy Stock Photo, p. 317; Amelie-Benoist/BSIP SA/Alamy Stock Photo, p. 325; michaeljung/Shutterstock, p. 346; Scott Cunningham/Merrill, p. 353; Karenoppe/Shutterstock, p. 367; Monkey Business/Fotolia, p. 378; Franco Lucato/Shutterstock, p. 412; Little Blue Wolf Productions/Corbis/Getty Images, p. 421; John Todd/AP Images, p. 441; Wang Hsiu-Hua/Fotolia, p. 456; Douglas J. Glass/Fotolia, p. 496

Cataloging-in-Publication Data is available on file at the Library of Congress.

ISBN 10: 0-13-489509-6
ISBN 13: 978-0-13-489509-3

10 2021

Preface

This is the seventh edition of *Teaching Students Who Are Exceptional, Diverse, and at Risk in the General Education Classroom*, now in MyEducationLab.

MyEducationLab is Pearson's newest way of delivering our respected content. Fully digital and highly engaging, MyEducationLab offers an immersive learning experience designed for the way today's students read, think, and learn. Enlivening course content with media interactives and assessments, REVEL empowers educators to increase engagement with the course to better connect with students.

MyEducationLab Offers

Dynamic content matched to the way today's students read, think, and learn, including:

- **Integrated Videos** Integrated within the narrative, videos empower students to engage with concepts and take an active role in learning. MyEducationLab's unique presentation of media as an intrinsic part of course content brings the hallmark features of Pearson's bestselling titles to life.
    - *Video Examples* include video of educators both in and out of the classroom, students talking about their experiences with adaptive technologies and in-class methods of teaching and learning, and parents discussing resources, adaptive technologies, and strategies they have learned to help their children at home. In each chapter, these skills and strategies tie back to relevant content and learning outcomes. These voices of real teachers telling their own stories about ways they help students, or real students talking about what has been effective for them in the general classroom, help students develop a deeper understanding about the impact of using special education skills and concepts.
    - *URLs* integrated throughout the text direct students to websites where they can enhance their knowledge about relevant topics, skills, tools, and strategies for teaching and learning.
- **Quizzing and Short-Answer Response Opportunities** Located throughout MyEducationLab, quizzing affords students opportunities to check their understanding at regular intervals before moving on. Quizzes are in multiple-choice and short-answer response formats.
    - *Check Your Understanding* multiple-choice assessment questions test students' knowledge of the content they have just read at the end of each major section. Feedback for the correct answer is provided.
- **Interactive Glossary** links bolded key terms in the text to glossary definitions, enabling students to read and comprehend with clarity without skipping concepts they do not understand.

New to This Edition

We have listened to our users and created a text that will be easier to use in the classroom and more engaging for students. The strength of the book continues to be its numerous learning activities addressing both elementary and secondary classrooms. Changes and enhancements include:

- Streamlined content that offers more strategies and more examples that bring our students into the classroom.

- Evidence-based research practices throughout the text that are based on the most current research and instructional strategies.
- A revised and updated Chapter 2 on response to intervention (RTI) or multitiered systems of support (MTSS) reflects the most current research and strategies. In addition, chapters throughout this text integrate and highlight information regarding understanding and using research-based practices within an RTI framework.
- Chapter 4 discusses the use of response to intervention to improve opportunities for linguistically and culturally diverse students and reduce their disproportionate representation in special education programs.
- In Chapter 6, we have significantly updated the information about identifying students with learning disabilities and ADHD. New research, strategies, and resources have also been included.
- Chapter 7 includes an enhanced section on the role of the speech and language pathologist as well as including a new strategy on how to describe practices you could suggest to the parents of a child with a speech or language disorder to support the child's communication.
- Chapter 8, in its discussion of targeting behavior problems, discusses how to implement functional behavioral assessment during any of the tiers of the RTI framework. Why and how this works are discussed.
- Chapter 10, "Teaching Students with Intellectual and Developmental Disabilities," has been updated significantly, with new research, sections, strategies, and definitions.
- Integration of the Common Core State Standards in English language arts including reading (Chapter 14), writing (Chapter 15), and listening as well as mathematics (Chapter 16). Specific applications of the standards for students with special needs are provided.

Our Approach

Today's teaching professionals are assuming considerably more responsibility for meeting the educational and behavioral needs of students from diverse backgrounds and with diverse learning needs. Teachers identify students with special needs as their greatest challenges and often their greatest rewards. Unfortunately, many general education teachers feel at a loss for finding strategies to use in educating their exceptional students. They are eager to provide appropriate instruction, yet often feel inadequately prepared to do so. Furthermore, teachers tell us that what they most want to learn are specific instructional practices that will make a difference for diverse learners, and that they want these practices to enhance the learning of all students in their classrooms.

The central theme of this book is that general education teachers can make a difference in the lives of all students, particularly students with special needs, by using the tools and strategies described in this text. What we think is particularly exciting about the recommended practices is that they improve outcomes for all learners in the classroom—not just students with special needs. Our confidence in the effectiveness of these practices comes from two important sources: (a) research documenting their effectiveness with a range of learners, and (b) our ongoing work in classrooms where these practices are successfully implemented. Many teachers whose stories appear throughout this book implement and extend the recommended practices.

Preservice teachers in our university classes, as well as practicing teachers, urged us to do more than describe curriculum adaptations; they encouraged us to provide the step-by-step procedures for how to implement curriculum adaptations in the classroom. After reading this book, prospective teachers will have more than increased knowledge about students with special needs—they will have the tools and confidence to adequately meet all of their students' academic and social needs. In addition to having the necessary background knowledge about individuals with disabilities, we think that users of this book will have the practice knowledge to improve outcomes for all learners in their classroom.

This seventh edition includes updated references to the latest research and legislation, allowing readers to look up the most recent studies on topics of interest. Throughout the text we have added new information and described instructional and behavioral practices that are evidence based. We provide innovative approaches to enhancing the teaching of diverse learners in general education classrooms.

A Focus on Applying Strategies

- Each chapter opens with an **Interview** that presents a teacher's, student's, or parent's story that directly relates to the central ideas of the chapter. Each of these stories also identifies issues and personal responses that set the tone for the material that follows.
- Each chapter closes with **Think and Apply** questions, activities, and dilemmas to challenge the reader to integrate and apply the materials presented.

In addition to the organizational features that open and close each chapter, the following features are included within chapters:

Tips for Teachers in every chapter offer specific advice, guidelines for teaching practice, and step-by-step procedures.

TIPS FOR TEACHERS 2.3

How Campus Leadership Team Members Facilitate RTI

Members of the decision-making team facilitate the RTI process in several ways, including:

- Reviewing progress-monitoring data of students in interventions and for grade levels and the school as a whole.
- Observing classroom lessons to ensure that research-based instruction is occurring.
- Providing professional development to teachers and other key educators.
- Assisting with data collection and monitoring.
- Facilitating instructional decision making.
- Providing material and human resources to implement the RTI process.
- Organizing intervention groups and monitoring their effectiveness.
- Interpreting screening, progress monitoring, and other assessment data.
- Communicating with key stakeholders to be sure instructional and behavioral plans across treatments are aligned.

The 60-Second Lesson features throughout all chapters present brief mini-lessons that provide specific, concrete examples of how a teacher can make a difference for students with disabilities or diverse needs in only 1 minute of time.

60-*SECOND* LESSON

HOMEWORK BUDDIES: THINK–PAIR–SHARE

School days can be long for both teachers and students. With so much activity going on, it can be easy for students to forget assignments or forget books or materials they might need to complete homework assignments. This is true for students who are in a self-contained class or in departmentalized classes when students move from room to room.

Activities for All Learners features present sample lessons that include objectives, procedures, and application suggestions for classroom implementation.

ACTIVITIES FOR ALL LEARNERS

Using a Timer to Change Behavior

Purpose: To increase appropriate behavior, such as on-task behavior, and to reduce inappropriate behavior, such as being out of seat

Materials: Kitchen timer

Procedures:

1. Show students the kitchen timer and indicate that you will be using it to cue students to look for on-task behavior in the class. Discuss with students what behaviors will be included (e.g., working, completing an assignment, asking a question, reading a text).
2. Indicate that the timer will ring at different intervals and that all groups or individuals who are on task when the timer rings will be awarded a point.
3. Set the timer initially for a range of times (from 5 to 10 minutes), and then for longer periods of time.

Source: Adapted from "The timer-game: A variable interval contingency for the management of out-of-seat behavior," by M. M. Wolf, E. L. Hanley, L. A. King, J. Lachowicz, & D. K. Giles, 1970, *Exceptional Children, 37*, 113–117.

***Tech* Tips** provide access to resources that will provide guidelines and advice about tools, skills, and teaching strategies.

TECH TIPS

Useful Tools for Students with Learning Disabilities

Web Resources for Teachers, Parents, and Students

CHADD (Children and Adults with Attention-Deficit/Hyperactivity Disorder) (www.chadd.org)

Attention Deficit Disorder Association (www.add.org)

LD Online (www.ldonline.org)

Keyboarding

Early on, students who have difficulty with handwriting, either for composition or note-taking—regardless of the reason—should be taught keyboarding. There are many excellent computer-based keyboarding tutorials:

MAVIS BEACON TEACHES TYPING from Broderbund (www.mavisbeacon.com)

This ever-popular product keeps users engaged and motivated through many different games and exercises.

Talking Word-Processing Programs

Talking word-processing programs can help young writers by speaking letters, words, and sentences as they are typed, thus providing auditory as well as visual feedback in the writing process.

WRITE: OUTLOUD 6 by Don Johnston Incorporated (www.donjohnston.com)

Search for Write: OutLoud 6 on the Don Johnston, Inc. site. This product provides struggling writers in grades 3 through 12 with auditory tools that will help them write more effectively.

Word-Prediction Software

Students receive a list of possible words after every letter typed and can choose the desired word; offers support for spelling and word choices, and can be individualized with custom word banks and topic dictionaries. Also includes built-in speech recognition.

CO:WRITER 7 from Don Johnston Incorporated (www.donjohnston.com)

On the home page for the Don Johnson Inc., click on the Co:Writer 7 tab, then learn more about this word-prediction software.

Podcasts

Mobile devices are not just for listening to music. Students can record lectures, download audio files to their devices, and listen to lectures while studying for tests or reviewing and editing notes.

LEARNING ALLY (FORMERLY THE RECORDINGS FOR THE BLIND AND DYSLEXIC®) (RFB&D) (http://www.learningally.org)

The RFB&D is an organization that provides books and other materials recorded for individuals who have learning disabilities or visual disabilities.

iPad/iPod™

applications include:

- Read2Go
- Typ-O HD
- Sentence Builder
- Dragon Dictation

Support Materials for Instructors

The following resources are available for instructors to download on www.pearsonhighered.com/educators. Instructors enter the author or title of this book, select this particular edition of the book, and then click on the "Resources" tab to log in and download textbook supplements.

INSTRUCTOR'S RESOURCE MANUAL AND TEST BANK 0-13-444784-0

The Instructor's Resource Manual and Test Bank includes suggestions for learning activities, additional Experiencing Firsthand exercises, supplementary lectures, case study analyses, discussion topics, group activities, and a robust collection of test items. Some items (lower-level questions) simply ask students to identify or explain concepts and principles they have learned. But many others (higher-level questions) ask students to apply those same concepts and principles to specific classroom situations—that is, to actual student behaviors and teaching strategies.

POWERPOINT™ SLIDES 0-13-444785-9

The PowerPoint™ slides include key concept summarizations that enhance learning. They are designed to help students understand, organize, and remember core concepts and theories.

TESTGEN 0-13-444787-5

TestGen is a powerful test generator that instructors install on a computer and use in conjunction with the TestGen testbank file for the text. Assessments may be created for print or testing online.

TestGen is available exclusively from Pearson Education publishers. Instructors install TestGen on a personal computer (Windows or Macintosh) and create tests for classroom testing and for other specialized delivery options, such as over a local area network or on the web. A test bank, which is also called a Test Item File (TIF), typically contains a large set of test items, organized by chapter and ready for use in creating a test, based on the associated textbook material.

The tests can be downloaded in the following formats:

TestGen Testbank file—PC
TestGen Testbank file—MAC
TestGen Testbank—Blackboard 9 TIF
TestGen Testbank—Blackboard CE/Vista (WebCT) TIF
Angel Test Bank (zip)
D2L Test Bank (zip)
Moodle Test Bank
Sakai Test Bank (zip)

Acknowledgments

We have many people to thank for their generous contributions of time, knowledge, experience, and sound advice. We are deeply grateful to the many teachers who have shared their classrooms, students, and experiences with us. In particular, we would like to extend our heartfelt thanks to the teachers and principals of Flamingo Elementary School and Henry S. West Laboratory School. We would also like to thank the many students in the teacher preparation programs at the University of Arizona, the University of Miami, and the University of Texas who have helped us better understand the important attitudes, knowledge, and skills necessary for new teachers preparing to teach diverse learners.

Just a few of the many people whose names should be in lights for their generous contributions to earlier editions of this book are: Mary Hinson, for sharing her valuable knowledge as a job developer and university instructor for the mainstreaming course for secondary teachers; Sharon Kutok, for sharing her valuable knowledge as a speech/language pathologist; Elba Reyes and Manuel Bello, for reviewing and providing insights on teaching students with cultural and linguistic diversity; Paulette Jackson, for providing expert assistance with manuscript preparation and permissions; and Jean G. Ulman, whose knowledge about technology and special education benefited the Tech Tips.

A special thanks to Sandra Bowen, Penny Rosenblum, and Andrea Morrison. Their expertise in educating students with hearing impairments, visual impairments, and mental retardation/severe disabilities, respectively, was a valuable resource. Sandra played an important role in writing the section on hearing impairments. Penny took on a similar role in writing the section on visual impairments in the same chapter. Andrea not only worked on the physical disabilities and health impairments section of the text, but also played a significant role in writing the chapter on developmental disabilities. We would also like to thank Mark F. O'Reilly, Jeff Sigafoos, and Giulio Lancioni for their contribution of the earlier editions of the chapter on autism.

Ae-Hwa Kim, Alison Gould Boardman, and Jane Sinagub assisted with all aspects of manuscript preparation, including expert editorial work and good judgment. Their contribution to the book is extensive. I would particularly like to recognize the careful and thoughtful work of Ae-Hwa Kim, who made a significant contribution to the third edition, and Alison Gould Boardman for her significant contributions to the fourth edition. Alison Gould Boardman provided valuable assistance with the Tips for Teachers, the Appendix, and text reflecting policy changes. Brianna Bednarski provided much-appreciated editorial assistance with the sixth edition. We also want to acknowledge Dr. Heather Garrison from East Stroudsburg University of Pennsylvania for preparing the Learning Outcome Quizzes as well as her work on the revised author supplements.

We also benefited from the suggestions and revisions of outstanding reviewers. Thank you for your generous assistance: Beverly Argus-Calvo, The University of Texas at El Paso; Manuel Barrera, Metropolitan State University; Sherry DeMik, Valparaiso University; Yeunjoo Lee, California State University–Bakersfield; and A. Helene Robinson, University of South Florida–Sarasota Manatee.

There are also a handful of individuals who each put their respective areas of research expertise to work for us in a close reading of just a single chapter in their specialty area. Susan Johnston of the University of Utah gave us assistance with the chapter on communication disorders. Kathleen Robins, Janice Day, and Cheryl Winston of the University of Utah provided commentary on the text about vision/hearing/physical challenges. Missy Olive of the University of Texas gave feedback regarding pervasive developmental disorders. Jeff Sigafoos of the University of Texas provided insights on the chapter on developmental disabilities. Alliete Alfano of the University of Miami provided an expert review of the chapter on visual impairments, hearing loss, physical disabilities, health impairments, and traumatic brain injury. Michel Miller, also of the University of Miami, provided valuable comments on the chapter covering students with developmental disabilities. Jennifer Langer-Osuna of the University of Miami offered insights on the chapter covering teaching mathematics. Like all authors, we were not always anxious to rewrite but soon realized the benefits from their helpful suggestions and resources.

The personnel at Pearson Education provided ongoing support for this book. Ray Short, Senior Editor, contacted us about writing the book initially and provided encouragement and continuous positive feedback. He was a wonderful resource when the going got tough, assuring us we were making fine progress. The third and fourth editions of the book benefited enormously from the caring and careful work of Virginia Lanigan. Upon the sudden death of our coauthor Candace Bos, Virginia was a source of social and professional support. She truly guided these editions through completion. We are very grateful to her.

The fifth, sixth, and seventh editions of the book benefited from the insights and suggestions of Ann Davis, editor, and Max Effenson Chuck, development editor. Ann Davis is an outstanding editor. We have worked with numerous editors across many publishers and Ann is simply remarkable. She has extraordinary insight and vision, and we consider ourselves extremely fortunate to work with her. Max was our guide throughout the significant revisions we undertook for this edition. We cannot imagine how to adequately thank her or acknowledge the significance of her insights, support, and very fine editorial suggestions. We think you'll agree that this edition is by far our best edition yet.

We also would like to give a very special thank you to our husbands for their steadfast support and personal sacrifices: Jim Dammann and Jerry Schumm.

—SRV

—JSS

Brief Contents

Contents

TEACHING STUDENTS WHO ARE EXCEPTIONAL, DIVERSE, AND AT RISK IN THE GENERAL EDUCATION CLASSROOM

1

Special Education and Inclusive Schooling

Learning Outcomes

1.1 Identify the laws, key provisions, and guidelines that govern special education and explain how these laws influence educational practices for individuals with disabilities.

1.2 Describe the responsibilities you have as a classroom teacher for students with special needs and the types of practices and adaptations you need to implement.

1.3 Discuss No Child Left Behind and its influence on testing accommodations for students with disabilities and the expanded laws regarding IDEIA, including early education and transition, then consider the instructional implications of implementing inclusion and other services provided in the continuum of services for students with disabilities.

INTERVIEW: ELIZABETH DILLER

Elizabeth Diller is a fifth-grade teacher at Cory Elementary School in an urban city in Texas. Elizabeth is an unusual teacher in that she has worked as both a special education teacher and a general education teacher. For the past 2 years, she has served as the lead teacher in a fifth-grade team. What she likes about her job is that she blends her expertise in special education with her new knowledge as a general education curriculum specialist. She assists the other fifth-grade teachers in developing instructional practices and using progress monitoring to inform instruction for all of the fifth-grade students, including those with identified disabilities. She also works with the response-to-intervention (RTI) team to screen and monitor the progress of students who are at risk for reading and math problems. Elizabeth says, "This is the perfect blend of leading classroom teachers to make appropriate adaptations for students with disabilities in their classrooms and having an opportunity to put the practices in place in my own classroom."

Elizabeth has been very successful at keeping students with disabilities in general education classrooms. She also has been a cheerleader for the RTI model of preventing academic difficulties and identifying students for special education in their school. Here is some of her advice for general education teachers working in RTI schools:

- Don't worry if you do not know everything about students with disabilities. Be willing to ask questions and to allow others to help. Many instructional practices that are effective with most students are also effective with students with disabilities.
- Remember that a couple of minutes of focused instructional support that provides additional opportunities for students with disabilities to practice can be very helpful. You don't need to wait until you have 20 minutes or more, 3 to 5 minutes throughout the day of individual guidance, feedback, and support make a big difference.
- Use ongoing progress-monitoring measures in reading and math to inform your instructional decision making.
- Ask the special education teacher, an experienced general education teacher, or the school psychologist to observe students with disabilities in your class. Ask them for advice to improve your instruction.
- Communicate frequently with parents and other professionals. My class publishes a newsletter every other week that is posted on our class website. If parents like, we print the newsletter and send it home. I also send home weekly notes to parents of students with disabilities to inform them of their child's progress. I frequently meet with other professionals such as the school psychologist and special education teachers to assure that I am providing appropriate instructional and behavioral supports.

Elizabeth further reflects, "Ever since I was little, I wanted to be a teacher. When I imagined myself as a teacher, I thought about helping students who needed me the most. I really feel most like a teacher when students who have difficulty learning make progress. I like that my classroom includes students with a range of disabilities. We all learn what we can do well and

CHAPTER OUTLINE

what we need help with, and we always know that there are classmates there to support us."

Introduction

Elizabeth's account reflects the views of this book. We recognize that teachers make a difference; that we must teach purposefully to empower all of our students to learn; that even small steps matter; and that if we set ambitious goals, provide research-based instruction, and monitor students' progress, we can ensure success for all learners in our classroom. The aim of this book is to offer you the knowledge, tools, and strategies that will empower you as a classroom teacher to skillfully, confidently, and successfully promote learning for all your students. This book takes a cross-categorical approach—that is, accommodations for exceptional learners are discussed in terms of their shared needs rather than in terms of their identification as members of a disability category. This helps you make instructional and behavioral decisions that benefit the majority of students with special needs.

The basic knowledge you need includes an understanding of the laws and procedures that govern special education and inclusion. This is where we begin.

1.1 EARLY AND RECENT FOUNDATIONS OF SPECIAL EDUCATION

Before the 1950s, many students with disabilities were excluded from attending public schools. Although children with more severe disabilities were forced either to stay home or to be institutionalized, students with mild or moderate learning problems often dropped out of school long before graduating (Pardini, 2002). Interestingly, students with disabilities continue to have a dropout rate that is twice as large as their peers without disabilities (Chapman, Laird, & KewalRamani, 2011). It may be difficult for you to imagine, but as recently as 1958, court cases ruled in favor of excluding students with disabilities from a public school education. In *Department of Public Welfare v. Haas* in 1958, the Supreme Court of Illinois maintained that the state's compulsory education laws did not require a "free public education for the 'feebleminded' or to children who were 'mentally deficient' and who, because of their limited intelligence were unable to reap the benefits of a good education" (Yell, 1998, p. 55). Eventually, however, the tide turned in favor of advocating for the education of all students.

1.1.1 Early Influences

Exclusion of students with disabilities from public education would not last forever. A landmark education case paved the way for future legislation that would protect the rights of individuals with disabilities to attend and benefit from public education. In *Brown v. Board of Education* in 1954, the Supreme Court ruled that school segregation by race was not constitutional, even if resources were allotted equally. This was the first time the federal government had advocated for students who experienced inequality and prejudice at school, and it set the path for future legislation for individuals with disabilities. See Figure 1.1 for more examples of court cases that have influenced the education of individuals with disabilities.

The Elementary and Secondary Education Act (ESEA) passed in 1965 initiated the role of the federal government in protecting and providing for students from disadvantaged backgrounds so that they would have equal access to the public education system. For example, one of the ESEA provisions established the free and reduced lunch system because children whose basic needs are not met (e.g., being hungry) are not able to benefit

FIGURE 1.1 Influential court cases

- *1971—Pennsylvania Association for Retarded Children (PARC) v. Commonwealth of Pennsylvania.* Challenged the constitutionality of excluding individuals with mental retardation from public education and training. The state was not allowed to "deny to any mentally retarded child access to a free public program of education and training."
- *1972—Mills v. Board of Education of the District of Columbia.* Another case in which handicapped children had been excluded from public schools. Similar to the *PARC* case, this suit required the state to provide "adequate alternative education services" as well as "prior hearing and periodic review of the child's status, progress, and the adequacy of any educational alternative" (348 F. Supp., at 878). In both the *PARC* and *Mills* cases, the courts required schools to describe the curricula, objectives, teacher qualifications, and supplemental services that were needed, areas that would later be influential during the drafting of P.L. 94-142.
- *1982—Board of Education of Hendrick Hudson Central School District v. Rowley.* Clarified the definition of a free and appropriate public education (FAPE). Amy Rowley was a deaf fifth grader who used an FM hearing aid that amplified words spoken by her teacher. She was achieving better than the average student in her class and communicated well with her peers. Although she may not have been achieving maximally and might have benefited from an interpreter, the court ruled that P.L. 94-142 requires states to provide sufficient, but not the best possible, support for students to benefit from a public education at a level typical of that of nondisabled peers.
- *1988—Honig v. Doe.* Benefited individuals with emotional and/or behavior disorders who have academic and social problems. Ruled that schools could not expel children for behaviors related to their disability.
- *1999—Cedar Rapids v. Garret F.* Garret was paralyzed from the neck down in an accident when he was age 4, but his mental capacities were unaffected. He required nursing services to attend his regular classes, and the court ruled that under IDEA students must be provided with the supplemental services they need to attend school at no extra cost to the parents.
- *2007—Winkelman v. Parma City School District.* The Supreme Court decided that parents may pursue IDEA claims on their behalf independent of their child's rights.

fully from instructional programs that are provided. A critical component of the ESEA for individuals with disabilities was the grant program that encouraged states to create and improve programs for students with disabilities. This program was later revised in 1970 as the Education of the Handicapped Act (P.L. 91-230) and continued support for state-run programs for individuals with disabilities, although it did not provide any specific guidelines for how to develop these programs or what they should look like.

For many students with disabilities, the initial goal of special education was to ensure that they were provided an opportunity to attend school and profit from education. Not until the passage of P.L. 94-142 in 1975 were schools required to ensure that all children, regardless of their disability, receive a free and appropriate public education. For students with learning disabilities, most of whom were already provided education within the general education system, their special needs would now be identified and they would be provided with a special education.

Initially, defining and providing a special education for students with disabilities were challenges for educators. Little was known about what an effective educational program for students with disabilities should look like. Many classroom teachers perceived that they did not have the knowledge or skills to provide these students with an appropriate education. We have made extraordinary progress in the last few decades and yet we continue to realize that many students with disabilities are not accessing the quality education they need (Vaughn, Zumeta, Wanzek, Cook, & Klingner, 2014).

1.1.2 Recent Influences

The Every Student Succeeds Act (ESSA) was signed by President Obama in December 2015 as a commitment to equal opportunity for all students. ESSA replace the No Child Left Behind Act (NCLB) that was enacted in 2002. ESSA includes many of the components of NCLB but provides additional opportunities for schools when students are not making adequate progress. Both are bi-partisan bills with a focus on improving educational outcomes for all students including students who have traditionally demonstrated low performance in academic areas. ESSA shifts students accountability from the federal government to state and local control where progress is monitored and sanctions determined. NCLB was enacted to provide a framework "on how to improve the performance of America's elementary and secondary schools while at the same time ensuring that no child is trapped in a failing school" (U.S. Department of Education, 2002b, p. 1). NCLB covers a wide range of areas, from improving teacher quality and supporting instruction for English language learners (ELLs) to efforts to keep schools safe and drug free. Following are the three areas of education that have been affected by NCLB:

- *Increased accountability.* In perhaps the cornerstone of NCLB legislation, students are required to take statewide assessments (e.g., tests) that are aligned with curriculum accountability standards (e.g., state-identified grade-level learning expectations in key curriculum areas such as reading and math). Furthermore, school districts are expected to make adequate yearly progress (AYP) in the areas that are tested. Adequate yearly progress is the amount of gain the school district negotiates with the state that it will make for students who are behind. It is the way the school district can determine whether it is closing the gap between students' current performance and their expected performance at that grade level. Unique to this legislation is the distinction that all students should be included *and* make adequate yearly progress in these high-stakes assessments, regardless of disability, socioeconomic status, language background, and race or ethnicity. Schools that fail to make adequate progress toward proficiency goals are subject to improvement and restructuring efforts as needed to assist them in meeting state standards. Students with disabilities and special education teachers are influenced by this increased accountability, as most students with disabilities will conform to these increased high expectations for performance on outcome assessments.
- *School choice.* Parents whose children attend schools that do not meet state accountability standards are given the opportunity to send their children to schools with higher performance records. Furthermore, there is more flexibility in how Title I funds (special funds allotted to schools with a large proportion of low-income families) are used, as well as support for charter schools (schools that develop proposals to use state funds but have independence from the local school district) that provide parents with additional educational options for their children. Critics of school choice raise the concern that charter schools might exclude students with special needs or allow all students to attend without providing the necessary services and resources that would help them succeed (Howe & Welner, 2002).
- *Greater flexibility for states, school districts, and schools.* A goal of NCLB is to provide states with greater flexibility in how they choose to use federal education funds (including providing a variety of state grant options in areas such as teacher quality, educational technology, and reading) as long as they demonstrate high standards of accountability.

Since it has been more than a decade since NCLB was passed into legislation, it is very likely that a revised version of NCLB will appear in the near future. Secretary of Education Arne Duncan provided a press release on the NCLB revision process (press@ed.gov; April 16, 2015) stating that he thought the following ideas were critical:

- Expand access to high-quality preschool
- Invest in innovation and scaling what works
- Assist all students in succeeding (including those with disabilities)
- Provide communities with the information they need to know if students are falling behind in school

1.1.3 IDEIA and the Vocational Rehabilitation Act

Legislation for individuals with disabilities has provided them with education, employment, housing, and other rights that they previously were denied because of their disabilities. You can imagine how important the following two landmark pieces of legislation have been. The Individuals with Disabilities Education Act (IDEA),

P.L. (Public Law) 94-142, and the Vocational Rehabilitation Act, P.L. 93-112, have significantly improved the opportunities for individuals with disabilities.

P.L. 94-142, originally referred to as the Education for All Handicapped Children Act, was enacted in 1975, later reauthorized and expanded as the Individuals with Disabilities Education Act (IDEA) in 1990, and most amended by the Individuals with Disabilities Education Improvement Act (IDEIA) in 2004 (with regulations published in August 2006 for school age youngsters) and in 2011 for babies and toddlers. We do not expect significant changes in the law before 2017. This legislation was designed to ensure that all children with disabilities receive an appropriate education through special education and related services. Figure 1.2 provides a summary of the history of laws governing special education.

1.1.4 Provisions and Guidelines for Implementing IDEIA

To ensure that the provisions of this legislation are adhered to, teachers must understand the basic premises that are at its foundation. The following primary provisions and guidelines characterize what schools and teachers must know and do (Turnbull, Stowe, & Huerta, 2008):

- *Zero reject/free, appropriate public education.* No child with disabilities can be excluded from education. This is commonly referred to as zero reject. Mandatory legislation provides that all children with disabilities be given a free, appropriate public education. Before IDEIA, school officials who felt that they were not equipped to address the special needs of particular students would not accept such students into their schools.
- *Child Find.* States are required to identify and track the number of students with disabilities and to plan for their educational needs. This is commonly called Child Find.
- *Age.* The law defines the ages that individuals with disabilities must be educated. IDEIA provides for special programs and services for all students with disabilities between the ages of 3 and 21. Infants and toddlers with developmental delays (birth to 2 years of age) are also eligible to receive early intervention services.
- *Nondiscriminatory evaluation.* A nondiscriminatory evaluation—an evaluation that does not discriminate on the basis of language, culture, and student background—must be provided for each individual identified for special education.
- *Individualized education program.* An individualized education program (IEP)—a plan developed to meet the special learning needs of each student with disabilities—must be written, implemented, and reviewed.
- *Least restrictive environment.* IDEIA defines the educational settings in which students are placed. The least restrictive environment is the setting most like that of students without disabilities that also meets each child's educational needs. Inherent in the least restrictive environment is the notion of continuum of services. Continuum of services means that a full range of service options for students with disabilities will be provided by the school system. These service options include self-contained classrooms, resource rooms, and homebound and general education programs.
- *Due process.* Due process not only ensures that everyone with a stake in the student's educational success has a voice, but also addresses written notification to parents for referral and testing for special education, parental consent, and guidelines for appeals and record keeping. IDEIA guarantees the right to an impartial hearing if appropriate procedures outlined by IDEIA are not followed and parents or schools believe that programs do not meet the student's educational needs.
- *Confidentiality of records.* IDEIA requires confidentiality of records. All records and documents regarding students with disabilities must remain both confidential and accessible to parents.

FIGURE 1.2 History of the federal laws for the education of learners who are exceptional

Year	Law
1965	Elementary and Secondary Education Act (ESEA) (Public Law 89-10) • Supports many initiatives that help low-income families access high-quality education programs • Includes provisions for free and reduced lunches and additional teachers in disadvantaged communities • Applies to children who need additional support to benefit from public school education programs
1973	Vocational Rehabilitation Act (VRA) (Public Law 93-112, Section 504) • Defines *handicapped person* • Defines *appropriate education* • Prohibits discrimination against students with disabilities in federally funded programs
1974	Educational Amendments Act (Public Law 93-380) • Grants federal funds to states for programming for exceptional learners • Provides the first federal funding of state programs for students who are gifted and talented • Grants students and families the right of due process in special education placement
1975	Education for All Handicapped Children Act (EAHCA) (Public Law 94-142, Part B) • Known as the Mainstreaming Law • Requires states to provide a free and appropriate public education for children with disabilities (ages 5 to 18) • Requires individualized education programs (IEPs) • First defined *least restrictive environment*
1986	Education of the Handicapped Act Amendments (Public Law 99-457) • Requires states to extend free and appropriate education to children with disabilities (ages 3 to 5) • Establishes early intervention programs for infants and toddlers with disabilities (ages birth to 2 years)
1990	Americans with Disabilities Act (ADA) (Public Law 101-336) • Prohibits discrimination against people with disabilities in the private sector • Protects equal opportunity to employment and public services, accommodations, transportation, and telecommunications • Defines *disability* to include people with AIDS
1990	Individuals with Disabilities Education Act (IDEA) (Public Law 101-476) • Renames and replaces P.L. 94-142 (EAHCA) • Establishes "people-first" language for referring to people with disabilities • Extends special education services to include social work, assistive technology, and rehabilitation services • Extends provisions for due process and confidentiality for students and parents • Adds two new categories of disability: autism and traumatic brain injury • Requires states to provide bilingual education programs for students with disabilities • Requires states to educate students with disabilities for transition to employment, and to provide transition services • Requires the development of individualized transition programs for students with disabilities by the time they reach the age of 16
1997	Individuals with Disabilities Education Act (IDEA) (Public Law 105-17) • Requires that all students with disabilities continue to receive services, even if they have been expelled from school • Allows states to extend their use of the developmental delay category for students through age 9 • Requires schools to assume greater responsibility for ensuring that students with disabilities have access to the general education curriculum • Allows special education staff who are working in mainstream classrooms to assist general education students when needed • Requires a general education teacher to be a member of the IEP team • Requires students with disabilities to take part in statewide and districtwide assessments • Requires states to offer mediation as a voluntary option to parents and educators to resolve differences • Requires a proactive behavior management plan to be included in the student's IEP if a student with disabilities has behavior problems • Limits the conditions under which attorneys can collect fees under IDEA
2004	Individuals with Disabilities Education Improvement Act (IDEIA) (Public Law 108-446) • Allows districts to use a response-to-intervention (RTI) model for determining whether a child has a specific learning disability, and no longer requires that a child have a severe discrepancy between achievement and intellectual ability to qualify (RTI is described in more detail later in this chapter) • Increases federal funds to provide early intervention services to students who do not need special education or related services • Eliminates use of short-term objectives in an IEP except for students who do not take statewide achievement assessments • Raises standards for special education licensure • Adopts policies designed to prevent the disproportionate representation of students in special education by race and ethnicity

- *Advocacy.* IDEIA requires advocacy for students without guardians. Advocates are assigned for individuals with disabilities who lack known parents or guardians.
- *Noncompliance.* IDEIA requires that states mandate consequences for noncompliance with the law.
- *Parent participation.* Parent participation and shared decision making must be included in all aspects of identification and evaluation of students with disabilities.

Teachers may wonder what some of the guidelines are that pertain to all educational settings. The following guidelines were developed by the U.S. Department of Education after the Individuals with Disabilities Education Improvement Act (2004) was passed to provide this information to school personnel. Critical guidelines include:

- Using person-first language. In other words, do not define a child by his or her disability. For example, say "students with learning disabilities" rather than "learning-disabled students" or "students with autism" rather than "autistic students."
- Requiring that transition services be included in the individualized education programs of all students by at least age 16. Transition services refers to providing activities on behalf of the student with the disability that promote an outcome-oriented process of supports from school to postsecondary activities that include further schooling, vocational training, and integrated employment.
- Providing for states, as well as school districts, to be sued if they violate the IDEIA.
- Including two new special education categories: traumatic brain injury and autism.
- Adding assistive technology as a support service.
- Promoting the involvement of students with disabilities in the general education curriculum.
- Requiring greater accountability for results so that students with disabilities are part of the accountability system.
- Requiring that the IEP not only describe the extent to which a student will be integrated, but also detail the aids and accommodations the student will receive within the general education classroom.
- Allowing states and local districts to use "developmental delay" eligibility criteria through age 9 instead of one of the specific disability categories so that students will not be classified too early.
- Providing further flexibility by allowing IDEIA-funded staff who work with students with disabilities in general education classrooms to work with others who need their help as well.
- Requiring states to include students with disabilities in assessments, and to provide appropriate modifications and develop alternative assessments for the small number of students who cannot participate in regular assessments.

In addition to these provisions and guidelines, the U.S. Department of Education (n.d.) maps out key features of the IDEIA that shape how the provisions and guidelines are implemented:

- *Evidence-Based Practice:* One of the significant requirements when Congress reauthorized IDEA in 2004 was the stipulation that students with disabilities receive services based on knowledge and practice from research—to the extent possible. Students with disabilities are vulnerable to receiving risky practices. Establishing research as the baseline for decision making for individuals with disabilities is a valuable guide.
- *Discipline:* The IDEIA allows schools to remove students with disabilities for serious bodily injury and adds new authority to consider discipline on a case-by-case basis.
- *Response to Intervention:* Schools must permit the use of alternative research-based procedures for determining whether a student has a severe learning disability and must not require use of a severe discrepancy.

- *Early Intervention Services:* Schools may provide academic and behavioral support for students not currently identified as special education students. They may use not more than 15% of the amount of special education money the local education agency (LEA) receives.
- *Evaluations and Individualized Education Programs:* Not all personnel need to be present in IEP meetings if the parents and school agree in writing. However, parents and key educators not present must be informed of any changes to the IEP.
- *Monitoring:* Emphasis is on improving educational results and functional outcomes for each student.
- *Highly Qualified Teachers:* Special education teachers must obtain state certification or pass the state special education teacher-licensing exam.
- *Private Schools:* Students have no individual rights to services and service plans; rather, an IEP is developed for individuals with disabilities.

What do classroom teachers and parents need to know about referral and identification for special education?

Follow the ten-step sequence for a quick rundown on what you and your students' parents need to know about referral and identification for special education:

Step 1. Teachers, parents, or other stakeholders (e.g., physicians) consider that the individual may be in need of possible special education and refer the child for evaluation. The evaluation must be completed within 60 days after parental permission is obtained.

Step 2. A full and individual evaluation is provided.

Step 3. Eligibility for special education is decided by a group of qualified professionals and the parents.

Step 4. The student is found eligible for services.

Step 5. The IEP meeting is scheduled, including parents and all qualified personnel.

Step 6. IEP meeting is held to inform the IEP and IEP is written.

Step 7. Services aligning with IEP are provided.

Step 8. Ongoing progress is measured and reported to parents.

Step 9. IEP is reviewed annually or more frequently if needed.

Step 10. Reevaluation occurs to assure progress and further determine services.

1.1.5 Provisions of the Vocational Rehabilitation Act

The **Vocational Rehabilitation Act** (P.L. 93-112) prevents any private organization that uses federal funds, or any local or state organization, from discriminating against persons with disabilities solely on the basis of the disability. This law made a significant difference in the provision of equal opportunities and services for individuals with disabilities because agencies that accept state or federal monies must comply with the law. It prohibits discrimination not only in public education, but also in the employment of persons with disabilities and in social and health services. Because of this law, many individuals with disabilities now have greater access to opportunities in the workplace, community services, and colleges and universities.

Take, for example, the case of Kathy Carter. "Access to facilities has opened up the world for me and Kathy," said Amy Carter, Kathy's mother.

> Since Kathy's mobility is limited to scooting around or the use of a wheelchair, there were many places we could not go. The movie theater closest to our house has a show upstairs where they often show children's movies. I either have to go with another adult who can help me get Kathy up the stairs or we can't go at all. I must say, I've noticed a big difference recently. The new shopping mall near our house is completely wheelchair accessible.

1.1.6 Continuum of Educational Services: Concept of Least Restrictive Environment

According to the IDEIA (P.L. 108-446), a continuum of educational services must be available for students with disabilities. This continuum of educational services means that students with disabilities must have a range of service options available to meet their individual needs from the full-time general education classroom to a special day school or residential facility to full-time inclusion in general education. In other words, the type of service provided to the student with a disability is not predetermined based on the services the district chooses to provide, but rather a full range of services (i.e., more to less inclusive) are considered and the most appropriate service that is the least restrictive is the service provided to the target student. Figure 1.3 shows the continuum of services in terms of the major placement alternatives.

FIGURE 1.3 **Continuum of educational services for students with disabilities**

Level I General education classroom with consultation from specialists:
Student functions academically and socially in full-time general education classroom. Specialists provide consultation to the classroom teacher and support to individual students as needed.

Level II General education classroom; cooperative teaching or co-teaching:
Special education teacher and classroom teacher co-plan and co-teach for part of school day. For entire school day, student is included in general classroom, where support services are provided.

Level III Part-time placement in special education classroom:
Student is placed in the general education classroom for part of the school day and in the special education classroom, usually the resource room, for a specified amount of time each day.

Level IV Full-time special education classroom in a general education school:
Student is educated in a special education classroom housed in a general education school. This arrangement—of being educated in the special education room so students have contact with general education peers only during nonacademic periods—may include part-time involvement with general education students for activities such as physical education and lunch.

Level V Special school:
Student is provided special education services in a special education school typically serving only students with disabilities.

Level VI Residential school, treatment center, or homebound instruction:
Student is provided special education services at home, or resides in a school or treatment center in which special education is provided.

Consideration for educational placement is dynamic and ongoing. Students' placements are continually reevaluated for opportunities to move to less restrictive environments. Fundamental to the law is the notion that students cannot be educated in more segregated settings simply because it is easier to do so. The principle behind the least restrictive environment is that students are best served in the settings (most like those of their nondisabled peers) in which they can learn, ideally moving to less and less restrictive settings. A checklist for determining the least restrictive environment is provided in Figure 1.4.

The majority of students with disabilities receive services in the general education classroom, with support services provided as necessary. For some students with disabilities, however, students' needs are best met in other settings. The decision must be made on a student-by-student basis, with any level on the continuum potentially serving as the least restrictive environment for a target student. For example, many parents of children

FIGURE 1.4 A checklist for determining the least restrictive environment (LRE)

- ✓ School personnel use ongoing data collected throughout the referral and placement process to determine the least restrictive environment.
- ✓ School personnel document procedures and practices used to maintain the student in the general education classroom.
- ✓ School personnel document the research-based practices, aids, services, and interventions used within the general education classroom.
- ✓ School personnel document the mechanisms used to accommodate the student in the general education classroom.
- ✓ School personnel provide an analysis of the social and academic benefits likely to occur from placement in a special education setting.
- ✓ School personnel document the negative behavioral and/or academic outcomes to other students if the student with disabilities is maintained in the general education classroom.
- ✓ School personnel assure that the student has maximum opportunity to interact successfully with students without disabilities throughout the day.
- ✓ School personnel determine whether the continuum of services is available to provide educational support to the student.

who are deaf prefer that they be educated in settings with other children who are deaf so that their children have opportunities to learn the culture and language of deafness.

Part-time placement in special education

Some students whose educational and social needs cannot be met solely within the general education classroom receive special education and related services (e.g., counseling, speech and language therapy, occupational or physical therapy, instruction, and so on) from specialists in settings outside the classroom that better meet their needs. Related services may be provided individually or in small or large groups. For example, many speech and language specialists prefer to provide language therapy to small groups of students with common language problems in a quiet setting outside of the classroom.

A common educational placement designed to meet the educational needs of students with disabilities outside the general education classroom is the **special education resource room**. The resource-room model provides specialized, individualized, and intensive instruction to meet students' needs. Reading, writing, and math are the three academic areas most frequently addressed by the special education teacher in the resource room. Students can work with the special education teacher, typically with a small number of other students, for as little as a few hours a week in an elementary school or one period a day in a secondary setting. Depending on their needs, students may work nearly full-time in a resource setting.

Some resource rooms are designed to meet the needs of students identified as having a particular kind of disability—learning disabilities, for example. Other resource rooms are designed to meet the needs of students with varying exceptionalities. The term *varying exceptionalities* refers to the placement of students who represent a range of disability categories (e.g., students with emotional disorders, learning disabilities, and/or physical impairments, and students who are gifted). An example of the use of a resource room within a response to intervention (RTI) model is when students with significant reading disabilities are provided a 50-minute daily treatment in the resource room setting.

Full-time placement in special education

The educational and social needs of some students cannot be met through part-time placement in the general education classroom. These students may be placed in a special education classroom located in a general education school. Students placed in full-time special education classrooms often attend elective classes (such as physical education, music, art, and vocational education) with their peers without disabilities. If there are no full-time special education classrooms in the home school, students may be transported to schools outside their neighborhood. Many educators and parents, believing that the relocation of students to another school interferes with the students' social and personal adjustment, discourage such placements. Students who are placed full-time in special education classes should be closely monitored so that they can be placed as quickly as possible in the general education classroom.

Special school or residential settings

When the problems of students with disabilities are so severe and complex that adequate education cannot be provided in general education classrooms, students may be placed in special schools. These schools may be part of the school system, or the system may contract with private schools that specialize in programs for students with significant special needs. One advantage of special schools is that total enrollment is usually small, with technical services and individual attention more easily provided. One disadvantage to the school system is cost: Special schools are expensive, and transportation also can be expensive. Disadvantages for students are that travel to and from the school can be time consuming and that they have limited opportunities to interact during the school day with children who do not have disabilities.

Homebound instruction

Students with health or physical problems that prevent them from attending school regularly and students who have been expelled from school may receive homebound instruction. The primary role of a **homebound teacher** is to provide direct instruction and to coordinate instructional programs between the school and the home. Although students with disabilities sometimes receive long-term homebound instruction, it usually is a short-term remedy until the student is able to return to school. Mariel Simpson explains:

> Over the past 8 years my son Jalena, who has spina bifida, has been operated on six times. After each of these operations, he needed to stay at home for 8 to 12 weeks to recover. I felt very fortunate to have the homebound teacher come to my home to work with Jalena so that he would not get too far behind in his schoolwork.

In addition to defining the continuum of services, special education laws also identify the types of related services to which students with disabilities are entitled. These **related services** include speech therapy, audiology, interpreting services, psychological services, physical therapy, occupational therapy, early identification and assessment, counseling (including rehabilitation counseling), medical services for diagnostic or evaluation purposes, school health services, transportation, social work services, and recreation, including therapeutic recreation. Orientation (including aid in traveling to, from, and around school) and mobility services are also included.

1.1.7 The Individualized Education Program (IEP)

Teachers are required by law to develop an **individualized education program (IEP)** for each student with special educational needs. The purpose of an IEP is to provide an appropriate education that meets the specialized needs of each student with disabilities. IEPs are developed and implemented by the **multidisciplinary team (MDT)**. What is the multidisciplinary team (MDT) and what purposes does it serve? The MDT determines whether the student has a disability and is eligible for special education services. If this is the case, the team then develops the IEP, which provides the foundation for establishing the educational program for the student. The MDT includes a representative of the local education agency, the classroom teacher, the special education teacher, parents or guardians, a person who can interpret the instructional implications of evaluation results, and, when appropriate, the student. Depending on the student's needs, the MDT also includes professionals from related services (such as social workers, speech and language pathologists, psychologists, and occupational therapists) and may include other professionals, such as doctors.

Each IEP must include the following information:

- The student's present levels of educational performance, including how the disability affects the student's involvement in the general curriculum.
- Measurable annual goals, including short-term objectives for students who take alternate assessments, enabling the child to participate in the general education curricula and meet other education needs resulting from the disability.
- Special education and related services to be provided to the student and a statement of the program modifications or supports for school personnel that will be provided for the student not only to attain annual goals and be involved in the general education curriculum, but also to participate in extracurricular and other nonacademic activities.
- An explanation of the extent, if any, to which the student will not participate with students without disabilities in the general education class and in extracurricular and other nonacademic activities.
- Individual modifications in the administration of statewide or districtwide assessments or an explanation of why those assessments are inappropriate for the student and what alternative methods will be used to assess the student. Figure 1.5 provides a sample of test accommodations that are relatively easy to implement.
- The Individualized Education Program (IEP) provides the opportunity to specify the related services the student with disabilities requires for a successful education.
- Projected date for the beginning of services and modifications and their anticipated frequency, location, and duration.
- How the student's progress toward annual goals will be measured.
- What method will be used to inform parents (as often as the parents of nondisabled students) of their child's progress toward annual goals and whether that progress is sufficient to enable their child to achieve the goals by the end of the school year.
- Transition services described under the applicable components of the student's IEP that focus on the appropriate course of study. At age 16, the needed transition services, including, when appropriate, a statement of the interagency responsibilities or any needed linkages, must be specified.

FIGURE 1.5 Test accommodations

- Extended testing time
- Additional rest breaks
- Writer/recorder of answers
- Reader
- Sign language interpreter (for spoken directions only)
- Selectable background and foreground colors
- Alternative test formats: audio recording, Braille, large print
- Large-print answer sheet
- Audio recording
- Audio recording with large-print figure supplement
- Audio recording with raised-line (tactile) figure supplement

Source: "Testing accommodations for test takers with disabilities or health-related needs," by Educational Testing Services, n.d., retrieved from http://www.ets.org/disabilities/accommodations

The role of the IEP for planning and assessment

The IEP is a method for planning and assessment that reflects the judgment and input of the school system, specialists, teachers, parents, and students themselves. The IEP is a safeguard not only for students but also for families and school systems. An example of an IEP is presented in Figure 1.6.

FIGURE 1.6 **Sample IEP**

Individualized Education Program

I. Demographic Information

Last	First	M.I.	Date	
Smith	John	E.	May 12, 2014	
Student I.D.	**Address**		**Home Phone**	**Work Phone**
2211100	23 Lakeview St. Collier, MN 32346		(459)555-5555	(459)555-5000
Date of Birth	**Grade Level**	**Home School**	**Program Eligibility**	
03-02-99	5	Lakeview Elementary	Learning Disabilities	

Reason for Conference: ☐ Staffing ☑ Review

II. Conference

Parent Notification

Attempt #1:	Attempt #2:	Attempt #3:
Letter: 3-02-10	Phone call: 3-13-10	Notice sent home with student: 3-22-10

Parent Response: Will attend as per phone call on 3-13-10

III. Present Levels of Educational Performance

John is a 5th grade student whose disability inhibits his ability to read required material. John can read 35/100 in two minutes from a 4.0 grade level paragraph and 45/100 in two minutes from a 3.0 grade level paragraph. John can answer 8/10 literal questions and 4/10 inference questions from a 4.0 grade level passage read to him.

IV. Annual Goals and Short-Term Benchmarks

1. John will increase reading fluency to the 4.0 grade level.
   John will read orally a passage at the 4.0 grade level in 2 minutes with 50 or more words correct.
   John will use correct intonation and prosody when reading orally a passage at the 4.0 grade level 50% of the time.
2. John will improve the percentage of accuracy when responding to literal and inferential questions.
   John will answer literal questions from a 4.0 grade level passage read to him with 75% accuracy.
   John will answer inferential questions from a 4.0 grade level passage read to him with 90–100% accuracy.

Describe the extent to which the student will not participate in general education settings and explain why the student cannot be placed in general education settings.

John will not participate in general education settings for language arts, science, and social studies instruction. John requires close supervision when completing tasks, high levels of assistance, and intensive, systematic instruction.

V. Related Services

Type of Service, Aid or Modification			Location	Time per day/week
Assistive Technology:	☐ Yes	☑ No		
Adaptive PE:	☐ Yes	☑ No		
Audiology Services:	☐ Yes	☑ No		
Counseling:	☐ Yes	☑ No		
Interpreter.	☐ Yes	☑ No		
Medical Services:	☐ Yes	☑ No		
Occupational Therapy:	☐ Yes	☑ No		
Orientation/Mobility:	☐ Yes	☑ No		
Physical Therapy:	☐ Yes	☑ No		
Psychological Services:	☐ Yes	☑ No		
Special Transportation:	☐ Yes	☑ No		
Speech/Lang. Therapy:	☑ Yes	☐ No	Self-contained class, 30 min./wk	

(continued)

FIGURE 1.6 Sample IEP (*continued*)

VI. Assessment Participation

Will the student participate in state and district assessments: ☑ Yes ☐ No

If yes, what accommodations or modifications will be provided?

☐ None ☑ Flexible Setting ☐ Flexible Presentation ☑ Flexible Scheduling
☐ Flexible Responding

If no, indicate why state and district assessments are inappropriate:

VII. Transition Planning/Statement

☑ Under 14: Transition planning not needed.

☐ 14–15 years old: Statement of transition services needed that focuses on student's course of study.

☐ 16 years old: Outcome statement that describes a direction and plan for the student's post-high school years from the perspective of student, parent, and team members.

VIII. Scheduled Report to Parents/Guardians

John's parents will be informed of progress toward his annual goals via parent/teacher conferences and interim report cards (4 times per year). Parents will be notified of goals that have been met and the rate of progress toward meeting all of the annual goals.

IX. Initiationl/Duration Dates

Special education and related services will initiate September 2014 (MM/YY), through June 2015 (MM/YY)

IX. Persons Attending Conference

Signature	Position	Date
Mary Smith	Parent	May 12, 2014
Jonathan Smith	Parent	May 12, 2014
Laura Jones	Special Education Teacher	May 12, 2014
Rafael Gonzalez	General Education Teacher	May 12, 2014
Larry Brick	LEA Representative	May 12, 2014
Harrison Washington	School Psychologist	May 12, 2014
John Smith	Student	May 12, 2014

IEPs are intended to serve as planning guides for the student with special needs, not as mere paperwork. IEPs provide guidelines for educators for the daily education of the individual. Because the writing and updating of the IEP can be time consuming and tedious, there are a number of commercial software programs available to help simplify the task, enabling the IEP to be discussed, agreed on, and printed all in one meeting. See the Tech Tips "IEP Resources" for a list of some of these programs.

Unfortunately, classroom teachers at the middle and secondary levels often do not participate in the IEP process and do not know which students in their classrooms have been identified as having special needs (Schumm & Vaughn, 1992), despite findings that

TECH TIPS

IEP Resources

The most useful IEP software programs allow teachers to select from skill sequences and author long-term and short-term objectives, freely customizing skills and objectives to meet individual needs. Often school systems or special education units adopt one particular system. You may find that to be the case in your school district. Some programs are installed on individual computers, whereas others are web-based programs. Web-based systems are especially useful because you can access the data from any online computer while maintaining security by the use of a password. It is also easier to move students' records along as they move from teacher to teacher and school to school.

Following is a list of IEP management software products and their producers, along with their primary web addresses:

SpedAssist IEP Management Solutions, by SPEDASSIST™ (http://www.spedassist.com)

Class/Bridge IEP Program, by Class/Bridge (www.classplus.com)

IEP Writer Supreme II, by Super School Software (www.superschoolsoftware.com)

when classroom teachers participate in IEP meetings, parents perceive the meetings as more beneficial (Martin, Marshall, & Sale, 2004). Carl Turner, a middle school teacher, put it this way:

> I know that Mike has an IEP and I read it at the beginning of the year, but I haven't really used it in my planning. There may be other students who have learning disabilities in my class, but I won't know until the special education teacher tells me.

IEP meeting attendees

Persons who are *required by law* to attend the IEP meeting include:

- A representative of the local education agency (LEA) who is knowledgeable about the special education program, the general curriculum, and the availability of the resources of the LEA.
- A school representative other than the teacher, such as a person designated by the school system.
- Parents or guardians, to ensure that they are informed and involved in the student's placement and progress.
- The student, when appropriate (involving students in the planning of their educational goals is often appropriate, particularly at upper elementary grades and secondary grades).
- The student's general and/or special education teacher (the teacher is involved in identifying realistic and appropriate educational goals for the student).
- An individual who can interpret the instructional implications of evaluation results.
- Others who the parents or school believe can help develop the IEP (as mentioned earlier, this may include representatives from a range of related services and professions, such as medicine, physical therapy, speech and language therapists, and psychology).

IDEIA 2004 allows one of the required individuals to be excused from attending an IEP meeting or to provide input in writing with the written consent of the parent. The intent of the IEP development and implementation is met when the key stakeholders at the school ensure that parents attend IEP meetings, making every reasonable attempt to contact parents and accommodate their schedules. This includes scheduling meetings at times that are convenient for parents, giving ample advance notice of the meeting, securing mutual agreement for the time and place of the meeting, meeting through phone calls or home visits if parents cannot attend, and providing a copy of the IEP to parents on request. If parent involvement cannot be obtained, the school should document all attempts to involve parents, including correspondence and a log of phone calls and visits. Some school districts have a placement specialist who takes responsibility for managing the placement and program development of students with IEPs. In other schools, the special education teacher takes this responsibility.

The role of the general education teacher in the IEP process varies because each school district handles IEP meetings a little differently. As the classroom teacher, however, you will be an important resource, as you will be providing information about the student's performance in your class and implementing many of the academic and behavioral suggestions.

Why are so many people involved in the development and monitoring of the IEP? Each person is at the meeting because he or she has knowledge and experience that can assist in designing the best educational program for the student. Not everyone knows the same things, so each person's contribution is unique and necessary. For example, the school psychologist often provides expertise on diagnostic test results and interpretation. You, however, are the expert on the curriculum for your content areas and grade levels. Your responsibility is to ensure that the goals that are designed to be implemented in your classroom reflect appropriate content, skills, and curriculum for students in your class. Everyone's knowledge of the student is useful to establish high, realistic behavioral and academic goals.

How can IEP meetings provide meaningful involvement for parents of children with disabilities? The purpose of including parents in the IEP meeting is to provide them with an opportunity to provide meaningful information to key educational stakeholders to positively influence the type and quality of their child's educational experience. Unfortunately, there are often unintentional negative consequences for parents attending the IEP meeting (Zeitlin & Curcic, 2014). As Zeitlin and Curcic summarize, many parents perceive the IEP meeting as depersonalized meetings where many decisions have been made prior to their involvement. They think there is too much focus on the paperwork and compliance and too little emphasis on genuine communication and understanding. Many parents also find the IEP meeting to be an emotional event, and for some the focus is on the deficits of their child and a tool to label them rather than a tool to help them improve. What can schools do to improve the process for parents?

- Use language that is understood by all participants including the parents. When professional language that is unfamiliar is used, be sure to explain it so the parents understand.
- Provide opportunities for the parents to engage, give their views, express questions, and provide feedback.
- In addition to the IEP document, provide a one- to two-page summary sheet of the key decisions made.
- Check with the parents to assure that they understand decisions made and how they will influence their child's education.

Determining appropriate accommodations and modifications

During the IEP conference, parents and professionals work together to identify appropriate accommodations and modifications that will assist the student in learning skills in class. It is important that general education teachers are included in the decisions regarding accommodations and modifications because they will take part in implementing them when students with disabilities are in the general education classroom. For example, if the IEP team decides that a student needs a highlighted textbook in science, someone must be available to do the highlighting or the accommodation cannot be carried out. Furthermore, effective communication systems must be in place so that all teachers and support personnel who will work with the student are aware of the accommodations and modifications that will be implemented (Cease-Cook, Test, & Scroggins, 2013).

Student involvement

By law, students need to attend the IEP meetings only if appropriate. In practice, too often students with disabilities do not attend these meetings, even when the students are in secondary-level settings. However, involving students in this decision-making process helps them develop a commitment to learning and a sense of responsibility and control over the decisions made regarding their learning, and may improve their likelihood of being employed after high school (Wehmeyer, 2015). Students can learn how to participate in their IEP meetings and identify learning needs when teachers assist them prior to the meeting through coaching and "mock" IEP meetings (Neale & Test, 2010).

Why do many students not attend the conference? When middle grade students with learning disabilities and their parents were interviewed, two major reasons were evident (Van Reusen & Bos, 1990). First, parents often are not aware that students can attend. Second, even when students are invited to attend, they choose not to because they feel that they do not know what to say or do, and they are afraid that the major topic of discussion will be "how bad they are doing."

A variety of methods can be used to increase the engagement of individuals with disabilities and their families in IEP planning. This is often called *person-centered planning*, or PCP. As the name suggests, PCP involves more than completing an IEP document that addresses a set of issues established by the school or district. The focus in PCP is on developing a more complete understanding of the individual with a disability and his or her family so that his or her specific needs and issues can be addressed (Keyes & Owens-Johnson, 2003). Even with thoughtful and inclusive planning, communication challenges may require facilitation. When this occurs, consider the following practices aimed at facilitating highly effective problem solving at IEP meetings (Mueller, 2009):

- Use a *neutral facilitator* who can listen and interpret fairly the messages from all participants.
- Establish the *agenda*, allowing everyone to contribute.
- Allow everyone *adequate time* to discuss their issues.
- Summarize *goals* and *solutions.*
- Provide a comfortable and *relaxed setting.*
- Agree that issues that are brought up but are not on the agenda will be "*parked*" on the side and revisited at the end of the meeting.
- Promote participation and *equity* among all voices at the meeting.

Teaching students how to participate in a meaningful way can increase their participation in IEP meetings (Kelley, Bartholomew, & Test, 2011; Mason, Field, & Sawilowsky, 2004; Myers & Eisenman, 2005). Thus, a component that often accompanies PCP is teaching students ways to become more actively engaged in their own educational planning. Van Reusen and his colleagues developed a self-advocacy strategy (I PLAN) designed to inform students and prepare them to participate in educational-planning or transition-planning conferences (Deshler & Schumaker, 2006; Van Reusen, Bos, Schumaker, & Deshler, 1994). Teachers can teach students this strategy in about 5 to 6 hours over a 1- to 2-week period. Findings show that secondary school students with learning disabilities who learn this strategy provide more information during IEP conferences than do students who are only told about the IEP conference but not taught the strategy. Figure 1.7 describes this strategy and how to teach it.

Focus on self-determination

Teaching students skills related to self-determination helps them become part of the decision-making process in developing their IEP or transition plans from school to work. Someone who is self-determined is actively involved in making decisions, knows what

FIGURE 1.7 I PLAN—An educational planning strategy

Purpose: The I PLAN strategy gives students the knowledge and skills to actively participate in their IEP or transition-planning conferences.

Students: The strategy is most effective with upper elementary, secondary, or postsecondary students who will be participating in an IEP or other educational planning meeting.

Group size: Small-group or large-group instruction.

Duration: 5 to 6 hours of instruction.

Description of strategy: The I PLAN strategy is taught in five steps. The first step is completed before the target conference (e.g., IEP meeting), and the remaining steps are practiced first and then implemented during the meeting.

The acronym I PLAN represents the first letter of each phase of the planning strategy (inventory, provide, listen, ask, and name):

1. *Inventory* your learning strengths, weaknesses, goals, interests, and choices for learning.
2. *Provide* your inventory information.
3. *Listen* and respond.
4. *Ask* questions.
5. *Name* your goals.

Instruction: Teachers focus on gaining commitment from students and encouraging them to actively participate both in learning the I PLAN strategy and in using their new knowledge and skills during the target meeting.

Source: Sharon R. Vaughn, Candace S. Bos, *Strategies for Teaching Students with Learning and Behavior Problems* , 8th ed., © 2012. Reprinted and electronically reproduced by permission of Pearson Education, Inc., Upper Saddle River, New Jersey.

he or she wants out of life, and is able to influence decisions about his or her life. Students with disabilities are able to identify the knowledge they would like to acquire, the academic and social skills they value, and the activities and experiences they would like to have. Although most parents recognize the value of decision making with even very young children, students with disabilities—particularly those with significant cognitive impairments—have often been treated as though they are unable to have a causal role in their own lives (Shogren et al., 2013). Marks (2008) argues that the reason self-determination is important for students with disabilities is the same as for other minorities—to prevent oppression. Although teachers and parents can play an important role in facilitating support for self-determination skills for individuals with disabilities, paraprofessionals also play an important role, as many of them have extensive contact with individuals with severe cognitive impairments in general education classrooms (Lane, Carter, & Sisco, 2012).

In a review of two decades of research, Test and his colleagues (2004) established that instruction in the following self-determination skills leads to positive outcomes for students with a wide range of disabilities:

- Decision making
- Self-advocacy
- Goal setting/attainment
- Problem solving
- Self-regulation
- Participation in IEP meetings
- Self-awareness

Students with disabilities who have positive self-determination are more likely to benefit from school and post-school opportunities. It is particularly important that students with disabilities are provided supports for developing their self-determination since they display lower levels of self-determination than their peers. Furthermore, when students with disabilities are provided appropriate interventions focused on positive self-determination, school-related outcomes are quite positive (Wehmeyer, 2015). Consider the following as you prepare your students to serve as self-advocates: (a) role-play their participation in meetings; (b) help them learn to problem solve; (c) provide them with information about their disability and their rights; (d) encourage them to have a mentor; (e) assist them in communicating their needs, wants, strengths, and weaknesses; and (f) encourage them to communicate effectively with all key educators about their educational needs.

The IEP Process

Most school districts have developed their own format and procedures for writing IEPs. All members of the team contribute to the IEP, which should include everyone's ideas about the students' educational goals and objectives—including in most cases the students' views. The person who most frequently incorporates what the team agrees on and writes the IEP is the special education teacher.

MyEdLab **Self-Check 1.1**

MyEdLab **Application Exercise 1.1:** IDEIA

1.2 RESPONSIBILITIES OF CLASSROOM TEACHERS

General education teachers often express concerns about the extent to which they need to know and understand the law as it pertains to individuals with disabilities. Leila MacArthur put it this way:

> As a classroom teacher, I'm concerned about all of the children in my classroom. I want to do as good a job as I can, but I also realize that I cannot know everything about every difficulty, learning and behavioral, that the children in my classroom will manifest. I know that I need to know who to contact when I have questions. But I suppose what is of the most interest to me is exactly what I'm responsible for and what I need to know so that I can successfully implement education programs for the students with special needs. Probably my biggest questions center on the law and what I need to do.

When asked what questions she had, Leila provided the following list:

- *Who is responsible for the IEP?* The multidisciplinary team is responsible for developing the IEP; the person who is principally responsible for the IEP, however, is the special education teacher. The general education teacher and the parent might be responsible for particular goals described in the IEP.
- *Can I be held responsible if a student in my class does not accomplish all of the objectives in the IEP?* The IEP is not a contract but rather an agreement by which the teacher undertakes the optimum educational procedures to help ensure that the student meets the IEP objectives. Teachers cannot be held responsible for students' lack of progress on IEP goals unless it can be proved that teachers have not made efforts to fulfill their responsibilities.
- *What if I was unable to attend the meeting at which the child's IEP was developed?* Obtain a copy of the student's IEP from the special education teacher or meet with the special education teacher to identify the IEP goals for which you are responsible.
- *What should I do if I feel a student is not making adequate progress on his or her IEP?* Collect appropriate data through progress monitoring, representative work samples, or behavioral observations. Communicate your findings to other members of the multidisciplinary team. Regular meetings with the special education teacher and other professionals who are providing services to the student will ensure that the student's progress is monitored. Also, meetings that involve parents or guardians will help you explain a student's progress and find ways to enhance his or her performance.

The IDEIA is a law aimed at enhancing the quality and equity of education for all students. The law requires reasonable expectations of teachers. Your role is to help students fulfill the goals in the IEP and to provide an appropriate education for all students (see Tips for Teachers 1.1).

TIPS FOR TEACHERS 1.1

How Can You Meet Your Special Education Responsibilities?

- Ask the special education teacher what reports are relevant to successful instruction of students with disabilities in your class; then read these reports.
- Ask appropriate professionals such as the special education teacher for suggestions for enhancing the learning of students with disabilities in your classroom.
- Ask appropriate professionals such as the special education teacher to co-teach your class or demonstrate lessons that show how his or her suggestions can be implemented.
- Attend relevant meetings related to the students with disabilities for whom you have responsibilities and use these meetings to communicate about students' progress and needs.
- Reexamine IEPs quarterly and check that you monitor the progress of students with disabilities in your classroom.
- Keep a folder of relevant work samples to document progress for each student with disabilities for whom you have responsibilities.
- Maintain parent contact through occasional phone calls and written notes.
- Meet regularly with the special education teacher. If he or she does not already work in your classroom, extend an invitation to come in and help you instruct students with special needs.
- If you are concerned about a student's progress, don't hesitate to inform all key personnel, including the appropriate administrator and special education teacher, as well as the student and parent(s).

Although knowledge of the law is important, you should also be aware of the resources available to you when you have questions and need further information. Many people in your school and district can help you. Experienced teachers report that their best resources are the special education teachers in their building, other teachers, the school psychologist, and the principal.

Octavio Gonzalez, a ninth-grade English teacher, has three students with disabilities in two of his five sections of English. These students receive support services during the school day from the special education teacher, and Octavio meets occasionally with the special education teacher to plan and get suggestions for accommodating their needs in his English class. Octavio comments:

> At first I was nervous about having students with disabilities in my class. One of the students has a learning disability, one student has serious motor problems and is in a wheelchair, and the third student has vision problems. Now I have to say that the adaptations I make to meet their special learning needs actually help all of the students in my class. I think that I am a better teacher because I think about accommodations now.

How do classroom teachers participate in the IEP process? What are three ways the teachers participate in the referral and planning process for students with special needs?

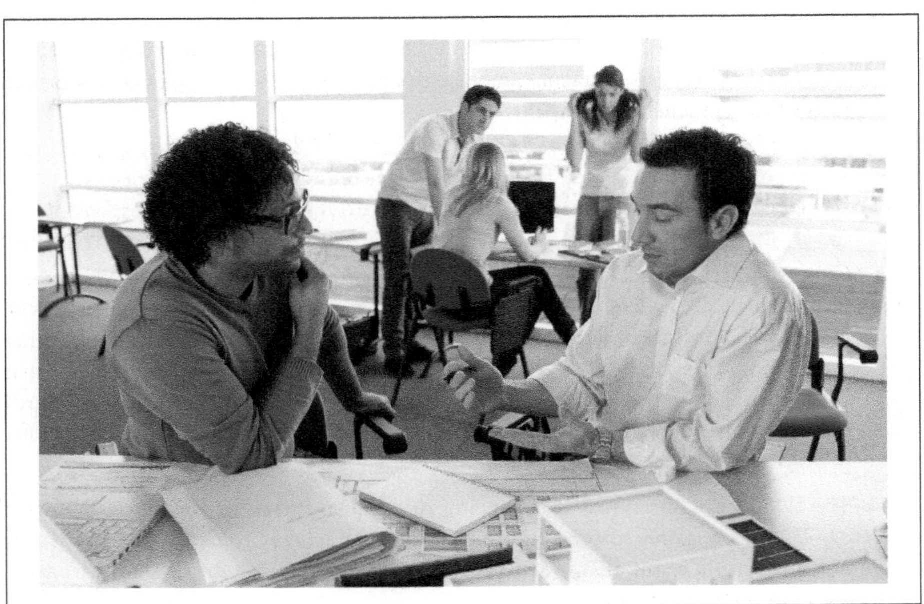

An eighth-grade teacher, Lin Chang, put it this way:

> At first I was worried that it would be all my responsibility. But after meeting with the special education teacher, I realized that we would work together and I would have additional resources if I needed them. Furthermore, I think more about keeping in touch with the parents so that they are always informed of progress. Doing all of this communication on the telephone is not always possible, so I send a lot of notes home.

MyEdLab
Video Example 1.1.
Watch this video, where you will see students with special needs in a general education setting. What do you notice about student involvement and the role of the teacher?

Monitoring the progress of students included in general education sometimes becomes the sole responsibility of the special education teacher, but this is not an effective procedure. Students with disabilities are more likely to benefit from collaboration between the special and general education teachers, with both teachers collecting curriculum-based measures and behavioral measures to determine students' needs. Our studies with middle and high school teachers reveal that obtaining access to students' IEPs and psychological reports (to be used to guide teacher planning for students with disabilities) may be difficult (Vaughn & Schumm, 1994). Teachers reveal that their best sources of information are parents, former teachers, or the students themselves (Schumm & Vaughn, 1992). Thus, middle and high school teachers need to consider adaptations that provide for the special learning needs of students with disabilities and also enhance instruction for all their students. It is also important to consider ways to transition older students with disabilities to work settings. The IEP can be an excellent tool for facilitating instructional decision making (Brooke & McDonough, 2008).

Remember, a few minutes of one-on-one purposeful teaching is an effective way to assess progress and provide directed instruction. We have found several accommodations general education teachers can make that not only assist students with disabilities in the general education classroom, but also enhance instruction for all students. These approaches, described in detail later in this book, are summarized in Tips for Teachers 1.2.

TIPS FOR TEACHERS 1.2

Adaptations for Students with Disabilities

- Treat all students with respect. Through your treatment of all students and your encouragement, assist all students in recognizing the assets of students with special needs.
- Consider ways to assure that students with special needs are in your classroom for key times, including instructional times, class bonding times, and other relevant periods where being part of the class is important. Coordinate your schedule with specialists who work with students in or out of your classroom (e.g., students don't leave or enter class in the middle of a lesson; specialists are in your classroom at times when they can be the most effective).
- Adapt effective classroom management strategies for students with special needs so that they are productively integrated into the classroom behavior routines but also have the specialized behavior supports that they require (e.g., time-out, point systems).
- Provide opportunities both socially and academically to be encouraging and positive with students, including looking for opportunities to recognize success academically and good behavior.
- Establish personal relationships with students (e.g., get to know students as individuals; determine student interests and strengths).
- Communicate frequently with included students (e.g., plan frequent short, one-on-one conferences and discuss potential modifications with students).
- Communicate with professionals and parents of included students (e.g., exchange notes and talk informally with parents; encourage parents to provide support for students' education).
- Establish expectations for all students and develop mechanisms for making these expectations known to students with clear steps for achieving them.
- Make adaptations for students when developing instructional plans. As you design instruction, assignments, or practice routines, consider ways to assure that students with disabilities can fully and meaningfully participate.
- Structure assignments and instructional opportunities to reduce frustration and improve learning.
- Teach test-taking skills, note-taking skills, and other practices that facilitate effective learning.
- Adapt instructional materials (e.g., different textbooks, supplemental workbooks).
- Use computers to enhance learning (e.g., as a tool for writing, as a tool for practicing skills).
- Monitor students' understanding by asking them to repeat or demonstrate directions or key ideas.

- Monitor students' understanding of concepts presented in class (e.g., attend to, comment on, and reinforce understanding of vocabulary, abstract ideas, key words, time sequences, and content organization).
- Provide one-on-one instruction through 60-second lessons and brief "check-ins" to assure students with disabilities are learning and getting appropriate feedback.
- Pair students with a classmate (e.g., to provide assistance with assignments, to provide models for behavior and academics, and for social support).
- Adjust grouping practices to involve students with disabilities successfully. For example, engage students in small-group activities with both mixed-ability grouping (different achievement levels) as well as same-ability groupings to target engagement and learning.
- Involve all students in whole-class activities providing opportunities to respond and participate.
- Provide extra time (e.g., schedule extra time for skill reinforcement and extra practice).
- Adapt pacing of instruction (e.g., break down materials into smaller segments; use step-by-step approaches).
- Design procedures for monitoring students' progress that engage students in keeping and recording progress. This can be done through a student's folder or progress chart.
- Provide students with ongoing feedback about their academic and social progress. This feedback can be (a) immediate and aligned with the activity, (b) ongoing in terms of periodic mini-meetings regarding progress (2 to 3 minutes), and (c) less frequent longer meetings to discuss academic and behavioral performance.
- Adapt assessments (e.g., use oral testing; give more time for tests; modify administration procedures; reduce the number of items; reduce the difficulty of items).
- Consider grading criteria and how they may need to be adapted for students with special needs.

Sources: Based on Heward, W. L. (2012). *Exceptional children.* Upper Saddle River, NJ: Pearson; and Schumm, J. S., & Vaughn, S. (1991). Making adaptations for mainstreamed students: General classroom teachers' perspectives. *Remedial and Special Education, 12*(4), 18–27.

1.2.1 Participating in the Referral and Planning Process

In November 2010, 35 years after the U.S. Congress enacted the Education for All Handicapped Children Act in 1975, the U.S. Department of Education issued a report on the status of educating individuals with disabilities (U.S. Department of Education, 2010). The report identified several ways in which students with disabilities are receiving improved services, including:

- Increasing the number of young children with disabilities receiving high-quality interventions, with the number of young children under 5 increasing by more than 35% in the last 10 years.
- Increasing the percentage of students educated in their neighborhood schools to 95%, thus assuring that the vast majority of students with disabilities attend schools where others in their neighborhood go to school near their homes.
- Increasing the reading scores of students with disabilities over the last 10 years by 20 points on the scale, whereas the scores of students without disabilities remained stable.
- Significantly increasing the number of students with disabilities graduating from high school and reducing the percentage of students with disabilities dropping out of high school.
- Doubling the percentage of students with disabilities enrolled in postsecondary programs and increasing the percentage of young adults with disabilities who are employed.

Approximately 14% of the school-age population receives special education services. These are students whose educational and social–emotional needs we do not expect can be met through traditional instructional procedures alone.

The term **disabilities** refers to conditions that include mental retardation, hearing impairments, vision impairments, speech and language impairments, learning disabilities, serious emotional disturbance, orthopedic impairments, other health impairments, autism, traumatic brain injury, deafness and blindness, and multiple disabilities. The classification of students into categories of disability is controversial. Many people believe that labels are necessary because they provide a common understanding of each student's needs and

FIGURE 1.8 **System of federal categories and percentage of students served (ages 6–21)**

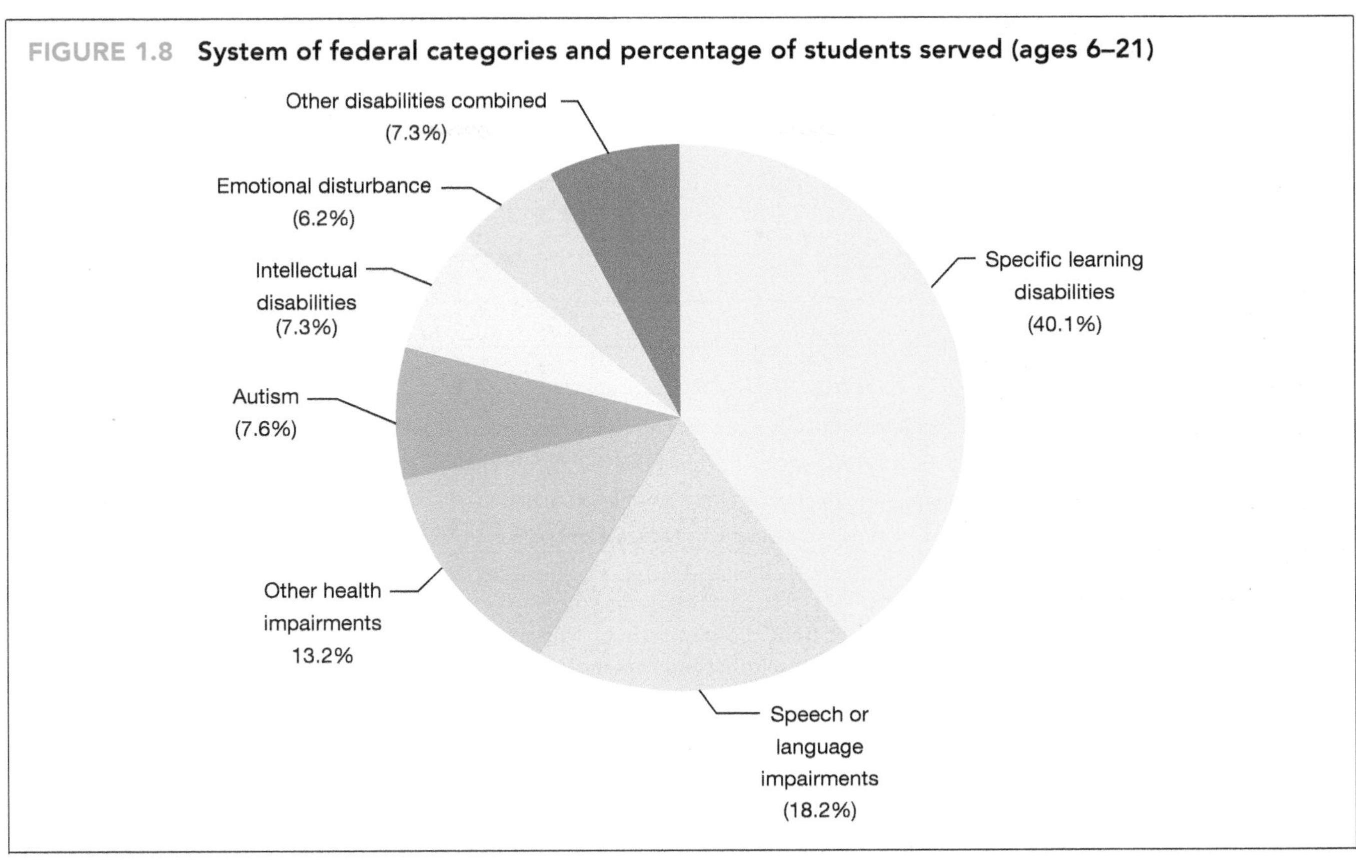

Source: "36th Annual Report to Congress on the Implementation of the Individuals with Disabilities Education Act, 2014, Washington, D.C. 2014. This report is available on the Department's website at: http://www.ed.gov/about/reports/annual/osep. Retrieved May 2015.

help to identify appropriate special education services. Others believe that the labels conjure up negative stereotypes, harm students' self-concepts, and cause confusion because each category subsumes many different defining characteristics. Regardless, labels and categories can be used in ways that are helpful as well as harmful. You need to consider how to think of the person first rather than the type of disability. Figure 1.8 shows the system of federal categories and the percentage (by category) of students who are provided with special education.

Students are identified as having special needs through a system of referrals. Students who have obvious disabilities (such as significant hearing, visual, or physical impairments or significant mental retardation) are usually referred and identified before age 5. For these children, the disabilities are often apparent to parents and pediatricians, and intervention begins early in the child's life. Classroom teachers or parents often identify students as having possible disabilities after they begin school.

The prereferral process

Response to intervention (RTI) has influenced the prereferral process. RTI refers to providing a validated (based on research) intervention to students in the instructional area of need before determining whether a student qualifies for special education services. A student's progress is monitored, and based on this progress additional intervention is provided before the student might be referred for special education. Prior to RTI, classroom teachers initiate referrals for assessment and appropriate intervention services.

Many schools have established school-based prereferral assistance teams (PATs) to facilitate assessment and identification of students with special needs. The PAT is a group of teachers and other key educators such as a school psychologist or reading

FIGURE 1.9 Prereferral for special education services

Directions: Please complete all sections of this form. The form should be sent to the Teacher Assistance Team. Complete and provide specific information that will assist the team in providing as much assistance as possible. Use behavioral descriptions whenever possible.

Teacher ______________________________

Grade/Class ______________________________

Date ______________________________

Student ______________________________

Age ______________________________

1. Describe what you would like the student to be able to do that he or she does not presently do.
2. Describe what the student does (strengths) and what he or she does not do (difficulties).
3. Describe what you have done to help the student cope with his or her problem.
4. Provide background information and/or previous assessment data relevant to the problem.

specialist from the same school who meet regularly to discuss the specific progress of students whom other teachers in the school have brought to their attention. This school-based problem-solving team is designed to help teachers by making classroom accommodations that maximize opportunities for students to succeed in the general education classroom or by identifying a treatment intervention to determine how the student responds. The idea is to determine whether this student needs additional instruction or has a special need. The model provides a forum in which classroom teachers can be part of the problem-solving process to ensure that all students in their classes receive appropriate services and that adequate information is available to determine whether students have a special need. Increasingly, students' responses to traditionally successful interventions are used as a data source to determine whether students have a special need. Research documents the value of having parents involved in this prereferral process, with overall improved quality of prereferral meetings and improved outcomes for students when parents are involved in the meetings and in providing interventions (Chen & Gregory, 2011).

Figure 1.9 provides an example of a form that can be used to assist with prereferral.

Currently, individuals who may need special education come to the school's attention because (a) a teacher or parent expresses concerns about the academic or behavioral functioning of the student, (b) a schoolwide screening test suggests possible learning or behavior problems, or (c) students at risk for problems have been provided interventions and haven't responded adequately to the intervention. Whether your school is using a more traditional approach to referral for special education identification or RTI, recommended practice is that students are provided research-based instructional intervention and adequate progress monitoring to adjust instruction prior to referral for special education. Sometimes the classroom teacher or educational specialist provides the instructional and behavioral support students' need.

Prereferral teams work toward the following goals:

- Providing suggestions to the classroom teacher.
- Identifying a secondary intervention that is associated with improved outcomes for most students.
- Implementing reasonable accommodations and modifications to meet students' academic and behavioral needs, document their results, and problem-solve alternative interventions.
- Assisting the teacher or parent with the referral process if necessary.

Although prereferral strategies take different forms in different school districts (Jimerson, Burns, & Van Der Heyden, 2007), most school districts use one of the following models:

- Response-to-intervention model
- Special-education-teacher-as-consultant model
- Problem-solving model

Response-to-intervention model

Individuals with learning disabilities have typically been identified based on practices that involve referral by the classroom teacher or parent followed by a complete battery of assessments designed to identify whether the student qualifies as learning disabled. There has been considerable concern about the appropriate use of IQ tests for all students, particularly for minority students, and the extent to which the traditionally used IQ–achievement discrepancy is an appropriate practice for identification of learning disabilities (Fletcher et al., 2011; Jimerson et al., 2007; Stuebing et al., 2012). In reaction to these concerns, a significant change in special education law about how students with specific learning disabilities are identified was made in IDEIA 2004. The law stipulates that a student with a learning disability may qualify for special education services if he or she has participated in but does not respond adequately to a scientific research–based intervention (for example, in reading or math).

What is IQ–achievement discrepancy, and what concerns are there about using it for identification? IQ–achievement discrepancy has been the common practice by which the IQ and standardized achievement scores of students referred for learning disabilities are used to establish whether a learning disability exists. A significant discrepancy (higher IQ scores than achievement scores on one or more relevant outcomes) occurs when an individual performs lower than would be expected based on his or her IQ, in one or more areas. Although the presence of an IQ discrepancy was considered a strong indicator of learning disabilities in the past, today there are several concerns about this practice:

- The discrepancy is difficult to determine with young children and may unnecessarily postpone identification until second grade or later.
- Many young children (ages 5 to 7) benefit greatly from prevention programs, particularly in reading.
- Formal IQ and achievement tests are expensive to administer and interpret, and the money may be better used to provide instruction.
- IQ tests provide little information on how to improve or alter instruction.

The most frequently suggested alternative to the IQ–discrepancy approach to identifying students with learning disabilities is the use of RTI. Using this approach:

- Students who respond adequately to the intervention and are able to make appropriate progress in the classroom are considered high responders to the intervention and are unlikely to require special education.
- Students whose response to the intervention is adequate but who continue to make less-than-adequate instructional gains in the general education classroom may qualify for special education.
- Students who make little progress when they are provided with research-based instructional methods are very likely to require special education.

The implementation of the RTI approach is relatively new, and therefore questions regarding who will provide the interventions and the extent to which validated instructional practices exist in fields other than reading still need to be addressed. Nevertheless, this approach appears to be a path for identification of learning disabilities that will soon be used by more and more school districts (Fuchs & Vaughn, 2012; Vaughn & Fuchs, 2003). See Figure 1.10.

FIGURE 1.10 Response to intervention

What does RTI look like in schools? Following is an example of RTI in practice. The three-tier reading model is designed to provide a safety net for struggling readers. The three-tier model is currently being used in more than ten states, with promising outcomes for readers at all proficiency levels.

- *It is January of Patrick's kindergarten year, and although most of his classmates have learned all the letter names and most of the letter sounds, Patrick is having difficulty. He identifies a few letter names and letter sounds but does not always remember them.*
- *It is April of second grade, and Mara, who has struggled since first grade with most reading-related tasks, seems to be falling further and further behind. She has difficulty decoding new words, and winter benchmark assessments show she is reading about 35 words a minute, whereas average readers are reading about 90 to 95 words a minute.*

The three-tier reading model meets the instructional needs of young readers, including those who are slow starters in kindergarten, like Patrick, and those who continue to struggle in the early elementary grades, like Mara. It is a prevention model designed to catch students early, *before* they fall behind, by providing the supports they need throughout the first 4 years of school. The model consists of three tiers, or levels, of intervention.

Tier 1: Core Reading Instruction in the Regular Classroom

Tier 1 consists of three components: (1) core classroom reading instruction provided to all students that is based on scientific reading research, (2) benchmark testing at three times during a year (fall, winter, spring) to determine instructional needs, and (3) ongoing professional development so that teachers are equipped to provide quality reading instruction to their students. In Tier 1 the classroom teacher provides the instruction. Students are at various levels of development in critical early reading skills. Some students are able to acquire the necessary skills through the standard instruction given by the teacher, whereas others require more intensive instruction in specific skill areas. Using flexible grouping and targeting specific skills, classroom teachers are often able to meet the needs of most of the students they teach.

Tier 2: Supplemental Instruction

For some students, focused instruction in the regular classroom setting is not enough. To get back on track, these students require supplemental instruction in addition to the time allotted for core instruction. Tier 2 meets the needs of these students by giving them an additional 30 minutes of intensive small-group reading instruction daily. The goal is to support and reinforce skills being taught by the classroom teacher. At this level of intervention, progress monitoring is used (twice a month) to ensure adequate progress is being made on target skills. Tier 2 instruction may be provided by the classroom teacher, a specialized reading teacher, or another teacher trained in Tier 2 reading methods.

Tier 3: Intensive Instruction

A small percentage of students who receive supplemental reading instruction (Tier 2) continue to have difficulty acquiring necessary reading skills. These students require instruction that is more explicit, more intensive, and specifically designed to meet their individual needs. For these students, two additional 30-minute sessions of specialized small-group reading instruction are provided with bimonthly progress monitoring of specific skills. The special education teacher or another specialist trained in Tier 3 intervention methods may provide the instruction.

Movement through the tiers is a dynamic process, with students entering and exiting each level of instruction as needed. Students with significant instructional needs do not need to wait and pass through Tier 2 in order to access more intensive interventions in Tier 3. Once a student acquires the target skills, he or she may no longer require supplemental instruction. The key components of the three-tier model are (1) the use of effective instruction, designed to meet the needs of students at each level, and (2) assessment procedures that measure current skills and growth over time and that are used to provide new instruction to individual students. In contrast to previous interventions for reading, the three-tier model provides a system that is responsive to students' changing needs.

Source: Based on *3-tier reading model: Reducing reading difficulties for kindergarten through third grade students*, by the University of Texas Center for Reading and Language Arts, 2008, Austin: Texas Education Agency; Fuchs, Fuchs, & Vaughn, 2014.

Consultant model

The special education teacher as a consultant is a traditional prereferral intervention model. Classroom teachers who have students with learning and behavioral difficulties and other disabilities in their classrooms frequently look to the special education teacher for advice and support. Teachers might ask the special education teacher to observe students in the classroom and in other settings to provide initial suggestions for assistance. The idea is that the special education teachers can provide instructional and behavioral supports and observe students' response, determining whether referral to special education might be warranted.

In a second consultant model, the special education teacher works part-time in general education classrooms to assist teachers with students who have been identified as requiring special education but whose needs generally can be met in the general education classroom. The special education teacher also assists teachers in implementing practices to enhance academic and social outcomes for students at risk for referral to special education. In this model, the special education teacher assumes instructional responsibility for selected students or a group of students and/or provides suggestions to the general education teacher to improve outcomes for students (Solis, Vaughn, Swanson, & McCulley, 2012).

TIPS FOR TEACHERS 1.3

Problem-Solving Guidelines for Team Meetings

- Present and review summary information about students from your prereferral form or notes.
- Identify the primary concern and describe interventions you and other teachers have tried.
- Brainstorm and evaluate ideas for potentially solving the problem.
- Select a goal to address the problem and identify objectives and procedures for solving it.
- Discuss suggestions with the classroom teacher and further refine your classroom intervention plan.
- Select an intervention or set of instructional or behavioral procedures and assure that they can be appropriately implemented.
- Develop a means of measuring the success of the intervention plan.
- Establish a date and time for a 15-minute follow-up meeting to evaluate the effectiveness of the plan.

Problem-solving model

This model provides initial strategies and support for classroom teachers before referring a student for assessment for special education services. Schools may benefit in several ways by using a problem-solving team:

- Classroom teachers have considerable knowledge and talent and can help one another meet the needs of targeted students.
- Classroom teachers can and do help many students with disabilities. Every effort should be made to meet students' needs in the classroom before referral for special education.
- Teachers who work together can solve more problems more effectively than teachers who work alone.
- Teachers can increase their skills and knowledge through solving the academic and social problems of students.

Members of the problem-solving team can include school psychologists, reading specialists, speech and language specialists, and other teachers with experience in effectively teaching students with academic or behavior problems.

During a problem-solving meeting, team members (using the guidelines in Tips for Teachers 1.3) participate in a problem-solving process that lasts approximately 30 minutes.

1.2.2 Adapting Instruction

In addition to participating in planning, prereferral, and referral procedures, classroom teachers must adapt curriculum and instruction to accommodate students' special needs (see Figure 1.11 for models for adapting instruction).

"What does it mean to adapt instruction for students with disabilities?" asked Anna Schmidt, a tenth-grade social studies teacher. "I have certain objectives I need to meet for all of my students. Does this mean I alter these objectives?" Anna's questions are relevant to issues related to effective interventions. Classroom teachers can greatly help their students with special needs by making adaptations that positively affect learning for all students in the classroom.

Many of the adaptations you make for students with disabilities will enhance learning for all students in your classroom. For example, Maria Arguelles, an eighth-grade teacher, develops an outline of her lectures. She projects this outline on a screen, pointing out her location in the outline as she presents key information. This procedure not only helps students with disabilities who have difficulty organizing information, taking notes, and identifying key ideas, but also enhances learning for all the students in her classroom.

FIGURE 1.11 Models for adapting instruction

A 3-year project involving nine elementary and middle schools in integrating students with moderate or severe disabilities into general education classrooms yielded guidelines for change at three phases: planning, implementation, and sustainability (Burstein, Sears, Wilcoken, Cabello, & Spagna, 2004).

Planning
Participants reported that the most essential features of planning for change are:

- ***Change process.*** Implement a plan for the change process that includes (a) building a commitment to change with teachers, administrators, and parents; (b) planning for change; and (c) providing support for change.
- ***Staff development.*** Opportunities to learn about inclusive practices provided motivation and preparation for change and gave participants the tools to meet the needs of students in inclusive settings.
- ***Collaborative activities.*** Collaborative planning and teaching allowed special education and general education teachers to benefit from the unique expertise that was brought by each group and to create a collaborative environment where meeting the special needs of students became a priority for all teachers.
- ***Commitment to change.*** Changing practices involved active participation of both administrators and teachers in activities such as making available (administrators) and using (teachers) funds for planning time, staff development, and site visits.

Implementation
Inclusion looked different from school to school and was determined by a variety of factors, including the following:

- ***Range of program options.*** There was great variation in the types of inclusive practices that occurred in schools. Some served all students with disabilities in general education classrooms and others offered a range of service options. The teachers, administrators, and parents at specific school sites determined how changes were implemented.
- ***School-site decision making.*** Although participants were satisfied with the changes that occurred, the inclusion models implemented looked very different from school to school. This reflects the site-level decision making that was made to address the specific needs of each school.
- ***Support services.*** Teachers, administrators, and parents required training in effective teaching practices and collaboration as well as resources such as materials and extra staff to effectively implement inclusive practices.

Long-Term Change
Suggestions for sustaining change were as follows:

- ***Leadership at the district level.*** Administrators must be committed to supporting long-term change and establishing systems to continue implementation.
- ***Teacher satisfaction.*** Teachers who see the benefits of the inclusion model for students and faculty in general and special education are likely to sustain the new practices.
- ***Ongoing support.*** The school district must maintain sufficient resources for ongoing staff development, collaborative planning, and classroom support.
- ***Monitor workload.*** Teachers were more likely to continue inclusive practices when they were not overloaded with too many students or too many responsibilities in the inclusion model.

Looking for students' strengths and ways to say "good job" also promotes learning for all students. Jane Gordon, a fourth-grade teacher, was a pro at this. She realized that motivation is the key to success, particularly for the students with disabilities in her classroom, and she put considerable effort into knowing the strengths and interests of each student and recognizing those strengths and interests whenever possible.

MyEdLab **Self-Check 1.2**

MyEdLab **Application Exercise 1.2:** Accommodations

1.3 NO CHILD LEFT BEHIND ACT, EXPANDING IDEIA, AND INCLUSION

The No Child Left Behind (NCLB) Act requires that at least 95% of students with disabilities participate in the statewide assessments that are used as standard measures of yearly progress for school-age children. However, in 2011, flexibility in NCLB was offered as a voluntary opportunity for state and local leaders to submit proposals for how they might be able to alter these requirements in exchange for rigorous state-level proposals.

1.3.1 Testing Accommodations for Students with Disabilities

Because NCLD requires annual yearly progress for students, the issues relating to testing accommodations are significant. Testing accommodations are designed to provide changes in testing to prevent a student's disability from interfering with determining his or her skills. According to the National Joint Committee on Learning Disabilities (NJCLD, 2004), the inclusion of students with disabilities in statewide assessments should "lead to informed teaching, improved learning, and the acquisition of needed literacy skills, learning strategies, and social skills that allow students with learning disabilities to access the general education curriculum" (pp. 67–68). The hope is that by including students in all parts of the statewide assessment process (e.g., curriculum alignment, test preparation, assessments, and public reporting of scores), teachers and schools will raise expectations and the quality of instruction for low-achieving students will increase performance in essential knowledge and skills (Thurlow & Kopriva, 2015; Ysseldyke et al., 2004).

In a review of the few studies that exist on high-stakes assessments and students with disabilities, Ysseldyke and colleagues (2004) determined that raising expectations for low-achieving students and increasing their participation in statewide assessments can yield positive results when students are given (a) appropriate and individualized accommodations and (b) improved instruction in the content that will be covered on the test. In these situations, students with disabilities gain greater access to the general curriculum and can do well on assessments (see Tips for Teachers 1.4).

Remember that each test has accommodations that are allowed as well as those that invalidate results. For example, it may not be acceptable to read out loud a passage that measures reading comprehension, but it may be okay to read out loud math questions. Also, some states allow reading aloud of specific parts of the test, for example, proper nouns or test questions, but not other parts of the test. Recommendations for considering accommodations on high-stakes assessments include the following (Cormier, Altman, Shyyan, & Thurlow, 2010; NJCLD, 2004; Thurlow & Kopriva, 2015):

- *Setting.* Is the student distracted by or distracting to other students? Is the student able to focus in a quiet classroom with twenty-five to thirty other children? Will alternative delivery or response forms be embarrassing to the student or disruptive to other students?
- *Administration.* Does the child need an alternate form of test (e.g., large print for a student with a vision impairment)? Does the student need the directions or questions read out loud?
- *Timing.* Does the student require extra time? Does the student need frequent breaks to maintain attention? Does the student perform better at certain times of the day than

TIPS FOR TEACHERS 1.4

Types of Accommodations Used to Facilitate Student Participation

What types of accommodations can be used to facilitate participation and success of students with disabilities? According to Salend (2008), accommodations can be organized into five categories:

1. Presentation mode—for example, clarifying and simplifying language, fewer items on a page
2. Response mode—for example, extra space on the page, lined or graph paper
3. Timing and scheduling—for example, shorter segments, more time
4. Setting accommodations—for example, individual administration, familiar setting
5. Linguistic accommodations—for example, respond in best language, provide context clues

Source: "Determining appropriate testing accommodations," by J. S. Salend, 2008, *Teaching Exceptional Children, 40*(4), 4–22.

at others? Should the order of the test sections be alternated to improve motivation or decrease anxiety (e.g., allowing the student to choose the order of the test sections)?

- *Computer-based testing.* The majority of studies reveal that students perform comparably on computer-based assessments and paper/pencil assessments, suggesting that computer-based assessments are an appropriate alternative for students with disabilities who prefer or require this accommodation.
- *Response.* Should the student respond orally rather than in writing? Does the student need assistance in recording answers (e.g., tracking answers from a test booklet to correctly bubbling responses on the answer sheet)?
- *Use of language or American Sign Language.* For students who are deaf and hard of hearing (SDHH) consider bridging the gap between a student's linguistic background and the language of the assessment by using American Sign Language (ASL) to present test items.
- *English language learners (ELLs) with disabilities.* Abedi (2014) notes that there is very little research on the types of accommodations that are effective for students with disabilities who are ELLs. He suggests that we consider: (a) linguistically modified tests, (b) native language or bilingual test booklets, and/or (c) computer-based testing.
- *Universal design.* As universal design for learning is applied to accommodations for testing, the principle is one of providing multiple means of presentation, expression, and engagement (Thurlow & Kopriva, 2015).

Classroom teachers should be aware of the test accommodations that are in place for each student and, as much as possible, should implement similar accommodations during test-preparation activities and for classroom-based assessments (see also Figure 1.5 on test accommodations). For example, a student who will be given breaks during the statewide assessment should also be allowed to take breaks during practice sessions or when taking long classroom-based assessments.

1.3.2 Expanding the Impact of the IDEIA

With the amendments, the impact of the IDEIA has expanded to include (a) services for infants, toddlers, and young children from birth to age 5 and (b) transition planning and services for adolescents as they move from high school to postsecondary education, adult life, and the world of work.

Early intervention and transition from early childhood to school

Part C of the IDEIA, or early intervention services, is a state-operated program established in 1986 to serve infants and toddlers (under age 3) and their families. Children who exhibit at least one of the following criteria and who need assistance are served:

- Diagnosed conditions (e.g., deafness)
- Development delays (e.g., not reaching developmental milestones for talking or walking)
- Children who are at risk but who do not currently exhibit a disability or delay (e.g., physical abuse, homelessness)

Early intervention services are comprehensive services that incorporate goals in education, health care, and social services. The emphasis for early intervention services is on supporting family members accessing resources and managing the care and environment of the infant or toddler with special needs. The important role the IEP plays in program planning for school-age students with disabilities is taken on, for children from birth to 3 years of age, by the **individualized family service plan (IFSP)**. As the name suggests, however, the IFSP broadens the focus to include not only the child but also the family members and their needs in supporting a young child with disabilities.

An IFSP must be designed to meet the needs of the child *and* the family. This plan should provide a coordinated array of services that may be provided directly to the child (e.g., speech therapy or occupational therapy) or may be provided to the family to assist the child (e.g., parent training, counseling, or case management). The following services are included:

- Screening and assessment
- Psychological assessment and intervention
- Occupational and physical therapy
- Speech, language, and audiology services
- Family involvement, training, and home visits
- Specialized instruction for parents and the target youngster
- Case management
- Health services that may be needed to allow the child to benefit from the intervention service

The IFSP is a family-oriented approach to designing an effective management plan for the youngster with disabilities. The IFSP must be developed by a multidisciplinary team and should include:

- A description of the child's level of functioning across the developmental areas: physical, cognitive, communicative, social or emotional, and adaptive.
- An assessment of the family, including a description of the family's strengths and needs as they relate to enhancing the development of the child with disabilities.
- A description of the major goals or outcomes expected for the child with disabilities and the family (as they relate to providing opportunities for the child).
- Procedures for measuring progress, including timelines, objectives, and evaluation procedures.
- A description of natural environments in which the early intervention services will be provided.
- A description of the early intervention services needed to provide appropriate help for the child and family.
- Specifically when the specialized intervention will begin and how long it will last.
- An appointed case manager.
- A specific transition plan from the birth-to-3 program into the preschool program.

If you are a kindergarten teacher, you probably will have the opportunity to teach young children who, having received early intervention services, are making the transition from preschool to your classroom. It is important to remember that for families and children with disabilities, these transitions are among the most significant times in their lives, filled with uncertainty and concern.

As a teacher, you can help parents of children with special needs by recognizing that their fears and concerns are expected and realistic and by providing information about your classroom and the school to help alleviate their concerns. You can also help to facilitate transition from preschool to kindergarten by doing the following:

- Attending the IEP or IFSP meeting before transition so that you are aware of the child's strengths, the goals planned, and the techniques and strategies that have been successful. You can meet the child's parents and current teachers, ask questions, and determine how this child's goals fit with goals for your other students.
- Meeting with the child's parents before the transition to learn about their goals for their child, the child's strengths and needs, and strategies they have found that help their child succeed in preschool.
- Setting up a regular means of communication with the child's parents and former teachers, particularly for the first several months. Invariably, questions will arise that can be answered easily by the parents and those who have been working with the child. Do not hesitate to use these resources.

MyEdLab
Video Example 1.2.

Watch as issues related to early childhood special education are discussed. How and why does focusing on preschool contribute to their transition to elementary school?

Section B of the IDEIA provides special education or related services to children in the range of 3 to 5 or 6 years old. At this stage, there is no longer any provision for children who are at risk, and children must exhibit a disability to receive services. However, the term *preschool child with a disability* is often used to avoid labeling very young children:

> **(B)** The term "child with a disability" for a child age 3 through 9 may, at the discretion of the State and the local education agency, include a child
>
> i. experiencing developmental delays, as defined by the State and as measured by appropriate diagnostic instruments and procedures, in one or more of the following areas: physical development, cognitive development, communication development, social or emotional development, or adaptive development; and
>
> ii. who, by reason thereof, needs special education and related services. (Sec. 602[3]; 34CFR 300.7)

Preschool children who qualify are provided with a free and appropriate education that is outlined in an individualized education program. Note that the IEP focuses on educational needs, whereas the IFSP does not. The 2004 revisions to the IDEA provide some flexibility for families; for example, children may continue to be served in an infant/toddler program with an IFSP (with educational goals added) after age 3 or move on to a designated preschool program.

Transition from school to work and other post-school activities

The 2004 amendments to the IDEA mandate transition planning and transition services for students from 16 years of age to age 21. In the IDEIA, transition services are defined as:

> a coordinated set of activities for a child with a disability, designed within a results-oriented process, that is focused on improving the academic and functional achievement of the child with a disability to facilitate the child's movement from school to post-school activities, including postsecondary education, vocational education, integrated employment (including supported employment), continuing and adult education, adult services, independent living, or community participation. (H.R. 1350, 602[34])

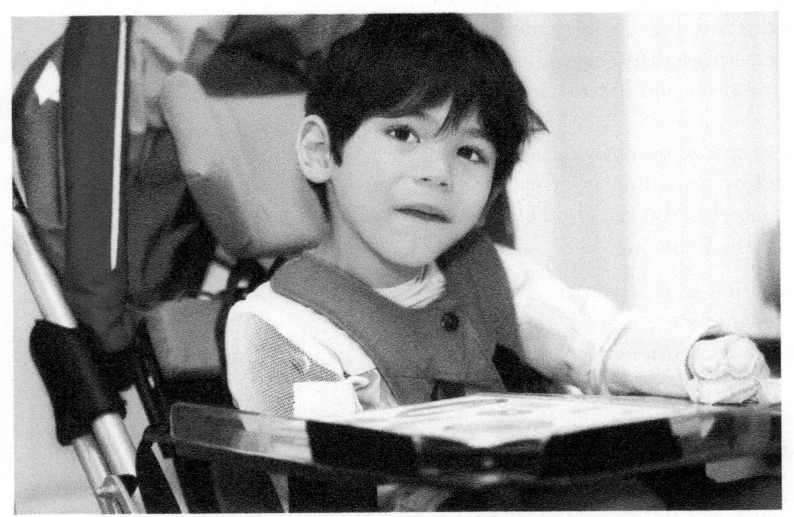

Why was IDEIA expanded to include eligibility for transition planning for individuals with disabilities from birth to age 21? In what transition activities might this student be involved when he is in high school?

The law also notes that these activities should be based on the student's strengths, preferences, and interests. The activities include instruction, community experiences, the development of employment and other adult-living objectives and, when appropriate, vocational evaluation, rehabilitation counseling, and the acquisition of daily living skills.

This emphasis on transition planning and services came in response to the growing concern about the number of students with disabilities who were unemployed or underemployed as adults and the limited emphasis on vocational education and adult living in many secondary programs for students with disabilities. A consistent finding is that workers with disabilities are twice as likely as workers without disabilities to be in contingent and part-time jobs. A study conducted by Schur (2003) reports that the primary explanation is health problems of individuals with disabilities that make traditional full-time jobs difficult or impossible for them to hold. Even though part-time jobs pay less, individuals with disabilities would not be able to work if it were not for these positions. Transition services for students with disabilities are even more important under the No Child Left Behind Act because the graduation rate is one of the criteria to determine if schools and districts meet performance criteria.

Individualized transition plan (ITP)

A key component of these transition services is the individualized transition plan (ITP) incorporated into the IEP. This transition plan includes the designation of "appropriate measurable postsecondary goals based upon age appropriate transition assessments related to training, education, employment, and, where appropriate, independent living skills" and should also state the transition services (including courses of study) needed to assist the child in reaching his or her goals, as indicated by H.R. 1350 and IDEIA 2004. An ITP addresses the student's preferences, interests, and needs; develops a plan 5 to 7 years prior to graduation; and encourages coordinated efforts between agencies, service providers, and vocational and rehabilitation services.

Specific goals for transition, followed by a list of classes and activities that would provide opportunities for students to meet these goals, are written into the IEP. Sample goals follow:

- By the end of the semester, Jason will develop the skills to complete job applications successfully (taught in career exploration class and by completing job applications with the job developer).
- By the end of the school year, Nancy will develop positive work habits (e.g., arriving on time, interacting with coworkers) (taught in career exploration class and during work experiences supported by the job developer).
- Within the next 3 years, Maria will develop computer skills in word processing, databases, and spreadsheets to the degree that she can effectively use them on a job (taught in computer classes and during work experiences supported by the job developer).
- Before the end of this school year, Jose will develop a monthly budget of expenses that reflects a realistic independent living arrangement, including rent, food, clothing, and other expenses, which will be reviewed by his parents and special education teachers.

Although students with disabilities are underrepresented in postsecondary education settings, students who continue on in school have greater access to employment opportunities and are more likely to get a job and earn a higher salary than those without a postsecondary education (Johnson, Thurlow, Cosio, & Bremer, 2005). High school teachers, specialists, counselors, and families can prepare students who plan to go on to college in the following ways (National Center on Secondary Education and Transition [NCSET], 2004; Torgerson, Miner, & Shen, 2004; Wood, Karvonen, Test, Browder, & Algozzine, 2004):

- Encourage students to actively participate in IEP meetings and in the development of the individual transition plan.
- Help students understand the nature of their disability and how it influences learning.
- Teach strategies for developing self-determination and advocacy.
- Support students in transition activities such as education planning and work–study to prepare for college.
- Help students and families find postsecondary settings that are supportive to students with special needs.
- Ensure that students take the courses and have the skills required for enrollment in college.

With the increased emphasis on transition, vocational education, and work experience opportunities during high school for students with disabilities, many districts have special education personnel who work in this area. Mary Hinson, a job developer at Catalina High School, is one such person. She comments on her job and the difference it makes in helping students:

> I believe that the work I do as a job developer makes the difference for many students with disabilities and lets them leave high school already employed and adjusted to the world of work. What I do is work with the students, their teachers, and parents to plan a program that allows them to develop job and independent living skills, take relevant course work both at the high school and at the community college, and have relevant work experiences. A big part of my job is developing partnerships with businesses that will provide initial training and "the first job" for students with disabilities.

Clearly, Mary has a different role from that of a typical special education teacher. If you teach in high school, you will want to take the time to find out about transition services and the job developers or persons in charge of transition planning and services. Knowing about a student's transition goals will help you tailor your accommodations so that they are relevant for the student's long-term career goals. For example, if a student with a learning disability is planning to enter the field of drafting, then emphasizing measuring skills in basic math classes and computer-assisted design in computer classes may be particularly beneficial for this student.

The philosophy of this book is that classroom teachers can help their students with disabilities by teaching "on purpose," that is, by being mindful and proactive in using opportunities to make a difference in these students' classroom experiences. See the 60-Second Lesson to learn more about how to incorporate this philosophy into your teaching.

60-*SECOND* LESSON

TEACHING ON PURPOSE

Contrary to common belief, purposively teaching students with special needs does not need to take a great deal of time. You can make a difference in only a minute. For example, think about having one or two 60-second lessons with each of your students with special needs every day. How is Darnell progressing on a given IEP objective? What directed feedback can you provide to Marlene to help her achieve her goals? To reflect the value of short, targeted lessons in classroom practice, a feature called "60-Second Lesson" provides an example in most chapters of this book.

1.3.3 Inclusion

How does inclusion relate to the continuum of services? **Inclusion**, the placement (from part-time to full-time) of students with disabilities in the general education classroom, is not required by law, but is often a means for providing an appropriate education in the least restrictive environment. The essential element of inclusion is shared responsibility on the part of all educators in the school for the student with disabilities.

The effectiveness of inclusion has been the subject of extensive discussion in the field of special education (Fuchs & Fuchs, 1994; Kauffman & Hallahan, 1995; Kavale & Forness, 2000; Zigmond, Kloo, & Volonino, 2009). On the basis of available evidence, many factors may influence the effectiveness of inclusion (e.g., the type and severity of disability, and services provided in inclusive settings). Thus, it is important to decide the placement of each student individually on the continuum of services based on his or her unique needs and to determine whether the student's special needs are adequately met.

In practice, the terms *mainstreaming* and *inclusion* can be used interchangeably. They can have very different meanings, however. **Mainstreaming** refers to the participation of students with disabilities in general education classrooms to the extent that is appropriate to meet their needs. Inclusion refers to the education of students with disabilities with their nondisabled peers, with special education supports and services being provided as necessary. Advocates of full inclusion believe that all students with disabilities should be educated in the general education classroom all the time (Stainback & Stainback, 1992). Pull-out services (e.g., special education resource-room models) are not options for full-inclusion advocates because students with disabilities are not educated entirely in the same setting (i.e., the general education classroom) as students without disabilities. A meta-analysis examining research studies on inclusion models indicates that inclusive settings can be effective for some, although not all, students with disabilities (Zigmond, 2003). For example, Salend and Duhaney (2007) reported that students with severe disabilities who were educated in inclusive settings demonstrated increases in skills acquired, time on task, and exposure to more extensive academic content than those educated in other settings. Also, students in inclusive settings had more friends, greater social acceptance, and higher self-concepts. Justice (2014) reported that for young students with disabilities language outcomes were affected by the language development of peers in their classroom. Of course, for many, the access to fully inclusive classrooms provides opportunities for academic and social growth for all learners (Florian, 2013).

Also, students in inclusive settings had more friends, greater social acceptance, and higher self-concepts. Justice (2014) reported that for young students with disabilities language outcomes were affected by the language development of peers in their classroom. Of course, for many, the access to fully inclusive classrooms provides opportunities for academic and social growth for all learners (Florian, 2013).

At issue is the extent to which a continuum of services is maintained. Earlier in this chapter, the range of educational options for students with disabilities (e.g., the self-contained special education classroom, homebound instruction, and resource room) was presented. This is the continuum of services that advocates of inclusion want to maintain. Advocates of full inclusion are concerned, however, that maintaining a continuum of services will prevent real integration of students with disabilities. The concern is that if the option for separation or pull-out from the regular classroom is available, educators will too easily choose it. Debate continues over the extent to which full inclusion should be required for all students with disabilities. We recognize that the central issue is the extent to which the academic and social progress of students with disabilities is monitored and adjustments provided if progress is not adequate. Figure 1.12 summarizes guidelines for responsible inclusion.

1.3.4 Accessing Information About Students

How do you learn everything you need to know about your students with disabilities? One of the most difficult aspects of working with students with disabilities is figuring out just what they need and what you need to do to help them be successful while they are in your classroom. The first step is accessing information about your students. At a minimum, teachers should have information about the student's educational and social–emotional needs and about the modifications and accommodations that are required for this student. Although it is important to participate in the IEP process and to read each student's IEP, it is also useful to have information that is easily accessible to you in your classroom.

One way to keep track of the needs of your students is to have a *program outline* for each student with disabilities that provides a quick overview of your students. Sometimes a special education teacher will make a program outline for each student, or you can create one yourself by looking at the IEP, assessment information from the schools, progress monitoring data, and reports provided by previous teachers. The focus of the outline is to provide a one- to two-page document that has the critical information you need to assure you are meeting the student's needs. Consider the following:

- Descriptive information about the student including disability and contact information for parent.
- Description of current and previous special education services.
- Description of instructional adaptations that are recommended.
- Assessment data related to academic performance.
- Assessment data related to social–emotional development.

FIGURE 1.12 Guidelines for responsible inclusion

Responsible Inclusion	Irresponsible Inclusion
The student comes first.	**The place comes first.**
The priority is the extent to which the student makes academic and/or social progress.	The priority is the place in which the student's education occurs.
Adequate resources are considered and provided for in inclusive classrooms.	**Resources are not considered before the establishment of inclusion.**
Both personnel and materials are required to develop and maintain effective inclusive classrooms.	Inclusion is established with little consideration for the necessary personnel and physical resources.
A continuum of services is maintained.	**Full inclusion is the only service-delivery model.**
A range of education programs is available to meet the unique needs of students with disabilities.	All students are placed in general education classrooms, regardless of their needs.
The service-delivery model is evaluated on an ongoing basis.	**The service-delivery model is not evaluated on an ongoing basis.**
The success of the service-delivery model is evaluated with consideration for the extent to which it meets the student's academic and social needs.	When problems occur, personnel are blamed rather than the model being evaluated.
There is ongoing professional development.	**Professional development is not part of the model.**
The curricula and instruction meet the needs of all students.	**Curricula and instruction that meet the needs of all students are not considered.**
Services provided to students are flexible.	**Services are defined and not readily altered.**
Teaching assistants provide in-class support that includes pairs and small groups of students.	**Teaching assistants support the student with a disability only.**
Instructional practices and behavioral approaches are recognized as good practice.	**Considerable variation in quality of practices is observed.**

Sources: "Responsible inclusion for students with learning disabilities," by S. Vaughn & J. S. Schumm, 1995, *Journal of Learning Disabilities, 28*(5), 267; and "Inclusive school placements and surplus/deficit in performance for students with intellectual disabilities: Is there a connection?" by N. L. Waldron & J. McLeskey, 2010, *Lifespan and Disability, XIII*(1), 29–42.

- Types of reinforcers and supports that are effective.
- Instructional goals and objectives.
- Students' likes and dislikes.

Items contained in the program outline are information on the disability, strengths and needs, IEP objectives, medical or other needs, grading accommodations, instructional modifications, and contact information. A second piece of useful information is an accommodation checklist (see Figure 1.13).

Usually part of the IEP, the checklist should be referenced during planning to ensure that you are providing the student with necessary support and access to the curriculum during your lessons.

1.3.5 Inclusion Issues

As previously mentioned, not everyone agrees on every aspect of the education of students with disabilities. Most educational professionals do support the access to a continuum of services for students with disabilities with an aim towards assuring students are in the general education classroom with their peers as much as possible. One issue that has aroused controversy is the view that all students with disabilities need to be educated in an inclusive setting—typically referred to as full inclusion. The argument is that students with disabilities need to be educated in the most normalized environment available and that extensive experience with persons without disabilities is essential to the social and academic growth of students with disabilities. The extent to which these experiences can be provided, while not abolishing required special education support services, should serve as the guiding principle (Fuchs, Fuchs, & Stecker, 2011).

FIGURE 1.13 **Accommodation Checklist**

Accommodation	Subject Area/Course
1. Highlighted texts	
2. Taped texts	
3. Simplified texts	
4. Manipulatives	
5. Note-taking assistance	
6. Access to study aid (e.g., number chart, map, dictionary)	
7. Peer buddy	
8. Peer tutor	
9. Assignment notebook	
10. Extended time on assignments	
11. Shortened assignments	
12. Alternate presentation format	
13. Small-group instruction	
14. Repeat directions	
15. Increased verbal response	
16. Check for understanding	
17. Frequent breaks	
18. Preferential seating	
19. Assistive technology (list technology)	
20. Calculator	
21. Study guides	
22. Extended time on tests	
23. Tests in special education classroom	
24. Oral tests	
25. Alternative tests	
26. Read-aloud tests	
27. Other ______________________	

The arguments presented in Figure 1.14 are really not for or against inclusion. All advocates believe that students with disabilities should be educated in general education settings to the extent possible. Actually, an examination of data from reports to Congress regarding placement practices for students with learning disabilities over the last 6 years revealed that such students are educated in increasingly less restrictive settings (U.S. Department of Education, 2007). However, the data do not provide insight into how schools have provided appropriate accommodations and support services to these students placed in less restrictive settings. Of concern is the extent to which specialized support services aimed at meeting the learning and behavior needs of students with disabilities should be available.

MyEdLab
Video Example 1.3.
Watch and listen to this student with special needs share his experiences in the general education classroom. Do you feel the supports and services that were put in place for this student were successful and, if so, how is this demonstrated?

Cortina Fernandez, a fourth-grade teacher, describes the strategy she uses successfully to incorporate students with disabilities into her general education classroom:

> First, I work very closely with the special education teacher. Before a student is placed into my classroom, I find out as much as I can about what the student likes, what they can do, what their academic strengths are, what they enjoy doing outside of school, and what they can teach me and other students in the classroom.

FIGURE 1.14 Arguments for full inclusion and maintenance of the continuum of services

ARGUMENTS FOR FULL INCLUSION

- Students with disabilities should be educated in general education classes all the time.
- Students with disabilities should not be pulled out of the general education classroom to receive specialized education.
- Benefits of placing students with disabilities in specialized classes, for either their academic or social growth, have not been adequately demonstrated.
- Comprehensive, professional development that prepares teachers to meet the educational and social needs of all students is required.
- All students with disabilities have the right to education in the most normalized setting—the general education classroom.

ARGUMENTS FOR MAINTAINING CONTINUUM OF SERVICES

- Students with disabilities should be educated in general education classes to the extent that this meets their educational and behavioral needs.
- Some students with disabilities need to have their educational needs met outside of the general education classroom for part or all of the school day. A continuum of services to meet the needs of students with disabilities is required.
- Benefits and pitfalls of full-inclusion models for all students with disabilities have not been empirically documented.
- General education teachers are inadequately prepared to meet the specialized needs of all students with disabilities.
- Inclusion is a philosophy, not a place. Students have the right to receive the appropriate educational services to fulfill their learning needs at the most suitable site.

Second, I find out what they need to know, where they are in terms of their academic progress, and what skills they need to learn, both academically and socially. I get this information from the student's IEP, from the previous teacher, usually the special education teacher, and, if possible, by interviewing the student and the parent before the student is placed into my classroom.

Third, I work with all of the students in my classroom to assure that every child is a member of our community. Our learning community provides support and assistance for every other member and provides social support as well. This ongoing philosophy maintains a classroom environment in which all children are accepted, an essential ingredient to the success for mainstreaming of students with disabilities. I also make the success of every student in the class the responsibility of every other student. While I'm the teacher in the classroom and take that responsibility seriously, our learning community is one in which each child teaches each other. Thus, it's important to find out what everyone knows and what everyone needs to know so we can all work together. I also closely monitor the progress of every student in my classroom, particularly students with disabilities. I frequently check in with them, make sure they know what they're doing, and assure that they are making expected progress.

Fourth, communication is essential to the successful mainstreaming of students with disabilities. This communication occurs between myself and all the specialists, myself and the parent, as well as myself and other students in my class. However, I do not feel the communication is solely a one-way street. I hold the special education teacher and other specialists responsible for communicating with me, as well as encourage the parents to talk to me as frequently as they feel necessary. In addition, communication is part of the responsibility of students. They need to inform me about what they are doing well and where they need help. I encourage this communication by being open and receptive when they want to talk to me. Successful mainstreaming is more than just what I do as a classroom teacher. It's how I think and how I convey this to all the students and teachers in my school.

MyEdLab **Self-Check 1.3**

MyEdLab **Application Exercise 1.3:** Individualized Transition Plan

1 SUMMARY

- The Individuals with Disabilities Education Improvement Act (IDEIA; which incorporates and extends P.L. 94-142) and the Vocational Rehabilitation Act (P.L. 93-112) are the two primary laws that have increased the opportunities and services available to individuals with disabilities. The IDEIA and the Vocational Rehabilitation Act changed the way students with special needs are educated. Among the provisions of the IDEIA is the concept of educational settings providing a continuum of services placing students in the least restrictive environment, meaning that students are best served in settings most similar to those of their peers without disabilities in which they can learn (ideally, moving to less and less restrictive settings). The individualized education program (IEP) is developed and implemented by the multidisciplinary team, the goal being the appropriate education of all students.
- Among the responsibilities of the classroom teacher are participating in the referral and planning process for students with special needs as well as working with other professionals such as those who participate on the teacher assistance team. Also important is understanding how to make adaptations to instruction to meet the needs of students with special needs.
- The IDEIA has been expanded to include services for young children (birth to age 5) and to incorporate transition planning and services for students in secondary schools. Inclusive education models include mainstreaming and full inclusion to promote appropriate placement of students with disabilities in the general education classroom.

THINK AND APPLY

1. Now that you have read Chapter 1, review Elizabeth's account of her experience at the beginning of this chapter. If you could talk with Elizabeth directly, what questions would you ask her? List any questions or concerns you currently have about teaching students with disabilities. Then, after you read each chapter, consult your list again and check off any questions that you can answer satisfactorily. File your personal inquiries in your teaching portfolio and record your answers as you progress through the book.
2. Sit in on an IEP meeting. Who were the participants? What roles did each participant play? Based on the roles of the participants, what role do you see yourself playing? The general education teacher? The special education teacher? Why?
3. Interview one or more teachers who have students with disabilities in their classrooms. Ask these teachers to identify any key practices they implement that they believe make a difference. Ask also what they wish they knew more about and what they will do to learn more. What resources do they find most helpful?

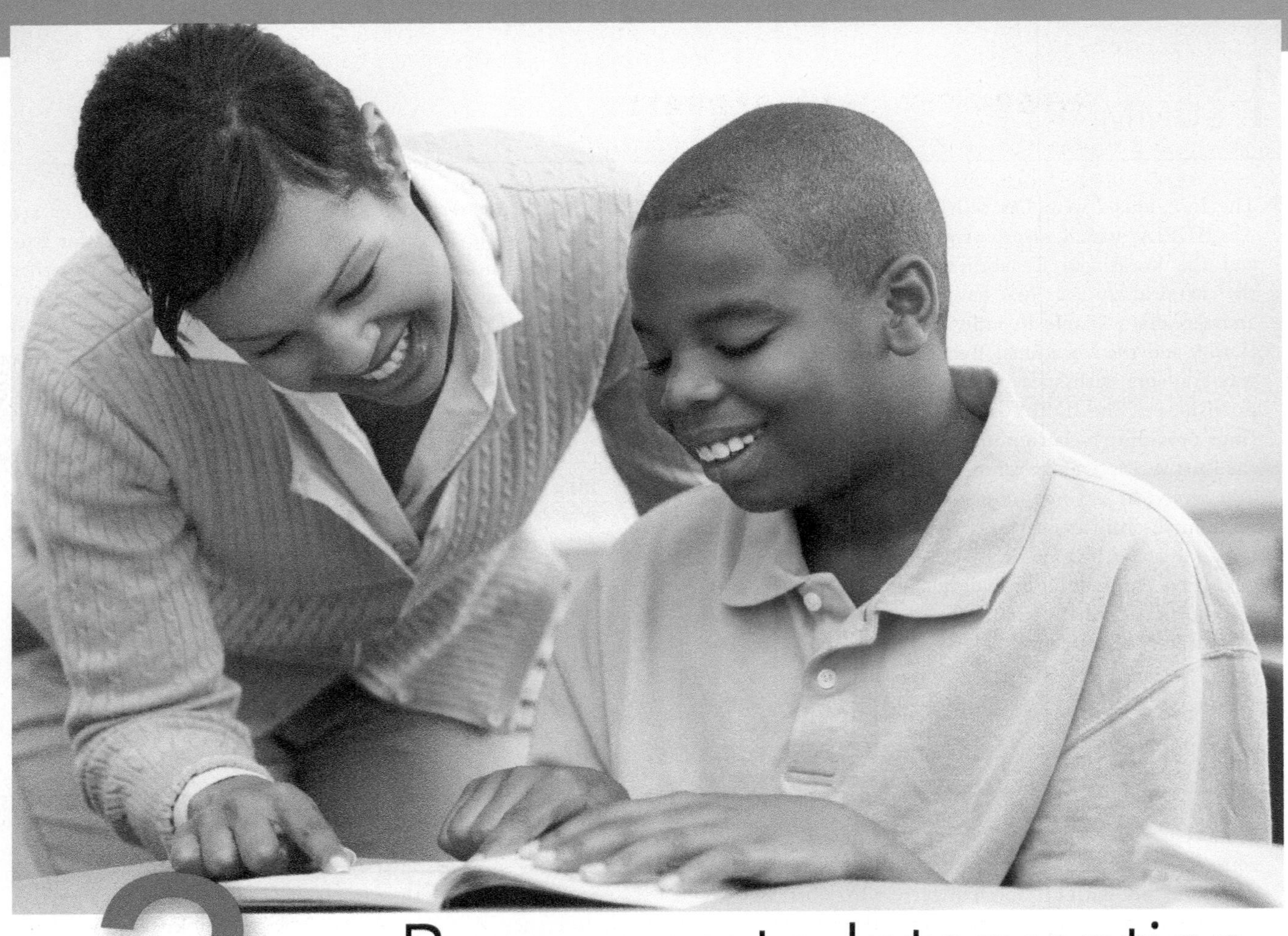

2 Response to Intervention and Multitiered Systems of Support: Developing Success for All Learners

Learning Outcomes

2.1 Provide a rationale for the importance of implementing a response to intervention (RTI) or multitiered systems of support (MTSS) model in schools and describe the issues that led to the development of RTI models.

2.2 Describe an RTI or MTSS model, including the components and implementation practices.

2.3 Provide a rationale for screening and progress monitoring, including how these practices influence decision making about interventions.

2.4 Discuss the approaches to implementing interventions for students within an RTI or MTSS model and consider issues such as culturally linguistically diverse students, the role of parents, and the role of the classroom teacher.

INTERVIEW: JANE JARRELL

Jane Jarrell has been a second-grade teacher at Horizon Elementary School for 6 years. She previously taught in two other states and as a veteran teacher has taught almost every grade from second through seventh. Because of her experience and training with students with special needs, she often has several students with disabilities in her class.

Jane makes the following comments:

> What I like about teaching at Horizon is the student population. I enjoy working with culturally and linguistically diverse students, and this school attracts a range of students from different socioeconomic groups as well as racial backgrounds. I also like that many of the teachers I work with have been here for more than 5 years and share the same passion I have for teaching. Additionally, the principal (Mr. Johnston) serves as the curriculum leader and provides new instructional directions. That's why when Mr. Johnston asked me to work with him and several other teachers to design the RTI model for their school, I was eager to participate.
>
> After reading the recommendations from the State Department of Education and checking online with several key resources (**RTI action network** [www.rtinetwork.org] and **National Association of State Directors of Special Education** [www.nasdese.org]), we established the following as our primary goals:
>
> a. Improve the overall instruction for all students in reading and math.
> b. Establish a schoolwide behavior support plan that would promote positive behavior throughout the school.
> c. Screen all students at least twice a year for learning difficulties in reading and math.
> d. Provide ongoing intervention for students with learning difficulties.
> e. Use data from students' response to intervention as a means of improving instruction and as an information source for referral and identification for special education.

Jane worked with the principal and a few other teachers to establish a mechanism for assuring that all educators in the school had the knowledge and skills to implement the RTI school model. This required ongoing professional development (e.g., collecting and using data to improve outcomes for students), establishing a guide for implementation (e.g., selecting and using screening tools, providing interventions across the grade levels), and determining how data would be collected to influence referral and placement in special education. Jane summarizes where they are this way: "I'm excited about having a schoolwide model that provides early and ongoing support to all students. I think we can really make a difference, and I have renewed commitment to making sure the reading and math instruction for all students is as successful as it can be."

Introduction

In this chapter, we use the terms *response to intervention* (RTI) and *multitiered systems of support* (MTSS) similarly for describing the issues

CHAPTER OUTLINE

and challenges of implementing response to intervention and multitiered systems of support. Furthermore, we discuss how practices implemented within RTI models can help you address the special needs of students with learning and behavior problems in your classroom. Many states refer to their models as RTI models, and several states refer to them as multitiered systems of support (e.g., Kansas and Florida). However, the general principles that are described in this chapter apply whether the term RTI or MTSS is applied.

As you think about your role as a classroom teacher, what are some of the challenges that you encounter? One concern that many teachers have is whether they are able to adequately meet the instructional needs of all the students in their classes. You are aware that whatever grade you are assigned to teach, the students in your class represent academic achievement levels that are on grade level, below grade level, and above grade level. Also, if you teach students in fifth grade or older, many of their instructional needs or learning gaps may be significant and they may have negative self-perceptions about their success as learners. Many educators perceive that although special education may be available to serve students with disabilities, there are many other students with learning needs who do not qualify for special education and yet require interventions to succeed in reading, writing, and math. What are some possible solutions to this dilemma? One solution that is recommended in the reauthorization of the Individuals with Disabilities Education Act (IDEA), the Individuals with Disabilities Education Improvement Act (IDEIA 2004), is to implement a **response-to-intervention (RTI)** model as a means of preventing learning and behavior difficulties. RTI is the recommended model for screening students and using their response to intervention as a data source to facilitate identifying students who need special education services (Fuchs & Vaughn, 2012).

Prior to IDEIA, how were students with learning disabilities identified? Students with learning disabilities were most often identified by determining their potential or ability, usually with an intelligence test, and comparing that with their academic achievement, typically measured by reading or math tests. One of the challenges with this approach is that students who were assessed as being low in both ability and achievement could not qualify for special education services unless they were so low they were determined to have a cognitive disability. This process had many difficulties, including (a) overreliance on IQ measures and (b) the requirement to wait for a discrepancy between IQ and achievement (e.g., math or reading performance), which might have meant that students would not be provided services until too late in their education.

RTI was presented in IDEIA as a potential solution to these difficulties. How does RTI address these challenges? School districts and/or state departments of education recommend that teachers use early screening and intervention as a means of determining students' success and thus subsequent needs. Students who are identified through screening as "at risk" are provided enhanced instruction, typically through what might be called a Tier 1 intervention. Students who respond well to these interventions do not require subsequent support, whereas students whose response to interventions (e.g., supplemental reading instruction for 30 minutes a day) is low may be provided additional supplemental instruction or an alternative more intensive intervention (Tier 3). In addition, the data gathered as a result of monitoring student progress, or **progress monitoring**, might be used to assist in the referral and identification for special education.

As a result of the recommended use of RTI, eligibility and identification criteria for the category of learning disability are described as follows (IDEIA 2004; reauthorization [614(b)(6)(A)-(B)]):

When determining whether a child has a specific learning disability:

- The LEA (local education agency) is not required to consider a severe discrepancy between achievement and intellectual ability.
- The LEA may use a process that determines if a student responds to scientific, research-based intervention as part of the evaluation.

Therefore, RTI may help identify students with learning disabilities by replacing discrepancy criteria and using students' responses to intervention as a source of information in the identification process.

2.1 PAST AND PRESENT CHALLENGES: THE NEED FOR RTI

In the past, when students first showed signs of struggling, the prevailing approach was to wait and hope that their progress would improve over time. The idea was that students might simply be slow to achieve academically because of normal developmental or experiential differences, and that it would be a disservice to assess them prematurely and place them in special education. Yet students who struggled were provided with few avenues for extra support. For many of these students, their instructional needs were not adequately addressed and they demonstrated even more significant learning problems in later grades. Also, young students who were evaluated for possible special education placement sometimes had not yet exhibited enough of a discrepancy between their ability and their achievement to qualify for special education services. For these reasons, this approach was often referred to as the "wait to fail" model.

RTI is different. All students are screened early, often as early as kindergarten, to identify at-risk students, and the progress is assessed frequently so that those students who do not seem to be making adequate progress are provided with timely interventions, before they have a chance to fall further behind. Thus, RTI is a *prevention and intervention model* at the younger grades, that is, preschool through grade 3. However, for students in older grades, grade 4 or above, including secondary grades, RTI is a remediation model whereby the focus is less on preventing academic and behavioral difficulties and more on remediating them. As you read this chapter, think about what these changes mean for classroom teachers and their students.

2.1.1 Previous Identification Procedures

Over the past 30 years, the field of learning disabilities has struggled with numerous challenges related to its definition and identification procedures. These challenges include:

- An increase of more than 200% in identification since the category was established—although in the last decade the prevalence of learning disabilities has been more stable.
- Questionable procedures regarding reliability of determining learning disabilities through emphasis on IQ–achievement discrepancy and processing disorders.

- Students identified using a "wait to fail" model rather than a prevention–early intervention model.
- Excessive subjectivity in student referral for services, with teachers' perceptions of students' performance often determining who was referred for special education. RTI provides data from response to intervention to influence referral and placement.
- Students' opportunities to learn not adequately considered during the referral and identification process.
- Considerable variation from state to state concerning identification procedures and prevalence rates for learning disabilities.
- Little emphasis on the use of research-based practices in content area instruction and identification procedures.
- An identification process that provides little information to guide instructional decision making.
- Problematic assessment practices, particularly for culturally and linguistically diverse students.
- Disproportionate numbers of culturally and linguistically diverse students inappropriately identified for and served in special education.

These challenges to the traditional model for identifying students with learning disabilities illustrate the importance of implementing an RTI or MTSS model as a means of screening, monitoring, intervening early, and using data for decision making regarding referral and placement in special education. RTI models resolve many of these challenges by providing early and ongoing screening of students with early intervention and using data to facilitate decision making for identification.

The overview in Table 2.1 compares identification of students with learning disabilities before IDEIA 2004 to the identification process with RTI.

2.1.2 Initiatives Influencing RTI

Over the past decade, several initiatives set the stage for changes in how we think about students with disabilities and RTI. First, in August 2001, the Office of Special Education Programs brought together leading researchers to discuss numerous issues related to identifying learning disabilities (Bradley, Danielson, & Hallahan, 2002). The team reached consensus on principles related to learning disabilities and the eventual use of RTI to facilitate more appropriate identification of students with learning disabilities:

- Learning disabilities is a valid construct that represents a lifespan disorder.
- Individuals with learning disabilities require a special education.
- The exact prevalence of learning disabilities is unknown; however, the rate is likely between 2% and 5%.
- The use of IQ–achievement discrepancy is not adequate for identifying students with learning disabilities.
- Linking processing disabilities to learning disabilities has not been adequately established; also, most processing disabilities are difficult to measure and link to treatment.
- The use of reliable and valid data from progress monitoring is a promising addition to identifying individuals with learning disabilities.
- Much is known about effective interventions for students with learning disabilities, and yet ineffective interventions continue to be used.

Second, the President's Commission on Excellence in Special Education held public hearings throughout the United States and received hundreds of written comments (*A New Era: Revitalizing Special Education for Children and Their Families*, 2002) about the state of special education in the nation's education system. The commission concluded that special educators were spending too much time on paperwork and not enough time teaching. The commission also noted that general education and special education seemed

Table 2.1 • Identifying Students with Learning Disabilities Prior to IDEIA 2004 and with RTI

PRIOR TO IDEIA 2004	RTI
No universal screening.	All students are screened.
Little progress monitoring or progress monitoring for special education students only.	Progress monitoring assesses whether at-risk and special education students are reaching goals—multiple data points are collected over an extended period of time across different tiers of intervention. Progress monitoring is used with all students with learning and behavior difficulties.
"Wait to fail" model—students frequently not provided with interventions until they have qualified for special education.	Students are provided with interventions at the first sign they are struggling; there is an increased focus on proactive responses to students' difficulties.
Focus on within-child problems or deficits.	Ecological focus. Systems approach to problem solving, focused on instruction and interventions varied in time, intensity, and focus.
Clear eligibility criteria (i.e., a child either did or did not qualify for special education services). Categorical approach—targeted, intensive interventions typically not provided unless a student was found eligible for special education.	Tiered model of service delivery with interventions provided to all students who demonstrate a need for support, regardless of whether they have a disability label.
Multidisciplinary team mostly made up of special education professionals; individual students typically referred by classroom teachers with academic and/or behavioral concerns.	Intervention or problem-solving teams include general and special educators; teams consider progress-monitoring data and all students who are not reaching benchmarks.
Reliance on assessments, particularly standardized tests.	Collaborative educational decisions based on ongoing school, classroom, and individual student data; adjustments to instruction/intervention based on data.
Assessment data collected during a limited number of sessions.	Multiple data points collected over time and in direct relationship to the intervention provided.
"Comprehensive evaluation" consisting mainly of formal assessments conducted by individual members of the multidisciplinary team, often the same battery of tests administered to all referred children.	"Full and individualized evaluation" relies heavily on existing data collected throughout the RTI process; evaluation includes a student's response to specific validated interventions and other data gathered through observations, teacher and parent checklists, and diagnostic assessments.
Learning disability (LD) construct of "unexpected underachievement" indicated by low achievement as compared to a measure of the child's ability (e.g., IQ–achievement discrepancy).	LD construct of "unexpected underachievement" indicated by low achievement and insufficient response to validated interventions that work with most students ("true peers"), even struggling ones.

Source: From S. Vaughn (2013), *Strategies for teaching students with learning and behavior problems*, Boston: Allyn & Bacon.

to be operating as two separate systems rather than as a coherent whole. In the report, the commission recommended shifting to a prevention model that takes into account the fact that students with disabilities are also part of general education, and that requires special and general educators to work together more closely.

Third, the National Research Council report on the disproportionate representation of culturally and linguistically diverse students in special education provided similar recommendations to those proposed by the Office of Special Education (Donovan & Cross, 2002). The council promoted widespread use of early screening and intervention practices and RTI models. The council's premise was that if schoolwide behavior and early reading programs help culturally and linguistically diverse students receive the support they need and improve their opportunities to learn, then the number of students who exhibit ongoing problems will decrease and the students who continue to struggle will more likely be those who require special education.

2.1.3 The Individuals with Disabilities Education Improvement Act (IDEIA 2004)

Using information from these initiatives, Congress passed the Individuals with Disabilities Education Improvement Act (IDEIA 2004). The new law promoted RTI as a means for preventing learning difficulties and furthering accurate identification of students with learning disabilities. Furthermore, Congress urged the use of *early intervening services* (EIS) to provide students with support as soon as they show signs of struggling. The IDEIA 2004:

- Recommends using alternative approaches to identifying students with learning disabilities, but does not require abandoning use of the IQ–achievement discrepancy criterion.
- Urges early screening and early intervention so that students who show signs of struggling do not fall further behind.
- Recommends a **multitiered intervention strategy** or **multitiered system of support (MTSS)**, which is a set of layers of instruction that increase in intensity (e.g., amount of instruction, group size) based on how well students are succeeding in a less intensive instructional format. The first tier in a multitiered intervention approach is typically the classroom instruction; the second tier is often additional targeted instruction that may be provided by the classroom teacher; and a third tier is provided for students whose response to Tier 2 was inadequate, requiring a more intensive instruction (e.g., longer amount of time, smaller group, and more customized instruction), often provided by a trained person or a specialist such as the special education teacher. Students with significant gaps in learning may bypass Tier 2 and receive intensive Tier 3 intervention.
- Provides flexibility in the number of tiers of support implemented. Schools and districts vary on the number of tiers of instruction in an MTSS model. Why is there variation in the number of tiers of instruction? Some schools and districts prefer to refer to each intervention cycle as a tier of support. For example, in some schools, students remain in Tier 2 as long as they are receiving adequate support. In other schools, students are provided a time framework for receiving Tier 2 support and then move to subsequent tiers if they need additional support. Districts may have as many as five or six levels of support, though the majority have three or four tiers of support.
- Asks districts to review practices to accelerate learning so that students make adequate progress in special education.
- Recommends ongoing systematic progress monitoring of students' responses to high-quality, research-based interventions. Progress monitoring provides frequent assessments of how students are learning target knowledge or skills to determine if their response to instruction is adequate.
- Requires better integration of services between general and special education.
- Emphasizes the role of context when referring, identifying, and serving students in special education.

Response-to-Intervention (RTI) overview by state

Figure 2.1 provides an overview of the practices related to RTI that are used by states. In addition to the information provided in Figure 2.1, Zirkel (2011) reports that fifteen states fully or partially require the use of RTI for identification of students with LD, including Colorado, Connecticut, Delaware, Florida, Georgia, Idaho, Illinois, Iowa, Louisiana, Maine, New Mexico, New York, Rhode Island, West Virginia, and Wisconsin.

There was a strong rationale in support of RTI practices for several reasons, but the primary reason is to provide early and intensive interventions to all students in need, not just those with disabilities, and to allow all students access to research-based education to improve their learning outcomes. A second reason was to provide better-integrated support and services for individuals with disabilities. For example, a student with a learning disability who is included in the general education classroom may also have a speech and language specialist, be taught in reading and math by the special education teacher, have opportunities during the day to work with the Title I reading teacher, and also meet with the school psychologist once or twice a month. One of the goals of RTI is to promote teacher collaboration, integrate services, and eliminate settings in which general

FIGURE 2.1 **Response-to-Intervention (RTI) model recommended by state**

GUIDANCE ON RTI	STATE MODEL DEVELOPED	DEVELOPING MODEL	NO MODEL SPECIFIED
California	Arizona	Alabama	Alaska
Illinois	Delaware	Arkansas	New Jersey
Maine	Florida	Colorado	South Carolina
Maryland	Georgia	Connecticut	
Massachusetts	Iowa	Hawaii	
Missouri	Kansas	Idaho	
North Dakota	Louisiana	Indiana	
Tennessee	Nebraska	Kentucky	
Texas	North Carolina	Michigan	
Virginia	Ohio	Minnesota	
	Oregon	Mississippi	
	Pennsylvania	Montana	
	Utah	Nevada	
	Washington	New Hampshire	
	West Virginia	New Mexico	
		New York	
		Oklahoma	
		Rhode Island	
		South Dakota	
		Vermont	
		Wisconsin	
		Wyoming	

Source: From "Implementation of response to intervention: A snapshot of progress," by S. Berkeley, W. N. Bender, L. G. Peaster, & L. Saunders, 2009, *Journal of Learning Disabilities, 42*(1), 85–95.

education teachers do "their thing" and special education teachers are quite separate and disconnected.

MyEdLab **Self-Check 2.1**

2.2 COMPONENTS OF RESPONSE TO INTERVENTION

RTI is considered an instructional model or framework for preventing learning difficulties in the early grades and a remediation framework for enhancing outcomes in academics and behavior in the older grades (upper elementary and secondary grades). What are the critical components of an RTI model or framework? Fundamentally, there are many frameworks for implementing RTI, not just one. However, within these multiple frameworks, there are critical components that everyone agrees are essential. These are:

- *Screening and progress monitoring.* To understand the role of screening and progress monitoring, consider, for example, that M. L. King elementary school screens all students at the beginning of the year to determine if they are on progress in reading and math. This screening takes about 5 to 10 minutes for reading and about the same time for math depending upon students' skills and is done individually by the classroom teacher. Teachers frequently assess the progress of at-risk students to ensure that the intervention is working to close learning gaps, usually every 2 or 3 weeks.

- *Implementation of effective classroom instructional practices so that all students have an opportunity to learn (Tier 1).* One of the fundamental components of an RTI framework is that classroom instruction is research-based and associated with high learning outcomes for the majority of students; thus, students who are not successful are not casualties of poor classroom instruction but have difficulties that require intervention.
- *Provision of secondary intervention (Tier 2).* This tier is for students who are not making adequate progress in the classroom. These students are provided additional instruction, ideally in small, homogeneous groups of three to five students, three to five times per week for 20 to 30 minutes each session. The purpose of the supplementary intervention is to provide additional instruction targeted at increasing proficiency in the target area of reading, math, or writing. It is important to remember that this instruction is in addition to and does not replace what students are currently receiving in their target area, for example, reading.
- *Provision of a more intensive individualized intervention (Tier 3).* This tier is for students for whom secondary intervention is inadequate. Some students do not benefit sufficiently even when provided a Tier 2 or secondary intervention. These students require an even more intensive intervention (e.g., longer instructional sessions, smaller group, instruction more specifically aligned with their learning needs).

What about students with disabilities? How are they provided specialized services within an RTI framework? Students who are considered for special education may be provided services within Tier 3 or within a fourth tier of intervention depending on the instructional framework used by the school or district. Their special education teachers may co-teach with the general education teacher, or model strategies that work with both special education students and at-risk students. Special education teachers also may assist with problem solving when at-risk students are not adequately responding to intervention. As specified in Chapter 1, students with disabilities are provided services as specified in their IEP and aligned with the continuum of services.

RTI is a schoolwide model that typically starts with students in kindergarten and may continue throughout the elementary grades or even into secondary grades in some districts. Although no one single model is accepted as the "gold standard," RTI models commonly include four key components (Fuchs, Fuchs, & Vaughn, 2008; Fuchs & Vaughn, 2012; Kovaleski & VanDerHeyden, 2013; Vaughn & Fuchs, 2003). What are the key components?

1. *Implement high-quality, research-based instruction matched to the needs of students.* Only instructional practices that generally produce high learning rates for students are used, as demonstrated by scientific research. The implementation of high-quality instructional practices as interventions is intended to increase the probability of positive student responses. Whether you are teaching reading or math at the elementary level or secondary content, the instructional programs, materials, and practices you use should be selected based on the best research available rather than your own ideology or perspective. The use of high-quality, research-based instruction is utilized across all tiers of instruction, including general classroom instruction.
2. *Monitor students' learning over time to determine their level and rate of performance (for ongoing decision making).* Educators periodically assess all students' learning to determine if they are making progress toward meeting expected benchmarks at a rate commensurate with their peers. Students who do not seem to be progressing are provided with extra assistance in the form of interventions targeted to their needs. What does this mean for you as an educator? Consider your expectations and goals for learning each week. Create a brief assessment that will help you determine

what students know about what you are teaching that week. At the end of the week (or two), use the assessment again to determine how much students have learned. Use this information for reteaching in Tier 1 and/or making decisions about additional intervention. In a more formal way, students' learning is monitored using reading and math assessments that are administered four to six times a year to all students and more frequently for students with learning difficulties.

3. *Provide interventions of increasing intensity when students continue to struggle.* Reducing group size, increasing time, and/or making sure that interventions are even more carefully customized to the students' instructional needs are all ways to increase the intensity of instruction. Providing additional opportunities for students to practice to automaticity also increases intensity. Determine what options for providing intervention are available. Typically, schools provide additional interventions for elementary students in math and reading. It may also be possible to provide additional supports in spelling and writing. For older students, additional reading classes or after-school tutoring may be available. As another option, consider how you might restructure and regroup students so that you can provide additional instruction to those students with the highest needs. Be sure to collaborate with after-school teachers to provide at-risk students with more opportunities to practice the strategies they are learning in intervention.
4. *Make educational decisions based on data.* Decisions about selecting instructional interventions, the intensity of the interventions (e.g., how much time each day and in what group size the intervention is provided), and the duration of the interventions (e.g., 2 weeks, 8 weeks) are based on students' responses to the interventions. As you examine students' performance based on data that is collected more frequently for students with more intensive needs (e.g., weekly or biweekly assessments), consider instructional adjustments that you could make to ensure that all students have improved outcomes. Also consider whether selected students would benefit from additional intervention instruction.

TECH TIPS

Using Technology to Implement RTI

A key objective of RTI is to select an instructional strategy to match a student's specific needs. Universal design, authoring software, and assessment software are aspects of technology that can facilitate RTI. The concept of universal design can be applied to instructional materials to meet the varied needs of all learners—appealing to different learning styles, methods of input, learner backgrounds, strengths, and abilities. Such classroom materials may have varying levels of difficulty, multiple means of input, various modes of presentation, and features to customize pace and feedback.

The following websites provide helpful information on RTI and tools for progress monitoring:

- **Intervention Central** (www.interventioncentral.org): useful free tools to implement the RTI model.
- **National Center on Student Progress Monitoring** (www.studentprogress.org): information about scientifically based progress-monitoring practices.
- **National Center on Intensive Interventions** (www.intensiveintervention.org): provides information about how to select and use intensive interventions for students with persistent academic and behavioral needs.
- **National Center on Response to Intervention** (www.rti4success.org): information on RTI and early intervention services.
- **Progress-Monitoring Tools** (http://www.rti4success.org/resource/progress-monitoring-tools-chart): provides commercially available progress-monitoring tools.
- **TechMatrix** (www.techmatrix.org): assists teachers in identifying educational or assistive technology for students in mathematics, reading, writing, and science.

Authoring software provides opportunities for teachers to customize lessons and simple assessments, such as the following program:

- **Classroom Suite 4** from Intellitools, Inc. (www.intellitools.com) includes a talking word processor, a math authoring component with digital manipulatives, and a multimedia authoring environment. The package includes many easy-to-use templates and customizable premade activities.

To learn about useful software and online assessment tools, see the Tech Tip "Using Technology to Implement RTI." These tools will help you better understand and implement an RTI model.

2.2.1 Progress Monitoring within the RTI Framework

Progress monitoring involves frequent and ongoing measurement of student knowledge and skills *and* the examination of student data to inform instruction. Used with a few students or the entire class, progress monitoring is essential to effective implementation of RTI because it allows key stakeholders, such as the classroom teacher and specialists, to determine the rate of growth students are making and to determine whether additional intervention is needed. Another critical purpose of progress monitoring is to use the data from students' performance to adjust instruction and influence the intensity of students' intervention (e.g., guide movement between the tiers of instruction). To better understand why and how to use progress monitoring, see Tips for Teachers 2.1.

2.2.2 Tiers of Intervention: Multitiered Systems of Support (MTSS)

Response-to-intervention models often describe levels of instruction or intervention in terms of "tiers." Typically, tiers represent the level of intensity of instruction provided to a student or group of students. However, the number of tiers—or layers of intensity offered to students with learning and behavior difficulties—is not specified. That is why the language of multitiered systems of support (MTSS) is often used.

TIPS FOR TEACHERS 2.1

Using Progress Monitoring in the Classroom

Why Use Progress Monitoring?

- To keep track of student learning
- To identify students who need additional help
- To assist in arranging small-group instruction
- To design instruction that meets individual student needs
- To refer and identify students for special education based on data gathered during progress monitoring
- To facilitate decisions about movement between tiers of instruction, e.g., from Tier 2 to Tier 3

How Do I Monitor Student Progress?

- Assess all students at the beginning of the year in the critical areas for their grade level.
- Use assessments to identify students who need extra help and to create goals for learning. Once you determine which students require extra help, you can plan small-group instruction and intervention.
- Monitor the progress of at-risk students in small groups more frequently (weekly or monthly) in the specific skill or area being worked on.
- Assess progress by comparing learning goals with actual student progress. Students who are making adequate progress should still be assessed approximately three times a year to ensure that they are learning and continue to achieve at grade level.

What Are the Benefits of Progress Monitoring?

- Increased learning because instructional decisions are based on student data
- Frequent progress monitoring that allows teachers to adjust instruction and stay on course to meet students' learning goals
- Improved instruction aligned with students' learning
- Improved accountability
- Better communication about student progress with family and other professionals
- Higher expectations for low-achieving students
- More accurate referral and identification for special education

The expectation is that most students will participate in Tier 1—which is high-quality, research-based instruction. Students with learning difficulties not meeting expectations move through Tiers 2 and 3 as the intensity of the interventions they receive increases. Some models include three tiers, and others include a fourth tier. In schools that have research-based reading programs in place, for example, approximately 80% of all learners make adequate progress in Tier 1, 15% to 20% may require some supplemental instruction in Tier 2, and about 5 to 6% need the intensive intervention implemented in Tier 3.

How do we make intervention more intense? One way is to decrease the number of students in a group to give them more opportunities for direct, explicit instruction. This allows students more opportunities to respond and receive immediate corrective feedback, and more opportunities to practice to automaticity. Other ways are to increase amount of time in the intervention sessions, for example, from 30 minutes to 40 minutes, or to increase the frequency of the sessions, for example, from five times a week to seven.

Primary instruction, Tier 1

What distinguishes Tier 1 from all of the other tiers of instruction? The primary distinction is that Tier 1 involves all students. For example, in a fourth-grade reading class, the reading instruction provided to all of the students in the class is referred to as Tier 1 instruction, or the math instruction provided to all seventh graders would be considered Tier 1 math instruction.

In Tier 1, general education teachers provide evidence-based instruction to all students in the class. The instruction must be evidenced-based so that when students are not making adequate progress and secondary intervention or Tier 2 instruction is provided, we know that the students have had an adequate opportunity to learn.

What do classroom teachers do during Tier 1 instruction? Classroom teachers or support personnel screen students using easy-to-administer screening measures that are selected for the grade level they are teaching. Typically, screening takes less than 10 minutes per student and can be done at the beginning, middle, and end of the year. Teachers use the screening data to form groups for small-group instruction. Students who are having difficulty in reading or math are administered progress-monitoring measures regularly to determine their progress. Teachers differentiate instruction as needed and strive to provide appropriate, effective instruction for their students. In some schools, classroom teachers are also responsible for providing Tier 2 interventions for students in their class with difficulties.

Secondary intervention, Tier 2

Tier 2 intervention is provided for those students who are not making adequate progress in Tier 1—in other words, those who are not making adequate progress in instruction. Tier 2 interventions are typically provided in small groups with the intention of providing additional instruction that will allow the student to make adequate progress in Tier 1 instruction without further intervention. Tier 2 interventions *supplement* rather than supplant the core curriculum taught in Tier 1 general education classrooms and are intended to reinforce the concepts and skills taught there. Yet the support that students receive in Tier 2 is still under the domain of general education. It is *not* special education. All children who appear to be struggling, as evidenced by their slow rate of progress and low assessment scores, are entitled to this support. Researchers refer to this consideration of both the rate of progress and absolute levels of learning as a dual discrepancy (Fuchs, Fuchs, & Speece, 2002; Hughes & Dexter, 2011).

MyEdLab
Video Example 2.1.
Watch this video and listen to an intervention specialist share her experiences about students with special needs. Do you think this specialist would be best working as a Tier 1, 2, or 3 intervention specialist and why?

Who provides the Tier 2 intervention? Practices for implementing Tier 2 intervention vary considerably by district and school. In some schools, personnel are hired and trained to provide the Tier 2 intervention to students while in other schools, classroom teachers are expected to provide the Tier 2 intervention. Teachers continue to monitor the progress of students while they are receiving Tier 2 support. Tier 2 interventions are provided for a fixed duration (e.g., 10 weeks). After this time, educators examine progress-monitoring results and other data to answer the following questions:

- Is the student making adequate progress and should he or she return to Tier 1–only instruction?
- Is the student making some but not sufficient progress to move to Tier 1, thereby necessitating that he or she receive another dose of Tier 2 intervention?
- Is the student making very little progress, thereby requiring either adjustments in her or his instruction (Tier 1 and Tier 2) or perhaps an adjustment in supplemental instruction so that the instruction is both more intense and customized (Tier 3)?

Tertiary intervention, Tier 3

Tier 3 intervention is provided to those students who continue to experience difficulties and show minimal progress during secondary or Tier 2 interventions or for students who demonstrate significant learning needs requiring Tier 3 or more intensive interventions immediately. Typically, the majority of students who require intervention benefit from Tier 2, or secondary interventions, and do not require a more customized intensive intervention (Tier 3). Tier 3 interventions are typically provided in smaller groups for a longer time period and more frequently than Tier 2 interventions. Usually students who are provided more intensive interventions such as Tier 3 continue in their Tier 1 instruction, but are not simultaneously provided Tier 2–type intervention. Depending on the number of tiers in the RTI model, this tier may or may not be special education. Tier 3 students receive explicit instruction individually or in small groups of two or three students. (See Figure 2.2 for a description of how Tiers 2 and 3 might compare.)

Additional tiers of intervention, Tier 4 and beyond

While the prevailing model for RTI is a three- or four-tier framework, there are schools and districts that provide even more tiers of instruction. The general idea is that each of these tiers of instruction refers to more intensive or responsive instructional levels designed to meet the learning or behavior needs of students. For some districts, each round of a Tier 2 type of intervention is referred to as Tier 2 even when students are provided the instruction for more than the typical 12 to 20 weeks. For other schools and districts, each round (e.g., 12 to 20 weeks of Tier 2 intervention) is sequentially numbered so that students may be in Tier 4 but still provided a secondary or Tier 2–type intervention; the Tier 4 indicates that they have been in intervention for an extensive time.

FIGURE 2.2 **How do Tier 2 and Tier 3 differ?**

	TIER 2 INSTRUCTION	TIER 3 INSTRUCTION
Daily instruction	20 to 30 minutes per day **(plus Tier 1)**	40 to 50 minutes per day **(plus Tier 1)**
Duration	10 to 12 weeks for 1 round **(1–2 rounds)**	10 to 12 weeks (the number of rounds of treatment varies based on students' needs and/or disabilities)
Group size	Small group	Smallest group possible/individual
Ongoing progress monitoring	Every 2 weeks	Weekly
Curriculum	Research-based—typically a standardized treatment	Research-based—typically customization of a standardized approach
Instructor	Classroom teacher or supervised instructional assistance	Specialist

MyEdLab **Self-Check 2.2**

MyEdLab **Application Exercise 2.1:** Implementing RTI

2.3 UNIVERSAL SCREENING AND PROGRESS MONITORING

Universal screening in reading and math is an essential component of RTI models at the Tier 1 level. Universal screening involves administering the same test to all students to determine who is likely to be at risk for academic difficulties, in the same way that schools have checked children's vision for years to screen students for potential problems. In many schools, screening is carried out three times a year: in the fall, winter, and spring. Screening instruments usually have few items and are short in duration. Screening is used to determine whether students are making adequate progress or additional testing is needed. Schoolwide academic screening was rarely implemented with previous models. Instead, it was typically the classroom teacher who first noticed that students were struggling and referred them for an evaluation. Invariably some students were overlooked. With universal screening, however, everyone is tested.

What is an example of universal screening? Texas provides universal screening in reading for all students in kindergarten through second grade. The classroom teacher conducts the screening, and the most frequently used screening measure is the Texas Primary Reading Inventory (TPRI, 2014; www.tpri.org) or in Spanish, Tejas LEE (www.tpri.org). The TPRI was developed and used to screen Texas students; this diagnostic instrument provides information on a student's reading/language arts development (from kindergarten through third grade). There is a quick screening that takes just a few minutes and is individually administered by the classroom teacher. Students' performance on the quick screen assists teachers in deciding whether a more diagnostic assessment would provide the necessary information to help teachers design instruction. The screening and assessment tool helps teachers decide for which of the critical elements in reading (e.g., phonics, fluency, and comprehension) the student needs additional instruction and even provides lessons to facilitate decision making about what instruction should be provided.

Universal screening is also a quick way to identify general performance levels and determine whether students are on track to developing proficiency in the fundamental skills of reading and math. We know much more than we used to about how to predict future reading levels, for example, using phonological awareness and rapid naming tasks. Thus, we can determine with some accuracy which students are at risk and require additional intervention (Spencer, Wagner et al., 2014). Foorman and Ciancio (2005) point out that "the purpose of early screening could be identifying students *not* at risk so that instructional objectives can be established for students potentially at risk" (p. 494). Screening also provides valuable information about class performance and identifies teachers who might need further professional development. Once students have been identified as needing additional assistance using a screening measure, interventions are provided.

Numerous assessments can be used as screening instruments (see Table 2.2 for a list of possible reading measures).

Some tests assess only one or two elements of reading (such as the C-TOPP, which only tests phonological processing), whereas others tap into several reading components. Some are quite quick to administer, such as the TOWRE, and others take much longer, such as the QRI-4 (Rathvon, 2004).

2.3.1 Using Screening to Make Educational Decisions

Screening is useful for providing quick information at the classroom or group level as well as at the student level. When all of the students in a school are screened, school administrators can examine assessment results for patterns across as well as within classrooms.

Table 2.2 • Possible Screening Measures for Reading

ASSESSMENT	PUBLISHER AND WEBSITE	GRADES OR AGES	ORAL LANGUAGE	PHONEMIC AWARENESS	PHONICS	WORD IDENTIFICATION	FLUENCY	VOCABULARY	COMPREHENSION	COMMENTS
AIMS web Curriculum-Based Measurement (CBM)	Edformation www .aimsweb.com	K–12	No	Yes	Yes	No	Yes	No	Yes	Offers web-based data management
Basic Early Assessment of Reading (BEAR)	Riverside www .riverpub.com	K–3	No	Yes	Yes	Yes	Yes	Yes	Yes	Pencil/ paper and computerized versions
Comprehensive Test of Phonological Processing (C-TOPP)	PRO-ED www .proedinc.com	K–3	No	Yes	No	No	No	No	No	Phonological processing only
Dynamic Indicators of Basic Early Literacy Skills (DIBELS)	Sopris West/ Cambium www .dibelsassessment .com	K–3, 4–6	No	Yes	Yes	No	Yes	No	Yes (4–6 only)	Grade 4–6 students assessed only in fluency and comprehension
Fox in a Box–2	CTB McGraw-Hill www.ctb.com	PreK–3	Yes	Yes	Yes	Yes	Yes	Yes	Yes	Includes pre-K
Qualitative Reading Inventory–4 (QRI-4)	Pearson Publisher	K–12	No	Yes	No	Yes	Yes	No	Yes	Informal assessment instrument
Slosson Oral Reading Test (SORT-R3)	Slosson www .slosson.com	K–12	No	No	No	Yes	No	No	No	Word ID only
Scholastic Reading Inventory (SRI)	Scholastic Teacher	K–12	No	No	No	No	No	No	Yes	Computer adaptive; includes data management system
Test of Early Reading Ability (TERA-3)	Pearson PRO-ED www.proedinc.com	Ages 3.6–8.6	No	No	No	Yes	No	Yes	Yes	Assesses letter knowledge and environmental print
Texas Primary Reading Inventory (TPRI)	Texas Education Agency www.tpri .org	K–2	Yes	Yes	Yes	Yes	Yes	Yes	Yes	Includes screening section and inventory section
Test of Word Reading Efficiency (TOWRE)	Pearson http:// ags.pearson. assessments.com	Ages 6.0–24.11	No	No	Yes	Yes	No	No	No	Pseudo-word reading and word ID only
Test of Silent Word Reading Efficiency-2 (TOSWRE, 2014)	Allen, Morey, Hammill; PRO-ED Publishers	6–24								

Although there are many advantages to early screening, screening measures in the early grades (kindergarten, first grade, and second grade) result in high levels of classification accuracy. Progress monitoring along with screening is needed to increase classification accuracy.

How can schoolwide screening assist schools? Problems that are widespread across grade levels can be identified and addressed through professional development. Or it could be that most of the students in the majority of classrooms do well, whereas in one or two classrooms a lot of students seem to be struggling. In this case, support at the teacher level, such as someone who can model research-based strategies or ways to increase student engagement, can improve student outcomes. When the data indicates a classwide problem for which it may be most appropriate to provide interventions at the class level. When only a few students are struggling relative to their peers, then problems seem to be at an individual level, and individual interventions are warranted.

2.3.2 Using Progress Monitoring to Assess Students' Response to Interventions

Whereas screening is used to assess *all* students to determine who might need additional support, progress monitoring is applied with individual students to assess their response to interventions. Like screening measures, progress-monitoring instruments are quick to administer and focus on targeted skills in the core curriculum. The purposes of progress monitoring are to closely monitor students' progress, to develop profiles of students' learning, and to assess the effectiveness of interventions so that changes can be made if necessary. These data can be quite useful if children continue to struggle and the decision is made to conduct a comprehensive evaluation of their strengths and needs. Progress-monitoring measures are administered frequently, perhaps once a month, or as often as once a week in some cases. For a list of steps to follow in completing progress monitoring, see Tips for Teachers 2.2.

2.3.3 Implementing Interventions

After schools establish an approach to screening and monitoring students' progress, it is important to have a schoolwide plan for how students will be provided appropriate interventions if they are behind in reading and math. Although specific interventions are

TIPS FOR TEACHERS 2.2

Conducting Screening and Progress Monitoring

When screening students and conducting progress monitoring:

- Screen all students in the beginning and middle of the year.
- Rank students by grade level and by classroom. In other words, compile assessment results so that patterns of achievement within classrooms and across classrooms at every grade level can be examined.
- Identify at-risk students in each grade or classroom.
- Set individual goals to close learning gaps with at-risk learners.
- Form small groups of students with similar goals and instructional needs for intervention.
- Use frequent progress monitoring with students identified as low achievers. Progress monitoring might occur monthly or as often as every week, particularly for students with the greatest learning needs in targeted skills (e.g., oral reading fluency).
- Students who score at adequate levels or higher on the screening instrument can be assessed less frequently, for example, three times a year (e.g., in the fall, winter, and spring).
- Create graphs that provide visual displays of students' progress.
- Evaluate progress-monitoring data regularly using a systematic set of decision rules to determine whether interventions seem to be effective for individual students.
- Revise interventions as necessary in response to the data.
- Communicate students' progress with parents.

discussed in the reading and math chapters of this book, there are also issues related to whether students receiving interventions are provided a standard protocol or a problem-solving approach. Some researchers recommend a standard treatment protocol approach for Tier 2–type interventions (Fuchs, Fuchs, & Vaughn, 2008), recognizing that when students do not respond to these research-based protocols, more customized instructional approaches may be necessary to intensify instruction (Fuchs, Fuchs, & Vaughn, 2014). Others prefer a problem-solving model (Marston, Muyskens, Lau, & Canter, 2003). As the National Association of State Directors of Special Education noted, "Some ... have suggested that multitier systems might use *either* a problem-solving method ... *or* a standard treatment protocol approach. This is an artificial distinction. All RTI systems must consider implementing the best features of both approaches" (Batsche et al., 2005; Castillo, Batsche et al., 2012).

2.3.4 Standard Treatment Protocol

Ms. Tackett was a fourth-grade teacher working in a school that used an RTI model. During her first year in the school, the principal provided training for all of the kindergarten through fifth-grade teachers on a reading intervention program that had been selected by the school district to be used with students who demonstrated reading difficulties. Ms. Tackett was informed that because all students who were at risk for reading problems were being provided the same intervention program (variation within grade level), the school was using a standard treatment protocol model.

With the **standard treatment protocol model**, the same empirically validated treatments are used for all children with similar problems using a trial of specified duration (Fuchs & Fuchs, 2006). The standard treatment protocol provides opportunities for the teacher to respond to the learning needs of students but defines the program or approach that will be used for all students with learning difficulties. The interventions are chosen from those that have an evidence base, and instructional decisions follow a standard protocol. Possible approaches might include explicit instruction in phonological awareness or in phonics skills, fluency or comprehension interventions, or computer programs. Specific research-based interventions for students with similar difficulties are provided in a standardized format to ensure conformity of implementation. Proponents argue that this is the most research based of the approaches to RTI and leaves less room for error in professional judgment (Fuchs & Fuchs, 2008). It is important to note that with the implementation of a standard protocol approach teachers are expected to:

- Select an approach that is based on research that aligns with the target population of students.
- Respond to the learning needs of students and adjust instruction in terms of practice and feedback to assure students are making progress.
- Implement interventions with fidelity, but consider the individual learning needs of students during the implementation.

2.3.5 Problem-Solving Model

Mrs. Denton was a second-grade teacher who was working at a school that was implementing an RTI model throughout the elementary grades. She was asked to attend professional development on how to implement the problem-solving approach to providing intervention for students in her class with reading and math difficulties.

The problem-solving model is a more individualized or personalized approach. For each child who is not progressing, a problem-solving team—comprised of the classroom teacher, school psychologist, special education teacher, and any other key educational stakeholders (e.g., parent, speech and language therapist)—meets to consider all of the data available so that they can come up with an intervention plan for the child. Interventions are planned specifically for the targeted student and are provided over a reasonable period of time. The process typically follows these steps:

1. *Define the problem.* Ms. Chung, a fourth-grade teacher, indicated that Thomas was not making progress in math. He seemed easily distracted, did not complete his math work during class, did not participate in team problem solving during math, and had incomplete math homework consistently. She was confident that Thomas was going to fail fourth-grade math. The problem-solving team suggested that the school psychologist observe Thomas during class and meet with him afterward.
2. *Analyze the problem.* After viewing Thomas in the class, the school psychologist asked Ms. Chung to provide samples of Thomas's work over the past month. Both agreed that Thomas would benefit from small-group instruction in math for about 30 minutes every day. They thought that Thomas was making some progress but it was too slow, and they identified that when he was working in a small group he paid more attention.
3. *Develop a plan.* Several other fourth-grade students lacked progress in math, so they were assembled in a group that met every day with one of the fourth-grade teachers. They identified the materials and instructional approach that would be used and selected a math progress-monitoring measure to use each week. Furthermore, the Tier 1 or classroom instruction was adjusted to better meet the needs of the student.
4. *Implement the plan.* Thomas started the additional math instruction the following week and received supplemental math instruction daily. His progress in math was monitored every week and the data were retained in a file.
5. *Evaluate the plan.* After 10 weeks, the problem-solving team determined that Thomas was making very good progress, and the team attributed it to the additional instruction he was receiving. They projected that after about 10 more weeks of supplemental intervention he would be caught up with his classmates. The team agreed that both the adjustments to the Tier 1–classroom instruction and the intervention (Tier 2) were effective.

This approach maximizes problem-solving opportunities by allowing teams to be flexible. Mrs. Denton appreciated that her professional expertise was valued but realized that it took considerable time to attend meetings with other professionals and design effective interventions for the students in her class who were behind in reading and math. Ms. Chung appreciated the contributions of the problem-solving team and its recommendation to involve the school psychologist. Together, she felt that they had come up with a successful intervention for Thomas.

2.3.6 Differences Between the Standard Protocol and Problem-Solving Models

Ms. Tackett, Mrs. Denton, and Ms. Chung all taught at schools that were implementing RTI models, yet Ms. Tackett was implementing a standard protocol intervention and Mrs. Denton and Ms. Chung were implementing a problem-solving intervention for the students in their classes requiring interventions. Research suggests that both of the models can be effective, and in fact, most sites implement a hybrid in which aspects of each model are used (Tacket, 2009).

The fundamental difference between the standard treatment protocol and the problem-solving model is the extent to which decision-making teams engage in analyzing individual student data before selecting and implementing interventions (Burns & Gibbons, 2013; Christ, Burns, & Ysseldyke, 2005). With a standard treatment protocol, there is little examination of the reasons for a child's struggles. The rationale is that for secondary interventions, there is considerable evidence about what interventions are effective, and the best strategy is to implement an effective intervention. In contrast, the problem-solving model is more flexible. The emphasis is on individualized, targeted interventions based on an analysis of the learning context, environmental conditions, and instructional variables as well as on a student's progress-monitoring and other assessment data (Spear-Swerling, 2015; Tilly, Reschly, & Grimes, 1999; http://iris.peabody.vanderbilt.edu/rti01_overview/chalcycle.htm.)

2.3.7 Decision-Making Teams (Campus or RTI Leadership Teams)

How is the RTI model implemented within schools? Who takes the leadership role for directing RTI? The answers to these questions vary by school and district. It is common to have a team of professionals who work together to guide the RTI process at the school level. Campus leadership teams might have one or more committees, and membership might be flexible, depending on the expertise needed. Some schools have committees that focus on each aspect of the RTI model: Assessment, Instruction, Intervention, and Professional Development. They provide input into the design of the campus RTI model, and use student data to progress monitor and evaluate its implementation. You may be asked to be a committee member to provide insights into curriculum expectations and suggestions for what interventions might be effective with students, or you may be asked only to attend meetings that are relevant to students you teach. It is likely that you will be asked to conduct screening measures of reading and math and to use progress-monitoring measures to determine at-risk students' ongoing progress.

Campus leadership teams comprise members with relevant expertise. Ideally teams may have an expert in the targeted area of concern (e.g., reading, mathematics, behavior); one in administering and interpreting results of screening measures; and, for students receiving special education services, a team member with expertise in learning disabilities.

The overall purpose of the leadership team is to ensure that the RTI model in the school is implemented effectively and that all students who need additional support are identified early, provided appropriate interventions, and monitored over time. See Tips for Teachers 2.3 for more about how team members facilitate the RTI process.

Mr. Chan works in an elementary school in California. He describes how his campus leadership team works:

> When the majority of a class is progressing and about 20% or fewer of the students differ from their peers in rate of progress, then the role of the team is to determine which Tier 2 interventions to implement with students who are slower to respond. When students who are receiving Tier 2 interventions continue to experience difficulty, the decision-making team convenes to determine which steps to take next. The team might decide to try different Tier 2 interventions, or perhaps more intensive Tier 3 interventions. The team might decide to initiate a more comprehensive evaluation for possible special education identification.

TIPS FOR TEACHERS 2.3

How Campus Leadership Team Members Facilitate RTI

Members of the decision-making team facilitate the RTI process in several ways, including:

- Reviewing progress-monitoring data of students in interventions and for grade levels and the school as a whole.
- Observing classroom lessons to ensure that research-based instruction is occurring.
- Providing professional development to teachers and other key educators.
- Assisting with data collection and monitoring.
- Facilitating instructional decision making.
- Providing material and human resources to implement the RTI process.
- Organizing intervention groups and monitoring their effectiveness.
- Interpreting screening, progress monitoring, and other assessment data.
- Communicating with key stakeholders to be sure instructional and behavioral plans across treatments are aligned.

Mr. Chan's experience is similar to that of other teachers who are in schools using an RTI framework. It is important to clarify when due process requirements are applied. For screening and interventions provided to students in the general education program, parent permission is not needed. However, parents must be informed if their child is receiving intervention, and kept informed of their child's progress. They have the right to request an evaluation for special education at any time. When students are suspected of having a disability, due process safeguards apply and parents must provide permission for an evaluation to take place.

MyEdLab **Self-Check 2.3**

MyEdLab **Application Exercise 2.2:** Problem-Solving Model

2.4 SPECIAL CONSIDERATIONS FOR IMPLEMENTING RTI

One of the important contributions of using a multitiered system in which students are provided primary (Tier 1), secondary (Tier 2), and tertiary (Tier 3) interventions is that it is possible to quickly identify when students are falling behind and provide additional intervention that is targeted to meet their needs. Fortunately, the majority of students respond well when provided additional intervention (Tier 2).

2.4.1 Responders and Nonresponders to Intervention

We refer to students who respond well to intervention as responders or high responders. These students may need additional intervention in the future but are generally able to maintain grade-level performance or near-grade-level performance with occasional Tier 2 intervention. An example of a good response is when the gap narrows between a student's rate and level of progress and that of her or his peers. In other words, the student seems to be catching up.

On the other hand, students who make minimal or no gains after being taught with high-quality, validated interventions are considered to be inadequately responding to intervention; in other words, they may be referred to as nonresponders, but technically they are low responders or inadequate responders because it is exceedingly uncommon that students have no response to an intervention. For these students, the gap keeps growing between them and their peers; these students may need more intensive long-term interventions, and if they continue to demonstrate low response, may benefit from referral and placement in special education. See Tips for Teachers 2.4 for some guidelines regarding what RTI can and cannot do.

Identifying Inadequate Responders

Students who respond inadequately to an intervention do not make expected progress even when instructed with a research-based approach. However, teachers must realize that not all students learn in the same way. They need to understand that although one student may respond well to a given research-based intervention, another student may not. Research can only help us make educated guesses about which instructional practices are most likely to benefit the greatest number of children. But even in the best research studies, some students might actually respond better to an alternative approach. Therefore, when a child does not seem to be responding to an instructional method, it is important to try a different approach. RTI researcher Amanda VanDerHayden defines nonresponders as "students for whom we have not yet found the right intervention" (personal

TIPS FOR TEACHERS 2.4

What RTI or Multitiered Systems of Support (MTSS) Can and Cannot Do

- RTI neither creates nor fixes learning disabilities. However, models such as multitiered systems of support or RTI provide a safety net for students who might end up in special education simply because they have not been provided adequate instruction or appropriate interventions prior to being referred for special education services.
- RTI or MTSS are dynamic models that allow students to move between levels of interventions depending on results of ongoing progress-monitoring and benchmark assessments. Thus, students are not "placed" in Tier 2 for multiple years without extensive consideration of their progress and how instruction might be modified to better meet their educational needs.
- The key to RTI and MTSS models is to provide effective instruction early to ensure that students are provided with the resources and support they need to become proficient learners.
- Successful implementation of RTI and MTSS requires all teachers to provide research-based instruction to ensure that students who are not adequately progressing need specialized instruction.
- Consider providing students the level of intensity of instruction they require rather than waiting for them to "pass through" successive tiers of instruction. In other words, if students have extensive needs, move them quickly into more intensive interventions.
- Develop guidelines for students in grades 4 to 8 that provide more intensive interventions quickly. Older students who have been provided RTI- or MTSS-type models in early elementary grades and are continuing to demonstrate significant problems benefit from more intensive interventions immediately.

communication, February 2006). (See Tips for Teachers 2.5 for help in identifying why children may not respond adequately to instruction.)

Figure 2.3 provides guidelines for implementing effective Tier 3 interventions.

2.4.2 Implementing Interventions

Teachers vary a great deal in how they apply different instructional approaches. How well a teacher implements a practice affects how well students learn (Al Otaiba & Fuchs, 2006; Spear-Swerling, 2015). This commonsense finding has important implications for anyone implementing RTI. How can you determine whether a research-based program was implemented well? Observing the teacher or interventionist is necessary to determine whether a program is well implemented and appropriate for students. A student may not be responding well to the program, but it may not necessarily be because the program is not appropriate for the student; it could be that the teacher may not be using it effectively. Maybe the teacher is struggling with classroom management and needs assistance in this

TIPS FOR TEACHERS 2.5

Identifying Why Children Do Not Respond to Instruction

Before concluding that a student is responding inadequately to an intervention and needs more intensive services, consider the following:

- Consider changing an instructional approach—even when it has been effective with many other students. It may need to be modified and more customized to the learning needs of the student in order to have positive results.
- The level of instruction might not be a good match for the child.
- The environment might not be conducive to learning.
- The teacher may not be aligning instruction well or engaging the student.
- The student may have social, emotional, or home issues interfering with learning.

FIGURE 2.3 **Guidelines for implementing effective intensive interventions**

- **Assure students have been provided research-based Tier 1 instruction.** Students who have been provided inadequate classroom instruction will require only intensive types of instruction like those in Tier 3 if they are multiple grade levels behind. Otherwise, supporting Tier 1 and Tier 2 instruction are the first steps.
- **Assure students have been provided with a research-based Tier 2 intervention.** Students requiring intensive interventions should either: (a) demonstrate significant learning needs that were not adequately addressed through Tiers 1 and 2, or (b) demonstrate significant learning problems that would benefit from more intensive intervention.
- **Use diagnostic and progress-monitoring data to determine students' instructional needs.** Students who are provided intensive interventions have previously received other interventions as well as progress-monitoring measures and assessments. Use this information to design and modify research-based approaches that are aligned with their instructional needs.
- **Use diagnostic measures to supplement information on students' needs.** When appropriate, use diagnostic measures to further determine students' learning needs and assist in designing the most effective instruction.
- **Provide daily, targeted instruction that is explicit, systematic, and with ample opportunities for students to demonstrate what they are learning with quality feedback.** Students in intensive interventions require very systematic and well-targeted instruction taking advantage of every opportunity for students to learn.
- **Provide very intensive instruction through small group size or one-on-one instruction.** Students who require intensive instruction will require learning groups that are very small so that they can have instruction specifically matched to their learning needs with increased opportunities for corrective feedback and practice to automaticity.
- **Provide intervention for as much supplemental time as possible.** Students with significant learning needs are unlikely to catch up with interventions provided for only 20 to 30 minutes a day.
- **If possible, provide additional and extended instructional sessions.** This may mean that some students are provided intensive interventions more than once per day, and for some students, before- or after-school interventions are required.
- **Vary the intervention practices to maximize effective outcomes.** Interventions may need to be varied to include more or less phonics instruction, the type of phonics instruction, more or less emphasis on narrative and information texts, and variation in levels of text encountered.
- **Students in grade 3 or higher with very low academic scores in reading or math relative to grade-level expectations may be better served if placed immediately in intensive interventions.** The rationale is that if students are in the upper elementary and secondary grades and are significantly behind, it may not be appropriate for them to be placed in less intensive interventions.
- **Communicate frequently with parents and other key stakeholders.** Parents and other key stakeholders will want to know the progress of students with significant problems and practices that they can implement to provide additional support.

Source: From "Why intensive interventions are necessary for students with severe reading difficulties," by S. Vaughn, C. A. Denton, & J. M. Fletcher, 2010, *Psychology in the Schools, 47*(5), 432–444; Vaughn, Zumeta et al (2014).

area before being able to focus more on instruction. In any case, it is important to explore what can be done to improve instruction (see Tips for Teachers 2.6).

Classroom observations are a valuable part of every RTI model (Vaughn & Fuchs, 2012; Vellutino et al., 2007). Vellutino and colleagues (2007) note that, "Intervention at this level is based on the assumption that many if not most struggling readers will be able to profit from relevant modifications in classroom literacy instruction, despite the fact

TIPS FOR TEACHERS 2.6

Determining Whether a Research-Based Intervention Was Implemented Appropriately

To determine whether a research based intervention is implemented appropriately:

- Examine the program to determine whether it has been validated with students like those in the class.
- Determine whether instruction is at an appropriate level for students (e.g., reading level of materials is appropriate for the target student).
- Identify whether the key components in the intervention program (e.g., phonemic awareness, fluency) align with the key components of instruction needed by the student.
- Establish whether teachers are sufficiently differentiating instruction to meet diverse student needs.

that they were (apparently) less well equipped than their normally achieving classmates to compensate for inadequacies in reading instruction" (p. 186). This recognition that many students struggle when their instruction is inadequate is an important one, with significant implications for culturally and linguistically diverse students who often are educated in high-poverty, high-needs schools in which teachers are sometimes not as qualified as those in more affluent schools (Harry & Klingner, 2006, 2014).

2.4.3 RTI for Students Who Are Culturally and Linguistically Diverse

RTI has the potential to improve outcomes for students who are culturally and linguistically diverse and to more accurately determine which of these students need special education services (Harry & Klingner, 2014; Klingner & Edwards, 2006). RTI practices that are responsive to the cultural and linguistic needs of students can assist teachers in determining whether students' progress is related to what they are being taught, their background experiences, or how they are being instructed. The success of RTI depends on the quality of the RTI team involved. Without sufficient knowledge about cultural and linguistic diversity, for example, educators implementing RTI may presume that a child who does not make progress at a certain pace must have a disability rather than recognizing that the child may need additional time and support while learning English. Educators may also equate cultural differences with cultural deficits, which may influence their interpretations of their diverse students' behaviors (Klingner & Solano-Flores, 2007).

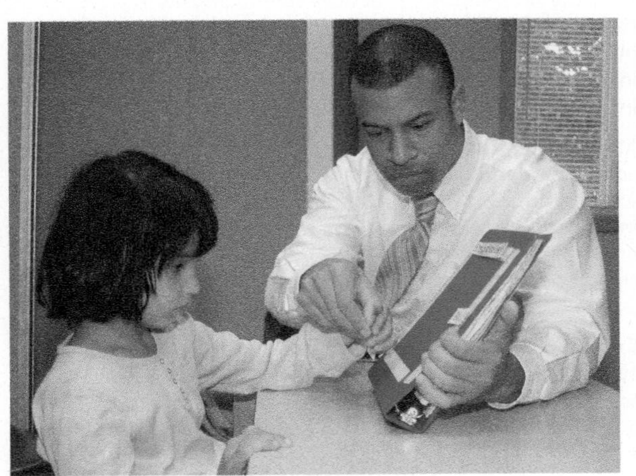

What can this teacher do to determine whether this child is one of the under-identified children with a learning disability or whether the language barrier is hindering this child's learning?

Although the process of learning to read in a child's second language is similar to learning to read in his or her first language, there also are important differences of which teachers may not be aware (August & Shanahan, 2006). Second language acquisition, best practices for English language learners (ELLs), and cultural variations should be considered when assessing student progress, designing interventions, and interpreting English language learners' responses to interventions.

RTI approaches that respond to the cultural and linguistic diversity of students focus on understanding external or environmental factors that affect their opportunity to learn in addition to personal factors. For RTI to work, team members must have expertise in cultural and linguistic diversity and be knowledgeable about interventions that have been effective with culturally and linguistically diverse students with different needs.

In implementing RTI approaches with ELLs, a significant challenge is determining students' knowledge and skills in their first language and then understanding their performance in their second language (English). For example, there are subgroups of students whose literacy knowledge and skills in their first language (e.g., Spanish) are adequate, but whose literacy skills in their second language (e.g., English) are low. These students have demonstrated the capacity to acquire reading skills and now require instruction so they can apply those skills to the acquisition of English literacy. Other students may have low literacy in both their first language and English because they have not received adequate instruction in either language. Still another group of students, the smallest group, demonstrates low literacy skills in both their first language and English even after receiving adequate instruction. For more on using RTI approaches with ELLs, see Tips for Teachers 2.7.

When students demonstrate reading or math difficulties, providing small-group intensive interventions that target their instructional needs and then monitoring their progress ensures that instruction is modified to meet the needs of students. To meet their needs, those working with ELLs should consider the following:

- ELLs benefit from teachers who are highly interested in ensuring that their students make adequate progress in reading or math and that they themselves have the knowledge and skills to provide appropriate instruction.

TIPS FOR TEACHERS 2.7

Using RTI or Multitiered Systems of Support (MTSS) with English Language Learners

To help determine how you can best provide instruction to your ELLs, consider the following questions:

- *What skills must educators have to effectively implement RTI for ELLs?* Having professional development provided to all educational stakeholders enhances knowledge and skills; however, a team of educators with knowledge is likely to be even more valuable. For example, a problem-solving team with knowledge and experience working with ELLs can be a resource to facilitate decision making and to design instructional supports. The more the team knows about the development of oral language, early literacy, students' home language, contextual considerations, and the cultural backgrounds of students, the more likely the team will make appropriate decisions about interpreting screening and assessment results and in designing appropriate interventions.
- *How is screening implemented with ELLs?* ELLs can be screened on the same early reading indicators as native English language speakers, including phonological awareness, letter knowledge, and word and text reading. Universal screenings must be conducted using native language and/or English measures that have demonstrated high validity and reliability. Provide instructional support to ELLs with low performance in reading areas even when oral language skills in English are low. Interventions should simultaneously address development of language and literacy skills in English.
- *How is progress monitoring effectively implemented with ELLs?* Monitor the progress of ELLs as frequently as you monitor the progress of all other students—a minimum of three times per year for students at grade level or above and three to six times per year for students at risk for reading problems. Consider students' accents and pronunciations when scoring English measures and provide appropriate interpretations when words are mispronounced. Do not penalize students for dialect features. Consider that students may be acquiring word meaning while acquiring word reading, and thus oral reading fluency may proceed at an expected rate early (while students are focusing on word reading) and then proceed at a lower-than-expected rate later when students are focusing more on word meaning.
- *How is primary instruction (Tier 1) provided to ELLs?* Set high but reasonable instructional expectations that provide ongoing instructional support to ensure that these expectations are met. The core reading program for ELLs should include consideration of the foundational skills such as phonemic awareness and phonics early in the reading process, with continued emphasis on vocabulary and concept building throughout the instructional process. Reading words accurately and with prosody, as well as reading for meaning and learning, are emphasized through listening comprehension early and then later through reading comprehension. Scaffold language and opportunities to respond. Scaffolding language includes paraphrasing key words, providing opportunities to extend answers, supporting language by using familiar synonyms (e.g., "that is also like …") and familiar antonyms (e.g., "that is also different from …"), teaching idioms, reframing students' responses, confirming aspects of the answer that are correct, and providing language supports to further explain aspects that require refinement.
- *How are secondary (Tier 2) and tertiary (Tier 3) interventions effectively implemented for ELLs?* Provide intensive reading interventions to ELLs demonstrating low reading skills immediately when needed. These interventions can be effectively implemented as early as first grade, as well as for more mature readers with reading difficulties. You do not need to wait for English oral language to improve before providing reading interventions. Maximize opportunities for vocabulary and language development during reading intervention. Use appropriate practices for building oracy skills and vocabulary development as well as reading skills.

Sources: Based on *Response to intervention in reading for English language learners,* by Sharon Vaughn and Alba Ortiz. The complete document is available on the NCLD website at www.ncld.org; and Baker, S., Lesaux, N., Jayanthi, M., Dimino, J., Proctor, C. P., Morris, J., … & Newman-Gonchar, R. (2014). Teaching Academic Content and Literacy to English Learners in Elementary and Middle School. IES Practice Guide. NCEE 2014-4012. *What Works Clearinghouse.*

- ELLs will be better served if teachers and school personnel do not expect or accept low performance and if they do not view students as undeserving of effective interventions.
- ELLs who exhibit learning disabilities may be underidentified and undertreated because school personnel may not have the knowledge and skills needed to identify and treat these students.
- Students benefit when school personnel are focused on meeting students' educational needs rather than on finding an external source to explain the educational needs. See Tips for Teachers 2.7.

2.4.4 Working with Families

Family involvement has been a required part of identifying and monitoring students with disabilities since the earliest version of the IDEA. Family involvement is required for all aspects of identifying students with disabilities—regardless of the model used. If schools

Video Example from YouTube

MyEdLab
Video Example 2.2.

Watch this video, "Response to Intervention: A Tiered Approach to Instructing All Students," to help you provide an overview of the RTI process that may be helpful when meeting with parents and families. How can you explain this process in terms of their children? https://www.youtube.com/watch?v=nkK1bT8lsOM

are using RTI models, families must be informed of and involved in the process. As mentioned earlier, families can request a formal evaluation for a disability at any time. A family should also be notified early in the RTI process that a child seems to be struggling and that the school plans to try specific interventions to help.

There are several ways school can inform families about their child's participation in the RTI process at least by Tier 2.

- Describing the RTI process in a written document that is provided to families in the home language.
- Providing families with a description of the intervention plan for their child that provides the amount of time, group size, who is providing the intervention, and a clear description of the focus of the intervention.
- Obtaining families' consent when their children are participating in extensive interventions, while not necessary, provides a good way to communicate with parents.
- Providing families with regular updates about their child's progress.

Sometimes students do not make enough progress in an intervention. The teacher knows this from checking the student's progress; however, parents may wonder about student's progress—particularly when it is inadequate. When this happens, it would be helpful to inform parents and to communicate how you are adjusting instruction. If the student is still not meeting goals, it may be useful to ask other teachers for ideas to solve the problem. Then if the student continues to struggle with learning, a school team may meet to figure out what is needed and meet with the parents to keep them informed. Several states have developed documents for parents to assist them in understanding RTI. See Tips for Teachers 2.8 for suggestions for parents when regarding RTI implementation.

2.4.5 Role of Teachers in an RTI Model

At a professional development session designed to improve teachers' knowledge of the RTI model at Sunset Elementary School, Mrs. Jacobs, a 20-year veteran teacher who had taught all grades from second through fifth grade, said, "I think I understand the basic principles of the RTI model, but I just don't understand what I'm supposed to do to facilitate implementation. What is my role?" Amanda VanDerHeyden (2009) indicates that

TIPS FOR TEACHERS 2.8

How to Explain to Parents About Effectiveness of RTI

Here is some information teachers may provide to parents about the effectiveness of RTI:

1. At any time, you have the right to request an evaluation for special education for your child. If you think your child has a learning disability. This is different from being at-risk. Your child does not have to wait until intervention is over. To do this, give a written request for the evaluation to the school. The school must respond to your request.
2. The school will begin the evaluation process. Your rights will be explained, and you will give written consent. Your child can continue to receive intervention.
3. The school will not evaluate your child. You will get a written explanation about why a disability is not suspected. Your child can continue to receive intervention.

- If the team decides that your child needs an evaluation for special education, you must give permission for this.
- After your child is evaluated, you and the school team will meet. The team may look at RTI information, such as what interventions were taught and how your child responded.
- You and the team will look at other information, too. Together, you will decide whether your child needs special education. RTI information also helps you and the team plan your child's instruction.

teachers and other school personnel need to establish procedures to accomplish the following:

- Identify students who need intervention. This is typically done using a schoolwide screening in which students who fail the screening at their grade level are considered at risk and provided secondary or tertiary intervention.
- Provide evidence-based interventions that effectively improve learning for the vast majority of students receiving the intervention. In many schools, the Tier 2–type intervention may be provided by the classroom teacher. This may occur in small groups or individually. In many schools, intervention for each grade level is scheduled at the same time so teachers can form groups of students with similar needs across classrooms. Sometimes teachers coordinate their Tier 2 instruction by working cooperatively with teachers in their same grade to provide intervention to a small group of students while the other teacher provides a large-class activity.
- Monitor the effects of the intervention to ensure that it positively influences learning. If the classroom teacher is providing the intervention, and if students in Tier 2 intervention are not making adequate progress, the teacher should consult with others, such as the special education teacher or school psychologist.
- Make decisions, in consultation with other key professionals, about the need for more or less intensive intervention so that monitoring students' progress through the tiers is possible.
- Meet regularly with interested stakeholders such as parents, other teachers, and school psychologists to facilitate successful interventions and identification of students who need special services.

Ms. Nigel is impressed with how the RTI model is working in her school. "I really like the way we screen students early to determine who needs additional support. I also like the fact that we have decided as a school which programs we will use for interventions depending upon the reading or math needs of students. However, the part that is so difficult for us is determining who and how students will be provided with the interventions they need. We never have enough teachers." How can you decide who provides interventions in your school? The teacher plays the most important roles in implementing an RTI model; the classroom teacher is responsible for implementing a research-based instructional program and is typically involved in screening students for academic or behavior problems as well. Because the primary focus of the RTI model is early identification of students who need additional assistance, the teacher is a critical link in ensuring that this happens. What if the classroom teacher has several students who require Tier 2 or secondary intervention and one or more students who require Tier 3 or more intensive interventions? Who provides these interventions? Effective school leaders know that it is critical for the most knowledgeable and effective teachers to provide intervention to the students with the greatest needs. Schools have different ways in which they provide interventions. In some schools, classroom teachers provide the Tier 2 interventions, while a specialist provides Tier 3. For example, in a school that has multiple teachers at each grade level, one of the teachers might provide the Tier 2 intervention while her students are participating in social studies or science with the remaining grade-level teachers. In other schools, well-trained and supervised teaching assistants provide the secondary intervention.

Once a student has been identified as needing additional assistance, the special education teacher may provide support for the implementation of interventions. The special education teacher plays several important roles in a multitiered RTI model. These include:

- Collaborating with general education teachers and providing consultation services.
- Providing professional development on and modeling implementation of research-based strategies.
- Helping to identify children with disabilities.

- Interpreting students' progress to determine if they are benefitting adequately from interventions or require more intensive interventions.
- Designing more intensive interventions that are aligned with the previous progress of students and their current needs.
- Communicating with families and key educational stakeholders to assure that participating students have programs that are aligned with classroom instruction.
- Working with other professionals such as the school psychologist and speech and language therapist to manage the RTI process for students with disabilities.
- Providing intensive interventions to Tier 3 students.
- Helping students requiring the most intensive interventions access the general education curriculum.

Special educators may work with struggling students who have not been labeled as having disabilities. In some ways these are similar to the roles special education teachers assumed in the past, and in other ways they are quite different. These shifting roles will require some fundamental changes in the way general education and special education personnel do their work (Burns, Griffiths, Parson, Tilly, & VanDerHeyden, 2007; Fuchs & Vaughn, 2012).

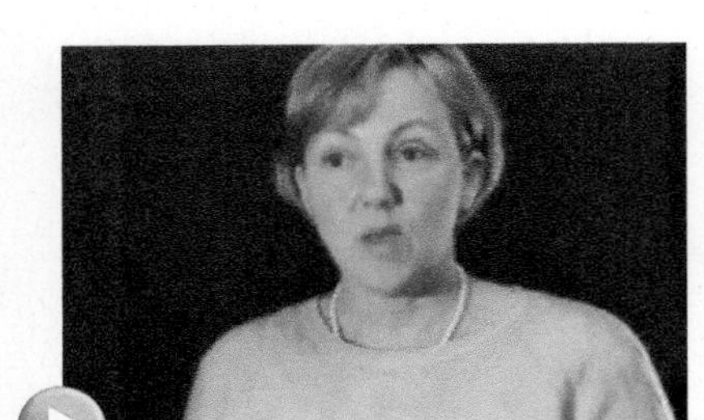

MyEdLab
Video Example 2.3.
Watch this video and listen as the speaker discusses the importance of collaboration between the general education teacher and the special education teachers across all three tiers for a child who is receiving Tier 3 instruction. As a general education teacher, what would your responsibilities be with regard to your student?

Collaborating and consulting

As with most effective school-based models, teachers in an RTI model collaborate with other professionals (e.g., English language development teacher, reading specialist, special education teacher, speech and language specialist) to provide students who have instructional or special needs with a seamless set of services. Special education teachers may still spend part of their day co-teaching or meeting with general education teachers as part of a collaborative consultation model. The purpose of these efforts is to make sure students with disabilities have access to the general education curriculum and can participate in the general education program to the extent they are able.

Another way that teachers collaborate is by serving on RTI problem-solving (or intervention) teams that consider progress-monitoring results and other data and make decisions about teacher and student needs. Teachers provide their expertise when planning interventions or assessments. They are most likely the team members with the greatest expertise about learning difficulties and can offer insights about individual cases.

See Tips for Teachers 2.9 for an example of how Marla conducts intensive interventions with her reading class.

2.4.6 Using RTI Data to Identify Students with Learning Disabilities

As you recall from the beginning of the chapter, one of the reasons Congress recommended using an RTI approach is that there was considerable concern about the validity of traditional practices for identifying students with learning disabilities (e.g., IQ–achievement discrepancy). For this reason, you are likely to work in a school or district that uses data from screening, progress monitoring, and other records related to students' progress in primary and secondary interventions to influence decision making about identifying students with learning disabilities.

Accrue data during progress monitoring

How might this work? There is no uniform procedure used in all states; however, many states are using data they accrue during progress monitoring of students in interventions to facilitate referral and decision making about whether students do or do not have a learning disability. When students have participated in targeted interventions at the Tier 2 or Tier 3 level and still do not seem to progress, the decision-making team may conclude that a comprehensive evaluation is needed to determine whether the students have learning disabilities. Not all researchers agree about how much and what

TIPS FOR TEACHERS 2.9

Using Intensive Interventions

Marla is teaching a 30-minute lesson to a group of second and third-grade students who are all reading at an upper-first- or a second-grade level. Progress-monitoring data indicate that all four students need to build their word study skills.

- During their first activity, the teacher asks students to review a previously taught word study component—words that end in "ide" or "ike." She asks students to take 1 minute to write all of the words they can think of that have the ide or ike rime, or, in other words, are in the same word families. Marla lets them know when time is up, and they count up all of the words they have listed. The student with the most words reads them aloud, while other students check their lists to see if they have written down any words not stated by the first student; if so, they then read these aloud. This is a quick warm-up activity that also serves as a review of previously learned material.
- Next Marla introduces two-syllable words that have an open, vowel–silent e pattern: be-side, a-like, lo-cate, fe-male, e-rase, do-nate, re-tire, ro-tate, pro-vide, and mi-grate. The last two are "challenge" words because they include blends. Before the lesson began, Marla had written the words on the whiteboard at the front of the classroom, each with a hyphen between syllables. Each student also has a list of the words at his or her desk, one row with the hyphens in each word and another without them. Marla directs students to count how many syllables they see in each word.
- Next she has them mark vowels and consonants. She asks the students what they notice about the first syllable in each word, and then what they notice about the second syllable in each word (i.e., that all have the vowel–silent e pattern). She points out that they have learned the syllables before, and probably recognize most of them. She asks them to look for syllables they know.
- Then together the students read the words. Marla explains and demonstrates what the words mean. For example, for the word *erase*, she erases a word on the board, and for *retire*, she reminds the students that one of their previous teachers has retired. Students practice reading the words, first with the entire group, and then taking turns with a partner.
- Marla then asks students to look at the story they are reading today. She reminds them of key words previously introduced that they will see in the story. She also asks them to look at the title and the key words and pictures and to make predictions about what they will read or learn. She continues with the lesson, providing students opportunities to read silently and aloud and to ask and answer questions about what they are reading.

Source: Fuchs, D., & Fuchs, L. S. (2006). Introduction to response to intervention: What, why, and how valid is it? *Reading Research Quarterly, 41*, 93–99.

kind of additional data are needed to make this determination. There are some educational leaders who think that students' response to intervention is adequate information and others who think that other data about the student (e.g., memory, cognitive processing) is needed to facilitate the decision making. In other words, the data collected should include information about the instructional environment as well as within-child factors. For example, within-child factors that have traditionally been the focus of determining whether a student had special needs include cognitive functioning, which can be measured by an IQ test; academic functioning, often assessed by individually administered tests in reading, math, writing, and spelling; or functioning on such processing measures as auditory and visual tasks. The change in perspective provides less emphasis on these within-child factors and more emphasis on how students are performing in the classroom, whether students are meeting the academic and social demands of their grade level, and whether the classroom environment is conducive to learning.

Administer formal, informal, and screening measures

Most experts agree that RTI data may not be sufficient to identify learning disabilities, but that RTI data should serve as the core of a comprehensive evaluation. It is likely that formal and informal measures of the child's academic skills will be administered in addition to the results of screening measures, progress-monitoring results, and other assessment data already collected. The focus should be to develop a profile that includes information about the student's strengths as well as areas of need. The special education teacher and/or other members of the team would observe the child in different contexts to better understand the instructional environment and how appropriate it seems, as well as under what conditions the student seems to thrive or struggle. Observations should include a focus on how well the child is doing in comparison with similar peers.

Possible psychological evaluation of intellectual ability

A psychologist may or may not conduct an evaluation of the student's intellectual ability and cognitive functioning. Just how this is done depends on the state's and district's policies and what the problem-solving team decides is useful data. If the team has concerns about the child's mental and emotional health, the psychologist also conducts assessments in this area. A social worker interviews the parents about the child's background and developmental milestones. The team collects additional information, such as the child's attendance patterns. The family members are involved in the process as valued team members.

Review and analyze material

The teacher then works with the team to review and analyze all relevant data to make decisions about the best course of action for the child. They develop an intervention plan and set learning and, if appropriate, behavioral goals. If the team determines that the student has a disability, then they develop an individualized educational plan (IEP).

2.4.7 Providing Interventions

Using a research-based approach to instruction means that the vast majority of students (typically 80%) will be meeting grade-level expectations. These students will not need additional interventions. However, in some schools, 20% to 40% of students will require secondary (Tier 2) or tertiary (Tier 3) interventions. What does this mean for the classroom teacher?

Depending on how your school is organized, you can expect to be involved in the delivery of the secondary interventions. This means that a subgroup of students will require additional instruction three to five times per week for 20 minutes or more. Typically, this instruction is provided in small groups by the classroom teacher, a paraprofessional, a reading or math teacher, or other educators trained to provide interventions. Because these students may need instruction that is closely aligned with their instructional needs, the teacher providing the additional instruction uses the data from progress monitoring to guide instruction. Teachers will adjust the pacing of the lesson, provide adequate differentiation, select appropriate materials, provide students with ongoing feedback, and allow students adequate opportunities to respond with guided feedback. Providing students with appropriate feedback is essential to effective interventions. There are several helpful resources to help you with interventions. Figure 2.4 identifies considerations for effectively implementing Tier 2 interventions. Tips for Teachers 2.10 provides some examples of how to provide this feedback.

In addition to the instruction provided by the general education teacher, the special education teacher works one-on-one or with small groups of students in reading, math, or other content areas. Instruction is intense, frequent, and of longer duration than at previous tiers in the RTI model. The special education teacher controls task difficulty and provides ongoing systematic and corrective feedback; progress monitoring continues.

2.4.8 Using RTI Models in Middle Schools and High Schools

Because RTI was designed as a prevention approach, it is typically considered to be most appropriate for implementation at the early elementary grades. However, some districts and school sites use RTI models with older students, particularly in grades 4 to 8.

FIGURE 2.4 **Guidelines for implementing effective Tier 2 interventions**

- **Implement universal screening to identify students at risk for learning problems.** Develop procedures for screening all students at least twice a year (beginning of year and middle of year) to determine students at risk for reading or math problems. Provide at-risk students with appropriate interventions.
- **Determine students' instructional needs.** Determine students' knowledge and skills related to relevant reading or math skills/knowledge expected at their grade level. For example, for reading it may be several of the following elements: phonemic awareness, alphabet knowledge, phonics, word reading, word or text fluency, vocabulary, spelling, and comprehension. Examples for math include: number knowledge, addition up to 20 or fractions.
- **Form small groups of students with similar learning needs.** For Tier 2 intervention, form groups of students with similar learning needs with group sizes as small as local resources will allow. Same ability groups allow the teacher to focus on the specific needs of students.
- **Provide daily, targeted instruction that is explicit, systematic, and provides ample practice opportunities with immediate specific feedback.** Identify the instructional content in small instructional units (e.g., 3 to 5 minutes per unit) for each lesson. Organize these instructional units into a cohesive lesson that is responsive to students' needs based on ongoing progress-monitoring data and curriculum goals for the grade level. Allow students to practice the target skills until they are proficient providing instructional feedback that adequately informs what they are doing well and what needs to be adjusted.
- **Focus on the reading or math skills that have the highest impact on learning based on students' current performance.** Do not try to teach everything during intervention. Based on the priority skills at that grade level, identify those skills that will assist the student in making the most rapid progress. Provide modeled examples before student practice. Scaffold instruction and make adaptations to instruction in response to students' needs and to how quickly or slowly students are learning.
- **Follow a systematic routine.** Establish and follow an instructional routine to maximize time on task and minimize lost time for intervention. Use clear, explicit, easy-to-follow procedures and sequence instruction so that easier skills are introduced before more complex ones.
- **Pace instruction quickly so students are engaged and content is covered.** Maximize student engagement, including many opportunities for students to respond. Provide students feedback on when they have mastered content to encourage engagement.
- **Provide ample opportunities for guided initial practice and independent practice.** Monitor student understanding and mastery of instruction frequently. Adapt instruction so that items are more difficult for some students and easier for other students.
- **Include frequent and cumulative reviews of previously learned material.** Review critical skills that have been previously taught and reteach, when necessary.
- **Ensure that students are performing tasks at the appropriate level of difficulty.** When students are reading text independently without teacher (or peer) guidance and support, levels of accuracy need to be very high. When students are reading text with teacher guidance and support, lower levels of accuracy may be appropriate. Reading accuracy levels vary from source to source. To calculate reading accuracy, divide the number of words read correctly by the total number of words read. Take into consideration:
    - Independent level: Texts in which no more than approximately one in twenty words is read incorrectly (accuracy level: 95% to 100%).
    - Instructional level: Texts in which no more than approximately one in ten words is read incorrectly. Students need instructional support from the teacher (accuracy level: 90% to 94%).
    - Frustration level: Texts in which more than one in ten words is read incorrectly (accuracy level: less than 90%).
- **Provide many opportunities for struggling readers to apply phonics and word study learning to reading words, word lists, and connected texts.**
    - Have students practice reading words and texts at the appropriate level of difficulty (usually instructional level under the direction of the teacher).
    - Include the reading of word cards or words in phrases or sentences to increase word recognition fluency (often used with high-frequency and irregular words and words that contain previously taught letter–sound correspondences or spelling patterns).
    - Include comprehension instruction that introduces new vocabulary words, incorporates graphic organizers, and teaches comprehension strategies explicitly.
- **Include writing to support reading and spelling.** Have students apply what they are learning about letters and sounds as they write letters, sound units, words, and sentences. Involve parents so they support students' efforts by listening to them read and practicing reading skills.
- **Conduct frequent progress monitoring (e.g., every 1 to 2 weeks) to track student progress and inform instruction and grouping.**
- **Monitor the implementation of the interventions to assure fidelity.** Fidelity refers to the alignment between the specified curriculum, lessons, or program and the instruction provided. Using research-based instructional approaches requires high levels of fidelity.

TIPS FOR TEACHERS 2.10

The Role of Appropriate Feedback

Following are examples of how to provide feedback to students:

- Nod, make eye contact with students, smile, and indicate approval.
- Use verbal praise that provides specific feedback about what the student did well.
- Pat the student on the arm to indicate that he or she answered a question correctly.
- Repeat the students' response, adjusting it to indicate the needed change, then ask the student to repeat the answer correctly.
- Write the student's response and then elaborate to extend or expand.
- Repeat the student's response and encourage other students to extend what was said.
- Ask students to write a response and then give specific feedback on what aspects are correct.
- Describe why the answer or work was correct.
- Describe what the student could say or do to make the answer more correct.
- Summarize what the key ideas were.
- Summarize what students should have learned.
- Ask students to identify what they learned.
- Advise students to start the task again.
- Ask another student to build on what a different student has said.
- Show students how to make specific corrections.
- Ask students to explain how their work is correct or incorrect.
- Ask students to show you from where in the text their answer was drawn.

Mr. Morris is one such teacher who worked at a middle school that is implementing an RTI model. As the science teacher, he was unsure what his role would be within the RTI model implemented at his school. He learned that all of the content teachers would be participating in professional development to enhance their knowledge and skills in providing vocabulary and comprehension instruction to their students. This was part of the school's Tier 1 instruction, and all content-area teachers (e.g., math, science, social studies, language arts) were participating.

His class consists of study groups supplemented with in-class modeling and coaching. Reading coaches, who are part of the research team, facilitate monthly study groups with content-area teachers, focus on effective practices for teaching students to read and comprehend academic (content-area) text, including research-validated instructional practices targeting vocabulary (e.g., providing examples and nonexamples of words, semantic feature analysis) and comprehension (e.g., question generation, summarization strategy instruction, strategic use of graphic organizers). Mr. Morris said, "At first I was skeptical, but then I learned some very practical strategies that were actually helpful to me in teaching all of the students. The emphasis is not on preparing content-area teachers to teach reading, but on giving them evidence-based instructional approaches to teach students vocabulary and comprehension in their specific content domain."

Mr. Morris went on to explain how his school uses RTI to provide secondary interventions for students identified as at risk for reading problems based on their low scores on the state assessment of reading. Selected teachers provide a standardized reading intervention to students who are at risk for reading problems but scored very close to grade-level expectations. Other teachers provide a more individualized approach to students with more significant difficulties. Figure 2.5 compares the differences between the standardized and individualized approaches used. Figure 2.6 provides guidelines for implementing RTI practices at the secondary level.

FIGURE 2.5 **Comparison between standardized and individualized interventions**

STANDARDIZED	INDIVIDUALIZED
Reduced instructional decision making by the teacher who follows the lessons as they are developed.	Increased instructional decision making based on student assessment results. Instructional lessons are modified to align with specific learning needs of students.
High control of materials used for instruction. Materials are based on previous research-based studies.	Lower control of materials used for instruction. Research-based materials are used but are customized to align with each student's instructional needs.
Instructional materials are well specified.	Low to moderate specification of curricula. Teacher has more flexibility about adapting materials for students.
Use of time specified for each component of instruction.	Flexibility in use of time to align time of instruction of each component (e.g., fluency) with each student's needs
High levels of fidelity to a single approach	Fidelity is difficult to assess, as the amount of time on each component varies in response to needs of students
Motivation results from success	Motivation considered in text selection and instructional practices
Systematic and explicit instruction	Systematic and explicit instruction
Fast-paced instruction	Fast-paced instruction
Ongoing progress monitoring	Ongoing progress monitoring

Source: From "Response to intervention with older students with reading difficulties," by S. Vaughn, M. Fletcher, D. J. Francis, C. A. Denton, J. Wanzek, J. Wexler, et al., 2008, *Learning and Individual Differences, 18*(3), 338–345.

FIGURE 2.6 **RTI guidance for secondary students with reading difficulties**

1. Secondary students are unlikely to require extensive screening to identify those with reading difficulties. When students enter middle and high school settings, they already have adequate testing to provide sufficient information on their reading to inform their need for additional reading instruction.
2. Reading interventions are necessary for many students with reading difficulties even after fifth grade. Middle and high schools are not too late to intervene, and secondary students benefit from interventions. However, many of the language and knowledge deficiencies that are associated with poor reading are unlikely to be readily and quickly remediated.
3. Focus the reading intervention on the specific reading problem. Most students at the secondary level have reading difficulties with words, reading and meaning, fluency, and comprehension. However, the depth of the problem in particular component areas, for example, reading comprehension, may be the most significant and benefit from being the focus of treatment. Consider whether students have reading difficulties at the word level, at the background-knowledge level, or with fluency, comprehension, or some combination of these, and design and provide treatment specifically to enhance their performance in the area(s) of need.
4. Consider how to build background knowledge as you focus on reading comprehension. Most older students with reading difficulties demonstrate reading comprehension difficulties because they have inadequate background knowledge about the text they are reading.
5. Improve vocabulary knowledge related to text and morphologically to increase knowledge of word meaning.
6. Schoolwide approaches to enhancing knowledge and vocabulary within content-area instruction (e.g., social studies, science) can enhance the limited background knowledge and vocabulary of students with significant reading problems.
7. Teaching comprehension strategies to older students with reading difficulties is beneficial but is unlikely to be sufficient to meet all of their needs for improved reading for understanding and learning.
8. Older students with significant reading problems are unlikely to make the large gains of younger students.
9. Reading comprehension is likely to improve at a slow rate for students with significant reading problems, and closing the gap between their reading comprehension and that of typical grade-level peers will likely require multiple years of intervention.

(continued)

FIGURE 2.6 RTI guidance for secondary students with reading difficulties (*continued*)

10. To better understand instructional conditions that could close the reading gap for struggling readers, we need studies of more intensive interventions. Mechanisms for intensifying interventions include increasing time, integrating cognitive processes, and organizing customized instruction responsive to students' learning needs.
11. There is little empirical support for more individualized approaches to teaching students with reading disabilities, and our limited research indicates that standardized approaches provide the same if not slightly better results for students with significant reading problems. However, students who respond inadequately to these standardized approaches may benefit from a more customized approach.
12. A districtwide plan for reading intervention from kindergarten through high school facilitates vocabulary, background knowledge, and reading comprehension for all students.

MyEdLab **Self-Check 2.4**

MyEdLab **Application Exercise 2.3:** Role of the General Education Teacher 

2 SUMMARY

- RTI addresses numerous challenges associated with past procedures for supporting student learning and identifying students with learning disabilities. Previous identification criteria focused on establishing a discrepancy between achievement and potential as measured with an IQ test. Yet this way of determining who qualified for special education turned out to be problematic for multiple reasons. Not all students who struggle and need special education demonstrate an IQ–achievement discrepancy. RTI provides an opportunity for schools to integrate a schoolwide approach to prevention and remediation of reading and math difficulties. As a schoolwide approach, RTI integrates school improvement. This entails coordinating screening, instruction, intervention, assessment, and progress monitoring as well as providing ongoing professional development.
- RTI includes several key components. The first is high-quality, research-based instruction that is well matched to students' needs and implemented with fidelity by skilled, caring teachers. Additional components include schoolwide screening to assess the learning levels of all students and progress-monitoring designed to assess individual students' learning over time. Thus, an important aspect of RTI is data-based decision making. Data are used to make decisions about which interventions to use, the intensity of interventions, and the duration of the interventions.
- Universal screening and progress monitoring are essential components of RTI. It is through these assessment procedures that data-base decisions can be made about which research-based instructional practices should be used to teach students. Screening is done as part of the first tier of an RTI model. All students are screened. Progress monitoring can also be part of the first tier, but it is an essential component of Tiers 2 and 3. The progress of all students who receive interventions targeted to their instructional needs is monitored frequently. The purposes of progress monitoring are to assess the effectiveness of the interventions so that changes can be made if necessary and also to develop a profile of the student's learning. These data can be quite useful when determining whether a student has a learning disability.
- Teachers play several important roles in an RTI model. The most important role they play is to provide high-quality, research-based instruction so that when students demonstrate low reading or math skills it is because they need additional instruction and not that their current instruction is adequate. They may also assist with screening, progress monitoring, and providing interventions. They collaborate with other educators (e.g., special education teacher, Title I teacher, school psychologist) and other service providers, offering consultation services and helping to identify children with disabilities. They also provide intensive interventions to special education students to help them reach learning objectives in targeted areas, such as in reading and/or math. In addition, they help special education students access the general education curriculum.

THINK AND APPLY

1. Some teachers are confused about different aspects of RTI and uncertain of how to deal with some of the challenges they are facing. For example, according to progress-monitoring data, more than half of the students in some classes are not reaching benchmarks. What should these teachers do?
2. RTI problem-solving meetings look very much like the child study team meetings of previous years, focused on possible reasons for a child's struggles from a deficit perspective. The teachers and other school personnel are not clear about how the RTI process is similar to and different from the prereferral process. How would you explain these differences?
3. School personnel are unclear about what it means to provide "evidence-based" or "research-based" instruction and the extent to which instruction should be differentiated to meet students' needs in the first tier. How would you explain this? Can you give an example of research-based instruction to illustrate how it is used?
4. When implementing RTI interventions, some researchers believe in the standard treatment protocol model, whereas others advocate for the problem-solving model. RTI proponents believe that both are needed. What is your stance on this issue, and what evidence supports your position?

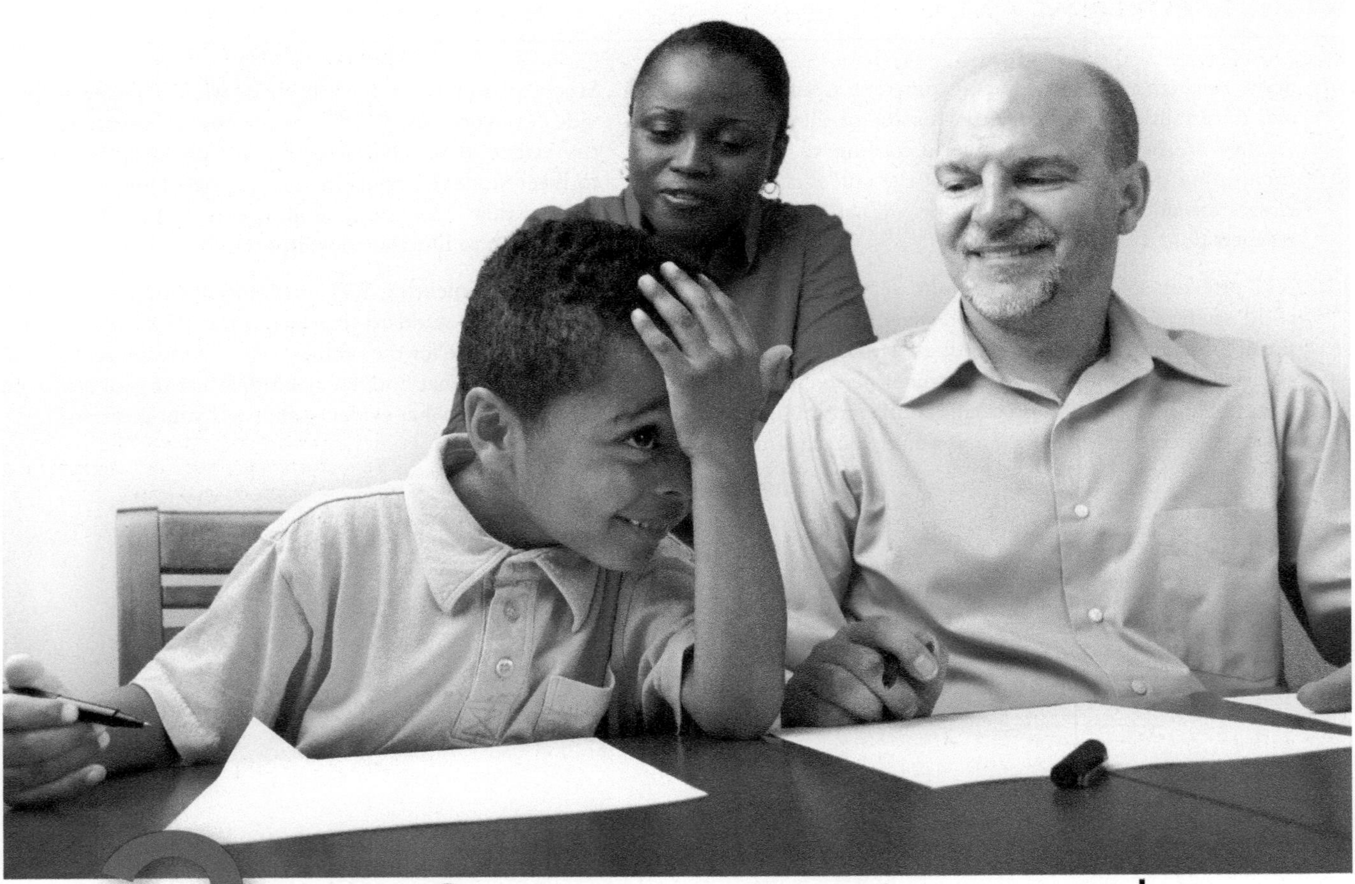

3 Communicating and Collaborating with Other Professionals and Families

Learning Outcomes

3.1 Describe skills necessary to communicate effectively with professional colleagues and families.

3.2 Identify different models that can be implemented to collaborate with other professionals and the conditions necessary for collaboration to succeed.

3.3 Discuss ways to foster positive home–school connections through homework, parent conferences, and other forms of communication.

INTERVIEW: MARGARET COX

Margaret Cox is one of two special education teachers at Henry S. West Laboratory School in Miami, Florida. "West Lab" is a professional development school in partnership with the University of Miami. A veteran teacher for nearly 40 years, Margaret has taught at West Lab for over a decade.

In that time the nature of her work has changed considerably. Initially, Margaret pulled out students identified for special education from the general education classroom to bring them to a resource room where she taught math and reading to her assigned students. Although Margaret coordinated curriculum with the general education teachers, she did have a great deal of autonomy in how she managed the resource room and in her dealings with parents of students with disabilities.

However, the movement toward inclusion of students with disabilities in the general education classroom has shifted the bulk of Margaret's work to the general education setting. Rather than teaching in her own resource room, Margaret is engaged in consultation, collaboration, and co-teaching models with several general education teachers in her school, depending on the needs of individual students. She is much more directly involved with teachers and their classrooms and has had to develop the flexibility to work with individuals with very different teaching styles.

In the past few years, Margaret's roles and responsibilities have been further altered due to the school's adoption of a response to intervention model. Students who do not master weekly learning "benchmarks" attend reteaching sessions with her. Margaret uses research-based interventions to help students master key concepts. This includes students who have not been identified for special education services. Thus, Margaret is now working directly with more students (and their families) than ever before.

Margaret has earned a reputation as the school's "learning specialist." In that capacity, she serves as a resource for her general education colleagues, providing research-based strategies, technology applications, and support in making adaptations to help all students learn. In her work with students, she provides strategies for learning or, as they would put it, "tips and tricks." She also provides parents with valuable suggestions for supporting learning in the home.

Margaret is very involved in supervising the University of Miami's students enrolled in teacher education programs. When students do their field experience rotation at West Lab, Margaret helps them understand her role as a collaborative professional in the school. She also provides suggestions for how they might work with a special educator assigned to their classroom:

> The special education teacher should not be a "wallflower in the classroom." He or she is another teacher who, in a sense, has been displaced from his or her classroom. What is great about inclusion is that students are not "stigmatized" by being sent to a special room. Learning support is

CHAPTER OUTLINE

right there—on the spot. What is challenging is that there is not always enough time for co-planning. Nonetheless, inclusion works best when the general education teacher views me as another teacher in the classroom, is prepared with specific instructional tasks for me to accomplish, is open to my suggestions for making adaptations, and is willing to make the effort to communicate.

Introduction

As a classroom teacher, your primary responsibility is to instruct your students. However, planning and instruction are only part of your job. As the interview with Margaret Cox exemplifies, increasingly teachers are required to work with other professionals and families and therefore need skills to communicate and collaborate effectively. The need for close collaboration is likely to increase as states and school districts implement response to intervention (RTI). The increasing diversity in our classrooms, including English language learners (ELLs), students with disabilities, and students who are gifted, requires collaboration with other professionals and the families of students. This chapter begins with general suggestions for effective communication. The chapter continues with pointers for collaborating with other professionals and then with guidelines and practices for working with the families of your students.

3.1 CRITICAL COMMUNICATION SKILLS

Whether you are an elementary or a secondary school teacher, you can expect to have encounters with many adults in the educational community of your school and school district. You will regularly work with administrators, the special education teacher, and other teachers at your school (Kampwirth & Powers, 2011; Murawski & Hughes, 2009). You might also interface with a variety of other professionals, including the school counselor, psychologist, nurse, Title I teacher, English as a second language (ESL) teacher, teacher of gifted students, and/or a paraeducator. You might have students in your class who need specialized services from the speech and language teacher or the occupational or physical therapist. In addition, you will also have interactions with family members of the students in your class.

Federal, state, and local school improvement goals continue to challenge many school professionals and require key stakeholders in educational units to join forces to meet accountability mandates. Some states also adopt benchmarks or specific student behaviors that indicate they have mastered a particular standard. An **educational standard** "is a statement that depicts what students should know and be able to do as a result of teaching and learning" (Conley, 2005, p. 5). Standards are intended to bring coherence and comprehensiveness to curricula and serve as curricular frameworks.

You may live in one of the over forty states that have adopted the Common Core State Standards (CCSS; www.corestandards.org). The CCSS are the result of a collaborative effort among states to develop uniform standards to have shared expectations for student performance, improved curricular focus, greater efficiency in development of materials and teacher preparation, and improved quality of assessments (Porter et al., 2011; Shanahan, 2015). The intent of the CCSS is to offer rigor and depth to the curriculum to better prepare students in the United States for college and careers for the future. Figure 3.1 presents a sequence of how the CCSS evolved.

Whether your state standards incorporate CCSS or not, you will work with colleagues to plan and implement curriculum to facilitate student mastery of your

FIGURE 3.1 Common Core State Standards: A brief timeline

- The standards movement was ignited by the 1983 report of the National Commission on Excellence in Education titled *A Nation at Risk*, which brought public attention to the state of education in the United States. Although controversial, the report did spawn school reform and the standards movement.
- The National Council of Teachers of Mathematics (NCTM) was the first professional organization to introduce standards for the teaching of mathematics (NCTM, 1989). Since that time, professional organizations representing other content areas have developed sets of standards as well.
- With the authorization of No Child Left Behind (2001), individual states adopted curriculum standards for school subjects.
- State and local curriculum standards were developed and were typically more detailed versions of professional standards. These state standards varied widely in terms of content and rigor.
- To rectify this variability, the National Governors Association Center for Best Practices and the Council of Chief State School Officers (CCSSO; www.corestandards.org) launched a state-led effort to draft CCSS in the areas of English language arts and reading (ELAR) and mathematics. The standards were developed in collaboration with teacher organizations (e.g., National Education Association, American Federation of Teachers), professional organizations (e.g., Council for Exceptional Children, National Council of Teachers of Mathematics, National Council of Teachers of English), and parent organizations (e.g., National Parent Teacher Association).
- The standards for English language arts and mathematics were released in 2010, and since that time over forty states have adopted them.
- Many states that have adopted the standards are still in the process of aligning the CCSS with their own state standards as well as classroom instruction, assessments, and requirements for teacher preparation.
- States are developing policies and procedures for implementing the standards for students with disabilities and students who are English language learners.
- Implementation of CCSS has launched a nationwide debate about their pros and cons.
    - Advocates maintain that having uniform standards across states will assure that students across the United States will have equal opportunity to be ready for the job and academic demands of the future. Supporters also maintain that educators have greater flexibility in planning activities for meeting these standards.
    - Critics cite concerns about teacher preparation for implementing standards, implications for assessment and accountability, and loss of state autonomy for educational matters. In addition, issues related to how best to address the needs of students with disabilities, English language learners, and students who are gifted and talented have been raised.

Sources: Darling-Hammond, L. (2007). Standards and accountability movement needs to push, not punish. *Journal of Staff Development, 28*, 47–50; Porter, A., McMaken, J., Hwang, J., & Yang, R. (2011). Common Core Standards: The new U.S. intended curriculum. *Educational Researcher, 40*(3), 103–116.; Ravitch, D. (1995). *National standards in American education: A citizen's guide*. Washington, DC: Brookings Institution. Shanahan, T. (2015). What teachers should know about Common Core. *The Reading Teacher, 68*(8), 583–588; Van Tassel-Baska, J. (2015). Arguments for and against the Common Core State Standards. *Gifted Child Today, 38*(1), 60–62.

state-designated learning goals for each grade level and/or subject area. Collaboration among professionals and the family members of children has been increasingly emphasized and encouraged since the Individuals with Disabilities Improvement Act of 2004 (IDEIA) and the advent of RTI. Consequently, teachers like Margaret Cox are beginning to work jointly with other professionals and students' family members in largely unprecedented ways. As Friend and Cook (2013) point out, collaboration among professionals and with families is mandated or implied in legislation pertaining to assessment, individualized education program (IEP) participation, placement, transition, development of behavior support plans, and mediation.

Successful collaboration among adults in the school community requires regular, ongoing communication, and a spirit of equity and mutual respect. In your position as a general education teacher, you will often take the lead in initiating such communication. Occasionally communication will take place face-to-face, other times by phone, through written communication, or, increasingly, through electronic means (Thompson, Mazer & Flood, 2015). Regardless of the mechanism, when teachers communicate effectively with other professionals and families with seemingly little effort, it is largely because they have developed the skills to do so. The following sections describe basic principles for communicating with your colleagues and also with the families of the students you teach. In addition, "The 7 Cs of Communication: Communication Skills Training" video provides general pointers for effective communication.

Video Example from YouTube

MyEdLab
Video Example 3.1.
Watch the YouTube video, "The 7 Cs of Communication: Communication Skills Training" for general pointers about effective communication. How might you apply these tips when working with your colleagues, students, and your students' parents? https://www.youtube.com/watch?v=v4OmXaihEp0

TIPS FOR TEACHERS 3.1

Facilitating Effective Communication and Acceptance

Lucia Corzo, a third-grade teacher, has been working with student families and professional colleagues for 12 years. Despite the frustrations and disappointments she encounters occasionally when communicating with key stakeholders, Lucia has learned that the benefits of learning from the perspective of others outweigh any negative aspects. When communicating one-to-one or in small groups, Lucia keeps a few general guidelines for effective communication that help her express acceptance and respect.

- Demonstrate respect for the diverse languages and cultures.
- Introduce parents to other members of the education team in a way that sets the tone for acceptance.
- Give all parties an opportunity to speak and be heard.
- Even when you are busy, take the time to let parents and colleagues know that you value them and that you are simply unable to meet with them at *this* time.
- Avoid giving advice unless it is requested. This does not mean that you can never give suggestions; however, suggestions should be given with the expectation that the person may or may not choose to implement them.
- Avoid providing false reassurances to colleagues or parents. Reassurances may make them and you feel better in the short run but are harmful in the long run. When things do not work out as you predicted, everyone can become disappointed and potentially lose trust.
- Ask specific questions. Unfocused questions make a consistent, purposeful conversation difficult to conduct.
- Avoid changing topics too often; you must monitor the topic and direct others to return to it.
- Avoid interrupting others or being interrupted. Interruptions disturb conversation and make effective collaboration difficult.
- Avoid using clichés. A cliché as a response to a problem situation makes the other person feel as though you are trivializing the problem.
- Avoid sarcasm. Sarcastic remarks can be easily misinterpreted and potentially insulting.
- Respond to colleagues and parents in ways that attend to both the content of their message and their feelings.
- Avoid jumping too quickly to a solution. Listening carefully and fully to the message will help you get at the root of the problem.

3.1.1 Acceptance

As the educational workforce and student demographics of our schools become more diverse, understanding and accepting personal perspectives becomes even more pertinent (Harry, 2008, 2011). Whether you are communicating with your colleagues or with the parents or guardians of the students you teach, conveying an attitude of acceptance is vital. Your fellow professionals can provide insights based on their specialized training. Family members can provide valuable information that will enable you to better understand and teach their child. Tips for Teachers 3.1 provides suggestions for facilitating effective communication and acceptance.

3.1.2 Listening

Your willingness to genuinely listen is important to being able to learn and to work effectively with others. **Effective listening** is more than waiting politely for someone to finish before you speak. You must hear the message the other person is sending and ask questions to clarify that you truly understand what others are saying. Effective listening involves the following elements:

- *Listening for the real content in the message.* The **real content** in the message is the main idea or the key information the person wants to convey.
- *Listening for the feelings in the message.* As you listen, consider what the message conveys about the person's feelings about the issue.
- *Restating content and reflecting feelings.* After the person has talked for a while, consider all that he or she has said. Then either ask a question to clarify what you know or restate the main idea to verify that what you heard is correct.
- *Allowing the speaker to confirm or correct your perception.* Give the speaker a chance to correct any misunderstanding you may have or to say more.

FIGURE 3.2 Effective listening: An example

Anna Martinez is the mother of Michael, a student with spina bifida and learning problems who has been placed full-time in a fifth-grade classroom. Michael's special education teacher, Joyce, works with him in the general education classroom for part of the school day. Anna made an appointment to meet with Joyce about her son's progress. Their conversation models effective listening.

Anna: (parent) I'm worried about Michael in this new program. I liked it better last year when I knew he was being pulled out of class and getting the help he needed. He seems to have a lot more work, and he complains about homework.

Joyce: (teacher) Let me see if I understand the problem. First, you are concerned about his progress in this new program, and second, Michael seems to have too much work. Is this right? Is there anything else you are concerned about?

Anna: Well, I can't help him with the work because I don't read English that well. He needs help when he comes home, and it can't be from me.

Joyce: The homework he is getting is too hard for him, and there isn't someone to help him at home.

Anna: That's right. He's going to flunk if he does not do his work, yet I can't help him with it, and we are both very worried about it.

Joyce: What if I met with Michael at the end of every day to ensure that he knows how to do his homework by himself? I could also meet with him in the morning before school to make sure he completes it and to help with what he doesn't know. How does that sound?

Anna: I would like to try that. That sounds good.

Joyce: Now let's get back to his placement this year. You indicated some concern about his being in the fifth-grade class all day.

Anna: No, it was really the homework in the class. If we solve that, it will be okay.

Joyce: Well, let's give this plan a try.

Figure 3.2 provides an example of a special education teacher listening effectively to a parent.

3.1.3 Questioning

Questions are an important part of the communication process and have multiple purposes. Questions can be used not only to teach, to establish relationships, to inquire, and to investigate, but also to bully or intimidate. Questions can be closed or open (Stockall, 2014). A closed question solicits a direct response and may be appropriate when obtaining factual information quickly. However, questions that solicit a quick response or a simple "yes" or "no" should be used sparingly. An open question allows a full range of responses (often beginning with "How," "What," or "Tell me about," for example) and discourages short "yes" or "no" answers. Following are several examples of open-ended questions:

- How do you explain the change in your son's behavior?
- What suggestions do you have about how I might help Mark get a better grade in social studies?
- Tell me your opinion about ways I might adjust my math instruction for Juan.
- How does what I've said about Tanika relate to her behavior at home?
- What do you suggest?
- How would you describe Gilbert's behavior?

Figure 3.3 provides an example of effective questioning. The teacher's questions give the parent a chance to consider the relationship between her child's behavior and what was occurring at home. This parent is also able to identify a change in the household that might be related to her child's poor performance. The parent and teacher collaborated to identify a possible solution and ultimately both felt better about their working relationship.

3.1.4 Staying Focused

Finding time to communicate with families and colleagues is often difficult. Therefore, it is important to use the time efficiently and effectively. Staying focused in your communication and keeping others focused is an important skill that contributes to successful collaboration. If you are meeting with an individual or a small group, having an agenda or checklist of

FIGURE 3.3 Effective questioning: An example

Antoinette Spinelli, a seventh-grade science teacher, was concerned about Naomi, who was not paying attention in class, seemed sleepy and uninterested, and was not completing assignments. She called Naomi's mother, explained the behavior, and let Naomi's mother give her point of view.

Antoinette (teacher): Naomi has not been paying attention in class and has generally seemed tired and disinterested. What do you think might be happening?

Tracey (parent): Well, I don't know. Maybe she just isn't that interested in science. I don't know why.

Antoinette: Well, the reason I'm concerned is that in the last few weeks Naomi has had more trouble focusing on her work and does not complete assignments as quickly as she has in the past. I wonder if you might be able to help me understand.

Tracey: Maybe it's because there have been so many people in the house the last few weeks. My family is visiting, and they were supposed to stay only one week and now they are starting on their third week. We really don't have room for all of them, so Naomi's had to give up her room. Maybe I need to make sure she is sleeping well enough.

items to discuss or accomplish can be helpful. Also, make an effort to limit distractions and interruptions in order to devote full attention to your exchange with others.

When talking with coworkers, it is tempting to steer the conversation to personal matters, situations of concern at the school, or even gossip. One thing you can do when someone has difficulty keeping to the topic is redirecting the individual, saying, for example, "Go back to talking about Katelyn. You were providing some suggestions for note-taking skills that might be helpful to her." Another thing you can do is remind him or her of the purpose of the meeting (for instance, "Jackie, let's stick to talking about our plans for content-area reading instruction").

When speaking with family members, some have so many problems of their own that they want to spend their time with you discussing their issues (including such personal problems as financial or marital difficulties) rather than the student's. When this occurs, a good strategy is to have ready a referral list for specialized assistance. It is your responsibility to remind parents that you cannot assist them with *these* problems and to suggest others (such as the school counselor) who can.

MyEdLab **Self-Check 3.1**

MyEdLab **Application Exercise 3.1:** Effective Communication

3.2 COLLABORATING WITH OTHER PROFESSIONALS

Collaboration among education professionals is occurring in schools across the nation (Murawski & Lochner, 2010; Solis, Vaughn et al., 2012). Greater collaboration (particularly among general and special education teachers) has grown out of increased awareness that students with disabilities are more likely to succeed if they receive targeted support services in the general education classroom. When professionals work in partnership and bring their expertise to the table, greater coherence results in planning and implementing academic and social goals for students. This section begins with an overview of collaboration with other professionals and continues with more detailed descriptions of various models designed to provide optimal learning opportunities for all students. In addition, specific suggestions for functioning with paraeducators are discussed.

3.2.1 Collaboration

Collaboration describes the interaction that is occurring when two are more people are working together as equal partners in activities, such as problem solving, student placement, instructional planning, and co-teaching (Friend & Bursuck, 2015). Collaboration is an umbrella term that includes a variety of models of interaction among professionals and

FIGURE 3.4 Benefits and challenges of consultation and collaboration models

BENEFITS	CHALLENGES
• Students with special needs are served in the classroom.	• Teachers need greater communication and problem-solving skills.
• Learning for all students is enhanced through spillover effects.	• Special educators' caseloads need to remain realistic.
• The social stigma of exceptionality is reduced.	• Expectations of results need to remain realistic.
• Teachers gain new knowledge and skills.	• Results need to be evaluated for effectiveness.
• Teachers develop a more integrated curriculum and instructional variety.	• Students need continued access to the continuum of services.
• Teachers share both the burdens and rewards of working with students with disabilities.	• Adequate funding, administrative support, and flexible scheduling need to be maintained.
• The importance of labels and categories of disability decreases.	
• Models work at all grade levels.	

other key stakeholders (Murawski & Hughes, 2009). The goal of collaboration is to achieve a dialogue among all persons who can provide support for the educational and social needs of students. For students with disabilities, the goal of collaboration models is to ensure that included students remain in the general education classroom while continuing to receive the accommodations they need for academic and social success.

Collaborating with other professionals can be rewarding and provides an opportunity to learn from people who have different training and experiences. It can also be demanding. In identifying myths and misunderstandings about professional collaboration, Friend (2005b) pointed out that collaboration does not come naturally to everyone. The professional preparation of teachers focuses primarily on working with students. Working with adults can be new territory—and can take skill, practice, and patience. Figure 3.4 outlines potential benefits of and challenges to collaboration.

Research on collaboration

With increased interest in including students with disabilities in general education classrooms full-time, there has also been movement toward working in cooperative ways using a variety of models. Research on collaboration has focused primarily on student and teacher perceptions of co-teaching models (Hang & Rabren, 2008; Solis, et al., 2012). Investigations of student (Dieker, 2001; Embury & Kroeger, 2012; King-Sears, Brawand, Jenkins, & Preston-Smith, 2014) and teacher (Cramer & Nevin, 2006; Kohler-Evans, 2006) perceptions of co-teaching indicate general favorability. However, research among both students and teachers underscored the importance of having clearly defined roles and responsibilities for each teacher. Students are often confused about why two teachers are in the classroom. Moreover, co-teachers can become frustrated if their role is reduced to something less than a full instructional partner (Embury & Kroeger, 2012; Keefe, Moore, & Duff, 2004). Research also indicates that a primary concern among teachers is lack of planning time (Solis et al., 2012).

There is a rich body of literature and practical resources related to collaboration. However, research data documenting the effectiveness of collaborative approaches for meeting the academic needs of students with disabilities is growing, but limited (Friend, Cook, Hurley-Chamberlain, & Shamberger, 2012; Scruggs, Mastropieri, & McDuffie, 2007; Sweigart & Landrum, 2015; Van Garderen, Stormont, & Goel, 2012). Research is particularly sparse at the secondary level (Magiera, Smith, Zigmond, & Gebauer, 2005; Nierengarten, 2013). Similarly, research on the efficacy of collaboration in RTI efforts is in its infancy (Martinez & Young, 2011; Murawski & Hughes, 2009; Perry, 2012). Therefore, it is recommended that teachers and administrators take a close look at their collaborative models through observation and self-reflection and make adjustments as needed (Murawski & Dieker, 2008; Murawski & Lochner, 2011).

Resources needed for collaboration

As research on teacher perceptions indicates, time is the most precious and necessary resource for effective collaboration. Unless time is built into teachers' and other professionals' schedules and workloads, collaboration simply cannot occur regularly. Also, if the special education teacher is going to work collaboratively with the social studies teacher, for example, both need to have a planning period at the same time. Although teachers can be resourceful in finding time to collaborate, administrative support is crucial. Here are ways some schools have resolved the challenge:

- Administrators designate a common time for collaborating professionals (e.g., all fourth-grade teachers who are members of the same team).
- School boards pay professionals for one extra time period each week that is used for collaboration or for meeting with parents.
- School districts provide early dismissal for students one day a week so that team members have a common planning time.
- Teachers schedule brief, but focused planning periods with one another as necessary.
- Administrators designate meeting rooms or other conference space for meetings among colleagues.
- Administrators provide workshops for faculty in how to run purposeful and results-oriented meetings.
- Administrators provide resources and professional development in web-based **collaborationware** tools to facilitate conferencing and collaboration on tasks such as planning and curriculum development (Charles & Dickens, 2012).

Administrators can also facilitate successful collaboration by providing an orientation session that sets expectations for implementation of the collaborative model in the school and answers basic questions about roles and responsibilities. For example, at the secondary level, when contact is to be made with parents for a meeting with the collaboration team, who contacts the parents and sets the agenda for the meeting? The orientation can also cover what paperwork is required and how it should be completed and submitted.

3.2.2 Collaboration Models

When Alexis Bourg began her 15-week student teaching assignment at Hancock Elementary School, her supervising teacher, Renee Ward, began introducing her to multiple specialists (e.g., special education teacher, speech therapist, school psychologist). Alexis soon found out that the nature and dynamics of the interaction with these specialists varied considerably. As a classroom teacher, your collaboration with other professionals is likely to take many forms. Different ways in which general education teachers might work collaboratively include consultation, teaming, co-planning, co-teaching, and co-assessing/co-grading.

MyEdLab
Video Example 3.2.
Watch this video to observe what happens in a meeting between a case manager and special education teacher as they discuss one of the teacher's struggling students. What suggestions did the teacher pick up from this conversation about different ways to present information for students who might struggle with vocabulary and spelling?

3.2.3 Consultation

For any professional, understanding the limits of personal expertise is imperative, and knowing when and how to solicit advice from colleagues with specialized training is important. From time to time you may feel the need to get input from a school counselor, psychologist, social worker, reading coach, or other specialist as you try to best serve the needs of students in your classroom. For example, in planning culturally responsive interventions in an RTI model, you may need to consult with a bilingual or English as a second language specialist (Klingner & Edwards, 2006a).

Consultation is an interactive process that enables people with diverse expertise to generate creative solutions to mutually defined problems. For example, a special

FIGURE 3.5 Consultation problem-solving worksheet

Collaborative Team Member Name and Position: ____________________

Team Member's Responsibilities Include: ____________________

____

Target Student's Name: ____________________

Problem Behavior Student Is Exhibiting: ____________________

____

Potential Interventions and Consequences Include: ____________________

____

Implemented Intervention: ____________________

Procedures Include: ____________________

____

Team Members Involved and Their Responsibilities: ____________________

____

Summary Evaluation of the Intervention: ____________________

____

Future Interventions/Objectives: ____________________

education teacher might consult with you about how to develop a behavior management plan for a child with a behavior disorder who is included in your classroom. Another instance might be a reading coach who consults with you regarding research-based interventions for a struggling reader in your classroom.

Consultation may be provided for an individual teacher, special education/general education teams, or other groups of teachers. Whatever the configuration of participants, the overall goal of consultation is to tap a consultant's professional expertise to assist a consultee or group of consultees in their efforts to resolve a particular problem or situation. Figure 3.5 is a worksheet that can be used to guide the problem-solving process.

Friend and Cook (2013) identify the following characteristics of consultation:

- *Triadic and indirect relationship.* Typically, consultation involves an expert (the consultant) and parents, teachers, and/or administrators (the consultee) in resolving a problem related to a particular student, group of students, or parent (the client). This triadic arrangement is indirect in that the client is not directly involved in consultation conversations and interactions.
- *Voluntariness.* Consultation should involve the voluntary participation of both the consultant and the consultee. Typically, consultation is initiated with a request from the consultee (Friend & Bursuck, 2015).
- *Expert and directional relationship.* The role of the consultant is to provide expertise and guidance in solving a classroom- or student-based problem.
- *Problem-solving process with steps or stages.* There are a number of models of consultation, mainly stemming from school psychology literature. Usually, models have steps or stages, although the stages are not always followed in a rigid manner.
- *Shared but differentiated responsibilities and accountability.* The responsibility of the consultant is to work with the consultee through the problem-solving process. Although a consultant may be available to provide support during implementation of an intervention, this is not always the case. The consultee has implementation responsibility if the consultee chooses to implement the intervention totally, partially, or at all.

Given the range of individual student needs in the classroom, an advantage of consultation is that it provides you with an efficient and effective way to meet those student needs. For example, if you have a student with a hearing impairment, a consultant might help you learn to implement appropriate assistive technology. A special education teacher might consult with you to implement an intervention for a student who has difficulty with phonemic awareness. A reading coach may demonstrate an intensive reading comprehension strategy to address the needs of children who do not meet benchmark standards with typical classroom instruction. In short, consultation can provide you with professional development to help students succeed.

One disadvantage of consultation is that the "directional relationship" can cause rifts. This is particularly true if a teacher feels that the "expert" is there to "fix" a problem or if the consultee is uncomfortable with the unevenness of expertise. However, if teachers develop a mind-set for learning and a positive attitude about seeking help to bring the best resources to the student, such disadvantages can be overcome.

3.2.4 Teaming

By definition, teams are groups with definite goals. This includes goals related to the assigned task as well as goals for the functioning of the group (Friend & Bursuck, 2015). In addition, by definition teams are groups consisting of committed members. This involves a commitment to the task at hand as well as a commitment to the educational well-being of students involved. As Beebe and Masterson (experts in the field of small-group communication) maintain, "All teams are small groups, but not all groups operate as a team" (2012, p. 6). What makes an effective team? Effective team efforts necessitate (a) focused leadership, (b) efficient procedures and rules, (c) clear definition of roles, (d) mutual understanding of issues related to accountability and responsibility, (e) active communication (both face-to-face and virtual), and (f) a mechanism for problem solving and conflict resolution (Beebe & Masterson, 2012; Richardson, 2005).

Teams differ in terms of formation (by administrators; by group members) and composition (multidisciplinary, groups of classroom teachers). They also differ in respect to duration (some are permanent, some short-term) and frequency of meetings. Finally, teams differ in terms of the scope of their work (schoolwide programs, focus on groups of children, focus on an individual child).

Your professional preparation as a classroom teacher, knowledge of the general education curriculum, and daily interactions with your students make you a valuable team member. There are a variety of teams in which you may be involved. You may be asked to serve on an RTI leadership team. RTI teams are multidisciplinary groups that review student assessment data, monitor student progress, and make recommendations for research-based interventions. Other multidisciplinary teams consisting of school professionals, student parents or guardians, and sometimes students collaborate to write and monitor students' IEPs.

Teachers in elementary and secondary settings frequently meet in teams for collaborative planning. For example, at Carver Elementary School the teachers work in grade-level teams to plan standards-based instruction in all subject areas. At Woodlawn Middle School, the special education teacher and the speech and language teacher specialist work in teams with the general education teachers to develop strategies for facilitating the vocabulary and concept learning of target students. Michelle Canner is a high school English teacher who has several students with learning disabilities in her classes. These same students are also in Jonathan Wood's social studies classes and Maria Rodriguez's science classes. The special education teacher and these three teachers established a collaborative team to meet the needs of the target students more effectively.

3.2.5 Co-Planning

Co-planning occurs when one or more professionals share the responsibility for constructing unit and/or lesson plans. For example, you might partner with a special education teacher to develop a long-range plan for teaching mathematics to a child with learning disabilities in your class. You may also work with grade-level or subject-area colleagues to develop lesson or unit plans based on specific standards. In long-range co-planning, the general education and special education teachers broadly plan their overall goals and desired outcomes for the class and for specific students with disabilities in the class. This co-planning of broad goals occurs quarterly (or more frequently if necessary). This planning fits in with the IEP of each student with disabilities.

In lesson co-planning, the general education and special education teachers plan specific lessons and desired outcomes for the week (Schumm, 2006; Schumm, Vaughn, & Harris, 1997). The teachers decide who will take the lead in the lesson, who will ensure that target students' needs are met, and who will provide individual or small-group instruction (Murawski, 2012). Figure 3.6 illustrates a form for daily co-planning.

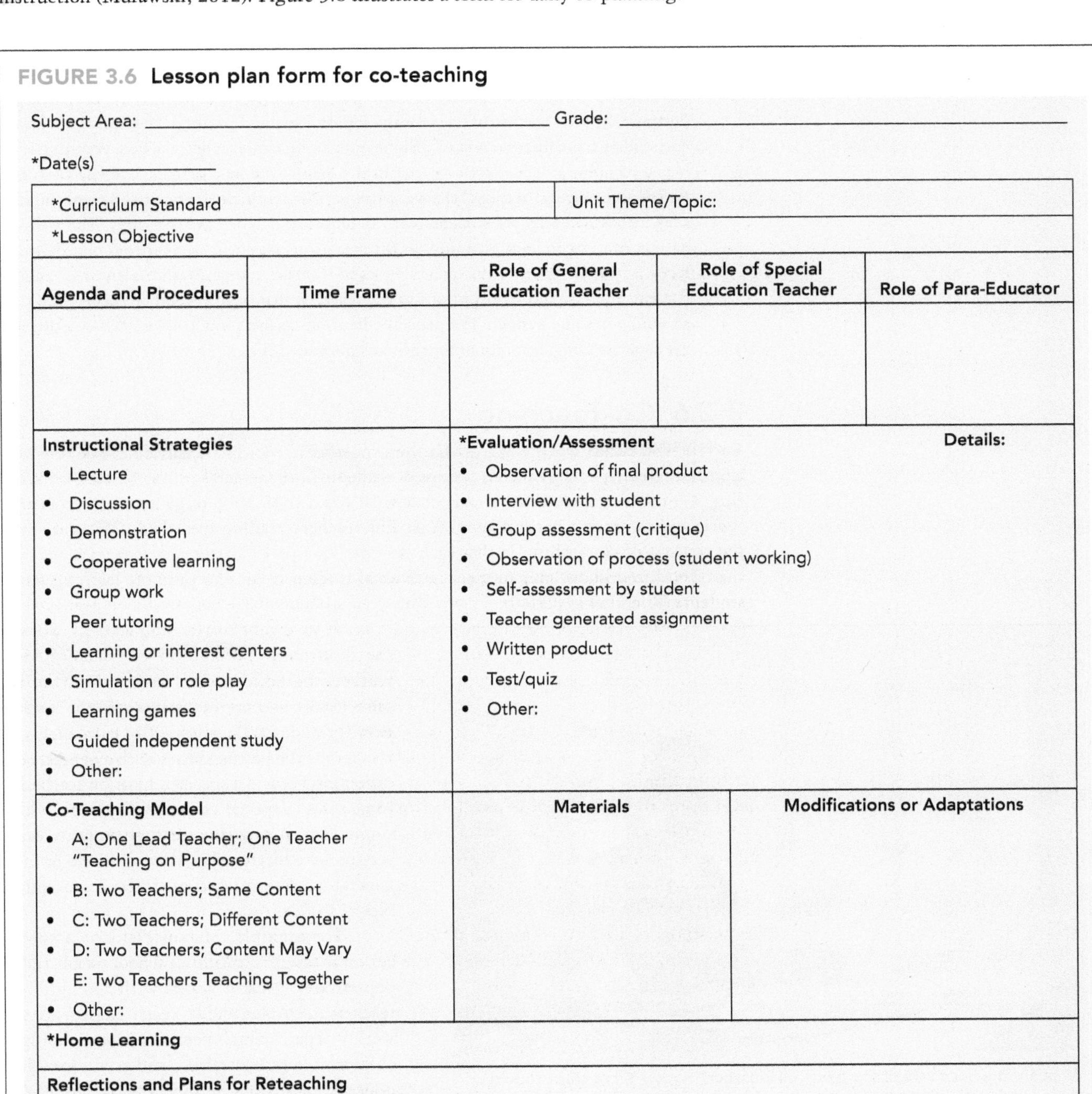

FIGURE 3.6 **Lesson plan form for co-teaching**

Subject Area: ______________________ Grade: ______________________

*Date(s) __________

*Curriculum Standard	Unit Theme/Topic:
*Lesson Objective	

Agenda and Procedures	Time Frame	Role of General Education Teacher	Role of Special Education Teacher	Role of Para-Educator

Instructional Strategies	*Evaluation/Assessment	Details:
• Lecture • Discussion • Demonstration • Cooperative learning • Group work • Peer tutoring • Learning or interest centers • Simulation or role play • Learning games • Guided independent study • Other:	• Observation of final product • Interview with student • Group assessment (critique) • Observation of process (student working) • Self-assessment by student • Teacher generated assignment • Written product • Test/quiz • Other:	

Co-Teaching Model	Materials	Modifications or Adaptations
• A: One Lead Teacher; One Teacher "Teaching on Purpose" • B: Two Teachers; Same Content • C: Two Teachers; Different Content • D: Two Teachers; Content May Vary • E: Two Teachers Teaching Together • Other:		

*Home Learning
Reflections and Plans for Reteaching

Finding the time for co-planning is often difficult, but it is critical for success (Murawski, 2012; Solis et al., 2012). Joyce Duryea, a special education teacher, has a set day and time for co-planning with each of the general education teachers with whom she is partnered. Meetings take place during the school day while students are in other classes, such as Spanish, art, or music. "We discuss the planning for the following week and how we can best work together," explains Joyce. Once a month, she and the other teachers go over the goals and objectives from the students' IEPs and discuss whether they are meeting goals or whether they need to switch over to another goal if the students have accomplished the one previously established. As Joyce puts it, "We discuss each student's progress in depth."

Pam Stover works with three general education teachers in the mathematics department at a high school. Finding time each day—or sometimes each week—to meet with each teacher is difficult. Pam and her colleagues have decided to use technology to foster communication:

> On teacher work days, I have 2-hour planning meetings with each math teacher. Fortunately, each teacher has a webpage for students and parents. The webpage outlines curriculum standards and related assignments for each month of the school year. In essence it is a planning calendar for everyone in the loop—students, parents, and the two of us. Before each teacher "releases" the webpage, we discuss curricular goals and think through adaptations necessary for students with disabilities included in the classes. The webpage has forced us to do joint planning. In the meantime, we email each other almost daily and focus primarily on any adjustments we need to make to our advance planning based on student progress and interruptions to the schedule that were beyond our control. We use an online grading system. The general education teachers input grades but consult with me about grading adaptations for the students with IEPs.

3.2.6 Co-Teaching

Co-teaching occurs when two teachers work together to coordinate curriculum and instruction and to teach heterogeneous groups of students in the general education classroom setting. Co-teaching partnerships can occur with any combination of general educators with special educators or other specialists (e.g., ESL teachers, reading specialists). What is key to the concept of co-teaching is that each partner has a particular area of expertise and uses that specialized knowledge to meet individual student needs and promote learning for all students (Friend et al., 2010).

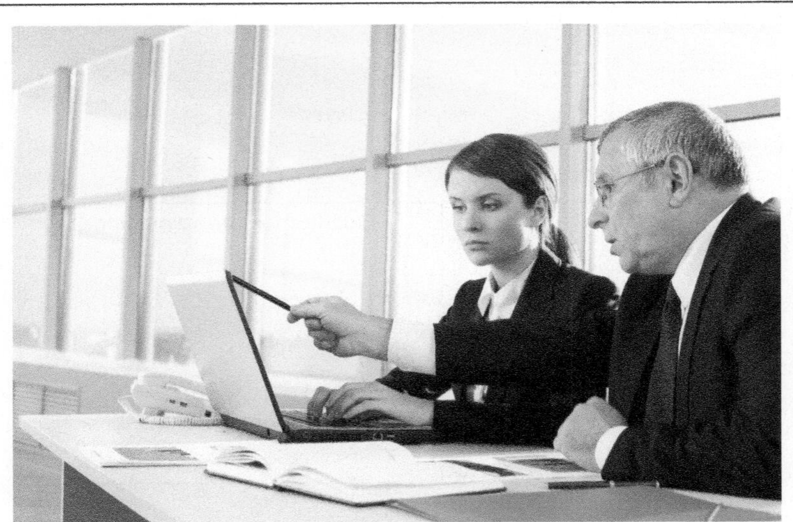

What are the hallmarks of the peer collaboration model? What steps should these teachers follow in planning and problem solving to achieve a successful peer collaboration?

How might co-teaching actually work in the classroom? For **lesson co-teaching**, two teachers are both in the classroom during the same lesson, and both participate in the instruction (Friend, 2007; Sileo, 2011). In inclusion classrooms the partnership is with a general education teacher and a special education teacher. In some cases, a special educator may work with a single general education teacher; in other cases, the special educator may work with two or more general education teachers (Villa, Thousand, & Nevin, 2008).

For example, Martin Fields is a special educator assigned to a high school social studies department. Martin works with five different teachers to co-plan and co-teach. Martin attends weekly departmental meetings to keep on top of curricular, administrative, and student-related issues. In addition, he meets with one teacher each school day either before, during, or after school to co-plan.

Co-teaching partnerships can occur with any combination of general educators with special educators or other specialists (e.g., ESL teachers, reading specialists). What is key to the concept of co-teaching is that each partner has a particular area of expertise and uses that specialized knowledge to meet individual student needs and promote learning for all students (Friend et al., 2010).

In inclusion classrooms the partnership is with a general education teacher and a special education teacher. In some cases, a special educator may work with a single general education teacher; in other cases, the special educator may work with two or more general education teachers (Villa, Thousand, & Nevin, 2008). For example, Martin Fields is a special educator assigned to a high school social studies department. Martin works with five different teachers to co-plan and co-teach. Martin attends weekly departmental meetings to keep on top of curricular, administrative, and student-related issues. In addition, he meets with one teacher each school day either before, during, or after school to co-plan.

Martin explains his role this way:

> I work in five general education classrooms. At first, some of my colleagues were unwilling to do anything but whole class, undifferentiated instruction. In some cases, I felt like an "assistant" or "teacher aide"—or worse "a fly on the wall." After our social studies team went through some extensive professional development, we identified ways to organize instruction within each person's comfort zone. I still have to be flexible enough to work with different classroom management styles and personalities, and that's OK. But our team members are all starting to see an impact on student learning with two teachers teaching.

Because lessons are co-planned, the specific roles and responsibilities of each teacher are mutually determined ahead of time. Sometimes the general education teacher works with the class as a whole, and the special education teacher adapts assignments for special-needs students, accommodating their learning needs or working with small groups of students. At other times, the class is divided into groups, and each teacher works with a different group. Sometimes the special education teacher takes the lead in providing instruction to the class while the general education teacher moves from student to student, conducting individual lessons or conferences. With careful planning, special education teachers might be present only during instructional support. During whole-group lecture time, the special education teacher might not be present. However, the special education teacher may be present for follow-up activities, completion of assignments, or reteaching. The roles of both teachers vary according to the goals of the lessons and the needs of the students.

Research indicates that in some co-teaching classrooms, teachers fall into a pattern of the general education teacher presenting a lesson and the special education teacher "grazing" or circulating around the room checking in on targeted students (Magiera & Zigmond, 2005; Scruggs et al., 2007; Weiss & Lloyd, 2003). In other situations, like that of Martin Fields, the role of the special educator is like that of a teaching assistant (Harbort et al., 2007; Murawski, 2009). In such cases, the impact of having two professionals in the classroom is diminished. The parity of two teachers—each with different training and set of professional tools—is imperative for successful co-teaching. One way to foster parity and to maximize student engagement and learning is to implement a variety of co-teaching models. The models differ in terms of teacher roles, grouping patterns, and/or content presentation (Solis, Vaughn, Swanson, & McCulley 2012). Descriptions of five models follow with elementary and secondary examples.

1. ***Model A—One Lead Teacher; One Teacher "Teaching on Purpose."*** One teacher takes primary responsibility for presenting the overall lesson to the whole class and the second teacher makes observations of student behavior and also "teaches on purpose." While observing, the second teacher can gather information about student engagement and participation, work habits, and needs for assistance. Teaching on purpose involves monitoring of student understanding through asking

targeted questions about key concepts and skills and/or examination of student work. Some teaching on purpose can occur on the spot to resolve misunderstandings—if it does not interfere with the flow of the lesson. The second teacher can also provide 1- to 5-minute mini-lessons for individual students or small groups of students who need additional help or reinforcement as a follow-up to the lesson. To assure parity among professionals, either the general education or special education teacher can take the lead role.

- As part of a unit on weather and climate, a class of fifth graders participated in a lesson on weather maps. After the class watched a DVD on different types of weather maps, the lead teacher led a discussion of the viewing. Students were then divided into five groups. Each group was given a different type of weather map (e.g., precipitation, satellite) and asked to develop a summary to describe the purpose of the map, how information was displayed, and how to interpret information from the map. While students were working in groups, the lead teacher was available to answer general questions from the groups when the group leader raised his or her hand and to reinforce rules for behavior during cooperative learning. The supporting teacher circulated around the room to make sure all students were participating and to clarify misconceptions. In addition, she reinforced the "big idea" of the lesson to targeted students who typically have difficulty with science concepts and connected what they were learning to daily life. At the end of the lesson, the supporting teacher met with a group of five targeted students she believed might need additional support. They met for 5 minutes to review the key concepts learned.
- During the course of a lecture and demonstration on how to determine latitude and longitude in a seventh-grade geography class, it became clear to both co-teachers that several students needed some assistance in learning the new concept. This included three students with learning disabilities and one ELL. While most students completed an independent follow-up activity, the special educator met with this small group and provided mnemonic strategies for remembering the difference between latitude and longitude.

2. ***Model B—Two Teachers; Same Content.*** In this model, both teachers teach the same content to small, mixed-ability groups of students. Sometimes referred to as parallel teaching (Friend & Bursuck, 2015), this format works well when complex new information is presented or when students need smaller groups to promote clarifying questions or discussion. After the small-group activity, the whole class can reconvene to recap key ideas from group sessions.
   - In a kindergarten classroom, the children are divided into two groups for a health lesson. Each teacher then conducts a demonstration to a small group of how to brush teeth using a model set of teeth and large toothbrush. Students then generate a list of rules for healthy dental care. The teacher writes the rules on sentence strip cards. The two groups then get back together to compare their rules and develop a master list.
   - After reading a textbook chapter on the War of 1812, an eleventh-grade U.S. history class is randomly divided into two groups. Each group is given a different article for supplemental reading on the topic. Each group then participates in a teacher-led discussion about whether or not the War of 1812 should be considered the second U.S. revolution. After the discussion, the groups present their position and describe how they integrated textbook and supplemental reading material. Finally, students vote pro or con on the issue (by secret ballot).
3. ***Model C—Two Teachers; Different Content.*** Students are placed in groups based on instructional needs. One group might focus on review and additional practice; a second group might engage in enrichment activities.
   - After teaching a lesson on contractions to a group of first graders, a review of student performance on homework revealed that six students were having

difficulty with the concept. Thus, one teacher worked with the six students who needed reteaching and guided practice. A second group worked with the other teacher to create a language experience story using contractions. The groups then came together and did a choral reading with the story the second group created.
   - Seventh graders in a math class were studying how to calculate the area of polygons. A pop quiz revealed that about half of the class had mastered the benchmark; the other half needed additional work. Two Internet-based programs were identified to address the needs of each group. One teacher remained in the general education classroom and projected the reteaching lesson on the Smart Board. The second teacher took her group to the computer lab and students worked independently on a web-based set of challenge problems.

4. ***Model D—Two Teachers; Content May Vary.*** This model includes multiple centers—some with teacher-led activities, some with student-led activities, and some with independent work. The groups may be composed of same- or mixed-ability students depending on the objectives of the lesson. This model includes reading groups and learning centers in which students are engaged in a variety of activities. It is sometimes referred to as **station teaching** (Friend & Bursuck, 2015).
   - In a third-grade reading/language arts class, group assignments are made based on interim reading assessments coupled with teacher judgment. Groups vary in number from three to six and are reconfigured after each interim assessment. Students rotate from center to center at regular intervals. Centers include two teacher-led guided reading centers, independent computer work, a writing center, and a word-work/spelling center.
   - In an eighth-grade math class, students are placed into three groups based on a benchmark test in dividing mixed fractions. One group works with the special education teacher to review steps and strategies to solve problems for the entire class period. The general education teacher meets with the other two groups (one at a time) to clarify questions. Students also demonstrate solutions of problems to other members of the group. When not meeting with the teacher, students work independently on word problems using division of mixed fractions.

5. ***Model E—Two Teachers Teaching Together.*** In this model, teachers divide up the agenda for teaching a lesson to a whole class. Teachers share responsibility for lecturing, demonstrating, modeling note-taking, and providing strategies for learning content. Some teachers comment that this is the most difficult model to implement. Initially, extensive planning is necessary to decide who does what. Eventually, co-teachers can develop a rhythm for teaching together.
   - A third-grade reading/language arts teacher describes a graphic organizer for narrative writing. Then her special education colleague and she provide a step-by-step demonstration on the Smart Board as they brainstorm together to complete the story map. Students then work in pairs to brainstorm about a narrative story on their own using the graphic organizer.
   - Co-teachers in a tenth-grade civics class co-lecture on the Bill of Rights. One teacher presents a set of PowerPoint® slides to introduce each. The other teacher leads a discussion about contemporary implications of each right.

For many teachers, co-teaching was not part of their professional preparation. Therefore, when asked to co-teach, teachers often need to adjust from working solo to working collaboratively on a regular, sometimes daily basis. Some teachers feel out of place in another teacher's classroom and find it difficult to determine how much control to take. Ongoing communication about how best to use the talents and expertise of each partner and explicit delineation of roles and responsibilities are imperative (Brown, Howerter, & Morgan, 2013; Schumm, Hughes, & Arguelles, 2001; Sileo, 2011). Want to learn more about co-teaching? The three-part series found on YouTube entitled "Successful Co-teaching: Keys to Team Development" includes excellent suggestions and examples.

3.2.7 Co-Assessment/Co-Grading

Co-assessment/co-grading occurs when two or more professionals are actively engaged in assessment data collection (e.g., screening, progress monitoring, diagnosis, etc.), evaluation, grading student performance, determining report card grades, and reporting student assessment outcomes and grades to parents or caregivers. As Murawski and Lochner (2011) point out, "Co-teachers should never view students as [a] 'my kids' and 'your kids' situation. This extends to assessment, evaluation, and grading as well" (p. 176).

Increasingly, co-assessment and co-grading are becoming more common (Conderman & Hedin, 2012). At the school level, multidisciplinary teams work collaboratively in assessment and evaluation of student performance. At the classroom level, co-teachers are active in all aspects of co-assessing—assessment and evaluation as well as co-grading. Consequently, it is important for professionals to develop assessment literacy (Avalos, Pazos-Rego, Cuevas, Massey, & Schumm, 2009; Popham, 2011, 2014). Assessment literacy involves an understanding of both formal and informal assessments and making instructional decisions based on assessment and student performance data (Mokhtari, Rosemary, & Edwards, 2008).

In a paper on comprehensive assessment and evaluation, the National Joint Committee on Learning Disabilities (2011) makes a case for distinction between the terms. The committee defines assessment as "the collection of data through the use of multiple measures, including standardized and informal instruments and procedures" (p. 3). Thus, data are collected using both formal and informal measures yielding qualitative or quantitative data about individual and groups of students. Evaluation is described as "the process of integrating, interpreting, and summarizing the comprehensive assessment data" (p. 3). Evaluation can also be referred to as data-based decision making.

MyEdLab
Video Example 3.3.
Watch this video as two special educators discuss how they assist teachers to modify classroom tests to accommodate students with special needs. What would you do to help students with special needs achieve the same results and outcomes as their general education peers?

There are a number of purposes for assessment and evaluation (Schumm & Arguelles, 2006):

- Initial screening for reading groups, instruction, or further assessment
- Diagnosis to determine individual strengths and challenges
- Monitoring to assure academic progress
- Determining appropriate placement in special education services or other student support systems
- Determining student outcomes to make decisions about promotion or graduation
- Evaluating the strengths and weaknesses of instructional programs
- Being accountable to key stakeholders at school, district, state, and national levels

How does collaboration with assessment and evaluation occur? The answer varies considerably by state, school district, and school. As a general education teacher, you will want to ask the following in terms of your role in the assessment and evaluation process:

- What is the process for each phase of assessment and evaluation (e.g., screening, diagnosis, progress monitoring, etc.) in my state, school district, and school?
- What assessment data will I be responsible for collecting?
- Which colleagues and professionals are involved in the assessment and evaluation process, and what are their roles and responsibilities in that process?
- What is the role of families and students in the assessment and evaluation process?

In thinking about co-teaching, grading is an important consideration when students with disabilities are in general education classrooms. Often the special education co-teacher makes adaptations to homework, assignments, and tests. How do these modifications affect the way students are graded? How can teachers align student grades with state standards and student performance on high-stakes tests? To what extent should students' motivation affect their grades? What about their persistence and their ability? How can these qualities be measured? These issues need to be openly discussed by teachers who have students with disabilities in their classrooms.

TIPS FOR TEACHERS 3.2

Questions to Ponder When Collaborating on Student Grades

When working with a colleague who is co-teaching with you, the following questions about managing student grades should be addressed at the beginning of the year and readdressed as necessary throughout the year:

- What is our classroom policy on grading? How will this be communicated to students? To families?
- When designing an assignment, what criteria will we use to grade the assignment? Who will do the grading?
- How will we evaluate student work when modifications are made for students with special needs?
- Who will record assignments in the standard and/or electronic gradebook?
- How will we determine final grades?
- How will we communicate grades to families? To administrators?

Standards-based grading and reporting have been offered as an alternative model for reporting students' strengths and areas in need of improvement (Jung & Guskey, 2007; Marzano, 2009; Munoz & Guskey, 2015). Recognizing the challenge of how best to evaluate and report the performance of students with disabilities in general education, school districts have begun to provide some clarity through the use of standards-based grading (Guskey & Jung, 2009; Iamarino, 2014; Munoz & Guskey, 2015). Standards-based grading involves an examination of individual curriculum standards; the process, product, and progress learning goals of the individual student; and the appropriate accommodations for the student as determined by the IEP. Depending on the situation, grading could occur on grade-level standards with accommodations and/or grading on modified standards. Although a great deal of work remains in the implementation of this practice in terms of logistics and equity, the promise of standards-based grading is that teachers, parents, and students are provided specific information about progress and instructional goals.

Grading procedures for students with disabilities are often an IEP item, and grading guidelines are written and agreed on during the development of the IEP. This means that students with special needs who are included in general education classrooms often do poorly in these classes. Even when students do their best, their grades are often in the failure range. Students with disabilities need grades that reflect more than the extent to which their performance compares with that of other students in the class. They need encouragement and reinforcement for their work and effort and reasonable accommodations in assessment and grading.

As in the case of co-assessment, grading policies differ considerably depending on local requirements. Nonetheless, policies for student grading are not always made clear, so it is important for teachers working together to communicate with one another and with administrators to ensure fair assessment and reporting of student performance (McLoughlin & Lewis, 2008). Tips for Teachers 3.2 provides some questions that need to be considered in thinking about how grading will be managed.

3.2.8 Collaborating with Paraeducators

In addition to collaborating with teachers and other specialists in your school, you may also be responsible for the supervision of **paraeducators**. Giangreco and his colleagues define paraeducators as "individuals who are trained to work with, and alongside, educators in classrooms and other educational settings to support the education of students with and without disabilities in a variety of capacities (e.g., physically, socially, instructionally)" (2008, p. 2). In recent years the role of paraeducators has become more prominent due largely from mandates of No Child Left Behind (NCLB) and IDEIA (Brock & Carter, 2013; Yell, 2016).

MyEdLab
Video Example 3.4.
Watch this video to see a paraeducator working with students in two settings: She is working with a small group of students by herself, and with an individual within a larger group of students led by the teacher. How is this paraeducator helping the teacher ensure that the needs of students are being met? What is the role of paraeducators and how can they help teachers ensure that the needs of all of their students are met?

Various terms are used to refer to paraeducators (e.g., paraprofessional, teacher assistant, teacher aide). Indeed, the National Education Association (NEA) lists over thirty job titles for support personnel (NEA, 2005). To recognize the important contributions of support personnel, some advocate the use of the term *paraeducator* (Nevin et al., 2009). However, it is recommended that teachers become familiar with locally accepted terminology (Giangreco et al., 2008) as well as local and state policies regarding paraeducators in the classroom.

This is particularly important in light of evidence indicating the overuse and misuse of paraeducators in the classroom (Giangreco, Doyle, & Suter, 2012; Giangreco, Suter, & Hurley, 2013). Research has documented that in many cases paraprofessionals are making educational decisions autonomously and implementing instruction without adequate supervision (Giangreco, Broer, & Suter, 2011). To assist teachers and administrators in the best ways to support paraeducators in their important work, resources have been designed to help school-based personnel (including paraeducators) evaluate their current status in terms of paraeducators' roles and responsibilities and set an action plan for improvement (Gerlach, 2014; Giangreco & Broer, 2003).

Although NCLB did mandate requirements for paraeducator credentials, states still vary in terms of credentialing of paraeducators. When a paraeducator is assigned to your class, it is important to learn about your colleague's educational background and experience and to provide guidance and modeling as needed. Ultimately, as the classroom teacher you are responsible for planning instruction. Stockall (2014) maintains that "the basic purpose of collaborating with paraprofessionals is protecting teachers' instructional time" (p. 198). If paraeducators do provide instruction, you are responsible for planning that instruction and monitoring student outcomes as a result of that instruction (Brock & Carter, 2013; Yell, 2016).

Professional resources for paraeducators

Fortunately, a growing body of professional resources is available for the professional preparation of paraeducators as well as the preparation of general and special education teachers for collaborating with these important members of the educational team. The National Education Association, National Resource Center for Paraprofessionals, the Paraprofessional Resource and Research Center, and National Clearinghouse for Paraeducator Resources all provide online professional resources. In addition, professional organizations such as the Council for Exceptional Children and the International Literacy Association have drafted guidelines for paraeducators.

Roles paraeducators can play to support you

If a paraeducator is assigned to your class, he or she can support you by working with individual or small groups of students, providing clerical support, assisting with behavioral issues, and planning family involvement activities. Often paraeducators reside in the same neighborhoods as your students and can serve as a "cultural broker" in helping you to understand and appreciate your students' home communities (Reuda & Genzuk, 2007). In schools serving students with ELLs, you may be assigned paraeducators to serve as interpreters with students and their family members.

A range of scenarios may occur in the case of students with disabilities. Depending on the student's IEP, the paraeducator may have duties related to instruction, behavior, safety, or physical needs (e.g., ambulation, toileting). In some cases, paraeducators may be assigned to a specific child; in other situations, they are assigned to an inclusion classroom consisting of a number of children with disabilities (Friend & Cook, 2013). Moreover, the paraeducator may be present in your classroom with or without a special education teacher. Regardless of the scenario, clear articulation about the roles and responsibilities of all adults involved is paramount.

What can you do as a general education teacher to assure successful collaboration with paraeducators? Much of what you have read in this chapter about communication and collaboration with other professionals applies with your partnership with paraeducators. In Tips for Teachers 3.3, Jamie DeFraites, a first-grade teacher in New Orleans, offers suggestions for successful partnerships with paraeducators.

TIPS FOR TEACHERS 3.3

Working with Paraeducators

Jamie's multicultural classroom includes eleven Vietnamese children and two Hispanic students who are English language learners. Jamie explains, "I love my class and was actually asked to loop to second grade—so I'll have the same students next year!"

Jamie is fortunate enough to work with two paraeducators, who join her classroom at different times during the day. One is a native speaker of Vietnamese; the other is a native speaker of Spanish. Here are Jamie's tips for working with paraeducators:

- Talk with paraeducators individually about personal interests and skills and try to match their duties with their strengths.
- Clarify roles, responsibilities, classroom routines, and expectations for student learning and behavior.
- Thank paraeducators at every opportunity—in the presence of the principal, parents, and students.
- Explain instructional strategies to them so that they can do more than grade papers—they can actually interact with children in small groups or individually.
- When assigning tasks, provide as much orientation as possible to make sure the paraeducators can be successful in what they do.
- Talk a great deal about what tasks you and the paraeducators like and dislike doing; all should agree to assume their share of unpleasant jobs.
- Plan a backup—what to do when there is nothing to do.
- Encourage paraeducators to get additional professional training. Let them know about workshops and other opportunities to learn.

3.2.9 Collaboration Issues and Dilemmas

At some time, most general education teachers will work with colleagues in consultation, teaming, co-planning, or co-teaching roles. Although research has yielded overall support from key stakeholders for collaborative teaching practices, it has also identified potential pitfalls and areas for improvement (Isherwood & Barger-Anderson, 2007; Murawski & Dieker, 2008; Rea, 2005). The following sections describe issues and dilemmas that frequently occur. Perhaps by considering these issues now, you will be able to work more effectively in future collaborative situations. Tips for Teachers 3.4 provides suggestions for collaborating with other professionals that can help you navigate such issues and dilemmas.

TIPS FOR TEACHERS 3.4

Collaborating with Other Professionals: It Takes More than Extrasensory Perception (ESP)

When working with other professionals, don't rely on extrasensory perception (ESP) to communicate. Successful collaboration necessitates more than a sixth sense. Based on their conversations with general and special education teachers and classroom observations, Schumm, Hughes, and Arguelles (2000) suggest that it takes ESP-Plus. The "plus" involves initial and ongoing conversations among key players regarding:

E—expectations, engagement, elasticity

- What are our **expectations** of each other? Of students? Of their families?
- How will each of us be **engaged?** What are our roles and responsibilities?
- How can we develop **elasticity** and learn to be flexible in our working with each other and our students?

S—skills, support, structure

- What **skills** do each of us bring to the table? How can we maximize our skills and talents?
- What **support** can we offer each other? What support and resources do we need from administration?
- How will we **structure** our collaborative efforts (e.g., classroom arrangements, planning, meeting times)?

P—professional development, pet peeves, parity

- What **professional development** do we need to enhance our partnership?
- What are each of our **pet peeves** and how can we work to avoid conflict?
- How can we establish **parity** and communicate that we are co-equal partners to administration, students, and families?

Source: Based on "Co-teaching: It takes more than ESP," by J. S. Schumm, M. T. Hughes, & M. E. Arguelles, 2000, in V. Risko & K. Bromley (Eds.), *Collaboration for diverse learners: Viewpoints and practices*, Newark, DE: International Reading Association.

Student ownership

When students with special needs are placed in general education classrooms for all or part of the day, both general education and special education teachers are responsible for their education. It is not uncommon, however, for teachers to claim "ownership" of or responsibility for some students and not others. Effective programs for all students require teacher attitudes that say, "All students are members of the learning community in my classroom, and I welcome them all."

A particular concern regarding student ownership may occur when paraeducators are assigned to a particular student. When the paraeducator remains in close proximity to a student with disabilities, the child's social relationships with the general education teacher and with other students can be stifled (Giangreco & Broer, 2007). Conversations about how best to promote social interactions and student independence should occur in IEP meetings.

Individual versus class focus

Traditionally, general education teachers at all grade levels plan instruction for the class as a whole rather than for individual learning needs (McIntosh, Vaughn, Schumm, Haager, & Lee, 1993; Mora-Harder, 2009; Schumm et al., 1995; Schumm, Moody, & Vaughn, 2000). This approach to planning reflects the need to cover the content for a subject area. Special education teachers, on the other hand, focus on meeting students' individual needs. This difference can lead to conflict. It is important for general–special education partners to discuss these differences and to consider together how to maximize differentiated professional training and skills for the benefit of all students in the classroom (Schumm, Hughes, & Arguelles, 2001; Sileo, 2011).

In recent years, one framework for designing instruction to meet the needs of all students in diverse educational settings has garnered attention among policy makers, researchers, and practitioners. This framework, Universal Design for Learning (UDL), emerged from the concept of universal design for products and architecture to bring access to individuals with disabilities. One commonly referenced example of universal design is that of curb cuts on sidewalks. The cuts were originally intended for persons using wheelchairs or walkers. However, the cuts also make life more convenient for folks using strollers or delivery carts. In other words, adaptations can make life easier for individuals with disabilities—but also for others as well.

The idea of universal design principle for education is similar (Hall, Meyer, & Rose, 2012; Rose & Gravel, 2010). With multiple ways of presenting content and multiple ways for students to demonstrate mastery, the needs of students with a wide range of learning differences can be met. This includes English language learners, students with disabilities, students identified as gifted, and struggling learners who do not receive additional services. The promise of UDL is that individual needs can be met within the general classroom setting using a wide range of adaptations—including the use of technology. Adaptations can be planned and implemented in three areas:

- Representation—presenting new skills and concepts in a variety of modes (including visual, auditory, and sensory materials) to accommodate different ways that students take in and comprehend information.
- Action and expression—providing alternate ways for students to access information and to show mastery of skills and concepts to accommodate individual differences in how students navigate in a classroom setting and demonstrate what they have learned.
- Engagement—offering appropriate ways to motivate students and opportunities for students to monitor their own learning to foster interest, independence, and student ownership in learning.

Content versus accommodation

When classroom teachers discuss planning and instruction, one of the most consistent themes is content coverage (Keefe et al., 2004; Kloo & Zigmond, 2008; Schumm et al., 1995). Classroom teachers feel they must cover more content to meet local and state standards and to ensure that students are prepared for the next grade level and for standardized tests. Moreover, Common Core State Standards lift the bar in terms of expectations for preparing students for college and the global workforce (Phillips & Wong, 2012).

Judy Schloss, a seventh-grade science teacher, admits, "I know that when I complete a science unit, some of the students understand the main concepts and others do not, but I do not have time to reteach. We just move on to new material." As a result of such moving on, many students, particularly students with learning problems, are introduced to a lot of material but learn little about any of it. As Ed Glover, a ninth-grade social studies teacher, says, "If I waited until the students got it, we would never be able to cover all the material."

The issue of content coverage directly influences the instruction of students with special learning needs, particularly now that they have greater access to the general education curriculum. You can imagine the difficulty you might have if you felt pressured to cover extensive amounts of content and at the same time felt pulled to meet the needs of individual students who failed to learn the material. To alleviate this situation, Margaret Cox (the special educator you read about at the beginning of this chapter) works with her general education colleagues to identify students—both with and without IEPs—who are in need of additional accommodations and/or reteaching to master standards in the critical areas of reading and mathematics.

Real world versus student's world

Some general education teachers think that treating all students fairly means treating them "the same." Making adaptations in homework or tests is perceived as providing undue advantage for some students. Furthermore, some general education teachers define their mission as preparing all students for the real world, where, they believe, accommodations and adaptations will not be made. Other general education teachers know that the best way to prepare students for the real world is to give them opportunities to be successful in their present world. Maria Pino, a secondary social studies teacher, explains, "My first responsibility is to help students feel successful in their present world—the world of the classroom. Making accommodations helps them feel that success. I also explain to them that employers are required by law to make reasonable adaptations for individuals with disabilities."

Successful collaborative teams emphasize the importance of establishing a community of teachers and learners who share and learn together (Hunt, Hirose-Hatae, Doering, Karasoff, & Goetz, 2000). The ability to collaborate successfully requires flexibility, respect for roles and responsibilities, and the ability to maintain a sense of humor (Schumm et al., 2001; Silio, 2011). Based on their experiences in collaborative classrooms and on their understanding of the literature on collaboration, Keefe et al. (2004) have offered the four "knows" of collaborative teaching: (a) know yourself, (b) know your partner, (c) know your students, and (d) know your "stuff."

In other words, think about your beliefs, goals, and teaching style in the context of working with a colleague to teach students in your class. This type of communication and cooperation requires time, effort, and commitment. However, the potential outcome of working together has benefits for teachers (e.g., developing mutual support, learning from one another's expertise) and students (e.g., enriched curriculum, scaffolding, reduced student–teacher ratios) (Murawski & Lochner, 2011; Sileo, 2011; Walsh & Jones, 2004).

MyEdLab **Self-Check 3.2**

MyEdLab **Application Exercise 3.2:** Collaboration

MyEdLab **Application Exercise 3.3:** Co-Teaching

3.3 WORKING WITH FAMILIES

The children you teach will represent a wide array of family compositions. While there are a number of definitions of "family," in general a family consists of individuals who are biologically or legally connected and who share a domestic relationship. This may include parents (biological, adopted, or foster), grandparents, stepparents, siblings and stepsiblings, legal guardians, or caretakers. Family units are highly influential in a child's physical, emotional, social, and academic well-being. This is particularly true for exceptional students, whose families serve multiple roles, including those of advocate and information source.

Parent or guardian involvement and collaboration are fundamental to the implementation of IDEIA (Turnbull, Turnbull, Erwin, Soodak, & Shogren, 2015). State and local regulations guide who can legally be involved in determining educational decisions for students. For example, some states include foster parents as decision makers; others do not. Rights for parents or guardians in the educational decision-making process include the following (Yell, 2016):

- They should be notified and their permission should be obtained before identification, evaluation, or educational placement of the child.
- They may request an evaluation when they think their child needs potential special education and related services.
- They may request an independent evaluation at public expense when they disagree with the educational evaluation of the school.
- They may request a reevaluation when they think their child's educational placement is no longer appropriate.
- They may request that their child be tested in his or her primary language.
- They may participate in the development of an IEP or individualized family service plan (IFSP), including placement.
- They may request a due-process hearing to resolve differences with the school.
- They should be informed about their child's progress at least as often as are parents or guardians of children without disabilities.

3.3.1 Family Collaboration

In addition to legal mandates for family involvement in the education of students with disabilities, two other forces have contributed to increased engagement on the part of parents, guardians, and other family members (Heward, 2013). One factor is increased advocacy for children with disabilities both individually and through involvement in family support groups and organizations (Turnbull et al., 2015). Another factor is a growing body of research indicating that family involvement has a positive impact on student academic and social outcomes (Epstein et al., 2009). Moreover, research in family involvement has underscored the importance of reaching out to families in "customer-friendly ways." Regularly communicating to parents, other family members, and caregivers that you truly care about your student, have high and reasonable expectations for their success, and treat all involved as you would like to be treated are as or more important than any program or home–school involvement "technique" that you might implement (Jeynes, 2011).

Culturally and linguistically diverse families

Taken together, these forces have created a climate for positive possibilities with home–school partnerships (Crosby, Rasinski, Padak, & Yildirim, 2014; Murray & Curran, 2008; O'Donnell & Kirkner, 2014). Although progress has been made in family involvement due to legal mandates and family advocacy, the ideal and reality of collaboration are far from being aligned, particularly when the needs of culturally and linguistically diverse and low-income families are concerned (Bower & Griffin, 2011; Gillanders, McKinney, & Ritchie, 2012; Harry, 2008, 2011). The overrepresentation of minorities in special education programs is an issue of national concern and challenges educators to consider how to interact with parents and their children in just and equitable ways (Donovan & Cross, 2002; Harry & Klingner, 2014). Families can bring a rich set of cultural and personal experiences to the educational process that can and should be heard (Moll, 2010; Protacio & Edwards, 2015). Developing patterns of behavior that tap these funds through commitment to the student, equality of power, and mutual trust and respect is key to successful collaborations (Blue-Banning, Summers, Frankland, Nelson, & Beegle, 2004; Harry, 2011). You as a classroom teacher play a key role in this process.

What can you do so that family members can serve as active, collaborative resources? Perhaps it is most important to recognize that home–school communication is a two-way street. As Hallahan, Kauffman, and Pullen (2015) put it, "It's critical to receive information *from* parents as well as to provide information *to* them" (p. 79). Your goal is working collaboratively for student success. Remember that most parents are doing the best they can. Parents do not wake up in the morning and decide, "I think today I will be a poor parent." Their values may be different than yours—and that is their right.

The role of families in the collaboration process

The advent of RTI makes it important for you to understand the role of families in collaboration with the process. As a general education teacher, you will be actively involved in communicating how the process works in your state, district, and school. Tips for Teachers 3.5 provides a list of potential questions you should be prepared to answer regarding RTI.

School systems have expended considerable effort to involve parents in their child's educational program. There are a range of ways that parents can become involved in their child's schooling: (1) parenting, (2) communicating, (3) volunteering, (4) home learning, (5) decision making, (6) collaborating with the community, and (7) advocacy for their child's emotional, social, and academic needs (Epstein, 1996; Young, Austin, & Growe, 2013). Parents, guardians, and other family members will vary considerably in terms of their motivation and capacity to become involved (Bower & Griffin, 2011). Nonetheless, teachers should be aware of school- and classroom-based ways to foster parent involvement and to provide leadership in promoting parent partnerships. Teachers also need to understand what parents are expecting from the relationship with their child's school.

To learn more about what parents think about essential components of successful partnerships, Blue-Banning et al. (2004) conducted individual and focus group interviews with 137 family members. Participants included parents representing a wide range of cultural and socioeconomic backgrounds and parents of children with and without disabilities. An analysis of the transcripts of interviews resulted in six indicators of successful partnerships: (a) communication, (b) commitment, (c) equality, (d) skills, (e) trust, and (f) respect. The authors concluded that parents viewed "common sense and ordinary human decency" to be the core of what parents want and expect (p. 183). Parents seemed less interested in elaborate, expensive programs and more interested in access to information and the

TIPS FOR TEACHERS 3.5

Ten Questions About RTI You Will Want to Answer for Parents

1. Is the school district currently using an RTI process to provide additional support to struggling students? If not, does the district plan to?
2. What screening procedures are used to identify students in need of intervention?
3. What are the interventions and instructional programs being used? What research supports their effectiveness?
4. What process is used to determine the intervention that will be provided?
5. What length of time is allowed for an intervention before determining if the student is making adequate progress?
6. What strategy is being used to monitor student progress? What are the types of data that will be collected and how will student progress be conveyed to parents?
7. Is a written intervention plan provided to parents as part of the RTI process?
8. Is the teacher or other person responsible for providing the interventions trained in using them?
9. When and how will information about a student's performance and progress be provided?
10. At what point in the RTI process are students who are suspected of having a learning disability referred for formal evaluation?

Source: From *Strategies for teaching students with learning and behavior problems* (p. 139), by S. Vaughn & C. S. Bos, 2015, Boston: Pearson.

quality of interactions with school personnel. The following section discusses family adjustment and the roles parents can play in supporting their children's education.

3.3.2 Family Adjustment

Family adjustment to having a family member with disabilities can vary considerably. In addition to concerns about health, safety, and academic achievement, family members can also have issues with denial, guilt, dealing with the public, hurt feelings, and stress (Hallahan et al., 2015). Parents of children with disabilities have many roles: caregiver, provider, teacher, counselor, behavior support specialist, parent of siblings without disabilities, marriage partner, information specialist, and advocate (Heward, 2013). These issues and roles can affect the parents, siblings, and extended family as well. Some families experience turmoil and suffering as a result of having a family member with disabilities, whereas others learn to cope (Seltzer, Greenberg, Floyd, Pettee, & Hong, 2001). Hallahan et al. (2015) point out that some families embrace the opportunity to learn about adjustment and equity through the experience of living with an individual with disabilities.

The needs of parents of children with disabilities are not static, but evolve and change over time (Turnbull et al., 2015). Moreover, the needs of your students and their families are likely to be highly diverse. Therefore, systematic, constant communication is imperative. In general, the needs of families with disabilities include the following:

1. ***Information exchange.*** Families need conferences, workshops, classroom information, progress reports, interpretations of their child's academic and social needs, and informal feedback about their child. Parents and guardians may need information about how to help a sibling cope with the disability of your student. Teachers can rarely provide too much information to parents (particularly parents of children with special needs, who are already aware of their child's differences).
2. ***Consumer and advocacy information.*** Family advocacy for students with disabilities and their families is a lifelong process that includes self-advocacy as well as advocacy for social, behavioral, academic, legal, and transitional support (Cohen, 2009). How can you help? First, you can listen carefully as family members advocate for the student's needs. Next, you can provide helpful information about local and online advocacy groups.
3. ***Counseling, therapy, and consultation.*** When family members request information about support groups, counseling, therapy, and other consultation services, what should you do? First, identify the information sources available from your school or school district, and keep them handy in a folder. Second, ask the school counselor or principal what procedures you should follow.
4. ***Family-coordinated service programs.*** Families need to be able to provide services to and receive services from other families through advisory councils, family-to-family networking, advocacy, and other options (Risko & Walker-Dalhouse, 2009).

Family is an important force in a student's learning and development. As a classroom teacher, fostering collaboration and communication with families is extremely important (Hallahan et al., 2015). The primary ways that you can facilitate this connection are through homework, parent conferences, and multiple forms of home–school communication. For online resources you can provide to parents, see the Tech Tips for parents of students with disabilities.

3.3.3 Homework

Homework (or *home learning*, as some school systems refer to it) gives involved family members a daily idea of your curriculum and instruction. Teachers assign homework for a number of reasons (Carr, 2013; Epstein & Van Voorhis, 2001):

- Practice (to help students strengthen skills learned in class)
- Preparation (to prepare for tests)

TECH TIPS

Helpful Resources for Parents of Children with Special Needs

There are a number of online resources that you can provide to parents to alert them to suggestions for how they can best advocate for their children. These sites also provide helpful tools and recommendations to parents of children with special needs.

- **Council for Exceptional Children** (www.cec.sped.org), the professional organization for special educators, has online resources for families.
- Exceptional Parent Magazine (www.eparent.com) offers vast online resources for parents of students with disabilities.
- **Parent Teacher Association** (www.pta.org) provides parents a voice in advocating for the safety and success of all children.
- **National Education Association** (www.nea.org) provides valuable resources for teachers in their collaborative efforts with parents.

- Participation (to increase involvement with learning activities)
- Personal development (to build a sense of responsibility and time-management skills)
- Parent–child relations (to increase involvement in home-learning activities)
- Parent–teacher communications (to inform parents about curriculum and student progress)
- Peer interactions (to promote student-to-student support and to prepare for collaborative learning activities)
- Policy (to conform to school and district mandates)
- Public relations (to communicate to parents what students are learning in school)
- Punishment (however, using homework for punishment is not particularly effective and can be counterproductive [Feldman, 2004])

Homework should not be assigned simply out of routine or "homework for homework's sake." It should be purposeful and directly tied to desired student outcomes (Marzano & Pickering, 2007). It is important to communicate to students and parents why you think homework is important and what positive outcomes it will have for students. This is particularly essential given the debate in both the professional literature and in the media regarding the validity of homework (Kohn, 2007; Sorrentino, 2013; Suskind, 2013; Watkins & Stevens, 2013).

Start the school year with a written policy statement that begins with a rationale for assigning homework (Cooper, 2001; Protheroe, 2009). Your policy statement should also include a set of expectations: what you expect of the student, what you expect of the parent, and what both the parent and the student can expect of you. Naturally, your policy should be consistent with the policy of your school or school district. However, whenever possible, involve parents in developing your policy statement. Tips for Teachers 3.6 provides an outline of issues to address in your policy statement.

Part of the controversy of homework is that it is often excessive in terms of the time it takes to complete (Pressman, Sugarman, Nemon, Desjarlais, Owens, & Schettini-Evans, 2015; Suskind, 2012). This is especially true in the case of teachers or administrators who feel the pressure to assure student performance on high stakes tests (Carr, 2013). Researcher Harris Cooper and his colleagues have conducted in-depth examinations of the research on homework (Cooper, 2001; Cooper, Robinson, & Patall, 2006). In reviewing the literature, Cooper recommends the "ten-minute rule," or "ten minutes per grade level per night" (2001, p. 36). Thus, a first grader would have 10 minutes of homework per night; a sixth grader 60 minutes of homework per night. This rule of thumb may need to be amended for students with disabilities, depending on the needs of the individual student. At the secondary level, research indicates that an hour of homework is sufficient. As Fernandez-Alonso, Suarez-Alvarez, and Muniz explain, "... it is not

Video Example from YouTube

MyEdLab
Video Example 3.5.

Watch the YouTube video, "Are Teachers Giving You Too Much Homework?" to learn more about the homework debate. What is your perspective based on current literature on this issue and based on your own experience? https://www.youtube.com/watch?v=7h1olTR3Klo

TIPS FOR TEACHERS 3.6

Communicating Homework Policy

What the Parent and Student Can Expect of You

- Create homework assignments that are meaningful and provide for independent practice of skills taught in class or enrichment of content covered in class.
- Write homework assignments on the board daily.
- Provide parents with a general homework schedule (e.g., Monday night, math and spelling; Tuesday night, math and composition).
- Inform parents about long-range projects in advance.
- Provide a system for reporting missing or late homework to parents and students.
- Grade homework in a timely fashion and provide feedback to students.

What You Expect of the Student

- Record homework assignments on an assignment sheet or in an assignment notebook.
- Complete homework assignments in a neat and timely manner.

What You Expect of the Parent

- Help the student set up a homework center.
- Help the student determine a regular homework schedule.
- Monitor and assist as necessary in the completion of homework.
- Write a note if confused about the assignment.

necessary to assign huge quantities of homework, but it is important that assignment is systematic and regular, with the aim of instilling work habits and promoting autonomous, self-directed learning" (2015, p. 9). See the 60-Second Lesson for a strategy that can help students get organized for homework.

60-*SECOND* LESSON

HOMEWORK BUDDIES: THINK–PAIR–SHARE

School days can be long for both teachers and students. With so much activity going on, it can be easy for students to forget assignments or forget books or materials they might need to complete homework assignments. This is true for students who are in a self-contained class or in departmentalized classes when students move from room to room.

At the beginning of the school year, assign each student a homework buddy—two students who sit close to each other. Then, at the end of each school day (in self-contained settings) or at the end of the class period (in departmentalized settings), do a think–pair–share (McTighe & Lyman, 1988).

1. Ask students to take out their homework assignment sheet.
2. Have each student think quietly about what the assignment is and what materials they will need to take home to complete the assignment.
3. Encourage the homework buddies to speak to each other to discuss both the assignment and what they will need to take home.
4. After buddies have conferred, ask the whole class if they have questions they were unable to resolve as a pair.

At first this routine may take more than 60 seconds, but eventually it will occur smoothly. Taking just a minute or two to get organized for homework will go a long way in helping students with disabilities succeed.

In addition to designing homework assignments that are purposeful, efficient in terms of length, and appropriate in terms of complexity, Vatterott (2010) offers two recommendations, ownership and aesthetic appeal. Assignments that foster student ownerships are those that consider student choice, interests, competence, and connection with the

What guidance can teachers provide to parents so they can help with their child's homework assignments?

subject matter. Assignments that are aesthetically appealing (e.g., include graphics, visuals, white space) encourage student engagement. The interactive nature of assignments involving technology can also motivate students to complete individual assignments, connect what they are learning to real-world evidence, and also to work with peers in collaborative projects (Roblyer, 2016).

Ongoing communication with parents about the time and effort it takes students to complete assignments at home can be helpful (Bryan & Burstein, 2004; Margolis, 2005). The goal of helping students with homework and providing an academic support system at home is to enable students to develop independent study skills. For this to happen, family members and teachers need to work together. One way you can help is to hold workshops in which families can learn skills for helping with home learning. Often, parents, guardians, and other family members want to help but are not certain how to do so (Hughes, Schumm, & Vaughn, 1999; Rodger, 2011). Providing home-based adults with specific strategies that are aligned with what you are doing in the classroom can improve rates of homework completion and possibly lead to higher academic outcomes (Patall, Cooper, & Robinson, 2008).

Many school districts have implemented student information systems (SISs) with online access for parents (Roblyer, 2016). Immediate access to grades, progress in meeting benchmarks and standards, attendance, and/or schedules can help parents stay on top of their child's progress and communicate with the school before it is too late. If you use an SIS, communicate to parents and students your schedule for posting grades so they have reasonable expectations about when information will be provided. If you do not have access to an online system, plan to send home regular progress reports providing information about performance on homework, class assignments, and tests. By taking 30 minutes every other week to complete a progress form, you can eliminate problems that arise when parents are uninformed about the student's progress until report cards are issued.

3.3.4 Planned and Unplanned Parent Conferences

Parent–teacher conferences provide a forum for a two-way conversation regarding student progress, goal setting, and problem solving (Hoerr, 2014). They provide you with a great opportunity to develop a partnership with parents and gain insights about the children you teach.

Schools vary considerably in terms of how conferences are scheduled. In some schools, entire days are set aside once or twice during the school year for conferences. In other situations, conferences are held only on an as-needed basis. When assigned to a new school, you'll want to find out early on about the expectations for parent–teacher conferences at your school and plan accordingly.

Parent–teacher conferences differ in terms of purpose and composition of participants. Some focus on general academic progress; others focus on a specific academic or behavioral issue. Conferences may occur with a single teacher, co-teachers, or multidisciplinary team. In respect to families, a single parent may attend or additional parents, family members, or family advocates may be present. At times you may want to include the student in the conference; this is particularly true with middle and high school students (Brodie, 2014; Buchino, 2011). If you think including the student is appropriate, talk with the parent first so that there are no surprises.

FIGURE 3.7 Sample note for parent conference

It's a Date

Dear Parent of ______________________________________,

Thank you for your response to my request for a meeting about your child. Your appointment has been set for ________________________ (time) on ________________________ (day), ________________________ (date).

I have set aside ________________________ minutes for our visit. If you will be bringing any guests, please let me know in advance. If this time is no longer convenient, please let me know.

Looking forward to seeing you,

____

Teacher's Name

In your role as a general education teacher, you may be responsible for scheduling the conference with all key stakeholders (e.g., colleagues and family members). Figure 3.7 is a sample letter teachers can send to parents to confirm a planned meeting.

Determine if your school provides child care and/or translators for parents who may be in need of such services. Also, if working parents cannot meet during the school day, find out about your school's policy on alterative scheduling for conferences.

Planned conferences require the same amount of attention and care as planning your instructional lessons (Dardig, 2008; *Educational Horizons Magazine*, 2012). There are measures that you can take before, during, and after a parent conference that will make the most out of the experience.

Before the Conference. To prepare for a planned conference:

- Review the student's materials, grades, and work progress.
- Meet with and learn the perspectives of other professionals who also work with the student.
- Review the student's folder, portfolio, and previous assessment information.
- Obtain samples of the student's most recent work.
- Make an outline of topics to discuss and prepare a copy for all attendees.
- Organize student assessment results and work samples in order of the outline.
- Create a comfortable setting (no small child chairs) that encourages engagement (a round table works well).

During the Conference. Welcome the parent with warmth and introduce all participating adults to each other. Review your outline and ask the parent if he or she has other items to discuss. Make notes of key ideas so that parents know you value their input (Hoerr, 2014). Begin and end the discussion by saying something positive about the child (Rose, 2005). During the conference, try not to use technical education language that may intimidate or insult the parent (Allen, Harry, & McLaughlin, 1993.). Make certain that you have communicated any concerns in a straightforward and sensitive manner, and solicit parent reactions and recommendations to address those concerns (Rose, 2005; Shalaway, 2005). At the end of the conference, summarize any decisions that were made and review any action plans. If necessary, set up a target date for follow-up by phone, by email, or in person.

After the Conference. After the conference, follow up with parents with a brief note or email thanking them for their participation and reminders about follow-up steps. Also, organize your files regarding the meeting for your records and, if necessary, for records that need to be submitted to administrators at your school.

TIPS FOR TEACHERS 3.7

Working Toward Effective Parent Conferences

- *Listen until they are finished.* As difficult as it may be to hear parents out, particularly when the statements they are making are inaccurate, the best way to begin the meeting is to allow them to say everything that is on their minds. Listening does not mean that you agree. Let them finish.
- *Take notes.* Write down key phrases the parents say, summarize key points, and jot down notes of things you want to remember to tell them. While you are doing this, be sure to maintain eye contact and composure.
- *Summarize their major concerns.* Your summary shows parents not only that you have been listening, but also that you care about what they say.
- *State your position calmly.* After you have listened thoroughly and let parents know that you understand their key points, state your position calmly and succinctly. If parents have inaccurate information, now is the time to provide accurate information. Be sure that they understand your point of view.
- *Come to closure.* Getting to closure differs according to the situation. Sometimes, for example, you hear a parent's concern and quickly find a solution. "Oh, Mrs. Garcia, Lucy can stay in during lunch while she is sick. That is no problem. Just be sure she remembers to bring her own lunch." At other times, an issue needs to be negotiated. "Well, Mrs. Garcia, I do not think that Lucy has too much homework. The main reason it takes her so long is that she does not work on her math homework during the time allotted at school. Let's first set up a plan to increase her working on math at school."

What happens when conferences are unplanned? Unplanned interactions with family members can happen at any time (Turnbull et al., 2011). For example, sometimes, at the end of the day, as students line up to go home, you may notice a parent waiting by the door to speak with you. It is not unusual for parents to approach you during a school's open house or another special event. Often, parents who come to school to talk with the teacher do so because they are concerned about something they have seen or heard. Their source of information might be their own child, who might not have told the story accurately. Avoid the temptation to resolve complex issues in an impromptu meeting. Recognize the importance of the issue and arrange a time to discuss the parent's concerns in a more appropriate setting, either by phone or in person. See Tips for Teachers 3.7 for suggestions that will help you alleviate parents' anxiety.

3.3.5 School-to-Home Communication

Family communication must be a part of your routine as a teacher. Communication with all parents and guardians is important, but it is particularly important with families of students with special needs. What are some ways to communicate? Written communication, phone calls, computer-mediated communication, and surveys are described in this section.

With respect to written communication, Nagro (2015) recommends that teachers take in account the needs and literacy levels of the target family audience. Factors such as font and print size selection, readability level of text, organizational features, structure and arrangement of presentation, and overall ease of reading should be attended to in creating messages for home. Many templates for parent notices, calendars, and so forth are now available online.

In the beginning of the year, it is a good idea to send home a note with students that introduces you and provides a means for parents to contact you. You might also want to send home a letter or bulletin before any long break (1 week or more) to alert parents of activities they can do with their children to reinforce learning while they are out of school or to introduce a new unit of study. Remember, parents want to receive notification about their child: things that are going well, progress reports, your expectations of their child, materials the child needs, problems (early on), and general ideas of how to help their child learn.

You can communicate with parents in many ways. Consider some of the following:

- "Good news" notes can be used to communicate effectively regarding the positive academic and behavioral progress of students.

- Student-written learning logs can document key concepts presented and discussed in class.
- Weekly and monthly calendars can be used to communicate key information and to record homework assignments. You can fill in events on a calendar and then copy and distribute it to students to take home. A fourth-grade teacher who regularly sends home a weekly calendar reports that it takes her about 10 minutes to create. Alternatively, you and the special education teachers you work with might decide to provide parents with a weekly list of accomplishments.
- Newsletters can be written by the teacher or by students. The purpose of a newsletter is to keep parents informed about what is happening in the classroom. You can use the newsletters to describe your classroom policies or coming events, elicit parent support for projects, or provide ideas for enrichment activities and home learning. Newsletters should not target the poor performance or behavior of a particular student. If your newsletter recognizes student accomplishments, be careful not to name certain students repeatedly while never mentioning others.
- Phone calls are an important and often effective means of communicating with parents. Make a list each week of several parents you want to contact with positive reports. Allow 3 to 5 minutes for each call, and make one call at the end of each day. Be sure to keep a phone log of parents contacted by phone during the year.

Computer-mediated communication is another way to touch base with parents (Thompson, Mazer, & Grady, 2015). Working parents often cannot come to school for meetings during the day, so email communication is a necessary alternative. Using email is great for providing parents with updates and clarifying questions about homework and other activities. Text messaging (or texting) and the use of social media are also being used with greater frequency. Increased use of smartphones has, in many cases, accelerated the frequency of school–home communication. Most schools now have websites that provide information about school policies, major events, and homework tips. Individual classroom webpages and teaching blogs are forums for teachers to communicate information about grading policies, homework and class assignments, major projects (such as a science fair), links to online resources, and field trips (Maloy, Verock-O'Loughlin, & Edwards, 2014). You can also use computer-mediated communication to post worksheets for downloading and to publish student writing.

Of course, major concerns and dilemmas should be resolved in face-to-face meetings or by phone. It is also important to communicate to parents your availability and guidelines for using electronic media. Spending your evenings or afternoons answering thirty emails, text messages, or social media messages might not be the best use of your time.

School districts and individual schools have very different policies and procedures for using computer-mediated communication with parents. These state and local policies are in place due to issues related to privacy, liability, and ethics (Lytle, 2011). Make certain that you are aware of the policies in your locality. With these state and local policies in mind, find out from parents and guardians the most efficient and effective way to communicate with them. Also, be aware that not all families will have access to computers, so other modes of communication need to be made available as well.

Still another way to foster communication is through parent interviews and surveys. Asking family members about their level of satisfaction with programs, curriculum, and services can give family members a voice, put key issues on the table, and lead to program improvement. Inclusion teams can conduct brief interviews or surveys to tap the concerns of family members and to use data to generate possible solutions and to identify necessary resources for program improvement (Salend & Duhaney, 2002).

MyEdLab **Self-Check 3.3**

MyEdLab **Application Exercise 3.4:** Working with Families

3 SUMMARY

- Successful collaboration among adults in the school community requires regular, ongoing communication and a spirit of equity and mutual respect. Developing communication skills, such as (a) acceptance, (b) effective listening, (c) appropriate questioning, and (d) maintaining focus, can facilitate effective and productive interactions in one-on-one and group settings.
- Greater collaboration among professionals has grown out of increased awareness that students with disabilities are more likely to succeed if they get targeted support services in the general education classroom. Different ways in which general education teachers might work with other professionals include (a) consultation, (b) teaming, (c) co-planning, (d) co-teaching, and (e) co-assessment/co-grading. For any collaboration model to be effective, several criteria must be in place, including (a) time to co-plan, (b) knowledge of the procedures involved in a particular model, and (c) a meeting location.
- Implementation of clear and consistent lines of communication with family members of students is vital for student success in school. A well-developed homework policy statement can set the stage for productive home-learning routines. Planned and unplanned conferences provide forums for partnerships with parents in setting goals, resolving problems, and monitoring student academic and social progress. In addition, regular exchanges using a variety of formats (e.g., letters, newsletters, phone calls, computer-mediated communication, and surveys) can build positive home–school connections.

THINK AND APPLY

1. Have you ever had a conversation during which you did not feel connected? Think about what the other person(s) did and what you did. Using the principles of effective listening identified in this chapter, make a checklist of things you should consider during a conversation (a) with parents and (b) with other professionals.
2. This chapter's Collaboration Issues and Dilemmas section lists four issues you might need to consider if you are involved in collaboration with another professional. Write your current feelings about each issue (student ownership, individual versus class focus, content versus accommodation, and real world versus student's world). What knowledge and experiences might support your perspectives? What knowledge and experiences might cause you to change your views?
3. Write a homework policy statement for an elementary or secondary classroom. Include in your statement the roles and responsibilities of the teacher, students, and parents.

4 Teaching Culturally and Linguistically Diverse Students

Learning Outcomes

4.1 Describe what you can do as a classroom teacher to learn about your own culture and your students' cultures and communities.

4.2 Define multicultural education and explain the ways you can incorporate multicultural education into your curriculum.

4.3 Identify common misconceptions about second language acquisition and explain what you can do to support English language learners in your classroom.

4.4 Explain how assessment of culturally and linguistically diverse students can be designed and implemented to ensure fairness and accuracy.

4.5 Provide examples of culturally responsive teaching practices that promote success for culturally and linguistically diverse students in your classroom.

INTERVIEW: KRISTINA ZAYAS-BAZAN

Kristina Zayas-Bazan is assigned to Kensington Park Elementary in South Florida for her 15-week associate teaching experience. On her first day of associate teaching, Kristina steps into a second-grade self-contained classroom full of twenty-seven smiling faces. All of her students are English language learners, but they represent a full range of English language proficiency.

Overwhelmed with thoughts of how she can productively divide her instructional time among the various learning needs of her diverse students, Kristina implements an interactive pedagogy style aimed to address all possible obstacles. First, through song, kinesthetics, and hands-on experiences, students will actively experiment with the English language in a nonthreatening social arena to further promote the acquisition process. Therefore, Kristina develops a morning routine when students sing, dance, and update the calendar on a daily basis, continually acquiring greater English vocabulary words and phrases through rhythm and rhyme.

Second, thinking about principles of culturally responsive teaching, Kristina creates a learning environment in which students trust her as a teacher, guide, and friend. Kristina encourages her students to take risks with the English language. Kristina's approach allows her to use the students' rich cultures as a stepping-stone on the path toward state and local curriculum goals. Even while Kristina respects the students' native language and traditions, students are simultaneously learning English.

Third, the emphasis on hands-on learning heightens students' educational motivation and interests. Through the continuous incorporation of manipulatives, visuals, and experiments, Kristina is able to relate abstract concepts to pertinent real-world situations that are compatible with the students' life experiences. As Kristina comments,

> My goal is to create a learning environment that complements the uniqueness of each student. Using strategies like that of rhyme, kinesthetics, hands-on experiences, visuals, and bilingual teaching, I am able to reach each and every one of my students regardless of their level of proficiency in English. For us, the English language is not a barrier because we did not let it become one. Via this setup, students smoothly venture down the language acquisition path without ever forgetting who they are or where they come from.

Introduction

Kristina not only teaches children who are new immigrants to the United States, but also, as a kindergartener, was a new immigrant herself. With this background, her focus is to bring her students the best of both worlds: the riches and value of their native cultures as well as the beauty and excitement of our increasingly diverse country. This chapter focuses on the growing diversity of schools and students in the United States. It also presents the key concepts associated with multicultural education, linguistic

CHAPTER OUTLINE

diversity, second-language learning, and bilingual education. The chapter continues with a presentation of issues regarding the fair and accurate assessment of diverse students. Finally, it discusses instructional strategies for educating students who are culturally and linguistically diverse. As you read this chapter, think about how the ideas presented by Kristina help create a classroom that facilitates the successful education of culturally and linguistically diverse students.

4.1 DIVERSITY IN CLASSROOMS

The United States is one of the most culturally diverse nations in the world. This diversity continues to increase as new immigrants relocate in the United States (Kent, 2015). Currently, the single race, non-Hispanic white population is approximately 62% of persons in the United States. The largest minority group is Hispanic or Latino (17% of the population), followed by Black or African American (13%), and then Asian (13%) (United States Census Bureau, 2015b). The United States Census Bureau (2012) projects that the percentage of minorities will grow from 37% of the population in 2012 to 57% of the population in 2060.

The United States Department of Education (2015a) reports that 51% of the students enrolled in public schools are White, 24% Hispanic, 16% Black, 5% Asian/Pacific Islander, 1% American Indian/Alaska Native, and 3% two or more races. Although the majority of these students are born in the United States, some of them are new immigrants or the children of immigrants and are emerging in their use of English. The federal government estimates that 22% of students enrolled in public schools speak a language other than English in the home and 5% have difficulty in speaking English (United States Census Bureau, 2015a).

Minorities constitute the majority of public school students in many of the country's largest school systems, including those of Miami, Philadelphia, Baltimore, and Los Angeles. Although many of these students do well in school, substantial numbers of students come from homes in which families live in poverty and parents are unemployed or underemployed, have little education and few technical skills, and may not be fluent in English (Aud, Fox, & KewalRamani, 2010). Furthermore, traditional education practice often does not provide a good match between the students' cultures and the curriculum and instructional practices (Ovando & Combs, 2012).

4.1.1 Achievement Disparities

The average achievement of African Americans, Native Americans, and Latino Americans is consistently lower than that of non-Hispanic White students (National Education Association, 2015). Although the achievement gaps between minority students and their White peers have narrowed in recent years, achievement gaps persist (United States Department of Education, 2014). The dropout rates are also higher for these groups of students. The dropout rates have declined considerably in the time span between 1990 and 2013 (from 12% to 7% for males; from 12% to 6% for females. However, the dropout rate for Hispanics is the overall highest at 12%, while African Americans drop out at a 7% rate and Whites at about a 5% rate (Krogstad, 2015; United States Department of Education, 2015b). The dropout rate for students from low-income families (11%) is higher than the rate of their peers from high-income families (3%).

A disproportionately high percentage of African Americans, Latino Americans, and Native Americans have been identified as having learning disabilities, mild mental retardation, and emotional or behavioral disorders (Harry & Klingner, 2014). Similarly, students from low-income families are more likely to be identified for special education services (Sullivan & Bal, 2013). In contrast, a disproportionately lower percentage of students from these cultural groups and economic groups have been identified for more advanced academic programs (Castellano & Frazier, 2010; Coleman & Shah-Coltrane,

2015). Clearly, educational equity for all students continues to be a challenge for our schools and society (Bicard & Heward, 2013).

Inaccurate explanations for the achievement gap are that parents just don't care or value education. These are misconceptions that do not even begin to address the issue (Ladson-Billings, 2007). "It is time to challenge these inherent fallacies and place students' academic struggles in the larger context of social failure, including health, wealth, and funding gaps that harm their school success" (Ladson-Billings, 2007, p. 316). Indeed, the reasons for the limited success of many students are complex and interrelated, but several factors should be considered (Salend, Duhaney, & Montgomery, 2002):

- Role models from minority groups are often limited in school, in that many teachers are European Americans, and limited mentor programs are available for these students to connect with leaders in their communities (Ford, Stuart, & Vakil, 2014).
- Discrimination against students from minority groups continues in assessment for and placement in advanced and gifted programs (Coleman & Shah-Coltrane, 2015; Hoover, 2012; Pereira & de Oliveira, 2015).
- Curriculum and educational practice are often not culturally responsive, with limited integration of information about different cultural groups into the curriculum (Gay & Kirkland, 2003; Harry & Klingner, 2014).
- Teaching styles might not match the learning styles of students from diverse cultures (Chamberlain, 2005; Ford et al., 2014).
- Greater percentages of students from minority groups live in poverty and their poverty levels are lower than those of European Americans (Jiang, Ekono, & Skinner, 2015; National Education Association, 2015).

The overrepresentation of minorities in special education has long been a dilemma for students, parents, and educators, with African American students identified at rates two to three times the rates of White students in some states (King, Artiles, & Kozleski, 2011). Although the explanations mentioned earlier for this persistent problem may or may not hold merit, the fact that students have been subject to misdiagnosis and inadequate instruction cannot be denied (Harry & Klingner, 2014). Response to intervention (RTI) holds great promise for minority students (Haager, 2007; Rinaldi & Samson, 2008). "We are encouraged by the potential of RTI models to improve educational opportunities for culturally and linguistically diverse students and to reduce their disproportionate representation in special education" (Klingner & Edwards, 2006, p. 115). For example, research indicates that there has been a decrease in referrals of African American students for special education services due to intellectual disabilities (Zhang, Katsiyannis, Ju, & Roberts, 2014). However, the same investigation detected an increase in the number of Hispanic students identified with learning disabilities.

The key components of RTI (i.e., early screening, high-quality core instruction, progress monitoring, and intervention with research-based instruction) are designed to promote early success in the acquisition of basic skills rather than the traditional "wait-to-fail" model (Brown & Doolittle, 2008; Haager, 2007). However, research in RTI—particularly as it pertains to culturally and linguistically diverse students—is in its early stages and much is yet to be learned about optimum assessment and instructional practices (Graves & McConnell, 2014; Haager, 2007; Klingner & Edwards, 2006).

4.1.2 Culturally Responsive Teaching

What can the classroom teacher do? Like Kristina, classroom teachers can strive to develop a **culturally responsive teaching (CRT)** style. What is culturally responsive teaching? Gay (2010) defines CRT as "using cultural knowledge, prior experiences, frames of reference, and performance styles of ethnically diverse students to make learning encounters more relevant and effective for them" (p. 31). Several elements that are consistently included in definitions of CRT include:

- High expectations for all students
- Active teaching that is engaging and responsive to students' learning

Video Example from YouTube

MyEdLab
Video Example 4.1.

Watch the YouTube video "Multiracial American Voices: Identity—Pew Research Center" to learn more about multiracial and biracial individuals. What can you as a classroom teacher do to help students share and embrace their cultural heritage? https://www.youtube.com/watch?v=l2WaNmhvEzo

- Using language that reflects cultural and linguistic sensitivity in your response to students
- Cultural and linguistic sensitivity
- Small-group instruction
- Positive perspectives on parents and families
- Student opportunities to respond to and lead discussion

CRT is particularly important in thinking about implementation of RTI models (Graves & McConnell, 2014; Klingner, Barletta, & Hoover, 2008; Taylor, 2008). However, teachers involved in all tiers of instruction must be prepared to teach in ways that will promote student engagement and address individual needs. Teachers and administrators should also use multiple assessment tools (including student observation) to ensure fair and accurate assessment. Developing an understanding of diverse cultures and cultural characteristics are two of the best steps in becoming a culturally responsive teacher.

4.1.3 Understanding Diverse Cultures

The United States is composed of a shared core culture and many subcultures (Banks, 2014). Students in our schools are influenced by this core culture, sometimes referred to as the **macroculture**. The United States is such a complex and diverse nation that its macroculture is somewhat difficult to describe, but Banks (2014) suggests the following key components:

- Equality, justice, and human dignity
- Individual versus group orientation
- Orientation toward materialism

At the same time, students are influenced by their home and/or regional cultures, or **microcultures** (Banks, 2014). Microcultures are often based on such factors as national origin, ethnicity, socioeconomic class, religion, gender, age, and disability. Sometimes the core values of the macroculture and microcultures are relatively similar, but in other cases, the microculture values are quite different from those of the macroculture (Banks, 2014). For example, the emphasis on individuality is generally not as important in African American, Latino American, and Native American ethnic communities as it is in the European American macroculture. Instead, these communities may place more importance on group and family values. Hence, teaching students to work together to complete assignments rather than compete with each other may be more culturally appropriate for students from these ethnic backgrounds (Cohen & Lotan, 2004; Toppel, 2015). In fact, cooperative learning activities that support equal status contact between majority and minority groups in pursuit of common goals have been shown to increase cross-ethnic friendships in classrooms and also increase academic success (e.g., Johnson & Johnson, 2009; Vaughn et al., 2011).

Another example of differences between the macroculture and various microcultures in the United States is the value given to **personalized knowledge** (i.e., knowledge that results from firsthand observation). This use of personalized knowledge and experiences that are acknowledged as ways to seed thinking and expanding understandings is also used to build leadership teams (Kundi & Nawaz, 2010). Although the macroculture values knowledge based on objectivity, and educational institutions emphasize abstract out-of-context knowledge, research on women's ways of knowing suggests that women value personalized knowledge (Belenky, Clinchy, Goldberger, & Tarule, 1986; Brown & Gilligan, 1993). In Carol Gilligan's classic book *In a Different Voice* (1982), she presents a moral framework for the importance of providing opportunities for various voices to be expressed.

Concerns have been raised about the potential bias in educational testing against certain microcultures within our society. Students who have been raised in microcultures that have not been aligned with the macroculture in which they are being educated may have different sets of knowledge and skills than those represented on intelligence or achievement tests. This results in the misidentification of minority students in special education placements, such as those with learning disabilities, mental retardation, and emotional or behavioral disorders (Harry, 2008; Hart, Cramer, Harry, Klingner, & Sturges, 2010; Samuels, 2007).

When the core values in the macroculture and microculture are different, teachers can help students understand and mediate differences between the cultures. To act as mediators, teachers need to learn about and incorporate the various microcultures and home communities into school life and the curriculum. For example, Luis Moll and his colleagues (e.g., Moll, 2010) conducted research in Tucson's barrio schools for a number of years. Moll's research and ethnographic methods of study provide strategies for teachers to integrate the home and school communities by building on the **funds of knowledge** found in students' home communities. Learning about the funds of knowledge in the students' home communities can help teachers to not overgeneralize characteristics that are often attributed to different cultural groups (Harry, Klingner, & Hart, 2005; Moll, 2015).

If you begin your teaching career in a school in which the students' home communities are neither your home community nor similar to your home community, you'll need to spend some time learning about your students' cultural backgrounds. One way to do this is to locate at least one person in the community who can serve as your cultural guide. This can often be a fellow staff member who is willing to teach you about the culture and community.

If it is appropriate and within school policy, visits to students' homes can allow you to talk with parents and other family members. This is an ideal opportunity to learn more about the students, the households, and the culture, including interests of the family, the role of the extended family, the way in which jobs are shared, and the ways in which literacy is used in the home.

Also, you'll need to be a learner in the classroom. Discuss with students your interest in learning about their cultures, including community activities. Information that can help guide your learning includes jobs of parents, their special skills and knowledge, special interests of students (at home and in the community), community activities, special occasions and holidays, family structure, and family responsibilities and relationships. Tips for Teachers 4.1 provides additional guidelines for working with culturally and linguistically diverse students.

TIPS FOR TEACHERS 4.1

Guidelines for Working with Culturally and Linguistically Diverse Students

- Develop cultural consciousness.
- Become aware of your own cultural background.
- Become aware of culture clashes.
- Develop knowledge of cultural variability and become knowledgeable about how culture influences the teaching/learning process.
- Hold high expectations for all students.
- Resist the blame game.
- Spend time reflecting on teaching practices.
- Gather information about your students.
- Develop an understanding of first- and second-language acquisition and the challenges students are likely to face in acquiring a second language.
- Develop an understanding of the interaction among language, culture, and disability.
- Teach the rules of the game, and at the same time respect students' cultural background.
- Adopt an integrated approach to instruction.
- Build trusting relationships with students and parents.
- Use a variety of strategies in educating culturally and linguistically diverse students.

MyEdLab
Video Example 4.2.

Watch this video, and note what the speaker says about the importance of looking within cultures and not just across cultures. How would you, as an educator, familiarize yourself with the cultural diversity represented by each child, family, and your community?

4.1.4 Understanding Cultural Characteristics

In learning about cultural influences, there is a tendency to make generalizations based on common beliefs about a culture. Culture is only one of the factors that influences our values and beliefs—there are many factors that contribute to who we are and how we think. Thus, we don't want to overgeneralize to all individuals in a particular microculture the typical beliefs and practices that characterize some of the individuals.

Cultural characteristics

Having some knowledge of students' cultural characteristics serves as a starting point for understanding individual students' behaviors and learning styles. This knowledge can keep teachers from misinterpreting students' actions. Culturally responsive teachers "recognize the differences between their students and themselves and strive to become nonjudgmental" (Cartledge et al., 2009, p. 18). Creating culturally responsive classrooms requires teachers to get to know students, their families, and their cultures. Díaz-Rico (2013) recommends that teachers use multiple resources to learn about the cultures of students in their classroom, including interviews with parents, students, and community members; printed materials; and websites.

Following are general areas and questions you can use to guide inquiry about the cultural characteristics of students in your classroom:

- *Time.* How do students perceive time? How is timeliness regarded in their cultures?
- *Space.* What personal distance do students use in interactions with other students and with adults? How does the culture determine the space allotted to boys and to girls?
- *Dress and food.* How does dress differ for age, gender, and social class? What clothing and accessories are considered acceptable? What foods are typical?
- *Rituals and ceremonies.* What rituals do students use to show respect? What celebrations do students observe, and for what reasons? How and where do parents expect to be greeted when visiting the class?
- *Work.* What types of work are students expected to perform in the home and community, and at what age? To what extent are students expected to work together?
- *Leisure.* What are the purposes for play? What typical activities are done for enjoyment in the home and community?
- *Gender roles.* What tasks are performed by boys? By girls? What expectations do parents and students hold for boys' and girls' achievement, and how do these differ by subject areas?
- *Status.* What resources (e.g., study area and materials, study assistance from parents and siblings) are available at home and in the community? What power do parents have to obtain information about the school and to influence educational choices?
- *Goals.* What kinds of work are considered prestigious or desirable? What role does education play in achieving occupational goals? What education level do the family and student desire for the student?
- *Education.* What methods for teaching and learning are used in the home (e.g., modeling and imitation, didactic stories and proverbs, direct verbal instruction)?
- *Communication.* What roles do verbal and nonverbal language play in learning and teaching? What roles do conventions such as silence, questions, rhetorical questions, and discourse style play in communication? What types of literature (e.g., newspapers, books) are used in the home, and in what language(s) are they written? How is writing used in the home (e.g., letters, lists, notes), and in what language(s)?
- *Interaction.* What roles do cooperation and competition play in learning? How are children expected to interact with teachers?
- *Behavior.* What are cultural expectations for appropriate behavior in school settings?
- *Family and Community.* What are effective and accepting ways to reach out and include families and community in my educational program?

Laurel Hopkins's first teaching assignment was in New Orleans. Much to her surprise, her students were primarily new immigrants who had recently come to the United States from Vietnam. As Laurel put it, "I had no idea there was such a large population of Vietnamese in New Orleans." Laurel was pleased to learn that her school had hired a Vietnamese woman, Ms. Nguyen, to work as a paraprofessional to assist with parent communication. Laurel had lunch once a week with Ms. Nguyen to learn more about how to respond to her students' needs. Ms. Nguyen helped Laurel with parent interviews so that she could gather important information about her students and their culture. "Ms. Nguyen was a treasure," explained Laurel. "Not only did I learn about customs and traditions, I also learned about some difficulties parents faced. For example, parents in the Vietnamese culture are honored and have authority. For some parents, having their own children know more English than they did posed a real problem."

The insights that Laurel Hopkins gained from Ms. Nguyen were important. For example, in some instances, there were differences among children and their families. Some were more Americanized than others who resisted Americanization. Laurel learned not to assume that cultural characteristics are common to all members of a cultural group. Rather, understanding characteristics served as a starting point in her education about the cultural diversity of the students she taught.

Cultural boundaries

Erickson (2005) defines a cultural boundary as "the presence of some kind of cultural difference" (p. 41). Cultural boundaries can occur at many levels, including when there are differences between the student and the teacher or between the student and the culture of schooling. For example, in the Haitian American culture, it is the custom to respect the work of the teacher and to put the responsibility of formal education in the hands of the teacher. Parental involvement in schooling is not typical for some families. When a teacher urges parental involvement, it would mean the crossing of a cultural boundary for parents. Teachers often ask why some cultural groups seem to cross cultural boundaries and succeed in school more easily than others do. In fact, global workforces and cross-cultural expectations in school and postsecondary education require all of us to be able to span diverse boundaries that allow us to develop and use cross-cultural identities (Yagi & Kleinberg, 2011). The classic work of anthropologist John Ogbu has shed light on cultural boundaries. Ogbu (1992, 2008) has suggested that some cultural groups seem to cross cultural boundaries more easily than other groups. Based on his comparative research, he classified cultural groups as autonomous minorities, immigrant or voluntary minorities, and caste-like or involuntary minorities:

- *Autonomous minorities* are considered minorities in a numerical sense; they include Jews, Mormons, and the Amish. In the United States, there are no non-White autonomous minorities.
- *Immigrant or voluntary minorities* are people who have moved to the new society or culture more or less voluntarily because they desire greater economic opportunities and political freedom. The Chinese and Punjabi Indians are representative examples in the United States.
- *Caste-like or involuntary minorities* are people who were brought to the United States or conquered against their will. Examples in the United States are African Americans, Native Americans, early Mexican Americans in the Southwest, and Native Hawaiians.

Ogbu (1992) suggests that voluntary groups experience initial (but not lingering) problems in school because of language and cultural differences. The involuntary minorities, on the other hand, usually experience greater, more persistent difficulties learning in school. This difficulty for involuntary minorities appears related to several factors:

- **Cultural inversion**, or the tendency to regard certain forms of behavior, events, symbols, and meanings as inappropriate because they are characteristic of European American culture.

- A collective identity, in opposition to the social identity of the dominant group, develops as the involuntary minorities are treated as subordinates by European Americans in economic, political, social, psychological, cultural, and language domains.

Hence, in an effort to retain their own identity and roots, students from involuntary minorities may be more oppositional and less motivated to learn in school. Ogbu (1992) explains, "They fear that by learning the White cultural frame of reference, they will cease to act like minorities and lose their identity as minorities and their sense of community and self-worth" (p. 10). In contrast, because voluntary minorities do not feel the need to protect their cultural identity, they do not perceive learning the attitudes and behaviors required for school success as threatening to their own culture, language, and identities. Instead they interpret such learning as *additive*, that is, adding to what they already have (Chung, 1992).

It is important to note that these are generalized types that include groups who may more appropriately "fit" a different type. For example, Cubans who fled Cuba during the 1960s were an involuntary minority, yet many acculturated and became quite successful in the Miami community.

James Cummins (1992), a leading scholar in bilingual education, suggests that the academic success of students from involuntary minority groups is related to the extent that schools reflect the following:

- Minority students' language and culture are incorporated into the school program.
- Minority community participation is encouraged as an integral component of children's education.
- Instruction (pedagogy) is used to motivate students to use language actively to generate their own knowledge.
- Professionals involved in student testing (assessment) become advocates for minority students by focusing primarily on ways in which students' academic difficulties are a function of interactions with and within the school context, instead of locating the problem within the students. (p. 5)

MyEdLab **Self-Check 4.1**

MyEdLab **Application Exercise 4.1:** Learning About Students' Diverse Cultures

4.2 MULTICULTURAL EDUCATION

Multicultural education is "a reform movement designed to make some major changes in the education of students. … Multicultural education incorporates the idea that all students—regardless of their gender, sexual orientation, social class, and ethnic, racial, or cultural characteristics—should have an equal opportunity to learn in school" (Banks, 2014, p. 1). Multicultural education originates with the civil rights movement in the 1960s and is closely linked to cultural diversity (Ariza, Morales-Jones, Yahya, & Zainuddin, 2006), fostering pride in minority cultures, assisting students in developing new insights into their cultures, reducing prejudice and stereotyping, and promoting intercultural understanding and understanding of cultural identity. In the fullest sense, multicultural education is a total rethinking of the way we conduct schooling in a diverse society within a democratic, civic framework (Lessow-Hurley, 2009).

4.2.1 Dimensions of Multicultural Education

Multicultural education is much more than a curriculum focused on learning about diverse cultures based on such parameters as gender, ethnicity, and race. It is a thread running through the total curriculum, not a subject to be taught (Gay, 2010; Tiedt & Tiedt, 2010). Banks (2014) suggests that multicultural education has five dimensions: content integration, knowledge construction, prejudice reduction, pedagogy that reflects equity, and an empowering school culture and social structure.

1. **Content integration** focuses on using examples and content from a variety of cultures and groups to illustrate concepts, principles, generalizations, and theories. Ethnic and cultural content is infused into the subject areas in a natural, logical way (Banks, 2014). For example, you can teach students about traditional dress and celebrations in many different cultures by discussing different holidays, the dress worn, and the reasons for the holidays and traditional dress. As a follow-up activity, students can interview their parents and other family members to learn about traditional dress and holidays celebrated by their families.
2. **Knowledge construction** refers to students learning about how implicit cultural assumptions, frames of reference, perspectives, and biases influence the ways in which knowledge is constructed. For example, the discovery of America by Europeans has two very different frames of reference when presented from the perspectives of the Native Americans and the Europeans. Similarly, the power of the mind over the body is viewed differently by Asian and European cultures.
3. **Prejudice reduction** is the idea that when misconceptions and stereotypes about diverse cultural and ethnic groups are dispelled, students can learn to develop an appreciation for individuals from backgrounds other than their own. Teachers can promote prejudice reduction through well-planned units and lessons that help students develop knowledge and positive images of a wide range of groups.
4. **Equity pedagogy** addresses how the teacher attends to the different learning styles of students and modifies teaching to facilitate the academic achievement of students from diverse cultures.
5. An **empowering school culture and social structure** promotes gender, racial, and social class equity. Establishing such a culture entails examining the school culture for biases and prejudices, developing strategies to alleviate them, and replacing them with opportunities that promote positive self-esteem for all students. An initial step in creating an empowering school culture is to have the staff share, learn about, and respect their own diversity.

A school's staff can learn about their school community through many of the activities used to help students learn about one another, such as sharing information about heritage, birthplace, family, traditional foods, and hobbies. For example, Stan Williams, the principal at an urban elementary school, takes time each year at the initial full-staff meeting for the staff to interview each other about their families, cultural backgrounds, areas of educational expertise, traditional foods, and hobbies. Then each interviewer uses the information garnered to introduce the interviewee to at least two other staff members. In the past, Stan has also displayed staff photos and profiles in the staff lounge. Stan comments, "When we take time [for] this activity, the staff immediately begins to learn about each other and find common interests that are fostered throughout the school year. It helps to create a sense of equality across all staff jobs (e.g., teachers, paraprofessionals, office staff, building maintenance staff)."

How can school culture empower all students to succeed? What student outcomes lead to the goal of creating a learning community in which students understand and respect diversity and have equal opportunity to academic success?

To implement multicultural education and integrate these dimensions successfully, teachers should conceptualize multicultural education as much more than a curriculum or a subject to teach. Several leaders in the field have suggested that viewing the school as a social system and studying and reforming the major variables is necessary to create a learning environment in which students have an equal chance for school success (e.g., Banks, 2014; Grant & Sleeter, 1993; Ladson-Billings, 2006; Nieto, 1994; Ogbu, 2008). Banks (2014) suggests that the following aspects of the school as a social system need to be considered:

- School staff: attitudes, perceptions, and actions
- Formalized curriculum and course of study
- School's preferred learning, teaching, and cultural characteristics
- Language and dialects of the school
- Instructional materials
- Assessment and testing procedures
- School culture and hidden curriculum
- The counseling program

As you study the schools in which you teach as social systems and as teaching and learning communities, consider these variables and determine the degree to which they foster the overarching goals of multicultural education. In other words, think about how you can create a learning community in which students have not only equal opportunities for academic success, but also an understanding of and respect for diversity.

4.2.2 Desired Student Outcomes

Given these dimensions of multicultural education and the overall goals, what are some desired student outcomes that lead to these goals? Multicultural teacher educators Tiedt and Tiedt (2006) suggest that students should be able to do the following:

- Identify a strong sense of self-esteem and express the needs and rights of others to similar feelings of self-esteem.
- Describe their own cultures, recognizing the influences that have shaped their thinking and behavior.
- Identify racial, ethnic, and religious groups represented in our pluralistic society.
- Identify needs and concerns universal to people of all cultures and compare cultural variations.
- Recognize, understand, and critique examples of stereotypic thinking and social inequities in real life and literature and develop solutions for altering their status.
- Discuss special gender-, ethnic-, age-, and disability-related concerns.
- Inquire multiculturally as they engage in broad thematic studies related to any field of study.

To achieve these outcomes, curricula must highlight cultural diversity. The next section discusses curricula for multicultural education.

4.2.3 Multicultural Curricula

Banks (2014) suggests that since multicultural education was introduced in the 1960s, curricular approaches to multicultural education have evolved, based on the degree to which diversity plays a central role in the curriculum. Banks identifies four approaches: contributions, additive, transformation, and social action (see Table 4.1).

Contributions approach

The contributions approach is characterized by the insertion of ethnic heroes and discrete cultural artifacts into the curriculum—adding culturally diverse inventors and their inventions to a thematic unit on inventions, for example.

This approach is the easiest to use but has several serious limitations. First, because the heroes are usually presented in isolation, students do not gain an overall

Table 4.1 • Banks's Approaches to Multicultural Curriculum Reform

APPROACH	DESCRIPTION	EXAMPLES	STRENGTHS	PROBLEMS
Contributions	Heroes, cultural components, holidays, and other discrete elements related to ethnic groups are added to the curriculum on special days, occasions, and celebrations.	• Famous Mexican Americans are studied only during the week of Cinco de Mayo (May 5). African Americans are studied during Black History Month in February but rarely during the rest of the year. • Ethnic foods are studied in the first grade with little attention devoted to the cultures in which the foods are embedded.	• Provides a quick and relatively easy way to put ethnic content into the curriculum. • Gives ethnic heroes visibility in the curriculum alongside mainstream heroes. • Is a popular approach among teachers and educators.	• Results in a superficial understanding of ethnic cultures. • Focuses on the lifestyles and artifacts of ethnic groups and reinforces stereotypes and misconceptions. • Mainstream criteria are used to select heroes and cultural elements for inclusion in the curriculum.
Additive	This approach consists of the addition of content, concepts, themes, and perspectives to the curriculum without changing its structure.	• Adding the book *The Color Purple* to a literature unit without reconceptualizing the unit or giving the students the background knowledge to understand the book. • Adding a unit on the Japanese American internment to a U.S. history course without treating the Japanese in any other unit. • Leaving the core curriculum intact but adding an ethnic studies course, as an elective, that focuses on a specific ethnic group.	• Makes it possible to add ethnic content to the curriculum without changing its structure, which requires substantial curriculum changes and staff development. • Can be implemented within the existing curriculum structure.	• Reinforces the idea that ethnic history and culture are not integral parts of U.S. mainstream culture. • Students view ethnic groups from Anglocentric and Eurocentric perspectives. • Fails to help students understand how the dominant culture and ethnic cultures are interconnected and interrelated.
Transformation	The basic goals, structure, and nature of the curriculum are changed to enable students to view concepts, events, issues, problems, and themes from the perspectives of diverse cultural, ethnic, and racial groups.	• A unit on the American Revolution describes the meaning of the revolution to Anglo revolutionaries, Anglo loyalists, African Americans, Indians, and the British. • A unit on 20th-century U.S. literature includes works by William Faulkner, Joyce Carol Oates, Langston Hughes, N. Scott Momaday, Saul Bellow, Maxine Hong Kingston, Rudolfo A. Anaya, and Piri Thomas.	• Enables students to understand the complex ways in which diverse racial and cultural groups participated in the formation of U.S. society and culture. • Helps to reduce racial and ethnic encapsulation. • Enables diverse ethnic, racial, and religious groups to see their cultures, ethos, and perspectives in the school curriculum. • Gives students a balanced view of the nature and development of U.S. culture and society. • Helps to empower victimized racial, ethnic, and cultural groups.	• The implementation of this approach requires substantial curriculum revision, inservice training, and the identification and development of materials written from the perspectives of various racial and cultural groups. • Staff development for the institutionalization of this approach must be continual and ongoing.

(*continued*)

Table 4.1 • Banks's Approaches to Multicultural Curriculum Reform (*continued*)

APPROACH	DESCRIPTION	EXAMPLES	STRENGTHS	PROBLEMS
Social Action	In this approach, students identify important social problems and issues, gather pertinent data, clarify their values on the issues, make decisions, and take reflective actions to help resolve the issue or problem.	• A class studies prejudice and discrimination in their school and decides to take actions to improve race relations in the school. • A class studies the treatment of ethnic groups in a local newspaper and writes a letter to the newspaper publisher suggesting ways that the treatment of ethnic groups in newspapers should be improved.	• Enables students to improve their thinking, value analysis, decision-making skills, and social-action skills. • Enables students to improve their data-gathering skills. • Helps students to develop a sense of political efficacy. • Helps students to improve their skills at working in groups.	• Requires a considerable amount of curriculum planning and materials identification. • May be longer in duration than more traditional teaching units. • May focus on problems and issues considered controversial by some members of the school staff and citizens of the community. • Students may be able to take few meaningful actions that contribute to the resolution of the social issue or problem.

Source: Reprinted with the permission of James A. Banks from pp. 262–263 of James A. Banks, "Approaches to multicultural curriculum reform," in James A. Banks & Cherry A. McGee Banks (Editors), *Multicultural education: Issues and perspectives* (6th edition, 2007, pp. 247–269). Hoboken, NJ: Wiley.

understanding of the role of ethnic and cultural groups in the United States. Second, this approach does not address issues such as oppression and discrimination. Instead, it reinforces the Horatio Alger myth in that ethnic heroes are presented with little attention paid to how they became heroes despite the barriers they encountered.

Additive approach

The **additive approach** is characterized by the addition of content, concepts, themes, and perspectives without changing the basic structure of the curriculum. Typical examples are adding books about different groups to the literature sets (e.g., Mildred Taylor's *Roll of Thunder, Hear My Cry*), adding a unit on Native Americans to an American history course, and adding a course on ethnic or gender studies to a high school curriculum. This approach offers better integration of multicultural perspectives than the contributions approach but does not result in a restructured curriculum. For example, including a unit on the Plains Indians in a U.S. history class will increase students' understanding of Native Americans, but not as clearly as will transforming the curriculum so that the movement to the West is viewed as both an expansion (from a European perspective) and an invasion (from a Native American perspective).

Transformation approach

In the **transformation approach**, the basic core of the curriculum is changed and the focus is on viewing events, concepts, and themes from multiple perspectives based on diversity. Banks (2014) suggests that

> When teaching a unit such as "The Westward Movement" using a transformation approach, the teacher would assign appropriate readings and then ask the students such questions as: What do you think the Westward movement means? Who was moving west—the Whites or the Native Americans? ... The aim of these questions is to help students to understand that the Westward movement is a Eurocentric term... . The Sioux did not consider their Homeland "the West" but the center of the universe. (p. 55)

In developing multicultural units, teachers need to identify the key concept and generalizations associated with that concept. Specific activities can then be planned so that students have the evidence to draw the generalizations and understand the key concept.

Social action approach

The social action approach incorporates all the elements of the transformation approach and also includes a cultural critique. Teaching units that use this approach incorporate a problem-solving process in which students make decisions and take actions related to the concept, issue, or problem being studied, following these steps:

1. Identify the problem or question (e.g., discrimination in our school).
2. Collect data related to the problem or question (e.g., what discrimination is, what causes discrimination, what examples are evident in our school).
3. Conduct a value inquiry and analysis (e.g., students examine and reflect on their values, attitudes, and beliefs related to discrimination).
4. Make decisions and establish a plan of social action based on a synthesis of the knowledge obtained in step 2 and the values identified in step 3.

As a teacher, you will undoubtedly use all four approaches to multicultural education, with the goal of primarily employing the transformational and social action approaches. Tips for Teachers 4.2 presents general strategies for integrating content about cultural groups into the school curriculum.

A successful curriculum incorporates opportunities to foster student achievement and cultural competence as well as help students recognize, understand, and critique current social inequities. Gloria Ladson-Billings illustrates how critical the role of culturally responsive teachers is in keeping the dreams of minority students alive (Ladson-Billings, 2009). Each of us has the opportunity to capitalize on the unique strengths each child brings to the classroom, remembering that a rigorous curriculum is one in which teachers demonstrate confidence that students can meet high expectations with adequate support and appropriate responses. Suggestions include the following:

- Integrate the family and community representatives into your classroom.
- Show respect for the knowledge and experiences of the range of learners in your classroom.
- Demonstrate high expectations and opportunities to succeed for all of the students in your class.

MyEdLab **Self-Check 4.2**

MyEdLab **Application Exercise 4.2:** Multicultural Curricula

TIPS FOR TEACHERS 4.2

Guidelines for Teaching Multicultural Content

- Improve your knowledge of cultural groups. Read books that survey the histories of cultural groups in the United States.
- Make sure that your room conveys positive images of various cultural groups (through bulletin boards, posters, literature, software, and so on).
- Plan time in which you and your students can learn about one another's cultural backgrounds.
- Be culturally conscious in selecting teaching materials. If the materials you use include stereotypes or present only one perspective, point out the limitations to the students.
- Use trade books, films, videotapes, websites, and recordings to supplement textbooks and to present more varied perspectives.
- Use literature to enrich students' understanding of cultural pluralism.
- Be sensitive to the developmental levels of your students when you select concepts, content, and activities. Use concrete, specific concepts and activities for students in early elementary grades. As students develop, focus on more abstract concepts and problem solving.
- Use group work to promote opportunities for student interaction and conversation.
- Make sure that not only classroom activities but also schoolwide activities (such as plays, sports, and clubs) are culturally integrated.

MyEdLab
Video Example 4.3.
In this video, students from different cultural backgrounds are being asked to share their experiences about what it was like for them when they were first learning to speak English. How would you, as an educator, adapt your teaching style or approach to help students from different cultural backgrounds to have a positive learning experience?

4.3 LINGUISTIC DIVERSITY AND SECOND-LANGUAGE ACQUISITION

Linguistic diversity is not new in the United States, with its rich history of immigration. Today, as in the past, many students live in homes in which the primary language spoken is not English. This trend is increasing rather than decreasing. José is a good example of such a student. At the age of 4, he emigrated with his parents and three siblings from a rural community in Mexico to an urban Spanish-speaking community in Texas. His parents spoke only Spanish when they arrived. Although he has some exposure to English and his father is taking a night course to learn English, José entered school at age 5 with Spanish as his first language and only a limited knowledge of his second language, English. This same scenario is true of children who emigrate from Central and South American countries, Asian and Pacific Island countries, and Eastern European countries.

The implications of this demography are that a growing number of students who enter school in the United States learn English as a second language in school. Between 1980 and 2013 the number of school-age children who spoke a language other than English at home increased from 4.7 million to over 11.7 million (United States Census Bureau 2015a). This represents approximately one in five school-age children. The teacher's knowledge of second-language acquisition and general instructional guidelines can help make school a success for students like José. However, many teachers hold misconceptions about how to teach ELLs (Gil & Bardack, 2010; Harper & de Jong, 2004). The four commonly held misconceptions outlined in Figure 4.1 can affect instruction in negative ways.

As Harper and de Jong argue, "unless teachers address these misconceptions, their curriculum, instruction, and assessment practices will only partially meet the needs of ELLs in their classrooms and will only superficially include ELLs in mainstream classes" (2004, p. 160).

4.3.1 Programs for Promoting Second-Language Acquisition

The programs for ELLs vary tremendously from state to state and even from school to school within a district. In some states, they allow **English only** unless the parents are able to obtain a waiver. English only means that students who are learning English are taught

FIGURE 4.1 Misconceptions and realities about the teaching of English language learners

- **Misconception 1:** Exposure and interaction will result in English language learning.
- **Reality:** Although there are similarities in learning a first and a second language, there are differences as well. In addition to exposure and interaction, ELLs need guided practice and frequent opportunities to learn a second language in both oral and written modes.
- **Misconception 2:** All ELLs learn English in the same way and at the same rate.
- **Reality:** Individual differences in English acquisition occur even though there are some predictable stages of second-language development. Many factors can influence different patterns and rates, including cultural differences, prior education in the first language, and whether the student was exposed to English orally first or in written form.
- **Misconception 3:** Good teaching for native speakers is good teaching for ELLs.
- **Reality:** Good teaching for native speakers is necessary but not sufficient for ELLs. Particularly at the secondary level, ELLs are often expected to have the prior knowledge, vocabulary, and reading and writing skills of their classmates in order to complete assignments and tests. Without adaptations and support, learning is difficult if not impossible.
- **Misconception 4:** Effective instruction means nonverbal support.
- **Reality:** Effective instruction means both verbal and nonverbal support. Providing students with visuals and physical prompts may be helpful, but students also need ample opportunity for formal and informal interactions with teachers, other school personnel, and their peers.

Source: Based on "Misconceptions about teaching English-language learners," by C. Harper & E. de Jong, 2004, *Journal of Adolescent & Adult Literacy, 48*, 152–153. Copyright © 2004 by the International Reading Association.

all of their subjects (e.g., math) in English and they learn to read and write in English (Menken, 2013). English language supports may be provided to these students as a separate class or through small-group instruction. English only policies continue to generate debate with some states considering adaptation of such practices based, in part, on growing evidence of the benefits of bilingual education (Gándara, 2015b; Reyes, Kenner, Moll, & Orellana, 2012).

The two general variations of programs are English as a second language and bilingual education. **English as a second language (ESL)** instruction has the acquisition of English as the goal, whereas the goal of **bilingual education** is to promote bilingualism or proficiency in both the first and second languages. "The most prominent characteristic that defines differences among programs in bilingual/ESL education is how much the primary language of the students is used for instruction" (Ovando & Combs, 2012, p. 36).

You will need to learn about programs that are available in your school and what your role is in the teaching of ELLs. You will also need to be familiar with the programs available in your school district so that you can articulate program possibilities to parents. In addition, you should know some other differences among programs, such as:

- Location—some instruction will take place in the general education classroom, whereas other instruction will be in a resource room or in a self-contained classroom.
- Staffing—some instruction is taught by the general education teacher, and other instruction is taught by an ESL specialist.
- Duration—placement may be either full time or part time.

In the following section various types of English as a second language and bilingual education programs are discussed. Keep in mind that program models do not always operationalize in pure forms and that often program models are combined or blended (Ovando & Combs, 2012; Varghese & Stritikus, 2013).

4.3.2 Instruction in English as a Second Language

English as a second language (ESL) instruction uses English to teach students, with limited emphasis on maintaining or developing proficiency in the student's first language. Instruction may be given during a specified instructional time (with students receiving the rest of their instruction in general education classrooms), or it may be integrated into content-area instruction (as is the case of sheltered English).

Sheltered English is a type of ESL instruction in which the goal is to teach English language skills at the same time that students are learning content-area knowledge (Ovando & Combs, 2012). Typically reserved for students who have some working knowledge of English, sheltered English employs direct experiences, hands-on learning, and meaningful context for instruction. As you will read later in this chapter, many sheltered English techniques can be helpful to you in daily instruction of ELLs.

Schools often use an ESL model when the non-English-speaking students are from several language groups or there are too few students from a common language group to support a bilingual education model. The ESL teacher is usually considered a resource teacher in that he or she works daily, or at least several times a week, with groups of students or whole classes of students for a specified instructional time. An ESL teacher may work in a pull-out program or, more commonly, in an inclusion model. In addition to instructional duties, the ESL teacher is usually responsible for assessing the students' language proficiency in English and, depending on the language, in their first language.

4.3.3 Bilingual Education

Bilingual education students may spend the entire day in classrooms designated as *bilingual classrooms*. These students are learning English and may be receiving content instruction in their first language, in English, or in both languages, according to their level of development in English. Frequently, bilingual education approaches are described as *transitional* or *maintenance*, depending on the degree to which the first language is developed and maintained.

The focus of **transitional bilingual education** or **early-exit transition** programs is to help students shift from the home language to the dominant language. In this form of bilingual education, students are taught in the home language with English as a second language and then they transition to English depending upon their performance in reading and math in their home language. These programs initially provide content-area instruction in students' native language along with ESL instruction. Students transfer from these programs as soon as they are deemed sufficiently proficient in English to receive all academic instruction in English (Díaz-Rico, 2013). The time taken for this transition from the students' first language to English varies, depending on the program. In programs in which literacy is taught in the first language, with other content taught in English, students may make the transition in 2 to 3 years. In other transition programs, at least 40% of the instruction is in the first language—including reading, language arts, math, and sometimes social studies or science—and students usually remain in the programs through fifth or sixth grade. When Gloria and Lidia, bilingual education teachers team teaching at Mission Way in southwest Arizona, were asked about their model of bilingual education, they described it as best fitting the transition model, with a relatively late transition to English (fourth to fifth grade). One of the reasons Gloria and Lidia chose to team teach was to better meet the needs of their students as they made the transition from skill and content instruction in Spanish to English. Gloria said,

> During grades 4 and 5, we transition the language of instruction to almost exclusively English. For us, the exception is reading and writing. In our literature-based reading program and writer's workshop, we continue to encourage the students to read some literature written in Spanish and to write some compositions in Spanish, although most instruction is in English. We also discuss the literature in Spanish. In this way, students do not lose those Spanish literacy skills that they have developed in the bilingual programs. We feel that this is important not only for them to stay connected to their home community, but also because being bilingual and biliterate are highly desired job skills.

Maintenance bilingual education, **developmental bilingual**, or **late-exit programs** are established to foster the students' first language and strengthen their sense of cultural identity while teaching the second language and culture (Díaz-Rico, 2013; Ovando & Combs, 2012). Maintenance programs typically provide native-language content-area instruction throughout the elementary grades, with the amount of native-language instruction decreasing as students progress through the program. This model values bilingualism and sees the learning of a second language as a positive addition for the students' cognitive development and life success. This model also places a strong emphasis on incorporating the students' culture and heritage into the instruction. A particularly compelling use of the maintenance bilingual model is in the education of Native Americans (Díaz-Rico & Weed, 2014), in which the goal is to increase the number of speakers of Native American languages and preserve their cultural and linguistic heritage.

Two-way immersion programs or **dual-language programs** have become an option for students learning English as a second language (Díaz-Rico, 2013) and for first-language English speakers to learn a second language such as Spanish. In two-way programs or dual-language programs, half the students are native speakers of English and the other half speak another language, usually Spanish. Instruction is in English half the time and in Spanish (or another second language) the other half. The goal is for all students to become fully bilingual and biliterate. Initial reports suggest that these dual-language models have the potential to improve language and learning for both English language learners as well as monolingual English speakers (Kim, Hutchison, & Winsler, 2015; Paradis, Genesee, & Crago, 2004). Indeed, the number of two-way immersion programs is increasing in popularity among parents and thus growing in number (Center for Applied Linguistics, 2015; Gándara, 2015a).

Although much is to be learned about the efficacy of ESL and bilingual programs of all kinds, some summaries of research have underscored the importance of initially teaching students to read in their home language, assuming there are print materials and appropriate teachers (Gándara, 2015a; Goldenberg, 2008; Rolstad, Mahoney, & Glass, 2005; Slavin & Cheung, 2005). As a classroom teacher, you can help students bridge the gap from first- to second-language learning by first understanding how a second language is acquired.

4.3.4 Framework for Second-Language Acquisition

Ellis (R. Ellis, 1985, 1994, 2005) provides a framework for second-language acquisition that can guide you in making accommodations for students whose first language is not English. Ellis suggests that five interrelated factors govern the acquisition of a second language, as discussed next.

Situational factors

The first factors in the framework are situational factors, which are related to the context or the situation (e.g., the learning environments) in which the second-language learning occurs. Students learn the second language in multiple learning environments—from relatives, friends, and neighbors who speak English; through ESL or bilingual education programs at school; and from peers in the classroom and on the playground.

Environments such as these can provide both formal teaching and more natural opportunities to acquire language. When José's uncle explains the concept "scientist" in Spanish and then pairs it with English, he is providing formal instruction. On the other hand, the instruction is much more natural when José and his uncle converse about what happened in school and his uncle provides José with words in English when José is searching for the English word. One goal of both bilingual education and ESL instruction is to create environments that are nonthreatening and in which students are willing to take risks and play with the language (Ovando & Combs, 2012; Vaughn & Gersten, 1998). Kristina, the associate teacher interviewed at the beginning of this chapter, encourages students to play with the language by experimenting with sounds, words, and syntactic construction. She makes these opportunities for discovery by encouraging experimentation.

Another situational factor that promotes second-language acquisition is an environment in which the students' first language and culture are respected and valued. The research consistently demonstrates that valuing students' first language is an important factor for student success (Carter & Chatfield, 1986; Jiménez et al., 2015; Lucas, Henze, & Donato, 1990; Stewart, 2013; Thomas & Collier, 1997). One important aspect of valuing the students' language is learning about their community's funds of knowledge and language.

Linguistic input

The second factor in the framework, linguistic input, refers to input received when reading or listening to a second language. Comprehensible input is a key factor for success (Krashen, 1985). Comprehensible input is a component of Specially Designed Academic Instruction in English (SDAIE), a set of instructional strategies many schools implement for students in early stages of English language learning (Díaz-Rico, 2013). Input is made more comprehensible by a number of strategies, including the following:

- Selecting a topic of conversation that is familiar to students
- Creating a context for what is being discussed
- Using simpler sentence construction
- Repeating important phrases
- Incorporating the students' first language into the instruction
- Emphasizing key words to promote comprehensible input

When teaching linguistically diverse students, it is important to consider the linguistic input. Tips for Teachers 4.3 presents guidelines and ideas for making input more understandable.

TIPS FOR TEACHERS 4.3

Guidelines for Making Input Understandable for Second-Language Learners

- Begin teaching new concepts by working from the students' current knowledge and incorporating the funds of knowledge from the students' communities.
- Use demonstrations and gestures to augment oral communication.
- To the degree possible, create the context in which the concepts occur. For example, when teaching about shellfish, visit an aquarium, watch a film depicting shellfish, or display shells in the classroom.
- Discuss connections between the concepts being taught and the students' home cultures.
- Encourage students to share the new vocabulary in their first language and incorporate the first language into instruction.
- If students share a common first language, pair more proficient second-language learners with less proficient peers, and encourage students to discuss what they are learning.
- Highlight key words and phrases by repeating them and writing them.
- Use simple sentence constructions, particularly to present a new or difficult concept.

Learner characteristics

The third factor affecting second-language acquisition or output is learner characteristics. Relevant learner characteristics include the age at which students learn a second language, their aptitude for learning language, their purposes and degree of motivation for learning the second language, their self-confidence in language learning, and their learning strategies.

Another important variable is the degree of acquisition of proficiency in the first language. Cummins (1991), in a review of research, concluded that the better developed the students' proficiency and conceptual foundation in the first language, the more likely they were to develop similarly high levels of proficiency and conceptual ability in the second language. He has referred to this as the common underlying proficiency, using the analogy of an iceberg to explain this hypothesis and relationship between first- and second-language acquisition (see Figure 4.2) and why proficiency in the first language complements proficiency in the second language (Cummins, 1981). As shown in Figure 4.2, both languages have separate surface features, represented by separate icebergs.

Below the surface and less visible, however, is the underlying proficiency common to both languages.

No matter which language the person is using, the thoughts that accompany the talking, reading, writing, and listening come from the same language core. One implication of this analogy is that individuals who are fluent in two languages have an advantage over monolingual individuals in that they have greater cognitive flexibility and a greater understanding of language.

FIGURE 4.2 Iceberg analogy of language proficiency

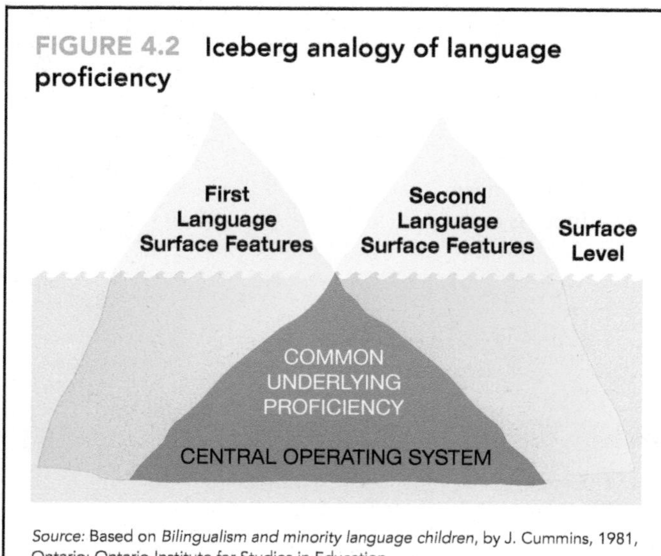

Source: Based on *Bilingualism and minority language children*, by J. Cummins, 1981, Ontario: Ontario Institute for Studies in Education.

4.3.5 The Learning and Developmental Process

The fourth factor addresses the learning and developmental process of second-language acquisition and learning. Cummins (1984) suggested that students generally acquire competency in the basic interpersonal communication skills (BICS) before becoming competent in cognitive academic language proficiency (CALP). The BICS, or social language, are the conversational competencies we develop with a second language—the greetings and small talk between peers that generally do not require much cognitive effort or social problem solving. The

CALP, or academic language, by contrast, refers to the more cognitively demanding language skills required for the new learning that occurs in school. In general, BICS develop in a second language before CALP. Cummins (1981) suggested that it takes 1 to 2 years to develop BICS but 5 to 7 years to develop competence in CALP.

Although these guidelines have been shown to vary widely depending on situational factors, linguistic input, and learner characteristics, they do have implications for teachers in general education classrooms. You might assume that because students can converse easily with you in their second language, they are ready to learn new concepts, strategies, and skills in the second language. This is not necessarily the case. For example, when Hoang Hy Vinh entered Sarah Miles's third-grade class, Sarah immediately noticed that he conversed easily with other students and with her. Vinh had emigrated from Vietnam 2 years before and had begun learning English through the school's ESL program. His parents, who took English in a night course, felt that learning English was important for their economic and personal success in the United States. Still, Vietnamese was the primary language spoken in the home.

As Sarah got to know Vinh, she realized that although his conversational skills were strong enough for him to be comfortable in the classroom community, he was not yet proficient in academic tasks such as reading and writing in English. She also found that for him to learn new concepts in social studies and science she needed to provide a lot of context. Sarah incorporated an extended segment on farming communities into a thematic unit on California, for example, because Vinh and several other students came from other Asian and Mexican farming communities. From the school and public libraries, she checked out books and magazines about farming and rural life in Mexico, Vietnam, and other Asian countries. The students also visited a California market, as well as Asian and Mexican food markets. They compared the foods from the markets and learned how those foods were grown in the three communities. For Vinh and other students from other cultures who were in the process of acquiring English as a second language, providing the link to their cultures helped to give them a context in which to build both their language and their cognitive skills.

This is an example of the context-embedded communication and instruction that Cummins (1981) and others (Chamot & O'Malley, 1994; Gersten & Jiménez, 1998; Reyes & Bos, 1998; Ruiz, Garcia, & Figueroa, 1996) recommend as facilitating second-language learning. As Ovando and Combs (2012) put it, "...good teachers will provide students with opportunities to develop both social *and* academic language in context" (p. 134).

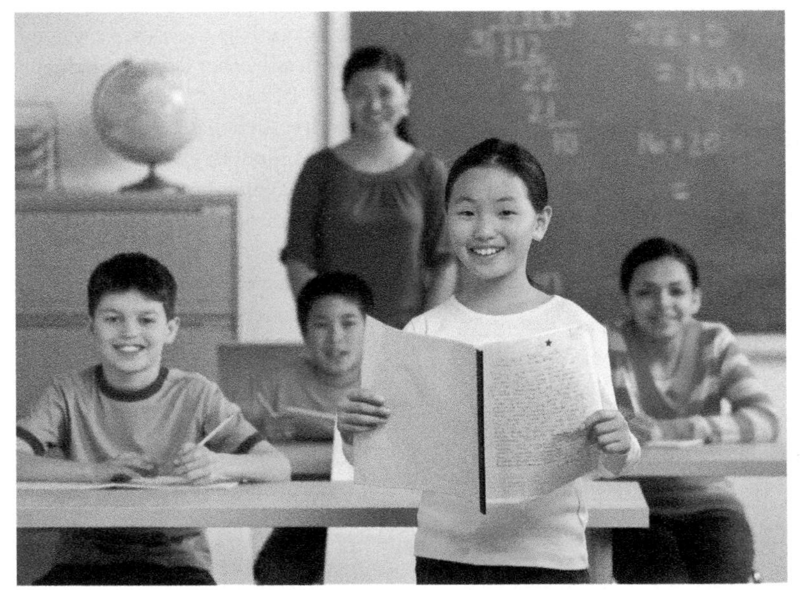

According to Ellis's framework for second-language acquisition, what five factors will influence this student's acquisition of English? What kinds of instructional activities for second-language acquisition might you recommend for this student based on effectiveness research?

4.3.6 Secondary Language Output

The fifth factor in the framework is secondary language output. Students may understand a language (listening and reading) but not be proficient in producing the language (speaking and writing). An important part of developing speaking proficiency is having the opportunity to engage in meaningful oral exchanges (in the classroom and the community) and to experiment with oral and written language in nonthreatening environments. Swain (1986) emphasized that not only comprehensible input but also opportunities for students to develop comprehensible output by oral practice with the language are important for acquiring a second language. Feedback from listeners and from self-monitoring enables second-language speakers to develop and fine-tune their oral language.

An important and noteworthy aspect of secondary language output is that receptive language skills typically develop before expressive language skills. As classroom teachers, we can facilitate students' use of expressive skills by giving them opportunities to express themselves in ways they perceive as safe and unthreatening. For example, "turn and talk" allows students to give their answers to a partner, and then the teacher can ask the student with better language skills to share the answer with the class.

4.3.7 Language Variation and Dialect

Language variation, which refers to the fact that language varies from place to place and from group to group, usually relates to the characteristics of groups of people (such as geographical region, social class, ethnic and cultural backgrounds, age, and gender). **Dialect** generally refers to language variations associated with a regional or social group of people. All English speakers use a dialect or variation of the English language. Think for a moment. Do you use the term *pop*, *soda*, *soda pop*, *tonic*, or some other term to label this popular type of drink? The answer depends on your dialect, which most likely relates to where you live and your cultural background. Dialect is also affected by age; for example, use of the term *icebox* rather than *refrigerator* is more evident in older people who grew up in times when iceboxes were used.

A wide range of dialects exists in the United States (Díaz-Rico, 2013). However, in general, there are four dialects that most people recognize: "(1) New York City, (2) New England, (3) the South, and (4) everyone else" (p. 330). Some other dialects include Louisiana French Creole and Hawaiian Creole, to name a few.

Language variation or dialects vary in several ways. Regional dialects tend to be distinguished by pronunciation and vocabulary features, whereas social and cultural dialects show variation not only in these areas but also in grammatical usage. Dialects also reflect conversation patterns. In a good, satisfying conversation in some speech communities, for example, speakers overlap one another's talk. In other communities, the listener waits for a break to enter a conversation, and the speaker is likely to stop talking when someone else starts speaking.

African American Vernacular English (AAVE) is a dialect used by some African Americans. It is the most prevalent native English vernacular dialect in the United States. As with any other language or dialect, there is great language variation among speakers of AAVE. Because of African Americans' historical status as an oppressed and involuntary minority, there has been a tendency to consider AAVE not as a valid language system but rather as random errors (Billings, 2005; Labov, Cohen, Robins, & Lewis, 1968). Like any other language, however, AAVE has an internally consistent linguistic infrastructure and set of grammar rules (Center for Applied Linguistics, 2008; Sealey-Ruiz, 2005; Varghese & Stritikus, 2013).

To be effective in teaching students with dialects other than your own, you need to expand your knowledge about dialects and how they affect learning (Adger, Wolfram, &

TIPS FOR TEACHERS 4.4

Strategies for Working with Students with Dialects

- Teach students pride in their community's dialect. Emphasize that no one dialect is the "right" way to speak.
- Support students in understanding the importance of communication over the accent.
- Explain that acquiring proficiency in formal English is a gradual transformation that is part of language learning.

Christian, 2007). It is important to recognize that students using AAVE or other dialects approach learning through differences in language, not deficits (LeMoine, 2001). In a supportive environment where home dialects are respected, students can learn to become **bidialectic** through learning the differences between their home dialect and that of the environment of school and the workplace (Ovando & Combs, 2012). See Tips for Teachers 4.4 for recommendations for working with students with dialects.

4.3.8 Historical Perspective on ESL Instruction and Bilingual Education

From the early 19th century to approximately the 1960s, a dominant belief was that bilingualism was detrimental to cognitive development and academic learning. Díaz (1983) summarized the research from before 1962, which built the case for bilingualism as a "language handicap." Researchers found that bilingual children had more limited vocabularies, more deficient articulation, and more grammatical errors than monolingual students. One interpretation was that bilingualism caused "linguistic confusion," which affected students' cognitive ability and academic performance. This research, overall, had many flaws. Bilingual and monolingual groups were not matched for other important variables such as socioeconomic status, for example, and tests for the intellectual functioning and learning of bilingual students generally were conducted in English, not in the first or more dominant language.

In 1962, a classic study was published that is now considered the turning point in the history of the relationship between bilingualism and cognition (Peal & Lambert, 1962). This research broke new territory in two respects: It overcame many methodological deficiencies, and it found that bilingualism has cognitive advantages over monolingualism. Researchers Peal and Lambert concluded that bilingualism provides greater cognitive flexibility, greater ability to think more abstractly, and greater ability to form concepts.

Subsequent research has shown that higher degrees of bilingualism are correlated with increased cognitive abilities in such areas as creativity, knowledge of how language works (*metalinguistics*), concept formation, and cognitive flexibility, and may even delay the onset of Alzheimer's disease symptoms (Bialystok & Shapero, 2005; Dreifus, 2011; Gándara, 2015a; Kroll, 2009). Of course, in our expanding multicultural and multilingual society, being bilingual also can help you secure a job. Bilingual education and teaching ESL for culturally and linguistically diverse students have evolved through the years. Figure 4.3 shows the chronology of this evolution in the United States.

What is interesting about this chronology is the way bilingualism has been tied to assimilation into American culture and therefore linked to political policy. Bilingualism in our schools and communities dates back to the early colonies. It was common among both the working and the educated classes for many official documents to be published in German and French as well as English. By the late 1800s, however, language restrictions were being placed on schools. Under strong political pressures to assimilate immigrants, bilingual education was virtually eradicated by the 1930s. After World War II, students from minority cultures were described as "culturally deprived" and "linguistically disabled."

In the early 1960s, however, bilingual education was reborn in Dade County, Florida, as Cuban immigrants requested bilingual schooling for their children. Programs were developed throughout the United States, under the authority of the Bilingual Education Act passed (as Title VII of the Elementary and Secondary Education Act) in 1968. Based on the law, suits were brought to ensure better services for students with cultural and linguistic diversities. The most noted case is *Lau v. Nichols*, in which the U.S. Supreme Court ruled that equal treatment is not merely providing students with the same facilities, textbooks, teachers, and curriculum when students do not understand English.

Although the Bilingual Education Act and the Civil Rights Act and their rules and regulations promoted equal access and bilingual education, political developments have moved the country back toward an assimilation philosophy. In 1981, Senator S. I. Hayakawa introduced a constitutional amendment to declare English the official language of the United States. This amendment was defeated, but a growing number of states have

FIGURE 4.3 **Developments in second-language and bilingual education in the United States**

Before 1914	Many community schools existed to teach a specific language, such as German. Saturday classes were common.
1918	World War I brought about reactions against Germany and a resurgence of patriotic feeling; use of "English only" in schools was legislated in many states.
1945	World War II led to realization of need for knowledge of foreign languages; teaching of foreign languages in schools was encouraged.
1958	Soviet launching of *Sputnik* shocked U.S. leaders, who then funded schools' efforts to promote key subject areas, including foreign languages.
1963	Dade County, Florida, initiated bilingual programs for Spanish-speaking Cuban children coming to Miami.
1964	Civil Rights Act forbade language-based discrimination.
1968	Bilingual Education Act: Title VII of the Elementary and Secondary Education Act promoted bilingual programs in the schools.
1971	Massachusetts Bilingual Education Act: A law mandating bilingual education for non-English-speaking children; Massachusetts was the first state to enact the law; other states followed.
1974	Bilingual Education Reform Act: Updated the 1968 law; mandated language instruction; added study of history and culture in bilingual programs.
1974	U.S. Supreme Court decision in *Lau v. Nichols* gave non-English-speaking students the legal right to instruction that enables them to participate in education process, and to bilingual instruction, as part of "equal educational opportunity."
1975	The U.S. Department of Education developed guidelines that specified approaches, methods, and procedures for educating students with limited proficiency in English. These "Lau remedies" were not enacted.
1981	Senator S. I. Hayakawa first introduced a constitutional amendment to declare English the official language of the United States. (It was defeated.)
1981	*Castenada v. Pickard* established a framework for determining whether school districts are in compliance with *Lau v. Nichols* decision. The framework for compliance included: Theory—Is the program based on sound theory? Implementation—Does the district have an implementation plan? Results—What kinds of results does the district intend to achieve from implementing the program?
1984	California voters passed a bill to publish ballots and other election material in English only.
1985	U.S. Secretary of Education William Bennett spoke out against federal bilingual education programs.
1994	Reauthorization of the Bilingual Education Act (Title VII of the Improving American Schools Act, formerly Elementary and Secondary Education Act): In this reauthorization, bilingualism was reconceptualized as a valuable national resource. Bilingual programs are no longer defined by types: maintenance, transitional, and immersion.
1994	Reauthorization of Improving American Schools Act resulted in language-minority students being eligible to receive Title I services, even if the source of disadvantage is determined to be language.
1998	The California state legislature passed the English for the Children Initiative that restricts the programs in which ELL students can participate, including the number of years to several years only and the types of programs to ESL programs.
1999	Proposition 227 passed in California, eliminating bilingual education programs.
2001	The Elementary and Secondary Education Act (ESEA) was reauthorized as the No Child Left Behind Act.
2006	The National Literacy Panel Report reviewing quantitative and qualitative research on literacy development of language-minority students. The American Institutes for Research releases results of a 5-year study of Proposition 227 impact indicating no difference between bilingual instructional practices compared to English-only practices.
2014	In California SG 1174 was passed to authorize a ballot item in November of 2016 to repeal most of the provisions of Proposition 227.
2015	The Elementary and Secondary Education Act (ESEA) was reauthorized as the Every Student Succeeds Act.

Sources: Based on *Multicultural teaching: A handbook of activities, information, and resources* (7th ed., pp. 16–20), by P. L. Tiedt & I. M. Tiedt, 2005, Boston: Allyn & Bacon; "Developing literacy in second-language learners: Report of the National Literacy Panel on Language-Minority Children and Youth," by D. August & T. Shanahan, 2006, Mahwah, NJ: Erlbaum; *Los Angeles Times* (June 4, 2014). Is bilingual education worth bringing back? Retrieved from http://www.latimes.com/opinion/editorials/la-ed-bilingual-education-proposition-227-repeal-20140605-story.html

passed what has been referred to as "English-only" legislation. In 2002, Congress repealed the Bilingual Education Act and subsumed the teaching of ELLs under the umbrella of No Child Left Behind (NCLB). The new law, Title II, the English Language Acquisition, Language Enhancement, and Academic Achievement Act, placed less emphasis on bilingual education, bilingualism, and biliteracy and greater emphasis on English language learning. Moreover, NCLB mandated the inclusion of ELLs in reporting of adequate yearly progress (AYP) as determined largely by performance on standardized tests.

These changes have resulted in continued controversy about the role of bilingual education in schools in the United States (Baker, 2011; Crawford, 2004; Cummins, 2011). Those who promote bilingual education offer the following justifications:

- It is the best way to attain the maximum cognitive development of ELL students.
- It is a means of achieving equal educational opportunity.
- It offers a means of easing the transition into the dominant language and culture.
- It is an approach to educational reform.
- It is a means of promoting positive interethnic relations.
- It is a wise economic investment to help ELL students become maximally productive in adult life for the benefit of themselves and society.

The reauthorization of the Elementary and Secondary Education Act (Every Student Succeeds Act, or ESSA) in December of 2015 will no doubt have an impact on the future of the teaching and formal assessment of ELL students in the United States. The reauthorized legislation de-emphasizes high-stakes testing, provides revisions to the timetable for including ELLs in high-stakes testing, makes commitment of federal funds to support English language instruction, and underscores the original intention of the Elementary and Secondary Education Act—to support students who are economically disadvantaged. How this legislation will be implemented in individual states and their programs for teaching ELLs remains to be seen.

MyEdLab **Self-Check 4.3**

MyEdLab **Application Exercise 4.3:** Framework for Second-Language Acquisition

4.4 ASSESSMENT OF STUDENTS WITH CULTURAL AND LINGUISTIC DIFFERENCES

Although progress has been made in many areas of teaching students with cultural and linguistic differences, the one area still in need of development is assessment (Abedi & Levine, 2013; Hurley & Tinajero, 2001; Klingner, 2003; Wagner, Francis, & Morris, 2005). As the Report of the National Literacy Panel on Language-Minority Children and Youth points out, assessment of diverse learners is complex and difficult (Garcia, McKoon, & August, 2006). The IDEIA 2004 demonstrates a growing awareness of the needs of students from different language backgrounds by mandating that assessments for special education services be conducted in the language and form that is most familiar to the student. Because school psychologists are often the key individuals in assessments for English language learners eligible for special education, O'Bryon and Rogers (2010) examined the assessment practices of bilingual school psychologists with ELLs. In this national survey, bilingual school psychologists perceived that they had "above-average" knowledge regarding second-language acquisition, but only 15% indicated that they took the lead in performing language proficiency assessments.

Assessment is particularly controversial with respect to mandated standardized tests and placement into special education (Cawthon, Leppo, Car, & Kopriva, 2013). The controversy about how best to include students with such differences in large-scale, standardized tests has escalated in recent years due to standards-based instruction, with most states participating in the Common Core Standards (Abedi & Levine, 2013). Moreover, the issue of identifying best practices in making adaptations to make high-stakes assessments more accessible for ELLs continues to be subject to debate (Cawthon et al., 2013; Heitin, 2014).

Abedi and Dietel (2004) of the National Center for Research on Evaluation, Standards, and Student Testing (CRESST) identify four reasons why standardized tests pose challenges for ELLs:

1. **Historically low ELL performance and slow improvements.** State tests show that ELL students' school performance is far below that of other students, oftentimes 20 to 30 percentage points, and usually shows little improvement over the years.
2. **Measurement accuracy.** CRESST research shows that the language demands of tests negatively influence accurate measurement of ELL performance. For the ELL student, tests measure both achievement *and* language ability.
3. **Instability of the ELL student subgroup.** The goal of redesignating high-performing ELL students as language-proficient students causes ELL high achievers to exit the ELL subgroup. The consequence is downward pressure on ELL test scores, worsened by the addition of new ELL students, who are typically low achieving.
4. **Factors outside of a school's control.** CRESST research shows substantial nonschool (e.g., home, community, and other contextual) effects on student learning even within ELL subgroups. Schools are therefore unable to control all factors related to student achievement. (p. 1)

Video Example from YouTube

MyEdLab
Video Example 4.4.

Watch the YouTube video "Authentic Assessment for English Language Learners" for ways to make assessment more culturally relevant. What are additional ways you can adapt assessment procedures and content to enable students to demonstrate what they have learned? https://www.youtube.com/watch?v=ehq0Yt9Atew

Although many factors may affect inappropriate student placement in special education, assessment does play a key role. It is often difficult for teachers, and in some cases experts in assessment, to discriminate between learning problems and language or cultural differences (Klingner, Barletta, & Hoover, 2008; Klingner & Eppolito, 2014; Wolf, Herman, & Dietel, 2010). However, becoming aware of the potential influence of language and culture on formal and informal assessment is a necessary first step. Ongoing professional development and consultation with colleagues with expertise in assessing diverse students are also important.

The role of the classroom teacher in preparing students for standardized tests is pivotal. It is important for you to learn the testing requirements for the diverse students in your state and possible accommodations that are allowable. Whether considering your role in administering standardized tests, interpreting test scores, or selecting and administering classroom assessment tools, principles of **culturally responsive assessment (CRA)** are vitally important. CRA is actually a collection of approaches that promote nondiscriminatory assessment practices (Cartledge et al., 2009). CRA is especially important in the monitoring of student progress that is recommended in RTI models (Fuchs, Stecker, & Fuchs, 2008) and in the research on effective instruction for ELLs. Tips for Teachers 4.5 provides suggestions for CRA.

TIPS FOR TEACHERS 4.5

Implementing Culturally Responsive Assessment

- Consider the testing environment and how it relates to students' prior experiences.
- Keep students' level of language proficiency in mind.
- Determine students' prior opportunities to learn the skill or concept.
- Implement appropriate accommodations (e.g., dictionary use, administration in first language, extended time).
- Use a variety of authentic assessments (e.g., checklists, performance tasks, group assessment).
- Align assessment with regular instruction and intensive interventions.
- Provide specific and frequent feedback.
- Involve students and families as active participants in the assessment process.

Sources: Based on *Literacy instruction for English language learners pre-k–12*, by D. M. Barone & S. H. Xu, 2008, New York: Guilford; and *Diverse learners with exceptionalities: Culturally responsive teaching in the inclusive classroom*, by G. Cartledge, R. Gardner, & D. Y. Ford, 2009, Upper Saddle River, NJ: Merrill/Pearson Education.

MyEdLab **Self-Check 4.4**

MyEdLab **Application Exercise 4.4:** Assessing Students with Cultural and Linguistic Differences

4.5 INSTRUCTIONAL GUIDELINES AND ACCOMMODATIONS FOR DIVERSE STUDENTS

As a teacher, you will have students from many cultures and students who are in the process of acquiring English as a second language or second dialect. You may or may not be familiar with the culture and language of these students. Moreover, their parents' views about schooling and the roles and responsibilities of parents and teachers (Edwards, 2012; Meyer, Bevan-Brown, Harry, & Sapon-Shevin, 2005), as well as their own experience in schools in the United States and elsewhere, may be very different from your own. It will be your responsibility to help all students feel comfortable in your class and to reach out to parents in culturally sensitive ways. To accomplish this, you can use culturally responsive teaching and best practices in teaching ELLs, discussed next.

4.5.1 Culturally Responsive Teaching to Accommodate English Language Learners

To promote learning, you should incorporate students' language and culture into the curriculum, demonstrate that you value their culture and language, have high expectations for all of your students, and make accommodations so that they can learn successfully. Culturally responsive teaching (CRT) involves teachers who "recognize the differences between their students and themselves and strive to become nonjudgmental" (Cartledge et al., 2009, p. 18).

Video Example from YouTube

MyEdLab
Video Example 4.5.
Watch the YouTube video, "Introduction to Culturally Relevant Pedagogy." What are some ways that you can help students link their culture and prior knowledge with what they are learning? https://www.youtube.com/watch?v=nGTVjJuRaZ8

Research into the characteristics of effective teachers of students with cultural and linguistic diversities indicates that such teachers:

- Have high expectations of their students and believe that all students are capable of academic success.
- See themselves as members of the community and see teaching as a way to give back to the community.
- Display confidence in their ability to be successful with students who are culturally and linguistically diverse.
- Provide explicit instruction to monitor students' progress, and provide immediate feedback.
- Integrate the students' native language and dialect, culture, and community into classroom activities to make input more relevant and comprehensible, to build trust and self-esteem, and to promote cultural diversity and cultural pluralism.
- Use curriculum and teaching strategies that promote coherence, relevance, progression, and continuity.
- Structure opportunities for students to use English.
- Challenge their students and teach higher-order thinking.

Throughout this chapter we have emphasized the importance of understanding the language and culture of your students. Involving the parents of culturally and linguistically diverse students in their children's education is the key to CRT (Edwards, 2004, 2012; Ford et al., 2014). Most parents want the very best for their children. However, some teachers may think that parents are not interested in their child's education because they do not get involved in school functions, parent conferences, or helping

TIPS FOR TEACHERS 4.6

Working with Parents from Diverse Backgrounds

- Be inviting and welcoming.
- Learn the correct pronunciation of the child's first name and of the family name, and learn a few words of the child's native language.
- When preparing your classroom and curriculum, make certain that the heritage of your students is reflected.
- Explore the best ways to communicate with parents.
- Do not talk down to parents; provide them with the respect you would expect as a parent.
- Enlist the support of a translator or encourage parents to bring a translator or person who can provide support to parent conferences.
- Do your best to provide written communication in the parents' native language.
- Interview parents to determine how they can be a resource at home or at school. All parents have time, treasure, or talent (funds of knowledge) to share in large or small ways.

their child with homework. There are many reasons parents do not get involved in traditional ways:

- Some parents do not feel comfortable in schools and are fearful of discrimination and disrespect.
- Others are not comfortable with the English language in either speaking or writing.
- Others may come from cultures in which the teacher has the responsibility of formal schooling and parents customarily do not get involved.
- Still others may have been educated in another system or might not have had the opportunity for schooling at all.

Tips for Teachers 4.6 offers general suggestions for teachers in working with parents from diverse cultural and linguistic backgrounds.

4.5.2 Best Practices in English Language Learning

A growing body of research is beginning to yield information about best practices in teaching ELLs (Baker et al., 2014; Goldenberg, 2008; Linan-Thompson & Vaughn, 2007). In recent years several summaries and syntheses of research have provided educators with important guidelines for instruction. Across these summaries several consistent themes are echoed (August & Shanahan, 2006; Baker et al., 2014; Francis, Rivera, Lesaux, Kieffer, & Rivera, 2006; Gersten & Baker, 2000): encourage strategic use of first language, build vocabulary with first language as a foundation, focus on meaning, and provide explicit skill instruction.

Encourage strategic use of first language

Students benefit when they are encouraged to develop proficiency in their first language even if it is not formally supported through bilingual education (Ovando & Combs, 2012). The issue of learning to read in the first language or English is a reoccurring question, and the research to date suggests that students perform better in reading when they learn to read in their first language (Goldenberg, 2008). To promote this, teachers can do the following:

- Encourage acquisition in first-language reading and writing while also learning to read and write in English.
- Encourage students to use their first language around school.

TECH TIPS

Software Programs and Web Resources for Culturally and Linguistically Diverse Learners

The array of software programs and resources for culturally and linguistically diverse learners keeps growing as the ELL population continues to grow. To help students and teachers with teaching and learning, try the following:

Little Explorers Picture Dictionary by Enchanted Learning Software (www.enchantedlearning.com/Home.html).

Little Explorers Picture Dictionary has more than 2,400 items in many different collections from English to Spanish, Portuguese, French, Dutch, German, Italian, Japanese, and more. Many of the pictures link to explanatory text, diagrams, and activities.

iPad/iPod™ translation applications include **translation+**, **Word/Roll ES**, **Compact English-Spanish Dictionary**, and **Spanish Phrasebook with Audio**.

In addition to these programs, you might check out the following web resources for dictionaries and translations in various languages:

- www.word2word.com
- https://translate.google.com
- www.freetranslation.com

When using online translators, just be aware that word-to-word translations of English may not be accurate because different languages have different grammatical structures.

- Provide opportunities for students from the same language group to communicate with one another in their first language (e.g., in cooperative learning groups, during informal discussions).
- Recruit people who can tutor students in their first language.
- Provide, in classrooms and the school library, books written in various languages.
- Incorporate greetings and information in various languages in newsletters and other official school communications.

For online programs that promote proficiency for culturally and linguistically diverse learners, see the Tech Tips "Software and Web Resources for Culturally and Linguistically Diverse Learners."

Build vocabulary with first language as a foundation

One way to teach vocabulary to ELLs is through cognates. Cognates are words in different languages that sound alike (homophones) or that look alike (homographs) and have roughly or exactly the same meaning. Cognates are very helpful when learning a new language because they make the process a little friendlier. We can say that cognates are "good friends." For example, words that end in *-ción* in Spanish tend to have cognates that end in *-tion* in English; *nación* means "nation," and *constitución* means "constitution." With all of these words looking and sounding alike, you might wonder why you don't speak four or five languages. This seems like a breeze, right? Wrong! Beware of *false cognates*, or "false friends." The term was first used by Koessler and Derocquigny in their 1928 book *Les faux amis ou les trahisons du vocabulaire anglais*. The title itself contains a false cognate and a true cognate: *trahisons* is not "treason" but "betrayal," and *vocabulaire* is "vocabulary" (Bello, 2007). Figure 4.4 provides samples of homographs, cognates, and false cognates. In addition to cognates, another effective strategy for teaching vocabulary is to focus on meaning.

In addition to teaching cognates, it is valuable to promote vocabulary development broadly as well as academic vocabulary (Baker et al., 2014; Lesaux, Kieffer, Faller, & Kelley, 2010). Academic vocabulary consists of those key words that help you understand and learn more about the content area you are studying. For example, in social studies, academic vocabulary includes words such as *feud*, *democracy*, and *agriculture*; whereas in science academic vocabulary includes words such as *cell*, *equilibrium*, and *vertigo*. Based on their review of research, Baker and colleagues (2014) recommend that selected academic vocabulary words should be taught intensively over several days using a variety of instructional strategies.

FIGURE 4.4 Homographs, cognates, and false cognates

Here are some exact Spanish–English homographs:

atlas	Atlas
popular	Popular
hospital	Hospital
metal	Metal
fatal	Fatal
hotel	Hotel
actor	Actor

There are many more words that, although not spelled exactly the same, are still understandable:

ácido	Acid
alfabeto	Alphabet
igual	Equal
familia	Family
plástico	Plastic

Here are some common Spanish–English false cognates:

- *Introducir* means to introduce into, to bring in, to place; to introduce friends, you will need to use presentar.
- You will be very embarrassed if you use *embarazada* in the wrong context; it means pregnant, as in "with child." Try *avergonzada/o* for embarrassed instead.
- *Delito* is not delightful; it is a crime. Use *delicia* or *encanto*.

Here are some tips on using cognates in a multicultural or foreign-language classroom:

- Take advantage of the students' prior knowledge of language.
- Ask questions such as "Does that sound/look like a word in Spanish/English?"
- Use the cognates in different contexts to facilitate understanding.
- Point out the homographic cognates to limited-English-proficiency students.
- Allow the students to repeat and get used to the homophonic cognates (e.g., *peace—paz, pleasure—placer*).
- Use words with the same roots to aid in learning others (e.g., *appear, disappear–aparecer, desaparecer*).
- Make generalizations about grammatical differences and similarities between the languages.
- Get the students to talk about words and language so that they are more aware of what they know.
- Create a wall of cognates and/or false cognates.
- Use cognates to introduce science lessons (e.g., biology prefixes and roots such as *epi, dermis, itis, geo,* and *lympho*).
- Use cognates to introduce lessons about (language) history, such as words that came into English during the Norman period (French and Latin terms) or Germanic period (Anglo-Saxon terms) and the differences between synonyms (e.g., *insane/crazy, autumn/fall*).

Source: "Using cognates," by M. Bello, 2007, in S. Vaughn, C. S. Bos, & J. S. Schumm, *Teaching students who are exceptional, diverse, and at risk in the general education classroom* (4th ed., p. 286), Boston: Allyn & Bacon.

Focus on meaning

Students who are acquiring English as a second language are focusing their attention not only on learning content and vocabulary but also on learning English. Depending on their level of language development, meaning is accessed in different ways. Following are stages of second-language development related to learning in content classes:

- *Low-beginning.* Students depend on gestures, facial expressions, objects, pictures, a phrase dictionary, and often a translator to understand or be understood. Occasionally, students comprehend words or phrases.
- *Mid-beginning.* Students begin to comprehend more, but only when the speaker provides gestural clues, speaks slowly, and uses concrete referents and repetitions. Students speak seldom and haltingly, show some recognition of written segments, and may be able to write short utterances.
- *High-beginning to low-intermediate.* Students comprehend more, but with difficulty. Students speak in an attempt to meet basic needs but remain hesitant and make frequent errors in grammar, vocabulary, and pronunciation. Students can read very simple text and can write a little (but writing is restricted in grammatical structure and vocabulary).
- *Mid-intermediate.* Students may experience a dramatic increase in vocabulary recognition, but idioms and more advanced vocabulary remain difficult. Students often know what they want to say but grope for acceptable words and phrases. Errors in

grammar, vocabulary, and pronunciation are frequent. Students can read text that is more difficult but still concrete and can write with greater ease than before.

- *High-intermediate to low-advanced.* Students begin to comprehend substantial parts of normal conversation but often require repetitions, particularly with academic discourse. Students are gaining confidence in speaking ability; errors are common but less frequent. Students can read and write text that contains more complex vocabulary and structures than before but experience difficulty with abstract language.
- *Mid-advanced.* Students comprehend much conversational and academic discourse spoken at normal rates but sometimes require repetition. Speech is more fluent and meaning is generally clear, but occasional errors occur. Students read and write with less difficulty materials commensurate with their cognitive development but demonstrate some problems in grasping intended meaning.
- *High-advanced.* Students comprehend normal conversation and academic discourse with little difficulty. Most idioms are understood. Students speak fluently in most situations with few errors. Students read and write both concrete and abstract materials and are able to manipulate the language with relative ease.

Although planning for culturally and linguistically diverse students takes some creative thinking and modifications of the curriculum, these students will broaden both your horizons and those of the class. In your planning, be sure to provide ample time for students to engage in meaningful conversations about topics related to language and culture. Tips for Teachers 4.7 will assist you in your planning.

See the 60-Second Lesson for a quick overview of how to teach a concept to second-language learners.

TIPS FOR TEACHERS 4.7

Strategies for Promoting Content and Second-Language Learning in General Education Classes

Beginning to Mid-Intermediate Proficiency Level

- Provide a supportive environment in which help is readily available to second-language learners.
- Establish consistent patterns and routines in the classroom.
- Use gestures, visuals, and demonstrations to present concepts.
- Connect content to students' home cultures.
- Simplify grammar and vocabulary.
- Slow the pace of presentation, enunciate clearly, and emphasize key concepts through gesture, facial expression, intonation, and repetition.
- Record your lectures or talks on tape, and make them available for students.
- Make copies of your notes, or have another student take notes, so that second-language learners can concentrate on listening.
- Build in redundancy by restating concepts in a simpler form, providing examples, and giving direct definitions.
- Extend wait time so that second-language learners have time to volunteer.
- Avoid forcing second-language learners to speak.
- Arrange cooperative learning so that students with the same first language work together.
- Encourage students to use their second language in informal conversations.
- Whenever possible, use tutors who speak the native language of the second-language learners.
- Alter criteria for grading.

High-Intermediate to Advanced Proficiency Level

- Add contextual support to your lesson (e.g., advance organizers, study guides, glossaries, videos/films).
- Take into account the linguistic demands of the content.
- Provide opportunities for students to write in the content area.
- Provide opportunities for second-language learners to practice critical thinking skills.
- Coach second-language learners in appropriate learning strategies for mastering content.

60-SECOND LESSON
TEACHING A CONCEPT TO SECOND-LANGUAGE LEARNERS

When students do not understand a concept, use one or more of the following strategies:

- Draw a picture.
- Have students with the same first language explain it in that language.
- Re-explain, but simplify the language.
- Demonstrate it.
- Provide examples and, if necessary, nonexamples (i.e., use of nonexamples is a typical strategy used in teaching concepts).

Source: Díaz-Rico, L. (2012). *Course for teaching English learners.* Boston: Allyn & Bacon.

Provide explicit skill instruction

At the beginning of this chapter you read about Kristina and her class of twenty-seven English language learners. Kristina quickly learned that her students not only had a range of English language proficiency, but also a range of prior schooling experiences. She also learned that what she learned in her teacher preparation program about explicit instruction was highly relevant to her classroom situation. Linan-Thompson and Vaughn (2007) define explicit instruction as "task-specific, teacher-led instruction that overtly demonstrates a task and can be used to teach students both basic and higher-order reading skills" (p. 6). Kristina realized that the principles of explicit instruction are also applicable when teaching skills in other content areas, such as map reading in social studies, computation in mathematics, and experiments in science. See Tips for Teachers 4.8 for an overview of ten general principles guiding effective instructional practice for second-language learners.

Think about the last time you were trying to learn a new skill. What helped you to learn the skill? Chances are you had a clear idea of what you needed to learn, why you needed to learn it, and steps in how to master the skill. That's explicit instruction. Explicit instruction of a skill begins with a description of what skill is to be learned and why. If necessary, specific instruction in relevant vocabulary helps the teacher and student to be "on the same page" and to foster understanding of the skill to be learned. The teacher then demonstrates or models the skill, breaking it down into steps if needed. A demonstration

TIPS FOR TEACHERS 4.8

General Principles for Effective Instruction with English Language Learners

1. Instruction emphasizes both a full repertoire of formulaic expressions and rule-based competence.
2. Meaning is the focus of instruction.
3. Form is also the focus of instruction.
4. Instruction needs to address both implicit and explicit knowledge of the second language.
5. Students acquire an internal grammar of the language and do not need extensive grammar instruction.
6. Learning a language requires considerable opportunities to receive language input in the second language.
7. Learning a language also requires extensive opportunities for output—to express yourself in the language.
8. Learning a language also requires opportunities to use both input and output in an interactive and contextually supportive manner.
9. Individual differences in language learning need to be considered, as all of us learn a second language at a different rate and with a different degree of difficulty.
10. Literacy supports oral language development and oral language development supports literacy development.

Sources: Based on *Instructed second language acquisition: A literature review,* by R. Ellis, 2005, Wellington, New Zealand: Research Division, Ministry of Education; and Teaching English language learners: What the research does—and does not—say, by C. Goldenberg, *American Educator,* Summer 2008, pp. 8–19.

is followed by guided practice, where the teacher provides support and re-explanations as needed. Finally, the student tries the new skill through independent practice. As Kristina put it, "When I use explicit instruction, my students catch on. Sure, some students need more practice than others. It's so exciting when they 'get it'!" As you read about the instruction activities, strategies, and methods included in this book, think about how you can apply the principles of explicit instruction in your planning.

MyEdLab **Self-Check 4.5**

MyEdLab **Application Exercise 4.5:** Explicit Instruction

4 SUMMARY

- The demographics of our nation and schools are changing, and the number of students with cultural and linguistic diversities is increasing. The macroculture represents the dominant culture of the United States; microcultures represent the students' home cultures. Learning about your students' home cultures and communities and integrating those cultures and communities into the curriculum is important to help them succeed in school and beyond.
- The goal of multicultural education is to change the structure of schools so that students from different cultural groups have an equal chance to achieve in school. Dimensions of multicultural education include content integration, knowledge construction, prejudice reduction, equity pedagogy, and an empowering school culture.
- When teaching students who are second-language learners, it is important to keep in mind individual differences, including prior educational experiences in the first language, needs for adaptation, and needs for verbal and nonverbal support.
- Assessment of diverse learners is complex and difficult. Culturally responsive assessment can facilitate fair and accurate assessment of students as they progress in learning skills and concepts.
- Culturally responsive teaching and use of best instructional practices can facilitate learning for students who are second-language learners. Best instructional practices include strategic use of a first language, building vocabulary with first language as a foundation, focus on meaning, and providing explicit skills instruction.

THINK AND APPLY

1. Now that you have read Chapter 4, think about the interview with Kristina Zayas-Bazan. What questions do you have for her about strategies for working with students who are culturally and linguistically diverse? Make a list of the questions and then ask them of an ESL or bilingual education teacher.
2. Visit a school known for its positive emphasis on multicultural education. Watch for evidence of cultural integration and an empowering school culture. Observe a lesson to see how the teacher builds on the students' cultural diversity.
3. In a job interview with a principal you are asked the following questions, "If a new immigrant with limited English proficiency were assigned to your class, what would you do to help the student become acclimated to your class? How would you support the student in his or her English language learning?"
4. Check out the website for your state department of education and school district. Research their policies and procedures for making adaptations for ELLs in the administration of assessments.
5. Select a unit you have taught or plan to teach. Review it for its focus on multicultural perspectives. Then, using one of the four approaches to multicultural education (contributions, additive, transformation, social action), modify the unit to include a stronger multicultural emphasis.

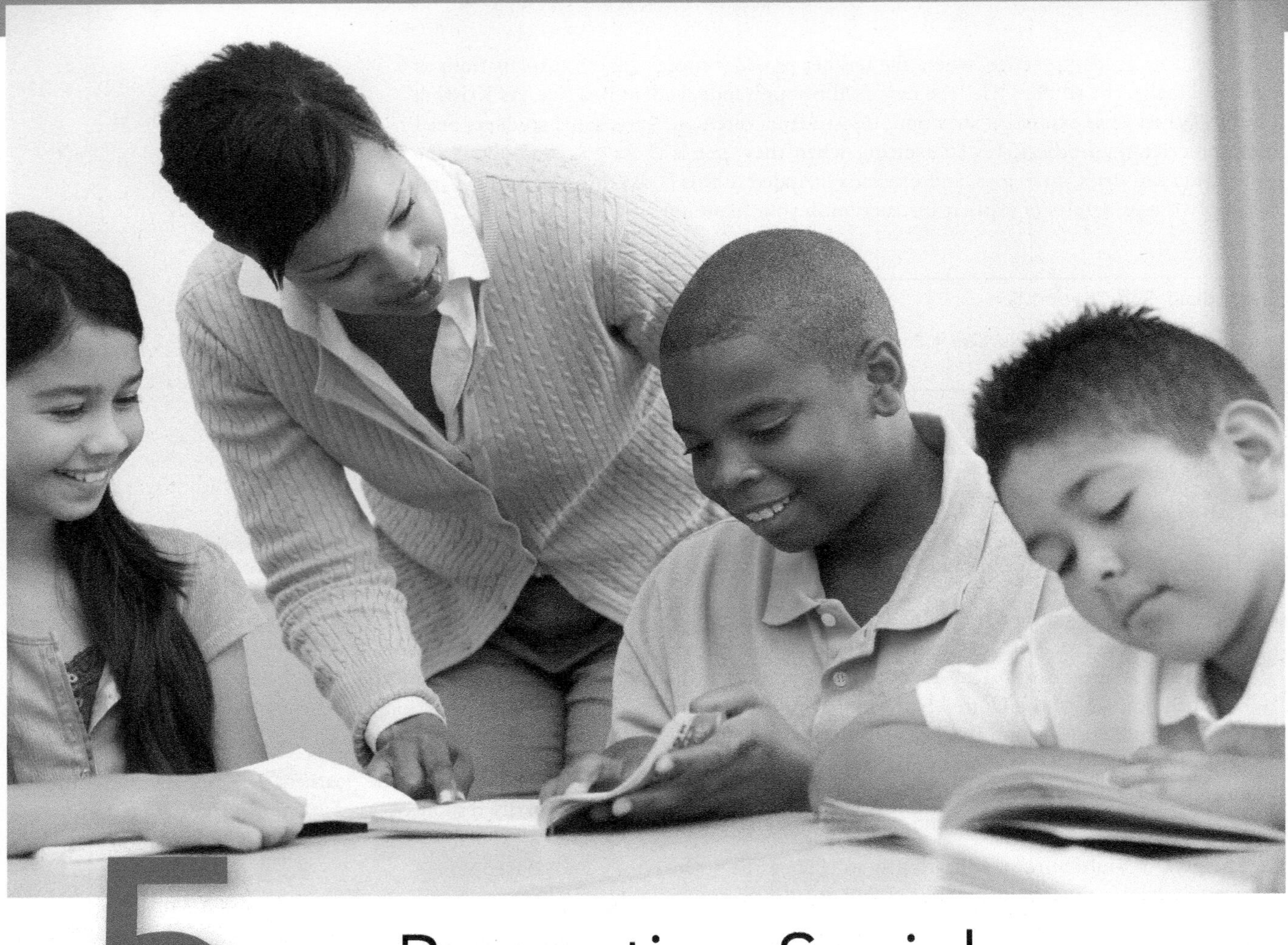

5 Promoting Social Acceptance and Managing Student Behavior

Learning Outcomes

5.1 Establish a classroom climate that promotes appropriate behaviors and acceptance of all students.

5.2 Promote acceptance of students with disabilities in your classroom.

5.3 Recognize bullying behavior and identify best practices for remedying bullying.

5.4 Identify factors to consider in teaching students from diverse cultural and linguistic backgrounds

5.5 Describe positive behavior supports (PBIS) and how to implement them within a Response to Intervention Framework.

5.6 Identify universal strategies in the classroom to help students recognize mistaken behaviors.

INTERVIEW: SAMANTHA DIETZ

Samantha Dietz has worked with the University of Miami Support Network for novice teachers to provide mentoring to alumni during the first 3 years of teaching. As a licensed clinical social worker and an expert in emotional and behavioral disorders, Samantha provides advice regarding general classroom management techniques as well as working with students with social emotional challenges.

Samantha uses a sociometric technique as a vehicle for a discussion of stressors that participants either have or are likely to experience. She asks the participants to move to one of four quadrants in a large assembly room. The quadrants represent four potential areas of stress for novice teachers: knowing their own subject, establishing positive school relationships (e.g., with administrators, parents), managing the general classroom, and dealing with problem behavior. From year to year the results are consistent. As Samantha describes it:

> For the most part, the participants place themselves in one of two quadrants—managing the general classroom or dealing with problem behavior. As a result of their undergraduate classes and student teaching experience, they feel they have a basic background for what they are about to encounter. They are excited and even thrilled about having their own classroom. However, there is still high anxiety about whether or not they will be able to handle the complexities of managing the range of behaviors they know they will encounter in the classroom. They are afraid of the unknown and even more concerned that some of the more serious behavior problems will be beyond their expertise.

This sociometric activity provides a mechanism for triggering discussions in small groups and with participants' individual mentors about their fears and concerns and also a platform for discussing ways to address these fears effectively. As the school year progresses, students are taught in follow-up sessions specific ways to identify problem areas, garner resources (both human and otherwise) to address those problems, and generate solutions. Samantha explains:

> Our goal is to help participants understand that their feelings are normal and natural. Eventually they learn from veteran teachers and from each other how to muster the self-confidence to take the risk to ask for help and advice. I've been labeled the "feel good" woman. Indeed our participants do feel good when they take the responsibility for their own professional growth and learn how to gather resources to do so.

Introduction

How can I set up my classroom so that I spend more time teaching and less time managing student behavior? How can I establish a classroom community where students work together and all students feel accepted and valued? How can I manage my classroom so that I can help my students

CHAPTER OUTLINE

recognize their strengths and learn to cope with personal challenges in behavior and learning? How can I help students with disabilities feel welcome and accepted in my classroom? In her work with novice teachers, Samantha is frequently asked these questions. This chapter provides practices for promoting student acceptance, managing student behavior, and providing positive behavior supports so that you will be prepared to conduct a classroom that enhances student learning.

This chapter begins with three sections that focus on ways to foster acceptance of all children in your classroom by establishing a respectful classroom climate. The chapter continues with an overview of a three-tier approach to implementing a system of positive behavior supports. The principles and practices you'll learn in this chapter will enable you to prevent and address most of the student behavior challenges elementary and secondary teachers encounter on a day-to-day basis.

5.1 ESTABLISHING A POSITIVE CLASSROOM CLIMATE

One of the first things Samantha Dietz recommends to novice teachers is starting the year off right by establishing a positive classroom climate that will be conducive to learning. Students who feel accepted by their teacher and classmates and are expected to treat others in the class with respect are far less likely to cause or experience problems. Consider that the classroom climate includes both physical and social elements.

5.1.1 Arranging the Physical Space

You cannot control certain aspects of the physical classroom climate. The condition of the building, the size of your classroom, the type of furniture, and the nature of the ventilation are examples of important elements in your environment that affect you and your students but over which you are likely to have little or no control.

You can, however, create an environment using classroom space and seating arrangements that communicate, "Learning happens here!" Look around your classroom or that of another teacher and evaluate whether the physical environment supports or detracts from students' ability to behave appropriately. The physical arrangement may have a significant effect on the classroom climate as well as on student behavior.

Interior designers often use paper scale models to plan room arrangements. You can use such a model to plan student seating (e.g., small-group pods, individual seats, pairs), computer work areas, and centers (Downing, 2007). Your seating arrangement should communicate that all students are part of the classroom and none are being "singled out." Nonetheless, some special considerations may be necessary for students who are easily distracted, have vision or hearing problems, or need to be in close contact with you or a paraprofessional. In addition, as you work on your model, create an organizational plan that will ensure smooth traffic flow from one activity to the next, easy access to instructional materials, and limitations to distractions.

Most students work best in organized, structured environments in which materials, equipment, and personal items are well maintained, neatly arranged, and presented in a predictable way. If you teach older students (not primary grades), you may want to establish a classroom committee of students who meet weekly to assess the classroom environment and address issues raised by students (perhaps in a student suggestion box). See Tips for Teachers 5.1 for other strategies for creating a structured environment.

Consider asking a student with disabilities to serve on the committee to assure all students' needs are considered.

TIPS FOR TEACHERS 5.1

Creating a Structured Physical Environment

- Keep the classroom uncluttered, clean, attractive, and uncrowded, especially in high-traffic areas (e.g., group work areas, space around the pencil sharpener, doorways, supply areas).
- Make sure necessary materials are accessible, organized, and stored appropriately.
- Ensure that the classroom is well ventilated and has appropriate lighting.
- Maintain an appropriate noise level. Consider which objects might be removed or changed to make the room less noisy.
- Arrange a quiet, no talk–no noise area for students who prefer to work with few distractions.
- Establish personal physical space, a desk, and materials for each student.
- Provide all students, especially those with special needs, easy access to the teacher and to instructional presentations and displays.
- Post a schedule that provides a predictable routine.
- Post classroom rules and consequences so that students can see them.

Source: From *Classroom management for elementary teachers* (9th ed.), by C. Evertson, & E. Emmer, 2013, Boston: Pearson.

Perhaps an even more important factor than the physical arrangement of the room is the procedures that you implement to create a classroom climate that is respectful and accepting of all students.

5.1.2 Creating a Respectful Learning Community

Your role as a teacher is to establish a classroom that is conducive for learning. To create a positive and productive learning community, consider the following guiding principles:

- *Recognize that students are children or adolescents first.* The best way to interpret this statement is that regardless of the special needs, backgrounds, or learning practices of students, they are all first and foremost individuals deserving of respect and consideration. Teachers who remember this look beyond the visible and less obvious ways in which students differ and respect their common needs and goals—to be accepted, recognized, and valued members of the community. An attitude that places children or adolescents first recognizes that students are more alike than different.
- *Focus on abilities.* To foster an accepting classroom climate, you must establish an environment in which teachers and students seek and use knowledge about the abilities and expertise of *all* class members. In Laureen Rankin's third-grade class, a picture of each student was framed in a decorated star and hung in the classroom. Attached to each star were lists of self- and teacher-identified strengths or abilities. In addition, all students were encouraged to recognize their fellow students' abilities (which, when identified, were added to the appropriate star).
- *Celebrate diversity.* Celebrating diversity means conveying to students the value of those who learn or behave differently, are physically challenged, speak other languages, or represent other cultural backgrounds. Sharon Andreaci, a sixth-grade teacher, considered the special needs of students as just that, *special*, and recognized students' unique qualities, whether it was their skillful use of a wheelchair or how they adapted technology to support their vision challenges.
- *Demonstrate high regard for all students.* Students know when teachers prefer particular students, even when teachers go out of their way to disguise their preference. Demonstrating high regard for all students means treating each of them as the most important student in the class. Carlos Rivera, a ninth-grade science teacher, recommends the following:

  Listen carefully and attentively to each student's responses, not just those of the brighter students. Look for ways to connect each student's response to what you are talking about now or in a previous lesson. Make eye contact with each student;

MyEdLab
Video Example 5.1.
Watch this video and pay attention to how two teachers promote positive behaviors and engage students in discussion about behaviors that are not always positive. Do you think these teachers were effective in engaging their students in making their own rules and, if not, what might you do differently in a class meeting for young children and discussions for older students?

do not always look at the brighter students. Be sure to call on each student at least every day. Get to know a few personal things about each student and check on them periodically.

- *Provide opportunities for students to work in mixed-ability groups, including peer pairing and cooperative groups.* Students prefer, and benefit from, opportunities to work with their peers in groups that represent a range of abilities. Be sure that each group member plays a genuine role in which he or she contributes to the group process. Particularly for students with disabilities, work to ensure that each student's role is active and linked to the group's success. For example, students can work in pairs in which a better reader works with a less skillful reader to reread text and answer questions. Students can also work in mixed-ability cooperative groups in which each student has a valued role in the group and contributes to the group product.

5.1.3 Engaging Students Through Class Meetings

Another way to improve the classroom climate is to engage students in taking responsibility for their classroom through class meetings. Class meetings are formal or informal meetings typically led by teachers to set mutual goals, solve problems, or plan activities (Saaty & Peniwati, 2013; Schaps, 2003). Joan McGinnis is a fifth-grade teacher who uses class meetings to involve students in the management of their class. Joan has a regularly scheduled Friday afternoon meeting that lasts from 15 to 30 minutes each week. She uses class meetings to solve crises and to deal with immediate problems. She also uses class meetings to prevent problems, identify potential or occurring problems, teach problem solving, and foster class responsibility for the cohesion and functioning of the classroom.

The format of the class meeting is much the same at both the elementary and secondary levels. You can start the class meeting by forming a circle so that everyone can see everyone else. Here's how Joan structures class meetings:

1. The first 5 minutes of the meeting are used for compliments and appreciations, which can be handled in several ways. Joan uses a *recognition box*, a decorated shoe box into which students and teachers place written recognitions of classmates or teachers who have done helpful or special things, such as helping a classmate, doing well on a paper, or ignoring someone who is bothering them. Recognitions also include personal information, such as winning a competition at a swim meet. When the class meeting starts, Joan passes the recognition box around the circle. Each student selects one slip until all the slips have been removed from the box. Students take turns reading the recognitions. This is also a chance for the teacher to provide positive feedback to the class.
2. The second part of the class meeting—follow-up on prior solutions—takes approximately 10 minutes. During this time, problems that had been brought up at previous meetings are discussed and evaluated. Students and teachers share their perceptions in answer to the following questions:
   - How frequently does the problem occur? More or less than before?
   - How well are people implementing the selected solution? Is this still a problem? Is the solution effective?
3. The third part of the meeting—new problems—takes approximately 10 minutes and gives students and teachers an opportunity to identify problems and work with the group to identify potential solutions to the problems. Joan cautions that it is important not to let this part of the meeting turn into a gripe session and to be sure not to allow students to complain about a specific student. Joan teaches all her students how to solve problems and encourages them to use those skills.

4. The fourth part of the meeting—future plans—takes just a couple of minutes. Joan describes this section of the meeting:

 I try to keep this part of the meeting very upbeat with an emphasis on future projects, school events, or field trips. I use this time to engage the students not just in the social plans of the class and school but also in my academic plans for the future weeks. If I have a special project planned, I use this time to introduce the new project to the students.

Even though Joan is an elementary school teacher, she recognizes that the same format can be used for middle and high school students as well. She comments on these meetings:

> I feel that it is an essential aspect of a successful classroom. The students in my room are not only better behaved, [but] they work more as a team. They take more responsibility for their own behavior as well as that of other students in the class. I think the benefits go way beyond classroom management and include academic gains as well. I guess you can tell I'm pretty enthusiastic about their function.

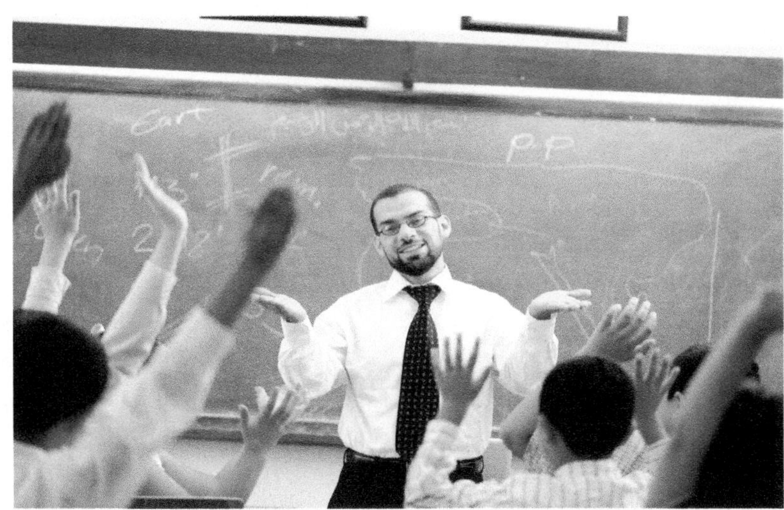

What instructional and management goals can be met throughout a class meeting format? How might class meetings increase students' stake in the day-to-day cohesion and operation of their classroom?

Class meetings can be successfully implemented with students in middle and high school. When the entire class is actively involved in solving problems and establishing procedures, there is a greater likelihood that the decisions will be remembered and implemented (Saaty & Peniwati, 2013). Furthermore, class meetings can serve as an excellent format for teaching adolescents to make good decisions, regulate their thinking, and solve problems (Baron & Brown, 2012). How often do these class meetings need to take place? In the beginning of the school year, teachers may want to have their class meetings more often (15 to 25 minutes of class time as often as once a week). However, after procedures and decisions are established, class meetings can occur less frequently (e.g., every 2 to 3 weeks). The rules previously reviewed for conducting class meetings are appropriate for students in secondary grades as well and include:

- Listen attentively while others are speaking.
- Appreciate the contributions that each person makes.
- Respect views whether they agree or disagree with yours.
- Give everyone the right to "pass" if they are not ready to comment.
- Make eye contact with persons when they are speaking.
- Stay on the topic.
- Ask questions that further the resolution of issues.
- Make decisions and summarize.

MyEdLab **Self-Check 5.1**

MyEdLab **Application Exercise 5.1:** Creating a Respectful Learning Community

5.2 INCREASING SOCIAL ACCEPTANCE OF STUDENTS WITH DISABILITIES

Judith Warner, a veteran tenth-grade teacher, is well respected by her students, their parents, and her fellow teachers for the effective way she manages students' behavior. She has experienced a great deal of success with teaching students with disabilities who are placed in her classroom. Judith indicates that the secret to her success is establishing a personal relationship with each student in her class:

> I value getting to know each of my students, what they are like, what they do outside of school, who is special to them at home and in their community, what their strengths are, and what makes them tick. I use this information to facilitate their adjustment to the classroom community and to establish a relationship with me that will influence our year together.

As she just described, Judith does a number of things to ensure that all of the students in her classroom are accepted:

1. ***She treats all students with respect.*** Her classroom is not segmented into those who know and those who do not. She genuinely communicates respect for each student and expects students to communicate respect for one another.
2. ***She teaches students concern for one another.*** The students in Judith's classes learn quickly that they are responsible for themselves and for one another.
3. ***She and her class point out students' abilities.*** Judith insists that when a negative statement is made about a student, something positive about that student must be said: "Yes, Myla [a student who uses a wheelchair] does slow us down going to lunch, but Myla is the class artist. She provides artistic guidance and gifts to all of us."

Conveying acceptance of all students in the classroom is an important responsibility of the classroom teacher. It is particularly important for you to demonstrate acceptance of students with disabilities. Remember that your students may have limited experience in meeting and interacting with students with disabilities. Students may perceive individuals with disabilities as different, resulting in pity, ridicule (Salend, 2004), or even bullying and teasing. Likewise, serving as an advocate for all of your students with other professionals is another critical role. Students with special needs may be more likely than other students in your class to receive negative judgments from others.

One way to help students experience social acceptance is to be aware of technological options open to them, such as those listed in the Tech Tips, "Using Technology to Promote Social Acceptance."

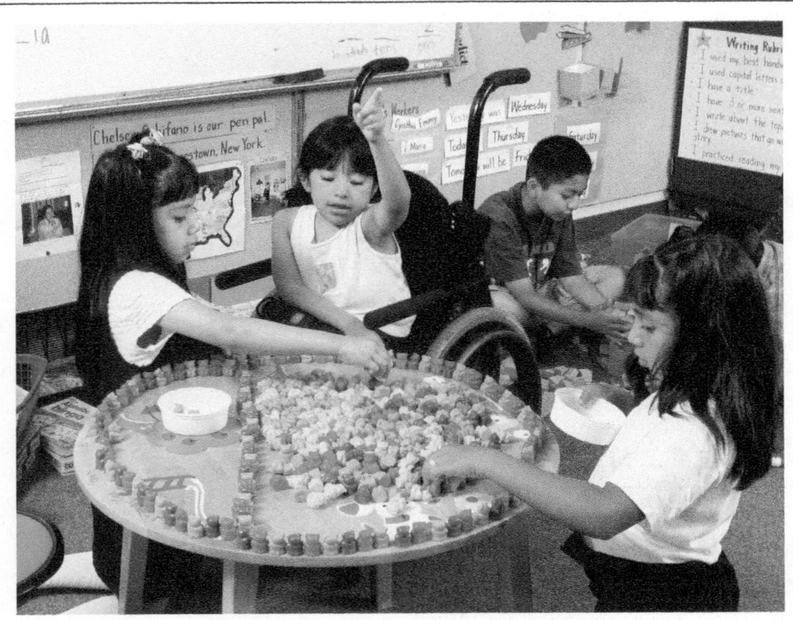

As a teacher, what is your role in promoting the social acceptance of students with disabilities? How will you model social acceptance for your students, and what other strategies will you use?

5.2.1 Enhancing Students' Self-Concepts

Ask parents what they most want for their children, and a frequent response is that they want their children to be happy. They want their children to like themselves and be proud of what they do and who they are. Another way to think about it is that parents want their children to have a good self-concept. What is self-concept? There are many terms used to describe self-concept, including self-esteem, self-perception, self-identity, self-awareness, and self-worth, to name a few. One way to think of self-concept is to consider it a way in which we use our cognition to appraise ourselves (Hattie, 2014).

How do you feel about yourself? Do you think you are a valuable person, worthy of love

TECH TIPS

Using Technology to Promote Social Acceptance

Teachers can use computers to enhance socialization skills by encouraging learners to work cooperatively at the computer. Activities that encourage students to make decisions and cooperate with other students can foster appropriate interaction, whether they are playing games or doing a research project together. Simulations, programs that require students to make real-life decisions, are popular options and include the following:

Community Success Go to Community Success by Tom Caine Associates at (http://caineassociates.com) This program is for K–12 students. It allows children to practice social skills and learn about appropriate and inappropriate behaviors in different situations with the help of realistic illustrations and auditory cues. There are forty-five activities that take place in a variety of settings.

and appreciation from others? Do you think you have friends and are liked by others? Do you think you do well in school or work and are likely to succeed? How do you feel about the way you look? What about your ability to play sports? Your answers to these questions provide insight into your self-concept. Individuals with positive self-concepts generally feel as though they are worthwhile and deserve the respect, recognition, and appreciation of others. They have positive feelings about themselves in multiple settings, including at school, with friends, and with family. They generally like the way they look and who they are. For example, students with positive self-concepts about their academic success are more likely to achieve more and get higher grades (Green, Liem, Martin, Colmar, Marsh, & McInerney, 2012; Hessels & Schwab, 2015).

Students who have disabilities face greater challenges to their self-concepts, as their characteristics set them apart from their mainstream peers. Because individuals who are at risk or those with disabilities often receive more negative feedback than other students do, their self-concepts may be lower, on the average, than those of other students (Sze & Valentin, 2007; Vaughn, Elbaum, & Boardman, 2001).

To help enhance the self-concepts of students with disabilities, teachers can:

- Hold all students to high standards, and then provide the encouragement and support students need to meet those standards. Consider how to provide them access to all high standards including state standards or Common Core standards (Haager & Vaughn, 2013). Teachers often have lower expectations for students who demonstrate learning and behavior problems than for other students. These lowered expectations, however unintentional, limit the opportunities available to these students as compared with those for whom we have high standards (Roach, Kurz, & Elliott, 2015).
- Discover students' talents, abilities, or interests, and recognize them personally. Identify the expertise of every student in your class. Expertise can be displayed in many ways, including in extracurricular activities such as sports or music. After all, students with disabilities demonstrate levels of self-concept similar to those of academically average students when their strengths are acknowledged (Kleinert, Miracle, & Sheppard-Jones, 2007).
- Provide opportunities for students who struggle academically to succeed in other ways. One parent described it this way: "The best thing that happened to my son is swimming. He joined a swim team when he was 6, and all his friends know he has won many swimming awards. No matter how discouraged he is about school, he has one area in which he is successful." As another example, students with epilepsy benefited from a karate program as a means of enhancing their self-concepts (Conant, Morgan, Muzykewicz, Clark, & Thiele, 2008).
- Recognize students' difficulties with learning or behavior, and explain their problems to them in a way they can understand. Sometimes, teachers and parents try to protect students and do not explain to them why they are having problems in school. An honest explanation (that they have attention problems, learning problems,

TIPS FOR TEACHERS 5.2

Providing Opportunities for Student Success

- When you correct papers, point out correct responses instead of focusing only on mistakes.
- Look for positive behavioral changes in students (e.g., hand raising, following directions) and let them know when you notice their appropriate behavior.
- Before students submit papers, ask them to look carefully to see whether they can find an error. Call on students to describe mistakes they find, and praise them for finding and correcting the mistakes. Point out that everyone makes mistakes and that with practice they can reduce the number and types of mistakes they make.
- Find opportunities for a student to "shine" in front of classmates. Even small recognitions are valuable.
- When a student with emotional or behavioral disorders asks for help, start by asking the student to find something pertaining to the task or assignment that he or she has completed successfully.
- Notice improvement. If the student usually gets three right on the weekly spelling test and this week gets five right, let the student know that you notice the change. Recognition of progress toward a goal motivates students more than recognition that comes only after the goal has been attained.

physical problems, etc.) often helps students understand why some things are more difficult for them than for other students. Group counseling can be an effective process for improving the self-concepts of middle school students with disabilities (Elbaum & Vaughn, 2001).

- Provide students an opportunity to write themselves letters about what they like about themselves and what they think they can do well. Allow them to identify areas they would like to target to make changes.

Tips for Teachers 5.2 gives suggestions for providing opportunities for student success.

MyEdLab **Self-Check 5.2**

MyEdLab **Application Exercise 5.2:** Enhancing Students' Self-Concepts

5.3 RECOGNIZING AND PREVENTING BULLYING

Bullying is when a student is the victim of aggressive behavior from others typically through verbal abuse, rumors, exclusion or even more aggressive acts. Schools and educators have reported that bullying and excessive teasing are a serious school problem, with 10% to 30% of students involved in bullying (Cook, Williams, Guerra, Kim, & Sadek, 2010; Luxenberg, Limber, & Olweus, 2013). Bullying often involves picking on or harming someone because he or she is "different." Students who are quiet, careful, sensitive, and cry easily are more susceptible to bullies, as are students who have a poor self-image or have few friends. Students with learning and behavior problems—particularly those who are anxious and withdrawn–are more likely to be bullied (Cook et al., 2010). In a survey of a random sample of U.S. students, as many as 23% of third graders and 15% of seventh and eighth graders report being bullied two to three times per month or more, with girls more often the recipient of bullying. Bullying most often occurs at recess or lunch time but also during class with the teacher present. More than 25% of the reports of bullying were described as occurring during class (Luxenberg, Limber, & Olweus, 2013).

Bullying is the most common form of aggression in youths, with more than 40% of students in grades 3 through 12 indicating that they were afraid of being bullied (Luxenberg, Limber, & Olweus, 2013). It is an intentional act and can result in mental and physical danger for the victim. Unfortunately, 25% of teachers do not perceive bullying as wrong and therefore rarely intervene, and most students perceive that schools do little to respond to bullying (Hoover & Stenhjem, 2005), though more than 90% indicate that they feel sympathy for students who are bullied (Luxenberg, Limber, & Olweus, 2013). When evidence of nonacceptance arises, teachers must serve as advocates to promote social acceptance. See the 60-Second Lesson.

60-SECOND LESSON

PROVIDING FEEDBACK FOR FUNCTIONAL BEHAVIOR

When working with students whose behavior is bothering you or other students, assume that they do not know that their behavior is bothersome. To address the behavior:

- Pull these students aside and tell them what they are doing and how it is affecting you or others.
- With older students, giving them feedback privately is important. It usually works.
- Some students have persistent behavior problems; understanding how these behaviors have been functional for the student will assist you in providing an appropriate treatment.

Intervening and not accepting bullying is an important role for teachers to play. What are research-based practices for intervening with bullying? A review of the research on bullying interventions (Merrell, Bueldner, Ross, & Isava, 2008; Ttofi & Farrington, 2011) revealed that interventions designed to prevent bullying influenced about one-third of the outcomes investigated and, for the most part, the interventions were much more effective in changing the attitudes and self-perceptions of participants and significantly less effective in altering the bullying behavior. The Olweus Bullying Prevention Program (http://www.violencepreventionworks.org/public/index.page) may be a useful program to reduce bullying (Ttofi & Farrington, 2011). See Tips for Teachers 5.3 for strategies for preventing bullying and teasing.

See Tips for Teachers 5.4 for a description of what competent schools do to prevent bullying and violence in their schools.

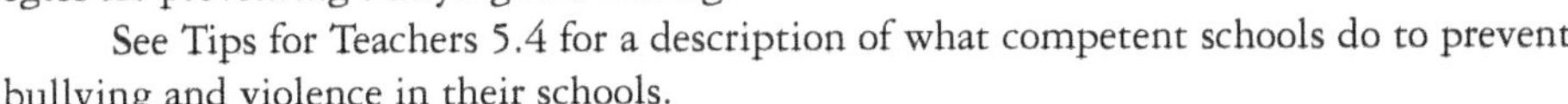

TIPS FOR TEACHERS 5.3

Preventing Bullying and Teasing of Individuals with Disabilities

As a classroom teacher, you have the responsibility to stop bullying in your classroom. Failure to recognize bullying or to stop it can have dire consequences for your students. The acronym STOP IT summarizes key steps you can take:

Stop bullying the moment you see it—intervene immediately.

Teach your students school rules regarding bullying, how to recognize bullying, and how to react when another student bullies.

Observe your students in the playground, lunchroom, hallways, and bus lines. Be vigilant for signs of bullying and work with colleagues to do the same.

Provide support for students who have been bullied and let them know that you are there to help.

Inform yourself about procedures for referring bullying to administrators and parents. Also, inform yourself about best practices in dealing with bullying.

Take necessary steps to deal with the bully and to provide him or her with positive support to overcome this pattern of behavior.

Source: Based on "What works and doesn't work in bullying prevention and intervention," by S. P. Limber, 2004, *Student Assistance Journal*, 16–19; and "A profile of bullying at school," by D. Olweus, 2003, *Educational Leadership*, *60*, 12–17. For a description of a bullying prevention program see: www.violencepreventionworks.org.

TIPS FOR TEACHERS 5.4

What Competent Schools Do to Prevent Bullying and Violence

1. Selecting and implementing a social skills curriculum schoolwide.
2. Establishing positive school and classroom social cultures emphasizing teaching and learning.
3. Using challenging and engaging teaching practices that maximize academic learning.
4. Positively monitoring student behavior and learning.
5. Acknowledging and reinforcing student success.
6. Taking active involvement of all students and family, faculty, and community members.
7. Using multiyear and multicomponent approaches to implementation.
8. Hiring adults who model the same positive social behaviors and values expected of students.

MyEdLab **Self-Check 5.3**

MyEdLab **Application Exercise 5.3:** Recognizing and Preventing Bullying

5.4 UNDERSTANDING BEHAVIOR MANAGEMENT IN CULTURALLY DIVERSE CLASSROOMS

Teachers often misinterpret the behavior of minority students and thus respond inappropriately to their behavior (Chamberlain, 2005; Harry & Klingner, 2014). The miscommunications between minority students and their teachers may cause misunderstandings that lead to discipline problems. For example, educators tend to have low expectations of poor, African American, Native American, and Hispanic students (e.g., Artiles, 2015; Donovan & Cross, 2002; Harry & Klingner, 2014). It is likely that teachers also hold low expectations for individuals with disabilities, and these low expectations influence the extent to which the teachers interact with these students. Students may be bored or perceive that there is little need to strive for success, so their behavior becomes increasingly problematic.

How might these low expectations influence how teachers manage these students' behavior? This question is particularly relevant because disproportionate numbers of students from minority groups are identified as needing special education, although many of them remain in the general education classroom for all or part of the school day (Donovan & Cross, 2002; Harry & Klingner, 2014). Teachers may have a prevailing view about the culture of the student and stereotype students representing particular cultural groups as likely to demonstrate particular behaviors (Artiles, 2015). Although little information is available about how teachers' attitudes might influence their treatment of students' behavior problems in their classrooms, there is little doubt that when teachers have lowered expectations for students, student motivation and learning are hampered. Because teachers are likely to expect students from traditionally underrepresented groups to be problematic, in an attempt to stop problems before they get out of control, they provide overcorrection for problems they might be willing to overlook in nonminority students. African American males are particularly vulnerable to disproportionate discipline by educators (Harry, Klingner, & Cramer, 2007; Townsend, 2000). The primary solution to the problem is awareness of the subtle and not-so-subtle ways in which these prejudices might influence the way you manage the behavior of students in your classroom. (See Tips for Teachers 5.5.)

TIPS FOR TEACHERS 5.5

Questions to Ask Yourself When Teaching Culturally Diverse Students

Keep the following questions in your desk, and read and reflect on them frequently:

- Who are the students I have the most difficulty managing? What socioeconomic, cultural, and linguistic background(s) do they represent? How does this affect my attitude?
- To what extent have I reached out and demonstrated genuine caring and respect to *all* students in my class?
- If students were asked to identify which students in the class I like best and least, what would they say? What does this say about me?
- How are students from traditionally underrepresented groups performing in my class? What behaviors do I demonstrate to promote their success?
- What steps am I taking to better engage all students in instruction and learning?
- How much do I know about the cultures and families of the students I teach? How do I integrate this knowledge in activities and opportunities in the classroom?

Following are cautions and considerations for improving management and understanding in your culturally diverse classroom (Chamberlain, 2005; Gay, 2010):

- Behaviors that are acceptable and encouraged in the home and the community may be incompatible with desirable school behaviors. In these cases, students may not only receive conflicting messages about their behavior, but also may be forced to choose between loyalty to home and community or to school. For example, in some immigrant homes, homework time is a group activity with lots of talking and interaction between parents and children. At school, students may be required to work quietly and independently—a direct contrast to what is encouraged at home.
- Teachers who understand the family and community can better understand students' behaviors and assist them with the transition to expected school behavior. For example, the teacher can talk with a student privately and say, "It is OK to be loud when you are with a group outside of school, but in school I expect you to use a very soft voice when working with your peers."
- Behaviors that are indicative of problems in one group of students might not be so in another. For example, teachers who know that some students might not ask for help may check frequently with these students to determine how they are proceeding. As another example, the behaviors of some students may be viewed as aggressive and acting out when the intention of the students is merely to fit in and be recognized.
- Some behaviors that students exhibit may be misinterpreted or attributed to the wrong factors by teachers who do not understand the students' culture or background. For example, students from some cultures are accustomed to clearly defined rules and regulations and may have difficulty interpreting more implicit rules; thus, their inability to follow classroom rules may be due to lack of understanding rather than defiance.
- Problem behaviors occur across cultural groups, with the highest reported behavior problems occurring in Puerto Rico and the lowest in Sweden (Crijnen, Achenbach, & Verhulst, 2014). Furthermore, across twelve cultures girls are more likely to have anxious and depressed symptoms and boys are more likely to have attention problems.

Finally, teachers may benefit from reflecting on their own attitudes and beliefs about race, culture, and ethnic diversity, and how these may influence their interactions with students and their families.

MyEdLab **Self-Check 5.4**

MyEdLab **Application Exercise 5.4:** Understanding Behavior Management in Culturally Diverse Classrooms

5.5 PROVIDING POSITIVE BEHAVIOR INTERVENTION SUPPORTS WITHIN A RTI FRAMEWORK

Sarah McCardle worked for a school district that utilized an RTI framework (see Chapter 2) for providing support services to students with behavior problems. The district used a similar model as a means of preventing academic difficulties. Within the RTI framework of services for students, the district provided training for Sarah and other teachers on how to use a problem-solving approach to preventing inappropriate behavior in the classroom and to teaching and reinforcing appropriate behavior.

In recent years, the principles of more traditional behavior management have been applied to schoolwide models for the prevention of problem behaviors, a system for monitoring student behavior, and a coordinated plan for dealing with problem behavior when it occurs. In place of individual and often disjointed classroom and school discipline procedures, a continuum of policies and procedures for all students is implemented throughout the school. This modification of behavior management principles is called **positive behavior intervention supports (PBIS)** (OSEP Technical Assistance Center on Positive Behavioral Interventions and Supports, 2009; Sugai, Simonsen, Bradshaw, Horner, & Lewis, 2014). PBIS is a problem-solving oriented, data-based, evidence-based, and systemic practice (Klotz & Canter, 2007; Sugai et al., 2014). PBIS for students with disabilities is not just good practice that is associated with reduced behavior problems (Horner et al., 2009); it's part of the law under the Individuals with Disabilities Improvement Act of 2004 (IDEIA 2004) as a recommended practice for dealing with challenging behavior in children. Moreover, PBS works hand-in-hand with the response to intervention (RTI) approach and facilitates a problem-solving model that involves collaboration and communication with all key stakeholders (administrators, teachers, students, and their families). Thus, individual teachers are not working alone in dealing with students with challenging behavioral issues.

5.5.1 Positive Behavior Intervention Supports as Prevention

Many schools today are coping with increasing numbers of behavior problems such as fighting and bullying, discontent among students, and general lack of discipline, even within what educational leaders describe as implementing a positive climate of support in the schools. This problem does not exist because teachers or administrators lack concern or caring for the issue. It occurs because a schoolwide consistent implementation of the positive behavior intervention support (PBIS) model has not taken place. A critical and pervasive finding is that these schools may have a plan for implementing PBIS but they have not successfully or consistently implemented the plan.

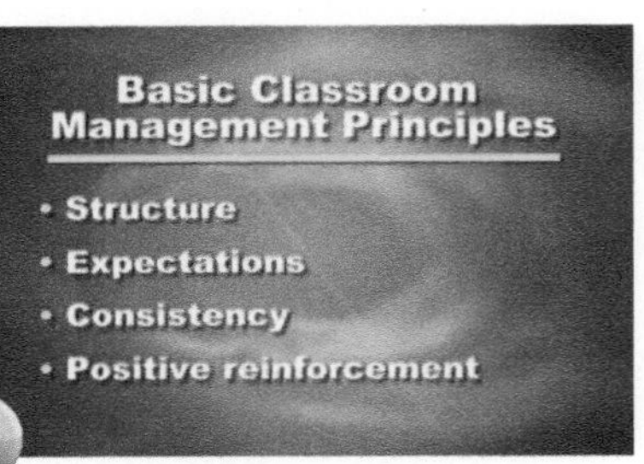

Basic Classroom Management Principles
• Structure
• Expectations
• Consistency
• Positive reinforcement

MyEdLab
Video Example 5.2.

Watch this video and pay attention to what this speaker has to say about the importance of establishing basic classroom management strategies and ways that teachers can implement the strategies for students with disabilities. Why is it so important for teachers in an inclusive setting to develop a classroom management plan for the entire class?

The focus of PBIS is on developing individualized interventions that occur within a coordinated schoolwide system that exercises principles of positive support throughout the day and across all classrooms to prevent behavior problems. This type of approach assures that when behavior problems occur, they can be addressed individually, as they are not a result of a dysfunctional approach to behavior management. The interventions emphasize preventing problem behaviors through effective educational programming to improve the individual's quality of life (Janney & Snell, 2008; Sandomierski, Kincaid, & Algozzine, 2009; Simonsen, Sugai, & Negron, 2008).

PBIS involves careful observation of circumstances and the purpose of the problem behavior. A significant number of negative behaviors can be dealt with by modifying the environment (e.g., who sits near a student, how a student is responded to). PBIS also emphasizes teaching appropriate behaviors to replace inappropriate behaviors in the target setting (Epstein, Atkins, Cullinan, Kutash, & Weaver, 2008; Janney & Snell, 2008).

Juan was a fifth-grade student who had a physical and cognitive disability, poor social skills, and difficulty interacting with peers. He hit other children and got into fights for no apparent reason. When Juan's teacher and the school counselor observed Juan's interactions with peers and his behaviors, they learned that hitting was Juan's way of saying, "Get off my back." He was sensitive to teasing, and students learned that they could get him very mad very easily by teasing him. Through PBIS, Juan was taught to say "Get off my back" and walk away instead of hitting. He was also taught to recognize teasing and to not let the other students control his behavior. Furthermore, the students primarily associated with teasing Juan were taught to have fun in other ways. All the teachers in the school reminded Juan to use his words instead of his hands to communicate. He was also taught other specific skills necessary for successful social interactions, such as joining a group and initiating and maintaining a conversation. All students were rewarded with tokens when Juan did not get into a fight or hit someone; thus, everyone was interested in seeing Juan's behavior improve. Teachers tried to pair Juan with other students during classroom activities to provide him with opportunities to practice his new skills.

In this case, Juan's behavior and the environment in which target behaviors occurred were observed. Once the causes, circumstances, and purposes of the behaviors were identified, the classroom teacher met with other teachers to discuss the issues and enlist their help in providing Juan with the support he would need. The teachers also developed a list of specific social skills to teach him. Over time, Juan's problem behaviors decreased, his social skills improved, and he made friends with a few students.

5.5.2 Schoolwide Positive Behavior Intervention Supports

Schoolwide positive behavior intervention supports (SWPBIS) is a model for conceptualizing how the entire school defines and participates in practices that reduce negative behaviors and increase positive behaviors. SWPBIS models begin with a **primary prevention model** in which the focus is on preventing behavior problems schoolwide (Sugai, Horner, & Gresham, 2002). All school personnel know the rules and expectations that are established and that a concerted effort is made to ensure that all students and their parents are aware of positive school behavior and rules.

Typically, an SWPBIS leadership team of administrators, teachers, and staff is established. This team coordinates efforts such as working with faculty to develop rules and expectations, providing professional development for teachers in evidence-based practices, examining student data (e.g., discipline referrals, suspensions, teacher ratings of behavior), monitoring progress of students identified for interventions, communicating rules and expectations to students and families, and evaluating the SWPBS plan on a regular basis. Although initially time consuming to establish, SWPBS yields high results over time, reduces behavior problems, and improves the school climate (Fairbanks, Simonsen, & Sugai, 2008).

The problem-solving team can cycle through several critical questions to determine whether effective decisions are being made (Scott, Alter, Rosenberg, & Borgmeier, 2010):

- What is predictable about the behavior?
- What is the most efficient and likely to be implemented research-based practice?
- How can key personnel achieve consistent implementation?
- Is it working?

Tips for Teachers 5.6 highlights the essential elements of an SWPBS approach.

Many schools are in the early stages of implementing SWPBIS plans. To change from a more traditional system of behavior management to one that is preventive and positive, the OSEP Center on Positive Behavioral Interventions and Supports (2009) suggests that schools must:

- Develop programs that consider behavioral issues for all students.
- Consider whether the behavioral practices recommended are empirically valid.

TIPS FOR TEACHERS 5.6

Essential Elements of a Schoolwide Approach

To change from a more traditional system of behavior management to one that is preventive and positive, schools need to (OSEP Center on Positive Behavioral Interventions and Supports, 2009; Reinke, Herman, & Stormont, 2013):

- Consider the needs of all children because every child needs some type of behavior support.
- Use research-based methods that have been validated and are relevant to the population.
- Work toward both academic and behavioral success for all students.
- Emphasize prevention first to create and maintain a safe and supportive school environment.
- Think beyond the school site to expand the use of effective PBS models to district, county, regional, and state levels.
- Collaborate with community agencies (e.g., education, juvenile justice, community mental health, family, and medical).
- Develop the schoolwide (including students, staff, and administration) use of team-building and problem-solving skills through instruction, high expectations, and reinforcement.
- Post classroom rules and make classroom expectations clear.
- Gain the class's attention before speaking.
- Provide high levels of specific positive feedback to individual students and to the class.
- Use a continuum of consequences to address rule violations.

- Consider the connections between academic and behavioral success.
- Approach behavior management from a prevention perspective.
- Involve all key stakeholders in the school, home, and community in developing team-building and behavioral problem-solving skills.

How will you know if your school is ready for PBIS? The Center on Positive Behavioral Interventions and Supports (2009) provides the following guidelines for ensuring that a school is prepared to implement an effective schoolwide PBIS model:

- Establish a leadership team consisting of administrators, teachers, support staff, specialists, and parents.
- Establish a commitment of support and active participation from the school administration and at least 80% of the staff.
- Conduct a self-assessment of the current schoolwide discipline system. Use the data to create an implementation action.
- Set up a system to collect discipline referrals and other relevant data on a regular basis to track progress and evaluate the effectiveness of schoolwide PBIS efforts.

It is not just up to the schools to implement PBIS; parents and other family members can get involved as well. Considerable evidence shows that PBS can be taught to and used by parents very effectively (Lucyshyn, Dunlap, & Albin, 2002). Parents and other family members have successfully engaged children with severe problem behaviors in alternative behaviors and modified contexts that no longer support the behavior problems. Much like general and special education teachers who have students with extreme behavior problems, parents can identify the behavior problems through assessment and then alter their feedback so that their child's behavior problems are no longer supported and thus become ineffective (Lucyshyn, Horner, Dunlap, Albin, & Ben, 2002). This yields more positive and constructive parent–child interactions. The Positive Behavior Interventions & Supports website (www.pbis.org) provides numerous guides and checklists for parents to assist in developing IEPS and working with schools.

5.5.3 Positive Behavior Intervention Supports and Response to Intervention

How does PBIS link to RTI? In the case of PBIS, the focus is less on academics and more on instruction of appropriate behavior; however, the application of the two models is similar.

- Tier 1 instruction involves applying universal strategies for creating a positive classroom climate and managing student behavior. These universal strategies for improving behavior are described in detail in the next section. Advocates of PBIS also recommend that universal strategies are lodged within a well-articulated schoolwide plan (Sandomierski et al., 2009; Simonson, Sugai et al., 2008). Key to the success of Tier 1 is setting expectations for positive behaviors, teaching those expectations to all students, and recognizing when students exhibit those behaviors (Fairbanks et al., 2008). When behavior challenges arise with individual students, teachers work with other professionals in the school to implement high-quality behavioral interventions. If those interventions are not successful, students may be in need of additional help.
- Tier 2 supports are provided for students who need additional support, individually or in small groups; these supports may take place inside or outside of the general education classroom (Fairbanks et al., 2008). Interventions can focus on social skills, counseling, or mentoring, depending on individual needs. Like academic interventions, it is recommended that evidence-based interventions for behavior are used to provide such support (Sandomierski et al., 2009). With Tier 2, students spend limited time away from the classroom, and progress monitoring is used to gauge students' growth and to determine whether Tier 3 intervention is necessary.
- Tier 3 intervention is at the individual level and is meant for students who have not made satisfactory progress with Tier 2 supports, have persistent or severe disciplinary infractions, or might endanger themselves or others. It involves more detailed assessment of student behavior and the development of an individual behavior improvement plan that may involve individual or group interventions and possibly alternative placements.

In the introduction to this chapter, Sarah McCardle emphasized the need for teachers to be proactive in gathering resources to address challenges in the classroom. The promise of PBIS within an RTI framework is that teachers will have expanded access to such resources and that, as a result, all students will be supported in becoming successful learners and productive citizens.

MyEdLab **Self-Check 5.5**

MyEdLab **Application Exercise 5.5:** Positive Behavior Supports

5.6 POSITIVE BEHAVIOR INTERVENTION SUPPORTS: UNIVERSAL STRATEGIES FOR MANAGING STUDENT BEHAVIOR

The foundation of effectively implementing PBIS is the schoolwide use of evidence-based practices for preventing behavior problems (Tier 1) and then appropriately treating less severe (Tier 2) behaviors as well as more severe behavior problems (Tier 3). A research synthesis of empirically based classroom management practices (Simonsen, Fairbanks, Briesch, Myers, & Sugai, 2008) determined that twenty practices are specifically associated with improved student behavior. These practices can be organized into four important categories that every teacher can use to improve their classroom management:

1. ***Maximize Organization and Structure.*** This means providing a highly predictable and well-defined set of procedures for how the classroom operates,

where materials are kept, how students move around in the classroom, when and how loudly students talk, and how assignments are managed and submitted.

2. ***Instruct, Review, Monitor, and Reinforce Expectations.*** Provide very clear and easily understood guidelines for behavior and teach the appropriate behaviors to students. Model the behavior you want to see and ask other students to model it for the class. Monitor the expectations that you establish and recognize when students are and are not meeting the expectations.
3. ***Engage Students Actively in Ways That Are Observable.*** Students need many opportunities to respond—either as a group, individually, in writing, or by indicating with hands up or down whether they are "with" the instruction. The rate of responding by students can also be increased by using response cards, peer tutoring, or guided notes.
4. ***Use a Continuum of Practices for Responding to Appropriate and Inappropriate Behavior.*** A continuum of practices refers to practices that are less intense (e.g., standing near students and lightly touching them on the shoulder) ranging to those that are more intense (e.g., developing a behavioral contract with a student).

You can build on the foundation of best-evidence practices in classroom management by looking for positive behaviors from students and recognizing them, using reinforcers to encourage positive behavior, establishing clear rules with known consequences, helping students to change inappropriate behavior, and recognizing students' mistaken goals. These basic principles are sometimes referred to as **universal strategies** (Anderson & Spaulding, 2007) in that they are used for all students in a classroom. Following these principles can avoid situations such as the following.

Glen Nichols, a seventh-grade science teacher, felt frustrated. One of his science classes included several students with disabilities, and he was interested in modifying his usual routine to ensure that they had an adequate opportunity to learn. He had spent considerable time preparing a science experiment for the laboratory, one he thought students would learn from and enjoy. He arranged the materials ahead of time, identified the key concepts he wanted to teach, and was optimistic that the lesson would go well. What happened? Glen described it this way:

> First of all, the students came to the lab and were more interested in who their lab partner would be than the topic. They seemed to have a more difficult time settling down than usual, and talking seemed to occur during the entire session. There were a few students who seemed to follow the procedures and get something out of it, but for the most part I think it was a waste of my time.

Glen understood well the content he was teaching, but was less able to manage student behaviors so that he could teach effectively. Glen is not alone. Many teachers identify classroom management not only as a cause of stress, but also as their reason for leaving the profession.

Glen was becoming increasingly frustrated and said so during lunch in the faculty lounge. Frank, a special education teacher, suggested that Glen needed to look for positive behaviors. Glen threw up his hands and said, "There weren't any! The poor behavior far outweighed the good." In response, Frank volunteered to videotape Glen's class and to view and discuss the lesson with Glen. When Glen examined the videotape of his lesson and Frank asked him to make a written list of student behaviors that he found acceptable, he noticed quite a few.

Glen, like many teachers, got into the habit of noticing and calling attention to *misbehavior* instead of noticing appropriate behavior and providing positive reinforcement. Frank asked him to list the behaviors he most wanted to see in his students. Glen was then asked to look for and say something positive to students who were performing those behaviors.

Another critical universal strategy is the promotion of **self-regulation**, teaching and modeling how to monitor behavior. Tips for Teachers 5.7 provides guidelines for how teachers can promote self-regulation with their students.

TIPS FOR TEACHERS 5.7

Promoting Self-Regulation

Learning to self-regulate your behavior—monitoring and giving yourself feedback about what and how you are doing—is an important element in supporting positive behavior. Examples include the following:

- Link students' behaviors to outcomes. "You moved away from Alex when he was talking loudly and you were able to go to recess."
- Support students in learning to use consequential thinking, in which they anticipate consequences and adjust their behavior accordingly. Teachers can ask questions like: "We are preparing to work in groups; what will happen if the groups get too rowdy or loud?"
- Provide examples of how you "regulate" your thinking and behavior. "I was distressed with the secretary for interrupting the class, but I realized she needed to locate a student so I adjusted my thinking."
- Encourage students to take responsibility for their successes and their failures. Discourage them from attributing their successes or failures to luck. Link their successes and failures to what they did or could do differently the next time.
- Ask students to establish goals for their learning, monitor their progress towards meeting those goals, and make adjustments to assure success.

5.6.1 Focusing on Positive Behaviors

Regardless of whether students are in Tier 1 (demonstrating appropriate behaviors the majority of the time), Tier 2 (exhibiting mild or infrequent behavior problems), or Tier 3 (exhibiting frequent or significantly challenging behavior), they require positive and specific feedback when they are behaving appropriately. Teachers tend to think they speak positively to students more often than they actually do. When someone counts the positive comments in the classroom, teachers are surprised at how few they actually made, particularly positive comments that are specific (e.g., great job finishing your math problems versus great job) (Reinke et al., 2013). McIntosh and colleagues (McIntosh, Vaughn, Schumm, Haager, & Lee, 1993) found that even teachers who were identified as effective and accepting of students with special needs made very few positive statements during a lesson. As third-grade teacher Nina Zaragoza explains: "At the end of the day, I think I have been so positive, calling out specific behaviors I like and describing the behaviors of students I want to see more of, yet I realize that with what I view as a nonstop positive onslaught, many students are still not getting enough positive feedback."

Positive feedback to students must be specific and must be presented immediately after you witness the target behaviors you want the students to continue (and other students to model). At the elementary level, teachers can comment on which students are displaying the desired behavior: "Mark, Jacob, and Cynthia are looking at me with their books open. I can tell they are ready. Who else knows what to do to show me they are ready?"

Elementary students find public recognition in front of the entire class more rewarding than do older students, who prefer to receive individual feedback that is more private. This does *not* mean that you should not have a positive attitude and look for appropriate behavior in older students. All students like to be told when they are doing something right. They all like a classroom in which the atmosphere is positive and upbeat and the teacher looks for good things, rather than only for bad behaviors. Teachers who provide appropriate feedback do so by helping students understand mechanisms for processing and regulating their learning and behavior so that they receive cues from the teacher (e.g., I raise my hand to indicate it is too noisy) and receive teacher support when they respond to these cues (Hattie & Timperley, 2007).

Several authors distinguish between positive feedback and encouragement (Dreikurs, Cassel, & Ferguson, 2004; Dreikurs, Grunwald, & Pepper, 1982). The primary difference is that **positive feedback** often provides some judgment from the teacher about the appropriateness of the behavior, whereas **encouragement** recognizes the behavior but does not provide teacher judgment. An example of positive feedback is a teacher saying,

"Shana is waiting in line quietly. Good job, Shana." An example of encouragement is to say, "I'm sure that you know how to stand in line when we get ready for lunch." Encouragement focuses on the process (Elliot & Dweck, 2013), as in the following: "The ending of this paper is quite strong. Can you reread the ending and consider how to improve the introduction?" Both encouragement and positive feedback are effective procedures for noticing what is positive about your students' behavior.

5.6.2 Using Reinforcers to Encourage Positive Behavior

Positive reinforcement is the presentation, following the target behavior, of a stimulus (a verbal response; a physical response, such as touching; or a tangible response, such as a reward) to maintain or increase the target behavior. Negative reinforcement is the removal of a stimulus to increase engagement in desirable behaviors. If a teacher rings a bell until the students are quiet, then the removal of the bell sound is a negative reinforcer for quieting student behavior. Because "negative" is often misinterpreted to mean "harmful," the implication is that positive reinforcement is good and negative reinforcement is bad, but this is not necessarily the case. The word *positive* in positive reinforcer refers to the presentation of an event that increases behavior and the word *negative* in negative reinforcer refers to the taking away or removal of an event (Kazdin, 2012). However, although negative reinforcement can be effective, positive reinforcement is the best way to increase desirable student behaviors.

Larrivee (2005) describes a hierarchy of reinforcers ranging from tangible or extrinsic rewards (e.g., raisins, stickers, school supplies) to internal or intrinsic rewards (student satisfaction). The hierarchy of reinforcers includes the following types:

- Consumable (raisins, crackers, jelly beans)
- Tangible (school supplies, toys)
- Token (stickers, checks, coupons)
- Activity (computer time, free time)
- Privilege (errands, line leader)
- Peer recognition (peer acceptance, approval)
- Teacher approval (recognition, praise)
- Self-satisfaction (motivation, seeing one's accomplishments)

Figure 5.1 provides a list of reinforcers that teachers can use to increase appropriate behavior.

In addition to thinking about the type of reward, you will also want to consider group versus individual rewards (Anderson & Spaulding, 2007). Lauren Angelo, a third-grade teacher, uses whole-class, small-group, and individual rewards. If all students bring in their homework, Lauren rewards her students by letting them dance to a favorite CD. Since starting this practice homework has improved to 100% completion. Lauren's students are seated in clusters of six seats, which she refers to as teams. Teams can earn points that lead to earning the right to work in independent centers. They earn points by following directions for independent or cooperative learning activities. Finally, Lauren uses individual rewards such as stickers, certificates, and stamps to acknowledge individual accomplishments on both academic and social goals.

For some additional suggestions for positive reinforcement, see Tips for Teachers 5.8.

Some teachers, particularly those who have students with exceptional behavioral problems in their classrooms, may need to establish a token system (or token economy). In a token system, students earn tokens (e.g., chips, points, tickets) for following classroom rules and meeting target behavioral objectives. Students can exchange the tokens for tangible and/or consumable rewards. Juanita Cowell is a middle-school teacher who has five students with special needs in her classroom. One of her students has difficulty staying on task, not disrupting others, and raising his hand when he has something to say. Unfortunately, several students seemed to be learning his "bad" behavior instead of his learning the good behavior of other students. Juanita had tried many of the reinforcers (such as adult, peer, and

FIGURE 5.1 **Reinforcers that can increase appropriate behavior**

ACTIVITIES

- Students can perform an activity they like (e.g., drawing) after they complete the desired activity (e.g., the activity during that class period).
- Students can perform their tasks on a computer.
- Students can perform their tasks with a partner they select.

ADULT APPROVAL

- Teacher provides verbal recognition that student is behaving appropriately (e.g., "John, you are following directions on this assignment.").
- Teacher provides physical recognition of appropriate student behavior. Teacher moves around classroom, touching the shoulders of students who are behaving appropriately.
- Teacher informs parents or other professionals of students' appropriate behavior. This can be accomplished orally or with "good news" notes.

PEER RECOGNITION

- Teacher informs other students of a student's appropriate behavior (e.g., "The award for Student of the Day goes to the outstanding improvement in behavior demonstrated by [student's name].").
- Students can place in a special box the names of students who have demonstrated appropriate behavior. These names can be read at the end of the week.
- A designated period of time is allocated at the end of the class period (high school) or day (elementary school) to ask students to recognize their fellow classmates who have demonstrated outstanding behavior.

PRIVILEGES

- Students are awarded free time after displaying appropriate behavior.
- Students are allowed to serve in key classroom roles after demonstrating outstanding behavior.
- Students are awarded passes that they can trade for a night without homework.

STUDENTS PROVIDE SELF-REINFORCERS

- Students give themselves points for behaving well.
- Students say positive things to themselves (e.g., "I'm working hard and doing well.").
- Students monitor their own behavior.

TOKENS

- Tokens are items (e.g., chips, play money, points) that can be exchanged for something of value.
- Use tokens to reward groups or teams in which students are behaving appropriately.
- Allow groups or individuals to accumulate tokens they can "spend" on privileges, such as no homework or free time.

TANGIBLES AND CONSUMABLES

- Tangibles are rewards, objects that students want, but usually not objects they can consume (e.g., toys, pencils, erasers, paper, crayons).
- Consumables are rewards that students can eat (e.g., raisins, pieces of cereal, candy).
- Tokens can be exchanged for tangible reinforcers or for consumable reinforcers.
- Tangible reinforcers or consumables can be used to reward the class for meeting a class goal.
- Tangible reinforcers or consumables may be needed to maintain the behavior of a student with severe behavior problems.

TIPS FOR TEACHERS 5.8

Suggestions for Positive Reinforcement

By using a menu of positive rewards, students can select and work toward specific activities or privileges that are particularly interesting to them. The following list gives examples of rewards that can be used to motivate students in the classroom:

- Read a story to the teacher or independently.
- Visit or help another class.
- Assist the teacher.
- Care for class pets, plants, etc.
- Pass out or collect materials.
- Write on erase boards, clean desks, or organize books.
- Help the custodian, in the school office, or in the lunchroom.
- Participate in an after-school activity.
- Decorate the classroom.
- Go to the library.
- Eat lunch with a teacher, the principal, or a favorite adult.
- Pick a friend to do an activity for a specified amount of time.
- Have free time to use specific supplies (e.g., computer, books on tape, music, art supplies).
- Sit in a special place (e.g., teacher's desk, next to friend) for a specified period of time.
- Tutor in class or with younger students.
- Take a short break.

- Get time to work on a special project.
- Omit specific assignments.
- Choose a free homework night.
- Have extra or longer recess.
- Take a turn as hall monitor or line leader.
- Use the teacher's materials (e.g., hole punch, paper cutter, dry erase pens).
- Keep score for a class game.
- Use technology such as a smart phone for a specified amount of time.

Additionally, the teacher can do the following as a reward:

- Display the student's work.
- Select the student as "Student of the Week."
- Remove the student's lowest grade.

activity reinforcers, as well as privileges), and although the class had more good days than bad, she was still concerned about the behavior of several students. She decided to establish a token system whereby she would place a token in a glass bank to indicate that the student was behaving appropriately. The tokens were deposited as follows:

- At the end of every period (usually about 50 minutes) if the student followed rules during the period.
- At the beginning of each new period if the student made a quiet transition to the new task.
- For exceptional student behavior, such as ignoring another student's interfering behavior or helping a student who was distracted get back to work.
- For successfully completing activities.

Juanita removed a token from the jar when rules were broken. The target student added up the tokens at the end of each day. If the student earned 10 tokens or more, a note was sent home. The number of tokens each day was recorded, and when the student reached 200 (approximately 10 days of good behavior), the student could exchange the tokens for a pizza party at lunch with two students of his or her choice. Juanita soon found that she could shake the jar as a signal to quiet down or as a warning that the student was about to lose a token.

Consider the following when implementing a token system (Doll, McLaughlin, & Barretto, 2013; Kazdin, 2012):

- Clearly identify the behavior(s) you want to change.
- Make the tokens readily available and easy to administer.
- Change tokens every several months, for example, use chips, fake money, points, tickets.
- Identify items, activities, or reinforcers that are highly rewarding for the student and that can be obtained by exchanging the tokens.
- Give regular opportunities to exchange the tokens.

When students have a clear incentive that is within reach, the token system is most effective. The token system may be more appropriate for students with more intensive or challenging behaviors and has been helpful for mimicking the real-life reinforcement system (money) for students with intellectual disabilities and/or autism (Matson & Boisjoli, 2009).

5.6.3 Establishing Clear Rules with Known Consequences

Effective management of student behavior requires clearly specified guidelines and consequences when students do not follow those guidelines. *Guidelines* in the classroom consist of procedures and rules (Brophy, 2003; Wentzel & Brophy, 2014). *Procedures* are classroom routines that occur at specified times and allow the classroom to run effectively. These procedures need to be taught to students and used consistently so that the classroom will run smoothly. Each teacher needs to establish procedures for record keeping (taking attendance, for example), passing out papers and materials, storing materials and books, collecting papers and materials, entering and leaving the room (alone and with the class), and making the transition between tasks.

Rules provide the structure for acceptable and unacceptable classroom behaviors. Like procedures, rules need to be taught explicitly. Instead of trying to develop a rule to govern every possible misbehavior, teachers can develop a few general rules that guide students in determining whether behavior is acceptable. These rules can be based on the teacher's criteria for what constitutes a behavior problem (Marzano & Marzano, 2009), as well as on schoolwide policies for rules and discipline. Effective management of students' behavior requires (Marzano, 2012):

- Establishing and enforcing rules and procedures
- Carrying out disciplinary actions
- Effective teacher to student relationships
- Maintaining an appropriate mental set that includes both with-it-ness and emotional objectivity

Some teachers involve students in determining class rules and consequences. Consequences are the repercussions associated with appropriate behavior (e.g., gaining a token) and inappropriate behavior (e.g., losing a token). When students are involved in the development of the consequences, the teacher needs to play an active role. Students often want to establish consequences far harsher than those established by the teacher. The following are examples of general rules:

- Raise your hand if you have something to contribute.
- Do not interfere with your fellow students' learning.
- Do not interfere with the teacher's instruction.
- Complete tasks and homework on time.
- Do not bring to school materials (e.g., toys, action figures) that interfere with your learning.

Some teachers show each new class the rules from the previous year and allow the current students to make changes.

Students need to know what the consequences are of not following a procedure or rule, and teachers need to be consistent in implementing consequences. Like many first-year teachers, Allison Frost had a hard time establishing and implementing consequences. She had difficulty anticipating the kinds of problems she would face and had limited experience in providing consequences for student behavior. She implemented a strategy in which consequences for breaking class rules were as closely related to the problem as possible. For example, students who interfered with their classmates' learning suffered the consequences of being removed from the group for a designated period of time.

Allison also established a system for classroom procedures. Every Friday, two students were selected to distribute and collect papers and materials during the following week. She identified these students by using a lottery system, with eligibility based on meeting weekly behavior goals. Also, so that students would understand what was expected of them, all students practiced procedures for transitions between centers, going to and from their classroom, and other routines. Rules were handled through the new token system she established. On Friday, she counted the number of tokens for the week, and students solved math problems about the number of tokens needed to win the prize.

5.6.4 Helping Students to Change Inappropriate Behavior

What should a teacher do when focusing on positive behaviors does not change the negative behaviors? Three alternative techniques are ignoring on purpose, time-out, and punishment. Effective procedures for implementing these techniques follow.

Ignoring on Purpose The goal of ignoring on purpose or planned ignoring is to eliminate (extinguish) a student's undesirable behavior, which is being reinforced through attention (Lewis, Lewis-Palmer, Newcomer, & Stichter, 2004). Many teachers and students unknowingly maintain the unwanted behaviors of students by attending to these behaviors. When teachers recognize their attention or the attention of fellow students is maintaining an undesirable behavior, they can plan to eliminate the attention. The strategy for elimination is called extinction. For example, a teacher might want to extinguish a student's behavior of shouting out. Having determined that telling the student to raise his hand provides the attention the student wants, the teacher decides to ignore the student (with the intention of reducing the behavior through ignoring on purpose).

Ignoring can be a very effective strategy to reduce undesirable behaviors but is harder to implement than most people think. Let's return to the example of the student who continually shouts out in class. If this student's behavior is reinforced not only by the attention of the teacher, but also by that of his classmates, then both teacher and classmates need to ignore the undesirable behavior. It is important for the teacher to understand that during extinction, the target behavior will increase in rate or intensity before decreasing. To be effective, this strategy requires patience and the ability to control reinforcement.

Time-out

Time-out occurs when the student is removed from the classroom situation. This eliminates the opportunity to receive reinforcement. In the classroom, the student receives reinforcement from classmates, the teacher, and, ideally, the environment. When a student is removed from this setting, he or she is no longer able to receive these reinforcers. The underlying principle behind the successful use of time-out is that the environment the student leaves must be reinforcing and the time-out environment must not. In general, the amount of time spent in time-out is gauged by a student's age—1 minute per year (i.e., a 6-year-old would have 6 minutes of time-out; Downing, 2007). Guidelines for implementing time-out in the classroom are provided in Tips for Teachers 5.9.

Punishment

Punishment is "the presentation or removal of a stimulus or event after a response, which decreases the likelihood or probability of that response" (Kazdin, 2001, p. 56). Punishment can take multiple forms, including the following (Axelrod, 2013; Downing, 2007):

- Verbal reprimands are short, targeted comments designed to address a specific misbehavior. Verbal reprimands used infrequently and to target specific behaviors

TIPS FOR TEACHERS 5.9

Guidelines for Implementing Time-out

- Use time-out only when other positive behavioral supports have not worked; it is a last resort.
- Discuss time-out procedures and applications with school administrators and parents before implementation.
- Provide students with information in advance about behaviors that will result in time-out.
- The amount of time the student is in time-out should be brief (between 15 and 20 minutes).
- Specify in advance the amount of time the student will be in time-out.
- Direct the student to go to time-out. If the student does not comply, the teacher should unemotionally guide the student to time-out.
- Implement time-out *immediately* following the inappropriate behavior.
- Establish contingencies in advance for the student who fails to comply with time-out rules.
- Do not leave the time-out area unmonitored.
- When time-out is over, the student should join his or her classmates.
- Look for opportunities to provide reinforcement for appropriate behavior after time-out.

can be effective particularly when paired with praise for appropriate behavior (e.g., Isaiah, stop pulling that string. Thank you for joining us by picking up your book and opening it.)

- Overcorrection refers to the act of having the student perform a duty or task to compensate for what happened (e.g., "Frank, you threw paper on the floor. During recess you can pick up paper in the school yard for 15 minutes."). It can also involve redoing an action in the correct manner for the purposes of practicing appropriate behavior (e.g., "Sarah, you ran into the room, did not pick up your writing journal, and started talking with Megan. Please walk into the room again and show me how we get ready for journal writing in the morning.").
- Response cost involves the loss of something tangible or intangible (e.g., "Samantha, because you were talking during independent work time, you will not be allowed to go to the computer center today."). Sometimes the teacher may use response cost for the entire class, for example, "You were so loud and disruptive during free time that we will terminate free time now."
- Time-out recognizes the social nature of youngsters and provides a period of time in a less reinforcing environment typically without reinforcers. Since time-out is so frequently used in schools, an extended description is provided in the previous section of this chapter.

Although punishment often reduces the undesired behavior, it does not ensure that the desired behavior will occur (Lee & Axelrod, 2005). For example, a student who is punished for talking in class might stop talking in that class, yet he or she might not attend to his or her studies for the remainder of the day.

Many educators argue against the use of punishment for these reasons:

- Punishment is often ineffective in the long run.
- Punishment often causes undesirable emotional side effects such as fear, aggression, and resentment.
- Punishment provides little information about what to do, teaching the individual only what *not* to do.
- The person who administers punishment is often associated with it and subsequently viewed as harsh or negative.
- Punishment frequently does not generalize across settings; therefore, it needs to be readministered.
- Fear of punishment often leads to escape behavior (e.g., running away, skipping class, reluctance to attend school).

Despite the many arguments against the use of punishment, parents and teachers frequently use it for the following reasons:

- They may be unfamiliar with the consequences of punishment.
- They are unable to effectively implement a more positive approach.
- It is often reinforcing to the person who administers it. When punishment rapidly changes the undesirable behavior, the person who implements the punishment is highly rewarded.

Punishment should be used as a last resort and when behaviors are harmful to a student or others. For example, Tracy Takamura, a second-grade teacher, felt she had no choice but to punish Monique Jackson, whose fighting on the playground was harmful to others. Despite Tracy's positive attempts to change her behavior, Monique continued to attack others when they did not do what she wanted. To address Monique's bullying, Tracy implemented the following procedures, which are necessary to make punishment effective:

- Tell the student ahead of time what the consequences will be the next time the student engages in the undesirable behavior.
- Deliver punishment immediately after the undesirable behavior (e.g., fighting) each time it occurs.

- Unless a sharp decrease in the frequency and intensity of the behavior occurs, the punishment is ineffective and should be altered.
- Identify and reinforce the appropriate behaviors of the target student.

Axelrod and colleagues (2013) suggest developing a school or district policy on punishment that includes:

- Preference for using positive behavior supports
- Team meetings when any form of punishment is being used to discuss alternatives
- Parental consent

Be aware that discipline procedures (e.g., school suspension) are different for a student whose infraction is related to his or her disability. For example, IDEIA 2004 includes limits on the number of days that a student can spend in an alternative placement after removal from the regular classroom. Check with your school counselor or special education teacher regarding the specific discipline procedures outlined in IDEIA 2004 that apply to students with disabilities. Table 5.1 provides a summary of behavioral techniques for increasing students' desirable behavior and decreasing undesirable behavior.

Recognizing students' mistaken goals

Rudolf Dreikurs, who was a follower of Alfred Adler and director of the Adler Institute, is well known for his contribution to understanding the classroom behavior of students (Dreikurs & Cassel, 1972; Dreikurs, Grunwald, & Pepper, 2013; Dreikurs et al., 2004). He believed that all behavior is purposeful and that teachers can more effectively deal with student behavior and misbehavior if they better understand that all of us fundamentally want to find a way to belong (Ferguson, 2010). After all, we are social beings and a primary drive is to belong and be accepted.

Table 5.1 • Summary of Behavioral Techniques to Moderate Students' Behaviors

PROCEDURES FOR INCREASING DESIRABLE BEHAVIORS	METHODS FOR DECREASING UNDESIRABLE BEHAVIORS
• ***Positive reinforcement:*** The application of a pleasurable consequence following the display of a desirable behavior. Positive reinforcement increases the target behavior that it follows. Positive reinforcement can be social (e.g., a smile, a pat on the back) or tangible (e.g., a sticker or food). • ***Negative reinforcement:*** The removal, following a behavior, of an unpleasant consequence that increases the likelihood of that behavior being maintained or increased. • ***Contract:*** An oral or written agreement between student and teacher that identifies the expected behavior and the consequences for exhibiting or not exhibiting that behavior. For example, the teacher and student write up the specific behavior to be demonstrated, how often it should occur, and the positive consequences of fulfilling the contract. • ***Premack principle:*** The Premack principle provides the opportunity for behaviors (acceptable to both teachers and students) to serve as reinforcers for behaviors that teachers want, as well as other behaviors that are acceptable to teachers but less acceptable to students.	• ***Extinction:*** The removal of positive reinforcement. For example, when a student shouts in class and other students laugh at this behavior, that laughter can be a positive reinforcer for the shouting behavior. In such cases, the teacher may want to have a class meeting when the target student is not present and elicit the cooperation of classmates, asking them to help reduce or extinguish the shouting behavior by not laughing when the student shouts. • ***Punishment:*** The application of an unpleasant or aversive consequence immediately following an undesirable behavior. In many cases, teachers think only of physical punishment. Other forms of punishment include any behavior that is extremely unpleasant or undesirable to the student and that reduces the occurrence of the student's target behavior. Sometimes staying after school or staying in the classroom during lunch is used as punishment. It is important for teachers to remember that a consequence is punishing only if it reduces the occurrence of the target behavior. • ***Time-out:*** The removal of a student from a positively reinforcing situation. Many teachers use time-out ineffectively, removing students from classroom situations that are not positively reinforcing. Also, time-out should be for a very specific period of time, not more than 15 to 20 minutes, and students should be told ahead of time when they will be allowed to return to the reinforcing situation.

The following principles form the foundation of Dreikurs's approach to discipline:

- Students (like the rest of us) are social beings, and their behaviors are attempts to be liked and accepted.
- Students can control their own behavior.
- When students display inappropriate behavior, they do so because they have the **mistaken goal** that it will get them the recognition and acceptance they want.
- Students make decisions about their behavior and when they display inappropriate behavior, they are making wrong decisions about how to get the teacher or students' attention and fit in with the community.
- Students' behavior is a way for them to exercise power, planning, and persistence to manipulate their own environment.

Many students learn that they can garner the acceptance and recognition they need by behaving appropriately and completing school tasks. Other students do not feel capable or worthy of obtaining recognition in these ways; they attempt to obtain the acceptance and recognition they need by displaying inappropriate behavior and not completing their school tasks. Over time, they begin to feel that the only way to get recognition is through inappropriate behavior.

Dreikurs identified four mistaken goals that categorize the behavior of most students:

1. Gain attention
2. Seek power or control
3. Seek revenge or get even
4. Display of inadequacy

According to Dreikurs, the best way to determine a student's mistaken goal is to identify what the student is doing and how you feel about or react to the behavior. Table 5.2 provides a description of a student's mistaken goal, the student's behavior, and the teacher's reaction.

Dreikurs indicates that the teacher's job is to identify the student's mistaken goal and to discuss it with him or her. Teachers also need to identify their own reaction to the student's behavior and how that might contribute to the student's mistaken goal. See Charles and Senter (2005) for further information on the application of Dreikurs's approach to classroom management. What can teachers do to assure that students' mistaken goals (misbehavior) develop into appropriate goals? Consider the following as you interact with students:

- *Recognize that students are social beings that want to belong.* Teachers who use encouragement providing awareness of the potential of each child to contribute and be a member of his or her community go a long way to reducing problem behavior.
- *Establish procedures for promoting cooperation within the class and in ways that include every child.* This cooperation can be through learning teams and pairs and can also include class meetings to solve problems recognizing the mistaken goals that students may have about how to be recognized and encouraged.

Table 5.2 • Students' Mistaken Goals

STUDENT'S GOAL	STUDENT'S BEHAVIOR	TEACHER'S FEELING
Attention	Repeats aversive behavior	Annoyed
Power	Refuses to stop behavior	Threatened, loss of control
Revenge	Becomes hostile, tries to hurt others	Hurt
Exhibition of inadequacy	Refuses to participate or cooperate	Helpless, gives up

- *Develop firm control over procedures and practices.* Classrooms that are too permissive and inconsistent promote feelings of lack of control in students, encouraging students to misbehave. Students want to belong to a community in which the expected procedures and practices are clear and enforced.
- *Implement logical consequences for misbehavior rather than arbitrary punishment.* When the class or selected students misbehave, recognize that they have inappropriate or mistaken goals (e.g., attention, power, revenge, or inadequacy). Encourage them to recognize their mistaken ideas about how to fit into the classroom community and provide consequences that relate to the misbehavior. For example, rather than extra homework for students who are excessively noisy in the classroom, provide a quiet time for them in which they practice not talking to each other for a designated time.

MyEdLab **Self-Check 5.6**

MyEdLab **Application Exercise 5.6:** Classroom Procedures

5 SUMMARY

- Your role as a teacher is to establish a classroom that is conducive for learning. Consider how you arrange the physical space to promote appropriate communication between students and allow you ready access to all students.
- Students who have disabilities, are at risk, or are exceptional face greater challenges to their self-concepts, as their characteristics may set them apart from their mainstream peers. As a classroom teacher, you can take steps to nurture positive self-concepts among all students in your classroom by identifying unique and positive contributions. Conveying acceptance of students with disabilities is an important part of your role as a teacher. You will serve as a model for your students and will help them learn to recognize the strengths and talents of their peers.
- Bullying is typified by verbal abuse, rumors, exclusion, or even more aggressive acts. Teachers can stop bullying through intervention and non-acceptances of such behaviors.
- Classroom behavior needs to be considered within a cultural context. Learn as much as you can about your students' families, values, and beliefs and allow this personal knowledge to influence your decisions about behavioral issues.
- Positive behavior support provides a schoolwide approach to preventing behavior problems by applying the universal strategies for behavior management.
- Universal strategies for behavior management include looking for the positive, using reinforcers to encourage positive behavior, establishing clear rules with known consequences, helping students to change inappropriate behavior, and recognizing students' mistaken goals.

THINK AND APPLY

1. As the interview with Samantha Dietz revealed, many preservice teachers identify classroom management as the issue they are most concerned about before teaching, and practicing teachers identify it as the issue with which they have the most difficulty. Interview five practicing teachers and ask the following questions: What classroom management strategies do you find most useful? What aspects of classroom management do you wish you knew more about? What advice about classroom management would you offer?
2. Establishing a climate for acceptance is key to creating a productive learning environment. What are some specific things you plan to do to create an accepting environment for culturally and linguistically diverse students in your classroom? Describe some ways you can promote acceptance of students with disabilities in your classroom; in other words, how would you manage this inclusive classroom?

3. Bullying behavior can often be challenging to identify and even more difficult for teachers to address. Describe two approaches you might consider using with young students who are bullying and two additional practices you might consider with students in secondary grades.
4. What are several considerations you would like to remember when teaching students from culturally and linguistically diverse families?
5. This chapter identified positive behavior supports for effective classroom management. List the strategies for positive behavior supports. Now add several others to the list, based on information provided in this chapter and from your own experience. Rank these strategies according to their importance to you. As you continue reading, return to your list of classroom management strategies and see whether there are any you would rewrite or reorder.
6. What are the mistaken behaviors that students might demonstrate and what would be an effective teaching practice for handling each one?

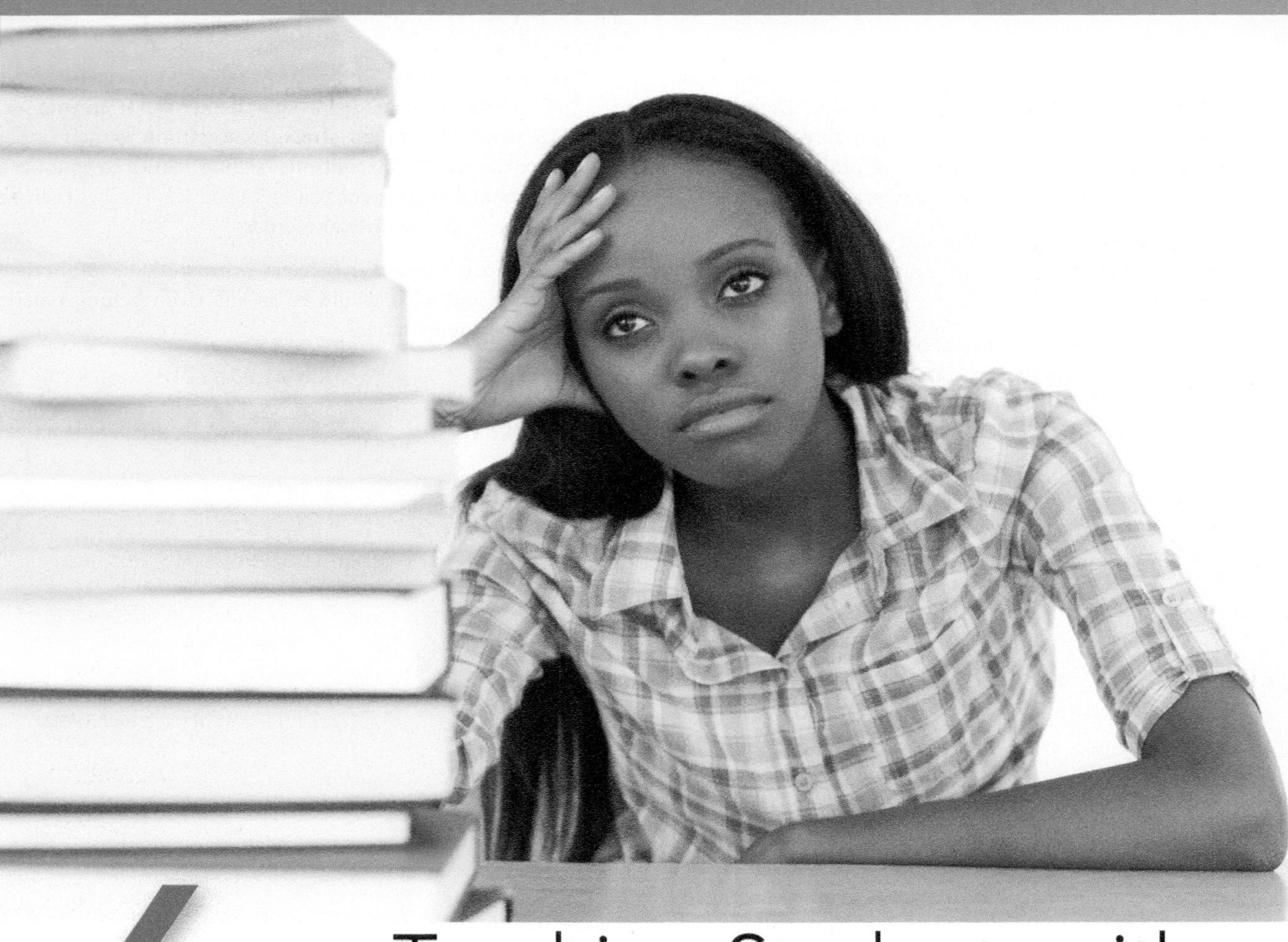

6 Teaching Students with Learning Disabilities and Attention Deficit Hyperactivity Disorder

Learning Outcomes

6.1 Identify the major components of the definition and criteria for determining a specific learning disability.

6.2 Describe the characteristics of students who have learning disabilities and their prevalence in the school-aged population.

6.3 Explain how identification of a learning disability is determined and the teacher's role in the identification process.

6.4 Illustrate possible techniques you could incorporate into your teaching to benefit students with learning disabilities.

6.5 Explain what attention deficit hyperactivity disorder (ADHD) is and how it might affect a student in school.

6.6 Describe the characteristics of students with hyperactive–impulsive-type ADHD and students with inattentive-type ADHD, and explain why it is so difficult to determine the prevalence of ADHD.

6.7 Explain how students are identified with ADHD.

6.8 Designate strategies you can use to help students with ADHD be successful in school.

INTERVIEW: TAMMY GREGORY

Tammy Gregory is a third-year teacher who has one student with learning disabilities, Adrian, and one student with attention deficit hyperactivity disorder, Lenny, in her class with twenty-six other second graders. Tammy is strongly committed to providing the most effective instruction and a supportive learning environment for all of her students. Adrian has a learning disability that is represented in the speed at which he processes information. He responds slower than other students, it takes him a while to process what the teacher and other students are saying, and he reads and performs math problems very slowly. When he writes, it takes him longer and he is often the last student to complete assignments.

Tammy regularly makes accommodations for Adrian so that he is a successful learner in her classroom. She may reduce the length of the assignment so that he can complete it in the time allowed. Tammy says, "The key is that Adrian understands and has mastered the skill. If he can demonstrate mastery answering five problems instead of ten problems in math, then he has learned and reached his goal." Although speed of processing can make Adrian appear slow and not very adept at many skills, his teacher has taken the time to learn about his interests and his strengths and to share these with the other students. It is not unusual to hear Tammy say to the class, "Check with Adrian on that. He's a real expert."

Tammy had more difficulties finding appropriate accommodations for Lenny, a student with attention deficit hyperactivity disorder. He moved constantly (even when sitting) and was always out of his seat, sharpening his pencil and talking to and bothering the other students. He rarely completed assignments. Tammy felt that Lenny could do much of the work but that his attention problems got in the way of his being a successful learner. To help Lenny, Tammy thought about and modified the structure of her classroom and schedule. Tammy reviewed the schedule each day with the entire class, ensuring that Lenny knew what was planned and expected of him. She provided a list of daily activities that Lenny checked off and asked him to rate himself on three criteria: paying attention, effort, and work completed.

Introduction

Think about Tammy's philosophy and practice of teaching students with learning disabilities and attention problems. To what extent do the practices she implements with Adrian and Lenny reflect the type of teacher you are or want to be? The first section of this chapter provides an overview

CHAPTER OUTLINE

of students with learning disabilities (LD), and the second section focuses on students with attention deficit hyperactivity disorder (ADHD). As you read, think about ways the strategies suggested for these students can also be used for other students in elementary and secondary classrooms.

6.1 LEARNING DISABILITIES

The disabilities of students who have visual impairments, are deaf or hard of hearing, or have overall cognitive delays are usually apparent. In contrast, you probably will not recognize students with **learning disabilities (LD)** in your classroom until you have the opportunity to see how they learn. Only in the last four decades have learning disabilities, sometimes referred to as the "invisible disability," been recognized in our schools. This section provides definitions and characteristics of learning disabilities, identification procedures, and suggestions for meeting the needs of students with LD in your classroom.

6.1.1 Definitions of Learning Disabilities

The issue of how to define learning disabilities has received considerable attention in the field since 1963, when Samuel Kirk suggested the term *specific learning disabilities* at the organizational meeting of the Learning Disabilities Association of America (LDA) (formerly called the Association for Children with Learning Disabilities [ACLD]). The LDA is a parent and professional organization that provides many resources related to learning disabilities. In the early 1960s, children with LD were referred to by such terms as *perceptually handicapped*, *brain-injured*, and *neurologically impaired* and were served in classrooms for students with intellectual disabilities or, in most cases, were not receiving any specialized services in the public schools.

For school-aged children, the definition of **specific learning disabilities** included in the Individuals with Disabilities Education Act (IDEIA, 2004) is most relevant. This disability category represents a heterogeneous group of students who, despite adequate cognitive functioning and the ability to learn some skills and strategies relatively quickly and easily, have great difficulty learning other skills and strategies. For example, students with specific reading disabilities may participate quite well in class discussions but have difficulty reading the text and taking tests. Other students may have great difficulty with math but have little difficulty with tasks that incorporate reading and writing.

Rules and regulations for IDEIA 2004 indicate that a multidisciplinary team may determine that a child has a specific learning disability if:

- The student does not achieve commensurate with his or her age and ability level in one or more of several specific areas when provided with appropriate learning experiences.
- The student has participated in but does not respond adequately to a scientific, research-based intervention (for example, in reading or math). In the updated definition, a child no longer needs to have a severe discrepancy between achievement and intellectual ability to qualify for a specific learning disability (Individuals with Disabilities Education Improvement Act of 2004, sec. 614[b][2], [3]).
- The student needs special education services.

A student is not regarded as having a specific learning disability if the deficit is primarily the result of any of the following:

- Visual, hearing, or motor disability
- Intellectual disability
- Emotional disturbance
- Environmental, cultural, or economic disadvantage
- Lack of appropriate instruction in reading

Children with specific learning disabilities have a disorder in one or more of the basic psychological processes involved in understanding or in using language, spoken or written, that may manifest itself in an imperfect ability to listen, think, speak, read, write, spell, or do mathematical calculations. These disorders include such conditions as perceptual handicaps, brain injury, minimal brain dysfunction, dyslexia, and developmental aphasia. Such terms do not include children who have learning problems that are primarily the result of visual, hearing, or motor handicap; of intellectual disability; of emotional disturbance; or of environmental, cultural, or economic disadvantage. The major components of this definition include the following:

- Difficulty with academic and learning tasks
- Discrepancy between expected and actual achievement that can be documented through low response to intervention
- Disorder in basic psychological processing
- Exclusion of other causes

In addition to the federal definition, you may also hear administrators, school psychologists, or other professions refer to the definition included in the American Psychiatric Association's *Diagnostic and Statistical Manual of Mental Disorders* (referred to as *DSM-5®*) (American Psychiatric Association, 2013). This recently updated manual provides guidelines for clinical diagnosis of mental disorders.

Video Example from YouTube

MyEdLab
Video Example 6.1.
Watch the YouTube video "You Are Not Alone" for challenges parents face when their child has difficulties in learning. What questions might you ask parents to gain further insights about what they are experiencing? https://www.youtube.com/watch?v=F5Qruysw2NA

MyEdLab **Self-Check 6.1**
MyEdLab **Application Exercise 6.1:** Definition of Learning Disabilities

6.2 CHARACTERISTICS OF STUDENTS WITH LEARNING DISABILITIES

Because learning disabilities are heterogeneous, it is difficult to list a set of characteristics that adequately describes all students with LD. Students with LD represent a broad range of linguistic, cultural, racial, and socioeconomic backgrounds (American Psychiatric Association, 2013). Thus, you will find that students with LD seem more different from one another than alike in relation to how they learn, but certain overriding characteristics will help you identify these students:

- *Unexpected difficulty* or low performance in one or more academic areas (unexpected in that your general impressions of the student would not lead you to predict that he or she would have difficulty).
- *Ineffective or inefficient information processing* or learning strategies in the area(s) of difficulty (ineffective in that students may demonstrate significant difficulties with memory, integrating ideas across text, or using learning strategies to make inferences).

Furthermore, the reasons for this low performance vary according to the academic strengths and weaknesses of the learner and the learning strategies he or she employs.

For example, Tamara and Manuel, two students in Carla Huerra's third-grade classroom, were identified as having specific learning disabilities and were reading and spelling at an early first-grade (primer) level. Both students have difficulty learning to recognize and spell words automatically when reading and writing, but the strategies they use are very different, as are the individualized education programs (IEPs) that Carla and the special education teacher, David Ross, use with each student.

Carla's observations reveal that Tamara has strong oral language skills. She capitalizes on these skills when she reads and uses the meaning and the syntax (word order or grammar) of the language as her primary strategies for figuring out unknown words. When she does not know a word, she skips it or substitutes a word that more or less makes sense. She shows little evidence of using phonics beyond using the initial sound to figure

What are some learner characteristics that might help you identify a student with possible learning disabilities? How might you work with an inclusion specialist or special education teacher to plan and design an education program to support such a student?

out unknown words. Carla notes that even though Tamara sees a word many times, either in context or written by itself, it is not easy for her to recognize it automatically so that it becomes part of her sight vocabulary. When Carla observes Tamara's writing, she notes that Tamara has wonderful ideas but spends much of her time asking other students how to spell words or changing what she was originally going to write so that she can use words she knows how to spell.

Like Tamara, Manuel has difficulty with reading and writing automatically. Manuel's reading is very slow and he sounds out the words (uses his phonic analysis skills). He is able to get a number of the individual sounds but has trouble blending them together to make a word. Although the words that result may not make sense, he does not seem to monitor this by going back and rereading. Manuel's writing also reflects his use of somewhat successful phonic analysis, in that even high-frequency, irregular words are spelled phonetically (e.g., "cum" for *come*, "wuz" for *was*).

In talking with David Ross, Tamara and Manuel's special education teacher, Carla learned that both students have visual-memory and auditory-processing difficulties that make it hard for them to learn to automatically recognize words. Each student, however, uses different strategies and strengths to compensate (i.e., Tamara relies on her strong oral language skills and Manuel relies on "somewhat successful" phonic analysis).

Together, Carla and David have planned and designed educational programs to support these students. For studying content areas such as science and social studies, Carla relies on using books written at different reading levels. She also allows students to demonstrate their knowledge through oral reports, posters, and pictures rather than only through traditional written reports and tests. During writers' workshops, Carla helps each student develop a spelling dictionary. For reading, Carla and David work together to help Tamara and Manuel expand the strategies they use to decode unknown words. For Tamara, this includes learning to use phonic analysis along with meaning to help her identify the unknown word. They are also helping Tamara to see similar spelling patterns in words (e.g., word families: *-ake*, *make*, *take*, *lake*). For Manuel, their help includes using repeated reading to get him to build fluency and take more risks when decoding words. Manuel is also learning to ask himself the question "Does this make sense?" to monitor his decoding and comprehension.

Figure 6.1 presents some characteristics that, although they might not apply to all students with LD, have helped signal to general education teachers which students might have specific learning disabilities.

Several of these characteristics refer to difficulties in attention. Students with LD often have difficulties with attention and, in some cases, hyperactivity. More than half of students with learning disabilities or behavior disorders also exhibit difficulties with attention problems (Pastor & Reuben, 2008). Although estimates vary (Owens, Cardoos, & Hinshaw, 2015), in general, boys are two times more likely to be diagnosed with attention deficit disorder than are girls (American Psychiatric Association, 2013). Although for some individuals, attention deficit continues into adulthood, the prevalence of attention deficit in adulthood declines substantially (American Psychiatric Association, 2013; Simon, Czobor, Bálint, Mészáros, & Bitter, 2009).

FIGURE 6.1 Signals for possible learning disabilities

Signals for learning disabilities are characteristics of students with learning disabilities. Because these students are a heterogeneous group, only certain signals will apply to any one student.

- Demonstrates unexpected low achievement in one or more academic area
- Has trouble understanding and following directions
- Has a short attention span; is easily distracted
- Is overactive and impulsive
- Has difficulty with handwriting and fine motor activities
- Has difficulty with visual or auditory sequential memory
- Has difficulty memorizing words or basic math facts
- Has difficulty allocating time and organizing work
- Has difficulty segmenting words into sounds and blending sounds
- Confuses similar letters and words, such as *b* and *d*, and *was* and *saw*
- Listens and speaks well, but decodes poorly when reading
- Has difficulty with tasks that require rapid naming of pictures, words, and numbers
- Is not efficient or effective in using learning strategies

6.2.1 Types of Learning Disabilities

Learning disabilities represent a group of disorders that cause students to have learning and academic difficulties. Currently, although no generally accepted classification systems exist for students with LD (Fletcher et al., 2007), types of learning disabilities have been discussed in the literature and used in medical and psychological reports for many years. Some of the most frequently used terms are *dyslexia*, *dysgraphia*, and *dyscalculia*.

- **Dyslexia** refers to severe difficulty in learning to read, particularly as it relates to phonological awareness, decoding, fluent reading, and spelling.
- **Dysgraphia** refers to severe difficulty in learning to write, including handwriting. Individuals with dysgraphia often struggle with accurate letter formation and writing fluently.
- **Dyscalculia** refers to severe difficulty in learning mathematical concepts and computation.

Dyslexia or significant reading difficulties are the most frequent academic challenge of students with LD. For students who are learning to read, evidence suggests that this problem is related to difficulties in phonemic awareness, developing the alphabetic principle, and fluent word reading (Wanzek & Vaughn, 2008). **Phonemic awareness** is the ability to blend, segment, and manipulate speech sounds (e.g., *trash* has four speech sounds or phonemes: *t-r-a-sh*). The **alphabetic principle** is learning how speech maps to print, or learning letter–sound relationships. Understanding letter–sound relationships allows students to decode unknown words by making the speech sounds associated with letters and then blending them together to make the word (e.g., *c-a-t* is *cat*). **Rapid naming** entails having children quickly name familiar objects, letters, or numbers. This skill is important in building reading fluency. Students with LD may also have difficulty with reading comprehension, and many students who have difficulty learning to read continue to have difficulty with decoding, which affects their reading comprehension. Examples of the types of reading disabilities frequently exhibited and the activities that teachers can use to instruct students are provided in Tips for Teachers 6.1.

Dysgraphia, or significant difficulties with writing, influence many students with learning disabilities who may read well but may have problems with written language (Harris, Graham, Mason, & Friedlander, 2008). These difficulties can occur in handwriting, spelling, productivity, writing mechanics, organization, and composition. Some students with learning disabilities have both dyslexia and dysgraphia and thus have significant problems learning to read and write. What are some of the warning signs of dysgraphia? They include: difficulty writing or drawing, difficulty writing letters,

TIPS FOR TEACHERS 6.1

Reading Difficulties and Suggestions for Instruction

Phonological Awareness

- Blending phonemes (e.g., blending sounds to make words such as /m/, /a/, /n/)
- Segmenting phonemes (e.g., this is the opposite of blending and requires identifying the sounds separately in a word; teacher says "not" and student says /n/, /o/, /t/)
- Integrating phonemic awareness with letters and print (e.g., as students are blending phonemes and segmenting phonemes, point to the letter, move the letters as tiles or blocks, or ask students to write, point to, or move the letters)

Phonics

- Letter–sound correspondence, letter combinations, affixes, and roots (e.g., examine a core reading program with a strong phonics strand and identify the key phonics elements taught at each grade level, determining which ones the student knows and doesn't know)
- Blending regular words (e.g., *fin, trump, sunshine, sailor*)
- Structural analysis to decode words (e.g., use prefixes such as *pre-* and *un-*, suffixes such as *-ly* and *-ed,* and key words to detect compound words)
- Strategies for decoding multisyllabic words (e.g., recognize the letter combinations that trigger multiple-syllable words, such as the "double letter" in *simmer* and endings such as *-ly* and *-ing*)
- Reading irregular words with extensive review (e.g., high-frequency irregular words such as *said, the, from, was*)
- Integrating phonics instruction with text reading and spelling (e.g., asking students to read words in context for which they know the phonics rules and asking students to use spelling to reinforce phonics rules)

Fluency

- Models of fluent reading (e.g., tapes of adult readers, older students, or better readers serving as models for reading the passages)
- Strategies for chunking text (e.g., phrasing and organizing text to read fluently)
- Rereading text with feedback (e.g., listening to students read and providing feedback about phrasing, prosody, and accuracy)

Vocabulary

- Oral discussions of new words and meanings (e.g., ask students to build word meanings through discussion)
- Instruction in specific word meanings for words used frequently in print (e.g., identify key words in text and preteach meanings using student-friendly descriptions)
- Practice making connections between related words (e.g., "*Gallop* describes how someone or something moves; what other words describe movement?")
- Repeated exposure to new vocabulary in a variety of contexts (e.g., words read in reading and language arts are encountered in other contexts)
- Strategies for determining word meanings independently (e.g., using context to understand word meaning)

Comprehension

- Generating questions (e.g., teach students to develop questions about what they read)
- Understanding features of text formats (e.g., story structure)
- Summarizing and generating main ideas (e.g., model and then practice finding the main idea and summarizing with different text types)

difficulty with legibility of words and sentences, concentrating so hard while writing that they forget the idea of what they want to write, and having a much better ability to tell a story than write a story.

Although not as prevalent as reading disabilities, substantial numbers of students with LD in elementary and secondary grades experience significant difficulties with mathematics, termed *dyscalculia* (Geary, 2010). Students may also have difficulty understanding the language used with numbers, such as understanding that when you have *fewer* coins, it means you have less or not as much. Difficulty may be in basic math calculations or more complex mathematical problem solving. Students with LD often require instruction in both basic math skills and math problem solving. What are some of the warning signs of dyscalculia? They include difficulty learning to count, difficulty connecting meaning to numbers, poor memory for numbers, difficulty doing simple word problems, being unfamiliar with math vocabulary, and having trouble with mental math.

6.2.2 Lifelong Outcomes for Individuals with Learning Disabilities

What are the lifelong outcomes for students with LD? There is no single answer for all students, but we do have evidence that some individuals with LD are quite successful in adult life and that they learn to adjust and make accommodations for their disabilities. Overall, however, students with LD have higher rates of unemployment and underemployment, fewer live independently, and fewer succeed in postsecondary programs than students in general. Also, many adolescents and adults with learning disabilities do not perceive that they are living the "quality" of life they would like to live. Why? For most of these individuals, the difficulties of schooling and thus applying learning to work settings are very challenging and discouraging.

What are the social and education factors that predict success for individuals with LD? Research indicates that successful adults with LD make realistic adaptations for their LD, take control of their lives, are goal oriented, and persist at these goals. Successful adults with LD have indicated that one or more significant people have supported their adjustments during school, postsecondary training, and young adult life (e.g., Gregg, 2009; Raskind, Goldberg, Higgins, & Herman, 1999), including engaging them in planning for the transition from middle and high school to other work or learning experiences (Mazzotti & Rowe, 2015; Neubert, 2003). Increased access to vocational training programs and support programs in colleges has also increased success, with many students with LD and ADHD performing on par with nondisabled students in college (Cortiella & Horowitz, 2014; Hamblet, 2014; Sparks, Javorsky, & Philips, 2004), although significantly higher numbers of adolescents and adults with learning disabilities are unemployed after completing schooling (Barkley, Murphy, & Fischer, 2010; Cortiella & Horowitz, 2014). Success after high school also means success in living independently, having positive relationships with coworkers, having friends, and enjoying family and community life (Ferguson & Ferguson, 2006).

Video Example from YouTube

MyEdLab
Video Example 6.2.

Watch the YouTube video "Famous People with Learning Disabilities," which shows examples of well-known individuals who have overcome learning challenges. Which of these persons would you like to read more about to learn about the struggles they experienced in learning? https://www.youtube.com/watch?v=xoeZAXUZbqQ&noredirect=1

6.2.3 Prevalence of Learning Disabilities

Today, more students are identified as having specific learning disabilities than any other type of disability. According to the Thirty-Sixth Annual Report to Congress on the Implementation of the Individuals with Disabilities Education Act (U.S. Department of Education, 2014), 8.4% of school-age children were identified as having disabilities, and just over 40% of this group, or approximately 3% of the school-age population, were identified as having specific learning disabilities. Formerly the fastest-growing disability category, the percentage of school-aged children identified as having a learning disability has steadily declined from 4.3% in 2003 to 3.4% in 2012. The National Center for Learning Disabilities suggests that this decline may be due to early screening and intervention, higher quality of reading instruction, and shifts in how individuals with LD are identified (Cortiella & Horowitz, 2014).

As a classroom teacher, you may notice that you have more boys than girls identified as having LD. Two-thirds of students with disabilities are males (Cortiella & Horowitz, 2014). Research on the genetic bases of dyslexia would suggest that the ratio of boys to girls should be more equal (Fletcher et al., 2007), even though males do have more of a biological vulnerability than females. Males may also be more vulnerable to referral and identification because boys generally exhibit more disruptive behaviors, including those associated with attention deficit disorder (Liederman, Kantrowitz, & Flannery, 2005).

MyEdLab **Self-Check 6.2**

MyEdLab **Application Exercise 6.2:** Dyslexia

6.3 IDENTIFICATION OF STUDENTS WITH LEARNING DISABILITIES

Determining that students have a learning disability has always been a difficult and somewhat controversial task. This is largely because it is challenging to distinguish between a learning problem and a learning disability. It is even more complex to determine if an English language learner experiences academic problems due to his or her status with language acquisition or if the student actually has a specific learning disability (Klingner & Eppollito, 2014). Furthermore, until relatively recently, most professionals believed that a discrepancy between intelligence quotient (IQ) and achievement was the sole or most significant criteria for learning disabilities.

6.3.1 Discrepancy between IQ and Achievement

Why is discrepancy between IQ and achievement no longer an appropriate criteria for identifying students with learning disabilities? What we have learned in the last few decades is that students with learning disabilities have an unexpected underachievement. This means that despite successes in many academic and cognitive areas, students have a significant learning problem. This unexpected underachievement is best diagnosed by using multiple data sources rather than relying on IQ–achievement discrepancy (Cortiella & Horowitz, 2014; Dennis et al., 2009; Francis et al., 2005; Stuebing et al., 2002). Concern was raised about the federal criteria using IQ–achievement discrepancy for determining a specific learning disability. The discrepancy is difficult to determine with young children and may unnecessarily postpone identification until second grade or later. At the same time, longitudinal research has demonstrated that 75% of students who do not learn to read by the third grade will continue to have reading disabilities throughout their schooling career (Wong, Graham, Hoskyn, & Berman, 2008). Moreover, questions have been raised about the appropriateness of traditional IQ and achievement assessment tools for students with cultural and linguistic differences (Klingner & Edwards, 2006). Thus, most states now allow multiple data sources for determining identification for learning disabilities, including response to intervention approaches (Berkeley, William, Peaster, & Saunders, 2009; Cortiella & Horowitz, 2014).

6.3.2 Response to Intervention

IDEIA 2004 includes the use of response to intervention (RTI) as an alternative to the traditional aptitude–achievement discrepancy approaches to identifying students with learning disabilities. Recall that RTI is a model for providing support to struggling readers in the primary grades at the intensity and level that is required to meet the needs of individual students. RTI provides a validated intervention to students in the instructional area of need before determining their qualifications for special education. Students who respond adequately to the intervention and are able to make appropriate progress in the classroom are unlikely to require special education. Students whose response to the intervention is low are very likely to require special education. Possible difficulties of the RTI approach include questions of who will provide the interventions and the extent to which validated instructional practices exist in fields other than reading, but this approach appears to be a path for identification of learning disabilities that will be taken by more and more school districts (Fuchs & Vaughn, 2012; Fuchs, Fuchs, & Vaughn, 2008; Vaughn & Fuchs, 2003).

Secondary science teacher Joseph Blankenship's ideas about learning disabilities are similar to those of many other teachers. He comments that initially these students may not seem different from other students. They participate in classroom discussions and may appear to understand the content covered. But as assignments are submitted and tests given, he quickly realizes that students with LD have difficulties with reading, writing, math, studying, and organizing their time. "What really surprised me was how poorly Michael wrote about what he learned and yet how well he would present it orally in class.

I found that if I just gave Michael a little extra time when taking tests and I didn't deduct points for his writing or spelling, he could do very well in summarizing the content he learned."

RTI neither creates nor fixes learning disabilities. However, models such as three-tier reading provide a safety net for students who might end up in special education simply because they have not been provided adequate instruction or appropriate interventions prior to being referred for special education services. RTI is a dynamic model that allows students to move between levels of interventions depending on results of ongoing progress monitoring and benchmark assessments. The key to the three-tier reading model and other RTI models is to provide effective instruction early to ensure that students are provided with the resources and support they need to become proficient readers.

6.3.3 Teachers' Role in the Identification Process

Most students with LD are identified because of difficulties with academic achievement. Teachers—usually the first professionals to notice the students' learning strengths and weaknesses and academic skills—play an important role in identifying students with LD. Louise Parra, a first-grade teacher, comments on the importance she places on being alert for students who may have LD:

> As a first-grade teacher, it is very important that I understand LD and keep alert for children who are not learning at the same rate or with the same ease that I would expect of them. If I notice these children in the first grade and begin collaborating with the special education teacher, other specialists, and the children's families, then I can assist in preventing these children from developing the poor self-esteem that frequently develops if they continue to fail and are not supported.

Of all the members of a prereferral or multidisciplinary team, classroom teachers and parents have the most experience with observing the child's behavior. Referral from the classroom teacher is one of the most important predictors of whether a student will be identified as having a learning disability. Tips for Teachers 6.2 provides suggestions for what classroom teachers should consider before referring a student who seems to have LD.

TIPS FOR TEACHERS 6.2

What to Consider in Referring Students Suspected of Having Learning Disabilities

- In which academic areas of learning (e.g., listening comprehension, oral expression, basic reading skills, reading comprehension, basic writing skills, written expression, math computation, math reasoning, and problem solving) is the student successful, and in which areas is the student having difficulties?
- What are the academic achievement levels in these areas, and what are representative examples of the student's work?
- How does the student compare with other students in the classroom in areas of success and difficulty?
- What factors (other than specific learning disabilities) might be contributing to the learning problems experienced by the student (e.g., frequent moves, absences, recent traumatic life events, vision or hearing impairments, emotional disorders)?
- Are the student's first language and language of instruction the same, or is the student learning academics while also acquiring a second language or dialect?
- What learning or compensatory strategies does the student currently use to aid in learning?
- How does the student perceive him- or herself as a learner, and what is the student's attitude toward school and learning?
- Have you provided effective instruction? If yes, did the student respond differently than most students (e.g., did not learn as well)?
- What strategies and accommodations have been tried, and how did they work?
- Has the student been provided supplemental instruction in either a very small group or one-on-one, and was the learning response still low?

FIGURE 6.2 Information shared by Jackie Darnell, the classroom teacher, at a multidisciplinary conference

Name: Cassandra **Age:** 10 **Grade:** Fifth

Literacy:

- Fourth- to fifth-grade level.
- Participates in literature discussion groups and can answer a variety of questions about the literature, including underlying theme and application questions.
- Can write a report with introduction and two supporting paragraphs.
- Spells at fourth-grade level, using phonic and structural analysis for unknown words.
- Can use a word processor to write and revise written work.

Progress monitoring data used to determine performance levels: Fall and winter benchmark testing.

RTI: No specialized intervention needed. Progress steady.

Math:

- Second-grade achievement level.
- Adds and subtracts with regrouping but makes computation errors in the process and with basic facts.
- Understands basic concept of multiplication but does not know basic facts or how to use for simple word problems.
- Has difficulty understanding simple one- and two-step word problems.
- Understands concept of multiplication as repeated addition. Does not compute multiplication problems.
- Demonstrates concept of simple fractions 1/2, 1/3, 1/4.
- Solves word problems. Errors are generally in computation and basic facts rather than problem representation.
- Describes math as least favorite subject.
- Struggles to learn basic math facts despite incentive program, coordination with parents, and use of computer programs at school.

Progress-monitoring data used to determine performance levels: Weekly tests in +, −, *, / (number correct out of 10).

RTI: 15-minute minimum daily small-group instruction. Progress minimal.

Social–Emotional:

- Well-liked by peers, both boys and girls.
- Quiet; does not ask for help when needed.
- Works well in cooperative groups but usually does not take leadership roles.
- Good sense of humor.

Jackie Darnell, a fifth-grade teacher, shared observations and information about a student, Cassandra, at a multidisciplinary conference, during which it was decided that, because of math disabilities, Cassandra was eligible for special education services (see Figure 6.2).

Jackie used a variety of assessments to collect information about Cassandra, including observations and analysis of work samples, curriculum-based assessments taken from the math curriculum and textbook, and informal math assessments Jackie designed to pinpoint skills on which students need to work to gain mastery. The information Jackie provided clearly identified her concerns in the area of math computation. She also provided information about strategies she had already tried with Cassandra. Documenting what has been tried and its success is key to justifying that a student needs special education services.

Because Cassandra enjoyed working on the computer, she and the special education teacher worked together to identify additional computer programs for Cassandra. In addition, the special education teacher planned to work with Cassandra on how to use a calculator and build skills in computation of multiplication problems. Both teachers also planned to use manipulatives (e.g., tokens, fraction cards, pegs) to build Cassandra's understanding of division and fractions.

MyEdLab **Self-Check 6.3**

MyEdLab **Application Exercise 6.3:** Identification of Students with Learning Disabilities

6.4 INSTRUCTIONAL TECHNIQUES AND ACCOMMODATIONS FOR STUDENTS WITH LEARNING DISABILITIES

No one instructional approach or technique is appropriate for all students with LD because students with LD are so diverse. In fact, many special education teachers describe having to be eclectic in their approaches to teaching to match the different learning patterns these students exhibit. The challenge of how best to teach students with LD has been exacerbated with the advent of higher state academic standards and state adoption of Common Core State Standards (McLaughlin, 2012). For some students, adaptations and modifications as part of ongoing instruction in the general education classroom may be sufficient. For others, more intensive, **specialized interventions** may be necessary (Fuchs et al., 2015; Fuchs, Fuchs, & Vaughn, 2014). Fuchs and colleagues (2015) define specialized interventions as those that include (a) explicit instruction using evidence-based practices and (b) ongoing progress monitoring to gauge student mastery. Collaboration with special education colleagues and reading specialists is necessary to implement specialized interventions.

Effective classroom teachers report that they must use their "best teaching practices" to teach students with LD. Len Hays, a seventh-grade English teacher, elaborates on best teaching practices:

> When I work with students who have been identified as having LD or demonstrate attention problems, it requires my best teaching. By this I mean that I must be very organized in the manner in which I present a literature unit or an English lesson. First, I give an overview of the lesson and explain the activities and what is expected of the students. I also make sure that when I lecture, I display the important information so that all students can see it. If I want the students to understand a process, such as how to revise an essay to add "color," then using a projector lets me demonstrate the process and my thinking as I edit. This allows me to model the questions I ask myself as a writer and to show the changes I make. It is also important that I organize the learning activities and working groups so that students have the opportunity to practice the skills that are the focus of the lesson. Whether we are working on editing skills or doing a critical analysis of a book, I always work to relate the learning to the students' daily lives. Finally, I try to be creative and humorous. That is just part of being a middle school teacher and dealing with adolescence.

Several instructional practices are associated with improved outcomes for students with learning disabilities. These instructional practices have emerged from more than a hundred studies (e.g., Fletcher et al., 2007; Swanson & Deshler, 2003; Vaughn & Bos, 2015).

On the basis of this work, several common practices were identified as powerful predictors of the academic success of students with LD:

- Controlling task difficulty (e.g., teaching at the student's instructional level and sequencing examples and problems to maintain high levels of student success)
- Teaching students with LD in small interactive groups of six or fewer students (e.g., students respond better when the instruction provides opportunities for them to practice and respond)

- Using graphic organizers and other visual displays to illustrate key ideas and concepts (e.g., students learn better when they have a picture or diagram to illustrate key ideas and concepts)
- Using a combination of direct instruction and cognitive strategy instruction (e.g., direct and explicit instruction is necessary but not sufficient for most students, and thus they benefit when teachers "think aloud" and illustrate how to think about the math or reading task)
- Providing modeling and "think-alouds" to demonstrate strategies and learning practices (e.g., describing how to perform a task is often insufficient, and thus teachers can show how to do tasks by talking aloud as they think through the task while they are doing it)
- Teaching students to self-regulate and self-monitor their learning and to "fix up" when they have learning problems (e.g., students can learn to ask themselves questions such as, "Did I check the problem twice to be sure the answer is right?" to benefit their learning)
- Providing opportunities for extended practice with feedback (e.g., students need lots of opportunities to practice what you want them to learn and to receive immediate feedback with instruction to support their learning).

6.4.1 Providing a Framework for Learning

Students are more successful when they have a good idea of where they are going. Research on the use of advance organizers (i.e., activities that orient students to the task and the materials) suggests that this is even more important for students with LD, learning problems, or limited background knowledge for the task being taught (Bulgren, Deshler, & Lenz, 2007; Dexter & Hughes, 2011; Kim, Vaughn, Wanzek, & Wei, 2004).

Colleagues at the University of Kansas identified steps for using advance organizers and concept maps to improve learning across the content area (Bulgren, 2006; Bulgren et al., 2007; Lenz, Deshler, & Kissam, 2003). When content-area teachers in middle and high schools used advance organizers and question exploration for learning, some adolescents with LD experienced significant improvements in both the quality and quantity of learning (Bulgren, Marquis, Lenz, Schumaker, & Deshler, 2009). Three factors seem important to the success of advance organizers. First, students with LD are taught how to listen for and use the advance organizer. For example, students might complete a worksheet (see Figure 6.3) as they listen to the teacher introduce each part of the advance organizer.

Second, after using the advance organizer worksheet, the teacher and students discuss the effectiveness of its use and how and when it might be used in various content classes. Third, before an advance organizer is presented, the teacher cues the students that it is going to be used. These advanced organizers can also assist students who are English language learners in orienting them to the big ideas and key academic vocabulary in learning content (Vaughn et al., 2009).

One critical aspect of the advance organizer is that it provides basic information or activates the students' background knowledge (refer to step 5 in Tips for Teachers 6.3).

Students with LD often have information about the topics, skills, or strategies being taught but do not automatically think about this information.

FIGURE 6.3 Headings and questions to include on an advance organizer worksheet

Advance Organizer Worksheet

Name:
Date:
What is the topic?

What is the framework or picture for the information?

What do I need to do or what are the assignments?

What do I need to learn?

What is the important vocabulary?

What are the due dates for the assignments and test?

Using thinking aloud and instructional conversations

One key to success for students with LD is to make the learning visible. Think back to your experiences as a student. How did you learn to find the

TIPS FOR TEACHERS 6.3

Steps in Using an Advance Organizer

1. Generate a big idea about the content.
   - Review the content for the weekly or 2-week unit.
   - Determine what the "big idea" is for that unit.
   - Present the big idea to students and make linkages to previous learning or readings.
2. Identify key vocabulary and concepts.
   - Preteach all proper names and places.
   - Identify the most important words and concepts students need to know and preteach them, connecting them to previous and future learning.
3. Provide an organizational framework.
   - Present an outline, list, or narrative of the lesson's content.
4. Provide background information.
   - Relate the topic to the course or to a previous lesson.
   - Relate the topic to new information.
   - Provide a springboard such as a picture, video, or other activity to activate student interest.
   - Clarify the concepts to be learned.
   - Clarify by examples or analogies.
   - Clarify by nonexamples.
   - Provide examples and illustrations and discuss possible misunderstandings.
5. Activate students' engagement to learn.
   - Point out relevance to students.
   - Be specific, personal, and believable.
6. Provide opportunities for students to work in pairs or cooperative groups to solve a problem related to what they are learning.
   - Teach students to work in pairs or cooperative groups by holding them individually accountable for their work as well as giving a team grade.
   - Provide a task that allows them to develop a product to share with the class.
7. Use assessment to determine ongoing learning.
   - Determine how much students know about what they are learning prior to teaching.
   - Assess along the way, providing immediate feedback about what they know and need to know.

main idea when you were reading? Many teachers traditionally used the technique of repeatedly asking students questions such as "What is the main idea of this story?" or "What is this story about?" These teachers mistakenly think that asking questions about what students have read is the same thing as teaching them to read for understanding. Students cannot be expected to infer how to find the main idea. Rather, intervention research on teaching reading comprehension and other cognitive processes has emphasized that teachers and students should model and discuss the **cognitive strategies** (i.e., thinking processes) they use for tasks such as finding the main idea of the story (e.g., Harris et al., 2008; Vaughn et al., 2011) and math problem solving (Krawec, Huang, Montague, Kressler, & de Alba, 2013; Pfannenstiel, Bryant, Bryant, & Porterfield, 2015). Teachers and students can use thinking aloud to comment on or make visible their thought processes as they are doing cognitive tasks such as finding the main idea. Teachers can use discussions (referred to as **instructional conversations**) to make visible the thinking processes needed for understanding (Klingner, Vaughn, & Boardman, 2007).

Mr. Waterhouse, a middle school science teacher, had numerous students with disabilities in his classroom. He frequently used "think-aloud" practices to help students identify key words and concepts and their meanings. For example, he would ask students to turn to a page in the science book and would say, "In paragraph 2, there is a key word, *mitosis*. Turn to page 139, paragraph 2, and find the word *mitosis*. I want you to listen to me read the paragraph aloud. As I read the paragraph, I am going to ask myself if there are any clues to help me understand what *mitosis* means. After I find the clues, I'm going to generate a description of mitosis. As I continue reading the text, I will look for additional information to confirm or modify the meaning I've established."

In the following dialogue, the teacher is helping students to better understand story elements using an instructional conversation to make learning more visible (Englert, Raphael, & Mariage, 1994). In this example, the teacher is working with two third-grade students who have partner-read a narrative story about a bear and are now telling the rest of the students about the story.

T: Tell us about the story.

Ann: [Begins by retelling random incidents from the story]

T: You already said we were going to talk about the characters, setting, and problem. Who are the characters in that story?

Dee: There is Brother Bear, Papa Bear, and Mama Bear. [Shows pictures from the book]

T: Who would you say is the main character?

Ann: They were all main characters because they were all together throughout the story.

T: When we try to figure out the main character, what is the question we ask ourselves?

Ann: What the author wants us to know.

T: Remember when we try to figure out the main character, we ask ourselves, "Who is..."

Ann: [Ann fills in] "... the story mostly about?"

T: Could you answer that question by saying it's mostly about everybody there? (p. 21)

Rather than providing the answer, the teacher is modeling what question to ask to determine who the main character is. Research on students with LD has consistently demonstrated that whether the teacher is teaching reading, math, or written expression, making the learning strategies visible improves learning significantly.

Teaching self-regulation and self-monitoring

By having students keep track of how well they are understanding or performing, students can gain incentives for learning and change their learning patterns to more effective ones. Research suggests that students with LD are not as adept as their peers at monitoring their own performance (e.g., Klingner et al., 2007; Lee, Palmer, & Wehmeyer, 2009), and effective teachers promote self-monitoring (Hacker, 2009; Hilden & Pressley, 2007; Pfiffner & DuPaul, 2015). One way to help students with LD is to teach them to ask themselves questions about their learning and performance. General questions that students can ask themselves include the following:

- What is my purpose for learning or doing this?
- What is my plan for doing this task?
- Does what I am learning, reading, or doing make sense?
- What do I already know about this topic?
- How am I doing with my work?
- What are the main points I am learning?
- How can I use this elsewhere?

The use of **self-monitoring** and graphing has been shown to be effective for students with learning and attention problems (e.g., Fletcher et al., 2007; Mason, 2009). For example, teaching students to self-monitor reading fluency can provide a means for them to set goals and see their progress. Students should read material written at their instructional to independent reading levels (e.g., word recognition 90% or greater). To calculate fluency, have the students use the following formula:

$$\frac{\text{Total words read} - \text{Errors}}{\text{Number of minutes of reading}} = \text{Words correct per minute}$$

Fluency information can be plotted onto graphs like the one shown in Figure 6.4.

Having students record their own progress serves as a motivation for reading, provides immediate feedback, and allows the students to set goals and see concrete evidence of their progress. Generally, for students with fluency problems, the goal should be an increase of one to two words correct per minute per week. However, use past performance to help students set goals.

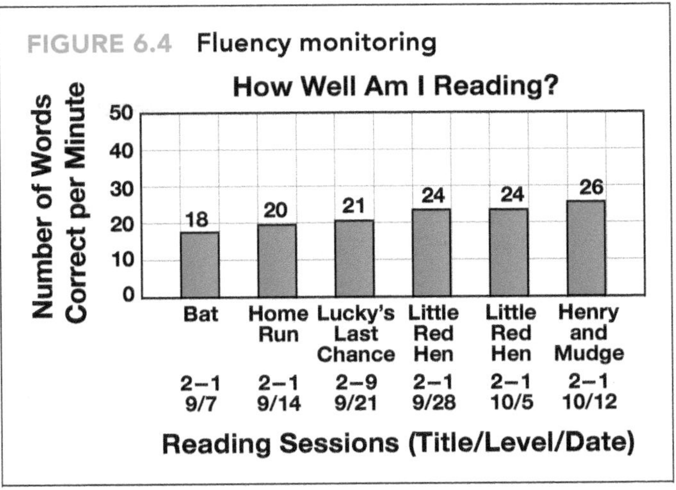

FIGURE 6.4 **Fluency monitoring**

Providing extended practice and application

Students with LD need extended practice and additional opportunities to apply their learning to ensure continued mastery. When teachers present complex materials and skills to adolescents with LD, extended practice with feedback is particularly important and helps to minimize difficulties with complex cognitive activities (Scammacca et al., 2007; Vaughn & Fletcher, 2012). To create these opportunities when other students in the class may not benefit from them, teachers must be adept at instructional management.

Sonya Rieden, a sixth-grade teacher, comments on the way she organizes her classroom to promote opportunities for extended practice and maintenance of skills and strategies:

> One of the most difficult aspects of teaching is juggling the grouping of students and scheduling of activities to ensure that students who need more time to learn have that opportunity available. Here is the way I do it. I select the skills/strategies based on students' needs, and we usually work on those skills/strategies for 1 to 3 weeks. I usually teach nine 10- to 15-minute lessons a week so that I focus on three skills/strategies at the same time. The students who are most academically at risk usually work on two of the three skills/strategies. This allows the students who need the most guidance to receive regular small-group instruction and to work consistently on a specific skill or strategy. In their learning folders students keep a list of these skills/strategies and space to record progress and to provide work samples. When I meet with students (either individually or in small groups), we review the skill/strategy list, update the records, monitor progress, and set goals. We prioritize activities and expected learning for the future.

Several other instructional principles that are important for students with LD and are helpful for many students include the following:

- Using learning tools and aids
- Adjusting workload and time
- Presenting information and having students demonstrate their learning in multiple ways
- Teaching students to use memory strategies

MyEdLab
Video Example 6.3.

Watch this video to observe how a teacher models and demonstrates the use of a graphic organizer to help students to recall and organize a lesson or activity that they had worked on previously. How could you use graphic organizers across disciplines to help all students, including those with disabilities, organize their ideas?

Using learning tools and aids

With new technology and its increasing availability, more students with reading, writing, and math disabilities are able to overcome their academic problems through the use of technologically based learning tools (Bryant & Bryant, 2012; Bowden, Johnston, & Beard, 2015; Marchel, Fischer, & Clark, 2015). What is assistive technology? It is any device, equipment, or system of support that helps students compensate for a learning disability. What are some examples of assistive technology tools?

- Abbreviation expanders
- Alternative keyboards

- Audio books and publications
- Electronic worksheets and learning activities
- Optical character recognition
- Portable word processors
- Proofreading programs
- Speech synthesizers and recognition programs
- Talking calculators
- Word-prediction programs

Also, with the use of technology, teachers are better able to organize their classrooms and to facilitate effective cooperative learning activities (see the Tech Tips, "Useful Tools for Students with Disabilities," to learn about some helpful programs and resources).

Computers, with their peripherals and programs, offer a number of effective tools for students, with new programs being created and older programs being updated. Some examples include:

- Students with handwriting and spelling disabilities have been helped by word processing programs with built-in spell checkers.
- Through speech synthesizers and software, students with reading and writing difficulties have had the opportunity to hear what they write and then to read along with the computer.

TECH TIPS

Useful Tools for Students with Learning Disabilities

Web Resources for Teachers, Parents, and Students

CHADD (Children and Adults with Attention-Deficit/Hyperactivity Disorder) (www.chadd.org)

Attention Deficit Disorder Association (www.add.org)

LD Online (www.ldonline.org)

Keyboarding

Early on, students who have difficulty with handwriting, either for composition or note-taking—regardless of the reason—should be taught keyboarding. There are many excellent computer-based keyboarding tutorials:

Mavis Beacon Teaches Typing from Broderbund (www.mavisbeacon.com)

This ever-popular product keeps users engaged and motivated through many different games and exercises.

Talking Word-Processing Programs

Talking word-processing programs can help young writers by speaking letters, words, and sentences as they are typed, thus providing auditory as well as visual feedback in the writing process.

Write: OutLoud 6 from Don Johnston Incorporated (www.donjohnston.com)

Search for Write: OutLoud 6 on the Don Johnston, Inc. site. This product provides struggling writers in grades 3 through 12 with auditory tools that will help them write more effectively.

Word-Prediction Software

Students receive a list of possible words after every letter typed and can choose the desired word; offers support for spelling and word choices, and can be individualized with custom word banks and topic dictionaries. Also includes built-in speech recognition.

Co:Writer 7 from Don Johnston Incorporated (www.donjohnston.com)

On the home page for the Don Johnson Inc., click on the Co:Writer 7 tab, then learn more about this word-prediction software.

Podcasts

Mobile devices are not just for listening to music. Students can record lectures, download audio files to their devices, and listen to lectures while studying for tests or reviewing and editing notes.

Learning Ally (formerly The Recordings for the Blind and Dyslexic®) (http://www.learningally.org)

The RFB&D is an organization that provides books and other materials recorded for individuals who have learning disabilities or visual disabilities.

iPad/iPod™ applications include:

- Read2Go
- Typ-O HD
- Sentence Builder
- Dragon Dictation

- Drill-and-practice programs for math facts, such as **Math Blasters Plus** (www.mathblaster.com), have provided students with the opportunity to review and practice their math facts in an interactive game format.
- Other learning tools that are recommended for students with LD include talking calculators, spell checkers, variable speed recorders, and electronic organizers.

Adjusting workload and time

Adjustments of workload and time allocations can be useful accommodations for students with LD. Workload adjustments can include both the amount of work given and the manner in which it is given. Reducing the amount of work may be a reasonable accommodation when the goal of an assignment or test is for the student to demonstrate mastery (and it can be demonstrated with less work). For example, if the purpose of a math assignment is to demonstrate mastery in using addition and subtraction with regrouping to solve verbal math problems, then completing the odd-numbered problems rather than all the problems may provide adequate evidence of mastery. This type of accommodation is reasonable for students who are slow in math computation because their knowledge of math facts is not at an automatic level. The accommodation of providing time extensions for tests or completion of large projects has also been helpful for students with LD.

Another way to adjust work is to divide it into smaller sections or tasks. Having students work on groups of five problems at a time rather than the complete set of twenty can make a task more manageable for the student and give the teacher additional opportunities to provide feedback and encouragement as each five-problem set is completed. Helping students to break a complex task, such as reading a book and writing a report, into smaller tasks and to develop a timeline for completing each task can also encourage successful task completion.

Presenting information in multiple ways

Students with LD may have difficulty processing information when it is presented in only one way. To assist these students, it is important to present the information in multiple ways. Bruce Ford, a ninth-grade science teacher, incorporates a number of activities, materials, and ways of presenting information as he plans a unit on cells:

> When I think about planning for biology class, I think about what are the key knowledge and skills that I want the students to understand and use. I know that if I just present the information using a lecture and have the students read the textbook, a good number of the students will not be able to access the information. So I find myself being creative and constantly on the lookout for additional resources that I can integrate into the unit. Right now, when we do the unit on cells, I have a great video from *Nova* that I use. I have also developed a study guide that I have students complete as we go through the unit. It incorporates pictures of cells and allows students to label the parts of the cell and their functions. It also includes Internet sites that provide accurate information on cells. The study guide provides the outline for my lecture notes. The study guide is critical because many of the students in my class cannot take adequate notes, and the study guide serves as a structure for their note-taking. One activity that I use is an experiment where students have to view cells during the reproduction cycle with a microscope. This activity allows the students to work in teams and develop a group report of their findings. I ask the students to be sure to include drawings. I have found that some of my students with LD excel at this activity.

By presenting information in multiple ways, teachers allow students to demonstrate their learning in multiple ways. This benefits many students, particularly because most students with LD have writing problems that are complex, multifaceted and can persist over time (Gillespie & Graham, 2015; Graham & Harris, 2009). A high school teacher who teaches students with LD explains: "The adolescents in my program do not

TIPS FOR TEACHERS 6.4

Demonstrating Learning in Multiple Ways

Ideas for Presenting Information

- Demonstrate the process or strategy.
- During lecture, write key points so that they are visible to students as you talk.
- During lecture, stop at natural breaks so that students, working in pairs, can discuss what they see as the major ideas.
- Use a graphic organizer or map to show the relationships among the ideas you are presenting.
- Use a video or movie that presents the key points.
- Have students listen to audio-recorded books.
- Have students conduct experiments to test hypotheses or discover relationships.
- Use pantomimes and skits to explain concepts.
- Have students role-play.
- Use computer simulations.
- Use manipulatives to demonstrate and then have the students use manipulatives.
- Use analogies, metaphors, and examples to further explain concepts.
- Have students use visualization and imagery to see ideas and their relationships.

Ideas for Demonstrating Learning in Math

- For students who have difficulties aligning numbers, use graph paper.
- Have students draw a visual representation of the story problem and then complete the math computation. Give partial credit for correct visual representation, even if the math computation is incorrect.
- Allow students who do not know their math facts to use math fact matrixes or calculators.
- Allow for time extensions.

Ideas for Demonstrating Learning in Content Areas

- Give tests orally and have students respond orally (students can record their responses). (The special education teacher or paraprofessional can often assist in this activity.)
- Allow time extensions on tests and projects.
- For projects, help students divide the project into steps and develop a timeline for completing each step.
- Have students use a picture or sequence of pictures to demonstrate understanding of a concept or process.
- Have students develop a skit or pantomime and present it to the class.
- Use word processing programs and spell checkers.

want to write. They do not even want to answer questions in writing. Writing a theme for a class is torture." Yet writing and tests are the major vehicles used to demonstrate learning. Also, they will have to write in almost every job they encounter, and certainly writing will be expected in postsecondary education. Modifying the manner in which students demonstrate learning enables students with LD to be more successful in the classroom. Tips for Teachers 6.4 suggests ideas for presenting information and demonstrating learning in multiple ways.

Teaching students to use memory strategies

Research has consistently demonstrated that students with LD are less effective at employing memory strategies than their peers (Hall, Kent, McCulley, Davis, & Wanzek, 2013; Swanson, 2009). This is particularly important when students with disabilities are included in general education classrooms where they are exposed to large amounts of information during content-area instruction. For the classroom teacher, this means that students with LD will not automatically use memory strategies such as rehearsing information they are learning, categorizing the information to make it easier to learn, using visual imagery to "see" the information mentally, and using acronyms to remember lists. By teaching students with LD how to organize and associate information, how to use mnemonic devices and key words, and how to use rehearsal strategies, you can help them remember information, whether they are beginning readers developing an automatic sight vocabulary or high school students studying for a science test. Take, for example, the use of acronyms to remember lists of information. The sentence "Kings play cards on fine green sofas" can help students remember the biological classification system:

Kingdom Phylum Class Order Family Genus Species

It is important not only to teach students memory strategies, but also to cue students to use their memory strategies when they work on a task. The 60-Second Lesson describes a fun way to have students develop acronyms.

60-*SECOND* LESSON

TEACHING STUDENTS TO DEVELOP ACRONYMS

One activity that students of all ages seem to enjoy and profit from is learning to develop and memorize acronyms for lists of information that must be learned. When you teach a list to students, have them form cooperative groups, with each group working on developing an acronym to help them remember the list. Then each group can report on its acronym.

Overall, key strategies for teaching students with LD include the following:

- Controlling task difficulty
- Teaching students with LD in small interactive groups of six or fewer students
- Using a combination of direct instruction and cognitive strategy instruction
- Providing a framework for learning
- Modeling processes and strategies with the use of thinking aloud and instructional conversations
- Teaching self-regulation and self-monitoring
- Providing opportunities for extended practice and application
- Using learning tools and aids
- Adjusting workload and time requirements
- Presenting information and having students demonstrate learning in multiple ways
- Teaching memory strategies

As a teacher, you will find that many of the strategies and accommodations suggested in this section will also assist English language learners with LD. In a position statement issued by the Division of Learning Disabilities of the Council of Exceptional Children (Klingner, Boele, Linan-Thompson, & Rodriguez, 2014), the importance of cultural and linguistically responsive teachers and instruction were also emphasized. Clearly these students will also need assistance with English language acquisition in a supportive learning environment. Students with attention deficit hyperactivity disorder as well as other learners will also benefit from these instructional practices.

MyEdLab **Self-Check 6.4**

MyEdLab **Application Exercise 6.4:** Teaching Techniques for Students with LD

6.5 ATTENTION DEFICIT HYPERACTIVITY DISORDER

Danny Moreira, a tenth-grade student, found out during the ninth grade that he has attention deficit hyperactivity disorder (ADHD):

> It has been an enormous relief to me, because all of my life I have been called names like "spaced out," "lazy," "hyper," and "daydreamer," yet I always knew that I was doing the best I could and that it was difficult for me to behave any other way. Ever since I was very young, I was very intense and had extra energy to work on areas of interest, but I also

> became easily bored and distracted. I've been reading and talking to my counselor about ADHD, and what they say is that people with ADHD have a hard time making friends. That has sure been true for me. I get bored with what people are saying. I interrupt. I am also somewhat impulsive so that if I am thinking something, I just blurt it out and sometimes I say the wrong thing. I've gotten much better and the friends I have now understand me. I must say, though, that finding out I had an attention deficit really took the weight off of me. I feel like I've had a boulder removed from my shoulders.
>
> School was a disaster for me, largely because I was so bored and the work all seemed so repetitive and tedious. I've only had one teacher who I felt understood me, Mrs. Golding, my third-grade teacher. I'll never forget her. For math, she would tell me I only had to do the problems until I got five in a row right, then I could stop. At recess she would help me get involved in games with other children and insist that I be included.

Students with attention deficit hyperactivity disorder have been identified for well over a century (e.g., Still, 1902), but only recently have we begun to address the educational implications of their disorder in schools. The terms *attention deficit disorder* (*ADD*) and **attention deficit hyperactivity disorder (ADHD)** have been used to describe students with this disability. Parent groups such as Children and Adults with Attention Deficit Disorders (CHADD) have applied pressure at the local, state, and national levels so that appropriate educational services would be developed for children with ADHD. Additionally, teachers and other school personnel, recognizing that students with ADHD come to school with behaviors that interfere with their successful learning, are increasingly requesting information that provides instructional guidelines that will help them meet the needs of students with ADHD. Linda Wellens, a veteran kindergarten teacher, explains her experiences with ADHD this way:

> I know that every year at least one of the students in my class will have serious attention problems. I don't mean the usual behaviors that a 5-year-old and 6-year-old display—I mean serious problems focusing on what we are doing, controlling themselves, and following directions even after everyone else in the room has caught on to the routines. I can usually tell after the first two weeks of school, but I try everything I can think of to structure the classroom for the child before I mention it to the parents or school counselor. I find that parents are relieved to discover that another adult has confirmed what they know about their child. Most of these parents are totally stressed out having to deal with the problems day and night and are looking for help.

What is the official definition of attention deficit hyperactivity disorder? The best source of information is the *Diagnostic and Statistical Manual of Mental Disorders* (referred to as *DSM-5*®), the foremost publication that addresses mental health disorders for children and adults (American Psychiatric Association, 2013). *DSM-5*® describes ADHD as a neurodevelopmental disorder with three "presentations": predominately inattentive presentation, predominately hyperactive/impulsive presentation, and combined presentation. Presentations are the symptoms that individuals might exhibit. In previous editions of the manual, "presentations" were referred to as "subtypes" of ADHD. This terminology was eliminated in *DSM-5*® due to complications with formal diagnosis of the disorder (Roberts, Milich, & Barkley, 2015) and the reality that symptoms may change over time (CHADD, 2013).

What are some signs of hyperactivity and impulsivity in students identified as having attention deficit hyperactivity disorder? What can you do to help students with ADHD in your classroom?

1. Teachers recognize "inattentivity" among students who are daydreamers who are often forgetful and easily distracted. Hallowell and Ratey (1995) describe these students as daydreamers, the kids—often girls—who sit in the back of the class and twirl their hair through their fingers while staring out the window and thinking long, long thoughts. These are the adults who drift off during

conversations or in the midst of reading a page. These are the people, often highly imaginative, who are building stairways to heaven in the midst of conversations, or writing plays in their minds while not finishing the day's work, or nodding agreeably and politely while not hearing what is being said at all. (p. 153)

2. Students who display hyperactive–impulsive behaviors have difficulty sitting still, talk out of turn, are the most challenging to parents and teachers, and are more likely to develop oppositional and defiant disorder or conduct disorder in adolescence.
3. Some students have features of both inattention and hyperactivity–impulsivity. Indeed, inattention and hyperactivity–impulsivity are highly related symptoms.

These characteristics of inattention and/or hyperactivity–impulsivity should be present in two or more settings (e.g., school, home, workplace). There should also be clear evidence that these characteristics significantly impair social, academic, or occupational functioning. The number of those symptoms and their impact on daily life determine the severity of the disorder: mild, moderate, or severe. In addition, there is evidence to suggest that ADHD often coexists with other conditions such as conduct disorder, depression, anxiety, and learning disabilities (American Psychiatric Association, 2013; Goldstein, 2009; Pliszka, 2015).

In previous editions of the diagnostic manual, focus was primarily on children with ADHD. Indeed, the guidelines indicated that evidence of symptoms should occur before the age of 7. Consequently, diagnosis of adolescents and adults with inattention and/or hyperactivity–impulsivity challenges was made more complicated. *DSM-5®* raised the age for documentation of symptoms to 12 and provides exemplars for how the disorder is manifest in adolescents and adults (CHADD, 2013).

Despite the increasing numbers of children, adolescents, and even adults who are clinically identified as having attention deficit disorder, there are some individuals who doubt the validity of attention disorders in children. Research studies provide compelling evidence that ADHD is a true disorder (American Academy of Child and Adolescent Psychiatry [AACAP], 2007, 2014; Barkley, 2015; CHADD, 2015). For example, magnetic resonance imaging (MRI) research has demonstrated decreases in blood flow in areas of the brain associated with attention in those with ADHD (CHADD, 2015; Roth & Saykin, 2004).

Despite compelling information scientifically documenting that ADHD is a true disorder, there are considerable myths and misunderstandings about ADHD.

What are some of the myths associated with ADHD?

- Skeptics believe that ADHD is not a real disorder and was "drummed up" by the pharmaceutical or psychiatric communities. Overwhelming evidence reports that ADHD is a real disorder with detrimental consequences for children, adolescents, and adults.
- Skeptics believe that ADHD is a disorder that only affects young children. ADHD affects individuals across the lifespan.
- Skeptics believe that the diagnosis of ADHD is overused and that many individuals who are labeled as having ADHD do not have the disorder. Although occasional misdiagnosis is possible with all disabilities, prevalence rates for ADHD vary from 3% to 5% (National Institute of Mental Health [NIMH], 2008).
- Skeptics adhere to the belief that ADHD diagnosis is just a practice used to overmedicate children. The increase in medication is likely a result of better diagnosis and treatment across the lifespan.
- Skeptics believe that ADHD is a result of poor parenting. ADHD is attributable to genetics in the vast majority of cases.
- Skeptics believe that all people lack focus and have a difficult time attending to school, but they need to fight through it. Individuals with ADHD have an excessive difficulty with focus and self-regulation.

Video Example from YouTube

MyEdLab
Video Example 6.4.

Watch the YouTube video "What It's Like to Have ADHD" to discover the impact that this disorder has on the daily lives of people. What skills could you teach your students to learn to cope with the challenges of inattention and/or hyperactivity? https://www.youtube.com/watch?v=Hl7Ro1PUJmE

- Uninformed individuals believe that children with ADHD are lazy or unwilling to try. ADHD has nothing to do with intelligence or willingness to work hard to succeed. Uninformed individuals may think that children use the ADHD diagnosis as an excuse for their inappropriate behavior. ADHD is a disability, and children need treatment to learn to cope better with their disability.

MyEdLab **Self-Check 6.5**

MyEdLab **Application Exercise 6.5:** Attention Deficit Hyperactivity Disorder (ADHD)

6.6 CHARACTERISTICS OF STUDENTS WITH ATTENTION DEFICIT HYPERACTIVITY DISORDER

Attention deficit hyperactivity disorder affects millions of children and adults. According to the diagnostic criteria of *DSM-5®* (American Psychiatric Association, 2013), identification requires evidence of onset of designated symptoms before the age of 12. There is general agreement that individuals with early onset of symptoms experience more severity and persistence over time, including into adulthood (Roberts, Milich, & Barkley, 2015). Parents and caregivers of toddlers and preschoolers may observe behaviors associated with ADHD early on. However, it is not unusual for most children before the age of 4 to get distracted or act impulsively (American Psychiatric Association, 2013; Barkley, 2013; National Institute of Mental Health, 2015), making early diagnosis complex. Most typically, preschool and elementary teachers are the first to observe children who display inattentive or hyperactive behaviors that are atypical (American Psychiatric Association, 2013; National Institute of Mental Health, 2015). The core characteristics of ADHD include the following:

- Feeling fidgety and restless
- Blurting out answers
- Having poor sustained attention and vigilance and being easily distracted
- Skipping from one incomplete task to the next, thus rarely completing work
- Being impulsive or having poor delay of gratification
- Being hyperactive or having difficulty regulating activity
- Exhibiting diminished rule-governed behavior
- Having increased variability of task performance

MyEdLab
Video Example 6.5.
Watch this video to observe student teachers who are discussing the characteristics of students with ADHD that they have observed in the general education classroom. Pay attention to their personal insights for accommodating these students. Can you think of any additional strategies that could be used to accommodate students with ADHD?

In the classroom, ADHD may manifest itself in a messy workstyle, careless mistakes, and misplacing needed items. Students with ADHD may have a difficult time persisting with a task until they finish it. Students with hyperactivity may jump from one task to the next, demonstrate a difficult time working quietly for a sustained period of time, and may display excessive talking or blurting out.

Even though preschool children may be diagnosed as having ADHD, some will not have the same diagnosis by later childhood or early adolescence (Riddle et al., 2013). These children may no longer be diagnosed with a disability or may develop LD as the academic tasks become more challenging. However, in the majority of those children in whom this early pattern of ADHD lasts for at least a year, ADHD is likely to continue into the school-age years, including adolescence. Parents describe these young children as restless, always on the go, acting as if driven by a motor, persistent in their wants, demanding of parental attention, and insatiable in their curiosity about their environment.

The common developmental features that distinguish ADHD from mild attention or hyperactive problems are the following:

- Onset in early childhood
- Chronic over time

TIPS FOR TEACHERS 6.5

Eight Tips Parents and Teachers Can Use to Explain ADHD to Children and Others

1. **Tell the truth.** This is the central, guiding principle. First, educate yourself about ADHD, and then put what you have learned into your own words, words the child can understand. Don't just hand the child a book or send the child off to some professional for an explanation. Explain it to yourself, after you have learned about it, and then explain it to the child. Be straightforward, honest, and clear.
2. **Use an accurate vocabulary.** Use accurate words even if they are technical. The child will carry the explanation you give him or her wherever he or she goes.
3. **Answer questions.** Solicit questions from students. Remember, children often have questions you cannot answer. Don't be afraid to say you don't know the answer. Then go find the answer.
4. **Be sure to tell the child what ADHD is not.** ADHD is not stupidity, retardation, defectiveness, badness, and so on.
5. **Give examples of positive role models.** Use role models either from history, such as Thomas Edison, or from personal experience, such as a family member (mom or dad).
6. **If possible, let others know the child has ADHD.** Let others in the classroom know (after discussing this with the child and parents), and let others in the extended family know. Again, the message should be that there is nothing to hide, nothing to be ashamed of.
7. **Caution the child not to use ADHD as an excuse.** Most kids, once they catch on to what ADHD is, go through a phase of trying to use it as an excuse. ADHD is an explanation, not an excuse. They still have to take responsibility for what they do.
8. **Educate others.** Educate the other parents and children in the classroom, as well as members of the extended family. The single strongest weapon we have to ensure that children get proper treatment is knowledge. Spread the knowledge as far as you can; there is still a great deal of ignorance and misinformation out there about ADHD.

- Generally pervasive behaviors across situations
- Deviance from age-based standards
- Increased likelihood of having another difficulty, such as a learning or psychiatric disorder

6.6.1 Teachers' Roles in Helping Others Understand ADHD

Typically, teachers notice that these students are restless, are inattentive, and have a difficult time with routines. Parents often confirm these observations. Tips for Teachers 6.5 describes what teachers and parents can do to understand ADHD and to help others such as family members and community personnel understand as well.

In the early elementary years, teachers often view these children as having "immature" behaviors and making slow academic progress. About 20% to 25% are likely to have difficulty learning how to read. The students struggle not only with phonological processing tasks, but also with overall regulation of their behavior and control over their learning related to both reading and behavior (Pliszka, 2015; Willcutt et al., 2010).

6.6.2 Working with Students Who Have ADHD

Research suggests that the key characteristic of ADHD lies in difficulty with behavioral inhibition or self-control (Barkley, 2015; Gevensleben et al., 2009). Behavioral inhibition or self-control refers to the ability to withhold a planned response, halt a response that has been started, protect an ongoing activity from interfering activities, and delay a response (Rubia, Oosterlaan, Sergeant, Brandeis, & van Leeuwen, 1998), and lack of behavioral inhibition or self-control is a predictor of youngsters who have more severe conduct disorders (Young et al., 2009). Preventing more significant behavior problems is an important reason why we need to teach self-regulation to students; we need to teach them to ask questions about their behavior and to talk to themselves as a means of regulating their behavior. Teachers note that children with ADHD have difficulty waiting their turn,

FIGURE 6.5 Promoting executive function or self-regulation

To promote students' self-regulation, or monitoring of their own behavior without adult supervision or direction, teachers may want to do the following:

1. **Provide task-related feedback.** Focus on the activity the students are engaged in and provide specific feedback about what parts of the activity students are doing well and how they could improve their performance on the activity. Avoid person-directed praise or comments such as "you are good at math." Instead, focus feedback specifically on task performance, "You have items number 1 through 3 correct; I can tell you worked hard and thought about them while you were working. Look at item number 5 and see how you might adjust it to make it more like item number 3."
2. **Link students' behaviors to outcomes.** "You remembered to take your worksheet home and do it. You also remembered to bring it back. Now you will get the entire recess time to play."
3. **Provide encouragement.** Because students with ADHD experience considerable failure, many are discouraged from attempting tasks that are difficult, even though they are capable of performing them successfully. Encourage and support their getting started and show them that they can be successful.
4. **Point out successes.** Discuss the academic tasks and social activities in which students experience success.
5. **Point out personal challenges and successes.** Discuss your own failures or difficulties, and express what you do to cope with these. Be sure to provide examples of when you persist and how persisting often but not always pays dividends.
6. **Encourage students to take responsibility for their successes.** "You received a B on your science test. How do you think you got such a good grade?" Encourage students to link studying and hard work with positive outcomes.
7. **Encourage students to take responsibility for their failures.** For example, in response to the question "Why do you think you are staying after school?" encourage students to take responsibility for what got them there. "Yes, I am sure Jason's behavior was hard to ignore, but what did you do that got you here?"
8. **Organize tasks to promote success.** Knowing students well and what they enjoy and are willing to do allows you to consider ways to organize their assignments and responsibilities so that they are more likely to succeed.
9. **Teach students to monitor their own successes.** Teach students how to use progress-monitoring procedures and charting to monitor their own successes, including behavioral successes (e.g., number of days at recess without a reprimand) and academic successes (e.g., number of days in which all assignments were completed).
10. **Teach students to use self-talk to control and guide their behavior.** Model for the student how you talk to yourself to keep you from getting into trouble, "The principal told us all to come early to the meeting and so I said to myself, 'I really don't want to do it, but if I go and participate I'll be able to ask the principal for a favor in the future.' "

refraining from interrupting conversations, delaying immediate gratification, working for long-term rewards, and resisting potential distractions when working (Barkley & Murphy, 2006; Wehmeier, Schacht, & Barkley, 2010). Learning to delay one's response to external stimuli permits the development of the executive functioning involved in self-control. **Executive functioning** is the ability to regulate one's thinking and behavior (also called self-regulation) through the use of working memory, inner speech, control of emotions and arousal levels, and analysis of problems and communication of problem solutions to others. For example, students can use **inner speech** to "talk to themselves" about various solutions when in the midst of solving a problem. Students with ADHD have problems in guiding their behavior in situations that demand the ability to follow rules or instructions. These students also have more limited persistent goal-directed behavior and can find it exceedingly difficult to stay focused on tasks that require effort or concentration but that are not inherently exciting (Barkley, 2015). Figure 6.5 provides suggestions on how to promote executive functioning or self-regulation with students.

As with learning disabilities, in the 1970s there was a common belief that children would outgrow ADHD as they reached adolescence and adulthood. Although there is evidence that outward signs of hyperactivity may be reduced, many individuals with ADHD continue to experience attentional problems in adolescence and adulthood. Approximately 50% to 65% of children diagnosed with ADHD are likely to continue to have the characteristics of ADHD as adults (Barkley, 2013). As in high school, at work, adults with ADHD may have significant problems with their ability to work independently of supervision, meet deadlines and work schedules, be persistent and productive in getting assigned work done, and interact cordially with fellow workers (Barkley & Benton, 2010). Perhaps one of the most distinctive characteristics of ADHD is the likelihood that

TIPS FOR TEACHERS 6.6

Ten Things Teens with ADHD Want Their Teachers to Know

1. I am not stubborn or stupid. I may be frustrated after struggling for so long, but I want and need your help to succeed in school—even if I don't always ask for it.
2. I may need help to organize my schoolwork. I really do complete my homework. I often lose papers, leave them at home, or can't find them when I need them.
3. ADHD is not an excuse. It is hard for me to do well in school. It helps when you ask me questions to guide my behavior and break the tasks down so I can accomplish them in parts.
4. I really do forget things. I'm not trying to be difficult. Sometimes I just don't remember.
5. I don't like to be singled out. Please talk to me in private about my behavior. Do not embarrass or humiliate me in front of the class. Don't advertise to everyone the modifications I need.
6. Sometimes I act without thinking. Help me navigate social and academic situations so that I can control my impulsive behavior.
7. It can be very hard for me to make friends. Cooperative learning and other organized activities that allow me to interact with my peers will help me make and maintain friendships.
8. I do better when I have a clearly organized plan and a routine to follow. If the routine changes, I may need more help than other students to adapt.
9. I am a person with feelings, needs, and goals. Include me in planning and decision making whenever possible.
10. Learn more about ADHD so you can understand the challenges I face every day at home and at school.

Source: Information from "12 things high school students with ADD/ADHD would like their teachers to know," by E. Bailey, 2005, retrieved from http://add.about.com.

it will co-occur with another disability and be associated with difficulties such as occupational and social functioning (Goldstein, 2009; Pliszka, 2015). Estimates are that as high as 84% of students diagnosed with ADHD also display oppositional and defiant behaviors with or without conduct disorders (Pliszka, 2015). Thus, students with ADHD frequently have other behavioral or academic difficulties. Because students with ADHD are much more likely than other students to have difficulties with their peers and to demonstrate problems that interfere with friendships (Centers for Disease Control and Prevention, 2015), we want to be aware of ways in which we can support positive peer relationships and enhance their friendship opportunities.

Tips for Teachers 6.6 lists ten things that adolescent students with ADHD would like their teachers to know about them.

6.6.3 Prevalence of Attention Deficit Hyperactivity Disorder

The Centers for Disease Control and Prevention provides prevalence estimates for ADHD, and they range considerably based on the state (Centers for Disease Control and Prevention, 2015). For example, Illinois, California, and Hawaii have prevalence rates of ADHD in children between ages 4 and 17 at below 7%, and states such as Ohio, Delaware, Indiana, and North Carolina have prevalence rates 11% or higher. It is important to note that these prevalence rates are based on parent reports of identification of ADHD. Recording the number of students with ADHD is difficult because there is no specific category for ADHD under the Individuals with Disabilities Education Improvement Act (IDEIA). Students with ADHD may be identified as having a health impairment or a secondary condition when ADHD and another disability (e.g., learning or emotional disabilities) coexist. Other students who do not qualify under IDEIA as students with ADHD do qualify under Section 504 of the Vocational Rehabilitation Act. Again, however, as in the case of IDEIA, the number of students with ADHD is not recorded.

With an overall prevalence of around 9%, prevalence estimates of students with ADHD are consistently reported at higher rates for males than for females, with parents reporting 13.2% of boys as having ADHD and 5.6% of girls (Centers for Disease Control and Prevention, 2015). It is difficult to determine why the rate is so much higher for boys, but there is some reason to believe that ADHD may manifest differently in girls than in boys and that the identification instruments are based on the behavioral manifestations of ADHD in boys. Oftentimes, girls with ADHD are more likely to be withdrawn and diagnosed as ADHD without hyperactivity (and thus less likely to be identified) than boys with ADHD, who are likely to be hyperactive and more aggressive.

MyEdLab **Self-Check 6.6**

MyEdLab **Application Exercise 6.6:** Characteristics of Students with ADHD

6.7 IDENTIFICATION AND ASSESSMENT OF STUDENTS WITH ATTENTION DEFICIT HYPERACTIVITY DISORDER

Unlike learning disabilities identification, initial identification of ADHD often involves a medical evaluation from a pediatrician, psychologist, or psychiatrist outside the school system. This evaluation should rule out other reasons for the student's behavior problems and evaluate the student's difficulty with attention and behavioral inhibition. This is usually accomplished through the use of interviews and/or the completion of behavioral rating scales by parents, teachers, and, when appropriate, the student. The information that you provide as a teacher can be helpful in determining whether attentional problems are severe enough to be identified as ADHD and how the attentional and behavioral problems are affecting the student in school both socially and academically. For example, keeping a record of the characteristics from the *DSM-5*® criteria that you observe in the child can be helpful in making the initial identification and in planning for accommodations.

Numerous rating scales have been developed specifically for the identification of ADHD (Venn, 2014). Conners 3™ is a frequently used scale that includes forms for parents and teachers to consider the behavior of a specific student and then rate items based on their knowledge of this student's behavior (Conner, 2009). Teachers and parents are asked to rate descriptive statements about the child's behavior based on presence of the behavior (not at all present, just a little present, pretty much present, very much present) or frequency of occurrence (never or rarely, sometimes, often, very often). Examples of behaviors include distractible, restless, always up, excitable, impulsive, excessive demands, unaccepted by peers, no sense of fair play, and fails to finish tasks. The assessment is normed for students ages 6 to 18.

Because the identification of ADHD is based on the perceptions of those rating the student, it is important to take into consideration cultural and ethnic factors that may result in the overdiagnosis or underdiagnosis of ADHD. Some students may have activity levels and behavioral patterns that are culturally and ethnically appropriate but differ significantly from those of majority-culture, same-age peers (Harry & Klingner, 2007). Teachers must be cautious in using and interpreting these behavioral assessments. Furthermore, although certain behaviors may occur more frequently owing to cultural influences, individuals vary widely within cultural groups. Instruments such as the Child Behavior Checklist: Direct Observation Form (Achenbach, 2000) allow for direct observation and comparison to peers from the same cultural group.

6.7.1 Eligibility for ADHD Services and Special Education Law

Two federal laws guarantee children with ADHD a **free and appropriate public education (FAPE)**: the Individuals with Disabilities Education Improvement Act (IDEIA) and Section 504 of the Rehabilitation Act of 1973 (Section 504). The two laws have different provisions for eligibility and services for students with ADHD, and it is important for parents and professionals to understand these differences. Whereas IDEIA mandates procedures for identifying students with disabilities and how services should be provided and monitored, Section 504 focuses on equity and access in all areas of life but does *not* detail how services will be provided. Following are brief descriptions of how the two laws influence services for students with ADHD.

IDEIA

IDEIA provides a mandate for special education for those students who meet the eligibility criteria for one or more disability *and* whose disability adversely affects their educational performance. ADHD is listed under the category "Other Health Impairment."

Evaluation and diagnosis of ADHD in the "Other Health Impairment" category is subject to the same referral and assessment procedures as other disabilities as specified in IDEIA. Examples of additional IDEIA provisions for a student with a disability are the development and regular evaluation of the IEP, parent participation and consent, procedures for handling suspensions and expulsions, and guidelines for determining how and where students are to receive special education services.

Section 504 of the Rehabilitation Act of 1973 Section 504 of the Rehabilitation Act of 1973 is a federal civil rights statute. It requires that schools do not discriminate against children with disabilities and that they provide children with reasonable accommodations (Murdick, Gartin, & Fowler, 2014). An individual is eligible for accommodations and services under Section 504 if he or she "has a physical or mental impairment that substantially limits one or more life activities" (Yell, 2016, p. 80). If it is determined that the ADHD substantially limits the ability to learn, the student meets the 504 eligibility criteria in schools that receive federal funding. Unlike in IDEIA, fewer regulations are placed on procedures for eligibility and services in Section 504. This makes 504 a more flexible and faster way for students to receive accommodations and services. Furthermore, students who may not meet eligibility criteria for a disability under IDEIA may still be eligible for 504. However, because IDEIA contains more specific guidelines for all aspects of referral, placement, and services, it may be more appropriate for students who require greater assistance and safeguards in order to succeed in school. CHADD (2015) provides resources for parents and professionals to understand the advantages and disadvantages of both laws and their influence on services for students with ADHD.

MyEdLab **Self-Check 6.7**

MyEdLab **Application Exercise 6.7:** Identifying Students with ADHD

6.8 INSTRUCTIONAL GUIDELINES AND ACCOMMODATIONS FOR STUDENTS WITH ATTENTION DEFICIT HYPERACTIVITY DISORDER

What are the characteristics of teachers who are effective in promoting the success of students with ADHD? According to Lerner and colleagues, "in many respects, they are simply good teachers" (Lerner, Lowenthal, & Lerner, 1995, p. 96). Lerner and colleagues (Lerner et al., 1995; Lerner & Johns, 2015) indicate that the following strategies help teachers work successfully with students who have ADHD:

- *Positive attitudes toward inclusion of students with ADHD.* These attitudes are reflected in the way teachers accept students and promote students' acceptance within the classroom community. Teachers have a significant influence on how students are perceived by others in the class. Even subtle preferences expressed by teachers are noticed by students and give them the "right" to like or not like certain students.

- *Ability to collaborate as a member of an interdisciplinary team.* Teachers who have students with ADHD in their classrooms have an opportunity to work with other professionals and family members who will be monitoring the students' academic and behavioral progress, response to medication, and self-esteem. Express interest in what you can do to promote the academic and social success of the students and ask professionals for ideas they think might make the instructional setting more productive.
- *Knowledge of behavior management procedures.* Most students with ADHD will demonstrate difficulty following directions, remembering routines, staying on task, and organizing themselves and their work. Behavior management skills are essential to adequately meet the needs of students with ADHD. If the behavior management practices that are typically effective with students are not effective with the student with ADHD in your class, ask a classroom management expert (e.g., school psychologist, special education teacher) to observe your classroom and provide suggestions.
- *Personal characteristics.* Teaching students with ADHD requires understanding, compassion, patience, concern, respect, responsiveness, and a sense of humor.

6.8.1 Educational Interventions

Although teachers often focus on providing interventions to students with ADHD that reduce inappropriate behaviors, these students benefit the most when behavioral interventions are accompanied by effective instruction designed to meet their individual learning needs (Salend, 2016; Salend, Elhoweris, & Van Garderen, 2003; U.S. Department of Education, 2008). Teachers should begin any educational intervention by planning. Maria Nahmias has served as a consultant to parents and teachers on how to effectively meet the needs of students with ADHD in the classroom, and Susan Stevens is a teacher and consultant with many years of experience working with students with ADHD. On the basis of their experiences, they recommend that teachers consider the following key points when planning **educational interventions** for students with ADHD (DuPaul & Stoner, 2003; Nahmias, 1995; Pfiffner & DuPaul, 2015; Stevens, 2001):

- *Use novelty in instruction and directions.* Highlight important instructions and key points with colored pens, highlighting markers, or felt-tip pens. Put key information in boldface or underline it. For example, have students highlight the operation signs on a math page before completing the page. Use oral cueing to identify key words or ideas in the directions.
- *Maintain a schedule.* As indicated earlier, students with ADHD have a difficult time learning rules and routines; therefore, it is critical that these be changed as infrequently as possible. Change is difficult for students to adjust to and often promotes behavior problems. Post rules and schedules in the room and on index cards on the students' desks.
- *Prepare students for transitions and provide support in completing transitions.* Alert students to upcoming transitions (e.g., "We'll be going to recess in 3 minutes. Finish what you are doing and put your materials away."). Provide guidance and encouragement as students complete transitions (e.g., "You have all your materials put away. All you need to do is line up when I call your table.").
- *Emphasize time limits.* Individuals with ADHD (adults even more so than children) have a poor concept of the time needed to complete tasks. Teach students to plan ahead and use the rule that to be considered "satisfactory," assignments are to be completed according to directions, with a passing grade, and turned in on time. Any adjustments in time should be arranged well before the deadline, not at the last minute.
- *Provide organizational assistance.* Provide guidelines for how students should maintain their desks, materials, and schedules. Provide opportunities at the beginning

of each week for students to organize, and then reward them for doing so. Ask students to keep a planner and a notebook for each of their classes and to write their assignments and due dates in the notebook.

- *Provide rewards consistently and often.* All students like to receive positive feedback about their performance and behavior; however, the frequency, intensity, and consistency of rewards need to be increased for students with ADHD. Whenever possible, involve the student in selecting the rewards.
- *Be brief and clear.* Think about instructions before stating them, and provide them as briefly and in as well organized a way as possible. Present the critical information in chunks so that it is more easily understood and remembered. Keep instructional lessons brief to maintain students' attention.
- *Arrange the environment to facilitate attention.* Consider where the student is sitting. Are other students who might promote good behavior and organizational skills sitting nearby? Are you able to quickly and easily maintain eye contact as well as physical contact with the student? Be sure to consider how to minimize distractions.
- *Provide optimal stimulation.* There is some support for the notion that optimal stimulation facilitates learning for students with ADHD. For example, students with ADHD who were provided with background music while doing arithmetic problems performed better than non-ADHD students under the same conditions (Abikoff, Courtney, Szeibel, & Koplewicz, 1996).
- *Allow for movement and postures other than sitting.* Arrange activities so that they include movement as part of the activity, such as writing, typing, drawing, or using manipulatives. Have students demonstrate their learning by using the board or overhead projector.
- *Promote active participation through effective questioning techniques.* Ask questions that promote student participation and provide feedback to the teacher about student learning. Effective questioning techniques include varying the types of questions to include high-level questions that require students to think critically about the material, adjusting question content for individual skill levels, using language that is understandable to students, pausing so that students have time to organize a response, valuing all responses so that not only the "correct" answer is acceptable, and rephrasing or summarizing student responses for the rest of the class.

Planning lessons for students with ADHD within the context of planning for the class as a whole is a challenge. The primary focus of planning should be on what accommodations are needed to make the lesson effective for all students, including students with ADHD. Table 6.1 lists types of problems frequently manifested by students with ADHD and also notes potential solutions.

A problem frequently noted by parents and teachers of students with ADHD is homework. Recent research suggests that there may be some medical reasons why students with ADHD have a more difficult time with postponed gratification (e.g., tasks such as homework) rather than those tasks that provide more immediate gratification, such as video games (Swanson, Baler, & Volkow, 2011). Students with attention problems have a difficult time recording assignments, knowing when they are due, and establishing an organizational sequence that enables them to complete the task on time. For this reason, homework record sheets are often developed and implemented by teachers and then monitored by parents.

Figure 6.6 provides an example of a daily assignment and homework log.

Tips for Teachers 6.7 provides guidelines that will help reduce the trauma often associated with homework for students with ADHD.

Tips for Teachers 6.8 lists some of the ways teachers can help children they suspect may have ADHD.

Table 6.1 • Educational Interventions

GOAL	SUGGESTIONS
Following Directions	Cue the student that you are going to provide directions: "Time to listen—I'm going to tell you what I want you to do." Cue the student as to how many parts he or she will be asked to follow in the directions: "There are three parts to these directions; you will need to do all three parts." Number the parts so that they are easily remembered: "First, I want you to write your name on the top of the paper. Second, I want you to cross out three problems you do not want to do, and third, I want you to finish the assignment before lunch."
Preventing Distraction	Establish work centers that are well defined and have minimal overlap with other work centers. Provide quiet centers for each activity. Provide specified time for noisy or more active centers. Work to eliminate the number of distractions in the room. Establish a work place in the room that is distraction-free.
Promoting Attention	Cue students when you want them to listen to you: "I'm going to say something you will need to know." Break work units into small parts and segments with one or two activities so students can finish them and then move on to the next work unit. Tell students how long you want them to work before a break: "I am going to ask you to work for 20 minutes on this reading task and then we will take a 3-minute break and walk around the room." Let the students know when they are listening and paying attention and that you appreciate it: "I like the way you are watching me and listening while I explain."
Promoting Remembering	Provide clear and limited directions that are easy to follow. Ask students to repeat directions after you state them. Ask students to repeat the key ideas you want them to learn.
Completing Assignments	Provide work assignments in manageable units (e.g., reduce the number of problems that students need to complete as long as they get a certain number of problems correct). Provide opportunities for assignments to be broken into smaller work units and turned in at earlier times so that the entire project is completed on time but in smaller units: The title of the book report is due, then the summary of the first chapter is due, and then the summaries of the remaining three chapters are due. Provide a model of the assignment when it is finished and illustrate how the final assignment can be broken into workable units to complete.
Reducing Impulsivity	Show students how to do the work, have a checklist for what they need to do, and have a reward system tied to the completion of all the steps.
Increasing Attention to Detail	Explain what details in the assignment are important. Provide an example of the assignment with those details completed correctly. Provide examples of assignments done well and ask the student to self-analyze the differences between their assignment and the one completed with appropriate attention to detail. Ask them how they would revise their assignment to be better aligned with expectations.
Improving Test Taking	Reduce test anxiety by telling students when tests will be given, how important they are, and how feedback will be given. If possible, give the student as much time as needed to complete each test. If possible, break the test into manageable units and give students a break after each unit. If possible, allow students alternative means of responding to the test.

6.8.2 Medication as One Aspect of Treatment for ADHD

The identification of ADHD in children frequently involves a pediatrician, psychologist, and/or psychiatrist. These professionals may recommend that the student be given medication as one aspect of treatment for ADHD. The most typical type of medication is **stimulant medication**, which includes Ritalin (methylphenidate). Other drugs that have been approved for youngsters (meaning that the drug has been tested by the U.S. Food and Drug Administration and decided to be safe) include amphetamine, methylphenidate, atomoxetine, dextroamphetamine, and dexmethylphenidate (National

FIGURE 6.6 **Daily assignment and homework log**

Student: ____________			**Week of:** ____________		
Day/ Subject	**Class Assignment**	**Finished** Y N	**Homework Assignment**	**Materials Needed**	**Finished** Y N
Special Projects			Materials/Clothes Needed		
Tests			Teacher/Parent Notes		

TIPS FOR TEACHERS 6.7

Guidelines That Help Reduce Trauma Associated with Homework for Students with ADHD

- *Keep homework assignments separate from unfinished classwork.* Unfinished classwork should remain in class. This helps students to differentiate between classwork and homework. If unfinished classwork becomes homework (as an add-on to the already assigned homework), students can easily become overwhelmed.
- *Establish routines for assigning, collecting, and evaluating homework so that students know what to expect.* Students are more likely to buy in to homework if they understand how it fits into the classroom routine.
  - *Consistency with homework is essential.* Decide which days during the week you will give homework and be consistent: You have homework in reading on Monday and Wednesday and homework in math on Tuesday and Thursday. To the extent possible, maintain this consistent schedule.
- *Use homework as practice for material that has already been taught.* Don't use homework as a means for teaching new information. Homework should be on the student's independent reading level and provide for review and practice.
- *Identify the minimum amount necessary to demonstrate learning.* Understanding and mastering the task are more important than completing an extensive amount of work. Consider shortening the task for these students. It is better that they do a small amount well than a lot of work poorly.
- *Provide timelines for tasks associated with long-term assignments.* Rather than telling students the date a long-term assignment is due, help them problem solve a timeline for completing the key components of the assignment. Pair them with a buddy or work cooperatively with parents to ensure that each component in the timeline is completed.
- *Homework folder.* Allow the student to design or select an attractive folder for homework. Use the folder as the location for homework that goes home and returns to school.
- *Involve families.* Communication with families (e.g., homework notebooks, recorded messages that state assignments, homework hotlines, email, websites) about both the value of homework as well as specific assignments and timelines helps families support students in completing work outside of school.

TIPS FOR TEACHERS 6.8

Ten Ways Teachers Can Help Students They Suspect Might Have ADHD

1. Discuss with other professionals such as the school psychologist or counselor to confirm the behaviors you are observing.
2. Discuss with the parents to determine whether they observe the same behaviors at home and other settings.
3. Ask other professionals to observe you and the students in your class to provide suggestions for how you might improve behavior and learning for the target students.
4. Get a formal diagnosis. Work with the school or choose a specialist who has knowledge and experience with ADHD. An evaluation should be able to determine other learning, psychological, or physical problems that may look like or coexist with ADHD.
5. If a diagnosis is made, gather information about medication and behavioral treatments. Write notes about how these interventions are working outside of school.
6. Play an active role in IEP or Section 504 plan development. Parents are valuable resources to professionals and can help design a program that works for the family and the school. Keep records of all documentation. This is especially important if parents and the school disagree at any point in planning or implementing services.
7. Work with the parents and school to identify problems and possible solutions. Parents and children with ADHD are protected by federal laws. If parents and the school cannot agree on services, try mediation; as a last result, consider a due-process hearing to ensure that the child with ADHD is getting the services and support he or she needs to be successful at school.
8. Consider seeking behavioral therapy or social skills training to support the students' behavior.
9. Organize the classroom schedule so that predictable routines are provided and made clear to all students.
10. When students break rules, respond to them in a calm and matter-of-fact way, reminding them of the rules and applying reasonable consequences. Although no one educational treatment package has been demonstrated to yield successful outcomes for all students with ADHD, the best treatment procedures to date are those that involve a range of instructional and behavioral supports and accommodations, which may be implemented in conjunction with medication (National Institute of Mental Health, 2015; Pfiffner & DuPaul, 2014).

Video Example from YouTube

MyEdLab
Video Example 6.6.
Watch the YouTube video "Treatments for ADHD: Medication, Behavior Therapy and the New AAP Guidelines" to learn about American Academy of Pediatrics recommendations for treatment of children with ADHD. What questions might you ask a pediatrician about children with ADHD? https://www.youtube.com/watch?v=PNSM6KrFxHI?

Institute of Mental Health, 2015). Between 65% and 75% of children with ADHD respond positively to a single medication, and this percentage increases if an alternative medication is introduced (Conner, 2015). However, medication is only one aspect of a treatment plan and should be paired with behavioral and/or academic interventions (National Institute of Mental Health, 2015; Smith & Shapiro, 2015; Swanson et al., 2011).

Many adults and parents are concerned about providing medications to children. It is important that a highly qualified physician as well as other well-trained personnel (e.g., psychologist or psychiatrist) be involved in decision making. However, youngsters who are provided either medication management alone or medication management with the services of a behavior therapist have demonstrated superior results as compared to youngsters who were provided routine community treatment or only behavioral intervention (National Institute of Mental Health, 2014; Smith & Shapiro, 2015).

The decision to use medication as one part of a treatment program can be a tumultuous one for parents who, unsure about the outcomes associated with medical treatment, fear negative side effects. As a teacher, you will want to monitor the positive and negative effects of medication and work with the parents so that the physician can be informed. It is not unusual for teachers to be asked to complete behavior rating forms as the physician works to adjust the medication dosage. Linda Wellens, a kindergarten teacher, comments:

> This year I had a student, Alex, who was identified as having ADHD with hyperactivity–impulsivity. His mother called me frequently to check on how he was doing in

Table 6.2 • Common Medications Used to Treat ADHD

MEDICATION	EFFECTS
Methylphenidate (better known by its brand name, Ritalin)	Methylphenidates are stimulant medications that help individuals with ADHD to concentrate and focus.
Concerta, Focalin, Metadate, and Methylin	These are all types of methylphenidate.
Atomoxetine (better known by its brand name, Strattera)	A nonstimulant medication for individuals with low response or who experience adverse reaction to stimulants.

school. He had been kicked out of three preschools before he even started kindergarten, and she was worried about how he would perform. Alex just couldn't sit still. He would try to stay in his seat and then would jump up and start playing with toys or building with blocks. He just seemed to need a frequent release. He was a handful, but I managed to set up a behavior modification program that was highly effective. One of the things that helped the most is that his parents and his behavioral pediatrician agreed that he would benefit from medication. Then we worked as a team to monitor his reaction and progress.

Stimulant medication works like a pair of eyeglasses, helping the individual to focus. It can also reduce the sense of inner turmoil and anxiety that is so common with ADHD. Stimulant medication works by adjusting a chemical imbalance that affects the neurotransmitters in the parts of the brain that regulate attention, impulse control, and mood (Conner, 2015).

See Table 6.2 for a list of common medications used to treat ADHD.

6.8.3 Teacher's Role in Monitoring Medication

As a classroom teacher, your role in monitoring the medication is important. Work with the parents and doctor to observe the following:

- Changes in impulsivity, attentiveness, activity level, frustration level, organizational skills, behavioral inhibition, and interest in schoolwork
- Changes in academic performance
- Changes related to changes in dosage of the medication
- Possible side effects (loss of appetite, stomachaches, sleepiness, headaches, mood changes, irritability)
- Duration of the medication dosage

The one thing all professionals agree on about treatment of ADHD with medication is that it should always be considered one component of an overall treatment plan (National Institute of Mental Health, 2015; Smith & Shapiro, 2015). Medical treatment is one part of a complete management and intervention program. School districts are prohibited from requiring a child to get a prescription for medications as a condition of school attendance or receiving services under IDEIA 2004. Schools, parents, the physician, and the counselor or psychologist all need to work as a team to develop a coordinated effort to meet the needs of students with ADHD.

MyEdLab **Self-Check 6.8**

MyEdLab **Application Exercise 6.8:** Instructional Guidelines and Accommodations for Students with ADHD

6 SUMMARY

- The term *learning disabilities* is used to describe a heterogeneous group of students who, despite adequate cognitive functioning, have difficulty with learning, particularly in academics. Dyslexia, dysgraphia, and dyscalculia are three types of learning disabilities that refer to extreme difficulty in learning to read, write, and do mathematics, respectively.
- Students with learning disabilities represent a range of characteristics that include low performance in one or more academic areas, unexpected low performance considering their overall ability, and ineffective or inefficient information processing.
- Evidence of discrepancy and achievement is no longer required when diagnosing a student as having a learning disability. Instead many professionals are using multiple criteria and data sources that are derived from traditional psychological testing that is typically administered to an individual by a school psychologist or diagnostician, data from teacher and parental observations and curriculum-based measures, and data based on students' response to intervention.
- Because the characteristics of students with learning disabilities are heterogeneous, the types of learning accommodations used for students with LD vary. Accommodations that generally assist students with learning disabilities include teaching the students at their instructional level, using interactive groups of six or fewer, and using a combination of direct instruction and cognitive strategy instruction. Other strategies that facilitate their learning include providing a framework for learning, modeling the processes and strategies, teaching self-regulation, providing opportunities for extended practice and application, using learning tools and aids, adjusting workloads and time requirements, presenting information and allowing students to demonstrate learning in multiple ways, and teaching students to use memory strategies.
- Attention deficit hyperactivity disorder (ADHD) refers to difficulty in attention and has two factors: inattention and hyperactivity–impulsivity. Students can display one or both of these factors.
- The core characteristics of ADHD are lack of behavior inhibition and difficulty with executive functioning, or the ability to regulate one's thinking and behavior. Other characteristics include poor sustained attention and vigilance, impulsivity with poor delay of gratification, hyperactivity and poorly regulated activity, diminished rule-governed behavior, and increased variability of task performance.
- Identification of ADHD often involves a medical evaluation from a pediatrician, psychologist, or psychiatrist outside the school system. This evaluation should rule out other reasons for the student's behavior problems and evaluate the student's difficulty with attention and behavioral inhibition. This is usually accomplished through the use of interviews and/or the completion of behavioral rating scales by parents, teachers, and, when appropriate, the student.
- Classroom interventions to assist students with ADHD include using novelty in instruction and directions, maintaining a schedule, providing organizational assistance, providing rewards consistently and often, communicating briefly and clearly, teaching students self-regulation, and arranging the environment to facilitate attention. In some situations, medication is another option. Teachers must work with parents and doctors to ensure they are aware of proper dosages.

THINK AND APPLY

1. Now that you have read this chapter, review Tammy's experiences in working with Adrian and Lenny. If you could talk to Tammy and the parents of Adrian and Lenny, what questions would you ask them to gain greater insights about the challenges that face children with LD, ADHD, or both?
2. Students with learning disabilities can exhibit an array of characteristics. Discuss the signals for possible learning disabilities listed in Figure 6.1 with a small group of classmates. Talk about whether you have seen children in classrooms display any of these signals and how they had an effect on student learning.
3. Go to the websites of your state department of education and local school district to find out their procedures for identification of students with LD. What questions would you pose to a school administrator or special education teacher to further clarify these procedures?
4. Select a lesson in which you are going to teach a new skill or strategy. Think about how you can modify the lesson

to provide more opportunities for you and the students to model or demonstrate the skill or strategy, and more opportunities for the students to practice the skill or strategy. Consider how you might make adjustments for students with learning disabilities.

5. This chapter provides a discussion of common myths associated with ADHD. Choose one of these "myths" and use multiple resources to prepare a response to a colleague or parent who might ask you about this aspect of ADHD.
6. Check the CHADD website. Identify resources that CHADD provides for parents and teachers to learn more about the characteristics of students with ADHD.
7. Work with a small group of your classmates to identify and review teacher rating scales that are used as part of the identification process for ADHD.
8. Prepare for an interview as a teacher with a principal in which you know one of the questions will be, "How do you plan to support the students with ADHD in your class?"

7 Teaching Students with Communication Disorders

Learning Outcomes

7.1 Describe what communication disorders are, in what areas of communication might students have difficulty, and what you might expect in terms of the percentage of students with communication disorders in your classroom.

7.2 Provide examples of some of the causes of communication disorders.

7.3 Identify signs to look for at school if students are having difficulty in language content, form, and/or use, and with whom you would work to determine whether a student needs further assistance in the area of communication.

7.4 Compare and contrast the guidelines and accommodations for working with students who have communication disorders.

7.5 Describe practices you could suggest to the parents of a child with a speech or language disorder to support the child's communication.

INTERVIEW: LORRI JOHNSON

Lorri Johnson is one of five third-grade teachers at Drexel Elementary School. In her class of twenty-seven students, one student (Samantha) has a communication disorder. Lorri also has two students with learning disabilities, one of whom receives support from both the speech and language pathologist and the special education teacher. Lorri has established a good relationship with both the special education teacher and the speech and language specialist so that she can integrate practices that promote the language and learning of her students with special needs.

Samantha is a student with a communication disorder who works with the speech and language pathologist, Nancy Meyers, for 30 minutes twice a week. Nancy and Lorri check with each other informally about once a week regarding Samantha's progress. Lorri's description of Samantha clearly shows that she understands Samantha's needs and makes accommodations to help her communicate successfully in the classroom. Lorri notes,

> The way I would describe Samantha is as a late bloomer when it comes to language. Early in the year, Nancy and I sat down with Samantha's file, and we discussed her history and needs. Samantha did not start talking until she was almost 3 years old. At age 4, Samantha began attending Head Start and was identified as a child with a speech and language disorder. She started working with a speech and language pathologist at that time. She has continued to receive services since then. Her sentences are short, and she continues to have difficulty producing complex sentence structures, does not use adjectives and adverbs to elaborate, and has significant difficulty with verb tenses and irregular verbs. Samantha also has a limited vocabulary when she speaks, and I am unsure if she is getting the concepts that I am teaching.
>
> I work to make my class successful for Samantha in several ways. First, I usually don't call on Samantha in large-class discussions unless she raises her hand. We have a deal that she can't use this rule to escape listening and learning and that I expect her to contribute to large-group discussions at least several times a day. But this way she gets to pick the opportunities. Second, I frequently "check for understanding" by asking students questions that allow me to determine whether they really are learning the key ideas of my instruction. To keep the class active, I have them use thumbs up, stand up, clap hands, and so on to indicate whether they understand. I think Samantha and the other students feel comfortable telling me they don't understand, for I encourage and praise them for the questions they ask. Third, I ask Samantha to take leadership roles that require her to talk when we work in small groups, and I encourage her to help other students when doing independent seatwork. Finally, through reading and writing, I can focus on the areas that are difficult for her in oral language. For example, we have been working on using adjectives to make our writing more interesting. Samantha has really improved in this area of writing, and now I am asking the students to take their new descriptive written language and use it more when they talk.

CHAPTER OUTLINE

I guess, overall, Samantha is a successful learner in my class, but I would like to know more about communication disorders so I can provide more encouragement and assistance.

Introduction

Many other teachers (both elementary and secondary) share Lorri's views that they know more about teaching reading and writing than they do about oral language. In this chapter, you will learn about the development of oral communication, the characteristics of students with communication disorders, strategies for identifying these students, and techniques for promoting oral communication and language development in general education classrooms. This chapter focuses on those areas and should provide you with a number of techniques and strategies for working with students who have communication disorders or other disabilities that result in delayed communication development.

7.1 COMMUNICATION DISORDERS

Communication is the process of exchanging ideas, information, needs, and desires (Owens, Farhella, & Metz, 2015). Both in school and in society, oral and written communication are powerful resources. We use communication to do the following:

- Develop and maintain contact and relationships with others
- Gain and give information
- Control and persuade
- Create and imagine
- Communicate feelings
- Monitor our own behavior when we talk to ourselves

Even though written communication plays a key role in school, speaking and listening are the most frequently used means of learning. Consequently, students with communication disorders may experience difficulties in many aspects of school, including both academically and socially (Joffe & Nippold, 2012).

The term **communication disorders** refers to students who demonstrate difficulties with exchanging knowledge, ideas, opinions, desires, and feelings (Owens et al., 2015). Communication is thought to be problematic when it deviates enough to interfere with the transmission of messages, stands out as being unusual or different, or produces negative feelings or responses. Communication disorders range in severity from mild to profound. They may be developmental or acquired through injuries or diseases that affect the brain. A communication disorder may be the primary disability, or it may be secondary to other disabilities (American Speech-Language-Hearing Association [ASHA], 2015). For example, students with learning disabilities and intellectual disabilities often have secondary language disabilities and receive services from a speech and language pathologist. A **speech and language pathologist (SLP)** is trained to provide screening, assessment, and treatment for students who have difficulties with speech (including pronunciation) as well as with language (including stuttering, inadequate language development, and poor use of syntax).

Video Example from YouTube

MyEdLab
Video Example 7.1.
Watch the YouTube video "ASHA President Judith Page: Identify the Signs of Communication Disorder" for an overview of communication disorders. What questions might you ask the American Speech-Hearing Association about the services the association provides for classroom teachers? https://www.youtube.com/watch?v=lDBPlUyvJ5c

When students enter school, they are expected to communicate by listening and speaking. Some students may have difficulty transmitting the message or information. Although many children "outgrow" early language difficulties, some children with delayed language development at age 2 continue to have communication problems throughout their preschool and school years. This is particularly true when early detection and intervention do not occur. Consequently, students may encounter difficulty with academics (especially reading and writing) and with social relationships as well (ASHA, 2011). Consider the following two examples. When Sarah entered kindergarten, her speech was so difficult to understand that both the teacher and the other students struggled to understand her. Sarah has difficulty with speech, or the vocal production of language. Jeffrey, by contrast, has difficulty understanding the messages of others and communicating messages to others. His speech (vocal production) is adequate, but the message is unclear. Jeffrey's difficulties have to do with communicating through using language. In the *Diagnostic and Statistical Manual of Mental Disorders* (*DSM-5*), communication disorders were divided into five broad categories: (1) speech disorders, (2) language disorders, (3) stuttering, (4) social communication disorder, and (5) other communication disorders (specified and unspecified) (American Psychiatric Association, 2013).

In what ways might developmental delays in language be manifested? What aspects of communication are important in identifying students with possible language-learning disabilities?

7.1.1 Speech Disorders

Individuals with **speech disorders** have difficulty with the verbal means of communication. The major components of speech are articulation, voice, and, fluency. *Articulation* has to do with the production of speech sounds, *voice* focuses on the quality of speech, including resonance, pitch, and intensity, and *fluency* refers to the flow and rhythm of language.

Speech sound disorders

Speech sound disorders (traditionally referred to as *articulation disorders*) occur when students are unable to produce the various sounds and sound combinations of language (ASHA, 2015; APA, 2013; Hulit, Fahey, & Howard, 2015). It is not unusual for SLPs to work with elementary-age children who have a delay in the development of articulation, because the ability to produce the speech sounds continues to develop through age 8. Learning to produce the speech sounds, no matter what the language, usually proceeds in a fairly consistent sequence, but there may be as much as a 3-year variance between the time early learners start producing a particular sound and the time late learners start producing the same sound. One of the last sounds that students learn is the "th" sound, so if students are 7 and still having difficulty with the sound but can pronounce all other sounds, then it may not be a cause for alarm. Figure 7.1 demonstrates the developmental progression of speech sounds and clarifies why many children enter school still in the process of learning to produce such sounds as /r/, /l/, /s/, /ch/, /sh/, /z/, /j/, /v/, /zh/, and voiced and voiceless /th/.

The production of speech sounds generally develops earlier in girls than in boys. Table 7.1 compares the development of girls and boys, noting the age at which 90% of girls and boys can articulate the sounds.

If you teach kindergarten through second grade, you will have the opportunity to hear these sounds developing in some of your students. Even if these sounds are not fully developed, children's speech, by the time they enter kindergarten, should be at least 90% intelligible.

Types of articulation errors include sound substitutions, omissions, additions, and distortions. The errors can occur at the beginning, middle, and/or end of words. Substitutions and omissions are the most common errors. In *substitutions*, one sound is

FIGURE 7.1 **Developmental sequence for the production of speech sounds**

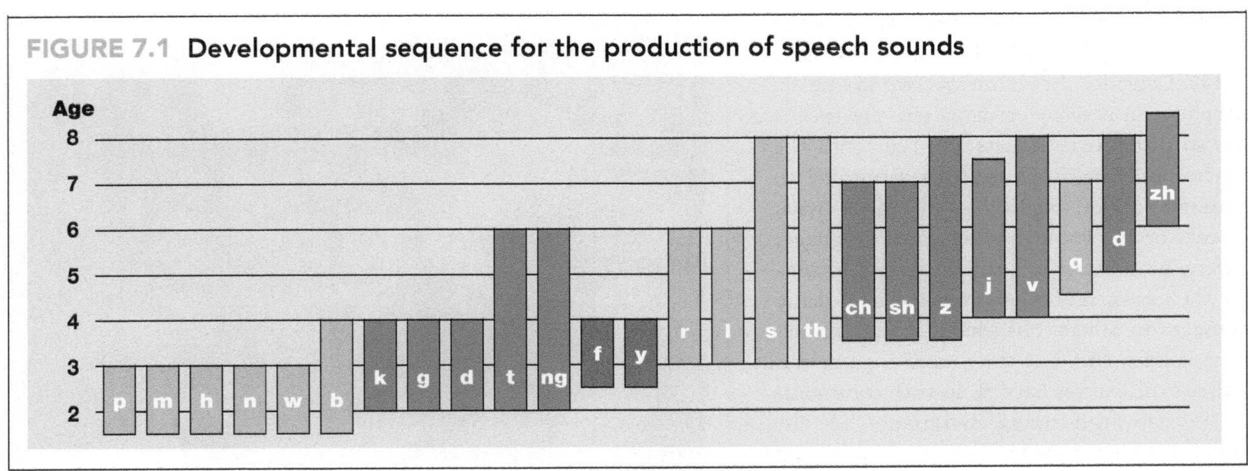

substituted for another. Common substitutions at the beginning of words include /w/ for /r/ (*wabbit* for *rabbit*), /t/ for /c/ (*tat* for *cat*), /b/ for /v/ (*balentine* for *valentine*), and /f/ for /th/ (*free* for *three*). *Omissions* occur when a sound is not included in a word. Because blends (two consonants that go together and make two separate sounds, such as /br/, /pl/, /cr/, and /gl/) are later in developing, many omission errors occur when young children or students with

Table 7.1 • Comparison of the Development of Speech Sound Production in Boys and Girls*

			BOYS		
AGE	**3**	**4**	**5**	**6**	**7**
	P	ng	y	zh	f
	B			wh	l
	M			j	r
	H				ch
	W				sh
	D				s
	N				z
	K				th (voiceless)
	T				v
	G				th (voiced)
			GIRLS		
AGE	**3**	**4**	**5**	**6**	**7**
	P	l	j	sh	s
	B	t	y	ch	z
	M			r	th (voiceless)
	W			zh	v
	D		f	f	th (voiced)
	N			wh	
	K				
	G				
	h				
	ng				

*The age at which 90% of boys and girls can articulate sounds. *Note:* Vowel sounds are produced correctly by 90% of all children by age 3. Consonant blends—/tr/, /bl/, /pr/, and so on—develop between ages 7 and 9.

Source: "Articulation disorders," by R. S. Work, 1994, in S. Adler & D. A. King (Eds.), *Oral communication problems in children and adolescents* (p. 3). Copyright© 1994 by Pearson Education. Reprinted by permission of the publisher.

communication difficulties leave off the second sound in the blend (e.g., *boo* for *blue*, *pity* for *pretty*). Final sounds also are commonly omitted, particularly the later-developing sounds such as /s/, /sh/, /z/, and voiced and voiceless /th/. For example, youngsters might say *mi* instead of *miss* or *mat* instead of *math*. As a classroom teacher, you must listen for children whose articulation might be developmentally delayed or whose articulation errors are so frequent that they significantly affect intelligibility. You will want to talk with the SLP and the parents of these children to learn more.

Articulation is affected not only by development but also by regional dialects and cultural uses. Variations or dialects of a language are products of historical, cultural, geographic, social, economic, ethnic, and political factors (Hegde, 2006; Owens, 2016). For example, Bostonians often use /er/ for /a/ (as in *idea/ider* and *data/dater*), and Southerners draw out vowels. We all speak a dialect of English—it is interesting to learn and appreciate the dialects of other English speakers.

How can a teacher determine whether students have an articulation disorder? When a student in your class has difficulty saying sounds that are said correctly by other students, the student may have an articulation problem. This is particularly true if the student's first language is English and the errors make it difficult for others to understand the child's speech. It is important to remember that some articulation errors are developmental and expected; many preschoolers have articulation errors that disappear over time. It is also important to recognize that some errors may be a result of the student's cultural background. For example, speakers of African American Vernacular English may substitute the /d/ sound for /th/, such as *dem* instead of *them*. This is not an articulation error.

Articulation of English sounds is also affected when students are learning English as a second language (ESL). Sounds made in one language might not be made in another language or might not be made in the same manner. As a classroom teacher, you must remember that differences in articulation due to regional or cultural dialects or English as a second language should not be considered disorders.

Voice disorders

Voice disorders relate to the quality of the voice itself. Voice disorders can occur when individuals experience difficulty in passing air from the lungs to the vocal chords (**phonation**) or through the throat, nose, or mouth (**resonance**).

Usually, three dimensions are considered:

- Quality (hoarse, breathy, hypernasal/hyponasal)
- Pitch (high or low, monotone)
- Intensity (loud or soft)

One common type of voice disorder found in school-age children is caused by the presence of **vocal nodules**. These nodules are the result of yelling and other forms of vocal abuse that affect voice quality. Vocal nodules, which develop because the vocal mechanism is used incorrectly or overused, are somewhat like calluses on the vocal folds. If the nodules become too large, students can lose their voices and require surgery. Generally, it takes consistent and prolonged abuse for nodules to develop, but it is important to provide students with information about good vocal hygiene, including:

- Keeping yelling to a minimum
- Breathing from the stomach
- Limiting time spent talking in noisy places
- Avoiding persistent and intense coughing

Few school-age children have the other types of voice disorders, such as those related to pitch and intensity. Should you notice students whose speech quality, pitch, and/or intensity seem to be affected, talk with your school's SLP.

Stuttering

Whereas articulation disorders involve difficulty with the production of sounds, fluency disorders involve difficulty with the rate and flow of speech. All of us are nonfluent to some degree when we communicate. We hesitate in the middle of sentences, break the flow of language with meaningless sounds and fillers (e.g., *ah*, *um*, *you know*, *like*), repeat parts of words, and speak quickly. We are more nonfluent in stressful, novel, or exciting situations. When we have difficulty thinking of a word, we may become dysfluent.

However, when a child's dysfluencies become more intense and are more problematic than the dysfluencies of normal speakers, the child might have a problem of fluency referred to as stuttering. Stuttering (or childhood onset-fluency disorder) is one of the most common types of fluency disorders in which sounds, syllables, or words are repeated or held in a manner that breaks the flow of speech (APA, 2013; National Institute on Deafness and Other Communication Disorders, 2014). About one in twenty children under the age of 5 demonstrate some form of stuttering. Typically, this goes away after the age of 5, but if it does not, then it is beneficial to refer the student to treatment by the speech and language specialist. Most young children, at different times during the preschool years, are nonfluent in a manner that resembles stuttering. Stuttering usually first appears between the ages of 2½ and 4, and for the vast majority of youngsters (approximately 75%), stuttering disappears by age 10. Boys are three to four times more likely to stutter than are girls (ASHA, 2015). While the exact cause of childhood onset-fluency disorder (stuttering) is not known, there is some evidence that the onset of stuttering is genetic in nature. Stuttering can also occur in school-aged children as a result of hearing loss, side effects of medications, or psychological conditions.

School-age language and social communication disorders

Language functions as an integral part of the communication process because it allows us to represent ideas using a conventional code. A person's ability to understand what is being communicated is referred to as comprehension or receptive language, whereas a person's ability to convey the intended message is referred to as production or expressive language.

Students with language disorders may have developmental delays in comprehension or receptive language. These students frequently ask for information to be repeated or clarified. In school, these students may have difficulties with following directions, understanding abstract concepts, and comprehending multiple meanings. Students with production or expressive language difficulties generally communicate less frequently than their peers. These students may have difficulty using correct grammar, thinking of the right word to convey meaning, and repairing communication when the listener doesn't understand.

To help us think about language disorders, language has been divided into content (semantics) and form (phonology, morphology, and syntax). Social communication disorders are related to difficulties with language use (pragmatics) (APA, 2013, 2015). It is the interaction of content, form, and use that creates language (Bloom & Lahey, 1978).

7.1.2 Language Content

Semantics refers to the meaning or content of words and word combinations we are communicating. When you teach a lesson (as in social studies or science), you are teaching concepts and the labels for those concepts (vocabulary). For example, students often ask for the label for an idea (e.g., "What is that?" or "What are you doing?"), and they ask about what a word means (e.g., "What is a penguin?" or "What does *freedom* mean?").

Teaching content focuses on teaching vocabulary, word categories and relationships, multiple meanings, and figurative language. Gloria Huerra, a high school social studies teacher, comments:

> Grouping words by categories and using relationship words (like *if ... then* and *because*) are often difficult for students with language impairments or for English language learners. It is also the multiple meanings of words and the figurative language that holds up

their learning. I consistently highlight these in our discussions of social studies. One way that I highlight them is by writing them so that they can be projected and visible to all students and then discussing them prior to reading. Then I cue the students to look for them when they read. We discuss them after reading by finding them in the text and reviewing their use.

7.1.3 Vocabulary

As students develop language, their vocabulary, or stock of words, and their ability to understand and talk about abstract concepts increase quickly. For example, children's speaking vocabulary, vocabulary that is used as part of their oral language, starts at age 2 with about 200 words. By the time students are 6 they have acquired about 10,000 words—although the range in words known is great, from 4,000 to 20,000. The number of words that students have in their receptive vocabulary, words they understand but may not use, is greater than that of their speaking vocabulary. By the age of 12, students' receptive vocabulary has increased to 50,000 words (Owens, 2016). In comparison, when technical words are discounted, average adult speakers use about 10,000 words in everyday conversation, and an estimated 60,000 to 80,000 words are known and used by the average high school graduate.

As Mary Armanti got to know Krista, a student with communication disorders in her third-grade class, she discovered that Krista's vocabulary was very limited. During sharing or small-group discussion, Krista used simple words and did not expand on her ideas (compared to the other students). Concerned about Krista's limited vocabulary, Mary worked with the SLP to develop some classroom strategies to increase Krista's vocabulary. These strategies included Mary elaborating on what Krista said—that is, to model for Krista how to use a more complex, richer vocabulary. For example, when Krista volunteered, "The egg hatched," as she watched a bird nest outside the classroom window, Mary elaborated on her statement: "Yes, the bird's egg just hatched. The new bird is so tiny and fuzzy."

The oral language of the students in your classes is influenced significantly by the oral language they are exposed to at home and at school (Spartis, 2015). Of the words in a child's vocabulary, 86% to 98% are words contained in their parents' vocabularies (Hart & Risley, 2003). Betty Hart and Todd Risley (2003) conducted more than 1,300 observations of forty-two families over a 2½-year-period. The families all had children who were learning to talk and were observed talking and interacting casually at home. By the age of 3, children had very different home language experiences. For example, the average child in a welfare family was exposed to 616 words an hour, the working-class child was exposed to 1,251 words an hour, and the average child in a professional family was exposed to 2,153 words an hour. Early language experience also predicted later language ability and school performance.

What can teachers do when students come to school with low language and vocabulary development? Teachers can advocate for intensive early intervention services for children and families to close the language gap between children from different types of families. Furthermore, teachers can provide direct and systematic instruction of word meanings as part of their everyday instruction. This includes general vocabulary as well as academic vocabulary or the words commonly used in school and in textbooks (Beach, Sanchez, Flynn, & O'Connor, 2015; Palumbo, Kramer-Vida, & Hunt, 2015).

Words selected for concentrated vocabulary instruction should include words from three tiers (Beck, McKeown, & Kucan, 2008, 2013). Tier 1 words include general vocabulary or words normally included in everyday conversation. While students typically pick such vocabulary through natural verbal interaction and reading, students with communication disorders may need more intensive focus on common, high frequency words. Tier 2 and 3 words constitute academic vocabulary. Tier 2 words are customary terms used across subject areas (e.g., examine, acquire, journal, theory). Tier 3 words represent technical vocabulary used in specific academic disciplines (e.g., in mathematics: equation, ratio, perimeter). Teaching Tier 2 and Tier 3 words using student-friendly language, in-depth discussion, word play, and writing connects can expand student word banks and support academic learning from text (Beach et al., 2015; Spies & Dema, 2014).

Word categories and word relationships

From kindergarten through twelfth grade, students' ability to learn to understand and organize words and concepts improves significantly (Owens, 2016). Students learn to group concepts by abstract features (such as animate and inanimate), spatial features, temporal relationships, or function. For example, in learning about fossils, students learn to simultaneously classify different types of fossils (e.g., trilobites, crinoids, brachiopods) according to plant/animal, extinct/not extinct, and location (e.g., sea, lakes, or land). By using semantic feature analysis, in which the categories or critical features are placed along one axis of a matrix and the specific vocabulary along the other axis, teachers can guide student discussion about the relationships among concepts and then visually represent those relationships. Relationships can be noted as positive, negative, or no relationship or can be rated as to the degree of relationship along a scale (see Figure 7.2).

Understanding the relationships among concepts is important to successful learning. Types of relationships include the following categories:

- Comparative (*taller than*)
- Spatial (*above, under*)
- Temporal–sequential (*before, first*)
- Causal (*because, therefore*)
- Conditional (*if ... then*)
- Conjunctive (*and*)
- Disjunctive (*either ... or*)
- Contrastive (*but, although*)
- Enabling (*so that, in order that*)

FIGURE 7.2 Semantic feature analysis for a chapter on fossils

RELATIONSHIP CHART							
	Type of Life		Location			Extinct?	
Important Words	**Plant**	**Animal**	**Sea**	**Lakes**	**Land**	**Extinct**	**Not Extinct**
Trilobites							
Crinoids							
Giant cats							
Coral							
Bryozoans							
Guide fossils							
Dinosaurs							
Fresh water fish							
Brachiopods							
Small horses							
Ferns							
Enormous winged bugs							
Trees							

Key:
+ = positive relationship
− = opposite or negative relationship
∘ = no relationship
? = uncertain

Teaching relationship vocabulary is important for students' understanding of content subjects such as science, social studies, and math.

Multiple meanings

Children also learn through context and instruction about the **multiple meanings** of words. For example, the word *bank* has several meanings and can function as both a noun and a verb:

- "Lou sat on the bank fishing."
- "You can bank on him to be there."
- "Put your money in the bank for now."
- "You can bank the basketball into the hoop."

Many students with communication disorders have more limited vocabularies, and their word meanings are generally more concrete and less specific than those of other students. These students also have greater difficulty understanding multiple meanings and when to apply which meaning.

Figurative language

Another area of language content, **figurative language**, represents abstract concepts and usually requires an inferential rather than a literal interpretation. Figurative language allows students to use language in truly creative ways and includes such uses as simile ("busy as a bee"), metaphor ("you are what you eat"), personification ("my laptop is my best friend"), and idioms ("my bad"). Students who are exposed to these types of language at home and through print acquire understanding of their meaning—other students, especially students who are acquiring English as a second language, may need to have them taught. The following types of figurative language may require explanation for some students:

- Idioms (e.g., "It's raining cats and dogs.")
- Metaphors (e.g., "She watched him with an eagle eye.")
- Similes (e.g., "He ran like a frightened rabbit.")
- Proverbs (e.g., "The early bird catches the worm.")

Figure 7.3 presents some common American English idioms.

Students with language disorders, students from other cultures or regions, and students for whom English is a second language may have difficulty with figurative language. Yet figurative language, particularly idioms, prevails in the classroom. Classroom research shows that teachers use idioms in approximately 11% of what they say. Understanding and using figurative language is associated with higher performance among adolescents on literacy measures (Dean Qualls, O'Brien, Blood, & Scheffner Hammer, 2003).

7.1.4 Language Form

Difficulties with the form of language are usually quite noticeable to classroom teachers. Students not only have difficulty pronouncing certain sounds and using prefixes, suffixes, and endings on words, but also use sentences that have poor word order and grammar. As was mentioned earlier, form refers to the structure of the language and includes phonology, morphology, and syntax.

Phonology

Phonology focuses on the sounds of language and the rules that determine how those sounds fit together. **Phonemes** are the smallest linguistic units of sound that can signal a meaning difference. In English there are approximately forty-five phonemes or speech sounds, classified as either consonants or vowels. (The section on speech sound disorders also includes information relevant to the development of phonemes.) The ability to listen

FIGURE 7.3 Common American English Idioms

See how many of the following idioms you know and can tell someone what they mean.

See if you can think of other idioms you know and add them to the list.

Animals

canary in a coal mine
drink like a fish
smart as a fox
a bull in a china shop
high on the hog
as stubborn as a mule
going to the dogs
playing possum
a bird in the hand is worth two in the bush
let the cat out of the bag
beat a dead horse
grinning like a Cheshire cat
dark horse
a leopard can't change his spots
thrown to the wolves
all bark and no bite

Body Parts

bite the bullet
flesh and blood
go out on a limb
break a leg
cast-iron stomach
chip on your shoulder
on the tip of my tongue
raised eyebrows
a slap on the wrist
turn the other cheek
put your best foot forward
an arm and a leg
put their heads together
kick the bucket

Colors

gray area
once in a blue moon
tickled pink
has a yellow streak
red-letter day
true blue

Games and Sports

ace up my sleeve
cards are stacked against me
got lost in the shuffle
keep your head above water
paddle your own canoe
ballpark figure
get to first base
keep the ball rolling
on the rebound
the ball is in your court

Foods

apple of my eye
eat crow
buy a lemon
nest egg
humble pie
a piece of cake
that takes the cake
a finger in every pie

Plants

heard it through the grapevine
resting on his laurels
shrinking violet
no bed of roses
shaking like a leaf
withered on the vine

Tools and Work

bury the hatchet
a drop in the bucket
has an axe to grind
everything but the kitchen sink
hit the nail on the head
add fuel to the fire
doctor the books
has a screw loose
a penny saved is a penny earned
hit the roof
nursing his wounds
sober as a judge

Vehicles

fix your wagon
like ships passing in the night
on the wagon
backseat driver
don't rock the boat
missed the boat
take a back seat
all in the same boat

Weather

calm before the storm
when it rains it pours
under the weather
haven't the foggiest
steal her thunder
come rain or shine
right as rain
throw caution to the wind

to and produce sounds is important not only for oral language but also for reading and writing (written language).

As students learn to decode unknown words while reading and to spell words as they write, one strategy they use is to "sound out the word" or "sound spell." Students who have difficulty generating rhyming words, segmenting words into their individual sounds, or producing individual sounds and then blending them together to make words often have difficulty using the "sound out" or "sound spell" strategies. These skills develop in the preschool and early elementary years as students experiment with sounds and sound patterns while they play with words and learn to read and write. These skills, referred to as **phonological awareness**, pertain to students' ability to recognize and segment the sounds of language and to distinguish these sounds through recognition, segmenting, deleting, and blending sounds. Youngsters who demonstrate difficulty with phonological awareness often have difficulty learning to read and spell. The reason is that hearing the sounds of language and distinguishing them allows you to map these sounds to letters and print and thus facilitates reading, writing, and spelling. This difficulty with phonological awareness has been identified as a strong predictor of later reading and spelling problems (Catts, Fey, Zhang, & Tomblin, 2001; Frost et al., 2008; Fumes & Samuelsson, 2010; Tambyraja, Farquharson, Logan, & Justice, 2015). Consequently, the ability to listen to and produce sounds plays an important role in the development not only of oral language but also of written language.

What are some of the ways in which phonological awareness can be improved?

- Phoneme isolation: What is the first sound in *milk*? What is the last sound in *bug*?
- Phoneme segmentation: Count the sounds in *fat*. Count the sounds in *lost*.
- Phoneme blending: Blend the following sounds into a word: c/a/p (cap); d/r/e/ss (dress)
- Phoneme deletion: Say the word as it changes when you delete a sound. Delete the /t/ in *trap* (*rap*); delete the /b/ in *brat* (*rat*).

Morphology

Whereas phonology focuses on sounds, morphology focuses on the rule system that governs the structure of words and word forms. And as phonemes are the smallest sound units, morphemes are the smallest units of language that convey meaning. There are two different kinds of morphemes: *free morphemes*, which can stand alone (e.g., *cat*, *run*, *pretty*, *small*, *inside*), and *bound morphemes* (prefixes, suffixes, and inflectional endings), which cannot stand alone but, when added to words, change their meaning. For example, *s* is a common morpheme in English that when used at the end of a noun changes it to plural. Students who understand both orally and in print that *cat* is singular and *cats* is plural have better understanding of what they hear and read. Another example is the prefix *re-*, which is often used to mean *do again*. Students who understand that *rewrite* means to write again will be able to generalize *re-* to other words and their meaning. Knowledge of morphology, or morphological awareness, is associated with student success in vocabulary development, decoding, spelling, and reading comprehension (Goodwin, Lipsky, & Ahn, 2012; Pacheco & Goodwin, 2013; Wolter & Pike, 2015).

Learning the different bound morphemes and their meanings can help elementary and secondary students to decode words, spell words, and determine the meaning of words. For example, students who do not recognize or know the meaning of the word *predetermination* can break it into the free morpheme *determine* (to decide) and the bound morphemes *pre-* (before) and *-tion* (denoting action in a noun). Then the students can decode the word and decide that the meaning of *predetermination* is "a decision made in advance."

Developmentally, inflectional endings are the easiest to learn, followed by suffixes and then prefixes (Owens, 2016). Although inflectional endings may be acquired through conversation, suffixes and prefixes usually require more direct instruction in both oral and written form. What does this mean for the teacher? Most students will learn how *-ing* and *-s* adjust the meaning of a word through listening and reading. However, they will require instruction in prefixes (e.g., *un-*, *re-*, *pre-*) to understand their meaning and use. This is also true for suffixes such as *-ful* and *-ment*. You can use the common prefixes, suffixes, and inflectional endings presented in Table 7.2 as a guide for teaching morphology.

Syntax

Syntax focuses on the rules that govern the order of words in sentences. During the school-age years, students continue to grow in their ability to use more complex sentence structures (Owens, 2016). Even though most students understand and generate basic sentences by age 5, first graders produce sentences that are neither completely grammatical (e.g., *He'll might go to jail*) nor reflect the syntactical complexities of the English language.

Students with language impairments and English language learners may experience difficulties in the area of syntax. Students who are learning English as a second language may understand complex syntax, particularly if similar syntax is found in their first language, but may be uncomfortable producing it.

Table 7.2 • Common Prefixes, Suffixes, and Inflectional Endings

DERIVATIONAL		INFLECTIONAL
PREFIXES	**SUFFIXES**	
a- (in, on, into, in a manner)	-able (ability, tendency, likelihood)	-ed (past)
bi- (twice, two)	-al (pertaining to, like, action, process)	-ing (at present)
de- (negative, descent, reversal)	-ance (action, state)	-s (plural)
ex- (out of, from, thoroughly)	-ation (denoting action in a noun)	-s (third person marker)
inter- (reciprocal, between, together)	-en (used to form verbs from adjectives)	-'s (possession)
mis- (ill, negative, wrong)	-ence (action, state)	
out- (extra, beyond, not)	-er (used as an agentive ending)	
over- (over)	-est (superlative)	
post- (behind, after)	-ful (full, tending)	
pre- (to, before)	-ible (ability, tendency, likelihood)	
pro- (in favor of)	-ish (belonging to)	
re- (again, backward motion)	-ism (doctrine, state, practice)	
semi- (half)	-ist (one who does something)	
super- (superior)	-ity (used for abstract nouns)	
trans- (across, beyond)	-ive (tendency or connection)	
tri- (three)	-ize (action, policy)	
un- (not, reversal)	-less (without)	
under- (under)	-ly (used to form adverbs)	
	-ment (action, product, means, state)	
	-ness (quality, state)	
	-or (used as an agentive ending)	
	-ous (full of, having, like)	
	-y (inclined to)	

Source: From *Language disorders: A functional approach to assessment and intervention* (5th ed., p. 444) by R. E. Owens, Jr., 2010, Boston: Allyn & Bacon. Copyright © 2010 by Allyn & Bacon. Reprinted by permission.

Regardless of the reason for the delay, one helpful strategy for identifying children's needs relative to syntax is to listen to the students' language and determine where they are in the developmental sequence. For example, Rebecca Blair, a third-grade teacher, noticed that several of her students with language-learning disabilities were not using the past participle (*has*/*have* + verb) during class discussions, on the playground, or during small-group discussions. She talked with Jean Gleason, the SLP, who agreed that this would be a good skill to work on, because all three students were able to use the simple past tense. To teach the skill directly, Rebecca interacted with the three students as they worked together to create and write a story in which she controlled the use of verb tense by requiring them to use the past participle. The story follows:

> Once upon a time, there was a very hungry boy named Jason. Jason decided that he would eat everything he could find in the refrigerator. All day long, he has gone to the refrigerator and eaten whatever food he could find. By the end of the day,
>
> Jason has eaten 3 pickles.
>
> Jason has eaten 5 olives.
>
> Jason has eaten 8 slices of cheese.
>
> Jason has eaten 25 grapes.
>
> Now Jason has a stomachache.

Table 7.3 • Development of Irregular Verbs

AGE IN YEARS	IRREGULAR VERBS
3–0 to 3–5	Hit, hurt
3–6 to 3–11	Went
4–0 to 4–5	Saw
4–6 to 4–11	Ate, gave
5–0 to 5–5	Broke, fell, found, took
5–6 to 5–11	Came, made, sat, threw
6–0 to 6–5	Bit, cut, drove, fed, flew, ran, wore, wrote
6–6 to 6–11	Blew, read, rode, shot
7–0 to 7–5	Drank
7–6 to 7–11	Drew, dug, hid, rang, slept, swam
8–0 to 8–5	Caught hung, left, slid
8–6 to 8–11	Built, sent, shook

Source: Information from "Children's development of irregular past tense verb forms," by K. Shipley, M. Maddox, & J. Driver, 1991, *Language, Speech, and Hearing Services in Schools, 22,* 115–122.

In discussing the story, Rebecca compared the simple past tense with the past participle and had the students think of other instances in which they could use the past participle. Rebecca had the students tell and write other stories with similar formats, and Jean, at the same time, worked on the same skill with the students. Rebecca also gave each student a quick "thumbs up" whenever she heard them use the past participle. Within 3 months, the past participle became part of their everyday language.

As sentence complexity increases, so does the average length of the sentences. During the early elementary grades, students also continue to increase in their ability to use irregular noun plurals (e.g., *mice, sheep, men*) and irregular verbs (see Table 7.3). In students with communication disorders and other disabilities, development of these irregular forms may be delayed.

Language use

The most important linguistic growth during the school-age years takes place in the area of language use, or pragmatics (Owens, 2016). Pragmatics refers to how the social context contributes to language use. For example, we learn to use language to greet others, to make requests, to inform others, and to communicate in any number of ways that are determined in large part by the social context. We also learn to adapt our language to the person we are talking to. We learn to use a different communication style with our fellow teachers than we use with our students and even different still with our families. During the school years, students become quite adept at using communication for a variety of functions. Students can use language to give and receive compliments, engage in role-playing, deal with conflicts, and ask for help. Students also learn to vary their communication style, or register, according to the listener's characteristics and knowledge of the topic. By the age of 13, students can switch from peer register to adult register (depending on the person with whom they are talking) and from formal register to informal register, depending on the setting and circumstances (McKinley & Larson, 1991; Owens, 2016).

Young children use language for such functions as gaining and holding attention, obtaining and giving information, directing and following others, expressing feelings, and role-playing. By adolescence, students demonstrate communication competence (Mobbs, Reed, & McAllister, 1993; Nippold, 1998; Owens, 2016; Wiig & Semel, 1984) in that they are able to do the following:

- Express positive and negative feelings and reactions to others
- Present, understand, and respond to information in spoken messages about people, objects, events, or processes that are not immediately visible

- Adjust their communication and vary it with different listeners
- Interpret social settings and adjust communication for these settings
- Take the conversational partner's perspective
- Comprehend the speaker's mood
- Comprehend nonverbal communication
- Understand and present complex messages
- Adapt messages to the needs of others
- Use clarification and repair in conversation
- On the basis of prior experience, approach verbal interaction with expectations of what to say and how to say it
- Relate a narrative cohesively and sequentially
- Communicate a point of view logically
- Select different forms of messages according to the age, status, and reactions of listeners
- Use sarcasm, humor, and multiple meanings
- Make deliberate use of figurative language

Individuals who experience difficulties with pragmatics and/or other aspects of social interaction or cognition may be diagnosed as having a **social communication disorder** (ASHA, 2015). Possible indicators of the disorder include problems with eye contact, body language, misreading emotions and communication cues of others, and conventions of social politeness. Social communication problems result in difficulties students may encounter in relationships with peers and adults in the school setting, at home, and beyond. Thus, professional diagnosis (with assessment sensitive to native language and cultural differences) and intervention are vital for the social, behavioral, and academic well-being of the student.

Language is used for many different communication activities. One activity that occurs frequently in school and in other settings is conversation. To determine whether students are having difficulty with the use of language, you can assess their conversational skills. See Tips for Teachers 7.1 for ideas on how to assess conversational skills.

Metalinguistics

Students who use **metalinguistics** can think about, analyze, and reflect on language, including how they use it and how it is used by others. Metalinguistics also involves understanding that language is a code for representing sounds, words, and ideas.

Young children learn to use language without really understanding how it operates and functions. They use the linguistic rules that govern language, but if you asked them

TIPS FOR TEACHERS 7.1

Assessing Your Students' Conversational Skills

Take a few minutes to think about several students you know or with whom you are currently working. Think about how they use language to communicate in social contexts.

- Do they vary their communication style depending on the listener?
- Do they present enough information for the listener to understand the message?
- If the listener is not understanding, do they take action to clarify what they said?
- Do they stay on topic?
- Do they take turns in listening and talking?
- Do they use appropriate body language and stand appropriate distances from others when they are talking?
- Do they say inappropriate or unrelated things during the conversation?

For students who do have difficulty with these areas, working on language use may be an appropriate goal.

to tell you about or explain the rules, they would have great difficulty. As children mature, however, they become more sophisticated language learners. They develop metalinguistic skills, or the ability to talk about and reflect on language as if it were an object. Berko Gleason (2001) notes that metalinguistics involves talking about words and language, seeing language as an entity separate from its function. Metalinguistics is the ability to judge the correctness of language and to correct it.

Teachers can use information about the development of metalinguistic skills to consider instruction in prereading and reading. These skills include ascertaining word boundaries in spoken and printed sentences, rhyming, making sound substitutions, segmenting words into syllables and sounds, and blending syllables and sounds into words. (One strategy teachers may use is to promote these skills through word games, as discussed in the 60-Second Lesson.)

60-*SECOND* LESSON

PROMOTING LANGUAGE THROUGH WORD GAMES

Often, teachers find themselves before or just after a transition with several minutes that need to be filled. Playing word games is a great way to fill the time and to promote language and metalinguistic skills. Listed here are several word games you and your students can play. You might want to make lists based on the words you generate from these games and post them for student reference.

For Younger Students

RHYMING WORDS. Select a word. Use a word from a word family (e.g., *-at, -ight, -an, -end*) to provide lots of opportunities for rhyming. Or have a student select a word. Then have the other students give rhyming words. You might want to write the words so that students can see the similarities between them. If you want students to select the words, put each word on a slip of paper and place them in a container such as a hat or jar, and then have students draw words from the container.

SOUND SUBSTITUTIONS. Select a word (e.g., *hat*). (Again, use of word-family words helps.) Say the word and write it on the board. Then ask students what word will be made if the first sound (e.g., /h/) is changed to another sound (e.g., /b/).

SYLLABLES. Have a student select a word and say it. Then repeat the word slowly and have the students clap once for each syllable in the word.

OPPOSITES. Select pairs of simple word opposites (e.g., *hot/cold, easy/hard, big/little, happy/sad*). Say one word from each pair and have students say the opposite.

For Older Students

ANTONYMS. Select pairs of word opposites (e.g., *cool/warm, hard/soft, cruel/gentle, empty/full, tame/wild*). Write one word from the pair on a card and put it in a container. Have a student draw a card, say the word, and have other students say or write the opposite word.

SYNONYMS. Select a word with several synonyms (e.g., *eat, pretty, pants, laugh*). Say one word and have students name as many synonyms as they can.

HOMONYMS. Select a word with at least one homonym (e.g., *fare, sale, male*). Say and spell one word and have students give the homonyms.

MULTIPLE MEANINGS. Select a word that has several meanings, write it on the board, and have students give examples of sentences that use the different meanings of the word (e.g., I have a *run* in my stocking. Let's go for a *run*. In the long *run*, it isn't very important. I have to *run* and pick up a sandwich.).

SUFFIXES. Select a suffix (e.g., *-tion*). Discuss its meaning and then have students provide examples of words that use this suffix (e.g., *determination, nomination, participation*). Have students also tell what the root word is. (You can play the same game with prefixes.)

As a teacher, you will want to talk about language, how it works, and the rules that govern language. Playing word games such as the ones suggested in the 60-Second Lesson is one way to build this type of language learning into those free moments during the day.

Research consistently demonstrates the reciprocal relationship between early reading and writing and the development of these metalinguistic skills (e.g., Fletcher, Lyon, Fuchs, & Barnes, 2007).

7.1.5 Prevalence of Communication Disorders

The prevalence of youngsters ages 3 to 17 with communication disorders is approximately 8% (Black, Vahratian, & Hoffman, 2015). Speech disorders are the most common, followed by language disorders, voice disorders, and swallowing. The number of students actually receiving services for speech or language disorders is reported at 21% (National Center for Educational Statistics, 2015). Why such a range from communication disorders to speech and language disorders? This is because many students receive speech services in preschool and in the early grades for disorders that are then readily corrected and they no longer receive services in the upper elementary grades. The vast majority of students, 87%, are included in the general education classroom for 80% or more of the school day (National Center for Educational Statistics, 2015). Thus, you, as a teacher, will likely be coordinating services for these students with the speech and language specialist. Of school-age children with communication disorders, most have difficulties in the areas of language and articulation. Within this population, communication disorders occur more often in boys than in girls (ASHA, 2008). Young students identified with speech and language disorders are also at much higher risk for psychiatric disorders, and this rate of association is even higher for girls with speech and language problems than boys (Beitchman, Nair, Clegg, Ferguson, & Patel, 2010).

MyEdLab **Self-Check 7.1**

MyEdLab **Application Exercise 7.1:** Speech Disorders

7.2 CAUSES OF COMMUNICATION DISORDERS

Communication disorders result from a wide spectrum of causes and often a combination of factors contribute to the disorder. Some disorders are due to physical causes. For example, the ability to perceive and/or articulate speech sounds (i.e., speech sound disorders) can be inhibited by a number of organic causes. Difficulty with auditory processing impacts perception of sounds. Physical conditions such as cleft palate and craniofacial disorders can have an effect on the production of sounds. Motor difficulties including paralysis, weakness, and apraxia (coordination of brain and speech production) are other potential causes. Voice disorders are typically physiological in nature, but can also result from infection.

Communication disorders can also arise from genetic factors or developmental disabilities that arise from birth. Others are acquired as a result of a stroke, brain injury, or disease such as cancer or AIDS. Difficulties with acquisition of receptive and expressive language proficiency and social language competency can arise from multiple cognitive impairments and genetics. Psychological disorders such as anxiety can trigger social communication disorders or selective mutism (refusal to speak in certain social situations). Environmental factors such as minimal verbal interaction with adults, peers, and siblings; abuse and neglect; and nutrition can also serve as contributors.

In some cases, communication disorders are a primary diagnosis. Such is the case with specific language impairment, a condition where young children experience language delays without symptoms of other developmental or hearing problems (National Institute on Deafness and Other Communication Disorders, 2015). Other times communication disorders are identified as a secondary diagnosis aligned with disabilities and disorders. In such cases, communication disorders are defined within the frameworks of those specific conditions. Communication disorders can be associated with other disabilities and disorders such as:

- Attention deficit hyperactivity disorder
- Autism spectrum disorder
- Cerebral palsy
- Developmental disability
- Hearing disorder
- Intellectual disability
- Learning disability
- Psychological/emotional disorders
- Traumatic brain injury

MyEdLab **Self-Check 7.2**

MyEdLab **Application Exercise 7.2:** Causes of Communication Disorders 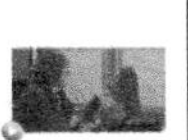

Video Example from YouTube

MyEdLab
Video Example 7.2.
Watch the YouTube video "Literacy Difficulties and SLI" to gain insights about how language disorders impact literacy learning. What questions would you pose to an SLP about how to support students like Stephanie in learning to read, write, and communicate? https://www.youtube.com/watch?v=CjF6rx-6KRY

7.3 IDENTIFYING STUDENTS WITH COMMUNICATION DISORDERS

Most students with communication disorders are identified in preschool or during the early elementary grades. However, some students remain unidentified as having a communication disorder—even into adolescence (Joffe & Nippold, 2012). As a teacher, consider the following steps if you suspect a student has a communication disorder:

- Talk with the speech and language specialist in your school district and ask her or him to schedule some time to observe the student in class and to interact with the student. The speech and language specialist is likely to recommend a hearing screening to determine whether there is interference in language development based on any hearing loss.
- Call the student's parents and ask them about the student's communication at home.
- Determine whether the student needs an evaluation. The evaluation for possible language delays or disorders often includes collecting a language sample. Sampling involves recording students as they interact, and then analyzing the students' utterances for characteristics such as mean length of utterance, types of utterances, vocabulary, topic maintenance, and turn taking.

7.3.1 Observe and Listen to Student Communication

One role that general education teachers play is that of observer and listener for students who have significant difficulty communicating. Particularly in the elementary grades, the classroom teacher spends more time with the students than any other individual in school. When Sharon Kutok, a SLP, spoke about what teachers should watch for, she commented, "Classroom teachers are good at identifying students with language disabilities. When identifying students with receptive language problems, typical teacher comments are 'When these students are listening to a presentation, they look away and don't focus. When I ask a question, they don't seem to know what is going on. I don't know if the students don't understand me or if they can't answer my question.'"

For expressive language difficulties, Sharon noted that "classroom teachers indicate that these students give answers that have no relationship to the question. They use short sentences or just words, and sometimes the words are out of order. Those are the kinds of symptoms that teachers notice when identifying students with language difficulties."

TIPS FOR TEACHER 7.2

Identifying a Student with Possible Language Disorders

Language Content

- Does the student comprehend and produce vocabulary as rich and varied as that of other students in the classroom?
- Does the student comprehend others' ideas and express his or her ideas as effectively as other students in the classroom?
- When talking, does the student have significant difficulty finding the word he or she wants to use (i.e., word-finding difficulties)?
- Does the student comprehend and use figurative language and multiple meanings of words similar to that of other students in the classroom?

Language Form

- Does the student mispronounce sounds or words and omit endings more than other students in the classroom do?
- Does the student comprehend and produce types of sentences similar to those of other students in the classroom?
- Is the student's language as elaborate and descriptive as that of other students in the classroom?
- Are the student's comprehension and production of grammatical rules similar to those of other students in the classroom?

Language Use

- Does the student use language for different purposes, including to gain attention, ask for and tell about information, express and respond to feelings, use imagination to understand and tell stories and jokes, express opinions and persuade, and for greetings, introductions, and farewells?
- Does the student take turns appropriately in conversations?
- Does the student initiate conversations?
- Does the student stay on topic during a conversation?
- Does the student have more than one style of interacting, depending on the listener, situation, and topic?
- Does the student recognize when the listener does not understand and act to clarify communication for the listener?

As a classroom teacher, you have the opportunity to observe students using language in the classroom (during both academic and social activities) as well as on the playground and during other activities such as art, music, and physical education. What should you look for in the area of language? Tips for Teachers 7.2 presents questions you can ask about your students to determine the possibility of difficulties with language.

Notice how the questions are grouped according to the three areas of language: form, content, and use. If a language delay is evident, you should consider making a referral to the speech and language pathologist.

7.3.2 Differentiate Between ELL Learning Curves and Language Disabilities or Disorders

Some of your students may be English language learners (ELLs) or have a first dialect that is other than Standard English. If so, it is important not to misinterpret a language *difference* for a language *disability* or *disorder.* Difficulties students experience in pronunciation, syntactical and grammatical errors, vocabulary development, and comprehension may stem from lack of fluency in English or fundamental differences in the linguistic structure of the student's first and second language—not from a communication disorder. Keep in mind that students acquire a second language at different rates. In addition, learning challenges students face may be a result of gaps in school attendance or access to education (Chu & Flores, 2011).

If you observe that a student is struggling to learn even when you implement culturally and linguistically appropriate practices, follow the procedures in your state or school district for next steps. A collaborative effort among school professionals and family members will be necessary to determine if the student's challenges are due to language difference or disability. Parents can be particularly helpful in providing information about family history, student's language development, and communication patterns of the student at home and in social situations.

Language assessment in the student's native language may be necessary to determine if there is a communication disorder. It is rare for a communication disorder to exist in one language and not the other. As you can imagine, assessment of this nature is sensitive and beyond the parameters of general education teacher responsibilities. However, culturally and linguistically sensitive assessment is vital to avoid misclassification of students and to provide optimum service to ensure student success.

MyEdLab **Self-Check 7.3**

MyEdLab **Application Exercise 7.3:** Identifying Students with Communication Disorders

7.4 INSTRUCTIONAL GUIDELINES AND ACCOMMODATIONS FOR STUDENTS WITH COMMUNICATION DISORDERS

Most students with communication disorders are educated in general education classrooms. Although these students may work (individually or in small groups) with an SLP several times a week for 30 minutes or so, they spend the rest of their school days with the classroom teacher and students. Consequently, students with communication disorders have many more opportunities to develop effective communication in the classroom than in the limited time spent with the SLP. As a classroom teacher, you will play a major role in facilitating the development of effective communication for these students.

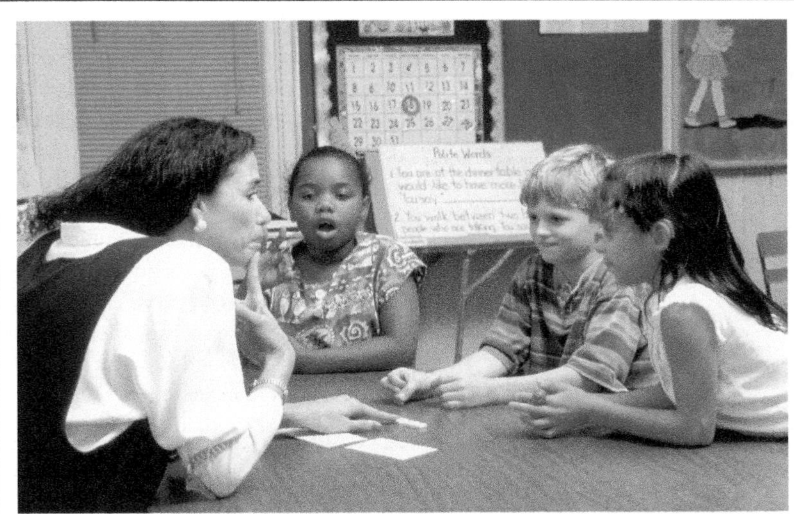

These students are working in a cooperative learning group. Which instructional accommodations described in this chapter might the teacher use for her students who have communication difficulties?

Speech and language pathologists are one of your best resources for ideas about facilitating speech and language development. The role of the school-based SLP has changed significantly within the past few decades due to legislative changes in special education. Traditionally, the SLP has used a clinical/medical model of assessment and intervention, treating students individually or in small groups in a separate therapy or resource room. Educational reform statutes such as the Education for All Handicapped Children Act of 1986 and the later Individuals with Disabilities Education Act (IDEA) and its 1997 and 2004 amendments have mandated increased participation of students with disabilities in the general education classroom. The roles and responsibilities of SLPs will vary due to differences in caseload (typically an average of about 50 per specialist), state or district regulations, and staffing needs (ASHA, 2014).

Speech and language pathologists now work closely with other school professionals and parents in a team model, using a combination of direct and indirect service methods to assist students with communication disorders. In addition to providing individual or group therapy, they may also collaborate with classroom teachers to develop modifications and strategies for students within the classroom. For instance, if you are implementing a Universal Design for Learning model in your classroom, an SLP may collaborate with you to identify and implement appropriate representation, action and expression, and engagement adaptations and AAC tools that will enhance learning for students with communication disorders as well as other students in your classroom (Ralabate, 2011; Ralabate, Currie-Rubin, Boucher, & Bartecchi, 2014).

MyEdLab
Video Example 7.3.
Watch the video to see how the language pathologist working with Mary Anne works with her to develop her language skills. As a general education teacher, how would you work with a speech pathologist to ensure that struggling students get the attention they need both at school and at home?

With their knowledge and professional expertise of oral language development and communication disorders, SLPs serve as valuable members of response to intervention (RTI) teams (Ehren, 2013; Squires, Gillam, & Reutzel, 2013; Watson, & Bellon-Harn, 2013). Depending on district and state guidelines, they may be involved in assessment or intervention facets at any tier of RTI, provision of professional development or consultation with teachers, or communicating with parents.

What can you do to secure support from the speech and language specialists for the students in your class? You can ask them to observe target students in your classroom and provide suggestions for enhancing their language and literacy. You can also ask them to provide model lessons in your class to guide you in providing more language support. You can also ask the speech and language specialist to meet with you and parents so that families have suggestions for improving communication skills at home as well as in the classroom.

7.4.1 Facilitating Speech Development

Generally, specific remediation of articulation errors, voice disorders, and stuttering is provided by the SLP. The major goal of the general education teacher is to provide opportunities for the student to communicate in the classroom using the most natural, supportive situations possible. If students are to generalize what they are learning in therapy, you will also need to work with the SLP to get specific information on the skills students are targeting and to discuss strategies you can use to help them generalize those skills. One such strategy is to develop a personal cueing system for students who have difficulty responding in a large group. Robert Encino, a seventh-grade science teacher, explains how he developed such a system with Kim:

> Kim was a student in my fifth period who stutters. I was aware that she often knew an answer and wanted to share her knowledge, but I was unsure of when she felt confident enough to do so. I met with Kim one day during planning period, and we agreed on a system where she would open her hand, palm-side up on her desk, if she wanted to respond. What I found was that this reduced her anxiety, and during the semester her hand was open more and more frequently. Eventually, we discontinued the system because she felt that she didn't need it any longer.

It is also important for students with speech disorders that the classroom be a safe environment in which to practice oral communication. Tips for Teachers 7.3 provides

TIPS FOR TEACHERS 7.3

Creating an Accepting Classroom Community for Students with Speech Disorders

- Create an atmosphere of ease and comfortable pacing. Avoid an atmosphere that creates time pressures and tensions.
- Listen in a calm and thoughtful manner to what students have to say. Allow time for students to finish their thoughts. Don't disregard ideas just because students have difficulty expressing them.
- Do not criticize or point out speech errors. You may, however, demonstrate correct speech by correctly repeating what the students said.
- Establish classroom rules that do not allow for ridicule of students or their speech errors.
- Take care not to place students with speech problems in situations in which their communication difficulties might interfere or be highlighted.
- Use flexible grouping so that students have opportunities to talk in small groups and with a partner.
- Allow time for students to respond. Students often need time to get their ideas organized and to plan their communication. Speech may be labored and slow.
- Develop cueing systems that allow students to let you know when they are comfortable responding.
- Read aloud in a slow, easy manner to give students an opportunity to practice fluency strategies or new sounds they are learning. Students become more fluent with multiple readings, so the use of repeated reading may be beneficial.
- Avoid competition among students, particularly when it highlights oral communication.

some strategies for helping to promote a classroom community that accepts and encourages meaningful student communication.

Augmentative and alternative communication systems

Some students with physical disabilities and other severe disabilities cannot communicate effectively through speech and therefore rely on augmentative and alternative communication (AAC) systems. AAC refers to ways (other than speech) that are used to send and receive messages. AACs attempt to compensate for, temporarily or permanently, the impairment and disability patterns of individuals with severe expressive and receptive language disorders. AACs provide a means for students with limited speech to augment their communication with peers and teachers in the classroom. For students with no speech, communication tools provide an alternative means to verbal interaction (Carpenter, Johnston, & Beard, 2015).

We all use AAC strategies such as facial expressions, gestures, and writing in our daily interactions. Such communication modes (as well as sign language) are unaided communication systems. Individuals with severe physical and/or cognitive disabilities use these strategies as well as individualized AAC tools and equipment, or aided communication systems (ASHA, 2015). The Tech Tips "Augmentative and Alternative Communication Tools" provides examples of augmentative and alternative communication tools that might be implemented in your classroom.

The AAC system that a student needs will likely be selected by the SLP with information provided by other specialists, the classroom teacher, the student, and the family. If a student in your classroom uses an AAC system, work collaboratively with the SLP to assure that you (and the paraeducator in the classroom) have the sufficient training to assist in implementation (Chung & Douglas, 2014; Douglas, 2012).

Video Example from YouTube

MyEdLab
Video Example 7.4.

Watch the YouTube video "Dear New Orleans by Steve Gleason" to see how AAC with eye tracking can be used for individuals with disabilities to communicate in powerful ways. What questions might you ask an SLP about how you can foster creativity in expression with students who use AAC devices? https://www.youtube.com/watch?v=K7ivpvixQG4

TECH TIPS

Augmentative and Alternative Communication Tools

A number of different augmentative and alternative technologies (AACs) are available that can assist students with communication disorders and pervasive developmental disorders.

Single Meaning Pictures

Mrs. Riley's Picture Cards
(http://mrsriley.com)

This online tool facilitates production of customized picture cards that can be used to teach vocabulary. Commercial card sets are also on the market, such as:

Tangible Object Cards from Adaptivation (http://www.adaptivation.com)

Communication Boards

One relatively simple communication solution for learners who cannot speak is the communication board. Typically, the user points to the desired symbol, word, or picture on the board. The communication board could be a laminated page or computer screen with pictures, words, or symbols to which the learner points, or a small book of pages the learner flips through to express needs or feelings.

Boardmaker Software Family by Mayer-Johnson (http://www.mayer-johnson.com)

This widely used series of software and online programs simplifies the creation of communication boards. They provide many useful templates and an extensive collection of picture communication symbols as well as text options for individuals with speech disorders who can read.

Proloquo Series by AssistiveWare (http://www.assistiveware.com)

This computer application for computers, tablets, and smartphones is designed to develop customized communication boards in either symbol-based or text-based formats.

Speech Generating Devices (SGDs)

Speech generating devices (SGDs) are electronic tools that use graphic, textual, or eye-tracking input to produce digital or synthetic speech. Advances in technology have resulted in SGDs that are increasingly more affordable and thus more accessible. Examples of SGDs include:

- **Maestro Dynavox** from Tobii Dynavox (http://www.dynavoxtech.com)
- **Accent 1400-M** from Prentke Romich (www.prentrom.com)

In addition, SGD apps for handheld electronic devices are also emerging. Work with the SLP or assistive technology resource person at your school to learn more about SGDs and how they might be implemented for students in your classroom. You may want to utilize technical support resources that are offered online and with company representatives in the use of these devices.

Video Example from YouTube

MyEdLab
Video Example 7.5.

Watch the YouTube video "Phyllis Hunter, president of PCH Consulting, on the Importance of Oral Language" for a discussion of the importance of oral language for academic success. What are some ways you can "level the playing field" in your classroom for students with challenges in their oral language development? https://www.youtube.com/watch?v=yY-cMpfFmgo

Methods for enhancing communication

There are two primary methods for augmenting communication: the *language representation method* and the *physical selection technique* (ASHA, 2015). The language representation method is a way of sending messages that requires good motor control and is for those individuals with speech-production problems who can communicate with symbols through speech, gestures, sign language, fingerspelling, writing, head shaking, eye blinks, and other gestures. Sometimes a communication device is used to register inputs. The physical selection technique is for individuals who lack adequate motor control and need to be taught to indicate symbols by pointing with body parts they can control (e.g., a stick held in the mouth, light beam mounted on a headband). When individuals have less control, the symbols can be presented to them by scanning and then asking, "Is this what you want—yes, no?" and through a small gesture such as blinking, the individual communicates intention.

Facilitating language development

Opportunities for teaching oral language abound during general education classroom activities—whether they occur in the classroom or in transition activities. As a classroom teacher, you have considerable opportunity to model and teach language. When you teach students new concepts and vocabulary in content-area subjects, you are developing oral language. When students learn how to give oral reports or retell a story, how to introduce themselves, or how to use irregular verbs, they are developing language skills.

Findings from the National Early Literacy Panel's (NELP) research synthesis underscored the importance of oral language in academic success in reading, writing, speaking, and listening (NELP, 2008; Shanahan & Lonigan, 2012). Early oral language development serves as the foundation for ongoing language development throughout the grades. Consequently, the Common Core State Standards (CCSS) as well as curriculum standards in many states that have not adopted CCSS include standards for language development.

CCSS has incorporated standards for grades 3 through 12 in three areas: Conventions of Standard English (i.e., grammar, usage, spelling, capitalization, punctuation), Knowledge and Use (i.e., style, sentence structure, formal and informal language), and Vocabulary Acquisition and Use (i.e., figures of speech, morphology, word relationships) (http://www.corestandards.org). For students in your classroom who have communication disorders or who have challenges in language and literacy learning, the SLP in your school can be a collaborator in designing adaptations and interventions to promote student success in meeting standards (ASHA, 2015).

What are some general guidelines you can use to facilitate language development in your classroom? Vaughn and Bos (2015) suggest the following guidelines to help shape your instruction.

Teaching language in purposive contexts

Whether you are teaching students causal relationships such as the effect of heat on water or how to request information by telephone, it is important to teach language in the context of meaningful activities. It is difficult to imagine teaching someone how to use a screwdriver or a needle and thread without having the tools at hand, demonstrating how to use them, and then letting students practice. The same is true for language. Hence, when you cannot create a "real" situation, use such techniques as simulations and role-playing to create authentic learning experiences. The Activities for All Learners feature explains how to use barrier games to teach language.

Teaching comprehension and production

Give students opportunities to develop both their understanding of (comprehension) and their ability to express (production) the new structures (form), vocabulary (content), and ways of using language (use) they are learning. When teaching the vocabulary associated with a new unit, you can provide students with opportunities not only to listen to explanations but also to discuss their knowledge of the vocabulary and to use the new terms in their discussion and writing. Vaughn and colleagues (2009) used a procedure in

ACTIVITIES FOR ALL LEARNERS

Using Barrier Games to Promote Language

Objectives: Helping students build their comprehension and production of descriptive language

Grades: Pre-K through grade 3

Materials: Blocks for building or paper and crayons for making a picture

It is not always possible to create authentic learning environments when you teach language, but we know that the best and quickest way to learn language is when it is purposeful and taught in context. One way to promote purposeful language and to help students build their comprehension and production of descriptive language, particularly locative prepositions, is to use barrier games. These games (frequently used by SLPs to teach prepositions) can be a great activity for the entire class or used as a filler activity after students complete their work.

Teaching procedure: Students work in pairs, with a barrier placed between them so that they cannot see each other's work.

- The lead student builds a simple structure or draws a simple design or picture. Then the lead student describes to the second student how to make what he or she has built or drawn.
- The second student is encouraged to ask questions when the directions are unclear.
- After the second student has finished his or her project, the barrier is removed, the two projects are compared, and differences are discussed. Then the roles are reversed.

Students can keep track of the number of projects that resemble the one that was presented to them orally. Another way to facilitate clearer communications is to provide a picture to one student and not to the second student. The student with the picture is given an allocated amount of time, perhaps 60 seconds, to talk about the picture without stating what it is. The second student guesses what it is based on the description.

which the teacher provides a stimulating question or dilemma and asks students to turn to their partners and discuss their response. They also prompt the students to use the key words or concepts that were being taught in the unit. Using this procedure, the teacher pauses at logical breaks in the lecture or discussion, the students discuss what they are learning (with a partner or in a small group), and then the teacher calls on selective members of the group to present their comments to the class.

Presenting new concepts

Critical to students' learning of new content or concepts is the use of effective teaching strategies. As you may recall from the earlier discussion of vocabulary development, students' knowledge of concepts grows exponentially during the school-age years. By using effective teaching strategies (see Tips for Teachers 7.4), you help students with language

TIPS FOR TEACHERS 7.4

Presenting New Language Concepts or Content

When teaching new language concepts or patterns, keep the following strategies in mind:

- Gear the activities to the students' interests and cognitive level.
- Get the students' attention before engaging in communication activities.
- Bombard the students with the concept or skill frequently throughout the day in a functional manner.
- When speaking, place stress on the target concept or language pattern.
- Pause between phrases or sentences so that the students have time to process the new concept or language pattern.
- Decrease the rate of presentation when first introducing the concept or language pattern.
- When introducing a new concept or language pattern, use familiar vocabulary that can be readily visualized.
- If possible, present the new concept or language pattern by using more than one input mode (e.g., auditory, visual, kinesthetic). Gestures and facial expressions that are paired with a specific language pattern often assist students in understanding the form. For example, giving a look of puzzlement or wonder when asking a question can serve as a cue to the students.
- Pair written symbols with oral language. For instance, demonstrating morphological endings such as -s (plurals) and -ed (past tense) can be done in writing. The students can then be cued to listen for what they see.

impairments and English language learners to gain the concepts and content necessary for success in content-area classes.

Demonstrating connections between concepts

One important way we learn about concepts is by understanding the relationships or connections between concepts. If you listen to a conversation in which a new idea is being explained, you'll undoubtedly hear statements such as "It's like," or "You can compare it to," or "It's like ... except that," or "It's almost the opposite of." These phrases all help students understand and see the connections between concepts. Because students with language problems have difficulty making such connections, it is important that you highlight them as you and the students discuss new concepts. For example, when Peggy, a first-grade teacher, was introducing the concept of "squirm" because it was important for understanding the book her students were to discuss and read, she asked the students, "What does *squirm* mean? Show me with your body how you can squirm. What other things can squirm? Now that we know what *squirm* is, what other words mean something similar to *squirm*? Is *squirm* similar to *wiggle*? What would be the opposite of *squirm*? If you weren't squirming, you would be __________."

At more advanced levels, when students make comparisons between books written by the same author, when they compare the relationships between addition and multiplication versus subtraction and division, and when they compare the similarities between the Korean and Vietnam Wars, the emphasis is on making connections. These kinds of discussions help students see the relationships between concepts and better understand semantic relationships (such as contrastives, comparatives, causals, and conditionals). The use of semantic feature analysis and other graphic organizers such as semantic maps and concept diagrams can help students see the relationships.

Using conversation

As students with language impairments work, think, and play in your classroom, you need to create opportunities for them to engage in conversations with you and with other students. One way to do this is to use discussion groups rather than a question-and-answer format for reviews of books and current events. Nancy Meyers, the SLP who works with Lorri Johnson, chose to work in Lorri's classroom while the literature groups meet. Once a week, she joins Samantha's literature group. As she listens and joins in the conversation about the book being discussed, Nancy has the opportunity to model the language patterns on which Samantha is working.

At least several times a week, engage students in conversation. This may take some forethought and effort on your part, for observational research has shown that classroom teachers, in general, are not as responsive to students with language impairments as they are to average and high-achieving students (Pecyna-Rhyner, Lehr, & Pudlas, 1990). Let the students direct the topics of these conversations, which need not be long and, in secondary settings, can be accomplished as students enter the room. Do not fire away questions but give students time to think, talk, and engage. Children like when adults "play with language" and are a little silly. Most important, be interested in the children and what they have to say.

Video Example from YouTube

MyEdLab
Video Example 7.6.
Watch the YouTube video "Asking Open-ended Questions and Using Wait-time—Overview" to learn more about using wait time. What are the benefits of using wait time for students with speech and/or language disorders? https://www.youtube.com/watch?v=y__p_Vyu-IE

Using wait time

When SLP Sharon Kutok talks about the most important principles in teaching students with language impairments, the first one she mentions is wait time. "For some students, waiting is important. A wait time as brief as 5 seconds gives students the opportunity to understand what has been said and to construct a response (Johnson & Parker, 2013). These students may have particular difficulty with form (e.g., syntax) and need the extra time to think about the form they should use in constructing their response."

Students who have difficulty with content may also have difficulty with word retrieval or word finding. A word-retrieval problem is like having the word on the tip of your tongue but not being able to think of it. Two examples demonstrate how difficulty with word retrieval can affect the flow of communication. The first conversation (about making an Easter basket) is a dialog between two third graders, one with typical language and the other with word-retrieval problems (Vaughn & Bos, 2012).

> ***Susan:*** Are you going to make, uh, make, uh, one of these things [pointing to the Easter basket on the bookshelf]?
>
> ***Cori:*** Oh, you mean an Easter basket?
>
> ***Susan:*** Yeah, an Easter basket.
>
> ***Cori:*** Sure, I'd like to, but I'm not sure how to do it. Can you help me?
>
> ***Susan:*** Yeah, first you need some, uh, some, uh, the things you cut with, you know.
>
> ***Cori:*** Scissors.
>
> ***Susan:*** Yeah, and some paper and the thing you use to stick things together with.
>
> ***Cori:*** Tape?
>
> ***Susan:*** No, uh, uh, sticky stuff.
>
> ***Cori:*** Oh, well, let's get the stuff we need.
>
> ***Susan:*** Let's go, to, uh, uh, the shelf, uh, where you get, you know, the stuff to cut up.
>
> ***Cori:*** Yeah, the paper, and let's also get the glue. (p. 76)

In the second example, an adolescent explains how to fix a tire:

> Well...to fix a tire...or your wheel...you gotta take the tire off...you gotta lift up...you jack up the car and use this thing...it's square metal wrench...to loosen the bolts...you know the nuts...then you take the wheel off the axle. First you ask the guy at the garage if he will fix the tire. You lock up the car so it won't...you put the car in gear so it stays put. (Chappell, 1985, p. 226)

It is clear from these two examples that wait time is important for students with word-retrieval problems. In addition to increasing wait time, strategies that teachers can use during classroom discussions include the following:

- Using multiple-choice formats so that students need recognize only one word in a group, rather than having to generate the word
- Providing a cue, such as the initial sound or syllable, the category name or function, a synonym or description, or a gesture demonstrating the word
- Restating a question so that it requires a yes-or-no response rather than an open-ended answer

By teaching students with word-finding problems to categorize words, make visual images of words, learn synonyms, use phonological-based vocabulary, and make word associations (e.g., *bread/butter, plane/fly*), you can help them recall words, thereby increasing the accuracy and fluency of their expressive language (German, Schwanke, & Ravid, 2011; Owens, 2008). Also, teachers can ask the students, "do you want me to give you a clue to the word?" This gives students a chance to make another association between the clue provided by the teacher and the word, increasing the likelihood that they will remember it.

Adjusting the pace

Students with language delays and other disabilities as well as English language learners often have difficulty comprehending what is being said during class, particularly in content-area classes. Teachers need to adjust the pace so that these students have time to process information. The flow of instruction does not have to suffer, but when you discuss new or difficult concepts or ideas, slow the pace and highlight key ideas by writing them on the board or using technology to project them. Reducing the amount of information in each segment is helpful. For instance, Bob Stern, a high school science teacher, used to introduce the terms for a new science chapter by writing them on the board and discussing them as a group when he introduced the chapter. After Bob noticed that his students with language problems listened to the first five words and recorded three of them in their science notebooks, he decided to chunk the words into groups of three to five, introducing them when they were needed.

Using self-talk and parallel talk

Students, particularly young students with language delays, need to hear language that is connected to activities. When teachers use self-talk, they describe what they are doing or thinking; in parallel talk, teachers describe what students are doing or thinking. As you and your students work or play, describe what everyone is doing. Maria Ferraro, a first-grade teacher who works in an inner-city school, regularly uses parallel talk and self-talk when she joins students at the different centers in her classroom:

> When I join a center, I try to sit down and join in the activities rather than asking students questions. My goal is to become part of the group. As I join in the activity, I describe what I am doing and what other students in the group are doing. For example, I might say, "José is making a clay animal. It's blue and right now he is putting a ferocious snarl on the animal's face. I wonder what kind of animal it is. I think I'll ask José." In this way, the students get to hear how words can describe what someone is doing, and it focuses the attention on José and the ongoing activities.

Using modeling

Modeling, using the oral language you want students to use, plays an important role in the process of learning language. Whether students are learning a new sentence structure, a new vocabulary, or a new function or use for language, modeling is a powerful tool. Consider this example. Sharon Kutok and Armando Rivera, the SLP and the eighth-grade English teacher at Vail Middle School, respectively, decided to improve their students' conversational skills during literature groups. Both Armando and Sharon were concerned about the number of students who did not clarify what they were saying when other students obviously did not understand (but did not request clarification).

To teach clarification skills, Armando and Sharon began discussing clarifying conversations. During their discussion, they role-played, first as students who could not effectively clarify what they were saying, and then as students who clarified effectively. They exaggerated the examples, and the students seemed to really enjoy their modeling. Next, Armando and Sharon joined the literature groups and continued to model as they participated in discussions. At the end of the period, they asked students to summarize what they had learned and whether they thought they could become more effective at clarifying what they said and asking others to clarify if they did not understand. During the next 2 weeks, Armando had the students in each literature group rate the group's effectiveness in clarification. When Sharon returned in 2 weeks, both teachers observed a difference in the students' discussions, particularly in their ability to clarify ideas and ask for clarification. The students also thought that their skills had improved. In discussing the change, both teachers and students agreed that the modeling Armando and Sharon had done on the first day was an important key to their learning.

Increased access to technology (including tablets, hand-held devices, digital cameras, and YouTube videos) has led to more frequent use of video modeling for students with communication disorders. Video monitoring involves the use of short video clips to demonstrate a number of desired behaviors including conversations, interactive behaviors, daily living skills, and vocabulary learning (Bellini & Akullian, 2007; Ely, Pullen, Kennedy, & Williams, 2015; Ganz, Earles-Vollrath, & Çook, 2011). Video self-modeling is a technique that engages the student in the production of the video (Rao, Hitchcock, Boisvert, Kilpatrick, & Corbiell, 2012). Video modeling is an excellent way to foster student engagement and to provide visual examples of effective communication.

Promoting language through expansion and elaboration

Language expansion is a technique used to facilitate the development of complex language form and content. By repeating what students say but in a slightly more complex manner, the teacher demonstrates how their thoughts can be more fully expressed. For example, Susie Lee, a first-grade teacher, is working to get Rob to use adverbs to describe his actions. As he finished several math problems, Rob reported, "I got the first one easy. The second one was hard." Susie replied, "Oh, you got the first one easily. That's good." Note that you do not want to imply that you are correcting the student; you are simply showing him or her a more complex way of expressing the thought. Note also that you should expand only one element at a time. Otherwise, the expansion will be too complex for the student to profit from it.

You can use language elaboration to build on the content of the student's language and provide additional information on the topic. For example, Chris, a fourth-grade student with language disabilities, was explaining that snakes have rough skin. Teacher Peggy Anderson elaborated on Chris's idea by commenting, "Yes, and snakes have smooth skin on their bellies and so do lizards. Are there other animals in the desert that have smooth skin on their bellies?"

Using language as an intrinsic motivator

Language is a powerful enabling tool and carries a great deal of intrinsic motivation for students. Rather than using praise (e.g., "I like the way you said that" or "Good talking"), you can capitalize on the naturally reinforcing nature of language. During a cooking activity, for example, teacher Jon Warner asked students, "How can we figure out how much two-thirds of a cup plus three-fourths of a cup of flour is?" After Lydia explained, Jon said, "Now we know how to figure that out. Shall we give it a try?" Later, Jon asked how to sift flour. After Randa explained, Jon said, "I've got it. How about the rest of you? Do you think you can sift the flour just the way Randa explained to us?" Instead of commenting on how "good" their language was and disrupting the flow of communication, Jon complimented Lydia and Randa by letting them know how useful the information was.

When students' purposes and intents are fulfilled because of their language, their language is naturally reinforcing, and students learn that language is a powerful tool for controlling their environment (Owens, 2016; Vaughn & Bos, 2015). Tips for Teachers 7.5 provides strategies for promoting effective communication in your classroom.

7.4.2 Using Effective Teaching Strategies for Language Intervention

As the classroom teacher, you are likely to have students in your class whose language development requires additional intervention. This is very similar to a response-to-intervention (RTI) model in which students require additional intervention (Tier 2 or Tier 3) to enhance their language development so that they can catch up with same-grade peers. Gillam and Loeb (2010) reviewed the literature on effective teaching strategies for language intervention and identified several key practices for instruction:

- ✓ *Intensity.* Extensive and highly focused time for language intervention is needed. This can occur by providing additional language intervention time during the school day or by adding language intervention after school or during the summer.
- ✓ *Active Attention.* Students benefit from language interventions that are engaging and thus maintain their interest. Signaling students to assure that they are attending and ready to learn, cueing them when they are not paying attention and recognizing them when they are paying attention, and providing them with feedback that is engaging about their learning assures that the language intervention is effective.
- ✓ *Feedback.* Students benefit from clear feedback about whether their responses are correct and then elaborations on this feedback to enhance learning. Direct and

TIPS FOR TEACHERS 7.5

Promoting Effective Communication in Your Classroom

- Use consistent verbal, visual, or physical cues to get attention (e.g., "1-2-3, eyes on me").
- Be brief and specific when giving directions.
- Use students' names when speaking with them.
- Use gestures and facial expressions to help convey meaning when speaking.
- Model courteous listening by not interrupting and promote listening without interrupting among students.
- Provide opportunities for students to use language and have that language work to accomplish goals.
- Allow time for students to respond.
- Allow students to speak for themselves (e.g., avoid completing students' thoughts or having a peer speak for another student).

indirect feedback are needed. An example of direct feedback is: "That's right, you remembered to sequence your story when you told it."

✓ *Reward.* Supporting internal motivation and recognizing learning and achievement through rewards is an essential feature of effective language intervention programs.

MyEdLab **Self-Check 7.4**

MyEdLab **Application Exercise 7.4:** Facilitating Speech Development

7.5 WORKING WITH PARENTS TO EXTEND LANGUAGE CONCEPTS

Children are more likely to learn new vocabulary and language structures when they are active participants in their learning and can practice new concepts in different contexts (home and school). The following are some suggestions for using newly learned language concepts in a variety of environments. Keep all language activities short and fun so that parents do not view communication as "homework." When planning language activities, be aware of cultural and linguistic differences in the home. If the family does not speak English, encourage the child to complete these activities in the language of the home.

FOR YOUNGER STUDENTS

- Send home a short description or picture of a recent classroom activity or field trip. Encourage the parents to ask open-ended rather than closed questions about the activity. For example, parents might ask: "I understand that you made a papier-mâché vase today. How did you do that?"
- Inform the parents of new vocabulary the child is learning. Have the child write a note to his or her family about what he or she learned. The child might say, "I learned the word *notorious* today."
- Have the child bring new words to class that he or she has heard at home. Create a word "treasure chest" and encourage the children to be vocabulary "hunters."
- Inform parents of new social language concepts that the child has practiced in class. Have the child describe the concept to his or her parents. For instance, the child might say, "I learned what to say if someone is bullying me." Encourage the parents to practice similar role plays with the child at home.
- When possible, have students ask their parents questions about topics the students are learning in class. For example, if you are discussing the food pyramid, have the children ask their families about favorite foods and set aside a time for them to report back to the class on their findings.
- To practice figurative language, have children tell jokes or word puns to their families at home.
- To practice asking questions and listening skills, have the students ask their families about hypothetical situations discussed in class. Themes may come from journal topics such as "What would you do if you had a million dollars?"
- Encourage parents to discuss books that they read to or with their children. Send home some tips to encourage discussion of a book (e.g., talk about the pictures; relate the story to the child's own experiences).

FOR OLDER STUDENTS

- Encourage families to let students take responsibility for communicating in the community by asking for help from a store clerk, ordering for themselves in a restaurant, or calling a business to ask for directions or store hours.
- Encourage parents to ask students to explain school assignments and homework and jointly come up with a plan for accomplishing tasks.
- Model and encourage following conversation rules such as turn taking, active listening, and topic maintenance.

- Listen to students' stories, goals, and needs and help them problem-solve solutions. Effective listening can open the door to conversations with adolescents who may be reluctant to share with their families.

Because some adolescents with language disorders may misunderstand what has been said or have difficulty understanding nonverbal cues, it is important that parents are clear with their messages, check for understanding, and are patient if the student becomes frustrated during a conversation. If something is very important, parents should communicate the information in words and with a written note and encourage students to do the same.

MyEdLab **Self-Check 7.5**

MyEdLab **Application Exercise 7.5:** Promoting Language Extension

7 SUMMARY

- Communication disorders include speech disorders, language disorders, stuttering, social communication disorders, and other communication disorders (specified and unspecified). Approximately 8% of students ages 3 to 17 have communication disorders. However, the percentages are higher among preschool and primary grade children whose early disorders are readily treated with intervention.
- Some communication disorders result from physical, genetic, developmental, psychological, or environmental causes. Others occur as a consequence of injury or disease. Communication disorders can be a primary disability or associated with other disabilities such as autism or hearing disorder.
- Although most students with communication disorders are identified in preschool or in the early grades, an important role classroom teachers play is to identify students who might have communication disorders and work with other specialists to determine effective classroom strategies. Your daily observations of a student's speech (articulation, voice, fluency and language content, form, or use) and social interactions are important sources of information that professional assessment experts will need for diagnosis. As you observe, keep in mind the importance linguistic and cultural differences play in communication. Language differences are not the same as language disorders.
- Classroom teachers play an important role in facilitating the development of language. The classroom is an ideal setting to use such language techniques as self-talk and parallel talk, expansion and elaboration, modeling, and conversations. For students with speech disorders, the classroom teacher's role is to create a nonthreatening environment in which the students can communicate. It is also important to adjust the pace and wait time. Communicate with a speech and language pathologist or assistive technology resource person in your school in respect to adaptations and ACC tools for students with communication disorders.
- Home–school connections are vital ongoing language development. When preparing language activities, keep them short and fun. If the family does not speak English, encourage the child to complete these activities in the language of the home.

THINK AND APPLY

1. Determine the questions or concerns you have about teaching students with communication disorders. Discuss your questions with your fellow students, your instructor, and a speech and language pathologist. Record your answers and file your personal inquiry in your teaching portfolio.
2. Examine the list of disabilities that may be comorbid with a communication disorder and choose one that interests you. Research that disability and identify the speech or language challenges that may be associated with the disability. Share your findings with your classmates.
3. Go to the websites of your school district and state to identify procedures for identification of students with communication disorders. Discover if there are checklists for classroom teachers to document observations of speech and language patterns of students. Also, see if there are guidelines for the observation of students who are English language learners.
4. When teaching or observing a teacher, consciously use the techniques of parallel talk, expansion, and elaboration. How does this affect the expressive language of the students whose language is typically less elaborated and complex?
5. Assume that you are a new teacher at Drexel Elementary School and Lorri Johnson is your teaching mentor. Make a list of two or three activities you might send home for practicing language content, form, and use. Provide these suggestions to your mentor teacher for feedback.

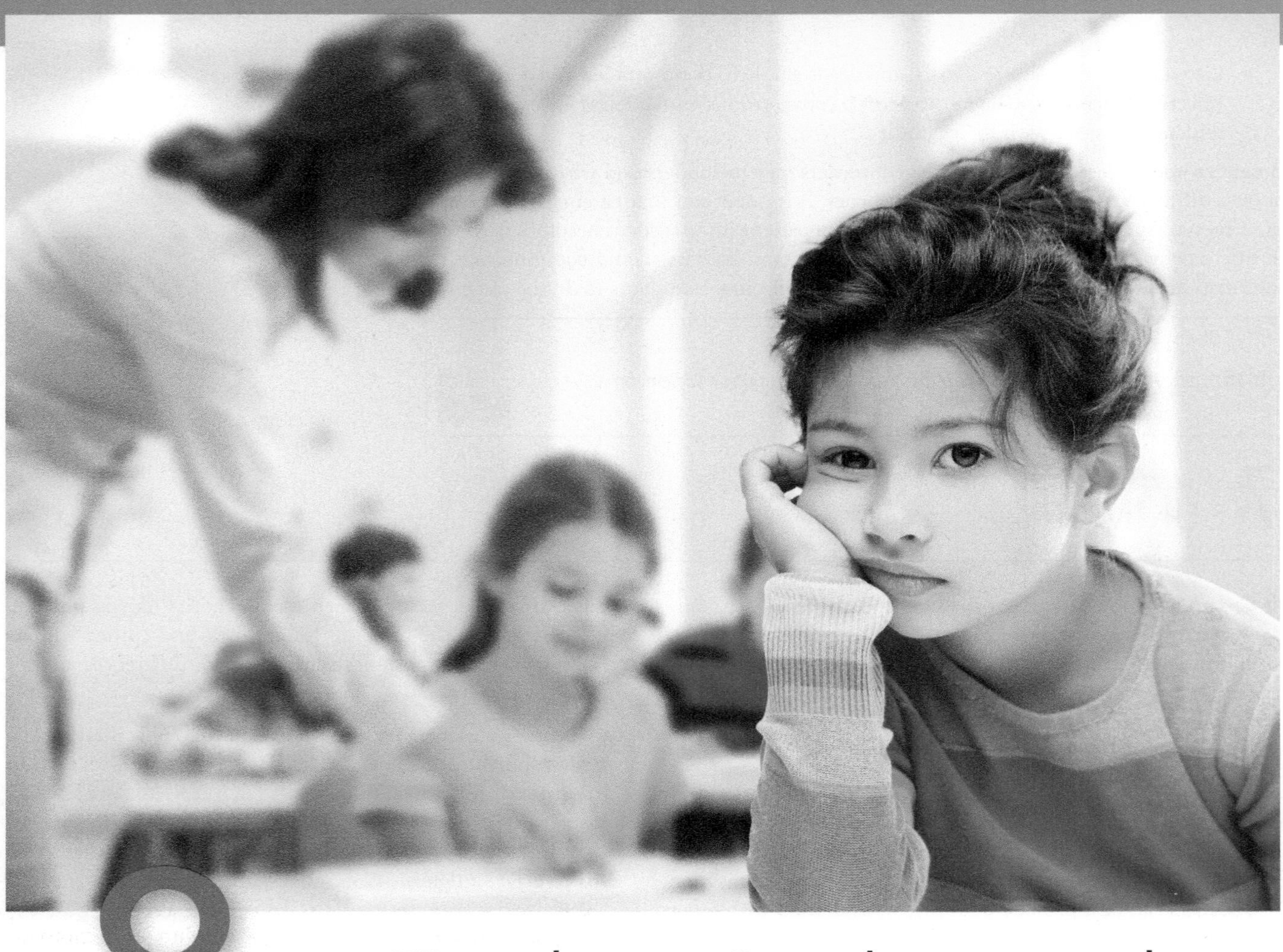

8 Teaching Students with Emotional and Behavioral Disorders

Learning Outcomes

8.1 Describe the characteristics of students with emotional or behavioral disorders and the percentage you would expect in your class.

8.2 Identify the causes of emotional and behavioral disorders, and how these disorders might be treated educationally and medically.

8.3 Describe the teacher's role in the identification and assessment of students with emotional or behavioral challenges.

8.4 Describe the practices teachers can implement to enhance the teacher–student relationship, including the types of positive behavior intervention supports (PBIS) that are likely to facilitate the social and academic development of students with emotional and behavioral problems.

INTERVIEW: ADALYN SALADRIGAS

Adalyn Saladrigas has been a middle school teacher for over 10 years. Adalyn holds certification in special education and has elected to focus on teaching students who are identified as emotionally and behaviorally disordered. She explains, "I love these kids—and have learned when to be tough, when to be strong, and when to be compassionate."

She has taught in self-contained classes of students with emotional and behavior disorders as well as in inclusion settings where she has co-taught with general education colleagues. After recently earning a graduate degree in educational leadership, her role at her current school, Ponce de Leon Middle Community School, has changed. Part of her role is as an administrative assistant. As such, she serves as a resource for teachers, parents, and students in terms of social and behavioral issues. Someone is always knocking on her door for advice on specific incidents as well as more chronic problems with an individual child or group of students. Her second role is as a consultant for individual students with disabilities who are included in general education classrooms. Adalyn describes services for students with emotional and behavior disorders at her school using positive behavioral intervention supports (PBIS) within an RTI framework:

> Many students are placed in general education classrooms with a co-teaching arrangement between the general and special education teacher. I work with key educational stakeholders such as the classroom teacher and the school psychologist to assess students' needs and assure that we have the appropriate positive interventions in place. I monitor students carefully and consult with parents and teachers about their progress and needs.

Adalyn relies on positive behavior supports when making recommendations to parents and teachers. She realizes that some students need specific instruction in how to behave in a variety of settings and how to get along with others. Often that is the curriculum they need to succeed at school and beyond.

Introduction

The relationships established between students with emotional and behavioral disorders (EBD) and their teachers are often among their more meaningful relationships. Sharon Andreaci, a sixth-grade teacher, describes a student with emotional problems who was included in her classroom part-time and spent the rest of the day in the special education resource room:

> Diana was her name, and you could just tell by looking at her that something was wrong. She had been raped by a member of her family, and she never seemed to recover. She would see spirits and think evil things were coming to get her. She would say very strange things to me and to other students in the class. I felt that the support she got that year from me and the [other] students ... really helped her feel better accepted. I have followed her in school and checked to see how she is doing. Now she is in a regular ninth-grade class and is participating in counseling.

CHAPTER OUTLINE

MyEdLab
Video Example 8.1.
Watch this video and identify the attitudes and practices that are useful for including students with behavior problems in general education settings.

General education teachers indicate that the students they feel are the most difficult to have in their classrooms are students who demonstrate serious emotional and behavioral disorders (Landers, Alter, & Servilio, 2008; Scott, Park, Swain-Bradway, & Landers, 2007). As Juana Lopez, a third-grade teacher, says, "Overall, my students are terrific and respond well to the lessons I plan and teach. But when my two students with behavioral problems are present, I really earn my paycheck." Even special education teachers like Adalyn Saladrigas find students with serious emotional and behavioral problems to be a challenge; yet, for teachers who understand and implement the types of instructional adaptations necessary to meet these students' educational needs, the results can be very satisfying. As many experienced teachers have reported, the positive impact their efforts have on their students' lives can greatly reward teachers and stay with them forever.

Although some students with EBD receive at least part of their educational program in self-contained special education classrooms or in specialized settings (e.g., alternative schools for students with specific problems, hospital settings), approximately 50% of students who are identified as having emotional or behavioral disorders spend more than 21% of their school day in general education classrooms (National Center for Educational Statistics, 2009). Therefore, general education teachers must be knowledgeable in the techniques and skills necessary to work with students with EBD.

8.1 UNDERSTANDING EMOTIONAL AND BEHAVIORAL DISORDERS

What does it mean to have an emotional or behavioral disorder? What types of behaviors would you expect to see? As with many other disabilities, there is no clear line between those who have emotional and behavioral disorders and those who do not. Often the question is decided by the severity and persistence of the problem. As a teacher, you will come in contact with students who display a range of emotional and behavioral problems. Be sure to consider whether the problems are severe, exhibited in particular contexts, and persistent despite typical interventions that usually help.

8.1.1 The Federal Government's Definition of Emotional and Behavioral Disorders

Like other areas of special education, the field of emotional and behavioral disorders has grappled with definitional issues. The definition of *emotional disturbance* influences who is identified, who is provided services, how we conduct assessments, and how policies are developed and implemented. Although definitions among professional groups may differ (e.g., psychiatrist, psychologist, educators), they do have some commonalities. In general, describing someone as having **emotional disorders** or **behavioral disorders** commonly refers to students whose behavior falls considerably outside the norm, is chronic in nature, and is socially or culturally unacceptable (Quay & Hogan, 2013). Numerous definitions exist, but the two most prevalent are the U.S. federal government definition and that of the Council for Exceptional Children's division, Council for Children with Behavioral Disorders (CCBD).

The federal government uses the term *emotional disturbance* in its criteria for placement of students in special education. The federal definition of emotional disturbance is provided in Figure 8.1.

FIGURE 8.1 The Federal Definition of Emotional Disturbance

The federal government defines "emotionally disturbed" as follows:

1. The term means a condition exhibiting one or more of the following characteristics over a long period of time and to a marked degree, which adversely affects educational performance including:
   A. An inability to learn that cannot be explained by intellectual, sensory, or health factors;
   B. An inability to build or maintain satisfactory interpersonal relationships with peers and teachers;
   C. Inappropriate types of behavior or feelings under normal circumstances;
   D. A general pervasive mood of unhappiness or depression; or
   E. A tendency to develop physical symptoms or fears associated with personal or school problems.
2. The term includes children who are schizophrenic. The term does not include children who are socially maladjusted, unless it is determined that they are emotionally disturbed.

Source: Building the legacy: IDEA 2004, U.S. Department of Education, 2004, retrieved from http://idea.ed.gov.

8.1.2 An Alternative Definition of Emotional and Behavioral Disorders

Critics of this definition point out that it is vague and ambiguous. Terms such as *satisfactory* or *inappropriate* can be interpreted in different ways in different contexts (Walker, Ramsey, & Gresham, 2004; Walker & Severson, 1992). A larger concern for many is the definition's exclusion of students who are socially maladjusted, but not emotionally disturbed. What does it mean to be socially maladjusted? Though difficult to clearly identify, typically social maladjustment is reserved for youngsters demonstrating a pattern of persistently violating societal norms. These students may be consistently truant, abuse substances, and demonstrate consistent trouble with authority. Unless these students also demonstrate emotional disturbance, they are not eligible for special education.

The CCBD definition was proposed as an alternative to the federal definition (see Figure 8.2). Advocates of this alternative point out that it couches emotional and behavior disorders in school, age, and ethnic/cultural contexts and focuses on early identification and intervention (Cullinan, 2004; Fallen, O'Keefe, & Sugai, 2012). Moreover, it incorporates the idea that students can have more than one disability, referred to as **comorbidity**. For example, Sam is a fourth-grade student who qualifies for services in two areas: learning disability and emotional disorder. This issue is important because many students with emotional and behavior disorders also have challenges in academic achievement.

FIGURE 8.2 Council for Children with Behavioral Disorders (CCBD) Definition of Emotional and Behavioral Disorders

1. The term "emotional" or "behavioral disorder" means a disability that is characterized by emotional or behavioral responses in school programs so different from appropriate age, cultural, or ethnic norms that the responses adversely affect educational performance, including academic, social, vocational, or personal skills; more than a temporary, expected response to stressful events in the environment; consistently exhibited in two different settings, at least one of which is school-related; and unresponsive to direct intervention in general education, or the condition of the child is such that general education interventions would be insufficient.
2. Inability to learn that includes significant difficulty maintaining satisfactory interpersonal relationships with peers and teachers.
3. Inappropriate behaviors and feelings under normal circumstances.
4. Pervasive mood of unhappiness or depression.
5. Excessive fears related to personal or school circumstances.

Source: www.CEC.sped.org/CCBD, June 26, 2015

Although it is not the responsibility of general education teachers to determine whether a student has an emotional or behavioral disorder, because teachers are on the front line, they may be involved in the initial identification of students for referral for possible special education placement. Indeed, general education teachers serve as the primary source for referrals for students with emotional or behavioral challenges (Gresham & Kern, 2004). General education teachers may also be responsible for teaching students with EBD while they are in the general education classroom, full- or part-time. Therefore, teachers must become familiar with local and state policies and procedures for such students.

8.1.3 Prevalence of Students with Emotional or Behavioral Disorders

Prevalence of students with emotional and behavioral disorders varies, depending on the criteria used to classify students. Higher prevalence rates are reported for mild emotional or behavioral disorders, and lower prevalence rates for more severe disorders. Current reports of the prevalence of emotional and behavioral disorders in the general population range from 6% to 10% of the school-age population (Kauffman & Landrum, 2013). However, these estimates are considerably higher than the percentage of students identified and provided school services as emotionally disturbed. Although almost half of the referrals for special services occur in the elementary grades, referrals peak with students in their early teens. These numbers are especially worrisome given the preponderance of evidence documenting the importance of early (at or before entrance to school) identification and intervention. Thus, students with emotional or behavioral disorders are regarded as underserved.

The following issues are reasons often provided for the underidentification of students with emotional and behavioral disorders (Kauffman & Landrum, 2013):

- Social stigma is associated with the label "seriously emotionally disturbed."
- Eligibility for categorization as emotionally disordered is not clearly defined.
- The identification process lacks uniformity.
- Co-morbidity can make identification difficult.
- A lack of funding may limit school districts' willingness to identify and provide services for these students.
- There is often a lack of appropriate services when students are identified, and identification limits a school's ability to take disciplinary action against misbehavior.
- Adequate assessment measures to facilitate identification are few, though recent screening measures hold promise.

Although most professionals agree that students with emotional and behavioral disorders are underidentified, there is less certainty as to why so many of the students who are identified are males. For decades, males have consistently outnumbered females in all prevalence reports for emotional disturbance (Quay & Hogan, 2013; Wagner, Kutash, Duchnowski, Epstein, & Sumi, 2005). Students from minority populations are also disproportionately represented in the emotional and behavioral disorders category (Fallen et al., 2012; Skiba et al., 2008). The issue of overrepresentation of minority students is complex and is viewed in terms of a combination of factors, including cultural bias, poverty, and the historical practice of segregation and discrimination in schools (Harry & Klingner, 2014). Recently, case studies of African American students identified as having emotional disturbance revealed several disturbing contributors (Hart, Cramer, Harry, Klingner, & Surges, 2010) to their identification, including:

- Inadequate instruction and behavior management prior to referral
- Exclusion of classroom contextual information from the decision-making process
- Evaluation process that was not objective

What is the prevalence rate of students with disabilities in juvenile correction services? A survey conducted by Quinn, Rutherford, Leone, Osher, and Poirier (2005) revealed that 33.4% of all youth in the juvenile justice system were receiving services for special education. This is more than four times as many as the number of students provided services in the public schools. Of the individuals in juvenile justice receiving special education services, the majority were identified as having emotional disturbances (47.8%), with the next largest group identified as having specific learning disabilities (38.6%). Most of these students exhibit significant difficulties with reading and writing as well as social and emotional difficulties.

8.1.4 Types and Characteristics of Emotional or Behavioral Disorders

As Adalyn Saladrigas has learned over the years, students with behavior disorders display a wide range of characteristics. Perhaps the most consistent characteristic of these students is their inability to maintain satisfying relationships with others (e.g., Kauffman, 2004). Nonetheless, there is a spectrum of emotional and behavioral characteristics that elementary and secondary educators may experience among their students.

Think about classrooms where you have observed or taught. Which students got your attention first: those who were quiet and withdrawn or those who were acting out and disturbing others? Not surprisingly, students who demonstrate such externalizing behaviors as aggression, hitting, lack of attention, and impulsivity are much more likely to come to the teacher's attention and therefore to be identified as behavior-disordered (Furlong, Morrison, & Jimerson, 2004). On the other hand, there are students who exhibit more internalizing behaviors that are less noticeable, such as shyness, withdrawal, depression, fears/phobias, and anxiety (Spielberger, 2013). Emotional and behavioral disorders can be classified broadly as externalizing or internalizing. Students who exhibit **externalizing behaviors** (e.g., conduct disorders, acting out, aggression, tantrums, and bizarre behaviors) tend to interfere with others. Students who exhibit **internalizing behaviors** (e.g., fear, immaturity, tenseness, withdrawal, worry) tend to be less disturbing to others but still very distressing to themselves and their families.

For example, two students identified for special education services were placed in Maribel Sterling's sixth-grade class. A special educator in the school, Greg Hauser, oriented Maribel to their individualized education programs (IEPs) and provided support for setting expectations and for positive behavioral supports. Their behavior patterns were strikingly different. Steven was excessively shy and reluctant to make friends or speak in class. In addition, completing tests and assignments caused Steven a great deal of fear and anxiety. Tara, on the other hand, had a long history of exhibiting aggressive behavior toward peers and defiance of teachers and administrators. When aggravated, Tara would throw tantrums and use language inappropriate at school. Tara was provided additional supports to learn practices for self-control. Maribel and Greg worked together to address ways to help Steven with his internalizing behaviors and Tara with her externalizing behaviors. Greg met with Maribel weekly to check on their progress and to make changes as needed. Greg realized that taking simple data on the number and

What internalizing behaviors might signal the possible presence of emotional or behavioral disorders? How would you identify signals for externalizing problems?

severity of target behaviors helped him make decisions about the effectiveness of the interventions.

Classifying students' behaviors as either externalizing or internalizing can be useful for classroom teachers.

1. First, it helps teachers become aware that students with internalizing problems also need help, even though they do not call attention to themselves in the same way as those with externalizing problems. It is important for classroom teachers to recognize the special needs of these students even though they might not interfere with instruction or the learning of others.
2. Second, identifying the type of behavior problem provides a framework for establishing a plan to help. It is important to note, however, that research has revealed overlap of both externalizing and internalizing behavior; thus, it is important to realize that the categories are not discrete (Kauffman & Landrum, 2013).

During your career as a teacher, you will have students who display a range of these behaviors, some mild and some severe. Understanding these categories will help you not only to more accurately describe your students' behavior to professionals, but also to respond appropriately to your students. One classification system frequently used by counselors, psychologists, and physicians is described next.

8.1.5 The *Diagnostic and Statistical Manual of Mental Disorders*

The **Diagnostic and Statistical Manual of Mental Disorders** classification system is based on the reference book of the same name, published by the American Psychiatric Association (APA). Currently in its fifth edition, the book is commonly referred to as the *DSM-5* (American Psychiatric Association, 2013). Its purpose is to provide a uniform nomenclature that clinicians and researchers can use to discuss, research, diagnose, and treat mental disorders. The book describes specific criteria necessary for the diagnosis of each disorder as well as symptoms, indicators of severity, and any variations of the disorder.

Counselors, psychologists, psychiatrists, and medical doctors who have had extensive training in diagnostic procedures generally use the *DSM-5*. Although teachers need not be fluent in its content, having it as a reference allows teachers to facilitate communication with school counselors, psychologists, and doctors who may use *DSM-5* disorder classification titles, symptoms, and codes.

Students with emotional and behavioral disorders frequently experience comorbidity, or the co-occurrence of more than one disability. Learning disabilities, attention deficit hyperactivity disorder (ADHD), and developmental disabilities can co-occur with emotional and behavioral disorders. The *DSM-5* can assist trained professionals in the detection of comorbidity. It can also be helpful in identifying particular types of emotional and behavioral disorders based on characteristics such as anxiety, mood, defiance, conduct and aggression, and socialized aggression. Mental health specialists also use *DSM-5* to identify rare conditions such as schizophrenia.

Anxiety

The term **anxiety** describes an affective disorder that involves extreme worry, fearfulness, and concern (even when little reason for those feelings exists). Students with significant anxiety avoid ordinary activities because of fear or anxiety. Simple reassurance is rarely effective. For example, Trent developed a fear of eating. Neither his parents nor teacher could convince him to eat solid food. His behaviors about resisting solid food persisted over an extended period of time and began to take a toll on his family life as well as his work in school. Trent was eventually diagnosed as having an **anxiety disorder**.

The National Institute of Mental Health (NIMH, 2009a) lists five primary types of anxiety disorder:

1. ***Generalized Anxiety Disorder***—reoccurring fears about everyday situations
2. ***Obsessive-Compulsive Disorder***—persistent thoughts about worrisome subjects (e.g., germs, objects out of order, safety) that result in ritual routines to alleviate those thoughts (e.g., hand washing, reorganizing objects, taking safety precautions)
3. ***Panic Disorder***—sudden onset of intense fear resulting in extreme mental and physical reactions
4. ***Posttraumatic Stress Disorder***—persistent anxiety resulting from a traumatic experience such as a death of a family member, natural disaster, or life-threatening experience
5. ***Social Phobia (or Social Anxiety Disorder)***—exaggerated fear of social situations and anticipations of nonacceptance and ridicule from others

Some students with anxiety disorder frequently withdraw from others and appear reclusive, preferring solitary activities. Withdrawn students are often timid or bashful around others—even people they know. In class, they may avoid participating in group work, volunteering, or answering questions. Some exhibit tendencies toward perfectionism and are afraid of making mistakes. Excessive fear and anxiety can have an impact on socialization and academic performance (Anxiety Disorders Association of America, 2015; Schoenfeld & Janney, 2008).

The Anxiety and Depression Association of America (www.adaa.org) provides guidelines about the myths, misconceptions, and folklore related to anxiety. For example, many people think that wearing a rubber band around your wrist and popping it whenever you have negative thoughts will make the negative thoughts go away. This is a myth and in fact could potentially increase the frequency of the negative thoughts. Others think that avoiding stress and discomfort will make the anxiety disappear. This is also not true. It is more important to gently and gradually participate in appropriate activities that are associated with anxiety.

Mood disorders

When asked what they want for their children, most parents say, "I want them to be healthy and happy." When children and adolescents are constantly irritable, sad, or fatigued, adults are naturally concerned about their well-being. Such was the case with Miriam Schatz, a tenth grader. Miriam was normally a well-adjusted, high-achieving student with a small but close circle of friends. Late in the fall semester, Miriam became increasingly sullen, withdrawn, and distracted. Her school attendance became irregular and her grades plummeted. Several of Miriam's teachers noticed these changes in her disposition and referred her to the school counselor. As secondary school teachers, they were accustomed to temporary mood changes among their students, but in Miriam's case the changes in her behavior were drastic and prolonged.

Many students with emotional and behavioral disorders are also prone to mood disorders. Disruptive mood dysregulation disorder (DMDD) is a relatively new diagnosis in mental health and refers to youngsters who have persistent irritability and/ or are angry most of the time. These youngsters may also display intensive temper tantrums that occur three or more times per week and are displayed in more than one place (American Academy of Child and Adolescent Psychology [www.aacap.org], June 24, 2015).

Mood disorders may develop into various types of depression. Depression involves prolonged and persistent feelings of dejection that interfere with life functioning (American Academy of Child and Adolescent Psychiatry [AACAP], 2014) and are associated with medical problems, particularly cardiovascular disease (Grippo & Johnson, 2009).

Bipolar disorder (formerly referred to as manic depression) is characterized by extreme mood swings (U.S. Department of Health and Human Services, 2015). These unpredictable mood swings can include "mania," which is excessive happiness, excitement, and increased energy and excitability, and also depressive symptoms such as sadness, anxiety, irritability, and even thoughts of death and suicide. All forms of mood disorders can vary in terms of frequency and degree. Some mood disorders are caused by genetic factors including abnormal brain circuits involving emotional processing, others by environment, and still others by a combination of genetic and environmental factors (Cancro, 2008; AACAP [www.aacap.org], June 24, 2015).

Mental health workers and educators have long realized that depression is a widespread, serious problem among children and adolescents, but it has only been in recent years that intensive attention has been focused on the disorder (NIMH, 2015). Whereas depression is more prevalent in adult women than men—women are 70% more likely to be depressed—young boys are as likely as girls to exhibit depression (e.g., Kovacs, Obrosky, & Sherrill, 2003). However, after the onset of puberty, depression in girls increases dramatically (Galambos, Leadbeater, & Barker, 2004). Slightly more than 3% of youngsters between 13 and 18 have depression (NIMH [www.NIMH.org], June 22, 2015). As girls with depression get older, they have an increased risk for acquiring eating disorders, whereas boys with depression may go on to exhibit aggressive behaviors and substance abuse (Kovacs et al., 2003). Youngsters with severe emotional problems who exhibit depressive symptoms are also more likely to use abuse substances, including illicit drugs, and to use multiple drugs (Wu et al., 2008). Teachers often have difficulty identifying students who are depressed (AACAP, 2015). This is particularly true at the middle and high school levels when students have multiple teachers. Consider that students who are bullied are much more likely to exhibit signs of depression, so you may want to pay particular attention to students who report bullying or appear to be victims (Fleming & Jacobsen, 2009). To recognize signs of depression in students, see Tips for Teachers 8.1.

Of particular concern is the fact that students who experience depression may grapple with thoughts of suicide. Indeed, suicide ranks third in leading causes of death among children ages 5 to 14 (AACAP, 2009b). A number of situations can trigger suicidal thoughts. Family conflict, changes in family situations, drug/alcohol abuse, and preexisting suicidal thoughts are among the conditions that may cause suicide among children and adolescents (AACAP, 2009b; Brent, Melhem, Donohoe, & Walker, 2009). The American Foundation for Suicide Prevention (2009) explains that suicide is preventable and that the emotional states that trigger suicide are often treatable. Suicide attempts by adolescents are frequently made to accomplish one or more of the following:

- Escape stress or stressful situations
- Demonstrate to others that they are desperate
- Hurt or get back at others
- Get others to adjust or modify their views

TIPS FOR TEACHERS 8.1

Recognizing Signs of Depression

The following behaviors may indicate depression:

- Acting sad, lonely, and apathetic
- Exhibiting low self-esteem or hopelessness
- Decreased interest in activities (particularly avoiding social experiences)
- Having chronic complaints about physical ailments, such as stomachaches or aching arms or legs, with no apparent cause
- Frequently being absent from school
- Talking of suicide or self-destructive behavior (e.g., cutting)
- Persistent boredom or low energy; loss of interest in activities
- Poor school performance
- Increased irritability, anger, or hostility
- Insomnia or sleep disturbances such as sleeping during the day and not at night

TIPS FOR TEACHERS 8.2

Suicide Warning Signs

Many adolescents provide warning signs that they are about to attempt suicide (AACAP [www.AACAP.org], October 2013; National Association of School Psychologists, 2001). Respond to these warning signs immediately and appropriately.

- *Suicide Notices.* All threats including verbal notices such as, "Don't worry you won't have me around much longer" should be considered as potential suicide threats. Suicide notes should be taken very seriously and reported to appropriate persons, including mental health professionals.
- *Previous Attempts.* Any student who has previously attempted suicide should be monitored carefully.
- *Depression.* Signs of depression including withdrawal and hopelessness may be concerns for risk for suicide.
- *Final Arrangements.* Students who exhibit signs that they are getting their affairs in order or making final arrangements, including giving away valuable items, preparing goodbyes, and so forth, may be suicidal risks.
- *Violent Behavior.* Extreme behaviors such as running away or signs of self-injury such as cutting and other inappropriately self-harmful behaviors may be signs of a suicide attempt.
- *Personality Changes.* Students who exhibit extreme changes in personality, appearance or persistently discussing how they are a bad person should be considered at risk.

In the unlikely event that a student reveals suicidal thoughts to a classroom teacher, that teacher must discuss the matter with the school counselor immediately. Also, if a student seems deeply depressed over a sustained period of time (over 2 weeks), seek advice from the school counselor as well. See Tips for Teachers 8.2 for a list of some of the suicide warning signs.

Defiance

It is not unusual for elementary and particularly secondary students to be defiant or disobedient from time to time. However, when students habitually question authority, intentionally misbehave and ignore rules, are temperamental and negative, and blame others for their actions, or when social and/or academic progress is inhibited as a result, such actions may indicate signs of an **oppositional defiant disorder (ODD)** (AACAP [www.aacap.org], July, 2013). ODD is a disorder that often occurs with other disorders, such as mood disorders and conduct disorders.

The onset of ODD often occurs before age 8 and frequently exacerbates with age (Hommersen et al., 2006); it is present in 1% to 16% of school-age children. In the case of Marcus Wagner, it all began in kindergarten. Each day after the pledge to the flag and a moment of silence, students recited their school's mission statement, which included language about being a good citizen and following rules. It didn't register with Marcus. Marcus spent most of the school day ignoring rules; talking back to his teacher, Megan O'Conner; and refusing to take blame for his actions. Given that defiant behavior is likely to persist, early diagnosis, intervention, and collaboration with parents is important (Downing, 2007).

The American Academy of Child and Adolescent Psychiatry (www.aacap.org, October 2013) identifies the following symptoms of ODD in children:

- Frequent temper tantrums
- Excessive arguing
- Excessive questioning of rules
- Active defiance of adults
- Deliberately annoying or upsetting people
- Blaming others for their mistakes
- Being spiteful and revenge seeking

What can teachers do to help students with ODD?

- Build on the positive, providing encouragement and support whenever possible.
- Take time out when you are in a conflict that is not readily resolving.
- Suggest that you discuss the issue again later and set a time to do so.

Students with ODD have trouble with power struggles, so you want to reduce the number of conflict situations you encounter. When providing consequences, consider ones that are reasonable and age appropriate.

8.1.6 Conduct and Aggression

Behaviors associated with misconduct and aggression can be covert (e.g., stealing, lying, burglary, use of drugs and alcohol) or overt (e.g., coercion, bullying, manipulation of others, escalated interactions with teachers, parents, and peers) (AACAP, 2015; Loeber et al., 1993). When students are consistent in ignoring the rights of others and are cruel, destructive, deceitful, or truant, they may be diagnosed as having a **conduct disorder**. Conduct disorder is the most common of the emotional and behavioral problems exhibited by school-age children. Some students with conduct disorders, like eighth-grader Derek Curtis, provoke peers into hitting them or others. When his teacher, Patrick Anthony, called Derek's home to describe his conduct, he discovered frustrated parents who feel that Derek is not as responsive to them as they would like.

The number and duration of risk factors the student experiences influences the likelihood that aggression and problem behaviors will continue throughout a student's lifetime (Mack, 2004). As a result of the multidimensional nature of conduct disorder, remediation, especially in older children and teens, is difficult and complex (AACAP, 2015). Although they typically have the cognitive skills to do well in school, students with conduct disorder often display low academic achievement.

Behavior management strategies and cooperation among the school counselor, psychologist, and parents are often effective for students with mild to moderate conduct disorder. For students with more extreme conduct disorder, however, such strategies may not be as effective and more dramatic measures may be required, such as removing the student from the classroom for all or part of the school day and moving the student into a special education setting where small class sizes and low student–teacher ratio are provided.

The American Academy of Child and Adolescent Psychiatry (August, 2013) identifies the following symptoms of conduct disorders in children:

- Aggression toward people and/or animals, including bullying, threatening, fighting, and cruelty
- Destruction of property (e.g., setting fire to property)
- Deception, lying, and stealing
- Serious breaking of rules, such as running away

8.1.7 Socialized Aggression

Antisocial behavior involves acts that can cause mental or physical harm to others or to the property of others. Although many people have intentionally or unintentionally engaged in some type of antisocial behavior at some point in their lives, the term **socialized aggression** refers to the repeated and routine display of such behaviors. Social aggression describes the behavior of youngsters who join a community of peers who are involved in a variety of delinquent acts, including bullying, thievery, and gang behavior. Adults may describe such individuals as hanging around with the wrong kinds of kids, displaying behaviors that are not typical of others in their age group, and engaging in behaviors such as harassing others and stealing and damaging property. These students may also cut classes or skip school.

Socialized aggression is also associated with **group behavior**; that is, these behaviors are displayed in the presence of other group members. Students with socialized

TIPS FOR TEACHERS 8.3

Key Points About Gangs

- Gangs can be highly organized and follow very specific rules and practices and can also be less structured and follow local rules.
- There are approximately 33,000 gangs with 1.4 million members in the United States.
- Gangs can have national affiliations or be local.
- Some gangs have allegiance to a particular color and other gangs do not.
- Gangs often do not have a clearly identified leader.
- Gangs usually have a particular area that they claim as their "turf."
- Gang members are typically male and may join gangs as young as age 8 but are typically 12 and older when they join the gang.
- Females are moving away from being girlfriends of gang members and are starting their own gangs.
- Gang members usually have a symbol to communicate to others that they are a member of that gang, for example, a handshake or other hand signal.
- Gangs typically are prone to violence and disrespect for authority. Between 48% and 90% of violent crimes are associated with gangs.

Source: (National Gang Report [https://www.fbi.gov/stats-services/publications/national-gang-report-2013/], 2013)

aggression often belong to gangs. Students' attraction to gang life is apparent in many inner cities as well as in suburban and rural areas and, since 2000, has been on the rise (Howell & Griffiths, 2015). Law enforcement agencies categorize gangs into the following four groups:

1. *Delinquent* youth gangs, which are loosely structured and recognize one another by the way they dress and look
2. *Turf-based* gangs, which are also loosely structured but committed to defending a reputation or neighborhood
3. *Crime-oriented* gangs or drug gangs, which engage in robbery, burglary, or sale of controlled substances for monetary gain
4. *Violent* hate gangs, whose members commit assaults or hate crimes against specific types of people

Students may be attracted to gangs due to a desire for companionship, acceptance, and success or for the perception of safety they believe may be afforded to them with gang membership (Howell & Griffiths, 2015; Thornberry, Huizinga, & Loeber, 2004). Many such students feel that they have not been accepted by traditional society. Teachers who work in suburban or rural settings may perceive that they will be "free" of gang activities and that gangs are something that occurs only in big cities or inner cities. Gangs are *not* just a problem for inner cities or students of a particular race or culture, or only for boys—gangs occur everywhere and they are flourishing in the United States. Tips for Teachers 8.3 provides some key points about gangs.

A high rate of overlap exists between conduct disorder, attention problems, and socialized aggression. For example, many students who have attention problems might also display behaviors associated with conduct disorder, such as aggression and acting out. See Tips for Teachers 8.4 to better understand how to respond to students' violent behaviors.

8.1.8 Schizophrenia

The National Institute of Mental Health (NIMH) defines schizophrenia as "a chronic, severe, and disabling brain disorder that has been recognized throughout recorded history" (NIHM [www.nimh.org], June 2015). It is one of a family of psychotic disorders. Schizophrenia is rare among children and typically emerges in the late teens or early 20s

TIPS FOR TEACHERS 8.4

Understanding Violent Behavior

- Take violent behavior at any age seriously. Do not dismiss it as a passing phase or because the child is very young.
- If a student displays violent behavior, contact the appropriate mental health professional or school psychologist. Work with the team of mental health specialists to conduct a functional behavior assessment to identify and address the needs of the child.
- Consider the following risk factors for violent behavior:

  Low frustration tolerance
  Frequent and easy loss of temper
  Previous aggressive behavior
  Victim of physical or sexual abuse
  Violence in the home

with most cases developing in adulthood (Konopasek & Forness, 2004). Individuals with schizophrenia experience hallucinations and delusions, and have disorders of both thought and movement (NIHM [www.nimh.org], June 2015). Individuals with schizophrenia demonstrate loss of contact with reality, including inappropriate actions and bizarre thought processes. Manuel Fuentes was a 17-year-old who believed that his mind was being controlled by aliens who had access to his thoughts and could control his behavior. He was prone to sudden outbursts and bizarre behaviors and frequently disrupted class by verbalizing bizarre interpretations of what he thought he was being told by aliens. Fortunately, treatment procedures (both with medication and social therapy) for schizophrenia have improved over the years and have allowed many individuals with the disorder to live productive lives (Lehman et al., 2004; see also "schizophrenia treatment" at http://www.psychcentral.com).

What are some of the behaviors associated with schizophrenia?

- Hallucinations in which they hear voices that others do not hear
- Delusions in which they believe, for example, that the waves from the television are controlling their mind
- Often do not make sense when they talk
- Lose touch with the reality of their setting

MyEdLab **Self-Check 8.1**

MyEdLab **Application Exercise 8.1:** Types of Emotional or Behavioral Disorders

8.2 CAUSES OF EMOTIONAL AND BEHAVIORAL DISORDERS

Our best understanding is that emotional and behavioral disorders result from both biological and environmental factors. In many cases, the causes of a disorder are complex and multiple. Because of the social nature of emotional and behavioral disorders, biological causes usually do not work independently of environmental causes. Typically, no one cause precipitates emotional and behavioral disorders (Hallahan et al., 2012).

8.2.1 Biological Causes

Three primary biological causes are potential contributors to emotional and behavioral disorders: brain disorders, genetics, and temperament (Hallahan et al., 2012; Heward, 2013; Pierangelo & Giuliani, 2007). Biological causes can work independently or in conjunction with each other.

1. Brain disorders can result from injuries, prenatal damage, infection, or other brain defects. Chemical imbalances can also affect the brain and nervous system.
2. Mental illness can have genetic roots. For example, depression is a disorder that tends to run in families, and maternal depression is a strong predictor of problem behavior in young children (Nelson, Stage, Duppong-Hurley, Synhorst, & Epstein, 2007).
3. Temperament is considered to be a biologically determined or inborn condition (Hallahan et al., 2012; Kagan & Snidman, 2004).

8.2.2 Environmental Causes

Environmental causes of emotional and behavioral disorders stem from unsettling circumstances in the home or community. What happens in the environment can affect students' quality of life, emotional well-being, and ultimately success or failure at school (Sacks & Kern, 2008). Sometimes these circumstances are temporary; at other times, they are an ongoing part of the student's life. Although the educational impact (both short term and long term) of environmental causes varies from student to student, it is important that you, as a teacher, create a classroom atmosphere that is a safe haven from the unpredictable circumstances affecting your students' lives.

Home conditions

Home conditions that can potentially affect student academic performance include family poverty, family instability, and family violence. According to the Children's Defense Fund (Children's Defense Fund [www.childrensdefense.org], 2015), one out of five children comes from a family living below the poverty level. The United States has the second highest child poverty rate of thirty-five industrialized countries. Students whose families live in poverty often come to school without their basic needs of food, clothing, shelter, and health care being met. The limitations that poverty places on families are likely to affect students' quality of life, level of stress, and performance in school (Children's Defense Fund [www.childrensdefense.org], 2015). Families with financial burdens often cannot afford educational materials, home computers, and extended vacations or day trips that broaden horizons and reduce stress. Older students may also have extended work responsibilities, such as caring for siblings or contributing to the family income.

One of the most common jolts to family stability is divorce. Divorce can cause students to become depressed and angry and can affect their desire to achieve in school (Wallerstein, Lewis, & Blakeslee, 2000). Although the emotional impact of divorce on individual children may vary, a divorce does cause inevitable changes in the home routine (Kelly & Emery, 2003). For example, after a divorce, children may have two homes instead of one, which can disrupt homework and study patterns, as well as such basic routines as getting dressed and ready for school.

Family stress and violence can create a volatile home situation that can result in child neglect and mental or physical abuse (Mattison, 2004). It is imperative that you follow local guidelines in reporting neglect and abuse. As a teacher, you have little control about what happens in the home; however, you can work with school counselors, social workers, and psychologists to provide parents and children with the support they need.

Community conditions

Every day we hear and read about risks to the safety of children in our communities. Millions of young people face life-threatening circumstances through neighborhood violence. Children who experience threats to their safety and well-being in their communities are at risk for having academic and socioemotional problems at school. Some safety risks are chronic and ongoing; others are the product of particular crises.

National tragedies continue to challenge our community and our teachers in how best to help students cope with safety issues that are beyond most of our experience. Well-publicized shootings at schools have undermined students' feelings of safety.

We can only begin to imagine the impact of our national tragedy of September 11, 2001. Traumatic natural disasters such as Hurricane Katrina resulted in high numbers of children in need of counseling and support. Organizations such as the Council for Exceptional Children (CEC) and the Association for Supervision and Curriculum Development (ASCD) provide updated resources to general and special education teachers for helping students through crises and trying times. Many schools are implementing violence-prevention and conflict-resolution programs to address these issues. It is imperative that you, as a classroom teacher, become familiar with your school district's procedures for student safety.

MyEdLab **Self-Check 8.2**

MyEdLab **Application Exercise 8.2:** Causes of EBD

8.3 IDENTIFICATION AND ASSESSMENT OF STUDENTS WITH EMOTIONAL AND BEHAVIORAL DISORDERS

Parents and other adults often recognize youngsters with severe emotional and behavioral disorders before they start attending school. These students may receive early treatment through a combination of educational interventions, medications, play therapy, and family counseling. Other students have emotional and behavioral disorders that remain latent until students are older. In some of these cases, the disorders become apparent once the students are in structured settings such as the school.

8.3.1 Initial Identification

MyEdLab
Video Example 8.2.
Watch this video and describe what you learned about what you might be able to do to facilitate a functional classroom setting for students with behavior problems.

Formal identification and assessment requires involvement of professionals who are specifically trained to do so (e.g., psychologists, physicians). As a classroom teacher, you may be involved in the initial identification process and, as a part of the response to intervention, universal screening, progress monitoring, and functional behavior assessment to determine appropriate levels of support.

Part of your responsibility as a classroom teacher is to handle the everyday situations when students do not meet established behavioral expectations. Realistically, you will encounter students with emotional or behavioral patterns that cause you concern and that warrant more intensive intervention and professional input. How should classroom teachers decide whether a student's behavior is problematic enough to warrant referral for more intensive interventions?

- *Behavior–age discrepancy.* The social and behavioral problems exhibited must be unusual or deviant for the student's age. For example, clinging to adults is common in very young children but is deemed inappropriate for school-age children.
- *Frequency of occurrence of the behavior.* Under stress, all people exhibit characteristics of emotional or behavioral disorders, such as whining, withdrawal, mood swings, or depression. These behaviors and feeling states are not considered problems if they occur only occasionally or as a result of a significant event, such as a car accident. However, frequent and extreme occurrence of these behaviors warrants referral.
- *Number of symptoms.* The display of one or more behavior problems at some time does not indicate that a person has an emotional or behavioral disorder, but students who frequently display several related symptoms should be considered for referral. The greater the number of symptoms, the greater the likelihood of a serious emotional disturbance. For example, Marla was occasionally depressed and unable to get out of bed without considerable prodding from her mother, but once

she got going and ready for school, she functioned the rest of the day with few problems. However, Kayla consistently exhibited signs of depression, including inability to go to school consistently, disinterest in school work, lack of interest in friends or participating in social situations, and consistent and ongoing thoughts of low self-esteem.

- *Inner suffering.* Signs of inner suffering include low self-esteem, less interaction with others, appearance of sadness or loneliness, and general malaise. Inner suffering interferes with learning, social relationships, and achievement.
- *Harm to others.* The student consistently harms others or animals intentionally and shows little remorse. These students seem indifferent to the feelings of others and do not seem affected by the effects of their cruelty on others.
- *Persistence of the behavior.* Persistence refers to the continuation of the emotional or behavioral problems over time, despite substantive efforts on the part of adults and the student to change the behaviors. A behavior problem is persistent when several types of interventions have not resulted in long-term change.
- *Self-satisfaction.* Students who appear to be generally happy with themselves reflect a measure of self-satisfaction. They show positive affect and the willingness to give and receive affection and pleasure. A lack of self-satisfaction contributes to problems that interfere with personal growth and development as well as academic and social success, but that might not signal the presence of an emotional or behavioral disorder.
- *Severity and duration of the behavior.* All dimensions of a student's behavior can be classified in terms of two important criteria: severity and duration. *Severity* refers to how extreme the problem is and the extent to which it varies from expected behavior. *Duration* (or persistence) refers to the length of time the problem has existed. A problem that persists over a long period is said to be *chronic.* Most students who are identified as having emotional or behavioral disorders must deal with their problems throughout their lifetimes.

When identifying a student with possible emotional or behavioral disorders, teachers need to be prepared to answer the following questions:

- How often does the behavior occur? How long has the problem persisted?
- Under what conditions does the behavior occur? To what extent does this behavior occur in different settings, such as the classroom, playground, or home?
- What are the *antecedents* of the behavior; that is, what events occur before the behavior is exhibited, triggering the behavior? What are the *consequences*; that is, what occurs as an outcome of the behavior after the student exhibits the behavior?
- Does the problem not arise in certain situations?
- To what extent does the student develop and maintain positive relationships with other people? Does the student seem happy or display satisfaction at any time?
- How severe is the problem? To what extent is the behavior deviant from that of other students of the same age?
- To what extent is this a problem in the relationship between you and the student or a problem within the student?
- What have you and/or the family done to reduce or eliminate the problem?

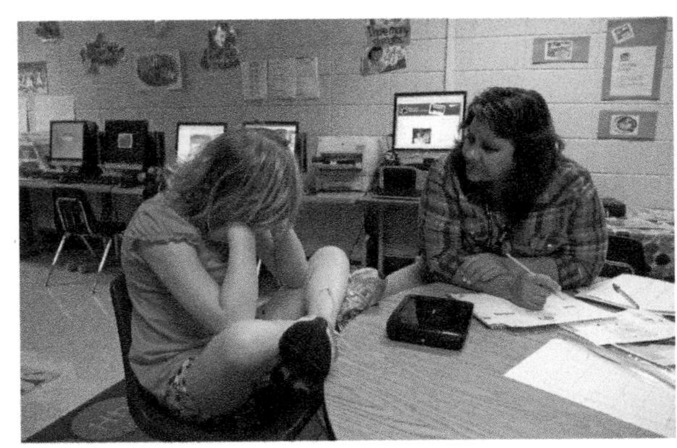

What criteria would you use to determine whether this student's behavior warrants referral for evaluation for the presence of an emotional or behavioral disorder?

Tips for Teachers 8.5 offers suggestions for gathering information before referring a student with possible emotional or behavioral disorders.

TIPS FOR TEACHERS 8.5

Making Referrals for Students with Emotional or Behavioral Disorders

- Keep an electronic or written journal that includes the dates, times, and contexts of student behaviors that you regard as deviant or bizarre.
- Be specific, using behavioral terms to describe what occurs. As much as possible, avoid including value judgments. For example, a journal entry might read "Mark got up from his seat, pushed John out of his chair, and then ran out of the room."
- Record any relevant information from parents, such as their descriptions of the student's behavior at home or telephone calls concerning the student. Keep parents informed of the problem, both in writing and by telephone.
- Record relevant information from other teachers or school personnel who know the student.
- Keep samples of the student's work in different subjects and a record of skills the student can and cannot perform. If the student's academic performance is inconsistent, note this as well.

8.3.2 Response to Intervention for Students with Emotional and Behavioral Disorders

Katie Newberg, a fifth-grade teacher, has the reputation among parents, fellow teachers, and her administrator as being highly organized. Year in and year out she creates a welcoming classroom that makes students want to learn, and they do. From the outset of this school year, Katie knew that she was working with a special group of children and that all of her attention to classroom organization, consistent following of rules, and predictable routines was not going to be enough to meet the needs of three students in particular: Mike, who exhibits disruptive behaviors; Carlton, who is often defiant and ignores rules; and Phoebe, who is extremely withdrawn and often is absent due to a great deal of anxiety about school. Katie kept careful anecdotal records on each child in preparation for meeting with parents and other school-based colleagues. Discussions with the school counselor, special education teacher, and parents led to the initial screening of the children and attempts to implement appropriate interventions. Nothing seemed to work. It was clear that each of her students needed additional support to make progress.

In Katie's case, Tier 1 of response to intervention (RTI) involved implementation of the following as part of a schoolwide positive behavioral interventions and support (PBIS) model: explicit teaching of rules and consequences, use of research-based universal strategies for general classroom management, and universal screening to identify students with special needs (Fairbanks, Simonsen, & Sugai, 2008; www.PBIS.org). Katie worked with parents and other professionals in the classroom to target problem behaviors and decide what additional positive behavioral supports might be appropriate for her to implement in the classroom.

Tips for Teachers 8.6 provides general research-based recommendations for interventions for children with emotional and behavioral disorders.

Ongoing monitoring of Mike, Carlton, and Phoebe indicated that more support was necessary. Thus, Tier 2 (or secondary) behavior interventions were launched. Tier 2 interventions are typically small-group interventions that can provide students with the self-control, self-monitoring, social, and self-management skills they need. The special educator, school counselor, and Katie met with each of the children's parents to identify concrete interventions for implementation. Katie's school uses a **check-in, check-out (CICO) procedure** where students earn points for appropriate behaviors in small-group instructional or mentoring sessions and in the classroom (Campbell & Anderson, 2008; Hawken & Horner, 2003; Maggin, 2015). (See Tips for Teachers 8.7 for more details on CICO.)

TIPS FOR TEACHERS 8.6

Recommendations for Effective Behavioral Interventions

1. Identify the specifics of the behavior and the conditions that prompt and reinforce it.
2. Modify the classroom learning environment to reduce problem behavior.
3. Teach and reinforce new skills to increase appropriate behavior and preserve a positive classroom climate.
4. Draw on relationships with professional colleagues and students' families.
5. Assess whether schoolwide behavior problems warrant adopting schoolwide strategies or programs.

To implement these recommendations consider:

- Linking assessment data of the student's behavior with interventions.
- Implementing interventions across settings and placements. For example, a behavior contract used in the special education classroom can also be used in a general class setting.
- Providing a range of interventions for improving behavior. The effect of a single intervention is likely to be short-lived.
- Using interventions that address not only the behavior related to a single disciplinary action, but also the related behaviors and contributing factors.
- Implementing interventions that are proactive, corrective, and instructive. In this way, interventions can support prosocial behaviors and the self-management strategies that students need to mediate their own behavior.
- Ensuring that interventions are developmentally appropriate and address the unique strengths and weaknesses of the individual.
- Accompanying student supports with parent education and family therapy.
- Devoting resources to early intervention to reduce the need for more extensive and expensive treatment later. Interventions are the most effective when provided early in life.
- Recognizing that the intensity and the duration of the intervention will vary depending on individual student needs.

Source: Epstein et al., 2008

All three students were monitored weekly for a period of 6 weeks. In that time, Mike's disruptive behavior began to subside as the result of the small-group interventions. Phoebe, although still somewhat withdrawn, demonstrated decreased absenteeism and increased participation in peer tutoring and small-group activities. However, Carlton's defiance and tendency to ignore rules continued to escalate. His aggressive behaviors (hitting, bullying) were endangering other students in the classroom. Moreover, his academic performance, particularly in reading, was an area that needed intervention as well.

TIPS FOR TEACHERS 8.7

Steps for Implementing Check-in/Check-out (CICO)

Check-in/check-out (CICO) serves as a way to conduct progress monitoring with students with emotional and behavioral disorders. It is a point system that serves as an ongoing report card of student behavior. Use the following steps to implement CICO:

Step 1 Understand how CICO fits into the overall positive behavior support program in your school and who serves as the CICO coordinator.

Step 2 Understand specifically what behaviors are being targeted for each student involved.

Step 3 Learn what school personnel will be involved with CICO for each student and if and how parents are to be involved.

Step 4 Review procedures for when points are to be recorded and reviewed, and when rewards are to be given.

Step 5 Evaluate the CICO plan with the CICO coordinator to decide if intervals for recording and reviewing need to be adjusted and whether selected rewards are appropriate.

At Katie's school, Tier 3 (or tertiary) interventions for students with emotional and behavioral issues begin with a comprehensive functional behavior assessment (see the following section). After a careful analysis of the externalizing behaviors Carlton displayed, a more intensive individual intervention program was deemed necessary. Specific replacement behaviors and academic objectives were targeted and taught to Carlton in one-on-one sessions. In Carlton's case, the school decided to employ multiple supports (family, teacher, school counselor, social worker, and school psychologist) to ensure consistency of intervention implementation at home, in school, and in community settings.

RTI is used in many schools and school districts. State and local guidelines coupled with the wide range of individual differences in student needs and local resources mean that the procedures at Katie's school might be different than your own—though the critical features discussed are likely represented in the RTI approach used in your school system. A great deal of research is needed to validate RTI practices at each tier for students with emotional and behavioral disorders. Consequently, schools may differ considerably at each tier in terms of

- Assessments, screening, and monitoring used
- Implementation of functional behavior assessment
- Interventions employed
- School personnel involved
- Venue for interventions (e.g., general education classroom, resource room)
- Decision points for placement in special education and IEP development

As part of your role as a general education teacher in the implementation of RTI, you will likely be involved in universal screening and progress monitoring as well as in functional behavioral assessment.

8.3.3 Universal Screening and Progress Monitoring

Key to RTI are the goals of early identification of emotional and behavioral disorders, appropriate intervention, and ongoing monitoring of student progress. Universal screening can provide quick information about which students may need additional academic supports. Screening of all students early in the school year can also be used to identify students who need emotional or behavioral supports. Recall that universal screening was introduced and discussed much earlier in the text.

Initial screening might involve basic student data: number of absences, discipline referrals, and teacher requests for additional support with a child. Information from previous years and schools may also be reviewed to provide archival data. Beyond that, you may be asked to complete a screening checklist or scale to provide additional information (Downing, 2007). Longitudinal research of students at risk for emotional and behavioral disorders indicates that teacher ratings are stable predictors of later identification (Montague, Enders, & Castro, 2005). Some commonly used rating scales are the Social Skills Rating System for Children and the Social Skills Improvement System (Gresham & Elliott, 2010; Gresham et al., 2011), Childhood Behavior Checklist (Achenbach & McConaughy, 2003), and Systematic Screening for Behavior Disorders (Walker et al., 2010). The brief ratings of target behaviors may also be a useful tool for screening and monitoring behavior problems (Direct Behavior Rating of Single Item Scale; Chafouleas, 2012). Individuals who are trained to do so using specific decision rules may be necessary for interpreting findings from such screening measures (Gresham, 2007). The National Center on Intensive Interventions provides a chart of screening and progress monitoring measures in the area of behavior disorders (www.intensiveintervention.org/chart/behavioral-progress-monitoring-tools; June, 26, 2015).

Universal screening should occur early in the school year to prevent escalation of potential problem behaviors, but not so early that teachers are not sufficiently able to report on the behaviors of their students.

When individual students have been identified as being in need of additional positive behavior supports, frequent progress monitoring is vital (Griffiths, VanDerHeyden,

Parson, & Burns, 2006). Monitoring can determine whether interventions can be discontinued, continued under similar or adapted conditions, or intensified. Monitoring of student progress should be coupled with an evaluation of intervention implementation fidelity, or the degree to which the intervention has been administered with consistency and according to prescribed guidelines (Gresham, 2007). The format used for progress monitoring should be aligned with the targeted objective and can involve observation, checklists, point systems, interviews, or logs and journals. If appropriate, parents can serve as partners in progress monitoring and students can become engaged in self-assessment. Data from progress monitoring should be reviewed systematically to make necessary adjustments in intervention. One process that works hand-in-hand with progress monitoring is functional behavioral assessment.

8.3.4 Developing a Functional Behavioral Assessment

New advances in assessment and intervention provide a wealth of information for teachers of students with emotional or behavioral disorders. In fact, much of the distress associated with these disorders can be minimized with the implementation of timely and appropriate interventions and supports. At school, an important component of identifying *and* addressing the needs of students with emotional or behavioral disorders is to develop a functional behavioral assessment (FBA). Functional behavioral assessments are a method of gathering data to design the most effective positive support plans and to monitor students' progress. As mandated by the Individuals with Disabilities Education Improvement Act (IDEIA), all students with disabilities who have significant behavior problems that interfere with either their own learning or the learning of other students must have an FBA.

An FBA and a behavioral improvement plan (BIP) are designed to identify behavior problems of students and to develop an intervention plan to treat these behavior problems. The procedures and practices for developing an FBA are not nearly as well defined as those for an IEP, and many school personnel use a variety of approaches for obtaining information and designing an FBA and a BIP. If students' behavior is interfering with their learning, the design and use of an FBA is required. Because it is much more likely that the FBA will assist students rather than interfere with their learning, when in doubt it is a good idea to develop an FBA and a BIP. As a general education teacher, you'll work with a special education colleague and possibly other professionals in the school to develop both.

According to Shippen, Simpson, and Crites (2003), there are several critical steps in designing an effective FBA, including:

- Defining the target behavior in behavioral terms. Clearly specify the behavior(s) you would like to see the student perform in observational terms that can be recorded and monitored.
- Collecting and monitoring the target behaviors through ongoing data collection that considers frequency, intensity, and rate.
- Recording the events and behaviors that precede and follow the target behavior. In this way, the antecedent, behavior, and consequences are noted.
- Developing a hypothesis of the conditions under which the target behavior occurs. This hypothesis guides the intervention plan.
- Developing an intervention plan that considers the antecedents and reinforcers and is built to test the hypothesis.

Although the FBA is often used in reaction to problem behaviors (as mandated in IDEIA), it is perhaps most effective when used to determine the educational needs of students before behavior has gotten out of control. It may also be used as part of an RTI model, to collect data and to track progress and the effectiveness of interventions before referral to special education (Ryan, Halsey, & Matthews, 2003). Figure 8.3 provides an example of a functional behavioral assessment.

FIGURE 8.3 Methods of Functional Behavioral Assessment (FBA)

Functional behavioral assessment (FBA) is a systematic process for gathering information to determine the relationships between a person's problem behavior and aspects of his or her environment. Through FBA, it is possible to identify specific events that predict and maintain behavior and to design a support plan that effectively addresses those variables. FBA methods can, and should, vary across circumstances but typically include *record reviews, interviews, social and behavioral rating forms,* and *direct observation.*

METHOD	SAMPLE SOURCES/TOOLS	EXAMPLES/PRODUCTS
Record reviews	Diagnostic/medical records, psychological reports, assessments from therapies, developmental profiles, social histories, previous behavior management plans, individualized education programs (IEPs), individualized family service plans (IFSPs), anecdotal records, incident reports, discipline referrals.	Sammy's records contained: History of allergies and asthma Some effective educational strategies used in the past Patterns of discipline referrals
Structured interviews	People who know the individual well and represent a range of environments (the person, family members, teachers, friends, direct service providers, etc.) may be interviewed. Some interview tools: *Functional Assessment Interview, Student-Directed Functional Assessment Interview* (O'Neill, Horner, Albin, Storey, & Sprague, 1997) *Motivational Assessment Scale* (Durand & Crimmins, 1988)	Interviews of Delores's family, friends, and job coach addressed her preferences for "low-key" settings, difficulty with dramatic changes in routine, and beliefs that she is motivated to avoid demanding social circumstances
Direct observation	Observations should be conducted across a variety of times and circumstances. Some observation tools: *ABC (Antecedent-Behavior-Consequence) Recording Scatterplot* (Touchette, MacDonald, & Langer, 1985) *Frequency Measures Across Conditions*	Scatterplot data indicate that Ben's biting is most likely to occur when he is getting ready to leave in the morning and immediately after lunch

FBA methods range from highly precise and systematic to relatively informal. Particular tools and strategies should be selected based on the circumstances, individuals involved, and goals of intervention. The goal of an FBA, regardless of which methods are used, is to answer certain questions:

1. Under what circumstances is the behavior most/least likely to occur (e.g., when, where, with whom)?
2. What outcomes does the behavior produce (e.g., what does the person get or avoid through his or her behavior)?

To answer these questions, the information gathered must be analyzed and summarized. Hypothesis (or summary) statements describe the specific patterns identified through the FBA and, if supported by the data, provide a foundation for intervention. A hypothesis statement must describe the behavior and surrounding conditions and be clear, comprehensive, and unbiased to be useful. Example: "When Steven finishes his work early, he makes noises and destroys his materials. His behavior prompts his supervisor to initiate an alternative activity."

Frequently Asked Questions

1. *When and why should a functional behavioral assessment be completed?* An FBA may be initiated when a person's behavior interferes with performance, progress, and/or participation within typical daily routines and environments. It is completed for the purpose of designing an effective intervention that will allow the person with challenging behavior to be successful across all circumstances.
2. *Who should do a functional behavioral assessment (e.g., what qualifications are needed)?* It is important to have individuals who are experienced and skilled in FBA, competent in promoting collaboration, and proficient in designing effective positive behavioral support strategies involved in the process. Such individuals may come from varying backgrounds (e.g., applied behavioral analysis, school psychology).
3. *Are there shortcuts (e.g., one-page forms) for conducting FBAs?* Yes and no. Various tools are available for data collection and synthesis. In many cases, an informal or abbreviated approach can lead to reasonable interventions. However, in other circumstances, a more comprehensive and systematic process is required. An appropriate FBA is one that is matched to the circumstances and leads to an effective behavioral support plan.
4. *What is the difference between functional behavioral assessment and functional analysis? Functional behavioral assessment* is a broad term referring to the information-gathering and hypothesis-development process. It can involve a variety of methods, including functional analysis. Functional analysis is a rigorous experimental procedure in which hypotheses are tested by manipulating antecedents and consequences to see what impact they have on behavior. Whereas functional analysis may be useful in some circumstances, it is not always necessary or appropriate.

Source: Based on *Methods of Functional Behavior Assessment.* Positive Behavioral Interventions and Support Technical Assistance Center; Behavioral Research and Training; 5262 University of Oregon; Eugene, OR 97403-5262; PBIS@oregon.uoregon.edu.

Using the FBA assessment

For a guide to understanding the practical use of FBA, consider the "Practical Functional Behavioral Assessment Training Manual" (Loman & Borhaier, www.PBIS.org, June 28, 2015). Designed for students with moderate (not severe) behavior problems, the practical approach to FBA organizes around the following key ideas:

- DEFINE behaviors in specific ways so that they can be reliably observed and measured
- ASK about the behavioral by interviewing key participants such as teachers, parents, students
- SEE the behavior by observing it in context

Hypothesize about why, when, and where the behavior occurs by summarizing what is learned from the previous tasks (e.g., defining, asking, and seeing).

The FBA is not a static procedure and can be implemented during any tier of RTI depending on individual needs; thus, FBA can occur across Tiers 1, 2, and 3 of the RTI framework even though it is most frequently used in its most extended way during Tier 3 or intensive intervention (Crone, Hawkin, & Horner, 2015). Through FBA, it is possible to identify specific events that predict and maintain behavior and to design a support plan that effectively addresses those variables. FBA methods can, and should, vary across circumstances but typically include *record reviews*, *interviews*, and *direct observation*. Thus, data sources to complete the FBA include:

- Observations during classroom instruction and free time such as lunch or recess. Because students typically exhibit different behaviors around different adults, it is a good idea to conduct observations in multiple settings.
- Student interview to learn more about the behaviors the student would like to change and to determine what the student's views are on why the behaviors persist and what might assist the student in rectifying the behaviors.
- Teacher interview to learn more about the behaviors the teacher would like to see changed and to determine the teacher's views of why the behaviors persist and what changes the teacher has made and is willing to make to change the behaviors.
- Parent interview to provide the perspective of another adult in addition to the teacher and insights into how the student's behaviors are exhibited in the home setting.
- Rating scales to determine which target behaviors are exhibited and the extent to which these behaviors compare with the behaviors of typical students.
- Team summaries and insights are used to put all of the data together and to develop hypotheses about the cause of the data and treatment plans.

In its most truncated form, FBA includes the following four steps (Crone, Hawken, & Horner, 2015):

Step 1. Interview teachers and other key personnel.

Step 2. Identify the function of the behavior.

Step 3. Hypothesize the cause or "why" of the behavior.

Step 4. Using a team-based process, design an intervention to change the behavior.

This more truncated approach to FBA is typically used when behavior problems are less intensive. For more intensive behavior problems, ones that might be classified as Tier 3, a more thorough FBA approach is provided. The critical feature of FBA is the use of data to generate plausible explanations for why the behavior occurs, assuming that all behavior is purposeful. Thus, closely linked with FBA is the provision of treatments and the collection of ongoing data to determine the effects of these treatments.

MyEdLab **Self-Check 8.3**

MyEdLab **Application Exercise 8.3:** Functional Behavioral Assessment

8.4 EFFECTIVE TEACHING PRACTICES FOR STUDENTS WITH EMOTIONAL OR BEHAVIORAL DISORDERS

Think about the teachers you remember most from your elementary and secondary classes who really cared about you, what you learned, and how well you liked school. Establishing good relationships with all students is important, but especially so for students with emotional and behavioral disorders. These students probably have had few positive relationships with adults and may act as if they dare you to care about them.

Teaching trust is the foundation for success with students with emotional and behavioral disorders. Students learn to trust you when you act in predictable ways and do what you say you are going to do. They also learn to trust you when they believe you will do what is best for them rather than what is best for you.

8.4.1 Guidelines and Accommodations for Students with Emotional or Behavioral Disorders

Remember that disliking the student's behavior is not the same as disliking the student, who needs your respect and caring. "Respect the student, dislike the behavior" is an important motto when you work with students with emotional and behavioral disorders. Think about the language you use when you reprimand students or enforce consequences for inappropriate behavior. Be sure you convince students that it is their behavior that is unacceptable, not the students themselves. Jason Landis, a high school English teacher, says it this way:

> When I provide feedback to students about their inappropriate behavior, I always talk about the behavior, and I let the student know that anyone who displays these behaviors will have consequences. For example, the other day in class, I needed to remind a student that no one swears in the class and those who swear will get a detention and therefore, here is your detention. Later on in the period, I encouraged the same student to respond to a question and provided positive feedback for the part of the answer he answered correctly.

Many teachers realize that understanding and recognizing the behaviors of students with emotional and behavioral disorders is the first step in providing appropriate interventions. Tips for Teachers 8.8 offers further suggestions for creating an appropriate emotional environment.

Although this first step is necessary, it is not sufficient. Positive behavior support is important for all of your students, but particularly for those who experience challenges emotionally, behaviorally, and socially (Hendley & Lock, 2007; Rafferty, 2007; Scott et al., 2007).

This section provides an overview of interventions and accommodations you can implement to provide positive behavior supports and to facilitate the social and academic growth of students with emotional and behavioral disorders. No single approach to intervention works for all students with severe emotional and behavioral problems. However, a systematic, well-organized plan and documentation of changes in behavior will help you determine whether an intervention is working, particularly when schoolwide prevention approaches are used (Chandler & Dahlquist, 2014; Reddy, Newman, De Thomas, & Chun, 2009). Keep in mind that some students with emotional and behavioral disorders may have comorbidity with learning disabilities or may otherwise have difficulty with making academic progress. Thus, we conclude with suggestions for academic adaptations.

TIPS FOR TEACHERS 8.8

Creating an Appropriate Emotional Environment

- *Respond to students' feelings and intentions* rather than to overt behavior. When students with emotional and behavioral disorders act out or become aggressive, your first reaction might be to respond with anger or hostility, but the student is really saying, "I'm hurting. Pay attention to me."
- *Listen.* Before responding, no matter how certain you are that the student is in the wrong, give the student an opportunity to explain and give his or her version of what occurred. You may not always agree with the interpretation, but by taking the time to listen you demonstrate caring and concern to the student. Listening is a sign of acceptance, an important first step in helping students.
- Develop a positive relationship with the student about one topic. All students are interested in and can succeed at something that you can recognize. Discover what this area is and what the student knows about it, and then make him or her the class expert.
- *Establish rules and consequences* to help provide the structure that students with emotional and behavioral disorders need.
- *Consider changes you can make.* Evaluate the classroom routines, instructional procedures, and discipline practices you use that may be contributing to the student's behavioral problems.
- *Catch the student being good.* You have many opportunities to recognize the student's inappropriate behavior. A greater challenge is to catch the student being good and to recognize that appropriate behavior several times a day.
- *Use humor* to build relationships and to decrease tension. Look for the fun in the way students relate to one another and to you.
- *Create an emotionally safe classroom* environment in which students accept one another's strengths and weaknesses and treat one another with respect and consideration.

8.4.2 Changing Behavior

The student behaviors that teachers most want to change are those they regard as undesirable, such as those that interfere with instruction, other students, or the student's learning. *Desirable behaviors*—those that enhance instruction, relations with others, and the student's success—are the behaviors teachers most want to see increased. Tips for

TIPS FOR TEACHERS 8.9

Promoting Desirable Behaviors and Decreasing Undesirable Ones

- Do not use threats; instead, issue consequences that you are prepared to execute if students do not behave appropriately. When you make remarks such as "You're going to do this math paper if you have to sit here all day," students soon learn that consequences are not real and that your words cannot be trusted.
- Establish consequences that do not punish you as well as your student. If you are overly stressed or inconvenienced by the consequence, you might resent the student (a circumstance that would surely interfere with the quality of the relationship you need to establish). For example, staying in at lunch, giving up your planning period, or driving the student home can punish you as much as the student.
- Listen and talk to your student but avoid arguing. If you are tempted to argue, recognize that you need a break and set another time to finish the discussion.
- Use logic, principles, and effective guidelines to make decisions. Do not flaunt your authority as a teacher to make students do something; always provide a clear sense of what is the right or best thing to do.
- Focus on the problems that interfere most; that is, ignore minor misbehaviors.
- Build into your instruction a strategy that shows students that the work they complete is necessary and meaningful.
- Avoid comparing a student with emotional or behavioral problems to other students. Comparisons do not help students understand and accept themselves or be understood and accepted by others.
- Resist the temptation to solve students' problems for them. Students need to learn how to resolve conflicts for themselves. The long-term goal of any behavior management strategy is to motivate students to behave appropriately and to shift the responsibility of "controlling behavior" from teacher to student.
- Recognize your feelings and do not let them control your behavior. When you are upset by a student's behavior in class, it is important not to respond by further upsetting the student. Never "strike back" by humiliating, embarrassing, or berating a student.
- Let your student know how many chances he or she has before a consequence will be applied (and do not add chances later). When you tell a student, "This is the last chance," and he or she continues to behave inappropriately, you need to follow through on whatever consequence was designated.

TIPS FOR TEACHERS 8.10

Fostering Change by Targeting Key Behaviors

- Whenever possible, involve students and parents in identifying the target behavior. In this way, you work at changing the behavior both at school and at home.
- As when making referrals, describe the behavior in as much detail as possible, including when and with whom it typically occurs.
- Get the student's input on the behavior, as well as his or her suggestions for what might help to reduce it.
- Describe the target behavior in writing, using the terms expressed by the student, the parent, and yourself so that everyone involved understands the problem.
- Establish a procedure for eliminating the behavior and providing positive consequences when the behavior does not occur. Involve parents in distributing positive consequences as well.

Teachers 8.9 provides guiding principles that will help you promote desirable behaviors and decrease undesirable ones.

Changing student behavior is a daunting task and it does not happen overnight. Give yourself positive feedback for what you do to enhance student learning and social functioning. Do not be too hard on yourself, especially when you make mistakes. At the end of the day, focus on the positive. Although there are limitations to what any effective teacher can do, there are always opportunities to be successful in teaching students with emotional and behavioral disorders. See Tips for Teachers 8.10 to learn about how to target key behaviors that you want to change.

Other techniques exist as well. Figure 8.4 provides an example of a behavior contract between a student and a teacher.

Good behavior game

One procedure that teachers may want to implement to positively affect behavior in their classroom is the Good Behavior Game (e.g., Flower et al. 2014). The Good Behavior Game is a mechanism for involving students in controlling their behavior as well as the behavior of their classmates. How does it work?

Step 1 Describe that the class is going to be divided into teams; for example, four teams of students with a mix of behavior challenges including class leaders, students with good behaviors, and students with behavior challenges.

Step 2 Describe that the class rules will be reviewed and revised in a class meeting. The teacher establishes a class meeting to specify with students the class rules and what types of behaviors indicate following rules and which ones indicate rule infractions.

Step 3 Students' teams are provided points when a member of the team does not follow a class rule. In other words, the teams try not to get points.

Step 4 At the end of the day, points are reviewed and groups that have fewer than the specified number of points, for example, 2 points, are provided with the reward. Rewards can vary and can consist of such things as reduced homework, more free time, access to class privileges, etc.

Teachers can make adjustments in the Good Behavior Game to suit their class. For example, teachers may want to count points and provide awards more frequently (e.g., at the end of a class period) or less frequently (e.g, at the end of a week). Teachers are also likely to want to adjust group composition after a specified amount of time, for example, every two weeks.

FIGURE 8.4 Sample student–teacher contract

Date: ______________

Ms. Gonzalez will draw a star next to Paul's name on the bulletin board and give Paul one point when he does any of the following in her classroom:

1. He raises his hand and waits for the teacher to call on him before talking.
2. He stays seated in his chair while working on class assignments.
3. When other kids in the class are bothering him, he tells the teacher about their behavior instead of yelling at and/or hitting the other kids.

After Paul has earned 12 points from his teacher, Ms. Gonzalez, he may select one of the following rewards:

1. He may have extra time to work on the computer.
2. He may serve as the teacher's assistant for a class period or longer.
3. He may be in charge of giving out passes for computer use and other class privileges.
4. He may serve as a peer tutor for a class or day.

After Paul has received 12 points, he begins earning the points again. Another reward will be given when 12 points have been earned.

I, Paul B. O'Brien, agree to the conditions stated above, and understand that I will not be allowed any of the rewards until I have earned 12 points by doing the activities stated above.

____

(student's signature)

I, Ms. Gonzalez, agree to the conditions stated above. I will give Paul one of the aforementioned reinforcers only after he has received 12 points.

____

(teacher's signature)

8.4.3 Resolving Conflicts and Promoting Self-Control

Dealing with conflict between students and between a student and a teacher is an ongoing issue for teachers at all grade levels. Conflicts are inevitable in a classroom community; they occur among all students, not just those who have emotional and behavioral disorders (Albrecht, 2008). Adalyn Saladrigas says, "With some of our students with emotional and behavioral disorders I can often see it coming on with their body language. In particular, when they clench their fists, something's going to happen." See Activities for All Learners to help students improve their behavior in class.

What about extreme cases? School districts have guidelines for procedures regarding restraining students. In general, the rule of thumb is—don't restrain unless you are specifically trained to do so. If a student seems violent, get other students out of harm's way and give the student time to decompress. Call security or an administrator according to policy in your building.

To assist students in resolving conflicts, Larrivee (2005) established a model for conflict resolution that teachers can use in class and that is applicable to most situations you will encounter.

See Figure 8.5 to learn more about Larrivee's suggestions for teachers to guide students in conflict resolution.

The idea is that students have a large number of strategies to apply individually or in combination in order to solve problems. Although all students can benefit from conflict-resolution strategies, this model is particularly effective for students who are easily frustrated or who become volatile when conflicts arise between or among peers. Teaching

ACTIVITIES FOR ALL LEARNERS

Using a Timer to Change Behavior

Purpose: To increase appropriate behavior, such as on-task behavior, and to reduce inappropriate behavior, such as being out of seat

Materials: Kitchen timer

Procedures:

1. Show students the kitchen timer and indicate that you will be using it to cue students to look for on-task behavior in the class. Discuss with students what behaviors will be included (e.g., working, completing an assignment, asking a question, reading a text).
2. Indicate that the timer will ring at different intervals and that all groups or individuals who are on task when the timer rings will be awarded a point.
3. Set the timer initially for a range of times (from 5 to 10 minutes), and then for longer periods of time.

Source: Adapted from "The timer-game: A variable interval contingency for the management of out-of-seat behavior," by M. M. Wolf, E. L. Hanley, L. A. King, J. Lachowicz, & D. K. Giles, 1970, *Exceptional Children, 37*, 113–117.

these techniques requires modeling, practice, feedback, and patience as students learn to recognize and support one another when they or their peers use strategies to solve problems.

In summary, conflict management skills involve proper communication from the teacher, who demonstrates and models the verbal communication expected. Views are expressed in a nonthreatening way and conflicts are anticipated before they escalate (Barsky, 2014).

FIGURE 8.5 Larrivee's model for conflict resolution

Group Work Solutions

- ***Compromising.*** Requires cooperation and also negotiation in order to find a workable solution. In a compromise, everyone gives up a little while still getting some of what he or she originally wanted.
- ***Sharing.*** Individuals decide to share for mutual benefit (e.g., working together to complete the assignment). This is a difficult concept for children to understand because it requires waiting for the benefit to occur in the future.
- ***Taking turns.*** A simple strategy; it is important to teach that the student who goes second has not "lost." It is often effective to let students decide the order in turn taking.
- ***Chance.*** Another strategy to alleviate a dispute around turn taking; flip a coin, draw straws, or use another method that leaves the resolution to chance.

Communication Strategies

- ***Apologizing.*** Admitting responsibility if you recognize that your behavior was wrong. It can also be a way to recognize the other person's feelings without having to take responsibility for causing the problem.
- ***Sending an I-message.*** Express how you feel without blaming the other person. For example, "I was angry when you used my book without asking."
- ***Active listening.*** This is the most difficult of the communication strategies. Active listening involves trying to understand how another person is feeling by listening carefully to what he or she says. This is particularly difficult because conflicts often arise when people do not listen or misinterpret what another person is trying to say.
- ***Self-talk.*** This strategy is a self-control method used to reduce stress or remain calm by engaging in rehearsed positive self-talk (e.g., "You are in control; don't lose it.").

Diffusing a Potentially Volatile Conflict

- ***Distracting/postponing.*** Attention on the conflict is diverted or postponed to diffuse a conflict. It allows students to cool off before addressing the conflict (e.g., "You know what, let's try this game again tomorrow.").
- ***Humor/exaggerating.*** Another strategy to diffuse a volatile situation is to poke fun at the situation or to engage in an exaggerated recounting in order to help students put their issues in perspective. These strategies should be taught with caution, as they can result in hurt feelings if all parties are not able to share in the "joke."
- ***Abandoning.*** If a person realizes he or she can't handle a situation, walking away may be the best way to exercise self-control.
- ***Seeking assistance.*** An individual or group should seek assistance if other conflict-resolution strategies are not working, if the situation is volatile, or if the problem is too complex to solve without help.

Source: Information from *Authentic classroom management: Creating a learning community and building reflective practice* (3rd ed.), by B. Larrivee, 2009, Boston: Allyn & Bacon.

8.4.4 Teaching Self-Monitoring Skills

By teaching students to identify their problem behaviors, to set personal goals, and to monitor their academic and social behavior, you also help them to develop self-control (Menzies, Lane, & Lee, 2009; Polsgrove & Smith, 2004; Vanderbilt, 2005). Setting and monitoring positive personal goals contribute to students' positive self-concept and higher self-esteem. What are the benefits of teaching self-monitoring strategies? Several of the advantages of self-monitoring are summarized below:

- It is feasible for teachers to implement and allows them additional time to work with students individually or small groups.
- Self-monitoring can help students improve academics as well as behavior.
- Because self-monitoring uses charting such as graphs and checklists, students are provided valuable feedback about how they are progressing.
- Students are provided with immediate feedback that can be used to adjust their behavior and/or learning goals.
- The focus is on individual improvement rather than comparisons with other students.

Self-monitoring has helped students with disabilities make positive behavior changes in a variety of areas, including improving on-task behavior (Hutchinson, Murdock, Williamson, & Cronin, 2000; Rock, 2005), decreasing aggressive behavior (Gumpel & Shlomit, 2000), improving other social behaviors such as peer interactions and cooperative behavior (McDougall, 1998), and improving academic performance (Levendoski & Cartledge, 2000; Rock, 2005). For example, Marcia Rock (2005) studied the use of a self-monitoring intervention in which elementary school students with EBD in inclusion math and reading classes were taught to self-monitor their attention to an academic task and their performance on the task. The strategy involved students in setting an individual performance goal for the lesson, creating a plan to achieve the goal, using self-talk to reflect during the lesson, and evaluating progress. To make the monitoring of appropriate behaviors concrete, teachers took pictures of students demonstrating on-task behavior. Students looked at the pictures of themselves periodically during class as a way to monitor and correct their behavior. The intervention helped students take control of their learning by supporting self-management skills that resulted in improved academic performance. The 60-Second Lesson feature, "Establishing Personal Goals" describes a simple activity for helping students establish personal goals.

60-*SECOND* LESSON

ESTABLISHING PERSONAL GOALS

Ask students to think of a person they admire. Ask them to consider one quality about the person they admire that they would like to have. Ask them to write the quality on an index card and keep in a prominent place. Throughout the year, ask students to look at the card and assess the extent to which they express the quality or trait for which they most want to be admired.

8.4.5 Teaching Self-Management Skills

Self-monitoring helps students to become more aware of their own behaviors. Self-management enables students to govern the reinforcers for their behaviors (Cooper, Heron, & Heward, 2007). Furthermore, teaching students self-management skills enables them to depend less on the teacher. In the basic principles of managing student behavior, much of the responsibility for targeting behavior, identifying reinforcers, and implementing a behavior change plan rests with the teachers. Self-management skills require that students learn some principles of behavior management and then implement the selected

MyEdLab
Video Example 8.3.

Watch this video and listen as a teacher asks her student to explain how a motivation tool, called a MotivAider, helps him manage and maintain good work habits. How many reinforcements did you notice that the teacher uses and how might you use this type of self-management strategy in other contexts?

reinforcers. Self-management requires a more active role from the student and a more collaborative role from the teacher.

Margarite Rabinsky is a fourth-grade teacher whose student, Eduardo Cora, was not completing assignments. Although Margarite worked closely with Eduardo to ensure that the assignments were not too difficult and that Eduardo understood how to complete them, he was still unsuccessful at turning in completed assignments on time. Deciding to involve Eduardo in a self-management plan, Margarite implemented the following steps for developing the plan:

1. ***Teacher and student identify and agree on the behavior to be changed.*** Margarite and Eduardo agreed on the behavior to change and put it in writing (see Figure 8.6).
2. ***Identify when and where the behavior most frequently occurs.*** Margarite stated, "First, let's think about what classes it occurs in most, and then let's think about whether there are certain days when it occurs." Eduardo volunteered that he started the week off pretty well and then felt he got worse on Thursday and Friday. Margarite indicated that she did not think he had difficulty with math, as he most frequently turned in his math work, but that he seemed to have trouble with social studies and science. Eduardo agreed, and they summarized this on the form.
3. ***Establish realistic goals for changing the behavior.*** Margarite and Eduardo discussed his behavior and then established the goals listed in Figure 8.6.
4. ***Identify a timeline showing how long the behavior change plan will be in effect.*** Because neither Margarite nor Eduardo had done this before, they decided to meet for 5 minutes every Friday to review the progress for the week and to have a longer meeting in 3 weeks to determine how effective the program had been.
5. ***Identify reinforcers and consequences.*** Margarite and Eduardo reexamined their goals and discussed what reinforcers should be provided if Eduardo met the goals. They also discussed consequences if the goals were not met. These reinforcers and consequences were written into the plan, as shown in Figure 8.6.

   Since Eduardo recognized that he started to fall apart during the end of the week, they planned to meet at the beginning of the school day on Thursday and Friday to check in about how to manage the day successfully.
6. *Self-evaluate the success of the program each day.* Margarite explained to Eduardo that he would be responsible, at the end of each day, for writing a brief evaluation of

FIGURE 8.6 **Self-management plan**

Name: Eduardo Cora

Target Behavior: Submit completed assignments to teacher on time or meet with teacher before assignment is due to agree on alternative date and time.

When Behavior Occurs: Mostly on Thursdays and Fridays

Where Behavior Occurs: Social Studies and Science

Goals:

1. Eduardo will write down assignments and due dates in a separate assignment book for each subject.
2. Eduardo will look at each assignment and be sure that he knows how to complete it. Eduardo will ask questions, as necessary.
3. Eduardo will tell the teacher ahead of time if an assignment is going to be late.

Timeline: Meet each Friday to review the progress on the plan, and then revise the plan in 3 weeks.

Reinforcer: Eduardo will receive 15 minutes of extra time to work on the computer each day his assignments are completed.

Evaluation: Eduardo will write a brief description of the program's success.

how effective the plan was for that day. Margarite observed a noticeable change in Eduardo's behavior after 1 week. After 2 weeks, Eduardo's behavior was more like the behavior of other students in the class. Though Eduardo would still have bad days, they were far less frequent.

8.4.6 Teaching Social Skills

Have you ever met someone who seems to know the right thing to say and do no matter what the situation might be? We often watch these people with envy as they move from person to person, always seemingly at ease. We refer to them as demonstrating good social skills or social competence. **Social skills** or **competence** are behaviors that promote effective relationships with others and appropriate responses to settings, persons, and communications, and, it should be added, while causing no harm to others. Social skills allow individuals to adapt and respond to the expectations of society. Social competence is a process that begins at birth and continues throughout life (Beauchamp & Anderson, 2010).

Many students with disabilities have difficulties with social skills (see Figure 8.7). This is particularly true for students with emotional and behavioral disorders, including students with autism (Michelson, Sugai, Wood, & Kazdin, 2013; Maag, 2006; Reichow & Volkmar, 2010).

Children with deficits in social skills may have difficulty with *acquisition* (they are simply unaware of the social skill), *performance* (they are aware of the skill, but don't know how to implement it), or *fluency* (they know how to implement the skill, but are awkward in doing so) (Gresham, Sugai, & Horner, 2001; Patterson, Jolivette, & Crosby, 2006). Consequences of having social skills deficits include alienation from peers, isolation, unsatisfying social relationships, academic failure, and difficulties in living independently as an adult (Maag, 2006).

Social skills training (SST) provides students with specific instruction in acquisition, performance, and fluency of social skills. SST is "a positive, proactive intervention, designed to teach specific social behavior by replacing negative behaviors with more desirable ones" (Patterson et al., 2006, p. 23). Although results of research on SST have been mixed (Cook, Gresham, Kern, Barreras, & Crews, 2008; Forness & Kavale, 1999; Gresham, Cook, Crews, & Kern, 2004; Gresham et al., 2001; Maag, 2006), there is still optimism about the potential for its success and recommendations for its continued research and development (Michelson et al., 2013; Trower & Hollin, 2013). Furthermore, social skills interventions that focus on social groups or video modeling have accumulated significant research suggesting their effectiveness (Reichow & Volkmar, 2010).

Numerous SST programs have emerged in recent decades, including a host of commercial SST curriculum products (Michelson et al., 2013). Although there are differences

FIGURE 8.7 Examples of social skills deficits

- Deficits in social perception and social cognition that inhibit students' abilities to interact with others
- Lack of consequential thinking
- Difficulty expressing feelings
- Difficulty in feeling empathy for others
- Difficulty delaying gratification (impulsive)
- Inappropriate grooming and hygiene
- Failure to understand and fulfill the role of listener
- Inability to take the perspective of another
- Less time spent looking and smiling at a conversational partner
- Unwilling to act in a social situation to influence the outcome
- Less likely to request clarification when given ambiguous or incomplete information
- Lack of self-confidence and tendency to portray learned-helplessness behaviors
- Aggressive or antisocial behaviors
- Tendency to talk more or less than peers
- More likely to approach teacher and ask inappropriate questions
- Less proficient in interpersonal problem solving
- Less proficient in planning for the future

FIGURE 8.8 Principles for conducting social skills training

1. *Develop cooperative learning.* Classrooms can be structured so there is a win–lose atmosphere in which children compete with one another for grades and teacher attention, or classrooms can be structured so children work on their own with little interaction between classmates, or classrooms can be structured for cooperative learning so children work alone, in pairs, and in groups, helping one another master the assigned material.
2. *Involve peers in the training program for low-social-status students.* An important function of social skills training is to alter the way peers perceive students identified as low in social status. Including popular peers in the social skills training program increases the likelihood that they will have opportunities to observe the changes in target students and to cue and reinforce appropriate behavior in the classroom.
3. *Use principles of effective instruction.* Teaching social skills requires implementing principles of effective instruction. These have been used and explained throughout this text and include obtaining student commitment, identifying target behavior, pretesting, teaching, modeling, rehearsing, role-playing, providing feedback, practicing in controlled settings, practicing in other settings, posttesting, and following up.
4. *Teach needed skills.* Many social skills training programs fail because youngsters are trained to do things they already know how to do. Social skills that learning- and behavior-disordered students frequently need to be taught include reading body language (e.g., what his or her body "says," gestures, eye contact, facial reactions), using greetings, initiating and maintaining a conversation, giving and accepting positive feedback, identifying feelings in self and others, and using problem-solving/conflict-resolution strategies. Perhaps the most consistent challenges for students with conduct disorders is anger and frustration management and conflict resolution. Focusing on managing these behaviors will yield big dividends in improving behavior.
5. *Teach for transfer of learning.* For social skills to generalize to other settings, the program must require the rehearsal and implementation of target skills across settings. Social skills training programs need to ensure that learned skills are systematically demonstrated in the classroom, on the playground, and at home. If skills are practices in isolated settings, for example, small groups not in natural settings, they are less likely to transfer.
6. *Empower students.* Many students with learning difficulties feel discouraged and unable to influence their learning. They turn the responsibility for learning over to the teacher and become "passive" learners. You can empower students by offering choices, providing them with opportunities to set goals and monitor progress towards those goals, teaching about consequences, documenting progress, and helping students to exercise control of what happens to them.
7. *Identify strengths.* Knowing something about the students' areas of strength might be helpful in identifying social contexts that may be promising for promoting positive peer interactions. Students with social skills deficits may benefit from acquiring strengths in athletic activities so they have areas of strength from which to build their social skills. Other areas such as hobbies or special interests can be presented in the classroom so that the student with difficulties with social relationships has an opportunity to be perceived as one who is knowledgeable. All students do something well—draw figures, video game, look up information on the computer—identify what it is and use it to highlight their strengths.
8. *Encourage reciprocal friendships.* Reciprocal friendship is the mutual identification as "best friend" by two students. Thus, a reciprocal friend is one that each student identifies as a good friend or best friend. Because it is unlikely that all youngsters in the classroom are going to like all the other students equally, the notion of developing a reciprocal friendship is a more realistic goal.

among programs, several principles of SST generalize across most programs (see Figure 8.8).

For such programs to be successful, they should (1) teach necessary social skills, (2) have an extended duration, (3) be sequenced and explicit, and (4) provide sufficient opportunities for practice in classroom settings (Duriak, Weissberg, & Pachan, 2010; Gresham, Van, & Cook, 2006; McIntosh & MacKay, 2008). Considering the emphasis on assuring that all students make annual progress in academic subjects such as reading and math, it is often difficult to find time during the school day for social skills training. What can teachers do? Successful social skills interventions have been implemented after school, improving students' self-perceptions and social behaviors (Durlak, Weissberg, & Pachan, & 2010).

As a classroom teacher, how might you be involved with SST? Because it is recommended that SST occur in natural settings with peers and adults involved (McIntosh & MacKay, 2008), you may be involved in teaching and reinforcing target social skills. Your school may have adopted a commercial program, or you can work with the special education teacher and/or school counselor to plan, implement, and evaluate social skills

ACTIVITIES FOR ALL LEARNERS

The ASSET Method for Teaching Social Skills to Secondary Students

Purpose: To develop the social skills of adolescents with special needs who demonstrate difficulties in social functioning

Materials: The leader's guide (Hazel, Schumaker, Sherman, & Sheldon, 1982, 2015) from the ASSET program provides instructions for running the groups and teaching the skills. Eight teaching sessions are provided on videotapes that demonstrate the skills. Program materials include skill sheets, home notes, and criterion checklists. Each lesson is taught to a small group of adolescents.

Procedure: Each social skill is taught by implementing the following nine-step procedure:

- **Step 1** *Review.* Previously learned skills are reviewed and homework is evaluated and integrated.
- **Step 2** *Explain.* The skill that is the focus of the lesson is explained and discussed.
- **Step 3** *Rationale.* A rationale for why the skill is important and why the students need to learn it is provided.
- **Step 4** *Example.* Examples of situations in which the skill can be used are provided. These examples relate directly to the experiences and interests of the students.
- **Step 5** *Examine.* A skills sheet that lists the component skills (refer to text for list of skills for following directions) is provided to each student.
- **Step 6** *Model.* Through videotapes that can be purchased with the curriculum, or as implemented by the teacher, the skills are demonstrated and modeled.
- **Step 7** *Verbal Rehearsal.* The procedure of verbally stating the components of each skill so that they can be learned by the student is implemented. The students practice saying the skill components and play games and engage in activities that teach them the skills.
- **Step 8** *Behavioral Rehearsal.* Students practice performing each subskill and overall skill, and demonstrate proficiency.
- **Step 9** *Homework.* Designed to enhance generalization, homework provides students with directed activities that allow them to practice the subskills and skills outside the classroom.

Source: ASSET: A social skills program for adolescents (Hazel, Schumaker, Sherman, & Sheldon, 2015), Research Press, Champaign, Illinois. "Group training for social skills: A program for court-adjudicated, probationary youths," by J. S. Hazel, J. B. Schumaker, J. A. Sherman, & J. Sheldon-Wildgen, 1982, *Criminal Justice and Behavior*, 9, 35–53.

interventions. The Activities for All Learners feature "The ASSET Method for Teaching Social Skills to Secondary Students" presents an example of an SST program for adolescents.

When developing social skills interventions, it may be important to consider the nature of children's friendships or social support outside of the school setting (Lane et al., 2003). Students with learning and behavior disorders who are not well accepted by their classmates may have friends in the neighborhood or within their families (e.g., cousins). Perhaps the most important point to remember is that because a child is not well accepted by peers at school does not necessarily mean that the child does not have effective social relationships outside of the school setting. Thus, getting input from key family members is important in planning social skills treatments.

First Step to Success (Walker et al., 2009) is an early intervention program designed to prevent antisocial and aggressive behaviors from becoming even more severe and allowing students to get a good start in school. Students are taught to recognize when they are exhibiting inappropriate behavior and to replace that behavior with an appropriate behavior. Peers and teachers are taught supportive behaviors to help the target student. Parents are also involved in learning communication, problem-solving, and limit-setting skills. The What Works Clearinghouse website recognized the research on First Step to Success as having positive effects on reducing problem behaviors.

8.4.7 Using Social Learning Strategies

Social learning also contributes to the success of students with emotional and behavioral disorders. **Social learning** involves observing and modeling or imitating the behavior of others (e.g., Bandura, 1971, 1973). To what extent can you expect students to imitate the appropriate behaviors of classmates, and what can you do to accelerate this process? Research suggests that students with emotional and behavioral disorders

TIPS FOR TEACHERS 8.11

Guiding Students to Learn Appropriate Behaviors from Classmates

- Identify student "models" and the behaviors that you want other students to emulate. For example, "Joaquin has his math book open to page 38 and is looking at me to indicate that he is ready. Who else can show me that they are ready?"
- Monitor whether the student with emotional or behavioral disorders follows the model. Look for approximations and provide positive reinforcement. For example, "Sheilah (student with emotional or behavioral problems) is getting her math book out. Thank you Sheilah."
- Provide frequent feedback when the student performs the desired behaviors. Look for as many chances as possible to recognize desirable behaviors.
- Students who view themselves as "like" a model are more likely than not to imitate desirable behaviors. You can facilitate this process by identifying ways in which students' behaviors are similar. For example, "Sheilah (student with emotional or behavioral disorder) and Joaquin are not talking while they are getting ready for the homework assignment. Good for them!"

are unlikely to imitate "better" behaviors in the classroom unless teachers provide directed experiences to promote this behavior (Kauffman & Landrum, 2009). Tips for Teachers 8.11 offers a strategy for guiding students to learn appropriate behaviors from classmates.

8.4.8 Implementing School-Based Wraparound

Students with behavior disorders and emotional disturbances are among the most highly segregated students with disabilities. Furthermore, systems operating independently of one another (e.g., schools, mental health agencies, juvenile justice) have repeatedly failed to adequately support individuals with EBD and their families (e.g., Eber & Keenan, 2004; Fries et al., 2012). In response, schools are starting to implement wraparound processes that provide coordinated services to students with emotional or behavior disorders and their families (Bruns, Walrath, & Sheehan, 2007; Eber, Breen, Rose, Unizycki, & London, 2008; Eber & Keenan, 2004; Nordness, 2005). Wraparound planning involves focusing on the actual needs of the students within their home–school community. It has been recommended as a process for Tier 3 interventions for the 1% to 2% of high-needs students with emotional and behavioral disorders and can be implemented within an RTI framework of supports (Eber et al., 2008; Miles et al., 2006).

Wraparound services can be used to provide supports that are coordinated through school, home, and community settings. Because wraparound planning considers the entire family, some supports may be included in the IEP (e.g., coordinating professionals who will implement interventions for the student), whereas others may not (e.g., parent training or support for siblings). Typically, a social worker, school counselor, or school psychologist will serve as the wraparound facilitator. As a classroom teacher, you may be a member of a wraparound team. Keep the following elements of successful wraparound systems of care in mind as you participate as a team member (Eber & Keenan, 2004):

- Use services that are based in the community.
- Individualize supports and services and base them on student strengths.
- Use culturally appropriate practices.
- Involve families as active participants.
- Collaborate with family, child, agencies, and community services to create a plan and provide services as a team (e.g., coordinate IEP planning with wraparound planning).
- Investigate flexible use of resources and funding.
- Involve the collaborative team in establishing goals and evaluating outcomes.
- Maintain a strong commitment to the wraparound system.

A wraparound facilitator or case manager will most likely be responsible for coordinating services. As a classroom teacher, you may be asked to be part of the wraparound team to ensure a systematic approach to address the needs of the student. The steps in providing wraparound services for students with emotional and behavioral problems include:

1. Identify a facilitator to work closely with the family, key community members, school personnel, and the student.
2. Reach out to key personnel and establish trusting relationships that support open exchange of information.
3. Guide the team through a series of meetings aimed at identifying the big needs for the students—for example, feeling accepted at home and school, providing support at home and school.
4. Develop a plan around these big needs and provide specific examples of what each key person can do to ensure achievement of the big needs.
5. Communicate frequently with key personnel about the success of meeting the big needs and make adjustments as needed.

How do wraparound services differ from special education services typically provided to students with emotional and behavioral disorders? The critical difference is that networks of key resources from all related educational, social, and mental health services work in a united way to communicate and develop effective services that connect solutions to the child and family. If there isn't improvement, then the team meets again and reconstructs an improved plan.

8.4.9 Adapting Instruction

Students with emotional and behavioral disorders (EBD) often have academic learning problems as well as behavior problems, although the academic problems are less frequently addressed for students with emotional and behavioral problems (Bruhn, Lane, & Hirsch, 2014; Ryan, Pierce, & Mooney, 2008). The relationship between EBD and academic failure has resulted in dropout rates for EBD students that are much higher than those of students with other disabilities (Cohen & Smerdon, 2009; Pierce, Reid, & Epstein, 2004). Moreover, requirements for schools to demonstrate academic progress places greater emphasis on the academic development of all students with disabilities, including those with emotional and behavioral disorders (Vannest, Temple-Harvey, & Mason, 2009).

MyEdLab
Video Example 8.4.
Watch this video and pay attention to the discussion between the general education teacher and special education teacher and listen to how they include students with emotional and behavioral disorders in the general education classroom. Of the many strategies discussed, which do you find the most important to ensuring successful inclusion of students with EBD?

An important factor that positively affects students with emotional and behavioral disorders is the extent to which they are busy in purposeful activities. Students need to view class activities as personally relevant and related to skills they need to learn. To engage their students, effective teachers need to explain to students *why* they are studying a topic, *why* they are given a particular assignment, and *how* their learning will contribute to their success as students and in the future.

Academic failure or frustration can exacerbate a student's emotional or behavioral disorder (Conroy, Sutherland, Snyder, Al-Hendawi, & Vo, 2009). Without creating a parallel program or watering down the curriculum, teachers can adapt and modify assignments and expectations so that students can succeed. One simple strategy is to look for opportunities to reinforce and reward students for what they know or have done correctly. Tips for Teachers 8.12 offers additional suggestions for giving students opportunities for success.

Adalyn Saladrigas loves her work, because she knows she is making a difference in the lives of the middle school students she teaches. Some students feel helpless and that their emotional reactions and behavioral patterns are beyond their control. Through positive behavior supports and through interactions with teachers and parents, she helps her students get in control of their lives. The stakes are high: academic failure, dropping out of school, decreased chances for professional success, and increased chances of substance

TIPS FOR TEACHERS 8.12

Adapting Instruction for Student Success

- *Use different groupings—individual, small groups, pairs, and large groups—to give students opportunities to acquire academic and social skills.* Students with emotional and behavioral disorders may have difficulty learning in whole-class instruction but do well in small-group or paired-learning situations. Also provide opportunities for students to be tutored and to serve as tutors themselves. Learning to work with others is an important skill for students with emotional and behavioral disorders. In a review of research, peer-mediated learning methods (cross-age, same-age, or classwide peer tutoring, and cooperative learning) were successful for students with emotional or behavior disorders in a range of academic subject areas and grade levels.
- *Use materials that will generate high interest.* When teachers design assignments to increase the likelihood of student success, it helps reduce incidences of inappropriate behaviors. Teachers can do this by using high-interest materials; for example, some students may enjoy working on computers, whereas others might like to write or use artistic means for approaching a task. Consequently, having students compose essays, practice skills on a computer, or illustrate responses may provide better motivation than more traditional activities.
- *Provide alternative ways for students to complete tasks and demonstrate learning.* For example, students might give oral recitations to describe what they know to other students who have already mastered the material. Allow students to express their individual learning-style preferences. For instance, some students work better standing up, others while sitting on the floor, and still others while sitting in beanbag chairs. As long as students are working, learning, and not interfering with the progress of others, providing appropriate alternatives for completing tasks makes sense.

Sources: "Evidence-based teaching strategies for students with EBD," by J. B. Ryan, C. D. Pierce, & P. Mooney, 2008, *Beyond Behavior,* 22–29; "Peer-mediated intervention studies on academic achievement for students with EBD: A review," by J. B. Ryan, R. Reid, & M. H. Epstein, 2004, *Remedial and Special Education, 25*(6), 330–341; and "Constant time delay: One way to provide positive behavioral support for students with emotional and behavioral disorders," by K. B. Stevens & A. S. Lingo, 2005, *Beyond Behavior,* 10–15.

abuse and incarceration (Crews et al., 2007). Success with her students is, in Adalyn's words, "priceless." See the Tech Tips, "Tools for Teaching Students with EBD," for additional online tools that Adalyn may have found helpful for students with EBD.

MyEdLab **Self-Check 8.4**

MyEdLab **Application Exercise 8.4:** Effective Teaching Practices for Students with EBD

TECH TIPS

Tools for Teaching Students with EBD

Many resources are available for teachers who have students with EBD in their classrooms. Some provide classroom activities and others provide teachers with resources and strategies.

PEGS, by STEPS Professional Development

INTERVENTION CENTRAL (www.interventioncentral.org), created by school psychologist and administrator Jim Wright of central New York. This site offers scientifically based online tools to help teachers promote positive classroom behaviors that enhance learning.

OSEP CENTER FOR POSITIVE BEHAVIORAL INTERVENTIONS AND SUPPORTS (www.pbis.org) provides current information related to research-based practices and schoolwide strategies for creating positive learning environments for all children.

8 SUMMARY

- Students with emotional and behavioral disorders exhibit behaviors that are significantly different from the norm and that persist over a long period. Typically, higher prevalence rates are reported for students with mild emotional or behavioral disorders, and lower rates for those with more severe disorders. Current estimates range from 6% to 10% of the school-age population. Students with emotional and behavioral disorders may exhibit problems in one or more of the following areas: anxiety, mood, defiance, conduct and aggression, socialized aggression, and immaturity.
- Emotional and behavioral disorders result from both biological and environmental factors. In many cases, the causes of a disorder are complex and multiple. Parents and other adults typically identify students with severe emotional and behavioral disorders. Other students have disorders that are latent or become apparent after school entry.
- As a classroom teacher, you may be involved with initial referrals for some students and with ongoing functional behavioral assessment and monitoring of progress for most students with emotional and behavioral disorders assigned to your classroom.
- Positive behavior supports for students with emotional and behavioral disorders often employ direct instruction focused on behavior change and include the teaching of (a) ways to change behavior, (b) conflict resolution and self-control, (c) self-monitoring skills, (d) self-management skills, (e) social skills, and (f) social learning strategies. For students with greater needs, you may be involved on a school wraparound team to provide more support. Students may also need academic adaptations to ensure success in meeting curricular objectives.

THINK AND APPLY

1. Adalyn Saladrigas has vast experiences in meeting the behavioral, social, and academic needs of students with emotional and behavioral disorders. If you could meet Adalyn, what would be some key questions you would ask about what she has learned from her experience?
2. Consider the many causes of behavior and emotional problems. Even though causes may seem outside of your control, what might you be able to do as a teacher to positively influence the educational setting for students with behavior problems?
3. Michelle is a student in your sixth-grade class. Michelle is aggressive and defiant to you and verbally abusive to her classmates. Several of the parents of children in your class have explained that Michelle is a bully and that their children are afraid to come to school because of her. Michelle is aware that school is a no-bullying zone, but despite your best attempts her behavior persists. Learn about the process for referring students like Michelle for special services for an emotional or behavioral disorder in your state and school district. What online resources are available for learning about your roles and responsibilities in this process? What are some Tier 1 and 2 interventions that may help change Michelle's behavior? How might the identification process work in your educational setting?
4. Describe the practices teachers can implement to enhance the teacher–student relationship, including the types of positive behavior intervention supports (PBIS) that are likely to facilitate the social and academic development of students with emotional and behavioral problems.

9 Teaching Students with Autism Spectrum Disorders/Pervasive Developmental Disorders

Learning Outcomes

9.1 Define autism spectrum disorders (ASDs) and describe the most prevalent characteristics of children with ASDs.

9.2 Determine the types of assessments that can be used to identify students with ASDs.

9.3 Examine the general instructional accommodations you could consider for students with an ASD.

9.4 Describe the types of severe challenging behaviors that might be expressed by students with ASD.

Contributors to this Chapter

Mark F. O'Reilly, University of Texas at Austin
Russell Lang, Texas State University–San Marcos
Jeff Sigafoos, Victoria University, New Zealand
Giulio Lancioni, University of Bari, Italy

CHAPTER OUTLINE

INTERVIEW: KELLY PAGE

Kelly Page is a public elementary school special education teacher in the Southwest. Her job involves supporting teachers and students within inclusive general education settings. She is responsible for ten students with a variety of disabilities. Several of these students are diagnosed with autism spectrum disorder (ASD). The interview starts by Ms. Page describing one of the students with ASD on her caseload.

> One of the students on my caseload is an 11-year-old boy named Carl who is diagnosed with ASD. He is considered high functioning because he has excellent language skills and can carry on a conversation. In fact, Carl has the ability to engage in conversations using words and constructs far above his age level. However, he only wants to talk about insects and spiders. He seems to know everything there is to know about bugs. For hundreds of different insects and spiders, he can tell you their Latin names, what they eat, and where they live. No matter what else you try to talk to him about he always seems to find a way to tie it back to this topic. When I started to work with him initially he had no classroom friends, struggled completing his schoolwork, and often got very upset. When plans changed at the last minute or when he did not want to complete his schoolwork, he would cry, scream, and occasionally try to leave the classroom without permission. On the playground, he would catch bugs and take them to show to people. The other children made fun of him and would not include him in their games. Carl attended general education classes and did excellent in Science, but he struggled in English. One of the more common tasks in English class was creative writing and Carl absolutely refused to participate. His English teacher saw no reason why such an intelligent student would not complete his work and would throw such a fit. She often wanted to punish Carl with bad grades and send him out of the classroom to go to the office. My initial goals for Carl included improving social skills, eliminating his tantrums, and improving his performance in English. The first priority was explaining to his English teacher that, even though Carl was a very bright child, he did have ASD and then to help her modify the creative writing assignments to be on Carl's level. Just because Carl excels in some areas does not mean he excels everywhere. In fact, the abstract thinking and imagination required in the creative writing assignments is exactly the type of thing some high-functioning individuals with ASD may struggle with.
>
> Another of my students is Erin. Erin also has ASD, but she and Carl are very different. Erin is a 5-year-old kindergartener with a dual diagnosis of intellectual disability and ASD. Erin currently spends half of

her day in a typical kindergarten class and the other half of her day working one-on-one with me. Erin does not have any functional language and often intentionally hits her head on solid objects when she gets upset. We try to block her from doing this, but she frequently gets in a hard hit. She has had a red bruise on her face and forehead for most of the year. I spend a lot of time worrying about her safety. Erin also waves her hands in front of her face pretty constantly and seems unaware of or disinterested in other people. Eye contact with Erin is rare and she will almost always turn her head or close her eyes if I try to make her look at me. Goals for Erin include simple self-help skills (toileting), requesting items with sign language, and reducing her self-injury. I noticed that head hitting seems to increase after she has worked on something for a few minutes. Specifically, if we work on sign language for too long, she gets really upset. I think head hitting may be Erin's way of asking for a break from work. I have decided to plan Erin's instruction so that she only works for brief periods of time and practices requesting only items she really likes, and when she starts to look like she may be about to get upset, I prompt her to sign for a break from work.

Introduction

Both Carl and Erin have been diagnosed with autism spectrum disorders (ASDs). Students with ASD have difficulty communicating or interacting socially with other people. Many of these students also have an intellectual disability. A lot of these students also engage in challenging behavior such as aggression, tantrums, and self-injury. They also tend to be rigid in terms of what they want to talk about and things they like to do. Like Carl and his insects, these students may also perseverate on specific topics and may get very upset when anyone interferes with their interests and activities. In this chapter, we first describe the characteristics of ASD and then outline the best ways to organize the curriculum to teach students with ASD.

9.1 DEFINITIONS AND CHARACTERISTICS OF AUTISM SPECTRUM DISORDERS/ ASPERGER SYNDROME AND PERVASIVE DEVELOPMENTAL DISORDERS

MyEdLab
Video Example 9.1.
Watch this video and pay attention as the speaker describes the characteristics of autism spectrum disorder. As a general or special educator, why is it important to have an understanding and working knowledge of this area of disability?

You will note that the chapter title mentions two conditions: ASD and pervasive developmental disorders. The term pervasive developmental disorder (PDD) is a diagnostic category used by the American Psychiatric Association to describe five related disabilities: autistic disorder or autism, Rett syndrome, childhood disintegrative disorder, Asperger syndrome, and pervasive developmental disorder–not otherwise specified (PDD–NOS) (American Psychiatric Association [APA], 2000; National Research Council [NRC], 2001). Autism spectrum disorders (ASDs) has recently become a popular term to describe a subgroup of PDD, namely, autism and Asperger syndrome.

Researchers have been studying the characteristics of people with ASDs and PDDs for nearly 70 years (e.g., Kanner, 1943), and the criteria for diagnosing these disabilities has changed several times (Fombonne, 2005; Matson, 2007; Matson, Belva, Horovitz, Kozlowski, & Bamburg, 2012). Before proceeding, we note terminology used in this chapter. With the publication of the fifth edition of the *Diagnostic and Statistical Manual for Mental Disorders* (*DSM-5*) from the American Psychiatric Association (2013), all former diagnostic labels related to ASD (e.g., autistic disorder, Asperger's syndrome, pervasive developmental disorder–not other specified, childhood disintegrative disorder) fall under the umbrella term of ASD. With the *DSM-5*, students with ASD are categorized into different levels of support depending on their challenges related to ASD. Level 1 requires the least amount of support. Level 2 requires substantial support and Level 3 requires very substantial support. Because this categorization system from the *DSM-5* is relatively new, the ASD terminology (e.g., Aspberger's, PDD) used by researchers before 2013 is still frequently utilized and will be used throughout the chapter. Regardless, the children on the spectrum that you will be teaching will still need the same supports and specialized instructional strategies discussed here.

The number of individuals diagnosed with ASD has risen dramatically in the last 15 to 20 years (Center for Disease Control [CDC], 2014). In 2006, approximately 211,610 students who were classified with autism received special education services in our schools. This is nine times more than the number of students receiving school services in 1994. The prevalence rates of ASD for children continue to increase dramatically in the United States [one in 88 (Center for Disease Control, 2008), one in 68 children (Center for Disease Control, 2014)]. It is unclear why there is such a rise in students diagnosed with ASD. The rise may be due to changes in diagnostic practices (Smith, Reichow, & Volkmar, 2015; Rutter, 2005) and the inclusion of autism as a special education category in the early 1990s. Nevertheless, some true rise in the rate of ASD cannot be firmly discounted. Despite widespread media attention, research has not found a connection between the measles-mumps-rubella vaccine and the increases in ASD (Demicheli, Rivetti, Debalini, Di Pietrantonj, & Robinson, 2013; Honda, Shimizu, & Rutter, 2005; Offit, 2008).

One of the main reasons for using the term *ASD* to describe autism and Asperger syndrome is that these disabilities incorporate many of the same symptoms and differ primarily in the severity of expression of those symptoms. The other categories of PDD are extremely rare (e.g., Rett syndrome, childhood disintegrative disorder) or may not be very clear, as in the diagnosis of pervasive developmental disorder–not otherwise specified (PDD–NOS). In this section, each of the five PDD categories is described along with accompanying information on the levels of support recognized under *DSM-5* that are associated with PDD categories described. However, the remainder of the chapter focuses on teaching students with ASD. There are quantitative and qualitative differences in the learning and behavioral characteristics exhibited by individuals who have each disability. Table 9.1 displays each disorder as well as the characteristics that set the disorders apart.

Table 9.1 • Comparison of Disabilities Across Developmental Areas

	SOCIAL INTERACTION	COMMUNICATION	STEREOTYPES	COGNITION
Autism ASD Levels 1–3	Little or no eye contact Autistic leading Unawareness of social situations	Little to no verbal communication Repetitive, echolalic, or robotic speech	Inflexible routines Motor repetitions (finger flapping, body rocking)	May have intellectual disability May have savant characteristics
Rett Syndrome, ASD Level 3	Loss of social skills within the first few years Loss of interest in social environment	Severely impaired expressive and receptive language	Develops hand movements such as hand wringing or hand washing between ages 5 and 30 months	Often associated with severe or profound intellectual disability
Childhood Disintegrative Disorder ASD Level 3	Loss of interest in environment but not until 2 to 10 years of age Lack of social or emotional reciprocity	Loss of language skills around 2 to 10 years of age Repetitive use of language Lack of make-believe play	Develops repetitive motor movements such as hand flapping and finger waving Restricted interests and activities	Usually associated with intellectual disability, as the loss of skills in all areas is progressive
Asperger Syndrome (Levels 1–3)	Lack of ability to read social cues Awkward eye contact Interest in social environment	No clinically significant delay in language Use of language (pragmatics) may be delayed (e.g., loudness or socially appropriate use)	Restricted areas of interest (e.g., preoccupation with a topic) Inflexible adherence to certain routines Repetitive motor movements	No clinically significant delay in cognition

Delays are usually noted in early childhood and may co-occur with intellectual disability. Currently, there is no identified cause for many of these disabilities. Given the lack of knowledge about cause, there are no empirically validated strategies for prevention or cure at this time.

9.1.1 Autism

Autism is a developmental disability that typically appears during the first 3 years of life. Although people diagnosed with autism are considered to have a severe disability, the range in ability level within this group is varied (NRC, 2001; Volkmar & McPartland, 2014). Some individuals with autism may function independently or almost independently. Under the current *DSM-5* categories the levels of support for students with autism can be anywhere from Level 1 (requiring support) to Level 3 (requiring the most intensive level of support).

To be diagnosed with autism, a child must have documented features in three areas:

1. ***Six or more of any combination of the following:***
   - Impairments in social interactions (e.g., poor eye contact, lack of responsiveness, inability to establish relationships)
   - Impairments in communication (e.g., no formal spoken language, robotic-sounding speech with little tone inflection, use of made-up gibberish words, and repeating exactly what has been heard)
2. ***Stereotypical behavior*** (e.g., body rocking, hand flapping, or fascination with objects or specific parts of objects)
3. ***Onset before age 3*** (note, this is not necessarily as a loss of skills but rather as an emergence of delay in skill development). The child must not meet criteria for Rett syndrome or childhood disintegrative disorder, in which loss of skills is reported before age 3.

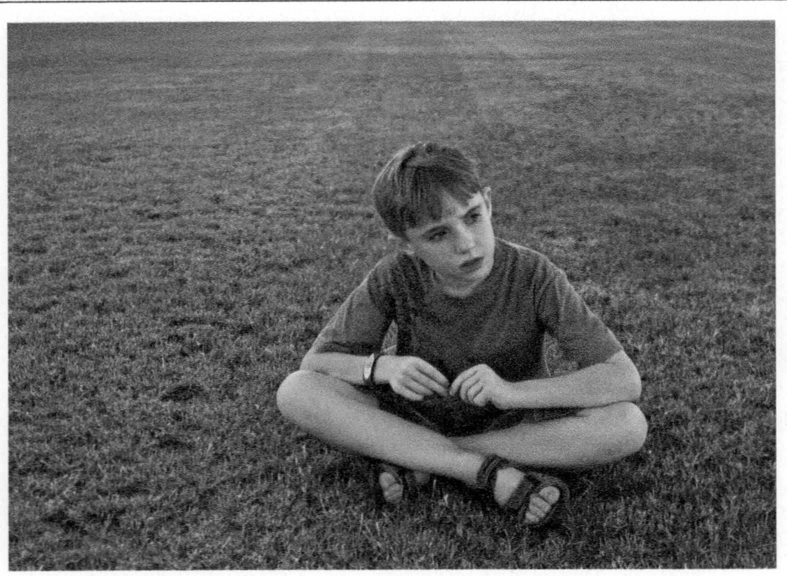

What physical behaviors do children with autism exhibit? What other impairments may occur in people diagnosed with autism?

The physical features and general appearance of people with autism might not suggest a disability. Rather, the disability is generally manifested in their language and their personal and social behavior. The Individuals with Disabilities Education Improvement Act (IDEA, 2004) defines *autism* as follows:

> A developmental disability significantly affecting verbal and nonverbal communication and social interaction, generally evident before age 3, that adversely affects a child's performance. Other characteristics often associated with autism are engagement in repetitive activities and stereotyped movements, resistance to environmental change or change in daily routines, and unusual responses to sensory experiences. The term does not apply if a child's educational performance is adversely affected primarily because the child has a serious emotional disturbance.

After having Terry, a student with autism, in his seventh-grade language block for several months, Thomas Salome expressed these thoughts:

> I was worried about how it would work with the other students; if it would take away time and attention from them. I was concerned that Terry would be a distraction to the students. But now that Terry has been part of our class for several months, I feel that the more he is in the classroom, the less the children even notice the noise or occasional outbursts. The students have learned that Terry does things that are not okay for them to do.

TIPS FOR TEACHERS 9.1

Working with Students with Autism

- *Don't let the behavior overwhelm you.* Develop a behavior management plan and implement small steps. Decide what behaviors you will put up with and what behaviors must stop, and target those.
- *Talk to the student's parents and other teachers.* Find out what works and what does not work with this student. For example, does the child like to be offered choices during the day (e.g., what to do next) or would the child prefer a more set schedule with a routine?
- *Systematically expect more and more of the student.* At first, it might be enough that the student sits with the class during circle time. However, over time you may require increased participation (e.g., answering questions).
- *Develop a picture and word schedule for daily activities.* Picture schedules may have photographs or drawings that represent activities that will occur during the day. Referencing this schedule may help the child understand what is coming next and transition between activities and environments more smoothly. This type of schedule will help you introduce changes in routine slowly and let the student know in advance that these changes are going to occur.
- *Use peers to help redirect the student's behavior.* Classmates can be a source of support for a student with ASD. They can help prompt appropriate behavior and even praise a student for his or her accomplishments.
- *Take ownership of the student.* Every child in your class is your responsibility and you have been entrusted with their education and well-being. Children with ASD can be challenging, but you will feel a deep sense of accomplishment when they make progress.

Tips for Teachers 9.1 presents Thomas's advice for working with students like Terry in the classroom.

9.1.2 Asperger Syndrome

Asperger syndrome is the next most common PDD. Under the current *DSM-5* categories, Asperger syndrome was incorporated under the category of ASD. The levels of support for students with Asperger syndrome will range from Level 1 (requiring support) to Level 3 (requiring the most intensive level of support). Despite serious impairments in social skills, abstract thinking, and the ability to relate to and identify emotions, these students are often in the normal IQ range and may have extensive verbal abilities. As a result, many people do not immediately recognize the child with Asperger syndrome in the classroom. Asperger syndrome is diagnosed by documenting behaviors in six different areas:

1. Qualitative impairment in social interaction (e.g., eye contact, failure to develop peer relationships) and lack of social or emotional reciprocity
2. Stereotypical behavior such as abnormal preoccupation with one or more areas of interest in either intensity or focus (e.g., Carl's interest in insects, discussed at the beginning of the chapter), inflexible adherence to routines or rituals, and stereotyped motor mannerisms (e.g., finger flapping)
3. Presence of impairment in a social, occupational, or vocational area (e.g., inability to get a job or make friends)
4. No clinically significant delay in language; in other words, in terms of vocabulary and semantics, language ability is comparable to a same-age peer without a disability, but speech may sound robotic or monotone
5. No clinically significant delays in cognition, self-help, adaptive skills (e.g., eating, dressing, toileting), or curiosity about the environment
6. Must not meet the criteria for schizophrenia, because schizophrenia would likely better explain the majority of the symptoms shared with Asperger syndrome

Because Asperger syndrome is not immediately obvious, this disability can create unique challenges for school systems and teachers (DePape & Lindsay, 2015; Portway & Johnson, 2005). If students with Asperger syndrome are overlooked and considered just to be quirky or immature, they are not likely to receive the supports and services they need. Without support, many of these students will experience social isolation, anxiety, and depression (DePape & Lindsay, 2015; Lang, Regester, Lauderdale, Ashbaugh, & Haring, 2010; Rayner, 2005). Parents of children with Asperger syndrome state that once school personnel understand the characteristics of Asperger syndrome, they do a better job of making accommodations and providing support (e.g., teaching social skills and modifying class assignments). In turn, these supports have a positive effect on these students' quality of life (Baric, Hellberg, Kjellberg, & Hemmingsson, 2015; Brewin, Renwick, & Schormans, 2008).

Consider the example of Rusty. Rusty is a 15-year-old boy who just started high school. In middle school, his teacher, Mrs. Garrett, was well aware of his Asperger diagnosis and made the minor accommodations necessary for him to make progress and feel successful at school. Among other things, Mrs. Garrett would explain complex directions for some assignments in very concrete terms, which Rusty was better able to understand. She would also offer Rusty slightly modified assignments to scaffold his learning experiences to better meet his current abilities and educational goals. However, now in high school, Rusty changes classes and has many teachers. Many of his new teachers are unaware of his diagnosis and think of Rusty as just a peculiar kid who fails to complete work or participate in class because of laziness. In his history class, Rusty is asked to work in a team of three students to prepare a presentation for the class. The topic of the presentation is how different people in different countries interpreted certain events during World War II. Rusty struggles to understand the topic and to recognize the frustration of the other members in his group. Ultimately, he is embarrassed and earns a poor grade. With slight modifications (e.g., allowing independent work and better explanation of the assignment), Rusty may have succeeded. However, because the teacher did not recognize the disability or understand its implications, Rusty experienced unnecessary failure.

9.1.3 Rett Syndrome

To be diagnosed with **Rett syndrome (RTT)**, a child must have normal prenatal and perinatal development, normal psychomotor development for the first 5 months, and normal head circumference at birth. The child also exhibits normal development in the following areas until a loss of skills occurs between 5 and 48 months. Under the *DSM-5*, children diagnosed with Rett syndrome are no longer part of the ASD diagnosis; rather, this is a separate disability category. The stated justification for this change is that "the disruption of social interaction may be observed during the regressive phase of RTT… however, after this period most individuals with RTT improve their social communications skills, and autistic features are no longer a major area of concern" (pg. 57, American Psychiatric Association, 2013). These students typically require the most intensive level of support (Level 3). These deficits include the following:

- Deceleration of head growth
- Loss of hand skills with subsequent development of stereotyped hand movements (e.g., hand washing or hand wringing)
- Loss of social engagement
- Poor gait or trunk movements
- Severely impaired receptive and expressive communication (Sigafoos et al., 2009)

This syndrome is extremely rare, occurring in approximately one in 10,000 live births, and occurs only in females (Katz et al., 2012). A genetic cause for Rett syndrome has been isolated. As these girls begin to regress developmentally, they exhibit symptoms that are superficially similar to autism (e.g., loss of communication skills). These children eventually suffer from multiple disabilities.

9.1.4 Childhood Disintegrative Disorder

To be diagnosed with **childhood disintegrative disorder**, a child must have a normal pattern of development through age 2. Between the ages of 2 and 10, the child must demonstrate a regression of skills in two of the following areas: language, social skills, adaptive skills, bowel or bladder control, play skills, and motor skills. The child must also exhibit delays in social interaction, communication, and stereotypical behaviors. Last, the child must not meet the criteria for any other PDD or schizophrenia. This is an extremely rare condition, occurring in approximately one in 50,000 live births (Chakrabarti & Fombonne, 2005; Frombonne, 2002). Under the *DSM-5*, children diagnosed with childhood disintegrative disorder are now diagnosed with ASD and typically require the most intensive level of support (Level 3).

9.1.5 Pervasive Developmental Disorder–Not Otherwise Specified

A child is diagnosed with **pervasive developmental disorder–not otherwise specified (PDD–NOS)** when delays are exhibited in social interaction or communication or if stereotypical behaviors develop and the child does not meet the criteria for another PDD. Essentially, the diagnosis is used when no other diagnosis seems appropriate but there are obvious delays for no apparent reason, such as traumatic birth or neurological development. Under the *DSM-5,* students previously diagnosed with PDD–NOS are now diagnosed with ASD with differing levels of support provided depending on need.

9.1.6 Characteristics of Students with ASD

Autism spectrum disorders thought of to exist along a continuum cover a wide range of abilities and difficulties, as described earlier in the chapter. Three core deficits are common to ASD: in social skills, in communication skills, and in repetitive behaviors and routines. Each student with ASD will possess these deficits to some degree. Being aware of these core areas of functioning can help you tailor your curriculum and instruction to the needs of a specific student.

MyEdLab
Video Example 9.2.
Watch this video for an example of positive peer support. Since many individuals with autism have challenges establishing positive relations with peers, identify ways you might use positive peer support to include students with autism in your classroom.

9.1.7 Social Skills

Students with ASD do not interact with other people in a typical fashion (Baric et al., 2015; NRC, 2001). In fact, they may not wish to interact with people at all. They can have difficulty interpreting the social cues of other people. For example, they may be unable to discriminate the different intentions of a wink versus a frown. They may appear not to notice other people at all and can give the impression that they are deaf. Other students with ASD may sincerely want to make friends and be social but lack core social skills to initiate, respond to, and maintain social interactions.

Additionally, students with ASD have difficulty seeing the world from the perspective of another person. They may be unable to "get in the head" of another person and recognize that other people have goals and feelings. This means that they may struggle to comprehend the behavior of other people. The social world may therefore be an unpredictable place for students with ASD. Unfortunately, this may lead to bullying (both being the bully and being the victim of bullying), anxiety, and/or depression (e.g., Baric et al., 2015; Didden et al., 2009; Lang, O'Reilly et al., 2010).

A related problem is that many students with ASD have difficulty regulating their emotions. They may engage in what appears to be spontaneous outbursts of aggression (hitting other students), self-injury (banging their heads), or sadness (weeping). This pattern can also impede social integration.

9.1.8 Communication Skills

Many children with autism do not talk at all, and others only develop extremely limited verbal language, which they use to make one-word requests (Tager-Flusberg & Kasari, 2013). Some of these children seem to pass the early milestones of language acquisition (e.g., babbling), but then they stop. Others may develop some language later, at age 9 or 10, for example.

Those who develop language may use it in unusual ways. Many use single words or phrases but do not combine these words and phrases into meaningful sentences. They may repeat what they hear verbatim, a condition called echolalia. For example, when you ask, "Would you like a cookie?" they might repeat, "Would you like a cookie?" instead of answering the question. Other students may have mild delays in language development or may, in fact, possess large or even precocious vocabularies, yet they have difficulty sustaining conversations with others. This last difficulty is typical of students with high-functioning autism and Asperger syndrome. A student with Asperger syndrome may be more than able to carry on a detailed monologue about a favorite topic (e.g., Carl and his insects, described at the beginning of the chapter) but will not give any other students an opportunity to engage in a conversation about the topic. They appear to talk *at* people and seem oblivious to any attempts at initiation by others. These students may also have difficulty interpreting the body language, tone of voice, and turn of phrase of other students.

Body language, including facial expressions, posture, orientation, and gestures, may not match what these students are saying. Tone of voice is often monotone, high-pitched, or robotic. Students with Asperger syndrome will often speak like adults and will not use the vocal nuances of their peer group. A child with Asperger syndrome may be expressing genuine interest in a topic or an individual but fail to accurately communicate this interest. For example, after hearing a joke they enjoyed instead of saying, "That was a cool joke, can you tell another?" they may instead say "I require a second amusing anecdote now." When making this sincere, yet peculiar and precocious request they might also fail to make eye contact and their voice and expression may make them appear bored or disinterested.

With such deficits in communication skills, these students can have difficulty expressing their wants and needs. They may therefore communicate their intent by other means such as grabbing, pulling, screaming, hitting, and self-injury. Young adults with high-functioning autism (i.e., those students with autism who do not have a diagnosis of intellectual disability or who may have mild levels of intellectual disability) or Asperger syndrome may become aware of these difficulties. This awareness that they are different can, in some instances, cause frustration, embarrassment, and social isolation, which may ultimately result in secondary psychiatric issues such as anxiety and depression.

9.1.9 Repetitive Behaviors and Routines

Many students with ASD engage in repetitive motor behaviors (NRC, 2001; Richler, Bishop, Kleinke, & Lord, 2007). These can be subtle (repeated head turning when they appear to be alone) or blatant (continuous and vigorous body rocking). Other typical types of repetitive motor behaviors include hand flapping, finger flicking, and tip-toe walking (Reed, Hirst, & Hyman, 2012). Children with ASD tend to demand strict adherence to a routine or consistency in the environment. For example, they will engage with certain toys but not play with them in a typical fashion. Instead of pretend play with toy cars, they may endlessly line them up in rows (e.g., Lang, O'Reilly et al., 2010). Any change in daily routines such as time, venue, and menu for meals; route to school; personal hygiene; and bedtime routines can result in challenging behavior. These children may also be intensely preoccupied with very specific interests such as train schedules, dinosaurs, or specific TV shows. These specific interests are referred to as "perseverative interests" because the student perseveres with them frequently and inappropriately (Wang, Parrila, & Cui, 2013).

It appears that such behaviors and routines may underpin consistency and predictability in the child's world. As a result, any attempt to interfere with the repetitive behaviors and routines can result in extreme upset and challenging behavior.

MyEdLab **Self-Check 9.1**

MyEdLab **Application Exercise 9.1:** Definition of Autism Spectrum Disorders 

9.2 IDENTIFICATION AND ASSESSMENT OF STUDENTS WITH AUTISM SPECTRUM DISORDERS

Children with severe ASD will most likely have a diagnosis before arriving in your classroom. However, it is also possible you may be involved in initial evaluations or screenings for ASD. If this is needed, you may be asked to document student performance in the areas of language, social, academic, or adaptive behaviors. You may even be asked to complete rating scales describing student behavior in your class. These rating scales are often simple and require little, if any, specialized knowledge to complete.

If you are not involved in the identification evaluation, you will certainly be involved in ongoing assessment and reevaluation. As a classroom teacher, you may be expected to monitor progress in areas in which delays are commonly reported. For example, you might have to monitor how a child with Asperger syndrome uses language in conversations and interacts with his or her peers. Keeping some sort of record or data concerning progress is paramount. For example, consider Carl's case described in the beginning of this chapter. Carl struggles with peer relationships. You might want to keep track of how often Carl interacts with his classmates without discussing insects. By simply making a note in a special folder at the end of the day detailing any interaction you witnessed, over time you may be able to gauge some progress. If his appropriate interactions increase, then you have some evidence that he may be making improvements in both controlling his perseverations and social skills (Lang & Page, 2011).

The assessment of contextual variables is also important for this population of students. A contextual variable is something that is unique to a particular situation, for example, the environmental differences between the classroom and the lunchroom and even the differences between one teacher and another. Students with ASD may learn something in one context but then fail to generalize the ability to another context (Lang, Sigafoos, Lancioni, Didden, & Rispoli, 2010; Otero, Schatz, Merrill, & Bellini, 2015). For example, during lunch, your student with autism may be able to demonstrate appropriate use of a napkin, but he may not be able to demonstrate this in home economics when his class is working on table manners. Additionally, a student's behavior may be substantially different in different environments (Lang et al., 2008; Lang, Machalicek et al., 2009). It is not uncommon for parents to say, "but my child never behaves that way at home." A well-prepared and organized teacher will keep a log documenting where students perform certain skills as well as under what conditions the skills are missing. This type of assessment can help you better understand exactly where, by whom, and the other contextual variables that may be important when teaching a particular student.

MyEdLab **Self-Check 9.2**

MyEdLab **Application Exercise 9.2:** Identification of Students with ASD

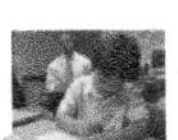

9.3 CURRICULAR AND INSTRUCTIONAL GUIDELINES FOR STUDENTS WITH AUTISM SPECTRUM DISORDERS

In this section, we outline some suggestions for organizing the curriculum and designing instruction for students with ASD. These guidelines are not exhaustive. To develop an effective instructional program for students with ASD, you should consider the key processes discussed in the following sections.

Later in this text you will read about the curricular and instructional guidelines for students with developmental disabilities that are equally applicable to students with ASD.

9.3.1 Assess Preferences

At the beginning of the school year, try to get a comprehensive picture of the students' likes and dislikes in terms of activities by conducting a preference assessment. A preference assessment form can be as simple as a piece of paper listing the items the student likes. Assess what contexts students find challenging. For example, some students might find that structured classroom tasks they complete individually are not a challenge, whereas cooperative learning might be. As part of this process, generate a list of items such as toys, foods, and activities that the students like. You can generate this list by interviewing parents and previous teachers and then tailor the emphasis to each student (Verschuur et al., 2011).

Preference assessments should be conducted at least two times during the academic year, because children's preferences change over time. Also, as you work with students, you may see changes in their preferred activities and items. This information will be invaluable when designing the classroom routine, selecting instructional strategies, and even when attempting to reduce challenging classroom behavior (Carnett et al., 2014; Kang et al., 2011).

9.3.2 Establish a Classroom Routine

When we discussed some of the difficulties experienced by students with ASD, we noted that they may be particularly challenged when a routine is absent or unpredictable. These students may be prone to challenging behavior when placed in a new classroom situation. It is important to establish a classroom routine quickly and to communicate this routine to the student.

When first establishing the classroom routine, consider the demands of the regular classroom routine, such as what the students are supposed to do when they first enter the classroom, when they go to lunch, and when they finish their work. The routine for the student with an ASD should fit within this larger routine as much as possible. When designing the routine, teachers should consider information regarding the student's high- and low-preference activities and then design the student's routine judiciously. For example, intersperse high- and low-preference activities. Do not expect the student to spend extended periods of time engaged in low-preference activities. Low- and high-preference activities should be evenly balanced. For example, consider Erin's case presented at the beginning of the chapter. Erin did not enjoy working on sign language, and if she is required to do this task for too long, she engages in challenging behavior. However, Erin does enjoy coloring and scribbling on paper. The teacher could use this information regarding Erin's enjoyment of coloring in attempts to reduce her challenging behavior. For example, the teacher could rotate between brief periods of sign language work with periods of coloring. Alternatively, the teacher could teach Erin signs to request coloring materials (Davis et al., 2009; Landers, Schlaug, & Wan, 2013), or she could allow Erin to color for an extended amount of time prior to working on sign language (Rispoli, O'Reilly et al., 2011).

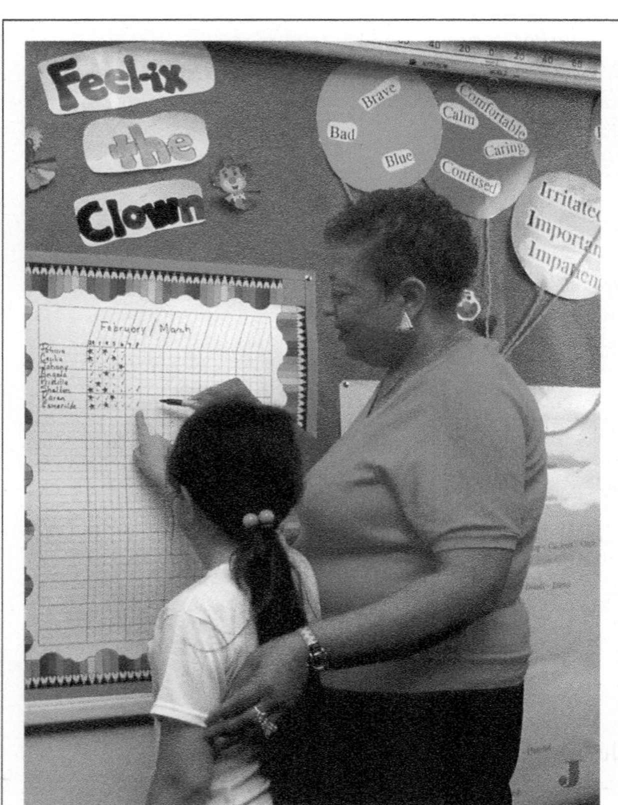

Why is it important to establish a classroom routine? How do daily routines benefit students with autism spectrum disorder?

Some students may experience difficulties transitioning from high-preference to low-preference activities. In these cases, it may be helpful to incorporate a neutral activity (i.e., something the child does not dislike, but is also not highly preferred) following a high-preference activity (e.g., coloring for Erin) and before a low-preference activity (e.g., sign language drills for Erin). When this is done, the child is not being asked to give up something enjoyable to do something he or she hates, and this eases the transition and may also reduce the likelihood of challenging behavior.

It is important to establish a routine as early as possible in the school year. The daily routine should be communicated to students through a daily schedule. This schedule can be presented to students in different formats. For the student with Asperger syndrome, the schedule can be written into a personal diary that the student carries with him or her. For the student with autism, the schedule could be posted on the wall with pictures attached identifying the daily activities and the times they will occur. At the beginning of each school day, you should review the activities on the schedule for that day with each individual student.

It is important to involve the student, as much as possible, in preparing this schedule. So, within the constraints of mandated classroom activities, the student could choose the sequence of activities for the day. Certain time periods may be left blank during the day. When a blank period arises, you might offer the student a choice between different activities. For example, consider Carl's case again. After English class, Carl could be scheduled for a preferred activity as a reward. Carl's teacher, Mrs. Page, could offer Carl two choices of how to spend his free time, perhaps playing on the computer or looking at an insect picture book. For higher-functioning students, it may be sufficient to simply offer the choices verbally. However, for some students, pictorial representations of the activities may more clearly explain the choices. In these instances, Carl could select the picture of the insect book to indicate his preference (Machalicek et al., 2009; Spooner, Ahlgrim-Delzell, Kemp-Inman, & Wood, 2014).

MyEdLab
Video Example 9.3.
Watch as this teacher works with a student with ASD on reading skills and following directions. What are the particular strategies that this teacher is using to promote learning?

This form of activity scheduling is an important antecedent intervention to enhance self-control and communication skills. It also reduces the probability of challenging behavior from students with ASD (Flannery & Horner, 1994; Lequia, Machalicek, & Rispoli, 2012; O'Reilly, Sigafoos, Lancioni, Edrishina, & Andrews, 2005). See Tips for Teachers 9.2 for more suggestions for working with students with ASD.

9.3.3 Teach Academic Skills

Sometimes overlooked, it's important to consider the instructional needs of students with ASD, particularly in core subjects such as reading. Taking time to think about the student's academic strengths and areas of need by reviewing data and work samples is an important first step. Recently technology-based educational apps have been designed to support learning for students with ASD have been gaining popularity. Despite the growing popularity, experts suggest using caution on relying solely on technology to support learning. Technology should be considered for use in conjunction with sound research-based instructional practices (Knight, McKissick, & Saunders, 2013). As a teacher, you should teach academic skills to students with ASD by utilizing explicit instructional routines and graphic organizers, teaching strategy instruction, and considering grouping practices such as cooperative learning and team-based learning. Make sure that you develop a comprehensive plan to determine the essential academic support needed to help them stay organized, make connections between concepts, and monitor their understanding over time (El Zein, Solis, Vaughn, McCulley, 2013). For example, during reading group the teacher might have a child with ASD use a self-monitoring checklist or graphic organizer to provide additional scaffolds of instructional and organizational support. Many of the instructional practices identified in the academic chapters addressing reading, writing, and mathematics are also appropriate for these students.

9.3.4 Teach Communication Skills

Communication skills are typically very difficult for students with ASD; consequently, it is essential that you develop a comprehensive plan that maps out the skills you plan to teach and how you are going to teach them. Once you have established your daily schedule for the student, it is helpful to target communication skills to teach during each activity, such as requesting preferred items or naming objects. For example, during snack time, Erin's teacher is going to teach the sign for popcorn (a preferred food) and have Erin use the sign to get her snack. Teaching in this way makes the skill relevant to the situation. A creative teacher will find a way to target at least one communication skill during every

TIPS FOR TEACHERS 9.2

Working with Students with ASD

- *Use picture and word schedules for daily activities.* Picture schedules may have photographs or drawings that represent activities that will occur during the day. Referencing this schedule may help the child understand what is coming next and transition between activities and environments more smoothly. This type of schedule will help you introduce changes in routine slowly, and let the student know in advance that these changes are going to occur.
- *Establish routines early in the school year.* Students with ASD often rely heavily on routines. Communicate clearly about any changes in the routine, and post them in your picture schedule.
- *Learn about augmentative and alternative communication.* Students with delays in social communication often use a different mode of communication. You may have students who use picture wallets, communication boards, or even voice output communication aids to communicate. Learn to feel comfortable using these devices.
- *Establish collaborative relationships with families.* Parents know their child best, and they can assist you when you have questions or concerns. Communicate regularly with parents so that they are aware of any changes in your class. Ask them to communicate to you about changes at home.
- *Be aware of your classroom environment.* Students with ASD may be hypersensitive to environmental conditions such as noise, lighting, and temperature. Become familiar with your individual students' needs and make adjustments to your classroom environment as needed.

scheduled activity (Koegel, Matos-Fredeen, Lang, & Koegel, 2012). Tips for Teachers 9.2 provides some useful strategies.

Massed trials strategy

Portions of the daily schedule might involve intensive instruction in communication skills using a massed trials strategy. A massed trials strategy means that the same instructional trial is repeated again and again to a predefined criterion of correct performance. For example, you might ask the child to name certain items that are presented individually on a table or to point to an item from an array of items presented simultaneously. Each trial begins with the teacher asking a question: "What is this?" or "Point to the ____." Initially, the teacher will immediately give the answer: "A doll." The student is expected to repeat the answer. As training progresses, the teacher systematically delays the answer to the question (e.g., by 2 seconds) in order to give the student the opportunity to respond independently. All of the student's correct responses receive reinforcement (reward) from the teacher. This reinforcement should be selected from the information obtained in the preference assessment described earlier. For example, if it was determined that Erin liked popcorn, using a small piece of popcorn as reinforcement during massed trials might be appropriate. Alternatively, for some children physical contact (e.g., high-five or a hug) and praise may be sufficient reinforcement.

Milieu or naturalistic instruction

Communication skills should also be taught as part of the ongoing natural context. This type of communication instruction is often called milieu or naturalistic instruction. These instructional strategies are similar to massed trials strategies. The main difference with milieu training is that the communication training occurs when there is a natural opportunity for the child to communicate. For example, at lunchtime the child could be presented with an empty glass. You hold the container of milk. The child motions toward the glass. You then present the container of milk with the request, "I want milk please." The student repeats the phrase and is then given the milk. The consequence of the request (receiving the milk) acts as a natural positive consequence of engaging in the request. No arbitrary consequences selected from the preference assessment are necessary using this strategy. Over time, you can delay using the phrase until the natural conditions (e.g., empty glass and container of milk) elicit the request spontaneously from the student (Koegel et al., 2012).

Augmentative and Alternative Communication (AAC)

Children with ASD often have profound language delays (Szatmari et al., 2014). Addressing communication difficulties is a common and often high-priority education goal. Communication can occur through gestures, facial expressions, and eye blinks, and through augmentative and alternative communication (AAC). AAC devices enhance communication by replacing or facilitating a speech. Low-technology AAC devices can involve pictures or drawings at which the student points to convey a message. High-technology AAC devices can provide voice output (speech synthesizers) and can be programmed with many messages (Rispoli, Franco, Van der Meer, Lang, & Camargo, 2010).

A communication board is one example of low-technology AAC. The essential elements are the board itself and the symbols or pictures. The board can be made of sturdy paper or an actual board, or it can be a regular or simplified computer keyboard or a computer screen. The symbols or symbol systems that are selected depend on the learner and the environment in which he or she is interacting. Symbols should be selected according to what students need and want to communicate. In constructing communication boards, Lewis (1993) suggests that the following questions need to be addressed:

- What choices will the student be able to make?
- How will the choices be represented on the board?
- How will the student make his or her selections?
- How many choices will be available, and how will they be arranged on the board?
- How will the communication board be constructed?

Figure 9.1 presents examples of common symbol systems, which include Core Picture Vocabulary (Johnson, 1985), Talking Pictures (Leff & Leff, 1978), Pic Syms (Carlson, 1984), Oakland Schools Picture Dictionary (Kirstein & Bernstein, 1981), Picture Communication Symbols (Johnson, 1985), and Blissymbols (Bliss, 1965).

Additionally, simply using the Internet to find and print relevant pictures may also be effective. This can be done easily by searching with Google © for keywords related to the picture needed and then clicking "Images" to find pictures.

The goals and strategies of communication instruction should be identical for students who do not speak and those who do speak. You will need to work closely with your speech and language pathologist and the student's family to find the best AAC solution for your student. To find the best solution for your student, you need to identify your communication goals for your student and present this information to the speech pathologist as you discuss the optimal AAC device for the student in question.

The communication skills chosen for instruction will depend on such factors as the level of the student's disability and family priorities. The communication skills of many students with ASD will be at what is described as a prelinguistic level. For example, the child may lead you to an area (e.g., locked cupboard) where a desired item is present (e.g., favorite toy). This leading behavior is common in ASD and is often referred to as autistic leading. It is important to identify these prelinguistic behaviors and replace them with more appropriate communication skills, such as orally requesting an item, using the instructional strategies previously described. Other children may not even present with prelinguistic behaviors, appearing almost comatose. For these students, rudimentary skills such as making and maintaining eye contact may need to be encouraged.

Because students with ASD tend not to efficiently generalize skills they have been taught, you will need to encourage generalization of the targeted communication skills in as many different environments as possible. One way to facilitate this is to involve parents as trainers. Parents spend more time with their children than you do and will have many opportunities to implement milieu or naturalistic strategies. Therefore, involving the parents in the process of teaching communication skills can be very beneficial. Parents can be effective teachers, and involving them in their child's instruction can have a positive effect on reducing the stress involved in interacting with their child (Lang, Machalicek et al., 2009).

See the Tech Tips, "Useful Tools for Teaching Children with Autism Spectrum Disorders," for information on computer programs that are helpful in instructing students with ASD.

FIGURE 9.1 **Picture symbol systems for communication boards**

Core Picture Vocabulary	Talking Pictures	Pic Syms	Oakland	Picture Communication Symbols	Blissymbols
Man					
Wash					
Want	No symbol				
Hello	No symbol		No symbol		
Happy	No symbol				
House					
Car					

Source: "Augmentative and alternative communication," by S. Glennen, 1992, in G. Church and S. Glennen (Eds.), *The handbook of assistive technology* (p. 100), San Diego, CA: Singular Publishing Group. Reprinted with permission.

9.3.5 Teach Social Skills

The distinction between communication skills and social skills is a somewhat arbitrary one. In a sense, one must possess adequate communication skills in order to engage socially with others. For the purposes of this chapter, **social skills** include the ability to initiate appropriate social interactions, respond to social initiations from others, and terminate social interactions appropriately.

A person is perceived to be socially competent by others if he or she is able to interact socially in an effective manner, generalize these interaction styles across multiple social situations, and maintain such interactions over time. Social skills targeted for instruction include the following:

- Initiating conversations with others
- Responding to initiations
- Maintaining conversations
- Responding to criticism

TECH TIPS

Useful Tools for Teaching Students with Autism Spectrum Disorders

Boardmaker software, by Mayer-Johnson, Inc.
(www.mayer-johnson.com)

In addition to using Boardmaker for communication boards, teachers have had success in helping learners with ASD with organization, structure, and expectations—for example, a visual calendar, sequential steps for specific activities, and visual signals to help learners with transitions.

PECS, by Pyramid Educational Consultants
(www.pecs.com)

The Picture Exchange Communication System (PECS) has received worldwide recognition for focusing on the initiation component of communication. The PECS system employs applied behavior analysis in conjunction with the development of functional communication skills that focus on the initiation of communication.

Early Learning, by Marblesoft
(www.marblesoft.com)

The Early Learning series of prereading programs for learners in preschool, early elementary, and special education classrooms teaches a variety of skills, including colors, shapes, numbers, letters, sorting, matching, problem solving, sequencing, beginning addition and subtraction, and counting money. These programs provide instruction in tiny steps, offer multiple levels of difficulty and various input methods, and generate a user profile. The teacher can specify the rate of advancing in difficulty, the amount of reinforcement and prompting, and how the program responds to wrong answers.

iPad/iPod™ applications include:

- ABC Data Pro
- Autism Apps
- MyFirstApp
- Calm Counter–Social Story and Anger Management Tool
- Touch Finger
- Touch Trainer
- Everyday Social Skills HD
- WhQuestions
- Conversation Builder
- Language Builder for iPad
- ChoiceBoard-Creator
- GoTalk Now, First-Then
- QuickCues

These skills have been taught within a multitude of social contexts such as play and leisure situations (e.g., initiating interactions with peers on the playground), the home environment (e.g., responding appropriately to parent initiations), and work settings (e.g., expanding interactions with coworkers). Strategies for teaching social skills are varied and can include verbal, gesture, and physical prompts; role-play; and a variety of self-management strategies (self-monitoring, self-instruction, and self-reinforcement).

You should focus your efforts on teaching social skills to students with ASD when they possess communication skills but fail to discriminate how to use these skills effectively with peers and others. In other words, social skills interventions should be a major focus for students with ASD who are higher functioning and students with Asperger syndrome. As mentioned earlier, many varying social skills intervention strategies are available; you need to select an intervention that will be maximally effective for your students. Remember that social skills deficits occur for a number of reasons, including the inability to understand the social context, such as the intentions, feelings, and perceptions of others. Therefore, many of the popular instructional strategies that focus primarily on teaching overt social skills without teaching the person to understand the perceptions of others may not be effective.

Two social skills teaching strategies that may prove helpful with these students are social problem solving and Social Story™ interventions. Both intervention strategies teach the student with ASD to understand the social context in addition to responding to or behaving appropriately in that social context.

Social problem solving

Social problem solving involves teaching the social skills you want your students to perform (e.g., maintaining appropriate distance from a person when initiating an interaction) as part of a generic process of engaging in social interactions. In other words, you will teach students a set of strategies to monitor or manage their own social skills in addition to the very specific social skills you want them to perform.

TIPS FOR TEACHERS 9.3

Using Social Problem-Solving Strategies

- Schedule two to three 30-minute periods during the first week of training to give the student ample exposure to the skill. Thereafter, you can provide brief feedback to the student during the regular classroom routine as he or she performs the social skill targeted during training.
- Teach the student to ask and answer a series of questions in relation to the social context in which the targeted social skill occurs.
- Teach the student to discriminate between important social cues by asking himself or herself, "What's happening here?" The student must then accurately describe the social situation.
- Help the student make decisions about how to behave by asking himself or herself: "What should I do?" These prompts help the student generate a series of alternative action plans and select the most appropriate social interaction for the current context. At this point, the student performs the overt social skill (e.g., initiating the conversation, responding to an initiation from another).
- The teacher or paraprofessional should role-play the social partner at this point of the training and give immediate feedback regarding the student's performance of the targeted social skill.
- Have the student evaluate the social interaction by asking, "What happened when I [description of how he or she behaved]?" The student is prompted to generate a description of the responses of other people in the social interaction and to evaluate whether these responses were positive or negative.

Numerous empirical studies have examined the effectiveness of teaching social problem solving to people with disabilities (e.g., Michelson, Sugai, Wood, & Kazdin, 2013; O'Reilly & Glynn, 1995; O'Reilly, Lancioni, & Kierans, 2000; O'Reilly et al., 2004, 2008). Replicating previous research from supported employment studies, O'Reilly and Glynn (1995) taught social problem-solving skills in school settings to students with disabilities who were socially withdrawn. After training, students learned to initiate appropriately with teachers. They also generalized the skills trained to the playground setting with peers. The results of this and similar studies indicate that social problem solving is a powerful strategy for teaching social skills that generalize to real-world settings and are maintained over time.

In school settings, teachers often teach these skills in an environment removed from the regular classroom context, because the training involves one-to-one rehearsal and feedback with the teacher or paraprofessional. This problem-solving strategy is taught using a combination of role-play, feedback, modeling, and verbal instruction with the teacher or a paraprofessional. See Tips for Teachers 9.3 for guidance on how to design this instruction.

9.3.6 Social Story Interventions

A **Social Story** is an individualized short story designed to clarify a particular social context, the perspectives of others in that context, and the social skills to be performed (Chan et al., 2011). In other words, a Social Story provides "information on what people in a given situation are doing, thinking, or feeling, the sequence of events, the identification of significant social cues and their meaning, and the script of what to do and say" (Chan & O'Reilly, 2008). Social Stories are usually developed based on a series of guidelines (Gray, 2000):

- Stories should be tailored to a student's comprehension level.
- A story may consist of a series of simple sentences and/or picture cues that describe the context and provide examples of desired responses, explain the perspectives of others, and explain the rules of social engagement.
- A Social Story should provide a description of a social context and social exchange and be directive in telling the student how to behave.

Social Stories usually use role-play, modeling, and feedback immediately before the target social situation in order to facilitate acquisition and generalization of the social skills.

FIGURE 9.2 Example of a social story used to decrease aggression during recess for Joey, a boy with ASD

Every day I go to recess with my class.

On the playground there are lots of fun things to do.

Sometimes I like to swing.

Sometimes I like to slide.

Sometimes I like to play with a ball.

When other kids are using the swings, slides, and balls, sometimes I get upset.

When I get upset, sometimes I want to hit.

Sometimes I hit the other kids.

My teachers and friends are sad when I hit.

When I want to slide, swing, or play ball and other kids are using them, I can wait my turn.

I can try to find another fun thing to do.

I don't have to hit.

If I want to swing but it is being used I can check the slide or balls.

If I want to slide and it is being used I can check the swing or balls.

If I want the ball and it is being used I can check the slide or swing. When I find something else fun to do my teachers and friends are happy.

I will find something else fun to do when the slide, swings, or balls are being used.

I will wait my turn.

I will use my quiet voice to tell Mom and Dad that I need help.

An example of a Social Story used to reduce aggression during recess for a student with ASD is included in Figure 9.2. The story can be read before going to the playground.

Selecting social skills for intervention

Take some time at the beginning of the school year to observe how your students with ASD interact with peers and others during the school day. Cue in to such skills as their ability to initiate social interactions, to respond to others' interactions, and to terminate interactions appropriately. Carefully examine their body language. Does body language match the intent of the verbal interactions? How is their social performance during structured versus unstructured parts of the school day? By making these careful observations, you may be able to develop a list of key social deficits and the social situations in which they occur. This information will form the basis of your social skills curriculum. When designing this curriculum, you should only target individual or small numbers of social skills at a time. Intervene using a problem-solving intervention strategy and then (unobtrusively) prompt performance of the target social skills throughout the school day. Once these skills begin to improve, target another set of social skills. Remember to involve paraprofessionals (see Tips for Teachers 9.4 for additional information on working with

TIPS FOR TEACHERS 9.4

Working with Paraprofessionals

- *Keep your paraprofessional informed.* Students may have quirks such as having tantrums when they are touched. Inform paraprofessionals about these and other unique characteristics of your students.
- *Educate your paraprofessional.* Paraprofessionals may have limited formal education. They may benefit from some tips on working with students with ASD.
- *Create a schedule.* Use a schedule to help your paraprofessional understand your classroom. If you are out of the class, the schedule can still be followed.
- *Communicate clearly.* Just as it is important to communicate clearly with parents, you should communicate regularly with your paraprofessional so that he or she is aware of minor changes in your classroom or with your students and their families.
- *Vary responsibilities.* Paraprofessionals may become frustrated when they are expected to supervise a student in the restroom day after day. Rotate staff responsibilities so that no person gets stuck with the "dirty work" on a regular basis.

paraprofessionals) and the students' families in training these social skills across settings, because these students do not generalize new skills without specific training (Otero et al., 2015; Rispoli, Neely, Lang, & Ganz, 2011).

MyEdLab **Self-Check 9.3**

MyEdLab **Application Exercise 9.3:** General Instructional Accommodations 

9.4 ADDRESSING CHALLENGING BEHAVIORS

Many students who are diagnosed with ASD engage in challenging behaviors. **Challenging behavior** is defined as behavior by a child that results in injury, causes damage to the physical environment, interferes with the acquisition of new skills, and/or socially isolates the child (Sigafoos, Arthur, & O'Reilly, 2003). Challenging behavior can include disruption, aggression, and self-injury. Disruptive behaviors that students most often exhibit include noncompliance, throwing materials, talking out of turn, and disturbing other students. **Aggression** can include any behavior that involves one student striking another (hitting, kicking, and biting). **Self-injury** includes behaviors in which a student injures him- or herself (e.g., head banging or eye poking).

Challenging behaviors are often a form of communication for students with disabilities. Specifically, students with disabilities engage in challenging behavior because it results in desired outcomes. Given their delays in language, communicating their wants and needs becomes more difficult, and thus challenging behavior becomes an effective form of communication. For example, consider Erin's case from the beginning of the chapter. Erin does not want to work on her sign language; however, she lacks the verbal ability to request a break from work. What Erin has learned is that if she engages in self-injury (head hitting), the teacher will give her a break. In this way head hitting is seen as a form of communication between Erin and her teacher in which Erin is in effect saying, "I do not want to do this." There are many possible messages that children with ASD communicate via challenging behavior. They may use challenging behavior to access a preferred item (Carl's insect book), gain adult attention, or escape from work. These consequences or outcomes of challenging behaviors are known as functions of behavior (Crone, Hawken, & Horner, 2015; Sigafoos et al., 2003). Tips for Teachers 9.5 provides recommendations for managing challenging behaviors.

TIPS FOR TEACHERS 9.5

Managing Challenging Behaviors

- *Understand why behaviors are occurring.* Students engage in challenging behavior for reasons, usually as a form of communication. A functional behavioral assessment will help you understand why the behaviors are occurring.
- *Be consistent.* All interventions should be implemented consistently so that the student understands what is expected on a daily basis.
- *Make sure that everyone is aware of the student's behavior intervention plan (BIP).* Challenging behaviors usually occur in all settings. Therefore, everyone, including bus drivers, secretaries, and parents, should implement intervention components.
- *Monitor challenging behavior closely.* It may be difficult to notice when a behavior decreases from fifty times a day to twenty-five times a day. Use systematic data collection and analysis to monitor your student's progress.
- *Avoid interventions without a research base.* Many common techniques intended to help reduce challenging behavior for children with ASD have been found by researchers to be ineffective and potentially dangerous. Be sure to only implement research-based interventions.

9.4.1 Using Functional Behavioral Assessment (FBA)

You can determine the function of a student's challenging behavior by completing a functional behavioral assessment (FBA). There are three steps to an FBA (see Tips for Teachers 9.5 for more information on how to handle challenging behavior):

1. Indirect assessments
2. Direct assessments
3. Functional analysis

Indirect assessments

These assessments should be completed before direct assessments. Indirect assessments include interviews with parents and previous teachers, as well as the completion of rating scales. These interviews and rating scales allow you to clearly describe the challenging behavior, along with some of the possible reasons for why it occurs.

Direct assessments

This type of assessment involves observing your student and documenting the sequence of behaviors around the challenging behavior. One example of a direct assessment is an ABC sequence chart. Observational assessment should be conducted during those times of the day when challenging behavior is most likely to occur; it should also be conducted for approximately five school days. Because of the intensity of this observational process, it may be best for a consultant, such as a behavior or ASD specialist, to conduct these observations.

An example of an ABC analysis for Manuel, a student with ASD and challenging behavior, is presented in Figure 9.3.

The ABC assessment presents data on Manuel's target behavior (head hitting) between 9:40 A.M. and 11:20 A.M. (the time of day when Manuel is most likely to engage in challenging behavior) during a given school day. Each time the target behavior occurs, the teacher places a check mark in the target behavior box (center column). The teacher then describes what happened immediately before the behavior. In the final column, the teacher describes what teachers, students, and anyone else in the classroom did in response to the student's behavior. Three incidents of the target behavior are included in Figure 9.3. You can see from this brief assessment that head hitting occurred when a task demand was placed on Manuel. When he engaged in head hitting, the task was removed. This brief assessment from this particular school day would seem to indicate that Manuel hit his head in order to communicate his desire to escape from demanding tasks.

FIGURE 9.3 An ABC analysis

Child: Manuel

Date and Time of Observation: April 4, 9:40–11:20 A.M.

What happened before the behavior	Target behavior	What happened after the behavior
Teacher says, "What word is this, Manuel?"	✓	Teacher moves away and asks another student.
Teacher points to a letter and asks, "What letter is this, Manuel?"	✓	Teacher moves on to a different topic with the class.
Teacher asks Manuel to open his book.	✓	Teacher does not persist but moves on to another student.

Source: Based on Adams, L., Gouvousis, A., VanLue, M., & Waldron, C. (2004). Social story intervention. Improving communication skills in a child with an autism spectrum disorder. *Focus on Autism and Other Developmental Disabilities, 19*, 87–94.

Functional analysis

If steps 1 and 2 do not clearly identify the function of your student's challenging behavior, you might need to seek the assistance of a behavioral specialist who can help you design and implement a functional analysis, step 3 of the FBA. A functional analysis consists of an experiment in which you manipulate one variable in your classroom to determine its effects on challenging behavior. All possible variables must be manipulated, and rates of challenging behavior must be compared across each condition. For example, if you think your student is trying to escape independent math or is trying to obtain peer attention, you have four manipulations to implement: getting out of math, not getting out of math, getting peer attention, and not getting peer attention. Because this third step of the FBA is time consuming and sometimes provokes more challenging behavior, it is often reserved for times when the function of behavior is not clear after steps 1 and 2 have been completed (Lydon, Healy, O'Reilly, & Lang, 2012).

9.4.2 Using Positive Behavioral Support

In the past, teachers and parents addressed challenging behavior by attending to the form of the behavior (e.g., hitting) rather than the function (e.g., obtaining teacher attention). The intervention was implemented after challenging behavior occurred. For example, when a student hit a peer, the teacher told the child to stop hitting. Hypothetically, this reprimand was intended to teach the student that hitting was not tolerated and thus help the student learn not to hit anymore.

Research has shown that these reactive procedures are not as effective at addressing challenging behaviors as the strategy of positive behavioral supports (Crone et al., 2015; Scheuermann & Hall, 2007). Positive behavioral supports comprise several key features. First, the approach is based on the sound behavioral science of human behavior. Second, interventions must be practical and based on FBA results. Interventions are implemented in a proactive manner rather than in a traditional reactive manner and focus on teaching new skills that foster independence, improve adaptive skills, or increase effective communication. For example, as opposed to putting a student in time-out (which may actually be a reward for students who are trying to escape from work!), a proactive approach might be to ensure the child has the ability to do the assigned work. If the child can do the work, he or she might not want to escape from it by going to time-out. These interventions also allow individuals with disabilities to access natural communities of reinforcement. Candy and other treats are not provided following the demonstration of a new skill such as talking (Koegel et al., 2012). Rather, an individual is taught to request food in the lunchroom where food is naturally available. Interventions are monitored through systematic data collection and analysis to determine intervention effectiveness (Bradshaw, Waasdorp, & Leaf, 2012).

Another feature of positive behavioral supports is the consideration of social values during the assessment and intervention processes. Behavior change should be observed across all environments of the child's day; it should be durable, lasting through the school and post-school years. Behavior change should be relevant and result in concomitant improvements in social behavior.

Over the years, Horner and his colleagues have conducted a series of studies on the use of positive behavioral supports with students who engaged in challenging behavior. In these studies:

- Teachers conducted functional behavioral assessments.
- A team approach to problem solving and intervention design involving many professionals and family members who know the child well was used.
- Teachers implemented practical and effective interventions.
- The students were taught new skills.
- Ongoing data collection and monitoring were used.

For example, Todd, Horner, and Sugai (2000) examined a fourth-grade student who was taught to self-monitor, self-evaluate, and self-recruit teacher attention. Teaching this student these skills resulted in a decrease in frequency of challenging behavior, an increase in on-task behavior, and an increase in task completion. Vaughn and Horner (1997) compared levels of challenging behavior when students received instruction during preferred and nonpreferred tasks and when teachers rather than students selected tasks. They reported that for two students, rates of challenging behavior were lower when students were able to select tasks, regardless of task preference. Last, Day, Horner, and O'Neill (1994) described an intervention in which students were taught alternative communication in place of challenging behavior. In this study, three participants engaged in challenging behavior to escape difficult tasks or to obtain preferred items. Once they were trained in an alternative communication, challenging behavior decreased and new communication increased.

You will note from this description of research on positive behavioral supports that many of the goals and strategies of positive behavioral support (e.g., to enhance self-control, choice making, communication training) were discussed earlier in this chapter. In fact, you may be able to prevent challenging behavior with many of these students if you use the strategies outlined earlier.

MyEdLab **Self-Check 9.4**

MyEdLab **Application Exercise 9.4:** Using Functional Behavioral Assessment (FBA)

9 SUMMARY

- PDD includes a number of disabilities, including autism, Asperger syndrome, Rett syndrome, childhood disintegrative disorder, and PDD–NOS. Both Rett and childhood disintegrative disorder are extremely rare. ASD is a subgroup of the PDD categories and includes autism and Asperger syndrome. Both of these diagnostic categories have similar symptoms but differ in terms of the severity of expression of these symptoms. The criteria for diagnosing these categories may soon be changing. The core difficulties experienced by students with ASD include communication and social skills deficits or excesses and rigidity of behavior patterns. These students may also engage in challenging behavior, including self-injury, aggression, and property destruction.
- Although teachers often know who those students are that have been identified with ASD, there may be others who they suspect may need additional supports. In both cases, teachers should document student performance in the areas of language, social, academic, or adaptive behaviors. In some cases, teachers are asked to complete rating scales describing student behavior. Documenting behaviors and monitoring progress helps teachers assess students' progress.
- Key processes for effective instruction for students with ASD include assessing preferences, establishing a classroom routine at the beginning of the year, teaching communication skills, and teaching social skills.
- Many students with ASD engage in challenging behavior. You must understand when, where, and why they engage in such behaviors. This can be accomplished using the FBA process. The results of the FBA can then be incorporated into a behavioral support plan that involves teaching communication skills and modifying the curriculum to make challenging behavior less necessary for the student.

THINK AND APPLY

1. Identify a special education teacher who works with students with autism and/or a parent of a child identified with autism. Ask them to tell you about the characteristics of the students with autism with whom they work (teacher) or the characteristics of their child (parent). Ask them to provide examples of activities the student(s) like or dislike. Ask them how they identify ways to incorporate what student(s) like or prefer into the student's routines.
2. Imagine a student with ASD who needs to learn how to make simple requests using sign language. The student's preference assessment reveals that he loves popcorn. How might you teach the student to request this during snack time using the milieu intervention strategy?
3. Imagine a student with ASD who engages in challenging behavior in class. What type of assessment should be done to determine why the student engages in this behavior? How will the results of this assessment be used to reduce the challenging behavior in the classroom?

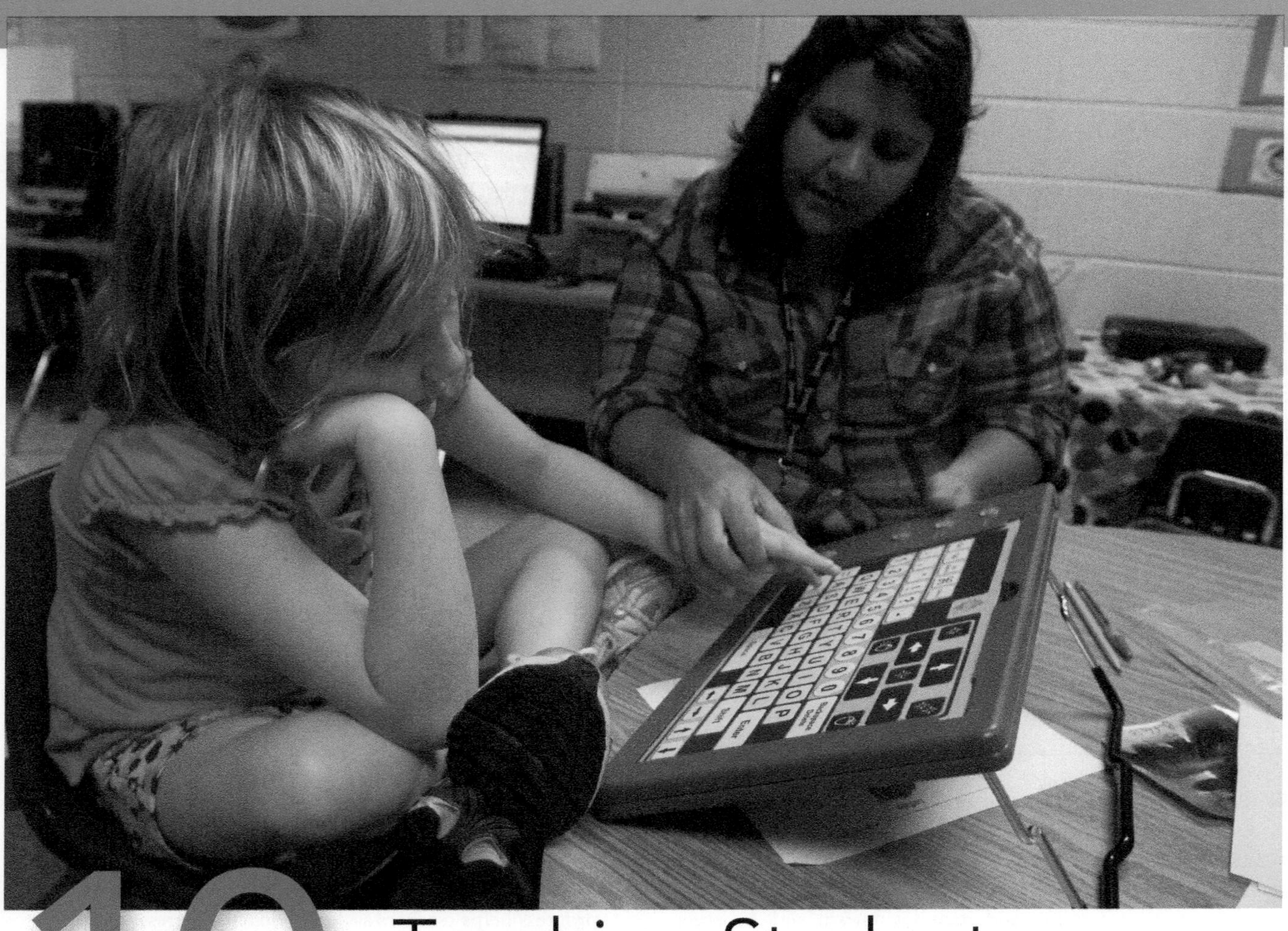

10 Teaching Students with Intellectual and Developmental Disabilities

Learning Outcomes

10.1 Describe the characteristics of individuals with intellectual and developmental disabilities and their prevalence in the school-age population.

10.2 Name some of the genetic, physical, and nonphysical causes of intellectual and developmental disabilities.

10.3 Explain how persons are identified as having an intellectual or developmental disability and, when applicable, the role of the classroom teacher in the identification process.

10.4 Identify some general guidelines that a classroom teacher can follow to plan for the academic and social needs of students with intellectual and developmental disabilities.

INTERVIEW: CHRIS JOHNSON

Three years ago, Chris Johnson's experience as a middle school teacher changed tremendously. For the first time, Chris was assigned a student with intellectual disabilities. Chris remembers his reaction on hearing that he would have Darrell, a student with mild intellectual disabilities, in his eighth-grade applied math class: "One of my main concerns was what am I going to do for Darrell? How am I possibly going to teach him anything? I don't have a special education degree. I feel as if I need one in order to teach him. How is Darrell going to fit in as a member of the class?"

To alleviate these feelings, Chris met with Darrell's special education teacher, Martha Anderson. They reviewed the applied math curriculum in relation to Darrell's individualized education program (IEP) goals and objectives. What they quickly realized was that many of Darrell's goals (including skills in measurement, making change, and using fractions and percentages) could be met within the general curriculum.

Each week, Chris discussed the activities and assignments with Martha, and she gave him ideas for modifications. Once a week, Martha worked in the room with Chris so that she could keep up with the curriculum and Darrell's progress. Martha uses math manipulatives and computer-assisted instruction to provide additional support in learning and applying new concepts. At the end of the first month, Chris said,

> Darrell is a member of our class, just like any of the [other] students. He works on math assignments, although I usually modify them by giving him less to complete, by allowing him to use manipulatives and a calculator, and in some cases giving him different assignments from the other students. Darrell has a great sense of humor and makes a contribution to a positive classroom environment.

By the end of the school year, Chris learned more about Darrell's strengths and challenges as a learner. He also developed genuine ways for Darrell to share his talents with his classmates and to build friendships. Chris also learned a great deal from Darrell's parents and how they worked to build a positive quality of life for their son. As a result of this experience, Chris not only volunteered to partner with Martha in teaching other students with disabilities, but also became involved as a volunteer with his local Best Buddies organization.

Introduction

Chris's initial concerns are those expressed by many general education teachers. Teachers want to give each student their best, but feel that they may not have sufficient knowledge and experience to provide students with intellectual and developmental disabilities with the support they need. Because the Individuals with Disabilities Education Improvement Act of 2004 (IDEIA, 2004) mandates access to the general education curriculum, you may have a student like Darrell in your classroom. The National Center for Educational Statistics (NCES) reports that approximately 92% of students with intellectual disabilities are placed

CHAPTER OUTLINE

in public schools (NCES, 2015) and 44% of students spend 40% or more of their time in general education classrooms. This chapter provides information about students with intellectual and developmental disabilities and presents guidelines you can use to support students with such disabilities in your classroom in their academic and social development. As Chris Johnson learned, working with students with intellectual and developmental disabilities can be both challenging and rewarding.

10.1 UNDERSTANDING INTELLECTUAL AND DEVELOPMENTAL DISABILITIES

The population of individuals who are considered to have developmental disabilities is quite heterogeneous. Developmental disabilities are mental or physical disabilities that impair the person's functioning in language, learning, mobility, self-care, or other important areas of living. These disabilities differ in severity from mild to profound. Students with developmental disabilities present a wide range of individual needs.

10.1.1 Definition of Intellectual and Developmental Disabilities

The Centers for Disease Control and Prevention (2015c) defines developmental disabilities as "a group of conditions due to an impairment in physical, learning, language, or behavior areas. These conditions begin during the developmental period, may impact day-to-day functioning, and usually last throughout a person's lifetime" (p. 1).

Developmental disabilities

Developmental disabilities are typically detected when parents and/or health care professionals recognize that a child is not meeting developmental milestones in one or more areas. In general, *developmental disability* is an umbrella term that can refer to a wide spectrum of intellectual disabilities and severe disabilities, including multiple or dual sensory disabilities. This chapter focuses primarily on students with intellectual disabilities.

Intellectual disabilities

Students with intellectual disabilities have limited cognitive functioning, which affects their learning. These students have slower rates of learning and are particularly challenged by complex and abstract tasks. Quite often students with intellectual disabilities may have challenges with adaptive behavior or the age-appropriate conceptual, social, and practical skills necessarily for daily living (American Association on Intellectual and Developmental Disabilities, 2013; Luckasson et al., 2002; Wehmeyer, Buntinx et al., 2008).

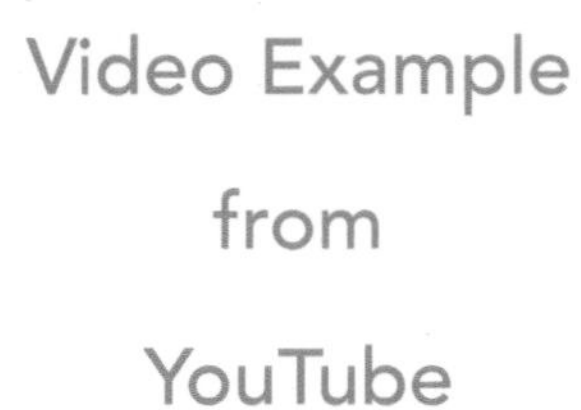

MyEdLab
Video Example 10.1.
Watch the YouTube video "More Alike than Different" to learn about the lives of adults with intellectual disabilities. What can you learn from these testimonies to support your students? https://www.youtube.com/watch?v=Jg2ZBPw2LyE

Students with intellectual disabilities are just like other students in your class in that they are members of families, have friends and neighbors, have personalities shaped by both their innate characteristics and their life experiences, and have aspirations to become adults, get jobs, and fall in love (Eidelman, 2011). In recent years, programs that enroll students with intellectual disabilities in college have been launched (Kleinert, Jones, Sheppard-Jones, Harp, & Harrison, 2012; Papay & Griffin, 2015; Plotner & Marshall, 2015; Taylor, 2013). Yet to be successful in academic settings at any level, students with intellectual disabilities need additional support and accommodations. In planning for this support, it is helpful for teachers to have some knowledge about intellectual disabilities and how they affect learning.

For decades, the term mental retardation was used in professional organizations and the federal government to refer to individuals with limitations in cognitive functioning. Individuals with disabilities, their families, and groups (such as the Special Olympics) advocated for a change to terminology that was less stigmatizing and disparaging (Lyle &

Simplican, 2015). Advocates promoted the use of the term *intellectual disabilities* to reflect a more optimistic view of the quality of life for individuals with cognitive challenges and to be more consistent with The World Health Organization's International Classification of Diseases.

In 2007, two major professional organizations changed their names. The American Association on Mental Retardation (AAMR) officially changed its name to the American Association on Intellectual and Developmental Disabilities (AAIDD). Similarly, the American Psychological Association's Division of Mental Retardation and Developmental Disabilities changed its name to Division of Intellectual and Developmental Disabilities.

This change in nomenclature resulted in an evolution of AAIDD's definition of the disability: "Intellectual disability is a disability characterized by significant limitations in both intellectual functioning and in adaptive behavior, which covers many everyday social and practical skills. This disability originates before the age of 18" (AAIDD, 2007, p. 1).

In the federal definition, IDEIA 2004 used the term *mental retardation*. However, this terminology was changed in 2010 when President Barack Obama signed legislation (Public Law 111-256) known as Rosa's Law. The original definition did not change, but the name of the disability was changed to *intellectual disabilities*. The federal law defines intellectual disabilities as "significant subaverage general intellectual functioning, existing concurrently with deficits in adaptive behavior and manifested during the developmental period, that adversely affects a child's education performance" [34 CFR 300.8(c)(6)]. The law is named in honor of Rosa Marcellino, a young girl with intellectual disabilities who championed the change in terminology in her home state of Maryland.

In the most recent edition of the American Psychiatric Association's *Diagnostic and Statistical Manual of Mental Disorders*, *DSM-5*, the term *intellectual disability* was also adopted (American Psychiatric Association, 2013). This change is important in that the *DSM-5* is typically used to refer to and diagnose disabilities and to determine eligibility for educational and vocational services, placement in residential facilities, and Social Security Disability (Papazoglou, Jacobson, McCabe, Kaufmann, & Zabel, 2014).

10.1.2 Characteristics of Students with Intellectual Disabilities

Maria Gort has taught in a fourth-grade inclusion class for over 10 years. In that time, she has had seven children with intellectual disabilities placed in her classroom. When asked to describe characteristics of these students, Maria commented, "Each student comes with different gifts and challenges academically and socially. My job is to work with my special education colleague and the child's parents to identify those gifts—and to build on them. We also identify challenges and develop strategies for coping and accommodating." As Maria has learned, not all students with intellectual disabilities exhibit the same intellectual, social, and behavioral characteristics. A discussion of the range of characteristics you might encounter follows.

Intellectual characteristics

Although students with intellectual disabilities have diverse learning characteristics, they generally learn slowly, often fail to notice relevant features of what is being taught, and do not demonstrate learned skills spontaneously (Heward, 2013). These students also have difficulty learning complex skills and abstract concepts, have difficulty making generalizations, and learn less overall than other students do. Many students with intellectual disabilities experience difficulties with memory, either remembering incorrectly or not remembering automatically, and attention when focusing on learning tasks (Hallahan, Kauffman, & Pullen, 2015).

You may notice that students with intellectual disabilities have communication challenges in such areas as comprehension, expressing what they have learned, or describing individual needs. Indeed, most students with intellectual disabilities demonstrate difficulties with expressive (speaking, writing) and receptive (listening, reading) language

TIPS FOR TEACHERS 10.1

Helping Students Develop Communication Skills

- *Give students a reason to communicate.* By anticipating the needs of students with intellectual disabilities, we often deprive them of reasons to communicate. Create situations that motivate students to communicate. For example, you might "accidentally" forget to give them their lunch tickets when the rest of the class receives their tickets, or have every student tell you about the drawing they just did before they can go out to recess. Working on communication skills during everyday activities is known to significantly increase students' desire to communicate.
- *Determine the best mode of communication.* Make sure that students have a way, as well as a reason, to communicate. Providing alternate modes of expression (e.g., drawing pictures, pointing to objects) can help them express what they know and want to say. If your students do not use speech, they should have an augmentative communication device. If your students do not have a mode of communication, talk with the school's speech and language pathologist or inclusion specialist about developing or purchasing one.
- *Give students a way to make choices.* Self-stick notes provide a quick and easy way to give students with disabilities on-the-spot choices (choosing a word to fill in the blank, choosing a color) to facilitate their participation in class. Just write the choices on the notes and stick them on the students' desks so that they can make the choices. To help students choose a partner, take pictures of all the students in the class (or use individual class photos) and paste them in a little book or on a board so that the student with a disability can choose the person with whom he or she wants to work on a class assignment.

that impact communication in academic and social situations. Tips for Teachers 10.1 provides suggestions for helping students with communication skills.

Social and behavioral characteristics

Students with intellectual disabilities can have friends and participate in social activities, but often have difficulties developing friendships. Such difficulties may be due to behaviors that deter interactions (e.g., limited communication skills, stereotypical behaviors, limited social judgment) or to lack of opportunity to practice social skills (Westling, Fox, & Carter, 2015). Students with intellectual disabilities are frequently naïve and gullible and thus are prone to risky or inappropriate behavior in their attempts to please others (Snell et al., 2009).

All students want acceptance from peers and just to "fit in." When placed in a general education classroom, students with intellectual disabilities have more opportunities to develop friendships and build solid social relationships (Hunt & McDonnell, 2009). However, those opportunities need to be fostered using specific strategies to promote social interactions (Carter & Hughes, 2009). One such strategy is Circle of Friends (see the Activities for All Learners feature).

Another challenge for general education teachers in working with students with intellectual disabilities is engagement. Even young children with intellectual disabilities have experienced failure in mastering new concepts and tasks. It is common for their motivation to learn to become deflated (Switsky, 2006). Frequently, they begin to think that they have no control over their own success or failure and do not see the link with personal effort and task completion (Raymond, 2012). To overcome this, promote

an attitude of "I can" do it and "I did" do it to help your students develop a sense of personal responsibility and accomplishment (Kleinert, Harrison, Fisher, & Kleinert, 2010).

Prevalence

The prevalence of persons with intellectual disabilities is difficult to determine because different definitions and methodologies are used to determine various conditions under this large umbrella (Stoneman, 2007). Generally, however, prevalence is estimated to be about 1% of the school population (NCES, 2015). According to the federal government, approximately 435,000 students with intellectual disabilities were eligible for IDEIA services (NCES, 2015).

ACTIVITIES FOR ALL LEARNERS

Providing School Support Through Circles of Friends

Purpose: To integrate students with disabilities into the general education classroom

Materials: Paper and writing/drawing implements

Procedure: In this activity, each student in the classroom completes a picture of his or her circles of friends, using the following steps:

1. Have students draw four circles.
   - In the first circle, students list the people closest to them, the people they love.
   - In the second circle, students list the people they really like (but not enough to put in the first circle).
   - In the third circle, students list groups of people they like or people they do things with (e.g., scouts, soccer team).
   - In the fourth circle, students list people who are paid to be in their lives (e.g., doctor, dentist).
2. After students have completed their own circles of friends, describe the circles for a fantasy person who is similar to the student who will be joining the class. For example, a student might have only Mom listed in the first circle, with the second and third circles empty. In the fourth circle are a number of doctors and therapists. Through discussion, talk with the students about how the student must feel and how this fantasy person is similar to the student with disabilities who is going to join the class.
3. Finally, the teacher and students plan how they can become part of the circles of friends for the student with disabilities through such activities as classroom ambassadors, telephone buddies, lunch buddies, and reading buddies.

Source: Based on Promoting educational equality for all students: Circles and maps, by M. Forest & E. Lusthaus, 1989, in S. Stainback, W. Stainback, & M. Forest (Eds.), *Educating all students in the mainstream of regular education* (pp. 45–57). Baltimore: Brookes.

MyEdLab **Self-Check 10.1**

MyEdLab **Application Exercise 10.1:** Characteristics of Students with Intellectual Disabilities

10.2 CAUSES OF INTELLECTUAL DISABILITIES

There are multiple causes of intellectual disabilities, including genetic, other physical causes, and nonphysical causes. Intellectual disabilities can be the consequences occurring before (prenatal), during (perinatal), or after (postnatal) birth (Hallahan et al., 2015). *The Educator's Diagnostic Manual of Disabilities and Disorders* (Pierangelo & Giuliani, 2007) lists fifty potential causes of intellectual disabilities using the following superordinate categories: chromosomal abnormalities, disorders of brain formation, metabolic disorders, maternal infections, fetal intoxicant exposure, gestational disorders, postnatal environmental problems, and other causes (e.g., postnatal conditions, intoxicants, or brain diseases). Although it is beyond the scope of this chapter to describe *each* of the potential causes, we will focus on some that you are most likely to encounter: chromosomal disorders, fragile X syndrome, and fetal alcohol syndrome.

Video Example from YouTube

MyEdLab
Video Example 10.2.
Watch the YouTube video "What Causes an Intellectual Disability?" to learn more about potential causes. While, as the video explains, some of these causes are chromosomal, others are environmental and may be potentially avoidable. Consider how might this change your own behavior? https://www.youtube.com/watch?v=dyjFJ19DF9Y&t=47s

10.2.1 Chromosomal Disorders

Chromosomal disorders are probably the best-known cause of intellectual disabilities. Down syndrome is one of the most common chromosomal disorders and is often what people think of when intellectual disability is mentioned. Down syndrome occurs in about one in 700 live births (Centers for Disease Control and Prevention, 2015d; National Down Syndrome Society, 2015). Individuals with Down syndrome typically experience mild to moderate intellectual disability and have strong promise for success in school and in the world of work with proper supports. Although they are prone to health problems such as congenital heart defects and thyroid conditions, with improved health care and reduced institutional placement, the life expectancy of individuals with Down syndrome has steadily increased (Presson et al., 2013).

Fragile X syndrome

Fragile X syndrome is the most common form of intellectual disability that is passed from parent to child (National Fragile X Foundation, 2012). The precise number of people with fragile X is unknown, however. The Centers for Disease Control and Prevention (CDC) estimates that one out of 5,000 boys are born with the disability (CDC, 2015a). Estimates of girls with fragile X are lower (National Fragile X Foundation, 2012). Individuals with fragile X syndrome can manifest a range of intellectual disabilities, from mild to severe. Their challenges can also include social and emotional difficulties, speech and language problems, and sensitivity to sensory input such as bright light or loud sounds. Some, but not all, males with fragile X syndrome have physical symptoms including an elongated face and large ears. The symptoms associated with fragile X syndrome are typically more severe with boys than with girls.

Fetal alcohol spectrum disorders

Fetal alcohol spectrum disorders (FASD), one of the top three known causes of birth defects, refers to a range of birth defects caused by the mother's drinking during pregnancy and is fast becoming the leading cause of intellectual disabilities. The prevalence figures are difficult to ascertain, but estimates are 0.2 to 1.5 babies with FASD for every 1,000 born (CDC, 2015b). The National Organization on Fetal Alcohol Syndrome (NOFAS) reports that the incidence may be even higher (NOFAS, 2014). Children with FASD may experience some degree of intellectual disabilities, delayed growth, psychosocial behavior problems, physical abnormalities, and speech and language problems. In addition to alcohol, maternal use of drugs or tobacco can also cause birth defects and potential intellectual disabilities (March of Dimes, 2010).

10.2.2 Other Causes of Intellectual Disabilities

Other causes of intellectual disability include physical (or biomedical) and nonphysical (social, environmental, educational) risk factors. Physical causes include infections, low birth weight, diseases (e.g., measles, meningitis), malnutrition, and exposure to toxins (Pierangelo & Giuliani, 2007). Nonphysical causes include various forms of child abuse (e.g., shaken baby syndrome) and neglect (e.g., inadequate health care), poverty (e.g., unsafe neighborhoods), lack of stimulation, and lack of opportunity to develop communication, social, and adaptive skills (Pierangelo & Giuliani, 2007). Determining the precise cause of an intellectual disability can be difficult in that a combination of physical and/or nonphysical causes may be involved. According to the National Institutes of Health, physicians identify a specific cause in only 25% of cases (NIH, 2015).

10.2.3 Comorbidity

Intellectual disabilities may co-occur with other psychological, medical or physical, and behavioral disabilities (Matson & Cervantes, 2013). Thus, students diagnosed with more than one disability (or comorbidity) may qualify for services in more than one area. Intellectual disabilities can be comorbid with a variety of disabilities such as autism spectrum disorders, attention deficit hyperactivity disorders, communication disorders, or deaf-blindness. Individuals with epilepsy or cerebral palsy may also have an intellectual disability. Disorders related to mood, anxiety, and depression can also co-occur with intellectual disabilities. In addition, health conditions such as sleep, digestion, and eating disorders may also occur.

MyEdLab **Self-Check 10.2**

MyEdLab **Application Exercise 10.2:** Causes of Intellectual Disabilities

10.3 IDENTIFICATION OF STUDENTS WITH INTELLECTUAL DISABILITIES

Before the passage of the Individuals with Disabilities Education Act (IDEA) in 1975, many students with intellectual and developmental disabilities were not allowed to attend public schools. This federal legislation required that educational services be provided for all students, including students with severe and profound disabilities. One result was the need for better methods of identification and assessment for educational purposes. With the passage of the IDEA amendments in 1986 (P.L. 99-457), these children became eligible to receive special education services as infants and toddlers and in preschool. More recent amendments in 2004 have ensured access to the general education curriculum.

For students with all but mild intellectual disabilities, initial identification is usually a medical diagnosis made at birth or shortly thereafter. For students with mild intellectual disabilities, initial identification often occurs during preschool when the child's rate of development in cognitive, language, and motor skills is not typical. For these students, the emphasis is on developmental and educational assessment, which usually includes measures of general intelligence and measures of adaptive behavior. Indeed, *DSM-5* (APA, 2013) requires assessment in both areas for diagnosis of an intellectual disability. Assessment is conducted by school psychologists or other professionals (e.g., private psychologists, psychiatrists) qualified to administer and interpret these measures. Some school districts may also require administration of an achievement test to ascertain performance in key academic areas (such as reading/language arts and mathematics).

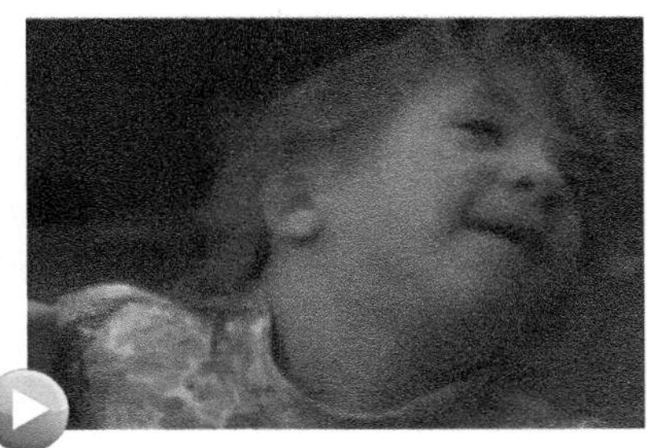

MyEdLab
Video Example 10.3.
Watch this video and listen to parents and the special education teacher of a child with intellectual disabilities discuss the child's early childhood experiences at home and at school. Why is the role that parents and family members play in the identification process so important?

10.3.1 Intellectual Functioning

Standardized intelligence tests are widely used to gauge eligibility for special education services. These instruments measure verbal, problem-solving, reasoning, and memory performance. Two commonly used measures are the Wechsler Intelligence Scale for Children-IV (Kaplan, Fein, Kramer, Delis, & Morris, R. 2004) and the Stanford-Binet Intelligence Scales (Roid, 2003). Intelligence tests yield an intelligence quotient (IQ) score. An average IQ score is 100. Individuals with an IQ score of 70 to 75 or below potentially may have limited cognitive functioning (AAIDD, 2013).

Although intelligence tests are commonly used to determine whether students have intellectual disabilities, some concerns have been raised. First, it can be difficult to know whether the tests accurately reflect the students' capacity to learn, particularly given their difficulty with communication and their delayed responses. Second, there is continuing concern regarding cultural influences and biases in tests of intellectual functioning (Klingner, Blanchett, & Harry, 2007; Venn, 2013). Factors influencing student performance on intelligence tests include family history and home life, duration of study in the United States, language proficiency, socioeconomic status, prior educational experiences, test-wiseness, and cultural background. Given the disproportionate representation of minorities (particularly African Americans and English language learners) in the number of students receiving special education services for developmental disabilities, issues related to equity and intelligence tests need continued exploration (Klingner et al., 2007; Sullivan, 2011).

10.3.2 Adaptive Behavior

Another area used to determine evidence of intellectual disability is the student's adaptive behavior (or adaptive functioning). Measures of adaptive behavior evaluate skills in a number of areas including communication, social skills, personal hygiene and grooming, work skills, and practical literacy and numeracy. Klingner and colleagues (2007) caution that assessment of adaptive behavior must be evaluated within a cultural context and that assessment should occur before placement in special education.

Two examples of adaptive behavior measures are the Diagnostic Adaptive Behavior Scale (DABS) (AAIDD, 2015) and the Vineland Adaptive Behavior Scales (Vineland-3).

The AAIDD designed DABS to assess conceptual, social, and practical skills domains. Unlike previous assessments normed only on individuals with impaired adaptive behaviors, DABS was normed on individuals with and without such challenges to compare performance on the assessment between the populations (Balboni et al., 2014). The Vineland Adaptive Behavior Scales (Vineland-3) (Sparrow, Balla, & Cicchetti, 2016) include protocols for interviewing the student as well as forms for parents (or caregivers) and teachers to complete as well.

10.3.3 Systems of Support

The notion of appropriate **systems of support** based on individual needs is critical to understanding appropriate instruction of students with intellectual disability (van Loon, Claes, Vandevelde, Van Hove, & Schalock, 2010). There are five dimensions where individuals with intellectual disabilities may need support:

1. intellectual functioning in school and in daily living;
2. adaptive behavior;
3. health;
4. participation in a variety of social, educational, and professional arenas; and
5. environmental and personal contextual factors (Wehmeyer, Buntix et al., 2008).

Systems of support across all five dimensions should be considered in planning for optimal functioning of individuals with intellectual disabilities. Systems of support coupled with appropriate assistive technology and evidence-based interventions can promote access to a variety of academic, social, and behavioral demands (Luckasson & Schalock, 2012).

The AAIDD publishes an assessment scale based on levels of support. The Supports Intensity Scale (Thompson et al., 2004) identifies the level of support individuals may need in home living, community living, lifelong learning, employment, health and safety, social interaction, and protection and advocacy. Case managers, psychologists, or social workers complete the scale by interviewing the individual with disabilities and key family members or caretakers to determine the needs for each of the support areas. The intent of this measure is to focus more on the supports needed to function as independently as possible.

10.3.4 Levels of Severity

Formerly, a traditional classification system based on an individual's "degree of retardation" was determined by intelligence test scores (i.e., mild: IQ scores of 50–55 to 70–75; moderate: IQ scores of 35–40 to 50–55; severe: IQ scores of 20–25 to 35–40; profound: IQ scores below 20–25) (APA, 2000). While some school districts may still use some form of this intelligence score scale for determining levels of severity, the *DSM-5* now uses a matrix to determine levels of severity. The matrix includes descriptors of performance in three domains: conceptual, social, and practical at four levels of severity: mild, moderate, severe, and profound. These levels of severity are determined by professionals with data gleaned from adaptive behavior assessment.

10.3.5 Teacher's Role in Identifying Students with Intellectual and Developmental Disabilities

As a classroom teacher, what is your role in the identification of students with intellectual disabilities or in their identification for special education services? Most students you teach will have been diagnosed by the time they reach your classroom. However, given that onset of the disability occurs during the developmental period up to the age of 18, there may be exceptions. For example, a child with fetal alcohol syndrome may not have been identified prior to entrance in the elementary school. Another example might be a student who experiences loss in cognitive functioning as a result of an illness such as meningitis.

If you observe a student in your classroom with persistent difficulties in learning tasks or adaptive behavior, begin documenting your observations quickly. Follow procedures in your school district about whom to contact first (e.g., the school principal, counselor) and when and how to approach parents about your concerns. You may be asked to participate in prereferral interventions to determine whether, with available supports, the student can function successfully. If your school implements a response-to-intervention (RTI) model, you may be asked to provide information of student performance during tiers of intervention. Once the referral process begins, administration and interpretation of findings from intelligence tests and adaptive behavior assessments will be the responsibility of a school psychologist or an independently contracted professional. You may be asked (along with parents) to provide input on the adaptive behavior assessments. You may also be asked to provide anecdotal records, student test scores, and work samples.

MyEdLab **Self-Check 10.3**

MyEdLab **Application Exercise 10.3:** Identification of Students with Intellectual Disabilities

10.4 INSTRUCTIONAL TECHNIQUES AND ACCOMMODATIONS FOR STUDENTS WITH INTELLECTUAL DISABILITIES

Teachers who have students with intellectual disabilities in their classrooms are asked to participate in their students' educational plans, work with the students, and communicate and work with the paraprofessionals and specialists who provide support. Douglas Akers, a fifth-grade teacher, has been working for several months with Amy, a student with Down syndrome, who is being included in general education classes for the first time. Reflecting on Amy entering his class, Doug comments:

> I wanted to establish a good rapport with Amy. I wanted her to take directions from me, not just to rely on her aide or the special education teacher. I wanted Amy to develop a relationship with me and feel comfortable coming to me or the other students for assistance. I knew this would take time because she has always been in a self-contained special education class. But now she does come to me with her work and with questions.

The instructional guidelines and accommodations discussed here will help you to include students with intellectual and developmental disabilities in your class and to develop a social support network that will facilitate these students' success.

In addition, you can access valuable information from the websites of nonprofit organizations. Numerous nonprofit organizations have been organized and broadened to address the needs of individuals with intellectual disabilities (e.g., American Association on Intellectual and Developmental Disabilities [www.aaidd.org]; the ARC of the United States, [www.thearc.org]; National Down Syndrome Society, [www.ndss.org]). Although their foci and missions vary, most organizations provide resources for research in addition to providing information for individuals with disabilities and their families as well as for teachers and the community at large. Most nonprofit organizations serve as advocacy groups for the individuals they represent and emphasize the supports needed to ensure a high quality of life.

10.4.1 Role of the General Education Teacher

At the beginning of this chapter, you read about the changes Chris Johnson experienced when Darrell was enrolled in his middle school class. With the help of his special education colleague, Chris learned there are three key roles that he could assume to guide students with disabilities:

1. Take ownership of students with disabilities by demonstrating that these students are members of the class and that they are valued (Downing &

What factors must be taken into account when planning instruction for students with severe or multiple disabilities?

Peckham-Hardin, 2007). When this happens, students with disabilities develop a sense of belonging and being accepted. For Chris and his class, Darrell was just another member of the applied math class.

2. Become familiar with the full range of goals and objectives on the student's IEP. Appropriate planning and adaptation for students with developmental disabilities requires careful analysis of tasks to be accomplished and some creativity (Downing & Peckham-Hardin, 2007). Having a strong command of the student's IEP makes planning more fluent and systematic.
3. A paraeducator or aide may be assigned to a student with disabilities for all or part of the school day. Your role is to plan curriculum and adaptations for all students in the classroom, frequently in collaboration with a special educator. Although paraeducators can be involved in the planning process, they should not take on that responsibility in isolation. Because most paraeducators do not have preparation in curriculum and instruction, their role is to supplement your planning and instruction (Giangreco, 2009; Pickett, 2008). With appropriate preparation and supervision, paraeducators can provide vital instructional roles (Keller, Bucholz, & Brady, 2007). When a student is assigned a paraeducator on a one-to-one basis, in-class isolation of the student with disabilities can result (Causton-Theoharis & Malmgren, 2005; Giangreco, 2009). Thus, you should also discuss specific strategies for using peer support and for developing meaningful interactions with peers to promote inclusion and formation of friendships (Hebdon, 2008).

10.4.2 Planning

Planning is critical for all students, but it is particularly so for students with intellectual disabilities, whose learning goals may differ from those of other students in the class. When Jeannette Robinson heard that she was going to have a student with moderate intellectual disabilities in her third-grade classroom (Steven), she was concerned that she would be responsible for writing lesson plans and making all the adaptations. She felt overwhelmed until she realized that it was a team process and that the special education teacher would help her plan. She said, "I'm so relieved. I feel much more positive now. I didn't know how I was going to do it."

Jeannette was planning a unit on weathering and erosion. During weekly planning time, Jeannette talked about the unit with the inclusion specialist who provided support for Steven. They decided that Steven's content goals would be to identify three types of weather (e.g., sunny, raining, and snowy) and how each might affect the earth's surface. Steven would participate in class demonstrations and experiments. A paraeducator would work with him on the general language and social goals stated on his IEP (e.g., working with others and sharing, communicating wants and feelings). The paraeducator also prepared materials for him to take home for home learning assignments.

Realizing that it is a team process and that everyone has knowledge to contribute is important. In the following sections, two approaches to planning are discussed: person-centered planning and functional, discrepancy, and task analysis.

Person-centered planning

Person-centered planning is a collaborative approach to planning for students with developmental disabilities in the school years and beyond (Claes, Van Hove, Vandevelde, van Loon, & Schalock, 2010). With person-centered planning the individual with disabilities works together with his or her support community (e.g., family, friends, school-based personnel) to construct a personal profile and to craft a vision for the future. For students with intellectual and developmental disabilities, it is important to plan beyond the students' school experiences, particularly as these students reach middle and high school. Person-centered planning for their transition into adult life in terms of vocation and adult living is critical to their success (Wehmeyer, Sands, Knowlton, & Kozleski, 2002). As part of the process, the student's circle of support map is developed by the student, family, educators, and other key support persons. As a classroom teacher, you may be involved in this process and in the process of aligning school-based curriculum with the transition goals.

The McGill Action Planning System (MAPS)

The **McGill Action Planning System (MAPS)** (Circle of Inclusion Project, 2002; Klein-Ezell, LaRusso, & Ezell, 2008; Lusthaus & Forest, 1987; Wells & Sheehey, 2012) is one example of such a planning system. The purpose of this planning activity is to foster relationships to improve the quality of life for people with severe disabilities and to facilitate participation in inclusive settings such as a general education classroom.

In the MAPS process, the student, his or her family and friends, and special and general educators establish a team. Because peers are important to the process, students from the classroom generally participate in the team (Hamill & Everington, 2002; Vandercook, York, & Forest, 1989). This team answers seven questions, using them to brainstorm methods to plan the student's future in an inclusive environment. Answers to the seven questions help to determine the goals and objectives. Figure 10.1 provides an example of the MAPS questions and ideas for Tyrone, a high-school student with severe intellectual disabilities.

FIGURE 10.1 MAPS questions and ideas generated for Tyrone

1. What is the individual's history?

   Tyrone developed meningitis shortly after birth, which resulted in brain damage. He learned to walk and talk much later than normal.

2. What is your dream for the individual?

   Tyrone will find a job in the community, where he can interact with many people, and a place to live with friends.

3. What is your nightmare?

   Tyrone will be alone after we (parents) pass away.

4. Who is the individual?

   Tyrone is a young man who loves music and talking to people. He is an only child. He is a sophomore in high school. He loves sports. He gets lonely and bored when alone for long periods of time.

5. What are the individual's strengths, gifts, and abilities?

   He loves to laugh and smiles a lot. He works hard. He has a great sense of humor. He's energetic. He is sensitive to others' moods.

6. What are the individual's needs?

   He needs friends his own age with whom to do things. He needs to be more assertive and ask for help when necessary. He needs to be more independent in food preparation and in getting around in the community.

7. What would the individual's ideal day at school look like, and what must be done to make it happen?

   A Circle of Friends should be done with Tyrone so that he has friends to meet when he gets off the bus and to hang out with during lunch and breaks. Tyrone should participate in some community-based instruction. Tyrone should take a Foods class.

Functional assessment, discrepancy analysis, and task analysis

Functional assessment, discrepancy analysis, and task analysis are important planning tools for determining the skills the students with developmental disabilities need to reach established goals. In a functional assessment, each goal or activity is broken into steps or subskills, and the student's present performance level is determined for each subskill or step in the activity. A discrepancy analysis reviews each specific step or skill and determines how the student does the step or skill compared to nondisabled peers. Next, a task-analysis (a further breakdown of each individual step or skill, with the necessary adaptations) is used as a guide to teach the step or skill to the student.

In Figure 10.2, a functional analysis and discrepancy analysis are shown for Marta, an eighth-grade student with moderate intellectual disability and cerebral palsy.

Notice how when Marta is unable to perform a step or skill, such as going to her locker, it is indicated in the third column (i.e., a discrepancy exists). From there, the teacher determines whether the student should be taught that particular step or skill or whether an adaptation should be made to help the student perform the skill. The fourth column shows the adaptations and instruction that will occur as a result of the functional assessment and discrepancy analysis.

The same goals can be assessed across the different environments in which the activities occur. Mary Hinson, Marta's high school job developer, assessed "arriving and getting started" as part of placing Marta in her first job in an office, which involved putting on labels and doing simple packaging. For a number of the steps, the adaptations made at school could easily be made in the workplace.

10.4.3 Assessment

Due to challenges individuals with intellectual disabilities have in oral and written communication, they often cannot express what they know or demonstrate what they can do in traditional ways. Accommodations may be necessary to enable students with these challenges to help you tap their mastery of content and skills. Authentic and alternative assessment can facilitate appropriate accommodations.

FIGURE 10.2 **Functional assessment and discrepancy analysis**

Student: Marta is an eighth-grade student with a moderate intellectual disability and cerebral palsy.
Activity: Arriving at school

STEPS OF THE ACTIVITY	STUDENT PERFORMANCE	DISCREPANCY ANALYSIS	TEACH OR ADAPT
1. Arrives at school by bus	+		
2. Goes to locker	–	Cannot propel herself	Peers will wait by bus
3. Opens locker	–	Doesn't remember combination	Use key lock
4. Gets notebooks, etc., out	–	Can't reach items	Put items in backpack on hook
5. Hangs out/does hair until class	–	Doesn't initiate conversations	Develop "Circle of Friends"
6. Goes to class when bell rings	–	Can't self-propel that far	Ask classmates to help
7. Listens to announcements in homeroom	+		
8. Raises hand to indicate will eat lunch	+		
9. Goes to first hour when bell rings	–	Doesn't know which class is at this time	Teach to review a picture schedule and ask for help

Code: + = can do step – = cannot do step

Authentic assessment

Authentic assessment makes a link between goals and objectives for your students and the documentation of progress toward meeting those goals and objectives (Layton & Lock, 2007). Many of the types of authentic assessment you read about in this book can be adapted for students with intellectual disabilities.

- Curriculum-based measurement and portfolio assessment are two approaches appropriate for students with developmental disabilities (Venn, 2013).

- Curriculum-based measurement (CBM) is a way to monitor ongoing growth in acquisition of basic skills and concepts. Frequent samples of student performance in mastering each step are obtained to gain an "academic yardstick" of student progress (Hall, Cohen, Vue, & Ganley, 2015).
- Portfolio assessment involves compilation of multiple artifacts or student work samples. Although somewhat cumbersome and time consuming, portfolios provide tangible evidence of student progress.

Alternate assessment

In addition to the authentic assessment tools you use in your class, you should also become familiar with alternate assessment policies in your state and school district for students with disabilities in meeting requirements for progress monitoring of mastery of standards as well as for high-stakes tests. In many cases, accommodations such as extended time will be sufficient for participation. For some students, additional procedures are necessary to provide fair and equitable assessment (Towles-Reeves, Kleinert, & Muhomba, 2009). These procedures may involve alternative presentation of directions and test content, equipment or materials, response modes, or setting [National Center on Educational Outcomes (NCEO), 2015]. NCEO (2015) lists three types of alternative assessments that might be implemented for high-stakes testing:

- **Alternate Assessments Based on Alternate Achievement Standards (AA-AAS)**—assessment for students with more severe intellectual disabilities based on modified versions of state standards.
- **Alternate Assessments Based on Modified Academic Achievement Standards (AA-MAS)**—assessment for students working on grade-level material who need additional time to master content.
- **Alternate Assessments Based on Grade-Level Achievement Standards (LAA-GLAS)**—assessment for students working on grade level who need different testing formats to demonstrate mastery of standards.

IDEIA and the Elementary and Secondary Education Act (ESEA) require that students with disabilities participate in high-stakes testing; however, individual states vary in terms of how alternative assessment occurs. The NCEO (http://www.cehd.umn.edu) includes a listing of state alternate assessment requirements, once you do a search for NCEOs on its website.

10.4.4 Curriculum Adaptations

In the past, students with intellectual disabilities have often been assigned low academic expectations and alternative instructional activities emphasizing life skills and adaptive behaviors (Friend, 2014). Although some educators have maintained that alternative instructional activities are appropriate to prepare students with intellectual disabilities for independent living and the world of work (Ayres, Lowrey, Douglas, & Sievers, 2011, 2012), others argue that with careful planning and adaptations, there is hope that the level of expectations can be raised and student mastery of grade-level standards is possible (Courtade, Test, & Cook, 2015).

The standards-based reform movement has strong implications for the academic outcomes of students with intellectual disabilities (Lee, Soukup, Little, & Wehmeyer,

2009; Saunders, Spooner, Browder, Wakeman, & Lee, 2013). The No Child Left Behind Act (NCLB, 2001) and the 2004 reauthorization of IDEA have mandated increased access to the general education curriculum for students with disabilities (Clarke, Haydon, Bauer, & Epperly, 2016; Hardman & Dawson, 2008). This includes requirements for students with disabilities to meet academic standards and, to the degree outlined in the student's IEP, to participate in high-stakes testing (Downing & Peckham-Hardin, 2007; Parrish & Stodden, 2009). The movement toward increased access to the general education curriculum for students with disabilities warrants changes in instruction that will enhance academic achievement (Clarke et al., 2016; Wakeman, Karvonen, & Ahumada, 2013).

In looking at the variables that contribute to successful access to the general education curriculum, researchers Lee et al. (2009) concluded that curriculum adaptations were extremely important for students with intellectual disabilities. Wolfe and Hall (2003) recommend that special education–general education teams use a **cascade of integration options**. As they put it, "This cascade of services highlights the need to individualize and base decisions for placement on the student's unique needs" (p. 56). The cascade of integration options can be used to guide teams in making decisions about the appropriate activities (same, similar, different), objectives (same, related, or unrelated), and settings (inside or outside the general education classroom) for instruction.

Two ways to modify curriculum in inclusive classrooms are multilevel curriculum and curriculum overlapping (Doyle & Giangreco, 2013). In both cases, students in the general education classroom participate in shared learning experiences based on designated state and/or local standards. This includes standards that states have outlined for individuals with disabilities as well as learning goals and outcomes set on the student's IEP.

Multilevel curriculum

With **multilevel curriculum**, all students are focused on the same instructional standard; however, expectations for level of content or skill mastery may differ based on individual needs. In the case of students with intellectual disabilities, many face difficulties with processing large amounts of information or complex or abstract ideas. Target standards can be modified in terms of number, use of technical vocabulary, and degree of concreteness. In the State of Florida, for example, state standards (based on Common Core State Standards) are accompanied with "access points" for students with identified special needs. Standards are written with three level of access points: independent, support, and participatory. Multilevel curriculum provides all students opportunities to engage in the general education curriculum with attainable goals.

Curriculum overlapping

On the other hand, when using **curriculum overlapping**, two or more curricular areas may be addressed during a single unit or lesson. This might include a combination of academic, functional, or behavioral objectives. For example, if a student's IEP addresses the need for interacting and responding to peers, participation in a cooperative learning group would offer the student an opportunity to simultaneously focus on an academic goal and communication skills.

10.4.5 Instructional Practices

Decades of research in teaching social, behavioral, and daily living skills has resulted in identification of effective instructional practices for teaching students with a full range of intellectual disabilities. A growing body of research has concluded that many of these practices are applicable to the teaching of academic skills and content as well (Browder, Wood, Thompson, & Ribuffo, 2014; Courtade et al., 2015). In addition, research in incorporation of these practices in inclusive settings is emerging as well (Hudson, Browder, & Wood, 2013). Using such practices as co-teaching, peer tutoring, and assistive technology, effective instruction in the general education setting is becoming more feasible, even for students with moderate to severe intellectual disabilities (Saunders et al., 2013). A description of some of these practices follows.

Systematic instruction

Systematic instruction works hand in hand with task analysis. Systematic instruction begins with the identification of a learning goal and steps taken to meet that goal. As the learning process continues, systematic prompting, fading of prompts, reinforcement of correct responses, and generalization to additional contexts occurs (Browder et al., 2014). Two examples of systematic instruction are constant time delay and least intrusive prompts (Browder Wood, Thompson, & Ribuffo, 2014; Saunders et al., 2013).

Constant time delay involves presentation of a target skill or concept simultaneously with a verbal, pictorial, or video prompt. For example, in teaching a new vocabulary word, a flash card with the target word would be presented along with a picture flash card as a memory prompt. Gradually the duration of time between the presentation of the prompt would be diminished and ultimately faded away.

Least intrusive prompts involve the presentation of prompts with increasing level of explicitness as needed. For example, the teacher, paraprofessional, or peer tutor might read a portion of a geography text followed by a comprehension question. If the student cannot answer the question, rereading of the text would occur. If that does work, more explicit prompts (choosing from three possible choices, presenting a pictorial representation of the correct answer) would be offered.

MyEdLab
Video Example 10.4.
Watch this video learn how this student with intellectual disabilities is receiving hands-on instruction from two different teachers. Based on what you learn of her enormous progress throughout the school year, do you think that this child could benefit from being placed in an inclusive setting and if so, what would be required?

Hands-on instruction

Hands-on, or experientially based, instruction relates learning to what students already know and uses real-life activities as teaching tools. This type of instruction provides greater opportunity for students with intellectual disabilities to be actively involved (Scruggs, Mastropieri, & Okolo, 2008). Learning centers, math manipulatives, science projects, art projects, and computers are examples of hands-on activities that give students with intellectual disabilities the opportunity to participate. Downing and Eichinger (2003) explain that working with materials helps students with intellectual disabilities learn how to follow directions and handle items in appropriate ways. Tips for Teachers 10.2 lists additional ways you can teach skills and strategies to students with intellectual disabilities.

TIPS FOR TEACHERS 10.2

Promoting Skills and Strategy Acquisition

- Engage students actively in learning.
- Teach the strategy or skill in small steps or segments.
- Teach students how to use the specific strategies.
- Check frequently for understanding and provide feedback.
- Use actual materials and real-life experiences or simulations.
- Provide concrete examples in instruction.
- Have students perform the skill or strategy repeatedly.
- Provide many examples and multiple contexts to promote generalization.
- Reinforce generalization.
- Use the skill or strategy in several different learning situations to promote generalization.
- Create learning environments that provide students with successful experiences.
- Limit the number of concepts presented.

TECH TIPS

Assistive Technologies for Students with Intellectual Disabilities

Once teachers become familiar with students' limitations due to their developmental disabilities, whether they are physical or intellectual, there are many sources for assistive devices. Finding the right tool for students can help them both reach their potential and become part of the classroom community. Sources include the following:

Enabling Devices

(http://enablingdevices.com) provides you with a wide array of products for individuals with disabilities, such as the Perceptual Motor Trainer, which helps teach hand–eye coordination, and the Slant Board, which helps with handwriting training.

Enable Mart

(www.enablemart.com) is where you can find assistive technologies, both hardware and software, that accommodate individuals with disabilities and communication disorders.

10.4.6 Strategies to Support Students in the General Education Classroom

A number of general strategies can be used to support students with intellectual disabilities in the general education classroom. In addition, assistive technologies (both low and high tech) can provide students with the support they need to participate in classroom activities. The Tech Tips, "Assistive Technologies for Students with Intellectual Disabilities," will provide you with tools that can help students with a variety of developmental disabilities.

Increasing a student's sense of belonging

The first key to success is creating a community to which the student with disabilities has a sense of belonging. Developing and implementing routines is one way to ensure a sense of belonging. When students can predict what is going to happen, they are more likely to feel a part of the classroom. Project PLAI (Promoting Learning through Active Interaction) (Chen, Alsop, & Minor, 2000) developed a set of routines for students with disabilities. Learning routines such as lining up, distributing materials, taking turns, and taking time for communication are important aspects of helping students feel at home in the classroom. Tips for Teachers 10.3 lists strategies to increase this sense of belonging.

TIPS FOR TEACHERS 10.3

Strategies to Increase Sense of Belonging

- Give the student the same things as the other students (e.g., desk, typical seating, locker, name on classroom charts).
- Demonstrate respect for the student by using age-appropriate language and being a good role model.
- Involve the student in the typical classroom routine.
- Work with your educational team and students to find ways for the student to participate actively in classroom activities.
- Consult with specialists for ideas, and express your concerns.
- Encourage students to find ways to increase learning opportunities for classmates who are challenged.
- Promote equality and interactions with other classmates (e.g., remember to use the word *friend* instead of *peer tutor*, and say "go together" rather than "take _____ with you."
- Make connections among students who have common interests (e.g., sports, animals) with students with disabilities to generate interaction.

Sources: "Strategies to help paraeducators promote peer interaction," by J. Causton-Theoharis & K. Malmgren, 2005, *Teaching Exceptional Children*, 37, 18–24; and *All together now*, by K. Frisbee & J. Libby, 1992, Concord, NH: Cubb Life.

Partial participation

An opportunity to participate should not be denied because a person cannot independently perform the needed skills; instead, individualized adaptations should be developed to allow participation and learning, even if of only part of the skill. The concept of partial or parallel participation assumes that an individual has the right to participate in all activities to the extent possible (Doyle & Giangreco, 2013). Active participation not only helps to maintain students' physical health, but also enhances their image, as peers see them partaking in a meaningful activity. Say, for example, that a class is working on writing sentences using correct punctuation. A classmate randomly selects three small pictures and places them on Heather's desk. Heather, a student with an intellectual disability, has to reach out and point to one of the pictures. Her goals are to reach and point, to look at her peer, and to make decisions in a timely fashion. The peer then holds up the picture for the class to see. The class writes a sentence about it, and Heather must answer a question about it.

Partial participation is one of many strategies you can use to foster engagement, but is not recommended as a sole pathway to include and instruct students with intellectual disabilities. It is recommended that partial participation should be used in conjunction with a task analysis so that participation is purposeful (Turnbull, Turnbull, Wehmeyer, & Shogre, 2012). It is also recommended that involvement of the student with disabilities be "status-enhancing" so that participation with peers is positive from both academic and social perspectives (Doyle & Giangreco, 2013).

Using routines to ensure safety

Teaching students with intellectual disabilities safety routines is vitally important (Kim, 2010; Mechling, 2008). Review emergency procedures with key personnel and with students. Students with intellectual disabilities may need direct, explicit instruction not only in emergency procedures, but also in day-to-day routines such as getting on the bus, crossing the street, and using telephones. Practice fire drills before an actual fire drill occurs to avoid confusion and emotional distress. If a student has a condition that may impede evacuation, a plan for emergencies should be documented in the IEP.

Peer support and peer tutoring

Peers may be the most underrated and underused human resource available in general education classrooms. Over 40 years of research have yielded positive academic and social outcomes for both tutees and their tutors (Bowman-Perrott, Davis, Vannest, Williams, Greenwood, & Parker, 2013). Nondisabled peers are often creative problem solvers and staunch supporters of students with intellectual disabilities (Carter, Cushing, Clark, & Kennedy, 2005; Stenhoff & Lignugaris/Kraft, 2007). Peer tutoring offers students greater verbal interaction, more frequent opportunities to respond and receive feedback, and increased opportunity for repetition in repeated reading and learning new skills (Hudson, Browder, & Jimenez, 2014).

It is important, however, that students not always take the role of "helping" a student with disabilities, which can get in the way of their developing a friendship. Initially, peer support and tutoring require adult facilitation as needs and strategies are identified, but adult participation should be reduced as friendships and tutoring routines develop. Tips for Teachers 10.4 provides general suggestions for making the most of working in pairs.

Tips for Teachers 10.5 presents steps for peers to provide survival skills support for students with intellectual disabilities.

Cooperative learning

Cooperative learning is an effective instructional method for including students with intellectual disabilities (Demchak, 2005; Hunt & McDonnell, 2009; Lee et al., 2009). In cooperative learning situations, the class is divided for learning activities into groups that have cooperative goals. Each student has a role, and it is important that each role

TIPS FOR TEACHERS 10.4

Making the Most of Working with Pairs

Set Procedures for Peer Tutoring

1. Give everyone a chance to be a tutor—every student has something to share with a peer.
2. Give the tutor very specific suggestions about what to teach and how to teach it.
3. Keep tutoring sessions short for students with short attention spans.

Set Procedures for Collaborative Pairs

1. Give specific guidelines about the responsibilities of each partner.
2. Hold each partner accountable for fulfilling responsibilities.
3. Give students the opportunity to work with a variety of partners.

Set Rules

1. Talk only to your partner.
2. Talk only about the assignment (project).
3. Use a low voice.
4. Cooperate with your partner.
5. Try to do your best.

Source: Used by permission of Douglas and Lynn Fuchs, Vanderbilt University.

is valued. Cooperative learning fosters interdependence and is a strong vehicle for bringing access to the general education curriculum to students with intellectual disabilities (Soukup, Wehmeyer, Bashinski, & Bovaird, 2007).

Barbara Mykel uses cooperative learning groups to support her fifth graders in reading social studies textbooks. She assigns students to mixed-ability groups and gives each student a role within that group. Two students take turns as readers; one leads the group in generating possible test questions, and one serves as a note taker. Kevin, a student with moderate intellectual disabilities, participates in these cooperative groups. Kevin serves as

TIPS FOR TEACHERS 10.5

Peer-Supported Strategy to Promote Classroom Survival Skills

Step	**Description**
Step 1	Peer tutors explain why the classroom survival skills are important to learn.
	Example: "In class when the bell rings, in seat when the bell rings, bring appropriate materials to class, greet the teacher, greet other students, ask questions, answer questions, sit up straight, pay attention to the teacher, acknowledge comments from other students."
Step 2	Peer tutors give one example for each survival skill.
	Example: "I am going to show you how you can teach yourself to be in class when the bell rings. You need to stop what you are doing outside of the classroom during recess and come to the class when the bell rings."
Step 3	Peer tutors give one counterexample for each survival skill.
	Example: "Staying in the cafeteria when the bell rings is not being in class when the bell rings."
Step 4	Peer tutors explain how to count and self-record survival skills.
	Example: "Were you in class when the bell rang? If you were in the class when the bell rang, mark Yes. If not, mark No."
Step 5	Peer tutors prompt for appropriate survival skills when necessary.
Step 6	Peer tutors provide feedback and praise for appropriate survival skills.

Source: Based on information from "The effects of peer delivered self-monitoring strategies on the participation of students with severe disabilities in general education classrooms," by G. H. Gilberts, M. Agran, C. Huges, & M. Wehmeyer, 2001, *Journal of the Association for Persons with Severe Handicaps, 26*(1), 25–36.

the announcer and makes sure that everyone in the group contributes possible test questions. The paraeducator, Gilbert Gomez, makes flashcards for later review with Kevin and for home learning.

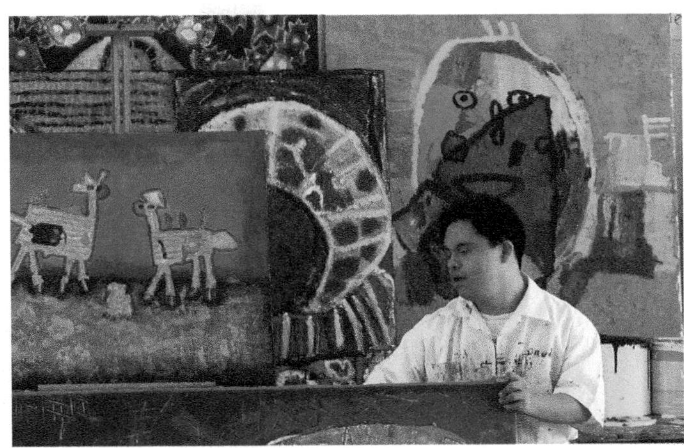

How would you identify the skills the student needs to succeed? What opportunities does this learning situation provide for the functional practice of these skills?

10.4.7 Providing Opportunities for Functional Practice

Students with intellectual disabilities may not independently make connections between what they are learning in school and their daily lives. Functional practice can help make those links. **Functional practice** is relevant practice to help students easily see the connection between what they are practicing and its use in real life. For example, you can incorporate into reading instruction activities that stress reading for fun or to obtain information needed for daily life. Tips for Teachers 10.6 provides information on how to incorporate functional tools and activities into the classroom.

Functional activities can often predict the degree to which students will function successfully as adults.

One aspect of functional practice in the teaching of students with intellectual disabilities is development of self-determination (Agran, Cavin, Wehmeyer, & Palmer, 2010; Sheppard & Unsworth, 2010; Wehmeyer, Martin, & Sands, 2008). **Self-determination** is the ability to make informed decisions that will lead to positive outcomes. Self-determination is important for transition to life beyond the school and ultimately for

TIPS FOR TEACHERS 10.6

Bringing Functional Tools and Activities into the Classroom

Following are some tools you can use to help make learning activities relevant:

- Directions (e.g., for cooking, building a model, repairing an appliance)
- Directional orientation and maps
- Menus
- Labels on foods, medicines, and clothing
- Telephone book
- Catalogs and advertisements (for selecting something to order)
- Schedules (e.g., bus, train, television)
- Signs
- Newspapers and magazines

Writing activities also can be centered on daily activities, such as:

- Sending an email to a friend
- Writing a letter to request something or to complain
- Writing a postcard or letter to a relative
- Making a shopping list
- Completing a job application or an application for a library card
- Ordering something by filling out a form
- Writing down a telephone message

Functional math activities include the following:

- Making change
- Counting money
- Making a purchase
- Using a checking account
- Using a credit card
- Budgeting money
- Telling and estimating time
- Reading a calendar
- Reading a thermometer
- Measuring
- Determining weight and height

quality of life (Carter, Lane, Pierson, & Stang, 2008). There are seven components of self-determination: (a) problem solving, (b) self-management, (c) decision making, (d) goal setting, (e) choice making, (f) self-awareness, and (g) self-advocacy (Bremer, Kachgal, & Schoeller, 2003). These domains may be represented on your student's IEP, and you'll need to work with your special education colleagues to implement systematic and intensive ways for your students to develop these skills, particularly with students in middle and high school (Kleinert et al., 2010; Sheppard & Unsworth, 2010; Shogren & Broussard, 2011).

10.4.8 Encouraging Family Involvement

Every teacher realizes the importance of family involvement in a student's education. In recent decades, research on families that include children with intellectual disabilities has expanded tremendously (Browder et al., 2014; Odom, Horner, Snell, & Blacher, 2007). Their parents, guardians, caretakers, and extended family members play key roles in determining the students' educational programs and their preparation for adult life. Knowing the family's goals for their child can help everyone work together as a team. Regular communication is the key to success. Moreover, if as a classroom teacher you can focus on a student's assets when communicating with parents, you can open the door to active problem solving to achieve mutual goals.

Turnbull, Turnbull, Erwin, Soodak, and Shogren (2010) talk about successful home–school partnerships as **reliable alliances**. Reliable alliances occur when there is mutual trust; ongoing communication; sensitivity to family culture, basic needs, and choices; and high yet realistic expectations. Keep in mind the influence of family culture on expectations (Harry & Klingner, 2014; Harry, Rueda, & Kalyanpur, 1999; Sparks, 2008).

As students with intellectual disabilities are increasingly included in general education classrooms, it is important that you learn strategies for accommodating these students in your class. You might need to adapt the curriculum or have the students work on goals that are not specified in the curriculum. As Chris Johnson discovered, a key to successful integration is collaboration with and support from the student's family as well as specialists who work with students such as Darrell. If you make time for co-planning and ongoing communication, you can help to ensure that students are successful and that you feel positive about the learning experiences of all the students in your class.

MyEdLab **Self-Check 10.4**

MyEdLab **Application Exercise 10.4:** Role of the General Education Teacher

10 SUMMARY

- Students with intellectual disabilities represent a diverse group of individuals with varied learning needs and abilities who, with proper supports, can improve their quality of life both in school and beyond. The challenges students with intellectual disabilities face can be physical, intellectual, and social and can vary from mild to severe. Generally, prevalence is estimated to be about 1% of the school population.
- There are multiple causes of intellectual disabilities, including genetic, physical, and nonphysical causes. These causes occur before, during, and after birth and during the developmental period of an individual's life up to the age of 18.
- Many students with intellectual disabilities will be identified for special services before entering your class. However, if you observe a student with persistent difficulties in learning tasks or adaptive behavior, follow your school district policies for providing support and, if necessary, determining what your role is in the referral process.
- As a general education teacher, you will be involved in the planning and implementation of adaptations and curriculum modifications for all students. Many planning systems and functional assessment and discrepancy analysis techniques are available to facilitate appropriate assessment and instruction. Using these systems and techniques as well as curricular adaptations, support strategies, functional practice, and input from families can help you provide high-quality instruction for students with intellectual disabilities.

THINK AND APPLY

1. Think about Chris Johnson's special education colleague Martha Anderson's role as an inclusion specialist in relation to your role as a classroom teacher. If one of Martha's students were to join your class, how would you plan, communicate, and work with Martha so that she could support both you and the student? List the questions you would want to ask Martha about the student's social, behavioral, and academic needs before he or she joined the class.
2. Intellectual disabilities result from numerous causes. Identify questions you have about the causes of intellectual disabilities and discuss those questions with a small group of your fellow students and then with your instructor.
3. Check your state and school district websites for information about how students with intellectual disabilities are identified for special education. Investigate the general education teacher's role in identification, in particular with response to intervention (RTI).
4. Check your state and school district websites for information about access to the general education curriculum for students with intellectual disabilities. Has your state or school district adapted curricular standards for students with intellectual disabilities? What requirements and accommodations are available for students with intellectual disabilities in your state's high-stakes testing?
5. Plan a lesson for one of your state's academic standards in your curriculum area. Include in your plan activities for partial or parallel participation for students with intellectual disabilities.

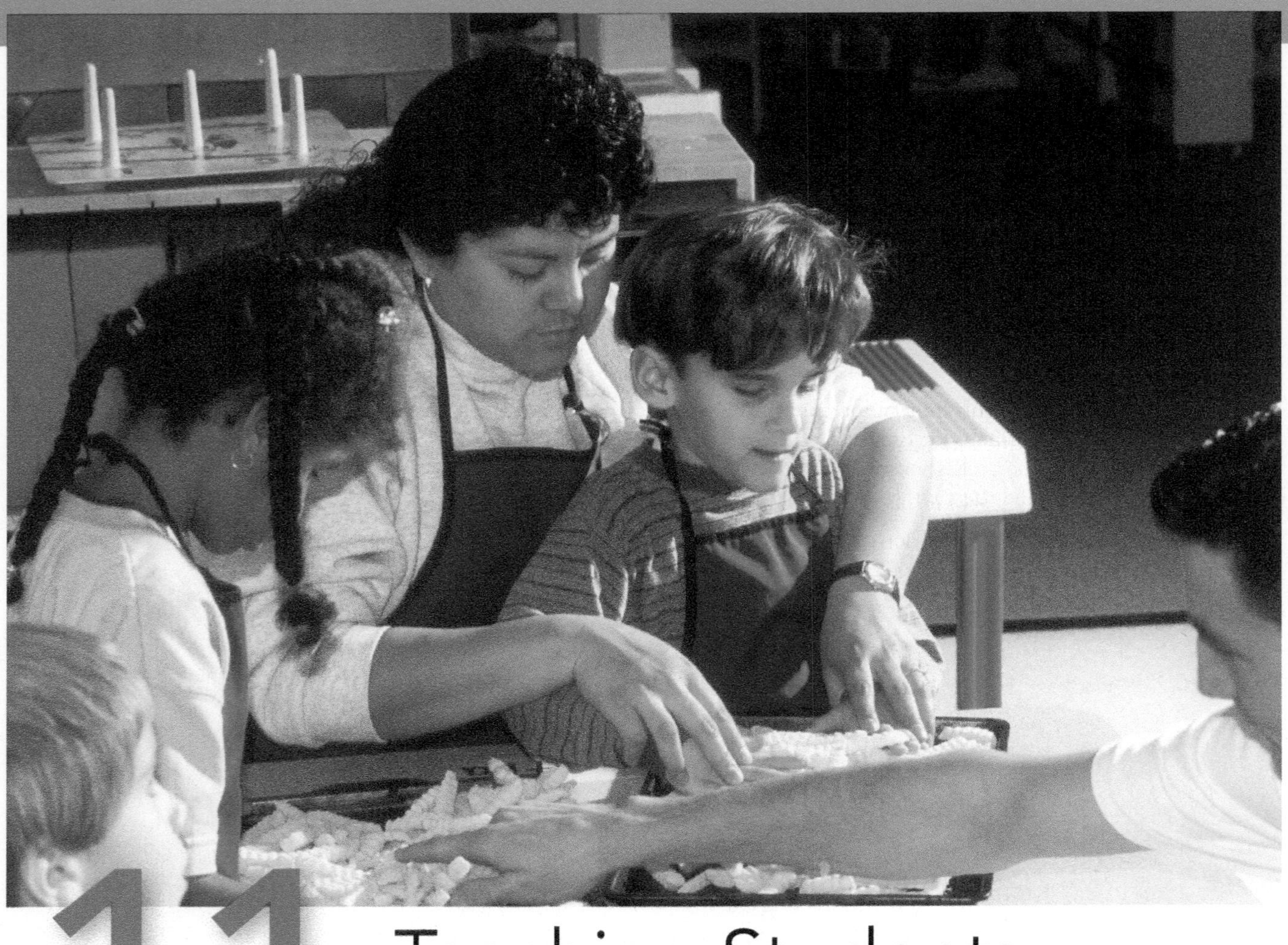

11 Teaching Students with Lower-Incidence Disabilities

Learning Outcomes

11.1 Describe *visual impairments* and how you might provide accommodations for students with visual impairments in your classroom.

11.2 Define *hearing impairments* and how you can provide accommodations for students with hearing impairments in your classroom.

11.3 Identify *physical disabilities, health impairments*, and *traumatic brain injury* and how you would take into consideration students with physical disabilities, health impairments, or traumatic brain injury when developing an education plan.

11.4 Explain *multiple and dual sensory disabilities* and how you can work with family members and other professionals to take a holistic approach to educating a student with multiple or dual sensory disabilities.

INTERVIEW: PEGGY KIRKLAND

Peggy Kirkland teaches fourth grade and has a group of twenty-five students. The school year got off to a great start and Peggy felt wonderful about the attitude and enthusiasm of all of her students. She knew it was going to be a terrific year. Shortly after the beginning of school, Peggy was told that one of her students, Kerri Albride, was hospitalized due to an accident at a playground near her home. Kerri sustained broken bones and injuries to the head. Doctors later confirmed that she had a traumatic brain injury.

Kerri was one of the most popular students in Peggy's class. She was a fluent reader, participated in class discussions, and had a large circle of friends. Her classmates were very upset when the accident occurred. Peggy asked the school counselor, Mark Romano, to meet with her students to help them cope with their concerns about Kerri.

After a long hospital stay and recuperation at home, Kerri finally returned to school. Physically, there was little change; the broken bones were healed. But a very different Kerri came back to fourth grade. Here are Peggy's observations:

> Other than slightly slurred speech, you really couldn't tell that Kerri might have some difficulties in making the adjustment back to school. But slowly other symptoms started to pop up. Kerri had trouble following directions, responding to questions, and reading. She got frustrated when she couldn't find the right words. Her problems weren't just academic; they were social as well. Kerri didn't see herself as being very different than she was before—at least socially. But we all noticed that her temperament was very different. Kerri would lash out at her classmates and they were bewildered by her actions. It soon became clear that we were going to have to continue to learn about what Kerri could and couldn't do and that it was going to take a team effort to help her adjust. It soon became clear to me that Kerri, her parents, her classmates, and I were all dealing with a loss for which we were not prepared.

Peggy was aware that she could not help Kerri or the other students she taught without support. The school counselor, Mark Romano, brought together a team that included Kerri's parents, the special education teacher, an occupational therapist, and a speech therapist. Kerri's physicians shared information that was useful for their planning. Together the team was able to develop an individualized education program (IEP) that addressed Kerri's academic and social needs. Peggy also talked with the team about how she could help her other students adjust to Kerri's changed behavior and how to set a positive classroom climate. Toward the end of the school year, Peggy observed:

> Kerri and her parents have many challenges ahead of them. What we all learned this year is the importance of teamwork. We're not sure if or when Kerri will recover fully. Her parents do have a strong support team that will help them along each step of the way.

CHAPTER OUTLINE

(continued)

CHAPTER OUTLINE
(*continued*)

Introduction

Peggy Kirkland is an experienced teacher who, from time to time, has had students with sensory (hearing and vision), physical, and health impairments in her classroom. Peggy recognizes that students have individual needs and may need support from other professionals. Individual needs vary in terms of the nature of their disability as well as the extent of their disability. Disabilities can vary in degree from minimal to mild, moderate, severe, or profound (Snyder & Dillow, 2015). In addition, some students may have needs based on more than one disability.

When you work with students with sensory, physical, or health impairments or disabilities, like Peggy you will likely be part of a team that includes you, the parents, the student, and other teachers and specialists. This chapter is divided into four sections: visual impairments; hearing loss or deafness/hardness of hearing; physical disabilities, health impairments, and traumatic brain injury; and multiple and dual sensory disabilities. You will learn about your role in the possible identification of special needs as well as strategies to promote student academic and social success.

The Common Core State Standards (CCSS) offer students with low-incidence disabilities greater access to grade-level standards than ever before. Advocates maintain that standards will lead the way to breaking the tradition of low-level expectations for students with disabilities (Hartle, 2011; Knight, Browder, Agnello, & Lee, 2010). Implementation of CCSS has been challenging for many schools (Fluery et al., 2014). However, teachers can improve access to CCSS standards by targeting appropriate standards and determining how to adapt text and enhance content to improve the instruction for students with low-incidence disabilities (Saunders, Spooner, Browder, Wakeman, & Lee, 2013). The Council of Chief State School Officers has published an Accommodations Manual to assist teachers in the planning and implementation of CCSS. Adaptations for both assessment and instruction are provided for a wide range of student characteristics and include suggestions for presentation of material, as well as options for student response, setting, and timing/scheduling.

11.1 STUDENTS WITH VISUAL IMPAIRMENTS

Think about classrooms you have visited and how many activities involve vision. According to the American Optometric Association (2011), as much as 80% of what children learn comes through visual input. This section's discussion of students with visual impairments focuses on appropriate instructional strategies you can use to support their learning. So that you can better understand their needs, the section begins with definitions of types of visual impairments, along with information about the characteristics, prevalence, and identification of students with visual impairments.

11.1.1 Definitions and Types of Visual Impairments

The visual system is a complex system that includes (a) the surrounding structures such as the skeletal structure of the face, the eyelid, and the tear system; (b) the eye globe itself, including each of the parts, such as the iris, lens, and retina; and (c) the neurological system, including the optic pathways and vision centers of the brain, such as the occipital lobes. In defining this system, Hallahan, Kauffmann, and Pullen (2012) note that visual impairments are typically defined within legal or educational frameworks.

Legal definitions

Have you ever stood in line in a school nurse's office to read a chart of letters of increasingly smaller size on a chart? Such a chart is a Snellen chart, a tool to gauge visual acuity or the ability to see detail clearly. Legal blindness is defined as a visual acuity of 20/200 with the best correction in the best eye or a visual field loss resulting in a visual field of 20 degrees or less. An individual with good vision can stand 200 feet away to read the largest line on the Snellen chart, whereas an individual who has a visual impairment of 20/200 must stand only 20 feet away to read the same line. Such an individual would be classified as legally blind and may be eligible for special services. Additionally, how well an individual can see using peripheral or side vision is called visual field. When someone experiences a significant visual field loss that leaves the person with a field of 20 degrees or less, he or she is then classified as legally blind (United States Social Security Administration, 2015) and can be eligible for tax benefits or special materials and resources.

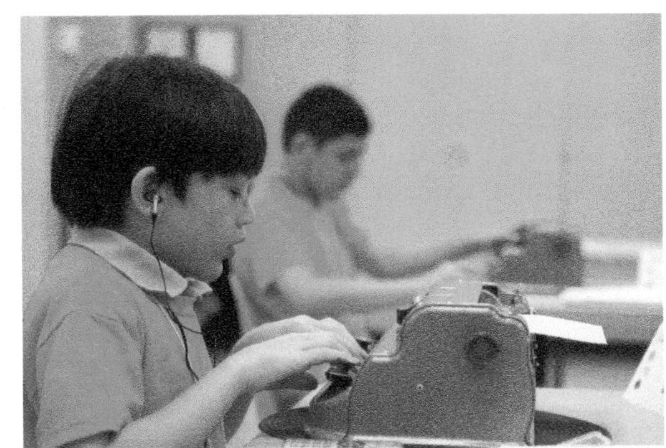

What low-tech and high-tech solutions available for students with vision impairments can students use in your classroom?

Some people who are classified as legally blind may be able to read standard print, see and identify the faces of friends and family, view objects at a distance, and discriminate details in objects or pictures. Others may have difficulty with these same tasks and may even have difficulty detecting objects, colors, and the location of light sources. Therefore, each individual's visual impairment is unique. Total blindness refers to a very small minority of individuals who have visual impairments and who are unable to see anything, including objects or light sources (Dandona & Dandona, 2006). Partial sight is a phrase that was previously used to specify individuals who had a visual acuity in the range of 20/70 to 20/200. This terminology is no longer used as widely as it once was (Corn & Lusk, 2010). Low vision is the term more typically used for individuals with visual acuity in that range who continue to have difficulty with vision even with corrective lenses (glasses) (Hallahan et al., 2012). Corn and Koenig (1996) define *low vision* as the preferred terminology for individuals who have an impairment and who with standard corrective lenses (glasses) continue to have "difficulty accomplishing visual tasks but can enhance [their] ability to accomplish these tasks with the use of compensatory visual strategies, low-vision and other devices, and environmental modifications" (p. 4).

Educational definition

An educational definition of visual impairment emphasizes academic tasks, particularly reading more and visual acuity less (Hallahan et al., 2012):

> *Visual impairment including blindness* means an impairment in vision that even with correction, adversely affects a child's educational performance. This term includes both partial sight and blindness. (IDEA 300.8 [c][13])

Causes of visual impairment

The many causes of visual impairment are usually grouped in the following three areas:

- Structural impairments (i.e., damage or impairment to one or more parts of the visual system)
- Refractive errors (i.e., an inability of the eye to focus the light rays onto the retina correctly)
- Cortical visual impairments (i.e., a problem with the neurological pathways, including reception and interpretation of the visual information) (Heward, 2009)

While vision impairment can occur anytime during life, the Centers for Disease Control and Prevention (CDC) reports that most children with vision impairment in the 3- to 10-year age range had causes that occurred in infancy (CDC, 2009b). Abnormal blood vessel growth or scarring of the retina of the eye were typical causes and more common among children with low birth weights (CDC, 2009b). Although it is helpful to know the cause of a student's visual impairment, it is more important to know how the student uses his or her vision to accomplish desired tasks.

11.1.2 Characteristics of Students with Visual Impairments

Even though a student with a visual impairment is more like sighted peers than different from them, a visual impairment has an impact on all aspects of development. Its effect on each student varies considerably (Mason & McCall, 2013). Children with visual impairments are thought to have a more difficult time developing basic concepts owing to their vision loss. Although the other senses help young children gain information about their world, a visual impairment will limit the range and scope of information available to the child. In its position statement on the educational needs of students with visual impairments, the American Foundation for the Blind (2009) states: "No other sense can stimulate curiosity, combine information, or invite exploration in the same way, or as efficiently and fully as vision. Students with visual impairments can and do succeed, but at different rates and often in different sequences" (p. 3).

Additionally, a young child will have difficulty learning from the activities of others (incidental learning) because the child might not be able to determine visually what someone, such as a teacher, is doing and what the results of the activity are (Arter, 2013). Preparing a simple snack is an example of such an activity. A child who has sight can watch a parent retrieve the food from the cupboard or refrigerator, prepare it, and then bring it to the child. A child who is visually impaired might not have access to any of this information because the child cannot see the location of the cupboard or refrigerator and might not even know what items are stored there. The child will not know how to prepare the food (e.g., spread peanut butter on bread) and will not know what utensils are needed. Finally, the child might not know how to open and close containers and will need repeated experiences to learn this skill.

Children with visual impairments typically reach developmental milestones in each of five developmental domains of cognition—concept development, communication, motor skills (fine and gross) and mobility, self-help, and social and emotional development. However, students may be delayed in these areas in the following ways:

- ***Concept development.*** Areas in which the child has not had a direct experience may be underdeveloped. In addition, children with visual impairments may not have access to clues such as color that can aid in conceptual development and vocabulary.
- ***Communication.*** There is general agreement that a visual impairment does not have a direct impact on oral language development (Rosel, Caballer, Jara, & Oliver, 2005). However, lack of access to appropriate adaptive materials may limit development in communication through the written word (Steinman, LeJeune, & Kimbrough, 2006).
- ***Motor skills and mobility.*** Children may be delayed in large (gross) motor skill development and may engage in fewer activities that use visual-motor skills (e.g., running, jumping, and kicking) (Wagner, Haibach, Pierce, & Lieberman, 2013). They may also have delays in fine motor skills (e.g., writing, cutting, and grasping small items). Moreover, issues related to safety may inhibit mobility and access to the physical environment.
- ***Self-help.*** If children have not been given responsibilities and guidance, they might not be able to fix a simple snack, independently select clothing, or dress themselves.
- ***Social skills.*** Children might not know when individuals are speaking to them. Additionally, children might be unable to see how others initiate interactions,

how they give nonverbal indications of their feelings and desires, and how peers are responding to interactions and common situations (Sacks, Lueck, Corn, & Erin, 2011; Zebehazy & Smith, 2011). As a result, children with visual impairments may also be more isolated than their sighted peers (Engel-Yeger & Hamed-Daher, 2013; Kelly & Smith, 2008) and less involved in after-school clubs, activities, and work opportunities.

It is important to remember that children with visual impairments need opportunities to directly interact with the environment. These children need to touch, listen, and explore new objects. They need to participate actively in all activities, have opportunities to talk about their experiences, and have opportunities to travel to and explore new environments. Teachers should provide additional time for these students to explore and ask questions about their environment and objects within the environment (Chen, 2014).

11.1.3 Prevalence of Students with Visual Impairments

Visual impairments are considered a low-incidence disability, which means that comparatively fewer students have visual impairments than have high-incidence disabilities such as learning disabilities. Most of the students with visual impairments placed in your class are likely to have some usable vision (Davis, 2013). The National Center for Education Statistics (2015) reports that during the 2011–2012 school year, approximately 28,000 students (ages 3–21) with vision impairments were served under the Individuals with Disabilities Education Improvement Act (IDEIA). Because students with visual impairments may also be classified under the umbrella of another disability, these numbers are not necessarily representative of children with visual impairments you might have in your classroom.

Approximately 29% of students with visual impairments are *visual* readers (use large print or some means of enlarging the print), 9% are *braille* readers (use braille for reading), and 9% are *auditory* readers (listen to tapes or others reading) (American Printing House for the Blind, 2010). The remaining students are either *prereaders* (young children) or *nonreaders* who, in addition to their visual impairment, have other disabilities (usually mental retardation) that interfere with their ability to read. The American Printing House for the Blind (2014) reports that 50,205 children with visual impairments attend public schools and 5,133 children attend residential schools for children with visual impairments. Note that the American Printing House for the Blind counts only children who are legally blind, so there are children with significant vision impairments (acuity better than 20/200) who are not reported in the preceding figures.

11.1.4 Identification and Assessment of Students with Visual Impairments

Although some students with visual impairments will be diagnosed before being part of your classroom, others may not. There are certain indicators that may help you identify students who need to be referred for evaluation. Following are common physical characteristics that might indicate visual impairments:

- Red-rimmed, swollen, or encrusted eyes
- Excessive blinking
- Itchy eyes
- Eyes that are tearing
- One or both eyes turn inward, outward, upward, or downward
- Extreme sensitivity to light
- Tilting or turning the head to one side to see an object
- Squinting
- Covering one eye to view an object

- Thrusting the head forward to view an object
- Headaches, fatigue, or dizziness after doing close work
- Tripping, bumping into objects, or appearing disoriented
- Recurring sties (i.e., inflamed swelling of the gland at the margin of the eyelid)

You may also observe some performance characteristics while students are reading, such as loss of place, omitting or inserting words or letters, or avoiding reading and writing tasks.

If you suspect that a student has a visual impairment, you should refer the student to the school nurse and the school or district's teacher who works with students who have visual impairments. To receive educational services from a special education teacher specializing in visual impairments, students must have a documented visual impairment. Written documentation in the form of an eye report is obtained from an ophthalmologist or optometrist.

After a student's visual impairment is identified, the special education teacher who specializes in visual impairments assesses the student's functional vision in multiple environments, including the academic setting. The **functional vision assessment** will include the student's ability to view objects at both near and distant points and the student's ability to sustain visual function throughout daily academic settings. Environmental conditions such as lighting, contrasts, optimal print size, seating preference, and visual features of the environment are part of a functional vision assessment. A **learning media assessment** to determine the student's dominant learning modality should also be included as part of the assessment battery. Compensatory skills assessments may also be appropriate to determine the services needed for the student. **Compensatory skills** include listening skills, orientation and mobility skills, social skills, and daily living skills. These important skills must be taught in the environments in which they will be used.

11.1.5 Instructional Guidelines and Accommodations for Students with Visual Impairments

Although most districts already provide adapted materials to students with visual impairments, the 2004 update of IDEA mandates that states adopt the National Instructional Materials Accessibility Standard (NIMAS) to provide appropriate instructional materials to individuals who are blind and to those with visual impairments. Fortunately, thanks to developments in technology, avenues for access to the general education curriculum are on the rise. The National Center for Accessible Instructional Materials (2015) has a website that lists resources for classroom teachers in its efforts to help students with a wide range of disabilities to access curriculum. In addition, the National Federation of the Blind (2015) maintains a website that presents a Technology Resource List. This list is updated regularly and provides information about resources available for students and adults with visual impairments.

The nonprofit organization Learning Ally (formerly known as Recordings for the Blind and Dyslexic) provides audio recordings of textbooks and other educational materials for individuals with disabilities. The organization is rapidly acquiring educational materials aligned with the Common Core State Standards (see www.learningally.org).

Some general education teachers feel apprehensive when they see the materials and equipment that a student with visual impairments needs in the classroom (Ajuwon, Sarraj, Griffin-Shirley, Lechtenberger, & Zhou, 2015). Ron Cross, an eighth-grade science teacher, was concerned when Diane, a special educator, and Brandy, his student, first indicated the materials and adaptations that Brandy would require. Brandy's equipment included the science textbook in braille (12 volumes) and an electronic brailler and braille paper (i.e., the machine and special paper used to write braille). During the year, Diane also provided tactile diagrams of cells and insects (i.e., diagrams that are raised and textured so that the features can be felt). Diane explained that the specialized equipment and materials would enable Brandy to succeed in science class.

General accommodations

In planning for students with visual impairments, teachers should think about auditory, tactile, and visual accommodations (Downing & Eichinger, 2011). Students may not have a wide range of visual images to draw from. Therefore, when giving directions or lecturing, you may need to activate the students' prior knowledge and vocabulary. You may also need to provide some auditory signs or cues to key students into vital information. Tactile accommodations include opportunities for students to touch and feel objects related to a learning activity. Children should be encouraged to touch with both hands and to have repeated opportunities to touch before, during, and after a lesson (Castellano, 2003). Visual accommodations include making certain that the student is seated in a way so as to get an unobstructed view, creating printed materials with appropriate font size, and writing in large letters on the board and interactive white board. Tips for Teachers 11.1 includes additional suggestions for students who have some usable vision.

Using braille devices

Some students may have some usable vision but rely on tactile and auditory information gained by using these learning channels. These students use braille, a system of embossed or raised dots that can be read with the tips of the fingers. The basic unit of braille is a cell that contains six dots in two vertical rows of three dots each. Combining the dots forms letters of the alphabet, numbers, punctuation marks, and contractions. Contractions are used to save space (for example, the entire word *understand* is written as ⠥⠝⠙⠑⠗⠎⠞⠁⠝⠙, whereas the contraction for *understand* takes up only four cells: ⠐⠥⠌⠯). When students learn braille, they learn to spell both the full and the contracted forms. Figure 11.1 gives examples of braille forms.

TIPS FOR TEACHERS 11.1

Modifying the Environment for Students with Visual Impairments

Physical Environment

- Announce your presence and identify yourself (e.g., "Hi, girls, it's Mr. Johnson. May I join your science group to see how you are working together?"). Also announce your departure (e.g., "Thank you, girls, for letting me join you. I'm going to check in with Ryan's group now.").
- Leave doors fully opened or closed and drawers closed so that the student does not run into them.
- Describe the locations of things, especially after rearranging the classroom. Start with the door and travel around the room systematically, noting locations.
- Provide an extra desk or shelf space for the student to store materials.
- Provide access to an outlet for audio equipment, braillers, lamp, or other electrical equipment.
- Allow early dismissal from class so that the student has time to travel to other classes.

Learning Environment

- Familiarize students with classroom materials (e.g., give them time to visually or tactually explore a globe before asking them to locate the longitude and latitude of a city).
- Have concrete examples students can touch (e.g., in science, have fossils, not just pictures of fossils).
- Provide lessons with tactual and auditory components, and adapt assignments so that students can participate.
- Consider lighting conditions. Some students do best with natural lighting; others do better with lamps. Backlighting reduces visibility, so avoid standing in front of a window when you present material to the class. Low contrast in materials and between backgrounds and foregrounds reduces visibility, so make sure the contrast is as high as possible.
- Provide written copies of any materials you use on the board or interactive white board. Say what you are writing as you do it.
- Allow a peer to take notes for the student, but check that the student is still paying attention and participating.
- Provide opportunities for students to work in groups, especially when the assignment has a visual component (e.g., conducting experiments in science class).
- Modify writing activities as necessary by allowing students to complete assignments over an extended time.

FIGURE 11.1 The braille alphabet

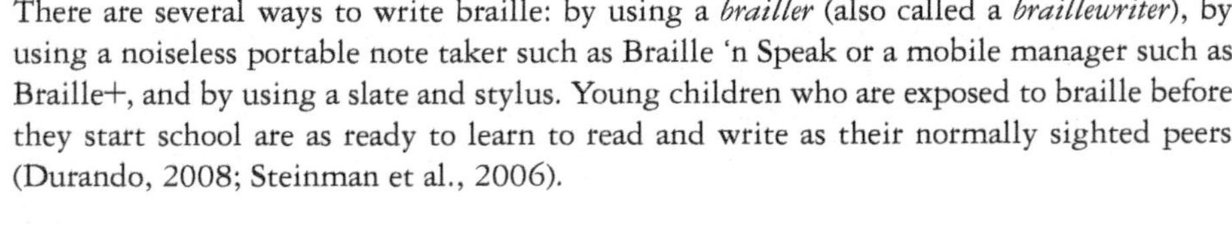

Source: Reprinted by permission of the National Braille Press © 2000.

There are several ways to write braille: by using a *brailler* (also called a *braillewriter*), by using a noiseless portable note taker such as Braille 'n Speak or a mobile manager such as Braille+, and by using a slate and stylus. Young children who are exposed to braille before they start school are as ready to learn to read and write as their normally sighted peers (Durando, 2008; Steinman et al., 2006).

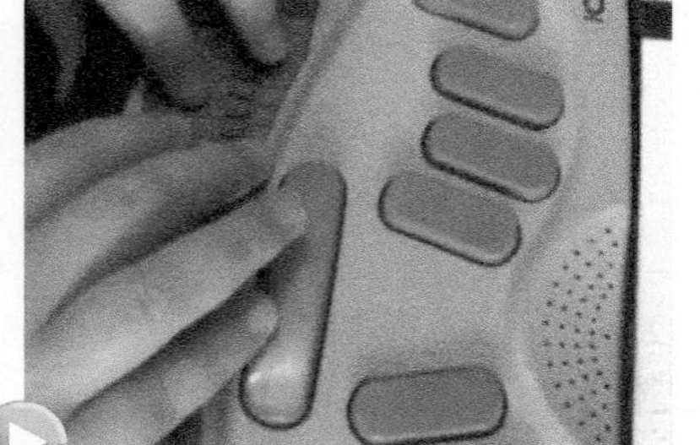

MyEdLab
Video Example 11.1.
Watch this video and notice the different types of accommodations available to students with visual impairments. As a classroom teacher, what kind of additional support is important in order for students to benefit most from these devices and accommodations?

Using orientation and mobility skills

Orientation and mobility specialists teach students with visual impairments to travel independently in their environments. "The goal is to enable the student to enter any environment, familiar or unfamiliar, and to function safely, efficiently, gracefully, and independently" (Hill & Ponder, 1976, p. 1). Consequently, it is not unusual for the student and specialist to work not only in school but also in the community.

The student needs to develop both orientation skills (which include understanding one's own body, one's position in space, and abstract concepts such as the layout of a city block) and mobility skills (which include going up and down stairs, crossing streets, and using public transportation) (Guth, Rieser, & Ashmead, 2010). The orientation and mobility specialist or the special education teacher who specializes in visual impairments can help you arrange your classroom to facilitate the student's mobility within the classroom and other key places in the school (e.g., cafeteria, library, bus loading zone, playground). In addition, students with visual impairments need to know procedures related to safety and emergencies (Clarke, Embury, Jones, & Yssel, 2014; Emerson & Corn, 2006).

The long cane is the mobility device most frequently used by individuals with visual impairments, including children. The cane has a handle (generally black or red); a shaft, which is white; and a red reflective material at the bottom of the shaft. The tip of the cane varies considerably, some being small and others quite large. The orientation and mobility specialist determines the type of tip used on the cane. If students have canes at school, they are taught to be responsible for their canes. Mobility specialists have shown them how to store their canes when not in use (sometimes by hanging the cane on a hook, other times by folding the cane and placing it in a school bag). The cane is not a toy and is used solely for the purpose of providing the visually impaired traveler with information about the terrain as he or she walks. Instruction from the orientation and mobility specialist is essential for the child with a visual impairment to develop the skills to be a safe and efficient cane user (Dias et al., 2015; Emerson & Corn, 2006).

Using optical, nonoptical, and instructional aids

Students who have difficulty seeing street signs, building numbers, and bus signs might use a *monocular*, an optical aid that magnifies a distant object. Other optical aids include many types of magnifiers—handheld, lighted, or with a stand—as well as prescription lenses (glasses or contacts). The special education teacher trained to work with students with visual impairments has learned techniques to employ in teaching students to use both distance optical devices such as the monocular and near optical devices such as magnifiers (Frances & Siu, 2015; Presley & D'Andrea, 2009).

Large print is another option for students with visual impairments. Large-print books are costly and difficult to store, and can sometimes embarrass the students. Reading large print may also be tiring, in that it requires exaggerated head movements and adaptive seating positions. The American Printing House for the Blind website provides guidelines for designing print documents.

Optical aids, by contrast, are more compact, less costly, and give students access to all materials (Corn, Wall, & Bell, 2000; Corn et al., 2002; Farmer & Morse, 2007). The key is to have the teacher who specializes in visual impairments assess the student's needs and abilities in multiple environments and provide appropriate training on all necessary equipment and devices.

General educators, parents, and special educators must not assume that all children with visual impairments need large print and will benefit from it. Many children with low vision are candidates for optical aids and should be evaluated by a doctor trained in low vision. Once optical aids are prescribed, teachers who are certified teachers of children with visual impairments need to provide students with instruction in how to use these devices. When selecting and preparing a text, teachers must make sure that it is clearly written, has adequate spacing between letters and words, and is on good-quality paper. Reducing the amount of background patterns on the page or providing good contrast between the color of the print and the color of the page is important (Kitchel, 2012).

Nonoptical aids also can help students to maximize visual potential. **Nonoptical aids** are devices that, although not prescribed by a doctor, promote efficient use of vision. Following are some examples of nonoptical aids:

- *Lamp* (provides additional light). Lamps with adjustable necks help to minimize glare.
- *Reading stand* (used to bring printed material closer to the eyes). Reduces poor posture and fatigue.
- *Bold-line paper* (makes writing easier for students with visual impairments). The American Printing House for the Blind manufactures writing paper, graph paper, and large-print paper with music staffs.
- *Hats and visors* (can help to reduce the amount of light). Helpful for students who are sensitive to light (photophobic).
- *Color acetate* (a plastic overlay that darkens print or increases contrast). Yellow is the color favored by many students with visual impairments.

Several nonoptical aids, available mainly from the American Printing House for the Blind, include the following:

- *Cranmer abacus*—an adapted device for the rapid computation of basic math functions, decimals, and fractions
- *Raised-line paper*—writing and graph paper with raised lines that can be followed tactually;
- rectangular templates designed to enable the writer to accurately place a signature, address an envelope, or write a check
- *Measurement tools*—items such as braille clocks, rulers, and measuring kits with raised marks

Testing accommodations

Classroom tests should be modified to make them accessible to students with visual impairments. Modifications may include assigning alternative items, orally reading sections of the test to the student, using large-print or braille answer sheets, providing real objects for items shown in pictures, or coloring pictures to make them easier to see. Tips for Teachers 11.2 provides some additional ideas for making accommodations for tests.

TIPS FOR TEACHERS 11.2

Accommodations for Tests in the General Education Classroom

- Provide test materials in the student's primary learning medium (e.g., braille, large print, audiotape).
- Allow extra time to complete test items.
- As a general rule, give students who read braille twice as much time as other students to complete a test.
- As a general rule, give students who read regular or large print time and a half to complete a test (e.g., if the time limit is 30 minutes, give them 45 minutes).
- Read written instructions to students with visual impairment to minimize the amount of reading they need to do (so as to reduce eye fatigue).
- Present test items orally if doing so will not compromise the integrity of the test.
- Allow students to write answers on the test material instead of a bubble sheet, or provide a large-print bubble sheet.

The special education teacher who works with the student with visual impairments is also an excellent resource for suggesting several simple testing accommodations.

MyEdLab **Self-Check 11.1**

MyEdLab **Application Exercise 11.1:** Students with Visual Impairments

11.2 STUDENTS WITH HEARING LOSS

You may have the opportunity to teach a student who is deaf or hard of hearing. Nancy Shipka, a fifth-grade math and science teacher who had that opportunity, worked with a special education teacher specializing in hearing loss and a sign language interpreter. Nancy had no idea what to expect when two students who were deaf joined her math and science classes. She was concerned not only that the students' academic performance would not measure up to that of the normally hearing students in her class, but also about working with a special education team. With the help of the special education team, however, Nancy worked with the students to determine where they should sit so that they could clearly see her, the interpreter, the interactive white board, and the computer monitor. She also learned to face the students directly when speaking and to vary her teaching methods, emphasizing hands-on activities and demonstrations. As part of her own education, Nancy came to understand that the role of the interpreter is one of facilitating communication. In this capacity, Nancy told the interpreter about difficult concepts ahead of time and also provided written summaries and class notes so that the interpreter would be prepared to sign difficult or technical concepts.

Like Nancy, you could also find yourself in a classroom with a student with hearing loss. If this is the case, you will have questions about how to best meet your student's needs. This section explains deafness, hearing loss, and how to best accommodate students with hearing loss.

11.2.1 Definitions and Types of Hearing Loss

Hearing loss, although often associated with aging, can occur at any time, including from birth. Hearing loss can occur as the result of several factors, including heredity, illness or disease, and excessive prolonged exposure to loud noises. Many of the causes of hearing loss in infants are unknown. Young children who are identified as having hearing loss before they learn language (2 to 3 years of age) are identified as prelingually deaf.

This early loss of hearing significantly affects language development. The U.S. Federal government provides definitions for deafness and hearing loss:

> *Deafness* means a hearing impairment that is so severe that the child is impaired in processing linguistic information through hearing, with or without amplification that adversely affects a child's educational performance. (IDEA 300.8[c][3])
>
> *Hearing impairment* means an impairment in hearing, whether permanent or fluctuating, that adversely affects a child's educational performance but that is not included under the definition of deafness in this section. (IDEA 300.8[c][5])

Hearing loss can occur in one ear (unilateral) or both ears (bilateral). It can be described by type and degree. The type of hearing loss depends on where it occurs in the ear. A hearing loss is referred to as **conductive** when the outer and middle ears do not transfer enough acoustic energy to the inner ear fluids. Blockage of the ear canal by congenital malformation, abnormalities of the middle ear structures, or otitis media (infection of the middle ear) are some of the causes of conductive hearing loss. Medicine or surgery may sometimes help with this type of hearing loss. A hearing loss is called **sensorineural** when there is damage to the cochlea (inner ear) or to the auditory nerve. This type of hearing loss is usually permanent. Hearing loss is called **mixed hearing loss** when the loss is both conductive and sensorineural.

By observing a person's responses to sounds the degree of hearing loss can be assessed. The intensity of a sound (loud versus quiet) is measured in **decibels** (dB); the frequency of the sound (high versus low) is measured in **hertz**. An audiologist tests and plots an individual's responses to sounds on a graph called an **audiogram**, a visual representation of an individual's ability to hear sound. Figure 11.2 shows a comparison of the frequency and intensity of various environmental and speech sounds, plotted on an audiogram (Stach, 1998).

As you can see from the diagram, the rustling sound of a palm tree is quiet (5 dB), whereas rock music is quite loud (100–110 dB). Speech sounds are somewhere in between in a configuration called the "Speech Banana."

What are some advantages and disadvantages of amplification systems for students with hearing loss? What communication alternatives are available for students who are deaf?

11.2.2 Characteristics of Students with Hearing Loss

Normal hearing falls within the range of 0–15 dB. Hearing losses are described by degree in terms such as *minimal*, *mild*, *moderate*, *severe*, and *profound:*

- 16–25 dB = minimal loss
- 25–40 dB = mild hearing loss
- 40–65 dB = moderate hearing loss
- 65–90 dB = severe hearing loss
- Greater than 90 dB = profound hearing loss

A person with a mild to moderate loss is usually referred to as being **hard of hearing**. Someone with a severe or profound loss is usually described as **deaf**.

Hearing loss affects normal speech and language development, which in turn affects reading development. Students who are deaf or hard of hearing may be significantly delayed in vocabulary development and reading skills. Some students who are deaf use vision as their primary mode of communication and learning. Other students who are deaf or hard of hearing develop communication and learning skills through the use of **residual hearing**, or the amount of hearing remaining after a hearing loss. Students with hearing losses to different degrees have difficulty accessing their environment and language system. Even though their vocal apparatuses function normally, they experience difficulty in

FIGURE 11.2 Comparison of the frequency and intensity of various environmental and speech sounds

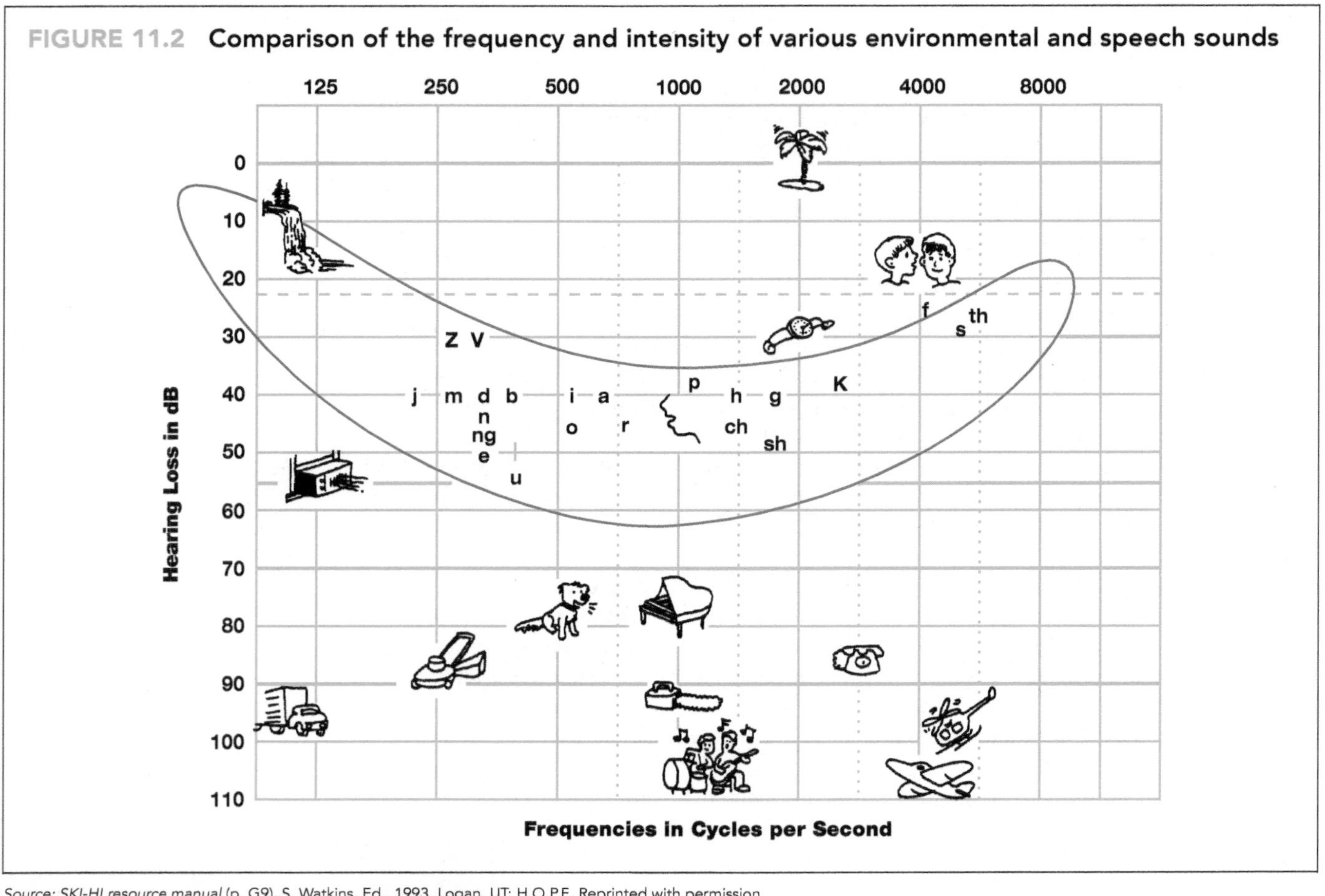

Source: SKI-HI resource manual (p. G9), S. Watkins, Ed., 1993, Logan, UT: H.O.P.E. Reprinted with permission.

learning to produce the speech sounds, because they might not get accurate or complete feedback from hearing the sounds they are producing. Many students who are deaf use American Sign Language (ASL) as their primary mode of communication. Other deaf or hard-of-hearing students use spoken English or a signed English system as their primary mode of communication. ASL is a visual, gestural language: It is not a visual representation of English, it is not a simplified language or communication system, and it is not a universal language. ASL has its own unique grammar and usage. Fingerspelling is a system for representing the English alphabet manually. Fingerspelling is used to "spell" names and proper nouns, as well as English words for which no sign exists. Typically, children acquire ASL and fingerspelling at the same time (Baker, 2010). Individuals who are native ASL signers use fingerspelling for 10% to 15% of their signed communication (Baker, 2010). Figure 11.3 shows the American fingerspelling alphabet.

Because many students and adults who are deaf speak a common language, ASL, and share similar backgrounds (in that they are deaf), they regard themselves as members of the Deaf culture. Members of the Deaf culture view hearing loss not as a disability but as a common characteristic among their members (Holcomb, 2012; Padden & Humphries, 2006).

11.2.3 Prevalence of Students with Hearing Loss

Since the implementation of the Individuals with Disabilities Education Act (IDEA), public schools have served more students with hearing loss than have state residential schools. On the basis of an annual survey of children and youth who are deaf or hard of hearing by the Gallaudet Research Institute (2011), which included 37,828 students,

FIGURE 11.3 **American fingerspelling alphabet**

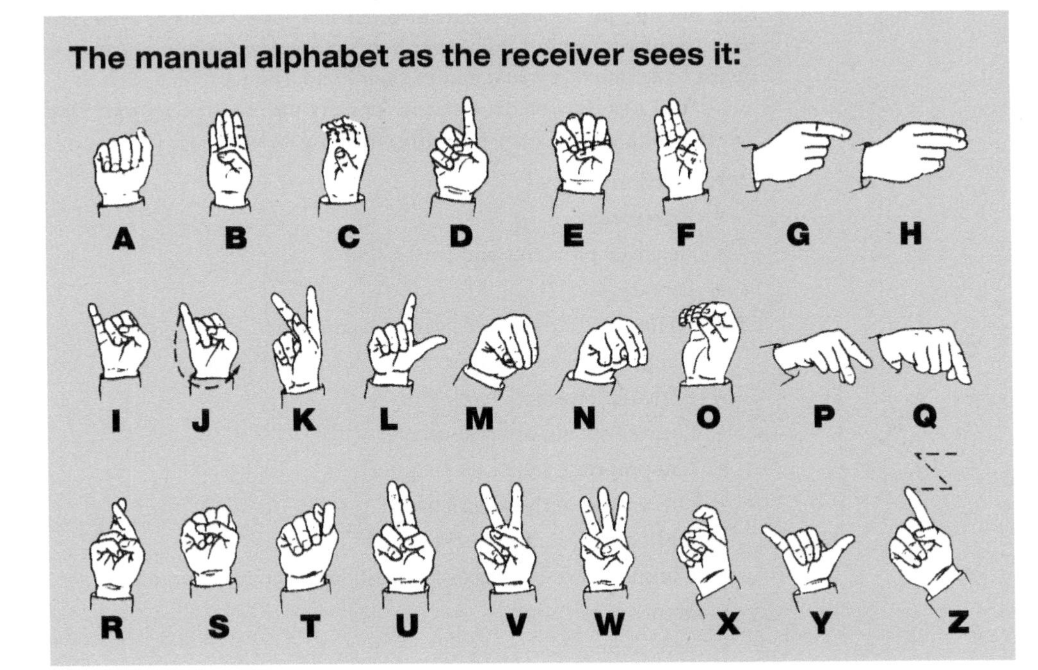

57% received instruction in the general education classroom and 11% received instruction in a resource setting. The remaining students were in special schools, home-schooled, or in self-contained classrooms. In the 2011–2012 school year, approximately 78,000 students with hearing impairments received special education services (National Center for Education Statistics [NCES], 2015).

11.2.4 Identification and Assessment of Students with Hearing Loss

Melanie Brooks, a kindergarten teacher, recalls her first experience of identifying a student with hearing loss. Chelsea had difficulty following directions, often asked that information be repeated, and had difficulty locating the speaker in group discussions. Melanie was also concerned about Chelsea's persistent colds, and she contacted the school nurse.

Together, the school nurse, Chelsea's parents, and Melanie began to identify ways to help Chelsea. They discovered that Chelsea had failed her kindergarten hearing screening and, by talking with her parents, the nurse, and Melanie, learned that Chelsea had incurred numerous ear infections as an infant and toddler. The district audiologist conducted further testing with Chelsea, discovering a mild to moderate hearing loss in both ears. To address the hearing loss, Chelsea was fitted with hearing aids. Melanie and the special education teacher specializing in hearing loss worked with Chelsea to provide resources and adaptations to help her learn better.

Some losses, particularly if they are mild to moderate ones, may be detected initially during kindergarten screening and by classroom teachers. Most moderate, severe, and profound hearing losses have already been detected and identified by the time students reach your class. Early identification and intervention are key to the development of language and learning for children with hearing loss (Pimperton & Kennedy, 2012; Tharpe et al., 2008). In 1993, the National Institutes of Health's (NIH) Consensus Development Conference on Early Identification of Hearing Loss concluded that all infants should be screened for hearing loss, preferably before hospital discharge. Currently all states and territories now have legislation requiring infant hearing screening (National Center for Hearing Assessment & Management, 2011). Although such screening is important, not all hearing loss occurs at birth and not all hearing losses are detected by a newborn hearing screening. Moreover, some children in your class may have been born before infant screening was mandated in their home state.

You may be able to assist in identifying children in your classroom with hearing loss by being aware of the following warning signs:

- Daydreaming
- Inattention
- Behavior problems and frustration
- Lethargy
- Failure to follow simple verbal commands
- Using verbal expressions of misunderstanding (e.g., "Huh?" and "I don't know")
- Articulation errors
- Limited speech or vocabulary
- Inappropriate responses to questions
- Difficulties with verbal tasks
- Difficulty decoding phonetically
- Unusual voice quality (soft, nasal, high pitch, monotonal)
- Mouth breathing
- Persistent colds
- Watching other students for instructional cues

11.2.5 Instructional Guidelines and Accommodations for Students with Hearing Loss

If you have a student with hearing loss in your classroom, you become an important member of a team that will make educational decisions that will affect that child. In addition to you, the team can include a special education teacher specializing in hearing loss, a sign language interpreter, the student, the parents, a speech and language pathologist, an audiologist, and other resource personnel.

Using amplification

Depending on the nature and extent of the hearing loss, students may use a **hearing aid** or an **implant**, which is a device inserted into the ear through surgery. Such devices do not regenerate hearing but amplify or give the sensation of hearing.

Even a mild hearing loss can have significant educational effects if it is not recognized. Lauren Resnick, a first-grade teacher, commented that she was surprised at the difference hearing aids made for Rider, a student in her class who had a mild hearing loss. When Rider was not wearing his hearing aids, he was often off task or seemed uninterested in class activities. With his hearing aids, however, he functioned like the other students in the class.

Technological advances provide many options in hearing aid selection. In classroom situations, hearing aids do have limitations. They may amplify all sounds in the environment, and the student may hear other noises (background and reverberation) in addition to the desired signal such as the teacher's voice. Although some hearing aids can greatly reduce these problems, many considerations must be taken into account in selecting and fitting amplification devices for children. To help create an environment that provides an optimum listening environment for children with hearing loss, teachers should try to reduce background noise and decrease the listening distance of the student to the speaker.

Implants are increasingly being used for individuals who cannot benefit from the use of hearing aids. As with hearing aids, the success of implantation is very individual. Different types of implants serve different individual needs and functions (Hear-it Org, 2011):

- *Middle ear implants* are for individuals with conductive or mixed hearing loss; they are microphones that transmit sound from the middle to the inner ear.
- *Cochlear (inner ear) implants* are for individuals who are profoundly deaf; the devices provide a sensation of hearing.
- *Bone-anchored implants* are for a variety of hearing losses; they conduct sound from an implant in the skull behind the ear to the inner ear.
- *Auditory brainstem implants* are for individuals who do not have adequate auditory nerves; they are electrodes applied to the brain stem that provide electric signals, leading to a sense of hearing and resulting in support for lipreading.

Making classroom accommodations

Accommodations for students must be individualized. Tips for Teachers 11.3 provides you with some general guidelines to help you meet the needs of your students with hearing loss.

As you plan your lessons, think of the consistent use of visuals for students with hearing loss not only in terms of instruction but also with respect to classroom management. Rule charts, daily schedules, and task organizers can help students become full participants in ongoing activities.

Using assistive technology

This system creates a favorable signal-to-noise ratio and accessibility to teacher instruction. The American Speech-Language-Hearing Association points out that the number and variety of types of assistive technology are vast and growing due to recent advances (American Speech-Language-Hearing Association, 2009). Amplified answering machines

TIPS FOR TEACHERS 11.3

Accommodating Students with Hearing Loss

Provide Preferential Seating

- Minimize listening distance by having the student sit near you. Seat students away from loud noises (e.g., high-traffic areas, doors, air-conditioning and heating units).
- Make sure the student can see you, the interpreter, and visual aids clearly.
- Eliminate glare from windows or lights.
- Minimize environmental noise.
- Use carpets, rugs, cork, and curtains to help absorb noise.
- Avoid unnecessary background noise (e.g., music, hallway noise).

Use Visual Clues and Demonstrations

- Face the student directly when you talk.
- Use an interactive white board so that you can face the student while you write.
- Use natural gestures.
- Use modeling to demonstrate how to do different procedures and tasks.
- Use pictures, diagrams, and graphic organizers.
- Provide opportunities for experiential learning.

Maximize the Use of Visual Media

- Provide closed-captioned television (see Tips for Teachers 11.4).
- Provide access to computers.
- Monitor the student's understanding.
- Ask the student to repeat or rephrase important information or directions.
- Reword statements for clarification.
- Provide written instructions and summaries.

Promote Cooperation and Collaboration

- Use peer and classroom tutors and note takers.
- Identify speakers in a group discussion.
- Inform interpreters of topics before class, and provide study guides or teaching.

TIPS FOR TEACHERS 11.4

Using Closed Captioning

Closed captioning is the process of encoding dialogue and sound effects from a program into readable text at the bottom of the television screen (similar to the subtitles in foreign films). *Decoders* are devices that enable you to view the words in a closed-captioning program.

In 1993 the federal Television Circuitry Decoder Act (passed in 1990) took effect. Thanks to this act, all televisions marketed in the United States must be capable of decoding closed-captioned signals. With this development, one does not need a special captioning machine to view closed-captioned text. How does this apply to the classroom?

Today, many films and Internet resources are captioned and available for use in the classroom. When you order a film or video, find out whether you can order it captioned. For more information, contact the Described and Captioned Media Program.

and telephones, paging systems, and wake-up alarms are examples of devices that your student's audiologist may recommend for use.

In classroom situations, students often use assistive listening devices (ALDs) such as personal FM (frequency modulation) units (Plumley, 2008). With a *personal FM unit*, the teacher wears a wireless microphone, and the student wears a wireless receiver incorporated with a hearing aid. The microphone amplifies the teacher's voice 12 to 15 dB above the classroom noise and is not affected by distance. A *sound field system* may be another option for a student with hearing loss in the classroom (Wilson, Marinac, Pitty, & Burrows, 2011). The teacher wears a small wireless microphone, and speakers are placed in strategic locations within the class.

In addition to ALDs, visual systems can be used in classrooms to promote learning for students with hearing impairments. Emails can be used for teacher-to-student or student-to-student communication (Lynne, 2007). Computerized speech recognition where computers transform human speech to print can be used to assist with composition and communication. Closed captioning with a television and CDs can also be used to improve access to the curriculum (see Tips for Teachers 11.4).

MyEdLab
Video Example 11.2.
Listen as the interpreter discusses her role with a student who is deaf and their interactions throughout the day. How might a teacher design a lesson plan so that the interpreter could follow along and identify key concepts?

Using interpreters and note takers

Sign language interpreters and note takers are valuable resources in the classroom. It is important that students who use a sign language system have an interpreter in the educational setting. Although an interpreter facilitates communication between the teacher and the student, the interpreter is not a substitute for you (the classroom teacher). Students may at first rely on the interpreter for answers and guidance but will learn to shift their confidence to you.

To understand the information being presented, students need to be visually attentive. By permitting these students to photocopy your lecture notes or a classmate's notes or by providing duplicating paper to a peer note taker, you allow them to focus all their attention on what is taking place in the classroom. Peer or adult note takers and tutors can also help to clarify and explain topics, preteach vocabulary, or review technical terms.

MyEdLab **Self-Check 11.2**

MyEdLab **Application Exercise 11.2:** Students with Hearing Loss

11.3 STUDENTS WITH PHYSICAL DISABILITIES, HEALTH IMPAIRMENTS, AND TRAUMATIC BRAIN INJURY

Students with physical disabilities, health impairments, and traumatic brain injury are a small but diverse group. Disabilities can range from asthma, a comparatively mild condition, to cerebral palsy, which may involve neurological impairment that affects mobility and other functional skills, to traumatic brain injury, which can vary greatly in its effect on learning and daily functioning.

One of Lanetta Bridgewater's second-grade students, Emma, has cerebral palsy and is unable to speak but understands what others are saying and is developing academic skills at a rate similar to that of her classmates. In planning and working with Emma, Lanetta worked closely with Susie Speelman, an inclusion support teacher. Among the strategies Lanetta and Susie used to facilitate Emma's successful inclusion in Lanetta's classes were taking time to plan together, making the classroom more accessible for Emma and her wheelchair, using technology (particularly assistive devices to enable Emma to make choices and demonstrate her understanding), and reducing the amount of work (so that Emma has enough time to respond).

11.3.1 Definitions and Types of Physical Disabilities, Health Impairments, and Traumatic Brain Injury

Students with significant physical disabilities, health impairments, and traumatic brain injury generally qualify for special education services under three IDEIA categories: orthopedic impairment, other health impairment, and traumatic brain injury. Under IDEIA 2004, **orthopedic impairment** is defined as

> a severe orthopedic impairment that adversely affects a child's educational performance. The term includes impairments caused by congenital anomaly (e.g., clubfoot, absence of some member, etc.), impairments caused by disease (e.g., poliomyelitis, bone tuberculosis, etc.), and impairments from other causes (e.g., cerebral palsy, amputations, and fractures or burns that cause contractures). (IDEA 300.8[c][8])

Orthopedic impairments represent a wide range of conditions. They may not only interfere with the students' coordination and mobility, but also affect their ability to communicate, learn, and adjust. Orthopedic impairments are frequently referred to in education circles as **physical disabilities** (Turnbull, Turnbull, & Wehmeyer, 2010). The two general categories of physical disabilities are orthopedic impairments and neuromotor impairments (Heward, 2009). Orthopedic impairments are directly related to the skeletal system (e.g., bones, joints). **Neuromotor impairment** is an abnormal performance caused by a dysfunction of the brain, spinal cord, and nerves, thereby creating transmission of improper instructions, uncontrolled bursts of instructions from the brain, or incorrect interpretation of feedback to the brain (Pierangelo & Giuliani, 2007). Some types of neurological impairments are seizure disorders, cerebral palsy, and spina bifida. Neuromotor impairments can also involve both the nerves and the muscles. Muscular dystrophy, polio, and multiple sclerosis are examples of this type of physical disability. Although the cause of the physical impairment may vary from student to student, many of the challenges they face in movement are similar (Pierangelo & Giuliani, 2007).

IDEIA also provides special education services for students with other health impairments. **Other health impairment** is defined as

> having limited strength, vitality, or alertness, including a heightened alertness to environmental stimuli, that results in limited alertness with respect to the educational environment, that is due to chronic or acute health problems such as asthma, attention deficit disorder or attention deficit hyperactivity disorder, diabetes, epilepsy, a heart condition, hemophilia, lead poisoning, leukemia, nephritis, rheumatic fever, sickle cell anemia, and Tourette syndrome; and adversely affects academic performance. (IDEA 300.8 [c][9])

Students with health impairments are characterized by their chronic or acute health problems that result in limited strength, vitality, or alertness. Two subgroups of students with health impairments are medically fragile and/or technologically dependent individuals (Cohen et al., 2011; Heward, 2009). **Medically fragile** children are at risk for medical emergencies on a regular basis and may also have progressive diseases such as cancer or AIDS. **Technologically dependent** students often require life support or specialized support systems such as ventilators.

With the 1990 amendments to IDEA, traumatic brain injury was identified as a category of disability and defined as

> an acquired injury to the brain caused by an external physical force, resulting in total or partial functional disability or psychosocial impairment, or both, that adversely affects a child's education performance. The term applies to open or closed head injuries resulting in impairments in one or more areas, such as cognition; language; memory; attention; reasoning; abstract thinking; judgment; problem-solving; sensory, perceptual, and motor abilities; psychosocial behavior; physical functions; information processing; and speech. The term does not apply to brain injuries that are congenital or degenerative, or brain injuries induced by birth trauma. (IDEA 300.8[c][12])

Common causes of traumatic brain injuries are motorcycle, automobile, and off-road vehicle accidents; sports injuries; and accidents from violence, such as gunshot wounds and child abuse (Faul, Xu, Walk, & Coronado, 2010; Langlois, Rutland-Brown, & Thomas, 2006).

11.3.2 Characteristics of Students with Physical Disabilities, Health Impairments, and Traumatic Brain Injury

During your teaching career, you undoubtedly will have students with physical disabilities, health impairments, and traumatic brain injury. This section describes some of the more prevalent of these disabilities.

Asthma

The chronic health condition that your students are most likely to experience in your classroom is asthma. Asthma is a persistent inflammation of the air passages that causes episodes of difficulty in breathing (American Lung Association, 2011). Asthma is the most common chronic condition among children. The American Lung Association (2011) reports that approximately 7 million children 18 years and younger have asthma and that 14 million school days a year are lost due to the condition. Asthma can be caused by allergies, but can also be caused by nonallergic factors such as stress, viruses, and smoke (Akinbami, Moorman, Bailey et al., 2012). As a classroom teacher, you will want to learn what triggers an asthma attack (e.g., exercise, chalk dust, carpets, odors, or fumes), any dietary restrictions, and procedures to follow if an episode occurs.

Cerebral palsy

Students with cerebral palsy constitute one of the largest groups of children with physical disabilities (Boyle et al., 2011). Cerebral palsy is caused by damage to the brain before or during birth. Conditions are classified according to the areas affected and the types of symptoms. The degree of severity varies and is often evidenced by lack of coordination, speech disorders, motor problems, and extreme weakness. Cerebral palsy generally has accompanying problems in such areas as learning, vision, hearing, cognitive functioning, skin disorders (because of pressure sores), and social and emotional growth (United Cerebral Palsy, 2011). The condition can interfere with head control, arm use, sitting positions, balance, posture, and mobility, and these problems can be exacerbated by fatigue and stress.

As a classroom teacher of a student with cerebral palsy, you will want to be aware of the student's level of fatigue and stress. Paul Nichols, a high school math teacher, mentioned that his student, Allison, appeared stressed during tests, particularly if they were long or timed.

> I noticed that whenever we had a timed test with essays, Allison would have difficulty sitting up and holding up her head. At first I thought it was just a way for her to try to get out of the test, so I tried to be firm with her. When I spoke to the physical therapist, he

mentioned that she may be tired or stressed and then he taught her some relaxation techniques. She is doing better but it is still a difficult time for her. I did explain to her that the timed part was not as important as doing the work, so now I give her extended time by allowing her to finish the test with the special education teacher during her resource period.

Spina bifida

Spina bifida, a birth defect that occurs when the spinal cord fails to close properly, often causes paralysis of parts of the body but seldom affects intellectual functioning (Best, 2010; Spina Bifida Foundation, 2009). Most students with spina bifida walk with difficulty and lack complete bladder and bowel control. Some students need to use a catheter, which necessitates training in hygiene and extra time during the day to take care of the catheter. Generally, the school nurse or a special education teacher provides this training if it has not already been provided. This type of support is often provided by a paraprofessional.

Epilepsy

The most common neurological impairment in school-age children is seizure disorders, or epilepsy. Epilepsy is characterized by a tendency to have two or more seizures—sudden, excessive, spontaneous, and abnormal discharges of neurons accompanied by alteration in motor function, sensory function, or consciousness that were not caused by some known medical condition (Epilepsy Foundation, 2015).

There are two major types of seizures. Absence seizures (petit mal) are characterized by short lapses in consciousness. Students may appear inattentive and often do not realize that they are having seizures. Tonic–clonic seizures (grand mal) are characterized by convulsions followed by loss of consciousness. Usually, a tonic phase, in which the muscles are rigid, is followed by a clonic phase, in which the arms and legs jerk. Often the student loses consciousness and awakens disoriented and tired. Hallahan and colleagues (2012) note that seizures differ in the following dimensions: duration, frequency, onset, movements, causes, associated disabilities, and control (e.g., through medication). Talk with your student's family to learn more about what you might expect in terms of the nature and type of seizures your student experiences.

Although these seizures usually last less than 5 minutes, they can be a frightening event for you and your students. Tips for Teachers 11.5 provides some pointers for handling this type of seizure.

If a student in your class has this type of seizure disorder, be sure to help the other students in the classroom understand the condition and respond appropriately to the student.

Muscular dystrophy

Muscular dystrophy is a chronic disorder characterized by the weakening and wasting of the body's muscles. People with muscular dystrophy progressively lose their ability to

TIPS FOR TEACHERS 11.5

How to Respond to a Student Having a Tonic–Clonic (Grand Mal) Seizure

- Ease the student to the floor and clear the area around him or her.
- Put something soft under the student's head to keep it from banging on the floor.
- Do not interfere with the seizure. Turn the student gently on his or her side, but do not put anything in the student's mouth, and do not try to hold his or her tongue.
- Have someone stay with the student until he or she is fully awake.
- Allow the student to rest afterward.
- Seek emergency assistance if the seizure lasts longer than 5 minutes or if the student requests it.

walk and effectively use their arms and hands (Muscular Dystrophy Association, 2009). There is no cure for muscular dystrophy at this time, and the only prevention is genetic counseling (the condition appears to run in families). Helping the student maintain independence through regular physical therapy, exercise, and necessary physical aids is important. School personnel need to be careful not to lift or pull a student with muscular dystrophy by his or her arms, because doing so may cause dislocation of limbs. Most students with muscular dystrophy have a diminished ability to walk by the age of 10 to 14, and teachers should be alert for signs of fatigue (Heward, 2009).

HIV and AIDS

Human immunodeficiency virus (HIV) is a condition that infects and eventually destroys cells in the immune system that protect the body from disease. A viral infection transmitted through bodily fluids, HIV is responsible for acquired immunodeficiency syndrome (AIDS) (CDC, 2009a). Most children with HIV/AIDS contracted the disease through their mothers: either before or during birth or through breastfeeding (CDC, 2007; United Nations Programme on HIV/AIDS, 2010). Adolescents may contract HIV/AIDS through sexual activity (CDC, 2008; United Nations Programme on HIV/AIDS, 2010). Fortunately, advances in the diagnosis and treatment of HIV/AIDS are helping individuals with the disease to live longer and healthier lives (United Nations Programme on HIV/AIDS, 2010).

Students infected with HIV may eventually experience loss of stamina, developmental delays, motor problems, progressive neurological defects, repeated bacterial infections, psychological stresses, and death. HIV progresses through stages. In the latency stage, which generally lasts from 2 to 10 years in children, there are no outward symptoms. As the disease progresses through the middle stages, individuals experience a general weakening of the immune system, which results in persistent fevers and infections. In the final stages, opportunistic infections increase in frequency and severity.

A report by the World Health Organization (2013) recommends that students with the infection should receive the same opportunities for education as other children with chronic illnesses. Most school districts have established policies regarding the inclusion of students with HIV in general education classrooms. This includes policies on confidentiality and disclosure (WHO, 2013). If students in your classroom are identified as having HIV, consult with individuals knowledgeable about these policies and work with the special education teacher and school nurse in planning for these students. One important question to ask is how the condition currently affects the student's physical and mental health. Students whose frequent absences are due to recurrent infections might need a homebound teacher. Students may also exhibit anxiety about their condition, about visits to the doctor, or about facing death (WHO, 2013).

By knowing and adjusting to the student's capabilities, you enable the student to participate more fully and successfully in classroom activities. For example, Shirley Meeder, an eighth-grade social studies teacher, found that she could adapt assignments for Joey, a student in the middle stages of HIV, by reducing the amount of work required, giving him the option of listening to the textbook on tape, having a note taker, and letting Joey take tests orally. These modifications helped Joey deal with his limited stamina. The special education teacher helped Shirley provide many of these accommodations. When Joey suffered from a prolonged infection, he received homebound instruction so that he could keep up with his classmates.

You may not be informed that a student in your class has HIV. Therefore, taking precautions when coming in contact with blood or other bodily fluids of any student is wise (Marotz, 2015). Keep latex gloves available in case a student in your class has a cut or other injury.

Traumatic brain injury

Because traumatic brain injury may occur at different developmental stages, with a wide variety of severity and complexities and various responses to recovery, the characteristics and educational needs of these students are unique (Best, 2010). Key points to consider about the characteristics of individuals with traumatic brain injury are the following:

- The degree of initial recovery from the injury will vary widely and require frequent review of the student's IEP.
- Memory, attention, and executive function difficulties are common.
- Slowed processing of information and faulty reasoning are common.
- Preinjury skills may be preserved but are not predictive of new learning abilities.
- Lowered social inhibition and judgment, lowered impulse control, depression, and overestimation of abilities are typical.
- Less initiative and motivation are typical, as is general fatigue.
- Services and supports are often needed in at least four areas: cognition, speech and language, social and behavioral skills, and physical functioning.

For example, when Justin returned to high school 3 weeks after being in a car accident in which he sustained a head injury, Claudia Ruiz, his math teacher, immediately recognized the changes in his cognitive functioning. His response time was slower, and concepts that had been easy for him to grasp were fuzzy and required reteaching. Claudia worked with the special education teacher to identify key concepts for Justin to relearn and new concepts to be reinforced. Over the next 3 months, Claudia recognized a significant change in Justin's learning patterns. His response time quickened, and he was able to learn new concepts at a faster rate. During these first 3 months, Claudia stayed in especially close contact with the special education teacher and Justin's parents so that she could facilitate the recovery of his cognitive functioning.

The following are typical behaviors associated with traumatic brain injuries:

- Lowered social inhibition, judgment, and impulse control
- Faulty reasoning
- Numerous cognitive processing difficulties
- Lowered initiative and motivation
- Overestimation of abilities
- Depression
- Flat affect with sudden outbursts
- Agitation and irritability
- Fatigue

(Brain Injury Association of America, 2015; National Dissemination Center for Children with Disabilities, 2006).

MyEdLab
Video Example 11.3.
In this video, a general education teacher and a special education teacher discuss the inclusion of a kindergartener with a traumatic brain injury in their general education classes. As a general education teacher, how could you work with the special education teacher to ensure that a student with a traumatic brain injury makes both academic and social progress throughout the year? What signs of progress would you look for?

11.3.3 Prevalence of Students with Physical Disabilities, Health Impairments, and Traumatic Brain Injury

Despite advances in medical research and treatment, in some areas of chronic health conditions (such as asthma) prevalence figures are actually on the rise (van der Lee, Mokkink, Grootenhuis, Heymans, & Offringa, 2007; Winer, Qin, Harrington, Moorman, & Zahran, 2012). Depending on how chronic health conditions are defined, prevalence figures vary from 0.22% to 44% of children in the United States (van der Lee et al., 2007). To further complicate prevalence figures, students with physical disabilities or health impairments may be identified in the system under another disability category, including multiple disabilities. National Center for Education Statistics (2015) figures indicate that in the 2011–2012 school year approximately 61,000 students with orthopedic impairments and 743,000 students with other health impairments received special education services under IDEIA.

The most common cause of disability and death for persons 45 years of age and under is traumatic brain injury (Centers for Disease Control and Prevention, 2016;

Fowler & McCabe, 2011). Although approximately 475,000 children and adolescents sustain a brain injury each year (Fowler & McCabe, 2011), the number of students who receive services under IDEIA is substantially less, approximately 26,000 (NCES, 2010). The occurrence of traumatic brain injury increases dramatically during adolescence (15 to 24 years of age) owing to increased participation in contact sports, greater access to and use of automobiles and motorcycles, more frequent use of racing and mountain bikes, and injuries from firearms. Boys are two to three times more likely to receive head injuries than girls (Langlois et al., 2006; Mahapatra, Kumar, & Kamal, 2012).

11.3.4 Identification and Assessment of Students with Physical Disabilities, Health Impairments, and Traumatic Brain Injury

Medical diagnosis usually provides the initial identification of physical disabilities, health impairments, and traumatic brain injury. Assessments are carefully designed to take into account these students' potential for delayed motor skills or problems staying on task for long periods of time. Remember that, as a classroom teacher and a member of the education team, you are a valuable resource.

Depending on the student, assessments in the following areas are often appropriate:

- Activities of daily living (personal hygiene, eating, dressing, using public transportation)
- Attention, concentration, initiation, or sustained effort
- Adaptations for learning (academic and physical adaptations to help students achieve academic success and independence)
- Communication (students' ability to express and understand language)
- Mobility (students' current and potential range and mode of mobility)
- Physical abilities and limitations (positioning and necessary adaptive equipment and techniques that facilitate students' independence)
- Psychosocial development (effects of impairment on students' social and emotional functioning)
- Transition skills (skills needed for a successful transition into and from school and between grade levels)

11.3.5 Instructional Guidelines and Accommodations for Students with Physical Disabilities, Health Impairments, and Traumatic Brain Injury

Three basic principles can help you accommodate students with physical disabilities, health impairments, and traumatic brain injury in your classroom:

1. ***Use others as resources.*** Call on the expertise of the student, parents, other school personnel, and others in health-related professions, as well as the student's classmates.
2. ***Be flexible in your planning.*** Be willing to make last-minute changes in response to day-to-day changes in the student's condition and readiness to learn.
3. ***Be ingenious and creative.*** One of the greatest rewards from working with students is helping them discover their strengths and ways to demonstrate them.

Making environmental modifications

In addition to the necessary accessibility modifications (e.g., wide aisles for wheelchairs, low drinking fountains, appropriate handles), other environmental modifications facilitate independence for students with physical disabilities, health impairments, and traumatic brain injury. Wright and Bigge (1991) discuss four types of environmental modifications:

- Changes in location of materials and equipment (e.g., so that students in wheelchairs can reach items independently)
- Work surface modifications (e.g., raising a desk so that a wheelchair fits under it)
- Object modifications (e.g., attaching clips to a student's desk to secure papers)
- Manipulation aids (e.g., using a page turner to reduce dependency on others)

Providing instruction for motor skills

For students with physical disabilities, health impairments, and traumatic brain injury, working on motor skills is an important component of their education program. Many activities that support motor skills can be incorporated easily into daily classroom activities, such as increasing control by looking at a classmate during cooperative learning activities or improving fine motor skills by drawing or writing. The special education teacher, occupational therapist, physical therapist, and adaptive physical education teacher can be valuable resources in integrating instruction in motor skills into the curriculum.

Promoting literacy development

Promoting literacy development (reading, writing, listening, and speaking) is very important for individuals with physical disabilities (Browder, Lee, & Mims, 2011; Johnston, McDonnell, & Hawken, 2008). It provides students access to language, a means to communicate their ideas, and a way to increase their experiences and knowledge. It also provides a lifelong pleasurable activity.

Facilitating literacy development includes such suggestions as the following:

- ***Positioning.*** Adaptive wheelchairs or other seating devices may act as barriers to the students' ability to see print and pictures. Position students so that they can see the print and pictures while listening. This helps them begin to make the connection between print and speech. Ideally, students should be situated in a way that allows them to help turn the pages so that they begin to recognize the left-to-right orientation of text. Following the text with a finger or a bookmark also helps a person develop this concept.
- ***Siblings and peers.*** Because children with physical disabilities might not have the ability to question and retell a story, the inclusion of peers or siblings during storytime could help make the storytime livelier. Parents have reported that children related text to real-life activities and asked and answered a greater variety of questions when peers or siblings were present. The other children also act as models for the child with disabilities.
- ***Print in the environment.*** Having print everywhere in the students' environment is important. Remember that for students with physical disabilities the print needs to be at eye level based on their adaptive equipment.
- ***Accessing literacy.*** Students with disabilities need a method by which to independently access storybooks, writing instruments, and other literacy-related items. These could be books on tape, podcasts, or switches to access computer programs for reading, writing, and drawing. Drawing and writing can be made easier with adaptive holders for the writing utensil. Taping the paper down or stabilizing items with Velcro also helps the student draw or write. Tips for Teachers 11.6 provides more quick and easy ideas for helping students become more independent and successful.

Educating classmates

For students with health impairments and physical disabilities, some of the most important modifications relate to informing other students in the class. Classmates, particularly

TIPS FOR TEACHERS 11.6

Promoting Independence for Students with Physical Disabilities

- Retrace or enlarge print with a dark marker to help students see material more clearly.
- Schedule study buddies to help a student with disabilities gather learning materials.
- Assign a classmate or ask for a volunteer to take or copy notes for a student with disabilities.
- Ask students for whom writing is difficult whether they would prefer an oral assignment or test.
- Ask the special education teacher to provide (or advise you on acquiring) materials for securing small objects. Velcro and a Dycem mat on a student's desk prevent books, calculators, pencil boxes, and the like from slipping off.
- Ask parents to provide a bandanna or sweatband, worn on the wrist, to help a student with limited control of facial muscles wipe off excess saliva.
- Arrange with the special education teacher for the assistance of a paraprofessional in moving a student from a wheelchair to a beanbag chair during floor activities so that the student can be both supported physically and seated on the same level as peers.

of younger students with rare diseases or severe disabilities, will most likely have limited knowledge and many questions. For example, Sexson and Madan-Swain (1993) found that students most often asked the following questions about a classmate with a health problem:

- What's wrong with the student?
- Is the disease contagious?
- Will (the student) die from it?
- Will the student lose anything (such as limbs, hair)?
- Should we talk about the student's illness or ignore it?
- What will other students think if I'm still friends with this student?

It may also be helpful to talk about how a student might be different when he or she returns from a prolonged absence or a traumatic brain injury. Using children's and juvenile literature can help your students to learn about different disabilities and how to support a student with a specific physical or health-related impairment (Prater & Dyches, 2008; Rieger & McGrail, 2015).

Dealing with chronic illness and death

During your teaching career, you may have a student in your class who is dying. Children in your class may also experience a death of someone close to them: a friend, family member, teacher, classmate, or pet. Open communication with the student, parents, counselor, and other members of the education team becomes very important so that you can deal with the student's feelings and fears in a consistent and open manner. You may work directly with the school counselor, but you need written permission from parents before you can contact a student's private counselor or psychologist. You will also want to work with the school counselor as you develop a plan for communicating with and supporting classmates as they deal with the illness and/or death of a friend. There are abundant resources, including websites, to turn to so you can learn more about how to support children, their classmates, and their families (e.g., The Dougy Center, The National Alliance for Grieving Children).

Interviews with children who are cancer survivors shed light on the needs of children who have a chronic illness (Bessell, 2001). Students emphasized how important attending school was to their sense of normalcy. A caring and understanding teacher and the acceptance of their peers were seen as particularly important. Teachers who made accommodations for their special needs were viewed positively. Homebound instruction can be necessary when students are in treatment or otherwise unable to attend school.

If this is the case, Bessell recommends that teachers make every effort to "keep students in the loop." Using technologies such as email and Skype can assist in keeping the communication flowing.

For decades, it has been recognized that individuals can go through stages as they move toward accepting death (Berner, 1977; Cassini & Rogers, 1990; Kübler-Ross, 1969). Although not all children go through all stages and some stages may be experienced simultaneously, knowledge of these stages can help you understand the behaviors and emotions that may be exhibited by a student who is dying. Moreover, for children stages may not occur in a predictable order (Goldman, 2013). The stages include the following:

- Shock and disbelief
- Crying (sometimes hysterical)
- Feelings of isolation and loneliness
- Psychosomatic symptoms, which may distract the student from the fatal condition
- Panic
- Guilty feelings that he or she is to blame
- Hostility or resentment toward others
- Resistance to usual routines and continuing to live
- Reconciliation and beginning acceptance of the inevitability of death
- Acceptance

Although the suggestions in Table 11.1 are from parents of children with cancer (Candlelighters Childhood Cancer Foundation, 1993), many apply also to children with other life-threatening illnesses, such as HIV/AIDS and cystic fibrosis.

Finally, the loss of the child will be a loss for you as well. Make certain that you have identified a support network that can assist you as you cope with your own grieving process (Hunt & Munson, 2005).

As you work with students who have visual, hearing, physical, or health impairments, your repertoire of teaching strategies and knowledge of classroom accommodations

Table 11.1 • Parents' View: What Teachers Should and Should Not Do for a Student with Cancer

HELPFUL TEACHERS	LESS HELPFUL TEACHERS
• Take time to learn about the treatments and their effects on school performance.	• Fail to learn about the disease and its effects and treatments.
• Demonstrate support for parents as well as student.	• Show fear about having the student in class.
• Listen to parents' concerns and fears.	• Allow other students to pity the student.
• Call or visit during absences.	• Fail to keep ongoing communication with parents and student during absences.
• Encourage classmates to call or write during extended absences.	• Ignore problems classmates have in adjusting to friend's disease.
• Before reentry, talk with the student about any fears or concerns.	• Before reentry, fail to share information about the student and the disease with classmates.
• Adjust lessons and assignments based on the student's endurance.	• Do not give the student the benefit of the doubt on assignments and homework.
• Follow parental and medical instructions regarding snacks, wearing a hat, bathroom visits.	• Make an issue of the student's differences in front of others.
• Treat the student as normally as possible and include the student in as many class activities as possible.	• Do not give the student an opportunity to attempt what others are doing.

and assistive technology will grow. With the help of a number of specialists, who can assist both you and the student, you should feel confident of success in educating your students.

MyEdLab **Self-Check 11.3**

MyEdLab **Application Exercise 11.3:** Accommodations for Students with Physical Disabilities

11.4 STUDENTS WITH MULTIPLE OR DUAL SENSORY DISABILITIES

While the presence of any one disability can pose challenges to the academic and social success of your students, coping with multiple or dual sensory disabilities adds even greater complexity (De Bortoli, Balandin, Foreman, Mathisen, & Arthur-Kelly, 2012; Arthur-Kelly, Foreman, Bennett, & Pascoe, 2008). With appropriate supports, students who face such life challenges can participate in the general education classroom and have access to the general education curriculum (Downing, 2008; Horn & Kang, 2012).

11.4.1 Definitions of Multiple and Dual Sensory Disabilities

Individuals with **multiple disabilities** have disabilities that are severe or profound, as well as one or more significant motor or sensory impairments or special health needs. For example, a person with severe intellectual disabilities might also have cerebral palsy or epilepsy (Moeschler et al., 2014; Westling & Fox, 2009). Examples of multiple disabilities include intellectual disabilities with physical disabilities (e.g., cerebral palsy, spina bifida, seizure disorders), intellectual disabilities with severe behavior disorders, and intellectual disabilities with a visual or hearing impairment. IDEIA 2004 defines *multiple disabilities* as

> concomitant impairments (such as mental retardation–blindness, mental retardation–orthopedic impairments, etc.), the combination of which causes such severe educational needs that cannot be accommodated in special education programs solely for one of the impairments. The term does not include deaf–blindness. (IDEA 300.8 [c][7])

Like all students, students with multiple disabilities have learning needs that require a *holistic* approach to education (an approach in which the student is viewed as a whole person). In determining educational goals and teaching strategies, professionals consider factors such as the student's emotions, cognitive processes, and other factors that interact with the environment to produce behavior (Downing, 2002; Horn & Kang, 2012).

Students with **dual sensory impairments** (also referred to as **deaf–blind**) present unique challenges in that the two main channels (auditory and visual) of receptive communication and learning are impaired. Although difficult to determine, the cognitive abilities of students with dual sensory impairments can vary from severe intellectual disability to giftedness. The life and work of Helen Keller drew international and long-lived attention to the potential of individuals with dual sensory impairments. Individuals who are deaf–blind may have diverse combinations of vision and hearing impairments with normal or gifted intelligence, or they may have additional mental, physical, and behavioral disabilities (Downing & Eichinger, 2003; Orelove et al., 2004; Ronksley-Pavia, 2015). IDEIA 2004 defines deaf–blindness as follows:

> *Deaf–blindness* means concomitant hearing and visual impairments, the combination of which causes such severe communication and other developmental and education needs that they cannot be accommodated in special education programs solely for children with deafness or children with blindness. (IDEA 300.8 [c][2])

Because these individuals do not receive clear and consistent information from either sensory modality, a tendency exists to turn inward. These individuals may appear passive, not responding to or initiating interactions with others.

11.4.2 Characteristics of Students with Multiple or Dual Sensory Disabilities

Individual needs of students with multiple or dual sensory disabilities vary tremendously depending on the nature and degree of their disabilities. As a student's IEP is developed, attention will focus holistically on academic needs, but also supports warranted in terms of physical mobility, social skills, and life skills. One area of support that is common among many students with multiple and dual sensory disabilities is communication skills.

Communication is important for students with multiple and dual sensory disabilities because it gives them some control over their environment and a way to fulfill their wants and needs. It is also an important key to being socially accepted. They might not acquire speech, or their speech might be difficult to understand for people who do not interact with them often (Arthur-Kelly et al., 2008; De Bortoli et al., 2012). Yet it is important to realize that a lack of speech does not preclude communication.

Communication can occur through gestures, facial expressions, eye blinks, and behavior and through augmentative and alternative communication. Low-technology devices can involve pictures or drawings at which the student points to convey a message. High-technology devices can provide voice output (speech synthesizers) and can be programmed with many messages. Ideas to help students with developmental disabilities develop communication skills are discussed in Tips for Teachers 11.7.

Because students are unable to express their desires or dislikes verbally, they express them through their behavior. They often engage in isolated inappropriate behaviors such as stereotypic or self-injurious behaviors. **Stereotypic behaviors** include rocking, flapping fingers, twirling or spinning objects, and grinding teeth. **Self-injurious behavior** may consist of head banging, scratching, or self-biting and is difficult to understand. One of several theories about why children exhibit these behaviors is that they are a means of communicating or regulating the child's own level of awareness (Helmstetter & Durand, 1991; Johnson, Baumgart, Helmstetter, & Curry, 1996).

TIPS FOR TEACHERS 11.7

Helping Students Develop Communication Skills

- *Give students a reason to communicate.* By anticipating the needs of students with intellectual and severe disabilities, we often deprive them of reasons to communicate. Create situations that motivate students to communicate. For example, you might "accidentally" forget to give them their lunch tickets when the rest of the class receives their tickets, or have every student tell you about the drawing they just did before they can go out to recess. Working on communication skills during everyday activities is known to significantly increase students' desire to communicate.

- *Determine the best mode of communication.* Make sure that students have a way, as well as a reason, to communicate. If your students do not use speech, they should have an augmentative communication device. If your students do not have a mode of communication, talk with the school's speech and language pathologist or inclusion specialist about developing or purchasing one.
- *Give students a way to make choices.* Self-stick notes provide a quick and easy way to give students with disabilities on-the-spot choices (choosing a word to fill in the blank, choosing a color) to facilitate their participation in class. Just write the choices on the notes and stick them on the students' desks so that they can make the choices. To help students choose a partner, take pictures of all the students in the class (or use individual class photos) and paste them in a little book or on a board so that the student with a disability can choose the person with whom he or she wants to work on a class assignment.

11.4.3 Prevalence of Students with Multiple and Dual Sensory Disabilities

The National Center for Education Statistics (2015) reports that during the 2011–2012 school year, 132,000 students with multiple disabilities received services under IDEIA. The number of students with deaf–blindness was far less, only 2,000 students.

11.4.4 Instructional Guidelines and Accommodations for Students with Multiple and Dual Sensory Disabilities

Because many students with multiple and dual sensory disabilities receive services from special education teachers and a variety of specialists (e.g., occupational or physical therapist, an adaptive physical education teacher, speech and language pathologist), effective teaming and communication are crucial (Downing, 2008). In **transdisciplinary teaming**, all members of the team work together and view the student holistically instead of working only on their area of specialty (Copeley & Ziviani, 2005; Orelove et al., 2004). Family members are also critical members of the team. All team members are aware of the student's goals and observe one another as they work with the student so that they can share and generalize successful techniques and strategies.

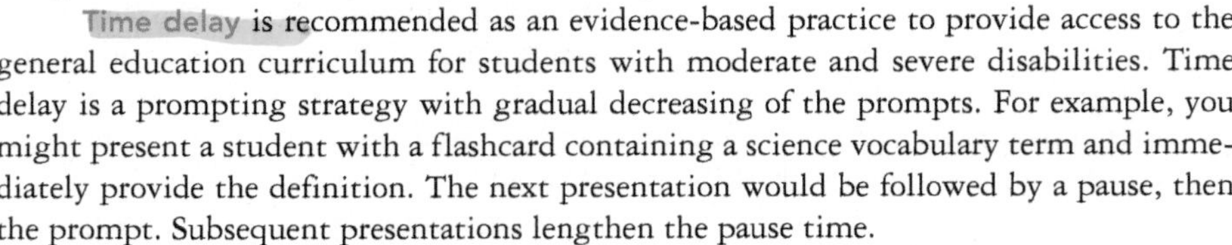

Time delay is recommended as an evidence-based practice to provide access to the general education curriculum for students with moderate and severe disabilities. Time delay is a prompting strategy with gradual decreasing of the prompts. For example, you might present a student with a flashcard containing a science vocabulary term and immediately provide the definition. The next presentation would be followed by a pause, then the prompt. Subsequent presentations lengthen the pause time.

Using assistive technology

The 2004 reauthorization of IDEA defines **assistive technology** as "any item, piece of equipment, or product system whether acquired commercially off the shelf, modified, or customized, that is used to increase, maintain, or improve functional capabilities of individuals with disabilities" (P.L. No. 108-466, Part A, Sec. 602, pp. 11–12). Assistive technology devices are particularly useful for increasing mobility, improving communication, gaining access to computers, performing daily living skills, enhancing learning, and manipulating and controlling the environment (Beard, Carpenter, & Johnston, 2011; Bryant & Bryant, 2011; Dell, Newton, & Petroff, 2011). By using such assistive technology as eye-gaze pointing, communication boards, and writing implements encased in plastic tubing or bicycle handle grips, for example, Lanetta's student, Emma, described earlier, is able to participate more fully in classroom life. The implementation of any assistive technology should be based on student needs as identified on the IEP. In thinking about the use of technology and assistive technology, consider these points (Bryant & Bryant, 2011; Green, 2011; Marino, Marino, & Shaw, 2006):

- Determine the people who are responsible for assistive technology at your school, district, or region and use them as resources.
- Check your school district policy on using equipment at home and on maintaining and repairing equipment.
- Ask for training on the equipment that your student will be using.
- Collaborate with others to share your knowledge and learn from them.

See the Tech Tips, "Assistive Technologies for Students with Lower-Incidence Disabilities," for more information on using these technologies.

TECH TIPS

Assistive Technologies for Students with Lower-Incidence Disabilities

When you are teaching children with special needs, you will make accommodations, based on individual needs, to enable those learners to accomplish the same work as their classmates who do not have disabilities. The computer empowers these children, more than any other population, to accomplish the same work in general education classes as their peers without disabilities. With appropriate accommodations, barriers to the general education curriculum imposed by a disability can be minimized or even eliminated. The following are suggestions.

Alternative Input

ALTERNATIVE KEYBOARDS

Big Keys (preschool ABC or QWERTY) (www.bigkeys.com)

FrogPad (one-handed) (www.frogpad.com)

Little Fingers (for small hands) (www.datadesktech.com)

PROGRAMMABLE KEYBOARD

IntelliKeys (six standard plug-and-play overlays, plus opportunities for customization) (www.ablenetinc.com)

ALTERNATIVE MOUSE DEVICES. For students unable to use a standard mouse device, explore small standard mouse, large and small trackball, trackpad, joystick device, and touch screen.

SINGLE SWITCHES. Activated by a single deliberate motion, switches offer full access to computers for persons unable to use any keyboard or mouse device. See the following sites for switches, switch interfaces, and switch software.

(enablingdevices.com)

(www.enablemart.com)

(www.ablenetinc.com)

(www.rjcooper.com)

SPEECH RECOGNITION (BOTH MACINTOSH AND WINDOWS)

(http://www.nuance.com)

ALTERNATIVE OUTPUT

Screen Magnification

(www.magnifiers.org)

SCREEN READER

Window-Eyes Windows

(www.gwmicro.com)

iPad/iPod" applications include:

- VoiceOver screen reader—built into iPad

MyEdLab **Self-Check 11.4**

MyEdLab **Application Exercise 11.4:** Students with Multiple and Dual Sensory Disabilities

11 SUMMARY

- Legal definitions of visual impairments are based on visual acuity and visual fields. Educational definitions are based on the student's ability to perform academic tasks. It is important when planning for a student with a visual impairment to consider the student's functional vision and to consider auditory, tactile, and visual accommodations.
- Definitions of hearing impairment include individuals who are deaf and those who are hard of hearing. Although most children with significant hearing loss are identified before beginning school, it is important to watch for signs of mild hearing loss. Arranging the classroom to reduce background noise and using interpreters and note takers provide means for students with hearing loss to better access the general education curriculum.
- Students who have physical disabilities, health impairments, and traumatic brain injury may need environmental modifications such as changes in location of materials, work surface modifications, object modification, and manipulation aids.
- When working with any students with disabilities, you will want to collaborate with specialists such as physical and occupational therapists, speech and language pathologists, assistive technology specialists, and school nurses and other medical professionals to develop a holistic approach to provide an optimal educational experience. This is particularly true for students with multiple and dual sensory disabilities.

THINK AND APPLY

1. In the opening interview, Peggy Kirkland was afraid that she lacked the knowledge and experience to work with students like Kerri. What systems are in place to help Peggy? Make a list of your questions, the people you would ask, and the meetings or activities you would plan before a student with disabilities joins your class.
2. Draw a diagram of a classroom. Indicate accommodations you might need to make for a student who is blind and for a student with a wheelchair.
3. Interview and observe a speech and a hearing specialist. Find out about the students with whom they work, their roles and responsibilities, and how they team with general classroom teachers.
4. Interview several adolescents or young adults with a physical disability, health impairment, or traumatic brain injury. Ask the following questions:
   - What impact does (the disability) have on your daily life?
   - How do your routines differ because of (the disability)?
   - How do others react to your disability?
   - What advice would you give classroom teachers about helping other students with (the disability)?

12 Differentiating Instruction and Assessment for All Learners

Learning Outcomes

12.1 Describe the standards-based movement and the challenges presented to teachers.

12.2 Identify several ways differentiated instruction can be implemented in classrooms.

12.3 List approaches you can use to assess the strengths and weaknesses of your textbook and differentiate reading assignments for students with reading difficulties.

12.4 Explain ways to differentiate assessment to meet the needs of all learners.

INTERVIEW: STEPHANIE BLUM AND CHRISTINE SHENG

"Our collaboration is much like a marriage. We spend more awake time with each other than our families. We think in terms of 'WE.' " In essence, this is how Stephanie Blum and Christine Sheng describe their co-teaching partnership of 7 years. They were matched during Stephanie's fifteenth year as a special educator and Christine's first year as a science teacher. When you come to the door of their classroom at Zelda Glazer Middle School in Miami, Florida, both names are on the door. They are equal partners.

Stephanie and Christine approach co-teaching as an opportunity to learn. Stephanie (whom students refer to as a learning specialist) has learned more about science curriculum; Christine has learned more about classroom management and adaptations for students with disabilities. They attribute their success to respectful and ongoing communication, ability to "adjust as we go," and a sense of humor.

Their eighth-grade science classes include students with disabilities as well as English language learners. State standards, local curriculum benchmarks, and a local pacing guide for content coverage determine their curriculum. This school year was particularly challenging in that a new science textbook was adopted that was aligned with the state's high-stakes test in science. Although Stephanie has noticed over the years that they are seeing fewer students with reading difficulties due to early intervention, they still face students with a range of learning needs in their classroom.

One aspect of their partnership that is particularly important is having a united front with regard to assessment. In preparing students for the high-stakes science assessment, Christine focuses on content and Stephanie focuses on teaching test-taking and study skills. Given that the science test involves math and reading as well as science content, they need to address gaps in these areas for some students. Grades are determined jointly and both are involved in the grading process. They jointly decide on alternate assessments, when needed. The products may vary based on individual needs—some might need to demonstrate what they know verbally rather than on paper. Others may need to diagram or draw what they know.

Introduction

Though it now seems almost effortless, many of the challenges encountered by all teachers working together in a co-teaching situation are ones that Stephanie and Christine have experienced. For many teachers, striking a balance between somewhat conflicting demands of meeting the needs of typical and advanced learners while also the special needs of students with disabilities can be daunting. This chapter begins with a discussion of the standards-based movement (e.g., Common Core State Standards) and the challenges it brings to teachers. Next, the chapter provides a definition of differentiated instruction and why it is necessary in today's diverse classrooms. It continues with concrete suggestions for preparing lessons and textbook readings that can accommodate a range of student needs. Finally, the chapter provides information about how you can differentiate assessment.

CHAPTER OUTLINE

12.1 STANDARDS-BASED INSTRUCTION

Like Stephanie and Christine in the opening interview, teachers are required to plan their instruction according to a set of standards determined by state or school district curriculum frameworks. Educational standards "are learning goals for what students should know and be able to do at each grade level" (Common Core State Standards Initiative, 2010). Some states also adopt benchmarks or specific student behaviors that indicate they have mastered a particular standard.

The standards movement was ignited by the 1983 report of the National Commission on Excellence in Education titled *A Nation at Risk*, which brought public attention to the state of education in the United States (Guthrie & Springer, 2014). With the authorization of No Child Left Behind (2001), individual states adopted curriculum standards for school subjects. State and local curriculum standards are typically more detailed versions of professional standards (Trujillo & Howe, 2015; Vacca, Vacca, & Mraz, 2011). In the past, these state standards varied widely in terms of content and rigor (Peterson & Hess, 2008). To rectify this variability, the National Governors Association Center for Best Practices (NGA Center) and the Council of Chief State School Officers (CCSSO) launched a state-led effort to draft Common Core State Standards in the areas of English language arts and reading (ELAR) and mathematics. Teacher organizations (e.g., National Education Association, American Federation of Teachers), professional organizations (e.g., Council for Exceptional Children, National Council of Teachers of Mathematics, National Council of Teachers of English), and parent organizations (e.g., National Parent Teacher Association) collaborated to develop the standards. Although controversial, the earlier report and release of the standards have prompted school reform (Butler, 2014; Guthrie & Springer, 2014; Marzano & Haystead, 2008; Trujillo & Howe, 2015). Standards are intended to bring coherence and comprehensiveness to curricula and serve as curricular frameworks.

12.1.1 The Release of the Common Core State Standards

NGA and CCSSO released the standards in 2010, and since that time, the majority of states have adopted them. To date, forty-two states have adopted the standards. In addition, states are developing policies and procedures for implementing the standards to students with disabilities and students who are English language learners. See the Common Core State Standards at www.corestandards.org for updates.

Figure 12.1 presents examples of Common Core Standards for sixth-grade ELAR and mathematics.

Potential benefits of the standards

The potential benefits of having uniform standards across states include: having shared expectations for student performance, improved curricular focus, greater efficiency in development of materials and teacher preparation, and improved quality of assessments (Porter et al., 2011). Proponents also pose that standards can form the basis for differentiating instruction based on individual student performance in relationship to each standard (Cooper & Kiger, 2009).

The intent of the Common Core State Standards is to offer rigor and depth to the curriculum to better prepare students in the United States for college and careers in adulthood.

Potential drawbacks to the standards

Critics of previous iterations of state standards argued that authentic learning and student engagement were dwindling (Certo, Cauley, Moxley, & Chafin, 2008). Some educators and students argued that standards are too high for some students and not high enough for others (Matus, 2009; Viadero, 2007). Still others observed that because of the sometimes-excessive number of standards, content coverage is gained while in-depth inquiry is

FIGURE 12.1 Sample Common Core State Standards for grade 6

Reading Standards for Literature

Key Ideas and Details

1. Cite textual evidence to support analysis of what the text says explicitly as well as inferences drawn from the text.
2. Determine a theme or central idea of a text and how it is conveyed through particular details; provide a summary of the text distinct from personal opinions or judgments.
3. Describe how a particular story's or drama's plot unfolds in a series of episodes as well as how the characters respond or change as the plot moves toward a resolution.

Craft and Structure

4. Determine the meaning of words and phrases as they are used in a text, including figurative and connotative meanings; analyze the impact of a specific word choice on meaning and tone.
5. Analyze how a particular sentence, chapter, scene, or stanza fits into the overall structure of a text and contributes to the development of the theme, setting, or plot.
6. Explain how an author develops the point of view of the narrator or speaker in a text.

Integration of Knowledge and Ideas

7. Compare and contrast the experience of reading a story, drama, or poem to listening to or viewing an audio, video, or live version of the text, including contrasting what they "see" and "hear" when reading the text to what they perceive when they listen or watch.
8. (Not applicable to literature)
9. Compare and contrast texts in different forms or genres (e.g., stories and poems; historical novels and fantasy stories) in terms of their approaches to similar themes and topics.

Range of Reading and Level of Text Complexity

10. By the end of the year, read and comprehend literature, including stories, dramas, and poems, in the grades 6–8 text complexity bands proficiently, with scaffolding as needed at the high end of the range.

Reading Standards for Informational Text

Key Ideas and Details

1. Cite textual evidence to support analysis of what the text says explicitly as well as inferences drawn from the text.
2. Determine a central idea of a text and how it is conveyed through particular details; provide a summary of the text distinct from personal opinions or judgments.
3. Analyze in detail how a key individual, event, or idea is introduced, illustrated, and elaborated in a text (e.g., through examples or anecdotes).

Craft and Structure

4. Determine the meaning of words and phrases as they are used in a text, including figurative, connotative, and technical meanings.
5. Analyze how a particular sentence, paragraph, chapter, or section fits into the overall structure of a text and contributes to the development of the ideas.
6. Determine an author's point of view or purpose in a text and explain how it is conveyed in the text.

Integration of Knowledge and Ideas

7. Integrate information presented in different media or formats (e.g., visually, quantitatively) as well as in words to develop a coherent understanding of a topic or issue.
8. Trace and evaluate the argument and specific claims in a text, distinguishing claims that are supported by reasons and evidence from claims that are not.
9. Compare and contrast one author's presentation of events with that of another (e.g., a memoir written by and a biography on the same person).

Range of Reading and Level of Text Complexity

10. By the end of the year, read and comprehend literary nonfiction in the grades 6–8 text complexity band proficiently, with scaffolding as needed at the high end of the range.

Mathematics

Ratios and Proportional Relationships

- Understand ratio concepts and use ratio reasoning to solve problems.

The Number System

- Apply and extend previous understandings of multiplication and division to divide fractions by fractions.
- Compute fluently with multi-digit numbers and find common factors and multiples.
- Apply and extend previous understandings of numbers to the system of rational numbers.

Expressions and Equations

- Apply and extend previous understandings of arithmetic to algebraic expressions.
- Reason about and solve one-variable equations and inequalities.
- Represent and analyze quantitative relationships between dependent and independent variables.

Geometry

- Solve real-world and mathematical problems involving area, surface area, and volume.

Statistics and Probability

- Develop understanding of statistical variability.
- Summarize and describe distributions.

Mathematical Practices

1. Make sense of problems and persevere in solving them.
2. Reason abstractly and quantitatively.
3. Construct viable arguments and critique the reasoning of others.
4. Model with mathematics.
5. Use appropriate tools strategically.
6. Attend to precision.
7. Look for and make use of structure.
8. Look for and express regularity in repeated reasoning.

Source: Common Core State Standards Initiative, retrieved from http://www.corestandards.org.

TIPS FOR TEACHERS 12.1

Making Standards-Based Instruction Work for You

1. Select—choose the standard you want to address.
2. Adopt or Adapt:
   - Adopt—use the standard as is to serve as the framework for your planning.
   - Adapt—adapt the standard to meet the needs of your students (e.g., teach one part of the standard, plan for adaptations for students with diverse needs).
3. Invent—use multiple resources to create innovative ways to address the standard in terms of lessons, assignments, and student assessment.
4. Assess—evaluate your approach to inform future planning.

Source: Information from *Connecting standards and assessment through literacy* by M. Conley, 2005, Boston: Allyn & Bacon.

lost (Certo et al., 2008; Marzano & Haystead, 2008). Time will tell whether or not the Common Core State Standards ameliorate these concerns.

12.1.2 Implementation of the Common Core State Standards

Tricia Ruf teaches mathematics and science at Lusher Charter School in New Orleans. Lusher is a K–12 school with an emphasis on art-based education. The school also has a strong environmental curriculum as well. Given that Lusher is a public school, teachers are responsible for teaching state standards and following a pacing guide for teaching and assessing curricular benchmarks. Tricia and her colleagues face the challenge of connecting state standards with the art-based school theme. How does Tricia do it?

Tricia explains that she plans collaboratively with other teachers at her grade level. They share resources and, at times, go "round robin" with labs and center activities. In other words, children go from teacher to teacher and experience as many as five labs during the math/science block. The teachers start their planning by determining what standard needs to be taught (such as arrays in multiplication) and then brainstorm and scour resources to link them to art or environmental themes. In the case of arrays, they came up with using the artwork of Andy Warhol. They used soup cans to demonstrate a mathematical array (for example, using 24 cans for an 8 × 3 array). The culminating project was that students created their own Andy Warhol–like array using pop-culture artifacts. Tips for Teachers 12.1 provides additional suggestions for how to make standards-based instruction work for you.

In addition, you will want to communicate the standards clearly to your students so that they will know what you expect them to learn. Marzano (2011) recommends that teachers have students express what they are expected to learn in their own words.

MyEdLab **Self-Check 12.1**

MyEdLab **Application Exercise 12.1:** Standards-Based Instruction

12.2 DIFFERENTIATING INSTRUCTION

Classrooms have students with a wide range of needs and abilities. The increased focus on inclusion of students with disabilities and students identified as gifted and talented in the general education classroom, as well as increased cultural and linguistic diversity, have increased the need to address the needs of a wide range of students.

In addition to issues related to individual student differences, there are a host of issues that can impact student success, including:

- Students' interests influence their content-area learning.
- Students' cultural backgrounds and prior knowledge influence their success learning a new content area.
- Foundation skills in reading, writing, and mathematics affect their access to deeper learning.
- The pace of instruction is too fast for some students and too slow for others.
- The level of conceptual complexity and density in some content areas is overwhelming for some students.
- Textbooks in content-area classes can be dull and encyclopedic.
- Content-area classes require both regular homework and assignments and long-term projects.
- Taking tests is a required component of many content-area classes.

One means to plan for individual student needs is differentiated instruction (DI). This section provides answers to questions teachers typically pose about DI:

- What is differentiated instruction?
- How can I differentiate assignments and homework to meet the learning needs of all of my students?
- How can I plan for differentiated instruction?
- How can I accommodate students who are gifted and talented?
- How can I differentiate instruction and still meet the ambitious goals of state standards?
- How does differentiated instruction relate to response to intervention?

12.2.1 What Is Differentiated Instruction?

The call for DI has come from a number of fields, including reading, special education, gifted education, teaching English as a second language, and multiple intelligences (Schumm & Avalos, 2009; Tomlinson, 2014). Consequently, a number of definitions for differentiated instruction have evolved and teachers often have misconceptions about what it is and what it entails. Schumm and Avalos (2009) offer the follow basic components of differentiated instruction:

- Differentiated instruction is both a philosophy of instructing students based on individual needs as well as instructional practices aligned with the philosophy.
- Differentiated instruction draws on a wide variety of practices (some research based, some not).
- Differentiated instruction at the secondary level can occur not only in the general education classroom, but also in advanced placement classes, resource rooms, or pull-out settings.

Carol Tomlinson, an expert in differentiated instruction, offers the following definition:

> A differentiated classroom offers a variety of learning options designed to tap into different readiness levels, interests, and learning profiles. In a differentiated class, the teacher uses (1) a variety of ways for students to explore curriculum content, (2) a variety of sense-making activities or processes through which students can come to understand and "own" information and ideas, and (3) a variety of options through which students can demonstrate or exhibit what they have learned. (Tomlinson, 2005, p. 1)

12.2.2 Components of Differentiated Instruction

Tomlinson (2008, 2014) identifies four key elements for teachers to consider in planning for differentiated instruction: content, process, products, and learning environment.

1. ***Content.*** What curriculum standards or benchmarks need to be taught? How can I sequence the components of the standard or benchmark in a way that is developmentally appropriate for each of my students?
2. ***Process.*** What activities and learning experiences will I plan to help each student master the standard or benchmark?
3. ***Products.*** What products will students provide that will demonstrate their mastery of the standard or benchmark?
4. ***Learning environment.*** How can I organize the classroom environment to active learning and student engagement?

Another way of thinking about differentiated instruction is that it involves curriculum enhancement and curriculum modification (Alquraini, Turki, & Gut, 2012). Curriculum enhancement involves no changes to the curriculum, and instead involves instructional strategies that make learning accessible for a wide range of students. For example, preteaching vocabulary and using graphic organizers are examples of curriculum enhancers.

Curriculum modification is more complex and is targeted to the individual needs of students. It includes both accommodation and adaptation. Accommodation involves no changes in curriculum requirements for students, but may involve modifications to how the material is presented and what is required of the student. For example, a student with learning disabilities might listen to an audiotaped version of a science textbook rather than completing the reading assignment. The student would take the same test as his or her peers, but in an oral format. Adaptations go one step further in that curriculum requirements might be altered. For instance, if students are working on a three-point essay in language arts class, a student with identified difficulties in writing may be assigned a paragraph writing activity. Accommodations and adaptations are more time consuming for teachers, but are critical for providing students with the support they need to succeed (Koga & Hall, 2004).

A learning contract is one mechanism for organizing DI. Learning contracts are particularly helpful when planning long-term assignments and research projects. With a learning contract, you identify target standards or objectives and then negotiate with students about the pathways and products they will produce to determine mastery.

12.2.3 Differentiated Instructing Using Flexible Grouping

As you implement DI in your classroom, you will want to plan for a variety of grouping patterns. Group size and membership should be flexible, with formats that change according to the goals of the lesson as well as your students' characteristics. Multiple grouping formats refer to a variety of grouping patterns.

Some schools group students by achievement level and others form mixed-ability classrooms. Quite often the decision of how to organize classes is a school or district decision. Even in "same-ability" classes, however, you will quickly note that students in your class have a range of differences to which you need to attend.

Two basic variables determine grouping patterns:

1. They can be categorized by group size: whole class, small group, pairs, and single student.
2. Group composition may be homogeneous grouping (students at similar achievement levels) or heterogeneous grouping (students at a wide range of achievement levels).

What might be some advantages of working in cooperative learning groups for students with special needs? What can teachers do to ensure that all group members get the most out of their group activity?

Depending on the purpose of the learning activity, you can branch beyond these two basic variables and group students by interest, skills to be learned, or prior knowledge of a topic. To mix things up a bit, you may give students time to create their own small groups for activities, such as discussing with classmates the books they read independently over the weekend.

For multiple grouping structures to be successful, careful planning is essential. The temptation becomes not to group at all, but instead to fall into the pattern of whole-class teaching followed by individual practice. As you think about a lesson, keep grouping in mind by asking yourself the following questions:

- What is the best grouping structure for teaching this lesson (e.g., small group, pairs, individual learning opportunities)?
- What is the best group size for follow-up activities (e.g., small groups of three to five, larger groups of six to eight)?
- What is the best composition of learners for each group with respect to student academic ability and work habits?
- What materials are needed for each group?
- Will the groups be teacher-led, student-led, or cooperative?
- What room arrangement is necessary for the grouping plan?
- When students move from one group to another, how can I ensure a quick and smooth transition?
- What issues related to students' behavior and social needs should I consider?

If you decide to have your students work cooperatively in small groups or in pairs, students may need explicit instruction in how to work together. In cooperative learning groups, students work together toward a common goal, usually to help one another learn academic material (Slavin, 2011; Vaca, Lapp, & Fisher, 2011). Working collaboratively, students must learn such lessons as how to give and receive help, how to listen and respond to the ideas of others, and how to complete a task as a team. Fundamental to the cooperative group is that all students participate and benefit—not that one or two students do all of the work. Teachers cannot assume that students (even in secondary settings) automatically know how to work in groups (Vaca et al., 2011). Most of the time, these skills need to be taught explicitly and practiced, just like skills in any other academic area. In addition, teachers should assess both group and individual participation and products.

12.2.4 Using Learning Stations to Differentiate Instruction

Learning stations or learning centers can be helpful in facilitating differentiated instruction at both elementary and secondary levels (Prevatte, 2007). Mykel Warren uses what she calls literacy stations during her reading/language arts block for her fourth graders. While Mykel works with one of her five guided reading groups, the other four groups work at computer, writing, skill practice, or vocabulary stations.

Hector Ruiz teaches eighth-grade mathematics. In the block scheduling at his middle school he sees each section of students for 2 hours every other day. The first hour is typically devoted to whole-class activities. During the second hour, students work in learning stations to practice previously taught curricular objectives, work in collaborative learning groups to solve math word problems, work on the computer with lessons based on individual needs, or work with Hector for reteaching of challenging new material. One center that students particularly like is the "Everyday Math" center, where Hector plans activities aligned with current instructional objectives and their application to relevant activities in students' lives.

Both Mykel and Hector recognize that in addition to providing students with opportunities for practice, exploration, and creativity, learning stations also help students learn how to work independently and cooperatively with their peers (Ediger, 2011). Both agree that the key to success of learning stations is to set clear expectations for student behavior and academic products are set. In addition, students need to feel they understand and can carry out the directions for working in the station. For more complex activities, Mykel and Hector recommend that teachers do a mini-demonstration before students go to the station.

The possibilities for learning stations are vast. General or special education teachers, paraeducators, volunteers, or students can lead stations. Stations can involve a wide range of technology applications. Stations can be routine (such as completing reading comprehension practice books) or can be topical (related to a specific objective being taught or reviewed). Stations can have set products to demonstrate student work or provide students with choices about how they will demonstrate their learning. Online resources for planning learning stations are readily available. For example, several websites such as Florida Center for Reading Research (www.FCRR.org) and The Meadows Center for Preventing Educational Risk (www.meadowscenter.org) provide teacher-developed learning center activities for elementary and secondary grades. Nonetheless, planning for efficient and effective learning stations takes time—and creativity. Tips for Teachers 12.2 provides a checklist for planning your learning stations.

Differentiating instruction is not easy. Stetson, Stetson, and Anderson (2007) followed a group of forty-eight teachers as they implemented DI for a year. Teachers reported that the benefits of DI in terms of student learning far outweighed the negative aspects. For teachers who have never experienced or seen DI firsthand, implementation can be tough. In addition, planning time can be an impediment. For those new to DI, Hall, Strangman, and Meyer (2011) recommend that you start out slowly, plan collaboratively, and seek out resources. Also, when you implement DI, survey your students about the types of differentiated learning experiences that help them learn and that they prefer (Kanevksy, 2011).

12.2.5 How Can I Differentiate Assignments and Homework?

Students' success or failure is often based on their performance on assignments and homework. But what about students with learning and behavior problems? Should they have

TIPS FOR TEACHERS 12.2

Checklist for Learning Stations

_____ Aligns with previously learned material so students can practice or extend learning.

_____ Provides a meaningful connection so students know why they are working in the learning station.

_____ Provides a task that can be modified to address a range of learners so all students can participate.

_____ The task can be completed during the designated work time—ranging from 15 to 20 minutes for primary students and 20 to 40 minutes for older learners.

_____ Provides feedback or correction so students quickly know how successful they were with their task.

_____ Provides adaptations for students who may have difficulty with the task.

the same assignments and tests as everyone else? What if a student cannot read? What if a student cannot work under timed conditions? What if a student has problems with attention and task completion?

Teacher surveys, interviews, and classroom observations indicate that teachers of all grade levels (elementary through high school) do not often make individual adaptations to homework, assignments, and tests (Ness, 2008; Schumm & Vaughn, 1991, 1992; Schumm et al., 1995). Constructing individual assignments and tests may not be feasible on a day-to-day basis and may not even be necessary.

Few topics in education generate as much heated discussion as homework (Vatterott, 2011). Whereas some argue that homework can be beneficial for all students in terms of reinforcing what was learned in school and in developing personal responsibility as a student (Marzaano & Pickering, 2007), others maintain that research evidence for homework (other than for secondary students) simply does not exist (Kohn, 2007). What is the evidence in favor of homework? At the middle and high school level, the amount of homework assigned is related to achievement, but this relationship is not significant at the elementary level (Cooper, Robinson, & Patall, 2006). However, there may be other attributes resulting from homework such as persistence, organization, and self-regulation.

It is likely that the school you work in will have a homework policy and it will be important to understand how this policy relates to individuals with disabilities so you can communicate that policy to students and their families. But there is more you can do to make assignments clear and comprehensible. Decades of research indicate that homework assignments for students with disabilities should be brief, focused on reinforcement of old material rather than new material, monitored carefully, and supported through parental involvement (Cooper, 2007; Cooper & Nye, 1994; Lynch, Theodore, Bray, & Kehle, 2009).

In no cases should homework involve practicing skills that were not addressed in class. This can only result in frustration for parents, students, and ultimately you. In their article entitled "High Quality Homework," Frey and Fisher (2011) list four primary purposes for homework. Keeping these purposes in mind will facilitate success for all students.

1. Developing fluency with skills and concepts already learned
2. Applying what they have learned to new situations
3. Reviewing previously learned skills and concepts
4. Extending what they know through research and other project-based activities

Class assignments and homework can be adapted for special learners so that they can experience success without undue attention being brought to their learning difficulties. The key to success is to make assignments appropriate in content, length, time required to complete, and skill level needed to accomplish the task (Warger, 2011). It is also important that students know how and where to get help when they get stuck.

The Center for Applied Special Technology (CAST) has developed Universal Design for Learning (UDL) guidelines to provide a framework for designing differentiated assignments and homework (CAST, 2012). Emphasis is on providing multiple means of representation, action and expression, and engagement. Representation refers to options for student learning through various types of perception (visual, auditory, haptic), language and symbols, and modes of comprehension. Action and expression means providing different ways to demonstrate learning and support in developing independent executive learning strategies such as goal setting. Engagement refers to various ways to trigger interest, effort, and self-regulation. The National Center on Universal Design for Learning (http://www.udlcenter.org) provides many resources and tutorials to help teachers implement UDL.

12.2.6 How Can I Plan for Differentiated Instruction?

Planning for the success of all students in your class involves careful consideration of the needs of individuals as well as those of the class as a whole. In most cases, teachers have a

Table 12.1 • Planning Systems for Differentiating Instruction

	SOURCE	DESCRIPTION	BENEFITS FOR STUDENTS WITH SPECIAL NEEDS
Planning Pyramid	Schumm, Vaughn, & Leavell, 1994; Schumm & Avalos, 2009	A three-tiered framework for planning instructional units and lessons for diverse learners. Key concepts are identified and appropriate assignments and adaptations are incorporated.	Serves as a tool to integrate learning for all students and as a way for special and general education teachers to coordinate planning and instruction.
Universal Design for Learning	National Center on Universal Design for Learning	A system for identifying appropriate goals, materials, methods, and assessments for all students.	Assignments and assessments are at an appropriate level of challenge. Exceptional students are viewed as participants, not outliers.
Curriculum Mapping	Jacobs & Johnson, 2009	A calendar-based system used to gather data about content, skill instruction, and assessment within and across grade levels in a school.	Specialists have a clear picture of what is going to be taught and when. Assists in planning of appropriate accommodations.
Concept Anchoring Routine	Deshler et al., 2001	A series of instructional methods to help students with disabilities master key concepts in the general education curriculum.	Helps students to connect new information with prior knowledge.

Sources: Universal design for learning guidelines, National Center on Universal Design for Learning, retrieved from http://www.udlcenter.org; "Making learning easier: Connecting new knowledge to things students already know," by D. Deshler et al., 2001, *Teaching Exceptional Children*, 33(4), 82–86. *The curriculum mapping planner: Templates, tools, and resources*, by H. H. Jacobs & A. Johnson, 2009, Alexandria, VA: Association for Supervision and Curriculum Development; "Responsible differentiated instruction for the adolescent learner: Promises, pitfalls, and possibilities," by J. S. Schumm & M. A., Avalos, 2009, in W. Blanton & K. Wood (Eds.) *Promoting literacy with adolescent learners*, New York: Guilford; and "Planning pyramid: A framework for planning for diverse student needs during content area instruction," by J. S. Schumm, S. Vaughn, & A. G. Leavell, 1994, *The Reading Teacher*, *47*(8), 608–62.

single lesson or unit plan and make adaptations, often on the spot to make learning accessible for individual students. The unfortunate consequence of "on-the-fly" adjustments is that adaptations become incidental, inconsistent, and (for students with disabilities) not representative of what is mandated on their individualized education programs (IEPs).

Numerous systems have been recommended for planning for DI (see Table 12.1). The planning pyramid, an excellent tool for co-planning in the general education classroom, is a framework for or a way of thinking about planning instruction to enhance learning for all students (see Figure 12.2).

FIGURE 12.2 Planning pyramid for a unit on Latin American countries

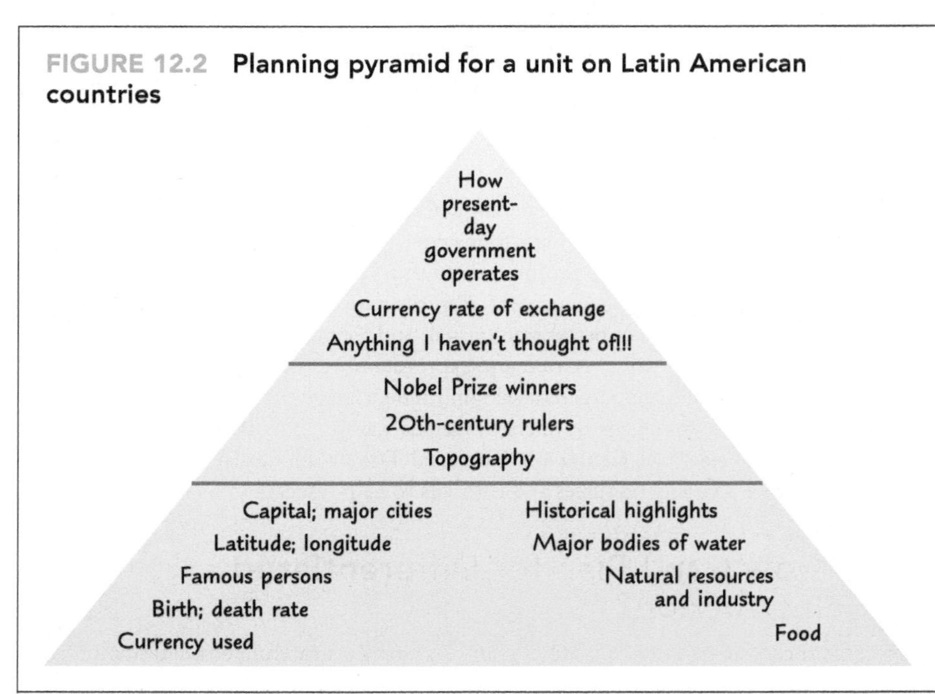

Schumm, Vaughn, and Harris (1997) reported that when teachers use the planning pyramid together, they develop a common mind-set about what all students will learn. They also can identify potential trouble spots as well as accommodations for students who may need them. Ruth Rogge, a special education teacher, adapted the planning pyramid for her weekly meetings with general education teachers (see Figure 12.3).

FIGURE 12.3 **Planning pyramid weekly lesson plan form**

Week of: ______________________________

General Educator: ______________________ Special Educator: ______________________

Overall Objective/State Standard ______________________________

____

Pyramid	Co-Teaching Model
	Monday ______________
	Tuesday ______________
	Wednesday ______________
	Thursday ______________
	Friday ______________

	General Educator Duties	Special Educator Duties
Monday		
Tuesday		
Wednesday		
Thursday		
Friday		

Materials/In-Class Assignments

Monday ______________________

Tuesday ______________________

Wednesday ______________________

Thursday ______________________

Friday ______________________

Homework Assignments

Monday ______________________

Tuesday ______________________

Wednesday ______________________

Thursday ______________________

Friday ______________________

Evaluation: ______________________________

TIPS FOR TEACHERS 12.3

Procedures for the Planning Pyramid

The primary component of the planning pyramid, degrees of learning, makes up the body of the pyramid and will help you and your co-teacher examine the content to be taught and decide how you will differentiate instruction for all learners.

Step 1: Examine your state or district curriculum guides or textbooks to identify key standards or objectives to be taught.

Step 2: Decide what will go in the base of the pyramid: the information that is essential for all students to learn. This section is guided by the question, "What do we want *all* students to learn?"

Step 3: Decide what will go in the middle part of the pyramid: the information that is next in importance. This section is guided by the question, "What do we want *most* students to learn?"

Step 4: Decide what you will put at the top of the pyramid: the information that will enhance basic concepts and facts about the topic or subject. This type of information will be acquired only by a few students who have an added interest in and a desire to learn more about the subject.

Step 5: Identify what grouping patterns would facilitate learning and what accommodations are necessary for individual learners.

Step 6: Discuss the roles and responsibilities of you and your co-teacher before, during, and after the lesson.

Source: Schumm et al., 1994, in *The Reading Teacher, 47*(8), 608–62, International Reading Association.

The pyramid is designed as a flexible tool that teachers can adjust to identify what needs to be taught and, based on student needs, how to teach it. Tips for Teachers 12.3 provides procedures for using the planning pyramid.

To be effective, you will need to take into consideration the degrees of learning—what and how much do you expect all, most, or some of your students to learn? Consider, for example, sixth-grade teacher Sara Hood, who used the planning pyramid to plan a 2½-week unit on Latin American countries for her middle school students. Sara has two students with learning disabilities in her class. One student, Carlos, has difficulty with decoding; another, Miriam, struggles with reading comprehension. Her state-adopted textbook is very difficult for these students, and her planning needs to include accommodations to help both students learn content. To prepare for the lesson, Sara examined the whole unit in the textbook and chose the fundamental ideas she wanted students to learn. The bottom of the pyramid listed topics that all groups would research and on which all students would be tested. The middle and top of the pyramid listed student-selected material.

MyEdLab
Video Example 12.1.
Watch this video and listen to what this teacher says about how she plans for differentiated instruction before preparing her lesson plans. What are some of her other thought processes as she is planning for differentiation and how does she incorporate the learning needs of all of her students?

One major concern Sara had in planning was finding activities that would keep her middle school students involved in learning and provide Carlos and Miriam the support they needed. To address these concerns, she planned to divide the classes into mixed-ability cooperative learning groups, each of which would select a country and present what they learned to the rest of the class. Sara provided the students with a checklist with her expectations for the cooperative learning groups' oral presentations in class. In the cooperative learning groups, material was read aloud to facilitate access to the information for Carlos. Also, groups worked together to identify key information, thus assisting Miriam with comprehension.

In addition to using cooperative learning groups to facilitate DI, Sara also planned to include differentiated assessment. In his IEP, Carlos is allowed to have tests administered orally. Thus, Sara's special education colleague administered his unit exam orally to Carlos. Miriam's IEP calls for extended time in taking tests, and the special educator facilitated that as well. Both Carlos and Miriam participated in their groups' oral presentations.

Planning is a critical component for successful DI in the general education classroom. The planning pyramid can serve as a framework for such planning—not only for students with learning and behavior problems, but also for students who are identified as gifted and talented.

12.2.7 How Can I Accommodate Students Who Are Gifted and Talented?

Consider the following quotation:

> Of all the students you are teaching in a given class, which group do you think will probably learn the least this year? It may surprise you to find that in a class that has a range of abilities (and which class doesn't?), it is the most able, rather than the least able, who will learn less new material than any other group. (Winebrenner & Espeland, 2000, p. 1)

How can this occur?

Think about Rick, a tenth-grade student who knows all the vocabulary for an English test at the beginning of the week. He gets a grade of 100% on the test, but has he learned anything?

Think about Mina, a sixth-grade student who is a voracious reader and is particularly interested in astronomy. She skims the chapter in her general science textbook, quickly gets its gist, and realizes that the content is basic and boring. The class lecture does not go beyond answering the end-of-chapter questions. Mina does not have the opportunity to share what she really knows and "tunes out" during class discussion. She gets a grade of 70% on a chapter test because she simply doesn't care about "proving" what she knows.

Think about Caroline, an eighth-grade student who has known all about the eight parts of speech since third grade. Even if she had forgotten the eight parts of speech in third grade, it wouldn't have mattered because they were also taught in fourth, fifth, sixth, and seventh grades. She gets a grade of 100% on a grammar unit test, but has she learned anything?

Think about Thaddeus. Thaddeus loves to draw and does so constantly at home and at school. Unfortunately, he would rather draw than do anything else, and his teacher frequently reprimands him for "doodling" rather than completing assignments.

You've got the picture. Frequently, students who are gifted or talented and other high-achieving students already know the material being covered in the general curriculum. Can you imagine spending 7 hours a day, 5 days a week, school year after school year, reviewing information you already know? Can you imagine having genuine artistic talent and not having the opportunity to develop that talent or to share it with others? Can you imagine repeated drilling on standards that you have already mastered (Rakow, 2012; Viadero, 2007)?

Characteristics of students who are gifted and talented

As a classroom teacher, you'll need to recognize the characteristics of students with extraordinary gifts and talents so that you can help identify students for special services and provide appropriate instruction for gifted students who are members of your class. There is disparity among states in terms of how giftedness is defined, how students are identified for gifted education services, and how services are provided (pull-out programs, full-time programs, inclusion programs) (Hallahan, Kauffman, & Pullen, 2015). There is a clear trend toward increased inclusion of students who are gifted and talented in the general education classroom (McGee, 2012; Petrilli, 2011). Thus, it is important that you investigate local policies and understand your role in identifying students with special gifts and talents and designing instruction that meets their needs.

MyEdLab
Video Example 12.2.
As you watch this video, pay attention to what the speaker says about the need to differentiate instruction for students who are gifted as well as students with disabilities. Based on what you learn, would you think any differently about designing your lesson plans to acknowledge students' diverse learning styles?

What you should also be aware of is that the gifted population is very diverse (Reis & Renzulli, 2009). Part of this diversity is due to definitional differences and local criteria for admission to gifted programs (Hallahan et al., 2015); part is due to individual academic, social, and emotional differences (Robinson, Zigler, & Gallagher, 2000); and part is due to the degree of giftedness (Ziegler & Heller, 2000). The response-to-intervention (RTI) model, designed as a framework for providing additional support to struggling learners, offers some guidance as well for meeting the needs of gifted and talented students in diverse classrooms (Johnsen, Parker & Farah, 2015).

Underidentified high-achieving students

Another group that is of particular interest to many general education teachers is that of high-achieving students who are not identified for special programs. Frequently, teachers will notice a child with extraordinary talents and abilities who might not meet state or school district criteria to qualify for a special program. It becomes the general education teacher's responsibility to provide such children with the support, encouragement, and stimulation they need to feel productive and successful.

As a general education teacher, you'll want to become familiar with policies and procedures for identifying and instructing students who are gifted and talented. In addition, you'll want to learn about what resources are available to you and to your students. You'll also want to learn about policies related to acceleration and enrichment. **Acceleration** refers to the procedure of moving students quickly through the grades or through the curriculum. With the idea that some students might not be socially ready for the demands of acceleration to higher grades, **enrichment** evolved as an alternative to acceleration. Gifted education programs in the United States have varied in their emphasis on acceleration or enrichment. In some cases, programs in general education have elected to incorporate elements of both.

It is easy to assume that capable learners are capable of creating their own ways to extend their learning. Quite the contrary, these students need to have support and scaffolding as well (Manning, Stanford, & Ruvek, 2010; Rakow, 2012). There are several approaches to DI for gifted students suggested in the literature. Two commonly recommended approaches for general education classrooms are curriculum compacting and the Parallel Curriculum Model.

Curriculum Compacting Experts in the field of gifted education suggest that general education teachers work cooperatively with teachers in gifted programs to compact the general education curriculum for gifted students (Renzulli, 2012). Many gifted and high-achieving students may already know concepts and skills at the outset of a lesson. **Curriculum compacting** provides students with the opportunity to demonstrate what they already know about a subject. Teachers can then eliminate content that is repetitive or review for students, replacing it with advanced learning experiences. To assess what your students know, see the 60-Second Lesson.

60-*SECOND* LESSON
ASSESSING PRIOR KNOWLEDGE

When you begin a new unit or topic, you need to find out what your students already know and what they need to learn. Finding out what students know will help you plan differentiated lessons and think about accommodations you might need for students with special needs. Some teachers skip this very important step because they don't want to take the time to construct a pretest. Here are some efficient ways to assess prior knowledge:

1. In a list of tasks organized by relative difficulty, identify the most difficult tasks and have students who are willing to take the challenge do them first. Allow students who demonstrate mastery to go on to a self-selected task. Students who are gifted or high achieving frequently get bored with undue repetition and practice. "Most difficult first" can help to circumvent this problem. This way of assessing prior knowledge (a way that takes little preplanning) is "most difficult first" (Winebrenner, 1992).
2. Put three or four structured questions that relate to the core of a lesson on the board or an overhead transparency. Have the students respond in writing to the questions.
3. Provide students with the topic of the lesson and have them generate as many ideas as they can about the topic within a brief time limit.

Curriculum compacting is a three-step identification process:

1. What the student already knows about a topic
2. What a student needs to learn
3. What adaptations or activities are appropriate for facilitating student learning

Parallel Curriculum Model Tomlinson et al. (2001) developed a framework for DI called the Parallel Curriculum Model (PCM). PCM takes into consideration four curriculum design components:

1. Core Curriculum—key concepts to be learned
2. Curriculum of Connections—making interdisciplinary linkages
3. Curriculum of Practice—supporting students in learning to think like a practitioner
4. Curriculum of Identity—helping students make personal meaning and clarification of what they are learning

The parallel curriculum components can be used together, separately, or in various combinations depending on the teacher's goals (Kaplan, Guzman, & Tomlinson, 2009). Like the planning pyramid, PCM forces teachers to think about what is important to learn and how to facilitate instruction for a wide range of student needs.

Although DI is a viable way to accommodate individual differences, the National Association for Gifted Children (www.NAGC.org) also offers some cautions and comments about the practice. Differentiated instruction should not mean "just more work" for advanced students. It should offer opportunities for both acceleration and enrichment. Thus, DI holds great promise, but involves careful planning and ongoing evaluation.

Best instructional practice

Van Tassel-Baska and Brown (2007) recommend some essential practices that are vital to teaching gifted students:

1. Using advanced subject matter taught at an accelerated rate
2. Using flexible grouping practices
3. Incorporating opportunities for higher-level thinking
4. Fostering inquiry in learning
5. Providing problem-solving opportunities related to real-world situations

Similarly, Maker and Schiever (2010) maintain that gifted students need access to differentiated content, learning processes, product outcomes, and learning environments. Kanevsky (2011) surveyed elementary and middle school students in both Canada and the United States to learn about their preferences for the types of instructional recommendations Maker and Schiever make for gifted students. Both students identified and not identified as gifted were included in the study. Findings indicated that in general both groups of students preferred similar practices for teaching and learning, but that students identified as gifted were more adamant about their preferences. For example, both groups liked practices such as self-pacing and choosing their own learning partners. Students identified as gifted felt more strongly about working independently some of the time, learning about complex topics, and creating their own products to demonstrate learning.

MyEdLab
Video Example 12.3.
Watch this video and listen to what the teacher says about the need to first establish a purpose for the lesson, followed by activities that can be incorporated to reach all learners. In the work station and class and the types of activities the teachers discussed, did you feel multiple intelligences were addressed?

How does differentiated instruction relate to response to intervention?

Megan Goodwell has been teaching fifth grade for 2 years. Over that span of time she has seen many educational innovations come and go. Her school had been actively engaged in professional development with DI. However, when Megan first learned about response to intervention (RTI), her first reaction was that this was yet another initiative to implement. As she learned more about RTI, Megan came to realize that it actually works hand-in-hand with DI to meet the needs of all learners.

As Allan and Goddard (2010) explain, RTI and differentiated instruction stem from different origins, but have goals that are very well aligned. RTI is a federal initiative intended to improve the identification process for students with special learning needs. All students (not just students with diagnosed disabilities) have access to ongoing screening and progress monitoring with more intensive instruction as needed. Differentiated instruction is a grassroots movement to help general education teachers meet a broad range of individual student needs—including the needs of students with learning challenges as well as high achieving and/or students identified as gifted and talented.

What Megan has come to learn is that differentiated instruction occurs at all tiers. Her Tier 1 instruction for her fifth graders includes flexible grouping as well as differentiated assignments based on students' needs and interests. With the onset of RTI, she now includes screening and progress monitoring. For students who do not respond to Tier 1 instruction, more intensive, "structural differentiated" approaches (or structures and resources beyond regular instruction) are implemented. Megan works with the school's reading coach to provide small-group instruction and more frequent progress-monitoring assessment.

RTI at the middle and high school levels offers challenges not inherent at the elementary level (Brozo, 2009; Lenski, 2011; Vaughn & Fletcher, 2012), such as:

- Students at secondary levels are more likely to be placed in departmentalized settings.
- Scheduling problems can inhibit time for Tier 2 and Tier 3 instruction.
- The pacing of instruction is much more rapid, with little time for review or reteaching.

There is a lot to be learned from research and practice about how best to provide tiered instruction for middle and high school students. Because students in both middle and high school settings may remain undiagnosed for special services, ongoing research in this area is warranted.

Much of what you read in this chapter about differentiated assessment and instruction can be incorporated into Tier 1 strategies. The steps you take to address individual needs through implementation of evidence-based strategies can form the foundation for RTI.

Because RTI in secondary settings is in its infancy, caution in implementation is warranted. You'll want to familiarize yourself with the legal requirements of RTI, engage in professional development to learn more about tiered instruction and progress monitoring, and develop strong communication with your peers (Canter, Klotz, & Cowan, 2008). You'll also want to know how Tiers 2 and 3 are implemented at your school and how and when student progress monitoring occurs (Burns, 2008). At the middle and high school levels, identifying and addressing student needs may offer students their last chance.

MyEdLab **Self-Check 12.2**

MyEdLab **Application Exercise 12.2:** Differentiating Instruction

12.3 DIFFERENTIATING READING ASSIGNMENTS

In your academic career, you've developed strategies for navigating reading assignments. Lots of practice and, perhaps, some direct instruction on how to read and learn from text have helped you along the way. For many students, required reading (especially textbooks) can be labor intensive (Wood, Lapp, Flood, & Taylor, 2008). This is certainly true for students who struggle with reading, but can also be true for some usually high-achieving students who have not learned approaches for efficient and effective reading.

The Common Core State Standards call for close and critical reading of a wide variety of texts to enable students to become college and career ready (Fisher & Frey, 2015; Wixson & Lipson, 2012). Teachers are encouraged to use both high-quality literature and informational texts (including primary sources) as well as other reading material (online sources, magazines, newspapers, etc.) (Jeger, 2012). Thus, it is critical that you understand the nature of text complexity and ways to help your students in becoming independent in reading increasingly complex and rigorous material (Fisher, Frey, & Lapp, 2012).

It is important to note that while the standards encourage rigor in the selection of classroom reading materials, the standards also support the need for adaptations for students with disabilities and English language learners.

This section shows you how to become familiar not only with the strengths and weaknesses of the reading materials you assign, but also with the ways in which students interact with and respond to the text. This section also contains effective techniques for making adaptations in reading assignments for special learners.

12.3.1 Familiarizing Yourself with the Texts

As a classroom teacher, you might not have the opportunity to select the reading material that is used in your content-area classroom. Typically, state selection committees decide on a limited number of state-adopted textbooks from which school districts can choose. At the district level, a district committee is often responsible for shortening the state-adopted list. At the school level, grade- or committee-level teams frequently choose the textbook. Chances are, you will inherit a textbook that someone else has chosen for you. To familiarize yourself with your textbook and supplemental reading materials, you need to consider text-based factors that contribute to the many challenges students encounter with reading: readability level and friendliness level.

Readability level

Traditionally, a text's level of difficulty is gauged by its **readability level**, expressed as a grade level. For example, you might hear a teacher say, "This science book is intended for tenth graders, but the readability level is eleventh grade." Readability levels are determined by applying one or more readability formulas to the text (e.g., Dale & Chall, 1948; Fry, 1977; Raygor, 1977). Such formulas are based on sentence complexity (measured by sentence length) and word difficulty (measured by word length and frequency). Keep in mind that readability levels are overall estimates of the level of difficulty and that within each text some passages might vary—in some cases by as much as three or four grade levels.

Another way to estimate the level of difficulty of a text is by **Lexile® levels**. The Lexile Framework® for Reading estimates the student's reading level and a text's readability level. If a student has the same Lexile level as the Lexile level of a text, the student should be able to read the book with 75% accuracy. Lexile scores range from 200L (beginning readers) to 1700L (advanced readers). To conform to the Common Core State Standards requirements for more rigor in text complexity, the Lexile grade bands have been adjusted to set higher expectations for each grade level (Finn, 2012).

Your teachers' manual will report the readability level and/or Lexile level of your text. Why is this important to know? Fran Hampton teaches tenth-grade biology. Some of her students are students with learning disabilities, some are English language learners, and a few are garden-variety poor readers who have not been placed in special services. The reading levels of her students range from about fourth-grade level to twelfth-grade level. The textbook has a stated readability level of tenth grade. Thus, Fran needs to make adaptations to the textbook to promote learning for all students in her classroom.

Friendliness level

In addition to the readability level, you should also become familiar with the text features included in your text that can support readers. **Friendly text** or **considerate text** is written and formatted in such a way that information can be extracted easily and support is available when the reader does not understand the text. The number of features included in the text that promote learning (such as headings and subheadings, vocabulary in boldface type, and chapter summaries) determine the degree to which text is considered friendly or considerate to the reader.

Familiarize yourself with the reading material you plan to use, and learn to recognize friendly text features that support student learning as well as areas in which you will need to intervene. Friendly text has *organization*, *explication*, *conceptual density*, *metadiscourse*, and *instructional devices*.

- *Organization* is the sequence in which the author presents information in the text. Organization includes the general structure of the text as well as consistency and connectedness of ideas.
- *Explication* is how the author explains ideas and teaches the reader. Explication includes necessary background information and examples.
- *Conceptual density* is the number of new vocabulary terms or concepts the author introduces.
- *Metadiscourse* is the degree to which the author "talks" to the reader. Metadiscourse includes direct explanations of how to learn from the text and how to connect ideas from one part of the text to another.
- *Instructional devices* are the number of learning tools the author provides. Examples of learning tools are a table of contents, marginal annotations, and a glossary.

At the beginning of the school year, Fran Hampton does a textbook walk-through with her students. She holds a class discussion about the friendly text features in their book and brainstorms about ways students can use those text features to prepare for class discussions, labs, and tests.

12.3.2 Understanding How Students Interact with and Respond to Text

As you examine the reading material you will be using, you should anticipate how you will need to supplement it. The ultimate judge of the readability and friendliness is the reader. The **FLIP chart strategy** helps students learn to evaluate text on their own (Schumm & Mangrum, 1991). ("FLIP" stands for friendliness, language, interest, and prior knowledge.) By filling out forms like the one shown in Figure 12.4, students learn what is comfortable for them individually as readers.

After students have completed the FLIP chart, you can learn (through class discussions and individual conferences) what is difficult for them in terms of text friendliness, language, interest, and prior knowledge. Students with reading and learning problems especially need to learn how to talk about the assigned reading and any problems they have with it. Classroom discussions based on the FLIP chart strategy also help students think as a group about effective strategies for coping with text they find difficult.

12.3.3 Making Adaptations

Suppose you learn that the textbook is too difficult for some of your students. What will you do? Many teachers resort to reading the text to students rather than asking them to read the text. Research indicates that most content-area teachers seldom implement adaptations for a number of reasons (Schumm & Vaughn, 1992; Schumm, Vaughn, & Saumell, 1992), such as the following:

1. Adapting reading assignments takes time, and teachers' time for planning and preparing for instruction is already limited.
2. Adaptations often slow down instruction, and teachers cannot cover as much material as they would like.
3. Some teachers think that making adaptations for the few students who need them is not fair to the high-achieving students who are ready to work at a faster pace.
4. Some teachers feel that they do not have the training they need to make adaptations. (Hall, 2005; Mallette, Henk, Waggoner, & Delaney, 2005)

Fortunately, with professional development and use of a broadening array of instruction resources, teachers can make the adaptations students want and need (Cantrell, Burns, & Callaway, 2009). Tips for Teachers 12.4 discusses components of the FIX strategy in greater depth: focus on the essay, identify problem areas, and execute revisions.

FIGURE 12.4 The FLIP chart

Title of assignment ______________________

Number of pages ______________________

General directions: Rate each of the four FLIP categories on a 1–5 scale (5 = high). Then determine your purpose for reading and appropriate reading rate, and budget your reading/study time.

F = Friendliness: How friendly is my reading assignment?

Directions: Examine your assignment to see if it includes the friendly elements listed below.

Friendly text features

Table of contents	Index	Glossary
Chapter introductions	Headings	Subheadings
Margin notes	Study questions	Chapter summary
Key terms highlighted	Graphs	Charts
Pictures	Signal words	Lists of key facts

1 __________ 2 __________ 3 __________ 4 __________ 5 __________

No friendly text features | Some friendly text features | Many friendly text features

Friendliness rating __________

L = Language: How difficult is the language in my reading assignment?

Directions: Skim the chapter quickly to determine the number of new terms. Read three random paragraphs to get a feel for the vocabulary level and number of long, complicated sentences.

1 __________ 2 __________ 3 __________ 4 __________ 5 __________

Many new words; complicated sentences | Some new words; somewhat complicated sentences | No new words; clear sentences

Language rating __________

I = Interest: How interesting is my reading assignment?

Directions: Read the title, introduction, headings/subheadings, and summary. Examine the pictures and graphics included.

1 __________ 2 __________ 3 __________ 4 __________ 5 __________

Boring | Somewhat interesting | Very interesting

Interest rating __________

P = Prior knowledge: What do I already know about the material covered in my reading assignment?

Directions: Think about the title, introduction, headings/subheadings, and summary.

1 __________ 2 __________ 3 __________ 4 __________ 5 __________

Mostly new information | Some new information | Mostly familiar information

Prior knowledge rating __________

Overall, this reading assignment appears to be at:

- a comfortable reading level for me
- a somewhat comfortable reading level for me
- an uncomfortable reading level for me

Source: "FLIP: A framework for textbook thinking," by J. S. Schumm & C. T. Mangrum, 1991, *Journal of Reading*, *35*, 120–124.

TIPS FOR TEACHERS 12.4

Fix It

Objective: To help students learn to revise their writing in a strategic way

Grades: Intermediate, middle school

Materials: Paper and pencil

Teaching Procedures:

1. Introduce the components of FIX strategy: **F**ocus on the essay, **I**dentify problem areas, E**x**ecute revisions by making additions, rearranging text, making deletions, and rewriting.
2. Model the use of the strategy and demonstrate how revisions are made.
3. Encourage students to memorize the strategy.
4. Provide opportunities for small group and independent practice.

Source: Based on "FIX: A strategic approach to writing and revision for students with learning disabilities," by C. K. Sherman & S. De La Paz, 2015, *Teaching Exceptional Children, 48*(2), 93–101.

12.3.4 Comprehension Canopy

Providing an advanced organizer to orient students to the expectations for the content in the unit of study can assist students of all learning levels (Vaughn et al., 2013). For example, an overarching question or series of key ideas that are returned to each lesson can help students tune into the most important elements of what they are expected to learn. Mrs. Roberts indicates that she uses overarching questions such as "How did the industrial revolution influence the quality of life of most workers?" as a means to help all students organize what they are learning during her two-week history unit.

Text highlighting

Students with comprehension problems have difficulty sifting out important information. Underlining or highlighting key points in assigned reading can help students attend to the most salient information (Santa, Havens, & Valdes, 2004; Wood & Wooley, 1986). As you read, highlight the information you think is most important. Then student or adult volunteers can use your book as a guide to highlight the same information in books for students with reading and learning disabilities. Keep in mind that this is an intermediate step. Students should also be taught how to highlight and identify key information on their own (Santa et al., 2004). You can use cooperative learning groups to support students in learning how to draw salient information from assigned reading. Students can work collaboratively to develop text coding or "text graffiti" systems using colored pens and sticky notes (Buehl, 2009).

Multiple sources

After you and your students have taken a careful look at your textbook, you might realize that you will need to go beyond the textbook to provide your students with alternative reading material. Living in a digital age requires students to learn skills for dealing with multiple sources of information (Bean, Readence, & Baldwin, 2008; Burniske, 2008; Wood et al., 2008). "No longer can we refer to traditional books alone as text. Now the term *text* has expanded to include print, graphic novels, art, music, digital and visual media, technical writings, popular culture such as music and television programs and characters, and Internet texts (webpages, blogs, instant messaging for example)" (Wood et al., 2008, p. 6).

Although Fran Hampton uses the textbook for her core curriculum, like more and more content-area teachers, she has begun using trade books (both fiction and nonfiction) and other reading materials (e.g., magazines and journals) to supplement content-area textbooks. Trade books and other alternative reading sources can be used to spark interest and to help students develop lifelong reading habits. In addition to informational books, she also uses historical fiction, biographies, and autobiographies as part of her planning to make the study of biology lively and relevant. Because informational trade books at lower readability levels have been produced in recent years, it's possible to locate books on the same theme at varying levels as a basis for classroom discussion (Fitzpatrick, 2008). Regardless of how you choose to integrate trade books in content-area instruction, try to select (or help your students select) books that are engaging and that will grab their interest, and don't forget to share your own enthusiasm for reading and learning beyond the textbook.

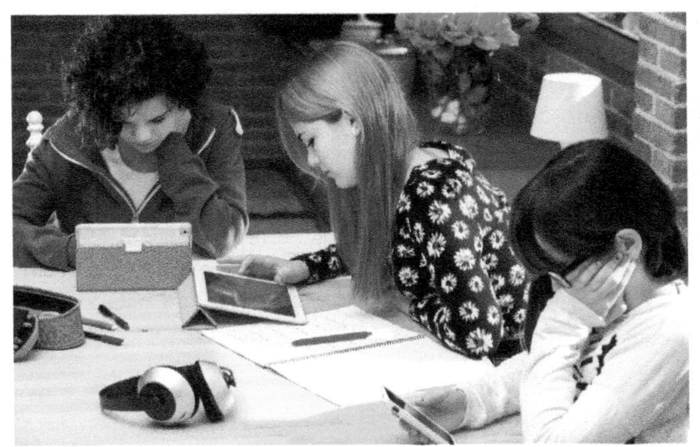

What are some ways that you can trigger student engagement using multiple sources?

Fran has not limited herself to traditional print media. She encourages students to use the Internet. Fran identifies appropriate websites and creates inquiry-based activities based on web content. Students work in teams using tablets or computers to complete the activity and then later to engage in class discussion about what they learned. She also encourages her students to find links to websites that can be useful in their research (e.g., *Nettrekker*). As Fran puts it, "I'm continuing to keep an open mind about multiple sources but do so with caution. On the one hand, my students are increasingly more tech savvy and motivated to use digital resources. On the other hand, I want to ensure that we use safe Internet practices." See the Tech Tips, "Using Technology to Support Learning in Content Areas," to learn about some available options.

TECH TIPS

Using Technology to Support Learning in Content Areas

Learners with difficulties in reading and comprehending written text often experience failure in content-area classes such as social studies and science. Although learners may be receiving support with their reading and writing skills, they also need support in their content-area classes. There are many programs and websites that you can use in the classroom or that students can use on their own, such as the following.

Read:OutLoud, by Don Johnston Incorporated
(www.donjohnston.com)

Cast E-Reader, by CAST, Inc.
(www.cast.org)

These programs read both websites and also books in many different formats.

Smithsonian's On-Line Museum
(www.smithsonian.org)

Virtual Tours of Museums, Exhibits, and Points of Special Interest
(www.virtualfreesites.com)

Bookshare—Books without Barriers, by Benetech
(www.bookshare.org)

Once students provide proof of a visual, learning, or physical disability, they can be eligible for online access to books, periodicals, newspapers, and textbooks.

Online Science Experiments

Physics Simulation
(www.myphysicslab.com)

Science Resources
(www.alline.org)

Social Studies for Kids
(www.socialstudiesforkids.com)

IPAD/IPOD™ applications include

- Science360 for iPad
- National Geographic Explorer
- My Birds of Prey HD
- UN CountryStats
- Art Authority for iPad, Civic Quotes
- History: Maps of the World
- Constitution for iPad
- US History Timeline (Free)
- USA Presidents (American President Life History)
- Maps.com US History Atlas
- iLearn Solar System: Making Science Fun
- Glossary of Geology & Earth Science

TIPS FOR TEACHERS 12.5

Suggestions for Recording Reading Assignments

Instead of recording an entire chapter verbatim, read the key sections and paraphrase the less important sections.

Code the text so that readers or listeners will know whether the person on the tape is reading or paraphrasing.

Provide a short advance organizer on the tape to help students get ready to read and listen.

Insert questions that readers or listeners can stop to think about.

Remind readers or listeners to stop periodically to think about what they have read.

Use a natural tone of voice and a comfortable reading rate. Have students experiment with recorded texts to see whether they comprehend better with or without the accompanying printed text.

Listening to learn

For over 60 years the nonprofit organization Learning Ally (formerly named Recording for the Blind & Dyslexic) has provided audiobook library services for students who have difficulty with traditional texts. The organization offers audiobooks to assist students who are blind, have low vision, or have learning disabilities. Its expanded website offers information for how to access recorded materials and suggestions for implementing them in your classroom.

With students increasingly using listening devices, including smartphones and tablets, in their daily lives, audiobooks are increasingly popular and acceptable to students. Students can listen to the books anywhere. If the material is not available through Learning Ally, Tips for Teachers 12.5 provides suggestions for recording reading assignments.

Boyle and colleagues (2002) recommend pairing the listening of recorded text with other learning strategies to get maximum results. In particular, they recommend the SliCK sequence to structure learning from recorded text. The steps in the SliCK strategy are as follows:

- Set up the playback device.
- Look ahead or preview the printed chapter and any organizational aspects of the audiobook to identify headings, subheadings, and key words.
- Comprehend the recorded text through careful listening and reading along with the text.
- Keep notes from the text for further review and to prepare for tests and classroom discussions.

Another key element that determines student success or failure is student assessment. Should students with disabilities have the same assessments and tests as everyone else? What if a student cannot read? What if a student cannot work under timed conditions? In the next section, you'll learn about key ideas in thinking about differentiating assessment.

MyEdLab **Self-Check 12.3**

MyEdLab **Application Exercise 12.3:** Making Adaptations

12.4 DIFFERENTIATING ASSESSMENT

In classrooms that include highly diverse learners, differentiated assessment should go hand in hand with differentiated instruction. Learners may have different assessment needs. For example, some students will need more diagnostic assessment based on your observations of their performance in class as well as initial screening results

(Lipson, Chomsky-Higgins, & Kanfer, 2011). Some students with challenges in learning basic skills may need more intensive and frequent progress monitoring than others (Fuchs, Fuchs, & Compton, 2012). For English language learners or students with disabilities, testing accommodations such as extended time, oral administration of the test, or the use of dictionaries may be appropriate (Salvia, Ysseldyke, & Bolt, 2013). Differentiated assessment involves the use of formal assessments and informal measures (Chapman & King, 2004; Wormeli, 2006b). It also involves accommodations and adaptations to meet individual needs. Tomlinson (2003) identifies four ways that assessment and instruction can be linked:

1. Preassessment is necessary to find out what each student knows and needs to learn.
2. Ongoing assessment is needed to monitor student learning during instructional units and to make adjustments as necessary.
3. Teachers identify multiple ways for students to demonstrate what they have learned.
4. Students become actively engaged in setting instructional goals and in self-assessment in meeting those goals.

This section begins with a discussion of formal assessment, including high-stakes testing and teacher-made tests. It continues with ideas for informal or alternative assessment, including suggestions for engaging students in self-assessment. The chapter concludes with ideas for assigning student grades.

12.4.1 Preparing Students for High-Stakes Tests

Large-scale assessment for all students, including students with disabilities and English language learners, is in place in all states. High-quality instruction that is direct and focused on concepts to be learned, clarification of student misunderstandings, attention to level of difficulty of assignments, and support to guide problem solving are some of the best practices to promote student achievement on high-stakes tests (Hollingworth, 2007; Vaughn, Gersten, & Chard, 2000). Additionally, now that tests are given electronically, students may need to learn strategies for navigating tests on tablets or computers.

Implementation of high-stakes tests varies considerably, especially among those students who qualify for accommodations. Other than providing high-quality instruction, how teachers prepare students for taking high-stakes tests depends on the nature of state-identified standards and the format of the examination used (Katsiyannis, Zhang, Ryan, & Jones, 2007). Kontovourki and Campis (2011) suggest that some teachers teach tests as a "genre." A test genre unit would include instruction in the vocabulary of testing, format of testing, analyzing responses to questions, and test-taking skills. Tips for Teachers 12.6 provides questions that can guide your thinking about how to prepare students for high-stakes tests. Some content areas are not included in statewide assessments. Nonetheless, teachers in all subject areas are increasingly being provided with professional development and resources to align their teaching in a way that promotes student achievement on tests in reading, writing, and mathematics. Tips for Teachers 12.6 also provides questions you can ask curriculum leaders in your school.

Your state, school district, and school may have policy statements and procedures for appropriate and ethical ways to prepare your students for high-stakes tests. As a classroom teacher, you should become familiar with those policies and procedures. You will also want to find out what adaptations or exam alternatives are available for which individual students in your class may be eligible (see Tips for Teachers 12.7) (Elbaum, 2007; Kettler, 2012).

12.4.2 Helping Students Develop Test-Taking Strategies

There is some evidence that helping students develop test-taking strategies can enhance performance on high-stakes tests (Carter, Hughes, & Wehby, 2005; Salend, 2011a), but

TIPS FOR TEACHERS 12.6

Questions That Will Guide You in Preparing Students for High-Stakes Testing

What standards are designated for students in my grade level?

How are standards aligned with district and school requirements?

What materials do I have that are aligned with the standards?

What is the format of the state exam?

Are there resources available to help me design my teacher-made exams to align with the format of the state test?

Does my state or district maintain a website with resources that can assist me in planning, assessment, and instruction?

When students do not seem to be making progress on state standards, what classroom interventions can I implement?

When classroom interventions do not work, are there resources for my students at the school or district level for more intensive intervention?

How can I integrate standards into my ongoing teaching to keep students motivated and engaged?

What accommodations or alternative assessments are available for students with disabilities or those who are English language learners?

Here are some questions you can ask of curriculum leaders in your school:

What is the format of high-stakes tests in our state?

What types of questions can I include in my class discussions and tests that support question formats used on state examinations?

What formats for writing assessment are used on our state assessments? In what ways can I incorporate those formats into my assignments and tests?

some are questioning the value of test preparation at the expense of focusing on core content (Welsh, Eastwood, & D'Agostino, 2014). Accommodations for English language learners and students with disabilities are an important consideration (Thurlow & Kopriva, 2014). While keeping local requirements in mind, Thurlow, Elliott, and Ysseldyke (2002) suggest three general ways a teacher can help students prepare for high-stakes tests: test-approach skills, test-taking skills, and test-preparedness skills.

TIPS FOR TEACHERS 12.7

Testing Adaptations

Teach students test-taking skills.

Give frequent quizzes rather than only exams.

Give take-home tests.

Test on less content than the rest of the class.

Change types of questions (e.g., essay to multiple choice).

Use tests with enlarged print.

Use black-and-white copies (versus dittos).

Highlight key words in questions.

Provide extra space on tests for answering.

Simplify wording of test questions.

Allow students to answer fewer questions.

Give extra help preparing for tests.

Give the actual test as a study guide.

Give practice questions as a study guide.

Give open-book and open-note tests.

Give tests to small groups.

Give extended time to finish tests.

Read test questions to students.

Allow use of learning aids during tests (e.g., calculators).

Give individual help with directions during tests.

Allow oral instead of written answers (e.g., tape recorders).

Allow answers in outline format.

Allow word processors.

Give feedback to individual students during the test.

Source: "Testing adaptations: A national survey of the testing practices of general education teachers," by M. Jayanthi, M. H. Epstein, E. A. Polloway, & W. D. Bursuck, 1996, *Journal of Special Education, 30,* 99–25.

1. Test-approach skills are skills that can help students get physically and mentally ready for exams. Sending flyers home to parents about the importance of sleep and nutrition can help prepare students physically. Salend (2011a) emphasizes the importance of reducing test anxiety. Teaching test-taking and test-preparedness skills will help alleviate student anxiety. However, the positive attitude you set in your classroom is vital for the reduction of anxiety. It is important to learn if students have a general anxiety disorder or if they have anxiety that is linked specifically to test-taking situations (Cassady, 2010). Talk with your school counselor about students who seem to have an unusually high level of anxiety about assessment—either formal or informal.
2. Test-taking skills are skills that students use during the examination (Flippo, Becker, & Wark, 2009; Strichart & Mangrum, 2010). You can help students develop test-taking skills by providing suggestions for taking specific types of tests (multiple-choice, true/false, matching, short-answer, essay) and by teaching testing vocabulary. Table 12.2 presents cue words related to essay examinations that can help students construct better answers on open-ended items on high-stakes tests.
3. Test-preparedness skills are skills related to knowing both the general content and the format of the test. Critics of high-stakes tests point out that teachers are reduced to "teaching to the test" and that instruction becomes stilted and narrow. Gulik (2003) warns, "A teacher should not engage in instruction that addresses only those portions of knowledge included on the test" (p. 2). Many teachers find

Table 12.2 • Instruction Cue Words for Answering Essay Questions

CUE	MEANING
Analyze	Break into parts and examine each part.
Apply	Discuss how the principles would apply to a situation.
Compare	Discuss differences and similarities.
Contrast	Discuss differences and similarities, stressing the differences.
Critique	Analyze and evaluate, using criteria.
Define	Provide a clear, concise statement that explains the concept.
Describe	Give a detailed account, listing characteristics, qualities, and components as appropriate.
Diagram	Provide a drawing.
Discuss	Provide an in-depth explanation. Be analytical.
Explain	Give a logical development that discusses reasons or causes.
Illustrate	Use examples or, when appropriate, provide a diagram or picture.
Interpret	Explain and share your own judgment.
Justify	Provide reasons for your statements or conclusion.
List	Provide a numbered list of items or points.
Outline	Organize your answer into main points and supporting details. If appropriate, use outline format.
Prove	Provide factual evidence to support your logic or position.
Relate	Show the connections among ideas.
Review	Provide a critical summary in which you summarize and present your comments.
State	Explain precisely.
Summarize	Provide a synopsis that does not include your comments.
Trace	Describe the development or progress of the idea.
Add your own instructions, cue words, and definitions!	

Source: Based on "Strategies for teaching students with learning and behavior problems" (4th ed., p. 326), by C. S. Bos & S. Vaughn, 2015, Boston: Allyn & Bacon. Copyright © 2015 by Pearson Education. Reprinted and electronically reproduced by permission of Pearson Education, Inc., Upper Saddle River, New Jersey.

this easier said than done (Schumm, Adelman, & McLeod, 2012). Guthrie and Wigfield (2000) offer suggestions for making connections between standards, test content, and student motivation:

Learning and knowledge goals. Set core learning goals that are co-developed by the teacher and the students.

Real-world interactions. Make connections between the academic curriculum and the personal experiences of learners.

Interesting subject content. Students will devote effort, attention, and persistence to topics that are enjoyable and intriguing.

Strategy instruction. Provide direct instruction, scaffolding, and guided practice.

Praise and rewards. Give informative compliments that make learners feel a sense of accomplishment and pride in their work.

Teacher-made tests

Tests are the primary means teachers use to determine whether students have learned new concepts and can apply them. Regular classroom tests can be teacher-made, department- or district-made, or come from supplemental textbook materials. If you use department-made, district-made, or textbook-made exams, read the exams thoroughly to make sure the content is representative of what you have covered in class or in reading assignments. It is a good idea to take the tests yourself as a way of reviewing test content. One of the primary steps you can take is to create student-friendly tests (Salend, 2011b).

Tests are also a way to find out what students need to learn and what they have learned. Pretests can be used to identify what students already know about a topic and help you plan for differentiated instruction. Tests can also be used for ongoing monitoring of student progress and for outcomes at the end of a lesson or unit. The best way to discover what students have learned is to construct student-friendly tests, adapt test administration and scoring as necessary, consider alternatives to testing (such as assessment portfolios), and teach test-taking skills. Student-friendly tests are considerate to the test taker in content and format. The content has been covered in class or assigned readings, and students have been told explicitly that they are responsible for learning it. The format is clear and easy to understand. To construct student-friendly tests, you must first decide what skills and concepts to include. The lesson- and unit-planning pyramids can be particularly helpful here; to complete them, you decide which concepts are most important and prioritize those concepts for instructional purposes. You know what you want all, most, and some of your students to know, and you have told them your expectations. You can cover those skills and concepts on the test. Avoid asking trivial or trick questions (Conderman & Koroghlanian, 2002; Salend, 2011b).

In a test format, directions should be clear and unambiguous, and items should be legible and properly spaced. Students should have sufficient room to place their answers and specific guidelines if answers are to be written on a separate sheet. Attention to format is important for all students but particularly for those who have difficulty reading and taking tests and those who are anxious about test-taking.

Even with student-friendly tests, students with learning problems may have difficulty reading tests, working within time constraints, or resisting distractions during a test. Other special learners may have physical needs that inhibit performance on a test (they may tire easily, for example). As you decide which, if any, adaptations to use, consider the material to be covered by the test, the test's task requirements (e.g., reading, taking dictation), and the particular needs of special learners. Consult with the special education teacher and other specialists in your school to get advice about the most appropriate adaptations for individual students.

The National Council on Educational Outcomes (2012) suggests five categories of accommodations for students with disabilities:

1. Presentation (e.g., reading the test aloud, large-print, providing individual help with directions)
2. Equipment and materials (e.g., dictionary, calculator, amplification devices)

3. Responses (e.g., oral responses, dictation, writing on test rather than using an answer sheet)
4. Setting (e.g., individualized setting, secluded space in the room)
5. Timing/Scheduling (e.g., extended time, testing over several days, breaks on an as-needed basis)

Your school district or state will have guidelines for allowable accommodations for students with disabilities and English language learners.

Alternative assessments

In addition to tests, alternative assessments can be used for preassessment, ongoing monitoring, and assessment of student outcomes at the end of a lesson or unit. The idea with alternative assessments is to offer students variety in terms of how they can demonstrate what they have learned and can do. The following are some examples of alternative assessments:

- Audio and video recordings, CD-ROMs, photographs
- Teacher, peer, and self-checklists
- Lists of books read
- Lists of accomplishments
- Samples of home learning
- Goals statements and record of goal attainment
- Journals and self-reflections
- Graphs of individual student progress
- Copies of passages read fluently

Both tests and alternative assessment artifacts can be organized into an assessment portfolio. **Assessment portfolios** are collections of work samples that document a student's progress (Wormeli, 2006a). You can use portfolios to provide tangible evidence of student performance over a period of time. Portfolios can include writing samples of all stages of the writing process and in all genres. Suggestions for developing assessment portfolios are included in Tips for Teachers 12.8.

TIPS FOR TEACHERS 12.8

Development of Assessment Portfolios

Develop a portfolio plan consistent with your purposes for the assignment.

Clarify what work will go into portfolios.

Start with only a couple of different kinds of entries and expand gradually.

Compare notes with other teachers as you experiment with portfolios.

Have as a long-term goal the inclusion of a variety of assessments that address content, process, and attitude goals across the curriculum.

Make portfolios accessible in the classroom. Students and teachers should be able to add to the collection quickly and easily.

Develop summary sheets or graphs that help to describe a body of information (e.g., "I can do" lists, lists of books read, or pieces of writing completed). Let students record these data when possible.

Work with the student to choose a few representative samples that demonstrate the student's progress.

Review portfolios with students periodically (at least four times during the school year). The review should be a time to celebrate progress and to set future goals.

Encourage students to review portfolios with a classmate before reviewing with the teacher. Students should help make decisions about what to keep.

In getting ready for a parent conference, have students develop a table of contents for the portfolio.

Source: A handbook for the K–12 reading resource specialist (pp. 119–120), by M. C. Radencich, P. C. Beers, & J. S. Schumm, 1993, Boston: Allyn & Bacon. Reprinted and electronically reproduced by permission of Pearson Education, Inc., Upper Saddle River, New Jersey.

FIGURE 12.5 **Charting student progress**

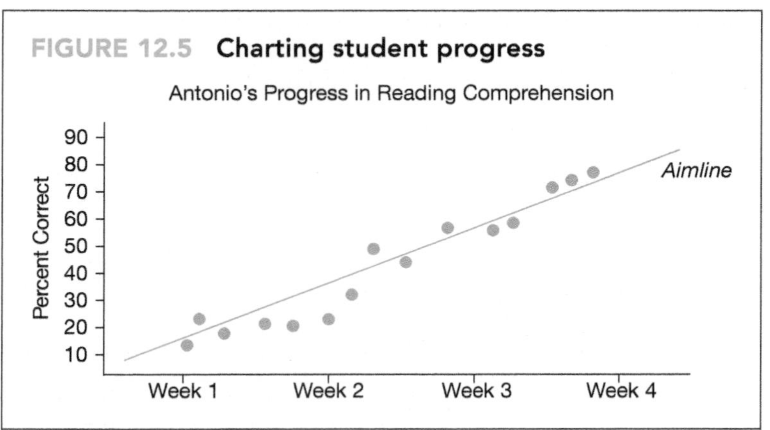

Assessment portfolios can be organized according to subject-area standards that students need to master. Students can gather evidence that demonstrates their progress in meeting standards and benchmarks. Thus, students can become actively engaged in self-assessment. For this to happen, students need to be aware of academic goals, criteria for mastery, and what constitutes adequate evidence (Andrade & Valtcheva, 2009; McMillan & Hearn, 2008). Checklist and self-reflection prompts can be used to get students actively engaged in gauging their progress in meeting goals (Wormeli, 2006a). Although students can become actively involved in monitoring their performance, their assessment should only represent a small portion (perhaps 5%) of their grade (Andrade & Valtcheva, 2009).

Students can become actively involved in charting their progress in meeting academic goals. Research indicates that teacher charting of progress results in positive student outcomes. The same is true when students chart their progress. What's even more powerful is when both teachers and students chart progress (Fuchs & Fuchs, 1986; Santangelo, 2009; Salvia et al., 2013).

Antonio is a fourth grader reading on a third-grade level. He needed to work on his reading comprehension. His teacher, Doris Walton, talked with Antonio about using commercial reading comprehension booklets at his instructional reading level during reading center time. Together they set a goal for Antonio to get a grade of 90% of the comprehension questions correct in 6 weeks (the aim line). Each time Antonio completed an exercise, Doris would grade it and work with Antonio to develop strategies for the types of reading comprehension questions that were difficult for him. Antonio charted his progress on a line graph. Figure 12.5 provides an example of a progress monitoring chart for Antonio.

12.4.3 Grading

Perhaps few other topics related to differentiated assessment and instruction generate more discussion than grading. Teachers, administrators, parents, and students struggle with what is fair in terms of individual student rights, equity among all students in the classroom, and accountability to state and local standards (Nunley, 2006; Wormeli, 2006a). Even though local policies are in place that address grading issues, there are no easy answers as to what is fair and equitable for all students.

In general, when differentiating assessment and grading, keep in mind what you want your students to know and be able to do to demonstrate mastery of a standard. The pathways that individual students take to mastery may be very different (Nunley, 2006). Students with an IEP may have an individualized grading system that documents progress in meeting educational or performance goals or defines an alternative grading scale (Conderman & Hedin, 2012). Salend (2011a) recommends that teachers might consider adaptations such as partial credit, bonus points, and test retakes to help students with disabilities and test anxiety to relieve tension associated with performance.

ACTIVITIES FOR ALL LEARNERS

Helping Students Use Rubrics

Objective: To help students learn to use rubrics effectively

Grades: Grades 6 and above

Teaching Procedures: To complete this activity, you will need a rubric and some student work samples. Give the students examples of high-quality work, average work, and less-than-satisfactory work, and have them complete the following **rubric** process:

Read the rubric and the material to be graded.

Use the rubric to give an initial score.

Bring a buddy to help you rate again.

Review the material together.

Identify and award the scores together.

Check the scores again.

Source: "RUBRIC—Teaching students to use grading rubrics," by C. W. Jackson, & M. J. Larkin, 2002, *Teaching Exceptional Children, 35,* 40–45.

One way to make your expectations and grading guidelines clear to students is through the use of rubrics or scoring guides. Such tools are increasingly being used to give students explicit information about expected performance on tests and assignments (Whittaker, Salend, & Duhaney, 2001; Wormeli, 2006a). Rubrics are of two general types: analytic rubrics (process-oriented instruments that break an activity into component parts) and holistic rubrics (product-oriented instruments used with parts that are interrelated) (Jackson & Larkin, 2002). Although the construction of rubrics does take some time, they typically streamline the grading process. Rubrics also make your expectations more tangible for students and their parents. The Activities for All Learners feature provides a strategy to help students become proficient in the use of rubrics.

As a classroom teacher, you will need to consider differentiated assessment as part of your overall planning process. Reutzel and Clark (2011) recommend that teachers first find out what assessments are required for screening, progress monitoring, diagnosis, and outcomes (both grades and on high-stakes tests). Planning for assessment begins with the school or state assessment calendar. It also includes inputting assessment results into a state or school district database, in addition to creating a teacher-made database to keep track of informal assessment data. One critical element of planning for assessment is logistics. How will you administer individual assessments when you have a class of twenty-one students? Finally, planning for assessment is facilitated by having a handy "assessment tool kit," including informal assessments that you collect over time.

MyEdLab **Self-Check 12.4**

MyEdLab **Application Exercise 12.4:** Differentiating Assessment

12 SUMMARY

- The standards-based movement has resulted in the creation of Common Core State Standards and implementation of those standards in many states. It is important that you become familiar with the standards for your subject area in the state where you plan to teach.
- Differentiated instruction has been identified as one means to plan for individual student needs. Differentiated instruction is both a philosophy of instructing students based on individual needs as well as instructional practices aligned with the philosophy.

- Textbook adaptations include study guides, highlighting, and alternative reading materials. You can become familiar with the strengths and weaknesses of your textbook by evaluating its subject-matter content, readability level, and friendliness level. One way to learn how your students interact with and respond to the textbook is to use the FLIP chart method.
- In classrooms that include highly diverse learners, differentiated assessment should go hand in hand with differentiated instruction. Assessment can be differentiated in terms of intensity, frequency, accommodations, and format. Differentiated assessment involves use of formal assessments and informal measures such as surveys, rubrics, checklists, projects, and home learning activities.

THINK AND APPLY

1. Now that you have read Chapter 12, think about how Stephanie and Christine met the challenges they faced in teaching their middle school students. What practices did they use? What additional strategies would you use in your own class?
2. On your state's department of education website, locate the instructional standards for your state in a subject area you plan to teach. Identify three standards and think about what challenges the standards might pose for high-, average-, and low-achieving students; for students with learning and behavior problems; for students who are English language learners; and for students who are gifted.
3. Work in a cooperative learning group to brainstorm the potential pitfalls of differentiated instruction and how you might overcome those pitfalls in your classroom.

13 Promoting Content Learning Through the Teaching and Learning Connection

Learning Outcomes

13.1 Describe ways to make lectures more student-friendly as well as how to support students in becoming more efficient in taking class notes.

13.2 Promote teaching and learning through questioning and classroom discussions.

13.3 Describe how graphic organizers can be used to enhance teaching and learning.

13.4 List ways to enhance lesson clarity by giving assignments that foster student responsibility for completing assignments.

13.5 Explain how to teach students effective practices for learning how to learn.

INTERVIEW: PATRICIA GRANDE, AMANDA REH, AND ANDREW DEMURO

Patricia Grande, Amanda Reh, and Andrew DeMuro completed their 15-week associate teaching (student teaching) experience. Faculty selected all three to receive awards for their excellence in associate teaching. Although their placements were very different in terms of grade level and school characteristics, they all learned strong lessons about the connection between how they teach and how their students learn.

Patricia taught kindergarten in a high-needs school. As she explained, "I didn't have a field placement in kindergarten, so this was a new experience for me. I had to learn how to teach in a way that was appropriate for their age and level of development." For example, when Patricia first made assignments, she provided directions with a number of steps. She quickly found that some students got one step, some got the second step, some got the third step, and some didn't know where to begin. "I learned to make assignments one step at a time to help them succeed." She was pleased to discover that much of what she learned about using graphic organizers with older students was appropriate for her kindergarten students as well.

Amanda was placed at a dual-language learning elementary school. She taught language arts and social studies to third graders in a diverse classroom that included students with disabilities (i.e., autism, emotional handicaps, attention deficit hyperactivity disorder) and one student who was limited English proficient. In the afternoon, she co-taught in a third-grade math and science class for students identified as gifted and talented. As she explains, "I experienced about every child discussed in the inclusion textbook." What came alive for Amanda during associate teaching was the importance of providing scaffolding in learning new strategies. She implemented literature circles in the morning class. Initially she modeled strategies for discussing narrative text. Then, she provided discussion steps on a handout. As the students became more proficient in using the steps, she removed the steps one at a time. When one step was missing, she asked what seemed to be gone and told the students to include that step as they always did. Gradually, the strategy steps became part of the routine in the literature circles and students developed independence in implementing the steps.

Andrew was placed in a high school in one of the most economically challenged neighborhoods in Miami. He taught American history and world history. The state was in the process of changing the order of what social studies subjects were taught at what grade. Thus, Andrew had ninth-, tenth-, and eleventh-grade students in his classes. He also had students who were strong readers and some who couldn't read very well. At the beginning of the semester, Andrew used a traditional routine consisting of lecture, discussion, and homework with textbook assignments. He was not confident that students were learning the material. As a result, he organized students into mixed-ability cooperative groups. Each day after a 5- to 10-minute overview, he had students work with carefully planned "discovery" activities to get them engaged with the material. Frequently students designed flowcharts, main-idea webs, and Venn diagrams to organize key concepts. Each lesson ended with a wrap-up activity to emphasize key concepts.

CHAPTER OUTLINE

Introduction

This chapter focuses on the teaching–learning connection, particularly in the content areas (e.g., social studies, science). As Patricia, Amanda, and Andrew realized in associate teaching experience, students need to be taught content material, but they also need to be taught how to learn the material. They have found it helpful in planning and in implementing plans to think about how to present content and assignments in class and how to explicitly prepare students to learn the material.

13.1 PREPARING LESSONS THAT PROMOTE ENGAGEMENT

Andrew (the social studies teacher in this chapter's interview) planned a big-bang lesson that students were not likely to forget. The lesson was on the Industrial Revolution and masses of workers moving from farm to factory, and involved a simulation of what it would be like to be a worker in a factory in that era. He set up stations with activities that involved completing somewhat complex assembly tasks. When a bell rang, students moved to another station. Each station had a "boss" or "overseer." Students became angry and frustrated until the bell rang and Andrew said they could have a break. However, soon the bell rang again and they went back to their stations. Andrew finally stopped the simulation and debriefed with the students. Andrew has developed a solid bag of tricks to get students actively engaged in a lesson. This section provides ideas for expanding your bag of teaching practices by (a) using prelearning activities, (b) creating listener-friendly lectures, (c) giving demonstrations, and (d) facilitating student learning through active listening and note-taking.

13.1.1 Getting Ready to Support Learning

Prelearning activities are strategies that teachers use to activate students' prior knowledge and to preteach vocabulary and concepts—essentially, to prepare students to learn. Lauren Lopez, who teaches ninth-grade science, describes her students as follows:

> Some of my students have traveled all over the world; others have never left their neighborhood. Some of my students have had solid instruction in science in the elementary grades; others have had none. The time I spend with prelearning activities sets the stage for learning and helps build common vocabulary. It saves lots of reteaching time.

Like Lauren, you can use purpose-setting activities and preteaching vocabulary to help students prepare to learn new information.

Purpose setting

Purpose-setting activities provide students with a reason for completing a reading assignment or for listening to a lecture. When teachers set a purpose for learning, students are guided through the reading and listening process and it improves the depth of their comprehension. Purpose-setting activities are important for all learners but particularly for students who have difficulties with attention and motivation. Although teachers often set a purpose for reading or listening, students can engage in purpose setting as well (Gunning, 2012). Tips for Teachers 13.1 provides guidelines for setting a purpose before you give a lecture or a reading assignment.

Preteaching vocabulary

In recent years, vocabulary instruction has taken a front seat in research and practice (Graves et al., 2014; McKeown & Curtis, 2014). Having an extensive vocabulary is linked to reading-comprehension competency and to academic success in general. Frequently,

TIPS FOR TEACHERS 13.1

Setting a Purpose for a Lesson

- Keep the purpose brief, but make it meaningful. Students become more actively involved in listening, reading, or participating in a classroom activity when they have a reason for doing so.
- Set a single purpose. When students are given too many purposes, they can lose their focus. If there is more than one purpose, focus on the most important one.
- Make certain that the purpose statement is not too narrow in scope and that it does not reveal too much content, which can actually inhibit comprehension.
- Have a regular purpose-setting instructional routine. For example, write the purpose for learning on the board or demonstrate how the purpose was set.
- After reading, begin the discussion asking students to state why they were doing the reading (i.e., restate purpose for reading).
- Help students learn how to set their own purposes. Talk about the importance of setting a purpose and how to develop purpose statements.
- Keep the written purpose statement in full view of students while they are participating in a class activity. Some students may need to be reminded about the purpose of the lesson.

Source: "The role of purpose in reading instruction," by W. E. Blanton, K. Wood, & G. B. Moorman, 1990, *The Reading Teacher, 43*(7), 486–493.

students with disabilities have vocabulary deficits that persist over time without adequate instruction (Wood, Mustian, & Cooke, 2012). Students who are English language learners often have gaps in their vocabulary knowledge, particularly with academic vocabulary in content-area subjects (Lesaux et al., 2014; Kelley, Lesaux, Kieffer, & Faller, 2010). Although a number of definitions of *academic vocabulary* exist in the literature, most definitions focus on terms that are specific to a given discipline or school subject or terms that are general and cross multiple disciplines (see Baumann & Graves, 2010 for a discussion). Nagy and Townsend (2012) provide a definition of academic vocabulary that is helpful for teachers and includes the following key elements:

- Specialized language of a discipline or profession (e.g., words used by a historian),
- Oral and written,
- Words that communicate understanding of the discipline (e.g., function in math).

The Common Core State Standards (www.corestandards.org) emphasize the importance of learning general academic vocabulary and vocabulary specific to various academic domains, as well as figurative language and connotations of words. The standards outline progressively more difficult goals throughout grades K through 12. Beck, McKeown, and Kucan (2013) suggest that vocabulary instruction should include words from three tiers. Tier 1 words are those students are likely to encounter frequently and are relatively easy to explain. Tier 2 words are terms used in multiple disciplines, but are not typically used in everyday conversation. Tier 3 words are discipline-specific and typically require more explanation and conceptual development.

Before beginning a unit or individual lesson, you can help students gain a better understanding of what they are about to read or hear through direct preteaching of a few key words. These are the most important words that the students need to know to understand the lesson or key ideas in the unit. Teaching too many new vocabulary words can confuse students. Preteaching these vocabulary words prior to conducting the lesson is helpful for all students, particularly those with limited prior knowledge of the topic.

In selecting the words you are going to preteach, begin by identifying the key ideas you want students to learn in a unit or lesson. Next, identify the key vocabulary related to expressing those key ideas that would be most helpful for your students to learn. Present the words enthusiastically using a variety of methods and materials and encourage them to identify other words of interest as they read. Presenting the words in context and linking with experiential background is helpful for all students, but particularly English language learners. Figure 13.1 provides a vocabulary instructional map as a sample of the ways in which key academic vocabulary can be taught.

FIGURE 13.1 Academic vocabulary map

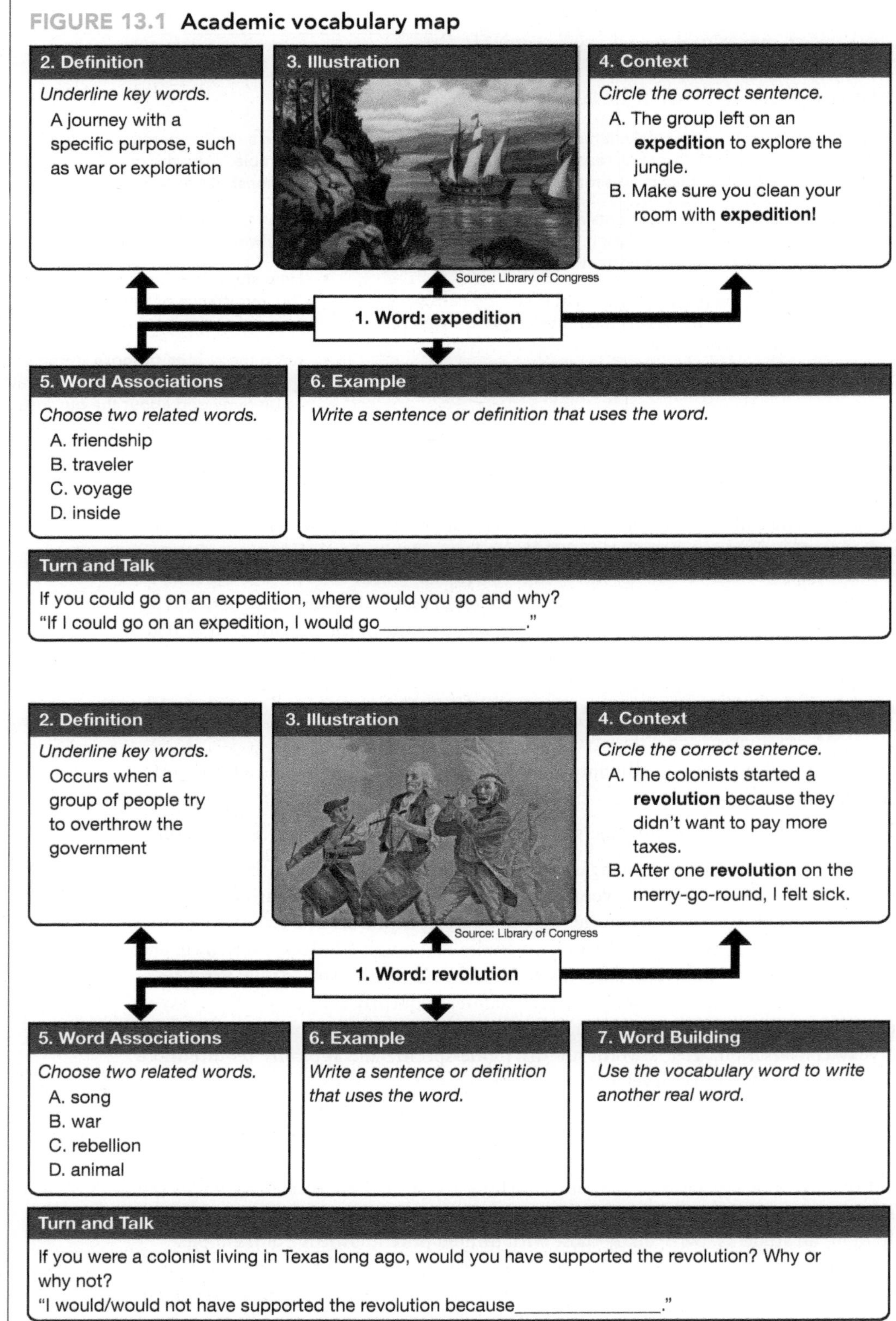

2. Definition

Underline key words.

A journey with a specific purpose, such as war or exploration

3. Illustration

Source: Library of Congress

4. Context

Circle the correct sentence.

A. The group left on an **expedition** to explore the jungle.

B. Make sure you clean your room with **expedition!**

1. Word: expedition

5. Word Associations

Choose two related words.

A. friendship
B. traveler
C. voyage
D. inside

6. Example

Write a sentence or definition that uses the word.

Turn and Talk

If you could go on an expedition, where would you go and why?
"If I could go on an expedition, I would go_______________."

2. Definition

Underline key words.

Occurs when a group of people try to overthrow the government

3. Illustration

Source: Library of Congress

4. Context

Circle the correct sentence.

A. The colonists started a **revolution** because they didn't want to pay more taxes.

B. After one **revolution** on the merry-go-round, I felt sick.

1. Word: revolution

5. Word Associations

Choose two related words.

A. song
B. war
C. rebellion
D. animal

6. Example

Write a sentence or definition that uses the word.

7. Word Building

Use the vocabulary word to write another real word.

Turn and Talk

If you were a colonist living in Texas long ago, would you have supported the revolution? Why or why not?
"I would/would not have supported the revolution because_______________."

13.1.2 Creating Listener-Friendly Lectures

Computer software and Internet sites are often described in terms of their "user-friendliness." When teachers, like website developers, keep the audience in mind and anticipate points of potential difficulty, the product is user-friendly. Listener-friendly lectures are lectures structured to facilitate listening and learning. Such lectures are not only well organized, but also help students discern what is most important and connect new ideas to what they already know. Well-designed lectures are particularly beneficial for students with learning disabilities, English language learners, and listeners with relatively limited language skills and/or little prior knowledge of the content.

The goal of lectures or instructional presentations is to enhance student understanding. One key to enhancing understanding is instructional clarity—the clear, direct, explicit presentation of information. The following contribute to instructional clarity (McCaleb & White, 1980; Stronge, Ward, & Grant, 2011).

Teacher's verbal knowledge

Teachers who have a strong verbal knowledge and command of the content are better able to provide instructional clarity.

Understanding—connecting new information with what students already know

Structuring—providing a clear format for the presentation, one that students can follow easily

Sequencing—arranging a presentation in a logical order

Explaining—defining key terms and providing examples as necessary

Presenting—delivering material in an articulate and lively manner with correct pacing, and using visual aids and multimedia as necessary

Clarity in presenting the most important information is necessary for all students but particularly for students who have difficulty with language or organizational skills or who have little prior knowledge of a topic. Instructional clarity is particularly important during lectures. Giving lectures is often necessary to generate interest in a topic, to provide information that is not included in textbooks, or to clarify or embellish textbook information. Although lectures tend to be overused, when used properly, they can be an effective way to teach. By improving your lectures, you help students improve their learning. See Tips for Teachers 13.2 for ideas on how to create listener-friendly lectures.

TIPS FOR TEACHERS 13.2

Tips for Creating Listener-Friendly Lectures

- Use advance organizers to provide an overview of the organization of the lecture.
- Use cue words or phrases to let students know what information is important (e.g., "It is important that you know," "The key information to remember is," "In summary").
- Repeat important information.
- Write important information on the board, the transparency, and a handout.
- Stress key points by varying the tone and quality of your voice.
- Number ideas or points (e.g., first, second, next, then, finally).
- Write technical words or words that are difficult to spell.
- Use a study guide that lists the major concepts, with space for students to add other information.
- Use pictures, diagrams, and semantic maps to show relationships among ideas.
- Provide examples and nonexamples of the concepts you are discussing.
- Ask questions or encourage discussion that requires students to relate the new information to ideas they already know (from their own background or your previous lectures).
- Stop frequently and have students work with partners to discuss what they have learned.
- Allow time at the end of a lecture for students to look over their notes, summarize, and ask questions.

Many teachers are using PowerPoint presentations to organize their lectures (Coleman, 2009; Parette, Hourcade, & Blum, 2011). PowerPoint can also be used to develop learning center or individualized activities. For example, Narkon, Wells, and Segal (2011) used PowerPoint to develop an "E-Word Wall" to help students with learning disabilities and autism in their vocabulary development. Leigh and Johnson (2004) recommend the following:

- When preparing PowerPoint presentations, give careful attention to font size and color and background color. The goal is for all students to be able to read the print clearly, even if they are sitting at the back of the room.
- Carefully plan the amount of information you provide on each slide—not too much information, not too little.
- When presenting the slides, don't go through them too quickly, particularly if students do not have handouts of the slides.

Kawasaki (2005) recommends the 10/20/30 rule for PowerPoint presentations. Use no more than 10 slides. Lecture for no more than 20 minutes (leaving the remaining time for discussion and follow-up activities). Use a font size no less than 30. While giving lectures, use cues to help students become more active listeners and better note takers (see Figure 13.2).

Another way to improve your presentations so students learn more is to implement the pause procedure (Armbruster, 2009; Bachhel & Thaman, 2014). The **pause procedure** is a technique that helps students learn more from lectures by keeping them engaged throughout

FIGURE 13.2 Using cues when giving lectures

Use the following list of cues to help students learn how to listen and watch for important information. Encourage students to listen and watch for additional cues and add them to the list. When integrating a content unit with a unit on note-taking, you can place the information presented in this activity on a handout or post it on a wall chart.

TYPE OF CUE	EXAMPLES
Organizational cues	"We will be discussing ..."
	"The topic I want to cover today ..."
	"There are (number) points I want you to be sure to learn ..."
	"The important relationship is ..."
	"The main point of this discussion is ..."
	Any statement that signals a number or position (e.g., first, last, next, then)
	"To review/summarize/recap, ..."
Emphasis cues: verbal	"You need to know/understand/remember..."
	"This is important/key/basic/critical."
	"Let me repeat this, ..."
	"Let me check, ... now do you understand?"
	Any statement that is repeated.
	Words are emphasized.
	Teacher speaks more slowly, loudly, or with more emphasis.
	Teacher stresses certain words.
	Teacher spells words.
	Teacher asks rhetorical question.
Emphasis cues: nonverbal	Information written on overhead or board.
	Information handed out in study guide.
	Teacher emphasizes point by using gestures.

Note: For more information, see "Notetaking strategy instruction," by S. K. Suritsky & C. A. Hughes, 1996, in D. D. Deshler, E. S. Ellis, & B. K. Lenz (Eds.), *Teaching adolescents with learning disabilities* (2nd ed., pp. 267–312), Denver: Love.

the process. During logical breaks in a lecture (approximately every 10 minutes), the teacher pauses for 2 minutes. During that time, pairs of students compare their notes to make certain that key concepts have been recorded. Students also ask each other questions to check for understanding. At the end of the 2 minutes, the teacher asks students whether they have any questions and whether any concepts need further discussion or clarification. After this quick monitoring for student understanding, the presentation continues.

13.1.3 Enhancing Lectures with Demonstrations

Demonstrations can be used to show students how to perform a skill, complete a task, or solve a problem. Demonstrations can be for the whole class, small groups, or individual students. They can be preplanned or can occur on the spot as part of interactive planning when students need more explanation. The key to demonstrations is that they must engage students, especially passive learners who will watch your demonstration and then forget every step of it. The important thing is to get students involved and thinking about what you are doing.

As with any lesson, before you give a demonstration be sure to set a purpose, define key vocabulary, and provide an overview or advance organizer of the presentation, including key things to observe (Good & Brophy, 2008). Also provide guidelines for student participation during the presentation. Should they take notes? Should they ask questions before, during, or after the demonstration (Good & Brophy, 2008)?

After the demonstration, ask students to summarize the steps, or have one or two students repeat the demonstration for the class. Bryant, Smith, and Bryant (2008) suggest adding two steps for giving demonstrations to students with learning problems using the **demonstration plus model strategy**:

1. After the students have viewed the demonstration, have a student perform each step, verbalizing each step as you did.
2. Have all students complete additional practice exercises independently, using the steps.

You can also improve a demonstration by describing your thinking as you move through the demonstration. Teacher **think-alouds** are a metacognitive strategy used to model how to think and learn (Fisher, Frey, & Lapp, 2011; Oczkus, 2009). Think-alouds are most frequently used to model reading processes, but they can also be used to model thinking during a demonstration. You can model how to make predictions, talk about tricky or confusing procedures, and verbalize how you plan to solve problems that arise.

13.1.4 Fostering Listening and Taking Notes in Class

Teachers typically base test material on assigned readings and on material presented in class. To perform well on tests, students often need to take notes to make a record of lecture content. However, some students face challenges in listening and taking notes. For example, research indicates that middle school students with learning disabilities take fewer and less accurate notes than their nondisabled peers (Boyle, 2010).

There is growing evidence that when students are actively engaged in taking notes, they retain more information than when complete sets of notes are simply handed to them (Austin, Lee, & Carr, 2004; Grabe, Christopherson, & Douglas, 2004–2005; Neef, McCord, & Ferreri, 2006).

Tinisha Robinson teaches seventh-grade civics. She uses class discussion or cooperative groups to have students generate a rationale for the importance of taking notes for school success. If students do not mention the following reasons, Tinisha points out that *note-taking*:

- Increases attention.
- Requires a deeper level of thinking because students must make sense of the information as they write down ideas.
- Requires students to process information at a deeper level, making learning and remembering information easier.

The Common Core State Standards (www.corestandards.com) require that students learn to integrate and evaluate information gleaned from a variety of sources. Thus, students will need strategies for how to summarize information presented in lectures, but also from other media and classroom discussions as well.

Guidelines for effective note-taking

Next, Tinisha teaches guidelines for effective note-taking, preparing students to implement practices before, during, and after a lecture. Following are some general guidelines.

Before the lecture, students can skim or read related sources to get ready to listen. Reviewing notes from the previous lecture is often helpful. During the lecture, students should both listen and write. For students with auditory, memory, or attention problems or difficulties with writing fluency, taking notes can be quite difficult. Developing good note-taking habits can help students overcome obstacles. Schumm (2001) offers the following suggestions for taking notes:

- Write down the date and title of each lecture.
- Don't worry about punctuation or grammar.
- Use abbreviations for speed and efficiency.
- Don't write down every word the teacher says.
- Record what the teacher puts on the board or includes in PowerPoint presentations or transparencies.
- Underline, circle, or star anything the teacher repeats or emphasizes.
- Don't write more than one idea per line.
- Listen for digressions (times when the teacher gets off the subject). It's okay to take a mental break during these—but listen for cues that the content from the lecture is starting up again.
- Write down any questions the teacher asks, because these are likely to appear on future tests.
- Don't cram your writing into a small space. Leave room to add more notes later.
- Put question marks by any points you don't understand. Check them later with the teacher. (p. 25)

Two-column note-taking is frequently recommended to provide structure for taking notes (Bean, Readence, & Baldwin, 2011; Pauk, 1989; Santa, Havens, & Valdes, 2004). Originally developed by Walter Pauk at Cornell University, two-column notes consist of a cue column, where students record main ideas or prompts, and a recording column, where students record details, examples, illustrations, and other key facts. Two-column notes can be used for taking notes during lectures but can also be used to take notes when reading textbooks (see Figure 13.3 for an example).

Guided note-taking is an effective way to provide students structure in learning how to take notes (Konrad, Joseph, & Itoi, 2011). Guided notes provide an outline of the lecture with spaces provided for students to write in key ideas. Graphic organizer frameworks may be inserted to help students organize the information. Teachers can also insert "cues" to guide students to key ideas, resources for completing activities or learning more about the topic, or engaging in metacognitive reflections.

After the lecture, students should clean up and review their notes within 24 hours. Because students may have trouble deciphering what they wrote or what they meant when they wrote something down, waiting a week or two to revise their notes or waiting until it is time to study for a test might be too late. Cleaning up notes involves reorganizing, supplementing notes with textbook information, and writing out abbreviations. It can also involve finding the correct spelling of key technical vocabulary words. Reviewing notes involves highlighting key ideas, writing notes to ask the teacher in class, and thinking about ways to remember important information for tests and class discussions. See also Figure 13.4 for listening and note-taking inventories students can use to guide their note-taking practice.

FIGURE 13.3 **Sample two column note-taking**

DATE: MAY 15	TOPIC: THE 3 BRANCHES OF U.S. GOVERNMENT
Key Concepts	**Notes**
Legislative Branch	
Houses	Senate; House of Representatives
Members	2 senators from each state
Major Duty	Representatives from each congressional district make laws
Executive Branch	
Members	President; Vice president
Major Duty	Members of the cabinet enforce laws
Judicial Branch	
Members	9 justices of the Supreme Court
Major Duty	Interprets laws

FIGURE 13.4 **Listening and note-taking inventory**

Part A: Listening Inventory

What kind of listener are you? Find out by taking this Listening Habits Inventory.

You'll need a piece of paper and something to write with. Number the paper from 1 to 12. For each statement, give yourself 2 points if you *always* do it, 1 point if you *sometimes* do it, and 0 points if you *never* do it.

1. I'm in my seat and ready to listen soon after the bell rings.
2. I don't do other things while the teacher is talking.
3. I don't talk with friends while the teacher is talking.
4. I listen carefully to directions.
5. I ask questions when I don't understand directions or other information the teacher presents.
6. I take notes when the teacher presents a lot of information.
7. I know when the teacher is making an important point.
8. If I catch myself daydreaming, I try to get back on track.
9. I look at the teacher when she or he is talking.
10. I concentrate on what the teacher is saying.
11. If someone else is keeping me from listening, I ask that person to stop talking. If this doesn't work, I ask the teacher to help or change my seat.
12. I spend more time listening than talking in class.

Scoring: Add up your points.
16–24 points: You're a good listener!
12–15 points: You need to be a better listener!
11 points or less: Huh?

Part B: Note-Taking Inventory

From time to time, it's smart to check the quality of your notes to see how you're doing. Then you'll know if you need to make any changes or improvements. Use this Note-Taking Inventory whenever you feel the need. Simply check it against that day's class notes.

You'll need a piece of paper and something to write with. Number the paper from 1 to 10. Give yourself 1 point for each item you find in your notes.

1. Date of lecture
2. Title of lecture
3. Writing neat enough for you to read (that's all that counts)
4. No more than one idea per line
5. Plenty of blank space to add extra ideas later
6. All main ideas brought up during class
7. All important details mentioned during class
8. All key terms and definitions given during class
9. Abbreviations used where necessary
10. No unnecessary words

Scoring: Add up your points.
9–10 points: You're a great note taker!
7–8 points: You're a good note taker.
5–6 points: You need to take better notes.
4 points or less: Make a note of this—practice, practice, practice.

Source: Schumm, J. (2001). *School power: Study skill strategies for succeeding in school* (pp. 23, 31).

TIPS FOR TEACHERS 13.3

Evaluating Students' Note-Taking Skills

- *Have students evaluate the effectiveness of their current note-taking skills.* Give a lecture from the content unit and have students take notes as usual. The next day give students an open-note quiz. Provide answers to the quiz and then ask students to evaluate the completeness, format, and legibility of their notes, as well as their ease of use for review. You can also have students review their listening and note-taking habits as a springboard for discussion.
- *Use recorded lectures to teach students to listen effectively and take notes.* Use a recording of your lecture so that students can listen and watch for cues you give to signal important information. When students notice a cue, stop the recording and replay it so that all the students can hear and see it.
- *Control the difficulty of the lectures.* Select the first unit of the year to teach note-taking. This unit usually contains simple information that was presented the previous year.
- *Discuss with students some ways to record notes* (e.g., record key ideas, not sentences; use consistent abbreviations; use an outline format; spell a word the way it looks or sounds). As a class, have students develop a set of abbreviations to be posted on a wall chart.
- *Teach students how to review their notes, add missing information, and clarify information that is unclear.* Have students, working as partners or in cooperative groups, use their notes to study for tests. Teach students how to use their notes to create questions, and then check to see that they can answer them.
- *Have students monitor their note-taking.* Have them keep track of how often they use their note-taking skills in your class (and others), and record how they are doing on tests and assignments (and the effect of their improved note-taking skills).

Source: School power: Study skill strategies for succeeding in school, by J. S. Schumm, 2001, Minneapolis, MN: Free Spirit.

Teaching Note-Taking

Teaching note-taking skills to students in your class is a good investment of time and effort. When you teach note-taking skills, keep in mind that students need to master four key areas (Gunning, 2012):

- ***Selectivity***—selecting the most important main ideas and details
- ***Organization***—showing how key ideas are related
- ***Consolidation***—shrinking the key ideas in a telegraphic style
- ***Fluency***—rapid and efficient note-taking

As you teach a unit, you can use the procedure in Tips for Teachers 13.3 to evaluate your students' note-taking skills and to introduce and teach alternative ways to take notes.

Students who are new to note-taking or who have some difficulties taking notes may need more support (Boyle, 2007, 2010). Students with more severe problems may need a note-taking buddy to assist with taking notes. For some students, graphic organizers such as Venn diagrams can help them better conceptualize lessons. For others, note-taking frames that accompany PowerPoint presentations provide a very structured framework for listening and taking notes. Giving students structured support may be necessary for some students, but teachers should keep in mind that too much support may hinder the goal of working toward independence.

MyEdLab **Self-Check 13.1**

MyEdLab **Application Exercise 13.1:** Preteaching Vocabulary

13.2 USING QUESTIONING AND DISCUSSION TO PROMOTE STUDENT ENGAGEMENT

Students in Tinisha Robinson's class come from a self-contained elementary school setting in sixth grade. So, at the beginning of the school year, her students need a lot of support and structure as they adapt to having multiple teachers. Her school has block scheduling, so Tinisha has long stretches of time (1 hour and 45 minutes) for each class. Tinisha explains,

> I don't want any passive learners in my classroom. I want them engaged and participating. But many of my students don't know how or are reluctant to take a risk to do so. I teach my students how to ask questions, how to be an active member in a group, how to listen, and how to take notes. When they leave my class, they have the tools to succeed.

This section begins with an overview of how Tinisha encourages active participation in class. It continues with a section on questioning and class discussions, with an emphasis on making the teaching–learning connection.

13.2.1 Encouraging Participation in Class

In Tinisha's class, nonparticipation is not an option: "I want my reluctant learners to become risk takers. I want my English language learners to practice their new language. I want my students who always seem to have the right answers [to] learn to listen to their peers." Tinisha talks with her students about her expectations for participating in general class discussions and group work.

Classroom discussions go beyond teacher questions and student responses. Genuine discussions provide opportunities for the expression of multiple points of view, critical thinking, and information seeking (Gambrell et al., 2011). Figure 13.5 provides some guidelines for students as they become active participants in classroom discussions.

Cooperative learning groups and student pairs can be excellent ways to promote class discussion. However, you cannot assume that students will automatically know how to work efficiently and effectively in small-group settings (Slavin, 2015).

Group discussion and collaboration are emphasized in the Common Core State Standards for Speaking and Listening (www.corestandards.org). Students are expected to come prepared to group discussions, set guidelines with their peers for group meetings, and participate actively as a speaker and listener while working in groups.

13.2.2 Questioning

When Grace Demming did her college field experience in urban high schools in the late 1990s, one of the most frequent instructional patterns she observed was questioning routines. Teachers asked questions; students gave answers. Grace remarked, "It was like watching a tennis match—back and forth; back and forth." The teacher asks questions and students answer, back and forth. When teachers "serve the ball" only to students who are most capable of supplying the answer, other students become mere spectators.

Meichenbaum and Biemiller (1998) talk about the "art of questioning" and compare it to a dance: "each partner needs to be attuned to the other, following the other's

FIGURE 13.5 Classroom discussions

Do ...

ask questions based on reading you've done ahead of time.
ask questions about what others say in class.
listen carefully to what others have to say.
add any information you may have to a point someone else makes.
share your knowledge related to the topic when this will enhance the discussion.
make statements or ask questions showing that you came to class prepared.
give yourself 3 to 5 seconds of thinking time before answering a question; your answers will be more accurate and interesting.
be kind when you disagree with what somebody else says.

Don't ...

make comments that take up too much class time.
make comments just to hear yourself talk.
make a habit of going off the subject.
interrupt others.
get into arguments.

Source: School power: Study skill strategies for succeeding in school (p. 37), by J. S. Schumm, 2001, Minneapolis, MN: Free Spirit Publishing, Inc.

lead" (p. 153). Questioning is important for helping you to monitor student understanding of content and also for understanding how students are processing what they learn. Good and Brophy (2008) write about the "diagnostic power" of questioning. Questioning can also be used to scaffold and support student learning.

Asking simple yes/no questions or "guess what I'm thinking" questions has little instructional value in the classroom. Effective questioning strategies include the following:

- Distribute questions evenly among all students.
- Make certain that questions are clearly stated.
- Ask a variety of question types—lower- and higher-order questions.
- Ask all kinds of students all kinds of questions.
- Give students specific feedback about their answers.
- Let students explain why an answer is right.
- Let students explain their thinking when they get an answer wrong.
- Sequence the questions in such a way that they provide structure for learning.
- Ask questions in a nonthreatening, natural way.
- Encourage students to ask questions of you and of one another.
- Make questions relevant to students and to real-world applications.

One of the most important aspects of question asking is to allow enough time after you ask the question for students to think about their answer and raise their hand. Most teachers wait less than a couple of seconds and then answer the question. What are they teaching their students? Students are learning that if they wait a brief time the teacher will do the difficult work of answering the question. Giving students 3 to 5 seconds to think about an answer results in more thoughtful answers, more elaborated responses, and greater likelihood of participation from a wide range of students. There are benefits to asking fewer questions and giving students more time to give thoughtful answers (Zwiers, 2008). See the 60-Second Lesson for more suggestions for questioning strategies.

60-SECOND LESSON

TECHNIQUES FOR TEACHING QUESTION ANSWERING

Scaffolded questioning: When a student answers a question incorrectly, rather than giving the student the correct answer or moving on to another student, provide scaffolded questioning to promote student learning. Scaffolded questioning is not asking questions that lead to the answer you have in your head. Rather, scaffolded questioning is a set of sequenced prompts that begins with general questions and then provides increased guidance. The goal is not just for the student to arrive at the right answer; it is also to help students learn strategies for problem solving and answering questions. Some examples of scaffolded questions are:

- What information do you need to answer this question?
- Do you need me to repeat the question?
- What are some key words in my question? How can the key words help you answer the question?
- Look at the graphic organizer we started at the beginning of the lesson. What information in the graphic organizer can help you answer the question?

Group responding: When reviewing material for a test or when helping students develop fluency in answering questions, group responding can be helpful. Choral or group responding occurs when the teacher asks the whole class a question and the entire class responds simultaneously. Group responding should be used judiciously because it is more difficult to monitor individual student responses.

Sources: Teaching reading comprehension processes (3rd ed.), by J. W. Irwin, 2007, Boston: Pearson; and *Nurturing independent learners: Helping students take charge of their learning*, by D. Meichenbaum & A. Biemiller, 1998, Newton, MA: Brookline Books.

TIPS FOR TEACHERS 13.4

Techniques for Stimulating Discussion

- Provide information to which students can respond or react.
- Summarize student comments or ask students to provide intermittent summaries.
- Ask questions that begin "I wonder…" or "What would happen if…"
- Make statements that encourage students to tell more about what they were thinking or to provide examples.
- Invite students to ask questions of one another.
- Do not be overly concerned with moments of silence or pausing. Give everyone time to think and to gather their thoughts.

13.2.3 Generating Classroom Discussions

When done well, classroom discussions can be stimulating for students and for teachers as well. However, leading classroom discussions can be challenging for teachers (Ezzedeen, 2008; Johnston, Ivey, & Faulkner, 2011; Zwiers, 2008). Effective classroom discussions involve not only setting a positive classroom environment that encourages participating and risk-taking, but also a great deal of planning (Johnston et al., 2011; Zwiers, 2008). The goal is to engage students in vibrant discussions (Bean, 1985), in which student participation is high, students' thinking is stimulated, and students have opportunities to connect what they are learning to their personal knowledge and experience. Vibrant discussions help students learn how to express ideas, justify positions, listen to the ideas of others, and ask for clarification when they don't understand (Kauchak & Eggen, 1993; Zwiers, 2008).

Your role in a discussion is that of moderator and encourager. As a moderator, you help the group to establish a focus and stay on the topic. As an encourager, you engage reluctant participants and make certain that students are free to express their points of view. To encourage vibrant discussions, try the alternatives to traditional questioning in Tips for Teachers 13.4.

Your role is also to listen genuinely and to attend not only to the content of student talk, but also to the process of how students are learning (Johnston et al., 2011).

MyEdLab **Self-Check 13.2**

MyEdLab **Application Exercise 13.2:** Encouraging Participation in Class

13.3 USING GRAPHIC ORGANIZERS

Rita Menendez uses graphic organizers almost every day. She regularly uses graphic organizers as part of her classroom presentations, but also teaches her students how to use them as learning tools. She even has students create and share their own graphic organizers. As Gallavan and Kottler (2007) explain, "Graphic organizers offer visual models that equip teachers and students with tools, concepts, and language to organize, understand, and apply information" (p. 117). This section begins with ideas for using graphic organizers in your teaching and continues with ways you can promote student learning using them.

MyEdLab
Video Example 13.1.
As you watch this video, listen to the speaker's description of a graphic organizer as a pictorial summary of text. Do you think this is an accurate description, and how else do you think that graphic organizers can be used effectively to meet the needs of all students in a classroom?

Graphic literacy is integrated in the Common Core State Standards. Students are expected to interpret information presented in increasingly complex forms (R.CCR.5) and use graphic displays in their own presentations.

Rita explains that she uses not only a variety of graphic organizers but also a variety of materials. "Sometimes I just use the white board, sometimes the interactive white board or PowerPoint, and sometimes overhead transparencies." Rita then adds, "Starting a lesson with a graphic organizer helps, but refining the organizer as we read or listen and using the organizer as a tool for reviewing what we have learned [are] important as well."

FIGURE 13.6 **A discussion web**

What Do You Think? After reading a minimum of three resources, state reasons for and against the building of artificial reefs.

No—State your reasons and provide evidence	**Yes—State your reasons and provide evidence**
Overall—What did you decide?	

For students with learning disabilities and other students with reading comprehension difficulties, graphic organizers provide a visual representation of key ideas in the text and the relationships among those ideas (Sabbatino, 2004). Using lines, arrows, and flow charts, graphic organizers can help students conceptualize key ideas. Indeed, research synthesis (Kim, Vaughn, Wanzek, & Wei, 2004) and meta-analysis (Dexter & Hughes, 2011) find evidence for support of the use of graphic organizers in terms of improved vocabulary and comprehension.

13.3.1 Discussion webs

The discussion web (Alvermann, 1991) is a graphic aid to help students prepare for classroom discussions in content-area classes. It provides a structure for *critical thinking*—as Figure 13.6 shows, the discussion web is designed to help students examine both sides of an issue.

The discussion web is appropriate for elementary and secondary students and can be used before and after lectures. Alvermann suggests the following procedure for implementing the discussion web:

- Prepare students for reading or listening by introducing key vocabulary, activating prior knowledge, and setting a purpose for reading.
- After students have read a selection or listened to a lecture, introduce the discussion web with a provocative question. For example, after giving a lecture about the First Amendment, you could ask, "Should rap music be censored?" Provide time for students to discuss the pros and cons of the issue in pairs and complete the discussion web as a team. Students should take turns filling in as many "Yes" and "No" statements as the team can generate.
- Regroup pairs of students into teams of four students, who then compare their discussion webs and build consensus on an answer to the question.
- Have the group select and record the strongest argument and the reason for their choice.
- Have a spokesperson from each group take 3 minutes to report the results, and give individual students with dissenting or unrepresented points of view an opportunity to state their positions.
- Assign students an individual activity in which they write a position statement about their point of view on the issue.

FIGURE 13.7 **Example of a semantic map**

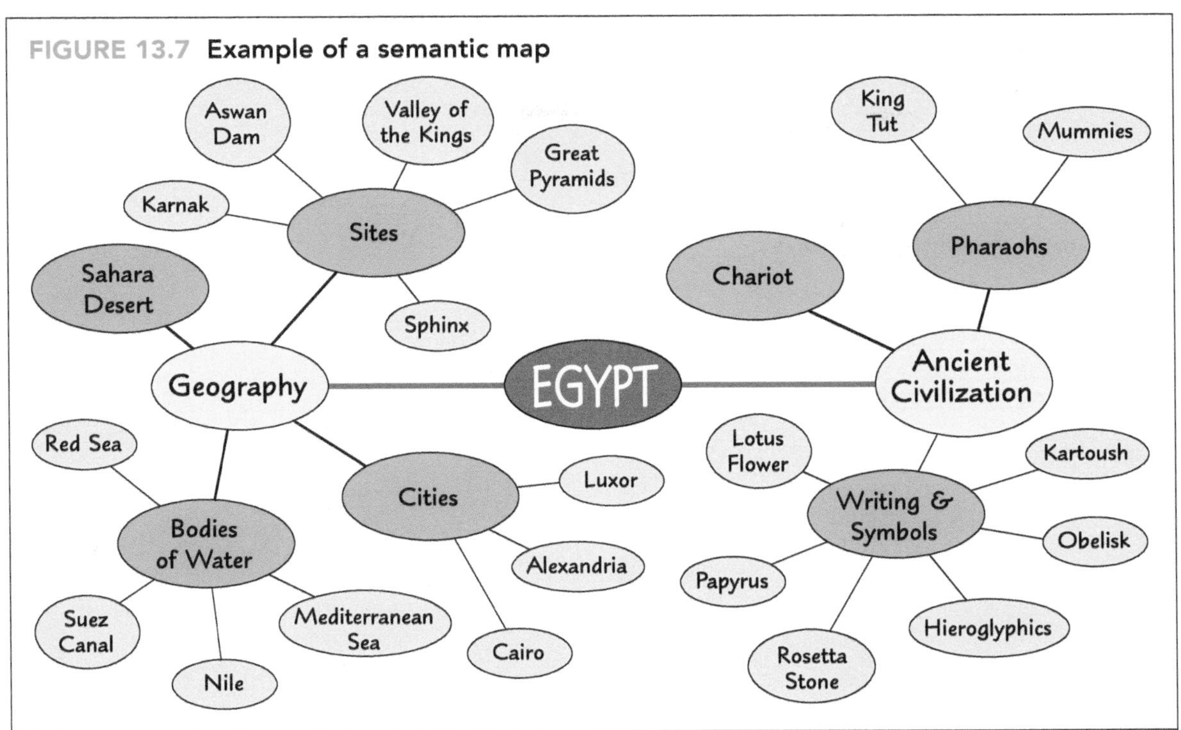

13.3.2 Semantic Maps

Providing students with visual representations of concepts and vocabulary to be learned is a powerful learning tool, particularly for special learners. One visual tool that is commonly used is a semantic map (Irwin, 2007; Pearson & Johnson, 1978), a visual aid that helps students see how ideas are related to one another and to what students already know.

Lists of words prepared in advance by the teacher or generated by students through teacher-guided brainstorming are placed on the board. After discussing the meanings of the words, students discuss how to cluster the words and work together to develop a map to represent visually the relationships that exist among the ideas. For example, Figure 13.7 shows a semantic map for the words for a chapter on Egypt. Students can use the map as a listening or reading guide. The map can also serve as a framework for postlistening and postreading discussions and as an aid for studying for tests or quizzes.

13.3.3 Concept Diagrams

Concept diagrams (Lenz & Deshler, 2004) are another way to introduce a lecture or reading assignment. A concept diagram (see Figure 13.8) is similar to a semantic map, but also helps students determine the definitions, characteristics, examples, and nonexamples of a concept.

Concept diagramming is time consuming. Select concepts with care. Choose those that are pivotal to the curriculum and that students need to understand thoroughly. See Tips for Teachers 13.5 for recommendations for creating concept diagrams.

13.3.4 Timelines

Timelines can be used to provide students with a way to visualize and sequence content-area information as they read, listen, and discuss. They can be used in math (e.g., sequences of events in word problems), science (e.g., seasons of the year), reading

FIGURE 13.8 Concept diagram

Concept Name: fossils

Definitions: Fossils are remains or prints of plants or animals who lived thousands of years ago which have been preserved in the earth.

Characteristics Present in the Concept:

Always	Sometimes	Never
remains or prints	frozen in ice	still alive
plants or animals	trapped in tar	still decaying
thousands of years old	crushed by water	
preserved in the earth	in volcanic ash	

Example:

- tigers in La Brea tar pits
- petrified forest in Arizona
- Siberian mammoth
- fish skeleton in limestone layers

Nonexample:

- your pet cat
- tree limbs and leaves in your yard
- elephant in Africa today
- fish in supermarket

Source: Vaughn, S., & Bos, C. (2012). *Strategies for teaching students with learning and behavior problems* (8th ed.). Copyright © 2014 by Pearson. Reprinted by permission.

(e.g., biographies or story plots), and art (e.g., timeline of classic art), and as a study skills tool (e.g., assignments for the month and activities needed to complete each assignment) (Fry & Kress, 2012). Timelines can be more than simple listings of facts on a horizontal black line (Kelly & Clausen-Grace, 2007). They can be illustrated or include photographs as well.

TIPS FOR TEACHERS 13.5

Creating Concept Diagrams

- Identify major concepts to teach.
- List important characteristics of the concepts. Think about whether each characteristic is always present, sometimes present, or never present.
- Locate examples and nonexamples of the concept.
- Construct a definition of the concept by naming the superordinate concept, its characteristics, and the relationships among characteristics.
- Introduce the concept diagram to students using an advance organizer.
- Elicit a list of key words or ideas that relate to the concept.
- Explain or review the parts of the concept diagram and their intended use.
- Name and define the concept with students.
- Discuss characteristics that are always present, sometimes present, and never present in the meaning of the concept.
- Discuss examples and nonexamples of the concept.
- Link the examples and nonexamples to the characteristics.

MyEdLab **Self-Check 13.3**

MyEdLab **Application Exercise 13.3:** Using Graphic Organizers

13.4 PROMOTING STUDENT SUCCESS WITH CLEAR ASSIGNMENTS AND TEACHING OF ORGANIZATIONAL SKILLS

In-class and homework assignments are staples in the teaching–learning connection. Assignments provide students with the opportunity to practice new skills and gain mastery of new concepts, and provide you with the opportunity to monitor student progress. This section begins with a discussion of how you can give clear assignments that promote student success. Next, it continues with specific ways you can develop student independence by teaching organizational and time-management skills and by teaching how to complete daily and long-term assignments.

13.4.1 Giving Assignments That Promote Student Success

Robert Pierre is a tenth-grade mathematics teacher. Robert grew up in the Little Haiti section of Miami and now teaches at the high school from which he graduated 5 years ago. Many of Robert's students are new immigrants to the United States. Many are still developing proficiency in English. Some attended school regularly in Haiti; others did not. Robert can identify with his students' struggles to learn, but he also serves as a role model of the merits of hard work and determination. Robert explains:

> My students know that they need to perform well on the state examinations if they are going to earn a college degree. It's a lot of pressure for them. At the beginning of the year I set guidelines (I call them Pierre's Pointers) for completing assignments and preparing for tests. I spend class time teaching them how to study so that we can bridge what's going on in class with what they are doing at home and on their own.

Spending class time teaching strategies for completing assignments, remembering information, and preparing for examinations can set the stage for what students do when they are on their own.

The most important aspect of making assignments is to give complete information. You need to let students know why the assignment is important, when it is due, what support they will have for completing the task, and the steps necessary for getting the job done. Having complete information helps to motivate students. The procedure in Tips for Teachers 13.6 can help you provide students with a complete set of directions.

TIPS FOR TEACHERS 13.6

Strategies for Giving Assignments

- Explain the purpose of the assignment. Stress what you expect students to learn and why learning the skill or concept is important. Connect the skill or concept to real-life applications.
- Explain in detail the procedures for completing the assignment. Ask one or two students to summarize the procedures to check for understanding.
- Get students started by modeling one or two problems or by providing an example.
- Describe the equipment and materials needed to complete the assignment.
- Anticipate trouble spots, and ask students how they might tackle difficult parts in the assignment.
- Tell students when the assignment is due.
- Explain how the assignment will be graded and how it factors into the overall grade for the class.
- Describe appropriate ways to get help or support in completing the assignment.
- For an in-class assignment, explain your expectations for student behavior while they complete the assignment and what students who finish early should do.
- Address student questions.

13.4.2 Developing Independence in Completing Assignments

You can probably predict reasons why students are not independent, successful learners. The reasons can be cognitive, cultural, communicative, educational, motivational, or organizational. For older students, family obligations, part-time jobs, and extracurricular activities can have an impact on study time. There can be a single reason or a complex web of reasons—over many of which you have little control.

Your students can also come up with a host of reasons:

- "There isn't enough time."
- "My teachers didn't prepare me for this level of work."
- "I don't have a quiet place to study at home."
- "I have to work after school."
- "I don't have a computer at home."

Many of the reasons you hear from students are beyond your control as well. Things you can control are (a) your focus on teaching students how to learn in your own classroom and (b) your advocacy for schoolwide strategy-learning programs. To make sure that strategy instruction is not superficial or inconsistent within and across classrooms, see Tips for Teachers 13.7 to learn about things you can do to support your students in becoming independent learners.

Classroom and homework assignments should be structured in such a way that they are purposeful and provide opportunities for students to practice, reinforce, or extend what was taught in school (Cooper, 2001). In addition, there should be definite rules about due dates and consequences for not meeting them (Good & Brophy, 2008). Most important, assignments should be checked, feedback provided, and intervention implemented as needed (Good & Brophy, 2008).

MyEdLab
Video Example 13.2.
Listen to the teacher in this video talk about the advantages of having her students use power outlining as an organizational strategy. What advantages does she mention and what organizational strategies have you found useful in your own studies that you would use with students to help them organize their thoughts before proceeding with tasks and assignments?

When students are habitually handing in assignments that are late or incomplete, you need to do some investigation to figure out whether the problem is with the level of difficulty of the work, clarity of directions, situations in the home, or personal learning or organizational issues. Students within all grade and achievement levels sometimes have problems with short-term assignments, long-term assignments, or both.

Getting organized for learning

Although students are typically receptive to learning organizational tips, some students will need more support and continuity in learning how to get organized. Failure to get organized can lead to lower grades and lack of academic progress. Some students with learning and behavior problems may need direct instruction in how to get organized (Anderson, Munk, Young, Conley, & Caldarella, 2008).

TIPS FOR TEACHERS 13.7

Helping Students to Become Independent Learners

- Teach strategies with sufficient depth and breadth.
- Integrate strategy instruction with ongoing content and curriculum.
- Get your students actively involved in assessing their strengths and challenges in learning strategies, setting goals for improvement, and monitoring their progress toward meeting those goals.
- Talk about personal responsibility and setting expectations for your students to meet.
- Teach your students about appropriate help-seeking behaviors.
- Communicate your expectations with parents and solicit their support as partners in learning.

FIGURE 13.9 Study habits checklist

Name ______________________ **Date** ______________

Rate each statement using higher numbers to indicate how well you perform on each statement: 2 = most of the time; 1 = some of the time; 0 = rarely.

STATEMENT

1. I keep track of my assignments and homework so I know what I need to do each night.
2. I understand the directions related to my homework assignments.
3. I keep the materials and resources I need to complete my assignments (e.g., books, papers).
4. I call my friends to find out what I am supposed to do.
5. I complete my homework on time.
6. My parents would describe me as having good study habits.
7. My friends would describe me as having good study habits.

To help students get organized, at the beginning of the school year, let parents know—through a letter, on your website, or on a class Facebook page, if you have one—that students will be assessing and thinking about modifying their home study environment to promote studying. After students complete a checklist (see Figure 13.9), have them meet in groups to discuss the results and their ideas for improving their study habits.

Meet with each student individually to summarize the results and to write one to three goals for improving the study environment, if warranted. Individual meetings are appropriate in that students may have personal or family issues they may not be willing to discuss in a group. For example, students whose parents are divorced may have two homes. Going back and forth between two different settings can pose logistical problems. Other students may not have access to a computer or other resources for learning in the home.

Have students report on their progress toward meeting their goals soon after the goals are set and several times each grading period thereafter. Also, alert students that you will be reviewing their notebooks for organization and will provide a list of recommended materials, including the following:

- Use a notebook or file folder so that pages can be added easily.
- Supply pouch and school supplies such as pens, pencils, erasers, calculator, hole punch, package of file cards, and ruler.
- Include labeled dividers—one for each class, plus others labeled "Schedules and Calendar," "Reference Information," "Notebook Dictionary," "Personal Word List," "Notebook Paper," "Graph Paper," and "Computer Paper."

Work with students to organize their notebooks, using the following suggestions:

- Include a semester calendar, weekly schedules, and to-do lists in the section on schedules and calendar.
- After the divider for each class, organize materials for that class (starting with class outline or syllabus).
- Date the notes and place them in order.
- In the personal word list, alphabetically list frequently misspelled words.

There are two inventories that will provide you with valuable information in guiding your students toward independence. The Study Habits Checklist (Figure 13.10) is one. The Help-Seeking Inventory (Figure 13.11) is the other inventory, which can be used as a guide for setting personal goals.

FIGURE 13.10 **Study habits checklist**

Name ______________________ Date ______________

Evaluate each statement by checking the column that describes your study habits.

STATEMENT	RARELY	GENERALLY	ALMOST ALWAYS
1. I set aside a regular time to study.			
2. I rarely allow interruptions during study time.			
3. I take short breaks when I get tired but return to work.			
4. I take a few minutes at the beginning to organize my study time.			
5. I begin with the hardest assignments.			
6. I finish one assignment before going on to the next one.			
7. I break long projects down into short tasks and work on the tasks over time.			
8. I begin studying for a test at least 3 days before the test.			
9. I have someone I can contact when I get stuck.			
10. I write down questions I need to ask the teacher.			

Source: Adapted from *Teaching study strategies to students with learning disabilities* (p. 356), by S. S. Strichart & C. T. Mangrum, II, 1993. Boston: Allyn & Bacon.

Using time-management strategies

Time management is the organization and monitoring of time so that tasks can be scheduled and completed in an efficient and timely manner. Effective time management includes the following:

- Identifying the tasks to be completed
- Estimating the time needed to complete the tasks
- Prioritizing the tasks
- Scheduling the time
- Working toward meeting deadlines
- Monitoring progress and adjusting deadlines or tasks
- Reviewing deadlines after task completion and adjusting schedules and priorities based on past performance

As a classroom teacher, long- and short-range planning are essential parts of your professional life—for both you and your students. Planning takes time; consequently, you will need to build a rationale that explains to students the importance of planning. Students will want to know why they need to take some time every month to do extended planning and to monitor their plans on a weekly or daily basis. Following are some suggestions for building a rationale:

- Scheduling your time helps you get jobs done so you have more time for fun and to spend with your friends.
- Parents will "get off your back" when they see you getting your work done on time.
- If you write down what you have to do, you don't have to try to remember everything.
- If you set a time to begin, it is easier to get started and not procrastinate.
- When you set a time frame for completing an assignment, it helps you focus on working toward your goal.
- When you have a schedule, you're less likely to let a short break become a long break.
- Being in control of time makes you feel like you have more control of your life.
- You can enjoy your free time more when your work is completed.

FIGURE 13.11 Help-seeking inventory

Purpose: To help you reflect on your help-seeking style.

Directions: Think of a time when you are studying and you are having some difficulty learning material or completing an assignment. Sometimes you might ask for help; other times you might not. These questions have to do with deciding whether to get some help. In each of the following situations, indicate how likely you are to ask for help. **Use a scale of 1–5, in which 1 is "Not at all likely" and 5 is "Very likely."**

How Likely Are You to Ask for Help When

1. You don't understand how to do a problem or exercise. 1 2 3 4 5
2. You need help with something the teacher already explained how to do. 1 2 3 4 5
3. You are having trouble during class and your teacher seems busy or in the middle of a lecture. 1 2 3 4 5
4. You are having trouble and your teacher seems to have too busy a schedule to meet with you outside of class. 1 2 3 4 5
5. You think you might get a bad grade if you don't get help. 1 2 3 4 5
6. You can't remember something that you need to know in order to do an assignment or problem. 1 2 3 4 5

Benefits of Help Seeking

7. I think that asking questions during class helps me learn. 1 2 3 4 5
8. I feel smart when I ask a question during class. 1 2 3 4 5
9. I think that asking teachers questions helps me learn. 1 2 3 4 5
10. I think that studying with friends helps me learn. 1 2 3 4 5
11. I think that asking friends for help enables me to learn. 1 2 3 4 5

Costs of Help Seeking

12. I think the teacher might think I'm dumb if I ask a question. 1 2 3 4 5
13. I think the teacher might think I'm unprepared if I ask a question. 1 2 3 4 5
14. I feel scared about asking questions during class. 1 2 3 4 5
15. I feel scared about asking questions outside of class. 1 2 3 4 5
16. I think the teacher will get angry with me if I ask a question. 1 2 3 4 5
17. I feel shy about asking questions. 1 2 3 4 5
18. I feel it's too much of a bother to ask questions. 1 2 3 4 5
19. I do not like to waste time seeking out help from teachers. 1 2 3 4 5
20. I think my friends might think I'm dumb if I ask for their help. 1 2 3 4 5
21. I do not like to waste time seeking out help from friends. 1 2 3 4 5

Help-Seeking Practices

22. I usually need a lot of help with my work. 1 2 3 4 5
23. I am aware of my teachers' office hours. 1 2 3 4 5
24. I have a listing of all teachers' office hours. 1 2 2 2 5
25. I have a telephone number of a fellow student from each class. 1 2 3 4 5
26. I have asked a fellow student in each class to take notes for me if I am absent and have agreed to do the same for that student in return. 1 2 3 4 5
27. I am aware of the free or low-cost tutoring services available to me on my campus. 1 2 3 4 5
28. I typically can monitor my learning and ask for help before it is too late. 1 2 3 4 5
29. Overall, how effective do you think your help-seeking behaviors and practices are with your fellow students?
    ________________ effective
    ________________ somewhat effective
    ________________ could be more effective
30. Overall, how effective do you think your help-seeking behaviors and practices are with teachers?
    ________________ effective
    ________________ somewhat effective
    ________________ could be more effective
31. My goals for help seeking this semester are:
    A. ______________________________
    B. ______________________________
    C. ______________________________

Sources: "Children's help-seeking in the classroom: The role of motivational factors and attitudes," by R. S. Newman, 1990, *Journal of Educational Psychology, 82*(1), 80; and "Children's reluctance to seek help with schoolwork," by R. S. Newman & L. Goldin, 1990, *Journal of Educational Psychology, 82*, 100.

FIGURE 13.12 To-do list: Daily planning worksheet

Things to do on ______________________________

Priorities	Daily Homework Assignments	Tasks to Be Completed for Long-Range Assignments
Social Media including texts	Flyers and Papers for Parents to Read/Sign	Clubs and Activities
Personal Activities	Home Chores/Tasks	Other

Source: School power: Study skill strategies for succeeding in school (p. 102), by J. S. Schumm, 2001, Minneapolis, MN: Free Spirit Publishing, Inc.

Teaching time management is easily integrated into any class. You can get your students started on time management through time-analysis exercises. Have student groups identify usual activities and estimate the time it takes to complete them. Distribute a blank schedule form to students, and have them use the form to keep track of their activities for 1 week. Also have students list each school assignment and note whether they had "too much time" (+), "the right amount of time" (×), or "too little time" (−) to complete it.

At the end of the week, have student groups review their schedules and compare how much time they spent on different activities such as sleeping, eating, studying, attending class, and so on. Also have students compare their estimates with the actual time it took to complete the activities. Usually students underestimate their time by about 50%.

Many middle schools and high schools provide students with academic calendars or assignment notebooks. If your school does not provide them, require your students to get a calendar and/or assignment notebook small enough to carry, but large enough to record assignments and due dates. Some students are beginning to use their cell phones or a portable computer for recording assignments. Regardless of the format students use, planning a schedule requires several steps:

1. Record due dates for assignments, tests, and other important projects.
2. Record regularly scheduled activities, study times, and personal times.
3. Identify complex tasks or projects, break them into smaller tasks, and determine the due dates for each smaller task.
4. Make a to-do list for each day (refer to Figure 13.12) so that you can see how you need to plan your time, particularly study time.
5. Set priorities; if there is a lot to do, make a list of everything and rank each task as high, medium, or low priority.

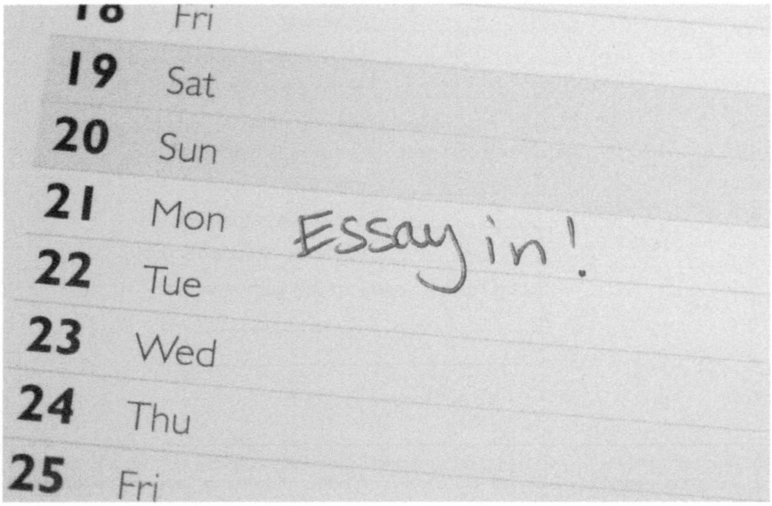

How can you assure that the assignments you make are clear and complete? What can you do to foster student independence in monitoring their assignments?

Monitoring task completion is the key to successful use of schedules and to-do lists. Following are some suggestions for monitoring:

- Have students spend about 5 minutes during the class period to update their schedules and cross off tasks they have completed. This can be done at the beginning of class when you are taking attendance.
- Meet with students, as necessary, to review their schedules and their monitoring.
- Have students adjust their schedules as necessary.

Using direct instruction for daily assignments

Jeremy Johnston was a bright, energetic eighth grader who was failing in school. His performance on tests was no less than a C, but he was failing because he seldom if ever handed in homework and rarely completed in-class assignments. When Jeremy's case was discussed during the middle school team meeting, the team discovered that Jeremy was having the same problem with short-term assignments across the board.

Students like Jeremy who have difficulty completing assignments may benefit from getting direct instruction in how to do so. The PROJECT strategy was developed for middle school students with learning disabilities to provide structure for assignment completion (Hughes, Ruhl, Schumaker, & Deshler, 2002, 2011). PROJECT leads students through steps that occur at school and at home. The strategy steps are as follows:

Prepare your assignment sheet.

Record and ask.

Organize.

- Break the assignment into parts.
- Estimate the number of study sessions.
- Schedule the sessions.
- Take your materials home.

Jump into it.

Engage in the work.

Check your work.

Turn in your work.

You can teach the PROJECT strategy in class. Also, let parents know through a flyer, letter, email, or on your website that you have taught the strategy and are encouraging your students to use the strategy for home learning.

Organizing and planning for long-term assignments

For many students, developing the skills to organize and plan long-term assignments and projects is new territory. Particularly in middle school, breaking big assignments down into manageable tasks, setting deadlines for those tasks, and seeing an assignment to completion is an essential learning process.

Michelle Miller is an eighth-grade language arts teacher. Each year she assigns a multiphase career project. First, students conduct a literature review on their career of choice and submit a three-page paper. Next, they construct an interview protocol to administer to someone in that career. After Michelle approves and grades the protocol, students interview their contact person and write a three-page summary of the experience. The final product is a 5-minute PowerPoint presentation that students give to the class. By embedding multiple due dates and assignments in the career project, Michelle can provide students support in developing a finished product of which they can be proud. Figure 13.13 is a project planning form you can use to assist students in planning long-term assignments.

MyEdLab **Self-Check 13.4**

MyEdLab **Application Exercise 13.4:** Developing Independence in Completing Assignments

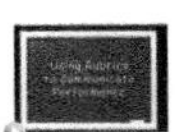

13.5 EFFECTIVE STRATEGY INSTRUCTION

Amanda, from the chapter-opening vignette, has learned that the time she spends teaching strategies for learning has big payoffs. Her students not only master the content, but also learn how to take more responsibility for their own learning. One way for students to

FIGURE 13.13 Project planning sheet

1. Decide on a project theme. **Date Done** ____________
2. Have the theme approved by your teacher. **Date Done** ____________

   Theme: ____

3. Make a list of things you need to do to complete your project. Rank them in the order they should be completed.

   Will Need Help With: **Who Will Help Me:**

4. Set deadlines for finishing each part of your project. Write the deadline dates on your calendar.

Task	Date Due	Date Done	Person Responsible

5. Make a list of materials you will need. Estimate how much they will cost.

Item	Cost

6. Send away for resource materials.

Resource Material	Date Requested	Date Received

7. Contact community resources.

Community Resource	Date Contacted	Result(s)

8. Visit the library.

Purpose of Visit	Date of Visit

9. Complete your project on schedule.

   Date Turned In: ____________ **Grade:** ____________

Source: Excerpted from *School power: Strategies for succeeding in school,* by Jeanne Shay Schumm, Ph.D., and Marguerite Radencich, Ph.D.

do this is to become more strategic in their learning. What is a learning strategy? **Strategies** are organized processes for understanding what you read, solving a problem, studying, or exercising behavioral controls. We all use strategies as a mechanism for helping us be more effective (Reid et al., 2013). Strategies are effective when they actively engage students in using **metacognition**, or their awareness of how they are using their thought processes and knowledge deliberately to affect a learning goal. This section begins with an overview of the goals of strategy instruction. It continues with guidelines for teaching strategies and concludes with strategies for improving memory, self-monitoring, and self-advocacy.

13.5.1 The Goals of Strategy Instruction

The goal of strategy instruction is to support students as they develop independence in completing learning tasks and eventually become skilled in their use. How can you help students in your class become strategic learners? One way is to incorporate strategy instruction into your instructional repertoire. When you teach strategies, keep in mind the teaching–learning connection. Most students need direct instruction and sufficient practice to learn how to learn. Following are key guidelines to keep in mind when planning for strategy instruction.

Guideline 1: Choose strategies carefully

There is a wide array of strategies from which you can choose. However, learning too many strategies can actually reduce their effectiveness. Why? Because students will consume too much of their cognitive capacity just remembering all of the strategies and have limited cognitive resources left to actually do the task.

So, which strategies should you select? See Tips for Teachers 13.8.

Guideline 2: Present content and strategies concurrently

Strategy instruction is not new. In fact, Frances Robinson (1941) introduced the reading strategy Survey, Question, Read, Recite, Review (SQ3R) in the 1940s! Often strategies are taught in isolation and students are on their own in determining when and how to use them. Most often they don't use strategies at all. You can increase the odds of your students' strategy use when you teach content and strategies concurrently (Bean et al., 2008). For instance, if a social studies teacher was teaching his high school seniors about the different types of bills that are introduced in Congress (e.g., enabling bill, amendment), he might also teach summarization strategies at the same time. Students would be assigned a textbook reading that provided an overview of each type of bill. Then students would write brief summaries of the essential components of each type of bill.

Guideline 3: Teach strategies in stages

Strategy instruction involves a gradual release of responsibility from the teacher to the learner (Buehl, 2009). The goal is to move from teacher-regulated to student-regulated use of strategies through scaffolded instruction (Buehl, 2009). There are different stages of strategy learning that lead to skilled, executive learning. If students learn a strategy only at a superficial level, they are not likely to use it on a regular basis. Yet, most students—including high-achieving students—appreciate learning "tricks" that will help them learn more efficiently and effectively.

TIPS FOR TEACHERS 13.8

Choosing Strategies to Meet All Students' Needs

- Most strategies are designed for a specific purpose; for example, to facilitate word reading or to help with anger management. Select a strategy that will help your students meet their instructional or behavioral goals.
- Select a research based strategy. Even so, the research base indicates it works with more students than a contrasting approach; however, it may not work with your target student. In selecting a strategy, think about the needs of the students in your classroom and whether your students are ready for the strategy in terms of their knowledge base and capacity. You might choose a few generic strategies to teach to the whole class in depth. Strategies to meet the needs of individuals or small groups of students can be taught in collaboration with a special education teacher or in small, teacher-led groups at appropriate times.
- For strategies to be useful for students, they must be presented in a memorable form. Strategies that are short and easy to remember are more likely to be internalized and actually used.
- The strategies you select must meet the "reality check" for you. Choose strategies that are consistent with the time, materials, and other resources you have available.

Sources: *Content area literacy: An integrated approach* (10th ed.), by T. W. Bean, J. E. Readence, & R. S. Baldwin, 2011, Dubuque, IA: Kendall/Hunt; *Teaching content to all: Evidence-based inclusive practices in middle and secondary schools*, by B. K. Lenz & D. D. Deshler, 2004, Boston: Pearson.

When introducing a strategy to your students, provide instruction and practice that will lead them to higher levels of strategy learning and ultimately to the automatic skill level as presented in the following stages:

1. **Stage 1:** *Awareness*—initially becoming introduced to a new strategy and the rationale for its use
2. **Stage 2:** *Knowledge*—developing insights about how the strategy works, when the strategy is most appropriate, and procedures for using the strategy
3. **Stage 3:** *Simulation*—trying the strategy out with simulated drills or exercises
4. **Stage 4:** *Practice*—trying the strategy out in actual reading and studying
5. **Stage 5:** *Skill*—making the strategy a part of a regular study routine

When Andrew Knox introduces a strategy to his freshman social studies classes, he builds in opportunities for students to move toward higher stages of strategy learning. For example, if Andrew were introducing the K-W-L strategy (Ogle, 1986), he would do the following:

- Provide an overview of the strategy, describe that its purpose is to activate prior knowledge, and give a pep talk about how the strategy can be helpful in promoting active reading and comprehension.
- Give an in-class lecture and demonstration to introduce the K-W-L strategy to develop general awareness of the steps and procedures involved.
- Use a think-aloud strategy to model using the strategy.
- Have his students take notes in their learning logs and participate in a class discussion about when and where to use the strategy.
- Have his students write a reflection in their logs to demonstrate knowledge (see Figure 13.14).

Students then would work in cooperative learning groups to try out K-W-L. For these simulations, Andrew would choose high-interest, low-vocabulary materials so that the focus is on the strategy itself. See the Activities for All Learners feature to learn about two types of K-W-L approaches.

13.5.2 Tools of Strategy Instruction

For additional student practice, Andrew would provide a strategy guide for students to gain independent practice in implementing the strategy in their homework. **Strategy guides** are graphic and questioning materials that provide support to students as they learn to use metacognitive strategies (Wood, Lapp, Flood, & Taylor, 2008). They can be used

FIGURE 13.14 Strategy satisfaction survey

Name of Student ______________________________

Name of Strategy ______________________________

How did you learn the strategy?

What was easy about using the strategy?

What was difficult about using the strategy?

How would you change the strategy to meet your learning needs?

Would you use the strategy in the future? If so, how?

Overall, how much did the strategy help you learn?

______________________ A lot

______________________ A little bit

______________________ Not at all

ACTIVITIES FOR ALL LEARNERS

K-W-L: Two Variations

Objective: To provide students with additional scaffolding as they read content-area material using two variations of K-W-L

Grade Level: Middle schools and above

Teaching Procedures: Although Donna Ogle's K-W-L is a popular teaching method used to activate students' prior knowledge, it lacks a clear description of school district standards and learner outcomes that are required in schools today.

1. To address this issue, Laura Alatorre-Parks devised K-W-E-L to teach her high school English students what the school district deemed they were expected to learn.
   - K-W-E-L is essentially the same as K-W-L; the critical difference is that K-W-E-L includes an in-depth discussion about district objectives or standards after the brainstorming (what I know and what I want to learn).
   - Alatorre-Parks also engages her students in planning how to merge their interests and wants with what they are expected to learn. She reports that this simple extension helps students to become more aware of what is expected of them and to develop a sense of ownership about their learning.
2. Another variation is K-W-H-H-L and was developed after Susan Szabo, a middle school reading specialist, conducted a content analysis of her students' K-W-L journals.
   - She learned that her students needed more structure in targeting essential material from text and in making personal responses to what they read.
   - She added two additional headers: H (hard words) to help students identify key vocabulary and H (heart) to have students reflect about content based on personal experience and emotional reactions.

Sources: "Aligning student interests with district mandates," by L. Alatorre-Parks, 2001, *Journal of Adolescent and Adult Literacy, 44*, 330–332; "K-W-L: A teaching model that develops active reading of expository text," by D. Ogle, 1986, *The Reading Teacher, 39*, 564–570; and "KWHHL: A student-driven evolution of the KWL," by S. Szabo, 2006, *American Secondary Education, 34*, 57–67.

independently or in small groups, as a class activity, or as a home learning assignment. Often strategy guides are teacher-developed; however, publishers are including them in supplementary text material such as workbooks (see Tips for Teachers 13.9).

See the Tech Tips, "Using Technology to Improve Study Skills," for some online resources that support study skills.

13.5.3 Memory Strategies

What is one of the most common frustrations expressed by teachers? Students knew the information yesterday and now they don't seem to remember it. Using memory strategies to learn information is critical for success in school. Students, particularly students with disabilities and those who are at risk, often have difficulty remembering critical information (Peng & Fuchs, 2014). Interestingly, students with learning disabilities have both verbal and mathematical memory problems. Sometimes students do not understand the information,

TIPS FOR TEACHERS 13.9

Developing Strategy Guides

- Analyze the learning task, think about student needs, and identify a strategy that will help students accomplish the task you have identified.
- Design guides that are graphically appealing, promote engagement, and foster higher-order thinking.
- Embed adaptations for English language learners and students with disabilities as necessary.
- Provide extension activities for students who want or need a "stretch."
- Introduce the guide with emphasis on (a) the task to be accomplished and (b) how the strategy will assist in accomplishing the task.
- Model the use of the strategy guide.
- If students need additional support, particularly for new strategies, have them work in cooperative learning groups or pairs to try out the guide.
- After completion of the guide, use a class discussion encouraging students to think about what was learned and how the strategy facilitated learning. Consider asking students for suggestions for how they might modify the strategy to be more effective for them in subsequent learning.

TECH TIPS

Using Technology to Improve Study Skills

Help and Tips for Standardized Tests

The Educational Testing Service
(www.ets.org)

Test Prep Review
(www.testprepreview.com)

Test Preparation Instruction
(www.magoosh.com)

Tips for All Areas of Study Skills

www.studytips.org

www.thegreatcourses.com

but in some cases, students may not perform well because they have difficulties retrieving information or because they do not use memory strategies to improve learning and recall.

As a classroom teacher, there are some general practices you can implement to enhance students' memory of what they learn in class:

- Cue students when important information is being presented.
- Encourage students to make connections between prior and new knowledge.
- Use visual aids such as semantic maps and diagrams to make the information more memorable.
- Limit the amount of information presented; group-related ideas.
- Control the rate at which information is presented.
- Provide time to review, rehearse, and elaborate on the information.
- Teach students how to use and apply memory strategies and devices.
- Give students an opportunity to paraphrase the information or practice the activity independently.
- Provide opportunities for distributed practice and encourage overlearning.

Distributed practice means breaking up the material to be learned into manageable chunks and then holding several short study sessions over a period of time. The opposite of distributed practice would be to try to learn a large amount of material in one sitting. **Overlearning** means learning to mastery. Sometimes students say, "I knew it last night and then forgot it during the test." Typically, when this happens, the student did not rehearse or practice the material a sufficient number of times to get to the point of mastery.

Direct teaching of memory strategies can enhance student performance on tests, vocabulary learning, and retention of key concepts (Rummel, Levin, & Woodward, 2003; Scruggs et al., 2008); however, not all approaches yield the same impact. For example, asking students to repeat information is not as effective at getting them to remember the information as having them do an action while learning the information (Yang et al., 2014).

Mnemonics

Mnemonic devices are memory-triggering techniques that help us remember and retrieve information by forming associations that do not exist naturally in the content. The word *mnemonics* is derived from the name of the Greek goddess of memory, Mnemosyne. There are several types of mnemonic devices recommended to promote student independent learning. Two of the most versatile mnemonic strategies are letter strategies and key word strategies (Fontana, Scruggs, & Mastropieri, 2007). Memory strategies (also known as mnemonic devices) are particularly helpful for students with learning disabilities, but may be helpful for other students—and for you!

Two types of **letter strategy** mnemonics are acronyms and acrostics. **Acronyms** are words created by joining the first letters of a series of words. Examples are *radar* (radio detecting and ranging), *scuba* (self-contained underwater breathing apparatus), and *laser* (light amplification by stimulated emission of radiation). **Acrostics** are sentences created by words that begin with the first letters of a series of words. A popular example of an acrostic is "Every good boy does fine," which represents the notes on the lines of the treble clef staff: E, G, B, D, F. By teaching students to construct acronyms and acrostics, sharing them in class, and then cueing students to use them when they study and take tests, you help them to learn and retrieve information.

The **FIRST-letter** mnemonic strategy is one strategy you can teach to help students construct lists of information to memorize and develop an acronym or acrostic for learning and remembering the information. The strategy includes an overall strategy (LISTS) and a substrategy for making a mnemonic device (FIRST). The steps in the overall strategy are as follows:

Look for clues. In class notes and textbooks, look for lists of information that are important to learn. Name or give a heading to each list.

Investigate the items. Decide which items should be included in the list.

Select a mnemonic device, using FIRST. Use the FIRST substrategy, explained shortly, to construct a mnemonic.

Transfer the information to a card. Write the mnemonic and the list on one side of a card and the name of the list on the other side of the card.

Self-test. Study by looking at the name of the list, using the mnemonic to recall the list.

To complete the selection step, students use the FIRST substrategy to design an acronym or acrostic:

Form a word. Using uppercase letters, write the first letter of each word in the list; see whether an acronym—either a recognizable word or a nonsense word—can be made.

Insert a letter(s). Insert letter(s) to see whether a word can be made. (Be sure to use lowercase letters so that you know they do not represent an item on the list—BACk, for example.)

Rearrange the letters. Rearrange the letters to see whether a word can be made.

Shape a sentence. Using the first letter of each word in the list, try to construct a sentence (an acrostic).

Try combinations. Try combinations of the preceding steps to generate the mnemonic.

This strategy can be taught in any content-area class, but it is particularly effective in science and social studies classes in which lists of information are to be learned. The strategy provides a systematic method for students to review text and class notes, construct lists, and develop acronyms and acrostics that help them remember and retrieve information.

The **key word strategy** is a research-based mnemonic that can be used to remember both vocabulary and concepts (Atkinson, 1975; Uberti et al., 2003). The method uses both verbal and visual cues to create images that prompt recall and retention. The key word method involves three steps:

1. Identify a target word or concept to be learned.
2. Identify a concrete, easily imagined "key word" that is either phonetically or semantically related to the target word.
3. Identify a visual image that links the key word to the meaning of the target word.

For example, in a social studies class the target word to be learned might be *archipelago*, or a group of islands. The target word is *archipelago*, the key word could be *arch*, and the visual image could be a series of islands connected by arches (see Figure 13.15).

The key word strategy can also be helpful in remembering facts and key information from text you are reading. What do students need to do?

- Underline or otherwise note the most important information in the passage.
- Write a summary of the key ideas or facts

MyEdLab
Video Example 13.3.
Watch how the teacher in this video gives several examples of mnemonic devices to help students to memorize key words. Did you find this strategy effective, and if so, how might you see yourself using this in your own teaching? If you did not find this strategy effective, why not?

FIGURE 13.15 **Key word example**

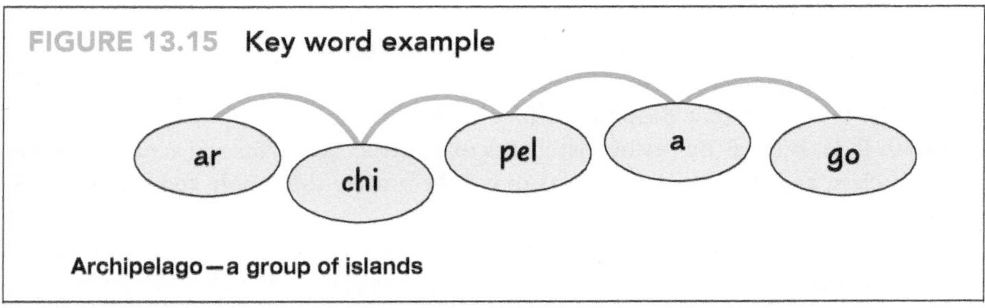

- Select a key word that will help you remember the big ideas and facts.
- Develop a mental picture that helps you think of the key word.

Although research has demonstrated the potential usefulness of mnemonic devices (Fontana et al., 2007; Kretlow, Lo, White, & Jordan, 2008), Lenz and Deshler (2004) offer one caution: If students do not make a final link between the memory prompt and the term or concept, the mnemonic can be troublesome. In addition, students may spend more time creating the mnemonics than actually rehearsing the material to be learned. Students need direct instruction in mnemonic strategies, but they also need time to reflect on what worked, what didn't work, and why. See the Activities for All Learners feature for more strategies for helping students absorb and retain information.

13.5.4 A Strategy for Self-Monitoring

Many students have difficulties with self-monitoring—closely monitoring their learning to purposively control and adjust what they know and how they are learning. Others have difficulty with self-determination—articulating what they want and need in appropriate ways so that they are in control of their own learning. Teaching students strategies related to self-initiative and personal organization can help with academic achievement. Moreover, teaching students how to assume personal responsibility can help them move beyond passivity and learned helplessness (Hallahan, Kauffman, & Pullen, 2015).

You can support your students' move toward assuming personal responsibility for their own learning by teaching strategies for goal setting and monitoring, organizational systems, time management, and self-advocacy.

Self-monitoring includes both self-evaluation and self-recording (Hallahan et al., 2015). Self-evaluation involves self-analysis and goal setting for either academic or behavioral tasks. Self-recording is written documentation of incremental progress made in meeting goals. Whether the task is working on finishing a term paper or saving enough money to buy a car, it is important to set goals, make a plan to accomplish the goals, and monitor progress.

Van Reusen and Bos (1992) developed a strategy that students can use for setting goals and monitoring progress. The strategy uses the acronym MARKER (it gives students a *mark* to work toward and is a *marker* of their progress) and includes the following steps:

Make a list of goals, set the order, and set the dates.

Arrange a plan for each goal and predict your success.

Run your plan for each goal and adjust if necessary.

Keep records of your progress.

Evaluate your progress toward each goal.

Reward yourself when you reach a goal, and set a new goal.

For each goal, students use a goal-planning sheet to answer the following questions:

- Can I describe my goal?
- What is the reason or purpose for the goal?
- Where am I going to work on and complete this goal?
- How much time do I have to complete the goal?

FIGURE 13.16 Goal-planning and monitoring sheet

Name: ______________________ Class: ______________________ Date: ______________________

1. Goal: ______________________
2. Reason(s) for working on goal: ______________________
3. Date to reach goal (due date): ______________________
4. Materials needed: ______________________
5. Steps used to reach the goal: ______________________
6. Progress toward the goal: Record in each box the date and progress rating.

	3—Goal reached	2—Good progress made	1—Some progress made	0—No progress made
Date / Rating				
Date / Rating				
Date / Rating				

7. Reward for reaching goal: ______________________

Source: Adapted from *Use of the goal-regulation strategy to improve the goal attainment of students with learning disabilities (final report)*, by A. K. Van Reusen & C. S. Bos, 1992, Tucson: University of Arizona.

- What materials do I need to complete the goal?
- Can I divide the goal into steps or parts? If so, in what order should I complete each step or part?
- How am I going to keep records of my progress?
- How will I reward myself for reaching my goal?

Students usually work on one to three goals at a time, keeping progress data on each goal (see Figure 13.16).

This strategy can be taught as a unit in almost any class but is particularly appropriate for social studies and life skills classes. When Van Reusen and Bos (1992) used this strategy with middle and high school students with learning disabilities and behavior disorders, they found that students accomplished more goals and gained a more informed perspective on their educational and personal goals.

For students in departmentalized settings, adjusting to different teaching styles and class requirements can be difficult. Setting course-specific goals can help students with the adjustment. Figure 13.17 provides a framework for analyzing courses and for setting course-specific goals.

13.5.5 Strategies for Self-Advocacy

Self-advocacy occurs when individuals effectively communicate and negotiate for their interests, desires, needs, and rights by making informed decisions and taking responsibility for those decisions (Kleinert, Harrison, Fisher, & Kleinert, 2010; Test, Fowler, Wood, Brewer, & Eddy, 2005). Self-advocacy is a subset of the skills, knowledge, and beliefs that constitute self-determination (Campbell-Whatley, 2008; Carter, Lane, Pierson, & Stang, 2008; Test, Fowler, Wood, Brewer, & Eddy, 2005). Other aspects of self-determination include choice making, decision making, and self-awareness, as well as providing opportunities for genuine friendships and meaningful activities (Kramer, 2015). Self-advocacy can be taught; there is evidence that direct instruction of these skills is beneficial to students with learning and cognitive disabilities (Brewer et al., 2005; Campbell-Whatley, 2008; Pocock et al., 2002; van Belle, Marks, Martin, & Chun, 2006).

FIGURE 13.17 Setting course-specific goals: Long-range task analysis

Purpose: To provide a structure with which to examine the demands and requirements of each of your courses this semester.

Directions: Make copies of this form and complete one for each of your courses.

Course number __________ Course title __________

Lectures

Does the teacher deliver content through class lectures?

_____ Yes _____ No

Are the lectures generally easy to understand?

_____ Yes _____ No

Is it easy to capture key vocabulary and ideas from the lectures?

_____ Yes _____ No

Is it easy to take notes from the lectures?

_____ Yes _____ No

Are the lectures presented in the same order as the information in the textbook?

_____ Yes _____ No

Are the lectures made up of information not presented in the text at all?

_____ Yes _____ No

Reading Assignments

Does the teacher have required reading assignments?

_____ Yes _____ No

Is the reading material generally easy to understand?

_____ Yes _____ No

Is it easy to capture key vocabulary and ideas from the reading material?

_____ Yes _____ No

Is it absolutely necessary to read the textbook in detail to prepare for class discussions?

_____ Yes _____ No

Is it absolutely necessary to read the textbook in detail to prepare for tests?

_____ Yes _____ No

Other Assignments

List other assignments for this course:

Quizzes and Examinations

Number of quizzes _____

Number of exams _____

Is the final exam cumulative?

_____ Yes _____ No

The format of the quizzes and examinations is typically

_____ multiple choice

_____ true/false

_____ identification/short answer

_____ essay

_____ other _____

Quizzes and examinations cover content from

_____ lectures

_____ reading assignments

_____ other _____

Course Analysis

Given the level of difficulty and my level of interest in this course, my goal for a grade in this course is _____

My other goals for this course are:

____

____

____

Source: Executive learning: Successful strategies for college reading and studying (pp. 79–81), by J. S. Schumm & S. A. Post, 1997, Upper Saddle River, NJ: Pearson. Adapted by permission of Pearson Education, Inc.

The I PLAN self-advocacy strategy helps students develop their advocacy skills (Van Reusen & Bos, 1990). This strategy is effective for older students who are becoming more independent learners.

The strategy consists of five steps. During the first step, students work in instructional groups to develop their own personal inventories (I). The remaining four steps in the strategy focus on the communication skills needed to present the information and advocate with teachers, parents, counselors, and others. These steps are presented, discussed, and then practiced through role-playing.

Inventories are created by each individual in instructional groups; these inventories focus on students' strengths, areas to improve or learn, goals, and choice for learning or accommodations.

Provide your inventory information.

Listen and respond.

Ask questions.

Name your goals.

Students also learn the following SHARE behaviors to promote positive communication:

Sit up straight.

Have a pleasant tone of voice.

Activate your thinking.

- Tell yourself to pay attention.
- Tell yourself to participate.
- Tell yourself to compare ideas.

Relax.

- Don't look uptight.
- Tell yourself to stay calm.

Engage in eye communication.

I PLAN and SHARE can be taught using role-playing activities. For example, two students could role-play how to communicate with a teacher when the student feels he or she needs an adaptation to complete a test or assignment. The whole class could then reflect on the role-play and make suggestions for improved communication.

MyEdLab **Self-Check 13.5**

MyEdLab **Application Exercise 13.5:** Strategy Instruction

13 SUMMARY

- Teachers can connect their teaching with student learning by using prelearning activities, preparing listener-friendly lectures, and teaching students how to listen and take notes in class.
- Teachers can improve student engagement by implementing vibrant discussions and using high-impact questioning techniques. Students benefit when teachers plan systematic ways for engaging their participation in class discussions and small-group learning situations, as well as how to generate their own questions.
- Graphic organizers can be powerful tools for teaching and learning. Use a variety of graphic organizers in your classroom lectures and presentations, and teach your students how they can use the organizers to organize and learn new material.
- You can help students become more independent in completing assignments by providing clear assignments. Providing opportunities to examine their study habits and help-seeking styles can guide students in setting academic and personal goals. Organizational systems, time management, and planning help students set the stage for efficient studying.
- The goal of strategy instruction is to support students in becoming independent in completing learning tasks. Most students need direct instruction and sufficient practice to become skilled in learning how to learn.

THINK AND APPLY

1. Reread the interview with Patricia Grande, Amanda Rey, and Andrew DeMuro at the beginning of this chapter and, using examples from this chapter, provide suggestions to them.
2. Develop a series of lesson plans you would use to introduce a strategy to your students. Include in your plans the stages of strategy learning, a strategy guide, and a metacognitive conversation.
3. Develop a graphic organizer for a topic of your choice, then explain how this will help to reach all of the students in your class.
4. Many teachers struggle with motivating students to turn in homework assignments on time. Explain your position on turning in homework and consequences for not turning in homework on time. How would you work with students and parents to improve your students' personal responsibility for homework completion?

14 Facilitating Reading

Learning Outcomes

14.1 Explain key concepts that guide reading instruction, basic components of reading curriculum, and reasons students struggle to become skilled readers.

14.2 Identify principles of effective reading instruction for struggling readers.

14.3 Present guidelines and teaching strategies can you implement for students who have difficulty with phonological awareness, letter–sound correspondence, and the alphabetic principle.

14.4 List guidelines and teaching strategies you can use to help your students identify words when they are reading.

14.5 Identify activities you can use to help your students become more fluent readers.

14.6 Apply strategies to help improve students' comprehension before, during, and after they read.

INTERVIEW: INES LEZCANO

Ines Lezcano is a third-grade teacher at Flamingo Elementary School in Miami, Florida. Of the twenty-nine students in her classroom, eight are originally speakers of languages other than English who have transitioned into speaking, reading, and writing in English. Four are children with learning disabilities (LD) who are in her class full time. Ines works with the special education teacher, Joyce Duryea, to plan for the reading and writing instruction of these four students. However, Joyce is a great support for all students because she co-teaches lessons and makes instructional adaptations for students with LD.

> For the last 2 years, I have also [had] a classroom in which most of the students with disabilities are placed. Even though I received a lot of support from Joyce, I was still concerned about whether or not I could adequately meet the academic needs of the students with LD in my classroom. What I've learned is that it can be done, but I've had to rethink my instructional practices—especially for reading. For my students who have reading skills that are substantially below those of the other students in my class, I keep on having to think, "How can I meet their needs and still keep things going for everyone else in the classroom?" I've figured out how to do this through multilevel activities, adaptations during whole-group activities, and small-group instruction.
>
> My favorite multilevel activity is classwide peer tutoring. During classwide peer tutoring, everyone is reading to a partner. I like it because the students really get involved and learn how to give each other help with their reading. This practice gives me an opportunity to work closely with students with reading disabilities. I also teach comprehension strategies such as finding the main idea or making a story map as multilevel activities. I teach the whole class the strategy and then have the students work in groups and practice using text that is appropriate for their reading levels.
>
> When I do give whole-class assignments in reading that I think are going to be hard for the students with reading problems, particularly with recognizing the words, I have to plan for adaptations. For example, sometimes we read a story from the basal reader. I have a listening station set up in my room so that my lowest readers can listen to an audiotape of the story. Volunteer readers from the fifth-grade class make the audiotapes of the stories. It's important to keep in mind how to give kids the support they need to do well.
>
> A few of my students need intensive instruction in decoding. To help them learn to read sight words, they work in the computer station daily with a sight word program. I have also found that phonics instruction for about 15 minutes a day really supports their reading. Joyce has helped me establish instructional goals and activities for the students with disabilities. We're monitoring their progress and really starting to see some growth.
>
> The reading [and] language arts block is my favorite time of the day. It's fun to see my students get excited about reading. It is also rewarding to watch their progress and to see how much more fluent and competent

CHAPTER OUTLINE

they're becoming as readers. It's a challenge to think about what each one needs, but I'm getting better at observing them and thinking of ways to help them become independent learners. I feel that during reading [and] language arts time I'm giving them the tools they need to be successful learners in all of their subjects.

Introduction

Ines values the interactive role that the special education teacher, Joyce, provides in designing and implementing instructional routines for all of her students, but especially those with disabilities. Both Ines and Joyce are on the lookout for strategies, instructional materials, and computer-assisted instruction that can make all students successful learners. Students with moderate to severe disabilities are frequently denied opportunities to learn to read and become participating members of our literate society, even though many of them are able to successfully learn to read or to make meaning from messages in our environment (Copeland & Keefe, 2007; Keefe & Copeland, 2011).

This chapter focuses on what general education teachers can do to provide effective instruction for students who struggle with learning to read. The chapter begins with an overview of concepts undergirding reading instruction, components of the reading curriculum, and an explanation of why some students struggle in learning to read. Next, current trends in reading instruction are described, followed by an outline of key principles of effective reading instruction for struggling readers. The next four sections provide suggestions for teaching components of reading instruction: phonological awareness and phonics, word identification, fluency, and comprehension.

14.1 READING INSTRUCTION

The goal of reading instruction is to provide students with the skills, strategies, and knowledge to read fluently and to understand and construct meaning from text for purposes of enjoyment and learning, whether reading a book, magazine, sign, pamphlet, email message, or information on the Internet. Reading is considered by many to be the most important area of education, and proficiency in reading is becoming even more critical in our technological society. Can you even imagine how difficult it would be to succeed not just in school but in life if you have difficulty reading? For example, consider a middle school boy with significant reading problems who explained that after he learned to read, what he really appreciated was being able to read the menu for lunch and not have to wait to look at the food. Skill in reading is a prerequisite for many of the learning activities in content-area classes such as social studies, science, and mathematics, and for successful employment and daily living.

Reading is one aspect of literacy. On its website, the International Literacy Association (ILA) (until 2015 known as the International Reading Association) defines *literacy* as "The ability to READ, WRITE, and COMMUNICATE connects people and empowers them to achieve things they never thought possible. It truly is the basis of who we are and how we interact with the world" (ILA, http://literacyworldwide.org). This broad definition of literacy incorporates communication skills in reading, writing, speaking, listening, and viewing. Current thinking about literacy education also recognizes the important role of digital literacy as well.

Like the ILS, many professional organizations have adopted "literacy" in their names (e.g., Association of Literacy Educators and Researchers [formerly Association of Reading Educators and Researchers]; Literacy Research Association [formerly National Reading

Conference]). Similarly, in many school districts the term *literacy* is used instead of *reading* to refer to the instructional period when communication competencies are taught, and teachers are sometimes called "literacy teachers" rather than "reading teachers." This chapter focuses primarily on reading instruction, recognizing that it is one aspect of literacy instruction and is connected to other components of written, oral, and visual communication. In this section, you'll read about the key concepts that underlie reading instruction, basic components of the reading curriculum, and reasons why some students have difficulty in learning to read.

14.1.1 Three Key Concepts Underlying Reading Instruction

Whether you become an elementary teacher, a reading or language arts teacher in middle or high school, or teach a content area such as social studies, science, or mathematics, three overarching concepts will be important to consider when you support students in reading:

1. *Reading is a skilled and strategic process in which learning to decode and read words accurately and rapidly is an essential feature.* Reading requires a variety of thinking skills and strategies, including those for recognizing words, sometimes called decoding or word perception. Reading entails using attention, perception, memory, and retrieval processes so that the reader can automatically identify or decode words. Readers use selective attention and perception coupled with their knowledge of the letter–sound relationships and context to help them automatically recognize the words. As students become proficient readers, they recognize most words with little effort. But as students are learning to read or when readers encounter unknown words, they use their knowledge of the alphabetic principle (how speech relates to print), phonological awareness skills (distinguishing the sounds in a word and being able to segment and blend them) (e.g., *-at*, *-ight*, prefixes, suffixes, syllables), and their decoding strategies (e.g., phonic analysis, structural analysis, context) to assist in decoding. When students have difficulty identifying words, they also have difficulty with fluency (reading quickly and smoothly) because so much effort is spent just on figuring out the words. When decoding is fluent, effort can be focused on comprehension. Therefore, one goal of reading instruction is to teach phonological awareness, the alphabetic principle, decoding, and fluency so that students decode quickly and effortlessly and attention can focus on comprehension (Moats, 2009).
2. *Reading entails understanding and constructing meaning from text and is dependent on the reader's active engagement and interpretation.* Reading also entails developing skills and strategies for understanding or constructing meaning from text (reading comprehension) and for monitoring understanding (comprehension monitoring). Understanding is influenced both by the text and by the readers' prior knowledge (Klingner, Vaughn, & Boardman, 2007; Valenica, Wixson, & Pearson, 2014). When readers read, the text does not simply convey ideas to the readers but stimulates readers to actively engage in the following comprehension strategies:

   - *Predicting* to make hypotheses about the meaning
   - *Summarizing* to put the major points in the text into their own words
   - *Questioning* to promote and check for understanding
   - *Clarifying* when concepts are not clear

   Effective readers regularly monitor their comprehension to determine whether they understand what they are reading. When they are not sure, they might decide to employ "fix-up" strategies such as rereading or reading on for further clarification, or they might decide not to worry about the confusion, depending on the purpose for reading. Hence, a second goal of reading instruction is to teach comprehension and comprehension-monitoring strategies.

3. *Reading is a socially mediated language-learning activity.* Because reading is a mode of communication, learning to read, like learning to listen, speak, and write, is socially mediated (Vygotsky, 1978). When students and teachers ask questions and discuss what they are reading, they share what they already know about the topic and integrate their knowledge with that of the text. When students and teachers talk about the reading process, they share the strategies they use to decode words and construct meaning, sometimes referred to as *instructional conversations* (Tharp, Estrada, Dalton, & Yamaguchi, 1999). Therefore, a goal of reading instruction is to use a social context in which to engage students in discussions about what they are reading and the reading process (Ivey, 2014; Snow, Porche, Tabors, & Harris, 2007).

14.1.2 Components of Reading Instruction

Depending on the student's level of development and needs, you will want to emphasize certain components. Yet at the same time you will need to integrate these components to obtain a balanced approach to teaching reading. Components of an effective and efficient reading program are depicted in Figure 14.1. Consider the following examples.

Stephanie is a third grader with a specific reading disability who receives reading instruction in her classroom and also works with the special education teacher on reading. She reads at a beginning level and is able to recognize only about thirty words. When she comes to a word she does not recognize, she sometimes attempts to sound out the word. However, she has difficulty remembering common letter–sound relationships. She also struggles to blend the sounds so she can generate a word that is close enough to the correct word that she can figure it out. Her reading instruction focuses primarily on building phonics skills and rapid reading of sight words. However, her instructional program also includes repeated and partner reading of instructional-level **decodable books** (i.e., books that primarily use words that reflect the phonic and word patterns she has already learned) to build fluency. She also listens to and discusses a wide variety of literature and content-area materials with her classmates to support her development of vocabulary and comprehension. It is important that Stephanie pairs reading and writing activities so that as she builds reading decoding skills, she works simultaneously on spelling. Similarly, as she develops an understanding of different types of text and genres (e.g., narratives such as folktales, adventure stories, and mysteries and expositions such as descriptions, comparisons/contrasts, persuasions), it is also important that she explores writing in different genres and different types of texts.

FIGURE 14.1 Components of reading and reading instruction

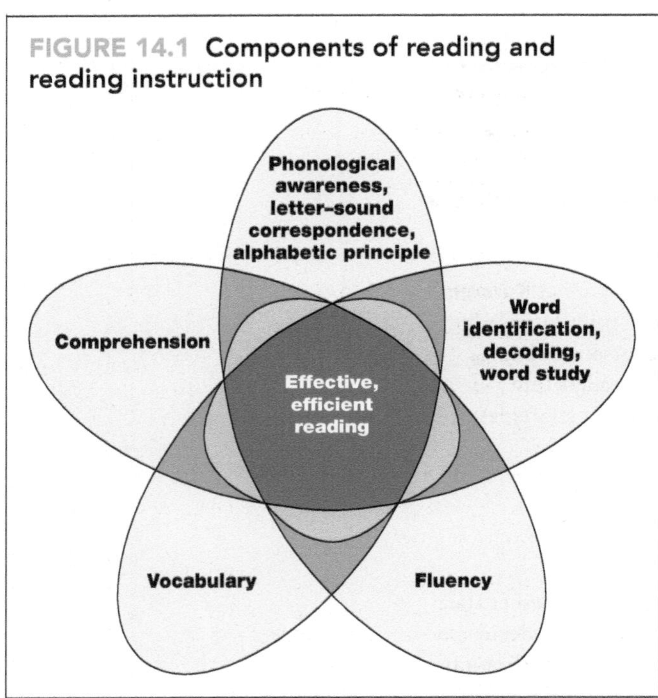

Source: Strategies for teaching students with learning and behavior problems (9th ed., Figure 7-1, p. 178), by S. Vaughn & C. Bos, 2015, Boston: Pearson. Copyright © 2015 by Allyn & Bacon. Reprinted by permission.

Manuel is an eighth grader who is reading at approximately the fourth-grade level. He entered school speaking both Spanish and English. He struggled with learning to read in Spanish because of his limited vocabulary knowledge and comprehension skills (e.g., getting the main idea, comprehension monitoring). He began reading in English during third grade and continued to struggle with vocabulary knowledge and comprehension and also had difficulty with decoding in English because its letter–sound relationships are not as regular as those in Spanish. As an eighth grader, he is taking English language arts from Ms. Gonzalez, who works with Manuel and a group of six students on building their vocabulary, comprehension, and advanced decoding skills. To build both decoding of multisyllabic words and vocabulary, they have learned to identify and separate prefixes and suffixes. They also learn the meaning of these affixes and of root words. For example, if the word is *construction,* they make a "struct" web with words such as *destruction*, *construct*, *reconstruction*, and *deconstruct*. For comprehension enhancement, Manuel and his classmates have been working with Ms. Gonzalez and the special education teacher to learn to use comprehension strategies. These include activities such as previewing the key words, headings, or pictures before reading and practices for identifying the main idea of what they read and then summarizing accurately what they've read or learned. The students work in collaborative learning groups, and they have been using social studies content to engage in close reading of text.

14.1.3 Learning Difficulties in the Process of Reading

Because reading is a complex process, it involves many areas of potential difficulties. As Figure 14.2 indicates, various interrelated factors influence whether students experience success in learning how to read.

A leading reading researcher, Keith Stanovich (1986), refers to this combination of factors as reciprocal causation—essentially a domino effect, in which an initial factor leads to a second factor, which leads to a third, and so on. For example, children who are not read to during their preschool years might not have the opportunity to become familiar with books and how print and sounds relate to each other, which may lead to greater challenges in learning how to read, which may lead to limited motivation to read, which may then result in the child not choosing to read and thus having less opportunity to practice reading skills and less opportunity to develop new concepts and vocabulary through reading.

As a classroom teacher, you must be sensitive to the factors that influence reading and to the individual needs of your students in their attempts to tackle this complex process. For example, some of the students in your classes will have overall low reading skills and will need instructional support in all of the critical elements of reading, including learning to read words, reading connected text, knowing what words mean, and understanding how to grapple with text to improve understanding. Other students may

FIGURE 14.2 **Factors that influence reading**

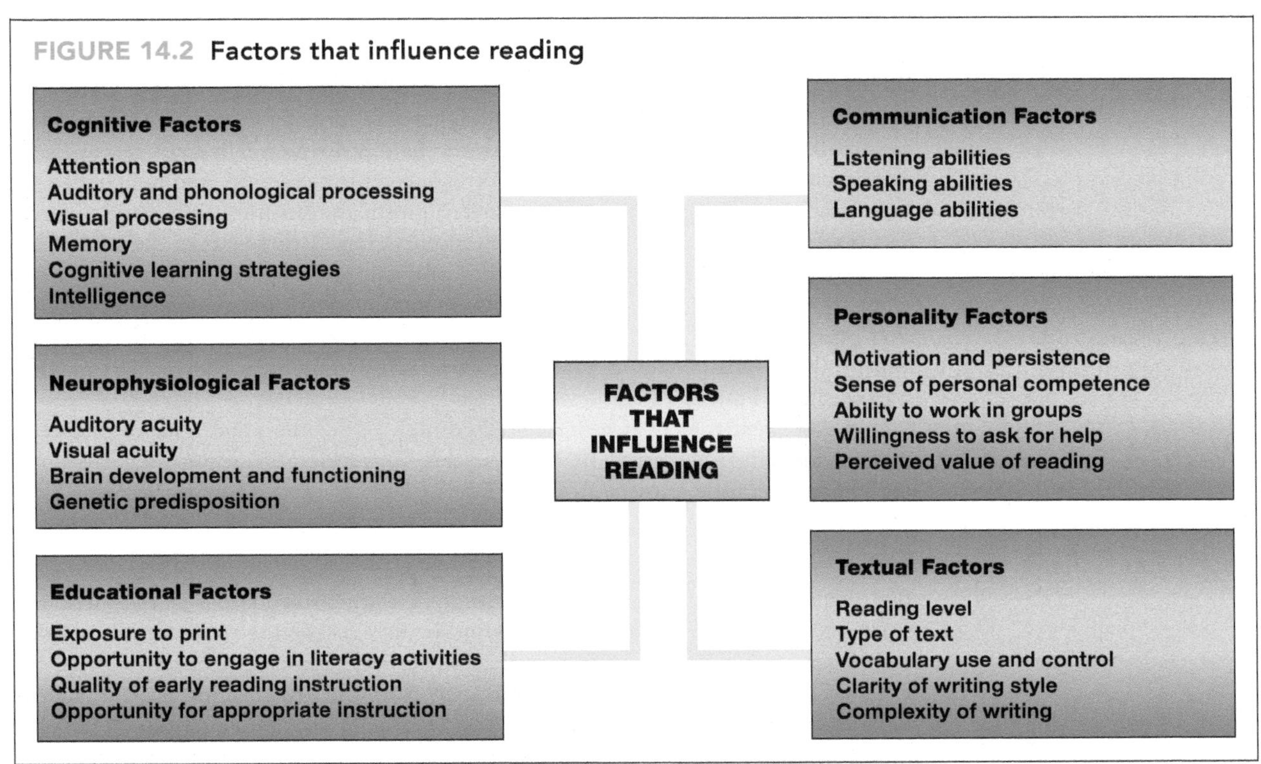

Cognitive Factors
Attention span
Auditory and phonological processing
Visual processing
Memory
Cognitive learning strategies
Intelligence
Neurophysiological Factors
Auditory acuity
Visual acuity
Brain development and functioning
Genetic predisposition
Educational Factors
Exposure to print
Opportunity to engage in literacy activities
Quality of early reading instruction
Opportunity for appropriate instruction
FACTORS THAT INFLUENCE READING
Communication Factors
Listening abilities
Speaking abilities
Language abilities
Personality Factors
Motivation and persistence
Sense of personal competence
Ability to work in groups
Willingness to ask for help
Perceived value of reading
Textual Factors
Reading level
Type of text
Vocabulary use and control
Clarity of writing style
Complexity of writing

Sources: Stanovich, 1986; Pressley & McCormick, 1995; Taylor, Harris, & Pearson, 1988; Johnston & Allington, 1991; Hiebert & Taylor, 1994.

only need support in learning the meanings of words and improving their comprehension. Still others will have inadequate word reading that interferes with their understanding of text. Identifying students' specific needs and then developing instructional programs that prioritize instruction in these areas leads to effective outcomes.

Teachers, administrators, researchers, parents, and policy makers have been concerned for decades about improving reading instruction. Fundamentally, there is nothing more important than learning to read and reading to learn. Although there is much agreement that learning to read is important, there have always been rather contentious discussions on how best to accomplish this goal. Historically, some researchers and practitioners have advocated a phonics first approach using basal readers while others supported exposure to naturally occurring text as the road to reading. National panels of experts have reviewed the research and written summaries of research-based practices for reading instruction. These committees were composed of national experts on reading research and a few selected practitioners and assembled two reports:

- The Committee on Prevention of Reading Difficulties in Young Children published the report *Preventing Reading Difficulties in Young Children* (Snow, Burns, & Griffin, 1998).
- The National Reading Panel (a panel charged by Congress to assess the research-based knowledge in teaching reading) published *Teaching Children to Read: An Evidence-Based Assessment of the Scientific Research Literature on Reading and Its Implications for Reading Instruction* (National Reading Panel, 2000).

Both reports stressed the importance of a balanced approach to teaching early reading, including the important role of phonological awareness and phonics instruction as well as the critical role that repeated reading plays in the development of reading fluency and the importance of teaching reading-comprehension strategies, vocabulary, and text structure. Even though these reports did not focus on individuals with disabilities, many of the practices recommended are also effective for these students (Boyle, 2008). This balanced approach to reading continues to be the norm in most reading programs. Two other trends have also emerged: standards-based instruction and professional collaboration in the teaching of reading.

14.1.4 Standards-based Instruction

For over 20 years, Jack Cassidy and his colleagues have surveyed twenty-five researchers to gain their opinions about "hot topics" in the field of literacy. The most recent survey (Cassidy, Grote-Garcia, & Ortlieb, 2015) revealed that close/deep reading, college and career readiness, digital/media/new literacies, high-stakes assessment, information/nonfiction texts, and text complexity are currently center stage largely due to the influence of the standards movement. This includes the Common Core State Standards and standards adopted by individual states. Indeed, the Common Core State Standards (see Figure 14.3) offer raised expectations for students at all grade levels in terms of how they read and respond (both verbally and in writing) to increasingly complex narrative and expository texts (Fisher & Frey, 2015).

Consequently, focus is being placed on high expectations and rigor to prepare all students for college and career literacy demands. This includes students with disabilities and English language learners.

14.1.5 Collaborating with Other Professionals

Traditionally, classroom teachers taught reading in relative isolation. Students with reading problems were pulled out for remediation in special education settings or with a Title 1 reading teacher. Collaboration and coordination between classroom teachers and other professionals was often inconsistent and incidental. With the advent of inclusion of students with disabilities in the general education classroom, and response to intervention as well as emphasis on standards-based instruction, schoolwide collaboration among school-level professionals has become more prevalent.

FIGURE 14.3 The Common Core Standards for English Language Arts: answers to relevant questions pertaining to reading instruction

What students are included in the Common Core Standards for English language arts?
Currently the standards are for students in grades K through12 for English language arts. The standards are designed for all learners, including English language learners and students with disabilities. Effective, research-based instructional practices can be implemented for assisting all students in accessing the general education curriculum and meeting the standards.

What are some of the critical features pertaining to reading in the Common Core Standards?
A critical component of effective reading instruction is the development of students' capacity to reading increasingly more challenging and difficult text. While the importance of reading text at an independent or instructional reading level is not negated, in grades 2 through 12 the standards require assignment of reading of longer and more complex, with developmentally appropriate guidance and support. In grades K and 1, teachers can introduce more complex text during teacher read-alouds.

What are some of the critical features pertaining to foundational reading skills in the Common Core Standards?
The standards recognize the importance of high-quality instruction of foundational reading skills in grades K through 5. This includes the teaching of phonological awareness, phonics, and fluency. The standards emphasize the importance of teaching all aspects of literacy in a coordinated way during the early grades (K through 2).

What are some of the critical features pertaining to close reading in the Common Core Standards?
The standards emphasize the importance of developing independence in developing critical and analytic reading proficiency during close reading of text. Specific instruction in how to analyze the author's message, craft, tone, and craft is recommended. In addition, students are required to learn how to evaluate information gleaned from their reading to develop arguments and written or oral presentations.

What are some of the critical features pertaining to disciplinary literacy in the Common Core Standards?
Disciplinary literacy involves the advanced literacy skills that facilitate learning in the areas of literature, science, social studies, and mathematics. Reading and responding in oral and written formats to a novel, scientific paper, biography of a historical figure, or math word problem involve very different types of literacy demands. Teaching of disciplinary literacy involves not only reader teachers, but those who teach content areas in elementary and secondary settings.

Sources: Common Core State Standards Initiative. (2016). Key shifts in English language arts. Retrieved from: http://www.corestandards.org/other-resources/key-shifts-in-english-language-arts/; International Reading Association Common Core State Standards (CCSS) Committee. (2012). *Literacy implementation guidance for the ELA Common Core State Standards* [White paper]. Retrieved from: http://www.reading.org/Libraries/association-documents/ira_ccss_guidelines.pdf

Collaborating with the special education teacher, teacher of English as a second language teacher, and grade-level team members will be important in implementing effective instruction (Hall, 2008). In addition, collaboration with the specialized literacy professional in your school is vital. **Specialized literacy professionals** are literacy leaders who serve in a variety of capacities depending on state, district, and school-based policies and procedures (Bean et al., 2015). The International Literacy Association position statement on specialized literacy professionals (International Literacy Association, 2015) identifies three general roles that vary in terms of focus and responsibilities.

1. *Reading/literacy specialist*—the focus of the reading/literacy specialist (sometimes referred to as interventionist) is on students with reading challenges. Responsibilities include direct instruction and assessment with students as well as collaboration with classroom teachers and other professionals to plan and implement literacy interventions.
2. *Literacy coach*—the focus of the literacy coach is on classroom teachers, including content-area teachers. Responsibilities include professional development for teachers, modelling of literacy strategies, and coaching and support for teachers as they implement literacy assessment and instruction.
3. *Literacy coordinator/supervisor*—the focus of the literacy coordinator/supervisor is on schoolwide, districtwide, or statewide literacy programs. Responsibilities include program development and evaluation, accountability to parents and the general public, and grant management.

These job titles as well as the professional credential requirements vary from region to region. Particularly in small schools, one professional may assume two or three of the roles described above (Bean et al., 2015). Therefore, it is advisable for you as a classroom teacher to find out who the literacy professionals are in your school, the nature of their roles and responsibilities, and how they can be an asset in your efforts to provide optimal instruction for struggling readers and writers. Renee Marx provides a good example of someone who could provide support.

As an educational diagnostician, Renee Webb is assigned to work in five different schools. Her primary forum for contact with classroom teachers is during School Building Level Committee meetings. The committee at each school consists of a general education teacher, school administrator, pupil appraisal specialist, and reading interventionist. Classroom teachers attend these meetings to gain input from the committee regarding students who are experiencing difficulty in one or more academic area. The committee then makes decisions about needs for additional assessment and/or intervention. Renee provides information about formal and informal assessments she has already conducted and recommendations for additional assessment and/or intervention.

Renee recognizes that her roles and responsibilities as a specialized literacy professional may vary within her state and school district. Nonetheless, she offers some general tips for classroom teachers in working with literacy professionals:

- Become familiar with the roles and responsibilities of literacy professionals in your school.
- Learn what you can do to facilitate their work and what resources they may offer to enhance your work as a classroom teacher.
- When attending meetings where cases of individual students are discussed, be prepared to provide documentation of what types of small group or individual interventions you have already provided.
- Find out what constitutes "evidence-based" interventions in your state, district, and school.

MyEdLab **Self-Check 14.1**

MyEdLab **Application Exercise 14.1:** Summarizing

14.2 EFFECTIVE READING INSTRUCTION FOR STRUGGLING READERS

It is important that you, as a classroom teacher, provide effective reading instruction and support for all your students, including those who struggle with reading. Features of effective reading instruction include the following:

- Establishing an environment to promote reading
- Using appropriate assessment so that you know the students' reading levels and what skills and strategies your students have mastered and need to develop
- Providing early intervention and intensive instruction when needed
- Providing ongoing support for older readers with reading difficulties
- Providing support for English language learners

14.2.1 Establishing an Environment to Promote Reading

Research has documented the importance of engaging in reading and reading with others for building vocabulary and reading skills (Guthrie, 2007; Klauda & Guthrie, 2015). Jane Saunders, a second-grade teacher in a culturally and linguistically diverse school, has a room that provides an environment filled with print that interests students and is readily available to them. When her second graders walk into the classroom on the first day of school, they feel right at home. There are curtains on the windows, a basket for writing supplies at the center of each cluster of four student desks, and a reading center with a couch and carpet for informal reading. The writing center has materials for making books.

The library center is well stocked with reading materials (e.g., newspapers, magazines, catalogs, brochures) and organized with books color-coded according to genre and reading level. The word study center has lots of activities and games for making words using different phonics elements, spelling patterns, and common prefixes and suffixes. The listening station has books on tape that can be used for reading along or for repeated reading to build fluency.

The social environment for reading is also critical. Jane plans times when students can engage in recreational reading. She also models reading by reading aloud to students daily and talking about the books with the students. She uses echo and choral reading so that students have more opportunities to practice their newly learned reading skills. Parents, grandparents, school personnel, and community leaders frequently visit Jane's class to read to students and to listen to students read. Reading is valued, reading is emphasized—reading happens!

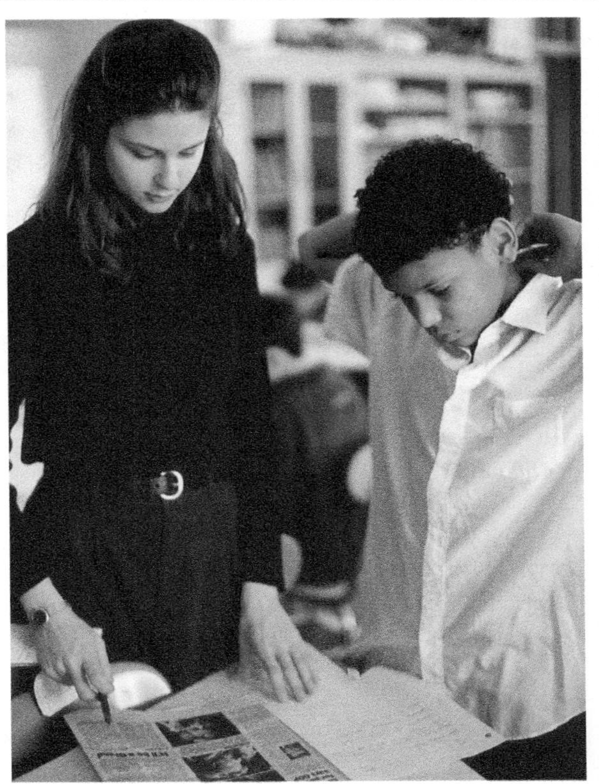

These students are using newspapers to find words with prefixes and suffixes. How might you use newspapers to teach skills in your classroom?

14.2.2 Assessment

Using appropriate assessment is important so that you understand students' reading levels and what skills and strategies your students have mastered and need to develop. Assessment can serve a number of functions (Schumm & Arguelles, 2006; Wixson & Valencia, 2011). Assessment can use used to:

1. Screen students to determine reading levels and instructional needs and to determine initial grouping for reading instruction.
2. Provide more in-depth diagnosis to pinpoint strengths and needs for more intensive interventions.
3. Monitor student response to instruction and progress in meeting learning goals.
4. Determine student end-of-semester and end-of-year outcomes in reading, typically with state-mandated testing.
5. Evaluate school reading programs.
6. Account to administrators, parents, policy makers, and the community at large.

As a classroom teacher, you will be most involved with screening, diagnosis, progress monitoring, and student outcomes with state mandated testing.

Typically, the assessment tools you use will be state or school-district approved. If you do get involved in selecting assessment tools, several critical aspects of assessments should be considered in choosing a test:

- The purpose of the testing (screening, progress monitoring, diagnostic, outcome)
- The specific information needed about the student's reading (specific skills assessment, reading level)
- The number of students being tested (whether you can test individually, in small groups, or in the whole class)
- The examiner's qualifications (whether the tester can acquire the skills to give highly specific tests)

Assessments that tell us specifically how a student is performing and what else he or she needs to know are referred to as **diagnostic assessments**. Some assessments help us to determine how the student's performance compares with that of other students of the same age or in the same grade. This gives us some idea of what students need to know to achieve grade-level performance. These assessments are referred to as **norm-based assessments**. Appropriate assessments can also allow us to monitor the progress of students and

TIPS FOR TEACHERS 14.1

Types of Assessment Resources

- *Comprehensive Test of Phonological Processing–Second Edition* (CTOPP-2; Wagner, Torgesen, Rashotte, & Pearson, 2012). The CTOPP is administered individually to students to determine their skill in phonological awareness and to guide the teacher in designing appropriate instruction. The test is designed for individuals between the ages of 4 and 24.
- *Dynamic Indicators of Basic Early Literacy Skills, Next Edition* (DIBELS *Next*; Good & Kaminski, 2010). The DIBELS consists of timed measures for grades K through 6: Letter Naming Fluency (automatic letter recognition); Initial Sound Fluency and Phoneme Segmentation Fluency (phonological awareness); Nonsense Word Fluency (alphabetic principle); Oral Reading Fluency (fluency); Retell Fluency (comprehension); and Word Use Fluency (vocabulary). There are twenty forms of each measure. The measures are individually administered and require 1 to 3 minutes each. Both English and Spanish versions are available on the DIBELS website (https://dibels.uoregon.edu).
- *Comprehensive Reading Assessment Battery* (CRAB; Fuchs, Fuchs, & Hamlett, 1989). The CRAB provides assessment in fluency and comprehension for students in grades K through 6. It takes 30 to 40 minutes to administer all sections of the test to an individual student.
- *Gray Oral Reading Test* (5th ed.) (Wiederholt & Bryant, 2012). This individually administered reading assessment gauges reading rate, accuracy, fluency, and comprehension. It is designed for individuals from age 6 to 23. Administration time is 20 to 30 minutes.
- *Gates–MacGinitie Reading Tests* (4th ed.) (MacGinitie, MacGinitie, Maria, Dreyer, & Hughes, 2006). This comprehensive reading assessment is designed for group administration. There are levels of the test available for grades K through 12 as well as for adults. The assessment requires 55 to 75 minutes to complete depending on the level.

MyEdLab
Video Example 14.1.
Watch the two teachers in this video provide corrective reading lessons to students who are struggling readers. What tier instruction do you think these students will need and how will that be implemented according to the RTI model?

determine whether their progress is on track and appropriate or whether we need to alter instruction to improve their performance. These assessments are referred to as *progress-monitoring assessments* or *curriculum-based measures.* Numerous assessments are available to meet specific needs. Tips for Teachers 14.1 describes some of these assessments.

Assessment plays an important role in the successful implementation of RTI. The critical elements of RTI include

- Universal screening
- Progress monitoring
- Early intervention in reading for students at risk for reading problems and ongoing assessment and intervention as needed

Assessment is discussed in this section, with instructional practices for teaching students with reading difficulties presented in the subsequent sections.

Preventing reading difficulties and appropriately serving students with reading disabilities requires an understanding of how to implement elements of response to intervention (RTI). (See Tips for Teachers 14.2.)

TIPS FOR TEACHERS 14.2

Questions to Ask About Students' Response to Intervention

How do you know if students are responding to instruction? The answers to several questions can provide valuable information for determining students' response to intervention:

- Have students received scientifically based reading instruction in the appropriate elements of reading (e.g., phonemic awareness and phonics for beginning readers, and fluency, vocabulary, and comprehension for all readers)?
- Have students received adequate opportunities to respond, obtain feedback, and see modeling and scaffolding to support their learning?
- How does the performance of students who are low responders compare with the performance of other students in the class?
- Have students received instructional opportunities in small groups to acquire reading proficiency?
- Have students been adequately engaged and had opportunities to select text of interest to read?
- Are progress-monitoring data available to show the slope of each student's progress?

Knowing the opportunities students have to learn and being able to examine their progress using data assists in determining the severity of the problem and designing interventions.

14.2.3 Screening

Screening is a mechanism for determining how students perform relative to their grade-level peers in order to determine whether further assessment or instruction would be beneficial. Most schools provide some measure to all students at each grade level at the beginning of the year to determine their relative standing in reading. These screening measures allow teachers to determine whether they have students who are reading considerably above grade level and also to determine whether students are below level. Often these screening measures assist teachers in grouping students for instruction, selecting texts at appropriate reading levels, and planning instruction.

14.2.4 Diagnosis

Diagnosis involves more in-depth assessment to determine individual instructional needs. At times you will conduct diagnostic tests independently, other times in collaboration with a school psychologist, special education teacher, or reading specialist.

Informal reading inventories are one tool classroom teachers use for diagnosing individual instructional needs (Walpole & McKenna, 2006). Using informal reading inventories, students read lists of words and passages that are leveled by grade, and retell or answer comprehension questions about the passages they have read. Typical criteria used for determining reading level are illustrated in Figure 14.4; students' answers to questions can help you determine whether students have received adequate instruction and thus whether their low response to reading instruction is a function of the exceptional needs of the student.

As a teacher, you not only can determine the independent, instructional, and frustration reading levels of the students, but also can gain insight into the decoding and comprehension strategies the students use when reading. There are a number of commercial IRIs on the market (see Nilsson, 2008 for a review), and many include additional informal assessments to pinpoint instructional needs in all areas of reading.

It is also vital for you to understand the reading levels of all of your students so you can select appropriate materials for instructional and recreational reading and make appropriate accommodations when students read complex texts (Fisher et al., 2012).

The following three guidelines provide a means for increasing the likelihood that students are reading appropriate materials:

1. The independent reading level is characterized by the students reading on their own without support from others.
2. The instructional reading level is the level at which instruction should occur. At this level, students are challenged by the reading and still need some support (e.g., preteaching words the students do not recognize automatically, teaching new vocabulary, making predictions about the story).
3. At the frustration reading level, the material is too difficult for the students to read with understanding even with assistance.

FIGURE 14.4 **Criteria for determining reading level**

	WORD RECOGNITION	WORD COMPREHENSION
Independent	95–100%	90% and above
Instructional	90–95%	75–90%
Frustration	Below 90%	Below 75%

14.2.5 Progress Monitoring

Progress monitoring, or curriculum-based measurement (CBM), is a means of measuring students' progress and highlights the close tie between curriculum and student performance (Christ, Cengiz, Long, & Monaghen, 2012; Salvia, Ysseldyke, & Bolt, 2013). It uses frequent (typically brief) samplings from the curriculum materials to assess students' academic performance (e.g., Deno, 1985). CBM has been used successfully in general education classrooms to increase word recognition, reading fluency, and reading comprehension (e.g., Fuchs, Fuchs, & Burish, 2000; Nese, Park, Alonzo, & Tindal, 2011). For example, to assess reading comprehension, students read passages at their instructional level and complete a maze task. For this task, the first sentence is left intact, but thereafter, every seventh word is deleted. Students select from three choices the one semantically correct word that fills in the blank. CBM provides ongoing data for making instructional decisions by considering:

- How performance is affected by changing the instructional level
- The rate of learning (as reflected by changes in the slope of the trend line) compared to the goal
- The variability in the consistency of the performance

The 60-Second Lesson provides procedures for monitoring student progress in fluency and comprehension.

60-SECOND LESSON

MONITORING STUDENT PROGRESS IN FLUENCY AND COMPREHENSION

1. Select two to three passages that are unfamiliar to the student and that are at the student's instructional or independent word-recognition levels. Make two copies of each passage of text you are using with the targeted student: one for recording errors and one for the student to read.
2. Tell the student: "When I say 'begin,' start reading aloud at the top of the page. Do your best reading. If you come to a word that you don't know, I'll tell it to you."
3. Have the student read for 1 minute. If the student does not read a word within 3 seconds, pronounce the word.
4. Follow along as the student reads and mark your copy by putting a slash (/) through words read incorrectly. This includes mispronunciations, substitutions, omissions, words pronounced after hesitations of more than 3 seconds, and reversals. Do not count insertions, self-corrections, or repetitions. Also note if the student is having difficulty with phrasing; ignoring punctuation; reading slowly, word-by-word, or laboriously; and/or has frequent extended pauses, false starts, sound-outs, and repetitions.
5. Note the last word read by the student when the 1 minute is up. If the student is in the middle of a sentence when the time has finished, have him or her finish the sentence but count only those words read up to the stop point.
6. Calculate fluency using the following formula:

   # of words read in 1 minute − # of errors = words correct per minute (WCPM)

   For example, if a student reads 83 words during a 1-minute sample and makes 6 errors, then the WCPM would be 83 minus 6 equals 77.

14.2.6 Using Data from Progress Monitoring

When working with struggling readers, progress monitoring provides the teacher with necessary data to inform decision making about grouping and instruction. Progress monitoring assists teachers in identifying students who are at risk for failing to acquire necessary skills and allows the teacher to monitor the progress students make in response to instruction. Two important aspects of progress monitoring measures are that (a) they should be predictive of later reading ability, and (b) they need to guide instruction.

14.2.7 Assessments Used for Accountability

Assessment includes measures state departments of education or school districts use to determine accountability to parents, the general public, and policy makers. Some states have developed their own assessments (e.g., State of Texas Assessments of Academic Readiness; Virginia Standards of Learning Tests). Other states have adopted assessments aligned with Common Core State Standards (i.e., The Partnership for Assessment of Readiness for College and Career [PARCC, www.parcconline.org]; Smarter Balanced Assessment Consortium [SBAC, www.smarterbalanced.org]) (Doorey, 2014; Shanahan, 2014). When matched to state standards or benchmarks in reading, these assessments can provide helpful information in determining what reading skills the students have developed. Although they are one source of information, it is important to remember that for struggling readers these assessments can be particularly difficult and might not provide a good picture of their reading achievement. Furthermore, standardized tests tend to focus on the "product" of reading and ignore salient factors that influence success or failure in literacy development (Afflerbach, 2016). These assessments are often called high-stakes tests in that student promotion, graduation, or placement in specialized programs were the consequence of test results.

The teacher's role in preparing students for assessment

What is your role in preparing students for state-mandated assessments? Obviously, you will need to be aware of your state standards for reading instruction and incorporate those standards into your daily planning. In addition, Shanahan (2014) recommends that teachers provide students with ample opportunities for reading throughout the school day, develop greater independence in reading and responding to text (orally and in writing), read text with a range of difficulty levels, and engage in rich discussions about text. It is also important to be familiar with accommodations that are approved for students with disabilities and English language learners.

The Every Student Succeeds Act (ESSA)

President Barack Obama signed the reauthorization of the bipartisan Elementary and Secondary School Education Act on December 10, 2015 (The White House, 2015). Now known as the Every Student Succeeds Act (ESSA), the act offers relief from some of the punitive aspects of high-stakes testing associated with its predecessor, No Child Left Behind (NCLB). In addition, the act mandates reduced time in testing, elimination of duplicate assessments, and greater autonomy for states. How individual state departments of education elect to restructure their accountability systems and how and when these changes will impact the classroom remains to be seen (National Education Association, 2016). States will also tackle the important issue of how to assure fair and equitable assessment of students with disabilities and English language learners (Abedi & Levine, 2013; Doorey, 2014). As a classroom teacher, you will want to follow these changes as they evolve in your state and engage in professional development activities to remain current.

14.2.8 Providing Early Intervention and Intensive Instruction

Early intervention programs address students' reading difficulties as soon as they become apparent. At Roma McCormick's school, where she is the reading specialist, kindergarteners and first graders who are not making adequate progress are enrolled in the school's

literacy support programs. These programs provide supplemental small-group and some one-on-one instruction in which students are grouped by level and needs. The programs emphasize teaching phonological awareness, letter–sound correspondences, decoding skills and word recognition, fluent reading, and vocabulary and oral language development. For grades 2 through 5, Roma asks teachers early in the school year to identify any students who are having difficulty with grade-level reading material. Roma confers with teachers to decide how to meet the needs of individual students in the general education classroom and in supplemental programs, if appropriate.

For students with special learning needs in reading, whole-class instruction can be treacherous. Therefore, it is important to find ways to provide instruction that is both appropriate for meeting individual students' needs and intensive enough for progress to occur. Research has demonstrated that a substantial number of students who are identified as initially having difficulty learning to read can profit from intensive small-group instruction or working as pairs in structured peer-tutoring formats (Begeny, Yeager, & Martinez, 2012; Elbaum, Vaughn, Hughes, & Moody, 2000; Fuchs, Fuchs, & Vaughn, 2014; Wanzek & Vaughn, 2007).

Reading instruction is appropriate and intensive when

- Students have a clear understanding of teacher expectations and the goals of instruction.
- Instruction provided matches the reader's instructional reading level and needs.
- Adequate texts are used that are engaging to the students and at their reading levels.
- Research-based instructional materials or strategies are implemented as intended (e.g., with fidelity).
- Duration of the intervention is sufficient to enable student mastery of instructional goals.
- Instruction is explicit and direct in the skills and strategies the reader needs in order to become proficient and more independent.
- Students are grouped appropriately, which includes ability-level grouping.
- Instruction includes frequent opportunities for responding with feedback.
- Student progress is monitored frequently and used to make instructional decisions.
- Teachers and peers support the students when necessary.

Teachers frequently ask, "What skills do I teach?" and "How do I decide what students to put in a particular skill group?" Tips for Teachers 14.3 provides some suggestions.

TIPS FOR TEACHERS 14.3

Flexible Grouping Strategies for Reading Instruction

- At the beginning of the school year, decide on the critical skills and strategies you want all students to learn by the end of the school year. Make a checklist of these skills, and place the list in each student's assessment portfolio. Keep a master list in your plan book or grade book.
- Base skills and strategies on your textbook series, school district curricular guides, and your own goals for reading and writing instruction.
- Schedule a regular time to meet with skill groups. Skill lessons can be whole class, small group, or for individual students, depending on student needs.
- Keep the membership of skill groups flexible. You may have a permanent group of low achievers that you meet with regularly, but include them as members of other groups as well.
- Do not limit skill and strategy lessons to low-achieving students only. Average and high-achieving students also need this instruction.
- Focus on a few skills or strategies each week, allowing some time in your schedule to teach skill lessons based on student requests and needs that arise from your daily observation of student work.
- Keep a record of the skill lessons you teach and which students participate in each lesson.

14.2.9 Providing Ongoing Support for Older Readers with Reading Difficulties

Maxine Ward is a middle school reading specialist in a large, urban school district and works with the special education teacher, Theresa Medina, to plan for students in need of intensive instruction. She also works with content-area teachers to imbed vocabulary and reading comprehension strategies in their lessons. Maxine explains that some of the students they teach have had persistent challenges with reading from the outset of their schooling. Others fared well in elementary school, but began to struggle when trying to read complex content-area textbooks. Still others are new immigrants to the United States who are in the initial stages of learning English and adapting to a very different school environment. Maxine has learned that ongoing, intensive, and individualized interventions as well as support for reading in their content-area classes are imperative to the academic progress of the students she teaches.

Provision of individualized or small-group instruction with skilled professionals and frequent progress monitoring may be necessary, but not sufficient to prepare students for reading challenging high school and college textbooks (Wilson, Faggella-Luby, & Wei, 2013; Solis, Miciak, Vaughn, & Fletcher, 2014). Continued research on both the content of instruction as well as the type of instructional practices implemented is warranted.

Many teachers of older students with reading difficulties or disabilities are eager to learn more about instructional programs that have been developed and tested specifically with older students. Fortunately, there is growing interest in research and development of instructional practices to meet this demand (Cassidy et al., 2015; Wood & Blanton, 2009). Deshler, Palincsar, Biancarosa, and Nair (2007) provide an overview of more than fifty programs that have been developed and evaluated with older students with reading difficulties/disabilities. These programs are rated based on content and research. If you are thinking about using a program, you might want to check to see whether they have reviewed it. Tips for Teachers 14.4 presents some strategies for teaching older students to read.

Teaching older students with significant reading difficulties to read is not substantively different from teaching younger students. Many of the practices you will read about in this chapter apply to older readers, with a few important exceptions. First, few older readers require instruction in phonological awareness. Second, phonics and other word–study practices are taught with more complex multisyllabic words as opposed to the single-syllable words used with younger children (Goodwin, 2016; Wilson, Faggella-Luby, & Wei, 2013). This way, students learn to read "big" words at a level that is not demeaning.

TIPS FOR TEACHERS 14.4

Strategies in Reading Instruction for Older Students

- *Be an advocate for nonreaders.* As a content-area teacher, you might not be able to teach these students to decode, but you can be an advocate for them as individuals and for nonreaders collectively.
- *Work collaboratively with other professionals in the school.* What resources are available to help you teach and for students to receive additional help?
- *Work out a plan for what you can reasonably do in your classroom.* Communicate the plan to administrators, other professionals, parents, and students, and follow it regularly.
- *Continue to make knowledge available to students who cannot adequately access knowledge through reading.* Students who cannot read the text for content-area instruction can be left out of learning without teachers who provide alternative ways for them to access the content. Teach key words, concepts, and principles orally and provide opportunities to review this knowledge. Allow for engaging and interactive activities to promote access to knowledge for students who read poorly.
- *Include in your plan ways to provide support for students to complete reading assignments and tests by using recordings, parent support, or peer support.* Work out a way to have assignments and tests read aloud to students if they cannot read them on their own.
- *Find out about and build on the strengths of nonreaders.* Make certain that in your class they have an opportunity to share their gifts and talents with classmates.

14.2.10 Providing Support for English Language Learners

Many of the critical content components that are essential for monolingual English speakers are effective for English language learners (ELLs). English language learners typically speak a language other than English in the home and are more comfortable listening and speaking in their home language. However, whether you are teaching them to read in their home language or English, the essential components of learning to read are also effective for these students. However, adaptations such as visual aids, physical activities, cooperative learning, or additional repetition and reinforcement may be necessary (August, McCardle, & Shanahan, 2014; Toppel, 2015).

ELLs benefit from having phonological awareness and, with guidance, can readily transfer their phonological awareness knowledge in their home language to English. They make progress with phonological awareness instruction when focus is placed on English sounds that are not present in their first language. They also benefit from instruction in phonics, fluency, and comprehension. If they are not yet successful readers in English, learning to use listening-comprehension strategies similar to reading-comprehension strategies will help them be more effective at understanding what they hear and then transferring this knowledge later to what they read. Perhaps the most important component is to adequately build vocabulary, concept, and comprehension knowledge.

Unfortunately, there is substantially more knowledge about teaching students with reading difficulties who are monolingual English students than there is about teaching students who are ELLs. However, there is a growing knowledge base to inform our instruction in early reading with ELLs (August et al., 2014; Baker et al., 2014; Denton, Anthony, Parker, & Hasbrouck, 2004; Linan-Thompson & Vaughn, 2007; Vaughn, Cirino et al., 2006; Verhoeven, 2011). A summary of findings reveals that

- English language learners who were given direct instruction in early reading in English benefited in the number of words read correctly per minute (Gunn, Biglan, Smokowski, & Ary, 2000).
- Bilingual students with significant reading problems who participated in twenty-two tutoring sessions in a systematic and explicit approach to phonics and word and sentence reading significantly improved on word identification when compared with control groups who did not receive this type of instruction (Denton et al., 2004).
- ELLs who were second graders at risk for reading disabilities participated in fifty-eight sessions (35 minutes each) of supplemental intervention in group sizes of one to three students (Linan-Thompson, Vaughn, Hickman-Davis, & Kouzekanani, 2003). Students in the treatment made gains on reading outcomes such as word attack, passage comprehension, phoneme segmentation, and oral reading fluency. Only three students achieved less than 6 months' growth during the 3-month intervention.
- In a study with young children with problems learning to read in English but who spoke Sylheti (a dialect from Bangladesh), students who participated in a phonics program rather than story reading made significant gains on phonics recognition and recall and writing sounds, as well as on reading words and reading nonwords (Stuart, 1999). Findings indicate that a more structured, systematic approach that includes phonics resulted in better outcomes for ELLs than interventions without these elements.
- Young bilingual students (Spanish/English) with low literacy skills taught to read in English made considerable gains over their first-grade year and maintained these advantages into second grade (Vaughn, Cirino et al., 2006; Vaughn, Mathes et al., 2006). Similarly, young bilingual students (Spanish/English) with low literacy and oral literacy skills taught to read in Spanish also made considerable gains, outperformed comparison students, and maintained these gains into second grade (Vaughn, Cirino et al., 2006; Vaughn, Linan-Thompson, Pollard-Durodola, Mathes, & Cardenas-Hagan, 2006).

TIPS FOR TEACHERS 14.5

Effective Instructional Practices for English Language Learners

- Consider the commonalities between reading instruction in English and the reading instruction that is provided in the student's native language (assuming native-language instruction has occurred).
- Identify procedures for instructing students in all of the critical elements of reading, including phonemic awareness, spelling, phonics, vocabulary, language development, fluency, and comprehension.
- Recognize that English is the most difficult language of all alphabetic languages to learn to read, and therefore many of the foundation skills such as spelling and phonics require more explicit and systematic instruction than they might in other alphabetic languages such as Spanish or Italian.
- Make connections between the home language and the language of instruction at school.
- Capitalize on every opportunity to use and promote language development during instruction and give opportunities for students to engage in higher-order questions.
- Promote all opportunities to teach and engage in vocabulary and concept building.
- Use peer pairing and cooperative groups to enhance learning.

Sources: August, D., McCardle, P., & Shanahan, T. (2014). Developing literacy in English language learners: Findings from a review of the experimental research. *School Psychology Review,* 43(4), 490-498; Linan-Thompson, S., & Vaughn, S. (2007). *Research-based methods of reading instruction for English language learners: Grades K-4.* Alexandria, VA: Association for Supervision and Curriculum Development; *Strategies for teaching students with learning and behavior problems* (9th ed., p. 181), by S. Vaughn & C. S. Bos, 2015, Boston: Allyn & Bacon.

In summary, good readers—whether they are monolingual English or English language learners—rely primarily on decoding words (understanding the sound-to-print correspondence or alphabetic principle). They do not rely primarily on context or pictures to identify words. When they use context, it is to confirm word reading or to better understand text meaning. Well-developed phonics instruction provides ELLs with the knowledge they need to develop the skills and strategies needed to effectively and efficiently establish a map for making sense of how English language works in print. As with monolingual students, phonics instruction is a piece of the reading instruction and not the entire program. Good phonics instruction is well integrated into language activities, story time, and small-group support to create a balanced reading program. Learning to read in languages in which the print is less consistently connected to sounds (such as English) takes longer than learning to read in languages that have more consistent orthographies (e.g., Spanish) (Seymour, 2006). Tips for Teachers 14.5 provides suggestions for teaching reading to ELLs.

MyEdLab
Video Example 14.2.
Watch this video and pay attention to ways in which the bilingual coordinator explains why it is so important that teachers get to know about each of their ELL students. How do they use this knowledge to plan their instruction to accommodate each student?

MyEdLab **Self-Check 14.2**

MyEdLab **Application Exercise 14.2:** Progress Monitoring

14.3 STRATEGIES FOR TEACHING PHONOLOGICAL AWARENESS AND PHONICS

Ms. Ramirez, a kindergarten teacher, partners with Ms. Harry, a special education teacher, to assist the students who are having the most difficulty learning letter–sound correspondence, separating words by syllables, and blending and segmenting phonemes. With these kindergarteners, the teachers work on reinforcing each letter–sound pair, for example, *b*, *ball*, /b/, and students participate in phonological awareness games and activities in which they count the number of syllables in words, count the sounds in simple words (e.g., *me* and *sit*), and create word families (e.g., *-it*, *sit*, *mit*, *bit*, *fit*, *hit*). At first, they had the students only listen when working on these phonological awareness activities. Now they are using letters to demonstrate how the syllables and sounds are related to print. Why do they do these activities? Children who develop *phonological awareness* early begin to read earlier and are more successful readers.

Ms. Harry also works with a small group of six students in Ms. Wenske's first-grade class who are having difficulty learning to read. Ms. Harry engages these students in such activities as listening and clapping the number of sounds in words to help them segment the sounds; saying each sound in a word slowly and then saying them fast to practice blending; and when spelling, having them say the word, then say the sounds, then say the first sound and write it, then say the first two sounds and write the second sound, and so on until they have spelled the word.

These teachers are directly teaching phonological awareness and phonics, which are associated with successful reading and spelling (Ehri, 2003; Lane & Pullen, 2015). Problems with phoneme blending, segmenting, and manipulating have been consistent predictors of difficulties in learning to read (Cavanaugh, Kim, Wanzek, & Vaughn, 2004; Manyak, 2008). Children who struggle with these skills are likely to be among the poorest readers and most likely to be identified as having a learning or reading disability (e.g., Snowling & Hulme, 2012; Melby-Lervag, Lyster, & Hulme, 2012). Hence, the first- and second-grade teachers are working with students to help prevent or lessen later reading disabilities.

14.3.1 Teaching Phonological Awareness

If phonological awareness is so important, how does it develop and how can it be taught? **Phonological awareness** involves understanding and demonstrating that spoken language can be broken down into smaller units (words, syllables, phonemes), which can be manipulated within an alphabetic system or orthography. Phonological awareness includes the skills of rhyming, alliteration, blending, segmenting, and manipulating.

- **Rhyming**: identifying similarities and differences in word endings
- **Alliteration**: identifying similarities and differences in word beginnings
- **Blending**: putting syllables or sounds together to form words
- **Segmenting**: dividing words into syllables and sounds
- **Manipulating**: deleting, adding, and substituting syllables and sounds

In general, children's awareness of the phonological structure of the English language develops from larger units of sounds (e.g., words in a sentence, syllables in a word) to smaller units (e.g., phonemes, or individual speech sounds in a word). Figure 14.5 presents a continuum for the development of phonological awareness, with examples.

FIGURE 14.5 Phonological awareness continuum

LATER DEVELOPING	
SKILL	**EXAMPLE**
Phoneme blending, segmentation, and manipulations	Blending phonemes into words, segmenting words into individual phonemes, and manipulating phonemes (e.g., deleting, adding, substituting, transposing) in spoken words
Onset-rime blending and segmentation	Blending/segmenting the initial consonant or consonant cluster (onset) from the vowel and consonant sounds spoken after it (rime)
Syllable blending and segmentation	Blending syllables to say words or segmenting spoken words into syllables
Sentence segmentation	Segmenting sentences into spoken words
Rhyme/alliteration	Matching the ending sounds of words/producing groups of words that begin with the same initial sound
EARLY DEVELOPING	

Source: Adapted from *First grade teacher reading academy*, Texas Center for Reading and Language Arts, Austin: University of Texas.

Skills such as rhyming and alliteration develop earlier, whereas skills such as blending, segmenting, and sound manipulation develop later. Activities that focus on individual sounds in words constitute phonemic awareness. It is these more advanced skills of phoneme blending, segmenting, and manipulating that are most related to success in learning to read (Ehri, 2004; Stanovich, 1992; Torgesen, Wagner, & Rashotte, 1994).

To teach rhyming and alliteration, use books that are based on rhyme and alliteration, such as *There's a Wocket in My Pocket* (Seuss, 1974) and *Each Peach Pear Plum* (Ahlberg & Ahlberg, 1979). You can have students create, say, and listen/look for rhymes, alliterations, and "silly sayings." To build blending and segmenting skills, you might want to use the Elkonin procedure (Elkonin, 1973). As a phonological task, students listen to a word and push a marker, block, or other small object into a printed square for each sound they hear (see the first row in Figure 14.6).

Many programs and resources are available for teaching phonological awareness and the alphabetic principle (see Tips for Teachers 14.6 for a selected list).

FIGURE 14.6 **Using the elkonin procedure to support phonemic awareness and the alphabetic principle**

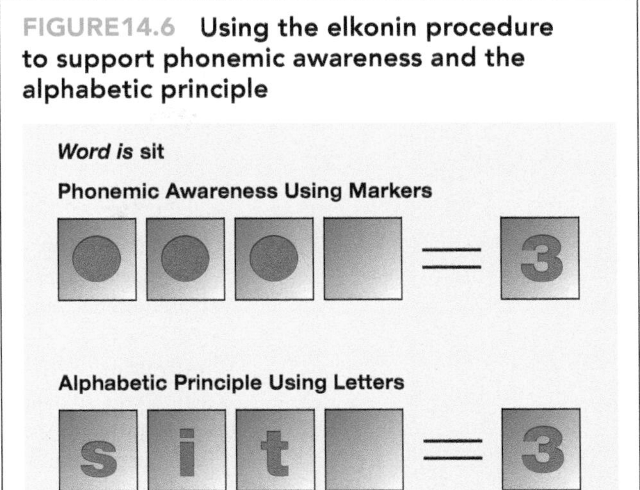

Source: Strategies for teaching students with learning and behavior problems (9th ed., Figure 7-2, p. 181), by S. Vaughn & C. S. Bos, 2015, Boston: Allyn & Bacon. Copyright © 2015 by Pearson. Reprinted by permission.

As students gain knowledge about the letter–sound relationships, they can push or write letters in the boxes (see the second row in Figure 14.6). This is one way to make an oral language activity more visible and kinesthetic. Other ways are tapping one finger to the thumb for each sound and watching your mouth in a mirror, feeling the facial movements by placing your fingers on your cheeks, and concentrating on how your mouth changes when different sounds are made.

General guidelines for teaching phonological awareness activities include the following (Vaughn & Bos, 2015):

- Consider the students' levels of development and tasks that need to be mastered.
- Model each activity.
- Use manipulatives and movement to make auditory/oral tasks more visible.
- Move from less to more difficult tasks, considering level of development (syllables, onset-rimes, phonemes), phoneme position (initial, final, medial), number of sounds in a word (*cat* is easier than *split*), and phonological features of the words

TIPS FOR TEACHERS 14.6

Selected Programs and Resources for Teaching Phonological Awareness and Phonics

- *Catching Readers, Grade K. Day-by-Day, Small-Group Reading Interventions* by Taylor, B. M. and Duke, N. K., 2011, Portsmouth, NH: Heinemann.
- *Peer-Assisted Learning Strategies* by Fuchs, D., & Fuchs, L. http://kc.vanderbilt.edu/pals/
- *Phonics They Use: Words for Reading and Writing* by Cunningham, P. M., 2017, Boston: Pearson.
- *Interventions for Reading Success* (2nd ed.) by Haager, D., Domino, J. A., and Windmueller, M. P., 2014, Baltimore, MD: Paul H. Brookes.
- *Speech to Print: Language Essentials for Teachers* (2nd ed.). by Moats, L. C., 2010, Baltimore, MD: Paul H. Brookes.
- *The Lindamood Phoneme Sequencing Program for Reading, Spelling, and Speech* (4th ed.) by Lindamood, P. A., and Lindamood, P., 2011, Austin, TX: PRO-ED.
- *Evidence-based Instruction in Reading: A Professional Development Guide to Phonemic Awareness* by Mraz, M., Rasinski, T., and Padak, N. D., 2008, Boston: Pearson.
- *Purposeful Play for Early Childhood Phonological Awareness* by Yopp, H., and Yopp, R. H., 2010, Huntington Beach, CA: Shell Education.
- *Words Their Way* (6th ed.) by Bear, D. R., Invernizzi, M., Templeton, S. and Johnston, F., 2015, Boston: Pearson.

(e.g., continuing consonants such as /m/, /n/, and /s/ are easier than stops or clipped sounds such as /t/, /b/, and /d/).

- Provide feedback and opportunities for practice and review.
- Make learning fun!

14.3.2 Teaching Phonics

Students who are able to distinguish the sounds in words and to segment and blend them orally (phonological awareness) are more likely to be successful in applying their knowledge to making connections between sounds and print. As students learn letter–sound correspondences and how to blend, segment, and manipulate sounds, it is important that they associate speech with print (Shaywitz, Morris, & Shaywitz, 2008; O'Connor, 2011), thereby learning the **alphabetic principle** (understanding that the sequence of letters in written words represents the sequence of sounds in spoken words). Almost all early reading programs are developed to teach letter–sound correspondence and phonics to students. There are also programs designed specifically for students with reading difficulties or disabilities:

- *Corrective Reading 2008* © (Engelmann et al., 2008)
- *Lindamood Phoneme Sequencing Program–LiPs*® (Lindamood & Lindamood, 2011)
- *Wilson Reading System*® (Wilson, 2004)
- *SpellRead*™ (PRO-ED, 2008)

Most programs that are designed to teach phonics to students with reading difficulties have these instructional features:

- Teach a core set of frequently used consonants and short vowel sounds that represent clear sounds and nonreversible letter forms (e.g., /a/, /i/, /d/, /f/, /g/, /h/, /l/, /n/, /p/, /s/, /t/).
- Begin immediately to blend and segment the sounds in order to read and spell the words and read the words in **decodable text** (i.e., text in which most of the words are composed of letter–sound correspondences that have been taught).
- Separate the introduction of letter sounds with similar auditory or visual features (e.g., /e/ and /i/, /m/ and /n/, /b/ and /d/).
- Use a consistent key word to assist students in hearing and remembering the sound (e.g., *b*, *ball*, /b/).
- Teach that some letters can represent more than one sound. For each letter, first teach the most frequent sound and then teach other sounds (e.g., /c/ in *cat,* then /s/ in *city;* /g/ in *gate*, then /j/ in *gem*).
- Teach that different letters can make the same sound, such as the /s/ in *sit* and *city*.
- Teach that sounds can be represented by a single letter or a combination of letters (e.g., /a/ in *make* and *rain*, /sh/ in *fish*) and may be represented in boxes with a dotted line.

F	I	S	H

- Color-code consonants and vowels so that the two categories of sounds are highlighted. Add a kinesthetic component by having students trace or write the letter as they say the sound.
- Have students use mirrors and feel their mouths to see and feel how sounds are different.

With respect to phonics instruction, research reviews (e.g., Ehri, 2004; National Reading Panel, 2000) make the following recommendations (also see Tips for Teachers 14.4):

- Systematic phonics instruction results in significant benefits in decoding and spelling for students in kindergarten through sixth grade.

- Synthetic phonics instruction (i.e., teaching students explicitly to convert letters into sounds and then blend the sounds to form recognizable words) was particularly effective for students with reading/learning disabilities and students from low-socioeconomic backgrounds.
- Although conventional wisdom has suggested that kindergarten children might not be ready for phonics instruction, this assumption was not supported by the research.
- Invented spellings should be encouraged, in that they help students develop the necessary phonological awareness skills for reading and spelling. Students should also be taught to transition to conventional spellings.
- Teaching of some phonics rules and generalizations can be helpful if they bring attention to spelling patterns. But learning rules is no substitute for practicing with spelling patterns.
- Teaching of onset-rimes and the blending and segmenting of sounds is particularly important for building decoding and spelling skills.
- Teachers need to be flexible in their phonics instruction to adapt to the strengths and needs of individual students.
- Systematic phonics is only one component, but a necessary one, of a total reading program.
- Students should be taught how to use their phonics rules in multisyllabic words.
- Teachers should spend enough time teaching and applying phonics rules to help students read new words but not too much time to detract from opportunities to read.

Teaching phonics is a key element in understanding the alphabetic principle and learning to read and spell words. However, programs that focus too much on teaching phonics and not enough on putting the rules of phonics to work by reading words automatically and understanding text are likely to be ineffective. Through modeling and discussion, students need to understand that the purpose for learning these relationships is to apply them to their reading and writing activities. For example, when students in Ms. Wanzek's class have trouble reading a word, she asks them to use the phonics rules they know to decode the word. When her student Michael was stuck on the word *happen*, she reminded him about the phonics rule he knew about dividing the word into syllables when two consonants are doubled in the middle of a word. He then was able to read "hap" and "pen" and put it together to read the word *happen*. Tips for Teachers 14.7 provides guidelines for teaching phonics.

See the Activities for All Learners feature for additional activities to use to encourage successful reading for all students.

TIPS FOR TEACHERS 14.7

Guidelines for Using Phonics Instruction

- Build on a child's foundation of phonological awareness and rich concept of how print functions.
- Use direct and systematic instruction, as follows (V = vowel; C = consonant):
  - Begin with simple VC (*in*) and CVC (*pet*) words, and then move to more complex sound patterns, such as CCVC (*slim*), CVCC (*duck*), CVCe (*make*).
  - Demonstrate and have the students point to each letter sound as they say the sound, and then have them sweep their fingers under the word when they say it fast.
  - Provide practice with feedback.
- Integrate phonics instruction into a balanced reading program.
- Teach only the most salient and needed patterns (e.g., silent *e*).
- Develop automatic word recognition so that students can devote their attention to comprehension rather than identifying words.

ACTIVITIES FOR ALL LEARNERS

Reading Activities for All Learners

1 Phonological Awareness Songs

Objective: To teach sound matching, isolation, blending, and segmentation

Grades: Kindergarten to third grade

Materials: Song sheets or poster with words to songs

Teaching Procedures:

1. For younger students, the singing and rhyming may occur only as a listening activity.
2. For older students, words and letters could be added using song sheets or posters with words to the songs.

2 Sound Matching Activity

(To the tune of "Jimmy Crack Corn and I Don't Care")

Teacher:

Who has an /m/ word to share with us?

Who has an /m/ word to share with us?

Who has an /m/ word to share with us?

It must start with the /m/ sound.

Child:

Man is a word that starts with /m/.

Man is a word that starts with /m/.

Man is a word that starts with /m/.

Man starts with the /m/ sound.

3 Sound Isolation Activity

(To the tune of "Old MacDonald Had a Farm")

What's the sound that starts these words:

Turtle, time, and teeth? (wait for a response)

T is the sound that starts these words:

Turtle, time, and teeth.

with a /t/, /t/ here, and a /t/, /t/ there,

Here a /t/, there a /t/, everywhere a /t/, /t/.

T is the sound that starts these words:

Turtle, time, and teeth.

(This can be used with medial and final sounds as well.)

4 Blending Activity

(To the tune of "If You're Happy and You Know It, Clap Your Hands")

If you think you know this word, shout it out!

If you think you know this word, shout it out!

If you think you know this word,

Then tell me what you've heard,

If you think you know this word, shout it out!

(Sound out a word slowly such as /m/-/a/-/n/ and have students blend the sounds to make a word.)

5 Sound Magic Game

Objective: To improve phonological awareness of beginning, medial, and ending sounds

Grades: Primary

Materials: List of one-syllable words

Teaching Procedures:

1. Decide whether you want to play Sound Magic with the whole class or with small groups of students.
2. Place all participating students in a circle.
3. Begin by introducing a one-syllable word.
4. Explain that you play the game by moving the word around the circle from person to person. To move the word, you make a new word by changing the beginning, middle, or end sound and say the new word out loud. For example, you might start out with the word *sit*. The first child might form the new word *hit*, the next child *hat*, the next child *mat*, and so on.
5. If a child can't think of a word in a reasonable period of time, the child can pass.
6. Keep going until there are three passes in a row.
7. Start again with a new word and with the next child.
8. The object of the game is to make new words out of one word and to break the group's record.

6 Compound Concentration

Objective: To give the students practice in identifying compound words and to illustrate how words may be combined to form compound words

Grades: Intermediate and secondary

Materials: thirty-six index cards ( ) on which the two parts of eighteen compound words have been written; make sure each part can only be joined with one other part

Teaching Procedures: Explain the game. Have the students shuffle the cards and place them face down in six rows with six cards each. Each player takes a turn at turning over two cards. The student then decides whether the two words make a compound word. If they do not, the cards are again turned face down and the next player takes a turn. If the words make a compound word, the player gets the two cards and turns over two more cards. The student continues playing until two cards are turned over that do not make a compound word. The game is over when all the cards are matched. The player with the most cards wins.

Adaptations: Students can match synonyms, antonyms, prefixes, suffixes, initial or final consonants, categories, and sight words.

7 How Short Can You Make It?

Objective: To improve summarizing skills

Grades: Intermediate grades and above

Materials: Any reading material

Teaching Procedures:

1. Decide whether to play this game as a whole-class or small-group activity.
2. Have students read a sentence or paragraph aloud or silently.
3. Give students time to think how to reduce the sentence or paragraph to its most important ideas, write down their reduction, and make edits as needed.
4. Have students "bid" on how short they can make it. For example, one student might say, "I can reduce it to six words"; another might say, "I can reduce it to four words."
5. The lowest bidder then reads his or her reduction. If the group agrees that it maintains all key ideas, then the lowest bidder gets to conduct the next round of bidding. If not, then necessary revisions are made and the teacher runs the next round of bidding.

8 WH-Game

Objective: To provide students practice in answering who, what, when, where, why, and how questions

Grades: All grades

Materials: (1) Generic game board, spinner or die, and markers. (2) WH cards: cards with "WH-Game" written on one side and one of these written on the other: Who, What, When, Where, Why, How. (3) Sets of story and article cards: copies of short stories and articles mounted on cards. There should be one set for each player. Select topics of interest for the students' age level.

Teaching Procedures: Explain the game to students or have them read the directions. First, the players set up the game. Next, they select a set of story or article cards. All players read the card and place it face down. Each player then takes a turn by throwing the die or spinning and selecting a WH card. The player must make up a question using the WH word and answer it correctly to move his or her marker the indicated number of spaces. If another player questions the validity of a player's question or answer, the players may look at the story or article card. Otherwise, these cards should remain face down during play. After ten questions have been asked using one story or article card, another set is selected. The students read this card, and the game continues. The first player to arrive at the finish wins.

Adaptations: Students may also work in pairs, with one person on the team making up the question and the other person answering it.

9 Comp Checks

Objective: To help students learn to monitor their own comprehension

Grades: All grades

Materials: Paper strips; assigned reading

Teaching Procedures:

1. As you prepare a reading assignment, think about the characteristics of the text, your purpose for having students read the assignment, and your goals for learning about students' response to the text.
2. Identify key comprehension-monitoring goals. For example, during a social studies reading assignment, you might want to know when a student is bored or confused, when a student thinks an idea is important, and when a student encounters a surprising new fact.
3. Brainstorm with students to create a code. For example, Bored = ^, Confused = ?, Important idea = *, Surprising fact = !.
4. While students read, have them record page numbers and codes on paper strips.
5. After reading, focus the discussion on what students found to be boring, confusing, important, and surprising.

Source: Strategies for teaching students with learning and behavior problems (9th ed.), by S. Vaughn & C. S. Bos, 2015, Boston: Pearson.

MyEdLab **Self-Check 14.3**

MyEdLab **Application Exercise 14.3:** Phonological Awareness

14.4 STRATEGIES FOR TEACHING WORD IDENTIFICATION

Reading words quickly and easily is one key to successful reading (Beck, 2006; Ehri, 2003). Successful readers identify words fluently and, if a word is unknown, have effective decoding strategies to decipher the word. Therefore, it is important that students develop a sight word vocabulary (i.e., the words that students recognize without conscious effort) and decoding strategies to support them when they encounter an unknown word including knowledge of common word patterns and morphological awareness.

14.4.1 Teaching Sight Words

A **sight word** is a word for which the student can recognize the pronunciation and meaning automatically. In reading words by sight, the words are processed quickly and accessed from information in memory. LaBerge and Samuels (1974) are two early researchers who developed the theoretical basis underlying the importance of fluency in reading instruction. They argue that it is important for students to develop automaticity (quick word recognition) so that they can focus on comprehension. Some students have difficulty with automatic recognition of words in print, particularly with high-frequency words—words such as *the*, *you*, *and*, and *was*—that serve as the basic glue of our language. According to Fry and Kress (2006), about 50% of written language contains 100 high-frequency words, such as those presented in Table 14.1.

Video Example from YouTube

MyEdLab
Video Example 14.3.
Watch the YouTube video "How to Teach Sight Words – Reading Lesson." How does this reading specialist introduce and reinforce the learning of sight words? https://www.youtube.com/watch?v=PSSbhgpOYDY

You can select words to teach on the basis of the materials the students are reading, words the students are having difficulty learning, key vocabulary from content-area textbooks, or high-frequency words from graded word lists. Consider two factors: usefulness (words that occur most frequently) and ease of learning (Gunning, 2011, 2016). The words *the*, *of*, *and*, *a*, *to*, *in*, *is*, *you*, *that*, and *it* account for more than 20% of the words that students will encounter. Nouns and words with distinctive shapes are generally easier to learn. See Tips for Teachers 14.8 for guidelines for teaching sight words, particularly those that are less predictable on the basis of phonics and spelling patterns (e.g., *was*, *want*, *come*).

When introducing new sight words, do so in isolation and in context. Keep in mind that most high-frequency words will be familiar to most students; however, ELLs may not have incorporated these words into their speaking vocabulary (Gunning, 2016).

Table 14.1 • The Instant (Sight) Words

THE FIRST 100 WORDS (APPROXIMATELY FIRST GRADE)				THE SECOND 100 WORDS (APPROXIMATELY SECOND GRADE)			
GROUP 1A	**GROUP 1B**	**GROUP 1C**	**GROUP 1D**	**GROUP 2A**	**GROUP 2B**	**GROUP 2C**	**GROUP 2D**
the	he	go	who	saw	big	may	ran
a	I	see	an	home	where	let	five
is	they	then	there	soon	am	use	read
you	one	us	she	stand	ball	these	over
to	good	no	new	box	morning	right	such
and	me	him	said	upon	live	present	way
we	about	by	did	first	four	tell	too
that	had	was	boy	came	last	next	shall
in	if	come	three	girl	color	please	own
not	some	get	down	house	away	leave	most
for	up	or	work	find	red	hand	sure
at	her	two	put	because	friend	more	thing
with	do	man	were	made	pretty	why	only
it	when	little	before	could	eat	better	near
on	so	has	just	book	want	under	than
can	my	them	long	look	year	while	open
will	very	how	here	mother	white	should	kind
are	all	like	other	run	got	never	must
of	would	our	old	school	play	each	high
this	any	what	take	people	found	best	far
your	been	know	cat	night	left	another	both
as	out	make	again	into	men	seem	end
but	there	which	give	say	bring	tree	also
be	from	much	after	think	wish	name	until
have	day	his	many	back	black	dear	call

Source: Reprinted by permission of Edward Fry, author.

TIPS FOR TEACHERS 14.8

Guidelines for Teaching Sight Words

- Teach the most frequently occurring words.
- Check to see that students understand the meaning, particularly if they have limited language, have a specific language disability, or are English language learners.
- Introduce these new words before students encounter them in text.
- Limit the number of words introduced in a single lesson.
- Reinforce the association by adding a kinesthetic component such as tracing, copying, and writing from memory.
- Introduce visually similar words (e.g., *where* and *were*, *was* and *saw*) in separate lessons to avoid confusion.
- Analyze words with students to discover if the word has a regular or irregular phonic pattern.
- When students confuse visually similar words (e.g., *what* for *when*), highlight the differences.
- Provide multiple opportunities, including games and computer-assisted instruction, for the students to read the words in text and as single words until they automatically recognize the words.
- Review words that have been previously taught, particularly if the students miscall them when reading text.

Sources: "Strategies for teaching students with learning and behavior problems" (9th ed.) by S. Vaughn, & C. S. Bos, 2015, Boston: Pearson; "Phonics they use" (7th ed.), by P. Cunningham, 2017, Boston: Pearson; "Creating literacy instruction for all students" (9th ed.) by T. G. Gunning, 2016, Boston: Pearson.

14.4.2 Teaching Decoding Strategies

What decoding or word-identification strategies do readers employ to decode words they do not know automatically? Research on teaching struggling readers, including those with specific reading disabilities, would suggest that five strategies are helpful in teaching these students to decode words. Figure 14.7 defines these five strategies, and each one of them is described in detail in the next sections.

14.4.3 Phonic Analysis

Identify and blend letter–sound correspondences into words. This is referred to as phonic analysis, which is the use of phonics to decode words. This strategy builds on the alphabetic principle and assumes that the students have basic levels of phonological awareness and knowledge of some letter–sound correspondences. Students with reading difficulties need systematic word-identification instruction, including phonics instruction.

14.4.4 Onset-Rime

Use common spelling patterns to decode words by blending. One salient feature of the English language is the use of spelling patterns, also referred to as onset-rimes, *phonograms*, or *word families*. When using spelling patterns to decode an unknown word, the students segment the word between the onset (/bl/ in the word *blend*) and the rime (*-end*) and then blend the onset and rime to make the word (*blend*). Figure 14.8 presents a list of thirty-seven common rimes that make almost 500 words (Wylie & Durrell, 1970).

FIGURE 14.7 Five strategies for decoding unknown words

1. *Phonic Analysis:* Identify and blend letter–sound correspondences into words.
2. *Onset-Rime:* Use common spelling patterns (onset-rimes) to decode words by blending the initial sound(s) with the spelling pattern or by using analogy.
3. *Structural Analysis and Syllabication:* Use knowledge of word structures such as compound words, root words, suffixes, prefixes, and inflectional endings and syllable types to decode multisyllabic words and assist with meaning.
4. *Syntax and Semantics:* Use knowledge of word order (syntax) and context (semantics) to support the pronunciation and confirm word meaning.
5. *Use Other Resources:* Use other resources such as asking someone or using a dictionary.

FIGURE 14.8 Common spelling patterns from primary-grade texts

	-ack	-ail	-ain	-ake	-ale
	-ame	-an	-ank	-ap	-ash
	-at	-ate	-aw	-ay — ell	
			-est		
	-eat				
	-ice	-ick	-ide	-ight	-ill
	-in	-ine	-ing	-ink	-ip
	-ir				
	-ock	-oke	-op	-ore	-or
	-uck	-ug	-ump	-unk	

Guidelines for teaching onset-rimes follow the same guidelines as those suggested for teaching phonic analysis, except that the word is segmented at the level of onset-rime rather than at the phoneme level.

14.4.5 Morphological Awareness

Morphological awareness is the use of knowledge of word structures such as compound words, root words, suffixes, prefixes, and inflectional endings and syllabication to decode and/or glean the meaning of multisyllabic words. It is sometimes referred to as **structural analysis** (Reutzel & Cooter, 2011). Between third and seventh grades, children learn from 3,000 to 26,000 words, most of them multisyllabic words encountered through reading; only a limited number are taught directly (Wysocki & Jenkins, 1987). Morphological awareness can also be used to identify root words, prefixes, suffixes, and inflectional endings, because (a) such analysis provides students with ways to segment longer, multisyllabic words into decodable (and meaningful) parts, and (b) it assists students in determining the meanings of words (Goodwin, Lipsky, & Ahn, 2012; Pacheco & Goodwin, 2013). Teaching students to use smaller meaningful units within a longer word can facilitate understanding the meaning of the whole word. This procedure is called chunking or Part-to-Whole strategy (Pacheco & Goodwin, 2013). For example, the word *unbelievable* can be segmented into three parts: *un–believe–able.* In the case of *unbelievable*, *un-* means "not," and *-able* means "is or can be." Hence, *un–believe–able*, means something that is not to be believed. When teaching students to divide words into meaning parts, begin with analyzing compound words. Teach high-frequency prefixes (e.g., *re-*, *pre-*, *un-*), suffixes (e.g., *-er/-or*, *-ly*, *-tion/-ion*, *-ness*, *-ful*), and inflection endings (e.g., *-s*, *-es*, *-ing*, *-ed*). See Tips for Teachers 14.9 for ideas and guidelines for teaching and reinforcing structural analysis.

TIPS FOR TEACHERS 14.9

Guidelines for Teaching and Reinforcing Structural Analysis

- Teach the meanings along with recognition of the meaning parts.
- Explain and demonstrate how many "big words" are just "smaller words" with prefixes, suffixes, and endings.
- Ask students to decode words they do not know by covering all but one part of the word and having them identify it, then uncovering the next part and identifying it, and so on.
- Create a class or student dictionary that has each word part, its meaning, and several example words.
- Use a word map to demonstrate how one root word can make a cadre of related words (see Figure 14.9).

FIGURE 14.9 **Root word map of friend**

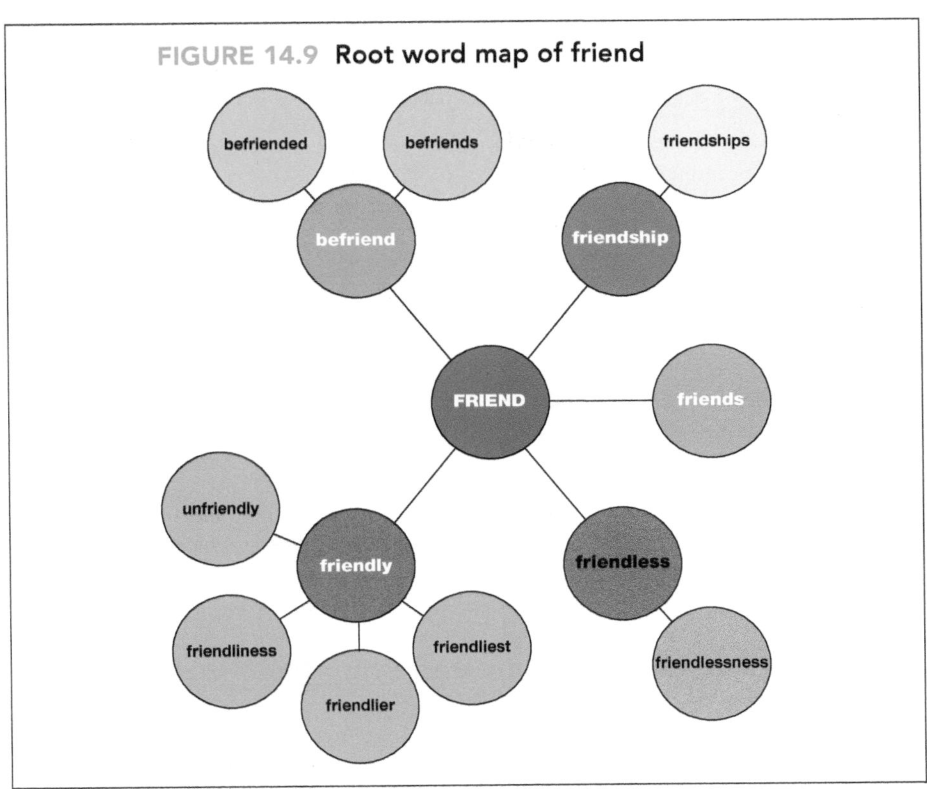

Dividing words by common syllable types, or syllabication, can also provide struggling readers with clues for decoding multisyllabic words. A high percentage of more than 600,000 English words can be categorized as one of six syllable types or a combination of different syllable types (Carreker, 1999; Knight-McKenna, 2008). English language learners also benefit from instruction in these syllable types (Goodwin et al., 2012; Vaughn, Mathes, Linan-Thompson, & Francis, 2005). By providing examples (listed in Table 14.2), you can lead students to discover the six types and how to apply them when decoding unknown words.

Table 14.2 • Six Types of Syllables

TYPE	DESCRIPTION/EXAMPLES
Closed (CVC)	Ends in at least one consonant; vowel is short.
	bed, lost, and, magnet, dap- in *dapple, hos-* in *hostel*
Open (CV)	Ends in one vowel; vowel is long.
	me, mo- in *moment, ti-* in *tiger, ta-* in *table*
Vowel–consonant–e (CVCe)	Ends in one long vowel, one consonant, and a final *e* that is silent.
	name, slope, five, -pite in *despite, -pete* in *compete*
Vowel team (CVVC)	Uses two adjacent vowels. Sounds of vowel teams vary.
	rain, sweet, -geal in *congeal, train-* in *trainer, bea-* in *beagle*
R-controlled (CV+r)	Vowel is followed by /r/, and vowel pronunciation is affected by /r/.
	fern, burn, car, forge, charter
Consonant–le (-C+le)	Unaccented final syllable with a consonant plus /l/ and silent *e*.
	-dle in *candle, -tle* in *little, -zle* in *puzzle*

14.4.6 Syntax and Semantics

Use knowledge of word order (syntax) and context (semantics) to support the pronunciation and confirm word meaning. Whereas students with reading difficulties often overrely on syntax and context to decode an unknown word, good readers use syntax and context for cross-checking their pronunciation and monitoring comprehension (Schumm, 2006). This is evident when students reread a word, phrase, or sentence because "it doesn't make sense." Key questions that students can ask are the following:

- Does that sound right here?
- Does that make sense?

14.4.7 Techniques for Teaching Decoding and Sight Words

Numerous programs and strategies have been developed for teaching decoding strategies and sight words. The techniques of making words, word sorting, and using word walls have been used by many teachers. Even secondary teachers who are instructing older students with reading disabilities are using word-analysis practices to bolster students' success at decoding and accurately reading words.

Making words, word sorting, and using word walls

A number of activities can be developed around making words, word sorts, and word walls. *Making Words* and *Words Their Way* were initially developed for students in the primary grades to develop sensitivity to manipulating sounds and building decoding strategies (Bear, Invernizzi, Templeton, & Johnston, 2015; Cunningham, 2017), but can also be used with upper elementary or middle school students who need to work on common spelling patterns, prefixes, and suffixes (Deshler, Palincsar, Biancarosa, & Nair, 2007; Scammacca et al., 2007) and with English language learners who can learn more about word meaning and word reading (Templeton et al., 2015). *Making Words* provides opportunities to construct words using magnetic letters, letter tiles, or laminated letters to see how words are affected. For example, the teacher might start with the sounds /s/, /t/, /r/, /n/, and /a/ and ask the students to do the following:

Teacher:

What two sounds make the word *at*?

Now add a letter sound to the beginning to make the word *sat*.

Remove the /s/. What one sound would you add to the beginning to make the word *rat?*

Now listen. We're going to make a three-letter word. Take off the /t/ sound at the end of the word. Now add the one sound that will make the word *ran*.

Using a specific set of letters (e.g., *a*, *c*, *h*, *r*, *s*, *t*), students make approximately fifteen words, beginning with two-letter words (e.g., *at*) and progressing to three-, four-, and five-letter words (e.g., *tar*, *cart*, *star*, *cash*) until the final "mystery word" is made (e.g., *scratch*). Students complete a three-step process that includes making words, word sorting, and making words quickly to build fluency. The whole sequence (including distribution of materials) takes about 30 minutes (see Activities for All Learners).

Using a word wall can reinforce students' learning to recognize and spell words (Hilden & Jones, 2012; O'Kelley, Wingage, Rutledge, & Johnston, 2014). The word wall is a large space dedicated to displaying word types that are the focus of the week's instruction. These word types can represent the phonics rules being learned, review previously learned phonics rules, and/or represent sight words that are the focus of instruction that week. Words can be displayed based on the sound units they represent (e.g., all words that end in "ay" are organized together), or they can be displayed in alphabetical order, or in whatever order makes sense based on the goals of

ACTIVITIES FOR ALL LEARNERS

Steps in Making Words

Objective: To improve students' ability to make words

Grades: Using simple words, such as *mat, him, it* (grades 1–3); using more complex words, such as *weather, marriage, champion* (grades 3–6)

Materials: Laminated letters, sentence strip board, word cards

Step 1. Teaching Procedures: Making Words Slowly (about 15 minutes)

- Students make twelve to fifteen words, using a set of individual laminated letters.
- The last word includes all the letters a student has been given that day. For example, a student might be given the letters "eudhnrt."
- Direct students to spell words such as *red, Ted, Ned, her, hut, rut,* and *under.* The final word would be *thunder.*
- After the students spell the words with their own letters, show or have a student show the correct spelling, using large letters and a sentence strip chart in the front of the room. Students correct their own work.

Step 2. Word Sorting (about 10 minutes)

- Put up on the sentence strip board word cards with all the words spelled that day.
- Ask students how some of the words are alike.
- Have a volunteer sort the words on the sentence strip board by putting all like words together (e.g., *fat, rat, sat*).
- Have the other students in the class then guess why those words are grouped together, which helps students focus on word patterns.

Step 3. Making Words Quickly (about 2 minutes)

- Have students write as many words as they can using the day's letters, writing the words in a "making words" log.
- Have students take 1 minute to write the date and the day's letters at the top of the page.
- When you say, "Go," they write words for 2 minutes.

This activity helps build fluency. Because each lesson starts with easy words and ends with more difficult words, all students in the class can work at their level.

instruction. When new words are added (usually five per week in the primary grades and ten per week in the upper grades), the teacher and students talk about the word pattern and its meaning, use the word in a sentence, and determine whether its spelling follows a regular or irregular pattern.

Word walls can also include technical vocabulary from content areas such as science and mathematics (Harmon, Wood, Hedrick, Vintinner, & Willeford, 2009; Hooper & Harmon, 2015; Southerland, 2011). Involve students in the selection of words to include on the wall (Harmon et al., 2009; Yates, Cuthrell, & Rose, 2011). Visual representations can be added to the word wall to assist in learning new vocabulary for all students, but particularly for English language learners (Jackson & Narvaez, 2013). Word walls can be used effectively with middle and high school students as well as elementary students (Vintinner, Harmon, Wood, & Stover, 2015).Keep in mind that word walls are intended to be an interactive teaching tool and not "wallpaper" (Hilden & Jones, 2012; Jackson & Naraez, 2013; Jasmine & Schiesl, 2009). You can review the words during the morning message or randomly when there are spare minutes in the school day. Students can use word walls to help them spell words they are writing and eventually learn to read and spell the words through repeated practice. Some teachers provide folders or word boxes in which students can retain the words they are working on in reading, vocabulary, or spelling. For students with visual tracking problems, an individual "mini-word wall" made out of a file folder can be kept in each student's desk. You can also use PowerPoint to create an E-word wall (Narkin, Wells, & Segal, 2011).

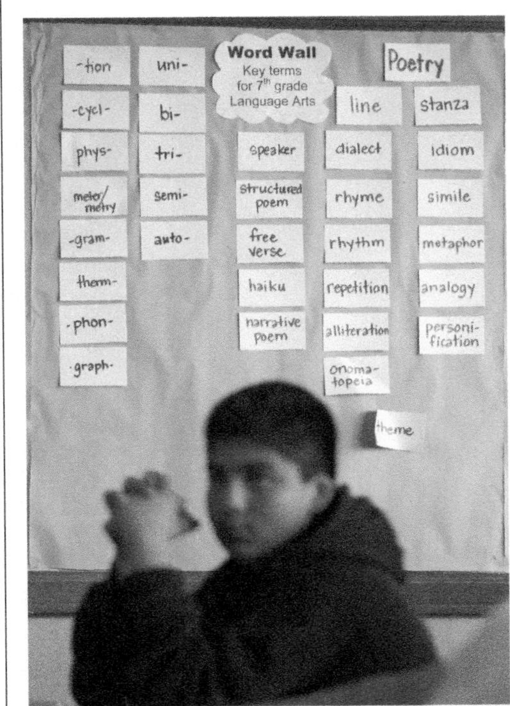

How can a teacher reinforce the use of the words students recommend for the word wall?

Using the DISSECT strategy

As students become more advanced in their reading, they begin to use structural analysis (e.g., compound words, prefixes, and suffixes) and syllabication to identify multisyllabic words. Lenz, Schumaker, Deshler, and Beals (1984) developed a strategy for secondary students with learning disabilities to approach multisyllabic words in a strategic way that has been validated through several research studies (e.g., Woodruff, Schumaker, & Deshler, 2002). This strategy, known by the acronym DISSECT, includes the following steps:

1. *D*iscover the word's context.
2. *I*solate the prefix. Students look at the beginning of the word to see whether the initial letters of the word match a prefix they know. If they do recognize a prefix, they isolate it (e.g., *pre/heat*). If students do not recognize a prefix, they proceed to step 3.
3. *S*eparate the suffix. Students look at the end of the word to see whether the letters match a suffix they know. If they do recognize a suffix, they separate it; if not, they go on to the next step.
4. *S*ay the stem.
5. *E*xamine the stem. Students dissect the stem into easy-to-pronounce parts, two or three letters at a time. When they can pronounce the whole word, students reread the whole sentence to check their understanding. If students still cannot figure out the word, they go on to the last steps.
6. *C*heck with someone.
7. *T*ry the dictionary.

DISSECT can be taught to your whole class. Students can then practice using the strategy in small groups or pairs. You may also want to put the steps for DISSECT on a poster in front of your room and remind students regularly about the steps.

MyEdLab **Self-Check 14.4**

MyEdLab **Application Exercise 14.4:** Word Identification

14.5 STRATEGIES FOR HELPING STUDENTS DEVELOP FLUENCY

Students are fluent in reading when they can recognize printed words quickly and effortlessly and are therefore able to focus more of their attention on comprehension. Fluency consists of multiple components: pace (slow or uneven rate), accuracy (with pauses, hesitations, repetitions, or incorrect pronunciations), prosody (expression and intonation), and correct phrasing (reading words in logical clause and sentence units) (McCormick & Zutell, 2011; Rasinski & Nageldinger, 2015). Because struggling readers often take longer and require more exposure to words in order to automatically recognize and rapidly recall words than do typical readers, it is important that fluency instruction provides multiple opportunities for practice (Wexler et al., 2008). In addition, students with challenges in reading can exhibit difficulty with one or more components of fluency. Use the suggestions in this section to help students become more fluent readers.

14.5.1 Using Response to Intervention (RTI) to Promote Fluency

Oral reading fluency is the number of words a student reads correctly in 1 minute. Typically, students are provided with grade-level passages and asked to read for 1 minute. The teacher then counts the number of words read correctly.

Monitoring the number of words students read correctly in a minute is frequently used in the lower grades (first through third grade) to monitor students' progress in reading. For this reason, it is also used as a means for determining how students with reading difficulties may be responding to interventions. For example, many schools screen students in first, second, and third grades using oral reading fluency to identify students who are at risk for reading problems. They then provide a standardized intervention to these students (four to five times per week) for 20 to 40 minutes per day over an 8- to 12-week period. During this intervention, students typically receive an oral reading fluency test every week or two so that the slope of their progress can be determined. Thus, based on students' overall progress and the extent to which they are closing the gap between their oral reading fluency prior to intervention and during intervention, a decision is made about participation in subsequent interventions.

To illustrate, Jeanine, a second grader, was making adequate progress in reading after she was placed in an intervention (more than two words correct per week gain on average) and appeared to be very close to meeting expected reading performance. Her teachers decided that it would be in her best interest to continue the intervention for another 10 weeks.

Max displayed a different pattern of learning. His overall progress was very low (less than one word correct per week on average), and teachers were concerned that he needed even more intensive intervention. They adjusted his instruction both in the classroom and in the intervention and provided one-on-one support to determine his RTI over time. Thus, oral reading fluency provided an important data source for decision making related to response to intervention. We know considerably less about the role of oral reading fluency and its application within RTI models with older readers.

14.5.2 Reading Aloud

Reading aloud is typically used at the elementary level to preview a book or model fluent reading (Hickman, Pollard-Durodola, & Vaughn, 2004; Kramer, McCabe, & Sinatra, 2012; Trelease, 1995; Swanson et al., 2011). Both narrative and expository texts can be used for read-alouds (Kramer et al., 2012; Stead, 2014). Reading aloud and previewing a book promote reading fluency in a number of ways:

- *Reading aloud models fluent reading.* For younger children, big books (books with large pictures and words that can be seen by the whole class) are ideal because they allow you to point to the text while reading and to use the pictures to create more interest in the story.
- *Students can become familiar with the story.* Reading aloud gives you the opportunity to preview the book (e.g., to discuss with the students the content of the story and to introduce difficult vocabulary).
- *Students can listen to and discuss books that may be too difficult for them to read.* Struggling readers may have listening comprehension that is several years more advanced than their reading comprehension due to difficulties with word recognition. This will allow them access to more advanced books and literature.
- *English language learners can improve their word knowledge and concept development.*
- *Less adept older readers can read books to young children and serve as cross-age tutors.*
- *Older readers can listen to audio books and then read those same texts as a way to improve reading fluency.*

Interactive read-alouds can provide an opportunity for teachers to interject lessons related to Common Core State Standards. For example, before, during, and after reading a story aloud you can interject questions about how the characters were introduced and developed, and how they interacted with each other.

Video Example from YouTube

MyEdLab
Video Example 14.4.
Watch the YouTube video "Increasing Your Students' Reading Fluency: Strategies that Work, Grades 1–3." How could you provide modeling and direct instruction for elements of reading fluency to older students? https://www.youtube.com/watch?v=8OVZYEGFfUk

14.5.3 Repeated Reading

Repeated reading consists of reading short, meaningful passages several times until a satisfactory level of fluency is reached (Chard, Ketterlin-Geller, Baker, Doabler, & Apichatabutra, 2009; Young, Mohr, & Rasinski, 2015). The general format for this reading procedure is to have the students repeatedly read short passages (50–200 words

Table 14.3 • Guidelines for Repeated Reading

GRADE	FALL	WINTER	SPRING
1	–	23–47	53–82
2	51–79	72–100	89–117
3	71–99	92–120	107–137
4	94–119	112–139	123–152
5	110–139	127–156	139–168
6	127–153	14.0–167	150–177
7	128–156	136–165	150–177
8	133–161	14.6–173	151–177

long) that are at the students' instructional to independent reading levels (90%–100% word recognition) until they reach a fluent reading rate.

The reading rate is most frequently measured by the words read correctly per minute (WCPM) and through observations of phrasing, smoothness, and pace. Having students read for 1 minute and then counting the total number of words read minus the incorrect words (e.g., mispronunciations, substitutions, omissions, and words pronounced after a hesitation of more than 3 seconds) provides the WCPM. Guidelines (words correct per minute) for reading fluency for grades 1 through 8 (Hasbrouck & Tindal, 2005) are presented in Table 14.3.

Consider, Jeff, a fourth-grade student with an instructional level at second grade, who reads the second-grade passage on whales at the rate of twenty-five words per minute. He and his teacher set a goal of Jeff reading the passage at fifty-five words per minute. It took him five repeated readings to reach this goal, and he graphed his progress.

A **phrased text lesson** is a variation of repeated reading than can be helpful for students who have difficulty with phrasing and intonation (Rasinski, Tildirim, & Nageldinger, 2011). In this, students are presented with a short passage with slash marks indicating logical pauses (similar to what public speakers might do in the speech script). The lesson begins with a teacher's oral reading of the passage demonstrating fluent, phrased reading. Students then reread the passage chorally, individually (in a low voice), and then in pairs. On the following day, the rereading steps are repeated, but students are given the passage *without* the slash marks.

14.5.4 Research Findings on Repeated Reading

Younger students reading below grade level who have used repeated reading have consistently demonstrated gains in both fluency and reading comprehension (Chard, Vaughn, & Tyler, 2002; Mastropieri, Leinart, & Scruggs, 1999; Meyer & Felton, 1999). However, older students with reading difficulties do not consistently benefit from repeated reading activities (Wexler, Edmonds, & Vaughn, 2008; Wexler, Vaughn, Edmonds, & Reutebuch, 2008; Wexler, Vaughn, Roberts, & Denton, 2010). Although many older students with reading disabilities demonstrate reading fluency challenges, we are still struggling to identify the most effective practices for these youngsters (Chard et al., 2009).

Instructional guidelines for using repeated reading

From these reviews of research, several instructional guidelines for using repeated reading are apparent (see Tips for Teachers 14.10).

You can incorporate repeated reading into whole-class or small-group routines. You can also pair students to read to each other. The secret to success is to keep it purposeful and fun (Cahill & Gregory, 2011). Selecting motivational readings (e.g., jokes, plays, song lyrics), reading into a recording device, and providing an audience can promote student engagement. The Tech Tips, "Technologies for Struggling Readers," provides ideas for using technology to support fluent reading.

TIPS FOR TEACHERS 14.10

Guidelines for Using Repeated Reading to Improve Fluency

- Use repeated reading with younger readers with reading difficulties to increase reading speed, accuracy, expression, and comprehension.
- Select text materials at the students' independent to instructional reading levels (90%–100% word recognition).
- Provide a good model reading of the passage before asking the student to read.
- Ask students to reread passages three to five times.
- Demonstrate how to use phrases so that students can also do multiple readings of phrases.
- Provide adult guidance and feedback during reading.
- Preteach words and phrases from the text.
- Model reading with expression.
- Use short, frequent sessions of fluency practice (10–15 minutes).
- Have students set goals and record progress.

TECH TIPS

Technologies for Struggling Readers

The computer is an ideal tool to help students learn phonological awareness and phonics, build fluency, increase their vocabulary and word recognition, and enhance comprehension. Some useful tools for achieving success include the following:

Phonics/Phonemic Awareness

Simon S.I.O. (Sounds It Out), **WordMaker**, Don Johnston Incorporated (www.donjohnston.com)

Earobics
(www.earobics.com)

Vocabulary and Word Recognition

Adjectives and Opposites, Words & Concepts Series, Swim, Swam, Swum: Mastering Irregular Verbs
(www.laureatelearning.com)

Reading Fluency and Comprehension

Start-to-Finish Publishing, Don Johnston Incorporated
(www.donjohnston.com)

Core content and literature series for older elementary and early adolescent students reading below grade level; includes comprehension and vocabulary quizzes, fluency recorder, books in two grade levels—2, 3 and 4, 5.

Lexia Reading
(www.lexialearning.com)

Individualized instruction in foundational reading skills for elementary students at all reading levels (Lexia Reading Core 5) and for older readers who are struggling in learning to read Lexia Strategies.

KidBiz
(www.achieve3000.com)

Provides high-interest nonfiction reading passages with related activities adjusted to student individual reading levels.

Additional Resources

Project Gutenberg
(www.gutenberg.org/catalog)

Thousands of free books in both audio and a variety of text formats that can be read aloud on the computer, iPad/iPod, Kindle device, and others.

iPad/iPod™ Applications

- Elkonin Boxes
- Kindergarten.com
- Meet the Sight Words
- The Electric Company Wordball!
- First Words: Deluxe
- Sentence Reading Magic
- Build a Word Express

14.5.5 Peer Tutoring

Two related practices, peer-assisted learning (PAL) (What Works Clearing House, 2012a, 2012b) and classwide peer tutoring (CWPT) (What Works Clearing House, 2007), promote the use of students working together to provide practice and feedback on improving reading fluency. In both approaches, students of different reading levels are paired, one average or high reader with one low reader. The reading material for the tutoring sessions can be a basal reader, trade book, or magazine; what is important is that the less able reader in the pair can read it easily. During peer-tutoring sessions, which last approximately 30 minutes, the pairs work through a sequence of structured activities in which partners read orally, share story retelling, and summarize what was read. Students earn points as they work through the series of activities. When reading, first the stronger reader reads aloud to serve as a model, and then the other reader reads.

There are many responsibilities for the teacher to ensure that peer tutoring is effective. It is important, for example, to teach students how to be both tutors/listeners and tutees/readers and provide role-play practice and feedback. For the tutors, give guidelines for how they should correct errors during oral reading (e.g., point out the word, pronounce the word, and have the tutee say the word) and the questions they should ask when the students have finished reading (e.g., What is the story about? What is happening in the story now? What do you think will happen next?). Many students are not experienced in providing effective feedback to their partners. Teachers can assist students by modeling the type of feedback that is helpful. For example, Mr. Zayer provides a list of phrases for students to use with each other to help shape positive and effective feedback (e.g., "you read that paragraph with no mistakes," "look at that word; read it again.").

Peer tutoring has been researched extensively in various school settings (e.g., McMaster, Shu-Hsuan, Insoon, & Cao, 2008; Leung, 2015). Results indicate that when the procedure is implemented consistently (three times a week over a period of 16 weeks), the amount of reading practice time increases substantially, and students of all ability levels improve in fluency and comprehension. Moreover, peer tutoring has the potential for positive social and behavioral benefits for all students—including those at risk for behavior and learning problems (Bowman-Perrott, Burke, Zhang, & Zaini, 2014).

MyEdLab **Self-Check 14.5**

MyEdLab **Application Exercise 14.5:** Developing Fluency

14.6 STRATEGIES FOR IMPROVING READING COMPREHENSION

Understanding, appreciating, and learning from what we read is the ultimate goal. For many students, however, reading the words is not enough to make understanding happen. Ms. Lockerson teaches a sixth-grade reading class for students who have reading problems and/or reading disabilities. She claims that the biggest problems she encounters are students who can read the words, albeit slowly, but do not understand what they read. "Even after they read a passage silently and then we reread the passage aloud, if I ask students what the passage is mostly about, there will be either few answers or incomplete answers." In this section of the chapter, we will discuss practices that Ms. Lockerson can use to enhance the understanding of the students in her class.

Students with reading difficulties need to learn specific ways to get ready for reading, to understand what they are reading while they read it, and to summarize and reflect on what they have read. In other words, many struggling readers need **comprehension strategies** to use before, during, and after reading (Klingner, Vaughn, & Boardman, 2015; RAND Reading Study Group, 2002). Students also need to learn strategies for dealing with both *narrative* and *expository* text (stories and informational writing, respectively) and to monitor their comprehension (comprehension monitoring).

Effective comprehension instruction includes many of the following features (e.g., Blachowicz & Ogle, 2008; Gersten & Baker, 2003; Klingner et al., 2015):

- *Activating background knowledge.* Thinking about what you already know about the topic and how your knowledge relates to what you are reading
- *Predicting.* Making predictions about what is going to happen or what will be learned from reading the text
- *Generating and answering questions.* Asking and answering relevant questions that promote understanding, such as who, what, when, where, why, and how questions
- *Clarifying.* Clarifying unclear concepts or vocabulary
- *Summarizing.* Determining the main ideas and important concepts related to the main idea
- *Using text structure.* Using knowledge of different text structures (e.g., narrative, expositions) as a framework for comprehension
- *Monitoring comprehension.* Checking for understanding and using fix-up strategies (e.g., rereading, clarifying a concept) to facilitate comprehension
- *Engaging text and conversations about reading.* Texts that are engaging and interesting and comprehension practices that involve students in conversations about what they read readily support understanding of the text

The Common Core State Standards as well as standards in individual states that have not been adopted by CCSS emphasize the importance of learning to read and learn from increasingly complex text. To facilitate proficiency in reading complex texts, students must develop skills in close reading of text and vocabulary knowledge.

14.6.1 Close Reading of Text

Close reading is the type of intensive, analytical reading that one is expected to become college and career ready (Snow & O'Connor, 2013). Close reading involves "an investigation of a short piece of text, with multiple readings done over multiple instructional lessons...students are guided to deeply analyze and appreciate various aspects of the text, such as key vocabulary and how its meaning is shaped by context; attention to form, tone, imagery, and/or rhetorical device..." (Brown & Kappes, 2012, p. 2). Key components of close reading lessons include:

- initial reading of a text (for basic comprehension)
- annotation or notetaking
- repeated readings (to analyze author's structure and style and to develop a deeper understanding and reaction to the text)
- text-based discussion
- responding to the text (Fisher & Frey, 2014, 2015; Shanahan, 2013)

Rereadings can vary in number (2, 3, or more) and be complete or partial. Close reading lessons can occur during literacy or content-area classes and with expository or narrative text. With ample teacher support, modelling, and developmentally appropriate activities, close reading can be taught in the primary grades. For example, in lower grades teachers can conduct the initial reading aloud and can conduct annotation. The earlier students are introduced to reading in depth, the more likely they will be to develop incremental proficiency and ultimately independence in dealing with the type of reading they will be expected to do in the future.

14.6.2 Vocabulary Knowledge

Vocabulary knowledge is also pertinent to student comprehension of text (Beck, McKeown, & Kucan, 2013). *Vocabulary* refers to the words a person understands and uses in listening, speaking, reading, and writing. Students can learn word meanings through direct and indirect experiences with oral and printed language. *Indirect experiences* that serve to increase student vocabularies include opportunities to engage in oral discussions of new experiences and new words that build on previous knowledge. For example, MaryAnn Radkin, a second-grade teacher, uses teacher read-alouds of narrative text in the morning and information text in the afternoon as a means of teaching new vocabulary words and concepts and encouraging students to use these new words as they talk about what they are hearing. She realizes that specifically teaching word meanings is necessary to increase student exposure to novel words (Brett, Rothlein, & Hurley, 1996; Seals, Pollard-Durodola, Foorman, & Bradley, 2007; Wiseman, 2011) and is most effective when words are selected and incorporated in text based on their usefulness in language and importance to comprehension (Beck et al., 2013). Juan Gonzalez, an eighth-grade science teacher, also preteaches key vocabulary and concepts before discussing new ideas or asking students to read text. He recognizes that students learn more about science when they know the meaning of the key words.

Following the initial introduction of words, students need repeated exposure to the new vocabulary in a variety of contexts to ensure significant reading gains (Manyak et al., 2014; Willis, 2008). Students will encounter novel words in print throughout their reading careers. Therefore, instruction in independent strategies for learning new word meanings is also necessary, such as using context (Hiebert & Kamil, 2005). Teachers should provide student-friendly definitions consisting of words that students know:

- Introduce a vocabulary word (e.g., *immigrant*), and ask students to repeat the word so that they know how to pronounce the word.
- Discuss the meaning of the word using synonyms, examples, and/or definitions (e.g., *immigrant* means "someone who comes from abroad to live permanently in another country").
- Test students on their understanding of the word by asking students to figure out positive or incorrect examples and to explain why. (Positive example of the word *immigrant:* "Tom's grandparents came to the United States from England in 1912. They lived in the United States until they passed away." Ask the students, "Are Tom's grandparents immigrants? Why or why not?" An example of an incorrect use of the word *immigrant:* "Recently, many international students came to the United States to study." Ask the students, "Are the international students immigrants? Why or why not?")

Each of the teaching techniques in this section focuses on teaching comprehension strategies and comprehension monitoring and can be used with a variety of texts. All of the strategies can be used to foster close reading of text and vocabulary knowledge. Tips for Teachers 14.11 provides instructions for using story retelling to enhance fluency.

TIPS FOR TEACHERS 14.11

Using Story Retelling to Enhance Fluency

Fluency is an excellent predictor of reading comprehension for classroom teachers because it provides a reasonable and feasible means for determining whether students understand what they read and whether they are likely to pass high-stakes reading comprehension tests. In addition, comprehension can be monitored by asking students to retell the most important parts of the text they have just read. One advantage to story retelling is that the teacher is able to learn a great deal about what the students understand and is able to determine what additional comprehension skills need to be taught.

1. Ask young students to read a brief passage (1 to 2 minutes) aloud. Ask older students to read a brief passage (1 to 2 minutes) silently. Select passages that are at the students' instructional or independent reading level.
2. Tell the students, "Start at the beginning and you tell me the story" (Lipson, Mosenthal, & Mekkelsen, 2004).
3. Score the story retelling based on the depth of information provided. Teachers may want to consider whether students mentioned characters, the story problem, events, problem resolutions, and/or story quality.

K-W-L strategy

K-W-L is a strategy used to help students become actively engaged in comprehension before, during, and after reading (Carr & Thompson, 1996; Ogle, 1986). The K-W-L strategy is based on research that underscores the importance of activating prior knowledge as a means of connecting what we know with what we are reading, and also in promoting engagement and comprehension-monitoring during reading. When using K-W-L, consider the following components:

1. Accessing what I Know
2. Determining what I Want to learn
3. Recalling what I Learned

During the Know step, teachers and students engage in a discussion about what they already know about a topic. This can be done very quickly and requires teachers to make linkages, align with the text they are reading, and build background knowledge. During the Want-to-learn step, teachers and students describe what they hope to learn from reading about the topic. Finally, during the Learned stage, teachers and students discuss what they learned after reading the passage and what information the passage did not provide. As with many reading-comprehension strategies, K-W-L can also be used as a listening-comprehension strategy before and after lectures. Ogle (1989) added a fourth column, "what we still want to know." Schmidt (1999) referred to it as K-W-L-Q, with the "Q" representing more questions. Figure 14.10 shows a K-W-L-Q worksheet you can use to help students learn this strategy.

14.6.3 Question—Answer Relationships Strategy

Is asking students questions after they read text the same as reading-comprehension instruction? Probably not. Though teacher's manuals and student workbooks, readers, and textbooks contain many comprehension questions for students to answer, these questions more often provide an index for the teacher of whether the student understood some element of the text. They may not help the student better understand the text. A more effective practice is to instruct students in how to develop good questions about what they read and to ask and answer these questions. Moving students into the role of developing the questions also teaches them to monitor their comprehension while they are reading and to think about what they read.

FIGURE 14.10 K-W-L-Q chart for pond and pond life

All About Ponds (K-W-L-Q)			
What We Know	**What We Want to Know**	**What We Learned**	**More Questions We Have**
Contains water	How does the pond get its water?	Underground springs and rain	Why do ponds die?
Smaller than a lake			What happens to a pond in winter?
Fish	What fish live in the pond?	Blue gill, trout, bass, catfish	
Ducks			
Frogs			
Muddy			
Algae	Why are ponds green and muddy?	Algae and other plants make it green	How do algae help or hurt a pond?
Insects on top	What insects live on the pond?	Dragonflies, mosquitoes, water fleas	

Source: Based on information from "KWLQ: Inquiry and literacy learning in science," by P. R. Schmidt, 1999, *The Reading Teacher*, 52, 789–792.

MyEdLab
Video Example 14.5.
In this video, the K-W-L strategy is presented. How do you think the strategy is used to promote reading comprehension and vocabulary?

For example, Simmons, Vaughn, and colleagues (Simmons & Vaughn, 2008; Swanson, Edmonds, Hairrell, Vaughn, & Simmons, 2011) developed question cards that they used to assist students in designing different types of questions during and after reading. Students learned to ask questions in which the answer was one word. For example, "Who was this story mostly about?" or "What country did the characters live in?" After students learned to ask questions that had one-word answers, they were taught to ask questions in which the answer was in the text but required more than one word to answer it. For example, "What happened after the dolphins were released in the gulf?" Students were then taught to ask questions that involved "why" and "how," requiring even more complex answers. Overall, students learned to think more about their text and their overall comprehension improved.

Pearson and Johnson (1978) developed a way to classify questions on the basis of the relationship between the question and the location of its answer. From this classification system, a strategy for teaching students how to answer different types of questions was also developed. This strategy, called the **question–answer relationships (QAR) strategy** (Raphael, 1982; Raphael, Highfield, & Au, 2012), helps students realize that when answering questions, they need to not only consider the text and their prior knowledge, but also use strategic behavior to adjust the use of each of these sources. As a result, student comprehension is enhanced (Simmonds, 1992).

The four question–answer relationships are based on the source of information and the types of reasoning involved:

1. *Right there.* Words used to create the question and words used for the answer are in the same sentence.
2. *Think and search.* The answer is in the text, but words used to create the question and those used for an appropriate answer are not in the same sentence.
3. *Author and you.* The answer is implied in the author's language, style, and tone.
4. *On my own.* The answer is found not in the text but in one's head on the basis of personal experience.

Teaching QAR involves having students learn to differentiate first between the two sources of information and then between the four question–answer relationships. Students also learn how to identify the types of questions they are trying to answer. Figure 14.11 presents a cue card students can use during instruction.

FIGURE 14.11 Question–Answer Relationships (QARs)

IN THE BOOK QAR

Right There

The answer is in the text, usually easy to find. The words used to make up the question and words used to answer the question are **right there** in the same sentence.

Think and Search (Putting It Together)

The answer is in the story, but you need to put together different story parts to find it. Words for the question and words for the answer are not found in the same sentence. They come from different parts of the text.

IN MY HEAD QAR

Author and You

The answer is not in the story. You need to think about what you already know, what the author tells you in the text, and how it fits together.

On My Own

The answer is not in the story. You can even answer the question without reading the story. You need to use your own experience.

Source: Adapted from "Teaching question–answer relationships, revisited," by T. E. Raphael, 1986, *The Reading Teacher, 39*(6), 519. Copyright by the International Reading Association.

Adapted from Raphael (1986), the following are procedures for introducing the QAR strategy to students from elementary to middle school:

1. On the first day you are introducing QAR, inform students that you are going to show them how questions and answers relate in text and how they can be developed to be increasingly difficult. Either read several short passages aloud or ask students to read them silently. Ask students to identify the type of QAR, the answer to the question, and the strategy they used for finding the answer. The progression for teaching should be from highly supportive to independent. In highly *supportive* teaching, the educator provides text, questions, answers, the QAR label for each question, and reasons the label is appropriate. In highly *independent* teaching, students generate their own questions, QAR labels, and reasons for their choices.
2. When students have a clear picture of the difference between "in my head" and "in the book," teach the next level of differentiation for each of the major categories. First, work on "in the book," then go to "in my head." The key distinction between the two "in my head" subcategories is "whether or not the reader needs to read the text for the questions to make sense" (Raphael, 1986, p. 519).
3. When students can use the QAR strategy effectively in short passages, gradually increase the length of the passages and the variety of reading materials. Review the strategy, model its use on the first question, and then have students use the strategy on the rest of the questions.
4. When students are proficient, use expanded or alternative QAR activities:
    - Have students work in pairs or cooperative learning groups, using QAR to answer comprehension questions.
    - Ask students to write stories with questions. Have other students determine the answer to each question and what kind of question it is.
    - Play a detective game in which students answer questions in their search for clues to solve the case and cite the source for their evidence.
    - Divide students into teams and have the teacher read a short passage, followed by questions. The teams earn points by answering questions and determining the QAR labels.

14.6.4 Questioning the Author

Questioning the Author (QtA) (Beck & McKeown, 2006) is an instructional conversation designed to provide engaging discussions about texts as though the author were present and contributing. QtA provides students with well-scaffolded instruction that supports students' thinking about text. It allows students to interact with each other as though the "author" were available for comment and conversation and also gives the students the opportunity to give the author feedback. Using QtA as a teaching strategy, the teacher has distinct goals and uses questions to assist students in reaching those goals. To use QtA, teachers should use the following steps:

1. Select text for students to read that is engaging and at an appropriate level. The text can be from traditional textbooks (e.g., social studies or science) or from other sources. Text that provides opportunities for students to engage in discussion is essential.
2. Make sure that students have some background knowledge of the topic they are reading about. The teacher can provide this information or have students do some prior reading. Background knowledge allows students to have an informed discussion about what they are reading.
3. Develop interesting questions that promote discussion and understanding of text. One of the primary goals is to promote students' thinking and to have them grapple with ideas and constructs while they read and then again after they read.

Students can explore ideas about the author and characters' purpose and point of view. Teachers can help guide these discussions by asking such questions such as "What is the author trying to tell us?" and "Why do you think the author is saying this?"

When effectively implemented, QtA can take students to a higher level of understanding.

14.6.5 Collaborative Strategic Reading

Collaborative strategic reading (CSR) is a multicomponent learning strategy that is typically used with students in grades 4 through 12 and combines essential reading-comprehension strategies that have been demonstrated as effective in improving students' understanding of text (Lederer, 2000; Palincsar, 1986; Rosenshine & Meister, 1994) with cooperative learning groups or paired learning. CSR takes advantage of the growing understanding that youngsters need to be taught and provided with specific strategies to enhance their understanding of text; however, students should not be overwhelmed with so many strategies that they are unable to decide which ones to use. CSR is based on reciprocal teaching (Palinscar & Brown, 1984) and teaches four strategies using the following steps: *preview* (i.e., predicting), *click and clunk* (i.e., questioning and clarifying), *get the gist* (i.e., summarization), and *wrap-up* (i.e., summarization). Preview is used only before reading the text and wrap-up only after reading the entire text. Figure 14.12 presents the four CSR steps with key questions students can ask as they complete the process.

1. ***Previewing.*** The goals of previewing are for students to (a) learn as much about the passage as they can in 2 to 3 minutes, (b) activate their background knowledge about the topic, (c) make predictions about what they will read, and (d) have their

FIGURE 14.12 **CSR's plan for strategic reading**

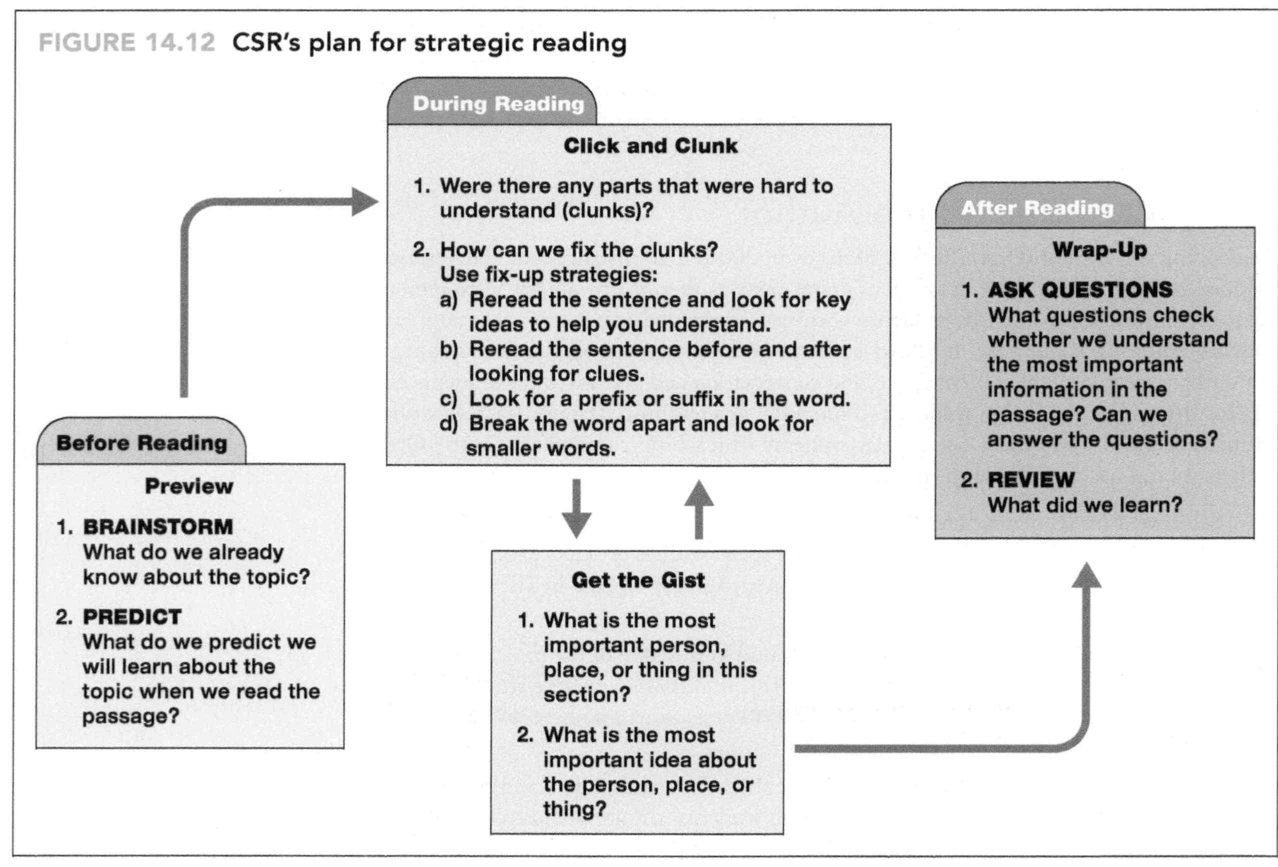
Before Reading
Preview
1. BRAINSTORM
What do we already know about the topic?
2. PREDICT
What do we predict we will learn about the topic when we read the passage?
During Reading
Click and Clunk
1. Were there any parts that were hard to understand (clunks)?
2. How can we fix the clunks?
Use fix-up strategies:
a) Reread the sentence and look for key ideas to help you understand.
b) Reread the sentence before and after looking for clues.
c) Look for a prefix or suffix in the word.
d) Break the word apart and look for smaller words.
Get the Gist
1. What is the most important person, place, or thing in this section?
2. What is the most important idea about the person, place, or thing?
After Reading
Wrap-Up
1. ASK QUESTIONS
What questions check whether we understand the most important information in the passage? Can we answer the questions?
2. REVIEW
What did we learn?

interest in the topic piqued and be engaged in active reading. In previewing, teach the students to check out the headings, key words, pictures, tables, graphs, and other key information. Jane Gordon, a sixth-grade teacher, uses previewing with her students by teaching them proper nouns and key words before they read. She then asks them to quickly examine the text and make sensible predictions about what they will read. If students make guesses that are not linked to the content of the text, she gives them feedback or asks them to justify their prediction.

2. ***Click and Clunk.*** Students "click and clunk" while reading each section of the text. "Clicks" refer to the portions of the text that make sense, and "clunks" are the portions about which comprehension isn't clear (e.g., students do not know the meaning of a word). Clicking and clunking is designed to help students monitor their comprehension and employ fix-up strategies to clarify their understanding. Clunk cards read as follows:
   - Reread the sentence and look for ideas that help you understand the word.
   - Reread the sentence leaving out the "clunk." What word makes sense?
   - Reread the sentences before and after the sentence with the "clunk."
   - Look for prefixes or suffixes in the word.
   - Break the word apart and look for smaller words you know.

Jane Gordon encourages her students to be "clunk experts" by identifying key words and ideas they don't know and working with their partners to uncover their meaning. Students learn to select clunks carefully, which helps them monitor their comprehension while they read.

3. ***Getting the Gist.*** Students learn to get the gist (get the main idea) by reading each section and then asking and answering in their own words and in ten words or less:
   - Who or what is it about?
   - What is most important about the who or what?

Teaching students to restate the most important point in ten words or less is a way of making sure they understood what they read. Students repeat the second and third steps for each paragraph or section of the passage. The students in Jane Gordon's class, for example, appreciate that they not only have to read the material, but also have to write a brief sentence about the main idea. Initially they had a difficult time figuring out what a paragraph was about, but Jane helped them by asking students

- To read or display their gists from commonly read material
- To provide support for aspects of the gist that were valuable
- To rewrite the gist

Over time, students improved in their gist writing.

4. ***Wrap-Up.*** During wrap-up, students formulate questions and answers about the key ideas from the entire passage and discuss what they have learned. The goal is to improve students' knowledge, understanding, and memory of what they read. For students with learning and language disabilities, it may be necessary to explicitly teach them to ask questions using the WH + How questions (*What?*, *When?*, *Where?*, *Why?*, and *How?*). Students can use the gists they have generated for the different sections to think about the most important information in the whole passage.

Cooperative learning groups

Once students have developed proficiency in applying the comprehension strategies through teacher-led activities, the students learn to use CSR in peer-led cooperative learning groups of about four or five students (Johnson & Johnson, 1989). Typical roles used during CSR include the following:

- *Leader.* Leads the group by saying what to read and what strategy to use next
- *Clunk expert.* Reminds students to use clunk strategies to figure out a difficult word or concept

- *Announcer.* Calls on different members to read and share ideas
- *Encourager.* Watches the group and gives encouragement and feedback
- *Reporter.* During the whole-class wrap-up, reports to the class the important ideas learned and favorite questions
- *Timekeeper.* Keeps time and lets the group know when it is time to move on

Roles should change on a regular basis. After students wrap up in their cooperative groups, a whole-class wrap-up is completed to give the teacher and groups the opportunity to report and discuss the content.

CSR has been used in diverse classrooms, including those with students with reading problems and English language learners, to help students in upper-elementary, middle, and high school read content-area materials more efficiently and effectively (Boardman, Buckley, Lasser, Klingner, & Annamma, 2015; Klingner & Vaughn, 1999, 2000; Klingner et al., 2007; Klingner, Vaughn, & Schumm, 1998; Vaughn & Klingner, 1999; Klingner & Vaughn, 2004; Vaughn, Klingner, & Bryant, 2001; Vaughn, Klingner et al., 2011). Tiffany Royal, a fifth-grade inclusion teacher, notes, "What I like best is that my students learn how to understand what they read while they improve their vocabulary. Also, it helps on our standardized achievement tests."

CSR offers a format for the close and careful reading recommended by the Common Core State Standards for reading. Moreover, when working in cooperative learning groups, students can discuss how what they read connects with what they have learned in class from lectures, media, and other readings to prepare for tests and projects.

MyEdLab **Self-Check 14.6**

MyEdLab **Application Exercise 14.6:** Strategies for Reading Comprehension

14 SUMMARY

- Reading is a key component of literacy education, and learning to decode, comprehend, and analyze text is a vital communication skill in our digital age. Classroom teachers need to be aware of the key concepts underlying reading instruction, the components of reading curriculum, and reasons why many students struggle in learning how to read.
- In planning and using effective reading instruction for struggling readers, teachers should establish an environment that promotes reading, use appropriate and ongoing assessment, use RTI strategies, provide intensive instruction, obtain early intervention, and provide ongoing support for older readers with reading difficulties.
- In the last decade, national, state, and local initiatives have emphasized balanced approaches to teaching reading and the use of research-based strategies for teaching students how to read. In addition, current trends include emphasis on standards-based instruction and professional collaboration in the teaching of reading.
- Students, especially struggling readers, need systematic instruction in phonological awareness, letter–sound correspondence, and decoding strategies, including phonics instruction. This instruction includes modeling and guided practice with feedback in context and with words in isolation. It is important that students develop a sight word vocabulary (i.e., the words that students recognize without conscious effort) and decoding strategies to support them when they encounter an unknown word, including knowledge of common word patterns and morphological awareness.
- Students are fluent in reading when they can recognize printed words quickly and effortlessly. Repeated reading, reading aloud to students, and classwide peer tutoring promote reading fluency. Fluency instruction should be integrated with instruction in word identification and comprehension.
- Asking students to predict and make connections with prior knowledge before reading, monitor their understanding during reading, and summarize key ideas after reading assists them in improving their comprehension.

THINK AND APPLY

1. Now that you have read Chapter 14, reflect about your own journey in learning to read. What parts of the reading curriculum were most difficult for you or other students in your family or classes? How does difficulty in learning to read impact your life or the lives of you family members of classmates?

2. Summarize current trends and issues in reading instruction. Discuss with your instructor and classmates what you now know and what you need to learn about these trends and issues.

3. Think about several students you have taught or are currently teaching who are struggling with reading. Which factors are influencing their learning? What components of the reading process pose the most problems for each student? What principles of effective reading instruction might you implement with these students?

4. Obtain copies of the elementary and middle school reading textbooks that your state or school district has adopted. Examine the scope and sequence of phonological awareness and phonics instruction from grade to grade to gain a better understanding of expected development of proficiency in this area of reading instruction.

5. Develop a plan for how you would use Word Walls in your classroom. Include procedures for development and maintenance of the Word Wall as well as related activities to make the Word Wall more meaningful and interactive. How would you adapt the Word Wall activities for English language learners and students with disabilities?

6. Go to the What Works Clearinghouse website. Use the website to identify research-based practices for teaching reading fluency.

7. Plan a lesson to teach a Common Core State Standard or your state standard in comprehension instruction for the grade level of your choice. Describe the follow-up activities, including the instructional grouping formats, you plan to use to reinforce learning and meet individual student needs. Describe how you will assess initial student understanding of the standard, monitor progress, and assess mastery.

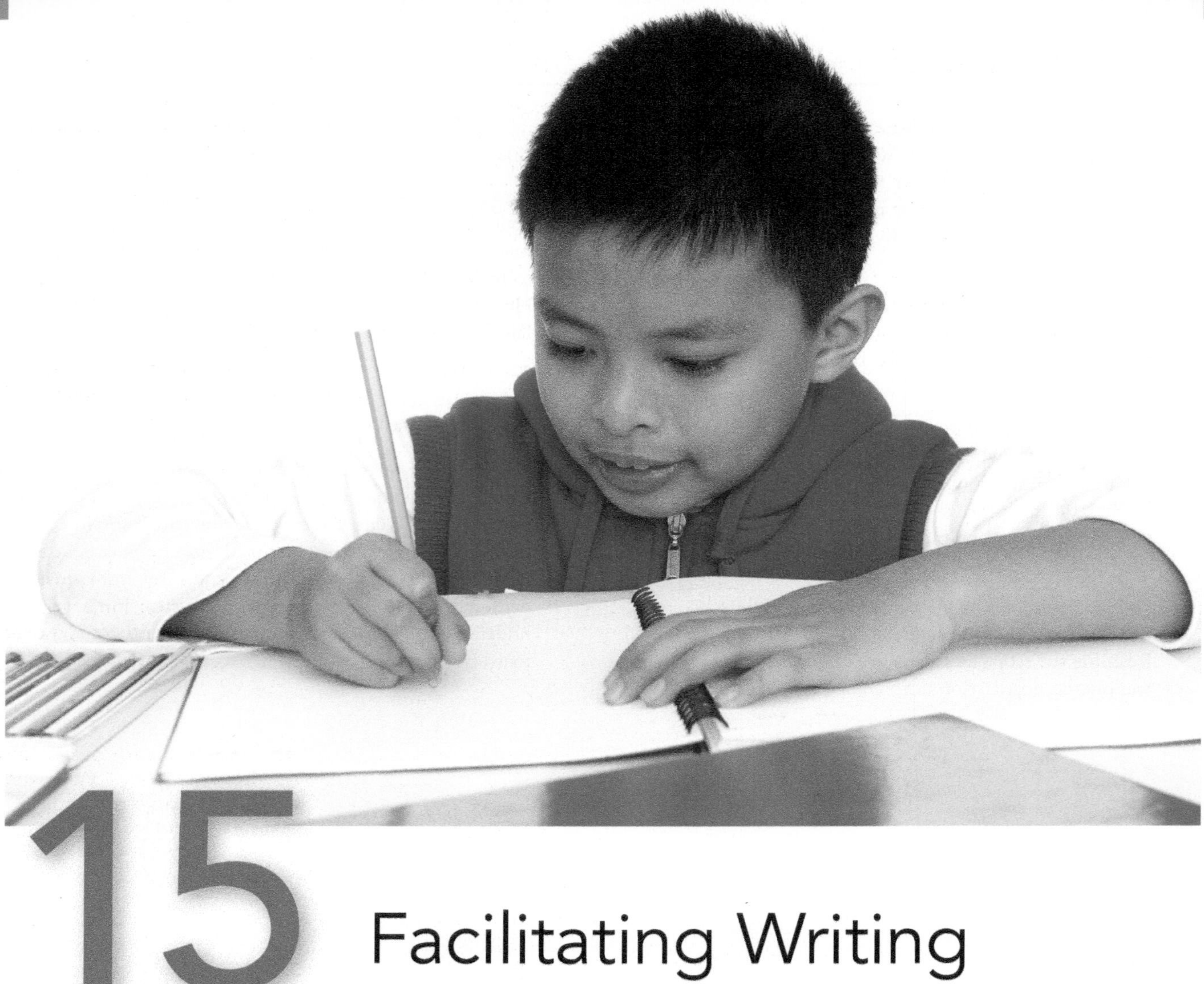

15 Facilitating Writing

Learning Outcomes

15.1 Describe current trends in writing curricula and instruction, and how they align with what you think about writing instruction.

15.2 Explain the advantages of teaching writing as a process, and how this process promotes effective writing instruction for all learners.

15.3 Identify practices can you implement to establish an environment that promotes writing.

15.4 Articulate what adaptations you could provide for students with challenges in prewriting and revising and how you might support struggling writers during conferencing.

15.5 Describe what instructional practices you could implement for students with difficulties in composing narrative, informational, and opinion/argument text.

15.6 Provide examples of strategies to support students with spelling difficulties.

15.7 Explain what you can do to support students in learning handwriting and keyboarding skills.

INTERVIEW: MICHELLE LANGLOIS

Michelle Langlois is a special education teacher who has worked for 5 years at the elementary level as an "inclusion" teacher providing instructional support to teachers and specialized instruction to students with disabilities in kindergarten through third grade. During the past year she decided to tackle a new challenge and accepted a transfer to a middle school, where she worked as a resource teacher with eighteen students with disabilities. Michelle was very confident about her successes in teaching writing at the elementary school but was less confident after her first year teaching middle school.

> Well I'm not sure who learned more this year, the students or me. I'm just kidding—I think—but it was a big learning experience for me. You see, when I taught elementary inclusion classes I worked cooperatively with a team of the kindergarten through third-grade teachers to establish writing centers that would give students experience in all of the elements of writing, including composing, editing, rewriting, and publishing. We all agreed that students needed time to practice the craft of writing and to learn that good writers read and rewrite their work and then receive feedback from others, including their classmates, before revising and publishing. We didn't just let students develop writing independently but provided explicit instruction in those critical skills associated with effective writing, including spelling, punctuation, and elements of grammar. However, we all seemed to agree on the procedures and shared a common language for how we talked about writing and instruction to students.
>
> I found that when I came to the middle school, many of the teachers were not accustomed to having the special education teacher be an active member of the team. I was hoping that I could extend many of the practices I used at the elementary level to establish and promote writing instruction across the content areas using research-based instructional practices that would promote writing for all learners but especially for students with disabilities. For example, we know that when students identify the topic they are writing about and use a graphic organizer to help them include critical ideas, key words, and important parts of the writing piece (e.g., introduction, summary), students produce better writing. I was encouraging all of the middle school teachers to work with me to identify common writing strategies we would all use—that way students could learn the new strategies and practice them across content areas. I was optimistic that I could then reinforce these instructional strategies by teaching and applying them in the resource room. I was not as successful at instituting these practices as I would like to have been, although I am optimistic that many of the teachers I worked with last year had a positive experience and that we will start off this next year with these teachers eager to continue our work together.

CHAPTER OUTLINE

(continued)

Introduction

Like many teachers who have acquired knowledge about effective instructional practices and are eager to share them with other teachers, Michelle found that the process works best when the professional development includes open communication and careful planning. In this chapter, you will first read about current trends in writing instruction. The chapter continues with an explanation of writing instruction as a process followed by strategies for creating a positive and productive physical and social environment for writing in the classroom. Next, the chapter continues with general suggestions for helping all students succeed in writing and specific suggestions for teaching composition of various genres, spelling, and handwriting/keyboarding.

15.1 CURRENT TRENDS IN WRITING CURRICULA AND INSTRUCTION

Michelle realized that research-based writing practices can be applied at both the elementary and the secondary level and are especially helpful to students with disabilities who are included in general education classrooms. However, there are competing issues, such as high-stakes assessment, that influence writing curricula. Writing instruction historically has taken a back seat to reading and mathematics instruction (Graham & Harris, 2013). However, there has been growing awareness of the importance of accomplished writing for personal communication as well as success in postsecondary education and the world of work. Current trends in writing curricula and instruction include

- Movement toward standards-based writing instruction and research-based practices
- Increased emphasis on assessment
- Emphasis on balanced and effective writing instruction for all students
- Implementation of writing practices that are based on research

15.1.1 Common Core Standards–Based Writing Instruction and Research-Based Practices

Teachers such as Michelle realize that they need to consider the writing standards of the Common Core English language arts (ELA) and reading standards as well as the standards in the state in which they teach. Approximately forty-two states, the District of Columbia, four U.S. territories, and the Department of Defense Education Activity are implementing Common Core State Standards (Common Core State-Standards Initiative, 2015). For a summary of the standards for writing, see Figure 15.1.

One way to ensure high-quality writing instruction is through the use of research-based practices. A growing body of knowledge exists that can be used by teachers to ensure success for students in learning to write (Graham, Harris & Santangelo, 2015)—even among students for whom learning to write is difficult, including students with learning disabilities (Gillespie & Graham, 2014) and English language learners (August, McCardle, & Shanahan, 2014). However, Baker, Gersten, and Graham (2003) emphasize the importance of teaching students strategies for composing text and for giving students specific feedback to help them improve their writing. Some of the research-based instructional practices for improving writing are provided in Tips for Teachers 15.1.

FIGURE 15.1 The Common Core Standards for English Language Arts: answers to relevant questions pertaining to oral and written language instruction

What are some of the critical features pertaining to writing in the Common Core Standards?

A critical component of effective English language arts instruction is the development of students' writing skills, which includes technically accurate composition and clearly stated views, ideas, reflections, and thoughts. One of the emphases of the writing standards is learning to write logical arguments that use good evidence, display sound reasoning, and integrate ideas. Writing is also a way to express opinions, provide information and explain ideas, increase understanding, and produce narratives. Like reading, writing is based on foundation skills and develops to the point that students can write clear and well-reasoned pieces. The Common Core Standards describe the writing goals expected at each grade level but do not specify the topics or curriculum for accomplishing these goals.

What are some of the critical features pertaining to speaking and listening in the Common Core Standards?

In addition to guidelines about the knowledge and skills needed to acquire proficiency in reading and writing, the standards also describe the increasingly complex expectations related to speaking and listening, including acquiring and expressing ideas orally and through media. Students are expected to engage in academic discussions with other students, the teacher, in small groups and in whole-class settings. Expectations also include the expression of informed views informally through discussion as well as formally through class presentations.

What are some of the critical features pertaining to language in the Common Core Standards?

Language expectations are encompassed within the reading and English language arts standards, and include the goal that students will develop increasingly proficient language skills demonstrated through improved vocabularies and language use. Students are expected to increasingly improve their knowledge of words and phrases and their meanings through direct instruction, reading, and attending to conversations that promote learning.

Source: Retrieved from: http://www.corestandards.org/other-resources/key-shifts-in-english-language-arts/; International Reading Association Common Core State Standards (CCSS) Committee. (2012). *Literacy implementation guidance for the ELA Common Core State Standards* [White paper]. Retrieved from: http://www.reading.org/Libraries/association-documents/ira_ccss_guidelines.pdf

15.1.2 Emphasis on Assessment and Progress Monitoring

Many states now require high-stakes writing tests that potentially affect student promotion and graduation from high school. The importance placed on student outcomes has spawned greater emphasis on ongoing student progress monitoring and providing students

TIPS FOR TEACHERS 15.1

Research-Based Writing Practices

- Teach students writing strategies that include planning, revising, and editing their compositions. Teachers can use planning formats that prompt students as follows: consider your topic, decide what the important ideas are about your topic, and determine your opening sentence. Revising is never fun, but students can learn to read their pieces aloud and to determine if there are parts that can be improved. They can also ask partners to read their pieces and ask questions that help them improve their writing.
- Help students to determine whether sentences are the right length and communicate clearly. Teach students how to determine if they have a run-on sentence that needs to be broken into multiple sentences. Also, teach students how to combine sentences to achieve more complex sentence types and to summarize texts.
- Provide opportunities for students to work together in pairs and groups toward cooperative written products to facilitate quality of composition.
- Establish goals for students' writing to improve outcomes, and establish procedures to monitor progress to achieve these goals.
- Give students access to and instruction in word processing to facilitate writing.
- Assist students in developing prewriting practices that help generate or organize ideas for writing.
- Use inquiry activities to analyze data related to writing reports.
- Use writing process approaches that provide extended time for writing and revision.
- Provide students with good models of writing to study and to compare with their own writing.
- Integrate writing as a tool to enhance content knowledge.

Sources: "A meta-analysis of writing instruction for adolescent students" by S. Graham & D. Perrin, 2007, *Journal of Educational Psychology, 99*, 445–476; and "Teaching writing: Balancing process and product," by G. E. Tompkins, 2012, Boston: Pearson.

FIGURE 15.2 Features of exemplary writing instruction

- A literate classroom environment where students' written work is prominently displayed, the room is packed with writing and reading material, and word lists adorn the walls.
- Daily writing with students working on a wide range of writing tasks for multiple audiences, including writing at home.
- Extensive efforts to make writing motivating by setting an exciting mood, creating a risk-free environment, allowing students to select their own writing topics or modify teacher assignments, developing assigned topics compatible with students' interests, reinforcing children's accomplishments, specifying the goal for each lesson, and promoting an "I can" attitude.
- Regular teacher–student conferences concerning the writing topic the student is currently working on, including the establishment of goals or criteria to guide the child's writing and revising efforts.
- A predictable writing routine where students are encouraged to think, reflect, and revise.
- Overt teacher modeling of the process of writing as well as positive attitudes toward writing.
- Cooperative arrangements where students help each other plan, draft, revise, edit, or publish their written work.
- Group or individual sharing where students present work in progress or completed papers to their peers for feedback.
- Instruction covering a broad range of skills, knowledge, [and] strategies, including phonological awareness, handwriting and spelling, writing conventions, sentence construction, text structure, functions of writing, and planning and revising.
- Follow-up instruction to ensure mastery of targeted writing skills, knowledge, and strategies.
- Integration of writing activities across the curriculum and the use of reading to support writing development.
- Instruction in use of strategies for summarizing text and developing a written response to text.
- Frequent opportunities for students to self-regulate their behavior during writing, including working independently, arranging their own space, and seeking help from others.
- Ample opportunities for students to develop proficiency with word processors for all aspects of the writing process.
- Teacher and student assessments of writing progress, strengths, and needs.
- Periodic conferences with parents and frequent communications with home about the writing program and students' progress as writers.

Sources: Information from "Prevention and intervention of writing difficulties for students with learning disabilities," by S. Graham, K. R. Harris, & L. Larsen, 2001, *Learning Disabilities Research and Practice, 16*, 74–84; "Research-based writing practices and the Common Core: Meta-analysis and meta-synthesis," by S. Graham, K. R. Harris, & T. Santangelo, 2015, *The Elementary School Journal, 115*(4), 498–522; "The Common Core State Standards and evidence-based educational practices: The case of writing," by G. A. Troia & N. G. Olinghouse, 2013, *School Psychology Review, 42*(3), 343–357.

with specific feedback about their performance. Although the debate about high-stakes tests will continue, the importance of learning to communicate through the written word using a variety of media and technologies remains. Students need feedback and monitoring to help them achieve success in written communication. Moreover, students with difficulties in writing need intensive and sustained interventions to improve their writing (e.g., Ferretti, Andrews-Weckerly, & Lewis, 2007; Gillespie & Graham, 2014). Figure 15.2 notes the features of exemplary writing instruction.

15.1.3 Progress Monitoring and Writing

Why is it a good idea to monitor the progress of students with writing difficulties? When teachers monitor students' progress on critical elements regularly (at least every 2 weeks), students are motivated to improve their writing and in turn make notable progress. Teachers record students' progress so that they, the students, and parents can see progress, such as the number of words written for younger children and the use of story elements and their quality in the narratives of older students.

Teachers monitor students' progress by noting:

- Advances in specific writing goals (e.g., number of words written per day, quality of writing, number of sentences that have been edited)
- Whether they can complete written projects
- How proficient they are at each element of the writing process (e.g., planning, composing, revising) and in the mechanics of writing (e.g., handwriting, spelling, punctuation)
- Whether they can apply the skills and knowledge to other contexts (e.g., at other times during the day or in content-area classes)
- How they explain the processes they are using

There are several approaches to progress monitoring, including observation, portfolios, quality ratings of writing goals, and number of words written based on skill-level criteria.

Using observations for progress monitoring

Effective writing instruction involves ongoing observations and feedback. Recording these observations systematically can serve as a progress-monitoring tool. For example, as students write, teachers notice what strategies they use to compose text (e.g., outline, notes, key words), reflect on the appropriateness of the task and teaching presentation, and keep written records to document student progress, such as notes, checklists, and samples of students' work. Teachers can observe students as they write and use conference times to assess and record their progress. By observing and examining writing processes and products, teachers can plan instruction to meet individual needs. Many teachers keep anecdotal records by creating a record sheet to quickly document students' progress on writing projects. They include a summary of what they observe, the date, and the context, and they list skills and writing strategies that need to be taught.

Using portfolios for progress monitoring

A **portfolio** is a folder that contains representative samples of a student's written work collected over a period of time, either in hard-copy or electronic form. Portfolios help teachers, families, and students document growth and development over the school year or selected time period. With older students, teachers may ask students to keep journals or writing folders documenting their progress in writing. Teachers may periodically review and select representative pieces to show writing development, and use this portfolio progress monitoring to establish writing goals for students.

Using words written per minute and rating scales to monitor students' progress

Another effective way to monitor students' progress is to record the number of letters (very young writers) or words students write in a minute. This task varies based on the age of the student.

Very Beginning Writers Ask beginning writers to write as many different letters or words as they can in 1 minute. Encourage those at the letter-writing stage to increase the number of words on their lists by using both upper- and lowercase letters; remind more skilled young writers that they can include the names of friends and places (proper nouns) in their lists as well. You can then monitor the number of correct letters or words written per minute to track student progress.

Beginning Writers Ask beginning writers to write as many words as they can in 1 minute. Have students complete this task every 2 weeks so that you can monitor their improvement, as well as note students whose lack of improvement suggests the need for further instruction.

Writers Ask students to think of a topic and then give them 1 minute to write as much as they can on that topic. Then either count the number of words written per minute or rate the overall quality on a scale of 1 to 5.

Advanced Writers Every 2 weeks, select a writing sample from students and rate it according to a 5-point scale using the criteria you are focusing on with each student during that 2-week period. For example, you may rate the writing sample on the number of improved edits, the clarity of the ideas, the use of correct punctuation, the number of idea units, the appropriate use of sentence structure, and so on. As students mature in their writing, the use of adjectives and vivid verbs, facility in editing and revising, and the overall quality of the writing can be monitored. It is important to focus on only one or two things at

Should children be encouraged to write before they can read or spell? Why or why not?

a time. After students demonstrate progress in the target areas, other elements of writing can be added. This way, progress is recorded, and students are not overwhelmed by the number of writing conventions that they need to monitor.

15.1.4 Response to Intervention and Writing

Documenting students' response to writing instruction is a useful way of providing valuable information that can assist in determining whether they require special education or, for those students already receiving special education, whether they are making adequate progress in writing. How might response to intervention be used for students with writing difficulties? Students with extreme writing challenges should be provided extra time each day (20 to 30 minutes) and extra instruction to determine whether their writing has improved. Teachers can maintain copies of students' writing to determine whether adequate progress in writing has occurred. Also, because writing requires time and feedback, consider ways to integrate writing throughout content-area instruction, such as in social studies, science, and math. If all teachers are focusing on the same writing goals and support is provided throughout the day for writing, improvements are more likely to occur.

15.1.5 Writing Rubrics and Portfolios

Writing rubrics and portfolios can be used to structure assessment. These tools are helpful for both teachers and students in that they serve as a gauge of student progress.

Writing rubrics

A **writing rubric** is a scoring guide that outlines expected performance on a written product. There are many variations of formats for rubrics (Flynn & Flynn, 2004; Tompkins, 2014), but most include levels of performance from unacceptable to proficient. Rubrics can be developed by teachers, and increasingly rubrics are part of required standards for writing. Textbook publishers are including more rubrics as supplemental material. Numerous rubrics and "rubric generators" are available online. Teachers and students can construct rubrics as well (see example in Figure 15.3). Often rubrics are accompanied by writing samples or exemplars that demonstrate different levels of performance.

Whatever the source, rubrics are best used to clarify what students are being expected to do and to provide a framework for self-, peer, and teacher evaluation. Rubrics can also be used to give guided feedback that will direct students in reaching higher levels of performance. It is useful for parents to be informed about the number of levels in your rubric (the more levels the better) and the meaning of the categories in the rubric (e.g., what you mean by "mechanical errors"), so that they can provide support to their youngsters at home.

Writing Portfolios What is the purpose of a writing portfolio? Portfolios provide evidence of development in the writing skills of each student. You can use several types of writing portfolios. Strickland, Galda, and Cullinan (2004) mention four types:

1. Showcase portfolios (featuring best work)
2. Documentation portfolios (include artifacts collected over a period of time)
3. Process portfolios (evidence of development of a single piece from beginning to end)
4. Evaluation portfolios (used to determine grades based on a predetermined set of standards)

The type of portfolio you use will depend on your state and district requirements and on your own decision about how you want to track student progress and report to parents and administrators. Tips for Teachers 15.2 provides suggestions for implementing writing portfolios in your classroom.

FIGURE 15.3 **Sample rubric for writing**

5 Excellent	4 Very Good Some revision would be beneficial	3 Adequate Considerable revision would be beneficial	2 Needs substantial revision	1 Revise completely or consider starting over
The purpose of your writing is clear and easy to read.	Your purpose is understandable.	Revise with a focus on improving the clarity of your overall purpose.	It is difficult to determine your purpose and goals.	Your purpose is unclear and errors are so significant that the paper is very challenging to read.
Paragraphs are well constructed; writing is original, clever, and/or well informed.	Most paragraphs are indented, have a main idea, and connect with paragraphs before and after.	Some paragraphs are well written and some need to be better organized and connected.	The main ideas within paragraphs are not clear and connections before and after paragraphs are not made.	Paragraphs are not well written and are not connected to one another.
Sentences are well organized and connected into effective paragraphs.	Most sentences are well organized within paragraphs.	Revision is required at the sentence level to assure that each sentence is clear and communicates effectively.	Complete thoughts are not represented in sentences.	Sentences are difficult to read and unclear.
Word choice is precise, interesting/unusual, and appropriate.	Reread to consider if there are selected word choices that could be improved.	Word choices are adequately considered but not precise or persuasive.	Needs revision for use of appropriate words.	Word choice is vague and redundant, with few well-chosen words.
Essentially free of grammatical and mechanical errors, including punctuation and spelling errors.	Grammatical and mechanical errors are uncommon and can be readily revised.	Grammatical and mechanical errors require revision so that ideas can be better understood.	Significant grammatical and mechanical errors make the paper difficult to read and understand.	Significant grammatical and mechanical errors indicate the need for complete revision.

TIPS FOR TEACHERS 15.2

Implementing Writing Portfolios

- Introduce the portfolio. Describe the purpose for the portfolio, intended use and audience, types of artifacts to include, and examples.
- Introduce the rubric or scoring guide. Explain how the portfolio will be evaluated and by whom (e.g., teacher, parent, peer, self).
- Explain guidelines for inclusion of artifacts, including electronic artifacts.
- Outline logistical and ethical issues: how materials will be housed and maintained, appropriate times and procedures for working on the portfolio, and who has access to materials.
- Assist the students in setting personal goals and planning artifacts/projects to meet those goals.
- Provide guided experiences for students to reflect on their work and to document those reflections.

Source: Adapted from *Assessment in the literacy classroom*, by M. E. Gredler & R. L. Johnson, 2004, Boston: Allyn & Bacon. Copyright © 2005 by Pearson Education. Adapted by permission of the publisher.

MyEdLab **Self-Check 15.1**

MyEdLab **Application Exercise 15.1:** Monitoring Progress

15.2 TEACHING WRITING AS A PROCESS

Think about some of your recent experiences as a writer. Perhaps you were writing a research paper for school. You might have been writing a letter or an email message to a friend. Maybe you were carefully crafting a letter of application for a job. Think about the process. To compose, you needed to do the following:

- Formulate your message in your head.
- Organize your ideas in a logical fashion.
- Think about the reader and how he or she might understand and react to the message.
- Choose words carefully to make the flow of language, or syntax, smooth.
- Select individual words to convey your meaning succinctly.
- Attend to your spelling, capitalization, and punctuation.
- Consider the appearance of the final product (the legibility or format of your handwriting, typing, or word processing).

As a teacher, you need to help your students write by considering these same factors.

15.2.1 Writing as an Interactive Process

Writers use the sounds, grammar, and meaning of our language system to **encode** (or to put language into print) and to communicate a message to the reader. In writing, as in reading, students may have problems with any aspect of the language system—with using language interactively and with using it fluently. In addition, students may have problems with the physical act of writing. For example, Grant Ellsworth, a fifth grader with learning disabilities, loves to tell stories, especially about fishing with his father, but he is reluctant when asked to write them. Grant is a poor speller and for some reason cannot get the hang of capitalization and punctuation rules. In addition, his handwriting is illegible, and he hasn't learned to use a keyboard. Writing a single sentence takes Grant so long that he soon loses his story and its intended meaning. Even though Grant can tell stories in an entertaining way, he cannot get them on paper.

Effective teachers understand what research has demonstrated: Students need to know the mechanics of writing if they are going to communicate effectively with others. Earlier instruction in writing often focused too much on the mechanics and too little on conveying meaning. It is also possible to focus too much on the meaning and too little on the mechanics. Successful teachers know that both are essential elements of successful writing (National Council of Teachers of English [NCTE], 2010). For example, Mrs. Zakibe, Grant's teacher, knows that she must ensure that Grant and all her students understand the rules of language, including capitalization, punctuation, and spelling, as well as the value of a well-organized story structure.

MyEdLab
Video Example 15.1.
In this video, we watch a teacher instruct an interactive writing activity in a kindergarten classroom. Do you think that this process would be helpful to students who struggle as writers? Why or why not?

When teachers implement effective intervention approaches that use both the conventions of writing, such as capitalization, punctuation, and sentence structure, and strategies for improving written expression, such as planning and composing, the results are positive (Gersten & Baker, 2000; Mason et al., 2010). Effective writing instruction requires the following critical points (Fearn & Farnan, 2001; Graham & Harris, 2009):

- Understanding that attention to the conventions of writing does not disrupt the flow of writing but is part of the discipline of writing, and thus does not inhibit growth in writing but facilitates it
- Understanding that even very young children can learn and perform simple conventions automatically
- Considering instructional needs and long-range goals when determining the emphasis on writing for students with disabilities to ensure that the amount of time in writing instruction aligns with students' needs

TIPS FOR TEACHERS 15.3

Checklist for Students to Support Their Writing

_______ I am clear about the writing assignment.

_______ I have a list of questions before I write and I am contacting the appropriate person to get answers.

_______ I have developed a timeline for when and how I will finish the written assignment.

_______ I have allowed time in my timeline for someone to read and respond to my paper and for me to make revisions.

_______ I have contacted and secured a reader for my paper.

_______ I have planned what I will write about, including my topic, my key ideas, and, if appropriate, an outline.

_______ I have thought about key words and important words I want to include in my writing.

_______ I reread my writing several times and thought about what others might understand and not understand.

_______ I reread and revised my writing several times, asking myself questions about what others might understand/not understand, whether punctuation was correct, and whether my word choices were the best I could do.

_______ I asked a good reader or writer to read my paper.

_______ I accepted feedback from a reviewer and made revisions.

_______ I determined whether my paper met the goals of the assignment.

_______ I edited my paper again and made sure that all of the mechanical elements were correct.

_______ I submitted the paper to the teacher and made additional revisions if needed.

- Focusing on teaching students to plan and think about their writing in ways that improve written outcomes
- Recognizing that students can learn metacognitive strategies to more effectively write, review their writing, and revise their writing

15.2.2 Writing as a Strategic Process

Because writing is such a complex task, successful writers need a strategy or plan for communicating ideas clearly. It is important to have systematic procedures for being successful and productive at each stage of the authoring process. Students, especially those with learning and behavior problems, often have difficulty not only planning their writing but also monitoring and regulating themselves while they write. Researchers have developed practices to improve writing both for students with disabilities and also for their classmates without disabilities (e.g., Graham et al., 2015; Harris, Graham, Friedlander, & Laud, 2013; Taft & Mason, 2011). Practices that can help students become more strategic writers are emerging in several areas, including learning the stages of the writing process, learning narrative and expository text structures, and getting systematic and specific feedback (Baker et al., 2003). Students may find a checklist like the one in Tips for Teachers 15.3 helpful for monitoring their writing.

15.2.3 Writing as a Process of Constructing Meaning

When writers compose, they need to keep potential readers in mind. Readers need to have background information and specific links (such as examples and definitions of new terms) to help them connect the new information with what they already know. In short, writers need to take responsibility for helping readers to construct meaning.

Students with writing difficulties might not understand the role of audience or potential readers or how to help readers construct meaning by providing background knowledge and using predictable story or informational writing structures. For example, Terry Macinello, a fifth grader, wrote a story about a recent trip but did not indicate where or why he went on his trip and gave only sketchy details of one event. In his narrative,

TECH TIPS

Technologies for Struggling Writers

Computer programs can help learners with written expression in many ways. The following programs are particularly useful in helping students master the writing process by giving them the tools necessary to compose with confidence.

Writing Process

Draft:Builder, Don Johnston Incorporated (www.donjohnston.com)

A talking organizer that helps structure the writing process from first ideas to first draft, including templates for a wide range of writing tasks, such as essay writing, book reports, and researching.

Inspiration, Inspiration Software, Inc. (www.inspiration.com)

Talking Word Processor

Write:Outloud, Don Johnston Incorporated (www.donjohnston.com)

Classroom Suite 4, IntelliTools, Inc. (www.intellitools.com)

Word-Prediction Software

Co:Writer, Don Johnston Incorporated (www.donjohnston.com)

Beginning Sentence Writing

Communicate: SymWriter, Widgit (www.widgit.com)

An easy-to-use symbol-supported word processor giving the student visual assistance and reinforcing meaning; includes a spell checker with symbol support and a speech function.

CONFUSING WORDS (www.confusingwords.com)

A collection of more than 3,000 words that are troublesome to readers and writers.

Using Microsoft Word's Built-in Features

Go to Word's "Preferences" menu and customize the following based on student needs:

AutoCorrect—Examine the options in AutoCorrect, Math AutoCorrect, AutoFormat as You Type, and AutoText.

Spelling and Grammar—Under Grammar, check all of the features that will produce the "squiggles" to prompt checking/correction in Writing Style.

iPad/iPod™ applications include:

- Abilipad
- Sentence Builder
- Sentence Maker
- Dictionary.com, Which Word?
- ESL Express: Words Frequently Confused
- Word Wit, Writing Prompts
- Kids Can Spell, SpellBoard
- ABC Sight Words Writing
- I Can Write 2
- Sight Words 1–100: Kids Learn

which had no distinguishable beginning, middle, or end, he referred to family members without letting the reader know who they were. Terry doesn't realize that when he writes a story, it is for someone to read, and thus he needs to fill in some gaps so that readers can understand and enjoy his story.

The majority of students with disabilities will benefit from effective instruction that assists them in progressing as writers. This requires instruction in thinking about text, planning, revision, and learning how to write differently for different writing purposes, such as description, persuasion, a letter, building an argument, or a narrative story.

Some students, like third grader Maya Bradley, get so wrapped up in basic writing skills (e.g., spelling, grammar, handwriting) that they lose track of the purpose of writing. When asked about good writing, Maya defines it as "when I am neat and get the words spelled right." Traditionally, teachers often spent more time teaching basic skills to students who struggle (Graham, Harris, Fink-Chorzempa, & MacArthur, 2003). However, all students need to be taught the purpose of writing as a way to communicate a message. As the Tech Tips, "Technologies for Struggling Writers," notes, technology can provide support for students in communicating their message.

Video Example from YouTube

MyEdLab
Video Example 15.2.
Watch the YouTube video "Donald Graves Tells Us How to Get a Writing Class Started." What do you think of Donald Graves's advice to teachers that in order to teach students to write, they should write themselves? https://www.youtube.com/watch?v=cZ_sXJKiiSA

15.2.4 Writing as a Student-Centered Process

The emphasis of a student-centered model of writing is on giving students ample opportunities to find personal meaning in what they write. Rather than being taught in isolation, as they are in more traditional models, skills are part of connected, meaningful experiences in communication. The work of Donald Graves (2003; Graves & Kittle, 2005) has provided a major contribution to the understanding of writing as a student-centered activity (Johnston & Goatley, 2014). His observations of children as they write reveal that even young children go through an interactive authoring process of prewriting, composing (drafting), and postwriting (revising, editing, and publishing), providing educators with the opportunity to implement strategies for increasing skills at each step of this process in the classroom.

Charles Schwartz teaches eighth-grade language arts using a student-centered model. Charles integrates reading, writing, speaking, and listening activities in his language arts program. To document students' progress in writing, Charles uses writing samples, self- and peer evaluations, and teacher observation checklists. His classroom looks like a writing workshop. Charles says that his role is to serve as a writing coach, providing not only encouragement but also direct skills instruction.

Although the student-centered model promotes creativity and student productivity, critics claim that teaching of skills is incidental, inconsistent, and not intensive enough for students who have problems learning to write. This chapter provides specific suggestions for making a student-centered model work for all students in your classroom by ensuring that the mechanics of writing are an essential feature of instruction.

15.2.5 Writing as a Socially Mediated Language-Learning Activity

To become more proficient writers, students must have social interactions with others to move forward (Vygotsky, 1978). Students who have experienced failure in learning to write may be reluctant to share their writing with teachers and peers because they are embarrassed about their lack of skill in writing mechanics. It is important, however, that students have the opportunity not only to share their writing but also to have that sharing focus on the intended meaning rather than on how many words are misspelled. It is also important for young writers to have time to talk with the teacher about composing strategies (Mason & Graham, 2008). For students who are English language learners, interacting with teachers and peers during the process of writing builds language fluency (Peregoy & Boyle, 2013).

MyEdLab **Self-Check 15.2**

MyEdLab **Application Exercise 15.2:** Writing Process

15.3 STRATEGIES FOR ESTABLISHING AN ENVIRONMENT THAT PROMOTES WRITING

From what you have already read about current trends and effective writing instruction, you can imagine the importance of planning the environment in which writing is taught. Gina Terry, a general education teacher, and her teaching partner, Galia Pennecamp, a special education teacher, have created a classroom environment that encourages their fourth-grade students to write. Gina and Galia have learned that the classroom's physical and social environment both need to be considered when teachers establish a writing community.

15.3.1 Physical Environment

As they planned the physical arrangement of their classroom at the beginning of the year, Gina and Galia decided to create a writer's studio in their co-taught classroom. The classroom setting should create a work atmosphere similar to that of a studio—one that promotes independence and in which students can easily interact (Graves, 2003). Gina and Galia felt that structuring their classroom as a studio was especially important for students who had already experienced failure in writing. The message they wanted to convey from day one was "This is a place for writers, and all of us are writers. Enjoy!"

A publishing center is set up for making books. Writing materials and supplies are plentiful and readily available to students. At the beginning of the year, Gina and Galia explain guidelines for using materials in responsible ways. In addition to individual writing folders for ongoing writing projects, each student has an assessment portfolio that serves as a record of his or her progress in writing. Individual folders and portfolios are located in a permanent place in the classroom, ready for student or parent conferences. Gina and Galia wanted the room arranged so that students could work together or individually. They planned spaces for writing conferences of small groups of students, teacher and student, and student and student.

Gina and Galia also realized that many students with disabilities would benefit from having technology and tools readily available to facilitate their writing. For this reason, the following tools and technologies were available in their classroom:

- Computer
- Charts and markers
- Paper with raised lines, highlighted lines, and so forth
- Adaptive grip for pencil or pen
- Word cards/word book/key words in a file
- Pocket dictionary
- Pocket thesaurus
- Electronic talking dictionary/thesaurus
- Voice-recognition software
- Keyboard with easy access
- Adaptive devices for students with disabilities, such as mouth stick/head pointer with alternate or standard keyboard
- Head mouse/head master with onscreen keyboard

Although not every classroom can be equipped with all of the tools that Gina and Galia were able to provide, there are still ways to establish an environment that is rich in literature and encourages writing.

Realizing that for students to write well, an environment of mutual trust and respect is essential, Gina and Galia posted the writing workshop's student guidelines (see Figure 15.4) in their classroom.

The guidelines these teachers follow to establish a social environment for a productive writing community are presented in Tips for Teachers 15.4.

TIPS FOR TEACHERS 15.4

Establishing a Social Environment for Productive Writing

- *Have students write every day for at least 30 minutes.* Students need time to think, write, discuss, rewrite, confer, revise, talk, read, and write some more. Good writing takes time.
- *Encourage students to develop areas of expertise.* At first, students will write broadly about what they know. With encouragement, however, they can become class experts in a particular area, subject, or writing form. Take the time to help students discover their own writing "turf."
- *Model the writing process.* Write with students in the classroom. Using an overhead or easel, teachers may share how they compose.
- *Share writing.* Include in the writing time an opportunity for the whole class to meet to read their writing to others and to exchange comments and questions.
- *Read to the students.* Share and discuss books, poems, and other readings. Young authors can learn from the writing of others.
- *Expand the writing community outside the classroom.* Place books published by your students in the library so that other students can use them and so that students can share their writing with other classes. Encourage authors from other classrooms to visit and read their writing.
- *Develop students' capacity to evaluate their own work.* Students need to develop their own goals and document their progress toward them. By conferring with the teacher, they will learn methods for evaluating their own work.
- *Slow the pace.* When teachers ask questions, they need to be patient, giving students time to answer.

FIGURE 15.4 Writing workshop

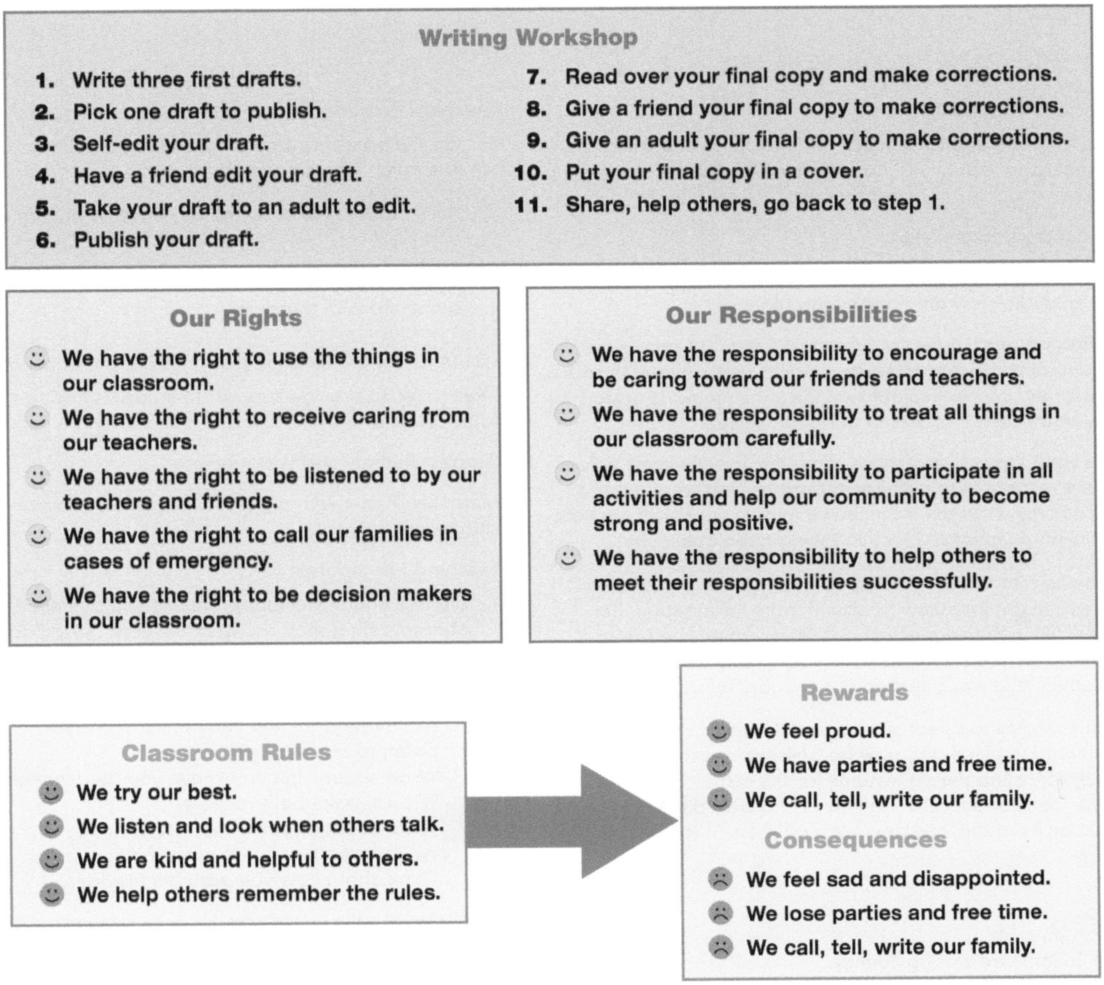

Writing Workshop

1. Write three first drafts.
2. Pick one draft to publish.
3. Self-edit your draft.
4. Have a friend edit your draft.
5. Take your draft to an adult to edit.
6. Publish your draft.
7. Read over your final copy and make corrections.
8. Give a friend your final copy to make corrections.
9. Give an adult your final copy to make corrections.
10. Put your final copy in a cover.
11. Share, help others, go back to step 1.

Our Rights

- We have the right to use the things in our classroom.
- We have the right to receive caring from our teachers.
- We have the right to be listened to by our teachers and friends.
- We have the right to call our families in cases of emergency.
- We have the right to be decision makers in our classroom.

Our Responsibilities

- We have the responsibility to encourage and be caring toward our friends and teachers.
- We have the responsibility to treat all things in our classroom carefully.
- We have the responsibility to participate in all activities and help our community to become strong and positive.
- We have the responsibility to help others to meet their responsibilities successfully.

Classroom Rules

- We try our best.
- We listen and look when others talk.
- We are kind and helpful to others.
- We help others remember the rules.

Rewards

- We feel proud.
- We have parties and free time.
- We call, tell, write our family.

Consequences

- We feel sad and disappointed.
- We lose parties and free time.
- We call, tell, write our family.

Source: "Writing workshop manual," by N. Zaragoza & S. Vaughn, 1995, unpublished manuscript.

15.3.2 Strategies for Conducting a Writing Workshop

If you were to visit Gina and Galia's classroom during their writing workshop, the first thing you would notice is the variety of activities. Some students would be working individually on a writing project; others would be working in small groups or pairs, generating ideas for a book or putting the final touches on a story. You would also observe that the teachers are busy. You might see Gina conferencing with a student. During conferencing, Gina's goals are related to the individual student and might include asking the student to read part of his or her writing aloud, commenting on what particular aspects of the writing are successful, and asking questions that "teach" the student to revise and adjust for improved writing. These conferences typically end with joint decisions about what the student will do next to improve the writing.

In addition to conferencing, you might see Gina or Galia teaching a mini-lesson on punctuation to a small group. You would discover that students often choose their own topics but also are expected to provide writing products that reflect a broad range of writing formats (e.g., letter to a pen pal, story, biography, opinion, argument). Also, students often have two or three writing projects in progress at a time. Some students have even elected to coauthor with a classmate. You would also note that amid all this activity, there is routine. Students seem to know exactly what to do and how to get help if they need it. See the Activities for All Learners feature for writing activities that can include all learners.

ACTIVITIES FOR ALL LEARNERS

Writing Activities for All Learners

Interview a Classmate

Objective: To give students practice in developing and using questions as a means for obtaining more information for the piece they are writing

Grades: Adaptable for all levels

Materials: Writing materials and a writing topic, a list of possible questions, an audio recording device (optional)

Teaching Procedures: Using the format of a radio or television interview, demonstrate and role-play "mock" interviews with sports, movie, music, and political celebrities. Give the students opportunities to play both roles, interviewer and interviewee.

1. Discuss what types of questions allow the interviewee to give elaborate responses (e.g., open questions) and what types of questions only allow the interviewee to give very brief answers (e.g., closed questions). Practice asking open questions.
2. Use a piece that you are writing as an example, and discuss whom you might interview to obtain more information. For example, "In writing a piece about what it might be like to go to the New York World's Fair in 1964, I might interview my grandfather, who was there, to obtain more information."
3. Ask the students to select an appropriate person to interview for their writing piece and to write possible questions. In pairs, the students refine their questions for the actual interview. The students then conduct the interviews and later discuss how information from the interview assisted them in writing the piece.

Flashwriting

Objective: To improve writing fluency

Grades: Intermediate and above

Materials: Paper and pencil, timer

Teaching Procedures:

1. Give students 1 or 2 minutes to think of a topic.
2. Start the timer and give students 5 to 10 minutes to flashwrite about the topic.
3. The goal is to keep writing about the topic. If ideas don't come, instruct students to just write, "I can't think of what to write," until an idea pops up.
4. At the end of the designated time, have pairs of students share their writing.
5. Have the pairs circle key ideas that might be worth developing during extended writing periods.

Sentence Stretching

Objective: To help students learn to elaborate simple sentences

Grades: Intermediate, middle school

Materials: Paper and pencil

Teaching Procedures:

1. On the board, write a simple sentence of two to four words—for example, "The king fell."
2. Have students expand the sentence by adding words and phrases.
3. If you choose, have students illustrate their expanded sentences and share with the class.

Up in the Air for a Topic

Objective: To provide support to students having problems with topic selection

Grades: Primary and intermediate

Materials: Poster with suggestions for topic selection, paper and pencil

Teaching Procedures:

1. During writing workshop, discuss topic selection and ask students what they do when they are "stuck" for a topic.
2. Present the following suggestions on a poster:
   Check your folder and reread your idea list.
   Ask a friend to help you brainstorm ideas.
   Listen to others' ideas.
   Write about what you know: your experiences.
   Write a make-believe story.
   Write about a special interest or hobby.
   Write about how to do something.
   Think about how you got your last idea.
3. Model or solicit examples for each suggestion, add students' other suggestions, and post the chart in the room for students to consult whenever they are "stuck" for a topic.

Finding the Topic by Using the Goldilocks Rule

Objective: To help students brainstorm for expository writing topics

Grades: Intermediate and above

Materials: Paper and pencil, timer

Teaching Procedures:

1. Describe the "Goldilocks procedure." Brainstorm as many ideas as possible in 5 minutes.
   Write down all ideas. Don't stop to read or judge them.
   Stop when timer goes off.

   Organize ideas into categories with the Goldilocks Rule:
   Too broad
   Too narrow
   Just right

   Choose a topic from the "just right" category.
2. Model the use of the Goldilocks procedure.
3. Try out the procedure as a whole-class activity.
4. Have students try out the procedure independently and then share their topics in small groups.

Tell It Again

Objective: To help students learn story elements

Grades: Primary, intermediate

Materials: Paper and pencil, crayons, markers

Teaching Procedure: Story retellings are a good way to determine which elements of a story are familiar (and unfamiliar) to your students. To help students "Tell It Again," follow these steps:

1. Provide a story for your students. It might be a story you read, a story they read independently or with a partner, or a story they heard on TV or on a video.
2. Decide on a retelling format. Students can retell the story by drawing pictures of major events (making a wordless picture book), rewriting and illustrating the story, dramatizing the story, or orally retelling the story to you or to a friend.
3. Keep tabs on the story elements your students include in their retellings. If a story element (such as setting, character, or plot) is missing, provide instruction (either individually, in small groups, or with the class as a whole) about one element at a time. Monitor that element in subsequent retelling assignments.

The RAFT Technique

Objective: To help students learn to vary their writing with respect to writer's role, audience, format, and topic

Grades: Intermediate and above

Materials: Paper and pencil

Teaching Procedures: The RAFT technique was developed by Santa (1988) to help secondary students write in the content areas. RAFT provides a framework for thinking about how to write for different purposes by varying the writer's role, audience, format, and topic. Here's how to teach it:

1. Explain the components of RAFT:
   Role of the writer. Who are you? A professor? A volcano? An ancient Egyptian?
   Audience. Who will be your reader? A friend? A famous athlete? A lawyer?
   Format. What form will your writing take? A brochure? A letter? A newspaper article?
   Topic. What topic have you chosen? Hazards of smoking? Need for gun control? How cheese is made?
2. Write R-A-F-T on the board or on a transparency. Brainstorm with students about possible roles, audiences, formats, and topics. Following is an example:
   R–Role = a liver
   A–Audience = alcoholic
   F–Format = script for TV commercial
   T–Topic = the ill effects of drinking
3. Have students work in cooperative groups to generate other RAFT ideas.
4. Have students work independently to complete a RAFT assignment.

Fix It

Objective: To help students learn to revise their writing in a strategic way

Grades: Intermediate, middle school

Materials: Paper and pencil

Teaching Procedures:

1. Introduce the components of FIX strategy: **F**ocus on the essay, **I**dentify problem areas, E**x**ecute revisions by making additions, rearranging text, deletions, and rewriting.
2. Model the use of the strategy and demonstrate how revisions are made.
3. Encourage students to memorize the strategy.
4. Provide opportunities for small-group and independent practice.

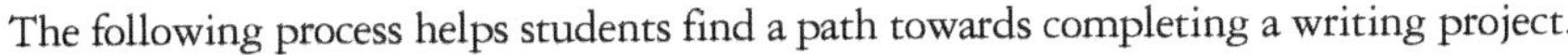

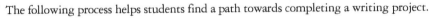

Source: School Power: Strategies for Succeeding in School, by J. S. Schumm, M. C. Radencich, & P. Espeland, 1992, Minneapolis: Free Spirit Publishing; "FIX: A strategic approach to writing and revision for students with learning disabilities," by C. K. Sherman & S. De La Paz, 2015, *Teaching Exceptional Children, 48*(2), 93–101.

The following process helps students find a path towards completing a writing project.

- *Prewriting.* During prewriting, a writer collects information about a topic by observing, remembering, interviewing, and reading.
- *Composing (or drafting).* When composing (or drafting), the author attempts to get ideas on paper in the form of a draft. The drafting process tells the author what he or she knows or does not know.
- *Postwriting.* In postwriting, the author revises, edits, and publishes the work.
  - During revising, the focus is on meaning; points are explored further, ideas are elaborated, and further connections are made.
  - When the author is satisfied with the content, editing takes place as the author reviews the piece line by line to determine whether each word is necessary. Punctuation, spelling, and other mechanical processes are checked.
  - The final element is publishing. If the author considers the piece a good one, it is published.

Video Example from YouTube

MyEdLab
Video Example 15.3.
Watch the YouTube video "Steve Graham: What Works in Teaching Writing." How can you use research-based practices to develop a positive and productive environment for writing in your classroom? https://www.youtube.com/watch?v=klabt03JQY4

MyEdLab **Self-Check 15.3**

MyEdLab **Application Exercise 15.3:** Establishing an Environment for Writing 

15.4 MAKING ADAPTATIONS FOR STRUGGLING WRITERS: TEACHERS' PRACTICES

How do teachers adapt writing instruction for struggling writers? In a survey of upper-elementary teachers (Gilbert & Graham, 2010) to determine their instructional writing practices, results included the following:

- Teachers spent about 15 minutes per day explicitly teaching writing.
- Students spent 25 minutes per day writing more than a paragraph.
- Teachers perceived that they were not well prepared to teach writing.
- Students mostly were asked to use writing as a means to explain what they were learning.

The majority of adaptations in supporting writing involve providing more instruction in basic writing skills. Graham and colleagues emphasized the importance of getting young writers off to a good start and the complexities they face in achieving a command of writing (Graham et al., 2013).

Students with writing problems differ in the degree to which components of the writing process are difficult for them. Many students with writing problems experience significant difficulty in editing and writing final copy because they have difficulty with mechanics. These students often produce well-developed stories that are hard to read because of the mechanical errors. Other students with writing problems have difficulty organizing during the composing stage and need to rethink the sequencing during revision. There is considerable agreement that students use the writing process best when they are taught explicitly how to use each of the elements (e.g., prewriting, revising, conferencing), as described next (Baker et al., 2003; Tompkins, 2014).

15.4.1 Prewriting: Getting Started

"What should I write about?" As a teacher, it's easy to say, "Write about what you did during your summer vacation," but the key to engaging students as writers is to have them select topics. Saying to students "Just write about anything" isn't enough. The following section shows how to help students approach topic selection.

15.4.2 Selecting Topics

How you prompt students to help them generate a list of topics they either know about or want to learn about varies somewhat by grade level. It is critical at each grade level that teachers provide students with some time to generate their own topics of interest in addition to writing about topics generated by the teacher.

For example, with elementary students, the teacher might say, "You know lots of things about yourself, about your family, and about your friends. You have hobbies and activities that you like to do. You have stories about things that have happened to you and to people you know. You have lots of things to share with others. I want you to make a list of things you would like to share with others through writing. Do not put them in any specific order—just write them down as you think of them. You will not have to write on all of these topics. The purpose of this exercise is to think of as many topics as you can. I will give you about 10 minutes. Begin."

Teachers may want to hold students accountable for writing in multiple genres. For example, you might say, "During this 6-week period, I need you to submit a completed composition in each of the following areas: story, opinion, and expository factual report on a topic of interest." For older students, teachers might provide descriptions of the different genres of writing, including personal biography, persuasion, sarcasm, humor, narrative story, and reporting, as a means to facilitate topic generation. Or, teachers might select one or more genres being discussed in class and provide writing examples of these genres, and then ask students to generate a list of topics that would fit each of the genres. Students can then select one genre and identify a specific topic they would like to write about.

One way to model brainstorming for a topic is for the teacher to write a list of things he or she does well, such as a hobbies, sports, or skills, using an LCD (liquid crystal display) or document projector so that students can follow along. The teacher then models his or her thought process while eliminating ideas and selecting one item from the list to write about. Students then develop their own "expert lists" (Tompkins, 2014) by writing as many topics as they can think of during the assigned time. When time is up, students can pick partners and share their topics, or topics can be shared with the entire group. Students may add any new topics they think of during the sharing step. Next, students select the three topics they are most interested in writing about and place their topic lists in their writing folders as a resource for future writing. Finally, students select one of their top three topics and begin writing.

15.4.3 Problems in Topic Selection

Maintaining a supply of writing topics is difficult for some students. When students tell you stories, ask them whether the stories generate a topic they might want to write about. When students read or you read to them, ask whether the reading has given them ideas for their own writing. If they were going to write a new ending for the story, how would they do it? If they were going to continue this story, what would happen? If they were going to add characters to the story, what types of characters would they add? Would they change the setting?

Some students want to repeat the same topic or theme, especially students with writing problems, who may find security in such repetition. In such cases, suggest that students use more precise words, add characters, or adjust the theme. These changes may assist them in progressing as writers while continuing to provide the security of sticking with a comfortable topic. With older students, it may be useful to provide them with choices about the topic they write about but limit the choices to align with instructional goals.

15.4.4 Planning

Prewriting entails developing a plan for writing. Planning for writing includes the following three steps:

1. ***Identify the intended audience.*** To make a writing project meaningful, the writer must identify the audience. Who will be the reader? The audience might be family, friends, businesspeople, politicians, teachers, potential employers—or oneself.
2. ***State a purpose for writing.*** The purpose for writing may be to inform, entertain, express an opinion, or present an argument. An example of a purpose statement is: "I am writing this story about my imaginary pet shark, Gums, to entertain my friends."
3. ***Decide on a format.*** Before writing begins, writers should have a general idea of how the piece will be structured. Although the structure may change during drafting and revision, this will provide an initial road map at the prewriting stage.

Some students are limited in text-organization skills because they have difficulty categorizing ideas related to a specific topic, providing advance organizers for the topic, and relating and extending ideas about the topic (Mason & Graham, 2008; Tomlinson, 2012). Some students lack strategies for planning or resist planning because it takes up too much time (Lassonde & Richards, 2013). As you teach the thinking process that goes into a piece of writing, you can model your own thinking as you move from topic selection; to planning for audience, purpose, and format; to drafting. During whole-class sharing time, you can also encourage students to describe how they generated topics and planned for their own writing.

15.4.5 Composing

The purpose of the composing stage is to develop an initial draft that will be refined later. Some teachers call this a *sloppy copy*. Many students with learning and behavior problems think of a topic and, without much planning, begin writing. Composing is also difficult for students who lack fluency in the mechanics of writing or in the physical act of writing (Datchuk, 2015; Scott & Vitale, 2003). During composing, you should assume the role of coach and encourage students to concentrate on getting their ideas on paper.

The purpose of revision is to make certain that the meaning is clear and that the message can be understood by others. *Editing* focuses mainly on mechanics, such as proofreading. After the students and teacher are happy with the content, it is time to finalize the correction of spelling, capitalization, punctuation, and language.

15.4.6 Editing

During editing, students circle words that might be spelled incorrectly, put boxes where they are unsure of punctuation, and underline sentences in which they feel the language may not be correct. Students are not expected to correct all errors, but are expected to correct known errors. Revising and editing are difficult tasks for all writers, especially beginning writers and students for whom writing is difficult. Getting the entire message down on paper the first time is difficult enough; making changes so that the piece is at its best and can be understood by others is a most formidable task.

15.4.7 Revising

Revising, which means attending to meaning and making adjustments to a written document, is an ongoing process. Through modeling and feedback, students will learn that they may need to revise once, twice, or more until their intended meaning is expressed clearly and completely. Most students with writing difficulties have difficulty revising their work. Teachers can do the following to support students in revising their work:

- Model the revision process for students by using your own writing and doing a "think-aloud" about how you revise. Display a draft of a written document you composed (e.g., a letter, an email, a paragraph) and say to students, "You can see the first draft of what I've written. Like you, I don't like to revise, but I know it will make my writing better and clearer. This is what I do. First, I reread it and think about whether I am communicating clearly the points that I think are important. After I make changes, I then reread it and wonder if I have used the most precise words, and then I edit several words to make my writing sharper. Then I reread and consider whether I have accurately used the mechanics of writing, including spelling, punctuation, and capitalization. My last step is to ask others to read it so I can use their feedback to further revise."
- Teach students that work "before writing" may help reduce the amount of revision needed later. Students should identify the topics and the big ideas that they intend to include. Also, students can make a list of words to include that will sharpen what they are writing. In addition, students should consider what their opening and closing points will be to tie the writing together.
- Students should be led to realize that although revising is often considered "work," it can actually be the most fun part of writing. This is the polishing step that can take a rough piece and make it beautiful.

Adolescents with disabilities can learn procedures such as *compare*, *diagnose*, and *operate* to assist them during the revision process. When teachers model, demonstrate, and provide feedback using the procedure described in Tips for Teachers 15.5, students' revisions and writing improve.

Peer editing

In addition to revising and editing their own work, students can serve as editors for the work of their peers. Peer editing can work several ways. One way is to have students edit

TIPS FOR TEACHERS 15.5

Teaching Students to Compare, Diagnose, and Operate

1. Compare and diagnose. Read your writing and consider the following:
   - Does it ignore the obvious points against my idea?
   - Does it have too few ideas?
   - Part of the essay doesn't belong with the rest.
   - Part of the essay is not in the right order.
2. Tactic operations.
   - Rewrite.
   - Delete.
   - Add.
   - Move.
3. Compare. Reread the paper and highlight problems.
4. Diagnose and operate.
   - This doesn't sound right.
   - This isn't what I intended to say.
   - This is an incomplete idea.
   - This part is not clear ____________________.
   - The problem is ____________________.

The following suggestions help students remove the mechanical barriers from their writing:

- Have students dictate their stories to improve the flow of their writing.
- Provide students with a list of key words and difficult-to-spell words to assist with writing and editing.
- Promote peer collaboration in editing.

Source: Information from "Mechanical obstacles to writing: What can teachers do to help students with learning problems?" by S. Isaacson & M. M. Gleason, 1997, *Learning Disabilities Research and Practice, 12*(3), 188–194.

their own work first and then ask a friend to edit it. Another way is to establish a class editor who is responsible for reading the material and finding mechanical errors. The role of class editor can rotate so that every student has an opportunity to serve in that capacity.

It is important that students not be too critical while revising and editing one another's work. You can communicate that the purpose of revising and editing is to support the author in developing a finished piece. You can also model acceptable ways to give feedback.

15.4.8 Publishing

Not all student writing is published; often only one in five or six pieces are published. **Publishing** means preparing a piece so that others can read it. Publication is often in the form of books with cardboard bindings decorated with contact paper or scraps of wallpaper. Books can include a picture of the author, a description of the author, and a list of books published by the author. Young children writing short pieces may publish every 2 weeks; older students who spend more time composing and revising publish less frequently.

Publishing is a way to confirm a student's hard work and share it with others. Publishing is also a way to involve others in school and at home with the students' writing. It is important for all students to publish, not just the best authors.

15.4.9 Sharing

Sharing work with others is important during all stages of the writing process. The author's chair (Graves & Hansen, 1983; Hall, 2014) is a formal opportunity to share writing. When Romain, a student who recently moved from Haiti to the United States, signed up for author's chair early in the school year, Galia and Gina were surprised. Romain, the most reluctant writer in their class, was also extremely self-conscious about not being able to spell. During author's chair, Romain sat on a special stool in a circle of peers and read his letter to an imaginary pen pal in Haiti. He described life in Miami and ended with a wish: "I hope that you are happy and have enough food to eat." It turned out that most of

Romain's story wasn't written at all—he held a paper in front of him and made up the letter as he spoke. But because Romain got a positive response from his audience about how well he communicated his ideas, he was encouraged to become a writer. The author's chair experience was his launching point. Using author's chair can be facilitated by having the student present the writing on a computer and then projecting it on an LCD so that all of the students can view the work at the same time (Labbo, 2004).

Setting rules for sharing

Teachers often need to set rules for students' behavior when a classmate is sharing work, whether it is with another student or with the class as a whole. Procedures for responding to the writing of others follows:

1. Listen until the author is finished (if the author is reading his or her work) or read the entire draft if you are reading the written work.
2. Make notes about what you like and think might be improved.
3. Start with the parts of the writing that you like. Ask the writer what could be done to make those parts even better.
4. Identify the parts of the writing you think could be improved. Provide specific suggestions, including what paragraphs connect well and which ones need transitions, which sentences are clear and which ones are unclear, which words might be replaced, and how mechanics could be improved.

Some students may be reluctant to share their writing with the whole class even when the teacher has established a supportive and inviting environment. Students who are naturally shy, have emerging proficiency in English, experience difficulties with reading and/or writing, or who have a written product that is highly personal in nature may feel uncomfortable under the spotlight (Hall, 2014). In such cases, alternative sharing opportunities (e.g., digital sharing, sharing in a small group) can be implemented.

15.4.10 Conferencing

The heart of the writing workshop—the student–teacher writing conference—is ongoing. The student comes to the writing conference prepared to read his or her piece, to describe problem areas, and to respond to questions. Students know that the teacher will listen and respond and that they will be asked challenging questions about their work. Questions should be carefully selected, with enough time allotted for the student to respond. Even though you may see many problems with the piece of writing, try to focus on only one or two specific areas. Some key points about conferencing with students are presented in Tips for Teachers 15.6.

MyEdLab
Video Example 15.4.
Watch the YouTube video "Give Great Writing Feedback." What can you do as a classroom teacher to give students feedback in positive ways and to teach students how to give and receive peer feedback? https://www.youtube.com/watch?v=JGFhbDO-UQ

Teaching writing skills

A frequently asked question is, "When do I teach skills?" This question is especially important for teachers whose students have poor writing skills to begin with. Prolific writing activities without help from a teacher will not lead to improvement (Gillespie & Graham, 2014; Graham & Perin, 2007).

Skills lessons can be taught to the class as a whole and then in small groups composed of students who need additional knowledge and practice with a specified skill. Skills lessons, or mini-lessons, should be brief (15 to 20 minutes), and the topics for these lessons should be based on the students' needs. Ideas for topics can come from your observations of student writing, requests for help, and data from writing conferences.

After teaching a skill and providing ample opportunities to practice it, help students to generalize and apply the skill in their daily writing. As Graham (1992) recommended for students with writing problems, skills are best taught in the context of "real" writing and have the most impact when they bring the greatest rewards in writing improvement.

TIPS FOR TEACHERS 15.6

Guidelines for Conducting a Writing Conference

Big Principles of a Writing Conference

- *Follow the student's lead during the conference.* Avoid starting with your critical feedback. Instead, start with a question and listen to the student: What do you think is working for you in this writing? Where are your challenges with this writing?
- *Listen to and accept what the student says.* When you talk more than the writer does during conferences, you are being too directive.
- *Ask questions that teach.* Ask students questions that help them understand what needs to be revised and what steps to take next with their writing.
- *Make conferences frequent and brief.* Although conferences can range from 30 seconds to 10 minutes, most last 2 to 3 minutes.
- *Listen to what students have written and tell them what you hear.* Learning to listen to what they are communicating from the perspective of a reader is essential for students to learn to make effective revisions.
- *Provide a few specific suggestions and set a plan with the student for revision.* Even when writing has many problems, it is best to pick a couple and establish a plan with the student for revision. Too many changes are overwhelming and discourage revision.

Suggestions to Compliment Writing

- I like the way your paper began in this way ...
- I like the part where ...
- I like the way you explained ...
- I like the order you used in your paper because ...
- I like the details you used to describe ...
- I like the way you used dialogue to make your story sound real. In particular, this section ...
- I like the action and the descriptive words you used in your writing, such as ...
- I like the facts you used, such as ...
- I like the way the paper ended because ...
- I like the mood of your writing because it made me feel ...

Questions and Suggestions to Improve Writing

- I got confused in the part about ...
- Could you add an example to the part about ...
- Could you add more to this part because ...
- Do you think your order would make more sense if you ...
- Do you think you could leave this part out because ...
- Could you use a different word for _________ because ...
- Is this paragraph on one topic?
- Could you write a beginning sentence to "grab" your readers?
- What happens in the end?
- Can you think of another word for "said"?

MyEdLab **Self-Check 15.4**

MyEdLab **Application Exercise 15.4:** Narrative Writing: Revising

15.5 STRATEGIES FOR TEACHING NARRATIVE, EXPOSITORY, AND OPINION/ARGUMENT WRITING

What types of writing do teachers address? Typically, teachers assist students in writing narratives, often thought of as the story structure of writing; expository writing, thought of as informational writing; and opinion/argument writing, and often considered the type of writing used to express a view and/or to present an evidence-based claim. The Common Core State Standards include standards for narrative, informational, and opinion writing in grades K through 5 and narrative, informational, and argument writing in grades 6 through 12. Many approaches to teaching writing are used generally across all writing genres, but there are several specific instructional practices that can be employed within each genre.

15.5.1 Narrative Writing

In the elementary grades and in middle school, students typically practice narrative writing (writing stories). For many students, story writing is not a problem. Through hearing and reading stories, they have learned the basic elements of a story and can incorporate them into their own storytelling and writing. Students with writing problems may be aware of story elements but may not incorporate them into their writing in a systematic way unless they are provided instructional support (Graham & Harris, 2006; MacArthur, Graham, & Fitzgerald, 2008). Students with writing problems may also exhibit the following problems when they compose stories:

- Lack of organization
- Lack of unity and coherence
- Lack of character development
- Incomplete use of story elements

Story webbing and direct instruction on the development of story elements are effective ways to address these difficulties.

Using story webs to plan

Story webs, or *maps*, were originally developed as visual displays to help students understand the structure of the stories they read. Stories are composed of predictable elements and have a characteristic narrative structure, or story grammar. Elements of stories include the setting, characters, a problem statement, the goal, the event sequence or episodes, and the resolution or ending. Using story webs such as the one shown in Figure 15.5, students can trace these elements when they read, plan, or write a story.

You can conduct mini-lessons on webbing with your whole class or just with students who need help with story planning. To introduce the story web, first talk about its components and model its use in planning a story. You might want to have students work together in small, mixed-ability groups to plan a group story.

FIGURE 15.5 An example of a story web

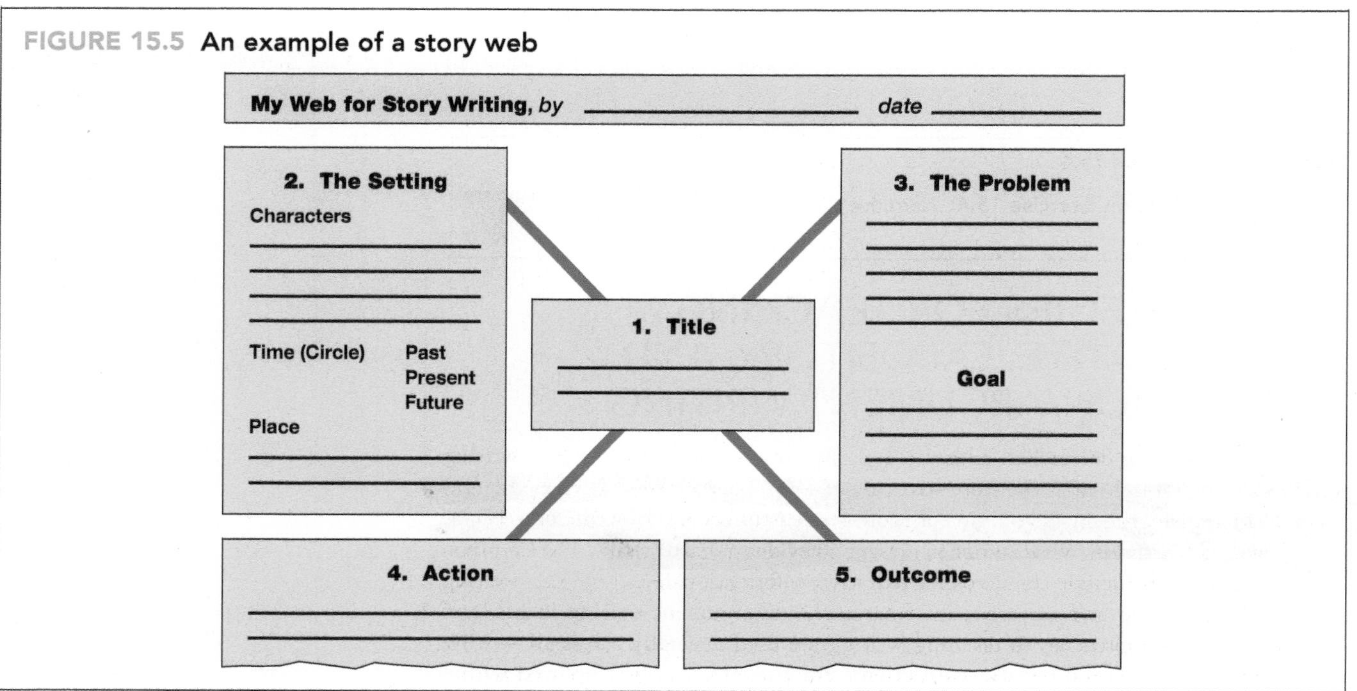

Source: "Teaching web-making as a guided planning tool to improve student narrative writing," by M. Zipprich, 1995, *Remedial and Special Education, 16*(1), 3–15, 52. Copyright © 1995 by PRO-ED, Inc. Reprinted by permission.

FIGURE 15.6 **Story check**

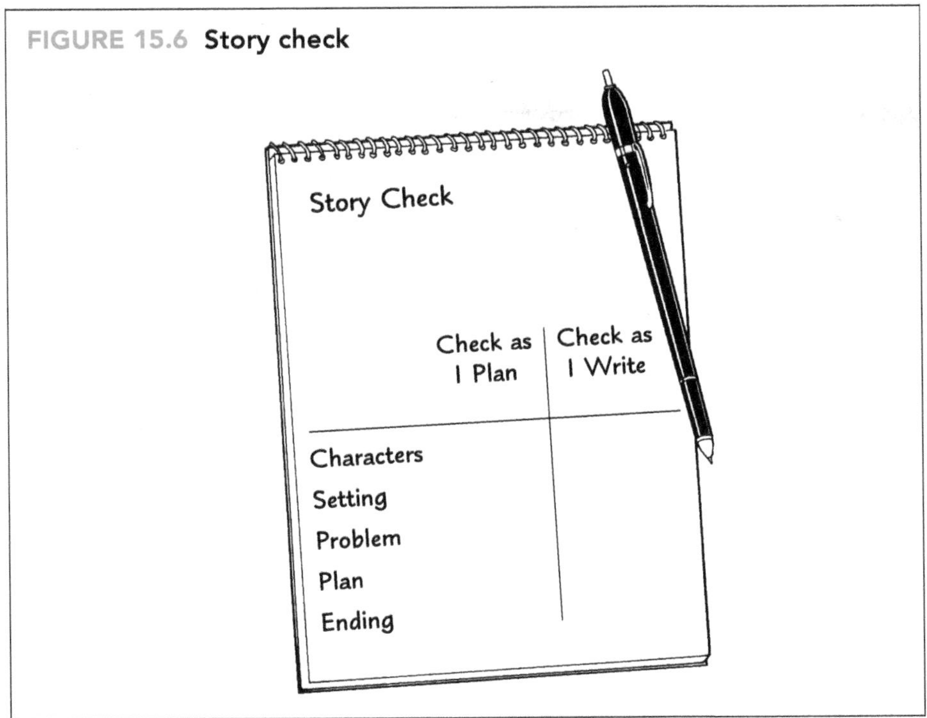

Source: "Using cues and prompts to improve story writing," by A. Graves & R. Hauge, 1993, *Teaching Exceptional Children, 25*(4), 38–45. Copyright 1993 by the Council for Exceptional Children. Reprinted with permission.

Some students might include a story element, such as a main character, in their stories but fail to develop the element fully. Graves and Hauge (1993) developed the cue sheet shown in Figure 15.6 to help students improve their story writing.

15.5.2 Expository Writing

Expository writing, or informational writing, once reserved for middle and upper grades, is now being included in the curriculum for even very young students. Expository writing poses particular difficulty for students with writing problems who may be unaware of the purpose of informational writing (Mason & Graham, 2008). What does expository writing do? This type of writing is used to explain, describe, present information, or instruct. There are many examples, such as newspapers, magazine articles, textbooks, essays, directions, guidebooks, and many of the articles on the web.

Tompkins (2014) describes several expository writing structures:

- *Description.* Students select a topic and provide characteristics, features, and examples related to the topic. What are some examples of description? Any topic in which students delineate information: World War II airplanes; the elephant life cycle; the sinking of the *Titanic.* What can teachers do to promote effective descriptive writing? Teach students to: (a) specify the topic, (b) identify sources, (c) organize key ideas, (d) identify key facts, and (e) list key words and technical terms.
- *Comparison:* Students select two or more related things and describe how they are alike and different. What are some examples of comparison? Any two or more people, events, places, or things that can be compared and contrasted: two historical leaders; two political parties; two or more events related scientifically or socially; two or more places; two or more ideas. What can teachers do to promote effective comparison writing? Teach students to: (a) use comparison words such as *different, like, same, similar, compared to, different from,* and *in contrast with*; (b) assist students in identifying related constructs to compare; (c) tell students to identify significant

ways in which the constructs are alike and different; and (d) provide written formats to model in which constructs are compared and contrasted.

- *Cause and Effect.* Students select an issue and discuss what caused or is related to the issue to explain why things happened as they did. Cause and effect can be used in social studies, English language arts, and science. What can teachers do to promote effective cause-and-effect writing? Teach students to: (a) identify an issue that requires explanation; (b) research the issue to better understand what caused the particular outcome, or why something happened; (c) look for counterarguments to build a stronger explanation; and (d) use terms such as *reasons*, *why*, *if*, *then*, *therefore*, *because*, *as a result of*, and *in addition to this point*.

15.5.3 Paragraph Writing

Whether students are writing narrative text or expository, many of them have difficulty organizing paragraphs to connect with previous and subsequent paragraphs. Students with writing problems often have difficulty developing coherent, logical paragraphs. The PLEASE strategy (Welch, 1992; Welch & Link, 1989) was developed to provide students with a step-by-step procedure for paragraph writing:

Pick the topic, audience, and paragraph type (cause/effect, compare/contrast, etc.).

List information about the topic.

Evaluate whether the list is complete and also determine how to order items in the list.

Activate your writing by starting with a topic sentence.

Supply supporting or detail sentences, using items from the list.

End with a strong concluding sentence, and evaluate the paragraph by revising and editing.

Developing coherent paragraphs is a challenge for many students. Consequently, this strategy is an effective tool to use with all writers.

15.5.4 Essay Writing

Students in secondary grades progress from writing paragraphs to writing well-developed essays. Some parents and educators resist what is referred to as "formulaic writing," or the five-paragraph essay. Formulas for developing a five-paragraph essay are variations on the same theme. For example, bing, bang, bongo: paragraph 1—list bing, bang, bongo; paragraph 2—write about bing; paragraph 3—write about bang; paragraph 4—write about bongo; paragraph 5—summarize bing, bang, and bongo. Despite resistance, many teachers find such formulas helpful in preparing students for standardized writing tests, particularly for students who need scaffolding and structure.

De La Paz and colleagues (De La Paz, 1999; De La Paz & Graham, 2002; De La Paz, Owen, Harris, & Graham, 2000; Harris, Graham, Mason, & Friedlander, 2008) have used two strategies effectively to facilitate improved essay writing for students with writing difficulties, PLAN and WRITE, as described next. Figure 15.7 provides a template for planning essays.

15.5.5 Opinion/Argument Writing

For some time, many state assessments and other high-stakes tests such as the ACT included persuasive writing components. Persuasive writing is a format in which the writer tries to convince or persuade the reader of his or her position or opinion. Persuasive writing is not mentioned in the Common Core State Standards. Rather, opinion writing is incorporated in standards in grades K through 5 and argument writing is included in standards in grades 6 through 12. Students begin with writing opinion pieces to take a point of view on a topic and to support that point of view with facts and details. In middle

FIGURE 15.7 **Informational essay planning**

KEY Theme or Idea

PEOPLE OR GROUPS

VOCABULARY

EVENTS

WHAT CHANGED?

school and high school students are expected to produce more sophisticated argument pieces using multiple data sources to provide evidence to support claims—and to incorporate opposing claims as well.

Writing opinion/argument essays involves planning and critical thinking. The most important activity is to consider the evidence and to consider the multiple views of persons interpreting the evidence. For example, when considering the effects of "climate change," consider the views of individuals who have different interpretations and how they build their arguments for their positions. This helps writers determine their own position and their own arguments.

For students to develop proficiency in opinion/argument writing, teacher modeling and peer support are important (Read, Landon-Hays, & Martin-Rivas, 2014). This is particularly true for English language learners (Ferlazzo & Hull-Sypnieski, 2014). To help all students compose well-developed and well-supported opinion/argument, consider using the STOP and DARE strategy (De La Paz & Graham, 1997; Ferretti & Lewis, 2013). Here are the steps:

1. ***Suspend judgment.*** First, ask students to suspend their own judgment about the topic, keep an open mind, and write a list of pros and cons about the topic. Use evidence to establish multiple perspectives.
2. ***Take a side.*** Next, ask students to decide which side they believe in most and for which they can build the best argument. Sometimes it is also useful for students to build a written argument for a position with which they don't agree.
3. ***Organize ideas.*** Tell students to reflect on their pro/con lists and identify the strongest points they can make to support their point of view. Have students identify points from the opposite side that they want to refute.

Video Example from YouTube

MyEdLab
Video Example 15.5.
Watch the YouTube video "Bubble Gum Letters: A Persuasive Writing Activity" and notice how the how the teacher works with her students to chart out ideas about why they want to break a rule about no bubble gum in school for just a day. Do you think this is an effective strategy for teaching persuasive writing, and if so, what about it did you feel was most effective, and if not, why not? https://www.youtube.com/watch?v=mweU8U6D798/

FIGURE 15.8 STOP and DARE cue cards

Step 1

Suspend judgment
Did I list ideas for both sides? If not, do this now.

Suspend judgment
Can I think of anything else?
Try to write more.

Suspend judgment
Another point I haven't considered is . . .
Think of possible arguments.

Step 2

Take a side
Place a "+" at the top of one box to show the side you will take in your essay.

Step 3

Organize ideas
Put a star next to ideas you want to use.
Choose at least ______ ideas to use.

Organize ideas
Did I star ideas on both sides?
Choose at least ______ arguments that you can dispute.

Organize ideas
Number your ideas in the order you will use.

Step 4

Plan more as you write
Remember to use all four essay parts:
Develop your topic sentence.
Add supporting ideas.
Reject possible arguments.
End with a conclusion.

Source: Information from "STOP and DARE: A persuasive writing strategy," by S. De La Paz, 2001, *Intervention in School and Clinic, 36,* 237. Copyright 2001 by PRO-ED, Inc.

4. ***Plan more as you write.*** As students refine and reorganize their essays, ask them to keep the components of DARE in mind (see the STOP and DARE cue card in Figure 15.8).

Writing opinion/argument essays can be incorporated into content areas such as science and social studies as well as reading or language arts. To give students experience and practice with this type of writing, find examples for them to consider—such as advertisements, commercials, blogs, tweets, letters to the editor, campaign speeches, and movie or book reviews.

MyEdLab **Self-Check 15.5**

MyEdLab **Application Exercise 15.5:** Persuasive Writing (Opinion/Argument Text)

15.6 TEACHING SPELLING SKILLS

Even in the age of computers with spell-check programs, learning how to spell is important. If a writer is bogged down with the spelling of even commonly used words, progress in writing is stymied. Students with spelling difficulties pause more often during writing, experience interruptions in their concentration during the writing process, and often limit word choice to words they feel more comfortable in spelling (Graham & Santangelo, 2014;

FIGURE 15.9 Characteristics of learners in five stages of development

Stage 1: Precommunicative Spelling
- Uses scribbles, letter-like forms, letters, and sometimes numbers to represent a message.
- May write from left to right, right to left, top to bottom, or randomly on the page.
- Shows no understanding of phoneme–grapheme correspondences.
- May repeat a few letters again and again or use most of the letters of the alphabet.
- Frequently mixes upper- and lowercase letters but shows a preference for uppercase letters.

Stage 2: Semiphonetic Spelling
- Becomes aware of the alphabetic principle that letters are used to represent sounds.
- Uses abbreviated one-, two-, or three-letter spelling to represent an entire word.
- Uses letter–name strategy to spell words (e.g., *U* for *you*).

Stage 3: Phonetic Spelling
- Represents all essential sound features of a word in spelling.
- Develops particular spellings for long and short vowels, plural and past-tense markers, and other aspects of spelling.
- Chooses letters on the basis of sound, without regard for English letter sequences or other conventions.

Stage 4: Transitional Spelling
- Adheres to basic conventions of English orthography.
- Begins to use morphological and visual information in addition to phonetic information.
- May include all appropriate letters in a word but reverse some of them.
- Uses alternate spellings for the same sound in different words, but only partially understands the conditions governing their use.
- Uses a high percentage of correctly spelled words.

Stage 5: Correct Spelling
- Applies the basic rules of the English orthographic system.
- Extends knowledge of word structure, including the spelling of affixes, contractions, compound words, and homonyms.
- Demonstrates growing accuracy in using silent consonants and doubling consonants before adding suffixes.
- Recognizes when a word doesn't "look right" and can consider alternate spellings for the same sound.
- Learns irregular spelling patterns.
- Learns consonant and vowel alternations, and other morphological structures.

Knows how to spell a large number of words.

Source: "An analysis for developmental spelling in GNYS AT WRK," by J. R. Gentry, 1982, *The Reading Teacher, 36*(2), 192–200. Copyright by the International Reading Association.

Sumner, Connelly, & Barnett, 2013). Many students with reading and other disabilities are poor spellers. Spelling, like reading, involves phonological awareness and morphological awareness (see Figure 15.9).

Spelling instruction is important for all students, but the students in your class are likely to differ in terms of their stages of development, the types of errors they make, and what skills they need to learn to become better spellers and thus more fluent writers. What instructional methods can you use to teach all your students to spell?

15.6.1 Approaches to Spelling Instruction

For decades, researchers and practicing educators have debated about the best way to teach spelling. The controversy boils down to the issue of whether learning how to spell is "caught" or "taught" (Gentry & Graham, 2010; Graham & Santangelo, 2014). Some contend that learning how to spell occurs naturally as students learn to read and write—or spelling is "caught" (Edelsky, 1990; Krashen, 1989, 2002). If spelling tests are incorporated, words are drawn from content area texts, novels, or student's self-selected words (Schlagal, 2013). Others advocate an approach to spelling instruction that includes systematic teaching of spelling patterns, generalizations, and word study—or spelling is "taught." In a recent analysis of the research literature, Graham and Santangelo (2014), found that systematic instruction in spelling for students in grades kindergarten through 12 resulted in improvements in spelling, but also in phonological awareness and reading. How spelling is taught varies considerably in the United States (Schlagal, 2013). Two typical instructional formats follow.

Mary Jacobs uses a traditional spelling instruction model in her third-grade class. All students in the class have the same third-grade spelling book. Each lesson in the speller focuses on a particular pattern (e.g., long vowels, short vowels, vowel plus *r*, prefixes). On Monday, Mary gives a spelling pretest on the week's fifteen new words, and for homework students write each word they missed five times. On Tuesday and Wednesday nights, students are assigned exercises in the spelling book. On Thursday night, they write one sentence using the word for each word on the list. On Friday during class, Mary gives students a spelling test on the fifteen words. Some teachers vary this traditional pattern by selecting words from the basal reader or from the current science or social studies unit. Keeping in mind that a "one size fits all" approach will frustrate students who are exceptional spellers and those who struggle with spelling, Mary plans appropriate adaptations to ensure positive learning experiences for all students.

Renee Blanter's school district has adopted an approach to spelling instruction based on individual developmental needs of students (Bear, Invernizzi, Templeton, & Johnston, 2015). At the beginning of the school year, students are administered a developmental spelling inventory and Renee analyzes student's mastery of phonological and morphological patterns. Renee forms instructional groups of students with similar developmental levels and instructional needs. The program Renee uses, *Words Their Way* (Bear et al., 2015), provides weekly lesson plans, materials for sorting words, games, and activities that students can use in small teacher-led groups, peer groups, and independently. Renee monitors student performance regularly to determine student progress and to restructure groups as necessary.

15.6.2 Spelling Instruction for Students with Learning Difficulties and Disabilities

How appropriate is explicit instruction in spelling for classrooms that include students of different academic levels? Many students who are good spellers know all the words at the beginning of the week and so have no real challenge. For students with learning difficulties, fifteen words may be too many to learn, feedback about their errors may be ineffective, and the amount of practice may be insufficient. In addition, traditional spelling instruction does not teach for transfer to new situations. Students often learn words from their spelling list and get 100% on the test, but misspell those same words in their compositions.

A review of spelling interventions (Wanzek et al., 2006) indicated that spelling practices that provide students with spelling strategies or systematic study and word practice methods yield the highest rates of spelling improvement. Instructional practice recommendations include:

1. ***A weekly list of words.*** Students perform better in spelling when they have a list of words each week that are related (e.g., same spelling patterns or thematically related), when they are required to demonstrate proficiency, and when they realize that spelling these words correctly in their writing is expected.
2. ***Error imitation and modeling.*** Students with learning disabilities need to compare each incorrectly spelled word with the correct spelling. The teacher copies the incorrect spelling and then writes the word correctly, calling attention to features in the word that will help students remember the correct spelling.
3. ***Unit size.*** Students with learning disabilities tend to become overloaded and have difficulty when they have to study several words at once. These students can learn to spell if the unit size of their assigned list is reduced to three words a day and if effective instruction is offered for those three words.
4. ***Modality.*** When studying words, students with learning disabilities learn equally well by (a) writing the words, (b) arranging and tracing letter shapes or tiles, and (c) typing the words on a computer. Most students prefer to practice their spelling words on a computer.
5. ***Computer-assisted instruction.*** Computer-assisted instruction (CAI) has been shown to be effective in improving the spelling skills of students with learning

disabilities. CAI software programs for spelling improvement often emphasize awareness of word structure and spelling strategies and make use of time delay, voice simulation, and sound effects.

6. ***Peer tutoring.*** A teacher's individual help is preferable, but structured peer tutoring can be a viable alternative. Students can be assigned a peer partner to practice writing the words with and without a prompt and can give each other feedback on the accuracy of the spelling.
7. ***Study techniques.*** Study techniques provide a format and standard procedure that help students with learning disabilities organize their study of spelling. Wheatley (2005) advocates strategic spelling rather than rote memorization of words.
8. ***Connecting spelling and word meaning.*** Students in the upper-elementary and secondary grades can learn to think about the meaning and spelling of common prefixes, suffixes, and roots (e.g., *-meter*, *tele-*, *oper-*) to assist them in better understanding what a certain word means and also in spelling it correctly.

Meredith Millan is a third-grade teacher whose three students with learning disabilities require that they receive specialized instruction. Meredith and the special education teacher have agreed that Meredith will assign students their weekly spelling words. Meredith has worked hard to integrate spelling instruction into her ongoing writing program. She likes the idea of having weekly spelling tests but knows that the range of student spelling levels in her class is too broad for all students to benefit from having the same words and the same number of words to learn. The following sections describe the way Meredith has structured her spelling program.

Selecting words

Meredith teaches spelling words that correspond with the phonics rules she is teaching in reading. For example, if she is teaching students the VCe rule (vowel, consonant, silent *e* as in *time*) as part of word study she also uses VCe word types for her spelling list. This allows her to connect reading and spelling rules and capitalize on the patterns of language (Carreker, 1999; Moats, 2000). This procedure can be used for older students as well. If students are progressing beyond rule-based instruction in reading, then spelling words can be selected from their writing errors or from key words used in their social studies and science instruction.

Each student in Meredith's class keeps a spelling log, which is a running list of words. At the beginning of the week, students select words from the log for the Friday spelling test and write the words on their homework sheets. Meredith and each student agree in advance on the number of words. Some students have five or six words, others as many as twenty. Meredith also assigns all students two to three words from the thematic unit they are studying at the time. Words that students misspell are taken from the edited drafts of their compositions. During a writing conference, Meredith not only discusses the words a student should add to his or her spelling log, but also asks, "Are there other words you really would like to learn to spell?" and adds them to the log.

Providing instruction and practice

Meredith provides spelling instruction and practice in four ways: through mini-lessons, student pairs, parental involvement, and collaboration with the special education teacher. Each week Meredith provides mini-lessons on spelling patterns. For example, she noticed that about twenty students were using *-ing* words in their writing and spelling them incorrectly. Meredith met with this group for 2 weeks, gave them mini-lessons on adding *-ing*, and included *-ing* words on their spelling tests.

Early in the school year, Meredith figured out that ten of her students needed more practice preparing for spelling tests. She decided to have these students work in pairs. The pairs met for 15 minutes three times a week, usually while other students were composing during writing workshop. Meredith involves parents in the spelling program in two ways. First, at the beginning of the year, she writes parents a letter about the spelling program and ways in which parents can help their child study for spelling tests. Second, she invites parents to add one or two words to the spelling list each week. Parents observe their children's writing at home and can pick up on important misspellings.

Two of the students with learning disabilities, Kara and Mitchell, needed additional help learning their words. In collaboration with Meredith, the special education teacher helped Kara and Mitchell learn and maintain new words by using individualized approaches to word study, including ensuring that the students knew the phonics patterns in the words and then using strategies for writing, checking, correcting, and rewriting spelling words until they were written correctly and automatically.

Monitoring student progress

There are basically three ways to assess student spelling: dictation, error-detection or proofreading tasks, and examination of student spelling in composition products (Hallahan, Lloyd, Kauffman, Weiss, & Martinez, 2005). She includes both dictation and error-detection formats as part of her weekly spelling tests. Meredith uses a spelling rubric in writing workshop (see Figure 15.10).

All students take their Friday spelling test during the same class period. Because it is not possible to give thirty-six students individual spelling dictation tests based on the words in their spelling logs, Meredith pairs the students so they can test each other. Students follow these strict guidelines during the test period:

- You can talk only to your partner and only about the test.
- You cannot give or receive information about how to spell words.
- You must take your test in ink—no erasing allowed.

FIGURE 15.10 Spelling rubric

Name: ______________________ **Date:** __________

Title of Writing Assignment: ______________ **Spelling Strategy Used:** __________

Spelling Rubric

CRITERIA	5	4	3	2	1
Circles all misspelled words	Student found and circled all misspelled words.	Student circled 75%–99% of misspelled words.	Student circled 50%–74% of misspelled words.	Student circled 25%–49% of misspelled words.	Student circled 1%–24% of misspelled words.
Accurately corrects all circled misspelled words	Student accurately corrected all circled misspelled words.	Student accurately corrected 75%–99% of circled misspelled words.	Student accurately corrected 50%–74% of circled misspelled words.	Student accurately corrected 25%–49% of circled misspelled words.	Student accurately corrected 1%–24% of circled misspelled words.
Always uses sounding-out, spell checker, dictionary, or similar words to spell words without help.	Student always used one of the taught spelling strategies to spell words correctly on his or her own.	Student almost always used one of the taught spelling strategies to spell words correctly on his or her own.	Student sometimes used one of the taught spelling strategies to spell words correctly on his or her own.	Student always used one of the taught spelling strategies to spell words correctly with some help from an adult.	Student sometimes used one of the taught spelling strategies to spell words correctly with some help from an adult.
Spells all words correctly in writing.	Student correctly spelled all the words in his or her writing.	Student correctly spelled 75%–99% of the words in his or her writing.	Student correctly spelled 50%–74% of the words in his or her writing.	Student correctly spelled 25%–49% of the words in his or her writing.	Student correctly spelled 1%–24% of the words in his or her writing.
Grade	/20 points	% =	Letter grade =		

Source: "No more Friday spelling tests? An alternative spelling assessment for students with learning disabilities," by K. A. Loeffler, 2005, *Teaching Exceptional Children, 37*, 24.

Meredith monitors the test process, collects and grades papers, and adds words missed to next week's spelling list.

Each week Meredith also gives an error-detection test with words representing phonics patterns she taught that week as well as review patterns. The test consists of twenty word pairs. Each word pair consists of a correctly and incorrectly spelled word. Students are directed to circle the correct spelling.

15.6.3 Principles of Effective Spelling Instruction

The following sections describe the principles of effective spelling instruction that Meredith observes. Any approach that is used with students who have spelling problems should include these principles.

Teaching spelling patterns

Learning to spell can be facilitated by understanding the patterns of our language. That is why early phonics instruction and later instruction in multisyllabic words helps students become better spellers. Thus, students benefit when they are taught common word patterns such as base words, prefixes, suffixes, consonants, consonant blends, digraphs, and vowel sound–symbol associations.

MyEdLab
Video Example 15.6.
In this video, we see a teacher using direct instruction for teaching spelling patterns. What does the teacher do to ensure that all students anticipate and engage in this lesson?

Teaching in small units

Teach students with spelling problems three words a day rather than four or five. In one study, students with learning disabilities who were assigned three words a day performed better than a control group of students with learning disabilities who were assigned four or five words (Bryant, Drabin, & Gettinger, 1981).

Providing sufficient practice and feedback

Give students opportunities to practice words each day, with feedback. Many teachers do this by having students work with spelling partners who ask them words and provide immediate feedback. Another procedure for self-correction and practice is presented in the 60-Second Lesson.

Selecting appropriate words

The most important strategy for teaching spelling is to make sure that students know how to read the word and already know its meaning. Selection of spelling words should be based on students' existing vocabularies.

Maintaining previously learned words

For students to be able to remember how to spell words, you must frequently assign (for review) words they have already learned, along with new words. Previously learned words must be reviewed frequently to be maintained.

Teaching for transfer of learning

After spelling words have been mastered, provide opportunities for students to see and use the words in different contexts.

Motivating students to spell correctly

Spelling can be interesting, linked to necessary skills such as writing, and monitored for success—all means to motivating students to spell correctly. Providing various games and activities, selecting meaningful spelling words, and giving examples of the use and need for correct spelling are strategies that help motivate students and give them a positive attitude about spelling. See the 60-Second Lesson for strategies to help students correct misspellings.

60-*SECOND* LESSON

PROCEDURE OF SELF-CORRECTION AND PRACTICE

To help students learn how to correct misspellings, try the following procedure:

1. Fold a paper into five columns, and write the correctly spelled words in the first column.
2. The student studies one word, folds the column back, and writes the word in the second column. The student then checks his or her spelling against the correctly spelled word in column 1.
3. After folding columns 1 and 2 back, the student writes the word in the third column. When the word is spelled correctly three times, the student moves on to the next word. The student continues until each word is spelled correctly from memory three times in a row.

Including dictionary training

Dictionary training (which includes alphabetizing, identifying target words, and locating the correct definition when several are provided) should be developed as part of the spelling program. Some teachers may decide to use computers to assist with this instruction.

MyEdLab **Self-Check 15.6**

MyEdLab **Application Exercise 15.6:** Spelling Instruction

15.7 TEACHING HANDWRITING AND KEYBOARDING SKILLS

Before computers, legible handwriting was a must. Even though children grow up using computers, learning how to write legibly is still important for students who are physically able. For most students, learning how to write legibly and fluently is a key to success in school. Indeed, many states have writing examinations that require students to write manually rather than using a computer.

15.7.1 Trends in Handwriting Instruction

In traditional handwriting instruction in the United States, students learn manuscript writing (printing) in the early grades and move to cursive writing (script) in the later grades (second or third, depending on the district). Clare Whiting, a second-grade teacher, teaches handwriting as a whole-class activity. To plan her lessons, she uses a commercial handwriting program that includes individual student booklets and extra worksheets to serve as models. Clare begins the school year by reviewing manuscript writing and then introduces the cursive alphabet after the first grading period. Clare assigns grades on the basis of her judgment of the legibility of students' handwriting.

Traditional handwriting instruction has been subject to controversy for several decades for several reasons. First, critics of traditional handwriting instruction say that spending valuable class time on developing legible handwriting is not time well spent, and that time could be better spent teaching students to keyboard. Second, some educators maintain that handwriting should be taught within the context of composition rather than during an isolated period of handwriting skill development. Third, some maintain that cursive writing is a practice from the past and is simply outdated (see Figure 15.11).

The Common Core State Standards do not include standards related to handwriting instruction. CCSS standards for keyboarding begin at grade 3. Consequently, states vary widely in terms of how and when handwriting is taught. De-emphasis on handwriting has caused concern among parents and teachers alike. In addition, emerging research has shed light on the importance of early handwriting instruction for development of literacy (Shanahan, 2014).

There are some advantages to learning early and well to print, as it corresponds more obviously with the print students read (Spear-Swerling, 2006). The research of

FIGURE 15.11 **Manuscript versus cursive**

MANUSCRIPT	CURSIVE
1. It more closely resembles print and facilitates learning to read.	1. Many students want to learn to write cursive.
2. It is easier for young children to learn.	2. Many students write cursive faster. Many adults object to students using manuscript beyond the primary grades.
3. It is more legible than cursive.	
4. Many students write manuscript at the same rate as cursive, and this rate can be significantly influenced through direct instruction.	
5. It is better for students with learning disabilities to learn one writing process well than to attempt to learn two.	

Berninger and colleagues underscores the advantages of handwriting instruction (Berninger, 2012; Berninger et al., 2006). Instruction in handwriting can improve letter perception, which then results in improved reading and spelling. Also, when children become more fluent in writing, the quantity and quality of their written composition improve. Thus, manuscript writing should be taught early on and maintained. Berninger (2012) also advocates for the teaching of cursive writing and eventually offering students the choice of which system works for them.

15.7.2 Students with Difficulty in Handwriting

Students with **dysgraphia** have severe problems learning to write, which may be associated with other learning problems in reading and math but may also be independent of other learning problems.

Poor handwriting, whether of students with dysgraphia or others, can include any of the following characteristics (Weintraub & Graham, 1998; Datchuk, 2015):

- Poor letter formation
- Letters that are too large, too small, or inconsistent in size
- Incorrect use of capital and lowercase letters
- Letters that are crowded and cramped
- Inconsistent spacing between letters
- Incorrect alignment (letters do not rest on a base line)
- Incorrect or inconsistent slant of cursive letters
- Lack of fluency in writing

With direct instruction and regular practice, most of these problems can be handled and corrected. There are six letters that account for 48% of the errors students make when forming letters: *q*, *j*, *z*, *u*, *n*, and *k* (Graham, Weintraub, & Berninger, 1998). It may be useful to spend more time teaching these letters and ensuring that students know how to connect them to other letters without changing their formation.

15.7.3 Principles of Effective Handwriting Instruction

It is important to address handwriting problems for several reasons. For one thing, illegible handwriting inhibits a student's ability to communicate. Lack of fluency with handwriting impacts the ability to complete written assignments in a timely manner and to take notes during class (Peverly, Garner, & Vekaria, 2014). In addition, handwriting problems are associated with reduced interest in writing and thus influence written expression. Also, students with handwriting difficulties spell worse than those without handwriting

TIPS FOR TEACHERS 15.7

Instructional Principles for Effective Handwriting

- Teach handwriting directly by using models and providing steps for letter formation that relate directly to the models.
- Give students with handwriting difficulties individualized instruction and feedback.
- Provide handwriting instruction with feedback several times a week for relatively brief periods (15 minutes) but provide feedback on handwriting throughout the instructional day.
- Teach brief handwriting lessons within the context of students' writing.
- Provide opportunities to practice handwriting through copying exercises and forming letters from memory.
- Have students evaluate their own handwriting and, when appropriate, the handwriting of others.
- Provide arrows to indicate the direction of correct letter formation.
- Use lined paper to model the letter formation.
- Gently guide students' hands so that they get immediate feedback about the motor task as well as letter formation.

problems even when spelling interventions are provided (Berninger et al., 1998). See Tips for Teachers 15.7 for some helpful strategies for teaching effective handwriting.

How can you help students who have difficulty with handwriting?

Handwriting involves both physical elements (fine-motor skills and visual-motor coordinating) and knowledge of letter names and formation (Datchuk, 2015). Although research does not strongly support motor skill exercises isolated from handwriting instruction, there are some simple steps you can use to facilitate the physical component of handwriting: correct posture, pencil grip, and paper position.

- *Posture.* Lower back touches the back of the chair and feet rest on the floor. The torso leans forward slightly in a straight line. Both forearms rest on the desk, with elbows slightly extended.
- *Pencil grip.* The pencil is held lightly between the thumb and first two fingers, about 1 inch above the point. The first finger rests on top of the pencil. The end of the pencil points toward the shoulder.

How can you help students who have difficulty with handwriting?

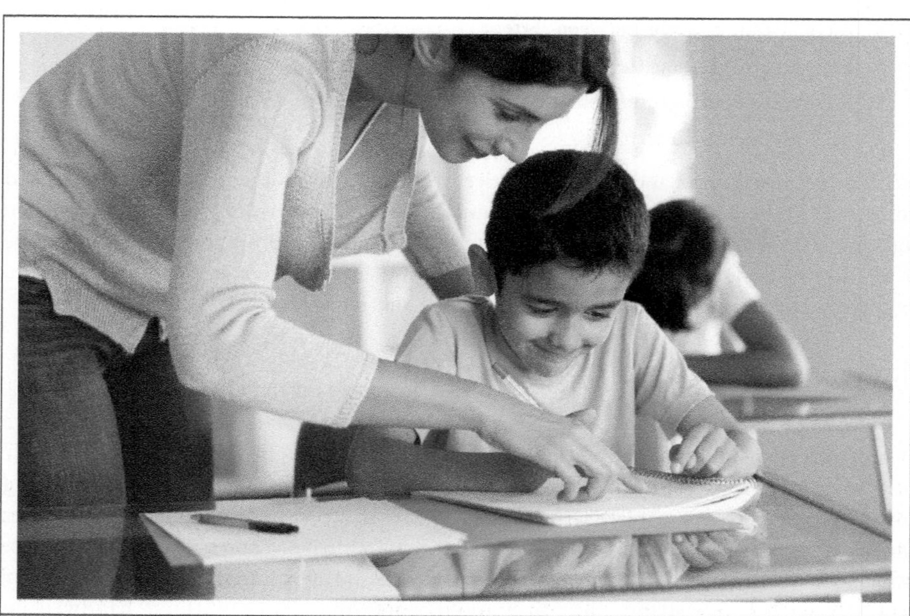

- *Paper position.* For manuscript writing, the paper is held straight in front of the writer, and the nonwriting hand holds the paper in place. For cursive writing, the paper is slanted counterclockwise for a right-hander and clockwise for a left-hander.

When planning copying exercises, keep in mind students who may have visual disabilities or difficulty in copying from a white board or projection screen. Some children with otherwise normal vision may have trouble switching from far to near vision or near to far vision. Provide a close model for the student's desk to accommodate the needs of students with general vision or visual tracking problems.

The bulk of handwriting instruction focuses on legibility, forming letters that are readable to others, and fluency, handwriting speed.

Legibility

Legibility is the most important goal of handwriting, and incorrect letter formation is the most common reason teachers identify students with handwriting challenges. Other problems with handwriting include: overall neatness (76%), spacing between words (66%), letter size (59%), letter formation (57%), alignment of letters (54%), and reversals (52%) (Graham et al., 2008). In general, it is best to teach letters that are easier to form first. Also, provide extended practice for the most frequently used letters (Gentry & Graham, 2010).

Teaching letter formation includes

- Identifying the critical features of the shapes of letters by comparing and contrasting them.
- Using physical prompts such as guiding the student's hand.
- Providing paper and materials that have the letters faded or with dots so that students have a model for tracing the letters.
- Giving students specific reinforcement for letters or parts of letters that are formed correctly and then giving specific feedback and correction for letters or parts of letters that need to be rewritten.

Hanover (1983) provided a system for teaching cursive writing based on the similarities of letters or letter families. Because students learn letters in groups with similar strokes, learning to write letters is easier. The position of the pencil when you start the letter and some of the significant "loops" or "shapes" used to form the letter allow you to teach letters with common shapes together. It makes sense that some letters can be taught in more than one family. Letter families in the Hanover method (Hanover, 1983) are shown here in the order recommended for teaching them:

e family: *e*, *l*, *h*, *f*, *k*

hump-shaped family: *n*, *m*, *s*, *y*

c family: *c*, *a*, *d*, *o*, *q*, *g*

hump family: *n*, *m*, *v*, *y*, *x*

back-tail family: *f*, *q*

front-tail family: *g*, *p*, *y*, *z*

One of the most effective ways to develop legibility is to provide a moving model. To provide a moving model, sit next to the student. As you form a letter or word, talk the student through the motions you are making. If the child writes with a different hand from you, have another child, a volunteer, or another teacher who writes with that hand provide the model. If you decide to have whole-class handwriting lessons, first provide a model by using the chalkboard or overhead projector; then circulate around the room, providing an individual moving model for students who seem to need the extra support. There is research indicating that students learn handwriting best from teachers who have had professional training in doing so (Berninger, 2012).

MyEdLab
Video Example 15.7.
In this video, the teacher is working on writing fluency with a small group of students. Why is writing fluency important to students' overall success and what strategies can be used to promote it?

15.7.4 Fluency

After students begin to master basic letter forms and their writing becomes more legible, the next goal is to learn to write quickly and with ease. Tom Reynolds helps students in his class improve their fluency through timed writings and journal writing.

Tom has three students in his fifth-grade class who have improved the legibility of their writing considerably during the school year but who still need to learn to write more quickly. He decided to group the three students together for timed writings. (In a timed writing, students copy a fifty-word passage and record the number of minutes the process takes.) When the group met for the first time, Tom showed them how to conduct a timed writing and keep records. For each student, he set up a folder with a collection of passages and a chart for recording progress. During this first meeting, Tom also explained that the idea is to work toward personal improvement, not to compete, and he talked about ways in which they could encourage one another. In time, the students could see that each was becoming a more fluent writer.

The daily 15-minute journal-writing activity Tom plans for all his students is a good way to enhance fluency. Because students know that their journals will not be graded for spelling or handwriting, they take risks and write more. Tom encourages students to evaluate their own journal writing and makes certain that students with fluency problems evaluate how much they write.

At the beginning of the year, Tom talked with the first-grade teacher, Helen Byers, and they decided to initiate a dialog journal activity (Atwell, 1984; Bode, 1989; Gambrell, 1985). A dialog journal is an ongoing written conversation between two students (or, in some cases, between a student and an adult). Each of Tom's fifth graders was paired with one of Helen's first graders. Once a week, the fifth graders visit the first-grade class and tell or read aloud a story to their first-grade partners. Then the pairs spend some time writing in a dialog journal.

Monitoring student progress

At the beginning and end of the school year, have students copy a short poem to get a sample of their handwriting and to indicate progress—you will be amazed at what you see. Hallahan and colleagues (2005) recommend using student writing samples on a variety of tasks to assess the legibility and fluency of their writing: freewriting, dictation, near-point copying, and far-point copying (see Table 15.1).

Perhaps one of the best ways to monitor students' progress in handwriting is to ask them to do two types of timed writing samples every 3 weeks. Writing for 1 minute by copying from a text is the first type of progress monitoring of handwriting. The second type is taking dictation or writing for 1 minute with the teacher reading sentences to students. Both types provide very valuable information about the progress of students in handwriting.

You can use the following criteria to determine students' progress in writing with each of the handwriting-monitoring exercises:

1. Count the number of words that students wrote in a minute and chart their progress over time.
2. Count the number of words that met high criteria for writing accuracy: (a) letter size and alignment is correct, (b) spacing is correct, and (c) letter formation is correct. You can also use the criteria to give feedback to students and to provide instruction.

15.7.5 Principles of Effective Keyboarding Instruction

Using the computer is frequently recommended as an adaptation for students who have difficulty with handwriting and spelling (Lerner, 2006). Using a word processor can be

Table 15.1 • Guidelines for Assessing Handwriting

	PURPOSE	DIRECTIONS	ACCURACY STANDARD	SPEED STANDARD
Freewriting	To provide a baseline for evaluating other tasks and for assessing programs	Identify the letters (i.e., alphabet) or words (e.g., names and familiar words) that the student can write readily. Direct the student to write the identified materials repeatedly, as quickly as possible.	95%–100%	60 characters per minute (cpm); 100 cpm, better
Dictation	To evaluate a student's production of writing when she or he does not know what will come next	Decide whether to test individual letters, words, or phrases. Identify items you are sure the student can write without requiring much thinking (e.g., "known" items); you can use the same item several times in a test. Direct the student to write items as you say them. Watch closely, and, as the student finishes an item, say the next one.	90%–100%	70% of standard for freewriting
Near-Point Copying	To evaluate a student's production of writing when she or he copies from materials on the desk	1. Familiar: Select highly familiar material for the student to copy. 2. Unfamiliar: Select material the student has not previously seen but that is at about the same difficulty level as in the familiar condition. Compare the performances to estimate the contribution of familiarity.	95%–100%	75%–80% of standard for freewriting
Far-Point Copying	To evaluate a student's production of writing when she or he copies from a distant source (e.g., the chalkboard)	1. Familiar: Select highly familiar material for the student to copy. 2. Unfamiliar: Select material the student has not previously seen but that is at about the same difficulty level as in the familiar condition. Compare the performances to estimate the contribution of familiarity.	90%–100%	75%–80% of standard for freewriting

Source: Adapted from *Learning disabilities: Foundations, characteristics, and effective teaching* (p. 412), by D. P. Hallahan, J. W. Lloyd, J. M. Kauffman, M. P. Weiss, & E. A. Martinez, 2005, Boston: Allyn & Bacon. Copyright © 2005 by Pearson Education. Reprinted by permission of the publisher.

beneficial in improving students' quality and quantity of writing, text organization, mechanics of writing, and motivation to write (Morphy & Graham, 2012). Learning to keyboard or type is essential for school success. Grade 4 is typically recommended for formal keyboarding instruction (see Table 15.2).

Many software programs are available for teaching keyboarding skills. Such programs can monitor student progress and give feedback about accuracy. However, they may be lacking in that students' fingering cannot be monitored directly. Direct instruction with feedback and sufficient time for practice are necessary. Although students may exhibit some frustration using word processing to compose, when keyboarding fluency develops the frustration often disappears.

Table 15.2 • Keyboarding Curriculum

	TOPIC	TIME FRAME	SKILL LEVEL ALPHABETIC COPY
Grade 1 or 2	Home keys	3–4 hours	Don't measure
Grade 2 or 3	1. Alphabetic keys and commonly used punctuation marks 2. Spelling words and other short activities	30–35 hours	20 wam*
Grade 4 or 5	1. Review alphabetic keys and introduce numbers and commonly used symbols. 2. Incorporate in language arts.	25 hours	30 wam
Grade 6 or 7 or 8	Review skills. Use skills in all language arts. Use for personal use, reports, essays, letters, etc.	min. of 1 semester—190 hrs 1 yr if preparing for vocational skill	40 wam
Grades 9–10	Introduction to business skills (word processing, database, spreadsheets, etc.)	1 semester	40–50 wam
Grades 11–12	Advanced business skills (word processing, database, spreadsheets, etc.)	1–2 semesters	50+

Note: Students can use word processing programs and microcomputers at any grade level where equipment is available.

* Words a minute—a standard word is five strokes, spaces, etc.

Source: "Typewriting/keyboarding instruction in elementary schools," L. W. Bartholome, 2003, retrieved from http://www.usoe.k12.ut.us/ate/keyboarding/Articles/Bartholome.

MyEdLab **Self-Check 15.7**

MyEdLab **Application Exercise 15.7:** Handwriting

15 SUMMARY

- Current trends in writing curriculum and instruction include (a) movement toward standards-based writing instruction, (b) increased emphasis on assessment, (c) emphasis on balanced and effective writing instruction for all students, and (d) implementation of writing practices that are based on research.
- As a process, writing (like reading) is (a) interactive, (b) strategic, (c) constructed by meaning, (d) student centered, and (e) socially mediated. To promote writing, teachers should teach the elements of the authoring process—prewriting, composing, revising, editing, and publishing—as well as effective strategies to use with each stage.
- Developing a positive and productive physical and social environment is vital for developing student confidence as writers. Establishing a writer's workshop in the classroom provides a framework for students to author written work and receive support and feedback to develop polished finished products.
- Students with writing problems differ in the degree to which components of the writing process are difficult for them. There is considerable agreement that students use the writing process best when they are taught explicitly how to use each of the elements (e.g., prewriting, revising, conferencing).
- Students need direct instruction in writing narrative, expository, and opinion/argument text patterns. Many approaches to teaching writing are used generally across all writing genres, but there are several specific instructional practices that can be employed within each genre.
- Spelling is an important tool for writers. Effective instruction for students with spelling problems includes teaching spelling patterns, teaching in small units, providing feedback and practice, selecting appropriate words, and maintaining previously learned words.
- Because handwriting is still necessary for success in school, students need specific instruction in how to write legibly and fluently. Handwriting assessment should include assessment of freewriting, dictation, near-point copying, and far-point copying. Instruction in the use of word processors, keyboarding, and adaptive technology can improve the quality and quantity of student writing.

THINK AND APPLY

1. Now that you have read Chapter 15, reread the interview with Michelle Langlois. What strategies does she use to plan a writing program that meets state standards and encourages student appreciation for the writing process?
2. Think about your own experience in learning about the process of writing. What instructional methods and procedures were most helpful? Least helpful? Develop a personal writing portfolio to share with your students. In your portfolio, include samples of your own writing from different phases of the authoring process. If possible, include some samples of your writing (and perhaps pictures of yourself) as a child. The portfolio will demonstrate to your students that you are a writer and will illustrate your own progress as a writer.
3. Develop a set of guidelines and procedures for implementing a writer's workshop in your classroom.
4. Work with a classmate (one as teacher; one as student) to role-play a writing conference. Then switch roles. Debrief by discussing positive ways to provide feedback to students.
5. Develop lesson plans for teaching narrative, informational, and opinion/argument text patterns. Incorporate models of each genre from children's or adolescent's literature in your plans.
6. Develop a presentation for parents describing how you teach spelling in your classroom and how parents can collaborate with you to support students in learning how to spell.
7. Plan an activity to teach a handwriting mini-lesson. Then, make a list of all the tools and technologies you might use to make accommodations and adaptations for students with disabilities who have difficulties writing.

16 Helping All Students Succeed in Mathematics

Learning Outcomes

16.1 Describe some of the current trends in math curriculum and instruction.

16.2 Identify some of the reasons students have difficulty with learning mathematics.

16.3 Articulate effective ways to assess students' instructional needs and monitor student progress in learning mathematics.

16.4 List some ways you can help students develop confidence and competence in math.

16.5 Identify the teaching strategies that are most important in helping all students acquire basic math skills.

16.6 Explain how teachers can ensure that students develop fluency and accuracy in math computational skills.

16.7 Give examples of how teachers can help students develop and use problem-solving strategies both in math and in other content areas.

INTERVIEW: RODNEY ROUZARD

Rodney Rouzard is a mathematics teacher at Ponce de Leon Middle School in Miami, Florida. He teaches general math to students in sixth, seventh, and eighth grade. Rodney completed his student teaching at the school and was eventually hired for a full-time position. Rodney's students have consistently shown improvement on state high-stakes exams, and recently the school district recognized him for his accomplishment. The state and federal accountability requirements and pressures for teachers to prepare students for high-stakes testing can be intimidating, but Rodney remains undaunted. When asked how he prepares his students for standardized tests, he offered some solid recommendations.

First, Rodney explains that his middle school students are developing abstract thinking skills. Therefore, he starts with concrete examples, supports students as they articulate their understanding of new concepts, and helps them derive their own definition or meaning of the topic at hand. For example, Rodney's unit on rational numbers (including negative integers) is centered on developing a personal budget. Students have a fictitious budget and they learn about negative numbers through the notion of debt. As Rodney observes, "They not only learn the concept of negative numbers, but also about financial responsibility. Using real-world examples makes it meaningful to my students. Students get frustrated and develop math anxiety if they don't see a connection to their life. The core of mathematics is logic. Concrete examples can help my students learn the concepts that underlie the topic at hand."

Second, Rodney also provides opportunities for regular practice with systematic feedback. Each class begins with what he calls a "bell ringer." The bell ringer is a problem posted on the white board that is a sample question from the state high-stakes test. "I encourage students just to try and not to be afraid of making mistakes. We analyze their mistakes so that they can learn from them. Math anxiety occurs when they don't feel competent. I provide enough practice and feedback to lead them to feel more confident. I also spend a great deal of time on test-taking strategies."

Third, Rodney recommends that teachers spend time familiarizing themselves with the high-stakes test. Not all state standards are covered equally on the exam. Rodney's school district has a pacing guide for curriculum coverage. However, he provides additional practice for those standards that are emphasized more heavily on the high-stakes exam.

Like most teachers today, Rodney is responsible for teaching state standards and for preparing students for exams. However, Rodney has managed to keep these responsibilities in balance with the larger goal of preparing his students to develop an understanding of the potential impact of mathematics on their academic careers and in their daily lives.

CHAPTER OUTLINE

(continued)

Introduction

The purpose of this chapter is to introduce procedures for effectively instructing students who have extraordinary problems learning mathematics. Think about how you felt about mathematics instruction. What do you think were some of the factors that influenced these feelings? Surely the teachers you had and the way mathematics was taught had a great deal of influence on how you feel about the subject today. Far too few students consider mathematics an exciting subject or are interested in careers in mathematics and related fields (e.g., science, technology, and engineering). Unfortunately, many students with and without disabilities perform poorly in mathematics because of low expectations for success and poor instruction (Carnegie Corporation of New York, Institute for Advanced Study, 2011; Fuchs et al., 2015; U.S. Department of Education, 2008, 2014). Still others do not succeed due to instructional practices that are not culturally relevant (Jackson, 2013) or sensitive to the needs of students who are learning the English language (Orosco, 2014).

This chapter begins with a presentation of current trends in mathematics curriculum and instruction. It continues with a discussion of reasons that students experience difficulty becoming proficient in math. The next two sections provide suggestions for assessment and progress monitoring of students followed by ideas for helping students become more confidence and competent in learning math. The last three sections provide specific ideas for teaching basic math skills, computation, and problem solving.

16.1 CURRENT TRENDS IN MATHEMATICS CURRICULUM AND INSTRUCTION

A central topic in education is mathematics instruction. This issue has been paramount for students with learning difficulties. There is growing national concern that students across all achievement groups are not faring well in mathematics compared with students in countries such as Belgium, Canada, England, Finland, Hungary, Japan, New Zealand, Scotland, and Sweden. Some think that the mathematics performance of students in the United States is related to the way in which mathematics is taught. In fact, the National Mathematics Advisory Panel (U.S. Department of Education, 2008) ignited increased focus on mathematics instruction in its conclusion that mathematics instruction is broken and needs to be fixed. The most important message the panel provides is to put "first things first"—meaning that students need to master important skills and knowledge sequentially.

16.1.1 Influences on Math Instruction

Mathematics instruction has been in a state of change over the past 30 years, with considerable emphasis on improving the quality of mathematics education in the United States (National Council of Teachers of Mathematics, 2014). The Mathematics Advisory Panel included outstanding research scientists in mathematics education in the United States who met and reviewed research on effective mathematics instruction. In its lengthy report (U.S. Department of Education, 2008), the Mathematics Advisory Panel offered six recommendations:

1. Streamline the mathematics curriculum so that only the most essential elements of mathematics instruction are taught. These essential elements include whole numbers, computational proficiency, measurement, geometry, and proficiency with fractions, including decimals, percentage, and negative fractions.

2. Use findings from rigorous mathematics research to (a) give students an early start in mathematics, (b) teach in ways that recognize the importance of both conceptual understanding of mathematics and fluency and automaticity in mathematical facts, and (c) recognize that persistence in teaching and learning mathematics (e.g., effort) is important, not just inherent talent.
3. Provide preservice and professional development for teachers of mathematics so that they are knowledgeable about math content as well as effective instructional practices.
4. Use both student-centered and teacher-directed instruction. Students with learning difficulties and disabilities respond positively to explicit instruction in mathematics.
5. Emphasize mathematics instruction that leads to success in algebra.
6. Read and implement findings from rigorous research on math instruction.

The History of the National Council of Teachers of Mathematics (NCTM)

The National Council of Teachers of Mathematics (NCTM), a professional mathematics instruction group, has been significantly influential in defining instructional core content in mathematics. In 1989, this group set curriculum standards for the development and implementation of mathematics curricula (NCTM, 1989). Since that time, NCTM has created professional standards (in 1991), assessment standards (in 1995), and, most recently, a set of standards that builds on the three previous standards documents (published in 2000), as summarized in Figure 16.1.

Since the NCTM standards were published, NCTM went one step further and created "Curriculum Focal Points," which are the topics in mathematics that are most important at each grade level. These related ideas, concepts, and skills define the key instructional practices for teachers for each grade (NCTM, 2006) and are available for each grade level from prekindergarten through grade 8. As a prospective or practicing teacher, these focal points may be useful to you as you select curriculum and design instruction for students with special needs. The organization also published a set of guidelines for teaching high school mathematics with an emphasis on reasoning and sense making (NCTM, 2009).

NCTM's involvement in the Common Core State Standards

Representatives from NCTM were involved with the drafting of the Common Core State Standards. In 2010, NCTM published *Making It Happen: A Guide to Interpreting and Implementing the Common Core State Standards for Mathematics* (NCTM, 2010). This publication, coupled with evolving online tools on the NCTM website, provides valuable resources for teachers as they plan lessons and activities to address the Common Core State Standards (for an overview, see Figure 16.2).

NCTM's response to lingering challenges in mathematics instruction

NCTM recognizes that while progress has been made in improvement of mathematics instruction, there is still work to be done. As a response to this lingering challenge, NCTM appointed a writing team and group of reviewers (both researchers and practitioners) to develop a blueprint for continued improvement. The resulting publication, *Principles to Actions: Ensuring Mathematics Success for All* (NCTM, 2014), addresses issues related to six guiding principles for teaching mathematics in kindergarten through twelfth grade classes: Teaching and Learning, Access and Equity, Curriculum, Tools and Technology, Assessment, and Professionals. The publication points out obstacles to achieving optimal instruction for each of the principles as well as suggestions for overcoming those obstacles.

FIGURE 16.1 NCTM standards 2000

Instructional programs for prekindergarten through grade 12 in the following areas should enable all students to use the following concepts:

1. Number and operations
   - Understand numbers, ways of representing numbers, relationships among numbers, and number systems
   - Understand meanings of operations and how they relate to one another
   - Compute fluently and make reasonable estimates
2. Algebra
   - Understand patterns, relations, and functions
   - Represent and analyze mathematical solutions and structures using algebraic symbols
   - Use mathematical models to represent and understand quantitative relationships
   - Analyze change in various contexts
3. Geometry
   - Analyze characteristics and properties of two- and three-dimensional geometric shapes, and develop mathematical arguments about geometric relationships
   - Specify locations and describe spatial relationships using coordinate geometry and other representational systems
   - Apply transformations and use symmetry to analyze mathematical situations
   - Use visualization, spatial reasoning, and geometric modeling to solve problems
4. Measurement
   - Understand measurable attributes of objects and the units, systems, and processes of measurement
   - Apply appropriate techniques, tools, and formulas to determine measurements
5. Data analysis and probability
   - Formulate questions that can be addressed with data and collect, organize, and display relevant data to answer them
   - Select and use appropriate statistical methods to analyze data
   - Develop and evaluate inferences and predictions that are based on data
   - Understand and apply basic concepts of probability
6. Problem solving
   - Build new mathematical knowledge through problem solving
   - Solve problems that arise in mathematics and in other contexts
   - Apply and adapt a variety of appropriate strategies to solve problems
   - Monitor and reflect on the process of mathematical problem solving
7. Reasoning and proof
   - Recognize reasoning and proof as fundamental aspects of mathematics
   - Make and investigate mathematical conjectures
   - Develop and evaluate mathematical arguments and proofs
   - Select and use various types of reasoning and methods of proof
8. Communication
   - Organize and consolidate their mathematical thinking through communication
   - Communicate their mathematical thinking coherently and clearly to peers, teachers, and others
   - Analyze and evaluate the mathematical thinking and strategies of others
   - Use the language of mathematics to express mathematical ideas precisely
9. Connections
   - Recognize and use connections among mathematical ideas
   - Understand how mathematical ideas interconnect and build on one another to produce a coherent whole
   - Recognize and apply mathematics in contexts outside of mathematics
10. Representation
    - Create and use representations to organize, record, and communicate mathematical ideas
    - Select, apply, and translate among mathematical representations to solve problems
    - Use representations to model and interpret physical, social, and mathematical phenomena

Source: Principles and standards for school mathematics, National Council of Teachers of Mathematics, 2000, retrieved from http://www.nctm.org/standards.

16.1.2 Mathematical Problem Solving

Mathematical problem solving is a major focus of the NCTM standards. When students with disabilities or math difficulties demonstrate challenges in mathematics problem solving, it is of particular concern because it interferes with students' access to higher-level math content and with applying math skills to everyday problems.

In an effort to determine how effective mathematical textbooks are in teaching math problem-solving standards to all students, Jitendra and colleagues (2005) reviewed five mathematical textbooks to determine the extent to which they addressed NCTM's problem-solving standards. These researchers also looked at the extent to which the texts provided design features associated with improved instructional outcomes for students with disabilities (e.g., prerequisite skills, teaching examples, practice problems, review, and feedback).

FIGURE 16.2 The Common Core Standards for mathematics: answers to relevant questions pertaining to mathematics instruction

WHAT ARE KEY SHIFTS IN COMMON CORE STANDARDS FOR MATHEMATICS (CCSS-M) WHEN COMPARED TO PREVIOUS STANDARDS?

The Common Core State Standards differ from previous mathematics standards in three respects. First, the CCSS-M focus on fewer topics per grade level. The goal is to provide greater depth of understanding and avoid tackling too many topics in a superficial manner. Second, the standards are designed to provide a coherent progression from grade to grade. The standards provide a foundation of learning at lower grade levels with reinforcement and extension of concepts through the grades. Third, the standards provide equal emphasis for math concepts, procedural skill and fluency, and application of mathematical knowledge and skills in the classroom and beyond.

How do the CCSS-M impact instruction for students with disabilities?

The CCSS-M provide rigorous guidelines for mathematical competencies students need to be college and career ready in the 21st century. Because students with disabilities now have greater access to the general education curriculum, they will also receive standards-based instruction with appropriate adaptations.

What are the mathematics concepts included in the CCSS-M?

Mathematical concepts in the CCSS-M include:

1. Counting and cardinality
2. Operations and algebraic thinking
3. Number operations in base ten
4. Number operations—fractions
5. Measurement and data
6. Geometry
7. Ratios and proportional relationship
8. The number system
9. Expressions and equations
10. Functions
11. Statistics and probability

Source: http://www.corestandards.org/other-resources/key-shifts-in-mathematics/; http://www.corestandards.org/math/

Most textbooks provided an adequate number of problem-solving opportunities for students. However, with respect to instructional design criteria that would enhance instruction and support learning for students with disabilities, the textbooks were rated quite low, with few textbooks meeting even three instructional design features. To best accommodate students with disabilities, these authors suggest that teachers will need to provide more specific and explicit instruction with additional examples as well as specific feedback.

Think about your own mathematics instruction when you were in school. Was the emphasis on worksheets and learning computation, or was it on problem solving and activities? Math educators suggest that an early emphasis on critical skills such as mathematical computational fluency is important, especially with opportunities to understand the computations conceptually and to apply them (U.S. Department of Education, 2008). In other words, it is not important to pick either mathematical computation or problem solving and application—students need to learn both.

16.1.3 Math Proficiency

The National Research Council (NRC) has conducted an examination of U.S. mathematics education from kindergarten through graduate study. This joint activity was conducted by the Mathematical Sciences Education Board, the Board on Mathematical Sciences, the Committee on the Mathematical Sciences, and the National Research Council. The extensive report resulting from the work of these committees not only outlines problems in mathematics education but also charts a course for remedying them. The suggestions that relate to students with learning and behavior problems are presented in Figure 16.3.

In addition to the guidelines in Figure 16.3, the NRC (2001) indicates that "mathematical proficiency" is the essential goal of instruction. What is mathematical proficiency? The aspects of mathematical proficiency are described here. As you read them, consider how you might integrate these ideas into your instruction for students with disabilities. Also, think about how you might document whether students are making progress.

- *Conceptual understanding* refers to understanding mathematic concepts and operations.
- *Procedural fluency* refers to being able to accurately and efficiently conduct operations and mathematics practices.

FIGURE 16.3 Recommendations from the National Council of Teachers of Mathematics

- Do not alter curricular goals to differentiate students; change the type and speed of instruction.
- Make mathematics education student oriented, not an authoritarian model that is teacher focused.
- Encourage students to explore, verbalize ideas, and understand that mathematics is part of their lives.
- Provide opportunities on a daily basis for students to apply mathematics and to work problems that are related to their daily lives. Relate what they are learning to real-life experiences.
- Teach mathematics so that students understand when they can estimate an answer and when they need to compute an exact answer.
- Teach problem solving, computer application, and use of calculators to all students.
- Teach students to understand probability, data analysis, and statistics as they relate to daily decision making, model building, operations, research, and application to computers.
- Shift from relying primarily on paper-and-pencil activities to use of calculators, computers, and other applied materials.

- *Strategic competence* refers to the ability to formulate and conduct mathematical problems.
- *Adaptive reasoning* refers to thinking about, explaining, and justifying mathematical work.
- *Productive disposition* refers to the ability to appreciate the useful and positive influences of understanding mathematics and how one's disposition toward mathematics influences success.

Despite this plea for additional emphasis on problem solving, computation is still an essential component of the math curriculum (Miller, Stringfellow, Kaffar, Ferreira, & Mancl, 2011; Van de Walle, Karp, & Bay-Williams, 2016). Some feel that students with learning problems potentially have the most to lose as the curriculum shifts away from computation and toward an emphasis on problem solving and teaching students to think mathematically; thus, the recent focal points for mathematics instruction (NCTM, 2006) provide an opportunity for teachers to identify the critical elements of instruction for their grade level and to determine whether students have mastered the previous focal points. This emphasis on the high-priority skills and practices at each grade level will ensure that the National Mathematics Advisory Panel's recommendation (U.S. Department of Education, 2008) to do first things first and to do the most important things at each grade level—not everything—can be accomplished.

For example, in fourth grade, the focal points (NCTM, 2006) emphasize that students demonstrate quick recall of multiplication and division facts and are very fluent with whole number multiplication. Fourth graders are also supposed to demonstrate understanding of decimals and the connection between decimals and fractions, as well as an understanding of area and how to determine the area of two-dimensional shapes. How can James Frist, a fourth-grade teacher with two students with disabilities, consider these math focal points for all of the students in his class, including his students with disabilities? Following are some guidelines to help James:

- Students with disabilities may be slower and require more practice, but they are not necessarily less accurate. Consider that the students with disabilities may need more time to complete the problem.
- Students with disabilities may need more support (e.g., additional instruction), to have the problem read to them, guidance about the key ideas to focus on, and

reminders about which operation to use. At the same time, however, they should have access to learning the same focal points in mathematics.

- When students work in pairs or groups, it is not uncommon that the students with disabilities are assigned passive and unimportant roles where they have little opportunity for learning and participating. Consider ways to alter this practice and to include them more actively in partner or group work.
- Students with disabilities may not have adequate fluency with basic math facts and may need additional practice and opportunities to acquire this proficiency.

Understanding why your students are having difficulty learning math will help you to better meet their needs. The following section offers specific information about why students struggle.

MyEdLab **Self-Check 16.1**

MyEdLab **Application Exercise 16.1:** Influences in Math Instruction

16.2 DIFFICULTIES IN LEARNING MATHEMATICS

As a teacher of mathematics in elementary, middle school, or high school, you are likely to encounter students with difficulties in learning mathematics. This includes students who have persistent problems in all aspects of the curriculum as well as students who perform adequately in some areas, but not in others (Gersten, Jordan, & Flojo, 2005). Students with disabilities such as behavior disorders, intellectual disabilities, and attention problems typically score below their same-age peers on measures of math achievement (Schulte & Stevens, 2015). Students with learning disabilities may have been diagnosed as having a specific mathematics learning disability or both mathematics disability and a reading learning disability (Shin & Bryant, 2015).

Some of their difficulties in mathematics relate to understanding the problem. In other instances, they lack the computation skills to adequately complete the problem. Typically, students with disabilities have difficulties with math facts, concepts, and procedures (Barnes et al., 2006; Doabler et al., 2012). Interestingly, not all of their difficulties in mathematics relate to their knowledge of math; some reflect other problems, such as difficulty in considering math problems from a "reasonable" perspective and difficulty with memory, perceptual skills, language, number reversals, and understanding symbols or operation signs (Bryant & Bryant, 2008; Bryant et al., 2003; Watson & Gable, 2012). Despite the significant difficulties many individuals with disabilities have with mathematics, they do not report lower self-perceptions of their math skills than average-achieving students (Montague & van Garderen, 2003).

Students who have both math and reading disabilities are more at risk than students with math disabilities alone (Jordan & Hanich, 2003; Shin & Bryant, 2015). This is because students with both reading and math disabilities have additional problems associated with processing symbols, text, and consequently word problems (Bryant & Bryant, 2008; Bryant, Bryant, & Hammill, 2000; Fuchs, Seethaler et al., 2008; Shin & Bryant, 2015).

16.2.1 Developmental Arithmetic Disorder

Students with developmental arithmetic disorder have significant difficulties learning arithmetic—difficulties that are unexpected given the students' overall cognitive functioning and academic performance in other subject areas. For example, Shawn is an undergraduate student with a significant arithmetic disorder. His performance in arithmetic was unexpectedly low given his overall cognitive performance. His difficulty in mathematics was also long lasting, not related to an area of mathematics or a particular teacher. Good teaching is likely to help students with developmental arithmetic disorder but probably not enough to ensure grade-level performance.

16.2.2 Nonverbal Math Difficulties

Johnson and Myklebust (1967) were the first to introduce the notion of **nonverbal math disabilities**. They were referring to a small group of students who displayed good reading and verbal expression but extreme difficulty with mathematics. Other problems associated with students who display nonverbal mathematics problems include the following:

- Social immaturity
- Disorientation
- Deficits in visual, motor, and self-help skills
- Problems estimating distance and time

Saje, a third-grade student with disabilities, was a successful reader but demonstrated significant difficulties in mathematics and was really a puzzle to his teacher, Theresa Ramirez. She could not figure out why, despite Saje's high verbal expression and good vocabulary, he continually mixed up old and new rules. He not only had problems in math but also was frequently inattentive and disorganized and avoided responsibility. No matter how often she reminded Saje to keep his math paper neat, the papers he turned in had frayed edges, had numbers all over the place (instead of problems written in neat columns), and were covered with eraser marks and holes. Theresa asked the special education teacher how to help Saje. The special education teacher worked with Saje, administered some tests, and explained to Saje's classroom teacher that he had a nonverbal math difficulty.

Although math would always be challenging for Saje, the special education teacher suggested some things that the classroom teacher could do to help him:

1. First, she taught only one mathematical principle at a time until Saje became masterful and fluent with that principle.
2. She used word games, songs, and other verbal activities to enhance instruction.
3. She devised organizational aids such as graph paper with large boxes that Saje could use to write numbers.
4. She provided Saje with items such as computers and audio recording devices as alternatives to pencil and paper.

Students who demonstrate nonverbal math difficulties are capable of acquiring meaningful understanding of mathematics and solving mathematical problems. Providing effective instructional accommodations such as the ones provided for Saje can improve their mathematical performance not only in your class, but in the future as well.

16.2.3 Math Difficulties and Effective Instruction

In this section, several student-based reasons why students can display poor math performance are discussed. Another reason that can be most readily corrected is the inappropriate or inadequate instruction in mathematics that many students receive.

Many professionals believe that the math difficulties among students with learning problems are compounded by ineffective instruction. Most teachers know how they learned to compute math problems but are not aware of alternative computation methods (e.g., they memorized multiplication tables successfully but are unfamiliar with adding numbers to resolve multiplication). Few teachers have procedures for using concrete approaches and how to successfully use manipulatives to teach computation. Fortunately, a growing body of research is providing guidelines for effective mathematics instruction for students with disabilities (Cole & Wasburn-Moses, 2010; Doabler et al., 2012; Doabler et al., 2015). To access a wide array of evidence-based resources and practices for teaching mathematics to student with disabilities, visit the Iris Center (http://iris.peabody.vanderbilt.edu). Tips for Teachers 16.1 provides a summary of guidelines for instructional practices for students with disabilities in a general education classroom.

TIPS FOR TEACHERS 16.1

Instructional Practices for Students with Disabilities

- Select appropriate, comprehensive math content.
- Select goals that establish high expectations.
- Teach prerequisite skills.
- Provide motivation and encouragement.
- Provide systematic and explicit instruction.
- Model calculation and problem-solving strategies and procedures.
- Set a purpose for learning.
- Provide real-world, culturally relevant, carefully sequenced examples.
- Provide scaffolding and support for English language learners.
- Teach students to understand math concepts.
- Allow time for guided and independent practice.
- Monitor the progress of students.
- Teach to strategies to solve problems.
- Teach to mastery.
- Promote a positive attitude toward math.
- Give specific feedback in a timely manner.
- Provide cumulative reviews.
- Teach students to generalize the math skills they learn.

Source: "Enhancing core mathematics instruction for students at risk for mathematics disabilities," by C. T. Doabler et al., 2012, *Teaching Exceptional Children*, 44(4), 48–57. Additional tips for teachers can be located at these websites: www.ldonline.org/ld_indepth/math_skills and www.superkids.com/aweb/tools/math.

16.2.4 Mathematics Learning for Linguistically and Culturally Diverse Learners

One of the basic tenets of NCTM is the importance of equity in teaching of mathematics (NCTM, 2014). This includes students with disabilities as well as students with cultural and linguistic differences. For students who are English language learners (ELLs), success in math learning is dependent on several factors (Orosco, 2014). Clearly, student proficiency in language affects comprehension of information presented and discussed in class and reading of math content in instructional materials and assessments. Both general and technical vocabulary knowledge pose challenges as well. Another factor that impacts math learning is the student's prior experiences in math learning and problem solving in the native language. Providing students with peer interactions, opportunities to use native language when appropriate, scaffolded instruction in vocabulary development, demonstration with visuals and manipulatives, and technology can give students the support they need to succeed.

Finally, both ELLs and native English speakers representing minority cultures may experience difficulties in math learning when instructional practices do not include materials and methods that are culturally relevant for them (Hernandez, Moreales, & Shroyer, 2013; Jackson, 2013). Culturally responsive instruction that incorporates activities and examples representing diverse cultures—including those of students in the classroom and community—provide opportunities for motivation and engagement. Many curricular materials may not provide examples that are geared to the context of a particular school community. Therefore, it is important that teachers know their students, know their community, and supplement the curriculum appropriately.

Video Example from YouTube

MyEdLab
Video Example 16.1.
Watch the YouTube video "The Importance of ELL Strategies—Immersion (Moises in Math Class)." What adaptation could this classroom teacher make in order to make math learning more accessible to Moises? https://www.youtube.com/watch?v=D6HUv2eFdLg

16.2.5 Teaching Students Who Are Mathematically Gifted

As a general education teacher, you will also need to be prepared to meet the instructional needs of students who are mathematically gifted. There is a debate about whether to accelerate the pacing of instruction for gifted students or to provide more in-depth enrichment instruction (Assouline, Colangelo, Heo, & Dockery, 2013).

TIPS FOR TEACHERS 16.2

Instructional Practices for Gifted Students

- Give preassessments so that students who already know the material do not have to repeat it, keeping instruction and activities meaningful. In the elementary grades, gifted learners still need to know their basic facts. If they do not, don't hold them back from other, more complex tasks, but continue to work concurrently on the basics.
- Create assessments that allow for differences in understanding, creativity, and accomplishment; give students a chance to show what they have learned. Ask students to explain their reasoning both orally and in writing.
- Choose textbooks that provide more enriched opportunities. Because most textbooks are written for the general population, they are not always appropriate for gifted students. Use multiple resources. No single text will adequately meet the needs of these learners.
- Be flexible in your expectations about pacing for different students. While some may be mastering basic skills, others may work on more advanced problems.
- Use inquiry-based, discovery learning approaches that emphasize open-ended problems with multiple solutions or multiple paths to solutions. Allow students to design their own ways to find the answers to complex questions. Gifted students may discover more than you thought was possible.
- Use a lot of higher-level questions. Ask "why" and "what if" questions.
- Provide units, activities, or problems that extend beyond the normal curriculum. Offer challenging mathematical recreations such as puzzles and games.
- Provide AP-level courses in calculus, statistics, and computer science, or encourage prepared students to take classes at local colleges if the supply of courses at the high school has been exhausted.
- Differentiate assignments. It is not appropriate to give more problems of the same type to gifted students. You might give students a choice of a regular assignment; a different, more challenging one; or a task that is tailored to interests.
- Expect high-level products (e.g., writing, proofs, projects, solutions to challenging problems).
- Provide opportunities to participate in contests such as Mathematical Olympiads for the Elementary School (grades 4 through 6), Math Counts (grades 7 through 8), the American Junior High School Mathematics Exam (grades 7 through 8), or the American High School Mathematics Exam (grades 9 through 12). Give feedback to students on their solutions. After the contests, use some of the problems as the basis for classroom discussions.
- Provide access to male and female mentors who represent diverse linguistic and cultural groups. They may be individuals within the school system, volunteers from the community, or experts who agree to respond to questions by email. Bring speakers into the classroom to explain how math has opened doors in their professions and careers.
- Provide some activities that can be done independently or in groups based on student choice. Be aware that if gifted students always work independently, they are gaining no more than they could do at home. They also need appropriate instruction, interaction with other gifted students, and regular feedback from the teacher.
- Provide useful, concrete experiences. Even though gifted learners may be capable of abstraction and may move from concrete to abstract more rapidly, they still benefit from the use of manipulatives and hands-on activities.

Additional tips for teachers can be located at the website of the National Association for Gifted Children (www.nagc.org).

Source: Adapted from "Teaching mathematics to gifted students in a mixed-ability classroom," by D. T. Johnson, April 2000, *ERIC Digest E594* (ERIC Document Reproduction Service No. ED441302). Reprinted by permission of the author.

VanTassel-Baska (2013) recommends curriculum design for differentiated instruction for gifted learners that includes acceleration, advanced curricular materials, emphasis on challenging skill and concept development, opportunities for creative expression, and engagement in projects and research. States and individual school districts vary considerably in terms of policies, programs, and curriculum for teaching academically gifted students.

As a classroom teacher, you will need to become familiar with resources (both curricular and human) available to meet the instructional needs of students who are advanced in mathematics. Tips for Teachers 16.2 provides some suggestions for meeting the needs of mathematically gifted students.

MyEdLab **Self-Check 16.2**

MyEdLab **Application Exercise 16.2:** Mathematics Learning for Linguistically and Culturally Diverse Learners

16.3 ASSESSMENT AND PROGRESS MONITORING

Effective math instruction involves checking students' work frequently and providing feedback. When students demonstrate math difficulties, their progress needs to be assessed by their classroom math teacher approximately every 2 weeks, and if students are not progressing adequately, accommodations including reteaching and guided practice need to be provided to ensure success. The math assessments used should align with the instructional curriculum.

16.3.1 Implementing Assessment and Progress Monitoring

Students in teacher Alex Chinn's fifth-grade class were asked to complete a worksheet to practice a new skill he had taught them for using dollar signs and decimal points in subtraction problems. Alex told the students to complete only the first problem. After they completed the problem, they were to consider whether the answer made sense and whether dollar signs and decimal points were used correctly. If so, they were to place a *C* next to the problem. If they were not sure whether the problem was correct, they were to mark it with a question mark (?); and if they thought the problem was wrong, they were to use a star (*). Alex moved quickly from student to student, checking the first problem and providing them with feedback and reinforcement: "Jacob, you were right, you did have the problem correct. Maxine, what are you unsure about? Now, look at it again. What do you think? Yes, that's right, it's correct. Beth, let's do this problem together." The teacher then guides the student by facilitating problem completion and then provides additional opportunities for the student to do similar problems independently.

16.3.2 Diagnosing Students' Learning Needs in Mathematics

When students have persistent difficulties in math that continue after teachers have made adequate instructional accommodations, teachers may need to provide further diagnosis to pinpoint the students' math learning needs. Jana is a first-year special education teacher. She is fortunate to work in a middle school with three other special education teachers who have been working at the school for several years and are used to team teaching. Jana's school administrator asked her whether she would be comfortable teaching mathematics to all of the students qualified for special education services. Because she is pretty good at mathematics herself, Jana thought this arrangement would give her an opportunity to learn to teach one content area very well. She quickly realized that her first task would be to determine the performance levels in mathematics of all her students. She also realized that she needed to select a measure that would tell her what students knew and did not know and also how they compared with other students in their grade. Although there is general information on a student's individualized education program (IEP) about his or her math performance, she wanted more precise, diagnostic information.

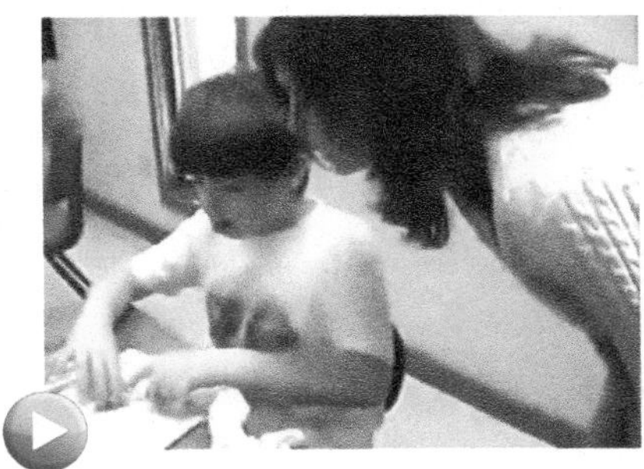

MyEdLab
Video Example 16.2.
In this video, some students are being identified as needing help as the rest of the class instruction is taking place. What would be the next step for those students who are falling behind in the general education math class to ensure that they can make adequate progress?

There are a number of ways in which Jana can obtain the information she needs to develop instructional programs for her students. One of the first questions Jana needs to address is whether she has the time to give an *individually administered assessment* or whether she needs to use a group-administered measure. For students with special needs, individually administered measures yield the most information for teachers. Second, Jana needs to decide whether the measure is designed for students in the age range of the students she is teaching. Table 16.1 provides a list of mathematics measures, states whether they are group or individually administered, and lists the age range for which they are appropriate.

Table 16.2 provides a list of mathematics measures suitable for progress monitoring.

Table 16.1 • Measures to Assess Mathematics Performance

TEST NAME	HOW ADMINISTERED	AGE/GRADE APPROPRIATE	OTHER INFORMATION
Comprehensive Math Assessment	Group	Grades 2–8	Based largely on the NCTM critical elements in mathematics instruction
Diagnostic Achievement Battery–3	Individual	Most grade levels	Provides normative data on student performance but not specific information for identifying strengths and weaknesses
Wide Range Achievement Test–4	Individual or Group	Most grade levels	Provides normative data on student performance but difficult to identify students' needs for instruction
Woodcock Johnson IV Tests of Achievement	Individual	Most grade levels	Provides normative data on student performance
Test of Early Mathematics Ability	Individual	Ages 3–9	Provides information to assist with designing and monitoring instruction
BRIGANCE Diagnostic Comprehensive Inventory of Basic Skills—Revised	Individual	Prekindergarten–grade 9	Provides information to assist with designing and monitoring instruction
Comprehensive Mathematical Ability Test	Individual	Grades 1–12	Provides information to assist with designing instruction
Key Math–3	Individual	Grades 1–12	Provides information to assist with designing instruction
Test of Mathematical Abilities–3	Individual	Grades 3–12	Provides information to assist with designing instruction
Math-Level Indicator: A Quick Group Math Placement Test	Group	Grades 4–12	Takes approximately 30 minutes, and because it is group administered, it quickly determines the performance levels of a large group of students; the problems are based on the NCTM standards

Source: Strategies for teaching students with learning and behavior problems (9th ed.), by S. Vaughn & C. Bos, 2015, Figure 11.1, p. 368, Boston: Pearson.

16.3.3 Using Response to Intervention: Identifying Students Who Need Help in Math

Math, like reading and writing, is an academic area where response to intervention (RTI) can be implemented (Bryant, 2014; Hunt & Little, 2014; Lembke, Hampton, & Beyers, 2012). One of the best ways to use RTI in mathematics is to screen students for math difficulties and then to provide them with early and intensive intervention to ensure their progress. In addition, ongoing progress monitoring provides data to develop individualized, intensive interventions (Powell & Stecker, 2014).

Table 16.2 • Progress Monitoring Measures for Mathematics

TEST NAME	WEBSITE	AGE/GRADE APPROPRIATE	CONCEPTS ASSESSED
Monitoring Basic Skills Progress	http://www.proedinc.com	Grades 1 and above	Math computation
Scholastic HMH Math Inventory	http://www.scholastic.com	Grades K–12	Computation concepts
Star Math	http://www.rennaissance.com	Grades 1–12	Computation application concepts
AIMSweb Systems	http://www.aimsweb.com	Grades K–8	Oral counting Number identification Quantity discrimination Missing number Basic skill areas

Source: Strategies for teaching students with learning and behavior problems (9th ed.), by S. Vaughn & C. Bos, 2015, Figure 11.2, p. 369, Boston: Pearson.

Many of the same principles that apply to the use of RTI in reading also apply to math, including the following:

- *Screening*—students can be screened to determine whether they have math problems in numeracy, math calculations, and/or problem solving.
- *Evidence-based math*—schools and districts can ensure that the math instruction for all students is based on the best research available.
- *Interventions*—when students have difficulties that are not adequately addressed through the evidence-based math program in the classroom, additional instruction through short-term interventions (10–20 weeks) can be implemented.
- *Progress monitoring*—students' progress in the classroom and in interventions can be documented to ensure that they are staying on track and meeting curriculum benchmarks.

16.3.4 Curriculum-Based Measurement

How can teachers best make decisions about whether students are learning mathematics effectively? Also, how can teachers monitor the progress of their students so that they can document the rate and progress students are making in mathematics? Perhaps the best way to determine student progress is to implement curriculum-based measurement (CBM), which is a method of determining whether the student is learning the curriculum that is taught (Deno, 1985; Fuchs et al., 2007; Koellner, Colsman, & Risley, 2014). Teachers prioritize the most important skills students need to learn each week and then assess students prior to and following instruction. These tests can be group-administered, teacher-developed assessments that can take as little as a few minutes to administer. Based on the findings from the pretest, teachers can identify what they need to teach all students and what they need to teach some students. Posttesting at the end of the week tells the teacher who needs additional instruction. CBM is becoming more widely used to make instructional decisions, particularly in light of RTI. Ongoing research to improve the technical quality of CBM procedures and instruments holds great promise for its use (Ball & Christ, 2012; Fuchs et al., 2007; Jitendra, Dupuis, & Zaslofsky, 2014; Montague, Penfield, Enders, & Huang, 2010; Yeo, Kim, Branum-Martin, Wayman, & Espin, 2012).

What is CBM for math? Simply stated, it is a way of documenting the extent to which the student is learning the critical elements you have targeted in the curriculum. To illustrate, consider the case of Ricky, a fifth-grade boy with learning and attention problems, who is struggling with math. His goals for the next 10 weeks are (a) to know all subtraction facts up to 100 automatically, (b) to quickly be able to do addition with regrouping word problems, and (c) to be able to use basic measurement terms such as *inches*, *feet*, and *yards* appropriately. Ricky's teacher, Mr. Rojas, pretested Ricky on all 100 subtraction facts in random order, timing him while he completed the worksheet. He then showed Ricky how to graph his performance in two ways: first, by graphing how long it took him to complete the worksheet, and second, by graphing the number of problems correct. Together they agreed that he would take a version of this test once every week to determine whether he could decrease the amount of time he needed to complete the test and increase the number of problems he got correct. Next, they established a schedule of work assignments and practice sessions. His teacher followed a similar procedure with measurement and problem solving to determine what Ricky knew and what he needed to know, and then he established a simple graph that Ricky could complete to monitor his progress. Ricky and his teacher frequently discussed Ricky's progress and modified assignments and instruction to facilitate his learning.

As a teacher, you may want to consider using a computerized application of CBM procedures, which is available for mathematics as well as for spelling and reading (Hosp, Hosp, & Howell, 2006). Remember, CBMs should be easy to administer, cost efficient, and sensitive to small changes in learning.

16.3.5 Assessing Students' Number Sense

One promising practice for monitoring the progress of young children in mathematics and identifying children who have mathematics difficulties or disabilities is by assessing their number sense (Gersten et al., 2005). Number sense refers to whether a student's understanding of a number and its use and meaning is flexible and fully developed. Although different definitions of number sense appear in the literature, NCTM indicates that number sense "develops as students understand the size of numbers, develop multiple ways of thinking about and representing numbers, use numbers as referents, and develop accurate perceptions about the effects of operations on numbers" (NCTM, 2000, p. 80). Thus, number sense includes knowledge of magnitude comparison (which number is larger or smaller), recognizing number sequences and patterns, relating a number to another number (anchoring with 5 or 10), and basic math operations. Along with fluent counting strategies, early number sense forms the foundation for learning math concepts such as place value and for problem solving (Gersten et al., 2005; Van de Walle et al., 2016).

In terms of assessment, number sense is particularly important because it assists teachers in determining which students currently have mathematical difficulty; it also serves as a predictor for students who may have learning difficulties in the future. Several informal measures can be used to determine students' early math knowledge (Clarke & Shinn, 2004; Fuchs et al., 2007):

1. ***Number identification.*** Students are asked to identify orally numbers between 0 and 20 when these are presented randomly on a piece of paper.
2. ***Number writing.*** Students are asked to write a number between 1 and 20 when the number is provided to them orally.
3. ***Quantity discrimination.*** Students are asked to identify which of two numbers is the larger (or smaller).
4. ***Missing number.*** Students are provided with a string of numbers and are asked to identify the number that is missing.
5. ***Computation.*** Students are asked to complete computations that are representative of their grade level. Students are provided 2 minutes to complete as many problems as possible.

Given the growing interest in the importance of number sense in early stages of math learning, commercial screening and progress-monitoring measures are beginning to become available. For example, *Assessing Student Proficiency in Early Number Sense* (*ASPENS*) is an instrument designed for children in kindergarten through first grade (Clarke, Gersten, Dimino, & Rolfhus, 2011). Appropriate assessments allow teachers to detect early signs of math difficulties and to make effective instructional decisions that influence students' performance.

MyEdLab **Self-Check 16.3**

MyEdLab **Application Exercise 16.3:** Assessment and Progress Monitoring 

MyEdLab
Video Example 16.3.
Watch this video to see a teacher engaging her students in math problem solving. What hands-on instructional activities does this teacher use to help her students develop competence and confidence in math?

16.4 HELPING STUDENTS IMPROVE IN MATH

As Rodney Rouzard tells his students, they can become proficient in mathematics if they develop competence and confidence. This section includes concrete ways that you can implement to develop competence and confidence among your students.

16.4.1 Being a Model in Math

Most of the time, a positive attitude toward math comes from effective instruction and the interest the teacher shows in mathematics. Tips for Teachers 16.3 offers suggestions for promoting positive attitudes toward math.

TIPS FOR TEACHERS 16.3

Promoting Positive Attitudes Toward Math

- Provide multiple opportunities for success.
- Select real-world problems that address issues of importance to the students.
- Be certain that students have the prerequisite skills to adequately solve the problem.
- Teach students to chart their progress—success is the best motivator.
- Provide calculators and other tools to support success.
- For complex problems, ask students to solve the problem in steps so that they get feedback as they proceed.
- When appropriate, encourage students to work with partners.

16.4.2 Evaluating the Mathematics Curricula

Considering the mathematical focal points by NCTM (2006) and the guidance provided by the National Mathematics Advisory Panel (U.S. Department of Education, 2008), it is likely that math curricula will be influenced and aligned with the math panel guidelines described in the section "Influences on Math Instruction." Students with disabilities and math difficulties will benefit from teachers who consider the following:

- *Students have difficulty reading the information provided.* Because the reading vocabulary is too difficult and the reading level is too high, students with math difficulties are able to learn very little by reading their math books. Consequently, teachers must provide supports that make the information accessible. For example, Max Diamond, a tenth-grade math teacher, assigned several pages of reading in the math textbook as homework. Realizing that several of his students would not be able to read and understand the text adequately, Max had these pages read into an audio recording device and made the results available to all students in his class.
- *Math concepts are often presented poorly.* Multiple concepts are introduced at one time, and information is often presented in a scattered fashion. For this reason, Dawn McQueen reorganizes the information in the math text so that she can teach computation skills to mastery rather than skipping around teaching many new ideas in 2 weeks. Dawn introduces only one concept at a time, teaching that concept until *all* students in her class (not just those with learning problems) learn it. Then she moves on to the next concept. Although Dawn follows a sequence of pages different from that presented in the book, she believes that her efforts are worthwhile because her students seem to understand better.
- *There are insufficient problems covering any one concept or operation and too few opportunities for application of knowledge learned.* The problems are not presented in enough different situations for students to learn and transfer what they know. Janice Kauffman, a sixth-grade teacher, addresses this problem by developing her own supportive materials to supplement the book. She also provides practice with problem solving, reasoning, and real-life applications that help students transfer their knowledge to real-life settings.
- *Students often do not have the necessary prerequisite skills assumed by the text (and so the next level is too difficult).* As Margaret Gardner plans each math unit she teaches, she spends considerable time considering the prerequisite skills students need to master the concept or operation she is teaching. After identifying these prerequisite skills, she tells students directly that she is looking to see whether they know them. She prepares activities and exercises so that she knows which students do and which do not possess the skills they need to move on to the next math concept or operation.

- *The pages and organizational format of the text vary considerably and make learning from the text difficult.* Linda Saumell, having recognized this problem, walks students through the text section by section, explaining the format to them.
- *Students have difficulty transferring knowledge to real problems.* Many of the steps necessary to help students transfer what they know mathematically to selected problems are not taught explicitly, and so students fail to perform correctly. With problem solving, for example, students often know how to do pieces of the problem but do not know how to assemble these pieces to correctly generalize what they know to the new problem.

To shape the mathematics curricula so that it accommodates the learning needs of all students, particularly students with learning problems, teachers need to adapt traditional math curricula to best meet the learning needs of students in their classrooms. The teachers just cited are successful in addressing inherent limitations, improving their students' potential for a positive outcome.

16.4.3 Using Curricular Programs for Students with Math Difficulties

Other than the basal curriculum books, math workbooks, and curriculum guidebooks published by many state departments of education, what curriculum resources are available to teachers? The following list provides brief descriptions of some resources that are helpful for students who have difficulty learning math.

- **Vmath Third Edition®** (Voyager Sopris Learning, 2009) was developed for students in grades 2 through 8 who may need extra instruction to meet mathematics learning goals. Vmath is designed at each grade level to assess and monitor the progress of students so that through a systematic approach to instruction, they can develop into independent learners in math and meet grade-level goals in math. VMathLive provides online practice with purposeful, motivating tasks.
- **Corrective Mathematics 2005** (Englemann, Carnine, & Steely, 2005) stresses direct instruction through a highly sequenced format that provides immediate feedback to students. The mathematics modules come with a detailed teacher's guide, workbooks, and other supplementary materials. The entire program is based on behavioral principles of learning and provides explicit instructions for the teacher. Particular focus is on problem areas for students with challenges in learning math.
- **The NCTM Navigation Series** is a series of graded and topical books with CD-ROMs published by NCTM from 2001 to 2009. The books (ranging from PK through twelfth grade) focus on activities for teaching algebra, geometry, numbers and operations, and the like, based on the NCTM principles and standards.
- **Key Math™-3 Essential Resources** is designed to provide interventions for students with math difficulties (Connolly, 2007). Materials include 350 lesson plans, instructional easels, interactive software, and progress-monitoring tools.
- **ETA/hand²mind** provides a variety of supplemental mathematics materials. This company specializes in math manipulatives that emphasize learning principles through hands-on learning. One of its earliest products was the Cuisenaire rods. Cuisenaire rods come in various lengths and colors and can be used to represent numbers. Students with disabilities can be taught to use Cuisenaire rods as manipulatives to facilitate their successful understanding of word problems. Over time, they are able to generalize the skills learned to similar problems when the rods are not used (Marsh & Cooke, 1996).
- **Saxon Math™** was designed for use in kindergarten through seventh grade (Larson, 2004) and eighth through twelfth grade (Saxon, 2003), and addresses math concepts with an emphasis on solving math problems. Strategies for solving math problems are scaffolded through step-by-step problem solving. The program provides guidelines for differentiating instruction and making connections with "real-world" applications and mathematics concepts.

TIPS FOR TEACHERS 16.4

Providing Feedback That Enhances Student Learning

Teachers are often reluctant to give feedback to students with disabilities, wondering whether they will do more damage than good. Specific feedback helps students learn when it is provided with teaching the student as the goal. Consider the following suggestions:

- Provide feedback informing students that their response is not accurate and cue them as to what is wrong. Give students an opportunity to try again. Recognize positively if students are successful in the next try. If not successful, provide even more instruction with another opportunity to demonstrate success.
- Remind students of what they know and have done successfully in the past that is related to the problem. Encourage them to use previous knowledge to solve the new problem.
- Ask students to monitor their problem resolution and reinforce them for checking and monitoring their learning.
- Provide readily available answers and feedback so that students wait a minimal amount of time after completing problems to know what they did right and what needs to be redone.

- **Number Worlds®** includes Tier 2 and 3 teacher-led interventions in mathematics for students in prekindergarten through eighth grade (Griffin, Clements, & Sarama, 2015). Program includes an assessment component as well as digital and hands-on supplements to provide motivational instructional and practice activities.

Being aware of these options equips teachers with alternatives for helping all students achieve some success in math. When necessary, working with the special education teacher can help teachers identify the best programs for struggling students.

16.4.4 Using Peers to Support Instructional Practice

An effective way to facilitate learning of mathematics for students with difficulties is to engage peers in the process. One way is through peer pairing, in which two students work together (usually a stronger student in math is paired with a less able student). Students are provided instruction by the teacher, and then student pairs complete designated problems. The idea is that by working together they can learn to solve problems effectively (Dion, Fuchs, & Fuchs, 2007; Gardner, Nobel, Hessler, Yawn, & Heron, 2007), as well as practice these problem-solving skills (Fuchs et al., 1997). Peer tutoring is effective not only for the student who is tutored, but also for the student who does the tutoring (Leung, 2015). Teaching not only helps enhance students' self-concept, but also helps them learn a great deal.

Another way for students to learn to communicate mathematically is through cooperative learning groups (Francisco, 2013). Cooperative learning occurs when the teacher divides the class into small groups (ordinarily three or four students per group), usually not based on ability, and asks these groups to work together to solve problems. When students hold joint discussions related to problem solving, they can build on each other's ideas, engage in critical thinking, and enrich their understanding of mathematics concepts.

Slavin, Madden, and Leavey (1984; Slavin, 1995) designed team-assisted individualization, in which individualized instruction is provided in a cooperative learning model. Each of the four or five students in the heterogeneous learning team is assigned individualized mathematics material at his or her own level. Students on the same team help one another with problems and also manage checking and record keeping for the individualized math materials. Students work independently, but teachers teach skills to groups of students who are at the same level by pulling them from various teams.

16.4.5 Using Teaching Tools and Methods for Improvement

Student proficiency in mathematics is improved when instruction is systematic and explicit (Doabler et al., 2015; Fuchs, Seethaler et al., 2008; Gersten et al., 2009; Hughes,

Witzel, Riccomini, Fries, & Kanyongo, 2014). Guidelines for systematic and explicit instruction include:

- Explicit instruction that not only involves highly organized, step-by-step presentations related to the specific target skill, but also provides information about why learning this skill facilitates student learning.
- Assurance that students understand the directions and the task demands. Periodic checks are necessary to determine whether students understand the directions, and the teacher must monitor students' progress.
- The systematic use of learning principles. This refers to maintaining and using positive reinforcement, providing varied practice, and ensuring motivation.
- The use of everyday examples that are understandable and make sense to a wide range of youngsters based on their own experiences.
- Clearly articulated models with scripted examples of how these models can be used to promote instruction.

What can teachers do to ensure that students will improve their math performance? Baker et al.'s (2002) synthesis of the research suggests the following:

- Collect ongoing progress-monitoring data to identify what students are learning and how quickly they are learning.
- Have peers assist one another in learning, applying, and reviewing math problems.
- Use explicit and systematic instruction in all elements of mathematics, including computation and problem solving. This type of instruction guides students through problems and calculations rather than relying on students to "figure it out" independently.
- Provide parents with information on how their children are performing and engage them as supporters and motivators for their children's progress in mathematics.

Teaching with math manipulatives

Math manipulatives are designed to help students learn about mathematics concepts through active engagement (Carbonneau, Marley, & Selig, 2013). A three-step sequence—concrete–representational–abstract (CRA)—is used to help students comprehend math concepts (Berkas & Pattison, 2007; Cole & Wasburn-Moses, 2010; Steele & Steele, 2003). The first step (concrete) involves direct experiences with math manipulatives. Students engage in manipulative and interactive opportunities to integrate the new mathematical concept. For example, you can use play money, blocks, rods, cereal, Legos, geometric shapes, or other representations to demonstrate understanding of the answer to a math problem. While they are using the manipulatives, encourage students to use both oral and written language to relate to the new mathematical vocabulary and concept. Keep in mind that math manipulatives can be hands-on, physical models or virtual (web or computer-based) (Satsangi & Bouck, 2015).

The second step (representational) moves students to a representation of the concept using symbols such as tally marks or pictures. During this step, encourage students to talk about what they have learned and to explain it to others. By recording or demonstrating what they have learned in meaningful ways, they can link their language to the mathematical algorithm.

In the third step (abstract), have students solve the problem using numbers and traditional math symbols. In addition, you can teach the steps for computing or problem solving with alternative solutions, and then solve problems in new and creative ways without using concrete or pictorial representations. Tips for Teachers 16.5 provides do's and don'ts for using math manipulatives effectively.

TIPS FOR TEACHERS 16.5

Do's and Don'ts for Using Math Manipulatives

Do

- Achieve a balance between providing sufficient modeling and allowing students the opportunity to explore new concepts.
- Organize materials and anticipate potential difficulties students might experience in using them.
- Allow sufficient space and time to allow for efficient and effective exploration.
- Set firm guidelines for use of materials and be consistent in following the guidelines.
- Be creative in selecting materials and think about how commercial and everyday objects can be used to motivate students.
- Develop an organizational system for distribution and storage of materials.

Don't

- Think that manipulatives are only for students in elementary grades. Manipulatives can be used to engage middle and high school students as well.
- Think that manipulatives are only for students with disabilities. Most students can benefit from hands-on and virtual manipulatives.

16.4.6 Teaching for Comprehension

Teach students to understand math concepts. Most instruction is provided to ensure that the answer is correct, the math computation has been accurately completed, or the math fact is memorized. Additional emphasis on ensuring that students understand the math process needs to be included in the math curriculum. Jan Hughes, a third-grade teacher, continually asks students to say in their own words what she has just said. During math problem solving, she often asks students to work in groups of three to write story problems that go along with an operation she has just taught. She continually thinks about ways to make the mathematics she teaches "real" to students. The following section describes ways to check for comprehension in math instruction.

Checking for comprehension

The Case of Trinette Be certain that students understand the meaning of an operation, not just the answer. Students who have memorized the facts by rote often operate with little understanding of what they are doing. For example, Trinette was asked to write the answer to the following math problem:

$$3 \times 2 =$$

Answering correctly, she wrote 6. But when Trinette's teacher asked her to illustrate the problem with pictures of flowers, this is what Trinette drew:

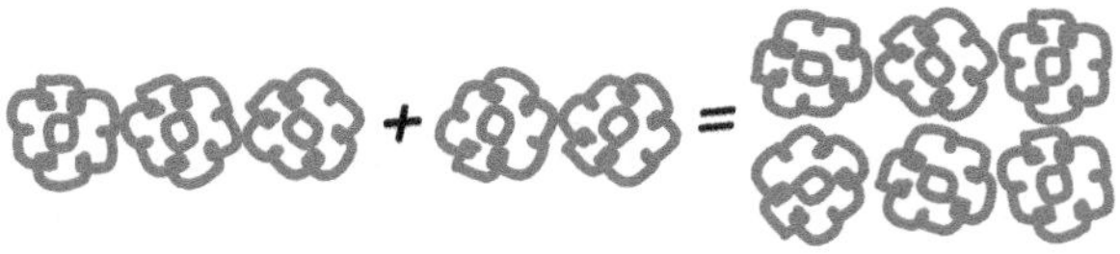

Trinette demonstrated that she did not understand the problem, although she had successfully memorized the answer and her facts.

The following drawing illustrates how rows of chips can be used to illustrate multiplication.

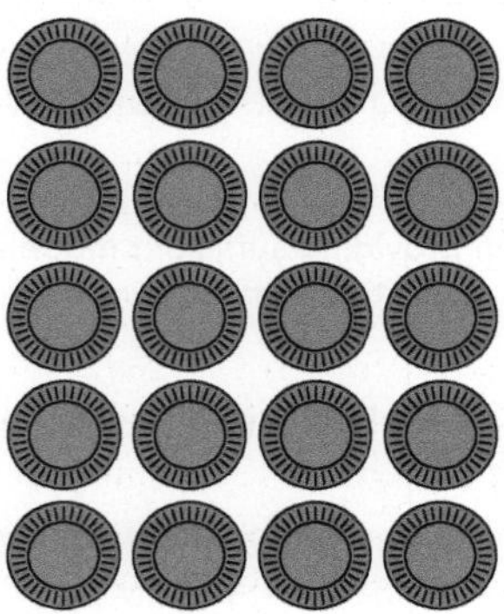

For example, ask, "How many 4s make 20?" "Fours are placed on the board ____ times."

$$4 \times \_\_\_\_ = 20$$

Other ways to check for comprehension include having students "talk aloud" about what is involved in solving a problem. Instead of letting them merely *read* the problem, ask them to *explain* what it means. For example, 63 − 27 could mean that someone had 63 pieces of gum and gave 27 pieces to a friend. Another strategy is to have one student explain the process to another student by using block manipulatives. For example, 24 + 31 is the same as adding 4 one-block pieces to 1 one-block piece and 2 ten-block pieces to 3 ten-block pieces. Some teachers use vocalization or have students close their eyes and use noises to illustrate operations. To illustrate multiplication, for example, the teacher and student might tap to indicate groups of six.

16.4.7 Using Constant Time-Delay Procedure

Constant time delay is a procedure for teaching math facts that provides for the systematic introduction of teacher assistance. This nearly errorless technique employs a controlling prompt to ensure the successful performance of the student (Gast, Ault, Wolery, Doyle, & Belanger, 1988; Stevens & Schuster, 1988; Swain, Lane, & Gast, 2015). In general, the procedure involves presentation of a stimulus (e.g., a word or math fact), after which the student is allowed a specific amount of time (e.g., 3 seconds) to provide the correct answer (e.g., read the word or answer the fact). If the student does not respond within the time allowed, a controlling prompt (typically a teacher modeling the correct response) is provided. The controlling prompt is a cue that ensures that the student will respond correctly (i.e., the word name or the answer to the problem is modeled). The student then repeats the teacher's model. Although correct responses before and after the prompt are reinforced, only correct responses given before the prompt count. The effectiveness of the constant time-delay procedure has been demonstrated with a variety of academic skills, students, and instructional arrangements, as demonstrated in the 60-Second Lesson (Mattingly & Bott, 1990; Schuster, Stevens, & Doak, 1990; Stevens & Schuster, 1987; Wolery, Cjybriwsky, Gast, & Boyle-Gast, 1991).

60-SECOND LESSON

USING THE CONSTANT TIME DELAY WITH MATH FACTS

- Ask a small group of students struggling with multiplication facts to join you at a small table.
- Show each student separately a math fact, allowing 3 seconds for them to respond.
- If they respond correctly within that time period, give them positive feedback.
- If they either respond incorrectly or not quickly enough, you can say, "The answer to 4 × 7 = 28. Can you say the problem and the answer?"

16.4.8 Providing Correction and Feedback

Immediate correction and feedback are essential to the success of students with math difficulties. Saying, "Orlando, the first six problems are correct, and then the third row is all wrong. Please redo them." is an example of insufficient feedback. Teachers often tell students which problems are correct and which are wrong and hope that this feedback is adequate. For students with learning problems, it is not. They need more sustained interaction to help them acquire not only the skills for identifying what they did wrong, but also the procedures for how to do it differently. The teacher must analyze the problem and also obtain sufficient information from the student to determine why the problem was not done correctly. A better model for correction and feedback is as follows: "Orlando, point to the problems you think are correct. Think about each problem before you point." (The teacher positively reinforces Orlando as he points to problems that are right.) "Yes, those are all correct. You did an excellent job with those. You started on the right, added them correctly, and carried numbers when you needed to."

When students are first learning a math concept or operation, teachers need to provide a great deal of assistance to ensure that students perform correctly. Over time, teachers need to systematically reduce the amount of help they give students.

16.4.9 Providing Practice

Practice is important if students are to exhibit high levels of accuracy consistently and across multiple problem types. Mastery occurs when students meet expectations for accuracy and speed in different types of problems. In operations, mastery refers to the ability to use multiple algorithms to solve an operation so that students truly learn (rather than memorize). Denise, a ninth-grade student, expresses her frustration this way: "I never seem to be able to really learn anything. Just when I feel like I'm starting to get it, we move on to a different thing. I wish I could just stay with something until I really get it." As a teacher, you need to know when there are students like Denise who need additional support.

Counting by numbers

Students are taught to "count by" numbers, beginning with 2, 10, and 5, and then 3, 4, 6, 7, 8, and 9. This is done by group counting, singing the numbers in sequence, writing the numbers, erasing some numbers in the sequence and having students fill them in, and having students work on worksheets with the count-by sequences.

After the students have learned to count by numbers, they can apply the strategy to multiplication by using the following steps:

1. Ask students to point to the number they can count by.
2. Make hash marks to represent the number on the other side of the multiplication sign.
3. When you count by the number, point to each of the hash marks. The last number said when you reach the end of the hash marks is the answer to the problem.

Games

Games can be an important way for students to practice mathematics skills (Shin, Sutherland, Norris, & Soloway, 2012; Ramani & Eason, 2015). Card, board, and computer games can promote positive attitudes about learning mathematics as well as increasing engagement and persistence (Shin et al., 2012). Commercial and teacher-made games can be linked to standards and can provide opportunities for differentiated instruction and practice (Trinter, Brighton, & Moon, 2015). Suggestions for using games in mathematics instruction include (Larson & Slaughter, 1984):

- *Choose games that reinforce present instruction.* Be sure that the selected game reinforces much of what students already know.
- *Consider the complexity of the game* so that students do not spend more time learning the game's procedures and rules than they spend learning the math-related material.

- *Foresee potential problems associated with games*, such as disruptive behavior and shouting out.
- *Provide an answer key if an adult is not available.*
- *Play at least one round of the game with students* to ensure that they understand the rules and procedures and are acquiring the mathematics skills desired.
- *Use aides or parent helpers to monitor the games.*

16.4.10 Adapting Instruction for Secondary Students with Math Difficulties

Older students with mathematical problems require instructional considerations to access and learn mathematics. Though the research base is better developed for teaching mathematics to younger students with learning difficulties, there are instructional practices with older students that are associated with improved outcomes. See Tips for Teachers 16.6 for some suggestions for teachers working with older students who have experienced years of challenge and frustration in learning math.

Many older students benefit from real-world problem solving that includes a game-like experience. Shaftel, Pass, and Schnabel (2005) provide an example of a game that gives adolescent students with learning disabilities an opportunity to use a checkbook and keep track of their expenses.

Teachers can create a game board on which each "space" has a real-life experience. Examples of these experiences include

- Pay rent for your apartment: \$300.
- Receive your monthly paycheck of \$800.
- Unexpected dental expense; pay \$180.

Each student is provided with a checkbook and checks. Students can all be given a designated amount of money at the beginning of the game. Based on where they land on the game board, they add or subtract money. After a specified period of time, the student with the most money in his or her checkbook is the winner.

TIPS FOR TEACHERS 16.6

Working with Older Students Who Have Experienced Frustrations Learning Math

- *Provide explicit instruction.* For many students, this means clearly identifying the steps in solving the problem, facilitating background knowledge and skills, and demonstrating clearly all aspects of problem resolution. One way teachers can improve explicit instruction is to determine whether they have made transparent to the learner all critical parts of solving the mathematical problem.
- *Provide a clear and sufficient number of examples; most commercial materials fall short in this area.* Students with learning difficulties benefit from more examples and nonexamples. This means showing them the application several ways. It is also useful to demonstrate a counterexample that illustrates a faulty application.
- *Give real-life applications for students.* Students with mathematical difficulties find math abstract and conceptually difficult to understand. For this reason, teachers who link the problems to real-life situations are more successful.
- *Provide ample opportunities to be successful.* Students with mathematical difficulties need not only lots of examples from the teacher, but also lots of opportunities to practice the different problem types until they master them. One of the critical difficulties experienced by students with math problems is that they never really master a problem type before they are introduced to something new.
- *Use cooperative learning activities, but include individual accountability as a key component.* Although cooperative learning (asking students to work in small groups with three to five other students in which they all attempt to solve the same problem) may be useful for students with mathematical difficulties because it provides them ready access to able students as models and guides, it also can have the negative consequence of leaving the target student out of the learning. Unless there is a focus on individual accountability, where every student is responsible for demonstrating learning, it is possible that cooperative groups can give students with mathematical difficulties a free ride.

Using real-world examples such as paying bills and keeping a checkbook heightens students' interest in doing math. It also shows them that there are important reasons to master math skills, as they really do need to use these skills in their everyday lives.

MyEdLab **Self-Check 16.4**

MyEdLab **Application Exercise 16.4:** Providing Practice

16.5 STRATEGIES FOR HELPING ALL STUDENTS ACQUIRE BASIC MATH SKILLS

Beginning mathematics instruction once focused on the acquisition of the basic math skills, saving problem solving for later in the math curriculum. We now realize that teaching basic skills and problem solving must be coordinated from the beginning of math instruction. Key components of basic math skills include the following:

- Prenumber
- Numeration
- Place value
- Fractions

16.5.1 Prenumber Skills

Many young students with learning problems come to school without the prenumber skills necessary for initial success in mathematics. This may be due to lack of exposure at home or preschool or developmental disabilities (Browder et al., 2012). Sonya Perez, a first-grade teacher, described her student Malcolm in this way: "When he came to my class, he knew how to count to 10, but he didn't know what he was doing. He didn't know what the numbers meant. As far as he knew, he could have been saying his ABCs." She realized that he first needed to learn one-to-one correspondence. Prenumber skills include one-to-one correspondence, classification, seriation, and patterning.

One-to-one correspondence

Students demonstrate understanding of one-to-one correspondence when they are able to determine that each object corresponds to another object. For example, when a student puts out cereal bowls for himself, his sister, and his mother, he learns that each bowl represents one person. Early humans used one-to-one correspondence to keep track of their accounts. For example, a man might have put a rock in a bucket to represent each bag of grain he gave to a neighbor. The following activities can be used to teach one-to-one correspondence:

- *Use everyday events to teach one-to-one correspondence.* Allow students with difficulties in this area to pass out materials. "Allison, please get one pair of scissors for each student in your group. Naja, you need to have a chair for each member of your group. How many chairs are there? How many more do you need?"
- *Use objects when you work with small groups of students who need help with one-to-one correspondence.* Give each student ten small blocks. Place three blocks in the center. Say, "I want you to place a block next to each one in the center. As you place a block, I want you to say the number. I will do the first one, and then you do what I did."
- *Give students a set of cards with pictures on each card.* Ask students to put the correct number of objects (e.g., pegs) on top of each number card. Reverse the task by giving objects to students and asking them to put the correct picture card next to the objects.

Classification

Classification, the ability to group or sort objects based on one or more common properties, is an important prenumber skill because it focuses students, making them attend to the common properties of objects and reduce large numbers of objects to smaller groups. Classification can be by size, color, shape, texture, or design. Most students are naturally interested in sorting and think that activities related to this prenumber skill are fun. Examples of such activities follow:

- Provide students with a bag of miscellaneous articles that vary in size, shape, and color. Ask students to sort the articles any way they like into an empty egg carton or empty plastic containers. After they finish, ask them to tell you the rules for sorting their articles. After they have had a chance to listen to others, give them a chance to sort the articles again and to explain their rules for sorting.
- Provide students with an empty egg carton and a box of small articles. Ask students to sort the articles by a single property, such as color. Now ask them whether there is another way in which they might be able to sort the articles. For example, ask them to consider size, texture, and so on.
- Ask students to work in small groups, and provide them with a bag of articles. Ask one student to sort several of the articles by a property. Then ask other students in the group to guess the property that qualifies the articles for the group.
- Use pictures for sorting tasks. Good pictures include ones that represent animals, foods, plants, and toys.
- Board games and bingo games can be played by sorting or classifying shapes, colors, and pictures.

Seriation

Seriation, the ability to rank objects according to the degree to which they possess a certain common characteristic, is similar to classification in that it depends on the recognition of common attributes of objects, but differs from classification in that the order in which objects are placed depends on the extent to which each object possesses the attribute. For example, seriation can occur by length, height, color, or weight. Sample activities for teaching seriation follow:

- Give students a long piece of string. Ask them to cut the string into pieces of various lengths. Then ask them to put the lengths in order from shortest to longest. Now ask students to work in groups of three. Have them use those same piles of string to create one long seriation, from shortest to longest. Continue to ask students to work in different groups to sort the string sizes.
- Ask students to work in groups of eight. In these groups, ask them to put themselves in order from shortest to tallest. Now ask them to put themselves in order from longest to shortest hair. Continue asking students to put themselves in seriation based on different attributes.
- Using a peg with various sizes of rings, ask students to put the rings on the peg from largest to smallest.
- Fill jars of the same size with different amounts of sand or water and ask students to put them in order.

See the Activities for All Learners feature later in the chapter for more activities.

MyEdLab
Video Example 16.4.
Watch this video to see a teacher providing instruction on mathematical patterns. What hands-on instructional activities does Ms. Adimoolah use to make learning patterns motivational and purposeful to all learners?

Patterning

Patterning is the ability to identify, duplicate, extend, and describe predictable sequences (Rittle-Johnson, Fyfe, Loehr, & Miller, 2015). Patterning is an important mathematical concept that is increasingly being recognized as critical to mathematic achievement and algebraic reasoning (Kidd et al., 2014). Pattern instruction includes both repeating (abbabb) and growing (a, ab, abc, abcd) patterns (Van de Walle et al., 2016).

In pre-kindergarten and kindergarten, teaching of patterning begins with recognition of patterns in the environment (e.g., stripes on the American flag, black and white keys on a piano). Activities involve duplicating patterns using blocks, shapes, or other objects in predictable patterns. Students also learn to continue or complete patterns and to generate "rules" for the pattern. As the students progress, numerical patterns of increasing difficulty are included in the curriculum.

16.5.2 Working with Numeration

Numeration is the understanding of numbers and their manipulations. Do not assume that because students can count or identify numbers that they understand the value and the meaning of the numbers. This is a mistake that many teachers and parents make.

Understanding numerals is an extremely important basic concept, one that throws many children into mathematical confusion early. A good example is Michelle, whose early experiences with math were positive. She learned to say, read, and write numbers with little or no difficulty. In first and second grade, she mastered addition and subtraction facts and did these problems easily. When Michelle was asked to do problems that involved addition with regrouping (adding numerals and then converting them to tens, hundreds, thousands, etc.), her lack of knowledge of numerals and their meaning quickly became evident. Following are examples of the way Michelle did some problems.

$$27 + 15 = 312$$
$$49 + 36 = 715$$

Why is extra practice in estimation and other basic math skills important for students with math difficulties? How can instruction in those skills be modified for students with learning problems?

As you can see from Michelle's answers, she remembered her math facts, such as $7 + 5$ and $2 + 1$, or $9 + 6$ and $4 + 3$, but did not understand what the numbers meant. Michelle added 7 plus 5 to get 12 and then 2 plus 1 to get 3, resulting in the answer 312; however, Michelle did not understand the importance of place value, nor did she "check" her answer by estimating a reasonable answer and determining if she was even close.

Understanding numeration and place value is necessary for progress in computation. Like Michelle, many students fail to make adequate progress in math because they do not understand the meaning of the numerals and the place value with which they are working. For example, students who understand the meaning of the numerals 25 and 17 would be less likely to make the following conceptual error:

$$25 - 17 = 12$$

Estimating

Many students with learning difficulties in math do not have a sense of how much a certain amount really is—what it means to have five dollars, for example, or how many eggs are in a dozen, or about what 15 and 15, added together, should equal. These students cannot check their answers to determine how far off they are because they do not have a good idea of what an answer that makes sense would be.

Estimating is something that can be done throughout the day and throughout the curriculum. For example, start the day by asking students to estimate how many children are absent. Estimation can be included in subject-matter content as well. You can use estimation in science and social studies, and even with art projects.

Students who do not understand the real meaning of numerals have difficulty applying computation to everyday problems. For example, when Michelle's teacher posed the following problem, Michelle did not understand how to begin to find the answer: "Let's pretend that you had three one-dollar bills and you were going to McDonald's to buy lunch. Let's pretend that your hamburger cost 89 cents, your French fries cost 74 cents, and your medium-sized Coke cost 69 cents. How much money would you have left to spend?"

Mistakes occur when students attempt problems that are entirely too difficult for them or when they do not understand the idea behind the problem. In such cases, the solutions students provide are totally unreasonable given the problem. One of the best ways to help students who demonstrate this problem is to continually ask them to think about the problem and estimate what their answer probably will be. For example, before computing the problem 24 plus 73, ask students what they would estimate the answer would be. If students have difficulty even identifying a reasonable response, help them round the two numbers up or down so they are easier to estimate. In the previous problem, students can round 24 up to 25 and 73 to 75. That way they can guess that the answer will be very close to 100. When students are taught to consider what a reasonable answer should be, they are better able to catch their mistakes. Estimation problems are particularly severe for students with disabilities who demonstrate low understanding of mathematical problems and the meaning of numbers (Lucangeli, Coi, & Bosco, 1997). For this reason, it is beneficial to provide students with opportunities to determine if answers "make sense" or could really be accurate. Techniques like reporting a students' answer and then asking students to "think about it" and indicate through "thumbs up" or "thumbs down" whether it is likely to be correct can be useful.

Understanding regrouping

Regrouping refers to converting from tens to ones or hundreds to tens, and so forth, so that borrowing can occur. Many children have difficulty with regrouping. Regrouping errors are less likely to occur when students understand numeration. The following are examples of regrouping errors:

$$39 + 27 = 516$$
$$56 - 18 = 42$$
$$41 - 24 = 23$$

Examine the errors students make and use the information to provide instruction. For example, some students subtract the smaller number from the larger number regardless of the problem. These students need practicing reading the entire number and determining which number is larger. Practicing reading numbers and stating which one is bigger or smaller may be helpful to them. Furthermore, students who consistently make errors in regrouping can practice subtracting smaller numbers (e.g., single-digit numbers) until they can do so automatically and correctly before subtracting more complex numbers.

Understanding zero

Students need to understand that zero is a number and means more than "nothing." In the number 30, for example, students need to understand that the number zero is a placeholder. For the number 306, students need to understand that there are 0 tens and that zero is serving as a placeholder.

16.5.3 Understanding Place Value

Before students can understand place value, they must understand numeration. Students who know the meaning of numbers will have far less difficulty understanding place value. For example, if a student knows what 56 actually means, then when someone talks about the tens place equaling 50, the student will not be confused. When someone talks about the ones place equaling 6 ones, the student will understand what is meant.

Grouping by ones and tens

To teach grouping, start with manipulatives (buttons, sticks, and blocks are useful), then move to pictures, and then numbers. Ask students to practice grouping by ones and tens. Students can also develop a table to record their answers, as follows:

Hundreds	Tens	Ones	Numerals
1	3	1	131
1	2	3	123
1	4	5	145

Use "ten blocks" and "single blocks" to represent numerals. For example, 35 can be represented as follows:

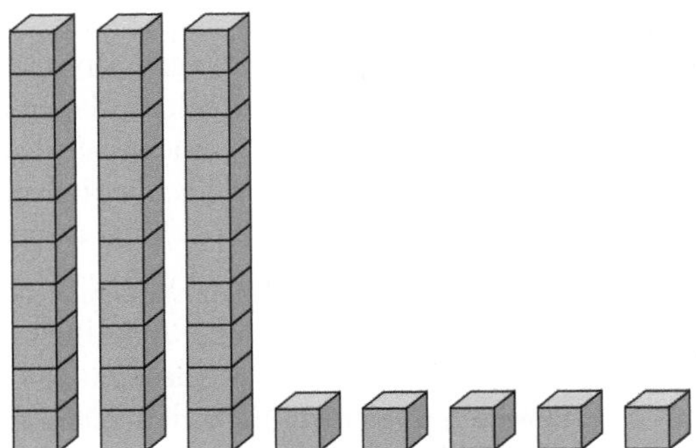

Naming tens

Teach students to identify numerals by the number of tens. For example, 6 tens is 60, 4 tens is 40, 8 tens is 80, and so on. Give students opportunities to count by tens and then name the number. For example, "Count by tens three times." "10, 20, 30." "Count by tens seven times." "10, 20, 30, 40, 50, 60, 70." Also give students opportunities to draw picture diagrams that represent the place values of tens and ones and to identify the number.

Place value beyond two digits

When students can accurately group and identify numbers at the two-digit level, introduce them to three- and four-digit numbers. It is a good idea to be certain that students have mastered the concept of two-digit place value before you introduce numerals and place value. Give students plenty of opportunity to group, orally name, and sequence three- and four-digit place values.

Because place value is a skill taught during the primary grades, older students who have not adequately learned the skill will have difficulty with computation and word problems and may have little opportunity to learn place value. Many of the games and activities designed to teach place value are aimed at young children and are less appropriate for older students. Tips for Teachers 16.7 provides sources of numbers from real-life context that may be useful for teaching place value to older students.

16.5.4 Learning Fractions

Although often thought of as one of the more difficult mathematical skills, fractions are actually introduced early in the mathematics curriculum. Children between the ages of 3 and 5 discover fractions when they begin to cook. "Pour in $^1/2$ cup of milk and $^1/3$ cup of raisins" is often a youngster's introduction to fractions. Sharing—as in "Give half of your cookie to your sister"—is also a good way for children to discover fractions.

TIPS FOR TEACHERS 16.7

Sources of Numbers for Teaching Place Value to Older Students

- An odometer
- Numbers from students' science or social studies texts
- Numbers from school population (e.g., number of first-year students, sophomores, juniors, seniors, and so on)
- Population data from town, county, state, or country
- Financial data page from the newspaper

The teaching of fractions, mirroring that of other computations, proceeds from concrete to abstract. Many manipulative aids can be used to teach fractions: colored rods, cardboard strips and squares, blocks, fractional circle wheels, cooking utensils such as measuring cups and spoons, and any unit divider (e.g., egg cartons and muffin pans).

Fractions frequently pose problems for students with learning problems (Newton, Willard, & Teufel, 2014). Students who have difficulty in learning fractions are likely to experience problems with higher-order mathematics such as algebra (Bottge, Ma, Gassaway, Butler, & Toland, 2014). They are unlikely to learn fractions unless they are taught directly and systematically (Engelmann et al., 2005). Such teaching includes the following:

- *Systematic practice in discriminating among different problem types.* Students with learning disabilities and behavior problems often confuse algorithms when they compute fractions. For example, when adding fractions the denominator stays the same, as in $^1/4$ plus $^3/4$ = $^4/4$ or 1. However, when dividing with fractions the denominator changes.
- *Separation of confusing elements and terminology.* Because much of the language of learning fractions is unfamiliar and confusing, students are more likely to learn fractions successfully when the language and concepts are clearly explained and illustrated.
- *Use of a wide range of elements to illustrate each concept.* Students have a difficult time generalizing beyond the number of examples provided by the teacher; therefore, by providing many different examples, you help students understand.

The teaching sequence for fractions, which ensures that each student can do certain work, is as follows:

1. ***Manipulate concrete models.*** Students must use fraction blocks and pegs and use instruments that require understanding of fractions (such as measuring cups, spoons, and rulers).
2. ***Match fractional models.*** Students must match halves, thirds, and fourths. One way to do this is to think about the role of fractions when dividing food such as pizza or pieces of cake.
3. ***Point to a fractional model when the teacher names a fraction.*** When the teacher says "half," the student selects a model of "half" from several answers.
4. ***Name a fractional unit when the teacher selects it.*** When the teacher points to a fractional unit such as a "fourth," the student names it.
5. ***Draw diagrams or use manipulatives to represent fractional units.*** When the teacher says or writes fractional units such as "whole," "half," and "third," the student uses manipulative drawings to represent these units.
6. ***Write fraction names when given fractional drawings.*** When the teacher shows the student a picture of a fractional unit, the student writes the name of the fraction.
7. ***Use fractions to solve problems.*** Fractions are very helpful for dividing the cost of a bill when eating out or when dividing food such as a pie.

MyEdLab **Self-Check 16.5**

MyEdLab **Application Exercise 16.5:** Learning Fractions

16.6 STRATEGIES FOR HELPING ALL LEARNERS ACQUIRE AND USE COMPUTATION SKILLS

The emphasis on problem solving from NCTM (2000) does not mean that students do not need to learn math computation. In fact, students will be unsuccessful problem solvers if they spend too much time on math computation. Developing fluency in addition, subtraction, multiplication, and division computational operations in the early grades provide a firm foundation for subsequent grades (Miller et al., 2011). You can help students with special needs, which often have difficulty with math computation, by addressing the following issues that present obstacles for these students.

16.6.1 Patterns of Common Computation Errors

The computation errors that students make fit certain patterns. Rourke (1993) identifies common types of mechanical arithmetic errors, described in the following sections. Tips for Teachers 16.8 has suggestions for helping students learn computational techniques.

TIPS FOR TEACHERS 16.8

Teaching Students Computational Strategies

1. **Use doubles.** Students know that 2 + 2 = 4, 3 + 3 = 6, and 5 + 5 = 10. With this basic information, they can easily compute related facts. For example, if 3 + 3 = 6, what is 3 + 4? Yes, it is one more.

2. **Count on.** Students do not need to resort to counting from 1 to solve math facts. They can learn to count on from the largest numeral in an addition fact. For example, 8 + 3 means counting on 3 more from 8, for a sum of 11. Students learn to count on 3 more from 8: "9, 10, 11." The answer is the last number they say after they have counted on the correct number. Students can use this same principle for subtraction. For example, when asked to solve the following problem:

   8 − 3 =

   they now count backward from eight, "7, 6, 5." Again, the last number is the answer.

3. **Use the commutative idea.** With addition and multiplication, the order of the numbers does not matter—it always yields the same answer. For example, 3 + 4 = 7 and 4 + 3 = 7. With multiplication, this is also true: 4 × 6 = 24 and 6 × 4 = 24. Give students many opportunities to use this principle to be sure they understand and apply it.

4. **Think one more or one less than a known fact.** When students know a math fact, teach them that they also know related math facts. For example, Guido knew that 6 + 7 = 13. When he was faced with the problem 6 + 8 = ________, he panicked. When his teacher told him that 8 is one more than 7, thus the answer is one more than 6 + 7 = 13, he was able to solve the problem quickly. Pictures such as the following can help to illustrate the principle:

   5 + 5 = 10 ♥♥♥♥♥ + ♥♥♥♥♥ =

   5 + 6 = ♥♥♥♥♥ + ♥♥♥♥♥♥ =

   5 + 4 = ♥♥♥♥♥ + ♥♥♥♥ =

5. **Using tens.** Students can learn that 10 + any single-digit number merely changes the 0 in the 10 to the number they are adding to it, as in the following examples:

   10 + 4 = 14
   10 + 8 = 18

6. **Using nines.** There are two strategies students can apply to addition facts that involve nines. First, they can think of the 9 as a 10 and then subtract 1 from the answer. In the following example, the student is taught to "think" of the 9 as a 10:

   9 + 6 think 10 + 6 = 16 − 1 = 15

   Second, students can think that whenever there is a 9 in an addition problem, the answer in the ones column is always one less than the number they are adding to the 9. For example:

   9 + 4 = 13   8 + 9 = 17   9 + 6 = 15

7. **Counting by twos, threes, fours, fives, and tens.** Beginning with 10, teach students to count by the number. This can be done with individual students or with a small group. It is sometimes helpful to develop a rhythm to the counting sequence:

   10 – 20 – 30 – 40 – 50 – 60 – 70 – 80 – 90 – 100

   After students can count by tens to 100, ask them to count aloud by 10 from two points other than 10 and 100. For example, "Count aloud from 20 to 80." After students have learned to count by tens, they should be taught to count by fives and then by twos, threes, and fours. Being able to count by multiples helps in addition, multiplication, and division. Multiplication facts can be taught by interpreting 3 × 4 as counting by threes four times. Division facts, such as 8 divided by 2, can be interpreted as "How many times do you count by twos before you reach 8?"

8. **Relationship between addition and subtraction and between multiplication and division.** After students learn addition facts, they can be shown the relationship between the addition facts and subtraction. For example, students who know 7 + 6 = 13 can learn the relationships between the known addition fact and the subtraction fact, 13 − 7 = ________. Whenever possible, reinforce this principle as students are working: "You know 8 + 4 = 12, so 12 − 4 must be ________." Give students known facts and ask them to form subtraction problems. These sample relationships can be used to teach multiplication and division facts.

Sources: Adapted from *Teaching mathematics to students with learning disabilities*, by N. S. Bley & C. A. Thornton, 2001, Austin, TX: PRO-ED; "Basic math facts: Guidelines for teaching and learning," by C. A. Thornton & M. A. Toohey, 1985, *Learning Disabilities Focus*, 1, 44–57; and *Teaching mathematics to children with special needs*, by C. A. Thornton, B. F. Tucker, J. A. Dossey, & E. F. Brazik, 1983, Menlo Park, CA: Addison-Wesley.

Spatial organization

Mistakes in spatial organization are those that occur because students misalign numbers in columns. These mistakes can occur when students copy problems incorrectly or as they solve problems. One way to help students correct misaligned numbers is to tell them to draw vertical lines through their numbers to ensure that ones, tens, and hundreds are all in the right place. Another way to help is to provide graph paper with large squares so that students can write the numbers in boxes and more easily align them.

Visual detail

Mistakes involving visual detail occur when students misread one aspect of the arithmetic problem—misreading a minus sign as a plus sign, for example, or disregarding a dollar sign. Because many of the problems that occur in mathematics can be easily corrected by the student, teach students to stop and reread the problem and their answers before they go to the next problem to be sure that they neither misread nor omitted something.

Procedural error

Procedural error occurs when students misapply a procedure from one arithmetic operation to another. For example, a student learns that $5 \times 5 = 25$, and when asked to complete the problem $5 + 5$, misapplies information from multiplication and writes the answer 25.

Failure to shift operations

A failure to shift operations occurs when students fail to move to another operation after completing one operation. This occurs in word problems that involve more than one step, such as subtraction and addition. To help students who demonstrate this problem, ask them to reread the problem and tell you whether more than one operation is involved. Ask them to identify the types of operations involved and to provide an example of each one. Ask them to tell you how they will monitor their process and determine how they will ensure accuracy in switching from one operation to the next.

Motoric problems

Mistakes resulting from motoric problems can occur when the students' writing is so difficult to read that it leads to errors in arithmetic. Many students with learning problems demonstrate such poor writing ability that it interferes with their ability to successfully perform arithmetic computations. These students have difficulty not only writing their numbers but also reading them. They often mistake their fives for threes, their twos for threes, and so on. Therefore, their calculations may be accurate, according to their interpretation of the number, but the answers are wrong because they have mistaken the number.

Memory problems

Mistakes resulting from memory problems occur when students forget or misremember a fact that leads to an error in arithmetic calculation. As a teacher, you can help students with learning problems by providing them with adequate time and frequent opportunities to rehearse and learn arithmetic facts.

Difficulty with zero

Difficulty with zero can lead to mistakes that occur when students do not understand the multiple meanings and uses of zero. Many students with learning problems learn that zero means "nothing," and they never really understand that zero is a number or the role of zero as a placeholder. The best way to help students who have difficulty with zero is to ensure that they understand how zero can be used as a placeholder. To facilitate understanding and adequate use of zero, you can teach a mini-lesson to a small group of students who demonstrate difficulty with this concept, such as the one described in the 60-Second Lesson.

60-SECOND LESSON
THE MEANING OF "ZERO"

In a 60-second lesson, the teacher might indicate that the term *zero* has several meanings.

- "What is one of the meanings of *zero*?" "Yes, zero means 'nothing.'"
- "If you have zero candy, you have no candy."
- "A different meaning of zero is as a placeholder when we are writing numbers. For example, in the number 100, the zeros tell us that the number is a LOT more than 1." The teacher can then delete the zero at the end of the number 100.
- The teacher then asks, "What number is this? Yes, the new number is 10. The zero at the end tells us that the number is more than 1 but a lot less than the previous number 100."

The teacher can then add additional examples.

16.6.2 Computation and Calculators

Calculators and other technological supports are part of everyday life for most adults. Thus, helping students develop fluency in their use is a practice that has gained support from the National Council of Teachers of Mathematics in its 2011 position statement on Calculator Use in Elementary Grades. If your instructional purpose is to practice calculation skills, technology use is not appropriate (Van de Walle et al., 2016). However, calculators are commonly used as an adaptation for students with disabilities in ongoing mathematics instruction and in some states as a support for students in taking standardized tests (Bouck & Bouck, 2008; Carpenter, Johnston, & Beard, 2015).

There is evidence that calculators assist in the acquisition of mathematics achievement (Center for Implementing Technology in Education, 2007). Reviews of the calculator research have drawn the following conclusions:

- Calculators for instructional purposes do not impede the acquisition of basic skills. In fact, calculators can increase skill acquisition.
- The advantages of using calculators are more obvious for problems that include computation than for problem solving.
- Students who use calculators on criterion tests produce higher achievement scores than students who do not.
- Studies indicate that students do not develop a negative attitude toward math because of calculator use. In fact, calculators improve students' attitudes toward mathematics.
- It is appropriate to introduce calculators at the same time that the paper-and-pencil methods are taught.
- Students can develop their own complex problems and then solve them with use of the calculator. This also serves to increase their self-concept about their math skills.

Students are more likely to be persistent in solving math problems and have a better attitude toward math when they use technology supports (Cawley, Foley, & Doan, 2003). The Tech Tips, "Using Technology to Master Math," provides examples of some of these supports.

MyEdLab **Self-Check 16.6**

MyEdLab **Application Exercise 16.6:** Strategies for Helping All Learners Acquire and Use Computation Skills

TECH TIPS

Using Technology to Master Math

Many educational software programs are designed to enhance mathematics instruction and learning, whether they provide students with reinforced practice, provide a better calculator, or enable teachers to create digital manipulatives to enhance lessons.

AAAMATH

(www.aaamath.com)

A web resource for math activities loaded with explanations, interactive practice, and games, along with teacher resources.

Classroom Suite 4, IntelliTools, Inc.

(www.mayer-johnson.com)

The math component of this suite contains many templates and tools that allow teachers to easily design custom activities.

FRS Talking Calculator (shareware for Macintosh)

(fastrabbitsoftware.com)

The National Library of Virtual Manipulatives

(http://nlvm.usu.edu)

This website (housed at Utah State University) is a valuable resource for computer-based manipulatives and games.

iPad/iPod™ applications include:

- Math Dictionary for Kids
- Math Bug Free
- Door 24 Plus
- Counting Caterpillar
- Team Umizoomi Math: Zoom into Numbers HD
- Visual Nerd Mobile Math
- Park Math HD
- Math Board
- Mathemagics–Mental Math Tricks
- Math Bingo

16.7 STRATEGIES FOR HELPING ALL STUDENTS DEVELOP PROBLEM-SOLVING SKILLS

Teaching problem-solving skills is an important aspect of effective math instruction. Mathematical word problems involve both the translation of linguistic statements and implementing appropriate mathematical solutions (Zheng, Flynn, & Swanson, 2012). Mathematical word problems play a prominent role in standards-based education as students learn to apply math concepts in real-world settings and also in learning science, technology, and engineering subject matter. While word problems are introduced in early grades, their role becomes more prominent in the middle and high school curriculum. There are several unifying components of mathematical problem solving:

- A mathematics knowledge base,
- An application of knowledge to new and unfamiliar situations, and
- An ability to actively engage in thinking processes and apply this knowledge base to problems.

Each of these components must be present in order to help all students understand how to develop problem-solving skills.

Math word problems (sometimes called story problems in elementary grades) offer challenges for students with a wide range of mathematic skills. However, for students with mathematics disabilities or students at-risk of mathematics disabilities, there are a number of factors beyond computational skills that interfere with solving math problems including text comprehension, lack of knowledge of mathematics vocabulary, memory, strategy planning, and execution.

A growing body of research has led to breakthroughs in the teaching of math word problems through the use of strategy instruction (e.g., Jitendra et al., 2015; Krawec et al.,

2012; Montague et al., 2011). With explicit instruction, students with MD (math disorder) and at-risk of MD can develop independence in solving math word problems. Key elements of strategy instruction include:

- Step-by-step presentation of strategy
- Teacher modeling of strategy
- Careful sequencing of problems (e.g., easy to difficult, concrete to abstract, single-step to multi-step)
- Use of visual representations such as diagrams
- Incorporation of opportunities for student verbalization and discussion of processes
- Scaffolding of instruction to work toward independence

Video Example from YouTube

MyEdLab
Video Example 16.5.
Watch the YouTube video "Classroom Close-up: Part 4: Third Grade Math Solutions." How can you use graphic organizers to help students become engaged in the problem solving process? https://www.youtube.com/watch?v=VW-XpG6u3Dk

16.7.1 Teaching Problem-Solving Strategies

When teaching story problems to students with learning and behavior difficulties, keep the following guidelines in mind (Vaughn & Bos, 2015):

- Be certain students can perform the arithmetic computation before introducing the computation in story problems.
- Develop a range of story problems that contain the type of problem you want students to learn to solve so that they have adequate opportunities to practice and learn the pattern of the story problem.
- Instruct with one type of problem until mastery is attained.
- Teach students to read through the word problem and visualize the situation. Ask them to read the story aloud and tell what it is about.
- Ask students to reread the story, this time to get the facts.
- Identify the key question. In the beginning stages of problem solving, students should write the key question so that it can be referred to when computation is complete.
- Identify extraneous information. Tell students to note that this information will not be used.
- Reread the story problem and attempt to state the situation in a mathematical sentence. The teacher plays an important role in this step by asking the students questions and guiding them in formulating the arithmetic problem.
- Tell students to write the arithmetic problem and compute the answer. Students can compute some problems in their heads without completing this step.
- Tell students to reread the key question and be sure that they have completed the problem correctly.
- Ask students whether their answer is likely, based on their estimate.

Because many students with disabilities benefit from cognitive problem-solving instruction, Montague and colleagues developed and researched a 7-step strategy for math problem solving called *Solve It!* Using explicit, scaffolded instruction, students learn to:

1. Read the problem for initial understanding. If students have difficulty reading, read the problem to them.
2. Ask students to think about and identify the key words in the problem using their own words. Guide students in putting the key parts of the problem in their own words.
3. Ask students to visualize the problem or draw it.
4. Help students determine a reasonable hypothesis for solving the problem.
5. Ask students to estimate an answer.

6. Provide guided instruction as students calculate the answer.
7. Determine the accuracy of the answer.

Mercer and Miller (1992) developed a procedure called FAST DRAW to teach the concrete–representational–abstract teaching principle advocated in mathematics instruction. The Strategic Math Series is the name of their program. Following is an explanation of the FAST DRAW strategy:

Find what you're solving for.

Ask yourself, "What are the parts of the problem?"

Set up the numbers.

Tie down the sign.

Discover the sign.

Read the problem.

Answer or draw a conceptual representation of the problem, using lines and tallies, and check.

Write the answer.

16.7.2 Integrating Math Problem Solving into the Curriculum

Problem solving does not have to occur only during math time; it is an interesting and fun activity to integrate into the rest of the curriculum as well. Integration of math problem solving into the curriculum does not take the place of explicit, systematic mathematics instruction (Shaughnessy, 2013), particularly for students with learning disabilities. However, such integration can teach more about the application of mathematics in a variety of academic and real-world contexts.

Video Example from YouTube

MyEdLab
Video Example 16.6.
Watch the YouTube video "Career Showcase for Students with Disabilities." How can experiences such as this conference benefit students with disabilities? https://www.youtube.com/watch?v=o3mKYZo7zXs

Mathematics problem solving can be incorporated in science education. In recent years, a great deal of attention has been placed on the importance of Science, Technology, Engineering, and Mathematics (STEM) education (U.S. Department of Education 2013). Indeed, access to higher education and jobs of the future for all students depends largely on increased student proficiency in these disciplines. Frequently, students with disabilities have difficulty transferring learning in one area to another (Basham & Marino, 2013). Therefore, opportunities for problem solving in multiple contexts are important. STEM education has taken on various definitions and instructional formats across the country (Shaughnessy, 2013). In some cases, STEM education involves increased emphasis on problem solving within academic areas. In other cases, it involves interdisciplinary activities. What is essential to STEM education is the development of engineering "habits of the mind" that facilitate problem-solving proficiency. As a classroom teacher, you will need to become familiar with STEM education in your state and school district and discover recommended ways to integrate problem solving in your lesson plans.

Math story problems are easy to integrate into the literacy curriculum as well. How? Take stories that children are reading or books that you are reading to the entire class and change the stories so that they include numbers and problems the students need to answer.

Joan Lindquist, a third-grade teacher, asked students the following questions about a story they were reading in class: "How many friends has Marcia told us about? How many friends does Linda have? Altogether, how many friends do they have? How many more friends does Linda have than Marcia?" Teachers can also add information to the stories and then ask children to solve word problems based on the additional information provided. They can then have students work in pairs to write their own word problems from the stories they are reading and have them read their word problems to the entire class so that the class can solve them.

In addition, word problems can be easily integrated into the social studies curriculum. When dates are discussed, ask students to compute how many years ago the event occurred. Ask students word problems about the age of central figures in the social studies lesson. Add numbers and information to the lesson and construct word problems. Integrating math into other content areas is an important means of promoting generalization of math concepts. See the Activities for All Learners feature for a variety of mathematics activities suitable for all learners.

ACTIVITIES FOR ALL LEARNERS

Mathematics Activities for All Learners

Slap It!!!

Objective: To provide practice in responding quickly to math

Grades: Second through eighth grade

Materials: A set of 4-inch by 6-inch cards on which the answers to math facts are written; cards can be established as answers to addition, subtraction, multiplication, or division facts

Teaching Procedures:

1. Students and teacher stand around a small table (preferably round), and teacher shows students the cards, each with a number (the answer to a math fact). Teacher spreads the cards (approximately 10) on the table with the number side up.
2. Students are told to keep both hands on the table until the teacher says, "Go." Students who lift either hand prior to the "go" signal are eliminated from that round of competition.
3. The teacher says a computation problem, followed by the word "go." For example, "6 × 7 = (go)."
4. Students slap the card that has the correct answer. The first hand on the card gets to keep the card. The student with the most cards gets to be the teacher next.

Adaptations:

1. Teachers can use the same game with word problems.
2. Teachers can use more than one computation during the game.

Measurement

Objective: To reinforce understanding of perimeter and area

Grades: Third grade and above

Materials: 1-inch graph paper, scissors, teacher-made table worksheet

Teaching Procedures:

1. Have students cut out squares of graph paper of different sizes: a 1-inch square, a 2-inch square, a 3-inch square, a 4-inch square, and a 5-inch square.
2. Measure the number of small squares in each large cutout square, and complete the following table:

edges	1	2	3	4	5	6
perimeter						
area						

3. Ask, "What happens to the perimeter and area each time the edges are doubled?"
4. Have students experiment with different-size squares and then complete the table.

Subtraction with Money

Objective: To introduce the concept of subtraction of three-digit numbers with regrouping, using play money

Grades: Third grade and above

Materials: Play money (20 one-dollar bills, 20 dimes, and 20 pennies for each student), place-value board for each student

Teaching Procedures:

1. Review: 100 pennies = 1 dollar
   10 pennies = 1 dime
   10 dimes = 1 dollar
2. Write example on the board: $5.36.
   −1.27
3. Student makes $5.36 on place-value board.
4. Teacher begins questioning: "You have 6 pennies; you have to give me 7 pennies. Do you have enough pennies?" "Can you trade something?" "That's right. 1 dime = 10 pennies. Take 1 dime from your dimes place and trade it for 10 pennies from your bank. Put the 10 pennies in the pennies place." "Now, how many pennies do you have?" "Can you take 7 pennies away? How many are left?" (Teacher writes 9 in the ones column.) "Can you take 1 dollar away? How many are left?" (Teacher writes 3 in the hundreds place.)
5. Give students ample guided practice with one trade before giving them independent practice in pairs. Encourage students to self-question while completing each step.

Modifications: When students become proficient in subtracting with one trade, provide examples of problems involving two trades.

"99"

Objective: To generalize and practice adding numbers in one's head or on paper

Grades: Intermediate to high school

Materials: Playing cards, paper, and pencils

Teaching Procedures:
Explain that the objective of this game is to add cards up to a score of 99. Establish the following rules:

Jacks and Queens = 10
Kings = 99
Nines = "free-turn" pass; to be used anytime
Fours = pass
Aces = 1
Other cards = face value

Each player is dealt three cards. The rest of the cards go face down on a draw pile. The players take turns discarding one card from their hands face up on a discard pile and drawing one card from the draw

(continued)

pile to put back in their hands. As a player discards his or her card, he or she must add the number from the card to any previous score acquired up to that point in the game and give the new score out loud. Note the exception: If a player plays a nine, he or she receives a free-turn pass. If a player plays a four, he or she has to pass a turn with no score. The first player to score higher than 99 loses the game.

The Value of Numbers

By Ae-Hwa Kim

Objective: To help students understand the value of numbers (ones value, tens value, and hundreds value)

Grade: Primary

Materials: (1) Popsicle sticks; (2) rubber bands to group the ice cream sticks; (3) a sign; (4) number cards; (5) three boxes to hold 1s, 10s, and 100s of popsicle sticks

Teaching Procedures:

1. Count the number of popsicle sticks.
2. Model putting a rubber band around a group of 10 sticks; then ask students to put a rubber band around each new group of 10 sticks.
3. Model putting 1s in the 1s box, 10s in the 10s box, and so on. Ask students to put 1s in the 1s box, 10s in the 10s box, and so on.
4. Show the students a sign that says "Thank you for the ________ popsicle sticks" (e.g., 157).
5. Model putting that number of popsicle sticks in the boxes; then ask students to put the number of popsicle sticks in the boxes.
6. Change the numbers on the sign again and again and allow students to practice grouping popsicle sticks according to the sign.

Shopping

Objective: To provide practice in addition, subtraction, and comparing prices (problem solving)

Grades: Upper elementary, junior high

Materials: (1) Newspaper from which to cut out various supermarket sale ads that include price per item; mount individual items on cardboard and cover them with clear plastic or just bring the ads; (2) made-up shopping lists to hand out to the class; (3) pencil and paper

Teaching Procedures:
Divide the class into small groups. Tell the students that their shopping list contains the items they will need this week. Assign each group a designated amount for groceries (e.g., $30). The object is to buy everything on the list and spend the least. Place on each desk the supermarket sale ads, each with the name of its store. Assist students in interpreting the math concepts from the advertisements (e.g., 3 kiwis for $.99). After students buy each item, they record the price and the store where they bought it. (It is easier if one student in each group buys the meats, one buys the dairy products, and so on.) When the students have bought all the items on the list, tell them to total their bills, calculate how much money they have left over, and be ready to present the results.

Work Backwards

Objective: To deepen understanding of word problems by creating a problem from the solution

Grade: Upper elementary and higher

Materials: Answer sheet, pens/crayons/manipulatives, blank sheets of paper

Teaching Procedures:

1. Show students the answer to a problem (e.g., Saul has 9 balloons left).
2. Discuss the "problem" with students. Establish that this is the answer, and they need to come up with a word problem that fits.
3. The word *left* suggests that this problem involves subtraction.
4. Brainstorm with student possible problems that fit this solution, such as "Saul had 10 balloons and he let 1 go. How many does he have left?" or "Saul had 47 balloons and he gave 38 to his friends. How many does he have left?"
5. Tell students to write the algorithm (10 – 1 = 9; 47 – 38 = 9) and draw a picture or use manipulatives to describe the problem.
6. Give students a list of answers and have them create word problems to go with each. Adjust the level or focus on specific skills by adding additional criteria to the task. For example, word problems must involve at least one two-digit number, use division, create a two-step word problem, and so on. This can be an individual, partner, or cooperative group activity.

Source: Reprinted with permission of the publisher, Teaching K–8, Norwalk, CT 06854. From the April 1993 issue of *Teaching K–8*; Adapted from *Strategies for teaching students with learning and behavior problems* (6th ed.), by C. Bos & S. Vaughn, 2006, Boston: Allyn & Bacon; Based on an activity in "Ice cream stick math," by C. Paddock, 1997, *Teaching Exceptional Children*, 24(2), 50–51; Adapted from *Strategies for teaching students with learning and behavior problems* (6th ed.), by C. S. Bos & S. Vaughn, 2006, Boston: Allyn & Bacon.

MyEdLab **Self-Check 16.7**

MyEdLab **Application Exercise 16.7:** Teaching Problem-Solving Strategies 

16 SUMMARY

- The current trend in mathematics instruction is to emphasize effective problem solving and to promote positive attitudes toward a broad view of mathematics, with less emphasis on rote memorization.
- Difficulties in mathematical problem solving may originate from cognitive factors, educational factors, personality factors, and neuropsychological patterns. Difficulties can also stem from less-than-adequate classroom instruction.
- Using RTI to identify students who are struggling with math includes assessing students to determine their progress and providing appropriately intensive instructional supports for students with math difficulties or disabilities.
- To improve students' confidence and competence in mathematics, teachers can be a mathematics "model," evaluate curriculum based on student needs, use specialized curricular resources, provide structure for peer support, and use proven teaching tools and methods such as manipulatives and providing specific feedback.
- Because basic skills must be mastered before higher-order problems can be taught and understood, mathematics instruction should begin at a concrete level and gradually move to increasingly abstract levels.
- Providing instruction in computational skills (i.e., addition, subtraction, multiplication, and division) helps students not only to be able to fluently and accurately compute solutions to computational problems but also to understand the meaning of these computations.
- Teaching problem-solving skills to both elementary and secondary students with math difficulties includes ensuring that they have a knowledge base about mathematics, including computation, geometry, and pre-algebra, as well as how to apply this knowledge to new problems and to actively engage in thinking processes applied to problems.

THINK AND APPLY

1. Go to the website for your state department of education. Read the state standards in mathematics for your state and locate recommendations your state approves for the assessment and instruction of students with disabilities.
2. Interview a special educator or math interventionist. Ask them about key methods, strategies, and materials they find most helpful for children with difficulties in learning mathematics.
3. Consider RTI in math at the elementary and secondary grades separately. For elementary, identify two activities you would expect to be engaged in on an ongoing basis to successfully implement an RTI model in your classroom. At the secondary level, if you are a math teacher, what role would you have in implementing RTI?
4. Think about your own experiences in learning mathematics. What were some instructional practices that helped you most and least? Discuss these experiences with a small group of your peers and generate a list of "best" practices to help students develop confidence and competence in learning mathematics.
5. Develop a lesson plan based on a Common Core State Standard or state standard of your choice. Include in your lesson plan a real-life application of the standard. Also plan for using manipulatives to teach the standard.
6. Develop a card, board, or computer game for students to practice computational skills.
7. Examine a mathematics text for the grade level of your choice. What strategies do the authors recommend for teaching problem-solving skills? What adaptations do they provide for students with disabilities?

Appendix

CEC Standards

CEC		
MAJOR CHAPTER HEADINGS	**KNOWLEDGE AND SKILL CORE STANDARD**	**ASSOCIATED SUBCATEGORIES**
PART 1: FOUNDATIONS		
CHAPTER 1 SPECIAL EDUCATION AND INCLUSIVE SCHOOLING		
Early Foundations of Special Education	**1.** Foundations	**ICC1K1** Models, theories, philosophies, and research methods that provide the basis for special education practice.
IDEA and the Vocational Rehabilitation Act	**1.** Foundations	**ICC1K5** Issues in definition and identification of individuals with exceptional learning needs, including those from culturally and linguistically diverse backgrounds.
Responsibilities of Classroom Teachers	**1.** Foundations	**ICC1K3** Relationship of special education to the organization and function of educational agencies.
Inclusion	**1.** Foundations	**ICC1K4** Rights and responsibilities of students, parents, teachers, other professionals, and schools related to exceptional learning needs.
CHAPTER 2 RESPONSE TO INTERVENTION: DEVELOPING SUCCESS FOR ALL LEARNERS		
Past and Present Challenges	**1.** Foundations	**GC1K3** Historical foundations, classic studies, major contributors, major legislation, and current issues related to knowledge and practice.
Components of Response to Intervention	**7.** Instructional Planning	**GC7K3** Interventions and services for children who may be at risk for learning disabilities.
Universal Screening and Progress Monitoring	**8.** Assessment	**ICC8K3** Screening, pre-referral, referral, and classification procedures.
Implementing Interventions	**7.** Instructional Strategies	**GC7K3** Interventions and services for children who may be at risk for learning disabilities.
Role of Teachers in an RTI Model	**8.** Assessment	**ICC8S6** Use assessment information in making eligibility, program, and placement decisions for individuals with exceptional learning needs, including those from culturally and/or linguistically diverse backgrounds.
CHAPTER 3 COMMUNICATING AND COLLABORATING WITH OTHER PROFESSIONALS AND FAMILIES		
Critical Communication Skills	**10.** Collaboration	**ICC10S3** Foster respectful and beneficial relationships between families and professionals.
Collaborating with Other Professionals	**10.** Collaboration	**ICC10K2** Roles of individuals with exceptional learning needs, families, and school and community personnel in planning of an individualized program.
Working with Families	**10.** Collaboration	**ICC10K3** Concerns of families of individuals with exceptional learning needs and strategies to help address these concerns.

CEC		
MAJOR CHAPTER HEADINGS	**KNOWLEDGE AND SKILL CORE STANDARD**	**ASSOCIATED SUBCATEGORIES**
CHAPTER 4 TEACHING CULTURALLY AND LINGUISTICALLY DIVERSE LEARNERS		
Diversity in Classrooms	**5.** Learning Environments and Social Interactions	**ICC5K8** Ways to create learning environments that allow individuals to retain and appreciate their own and each others' respective language and cultural heritage.
Multicultural Education	**5.** Learning Environments and Social Interactions	**ICC5K7** Strategies for preparing individuals to live harmoniously and productively in a culturally diverse world.
Linguistic Diversity and Second-Language Acquisition	**6.** Communication	**ICC6K1** Effects of cultural and linguistic differences on growth and development.
Assessment of Students with Cultural and Linguistic Differences	**8.** Assessment	**ICC8S6** Use assessment information in making eligibility, program, and placement decisions for individuals with exceptional learning needs, including those from culturally and/or linguistically diverse backgrounds.
Instructional Guidelines and Accommodations for Diverse Students	**6.** Communication	**ICC6S2** Use communication strategies and resources to facilitate understanding of subject matter for students whose primary language is not the dominant language.
CHAPTER 5 MANAGING STUDENT BEHAVIOR AND PROMOTING SOCIAL ACCEPTANCE		
Establishing a Positive Classroom Climate	**5.** Learning Environments and Social Interactions	**ICC5K2** Basic classroom management theories and strategies for individuals with exceptional learning needs.
Increasing Social Acceptance of Student with Disabilities and Exceptional Learners	**4.** Instructional Strategies	**ICC5S1** Create a safe, equitable, positive, and supportive learning environment in which diversities are valued.
Understanding Behavior Management in Culturally Diverse Classrooms	**5.** Learning Environments and Social Interactions	**ICC5S1** Create a safe, equitable, positive, and supportive learning environment in which diversities are valued.
Practices for Providing Positive Behavior Support within a Three-Tier Framework of Services	**7.** Instructional Planning	**GC7S1** Plan and implement individualized reinforcement systems and environmental modifications at levels equal to the intensity of the behavior.
Positive Behavior Support: Universal Strategies for Managing Student Behavior	**1.** Foundations	**GC1K9** Theory of reinforcement techniques in serving individuals with disabilities.
PART 2: TEACHING STUDENTS WITH SPECIAL NEEDS		
CHAPTER 6 TEACHING STUDENTS WITH LEARNING DISABILITIES AND ATTENTION DEFICIT HYPERACTIVITY DISORDER		
Learning Disabilities	**3.** Individual Learning Differences	**GC3K1** Impact of disabilities on auditory and information processing skills.
Attention Deficit Hyperactivity Disorder	**3.** Individual Learning Differences	**ICC3K1** Effects an exceptional condition(s) can have on an individual's life.
CHAPTER 7 TEACHING STUDENTS WITH COMMUNICATION DISORDERS		
Communication Disorders	**2.** Development and Characteristics of Learners	**ICC2K1** Typical and atypical growth and development.
Prevalence of Communication Disorders	**9.** Professional and Ethical Practice	**ICC9S10** Access information on exceptionalities.

CEC		
MAJOR CHAPTER HEADINGS	**KNOWLEDGE AND SKILL CORE STANDARD**	**ASSOCIATED SUBCATEGORIES**
Identifying and Assessing Students with Communication Disorders	**10.** Collaboration	**ICC10S9** Communicate with school personnel about the characteristics and needs of individuals with exceptional learning needs.
Instructional Guidelines and Accommodations for Students with Communication Disorders	**6.** Communication	**ICC6S1** Use strategies to support and enhance communication skills of individuals with exceptional learning needs.
Working with Parents to Extend Language Concepts	**4.** Instructional Strategies	**ICC4S4** Use strategies to facilitate maintenance and generalization of skills across learning environments.
CHAPTER 8 TEACHING STUDENTS WITH EMOTIONAL AND BEHAVIORAL DISORDERS		
Definitions of Emotional and Behavioral Disorders	**1.** Foundations	**GC1K1** Definitions and issues related to the identification of individuals with disabilities.
Prevalence of Students with Emotional or Behavioral Disorders	**2.** Development and Characteristics of Learners	**GC2K4** Psychological and social-emotional characteristics of individuals with disabilities/disorders.
Types and Characteristics of Emotional or Behavioral Disorders	**1.** Foundations	**GC1K2** Models and theories of deviance and behavior problems.
Causes of Emotional and Behavioral Disorders	**2.** Development and Characteristics of Learners	**GC2K1** Etiology and diagnosis related to various theoretical approaches.
Identification and Assessment of Students with Emotional and Behavioral Disorders	**8.** Assessment	**GC8S4** Assess reliable method(s) of response of individuals who lack typical communication and performance abilities.
Teaching Guidelines and Accommodations for Students with Emotional or Behavioral Disorders	**7.** Instructional Planning	**GC7K1** Integrate academic instruction and behavior management for individuals and groups with disabilities.
CHAPTER 9 TEACHING STUDENTS WITH AUTISM SPECTRUM DISORDERS/PERVASIVE DEVELOPMENTAL DISORDERS		
Definitions of Autism Spectrum Disorders/Asperger Syndrome and Pervasive Developmental Disorders	**2.** Development and Characteristics of Learners	**ICC2K6** Similarities and differences among individuals with exceptional learning needs.
Characteristics of Students with Autism Spectrum Disorders/Asperger Syndrome	**2.** Development and Characteristics of Learners	**ICC2K2** Educational implications of characteristics of various exceptionalities.
Identification and Assessment of Students with Autism Spectrum Disorders	**8.** Assessment	**GC8S3** Select, adapt, and modify assessments to accommodate the unique abilities and needs of individuals with disabilities.
Curricular and Instructional Guidelines for Students with Autism Spectrum Disorders	**6.** Communication	**ICC6S1** Use strategies to support and enhance communication skills of individuals with exceptional learning needs.
Addressing Challenging Behaviors	**5.** Learning Environments and Social Interactions	**ICC5K6** Strategies for crisis prevention and intervention.

CEC		
MAJOR CHAPTER HEADINGS	**KNOWLEDGE AND SKILL CORE STANDARD**	**ASSOCIATED SUBCATEGORIES**
CHAPTER 10 TEACHING STUDENTS WITH INTELLECTUAL AND DEVELOPMENTAL DISABILITIES		
Definition of Intellectual and Developmental Disabilities	**1.** Foundations	**ICCIKI** Models, theories, philosophies, and research methods that provide the basis for special education practice.
Types of Intellectual Disabilities	**1.** Development and Characteristics of Learners	**ICC2K2** Educational implications of characteristics of various exceptionalities.
Characteristics of Students with Intellectual Disabilities	**1.** Development and Characteristics of Learners	**ICC2K2** Educational implications of characteristics of various exceptionalities.
Prevalence and Identification of Students with Intellectual Disabilities	**7.** Instructional Planning	**ICC7S4** Use functional assessments to develop intervention plans.
Instructional Techniques and Accommodations for Students with Intellectual Disabilities	**7.** Instructional Planning	**ICC7S4** Use functional assessments to develop intervention plans.
CHAPTER 11 TEACHING STUDENTS WITH LOWER-INCIDENCE DISABILITIES		
Students with Visual Impairments	**7.** Instructional Planning	**ICC7S9** Incorporate and implement instructional and assistive technology into the educational program.
Students with Hearing Loss	**5.** Learning Environments and Social Interactions	**GC5S2** Use and maintain assistive technologies.
Students with Physical Disabilities, Health Impairments, and Traumatic Brain Injury	**9.** Professional and Ethical Practice	**ICC9S3** Act ethically in advocating for appropriate services.
Students with Multiple or Dual Sensory Disabilities	**9.** Professional and Ethical Practice	**IC9S3** Act ethically in advocating for appropriate-services.
PART 3: TEACHING PRACTICES		
CHAPTER 12 DIFFERENTIATING INSTRUCTION AND ASSESSMENT FOR ALL LEARNERS		
Standards-Based Instruction	**7.** Instructional Planning	**ICC7K2** National, state or provincial, and local curricula standards.
Differentiating Instruction	**2.** Development and Characteristics of Learners	**ICC2K5** Similarities and differences of individuals with and without exceptional learning needs.
Differentiating Reading Assignments	**4.** Instructional Strategies	**GC4S11** Use instructional methods to strengthen and compensate for deficits in perception, comprehension, memory, and retrieval.
Differentiating Assessment	**4.** Instructional Strategies	**GC4K2** Strategies to prepare for and take tests.
CHAPTER 13 PROMOTING EXCELLENCE THROUGH THE TEACHING AND LEARNING CONNECTION		
Preparing Lessons That Promote Engagement	**5.** Learning Environments and Social Interactions	**ICC5S4** Design learning environments that encourage active participation in individual and group activities.
Using Questioning and Discussion to Promote Student Engagement	**4.** Instructional Strategies	**ICC4S4** Use strategies to facilitate maintenance and generalization of skills across learning environments.
Using Graphic Organizers	**4.** Instructional Strategies	**ICC4S4** Use strategies to facilitate maintenance and generalization of skills across learning environments.

CEC		
MAJOR CHAPTER HEADINGS	**KNOWLEDGE AND SKILL CORE STANDARD**	**ASSOCIATED SUBCATEGORIES**
Promoting Student Success with Clear Assignments and Teaching of Organizational Skills	**5.** Learning Environments and Social Interactions	**ICC5S4** Design learning environments that encourage active participation in individual and group activities.
Effective Strategy Instruction	**4.** Instructional Strategies	**ICC4S4** Use strategies to facilitate maintenance and generalization of skills across learning environments.
CHAPTER 14 FACILITATING READING		
Current Trends in Reading and Reading Instruction	**7.** Instructional Planning	**ICC7K1** Theories and research that form the basis of curriculum development and instructional practice.
Effective Reading Instruction for Struggling Readers	**8.** Assessment	**ICC8S8** Evaluate instruction and monitor progress of individuals with exceptional learning needs.
Strategies for Teaching Phonological Awareness and Phonics	**4.** Instructional Strategies	**GC4S14** Implement systematic instruction in teaching reading comprehension and monitoring strategies.
Strategies for Teaching Word Identification	**4.** Instructional Strategies	**GC4S16** Implement systematic instruction to teach accuracy, fluency, and comprehension in content-area reading and written language.
Strategies for Helping Students Develop Fluency	**4.** Instructional Strategies	**GC4S4** Use reading methods appropriate to the individual with learning disabilities.
Strategies for Improving Reading Comprehension	**4.** Instructional Strategies	**GC4S16** Implement systematic instruction to teach accuracy, fluency, and comprehension in content-area reading and written language.
Strategies for Teaching Older Readers with Reading Difficulties	**4.** Instructional Strategies	**GC4S4** Use reading methods appropriate to the individual with learning disabilities.
Putting It All Together	**4.** Instructional Strategies	**GC4S16** Implement systematic instruction to teach accuracy, fluency, and comprehension in content-area reading and written language.
CHAPTER 15 FACILITATING WRITING		
Current Trends in Writing Curricula and Instruction	**7.** Instructional Planning	**ICC7K1** Theories and research that form the basis of curriculum development and instructional practice.
Teaching Writing as a Process	**4.** Instructional Strategies	**GC4S16** Implement systematic instruction to teach accuracy, fluency, and comprehension in content-area reading and written language.
Strategies for Establishing an Environment That Promotes Writing	**5.** Learning Environments	**ICC5S4** Design learning environments that encourage active participation in individual and group activities.
Strategies for Conducting a Writing Workshop	**4.** Instructional Strategies	**GC4S15** Teach strategies for organizing and composing written products.
Making Adaptations for Struggling Writers: Teachers' Practices	**4.** Instructional Strategies	**ICC4S3** Select, adapt, and use instructional strategies and materials according to characteristics of the individual with exceptional learning needs.
Strategies for Teaching Narrative, Expository, and Persuasive Writing	**4.** Instructional Strategies	**GC4S15** Teach strategies for organizing and composing written products.
Strategies for Teaching Expository Writing	**4.** Instructional Strategies	**GC4S10** Identify and teach basic structures and relationships within and across curricula.

CEC		
MAJOR CHAPTER HEADINGS	**KNOWLEDGE AND SKILL CORE STANDARD**	**ASSOCIATED SUBCATEGORIES**
Teaching Spelling Skills	**6.** Communication	**GC6S2** Teach strategies for spelling accuracy and generalization.
Teaching Handwriting and Keyboarding Skills	**6.** Communication	**GC6S4** Teach methods and strategies for producing legible documents.
CHAPTER 16 HELPING ALL STUDENTS SUCCEED IN MATHEMATICS		
Current Trends in Mathematics Curricula and Instruction	**7.** Instructional Planning	**ICC7K1** Theories and research that form the basis of curriculum development and instructional practice.
Difficulties in Learning Mathematics	**2.** Development and Characteristics of Learners	**ICC2K2** Educational implications of characteristics of various exceptionalities.
Assessment and Progress Monitoring	**8.** Assessment	**ICC8S6** Use assessment information in making eligibility, program, and placement decisions for individuals with exceptional learning needs, including those from culturally and/or linguistically diverse backgrounds.
Helping Students Improve in Math	**4.** Instructional Strategies	**GC4K6** Methods for increasing accuracy and proficiency in math calculations and applications.
Strategies for Helping All Students Acquire Basic Math Skills	**4.** Instructional Strategies	**GC4K6** Methods for increasing accuracy and proficiency in math calculations and applications.
Strategies for Helping All Learners Acquire and Use Computation Skills	**4.** Instructional Strategies	**ICC4S3** Select, adapt, and use instructional strategies and materials according to characteristics of the individual with exceptional learning needs.
Strategies for Helping All Students Develop Problem-Solving Skills	**4.** Instructional Strategies	**ICC4S2** Teach individuals to use self-assessment, problem solving, and other cognitive strategies to meet their needs.

Glossary

A

Absence seizures (petit mal) A type of seizure characterized by short lapses in consciousness

Academic language or vocabulary Refers to the more cognitively demanding language skills required for the new learning that occurs in school

Acceleration The procedure of moving students quickly through the grades or through the curriculum

Accommodation Involves no changes in curriculum requirements for students, but may make modifications to how the material is presented and what is required of the student

Accountability standards State identified grade-level learning expectations in key curriculum areas such as reading and math

Acquired immunodeficiency syndrome (AIDS) A viral infection transmitted through bodily fluids that may eventually cause a loss of stamina, developmental delays, motor problems, progressive neurological defects, repeated bacterial infections, psychological stresses, and death

Acronyms Words created by joining the first letters of a series of words

Acrostics Sentences created by words that begin with the first letters of a series of words

Adaptations Might involve changes in curriculum requirements

Adaptive behavior Refers to the effectiveness or degree with which individuals meet the standards of personal independence and social responsibility expected for the person's age and cultural group

Additive approach A strategy characterized by the addition of content, concepts, themes, and perspectives without changing the basic structure of the curriculum

Adequate yearly progress (AYP) The amount of gain the school district negotiates with the state that it will make for students who are behind

Advance organizer Information presented in advance of and at a higher level of generality, inclusiveness, and abstraction than the learning task itself

Advocacy One of the primary characteristics of the Individuals with Disabilities Education Act, which involves the assignment of representatives (advocates) for individuals with disabilities who lack parents or guardians

African American Vernacular English (AAVE) A dialect used by some African Americans; it is the most prevalent native English vernacular dialect in the United States

Aggression A form of behavior characterized by hostile or destructive actions

Alliteration The repetition of beginning sounds in words; one aspect students can use to identify similarities and differences in words

Alphabetic principle The use of the letters of the alphabet to form words

Alternate assessment State and school district policies for students with disabilities in meeting requirements for high-stakes tests

American Sign Language (ASL) A visual, gestural language

Analytic rubrics Scoring guides for evaluating student work that is made up of component parts of the activity and a scoring method to indicate level of performance on each part

Antisocial behavior Acts that can cause mental or physical harm to others or to their property

Anxiety A type of problem behavior involving extreme worry, anxiousness, or depression

Anxiety disorder A disorder that involves extreme worry, fearfulness, and concern (even when little reason for those feelings exists)

Articulation disorders Occur when students are unable to produce the sounds and sound combinations of language

Asperger syndrome A disorder in which the individual has a normal IQ and language development but also exhibits autistic-like behaviors and marked deficiencies in social and communication skills

Assessment The collection of data through the use of multiple measures, including standardized and informal instruments and procedures

Assessment literacy An understanding of both formal and informal assessments and making instructional decisions based on assessment and student performance data

Assessment portfolios Collections of work samples that document student progress in one or more subject areas

Assistive listening devices Tools that aid in the process of hearing

Assistive technology Any item, piece of equipment, or product system whether acquired commercially off the shelf, modified, or customized, that is used to increase, maintain, or improve functional capabilities of individuals with disabilities

Attention deficit hyperactivity disorder (ADHD) A disorder consisting of two subtypes of behavior: inattention and hyperactivity–impulsivity

Audiogram A visual representation of an individual's ability to hear sound

Augmentative and alternative communication (AAC) systems Systems that attempt to facilitate and compensate for, temporarily or permanently, the impairment and disability patterns of individuals with severe expressive and/or language comprehension disorders

Authentic assessment Assessment that makes a link between goals and objectives for your students and documentation of progress toward meeting those goals and objectives

Authoring process A cycle of prewriting, composing (drafting), and postwriting (revising, editing, and publishing)

Autism A developmental disability characterized by extreme withdrawal and communication difficulties

Autism spectrum disorders (ASDs) A subgroup of pervasive developmental disorders, namely, autism and Asperger syndrome

Autistic leading Leading behavior that is common in autism

Automaticity Automaticity in decoding refers to recognizing the words on sight

B

Basic interpersonal communication skills (BICS) The conversational competencies that develop with a second language

Behavioral disorders Behavior that falls considerably outside the norm

Behavioral improvement plan (BIP) A plan designed to identify behavior problems of students and to develop an intervention plan to treat these behavior problems

Behavioral inhibition The ability to withhold a planned response, halt a response that has been started, protect an ongoing activity from interfering activities, or delay a response

Big books Books with large pictures and words that can be seen by a whole class and used for shared reading activities

Bilingual education An educational program involving instruction in two languages, the goal being to promote bilingualism (proficiency in both languages)

Bipolar disorder A type of depression characterized by extreme mood swings

Blending Putting sounds or phonemes together to form words

Braille A system of embossed or raised dots that can be read with the tips of the fingers

Bulletin A way to communicate with parents

C

Cascade of integration options The options special education/general education teams use to individualize and make instructional decisions based on a student's specific needs

Cerebral palsy Results from damage to the brain before or during birth; conditions are classified according to the areas affected and the types of symptoms

Challenging behavior A pattern of inappropriate behavior that interferes with learning or social situations

Charter schools Schools that develop proposals to use state funds but have independence from the local school district

Check-in, check-out (CICO) procedure A procedure where students earn points for appropriate behaviors in small-group instructional or mentoring sessions and in the classroom

Child Find A requirement that each state identify and track the number of students with disabilities and plan for their educational needs

Childhood disintegrative disorder A neurologic condition generally classified in the pervasive developmental disorders (PDDs) that is characterized by normal development through age 2 followed by a severe deterioration of mental and social functioning, with regression to a state suggestive of autism

Children with specific learning disabilities Those children who have a disorder in one or more of the basic psychological processes involved in understanding or in using language, spoken or written, that may manifest itself in an imperfect ability to listen, think, speak, read, write, spell, or do mathematical calculations

Class meetings Meetings that include all students in the class, as well as the teacher; used to foster students' involvement in the management of their classes

Classification The ability to group or sort objects by one or more common properties

Classroom routine The organization of classroom activities throughout the school day

Classroom web pages An individual classroom web page that provides information about the calendar, major events, and homework tips

Classwide peer tutoring (CWPT) Students of different reading levels are paired (one average or high and one low) and read materials that can be easily read by the less able reader in the pair

Co-assessment/co-grading Occurs when two or more professionals are actively engaged in assessment data collection, evaluation, grading student performance, determining report card grades, and reporting student assessment outcomes and grades to parents or caregivers

Cognitive academic language performance (CALP) Refers to the more cognitively demanding language skills required for the new learning that is characteristic of school settings

Cognitive strategies Thinking processes used by students to complete their academic work

Collaboration A style for direct interaction between at least two coequal parties voluntarily engaged in shared decision making as they work toward a common goal

Collaborative strategic reading (CSR) A multicomponent learning strategy that combines essential reading comprehension strategies that have been demonstrated as effective in improving students' understanding of text

Collective identity An identity that develops as the involuntary minorities are treated as subordinates by European Americans in economic, political, social, psychological, cultural, and language domains

Common underlying proficiency The phenomenon that the better developed the students' first language proficiency and conceptual foundation, the more likely they are to develop similarly high levels of proficiency and conceptual ability in the second language

Communication board An example of augmentative communication that includes the board itself and symbols or pictures

Communication disorders Difficulties with the transfer of knowledge, ideas, opinions, and feelings

Comorbidity The idea that students can have more than one disability

Compensatory skills Skills needed for independence, which may include the use of Braille, a slate and stylus, or an abacus

Composing Process in which the author attempts to get ideas on paper in the form of a draft

Comprehensible input Refers to input received and made understandable when listening to or reading in a second language

Comprehensible output Output that is transmitted and made understandable when speaking

Comprehension A person's ability to understand what is being communicated

Comprehension monitoring Refers to monitoring understanding

Comprehension strategies Techniques designed to improve students' understanding of text

Computational Arithmetic Program A program that provides 314 worksheets to teach basic math skills in grades 1 through 6

Concept diagram A way to introduce a lecture or reading assignment (similar to a semantic map) that also helps students determine the definitions, characteristics, examples, and nonexamples of a concept

Conduct disorder Includes behaviors such as hitting, fighting, throwing, temper tantrums, and acting defiant or disobedient, and characteristics such as being irritable or overactive, difficult to get along with, uncooperative, inconsiderate, resistive, jealous, quarrelsome, distractible, teasing, irresponsible, and inattentive

Conductive hearing loss Hearing loss when the outer and middle ears do not transfer enough acoustic energy to the inner ear fluids

Conferencing An ongoing student–teacher meeting prepared to read the student's writing piece, to describe problem areas, and to respond to questions

Confidentiality of records The requirement of the Individuals with Disabilities Education Act that all records and documents regarding students with disabilities remain undisclosed to the public but accessible to parents

Consequences The ramifications of not following classroom guidelines

Considerate text Text that is written and formatted in such a way that information can be extracted easily, with support available when the reader does not understand

Constant time delay A procedure for teaching math facts that provides for the systematic introduction of teacher assistance

Consultation An interactive process that enables people with diverse expertise to generate creative solutions to mutually defined problems

Content The semantics of language

Content integration Focused use of examples and content from different cultures and groups to illustrate concepts, principles, generalizations, and theories

Context-embedded communication and instruction Providing a link between students' culture, the instruction they receive, and the mode in which they receive it

Continuum of services A full range of service options for students with disabilities, provided by the school system

Contributions approach Characterized by the insertion of ethnic heroes and discrete cultural artifacts into the curriculum

Cooperative learning Groups in which students work together toward a common goal, usually to help one another learn academic material

Cooperative learning groups Groups of students working together toward a common goal, usually to help one another learn academic material

Corrective Mathematics 2005 A math program that requires only minimal reading skills and provides remedial math for students in grades 3 through 12

Co-planning Occurs when one or more professionals collaborate to construct unit and/or lesson plans

Co-teaching Occurs when general and special education teachers work together to coordinate curriculum and instruction and to teach heterogeneous groups of students in the general education classroom setting

Cultural characteristics Traits or aspects that characterize a particular culture

Cultural inversion The tendency to regard certain forms of behavior, events, symbols, and meanings as inappropriate because they are uncharacteristic of European-American culture

Culturally responsive assessment (CRA) A collection of approaches that promote nondiscriminatory assessment practices

Culturally responsive teaching (CRT) Using the cultural knowledge, past experiences, and learning styles of diverse students to make learning more appropriate and effective for them

Curriculum compacting Provides students with the opportunity to demonstrate what they already know about a subject by eliminating repetitive or review content and replacing it with advanced learning experiences

Curriculum enhancement Involves no changes to the curriculum, but involves instructional strategies that promote learning for all students

Curriculum modification Modifications targeted to individual needs of students

Curriculum-based assessment (CBA) A way to monitor ongoing progress in acquisition of basic skills

Curriculum-based measurement (CBM) A means of measuring student progress that highlights the close tie between curriculum and student performance

Cursive writing Script writing typically introduced in third grade

Cybaries Cyber libraries

D

Data-based decision making Another term for evaluation (the process of integrating, interpreting, and summarizing the comprehensive assessment)

Deaf Describes a person with a severe or profound loss of hearing

Deaf–blind Also known as dual sensory impairment; involves impairments in the two main channels (auditory and visual) of receptive communication and learning

Decibel Intensity of a sound (loud versus quiet) measurement

Decodable books Books that primarily use words that reflect the phonic and word patterns already learned

Decodable text Text in which most of the words are composed of letter–sound correspondences that have been taught

Decoding A strategy for recognizing words

Demonstration plus model strategy A strategy for giving demonstrations to students with learning problems that includes completion of the demonstration, having a student perform each step, verbalizing each step as the teacher did, and having all students complete additional practice exercises independently, using the steps

Depression A mental illness characterized by prolonged and persistent feelings of sadness, irritability, or anxiety that interfere with life functioning

Developmental arithmetic disorder Refers to students who have significant difficulties learning arithmetic (difficulties that are unexpected, given the students' overall cognitive functioning and/or academic performance in other subject areas)

Developmental disability Refers to a disability that is attributable to mental retardation or related conditions that include cerebral palsy, epilepsy, autism, or other neurological conditions when such conditions result in impairment of general intellectual functioning or adaptive behavior similar to that of a person with mental retardation

Diagnostic and Statistical Manual of Mental Disorders A reference book published by the American Psychiatric Association

Diagnostic assessments Assessments that tell us specifically how a student is performing and what else he or she needs to know

Dialect Refers to language variations associated with a regional or social group of people

Dialog journal An ongoing written conversation between two students (or in some cases between a student and an adult)

Difficulty with zero Refers to students' misunderstanding of the multiple meanings and uses of zero that causes errors in arithmetic

Direct assessment Assessment that involves observing students and documenting the sequence of behaviors around challenging behavior

Disabilities Conditions that include mental retardation, hearing impairments, vision impairments, speech and language impairments, learning disabilities, serious emotional disturbance, orthopedic impairments, other health impairments, autism, traumatic brain injury, deafness and blindness, and multiple disabilities

Discrepancy analysis A review of each specific step or skill and determination of how a student does the step or skill compared to what is expected

Discussion web A graphic aid to help students prepare for classroom discussions in content-area classes

DISSECT A learning strategy for secondary students with learning disabilities to approach a multisyllable word in a strategic way

Distributed practice The practice of breaking up the material to be learned into manageable chunks and then having several short study sessions over a period of time

Down syndrome One of the most common chromosomal disorders, usually associated with mental retardation

Drafting See **Composing**

Dual sensory impairments Refers to impairments in the two main channels (auditory and visual) of receptive communication and learning

Due process Ensures that everyone with a stake in the student's educational success has a voice; also addresses written notification to parents for referral and testing for special education, parental consent, and guidelines for appeals and record keeping

Dyscalculia Severe disability in learning mathematical concepts and computation

Dysfluent Difficulty with the rate and flow of speech

Dysgraphia Severe difficulty learning to write (including handwriting)

Dyslexia Severe difficulty learning to read, particularly as it relates to decoding

E

Early intervention services Comprehensive services that incorporate goals in education, health care, and social services

Early-exit transitions Transition programs in which at least 40% of the instruction is in the first language

Echolalia Repeating what was heard verbatim

Editing The process that takes place as the author reviews the written work line by line to determine whether the overall content is appropriate and the mechanics are correct

Educational interventions Special strategies for meeting the diverse needs of students

Educational placement The type of educational setting in which a particular student is instructed; examples include general education classrooms, resource rooms, special schools, and other types of settings

Effective listening Requires hearing the message being sent and often requires asking questions to clarify the true message being sent

Elaboration Teacher extension of language that builds on the content of the student's language and provides additional information on the topic

Emotional disorders Behavior that falls considerably outside the norm

Empowering school culture and social structure A culture that promotes gender, racial, and social class equity

Encode To change written language to symbols; to write

Encoding function The physical act of taking notes promotes student engagement and learning

Encouragement Teacher recognizes a behavior but does not provide judgment

English as a Second Language (ESL) Teaching English as a second language, with limited emphasis on maintaining or developing proficiency in the student's first language

English language learners (ELLs) Students for whom English is a second language

English only Students who are learning English are taught all of their subjects in English and they learn to read and write in English

Enrichment Adding breadth and depth to the traditional curriculum

Environmental accommodations Changes made to the physical learning environment so that each student can participate successfully

Epilepsy A condition characterized by the tendency to have recurrent seizures caused by sudden, excessive, spontaneous, and abnormal discharges of neurons accompanied by alteration in motor function and/or sensory function and/or consciousness

Equity pedagogy Attending to different teaching and learning styles and modifying teaching to facilitate the academic achievement of students from diverse cultures

ETA/Cuisenaire A company that provides a variety of supplemental mathematics materials, specializing in math manipulatives that emphasize learning principles through hands-on learning

Evaluation The process of integrating, interpreting, and summarizing the comprehensive assessment data

Executive functioning Refers to the ability to regulate one's thinking and behavior through the use of working memory, inner speech, control of emotions and arousal levels, and analysis of problems and communication of problem solutions to others

Executive learner A student who is aware of personal learning strengths and challenges, understands tasks to be accomplished, has a repertoire of learning strategies, and has developed help-seeking behaviors

Expansion A technique used to facilitate the development of more complex language form and content

Explicit instruction Task-specific, teacher-led instruction that overtly demonstrates a task and can be used to teach students both basic and higher-order reading skills

Expository writing Informational writing

Expressive language A person's ability to convey the intended message

External storage function One of two purposes of note-taking; students take notes to record what was presented and discussed in class; this record can be used for preparing for tests and class discussions

Externalizing behaviors Behaviors such as aggression, hitting, and shouting that are readily observable and tend to affect others

Extinction The elimination of a student's undesirable behavior by removing reinforcers

F

Facilitator The teacher who guides his or her peer through the process and helps to generate solutions

Failure to shift operations Occurs when the student fails to move to the next operation after completing a previous operation

Family adjustment A family's changes in response to having a child with severe disabilities, mental retardation, or physical disabilities

FAST DRAW A type of mnemonic used to teach the concrete-representational-abstract teaching principle advocated in mathematics instruction (Find what you're solving for; Ask yourself "What are the parts of the problem?"; Set up the numbers; Tie down the sign; Discover the sign; Read the problem; Answer or draw a conceptual representation of the problem, using lines and tallies, and check; Write the answer)

Fetal alcohol spectrum disorder (FASD) One of the top three known causes of birth defects, it refers to a range of birth defects caused by the mother's drinking during pregnancy and is fast becoming the leading cause of intellectual disabilities

Fetal alcohol syndrome (FAS) Refers to a spectrum of birth defects caused by the mother's drinking during pregnancy

Fidelity The degree to which an intervention has been administered with consistency and according to prescribed guidelines

Figurative language Represents abstract concepts and usually requires an inferential rather than literal interpretation

Fingerspelling A system for manually representing the English alphabet

FIRST-letter A mnemonic strategy in which students construct lists of information to memorize and develop an acronym or acrostic for learning and remembering the information

FLIP Chart Strategy Helps students learn to evaluate the difficulty of text on their own by examining text friendliness and language as well as their interest in and prior knowledge of the topic

Fluency The ability to recognize printed words quickly

Form The phonology, morphology, and syntax of language

Fragile X syndrome The most common form of intellectual disabilities that is passed from parent to child

Free appropriate public education (FAPE) The legal mandate that all children with disabilities be given a free and appropriate public education

Friendly text A text that features elements that support student learning

Frustration reading level The reading level at which students have difficulty reading even with assistance, because reading materials are too difficult

Full inclusion A movement that advocates educating all students with disabilities in the general education classroom full time

Functional analysis Involves analysis of the skills needed to complete a particular activity or task

Functional assessment Assessment in which each goal or activity is broken into steps or subskills, and the student's present performance level is determined for each subskill or step in the activity

Functional behaviorial assessment A method of gathering data to design the most effective positive support plans and to monitor their progress

Functional practice Relevant practice that helps students to easily see the connection between what they are practicing and its use in real life

Functional vision assessment Assessment that includes the student's ability to view at both near and distant points and to sustain visual function throughout daily academic settings

Funds of knowledge The information and resources available in the student's home community

G

Gangs Groups of individuals working to unlawful or antisocial ends

Graphic organizer A visual framework used to assist students in organizing information or making connections between concepts

Group behavior Behaviors displayed in the presence of other group members

H

Hanover method A system for teaching cursive writing based on the similarities of letters or letter families

Hard of hearing Describes a person with a mild to moderate loss of hearing

Hearing aid A device that amplifies hearing

Help-seeking behaviors A set of behaviors that exhibit a student's skill in seeking assistance in appropriate and effective ways

Hertz Frequency of the sound (high versus low) measurement

Heterogeneous grouping Groups consisting of students at a wide range of achievement levels

High responders Students who respond well to intervention

High-frequency words Words that occur frequently in spoken language and in written text

Holistic rubrics Scoring guides for evaluating a student product; the scoring method indicates level of performance on the product as a whole

Homebound teacher A teacher who provides direct instruction and coordinates instructional programs between the school and the home

Homogeneous grouping The practice of putting students at approximately the same achievement level together for instruction (also called *same-ability grouping*)

Human immunodeficiency virus (HIV) A virus that infects and eventually destroys cells in the immune system that protect the body from disease

Hyperactivity–impulsivity Refers to a group of behaviors associated with restlessness, excess motor activity, and an inability to control one's own actions

I

I PLAN A strategy for developing student self-advocacy skills during IEP or transition planning conferences; the plan includes five steps: Inventory your learning strengths, weaknesses, goals, interests, and choices for learning; Provide your inventory information; Listen and respond; Ask questions; Name your goals

Ignoring on purpose A method of eliminating a student's undesirable behavior by purposely removing the teacher's and other students' attention to that behavior

Immaturity Behaviors that include lack of perseverance, failure to finish tasks, short attention span, poor concentration, and frequent daydreaming or preoccupation

Implant A device inserted into the ear through surgery

Inattention Refers to difficulty sustaining attention

Inclusion The situation in which students with disabilities are educated with their nondisabled peers, with special education supports and services provided as needed

Independent reading level The reading level at which students read on their own without support from others

Indirect assessments Assessments providing information about student strengths and needs that do not involve direct observation or direct contact with the student

Individualized education program (IEP) A written plan, developed to meet the special learning needs of each student with disabilities

Individualized family service plan (IFSP) A plan, for children from birth to 3 years of age, developed to meet not only the special needs of each student with disabilities but also those of his or her family

Individualized transition plan (ITP) A plan, for students from 16 years of age (or 14 years and even younger, if appropriate) to age 21, that states what transition services are necessary and, when appropriate, includes a statement of the interagency responsibilities and linkages

Individuals with Disabilities Education Act (IDEA) Legislation designed to ensure that all children with disabilities receive an appropriate education through special education and related services

Informal reading inventory An individually administered reading assessment designed to help a teacher determine a student's reading instructional needs. The student reads lists of words and passages that are leveled by grade and retells or answers comprehension questions about the passages

Initiator The teacher who addresses the problems to his or her peer

Inner speech Talking to one's self about various solutions when in the midst of solving a problem

Instructional clarity The clear, direct, and explicit presentation of information

Instructional conversations Conversations between students and teachers on the reading process (e.g., sharing the strategies the students use to decode words and construct meaning)

Instructional reading level The reading level at which instruction should occur and at which students are challenged by the reading but still need some support

Intellectual disabilities Limited cognitive functioning, which affects learning

Internalizing behaviors Behaviors such as shyness, withdrawal, or depression that tend to be less readily observable and negatively affect the individual exhibiting the behaviors

K

Key Math 3 Essential Resources A program designed to diagnose math difficulties and provide remedial practice

Key word strategy A mnemonic strategy that uses both verbal and visual cues to create images to prompt recall and retention of information

Knowledge construction Refers to students' learning about how implicit cultural assumptions, frames of reference, perspectives, and biases influence the ways that knowledge is constructed

K-W-L strategy A strategy (based on research underscoring the importance of activating prior knowledge before reading) to help students become actively engaged in comprehension before, during, and after reading

L

Language disorders A major area of communication disorders

Language variation Refers to the fact that language varies from place to place and from group to group

Late-exit transitions Programs that foster the students' first language and strengthen their sense of cultural identity while teaching the second language and culture

Learner characteristics The third factor affecting second-language acquisition or output; includes the age at which students learn a second language, their aptitude for learning language, their purposes and degree of motivation for learning the second language, their self-confidence in language learning, and the learning strategies they have for learning language

Learning contract A contract that identifies target standards or objectives and allows the teacher to negotiate with students about the pathway and products they will produce to determine mastery

Learning media assessment An assessment to determine a student's dominant learning modality

Least restrictive environment The instructional setting most like that of nondisabled peers that also meets the educational needs of each student with disabilities

Legal blindness The visual impairment of an individual who with the best possible correction in the better eye has a measured visual acuity of 20/200 or worse or a visual field restricted to 20 degrees or less

Lesson co-planning Collaboration of general and special education teachers to plan activities for students

Lesson co-teaching Teaching in which the special education and general education teachers are both in the classroom during the same lesson and both participate in the instruction

Letter A way to communicate with parents

Letter strategy A type of mnemonics

Lexile levels An estimate of a student's reading level and a text's readability; levels can range from 200 for beginning readers to over 1700 for advanced text

Linguistic input Input received when listening or reading in a second language

Long-range co-planning Planning in which the general education and special education teachers broadly plan their overall goals and desired outcomes for the class and for specific students with disabilities in the class

Low incidence A disability that comparatively fewer students have than have high-incidence disabilities

Low vision Describes an individual who is either partially sighted or legally blind

M

Macroculture The core culture in a school

Mainstreaming The participation of students with disabilities in general education classrooms to the extent appropriate for meeting their needs

Maintenance bilingual education Education that attempts to foster the students' first language and strengthen their sense of cultural identity

Making words A whole-class guided activity that helps students develop phonological awareness and become more sensitive to common spelling patterns

Manipulating A type of phonological awareness skill: deleting, adding, and substituting syllables and sounds

Manuscript writing Print writing

MARKER A strategy for setting goals and monitoring progress: **M**ake a list of goals, set the order, and set the dates; **A**rrange a plan for each goal and predict your success; **R**un your plan for each goal and adjust if necessary; **K**eep records of your progress; **E**valuate your progress toward each goal; **R**eward yourself when you reach a goal, and set a new goal

Massed trials strategy A technique whereby the same instructional trial is repeated again and again to a predefined criterion of correct performance

Mastery Meeting accuracy, speed, and knowledge expectations

Mathematical difficulties Students who find math abstract and conceptually difficult to understand

McGill Action Planning System (MAPS) A planning activity that fosters relationships in order to improve the quality of life for persons with severe disabilities while facilitating participation in inclusive settings

Medically fragile A subgroup that has emerged within the health disabilities, characterized by an individual being at risk for medical emergencies on a regular basis and often requiring life support or specialized support systems such as ventilators

Memory problems Forgetting or misremembering a fact; lead to errors in arithmetic calculation and other areas

Memory strategies Mental techniques for increasing students' abilities to memorize information and utilize information in memory

Mental retardation Limited intellectual functioning that affects an individual's learning

Metacognition Knowledge of one's knowledge, processes, and cognitive and affective states; and the ability to consciously and deliberately monitor and regulate one's knowledge, processes, and cognitive and affective states

Metacognitive conversations Brief classroom discussions about specific learning tasks and how best to accomplish those tasks

Metalinguistics Involves thinking about, analyzing, and reflecting on language as an object in much the same way one reflects on a table or a friend

Microcultures Home cultures based on such factors as national origin, ethnicity, socioeconomic class, religion, gender, age, and disability

Milieu instruction Communication training occurring during natural opportunities for children or students to communicate

Mistaken goal Evidenced when students display inappropriate behavior because they believe it will get them the recognition and acceptance they desire

Mixed hearing loss Hearing loss that is both conductive and sensorineural

Mnemonic devices Memory-triggering techniques used to help remember or retrieve information by forming associations that do not exist naturally in the content

Mobility skills Skills such as going up and down stairs, crossing streets, and using public transportation

Modeling A technique for teaching language that involves following examples illustrated by others

Mood disorders Disorders that include various types of depression

Morpheme The smallest unit of language that conveys meaning

Morphology Word study that focuses on the rule system that governs the structure of words and word forms

Motoric problems Difficulty of writing and reading numbers

Moving model Modeling for students how to form letters and words in order to develop their legibility

Multicultural education An educational reform movement whose major goal is to change the structure of educational institutions so that female students; exceptional students; and students who are members of diverse racial, ethnic, and cultural groups have an equal chance to achieve in school

Multidisciplinary team (MDT) A group that usually includes a representative of the local education agency, the classroom teacher, the special education teacher, parents or guardians, and, when appropriate, the student; together they develop and implement the IEP

Multiliteracies Skills for dealing with multiples sources of information

Multiple disabilities The combination of severe or profound mental retardation and one or more significant motor or sensory impairments and/or special health needs

Multiple grouping formats The use of a variety of grouping patterns

Multiple intelligences The theory that human beings are capable of exhibiting intelligence in eight domains: linguistic, logical–mathematical, spatial, musical, bodily—kinesthetic, interpersonal (i.e., discerning and responding to the needs of others), intrapersonal (i.e., having detailed and accurate self-knowledge), and naturalistic (i.e., differentiating between living things and accurate knowledge of the natural world)

Multiple meanings Applies to words that have more than one meaning

Multitiered intervention strategy A set of layers of instruction that increase in intensity (e.g., amount of instruction, group size) based on how well students are succeeding in a less intensive instructional format

Muscular dystrophy A chronic disorder characterized by the weakening and wasting of the body's muscles

N

Narrative writing The writing of stories

Naturalistic instruction Communication skills taught as part of the ongoing natural context

NCTM Navigation Series Refers to a series of graded and topical books that focus on teaching algebra, geometry, numbers, and operations based on the NCTM principles and standards

Negative reinforcement The removal of a stimulus to increase responding

Neuromotor impairment An abnormal performance caused by a dysfunction of the brain, spinal cord, and nerves, thereby creating transmission of improper instructions, uncontrolled bursts of instructions from the brain, or incorrect interpretation of feedback to the brain

No Child Left Behind Act (NCLB) of 2001 An act that provides a framework on how to improve the performance of America's elementary and secondary schools while at the same time ensuring that no child is trapped in a failing school

Noncompliance Failure to comply with the law; the Individuals with Disabilities Act requires that states mandate consequences for noncompliance

Nondiscriminatory evaluation An evaluation that does not discriminate on the basis of language, culture, and student's background; must be provided for each individual who is assessed for special education

Nonoptical aids Devices that, although not prescribed by a doctor, promote efficient use of vision

Nonresponders Students who make minimal or no gains after being taught with high-quality, validated interventions

Nonverbal math disabilities Students who display good reading and verbal expression but who have extreme difficulty with mathematics

Norm-based assessments Assessments used to determine how a student's performance compares with other students of the same age or in the same grade

Number sense Whether a student's understanding of a number and its use and meaning is flexible and fully developed

Numeration The understanding of numbers and their manipulations

O

One-to-one correspondence A situation in which each object corresponds to another object

Onset-rime Onset is the word's initial consonant or consonant combination (e.g., /g/), and rime is the rhyming part of the word (e.g., /et/)

Open question A question that allows a full range of responses and discourages short "yes" or "no" answers

Oppositional defiant disorder (ODD) A disorder in which students habitually question authority, intentionally misbehave and ignore rules, are temperamental and negative, and blame others for their actions or when social and/or academic progress is inhibited as a result

Oral reading fluency The number of words a student reads correctly in one minute

Orientation skills Includes understanding one's own body, one's position in space, and physical concepts such as the layout of a city block

Orthopedic impairment Includes deficits caused by congenital anomaly (e.g., clubfoot, absence of some member), impairments caused by disease (e.g., poliomyelitis, bone tuberculosis), and impairments from other causes (e.g., cerebral palsy, amputations, and fractures or burns that cause contractures)

Other health impairments (OHI) Limited strength, vitality, or alertness (caused by chronic or acute health problems such as heart condition, tuberculosis, rheumatic fever, nephritis, asthma, sickle-cell anemia, hemophilia, epilepsy, lead poisoning, leukemia, or diabetes) that adversely affects a student's educational performance

Overcorrection The act of having a student perform a duty or task to compensate for what happened

Overlearning The continued study or practice of new content after initial proficiency levels are reached in order to reinforce the learned content; learning to mastery

P

Paraeducator Individuals who are trained to work with, and alongside, educators in classrooms and other educational settings to support the education of students with and without disabilities in a variety of capacities

Parallel Curriculum Model (PCM) A framework for differentiated instruction that takes into consideration four curriculum design components

Parallel talk A process in which the teacher describes what students are doing or thinking

Parallel teaching Both teachers teach the same content to small, mixed-ability groups of students

Parent interviews A way to foster communication by asking family members about their level of satisfaction with programs, curriculum, and services

Parent participation Involvement of parents in all aspects of identifying and evaluating students with disabilities, including decision making

Partial or parallel participation A concept that assumes that an individual has the right to participate, to the extent possible, in all activities

Partial sight Describes an individual who with best possible correction in the better eye has a measured visual acuity between 20/70 and 20/200

Pause procedure A technique in which, during logical breaks in a lecture (approximately every 10 minutes), the teacher pauses for 2 minutes to allow pairs of students to compare their notes to make certain that key concepts have been recorded

Peer collaboration model A model designed for classroom teachers to work with one or two other teachers

Peer editing Process in which students revise and edit each other's work

Peer-assisted learning (PAL) An instructional practice promoting the use of students working together to provide practice and feedback on improving reading fluency; higher and lower readers are paired together and work through a series of structured activities. *See* **Classwide peer tutoring (CWPT)**

Perinatal During birth

Personalized knowledge Knowledge that results from firsthand observation

Person-centered planning Planning for students' transition into adult life in terms of vocation and adult living

Person-first language Language that does not define a child by his or her disability

Persuasive writing A writing format in which the writer provides evidence in order to convince or persuade the reader of his or her position or opinion; writing persuasive essays involves planning and critical thinking

Pervasive developmental disorder (PDD) A disorder characterized by impairments in social interaction and verbal and communication skills, a limited number of interests, imaginative activity, and activities that tend to be repetitive

Pervasive developmental disorder–not otherwise specified (PDD-NOS) A disorder in which a child exhibits stereotypical behaviors or delays in social interaction or communication, but does not meet the criteria for another PDD

Phoneme The smallest unit of speech sound

Phonemic awareness The understanding of how to listen to and produce sounds

Phonic analysis Identifying and blending letter–sound correspondences into words

Phonological awareness Possession of skills such as rhyming, alliteration recognition, blending, and segmentation

Phonology Focuses on the sounds of language and the rules that determine how the sounds fit together

Physical disabilities Orthopedic impairments and neuromotor impairments

P.L. 94-142 This legislation, designed to ensure that all children with disabilities receive an appropriate education through special education and related services, was originally referred to as the *Education for All Handicapped Children Act*, enacted in 1975, and later reauthorized and expanded as the Individuals with Disabilities Education Act (IDEA)

Planned ignoring A strategy to eliminate (extinguish) a student's undesirable behavior, which is being reinforced through attention, by ignoring

PLEASE strategy A strategy developed to provide students with a step-by-step procedure for paragraph writing

Portfolio A record of a student's progress in writing

Portfolio assessment Assessment that involves compilation of multiple artifacts or student work samples

Positive behavioral intervention support (PBIS) The modification of behavior management principles applied in various community settings with supports to reduce problem behaviors and develop appropriate behaviors that lead to enhanced social relations and lifestyle

Positive feedback Recognizing a student behavior by providing some judgment about the appropriateness of the behavior

Positive reinforcement The presentation of a stimulus (verbal response, physical response such as touching, or tangible response such as a reward) following the target behavior to maintain or increase the target behavior

Postnatal After birth

Postwriting Process in which authors revise, edit, and publish their written work

Pragmatics The purposes or functions of communication or how we use language to communicate

Preference assessment An assessment of students' likes and dislikes

Prejudice reduction The dispelling of misconceptions and stereotypes about diverse cultural and ethnic groups

Prelearning activities Strategies teachers use to activate students' prior knowledge and to preteach vocabulary and concepts—essentially, to prepare students to learn

Prelinguistic level The communication skills of many students with autism, such as autistic leading

Prenatal Before birth

Prereferral assistance team (PAT) A group of teachers from the same school who meet regularly to discuss the specific progress of students brought to their attention by other teachers in the school

Prewriting Process in which a writer collects information about a topic through observing, remembering, interviewing, and reading

Primary prevention model A model in which the focus is on preventing behavior problems schoolwide

Procedural error Misapplying a procedure from one arithmetic operation to another

Production A person's ability to convey the intended message

Progress monitoring The frequent assessment of academic performance used to evaluate the effectiveness of instruction for students. *See* **Curriculum-based measurement (CBM)**

Progress report A letter sent to parents

PROJECT A multi-step strategy for completing assignments: Prepare your assignment sheet; Record and ask; Organize; Jump into it; Engage in the work; Check your work; Turn in your work

Prompt A situation and directions for writing an essay

Publishing Preparing a written work in a way that enables others to read it

Pull-out services Programs in which children are pulled out of their general education classroom for supplemental instruction in basic skills

Punishment The opposite of reinforcement, in that it follows a behavior and decreases the strength of the behavior or the likelihood the behavior will continue to occur

Purpose-setting activities Activities that give students a reason to complete a reading assignment or listen to a lecture

Q

Question–answer relationships (QAR) strategy A strategy for teaching students how to answer different types of comprehension questions

R

Rapid naming Tasks such as naming a series of random numbers or letters

Rating scales Data source used to determine which target behaviors are exhibited and the extent to which these behaviors compare with the behaviors of typical students

Readability level The level of difficulty of a textbook

Reading comprehension The ability to understand individual words, phrases and clauses, sentences, paragraphs, and larger units of text

Real content The main idea or key information that someone wants to convey

Receptive language A person's ability to understand what is being communicated

Receptive vocabulary Words that children understand the meaning of but may not use in their oral language

Reciprocal causation The combination of factors related to a student's reading problems

Register A language style the speaker uses to communicate to meet the needs or expectations of the speaker; includes such features as choice of words, sentences, intonation, and formality

Regular Education Initiative (REI) A concept that promotes coordination of services between regular and special education

Reinforcement Rewards from the teacher

Related services The types of services to which students with disabilities are entitled, including speech therapy, audiology, psychological services, physical therapy, occupational therapy, recreation, early identification and assessment, counseling, medical services for diagnostic or evaluation purposes, school health services, transportation, and social work services

Reliable alliances Home/school partnerships that occur when there are mutual trust; ongoing communication; sensitivity to family culture, basic needs, and choices; and high yet realistic expectations

Repeated readings Process of reading passages over and over again to develop fluency in reading

Repetitive motor behaviors Physical movements that are continuously repeated; examples are rocking, hand flapping, or rapid blinking

Residual hearing Usable hearing

Responders Students who respond well to intervention

Response cost Punishment that involves the loss of something tangible or intangible

Response to intervention (RTI) The practice of making educational decisions for students based on the student's level of performance and rate of progress after receiving high-quality, validated instruction or intervention

Rett syndrome An extremely rare disorder that primarily affects females, characterized by the following symptoms occurring between 5 and 48 months: deceleration of head growth, loss of hand skills with subsequent development of stereotyped hand movements, loss of social engagement, poor gait or trunk movements, and severely impaired receptive and expressive communication

Revising Stage of writing during which points are explored further, ideas are elaborated on, and further connections are made

Rhyming Identifying similarities and differences in word endings

RUBRIC A strategy for helping students learn to use rubrics effectively: Read the rubric and the material to be graded; Use the rubric to give an initial score; Bring a buddy to help you rate again; Review the material together; Identify and award the scores together; Check the scores again

Rubrics A tool that is increasingly being used to give students explicit information about expected performance on tests and assignments

S

Saxon Math A K–12 math program addressing math concepts with a scaffolded approach and an emphasis on solving math problems

Schizophrenia A chronic, severe, and disabling brain disorder

Schoolwide positive behavior support (SWPBS) A model for conceptualizing how the entire school defines and participates in practices that reduce negative behaviors and increase positive behaviors

SCORE A A type of mnemonic used to identify the writing steps (Select a topic; Create categories; Obtain reference tools; Read and take notes; Evenly organize the information using notecards; Apply writing process steps)

Scoring guides Guidelines indicating what students should know and be able to do to demonstrate mastery of a standard

Secondary language output The level of proficiency in producing (speaking and writing) a language

Segmenting Process of dividing ideas into words and words into syllables and individual phonemes

Self-advocacy Occurs when individuals effectively communicate and negotiate for their interests, desires, needs, and rights

Self-determination A set of skills related to development of independence in setting and reaching goals including self-advocacy, choice making, decision making, and self-awareness

Self-evaluation Student self-analysis and goal setting for academic or behavioral tasks

Self-injurious behavior Behavior that may consist of head banging, scratching, or self-biting

Self-injury A behavior that may consist of head banging, scratching, or biting oneself

Self-monitoring Keeping track of how well one is understanding or performing by oneself

Self-recording Written documentation of incremental progress in meeting academic or behavioral goals

Self-regulation Monitoring and giving yourself feedback about what and how you are doing

Self-talk A technique in which the teacher describes what he or she is doing or thinking

Semantic feature analysis A vocabulary-enhancement procedure that involves the placement of categories or critical features along one axis and the specific vocabulary along the other axis

Semantic map A prelearning activity for increasing students' comprehension

Semantics The content of language

Sensorineural hearing loss A hearing loss that occurs when there is damage to the cochlea (inner ear) or to the auditory nerve

Seriation The ability to rank objects according to the degree to which they possess a certain common characteristic

Severe disabilities Conditions that significantly affect typical life activities

SHARE A multi-step strategy for promoting positive communication: **S**it up straight; **H**ave a pleasant tone of voice; **A**ctivate your thinking; **R**elax; **E**ngage in eye communication

Sheltered English A type of ESL instruction in which the goal is to teach English language skills at the same time that students are learning content-area information

Sight word Words that are recognized immediately upon seeing them

Sight word association procedure (SWAP) A learning technique that helps students associate spoken words with their printed forms

Silent or nonverbal period A time during which children are absorbing information and language that they cannot demonstrate or do not yet feel comfortable demonstrating

Situational factors Factors related to the context or situation in which the second-language learning occurs

Social action approach An approach that incorporates all the elements of the transformation approach but also includes cultural critique and problem solving that require students to make decisions and take actions related to the concept, issue, or problem being studied

Social language Part of the conversational competencies we develop with a second language—the greetings and "small talk" between peers, which generally do not—require much cognitive effort or social problem solving

Social learning Involves observing and modeling or imitating the behavior of others

Social problem solving Social skill instruction taught within the process of engaging in social interactions and involving a set of strategies students learn to monitor or manage their own social skills

Social skills or competence The ability to initiate appropriate social interactions, respond to social initiations from others, and terminate social interactions appropriately

Social skills training (SST) Training that provides students with specific instruction in acquisition, performance, and fluency of social skills

Social Story An individualized short story designed to clarify a particular social context, the perspectives of others in that context, and the social skills to be performed

Social Story interventions Social skill instruction involving individualized short stories designed to clarify a particular social context, the perspectives of others in that context, and the social skills to be performed

Socialized aggression Routinely engaging in antisocial behavior

Speaking vocabulary Vocabulary that is used as part of children's oral language

Special education resource room A placement outside the general education classroom where students with disabilities receive specialized, individualized, and intensive instruction to meet their needs

Specific learning disabilities Represents a heterogeneous group of students who, despite adequate cognitive functioning and the ability to learn some skills and strategies quickly and easily, have great difficulty learning other skills and strategies

Speech and language pathologist A person trained to provide screening, assessment, and treatment for students who have difficulties with speech (including pronunciation) as well as with language (including stuttering, inadequate language development, and poor use of syntax)

Speech disorders Disorders that involve unintelligible or unpleasant communication

Spina bifida A birth defect that occurs when the spinal cord fails to close properly

Spiral curriculum Occurs when the same skills (e.g., mathematics skills) are woven into every year of school and students continually repeat knowledge acquisition in the same area

Standard English language learners (SELLs) Learners who approach learning through differences in language, not deficits

Standard treatment protocol model The same empirically validated treatments are used for all children with similar problems

Station teaching This model includes multiple centers—some with teacher-led activities, some with student-led activities, and some with independent work. The groups may be composed of same- or mixed-ability students depending on the objectives of the lesson. This model includes reading groups and learning centers in which students are engaged in a variety of activities

Stereotypic behavior Behaviors that characterize a disorder or condition such as rocking, flapping fingers, twirling or spinning objects, and grinding teeth

Stimulant medications Medications that are frequently used in the treatment of attention deficit and hyperactivity disorders

Stimulus Something that incites activity or attention

STOP and DARE strategy A multi-step strategy for persuasive writing: **S**uspend judgment; **T**ake a side; **O**rganize ideas; **P**lan more as you write; **D**evelop your topic sentence; **A**dd supporting ideas; **R**eject possible arguments; **E**nd with a conclusion

Story webs Visual displays developed to help students understand the structure of the stories they read

Strategies Step-by-step cognitive processes and plans for reading, studying, and problem solving

Strategy guides Graphic and questioning materials that provide support to students as they learn to use metacognitive strategies

Structural analysis Analysis involving the use of root words, prefixes, and suffixes to determine the pronunciation and meaning of a word, including multisyllable words and merged words such as compounds (*buttermilk, pancake*) and contractions (*don't, can't*)

Student-centered model An educational model in which students have ample opportunity to create personal meaning from what they are reading and writing

Student interview A data source to learn more about the behaviors the student would like to change and to determine what the student's views are on why the behaviors persist and what might assist the student in rectifying the behaviors

Stuttering The most common fluency disorder, involving an interruption of the forward flow of speech

Surveys A way to foster communication with parents

Syllabication Dividing words by common syllable types

Syntax The rules that govern the order of words in sentences

Systems of support A coordinated set of services and accommodations matched to the student's needs

T

TAG A strategy for students to provide each other with feedback about their writing

Talent pool approach Procedure used to avoid overlooking students with exceptional talents and abilities who might not be identified through IQ tests or teacher nominations alone

Task analysis A breakdown of each individual step or skill, with the necessary adaptations, that will be used as a guide for teaching the step or skill to the student

Teacher interview A data source to learn more about the behaviors the teacher would like to see changed and to determine the teacher's views of why the behaviors persist and what changes the teacher has made and is willing to make to change the behaviors

Teaming The formal work groups that have clear goals and committed members

Team-assisted individualization Provision of individualized instruction within a cooperative learning model

Technologically dependent Requiring life support or specialized support systems such as ventilators

Test-approach skills Skills that can help students get physically and mentally ready for exams; sending flyers home to parents about the importance of sleep and nutrition can help prepare students physically

Test-preparedness skills Skills related to knowing both the general content and the format of an exam

Test-taking skills Skills that students use to complete an examination in a timely and effective way

Think-alouds A way to model how to think and learn

Tiers The level of intensity of instruction provided to a student or group of students

Time delay An evidence-based practice to provide access to the general education curriculum for students with moderate and severe disabilities

Time-out Time during which the student is removed from the opportunity to receive reinforcement

Title I funds A federally funded program that provides financial assistance for schools with high numbers or percentages of students from low-income families; funds must be used to provide services for students who have demonstrated academic difficulties or are at risk of academic difficulties

Token system A system in which students receive tokens in exchange for meeting classroom objectives and can exchange the tokens for rewards

Tonic–clonic seizures A type of seizure that is characterized by convulsions followed by loss of consciousness

Total blindness Refers to a very small minority of individuals who have visual impairments and who are unable to see anything, including objects or light sources

Tracked The practice of placing students with similar needs together for extended periods of the school day

Transdisciplinary teaming The teaming of a group of experts who work together and view the student as a whole instead of working independently in a single specialty area

Transformation approach An approach in which the basic core of the curriculum is changed, and goals focus on viewing events, concepts, and themes from multiple perspectives, based on diversity

Transition services Services that provide activities on behalf of the student with the disability that promote an outcome-oriented process of supports from school to postsecondary activities that include further schooling, vocational training, and integrated employment

Transitional bilingual education A program that helps students shift from the home language to the dominant language

Traumatic brain injury An injury to the brain, caused by an external physical force, that causes total or partial functional disability or psychosocial impairment, or both, which adversely affects a student's educational performance

TREE method A type of mnemonic used to plan an essay (write a Topic sentence; think of Reasons to support the topic sentence; Examine your reasons; think of an Ending or conclusion)

Tutoring A systematic plan for supplementing the student's educational program

Two-way bilingual programs A program in which half the students are native speakers of English and the other half speak another language, usually Spanish. Instruction is delivered in English half the time and in the other language the other half

U

Universal screening Screening that administers the same test to all students to determine who is likely to be at risk for academic difficulties

Universal strategies Basic principles of managing student behavior

V

VCe rule Vowel, consonant, silent e as in "time"

Verbal reprimands Short, targeted comments designed to address a specific misbehavior

Vibrant discussions Discussions in which student participation is high, students' thinking is stimulated, and students have opportunities to connect what they are learning to their personal knowledge and experience

Visual acuity The clarity with which an individual can see an object from a distance of 20 feet

Visual detail Ability to perceive details in the visual field; difficulties in this area may lead to academic problems such as misreading an aspect of an arithmetic problem

Visual field How well an individual can see using peripheral or side vision

Vmath A curricular program developed for students in grades 3 through 8 who may need extra instruction to meet mathematics learning goals. Vmath is designed at each grade level to assess and monitor the progress of students so that through a systematic approach to instruction, they can develop into independent learners in math and meet grade-level goals in math

Vocabulary An individual's working knowledge of words

Vocal nodules Nodules that develop because the vocal mechanism is used incorrectly or overused

Vocational Rehabilitation Act This act (P.L. 93-112) prevents any private organization that uses federal funds, or any local or state organization, from discriminating against persons with disabilities solely on the basis of those disabilities

Voice disorders Disorders that relate to the quality of the voice itself

W

Wait time Time provided to allow students to understand what has been said and to construct a response

Websites School websites that provide information about the calendar, major events, and homework tips

Within-child factors Factors that have traditionally been the focus of determining whether a student has special needs, such as cognitive functioning, academic functioning, or functioning on such processing measures as auditory and visual tasks

Word identification A strategy for recognizing words involved in reading

Word retrieval Finding words from memory

Word wall A large, permanent bulletin board to which words are added each week and grouped in alphabetical order; used for word recognition and spelling

Wraparound Processes that provide coordinated services to families and students with emotional or behavior disorders

Wraparound facilitator A case manager responsible for coordinating services

Writing rubrics Scoring guides that outline expected performance on a written product

Z

Zero reject An element of IDEA that states that no child with disabilities can be excluded from receiving a free and appropriate education

References

AACAP. (2004). *The depressed child.* Retrieved from http://aacap.org/publications/factsfam/depressed.htm

Abedi, J. (2014). English language learners with disabilities: Classification, assessment, and accommodation issues. *Association of Test Publishers, 10*(2), 1–30.

Abedi, J., & Dietel, R. (2004). *Challenges in the No Child Left Behind Act for English language learners.* Los Angeles: National Center for Research on Evaluation, Standards, and Student Testing.

Abedi, J., & Levine, H. G. (2013). Fairness in assessment of English learners. *Leadership, 42*(3), 26–38.

Abikoff, H., Courtney, M. E., Szeibel, P. J., & Koplewicz, H. S. (1996). The effects of auditory stimulation on the arithmetic performance of children with ADHD and nondisabled children. *Journal of Learning Disabilities, 29*(3), 238–246.

Achenbach, T. M. (2000). *Achenbach system of empirically based assessment.* Burlington: University of Vermont.

Achenbach, T. M., & McConaughy, S. H. (2003). The Achenbach system of empirically based assessment. In C. R. Reynolds & R. W. Kamphaus (Eds.), *Handbook of psychological and educational assessment of children: Personality, behavior, and context* (2nd ed., pp. 406–432). New York: Guilford Press.

Adams, L., Gouvousis, A., VanLue, M., & Waldron, C. (2004). Social story intervention: Improving communication skills in a child with an autism spectrum disorder. *Focus on Autism and Other Developmental Disabilities, 19,* 87–94.

Adger, C. T., Wolfram, W., & Christian, D. (2007). *Dialects in schools and communities.* Mahwah, NJ: Erlbaum.

Adler, L. (2006). *Scattered minds: Hope and help for adults with attention deficit hyperactivity disorder.* New York: Putnam.

Adler, L., Barkley, R. A., & Newcorn, J. (2008). ADHD and comorbidity in adults. *Journal of Clinical Psychiatry, 69,* 1328–1335.

Afflerbach, P. (2016). Reading assessment: Looking ahead. *The Reading Teacher, 69*(4), 413–419.

Afflerbach, P., Pearson, P. D., & Paris, S. G. (2008). Clarifying differences between reading skills and reading strategies. *The Reading Teacher, 61,* 364–373.

Agran, M., Cavin, M., Wehmeyer, M., & Palmer, S. (2010). Promoting active engagement in the general education classroom and access to the general education curriculum for students with cognitive disabilities. *Education and Training in Autism and Developmental Disabilities, 45*(2), 163–174.

Ahlberg, J., & Ahlberg, A. (1979). *Each peach pear plum.* New York: Viking Press.

Ajuwon, P. M., Sarraj, H., Griffin-Shirley, N., Lechtenberger, D., & Zhou, L. (2015). Including students who are visually impaired in the classroom: Attitudes of preservice teachers. *Journal of Visual Impairment & Blindness* (Online), *109*(2), 131.

Akinbami, L. J., Moorman, J. E., Bailey, C., et al. (2012). Trends in asthma prevalence, health care use, and mortality in the United States, 2001–2010. NCHS data brief, no 94. Hyattsville, MD: National Center for Health Statistics.

Al Otaiba, S., & Fuchs, D. (2006). Who are the young children for whom best practices in reading are ineffective? *Journal of Learning Disabilities, 39,* 414–431.

Alatorre-Parks, L. (2001). Aligning student interests with district mandates. *Journal of Adolescent and Adult Literacy, 44*(4), 330–332.

Albrecht, S. F. (2008). Time away: A skill-building alternative to discipline. *Preventing School Failure, 53,* 49–55.

Algozzine, B., Browder, D., Karvonen, M., Test, D. W., & Wood, W. M. (2001). Effects of interventions to promote self-determination for individuals with disabilities. *Review of Educational Research, 71,* 219–277.

Allan, S. D., & Goddard, Y. L. (2010). Differentiated instruction and RTI: A natural fit. *Educational Leadership, 68*(2). Retrieved from http://www.ascd.org/publications/educationalleadership/oct10/vol68/num02/Differentiated-Instruction-and-RTI@-A-Natural-Fit.aspx

Allen, N., Harry, B., & McLaughlin, M. (1993). *The parent-professional partnership: African-American parents' participation in the special education process.* Final Report, Grant No. H023C901254. College Park, MD: Institute for the Study of Exceptional Children and Youth, Department of Special Education, University of Maryland College.

Alper, S., Schloss, P., & Schloss, C. (1994). *Families of students with disabilities.* Boston: Allyn & Bacon.

Alquraini, Turki; Gut, Dianne (2012). Critical components of successful inclusion of students with severe disabilities: Literature review. *International Journal of Special Education, 27*(1), 42–59.

Alter, P. J., Wrick, A., Brown, E. T., & Lingo, A. (2008). Improving mathematics problem solving skills for students with challenging behavior. *Beyond Behavior, 17*(3), 2–7.

Alvermann, D. E. (1991). The discussion web: A graphic aid for learning across the curriculum. *The Reading Teacher, 45*(2), 92–99.

American Academy of Child & Adolescent Psychiatry. (2007). Practice parameters for the assessment and treatment of children and adolescents with attention-deficit/hyperactivity disorder. *Journal of the American Academy of Child and Adolescent Psychiatry, 46*(7), 894–921.

American Academy of Child and Adolescent Psychiatry. (2009a). Facts for families: Children with oppositional defiant disorder. Retrieved from http://www.aacap.org/cs/root/facts_for_families/children_with_oppositional_defiant_disorder

American Academy of Child & Adolescent Psychiatry. (2009b). Facts for families: The depressed child. Retrieved from http://www.aacap.org/cs/root/facts_for_families/the_depressed_child

American Academy of Child & Adolescent Psychiatry. (2010). Facts for families: Conduct disorder. Retrieved from http://www.aacap.org/cs/root/facts_for_families/conduct_disorder

American Academy of Child and Adolescent Psychiatry. (2014). ADHD Resource Center. Retrieved from: http://www.aacap.org/AACAP/Families_and_Youth/Resource_Centers/ADHD_Resource_Center/Home.aspx

American Academy of Pediatrics. (2001, 2007). Policy statement: American Academy of Pediatrics: Education of children with human immunodeficiency virus infection. Retrieved from http://www.aappolicy.aappublications.org/cgi/content/full/pediatrics;105/6/1358

American Association of Intellectual and Developmental Disabilities. (2009a). Diagnostic Adaptive Behavior Scale. Retrieved from http://www.aamr.org/content_106.cfm?navID=23

American Association of Intellectual and Developmental Disabilities. (2009b). FAQs on intellectual disability. Retrieved from http://www.aamr.org/content_104.cfm?navID=22

American Association of Intellectual and Developmental Disabilities. (2009c). What is the Supports Intensity Scale? Retrieved from http://www.siswebsite.org/

American Association of Intellectual and Developmental Disabilities. (2013). Definition of intellectual disability. Retrieved from http://www.aaidd.org/intellectual-disability/definition

American Association on Intellectual and Developmental Disabilities. (2012). FAQ on AAIDD's new Diagnostic Adaptive Behavior Scale. Retrieved from http://www.aaidd.org/content_107.cfm

American Association on Mental Retardation. (2002). *Mental retardation: Definition, classification, and systems of support* (10th ed.). Washington, DC: Author.

American Foundation for Suicide Prevention. (2009). Warning signs of suicide. Retrieved from http://www.afsp.org/index.cfm?page_id=0519EC1A-D73A-8D90-7D2E9E2456182D66

American Foundation for the Blind. (2007). Estimates of severely visually impaired children. Retrieved from http://www.afb.org/Section.asp?SectionID

American Foundation for the Blind. (2009). Educating students with visual impairments for inclusion in society. Retrieved from http://www.afb.org/Section.asp?SectionID

American Lung Association. (2009). Asthma & children fact sheet. Retrieved from http://www.lungusa.org/site/pp.asp?c=dvLUK9O0E&b=44352

American Lung Association. (2011). Back to school with asthma: Time to prepare. Retrieved from http://www.lung.org/about-us/our-impact/top-stories/back-to-school-with-asthma.html

American Optometric Association. (2009). *School-aged vision: 6 to 18 years of age.* Retrieved from http://www.aoa.org/X9451.sml?prt

American Optometric Association. (2011). *Ready for school: Children's vision.* St. Louis: Author. Retrieved from http://www.aoa.org/documents/RFS%20The%20Equation%20is%20Simple.pdf

American Printing House for the Blind. (2007). Distribution of eligible students. Retrieved from http://www.aph.org/fedquotpgm/dist07.html

American Printing House for the Blind. (2010). *Annual report.* Louisville, KY: Author.

American Printing House for the Blind. (2014). Annual Report: Distribution of Eligible Students Based on the Federal Quota Census. Retrieved from http://www.aph.org/federal-quota/dist14.html

American Psychiatric Association. (2012). DSM-5: The future of psychiatric diagnosis. Retrieved from http://www.dsm5.org/Pages/Default.aspx

American Psychiatric Association. (2013). *Diagnostic and statistical manual of mental disorders: DSM-IV-TR* (4th ed., text rev.). Washington, DC: Author.

American Psychiatric Association. (2013). *Diagnostic and Statistical Manual of Mental Disorders (DSM-5®).* American Psychiatric Pub.

American Psychiatric Association. (2013). *Diagnostic and statistical manual of mental disorders (DSM-5®).* Washington, DC: Author.

American Psychiatric Association. (2013). *Diagnostic and statistical manual of mental disorders* (5th ed.). Washington, DC: American Psychiatric Association.

American Speech-Language-Hearing Association. (2005). Retrieved from http://www.asha.org/default.htm

American Speech-Language-Hearing Association. (2006). *2006 schools survey report: Caseload characteristics.* Rockville, MD: Author.

American Speech-Language-Hearing Association. (2008). *Incidence and prevalence of communication disorders and hearing loss in children.* Retrieved from http://www.asha.org/members/research/reports/children.html

American Speech-Language-Hearing Association. (2009). Assistive technology. Retrieved from http://www.asha.org/public/hearing/treatment/assist_tech.htm

American Speech-Language-Hearing Association. (2011). *Parents: Don't hope your your child will just outgrow an early language problem.* Retrieved from http://www.asha.org/About/news/Press-Releases/2011/Parents—Don-t-Hope-Your-Child-Will-Just-Outgrow-An-Early-Language-Problem.htm

American Speech-Language-Hearing Association. (2014). *2014 schools survey. Survey summary report: Number and type of responses, SLPs.* Retrieved from http://www.asha.org/uploadedFiles/2014-Schools-Survey-SLP-Frequency-Report.pdf

American Speech-Language-Hearing Association. (2015). *Augmentative and Alternative Communication (AAC).* Retrieved from http://www.asha.org/public/speech/disorders/AAC/

American Speech-Language-Hearing Association. (2015). *Augmentative communication: A glossary.* Retrieved from http://www.asha.org/public/speech/disorders/AAC-Glossary/

American Speech-Language-Hearing Association. (2015). *Definitions of communication disorders and variations.* Retrieved from http://www.asha.org/policy/RP1993-00208/

American Speech-Language-Hearing Association. (2015). *Social communication disorders in school-age children.* Retrieved from http://www.asha.org/PRPSpecificTopic.aspx?folderid=8589934980§ion=Overview

American Speech-Language-Hearing Association. (2015). *Stuttering. Retrieved from* http://www.asha.org/public/speech/disorders/stuttering/

Amrein, A. L., & Berliner, D. C. (2002, March 28). High-stakes testing, uncertainty, and student learning, *Education Policy Analysis Archives, 10*(18). Retrieved from http://www.epaa.asu.edu/epaa/v10n18/

Anderson, C. M., & Spaulding, S. A. (2007). Using positive behavior support to design effective classrooms. *PBS in the Classroom*, 27–31.

Anderson, D. H., Munk, J. A. H., Young, K. R., Conley, L., & Caldarella, P. (2008). Teaching organization skills to promote academic achievement in behaviorally challenged students. *Teaching Exceptional Children, 40*(4), 6–13.

Andrade, H., & Valtcheva, A. (2009). Promoting learning and achievement through self-assessment. *Theory into Practice, 48*, 12–19.

Anxiety Disorders Association of America. (2009). Anxiety disorders in children and teens. Retrieved from http://www.adaa.org/GettingHelp/FocusOn/Children&Adolescents.asp

Archer, A. I., Gleason, M. M., & Vachon, V. L. (2003). Decoding and fluency: Foundation skills for struggling older readers. *Learning Disabilities Quarterly, 26*, 89–101.

Archer, A. L., Gleason, M. M., & Vachon, V. (2005). *REWARDS reading excellence: Word attack & rate development strategies.* Longmont, CO: Sopris West Educational Services.

Ariza, E. N., Morales-Jones, C. A., Yahya, N., & Zainuddin, H. (2006). *Why TESOL? Theories and issues in teaching English to speakers of other languages in K–12 classrooms* (3rd ed.) Dubuque: IA: Kendall/Hunt Publishing.

Armbruster, B. (2009). Notetaking from lectures. In R. F. Flippo & D. C. Caverly (Eds.), *Handbook of college reading and study strategy research* (2nd ed., pp. 220–248). New York: Routledge.

Armbruster, B. B., & Anderson, T. H. (1988). On selecting "considerate" content area textbooks. *Remedial and Special Education, 9*, 47–52.

Armstrong, T. (2003). *Multiple intelligences of reading and writing: Making the words count.* Alexandria, VA: Association for Supervision and Curriculum Development.

Arndt, S. A., Konrad, M., & Test, D. W. (2006). Effects of the self-directed IEP on student participation in planning meetings. *Remedial and Special Education, 27*, 194–207.

Arter, C. (2013). *Children with visual impairment in mainstream settings.* New York: Routledge.

Arter, J., & McTighe, J. (2000). *Scoring rubrics in the classroom: Using performance criteria for assessing and improving student performance.* Thousand Oaks, CA: Corwin Press.

Arthur-Kelly, M., Foreman, P., Bennett, D., & Pascoe, S. (2008). Interaction, inclusion and students with profound and multiple disabilities: Towards an agenda for research and practice. *Journal of Research in Special Education Needs, 8*, 161–166.

Artiles, A. J. (2015). Beyond responsiveness to identity badges: Future research on culture and disability and implications for response to intervention. *Educational Review*, 67(1), 1–22.

Assouline, S. G., Colangelo, N., Heo, N., & Dockery, L. (2013). High-ability students' participation in specialized instructional delivery models: Variations by aptitude, grade, gender, and content area. *Gifted Child Quarterly*, 57(2) 135–147.

Asthma and Allergy Foundation of America. (2005). Asthma overview. Retrieved from http://www.aafa.org/display.cfm?id=8&cont=6

Asthma and Allergy Foundation of America. (2009). Asthma overview. Retrieved from http://www.aafa.org/display.cfm?id=8

Atkinson, R. C. (1975). Mnemotechnics in second-language learning. *American Psychologist, 30*, 821–828.

Attwood, T. (2000). Strategies for improving the social integration of students with Asperger syndrome. *Autism, 4*, 85–100.

Atwell, N. (1984). Writing and reading literature from the inside out. *Language Arts, 61*, 240–252.

Aud, S., Fox, M. A., & KewalRamani, A. (2010). *Status and trends in the education of racial and ethnic minorities* (NCES 2010-015). Washington, DC: National Center for Education Statistics.

August, D., & Shanahan, T. (2006). *Developing literacy in second-language learners: Report of the National Literacy Panel on Language-Minority Children and Youth.* Mahwah, NJ: Erlbaum.

August, D., McCardle, P., & Shanahan, T. (2014). Developing literacy in English language learners: Findings from a review of the experimental research. *School Psychology Review, 43*(4), 490–498.

Austin, J., Lee, M., & Carr, J. (2004). The effects of guided notes on undergraduate student recording of lecture content. *Journal of Instructional Psychology, 31*, 314–320.

Austin, V. L. (2001). Teachers' beliefs about co-teaching. *Remedial and Special Education, 22*, 245–254.

Avalos, M. A., Pazos-Rego, A., Cuevas, P. D., Massey, S. R., & Schumm, J. S. (2009). *Cases and standards-based rubrics for candidate assessment and program evaluation in reading education.* Newark, DE: International Reading Association.

Axelrod, S. (Ed.). (2013). *Effects of punishment on human behavior.* New York: Academic Press.

Ayllon, T. (1999). *How to use token economies and point systems.* Austin, TX: PRO-ED.

Ayres, K. M., Lowrey, K. A., Douglas, K. H., & Sievers, C. (2011). I can identify Saturn but I can't brush my teeth: What happens when the curricular focus for students with severe disabilities shifts. *Education and Training in Autism and Developmental Disabilities, 46*(1), 11–21.

Ayres, K. M., Lowrey, K. A., Douglas, K. H., & Sievers, C. (2012). The question still remains: What happens when the curricular focus for students with severe disabilities shifts? A reply to Courtade, Spooner, Browder, and Jimenez. *Education and Training in Autism and Developmental Disabilities, 47*(1), 14–22.

Baca, L. M., & Cervantes H. T. (Eds.). (1989). *The bilingual special education interface* (2nd ed.). Columbus, OH: Merrill.

Bachhel, R., & Thaman, R. G. (2014). Effective use of pause procedure to enhance student engagement and learning. *Journal of Clinical and Diagnostic Research: JCDR, 8*(8), XM01.

Baker, C. (2011). *Foundations of bilingual education and bilingualism.* Clevedon, England: Multilingual Matters.

Baker, S. (2010). The importance of fingerspelling for reading. Visual language & visual learning: Research brief. Retrieved from http://vl2.gallaudet.edu/assets/section16/educator3.pdf

Baker, S., Gersten, R., & Graham, S. (2003). Teaching expressive writing to students with learning disabilities: Research-based applications and examples. *Journal of Learning Disabilities, 36*, 109–123.

Baker, S., Gersten, R., & Lee, D. (2002). A synthesis of empirical research on teaching mathematics to low-achieving students. *The Elementary School Journal, 103*(1), 51–73.

Baker, S., Lesaux, N., Jayanthi, M., Simino, J., Proctor, C. P., Morris, J., Gersten, R., Haymond, K., Kieffer, M. J., Linan-Thompson, S., & Newman-Gonchar, R. (2013). *Teaching academic content and literacy to English learners in elementary and middle school.* Washington, DC: National Center for Education Evaluation and Regional Assistance (NCEE), Institute of Education Sciences, U. S. Department of Education. Retrieved from the NCEE website: http://ies.ed.gov/ncee/wwc/publications_reviews.aspx.

Balboni, G., Tasse, M. J., Schalock, R. L., Borthwick-Duffy, S. A., Sreat, S., Thissen, D., Widaman, K. F., Zhang, D., & Navas, P. (2014). The Diagnostic Adaptive Behavior Scale: Evaluating its diagnostic sensitivity and specificity. *Research in Developmental Disabilities, 35*(11), 2884–2893.

Ball, C. R., & Christ, T. J. (2012). Supporting valid decision making: Uses and misuses of assessment data within the context of RTI. *Psychology in the Schools, 49*(3), 231–244.

Bambara, L. M., Wilson, B. A., & McKenzie, M. (2007). Transition and quality of life. In S. L. Odom, R. H. Horner, M. E. Snell, & J. Blacher (Eds.), *Handbook of developmental disabilities* (pp. 271–389). New York: Guilford Press.

Bandura, A. (1971). *Psychological modeling.* Chicago: Aldine/Atherton.

Bandura, A. (1973). *Aggression: A social learning analysis.* Englewood Cliffs, NJ: Prentice Hall.

Banks, J. A. (2008). *An introduction to multicultural education* (4th ed.). Boston: Pearson.

Banks, J. A. (2014). *An introduction to multicultural education* (5th ed.). Boston: Pearson.

Banks, J. A. (2015). *Cultural diversity and education: Foundations, curriculum, and teaching* (6th ed.). Boston: Pearson.

Baric, V. B., Hellberg, K., Kjellberg, A., & Hemmingsson, H. (2015). Support for learning goes beyond academic support: Voices of students with Asperger's disorder and attention deficit hyperactivity disorder. *Autism*, doi:1362361315574582.

Barkley, R. A. (1998). *Attention-deficit hyperactivity disorder: A handbook for diagnosis and treatment* (2nd ed.). New York: Guilford Press.

Barkley, R. A. (2000). *Taking charge of ADHD: The complete, authoritative guide for parents* (rev. ed.). New York: Guilford Press.

Barkley, R. A. (2005). *Attention-deficit hyperactivity disorder: A handbook for diagnosis and treatment* (3rd ed.). New York: Guilford Press.

Barkley, R. A. (2008). *Attention-deficit hyperactivity disorder: A handbook for diagnosis and treatment* (4th ed.). New York: Guilford Press.

Barkley, R. A. (2013). *Taking charge of ADHD* (3rd ed.). New York: Guilford.

Barkley, R. A. (2015). Executive functioning and self-regulation viewed as an extended phenotype: Implications of the theory for ADHD and its treatment. In R. A. Barkley (Ed.), *Attention-deficit hyperactivity disorder: A handbook for diagnosis and treatment* (4th ed., pp. 405–434). New York: Guilford.

Barkley, R. A., & Benton, C. M. (2010). *Taking charge of adult ADHD.* New York: Guilford.

Barkley, R. A., & Murphy, K. R. (1998). *Attention-deficit hyperactivity disorder: A clinical workbook* (2nd ed.). New York: Guilford Press.

Barkley, R. A., & Murphy, K. R. (2006). *Attention-deficit hyperactivity disorder: A clinical workbook* (3rd ed.). New York: Guilford Press.

Barkley, R. A., Murphy, K. R., & Fischer, M. (2008). *ADHD in adults: What the science says.* New York: Guilford Press.

Barnes, M. A., Wilkinson, M., Khemar, E., Boudescuie, A., Dennis, M., & Fletcher, J. M. (2006). Mathematics errors in spina-bifida. *Journal of Learning Disabilities, 39*(2), 174–187.

Baron, J., & Brown, R. V. (Eds.). (2012). *Teaching decision making to adolescents.* New York: Routledge.

Barraga, N. C., & Erin, J. N. (2001). *Visual handicaps and learning* (3rd ed.). Austin, TX: PRO-ED.

Barron, A. E., & Wells, J. A. (2008). School web sites: Essential communication tools. *Principal, 87*(4), 62–63.

Barsky, A. (2014). *Conflict resolution for the helping professions.* Oxford, United Kingdom: Oxford University Press.

Bartholome, L. W. (2003). Typewriting/keyboarding instruction in elementary schools. Retrieved from http://www.usoe.k12.ut.us/ate/keyboarding/Articles/Bartholome

Basham, J. D., & Marino, M. T. (2013). Understanding STEM education and supporting students through universal design for learning. *Teaching Exceptional Children, 45*(4), 8–15.

Batsche, G., Elliott J., Graden, J. L., Grimes, J., Kovaleski. J. F., Prasse, D., Reschly, D., Tilly, W. D. (2005). *Response to intervention: Policy considerations and implementation.* Alexandria, VA: National Association of State Directors of Special Education.

Baumann, J. F., & Graves, M. F. (2010). What is academic vocabulary? *Journal of Adolescent & Adult Literacy, 54*(1), 4–12.

Beach, K. D., Sanchez, V., Flynn, L. J., & O'Connor, R. E. (2015). Teaching academic vocabulary to adolescents with learning disabilities. *Teaching Exceptional Children, 48*(1), 36–44.

Beach, R. W. (2011). Issues in analyzing alignment of language arts Common Core Standards with state standards. *Educational Researcher, 40*(4), 179–182.

Bean, R. M., Kern, D. Goatley, V., Ortlieb, E., Shettel, J. Calo, K., Marinak, B., Sturtevant, E., Elish-Piper, L., L'Allier, S., Cox, M. A., Frost, S., Mason, P., Quatroche, D., & Cassidy, J. (2015). Specialized literacy professionals as literacy leaders: Results of a national survey. *Literacy Research and Instruction, 54*(2), 83–114.

Bean, T. W. (1985). Classroom questioning: Directions for applied research. In A. C. Graesser & J. Black (Eds.), *Psychology of questions* (pp. 335–358). Hillsdale, NJ: Erlbaum.

Bean, T. W., Readence, J. E., & Baldwin, R. S. (2008). *Content area literacy: An integrated approach* (9th ed.). Dubuque, IA: Kendall/Hunt.

Bean, T., Readence, J., & Baldwin, S. (2011). *Content-area literacy: Reaching and teaching the 21st century adolescent.* Huntington Beach, CA: Teacher Created Materials.

Bear, D. R., Helman, L., Invernizzi, M., & Templeton, S. R. (2007). *Words their way with English learners: Word study for spelling, phonics, and vocabulary instruction.* Upper Saddle River, NJ: Merrill/Prentice Hall.

Bear, D. R., Invernizzi, M., Templeton, S., & Johnston, F. (2008). *Words their way: Word study for phonics, vocabulary, and spelling instruction* (4th ed.). Upper Saddle River, NJ: Merrill/Prentice Hall.

Bear, D. R., Invernizzi, M., Templeton, S., & Johnston, F. (2015). *Words their way: Word study for phonics, vocabulary, and spelling instruction* (6th ed.). Boston: Pearson.

Beard, L. A., Carpenter, L. B., & Johnston, L. B. (2010). *Assistive technology: Access for all students.* Austin, TX: Pearson.

Beauchamp, M. H., & Anderson, V. (2010). SOCIAL: An integrative framework for the development of social skills. *Psychological Bulletin, 136*(1).

Beck, I. L. (2006). *Making sense of phonics.* New York: Guilford Press.

Beck, I. L., & McKeown, M. G. (2006). *Improving comprehension with questioning the author.* New York: Scholastic.

Beck, I. L., McKeown, M. G., & Kucan, L. (2002). *Bringing words to life.* New York: Guilford Press.

Beck, I., McKeown, M., & Kucan, L. (2008). *Creating robust vocabulary: Frequently asked questions and extended examples.* New York: Guilford.

Beck, I., McKeown, M., & Kucan, L. (2013). *Bringing words to life: Robust vocabulary instruction* (2nd ed.). New York: Guilford.

Beebe, S., & Masterson, J, T. (2012). *Communicating in small groups: Principles and practices* (11th ed.). Boston: Allyn & Bacon.

Begeny, J., Yeager, A., & Martinez, R. (2012). Effects of small-group and one-on-one reading fluency interventions with second grade, low-performing Spanish readers. *Journal of Behavioral Education, 21*(1), 58–79.

Beitchman, J. H., Nair, R., Clegg, M., Ferguson, B., & Patel, B. (2010). Prevalence of psychiatric disorders in children with speech and language disorders. *Journal of the American Academy of Child Psychiatry, 25*(4), 528–535.

Belenky, M. F., Clinchy, B. M., Goldberger, N. R., & Tarule, J. M. (1986). *Women's ways of knowing: The development of self, voice, and mind.* New York: Basic Books.

Bellini, S., & Akullian, J. A meta-analysis of video modeling and video self-modeling interventions for children and adolescents with autism spectrum disorders. *Exceptional Children, 73*(3), 264–287.

Bello, M. (2007). Using cognates. In S. Vaughn, C. S. Bos, & J. S. Schumm (Eds.), *Teaching students who are exceptional, diverse, and at risk in the general education classroom* (4th ed., p. 286). Boston: Allyn & Bacon.

Bereiter, C., Hilton, P., Rubinstein, J., & Willoughby, S. (1998). *SRA math explorations and applications,* Level 5 (teacher ed.). Boston: McGraw Hill.

Berkas, N., & Pattison, C. (2007). Manipulatives: More than a special education intervention. Retrieved from http://www.nctm.org/news/content.aspx?id=12698

Berkeley, S., Mastropieri, M. A., & Scruggs, T. E. (2011). Reading comprehension strategy instruction and attribution retraining for secondary students with learning and other mild disabilities. *Journal of Learning Disabilities, 44*(1), 18–32.

Berkeley, S., William, N. B., Peaster, L. G., & Saunders, L. (2009). Implementation of response to intervention: A snapshot of progress. *Journal of Learning Disabilities, 42*(1), 85–95.

Berko Gleason, J. (2001). *The development of language* (5th ed.). Boston: Allyn & Bacon.

Berner, R. (1977). What parents and teachers should know about death education. *DOPHHH Journal, 3,* 17–21.

Berninger, V. W., Rutberg, J. E., Abbott, R. D., Garcia, N., Anderson-Youngstrom, M., Brooks, A., & Fulton, C. (2006). Tier 1 and Tier 2 early intervention for handwriting and composing. *Journal of School Psychology, 44*(1), 3–30.

Berninger, V. W. (2012). Strengthening the mind's eye: The case for continued handwriting instruction in the 21st century. *Principal,* 28–31.

Berninger, V. W., & Wolf, B. (2009). *Helping students with dyslexia and dysgraphia make connections: Differentiated instruction lesson plans in reading and writing.* Baltimore: Brookes Publishing Company.

Berninger, V., Abbott, R., Rogan, L., Reed, E., Abbott, S., Brooks, A., Vaughan, K., & Graham, S. (1998). Teaching spelling to children with specific learning disabilities: The mind's ear and eye beat the computer or pencil. *Learning Disability Quarterly, 21*(2), 106–122.

Bessell, A. G. (2001). Children surviving cancer: Psychosocial adjustment, quality of life, and school experience. *Exceptional Children, 67*(3), 345–359.

Best, S. J. (2010). Physical disabilities. In *Teaching individuals with physical, health, and multiple disabilities* (6th ed., pp. 32–58). Upper Saddle River, NJ: Prentice Hall.

Bialystok, E., & Shapero, D. (2005). Ambiguous benefits: The effect of bilingualism on reversing ambiguous figures. *Developmental Science, 8*(6), 595–604.

Bicard, S. C., & Heward, W. L. (2013). Education equality for students with disabilities. In J. A. Banks, & C. A. M. Banks (Eds.), *Multicultural education: Issues and perspectives* (8th ed.), pp. 245–266. Hoboken, NJ: Wiley.

Bigge, J. L., Best, S. J., & Heller, K. W. (2001). *Teaching individuals with physical, health, and multiple disabilities* (4th ed.). Upper Saddle River, NJ: Merrill/Pearson.

Billings, A. C. (2005). Beyond the Ebonics debate: Attitudes about Black and Standard American English. *Journal of Black Studies, 36,* 68–81.

Blachman, B. A. (2000). Phonological awareness. In M. L. Kamil, P. B. Mosenthal, P. D. Pearson, & R. Barr (Eds.), *Handbook of reading research* (Vol. 3, pp. 251–284). Mahwah, NJ: Erlbaum.

Blachowicz, C., & Ogle, D. (2008). *Reading comprehension: Strategies for independent learners.* New York: Guilford.

Blanton, W. E., Wood, K., & Moorman, G. B. (1990). The role of purpose in reading instruction. *The Reading Teacher, 43*(7), 486–493.

Bley, N. S., & Thornton, C. A. (2001). *Teaching mathematics to students with learning disabilities* (4th ed.). Austin, TX: PRO-ED.

Bliss, C. (1965). *Semantography.* Sydney, Australia: Semantography Publications.

Block, C. C., & Israel, S. E. (2004). The ABCs of performing highly effective think alouds. *The Reading Teacher, 58,* 154–167.

Block, C. C., Morrow, L. M., & Parris, S. R. (2008). *Comprehension instruction: Research-based best practices.* New York: Guilford.

Bloom, L., & Lahey, M. (1978). *Language development and language disorders.* New York: Wiley.

Blue-Banning, M., Summers, J. A., Frankland, H. C., Nelson, L. L., & Beegle, G. (2004). Dimensions of family and professional partnerships: Constructive guidelines for collaboration. *Exceptional Children, 70*(2), 167–184.

Boardman, A., Buckley, P., Lasser, C., Klingner, J., & Annamma, S. (2015). The efficacy of Collaborative Strategic Reading in middle school science and social studies classes. *Reading & Writing, 28*(9), 1257–1283.

Bode, B. A. (1989). Dialogue journal writing. *The Reading Teacher, 42,* 568–571.

Bos, C. S., & Vaughn, S. (2002). *Strategies for teaching students with learning and behavior problems* (7th ed.). Boston: Allyn & Bacon.

Bos, C. S., & Vaughn, S. (2006). *Strategies for teaching students with learning and behavior problems* (6th ed.). Boston: Allyn & Bacon.

Bottge, B. A., Ma, X., Gassaway, L., Butler, M., & Toland, M. D. (2014). Detecting and correcting fractions computation error patterns. *Exceptional Children, 80*(2), 237–255.

Bouchard, D., & Tetreault, S. (2000). The motor development of sighted children and children with moderate low vision aged 8–13. *Journal of Visual Impairment and Blindness, 94*(9), 564–573.

Bouck, E. C., & Bouck, M. K. (2008). Does it add up? Calculators as accommodations for sixth grade students with disabilities. *Journal of Special Education Technology, 23*(2), 17–31.

Bowden, L. A., Johnston, L. B., & Beard, L. A. (2015). *Assistive technology: Access for all students.* Boston: Pearson.

Bower, H. A., & Griffin, D. (2011). Can the Epstein model of parental involvement work in a high-minority, high-poverty elementary school? A case study. *Professional School Counseling, 15*(2), 77–87.

Bowman-Perrott, L., Burke, M. D., Zhang, N., & Zaini, S. (2014). Direct and collateral effects of peer tutoring on social and behavioural outcomes: A meta-analysis of single-case research. *School Psychology Review, 43*(1), 260–285.

Bowman-Perrott, L., Davis, H., Vannest, K., Williams, L., Greenwood, C., & Parker, R. (2013). Academic benefits of peer tutoring: A meta-analysis review of single-case research. *School Psychology Review, 42*(1), 39–55.

Boyle, C. A., Boulet, S., Schieve, L. A., Cohen, R. A., Blumberg, S. J., Yeargin-Allsopp, M., & Kogan, M. D. (2011). Trends in the prevalence of developmental disabilities in U.S. children, 1997–2008. *Pediatrics,* peds-2010.

Boyle, E. A., Washburn, S. G., Rosenberg, M. S., Connelly, V. J., Brinckerhoff, L. C., & Banerjee, M. (2002). Reading's SLICK with new audio texts and strategies. *Teaching Exceptional Children, 35,* 50–55.

Boyle, J. R. (2007). The process of note taking: Implications for students with mild disabilities. *The Clearing House, 80,* 227–230.

Boyle, J. R. (2008). Reading strategies for students with mild disabilities. *Intervention in School and Clinic, 44,* 3–9.

Boyle, J. R. (2010). Note-taking skills of middle school students with and without learning disabilities. *Journal of Learning Disabilities, 43*(6), 530–540.

Boyle, J. R., & Weishaar, M. (2001). The effects of notetaking on the recall and comprehension of lecture information for high school students with learning disabilities. *Learning Disabilities Research and Practice, 16,* 133–141.

Boyle, O. F. & Peregoy, S. F. (2005). *Reading, writing, and learning in ESL: A resource book for K–12 teachers* (7th ed.). Boston: Pearson.

Bradley, D. H. (2001). 20 ways to help students who struggle with writing become better writers. *Intervention in School and Clinic, 37,* 118–121.

Bradley, R., Danielson, L., & Doolittle, J. (2005). Response to intervention. *Journal of Learning Disabilities, 38,* 485–486.

Bradley, R., Danielson, L., & Hallahan, D. P. (2002). *Identification of learning disabilities: Research to practice.* Mahwah, NJ: Erlbaum.

Bradshaw, C. P., Waasdorp, T. E., & Leaf, P. J. (2012). Effects of school-wide positive behavioral interventions and supports on child behavior problems. *Pediatrics, 130*(5), doi:e1136-e1145.

Brain Injury Association of America. (2015). Improving awareness and understanding of brain injury. Retrieved from http://www.biausa.org/biaa-advocacy.htm

Bremer, C. D., Kachgal, M., & Schoeller, K. (2003). Self-determination: Supporting successful transition. *Research to Practice Brief, 2,* 1–6.

Brent, D., Melhem, N., Donohoe, B. & Walker, M. (2009). The incidence and course of depression in bereaved youth 21 months after the loss of a parent to suicide, accident, or sudden natural death. *American Journal of Psychiatry, 166,* 786–794.

Brett, A., Rothlein, L., & Hurley, M. (1996). Vocabulary acquisition from listening to stories and explanations of target words. *Elementary School Journal, 96*(4), 415–422.

Brewer, D. M., Fowler, C. H., & Test, D. W. (2005). A content and methodological review of self-advocacy intervention studies. *Exceptional Children, 72,* 101–125.

Brewin, B. J., Renwick, R., & Schormans, A. F. (2008). Parental perspectives of the quality of life in school environments for children with Asperger syndrome. *Focus on Autism and Other Developmental Disabilities, 23,* 242–252.

Brock, M. E., & Carter, E. W. (2013). A systematic review of paraprofessional-delivered educational practices to improve outcomes for students with intellectual and developmental disabilities. *Research and Practice for Persons with Severe Disabilities, 38,* 211.

Brodie, B. (2014). Student-led conferences: Personalization in practice. *Principal Leadership, 15*(1), 34–47.

Brooke, V., & McDonough, J. T. (2008). The facts ma'am, just the facts. *Teaching Exceptional Children, 41*(1), 58–65.

Brophy, J. E. (2003). *Teaching problem students.* New York: Guilford Press.

Browder, D. M., Jimenez, B. A., Spooner, F., Saunders, A., Hudson, M., & Bethune, K. S. (2012). Early numeracy instruction for students with moderate and severe developmental disabilities. *Research and Practice for Persons with Severe Disabilities, 37*(4), 308–320.

Browder, D. M., Lee, A., & Mims, P. (2011). Using shared stories and individual response modes to promote comprehension and engagement in literacy for students with multiple, severe disabilities. *Education and Training in Autism and Developmental Disabilities*, 339–351.

Browder, D. M., Trela, K., Gibbs, S. L., Wakeman, S., & Harris, A. A. (2007). Academic skills: Reading and mathematics. In S. L. Odom, R. H. Horner, M. E. Snell, & J. Blacher (Eds.), *Handbook of developmental disabilities* (pp. 292–309). New York: Guilford Press.

Browder, D. M., Wood, L., Thompson, J., & Ribuffo, C. (2014). *Evidence-based practices for students with severe disabilities* (Document No. IC-3). Retrieved from University of Florida.

Brown, J. E., & Doolittle, J. (2008). A cultural, linguistic, and ecological framework for response to intervention with English language learners. *Teaching Exceptional Children, 40*, 66–72.

Brown, L. M., & Gilligan, C. (1993). Meeting at the crossroads: Women's psychology and girls' development. *Feminism Psychology, 3*(1), 11–35.

Brown, N. B., Howerter, C. S., & Morgan, J. J. (2013). Tools and strategies for making co-teaching work. *Intervention in School & Clinic, 49*(2), 84–89.

Brown, S., & Kappes, L. (2012). *Implementing the Common Core State Standards: A primer on "close reading of text"*. Washington, DC: Aspen Institute.

Brozo, W. G. (2009). Response to intervention or responsive instruction? Challenges and possibilities of response to intervention for adolescent literacy. *Journal of Adolescent and Adult Literacy, 53*(4), 277–281.

Bruns, E. J., Walrath, C. M., & Sheehan, A. K. (2007). Who administers wraparound? An examination of the training, beliefs, and implementation supports for wraparound providers. *Journal of Emotional and Behavioral Disorders, 15*, 156–168.

Bryan, T., & Burstein, K. (2004). Improving homework completion and academic performance: Lessons from special education. *Theory into Practice, (43)*3, 213–219.

Bryant, B. R., & Bryant, D. P. (2008). Introduction to the special series: Mathematics and learning disabilities. *Learning Disability Quarterly, 31*(1), 3–8.

Bryant, D. P. (2014). Tier 2 intervention for at-risk first-grade students within a response-to-intervention model of support. *School Psychology Review, 43*(2), 179–184.

Bryant, D. P., & Bryant, B. R. (2012). *Assistive technology for people with disabilities* (2nd ed.). Boston: Pearson.

Bryant, D. P., Bryant, B. R., & Hammill, D. (2000). Characteristic behaviors of students with LD who have teacher-identified math weaknesses. *Journal of Learning Disabilities, 33*, 168–177, 199.

Bryant, D. P., Bryant, B. R., Gersten, R. M., Scammacca, N. N., Funk, C., Winter, A., Shih, M., & Pool, C. (2008). The effects of tier 2 intervention on the mathematics performance of first-grade students who are at risk for mathematics difficulties. *Learning Disability Quarterly, 31*(2), 47–63.

Bryant, D. P., Goodwin, M., Bryant, B. R., & Higgins, K. (2003). Vocabulary instruction for students with learning disabilities: A review of the research. *Learning Disabilities Quarterly, 26*, 117–128.

Bryant, D. P., Hartman, P., & Kim, S. A. (2003). Using explicit and systematic instruction to teach division skills to students with learning disabilities. *Exceptionality, 11*(3), 151–164.

Bryant, D., & Bryant, B. (2003). *Assistive technology for people with disabilities*. Boston: Allyn & Bacon.

Bryant, N. D., Drabin, I. R., & Gettinger, M. (1981). Effects of varying unit size on spelling achievement in learning disabled children. *Journal of Learning Disabilities, 14*(4), 200–203.

Bryant, P. D., Smith, D. D., & Bryant, B. R. (2008). *Teaching students with special needs in inclusive classrooms*. New York: Pearson.

Buchino, M. A. (2011). Student-led conferences give junior high students insights into their academic strengths and challenges. *Momentum, 42*(4), 54–56.

Buehl, D. (2009). *Classroom strategies for interactive learning* (3rd ed.). Newark, DE: International Reading Association.

Bulgren, J. A. (2006). Integrated content enhancement routines: Responding to the needs of adolescents with disabilities in rigorous inclusive secondary content classes. *Teaching Exceptional Children, 38*(6), 54–58.

Bulgren, J. A., Marquis, J. G., Lenz, B. K., Schumaker, J. B., & Deshler, D. D. (2009). Effectiveness of question exploration to enhance students' written expression of content knowledge and comprehension. *Reading & Writing Quarterly*, 25(4), 271–289.

Bulgren, J., Deshler, D. D., & Lenz, B. K. (2007). Engaging adolescents with LD in higher order thinking about history concepts using integrated content enhancement routines. *Journal of Learning Disabilities, 40*(2), 121–133.

Burnette, J., & Peters-Johnson, C. (2004). *Thriving as a special educator: Balancing your practices and ideals.* Reston, VA: Council for Exceptional Children.

Burniske, R. W. (2008). *Literacy in the digital age.* Thousand Oaks, CA: Corwin Press.

Burns, M. K. (2008). Response to intervention at the secondary level. *Principal Leadership, 8*, 12–15.

Burns, M. K., & Gibbons, K. (2013). *Implementing response-to-intervention in elementary and secondary schools: Procedures to assure scientific-based practices*. Routledge.

Burns, M. K., & Gibbons, K. (2013). *Implementing response-to-intervention in elementary and secondary schools: Procedures to assure scientific-based practices*. Routledge.

Burns, M. K., Griffiths, A., Parson, L. B., Tilly, W. D., & VanDerHayden, A. (2007). *Response to intervention: Research for practice.* Alexandria, VA: National Association of State Directors of Special Education.

Burstein, N., Sears, S., Wilcoken, A., Cabello, B., & Spagna, M. (2004). Moving toward inclusive practices. *Remedial and Special Education, 25*(2), 104–116.

Butler, T. A. (2014). School leadership in the 21st century: Leading in the age of reform. *Peabody Journal of Education, 89*(5), 593–602.

Cahill, M. W., & Gregory, A. E. (2011). Putting the fun back into fluency instruction. *The Reading Teacher, 65*(2), 127–131.

Cambium Learning Voyager. (2009). *Vmath.* Dallas, TX: Author.

Campbell, A., & Anderson, C. M. (2008). Enhancing effects of check-in/check-out with function-based support. *Behavior Disorders, 33*, 233–245.

Campbell, J. (2007). Understanding the emotional needs of children who are blind. *Journal of Visual Impairment and Blindness, 101*, 351–355.

Campbell-Whatley, G. D. (2008). Teaching students about their disabilities: Increasing self-determination skills and self-concept. *International Journal of Special Education, 23*, 137–144.

Cancro, R. (2008). Depression. *The Exceptional Parent, 38*, 67–68.

Candlelighters Childhood Cancer Foundation. (1993). Advice to educators (adapted from a survey by A Wish with Wings). In *Educating the child with cancer* (pp. 21–22). Bethesda, MD: Author.

Cangelosi, J. S. (2004). *Classroom management strategies: Gaining and maintaining students' cooperation.* Hoboken, NJ: Wiley.

Canter, A. (2006). Problem solving and RTI: New roles for school psychologists. *NASP Communiqué, 34*(5). Retrieved from http://www.nasponline.org/publications/cq/cq345rti.aspx

Canter, A., Klotz, M. B., & Cowan, K. (2008). Response to intervention: The future for secondary students. *Principal Leadership, 8*, 12–15.

Cantrell, S. C., Burns, L. D., & Callaway, P. (2009). Middle- and high-school content area teachers' perceptions about literacy teaching and learning. *Literacy Research and Instruction, 48*, 76–94.

Carbonneau, K. J., Marley, S. C., & Selig, J. P. (2013). A meta-analysis of the efficacy of teaching mathematics with concrete manipulatives. *Journal of Educational Psychology, 105*(2), 380–400.

Carlberg, C., & Kavale, K. (1980). The efficacy of special versus regular class placement for exceptional children: A meta-analysis. *The Journal of Special Education, 14*, 295–309.

Carlisle, J., & Rice, M. (2002). *Improving reading comprehension: Research-based principles and practices.* Baltimore, MD: York Press.

Carlo, M. S., August, D., McLaughlin, B., Snow, C., Dressler, C., Lippman, D., Lively, T. J., & White, C. E. (2008/2009). Closing the gap: Addressing the vocabulary needs to English-language learners in bilingual and mainstream classrooms. *Reading Research Quarterly, 39*(2), 188–215.

Carlson, R. (1984). *Picsyms categorical dictionary.* Lawrence, KS: Baggeboda Press.

Carnegie Corporation of New York, Institute for Advanced Study. (2011). The opportunity equation: Transforming mathematics and science education for citizenship and the global economy.

Carnett, A., Raulston, T., Lang, R., Tostanoski, A., Lee, A., Sigafoos, J., & Machalicek, W. (2014). Effects of a perseverative interest-based token economy on challenging and on-task behavior in a child with Autism. *Journal of Behavioral Education, 23*(3), 368–377. http://dx.doi.org/10.1007/s10864-014-9195-7

Carpenter, L. A. B., Johnston, L., & Beard, L. A. (2015). *Assistive technology: Access for all students* (3rd ed.). Boston, MA: Pearson.

Carpenter, L. B., Johnston, L. B., & Beard, L. A. (2015). *Assistive technology: Access for all students* (3rd ed.). Boston: Pearson.

Carr, N. S. (2013). Increasing the effectiveness of homework for all learners in the inclusive classroom. *School Community Journal, 23*(1), 169–182.

Carr, S. C., & Thompson, B. (1996). The effects of prior knowledge and schema activation strategies on the inferential reading comprehension of children with and without learning disabilities. *Learning Disability Quarterly, 19*(1), 48–61.

Carreker, S. (1999). Teaching reading: Accurate decoding and fluency. In J. R. Birsh (Ed.), *Multisensory teaching of basic language skills* (pp. 141–182). Baltimore: Paul H. Brookes.

Carroll, J. (1964). *Language and thought.* Upper Saddle River, NJ: Prentice-Hall.

Carter, E. W., Cushing, L. S., Clark, N. M., & Kennedy, C. H. (2005). Effects of peer support interventions on students' access to the general curriculum and social interactions. *Research and Practice for Persons with Severe Disabilities, 30*, 15–25.

Carter, E. W., Hughes, C., & Wehby, J. (2005). Preparing adolescents with high-incidence disabilities for high-stakes testing with strategy instruction. *Prevention of School Failure, 49*, 55–62.

Carter, E. W., Hughes, C., Guth, C. B., Copeland, S. R., & MacLean, W. E., Jr. (2005). Factors influencing social interaction among high school students with intellectual disabilities and their general education peers. *American Journal on Mental Retardation, 110*(5), 366–377.

Carter, E. W., Lane, K. L., Pierson, M. R., & Stang, K. K. (2008). Promoting self- determination for transition-age youth: Views of high school general and special educators. *Exceptional Children, 75*, 55–70.

Carter, T. P., & Chatfield, M. L. (1986). Effective bilingual schools: Implications for policy and practice. *American Journal of Education, 5*(1), 200–234.

Cartledge, G., Gardner, R., & Ford, D. Y. (2009). *Diverse learners with exceptionalities: Culturally responsive teaching in the inclusive classroom.* Upper Saddle River, NJ: Merrill/Pearson.

Cash, R. E., & Cowan, K. C. (2006). Mood disorders: What parents and teachers should know. *Communique, 35*, 1–4.

Cassady, J. C. (2010). Test anxiety: Contemporary theories and implications for learning. In J. C. Cassady (Ed.), *Anxiety in schools: The causes, consequences, and solutions for academic anxieties* (pp. 7–26). New York: Peter Lang.

Cassidy, J., Grote-Garcia, S., & Ortlieb, E. (September/October, 2015). What's hot in 2016; Recognizing new trends and celebrating 20 years of data. *Literacy Today*, 12–16.

Cassidy, J., Ortlieb, E., & Shottel, J. (2011). What's hot for 2011. *Reading Today, 28*(3), 1, 6–8.

Cassini, K. K., & Rogers, J. L. (1990). *Death in the classroom.* Cincinnati, OH: Griefwork.

Castellano, C. (2003). Tips for classroom teachers. Retrieved from http://www.blindchildren.org/textonly/to_edu_dev/3_5_4.html

Castellano, J. A. (2003). *Special populations in gifted education: Working with diverse gifted learners.* Boston: Allyn & Bacon.

Castellano, J., & Frazier, A. D. (2010). *Special populations in gifted education: Understanding our most able students from diverse backgrounds.* Waco, TX: Prufrock Press.

Castillo, J. M., Batsche, G. M., Curtis, M. J., Stockslager, K., March, A., Minch, D., & Hines, C. (2012). Problem Solving/Response to Intervention evaluation tool technical assistance manual–revised.

Catts, H., Fey, M., Zhang, X., & Tomblin, B. (2001). Estimating the risk of future reading difficulties in kindergarten children: A research-based model and its clinical implementation. *Language, Speech, and Hearing Services in Schools, 32*(1), 38–50.

Causton-Theoharis, J., & Malmgren, K. (2005). Building bridges: Strategies to help paraprofessionals promote peer interaction. *Teaching Exceptional Children, 37*, 18–24.

Cavanaugh, C. L., Kim, A., Wanzek, J., & Vaughn, S. (2004). Kindergarten reading interventions for at-risk students: Twenty years of research. *Learning Disabilities: A Contemporary Journal, 2*(1), 9–21.

Cawley, J. F., Foley, T. F., & Doan, T. (2003). Giving students a voice in selecting arithmetical context. *Teaching Exceptional Children, 36*, 8–17.

Cawthon, S. W., Winton, S. M., Garberoglio, C. L., & Gobble, M. E. (2011). The effects of American Sign Language as an assessment accommodation for students who are deaf or hard of hearing. *Journal of Deaf Studies and Deaf Education, 16*(2), 198–211.

Cawthon, S., Leppo, R., Carr, T., & Kopriva, R. (2013). Toward accessible assessments: The promises and limitations of test item adaptations for students with disabilities and English language learners. *Educational Assessment, 18*, 73–98.

Cease-Cook, J., Test, D. W., & Scroggins, S. (2013). Effects of the CD-Rom version of the self-advocacy strategy on quality of contributions in IEP meetings of high school students with intellectual disability. *Education and Training in Autism and Developmental Disabilities, 48*(2), 258–268.

Center for Applied Linguistics. (2008). Dialects. Retrieved from http://www.cal.org/topics/dialects/aae.html

Center for Applied Linguistics. (2015). *Directory of two-way immersion programs in the United States.* Retrieved from http://www.cal.org/twi/directory/

Center for Applied Special Technology. (2012). Universal design for learning. Retrieved from http://www.cast.org/about/index.html

Centers for Disease Control and Prevention (2016). *TBI: Get the Facts.* Retrieved from https://www.cdc.gov/traumaticbraininjury/get_the_facts.html

Center for Disease Control. (2008). *Data and statistics: Autism spectrum disorder.* Retrieved from National Center on Birth Defects and Developmental Disabilities website: http://www.cdc.gov///.html#prevalence

Center for Disease Control. (2014). *Data and statistics: Autism spectrum disorder.* Retrieved from National Center on Birth Defects and Developmental Disabilities website: http://www.cdc.gov///.html#prevalence

Center for Implementing Technology in Education. (2007). Beyond "getting the answer": Calculators help learning disabled students get the concepts. Retrieved from http://www.ldonline.org/article/19274/

Centers for Disease Control and Prevention. (2007). Mother-to-child (perinatal) HIV transmission and prevention. Retrieved from http://www.ced.gov/hiv

Centers for Disease Control and Prevention. (2008). HIV/AIDS among youth. Retrieved from http://www.ced.gov/hiv

Centers for Disease Control and Prevention. (2009a). Autism spectrum disorders, 2009. Retrieved from http://www.cdc.gov/ncbddd/autism/index.html

Centers for Disease Control and Prevention. (2009b). Developmental disabilities. Retrieved from http://www.cdc.gov/ncbddd/dd/dd1.html

Centers for Disease Control and Prevention. (2009c). Basic information. Retrieved from http://www.cdc.gov/hiv/topics/basic/print/index.htm

Centers for Disease Control and Prevention. (2009d). Vision impairment. Retrieved from http://www.ced.gov/ncbddd/dd/vision3.htm

Centers for Disease Control and Prevention. (2011a). ADHD: Data and statistics. Retrieved from http://www.cdc.gov/ncbddd/adhd/data.html

Centers for Disease Control and Prevention. (2011b). What are developmental disabilities? Retrieved from http://www.cdc.gov/ncbddd/dd/default.htm

Centers for Disease Control and Prevention. (2012). Autism spectrum disorders, 2009. Retrieved from http://www.cdc.gov/ncbddd/autism/index.html

Centers for Disease Control and Prevention. (2015a). Data & statistics. Retrieved from http://cdc.gov/ncbddd/fxs/data.html

Centers for Disease Control and Prevention. (2015b). Data & statistics: Prevalence of FASDs. Retrieved from http://cdc.gov/ncbddd/fasd/data.html

Centers for Disease Control and Prevention. (2015c). Facts about developmental disabilities. Retrieved from http://www.cdc.gov/ncbddd/dd/developmentaldisabilities/facts.html

Centers for Disease Control and Prevention. (2015d). Facts about Down syndrome. Retrieved from http://www.cdc.gov/ncbddd/birthdefects/downsyndrome.html

Certo, J. L., Cauley, K. M., Moxley, K. D., & Chafin, C. (2008). An argument for authenticity: Adolescents' perspectives on standards-based reform. *The High School Journal, 91*, 26–39.

CHADD. (2005). Retrieved from http://www.chadd.org

CHADD. (2011). Retrieved from http://www.chadd.org

CHADD. (2015). Section 504 in public schools. Retrieved from: http://www.chadd.org/Understanding-ADHD/Parents-Caregivers-of-Children-with-ADHD/School-and-ADHD/Section-504-in-Public-Schools.aspx

Chafouleas, S. M., Sanetti, L. M. H., Kilgus, S. P., & Maggin, D. M. (2012). Evaluating sensitivity to behavioral change across consultation cases using Direct Behavior Rating Single-Item Scales (DBR-SIS). *Exceptional Children, 78*, 491–505.

Chamberlain, S. P. (2005). Recognizing and responding to cultural differences in the education of culturally and linguistically diverse learners. *Intervention in School and Clinic, 40(4)*, 195–211.

Chamot, A. U., & O'Malley, J. M. (1994). *The CALLA handbook: Implementing the cognitive academic language learning approach.* Reading, MA: Addison-Wesley.

Chan, J. M., & O'Reilly, M. F. (2008). A social stories intervention package for students with autism in inclusive classroom settings. *Journal of Applied Behavior Analysis, 41*, 405–409.

Chan, J. M., Lang, R., Rispoli, M., O'Reilly, M. F., Sigafoos, J., & Cole, H. (2009). Use of peer-mediated interventions in the treatment of autism spectrum disorders: A systematic review. *Research in Autism Spectrum Disorders, 3*, 876–889.

Chan, J. M., O'Reilly, M., Lang, R., Boutot, A., Baker, W., White, P., & Pierce, N. (2011). Evaluation of a social stories intervention implemented by pre-service teachers for students with autism in general education settings. *Research in Autism Spectrum Disorders, 5*, 715–721.

Chandler, L. K., & Dahlquist, C. M. (2014). *Functional assessment: Strategies to prevent and remediate challenging behavior in school settings.* Upper Saddle River, NJ: Pearson.

Chapman, C., & King, R. (2004). *Differentiated assessment strategies: One tool doesn't fit all.* Thousand Oaks, CA: Sage.

Chapman, C., Laird, J., Ifill, N., & KewalRamani, A. (2011). Trends in high school dropout and completion rates in the United States: 1972–2009. Compendium Report. NCES 2012-006. *National Center for Education Statistics.*

Chappell, G. (1985). Description and assessment of language disabilities of junior high school students. In C. Simon (Ed.), *Communication skills and classroom success: Assessment of language-learning disabled students.* San Diego, CA: College-Hill.

Chard, D. J., & Dickson, S. V. (1999). Phonological awareness: Instructional and assessment guidelines. *Intervention in Clinic and School, 34*(5), 261–270.

Chard, D. J., Ketterlin-Geller, L. R., Baker, S. K., Doabler, C., & Apichatabutra, C. (2009). Repeated reading intervention for students with learning disabilities: Status for the evidence. *Exceptional Children, 75*(3), 263–281.

Chard, D. J., Vaughn, S., & Tyler, B. (2002). A synthesis of research on effective interventions for building reading fluency with elementary students with learning disabilities. *Journal of Learning Disabilities, 35*(5), 386–406.

Charles, C., & Senter, G. (2005). *Building classroom discipline* (8th ed.). Boston: Allyn & Bacon.

Charles, K. J., & Dickens, V. (2012). Closing the communication gap: Web 2.0 tools for enhanced planning and collaboration. *Teaching Exceptional Children, 45*(2), 24–32.

Charman, T., Drew, A., Baird, C., & Baird, G. (2003). Measuring early language development in pre-school children with autism spectrum disorder using the MacArthur Communicative Development Inventory (Infant Form). *Journal of Child Language, 30*, 213–236.

Checkley, K. (1997). The first seven … and the eighth: A conversation with Howard Gardner. *Educational Leadership, 55*, 8–13.

Chen, D. (Ed.). (2014). *Essential elements in early intervention: Visual impairment and multiple disabilities.* New York: American Foundation for the Blind.

Chen, D., Alsop, L., & Minor, L. (2000). Lessons from Project PLAI in California and Utah: Implications for early intervention service to infants who are deaf-blind and their families. *Deaf-Blind Perspectives, 7*, 1–9.

Chen, W. B., & Gregory, A. (2011). Parental involvement in the prereferral process implications for schools. *Remedial and Special Education, 32*(6), 447–457.

Chiappone, L. L. (2006). The wonder of words: Learning and expanding vocabulary. In J. S. Schumm (Ed.), *Reading assessment and instruction for all learners* (pp. 297–332). New York: Guilford Press.

Children's Defense Fund. (2008). *State of America's children 2008.* Washington, DC: Author.

Children's Defense Fund. (2009). About child poverty. Retrieved from http://www.childrensdefensefind.org/help-americas-children/ending-child-poverty/about.html

Children's Educational Services, Inc. (1987). *Test of Oral Reading Fluency.* Minneapolis, MN: Author.

Christ, T. J., Burns, M. K., & Ysseldyke, J. E. (2005). Conceptual confusion within response-to-intervention vernacular: Clarifying meaningful differences. NASP *Communiqué, 34*(3). Retrieved from http://www.naspon-line.org/publications/cq/cq343rti.aspx

Christ, T. J., Cengiz, Z., Long, J. D., & Monaghen, B. D. (2012). Curriculum-based measurement of oral reading: Quality of progress monitoring outcomes. *Exceptional Children, 78*(3), 356–373.

Christenson, S. L., Ysseldyke, J. E., & Thurlow, M. L. (1989). Critical instruction factors for students with mild handicaps: An integrative review. *Remedial and Special Education, 10*(5), 21–31.

Christodoulou, J. A. (2009). Applying multiple intelligences. *School Administrator, 66*, 22–26.

Chung, J. P-L. (1992). The out-of-class language and social experience of a clique of Chinese immigrant students: An ethnography of a process of social identity information. Unpublished doctoral dissertation, State University of New York, Buffalo.

Chung, Y., & Douglas, K. H. (2014). Communicative Competence Inventory for students who use augmentative and alternative communication. *Teaching Exceptional Children, 47*(1), 56–68.

Circle of Inclusion Project. (2002). The MAPS process: Seven questions. Retrieved from http://www.circleofinclusion.org/english/guidelines/modulesix/a.html

Claes, C., Van Hove, G., Vandeveide, S., van Loon, J., & Schalock, R. L. (2010). Person-centered planning: Analysis of research and effectiveness. *Intellectual and Developmental Disabilities, 48*(6), 432–453.

Clarke, B., & Shinn, M. R. (2004). A preliminary investigation into the identification and development of early mathematics curriculum-based measurement. *School Psychology Review, 33*, 234–248.

Clarke, B., Gersten, R., Dimino, J., & Rolfhus, E. (2011). Assessing student proficiency in early number sense (ASPENS). Retrieved from http://store.cambiumlearning.com/cs/Satellite?c=CLG_Product_C&childpagenae=Store%2FStore_Layout&cid=1277944479287&pagename=Store_Wrapper&rendermode=previewnoinsite

Clarke, L. S., Embury, D. C., Jones, R. E., & Yssel, N. (2014). Supporting students with disabilities during school crises: A teacher's guide. *TEACHING Exceptional Children, 46*(6), 169–178.

Clarke, L. S., Haydon, T., Bauer, A., & Eperly, A. C. (2016). Inclusion of students with an intellectual disability in the general education classroom with the use of response cards. *Preventing School Failure, 60*(1), 35–42.

Coelho, E. (1994). Social integration of immigrant and refugee children. In F. Genesee (Ed.), *Educating second language children: The whole child, the whole curriculum, the whole community* (pp. 301–328). Cambridge, England: Cambridge University Press.

Cohen, E. G., & Lotan, R. (2004). Equity in heterogeneous classrooms. In J. A. Banks & C. A. M. Banks (Eds.), *Handbook of research on multicultural education* (2nd ed., pp. 736–750). San Francisco: Jossey-Bass.

Cohen, E. G., & Lotan, R. (2015). Equity in heterogeneous classrooms. In R. A. Barkley (Ed.), *Attention-deficit hyperactivity disorder: A handbook for diagnosis and treatment* (4th ed., pp. 736–750). New York: Guilford.

Cohen, E., Kuo, D. Z., Agrawal, R., Berry, J. G., Bhagat, S. K., Simon, T. D., & Srivastava, R. (2011). Children with medical complexity: an emerging population for clinical and research initiatives. *Pediatrics, 127*(3), 529–538.

Cohen, J. S., & Smerdon, B. A. (2009). Tightening the dropout tourniquet: Easing the transition from middle to high school. *Preventing School Failure, 53*, 177–184.

Cohen, M. (2009). *A guide to special education advocacy: What parents, clinicians, and advocates need to know*. PA: Jessica Kingsley Publishers.

Cole, J. E., & Wasburn-Moses, L. H. (2010). A special educator's guide to understanding and assisting with inquiry-based teaching in mathematics. *Teaching Exceptional Children, 42*(4), 15–20.

Coleman, M. (2009). PowerPoint is not just for business presentations with college lectures: Using PowerPoint to enhance instruction for students with disabilities. *Teaching Exceptional Children Plus, 6*(1), 13.

Coleman, M. R., & Shah-Coltrane, S. (2015). Children of promise: Dr. James Gallagher's thoughts on underrepresentation within gifted education. *Journal for the Education of the Gifted, 38*(1), 70–76.

Collaboration for Effective Educator, Development, Accountability, and Reform Center website: http://ceedar.education.ufl.edu/tools/innovation-configurations/

Collier, V. P., & Thomas, W. P. (2004). The astounding effectiveness of dual language education for all. *NABE Journal of Research & Practice, 2*(1), 1–19.

Collins, B. C., Hager, K. L., & Galloway, C. C. (2011). Addition of functional content during core content instruction with students with moderate disabilities. *Education and Training in Autism and Developmental Disabilities, 46*(1) 22–39.

Common Core State-Standards Initiative. (2015). Standards in your state. Retrieved from http://www.corestandards.org/standards-in-your-state/

Conant, K. D., Morgan, A. K., Muzykewicz, D., Clark, D. C., & Thiele, E. A. (2008). A karate program for improving self-concept and quality of life in childhood epilepsy: Results of a pilot study. *Epilepsy & Behavior, 12*(1), 61–65.

Conderman, G., & Hedin, L. (2012). Purposeful assessment practices for co-teachers. *Teaching Exceptional Children, 44*(4), 18–27.

Conderman, G., & Koroghlanian, C. (2002). Writing test questions like a pro. *Intervention in School and Clinic, 38*, 83–87.

Conley, M. W. (2005). *Connecting standards and assessment through literacy*. Boston: Allyn & Bacon.

Conner, C. K. (2008). *Attention deficit hyperactivity disorder in children and adolescents: The latest assessment and treatment strategies*. Kansas City, MO: Compact Clinicals.

Conner, D. F. (2015). Stimulant and nonstimulant medications for childhood ADHD. In R. A. Barkley (Ed.), *Attention-deficit hyperactivity disorder: A handbook for diagnosis and treatment* (4th ed., pp. 666–685). New York: Guilford.

Conner, D. J., & Bejoian, L. M. (2006). Pigs, pirates, and pills: Using film to teach the social context of disability. *Teaching Exceptional Children, 39*, 52–60.

Connolly, A. J. (1998). *Key math-revised: A diagnostic inventory of essential mathematics*. Circle Pines, MN: American Guidance Service.

Connolly, A. J. (2007). *Key Math™-3*. Minneapolis: Pearson.

Conroy, M. A., Sutherland, K. S., Snyder, A., Al-Hendawi, M., & Vo, A. (2009). Creating a positive classroom atmosphere: Teachers' use of effective praise and feedback. *Beyond Behavior*, 18–26.

Cook, C. R., Gresham, F. M., Kern, K., Barreras, R. B., & Crews, S. D. (2008). Social skills training for secondary students with emotional and/or behavioral disorders. *Journal of Emotional and Behavioral Disorders, 16*, 131–144.

Cook, C. R., Williams, K. R., Nancy, G., Kim, T. E., & Sadek, S. (2010). Predictors of bullying and victimization in childhood and adolescence: A meta-analytic investigation. *School Psychology Quarterly, 25*(2), 65–83.

Cook, L., Eignor, D., Steinberg, J., Sawaki, Y., & Cline, F. (2014). Using factor analysis to investigate the impact of accommodations on the scores of students with disabilities on a reading comprehension assessment. *Association of Test Publishers, 10*(2), 1–33.

Cooper, H. (2001). *The battleground over homework: Common ground for administrators, teachers, and parents* (2nd ed.). Thousand Oaks, CA: Corwin Press.

Cooper, H. M. (2007). *The battle over homework: Common ground for administrators*. Thousand Oaks, CA: Corwin Press.

Cooper, H., & Nye, B. (1994). Homework for students with learning disabilities: The implications of research for policy and practice. *Journal of Learning Disabilities, 27*(8), 470–479.

Cooper, H., Robinson, J. C., & Patall, E. A. (2006). Does homework improve academic achievement? A synthesis of research, 1987–2003. *Review of Educational Research, (76)*(1), 1–62.

Cooper, J. D., & Kiger, N. D. (2009). *Literacy: Helping students construct meaning* (7th ed.). Boston: Houghton Mifflin.

Cooper, J. O., Heron, T. E., & Heward, W. L. (2007). *Applied behavioral analysis* (2nd ed.). Upper Saddle River, NJ: Merrill/Pearson.

Cooper, P., & Bilton, K. M. (2002). *Attention deficit/hyperactivity disorder: A practical guide for teachers* (2nd ed.). Great Britain: David Fulton Publishers.

Copeland, S. R., & Keefe, E. B. (2007). *Effective literacy instruction for students with moderate or severe disabilities*. Baltimore, MD: Paul H. Brookes.

Copley, J., & Ziviani, J. (2005). Assistive technology assessment and planning for children with multiple disabilities in educational settings. *The British Journal of Occupational Therapy, 68*(12), 559–566.

Cormier, D. C., Altman, J. R., Shyyan, V., & Thurlow, M. L. (2010). A summary of the research on the effects of test accommodations: Technical Report 56. Minneapolis: University of Minnesota, National Center on Education Outcomes.

Corn, A. L., & Koenig, A. J. (1996). Perspectives on low vision. In A. L. Corn & A. J. Koenig (Eds.), *Foundations of low vision: Clinical and functional perspectives* (pp. 3–25). New York: American Foundation for the Blind.

Corn, A. L., & Koenig, A. J. (2002). Literacy instruction for students with low vision: A framework for delivery of instruction. *Journal of Vision Impairment and Blindness, 96*, 305–321.

Corn, A. L., & Koenig, A. J. (Eds.). (1996). *Foundations of low vision: Clinical and functional perspectives*. New York: American Foundation for the Blind.

Corn, A. L., & Wall, R. S. (2002). Access to multimedia presentations for students with visual impairments. *Journal of Visual Impairment and Blindness, 96*, 197–211.

Corn, A. L., Wall, R. S., Jose, R. T., Bell, J. K., Wilcox, K., & Perez, A. (2002). An initial study of reading and comprehension rates for students who received optical devices. *Journal of Visual Impairment and Blindness, 96*, 322–334.

Corn, A. L., Wall, R., & Bell, J. (2000). Impact of optical devices on reading rates and expectations for visual functioning of school-age children and youth with low vision. *Visual Impairment Research, 2*, 33–41.

Cortiella, C. (2006). A parent's guide to response to intervention. National Center for Learning Disabilities. Retrieved from http://www.ncld.org/images/stories/downloads/parent_center/rti_final.pdf

Cortiella, C. (2009). The state of learning disabilities. National Center for Learning Disabilities. Retrieved from http://www.LD.org/stateofld

Cortiella, C., & Horowitz, S. H. (2014). *The state of learning disabilities: Facts, trends, & emerging issues*. New York: National Center for Learning Disabilities.

Cotton, K. (2001). *Teaching composition: Research on effective practices*. Portland, OR: Northwest Regional Educational Laboratory.

Council for Exceptional Children. (2003). *What every special educator must know. Ethics standards, and guidelines for special educators* (5th ed.). Arlington, VA: Author.

Council for Exceptional Children. (2015a). CEC commends congress on the passage of Every Student Succeed Act. Retrieved from: http://www.cec.sped.org/~/media/Files/News/20151209%20ESSAStatementCECHeiden.pdf

Council for Exceptional Children. (2015b). CEC's summary of selected provisions in Every Student Succeeds Act (ESSA). Retrieved from http://cecblog.typepad.com/files/cecs-summary-of-selected-issues-in-every-student-succeeds-act-essa-1.pdf

Council for Exceptional Children. (n.d.). Response-to-intervention: The promise and the peril. Retrieved from http://www.cec.sped.org/AM/Template.cfm?Section=Home&CONTENTID=8427&TEMPLATE=/CM/ContentDisplay.cfm

Courtade, G. R., Test, D. W., & Cook, B. G. (2015). Evidence-based practices for learners with severe intellectual disability. *Research and Practice for Persons with Severe Disabilities, 39*(4), 305–318.

Courtade, G., & Browder, D. M. (2011). *Aligning IEPs to the Common Core Standards for students with moderate and severe disabilities*. Verona, WI: Attainment Company.

Courtade, G., Spooner, F., Browder, D., & Jimenez, B. (2012). Seven reasons to promote standards-based instruction for students with severe disabilities: A reply to Ayres, Lowrey, Douglas, and Sievers. *Education and Training in Autism and Developmental Disabilities, 47*(1), 3–13.

Cox, P., & Dykes, M. (2001). Effective classroom adaptations for students with visual impairments. *Teaching Exceptional Children, 33*, 68–74.

Cramer, E., & Nevin, A. (2006). A mixed methodology analysis of co-teacher assessments. *Teacher Education and Special Education, 29*(4).

Crawford, J. (2004, September). No Child Left Behind: Misguided approach to school accountability for English language learners. Paper presented at the Center on Educational Policy's Forum on Ideas to Improve the NCLB Accountability Provisions for Students with Disabilities and English Language Learners. Retrieved from http://www.cep-dc.org/pubs/Forum14September2004/CrawfordPaper.pdf

Crews, S. D., Bender, H., Cook, C. R., Gresham, F. M., Kern, L., & Vanderwood, M. (2007). Risk and protective factors of emotional and/or behavioral disorders in children and adolescents: A mega-analytic synthesis. *Behavior Disorders, 32*, 64–77.

Crijnen, A. A., Achenbach, T. M., & Verhulst, F. C. (2014). Problems reported by parents of children in multiple cultures: The Child Behavior Checklist syndrome constructs. *Journal of Psychoeducational Assessment, 32*, 699–709.

Crone, D. A., Hawken, L. S., & Horner, R. H. (2015). *Building positive behavior support systems in schools: Functional behavioral assessment*. New York: Guilford Publications.

Crosby, S. A., Rasinski, T., Padak, N., & Yildirim, K. (2015). A 3-year study of a school-based parental involvement program in early literacy. *The Journal of Educational Research, 108*(2), 165–172.

Cullinan, D. (2004). Classification and definition of emotional and behavioral disorders. In R. B. Rutherford, M. M. Quinn, & S. R. Mathur (Eds.), *Handbook of research in emotional and behavioral disorders* (pp. 32–53). New York: Guilford Press.

Cummins, J. (1981). *Bilingualism and minority language children*. Toronto, Ontario: Institute for Studies in Education.

Cummins, J. (1984). *Bilingualism and special education: Issues in assessment and pedagogy*. Clevedon, England: Multilingual Matters.

Cummins, J. (1991). Interdependence of first- and second-language proficiency in bilingual children. In E. Bialystok (Ed.), *Language processing in bilingual children*. Cambridge, England: Cambridge University Press.

Cummins, J. (1992). The empowerment of Indian students. In J. Reyhner (Ed.), *Teaching American Indian students* (pp. 1–12). Norman, OK: University of Oklahoma Press.

Cummins, J. (2011). Literacy engagement: Fueling academic growth for English learners. *The Reading Teacher, 65*(2), 142–146.

Cunningham, P. M. (2000a). *Phonics they use: Words for reading and writing* (3rd ed.). New York: Longman.

Cunningham, P. M. (2000b). *Systematic sequential phonics they use: For beginning readers of any age*. Greensboro, NC: Carson-Dellosa.

Cunningham, P. M. (2008). *Phonics they use: Words for reading and writing*. Upper Saddle River, NJ: Pearson.

Cunningham, P. M. (2017). *Phonics they use: Words for reading and writing* (7th ed.). Boston: Pearson.

D'Andrea, F. M., & Farrenkopf, C. (2000). *Looking to learn: Promoting literacy for students with low vision*. New York: AFB Press.

Dabkowski, D. M. (2004). Encouraging active parent participation in IEP team meetings. *Teaching Exceptional Children, (36)*(3), 34–39.

Dale, E., & Chall, J. (1948). A formula for predicting readability. *Educational Research Bulletin, 27*, 37–54.

Daly, P. M., & Ranalli, P. (2003). Using Countoons to teach self-monitoring skills. *Teaching Exceptional Children, 35*(5), 30–35.

Dandona, L., & Dandona, R. (2006). Revision of visual impairment definitions in the International Statistical Classification of Diseases. *BMC medicine, 4*(1), 7.

Dardig, J. C. (2008). *Involving parents of students with special needs: 25 ready to-use strategies*. Thousand Oaks, CA: Corwin Press.

Darling-Hammond, L. (2007). Standards and accountability movement needs to push, not punish. *Journal of Staff Development, 28,* 47–50.

Datchuk, S. (2015). Teaching handwriting to elementary students with learning disabilities: A problem-solving approach. *Teaching Exceptional Children, 48*(1), 19–27.

Davey, B. (1983). Think-aloud: Modeling the cognitive processes of reading comprehension. *Journal of Reading, 27,* 44–47.

Davis, P. (2013). *Including children with visual impairment in mainstream schools: A practical guide.* London, England: David Fulton Publishers.

Davis, T. N., O'Reilly, M. F., Kang, S., Rispoli, M., Lang, R., Machalicek, W., Chan, J. M., Lancioni, G., & Sigafoos, J. (2009). Impact of presession access to toys maintaining challenging behavior on functional communication training: A single case study. *Journal of Developmental and Physical Disabilities, 21,* 515–521.

Day, H. M., Horner, R. H., & O'Neill, R. E. (1994). Multiple functions of problem behaviors: Assessment and intervention. *Journal of Applied Behavior Analysis, 27,* 279–289.

De Bortoli, T., Balandin, S., Foreman, P., Mathisen, B., & Arthur-Kelly, M. (2012). Mainstream teachers' experiences of communicating with students with multiple and severe disabilities. *Education and Training in Autism and Developmental Disabilities,* 236–252.

De La Paz, S. (1999). Self-regulated strategy instruction in regular education settings: Improving outcomes for students with and without learning disabilities. *Learning Disabilities Research, 14*(2), 92–106.

De La Paz, S., & Graham, S. (1997). Effects of dictation and advanced planning instruction on the composing of students with writing and learning problems. *Journal of Educational Psychology, 89*(2), 203–222.

De La Paz, S., & Graham, S. (2002). Explicitly teaching strategies, skills, and knowledge: writing instruction in middle school classrooms. *Journal of Educational Psychology, 94*(4), 687–698.

De La Paz, S., Owen, B., Harris, K. R., & Graham, S. (2000). Riding Elvis' motorcycle: Using self-regulated strategy development to PLAN and WRITE for a state writing exam. *Learning Disabilities Research & Practice, 15*(2), 101–109.

De La Paz, S., Swanson, P. N., & Graham, S. (1998). The contribution of executive control to the revising by students with writing and learning difficulties. *Journal of Educational Psychology, 90*(3), 448–460.

Dean Qualls, C., O'Brien, R. M., Blood, G. W., & Scheffner Hammer, C. (2003). Contextual variation, familiarity, academic literacy, and rural adolescents' idiom knowledge. *Language, Speech, and Hearing Services in Schools, 34,* 69–79.

Degutis, L. C. (2012). Brain injury—No longer the silent epidemic. Retrieved from http://blogs.cdc.gov/ncipc/2012/03/16/brain-injury/?s_cid=rss_injury405

Dell, A. G., Newton, D., & Petroff, J. (2008). *Assistive technology in the classroom: Enhancing the school experiences of students with disabilities.* Upper Saddle River, NJ: Merrill/Pearson.

Dell, A. G., Newton, D., & Petroff, J. (2011). *Assistive technology in the classroom* (2nd ed.). Upper Saddle River, NJ: Merrill.

Demchak, M. A. (2005). Teaching students with severe disabilities in inclusive settings. In M. L. Wehmeyer & M. Agran (Eds.), *Mental retardation and intellectual disabilities: Teaching students using innovative and research-based strategies* (pp. 57–77). Washington, DC: American Association on Mental Retardation.

Demicheli, V., Rivetti, A., Debalini, M. G., Di Pietrantonj, C., & Robinson, J. (2013). Cochrane in context: Vaccines for measles, mumps and rubella in children. *Evidence-Based Child Health: A Cochrane Review Journal, 8*(6), 2239–2242. Retrieved from http://dx.doi.org/10.1002/ebch.1949

Demmert, W. G. (2005). The influences of culture on learning and assessment among Native American students. *Learning Disabilities Research & Practice, 20,* 16–23.

Dennis, M., Francis, D. J., Cirino, P. T., Schachar, R., Barnes, M. A., & Fletcher, J. M. (2009). Why IQ is not a covariate in cognitive studies of neurodevelopmental disorders. *Journal of the International Neuropsychological Society, 15*(3), 331–343.

Deno, S. L. (1985). Curriculum-based measurement: The emerging alternative. *Exceptional Children, 52,* 219–232.

Denton, C., Anthony, J. L., Parker, J., & Hasbrouck, J. (2004). Effects of two tutoring programs on the English reading development of Spanish-English bilingual students. *Elementary School Journal, 104,* 289–305.

DePaepe, P., Garrison-Kane, L., & Doelling, J. (2002). Supporting students with health needs in schools: An overview of selected health conditions. *Focus on Exceptional Children, 35,* 1–24.

DePape, A. M., & Lindsay, S. (2015). Lived experiences from the perspective of individuals with autism spectrum disorder: A qualitative meta-synthesis. *Focus on Autism and Other Developmental Disabilities,* doi:1088357615587504.

Deshler, D. D., & Schumaker, J. B. (2006). *Teaching adolescents with disabilities: Accessing the general education curriculum.* Thousand Oaks, CA: Corwin Press.

Deshler, D., Palinscar, A. S., Biancarosa, G., & Nair, M. (2007). *Informed choices for struggling adolescent readers: A research-based guide to instructional programs and processes.* Newark, DE: International Reading Association.

Deshler, D., Schumaker, J., Bulgren, J., Lenz, K., Jantzen, J., Adams, G., Carnine, D., Grossen, B., Davis, B., & Marquis, J. (2001). Making learning easier: Connecting new knowledge to things students already know. *Teaching Exceptional Children, 33*(4), 82–86.

Dettmer, P., Thurston, L. P., & Dyck, N. J. (2005). *Consultation, collaboration, and teamwork for students with special needs* (5th ed.). Boston: Pearson Education.

Dettmer, P., Thurston, L. P., Knackendoffel, A., & Dyck, N. J. (2008). *Collaboration, consultation, and teamwork for students with special needs* (6th ed.). Boston: Pearson.

Devine, T. G., & Kania, J. S. (2003). Studying: Skills, strategies, and systems. In J. Flood, D. Lapp, & J. R. Squire (Eds.), *Handbook on research on teaching the English language arts* (2nd ed., pp. 942–954). Mahwah, NJ: Erlbaum.

Dexter, D. D., & Hughes, C. A. (2011). Graphic organizers and students with learning disabilities: A meta-analysis. *Learning Disability Quarterly, 34*(1), 51–72.

Dias, M. B., Teves, E. A., Zimmerman, G. J., Gedawy, H. K., Belousov, S. M., & Dias, M. B. (2015). Indoor navigation challenges for visually impaired people. *Indoor Wayfinding and Navigation,* 141.

Diaz, R. (1983). Thought and two languages: The impact of bilingualism on cognitive development. *Review of Research in Education, 10,* 23–34.

Díaz-Rico, L. (2004). *Teaching English learners: Strategies and methods.* Boston: Allyn & Bacon.

Díaz-Rico, L. (2005). *Teaching English learners: Methods and strategies,* MyLabSchool edition. Boston: Allyn & Bacon.

Diaz-Rico, L. (2012). Course for teaching English learners. Boston: Allyn & Bacon.

Díaz-Rico, L. (2013). *Strategies for teaching English learners* (3rd ed.). Boston: Pearson.

Díaz-Rico, L., & Weed, K. Z. (2002). *The crosscultural, language, and academic development handbook: A complete K–12 reference guide* (2nd ed.). Boston: Allyn & Bacon.

Díaz-Rico, L., & Weed, K. Z. (2014). *The crosscultural, language, and academic development handbook: A complete K–12 reference guide* (5th ed.). Boston: Pearson.

Didden, R., Scholte, R., Moor, J., Korzilius, H., Vermeulen, A., O'Reilly, M., Lang, R., & Lancioni, G. (2009). Cyberbullying among students with mild to borderline intellectual disability and/or developmental disorders who visit a special school. *Developmental Neurorehabilitation, 12,* 146–151.

Dieker, L. A. (2001). What are the characteristics of "effective" middle and high school co-taught teams for students with disabilities? *Preventing School Failure, 46,* 14–23.

Dillon, J. (1979). Alternatives to questioning. *High School Journal, 62,* 217–222.

Dion, E., Fuchs, D., & Fuchs, L. S. (2007). Peer-mediated programs to strengthen classroom instruction: Cooperative learning, reciprocal teaching, classwide peer tutoring, and peer-assisted learning strategies. In L. Flonan (Ed.), *Handbook of special education* (pp. 450–459). London: Sage.

DiVesta, E. J., & Gray, G. S. (1972). Listening and notetaking. *Journal of Educational Psychology, 64,* 321–325.

Dixon, D. R. (2007). Adaptive behavior scales. In J. L. Matson (Eds.), *International review of research in mental retardation: Vol. 34. Handbook of persons with disabilities* (pp. 99–140). San Diego, CA: Elsevier.

Doabler, C. T., & Fien, H. (2013). Explicit mathematics instruction: What teachers can do for teaching students with mathematics difficulties? *Intervention in School and Clinic, 48*(5), 276–285.

Doabler, C. T., Baker, S. K., Kosty, D. B., Smolkowski, K., Clarke, B., Miller, S. J. & Fien, H. (2015). Examining the association between explicit mathematics instruction and student mathematics achievement. *The Elementary School Journal, 115*(3), 303–333.

Doabler, C. T., Cary, M. S., Junghohann, K., Clarke, B., Fien, H., Baker, S., Smolkowski, K., & Chard, D. (2012). Enhancing core mathematics instruction for students at risk for mathematics disabilities. *Teaching Exceptional Children, 44*(4), 48–57.

Doll, C., McLaughlin, T. F., & Barretto, A. (2013). The token economy: A recent review and evaluation. *International Journal of Basic and Applied Science, 2*(1), 131–149.

Donaldson-Pressman, S., Jackson, R., & Pressman, R. M. (2014). *The learning habit: A groundbreaking approach to homework and parenting that helps our children succeed in school and life.* New York: Penguin Group.

Donovan, M. S., & Cross, C. T. (2002). *Minority students in special education and gifted education.* Washington, DC: National Academy Press.

Doorey, N. (2014). The Common Core assessments: What you need to know. *Educational Leadership, 71*(6), 57–60.

Douglas, S. N. (2012). Teaching paraeducators to support the communication of individuals who use augmentative and alternative communication: A literature review. *Current Issues in Education, 15*(1), 1–12.

Downing, J. A. (2007). *Students with emotional and behavioral problems: Assessment, management, and intervention strategies.* Upper Saddle River, NJ: Merrill/Pearson.

Downing, J. E. (2002). *Including students with severe and multiple disabilities in typical classrooms: Practical strategies for teachers* (2nd ed.). Baltimore, MD: Paul H. Brookes.

Downing, J. E. (2005). *Teaching literacy to students with significant disabilities: Strategies for the K–12 inclusive classroom.* Thousand Oaks, CA: Corwin Press.

Downing, J. E. (2008). *Including students with severe and multiple disabilities in typical classrooms: Practical strategies for teachers.* Baltimore, MD: Paul H. Brookes.

Downing, J. E., & Peckham-Hardin, K. D. (2007). Inclusive education: What makes it a good education for students with moderate to severe disabilities? *Research and Practice for Persons with Severe Disabilities, 32,* 16–30.

Downing, J., & Eichinger, J. (2003). Creating learning opportunities for students with disabilities in inclusive classrooms. *Teaching Exceptional Children, 36,* 26–31.

Downing, J., & Eichinger, J. (2011). Instructional strategies for learners with dual sensory impairments in integrated settings. *Research and Practice for Persons with Severe Disabilities, 36*(3–4), 150–157.

Doyle, C., & Timms, C. (2014). *Child Neglect and Emotional Abuse: Understanding, Assessment and Response.* Thousand Oaks, CA: Sage Publications.

Doyle, M. B., & Giangreco, M. (2013). Guiding principles for including high school students with intellectual disabilities in general education classes. *American Secondary Education, 42*(1), 57–72.

Dreifus, C. (May 30, 2011). The bilingual advantage. *The New York Times.*

Dreikurs, R., & Cassel, P. (1972). *Discipline without tears.* New York: Hawthorn.

Dreikurs, R., Cassel, P., & Ferguson, E. D. (2004). *Discipline without tears: How to reduce conflict and establish cooperation in the classroom.* Hoboken, NJ: Wiley.

Dreikurs, R., Grunwald, B. B., & Pepper, F. C. (1982). *Maintaining sanity in the classroom: Classroom management techniques* (2nd ed.). New York: Harper & Row.

Dreikurs, R., Grunwald, B. B., & Pepper, F. C. (2013). *Maintaining sanity in the classroom: Classroom management techniques.* Philadelphia, PA: Taylor & Francis.

Dunlap, G., & Carr, E. G. (2007). Positive behavior support and developmental disabilities: A summary and analysis of research. In S. L. Odom, R. H. Horner, M. E. Snell, & J. Blacher (Eds.), *Handbook of developmental disabilities* (pp. 469–482). New York: Guilford Press.

Dunn, C., Chambers, D., & Rabren, K. (2004). Variables affecting students' decisions to drop out of school. *Remedial and Special Education, 25*(5), 314–323.

DuPaul, G. J., & Stoner, G. (2003). *AD/HD in the schools: Assessment and intervention strategies* (2nd ed.). New York: Guilford Press.

Durand, V. M., & Drimmins, D. B. (1988). Identifying the variables maintaining self-injurious behavior. *Journal of Autism and Developmental Disorders, 18*(1), 99–117.

Durando, J. (2008). A survey on literacy instruction for students with multiple disabilities. *Journal of Visual Impairment and Blindness, 102,* 40–45.

Durkin, D. D. (1978–1979). What classroom observations reveal about reading comprehension instruction. *Reading Research Quarterly, 14,* 481–533.

Durlak, J. A., Weissberg, R. P., & Pachan, M. (2010). A meta-analysis of after-school programs that seek to promote personal and social skills in children and adolescents. *American Journal of Community Psychology, 45*(3–4), 294–309.

Eber, L., & Keenan, S. (2004). Collaboration with other agencies: Wraparound and systems of care for children and youths with emotional and behavioral disorders. In R. B. Rutherford, M. M. Quinn, & S. R. Mathur (Eds.), *Handbook of research in emotional and behavioral disorders* (pp. 502–516). New York: Guilford Press.

Eber, L., Breen, K., Rose, J., Unizycki, R. M., & London, T. H. (2001). Wraparound as a tertiary level intervention for students with emotional/behavioral needs. *Teaching Exceptional Children, 40,* 16–22.

Edelsky, C. (1990). Whose agenda is this anyway? A response to McKenna, Robinson, and Miller. *Educational Researcher, 19,* 7–22.

Ediger, M. (2011). Learning stations in the social studies. *College Student Journal, 131*(3), 467–470.

Educational Horizons Magazine. (2012). Parent-teacher conferences: A tip sheet for teachers. *Educational Horizons Magazine, 90*(3), 23–24.

Educational Testing Service. (2008). Addressing achievement gaps: The language acquisition and education achievement of English-language learners. *Policy Notes, 16,* 1.

Edwards, P. A. (2004). *Children's literacy development: Making it happen through school, family, and community involvement.* Boston: Allyn & Bacon.

Edwards, P. A. (2012). *Tapping the potential of parents.* New York: Scholastic.

Egley, A., & O'Donnell, C. E. (2009, April). Highlights of the 2007 national youth gang survey. *OJJDP Fact Sheet.* Retrieved from https//www.ncjrs.gov/pdffiles1/ojjdp/225185.pdf

Ehren, B. J. (2013). Expanding pockets of excellence in RTI. *The Reading Teacher, 66*(6), 449–453.

Ehri, L. C. (2003). Systematic phonics instruction: Findings of the National Reading Panel. Paper presented at the invitational seminar organized by the Standards and Effectiveness Unit, Department for Education and Skills, British Government, London, England.

Ehri, L. C. (2004). Learning to read words. *Scientific Studies of Reading, 9*(2), 167–188.

Eidelman, S. M. (2011). The times they are a changing: Special Olympics and the movement toward valued lives and inclusion. *Intellectual and Developmental Disabilities, 49*(5) 403–406.

Elbaum, B. (2007). Effects of an oral testing accommodation on the mathematics performance of secondary students with and without learning disabilities. *Journal of Special Education, 40*(4), 218–229.

Elbaum, B., & Vaughn, S. (2001). School-based interventions to enhance the self-concept of students with learning disabilities: A meta-analysis. *Elementary School Journal, 101*(3), 303–329.

Elbaum, B., Vaughn, S., Hughes, M., & Moody, S. W. (2000). How effective are one-to-one tutoring programs in reading for elementary students at risk for reading failure? A meta-analysis of the intervention research. *Journal of Educational Psychology, 92,* 605–619.

Elbaum, B., Vaughn, S., Hughes, M., Moody, S. W., & Schumm, J. S. (2000). How reading outcomes of students with disabilities are related to instructional grouping formats: A meta-analytic review. In R. Gersten, E. Schiller, & S. Vaughn (Eds.), *Contemporary special education research* (pp. 105–135). Mahwah, NJ: Erlbaum.

Elhoweris, H., Mutua, K., Alsheikh, N., & Holloway, P. (2005). Effect of ethnicity on teachers' referral and recommendation decisions in gifted and talented programs. *Remedial and Special Education, 26,* 25–31.

Eli, E., Pullen, P. C., Kennedy, M. J., & Williams, M. C. (2015). A multimedia tool to deliver professional development of vocabulary development. *Journal of Special Education Technology, 30*(1), 59–72.

Elkonin, D. B. (1973). U.S.S.R. In J. Downing (Ed.), *Comparative reading* (pp. 551–579). New York: Macmillan.

Elliot, A. J., & Dweck, C. S. (Eds.). (2013). *Handbook of competence and motivation.* New York: Guilford Publications.

Ellis, R. (1985). *Understanding second language acquisition.* Oxford, England: Oxford University Press.

Ellis, R. (1994). *The study of second language acquisition.* Oxford, England: Oxford University Press.

Ellis, R. (2005). *Instructed second language acquisition: A literature review.* Research Division, Ministry of Education, PO Box 1666, Wellington, New Zealand.

Embury, D. C., & Kroeger, S. D. (2012). Let's ask the kids: Consumer constructions of co-teaching. *International Journal of Special Education, 27*(2), 102–112.

Emerson, R. S. W., & Corn, A. L. (2006). Orientation and mobility content for children and youths: A Delphi approach pilot study. *Journal of Visual Impairment and Blindness, 100,* 331–342.

Emmer, E., & Stough, L. (2001). Classroom management: A critical part of educational psychology, with implications for teacher education. *Educational Psychologist, 36,* 103–112.

Emmer, E., Everston, C., & Worsham, M. E. (2009). *Classroom management for elementary teachers* (8th ed.). Boston: Allyn & Bacon.

Emmer, E., Evertson, C., Sanford, J. P., Clements, B. S., & Worsham, M. E. (1989). *Classroom management for secondary teachers* (2nd ed.). Upper Saddle River, NJ: Prentice-Hall.

Engelmann, S., & Carnine, D. (1992). *Early corrective mathematics.* Columbus, OH: McGraw Hill.

Engelmann, S., Carnine, D., & Steely, D. (2005). *Corrective mathematics.* Columbus, OH: McGraw Hill.

Engelmann, S., Meyer, L., Carnine, L., Becker, W., Eisele, J., & Johnson, G. (1999). *Corrective reading program.* Columbus, OH: SRA/McGraw-Hill.

Engel-Yeger, B., & Hamed-Daher, S. (2013). Comparing participation in out of school activities between children with visual impairments, children with hearing impairments and typical peers. *Research in Developmental Disabilities, 34*(10), 3124–3132.

Englemann, S., et al. (2008). *Corrective reading 2008©.* East Desoto, TX: SRA/McGraw Hill.

Englert, C. S., Berry, R., & Dunsmore, K. (2001). A case study of the apprenticeship process: Another perspective on the apprentice and the scaffolding metaphor. *Journal of Learning Disabilities, 34*(2), 152–171.

Englert, C. S., Raphael, R. E., & Mariage, T. V. (1994). Developing a school-based discourse for literacy learning: A principled search for understanding. *Learning Disability Quarterly, 17,* 2–32.

Englert, C. S., Raphael, T. E., Anderson, L. M., Anthony, H. M., Fear, K. L., & Gregg, D. D. (1988). A case for writing intervention: Strategies for writing informational text. *Learning Disabilities Focus, 3*(2), 98–113.

Epilepsy Foundation. (2009). About epilepsy. Retrieved from www.epilepsyfoundation.org/about/

Epilepsy Foundation. (2015). *About epilepsy: The basics.* Retrieved from http://www.epilepsy.com/learn/about-epilepsy-basics.

Epstein, J. L. (1996). *Partnership-2000 schools manual.* Baltimore, MD: Johns Hopkins University.

Epstein, J. L., & Van Voorhis, F. L. (2001). More than minutes: Teachers' roles in designing homework. *Educational Psychologist, 36*(3), 181–193.

Epstein, J. L., Sanders, M. G., Sheldon, S. B., Salinas, K. C., Jansorn, N. R., Van Voorhis, F. L., Martin, C. S., Thomas, B. G., Greenfield, M. D., Hutchins, D. J., & Williams, K. J. (2009). *School, family, and community partnerships: Your handbook for action* (3rd ed.). Thousand Oaks, CA: Corwin Press.

Epstein, M., Atkins, M., Cullinan, D., Kutash, K., & Weaver, R. (2008). *Reducing behavior problems in the elementary school classroom.* Washington DC: Institute of Education Sciences National Center for Education Evaluation and Regional Assistance.

Epstein, M., Atkins, M., Cullinan, D., Kutash, K., and Weaver, R. (2008). Reducing Behavior Problems in the Elementary School Classroom: A Practice Guide (NCEE #2008-012).

Erickson, F. (2005). Culture in society and in educational practices. In J. A. Banks & C. M. Banks (Eds.), *Multicultural education: Issues and perspectives* (5th ed., pp. 31–60). Hoboken, NJ: Wiley.

Erickson, R. N., Ysseldyke, J. E., & Thurlow, M. L. (1997). Neglected numerators, drifting denominators and fractured fractions: Determining participation rates for students with disabilities in statewide assessments. *Diagnostique, 23*(2), 105–116.

Ervin-Tripp, S. (1974, June). Is second language learning like the first? *TESOL Quarterly, 8,* 111–127.

Eunice Kennedy Shriver National Institutes of Child Health and Human Development. (2012). Fragile X syndrome. Retrieved from http://www.nichd.nih.gov/health/topics/fragile_x_syndrome.cfm

Evertson, C., Emmer, E., & Worsham, M. (2006). *Classroom management for elementary teachers* (7th ed.). Boston: Allyn & Bacon.

Evmenova, A. S., & Behrmann, M. M. (2011). Research-based strategies for teaching content to students with intellectual disabilities: Adapted videos. *Education and Training in Autism and Developmental Disabilities, 46*(3) 315–325.

Ezzedeen, S. R. (2008). Facilitating class discussions around current and controversial issues: Ten recommendations for teachers. *College Teaching, 56,* 230–236.

Fairbanks, S., Simonsen, B., & Sugai, G. (2008). Classwide secondary and tertiary tier practices and systems. *Teaching Exceptional Children, 40,* 44–52.

Fallon, L. M., O'Keeffe, B. V., & Sugai, G. (2012). Consideration of culture and context in school-wide Positive Behavior Support: A review of current literature. *Journal of Positive Behavior Interventions,* 1098300712442242.

Farmer, J., & Morse, S. E. (2007). Project Magnify: Increasing reading skills in students with low vision. *Journal of Visual Impairment and Blindness, 101,* 763–768.

Faul, M., Xu, L., Wald, M. M., & Coronado, V. G. (2010). Traumatic brain injury in the United States: Emergency department visits, hospitalizations and deaths, 2002–2006. Atlanta, GA: Centers for Disease Control and Prevention, National Center for Injury Prevention and Control.

Fearn, L., & Farnan, N. (2001). *Writing effectively: Helping children master the conventions of writing.* Boston: Allyn & Bacon.

Feldman, S. (2004). The great homework debate. *Teaching PreK–8, 34*(5).

Ferguson, E. D. (2010). Adler's innovative contributions regarding the need to belong. *The Journal of Individual Psychology, 66*(1), 1–7.

Ferguson, P. M., & Ferguson, D. L. (2006). The promise of adulthood. In M. E. Snell & E. Brown (Eds.), *Instruction of students with severe disabilities* (6th ed.). Upper Saddle River, NJ: Merrill/Pearson.

Ferlazzo, L., & Hull-Sypnieski, K. (2014). Teaching argument. *Educational Leadership, 71*(7), 66–69.

Fernandez-Alonso, R., Suarez-Alvarez, J., & Muniz, J. (2015, March 16). Adolescents' homework performance in mathematics and science: Personal factors and teaching practices. *Journal of Educational Psychology.* Advance online publication: http://dx.doi.org/10.1037/edu0000032

Ferrell, K. A. (1996). Your child's development. In M. C. Holbrook (Ed.), *Children with visual impairments* (pp. 73–96). Bethesda, MD: Woodbine House.

Ferrell, K. A. (2000). Growth and development of young children. In M. C. Holbrook & A. J. Koenig (Eds.), *Foundations of education: Instructional strategies for teaching children and youth with visual impairments* (Vol. I, 2nd ed., pp. 135–160). New York: AFB Press.

Ferretti, R. P., & Lewis, W. E. (2013). Best practices in teaching argumentative writing. In S. Graham, C. A. MacArthur, & J. Fitzgerald (Eds.). *Best practices in writing instruction* (2nd ed.) (pp. 113–140). New York: Guilford.

Ferretti, R. P., Andrews-Weckerly, S., & Lewis, W. E. (2007). Improving the argumentative writing of students with learning disabilities: Descriptive and normative considerations. *Reading & Writing Quarterly, 23*(3), 267–285.

Ferriter, W. M., Ramsden, J., & Sheninger, S. (2011). *Communicating and connecting with social media.* Bloomington, IN: Solution Tree and the National Association of Elementary School Principals.

Fiffner, L. J., & DuPaul, G. J. (2015). Treatment of ADHD in school settings. In R. A. Barkley (Ed.), *Attention-deficit hyperactivity disorder: A handbook for diagnosis and treatment* (4th ed., pp. 596–529). New York: Guilford.

Finn, C. E. (2012). Text complexity grade bands and Lexile® bands. Retrieved from http://lexile.com/using-lexile/

lexile-measures-and-the-ccssi/text-complexity-grade-bands-and-lexile-ranges/

Fisher, D., & Frey, N. (2014). Closely reading informational texts in the primary grades. *The Reading Teacher, 68*(3), 222–227.

Fisher, D., & Frey, N. (2015). Contingency teaching during close reading. *Reading Teacher, 68*(4), 277–286.

Fisher, D., & Frey, N. (2015). Improve reading with complex texts. *Kappan, 96*(5), 56–61.

Fisher, D., Frey, N., & Lapp, D. (2011). Coaching middle-level teachers to think aloud improves comprehension instruction and student reading achievement. *The Teacher Educator, 46*(3), 231–243.

Fisher, D., Frey, N., & Lapp, D. (2012). *Text complexity: Raising rigor in reading.* Newark, DE: International Reading Association.

Fitzpatrick, D. (2008). Constructing complexity: Using reading levels to differentiated reading comprehension activities. *English Journal, 98,* 57–65.

Flannery, K. B., & Horner, R. H. (1994). The relationship between predictability and problem behavior for students with severe disabilities. *Journal of Behavioral Education, 4,* 157–176.

Fleming, L. C., & Jacobsen, M. P. H. (2009). Bullying and symptoms of depression in Chilean middle school students. *Journal of School Health, 79*(3), 130–137.

Fletcher, J. M., Lyon, G. R., Fuchs, L. S., & Barnes, M. A. (2007). *Learning disabilities: From identification to intervention.* New York: Guilford Press.

Fletcher, J. M., Stuebing, K. K., Barth, A. E., Denton, C. A., Cirino, P. T., Francis, D. J., & Vaughn, S. (2011). Cognitive correlates of inadequate response to reading intervention. *School Psychology Review, 40*(1), 3–22.

Fleury, V. P., Hedges, S., Hume, K., Browder, D. M., Thompson, J. L., Fallin, K., … & Vaughn, S. (2014). Addressing the academic needs of adolescents with autism spectrum disorder in secondary education. *Remedial and Special Education, 35*(2), 68–79.

Flexer, C. (2000). The startling possibility of sound field. *Advance for Speech-Language Pathologists and Audiologists, 36,* 5, 13.

Flippo, R. F., Becker, M. J., & Wark, D. M. (2009). Test taking. In R. F. Flippo & D. C. Caverly (Eds.), *Handbook of college reading and study strategy research* (2nd ed., pp. 249–286). New York: Routledge.

Florian, L. (2013). Special education in the era of inclusion: The end of special education or a new beginning? *Special Education, 7*(2).

Florida Center for Reading Research. (2006). Student center activities, grades 2–3. Retrieved from http://www.fcrr.org/Curriculum/studentCenterActivities23.shtm

Florida Center for Reading Research. (2007). Student center activities, grades 4–5. Retrieved from http://www.fcrr.org/curriculum/studentCenterActivities45.shtm

Florida Center for Reading Research. (2008). Student center activities, grades K–1. Retrieved from http://www.fcrr.org/curriculum/studentCenterActivities.shtm

Florida Department of Education. (2005). Types of writing prompts. Retrieved from http://www.firn.edu/doe/sas/fw/fwapprmp.htm

Flower, A., McKenna, J. W., Bunuan, R. L., Muething, C. S., & Vega, R. (2014). Effects of the good behavior game on challenging behaviors in school settings. *Review of Educational Research,* 0034654314536781.

Flynn, L. A., & Flynn, E. M. (2004). *Teaching writing with rubrics.* Thousand Oaks, CA: Corwin Press.

Fombonne, E. (2005). The changing epidemiology of autism. *Journal of Applied Research in Intellectual Disabilities, 18,* 281–294.

Fontana, J. L., Scruggs, T., & Mastropieri, M. A. (2007). Mnemonic strategy instruction in inclusive secondary social studies classes. *Remedial and Special Education, 28,* 345–355.

Foorman, B. R., & Ciancio, D. J. (2005). Screening for secondary intervention: Concept and context. *Journal of Learning Disabilities, 38*(6), 494–499.

Ford, B. A., Stuart, D. H., & Vakil, S. (2014). Culturally responsive teaching in the 21st century inclusive classroom. *The Journal of the International Association of Special Education, 15*(2), 56–62.

Forest, M., & Lusthaus, E. (1989). Promoting educational equality for all students: Circles and maps. In S. Stainback, W. Stainback, & M. Forest (Eds.), *Educating all students in the mainstream of regular education* (pp. 45–57). Baltimore, MD: Paul H. Brookes.

Forness, S., & Kavale, K. (1999). Teaching social skills in children with learning disabilities: A meta-analysis of the research. *Learning Disability Quarterly, 19,* 2–13.

Foulk, D., Gessner, L. J., & Koorland, M. A. (2001). Human immunodeficiency virus/acquired immune deficiency syndrome (HIV/AIDS): Content in introduction to exceptionalities textbooks. *Action in Teacher Education, 23,* 47–54.

Fowler, M. (1992). *CH.A.D.D. educator's manual: An in-depth look at attention deficit disorders from an educational perspective.* Plantation, FL: Children and Adults with Attention Deficit Disorders.

Fowler, M., & McCabe, P. C. (2011). Traumatic brain injury and personality change. *Communique, 39*(7), 4, 6, 8, 10.

Fowler, S. A., Schwartz, I., & Atwater, J. (1991). Perspective on the transition from preschool to kindergarten for children with disabilities and their families. *Exceptional Children, 58,* 136–145.

Frances Mary, D. A., & Siu, Y. T. (2015). Students with visual impairments: Considerations and effective practices for technology use. *Efficacy of Assistive Technology Interventions (Advances in Special Education Technology, Volume 1)Emerald Group Publishing Limited, 1,* 111–138.

Francis, D. J., Fletcher, J. M., Stuebing, K. K., Lyon, G. R., Shaywitz, B. A., & Shaywitz, S. E. (2005). Psychometric approaches to the identification of LD: IQ and achievement scores are not sufficient. *Journal of Learning Disabilities, 38*(2), 98–108.

Francis, D. J., Rivera, M., Lesaux, N., Kieffer, M., & Rivera, H. (2006). *Practical guidelines for the education of English learners: Research-based recommendations for instruction and academic interventions* (No. 2). Portsmouth, NH: Center on Instruction.

Francisco, J. M. (2013). Learning in collaborative settings: students building on each other's ideas to promote their mathematical understanding. *Education Studies in Mathematics, 82,* 417–438.

Frazier, T. W., Youngstrom, E. A., Speer, L., Embacher, R., Law, P., Constantino, J., et al. (2012). Validation of proposed DSM-5 criteria for autism spectrum disorder. *Journal of American Academy of Child & Adolescent Psychiatry, 51,* 2–40.

Fredrickson, N., & Turner, J. (2003). Utilizing the classroom peer group to address children's social needs: An evaluation of the Circle of Friends Intervention Approach. *The Journal of Special Education, 36,* 234–245.

French, N. K. (n.d.) Maximizing the services of paraeducators. CEC Today. Retrieved from http://www.cec.sped.org/AM/Template.cfm?Section=Home&TEMPLATE=/CM/ContentDisplay.cfm&CONTENTID=12850&CAT=none

Frey, N., & Fisher, D. (2011). High-quality homework: Good homework follows in-class instruction and feedback to reinforce and broaden learning. Retrieved from http://www.nassp.org/Content/158/PLOct11_instrucldr.pdf

Friend, M. (2005a). *Special education: Contemporary perspectives for school professionals.* Boston: Allyn & Bacon.

Friend, M. (2005b). Thoughts on collaboration for the 21st century school professionals … Moving forward or lost in space? Retrieved from http://www.ctserc.org/initiatives/teachandlearn/mfriend.shtml

Friend, M. (2007). The coteaching partnership. *Educational Leadership, 64*(4), 48–52.

Friend, M. (2011). *Special education: Contemporary perspectives for school professionals.* Boston: Pearson.

Friend, M., & Bursuck, W. D. (2002). *Including students with special needs: A practical guide for classroom teachers* (3rd ed.). Boston: Allyn & Bacon.

Friend, M., & Bursuck, W. D. (2012). *Including students with special needs: A practical guide for classroom teachers* (6th ed.). Boston: Pearson.

Friend, M., & Bursuck, W. D. (2015). *Including students with special needs: A practical guide for classroom teachers* (7th ed.). Boston: Pearson.

Friend, M., & Cook, L. (2010). *Interactions: Collaboration skills for school professionals* (6th ed.). Boston: Allyn & Bacon.

Friend, M., & Cook, L. (2013). *Interactions: Collaboration skills for school professionals* (7th ed.). Boston: Allyn & Bacon.

Friend, M., & Hurley-Chamberlain, D. (n.d.). Is co-teaching effective? CEC Today. Retrieved from http://www.cec.sped.org/AM/Template.cfm?Section=Home&CONTENTID=7504&TEMPLATE=/CM/ContentDisplay.cfm&CAT=none

Friend, M., Cook, L., Hurley-Chamberlain, D., & Shamberger, C. (2010). Co-teaching: An illustration of the complexity of collaboration in special education. *Journal of Educational and Psychological Consultation, 20,* 9–27.

Fries, D., Carney, K. J., Blackman-Urteaga, L., & Savas, S. A. (2012). Wraparound services infusion into secondary schools as a dropout prevention strategy. *NASSP Bulletin, 96*(2), 119–136.

Frombonne, E. (2002). Prevalence of childhood disintegrative disorder. *Autism, 6,* 149–157.

Frose, V. (1981). Handwriting: Practice, pragmatism, and progress. In V. Frose & S. B. Straw (Eds.), *Research in the language arts: Language and schooling* (pp. 227–243). Baltimore: University Park Press.

Frost, S. J., Landi, N., Menci, W. E., Sandak, R., Fulbright, R. K., Tejada, L., …& Pugh, K. R. (2009). Phonological awareness predicts activation patterns for print and speech. *Annals of Dyslexia, 59*(1), 78–97.

Fry, E. B. (1977). Fry's readability graph: Clarifications, validity, and extension to level 17. *Journal of Reading, 21,* 242–252.

Fry, E. B., & Kress, J. E. (2006). *The reading teacher's book of lists.* San Francisco: Josey-Bass.

Fry, E. B., & Kress, J. E. (2012). *The reading teacher's book of lists* (Vol. 55). San Francisco: John Wiley & Sons.

Fry, E. B., Kress, J. E., & Fountoukidis, D. L. (2003). *The reading teacher's book of lists* (4th ed.). Upper Saddle River, NJ: Prentice Hall.

Fry, R., & Gonzalez, F. (2008). One-in-five and growing fast: A profile of Hispanic public school students. Retrieved from http://pewresearch.org/pubs/937/

Fuchs, D., & Fuchs, L. (n.d.). *Peer-assisted learning strategies.* Retrieved from http://kc.vanderbilt.edu/pals/

Fuchs, D., & Fuchs, L. S. (1994). Inclusive school movement and radicalization of special education reform. *Exceptional Children, 60,* 294–309.

Fuchs, D., & Fuchs, L. S. (2006). Introduction to response to intervention: What, why, and how valid is it? *Reading Research Quarterly, 41*(1), 93–99.

Fuchs, D., & Fuchs, L. S. (2014). Rethinking service delivery for students with significant learning problems developing and implementing intensive instruction. *Remedial and Special Education,* 0741932514558337.

Fuchs, D., Fuchs, L. S. & Vaughn, S. (2014). What is intensive instruction and why is it important? *Teaching Exceptional Children, 46*(4), 13–18.

Fuchs, D., Fuchs, L. S., & Burish, P. (2000). Peer-assisted learning strategies: An evidence-based practice to promote reading achievement. *Learning Disabilities Research and Practice, 15*(2), 85–91.

Fuchs, D., Fuchs, L. S., & Compton, D. L. (2012). Smart RTI: A next-generation approach to multilevel prevention. *Exceptional Children, 78*(3), 263–279.

Fuchs, D., Fuchs, L. S., & Stecker, P. (2011). The "blurring" of special education in a new continuum of general education placements and services. *Exceptional Children, 76*(3), 301–323.

Fuchs, D., Fuchs, L. S., & Vaughn, S. (2014). What is intensive instruction and why is it important? *Teaching Exceptional Children, 46*(4), 13–18.

Fuchs, D., Fuchs, L. S., & Vaughn, S. (2014). What is intensive instruction and why is it important? *Teaching Exceptional Children, 46*(4), 13–18. doi:10.1177/0040059914522966

Fuchs, D., Fuchs, L. S., & Vaughn, S. (2014). What is intensive instruction and why is it important? *Teaching Exceptional Children, 46*(4), 13–18. doi:10.1177/0040059914522966

Fuchs, D., Fuchs, L. S., & Vaughn, S. (2014). What is intensive instruction and why it is important? *Teaching Exceptional Children, 46*(4), 13–18.

Fuchs, D., Fuchs, L. S., & Vaughn, S. (Eds.). (2008). *Response to intervention: A framework for reading educators.* Newark, DE: International Reading Association.

Fuchs, D., Mock, D., Morgan, P. L., & Young, C. L. (2003). Responsiveness to intervention: Definitions, evidence, and implications for the learning disabilities construct. *Learning Disabilities Research & Practice, 18,* 172–186.

Fuchs, D., Stecker, P. M., & Fuchs, L. S. (2008). The role of assessment within the RTI framework. In D. Fuchs, L. S. Fuchs, & S. Vaughn (Eds.), *Response to intervention: A framework for reading educators* (pp. 27–49). Newark, DE: International Reading Association.

Fuchs, L. S., & Fuchs, D. (1986). Effects of systematic formative evaluation: A meta-analysis. *Exceptional Children, 53,* 199–208.

Fuchs, L. S., & Fuchs, D. (1992). Identifying a measure for monitoring student reading program. *School Psychology Review, 21*(1), 45–58.

Fuchs, L. S., & Fuchs, D. (2003). Enhancing the mathematical problem solving of students with mathematics disabilities. In H. L. Swanson, K. R. Harris, & S. Graham (Eds.), *Handbook of learning disabilities* (pp. 306–322). New York: Guilford Press.

Fuchs, L. S., & Vaughn, S. (2012). Responsiveness-to-intervention: A decade later. *Journal of Learning Disabilities, 45*(3), 195–203.

Fuchs, L. S., & Vaughn, S. (in press). Responsiveness-to-intervention: A decade later. *Journal of Learning Disabilities.*

Fuchs, L. S., Fuchs, D., & Hamlett, C. L. (1990). Curriculum-based measurement: A standardized, long-term goal approach to monitoring student progress. *Academic Therapy, 25*(5), 615–632.

Fuchs, L. S., Fuchs, D., & Speece, D. L. (2002). Treatment validity as a unifying construct for identifying learning disabilities. *Learning Disability Quarterly, 25,* 33–45.

Fuchs, L. S., Fuchs, D., Compton, D. L., Bryant, J. D., Hamlett, C. L., & Seethaler, P. M. (2007). Mathematics screening and progress monitoring at first grade: Implications for response to intervention. *Exceptional Children, 73*(3), 311–330.

Fuchs, L. S., Fuchs, D., Compton, D. L., Wehby, J., Schumacher, R. F., Gersten, R., & Jordan, N. C. (2015). Inclusion versus specialized intervention for very-low-performing students: What does access mean in an era of academic challenge? *Exceptional Children, 81*(2), 134–157.

Fuchs, L. S., Fuchs, D., Hamlett, C. L., Phillips, N. B., & Bentz, J. (1994). Classwide curriculum-based assessment: Helping general educators meet the challenge of student diversity. *Exceptional Children, 60,* 518–537.

Fuchs, L. S., Fuchs, D., Hamlett, C. L., Phillips, N. B., Karns, K., & Dutka, S. (1997). Enhancing students' helping behavior during peer-mediated instruction with conceptual mathematical explanations. *Elementary School Journal, 97,* 223–250.

Fuchs, L. S., Fuchs, D., Hamlett, C. L., Walz, L., & Germann, G. (1993). Formative evaluation of academic progress: How much growth can we expect? *School Psychology Review, 22,* 27–48.

Fuchs, L. S., Seethaler, P. M., Powell, S. A., Fuchs, D., Hamlett, C. L., & Fletcher, J. M. (2008). Effects of preventative tutoring on the mathematical problem solving of third-grade students with math and reading difficulties. *Exceptional Children, 74*(2), 155–173.

Fuchs, L., Compton, D., Fuchs, D., Paulsen, K., Bryant, J. D., & Hamlett, C. L. (2005). The prevention, identification, and cognitive determinants of math difficulty. *Journal of Educational Psychology, 98*(1), 29–43.

Fuchs, L., Fuchs, D., & Hamlett, C. (1989). Monitoring reading growth using student recalls: Effects of two teacher feedback systems. *Journal of Educational Research, 83,* 101–111.

Furnes, B., & Samuelsson, S. (2010). Phonological awareness and rapid automatized naming predicting early development in reading and spelling: Results from a cross-linguistic longitudinal study. *Learning and Individual Differences, 21*(1), 85–95.

Furlong, J. J., Morrison, G. M., & Jimerson, S. (2004). Externalizing behaviors of aggression and violence and the school context. In R. B. Rutherford, M. M. Quinn, & S. R. Mathur (Eds.), *Handbook of research in emotional and behavioral disorders* (pp. 243–261). New York: Guilford Press.

Galambos, N. L., Leadbeater, B. J., & Barker, E. T. (2004). Gender differences in and risk factors for depression in adolescence: A 4-year longitudinal study. *International Journal of Behavioral Development, 28*(1), 16–25.

Galambos, S., & Goldin-Meadow, S. (1990). The effects of learning two languages on metalinguistic development. *Cognition, 34,* 1–56.

Gallaudet Research Institute. (2008). *Regional and national summary report of data from the 2006–2007 annual survey of deaf and hard of hearing children and youth.* Washington, DC: GRI, Gallaudet University.

Gallaudet Research Institute. (April 2011). *Regional and national summary report of data from the 2009–10 annual survey of deaf and hard of hearing children and youth.* Washington, DC: GRI, Gallaudet University.

Gallavan, N. P., & Kottler, E. (2007). Eight types of graphic organizers for empowering social studies students and teachers. *The Social Studies, 98*(3), 117–123.

Gambrell, L. B. (1985). Dialogue journals: Reading-writing interaction. *The Reading Teacher, 38,* 512–515.

Gambrell, L. B., Hughes, E. M., Calvert, L., Malloy, J. A., & Igo, B. (2011). Authentic reading, writing, and discussion. *The Elementary School Journal, 112*(2), 234–258.

Gándara, P. (2015a). Rethinking bilingual education. *Educational Leadership, 72*(6), 60–64.

Gándara, P. (2015b). *The impact of English-only instructional policies on English learners.* Retrieved from http://www.colorincolorado.org/article/impact-english-only-instructional-policies-english-learners

Ganz, J. B., Earles-Vollrath, T. L., & Cook, K. E. (2011). Video modeling: A visually based intervention for children with autism spectrum disorder. *Teaching Exceptional Children, 43*(6), 8–19.

Garcia, G., McKoon, G., & August, D. (2006). Language and literacy assessment of language-minority students. In D. August & T. Shanahan (Eds.), *Developing literacy in second-language learners: Report of the National Literacy Panel on Language-Minority children and youth* (pp. 597–624). Mahwah, NJ: Erlbaum.

Gardner, H. (1983). *Frames of mind.* New York: Basic Books.

Gardner, H. (1999). *Intelligence reframed. Multiple intelligences for the 21st century.* New York: Basic Books.

Gardner, H. (2006). *Multiple intelligences: New horizons.* New York: Basic Books.

Gardner, H., & Hatch, T. (1989). Multiple intelligences go to school: Educational implications of the theory of multiple intelligences. *Educational Researcher, 18*(8), 4–9.

Gardner, R. III, Nobel, M. M., Hessler, T., Yawn, C. D., & Heron, T. E. (2007). Tutoring system innovations: Past practice to future prototypes. *Intervention in School and Clinic, 43*(2), 71–81.

Gaskins, I. W. (1996). *Word detectives: Benchmark extended word identification program for beginning readers.* Media, PA: Benchmark School.

Gast, D., Ault, M., Wolery, M., Doyle, P., & Belanger, S. (1988). Comparison of constant time delay and the system of least prompts in teaching sight word reading to students with moderate retardation. *Education and Training in Mental Retardation, 23,* 117–128.

Gay, G. (2004). The importance of multicultural education. *Educational Leadership, 61,* 30–35.

Gay, G. (2010). Acting on beliefs in teacher education for cultural diversity. *Journal of Teacher Education, 61*(1–2), 143–152. doi: 10.1177/0022487109347320

Gay, G., & Kirkland, K. (2003). Developing cultural critical consciousness and self-reflection in preservice teacher education. *Theory into Practice, 42,* 181–187.

Geary, D. C. (2003). Learning disabilities in arithmetic: Problem-solving differences and cognitive deficits. In H. L. Swanson, K. R. Harris, & S. Graham (Eds.), *Handbook of learning disabilities* (pp. 199–212). New York: Guilford Press.

Geary, D. C. (2010). Mathematical disabilities: Reflections on cognitive, neuropsychological, and genetic components. *Learning and Individual differences, 20*(2), 130–133.

Genesee, F., Paradis, J., & Crago, M. B. (2004). *Dual language development & disorders: A handbook on bilingualism & second language learning.* Baltimore, MD: Brookes.

Gentry, J. (1982). An analysis of developmental spelling in "GNYS AT WRK". *The Reading Teacher, 36*(2), 192–200.

Gentry, J. R. & Graham, S. (2010) Creating better readers and writers. Retrieved from https://www.zaner-bloser.com/sites/default/files/public/pdf/HW_CreatingBetterReadersandWriters.pdf

Gerber, P. J., & Popp, P. A. (1999). Consumer perspectives on the collaborative teaching model: Views of students with and without LD and their parents. *Remedial and Special Education, 20*(5), 288–297.

Gerlach K. (2014). *Let's team up! A checklist for teachers, paraeducators, and principals.* Naples, FL: National Professional Resources, Inc.

German, D. J., Schwanke, J. H., & Ravid, R. (2011). Word finding difficulties: Differentiated vocabulary instruction in the speech and language room. *Communications Disorders Quarterly.* Advanced online publication. doi: 10.1177/1525740111405840

Gersten, R. M., & Jiménez, R. T. (Eds.). (1998). *Promoting learning for culturally and linguistically diverse students.* Belmont, CA: Wadsworth.

Gersten, R., & Baker, S. (2000). What we know about effective instructional practices for English-language learners. *Exceptional Children, 66*(4), 454–470.

Gersten, R., & Baker, S. (2003). English-language learners with learning disabilities. In H. L. Swanson, K. R. Harris, & S. Graham (Eds.), *Handbook of learning disabilities* (pp. 94–109). New York, NY: Guilford Press.

Gersten, R., Chard, D. J., Jayanthi, M., Baker, S. K., Morphy, P., & Flojo, J. (2009). Mathematics instruction for students with learning disabilities: A meta-analysis of instructional components. *Review of Educational Research, 79*(3), 1202–1242.

Gersten, R., Jordan, N. C., & Flojo, J. R. (2005). Early identification and interventions for students with mathematics difficulties. *Journal of Learning Disabilities, 38*(4), 293–304.

Gevensleben, H., Holl, B., Albrecht, B., Vogel, C., Schlamp, D., Kratz, O., …Heinrich, H. (2009). Is neurofeedback an efficacious treatment for ADHD? A randomized controlled clinical trial. *The Journal of Child Psychology and Psychiatry, 50*(7), 780–789.

Gewertz, C. (2012). Educators in search of common-core resources. *Education Week, 31*(22), 1–11.

Ghousseini, H. (2015). Core practices and problems of practice in learning to lead classroom discussions. *The Elementary School Journal 115*(3), 335–357.

Giangreco, M. F. (2009). *Critical issues brief: Concerns about the proliferation of one-to-one paraprofessionals.* Arlington, VA: Council for Exceptional Children, Division on Autism and Developmental Disabilities. Retrieved from http://www.dddcec.org/positionpapers.htm

Giangreco, M. F., & Broer, S. (2007). School-based screening to determine overreliance on paraprofessionals. *Focus on Autism and Other Developmental Disabilities, (22)*3, 149–158.

Giangreco, M. F., & Broer, S. M. (2003). *Guidelines for selecting alternatives to overreliance on paraprofessionals.* Burlington: University of Vermont, Center on Disability and Community Inclusion. Retrieved on August 10, 2015 from http://www.uvm.edu/~cdci/evolve/evolvegsa.pdf.

Giangreco, M. F., Broer, S. M., & Suter, J. C. (2011). Guidelines for selecting alternatives to overreliance on paraprofessionals: Field-testing in inclusion-oriented schools. *Remedial and Special Education, 32*(1), 22–38.

Giangreco, M. F., Cichoski-Kelly, E., Backus, L., Edelman, S. W., Tucker, P., Broer, S., & Cichoski-Kelly, C. (2008). Developing a shared understanding: Paraeducator supports for students with disabilities in general education. *TASH Newsletter, 25*(1), 21–23.

Giangreco, M. F., Cloninger, C. J., & Iverson, V. (1998). *Choosing outcomes and accommodations for children: A guide to educational planning for students with disabilities (COACH)* (2nd ed.). Baltimore, MD: Paul H. Brookes.

Giangreco, M. F., Doyle, M. B., & Suter, J. C. (2012). Constructively responding to requests for paraprofessionals: We keep asking the wrong questions. *Remedial & Special Education, 33*(6), 362–373.

Giangreco, M. F., Edleman, S. W., & Broer, S. M. (2001). A guide to schoolwide planning for paraeducator supports. Unpublished manuscript, Vermont.

Giangreco, M. F., Suter, J. C., & Hurley, S. M. (2013). Revisiting personnel utilization in inclusion-oriented schools. *Journal of Special Education, 47*(2), 121–132.

Gil, L., & Bardack, S. (2010). *Common assumptions vs. the evidence: English language learners in the United States.* Washington, DC: American Institutes for Research.

Gilbert, J., & Graham, S. (2010). Teaching writing to elementary students in grades 4–6: A national survey. *The Elementary School Journal, 110*(4), 494–518.

Gillam, R., & Loeb, D. (2010, January 19). Principles for school-age language intervention: Insights from a randomized controlled trial. *American Speech-Language Association Leader.*

Gillanders, C., McKinney, M., & Ritchie, S. (2012). What kind of school would you like for your children? Exploring minority mothers' beliefs to promote home-school partnerships. *Early Childhood Education, 40,* 285–294.

Gillespie, A., & Graham, S. (2014). A meta-analysis of writing interventions for students with learning disabilities. *Exceptional Children, 80*(4), 454–473.

Gilligan, C. (1982). *In a different voice: Psychological theory and women's development.* Cambridge, MA: Harvard University Press.

Gillon, G. T. (2007). *Phonological awareness from research to practice.* New York: Guilford Press.

Glass, T. F. (2004). What gift? The reality of the student who is gifted and talented in public school classrooms. *Gifted Child Today, 27,* 25–29.

Goldenberg, C. (2008, Summer). Teaching English language learners: What the research does—and does not—say. *American Educator,* 8–19.

Goldman, L. (2013). *Life and loss: A guide to help grieving children.* New York, NY: Routledge.

Goldstein, S. (January, 2009). Research briefs: Comorbidity in AD/HD. *Attention* (32–35).

Gonzales, J. E., Vannest, K. J., & Reid, R. (2008). Early classification of reading performance in children identified or at risk for emotional and behavioral disorders. *The Journal of At-Risk Issues, 14,* 33–40.

Good, R. H., & Kaminski, R. A. (2010). DIBELS next assessment manual Eugene, OR: Dynamic.

Good, R. H., Kaminski, R. A., Smith, S., Laimon, D., & Dill, S. (2003). *Dynamic indicators of basic early literacy skills* (6th ed.). Eugene: University of Oregon.

Good, T. L., & Brophy, J. E. (2008). *Looking in classrooms* (10th ed.). Boston: Allyn & Bacon.

Goodwin, A. P., (2016). Effectiveness of word solving: integrating morphological problem-solving within comprehension instruction for middle school students. *Reading and Writing, 29*(1), 91–116.

Goodwin, A., Lipsky, M., & Ahn, S. (2012). Word detectives: Using units of meaning to support literacy. *The Reading Teacher, 65*(7), 461–470.

Grabe, M., Christopherson, K., & Douglas, J. (2004–2005). Providing introductory psychology students access to online lecture notes: The relationship of note use to performance and class attendance. *Journal of Educational Technology Systems, 33,* 293–308.

Graham, S. (1992). Helping students with LD progress as writers. *Intervention in School and Clinic, 27,* 134–144.

Graham, S., & Harris, K. (2009). Almost 30 years of writing research: Making sense of it all with The Wrath of Khan. *Learning Disabilities Research & Practice, 24*(2), 58–68.

Graham, S., Harris, K. R., & Larsen, L. (2001). Prevention and intervention of writing difficulties for students with learning disabilities. *Learning Disabilities Research and Practice, 16,* 74–84.

Graham, S., & Harris, K. R. (2003). Students with learning disabilities and the process of writing: A meta-analysis of SRSD studies. In H. Swanson, K. R. Harris, & S. Graham (Eds.), *Handbook of learning disabilities* (pp. 323–344). New York: Guilford Press.

Graham, S., & Harris, K. R. (2006). Preventing writing difficulties: Providing additional handwriting and spelling instruction to at-risk children in first grade. *Teaching Exceptional Children, 38,* 64–66.

Graham, S., & Harris, K. R. (2013). Designing an effective writing program. In S. Graham, C. A. MacArthur, & J. Fitzgerald (Eds.). *Best practices in writing instruction* (2nd ed.) (pp. 3–25). New York: Guilford.

Graham, S., & Perrin, D. (2007). A meta-analysis of writing instruction for adolescent students. *Journal of Educational Psychology, 99,* 445–476.

Graham, S., & Santangelo, T. (2014). Does spelling instruction make students better spellers, readers, and writers? A meta-analysis review. *Reading & Writing, 27*(9), 1703–1743.

Graham, S., Berninger, V., Weintraub, & Schafer, W. (1998). Development of handwriting speed and legibility in grades 1–9. *Journal of Educational Research, 92*(1), 42–52.

Graham, S., Harris, K. R., & Santangelo, T. (2015). Research-based writing practices and the Common Core: Meta-analysis and meta-synthesis. *The Elementary School Journal, 115*(4), 498–522.

Graham, S., Harris, K. R., Fink-Chorzempa, B., & MacArthur, C. (2003). Primary grade teachers' instructional adaptations for struggling writers: A national survey. *Journal of Educational Psychology, 95,* 279–292.

Graham, S., Harris, K. R., Mason, L., Fink-Chorzempa, B., Moran, S., & Saddler, B. (2008). How do primary grade teachers teach handwriting: A national survey. *Reading & Writing: An Interdisciplinary Journal, 21,* 49–69.

Graham, S., MacArthur, C. A., & Fitzgerald, J. (2013). *Best practices in writing instruction* (2nd ed.). New York, NY: Guilford Press.

Graham, S., MacArthur, C. A., & Fitzgerald, J. (Eds.) (2007). *Best practices in writing instruction.* New York: Gilford.

Graham, S., Weintraub, N., & Berninger, V. W. (1998). The relationship between handwriting style and speed and legibility. *The Journal of Educational Research, 91*(5), 290–297.

Grant, C. A., & Sleeter, C. E. (1993). Race, class, gender, and disability in the classroom. In J. A. Banks & C. A. Banks (Eds.), *Multicultural education: Issues and perspectives* (2nd ed., pp. 48–67). Boston: Allyn & Bacon.

Graves, A. W., Valles, E. C., & Rueda, R. (2000). Variations in interactive writing instruction: A study in four bilingual special education settings. *Learning Disabilities Research & Practice, 15*(3), 1–9.

Graves, A., & Hauge, R. (1993). Using cues and prompts to improve story writing. *Teaching Exceptional Children, 25,* 38–45.

Graves, D. H. (1985). All children can write. *Learning Disability Focus, 1*(1), 36–43.

Graves, D. H. (2003). *Writing: Teachers and children at work* (rev. ed.). Portsmouth, NH: Heinemann.

Graves, D., & Hansen, J. (1983). The author's chair. *Language Arts, 60*(2), 176–183.

Graves, D., & Kittle, P. (2005). *Inside writing how to teach the details of the craft.* Portsmouth, NH: Heinemann.

Graves, E., & McConnell, T. (2014). Response to intervention: Providing reading intervention to low income and minority students. *The Educational Forum, 78*(2), 88–97.

Graves, M. F., Baumann, J. F., Blachowicz, C. L. Z., Manyak, P., Bates, A., Cieply, C., … & Von Gunten, H. (2014). Words, words everywhere, but which ones do we teach? *The Reading Teacher, 67*(5), 333–346.

Gray, C. (2000). *The new social story book.* Arlington, TX: Future Horizons.

Gredler, M. E., & Johnson, R. L. (2004). *Assessment in the literacy classroom.* Boston, MA: Allyn & Bacon.

Green, J. (2011). *The ultimate guide to assistive technology in special education: Resources for education, intervention, and rehabilitation.* Waco, TX: Prufrock Press.

Green, J., Liem, G. A. D., Martin, A. J., Colmar, S., Marsh, H. W., & McInerney, D. (2012). Academic motivation, self-concept, engagement, and performance in high school: Key processes from a longitudinal perspective. *Journal of Adolescence, 35*(5), 1111–1122.

Gregg, N. (2009). *Adolescents and adults with learning disabilities and ADHD: Assessment and accommodation.* New York: Guilford.

Gresham, F. M. (2007). Response to intervention and emotional and behavioral disorders: Best practices in assessment for intervention. *Assessment for Effective Intervention, 32,* 214–221.

Gresham, F. M., & Elliot, S. N. (2008). *Social skills improvement—Rating scales manual.* Minneapolis, MN: Pearson Assessments.

Gresham, F. M., & Kern, L. (2004). Internalizing behavior problems in children and adolescents. In R. B. Rutherford, M. M. Quinn, & S. R. Mathur (Eds.), *Handbook of research in emotional and behavioral disorders* (pp. 262–281). New York: Guilford Press.

Gresham, F. M., Cook, C. R., Crews, S. D., & Kern, L. (2004). Social skills training for children and youth with emotional and behavior disorders: Validity considerations and future directions. *Behavioral Disorders, 30,* 32–46.

Gresham, F. M., Elliott, S. N., Cook, C. R., Vance, M. J., & Kettler, R. (2010). Cross-informant agreement for ratings for social skill and problem behavior ratings: An investigation of the Social Skills Improvement System—Rating Scales. *Psychological Assessment, 22*(1), 157–166.

Gresham, F. M., Elliott, S. N., Vance, M. J., & Cook, C. R. (2011). Comparability of the Social Skills Rating System to the Social Skills Improvement System: Content and psychometric comparisons across elementary and secondary age levels. *School Psychology Quarterly, 26*(1), 27.

Gresham, F. M., Sugai, G., & Horner, R. H. (2001). Interpreting outcomes of social skills training for students with high-incidence disabilities. *Exceptional Children, 67*(3), 331–344.

Gresham, F. M., Van, M. B., & Cook, C. R. (2006). Social skills training for teaching replacement behaviors: Remediating acquisition deficits in at-risk students. *Behavioral Disorders 31,* 363–377.

Griffin, H., Williams, S., Davis, M., & Engleman, M. (2002). Using technology to enhance cues for children with low vision. *Teaching Exceptional Children, 35,* 36–42.

Griffin, S., Clements, D., & Sarama, J. (2015). *Number Worlds®.* Richmond, VA: McGraw-Hill.

Griffin-Shirley, N., Trusty, S., & Rickard, R. (2000). Orientation and mobility. In A. J. Koenig & M. C. Holbrook (Eds.), *Foundations of education: Instructional strategies for teaching children and youth with visual impairments* (Vol. 2, 2nd ed., pp. 529–568). New York: AFB Press.

Griffiths, A., VanDerHeyden, A. M., Parson, L. B., & Burns, M. K. (2006). Practical applications of response-to-intervention research. *Assessment for Effective Intervention, 32,* 50–56.

Grippo, A. J., & Johnson, A. K. (2009). Stress, depression, and cardiovascular dysregulation: A review of neurobiological mechanisms and the integration of research from preclinical disease models. *Stress, 12*(1), 1–21.

Guerin, A., & Murphy, B. (2015). Repeated reading as a method to improve reading fluency for struggling adolescent readers. *Journal of Adolescent and Adult Literacy, 58*(7), 551–560.

Gulik, C. (2003). Preparing for high-stakes testing. *Theory into Practice, 42*(1), 42–50.

Gumpel, T. P., & Shlomit, D. (2000). Exploring the efficacy of self-regulatory training as a possible alternative to social skills training. *Behavioral Disorders, 25,* 131–141.

Gunn, B., Biglan, A., Smokowski, K., & Ary, D. (2000). The efficacy of supplemental instruction in decoding skills for Hispanic and non-Hispanic students in early elementary school. *The Journal of Special Education, 34*(2), 90–103.

Gunning, T. G. (2003). *Building literacy in the content areas* (6th ed.). Boston: Allyn & Bacon.

Gunning, T. G. (2011). *Reading success for all students: Using formative assessment to guide instruction and intervention.* San Francisco, CA: Wiley.

Gunning, T. G. (2012). *Building literacy in secondary content area classrooms.* Allyn & Bacon.

Gunning, T. G. (2013). *Creating literacy instruction for all students.* Boston: Pearson.

Gunning, T. G. (2016). *Creating literacy instruction for all students* (9th ed,). Boston: Pearson.

Guskey, T. R., & Jung, L. A. (2009). Grading and reporting in a standards-based environment: Implications for students with special needs. *Theory into Practice, 48*(1), 53–62.

Guth, D. A., Rieser, J. J., & Ashmead, D. H. (2010). Perceiving to move and moving to perceive: control of locomotion. In W. R. Wiener, R. L. Welsh, & B. B. Blasch (Eds.), *Foundations of orientation and mobility* (Vol. 1, 3rd ed.). New York: AFB Press.

Guthrie, J. T. (2007). *Engaging adolescents in reading.* Thousand Oaks, CA: Corwin Press.

Guthrie, J. T., & Klauda, S. L. (2014). Effects of classroom practices on reading comprehension, engagement, and motivations for adolescents. *Reading Research Quarterly, 49*(4), 387–416.

Guthrie, J. T., & Wigfield, A. (2000). Engagement and motivation in reading. In M. T. Kamil, P. T. Mosenthal, P. D. Pearson, & R. Barr (Eds.), *Handbook of reading research* (Vol. III, pp. 403–422). Mahwah, NJ: Erlbaum.

Guthrie, J. W., & Springer, M. G. (2014). A nation at risk revisited: Did "wrong" reasoning result in "right" results? At what cost? *Peabody Journal of Education, 79*(1), 7–35.

Guyer, B. P. (Ed.). (2001). *ADHD: Achieving success in school and life.* Boston: Allyn & Bacon.

Haager, D. (2007). Promises and cautions regarding response to intervention with English language learners. *Learning Disabilities Quarterly, 30,* 213–218.

Haager, D., & Vaughn, S. (1995). Parent, teacher, peer, and self-reports of the social competence of students with learning disabilities. *Journal of Learning Disabilities, 28*(4), 205–215.

Haager, D., Domino, J. A., & Windmueller, M. P. (2014). *Interventions for Reading Success* (2nd ed.). Baltimore, MD: Paul H. Brookes.

Haager, D., Klingner, J. K., & Vaughn, S. (2007). *Evidence-based reading practices for response to intervention.* Baltimore: Paul H. Brookes.

Hacker, D. J. (1998). Definitions and empirical foundations. In D. J. Hacker, J. Dunlosky, & A. C. Graesser (Eds.), *Metacognition in theory and practice* (pp. 1–23). Mahwah, NJ: Erlbaum.

Hacker, D. J. (2009). *Handbook of metacognition in education.* New York: Taylor & Francis.

Hakuta, K. (1974). A report on the development of grammatical morphemes in a Japanese girl learning English as a second language. *Working Papers in Bilingualism* (Vol. 4, pp. 18–44). Toronto: OISE Press.

Haley, M. H., & Austin, T.Y. (2004). *Content-based second language teaching and learning: An interactive approach.* Boston: Allyn & Bacon.

Hall, A. H. (2014). Beyond the author's chair: Expanding sharing opportunities in writing. *The Reading Teacher, 68*(1), 27–31.

Hall, C., Kent, S. C., McCulley, L., Davis, A., & Wanzek, J. (2013). A new look at mnemonics and graphic organizers in the secondary social studies classroom. *Teaching Exceptional Children, 1*(46), 47–55.

Hall, L. A. (2005). Teachers and content area reading: Attitudes, beliefs, and change. *Teaching and Teacher Education, 21,* 403–414.

Hall, S. L. (2008). *A principal's guide: Implementing response to intervention.* Thousand Oaks, CA: Corwin Press.

Hall, T. (2002). *Differentiated instruction.* Wakefield, MA: National Center on Accessing the General Curriculum. Retrieved from http://www.cast.org/publications/ncac/ncac_diffinstruc.html

Hall, T. E., Cohen, N., Vue, G., & Ganley, P. (2015). Addressing learning disabilities with UDL and technology: Strategic reader. *Learning Disabilities Quarterly, 38*(2), 72–83.

Hall, T. E., Meyer, A., & Rose, D. H. (Eds.). (2012). *Universal design for learning in the classroom: Practical applications (What works for special needs learners).* New York: Guilford Press.

Hall, T., Strangman, N., & Meyer, A. (2011). *Differentiated instruction and implications for UDL implementation.* Wakefield, MA: National Center on Accessing the General Curriculum. Retrieved from http://aim.cast.org/learn/historyarchive/backgroundpapers/differentiated_instruction_udl

Hallahan, D. P., Kauffman, J. M., & Pullen, P. C. (2009). *Exceptional learners: An introduction to special education.* Boston: Pearson.

Hallahan, D. P., Kauffman, J. M., & Pullen, P. C. (2012). *Exceptional learners: An introduction to special education* (12th ed.). Boston: Pearson.

Hallahan, D. P., Kauffman, J. M., & Pullen, P. C. (2015). *Exceptional learners: An introduction to special education* (13th ed.). Boston: Pearson.

Hallanan, D. P., Lloyd, J. W., Kauffman, J. M., Weiss, M. P., & Martinez, E. A. (2005). *Learning disabilities: Foundations, characteristics, and effective teaching.* Boston: Allyn & Bacon.

Hallowell, E. M., & Ratey, J. J. (1995). *Driven to distraction: Recognizing and coping with attention deficit disorder from childhood through adulthood.* New York: Touchstone.

Hamblet, E. C. (2014). Nine strategies to improve college transition planning for students with disabilities. *Teaching Exceptional Children,3*(46), 53–59.

Hamill, L., & Everington, C. (2002). *Teaching students with moderate to severe disabilities: An applied approach for inclusive environments.* Upper Saddle River, NJ: Pearson.

Hamstra-Bletz, L., & Blote, A. W. (1993). A longitudinal study on dysgraphic handwriting in primary school. *Journal of Learning Disabilities, 26,* 689–699.

Hang, Q., & Rabren, K. (2008). An examination of co-teaching: Perspectives and efficacy indicators. *Remedial and Special Education, 30*(5), 259–268.

Hannon, E. (2015). *The Effects of Positive Reinforcement Using a Group Token Economy System to Increase Prosocial Behavior in an Inclusive Early Childhood Classroom* (Doctoral dissertation, Caldwell College).

Hanover, S. (1983). Handwriting comes naturally? *Academic Therapy, 18,* 407–412.

Harbort, G., Gunter, P. L., Hull, K., Brown, Q., Venn, M. L., Wiley, L. P. & Wiley, E. W. (2007). Behaviors of teachers in co-taught classes in a secondary school. *Teacher Education and Special Education, 30*(1), 13–23.

Hardman, M. L., & Dawson, S. (2008). The impact of federal public policy on curriculum and instruction for students with disabilities in the general classroom. *Preventing School Failure, 52,* 5–11.

Harmon, J. M., Wood, K. D., Hedrick, W. B., Vintinner, J., & Willeford, T. (2009). Interactive word walls: More than just reading the writing on the walls. *Journal of Adolescent & Adult Literacy, 52*(5), 398–408.

Harper, C., & de Jong, E. (2004). Misconceptions about teaching English-language learners. *The Reading Teacher, 48,* 152–153.

Harris, K. R., Graham, S., Friedlander, B., & Laud, L. (2013). Bring powerful writing strategies into your classroom! Why and how. *The Reading Teacher, 66*(7), 538–542.

Harris, K. R., Graham, S., Mason, L. H., & Friedlander, M. A. (2008). *Powerful writing strategies for all students.* Baltimore, MD: Paul H. Brookes.

Harry, B. (2008). Collaboration with culturally and linguistically diverse families: Ideal versus reality. *Exceptional Children, 74*(3), 372–388.

Harry, B. (2011). Reciprocity and humility in Wonderland. *Learning Disability Quarterly, 34*(3), 191–193.

Harry, B., & Klingner, J. (2006). *Why are so many minority students in special education? Understanding race and disability in schools.* New York: Teachers College Press.

Harry, B., & Klingner, J. (2007a). Discarding the deficit model. *Educational Leadership, 64,* 16–21.

Harry, B., & Klingner, J. (2014). *Why are so many minority students in special education? Understanding race and disability in schools (2nd ed.).* New York: Teachers College Press.

Harry, B., & Klingner, J. K. (2007b). *Case studies of minority student placement in special education.* New York: Teachers College Press.

Harry, B., Klingner, J. K., & Hart, J. (2005). African American families under fire: Ethnographic views of family strengths. *Remedial and Special Education, 26,* 101–112.

Harry, B., Klingner, J., & Cramer, E. (2007). *Case studies of minority student placement in special education.* New York: Teachers College Press.

Harry, B., Rueda, R., & Kalyanpur, M. (1999). Cultural reciprocity in sociocultural perspective: Adapting the normalization principle for family collaboration. *Exceptional Children, 66,* 123–136.

Hart, B., & Risley, T. R. (2003). The early catastrophe: The 30 million word gap by age 3. *American Educator, 27*(1), 4–9.

Hart, J. E., Cramer, E. D., Harry, B., Klingner, J. K., & Surges, K. M. (2010). The continuum of "troubling" to "troubled" behavior. *Remedial and Special Education, 31*(3), 148–162.

Hartle, J. (2011, March). Ensuring equal education for blind children: Setting standards that promote excellence. *Braille Monitor,* 54(3). Retrieved from http://www.nfb.org/Images/nfb/Publications/bm/bm11/bm1103/bm1103tc.htm

Hasbrouck, J., & Tindal, G. (2005). *Oral reading fluency: 90 years of measurement.* Eugene, OR: Behavioral Research & Teaching.

Hattie, J. (2014). *Self-concept.* East Sussex, England: Psychology Press.

Hattie, J., & Timperley, H. (2008). The power of feedback. *Review of Educational Research, 77*(1), 81–112.

Hawken, L. S., & Horner, R. (2003). Evaluation of a targeted group intervention with a schoolwide system of behavior support. *Journal of Positive Behavior Interventions, 9,* 94–101.

Hazel, J. S., Schumaker, J. B., Sherman, J. A., & Sheldon-Wildgen, J. (1982). Group training for social skills: A program for court-adjudicated, probationary youths. *Criminal Justice and Behavior, 9,* 35–53.

Hear-it Org. (2009). Implants. Retrieved from http://hear-it.org/printpage.dsp?printable=yes&page=2021

Hear-it. (2011). Implants. Retrieved from http://www.hear-it.org/Implants

Heath, M. A., Leavy, D., Hansen, K., Ryan, K., Lawrence, L., & Sonntag, A. G. (2008). Coping with grief: Guidelines and resources for assisting children. *Intervention in School and Clinic, 43,* 259–269.

Hebdon, H. M. (2008). The use of one-on-one paraprofessionals in the classroom: Does this assistance help to build necessary life skills? *The Exceptional Parent, 38,* 88–89.

Hedge, M. N. (1998). *Coursebook on aphasia and other neurogenic language disorders* (2nd ed.). Florence, KY: Thomson Learning.

Hedge, M. N. (2006). *Coursebook on aphasia and other neurogenic language disorders* (3rd ed.). Independence, KY: Cengage Learning.

Heitin, L. (2014). Testing plans differ on accommodations. *Education Week, 33*(29), 30–33.

Helman, L. A., & Burns, M. K. (2008). What does oral language have to do with it? Helping young English-language learners acquire a sight vocabulary. *The Reading Teacher, 62,* 14–19.

Helmstetter, E., & Durand, V. M. (1991). Nonaversive interventions for severe behavior problems. In L. Meyer, C. Peck, & L. Brown (Eds.), *Critical issues in the lives of people with severe disabilities* (pp. 559–600). Baltimore, MD: Paul H. Brookes.

Hendley, S. L., & Lock, R. H. (2007). 20 ways to … use positive behavior support for inclusion in the general education classroom. *Intervention in School and Clinic, 42,* 225–228.

Henry, M. (1997). The decoding/spelling curriculum: Integrated decoding and spelling instruction from pre-school to early secondary school. *Dyslexia, 3,* 178–189.

Hernandez, C. M., Morales, A. R., & Shroyer, M. G. (2013). The development of a model of culturally responsive science and mathematics teaching. *Cultural Studies of Science Education, 8,* 803–820.

Heward, W. L. (2009). *Exceptional children: An introduction to special education* (9th ed.). Upper Saddle River, NJ: Merrill/Pearson.

Heward, W. L. (2013). *Exceptional children: An introduction to special education* (10th ed.). Upper Saddle River, NJ: Merrill/Pearson.

Hiatt-Michael, D. B. (Ed.). (2007). *Promising practices for teachers to engage families of English language learners.* Charlotte, NC: Information Age Publishing.

Hickman, P., Pollard-Durodola, S., & Vaughn, S. (2004). Storybook reading: Improving vocabulary and comprehension for English language learners. *The Reading Teacher, 57*(8), 720–730.

Hiebert, E. H. (2005). *Teaching and learning vocabulary: Bringing research to practice.* Mahwah, NJ: Erlbaum.

Hiebert, E. H., & Kamil, M. L. (2005). *Teaching and learning vocabulary: Bringing research to practice.* New York: Routledge.

Hiebert, E. H., Taylor, B. M. (1994). *Getting ready right from the start. Effective early literacy interventions.* Old Tappan, NJ: Allyn & Bacon.

Hilden, K. R., & Pressley, M. (2007). Self-regulation through transactional strategies instruction. *Reading & Writing Quarterly, 23*(1), 51–75.

Hilden, K., & Jones, J. (2012). Classroom word walls: Is yours a tool or a decoration? *Reading Today, 29*(4), 9–10.

Hill, E. W., & Ponder, P. (1976). *Orientation and mobility techniques.* New York: American Foundation for the Blind.

Hoerr, T. R. (2014). Tips for better parent–teacher conferences. *Educational Leadership, 71*(7), 86–87.

Hofmeister, A. M. (1989). Teaching problem-solving skills with technology. *Educational Technology, 29*(9), 26–29.

Holburn, S., & Cea, C. D. (2007). Excessive positivism in person-centered planning. *Research and Practice for Persons with Severe Disabilities, 32,* 167–172.

Holcomb, T. K. (2012). *Introduction to American deaf culture.* New York: Oxford University Press.

Hollingworth, L. (2007). Five ways to prepare for standardized testing without sacrificing best practice. *The Reading Teacher, 61*(4), 339–342.

Holschuh, J. P., & Aultman, L. P. (2009). Comprehension development. In R. F. Flippo & D. C. Caverly (Eds.), *Handbook of college reading and study strategy research* (2nd ed., pp. 121–144). New York: Routledge.

Hommersen, P., Murray, C., Ohan, J. L., & Johnston, C. (2006). Oppositional defiant disorder rating scale: Preliminary evidence of reliability and validity. *Journal of Emotional and Behavioral Disorders, 14,* 118–125.

Honda, H., Shimizu, Y., & Rutter, M. (2005). No effect of MMR withdrawal on the incidence of autism: A total population study. *Journal of Child Psychology and Psychiatry, 46,* 572–579.

Hooper, J., & Harmon, J. (2015). The many faces of word walls in middle school science classrooms: Variability in function and content. *Science Scope, 38*(6), 54–59.

Hoover, J. J. (2012). Reducing unnecessary referrals: Guidelines for teachers of diverse learners. *Teaching Exceptional Children, 44*(4) 399–407.

Hoover, J., & Stenhjem, P. (2005). Bullying and teasing of youth with disabilities: Creating positive school environments for effective inclusion. *Issue Brief: Examining Current Challenges in Secondary Education and Transition, 2*(3), 1–6.

Horn, E., & Kang, J. (2012). Supporting young children with multiple disabilities what do we know and what do we still need to learn? *Topics in Early Childhood Special Education, 31*(4), 241–248.

Horner, R. H., Sugai, G., Smolkowski, K., Eber, L., Nakasato, J., Todd, A. W., & Esperanza, J. (2009). A randomized, wait-listed controlled effectiveness trail assessing school-wide positive behavior support in elementary schools. *Journal of Positive Behavior Interventions, 11*(3), 133–144.

Hosp, J. L., & Reschly, D. J. (2004). Disproportionate representation of minority students in special education: Academic, demographic, and economic predictors. *Exceptional Children, 70,* 185–199.

Hosp, M. K., Hosp, J. L., & Howell, K. W. (2006). *The ABCs of CBM: A practical guide on curriculum-based measurement.* New York: Guilford.

Hourcade, J. J., & Bauwens, J. (2002). *Cooperative teaching: Rebuilding and sharing the schoolhouse* (2nd ed.). Austin, TX: PRO-ED.

Howe, K. R., & Welner, K. G. (2002). School choice and pressure to perform déjà vu for children with disabilities? *Remedial and Special Education, 23,* 212–221.

Howell, J. C., & Griffiths, E. (2015). *Gangs in America's communities.* Thousand Oaks, CA: Sage Publications.

Hudson, M. E., Browder, D. M., & Jimenez, B. A. (2014). Effects of a peer-delivered system of least prompts intervention and adapted science read-alouds on listening comprehension for participants with moderate intellectual disability. *Education & Training in Autism & Developmental Disabilities, 49*(1), 60–77.

Hudson, M. E., Browder, D. M., & Wood, L. A. (2013). Review of experimental research on academic learning by students with moderate and severe intellectual disability in general education. *Research & Practice for Persons with Severe Disabilities, 38*(1), 17–29.

Hudson, P., & Glomb, N. (1997). If it takes two to tango, then why not teach both partners to dance? Collaboration instruction for all educators. *Journal of Learning Disabilities, 30*(4), 442–448.

Huebner, K. M. (2000). Visual impairment. In M. C. Holbrook & A. J. Koenig (Eds.), *Foundations of education. Volume I: History and theory of teaching children and youths with visual impairment* (2nd ed., pp. 55–76). New York: AFB Press.

Hughes, C. A., & Dexter, D. D. (2011). Response to intervention: A research-based summary. *Theory into Practice, 50*(1), 4–11.

Hughes, C. A., Ruhl, K. L., Schumaker, J. B., & Deshler, D. D. (2002). Effects of instruction in an assignment completion strategy on the homework performance of students with learning disabilities in general education classes. *Learning Disabilities Research and Practice, 17,* 1–18.

Hughes, C. A., Ruhl, K. L., Schumaker, J. B., & Deshler, D. D. (2011). The assignment completion strategy. *Focus on Exceptional Children, 44*(2).

Hughes, C., & Dexter, D. D. (2015). The use of RTI to identify students with learning disabilities: a review of the research. Retrieved from: http://www.rtinetwork.org/learn/research/use-rti-identify-students-learning-disabilities-review-research

Hughes, E. M., Witzel, B. S., Riccomini, P. J., Fries, K. M., & Kanyongo, G. Y. (2014). A meta-analysis of algebra interventions for learners with disabilities and struggling learners. *The International Association of Special Education, 15*(1), 36–47.

Hughes, M. T., Schumm, J. S., & Vaughn, S. (1999). Home literacy activities: Perceptions and practices of Hispanic parents of children with learning disabilities. *Learning Disability Quarterly, 22,* 209–222.

Hulit, L., & Howard, M. (2006). *Born to talk: An introduction to speech and language development* (4th ed.). Boston: Allyn & Bacon.

Hulit, L., Fahey, K. R., & Howard, M. (2015). *Born to talk: An introduction to speech and language development* (6th ed.). Boston: Pearson.

Hunt, J. H., & Little, M. E. (2014). Intensifying interventions for students by identifying and remediating conceptual understandings in mathematics. *Teaching Exceptional Children, 46*(6) 187–196.

Hunt, N., & Munson, L. J. (2005). Teachers grieve: What can we do for our colleagues and ourselves when a student dies? *Teaching Exceptional Children, 37,* 48–51.

Hunt, P., & McDonnell, J. (2009). Inclusive education. In. S. L. Odom, R. H. Horner, M. E. Snell, & J. Blacher (Eds.). *Handbook of development disabilities* (pp. 269–291). New York: Guilford Press.

Hunt, P., Hirose-Hatae, A., Doering, K., Karasoff, P., & Goetz, L. (2000). "Community" is what I think everyone is talking about. *Remedial and Special Education, 21,* 305–317.

Hurley, S. R., & Tinajero, J. V. (Eds.). (2001). *Literacy assessment of second language learners.* Boston: Allyn & Bacon.

Hutchinson, N. L. (1993). Effects of cognitive strategy instruction on algebra problem solving of adolescents with learning disabilities. *Learning Disability Quarterly, 16,* 34–63.

Hutchinson, S. W., Murdock, J. Y., Williamson, R. D., & Cronin, M. E. (2000). Self-recording plus encouragement equals improved behavior. *Teaching Exceptional Children, 32*(5), 54–58.

Iamarino, D. L. (2014). The benefits of standards-based grading: A critical evaluation of modern grading practices. *Current Issues in Education, 17*(2), 1–10.

Idol, L. (2002). *Creating collaborative and inclusive schools.* Austin, TX: PRO-ED.

Igo, L. B., Riccoinini, P. J., Bruning, R. H., & Pope, G. G. (2006). How should middle-school students with LD approach online note taking? A mixed-methods study. *Learning Disability Quarterly, 29,* 89–100.

Individuals with Disabilities Education Act (IDEA) Data. (2004). Number of children served under IDEA Part B by disability and age group, 2006. Retrieved from https://www.ideadata.org/arc_toc8.asp#partbCC

International Literacy Association. (2015). *The multiple roles of school-based specialize literacy professionals* [Research brief]. Newark, DE: Author.

Irwin, J. W. (2007). *Teaching comprehension processes* (3rd ed.). Boston: Allyn & Bacon.

Isaacson, S., & Gleason, M. M. (1997). Mechanical obstacles to writing: What can teachers do to help students with learning problems? *Learning Disabilities Research and Practice, 12*(3), 188–194.

Isherwood, R. S., & Barger-Anderson, R. B. (2007). Factors affecting the adoption of co-teaching models in inclusive classrooms: One school's journey from mainstreaming to inclusion. *Journal of Ethnographic and Qualitative Research, 2,* 121–128.

Ivey, G. (2014). The social side of engaged reading for young adolescents. *The Reading Teacher, 68*(3), 165–171.

Jackson, C. (2013). Elementary mathematics teachers' knowledge of equity pedagogy. *Current Issues in Education, 16*(1), 1–13.

Jackson, C. W., & Larkin, M. J. (2002). RUBRIC—Teaching students to use grading rubrics. *Teaching Exceptional Children, 35,* 40–45.

Jackson, J., & Narvaez, R. (2013). Interactive word walls. *Science and Children, 51*(1), 42–49.

Jacobs, H. H., & Johnson, A. (2009). *The curriculum mapping planner: Templates, tools, and resources.* Alexandria, VA: Association for Supervision and Curriculum Development.

Janney, R., & Snell, M. E. (2008). *Behavior support: Teachers' guides to inclusive practices* (2nd ed.). Baltimore, MD: Paul H. Brookes.

Jasmine, J., & Schiesl, P. (2009). The effects of world walls and word wall activities on the reading fluency of first grade students. *Reading Horizons, 49*(4), 301–314.

Jayanthi, M., Epstein, M. H., Polloway, E. A., & Bursuck, W. D. (1996). Testing adaptations: A national survey of the testing practices of general education teachers. *Journal of Special Education, 30,* 99–25.

Jeger, P. (2012). Complex text, reading, and rigor using technology to support the dramatic changes in the Common Core State Standards. *Library Media Connection, 30*(5), 30–32.

Jeynes, W. H. (2011). Parental involvement research: Moving to the next level. *School Community Journal, 21*(1), 9–18.

Jiang, Y., Ekono, M., & Skinner, C. (2015). *Basic facts about low-income children.* Retrieved from http://www.nccp.org/publications/pub_1099.html

Jiménez, R. T., David, S., Pacheco, M., Risko, V. J., Pray, L., Fagan, K., & Gonzales, M. (2015). Supporting teachers of English learners by leveraging students' linguistic strengths. *The Reading Teacher, 68*(6), 406–412.

Jimerson, S. R., Burns, M. K., & Van Der Heyden, A. M. (2007). *Handbook of response to intervention: The science and practice of assessment and intervention.* New York: Springer.

Jitendra, A. K., Dupuis, D. N., & Zaslofsky, A. F. (2014). Curriculum-based measurement and standards-based mathematics: Monitoring the arithmetic word problem-solving performance of third-grade students at risk for mathematics difficulties. *Learning Disability Quarterly, 37*(4), 241–251.

Jitendra, A. K., Griffin, C., Deatline-Buchman, A., Dipipi-Hoy, C., Sczesniak, E., Sokol, N. G., & Xin, Y. P. (2005). Adherence to mathematics professional standards and instructional design criteria for problem-solving in mathematics. *Exceptional Children, 71*(3), 319–337.

Jitendra, A. K., Petersen-Brown, S., Lein, A. E., Zaslofsky, A. F., Kunkel, A. K., Jung, P., & Egan, A. M. (2015). Teaching mathematical word problem solving: The quality of evidence for strategy instruction priming the problem structure. *Journal of Learning Disabilities, 48*(1), 51–72.

Joffe, V. L., & Nippold, M. A. (2012) Progress in understanding adolescent language disorders. *Language, Speech, and Hearing Services in Schools, 43,* 438–444.

Johnsen, S. K., Parker, S. L., & Farah, Y. N. (2015). Providing services for students with gifts and talents within a response-to-intervention framework. *TEACHING Exceptional Children, 47*(4), 226–233.

Johnson, D. (2000). *Teacher web pages that build parent partnerships.* Mankato, MN: MultiMedia Schools. Retrieved from http://www.infotoday.com/MMSchools/sep00/johnson.htm

Johnson, D. J., & Myklebust, H. R. (1967). *Learning disabilities: Educational principles and practices* (Report No. EC–001–107). New York: Grune & Stratton, Inc. (ERIC Document Reproduction Service No. ED 021 352)

Johnson, D. R., Thurlow, M., Cosio, A., & Bremer, C. D. (2005). High school graduation requirements and students with disabilities. *Information Brief* (NCSET publication), *4*(2).

Johnson, D., & Johnson, R. (1989). Cooperative learning: What special education teachers need to know. *Pointer, 33*(2), 5–10.

Johnson, D., & Johnson, R. (2009). An educational success story. *Educational Researcher, 38*(5), 365–379.

Johnson, J. M., Baumgart, D., Helmstetter, E., & Curry, C. A. (1996). *Augmenting basic communication in natural contexts.* Baltimore, MD: Paul H. Brookes.

Johnson, N., & Parker, A. T. (2013). Effects of wait time when communicating with children who have sensory and additional disabilities. *Journal of Visual Impairment and Blindness, 107*(5), 363–374.

Johnson, R. (1985). *The picture communication symbols: Book II.* Solana Beach, CA: Mayer-Johnson.

Johnston, L., Beard, L., & Carpenter, L. B. (2007). *Assistive technology: Access for all students.* Upper Saddle River, NJ: Merrill/Pearson.

Johnston, P. H., Ivey, G., & Faulkner, A. (2011). Talking in class: Remembering what is important about classroom talk. *Reading Teacher, 65*(4), 232–237.

Johnston, P., & Allington, R. (1991). Remediation. In R. Barr, M. L. Kamil, P. Mosenthal, & P. D. Pearson (Eds.), *Handbook of reading research* (Vol. 2, pp. 984–1012). New York: Longman.

Johnston, P., & Goatley, V. (2014). Research making its way into classroom practice. *The Reading Teacher, 69*(4), 245–250.

Johnston, S. S., McDonnell, A. P., & Hawken, L. S. (2008). Enhancing outcomes in early literacy for young children with disabilities: Strategies for success. *Intervention in School and Clinic, 43,* 210–217.

Jones, B., & Walsh, J. M. (2004). New models of cooperative teaching. *Teaching Exceptional Children, 36*(5), 14–20.

Jordan, N. C., & Hanich, L. B. (2003). Characteristics of children with moderate mathematics deficiencies: A longitudinal perspective. *Learning Disabilities Research & Practice, 18*(4), 213–221.

Ju, S., Zhang, D., & Katsiyannis, A. (2013). The causal relationship between academic self-concept and academic achievement for students with disabilities. An analysis of SEELS data. *Journal of Disability Policy Studies, 24*(1), 4–14.

Jung, L. A., & Guskey, T. R. (2007). Standards-based grading and reporting: A model for special education. *Teaching Exceptional Children, 40*(2), 48–53.

Justice, L. M., Logan, J. A., Lin, T. J., & Kaderavek, J. N. (2014). Peer effects in early childhood education testing the assumptions of special-education inclusion. *Psychological Science,* 0956797614538978.

Kagan, J., & Snidman, N. C. (2004). *The long shadow of temperament.* Cambridge, MA: Harvard University Press.

Kamens, M. W., Loprete, S. J., & Slostad, F. A. (2003). Inclusion classrooms: What practicing teachers want to know. *Action in Teacher Education, 25*(1), 20–26.

Kamins, M. L., & Dweck, C. S. (1999). Person versus process praise and criticism: Implications for contingent self-worth and coping. *Developmental Psychology, 35*(3), 835–847.

Kampwirth, T. J., & Powers, K. M. (2011). *Collaborative consultation in the schools: Effective practices for students with learning and behavioral problems* (4th ed.). Boston: Prentice Hall.

Kanevsky, L. (2011). Differential differentiation: What types of different do students want? *Gifted Child Quarterly, 53*(4), 279–299.

Kang, S., O'Reilly, M., Fragale, C., Aguilar, J. M., Rispoli, M., & Lang, R. (2011). Evaluation of the rate of problem behavior maintained by different functions across preference assessments. *Journal of Applied Behavior Analysis, 44*, 835–846.

Kanner, L. (1943). Autistic disorders of affective contact. *Nervous Child, 2*, 217–250.

Kaplan, E., Fein, D., Kramer, J., Delis, D., & Morris, R. (2004). *Wechsler Intelligence Scale–Fourth Edition*. San Antonio, TX: Pearson.

Kaplan, S. N., Guzman, I., Tomlinson, C. A. (2009). *Using the parallel curriculum in urban settings: Grades K–8*. Thousand Oaks, CA: Corwin Press.

Katsiyannis, A., Zhang, D., Ryan, J. B., & Jones, J. (2007). High-stakes testing and students with disabilities. *Journal of Disability Policy Studies, 18*, 160–167.

Katz, D. M., Berger-Sweeney, J. E., Eubanks, J. H., Justice, M. J., Neul, J. L., Pozzo-Miller, L., … & Mamounas, L. A. (2012). Preclinical research in Rett syndrome: setting the foundation for translational success. *Disease Models & Mechanisms, 5*(6), 733–745. Retrieved from http://dx.doi.org/10.1242/dmm.011007

Kauchak, D., & Eggen, P. (1993). *Learning and teaching: Research-based methods* (2nd ed.). Boston: Allyn & Bacon.

Kauffman, J. M. (2004). *Characteristics of emotional and behavioral disorders of children and youth* (8th ed.). Upper Saddle River, NJ: Merrill/Pearson.

Kauffman, J. M., & Hallahan, D. P. (1995). *The illusion of full inclusion: A comprehensive critique of a special education bandwagon*. Austin, TX: PRO-ED.

Kauffman, J. M., & Landrum, T. J. (2009). *Characteristics of emotional and behavioral disorders of children and youth* (9th ed.). Upper Saddle River, NJ: Merrill/Pearson.

Kauffman, J. M., Brigham, F. J., & Mock, D. R. (2004). Historical and contemporary perspectives on the field of emotional and behavioral disorders. In R. B. Rutherford, M. M. Quinn, & S. R. Mathur (Eds.), *Handbook of research in emotional and behavioral disorders* (pp. 15–31). New York: Guilford Press.

Kavale, K. A., & Forness, S. R. (2000). History, rhetoric, and reality: Analysis of the inclusion debate. *Remedial and Special Education, 17*, 217–225.

Kavale, K. A., Mathur, S. P., & Mostert, M. P. (2004). Social skills training and teaching social behavior to students with emotional and behavioral disorders. In R. B. Rutherford, M. M. Quinn, & S. R. Mathur (Eds.), *Handbook of research in emotional and behavioral disorders* (pp. 446–461). New York: Guilford Press.

Kawasaki, G. (2005, December 30). The 10/20/30 rule of PowerPoint. Retrieved from http://blog.guykawasaki.com/2005/12/the_102030_rule.html

Kazdin, A. E. (2001). *Behavior modification in applied settings* (6th ed.). Belmont, CA: Wadsworth.

Kazdin, A. E. (2012). *Behavior modification in applied settings* (7th ed.). Long Grove, IL: Waveland Press.

Keefe, E. B., & Copeland, S. R. (2011). What is literacy? The power of a definition. *Research and Practice for Persons with Severe Disabilities, 36*(3–4), 92–99.

Keefe, E. B., & Moore, V. (2004). The challenge of co-teaching in inclusive classrooms at the high school level: What the teachers told us. *American Secondary Education, 32*(3), 77–88.

Keefe, E. B., Moore, V., & Duff, F. (2004). The four "knows" of collaborative teaching. *Teaching Exceptional Children, 36*, 36–42.

Keller, C. L., Bucholz, J., & Brady, M. P. (2007). Yes, I can! Empowering paraprofessionals to teach learning strategies. *Teaching Exceptional Children, 39*, 18–23.

Kelley, J. G., Lesaux, N. K., Kieffer, M. J., & Faller, S. E. (2010). Effective academic vocabulary instruction in the urban middle school. *Reading Teacher, 64*(1), 5–14.

Kelley, K. R., Bartholomew, A., & Test, D. W. (2011). Effects of the self-directed IEP delivered using computer-assisted instruction on student participation in educational planning meetings. *Remedial and Special Education*. Advanced online publication. doi: 10.1177/0741932511415864

Kelly, J. B., & Emery, R. E. (2003). Children's adjustment following divorce: Risk and resilience perspectives. *Family Relations, 52*, 352–362.

Kelly, M. J., & Clausen-Grace, N. (2007). *Comprehension should be silent: From strategy instruction to student independence*. Newark, DE: International Reading Association.

Kelly, S. M., & Smith, T. J. (2008). The digital social interactions of students with visual impairments: Findings from two national surveys. *Journal of Visual Impairment and Blindness, 102*, 528–539.

Kent, L. (2015). *5 facts about America's students*. Retrieved from http://www.pewresearch.org/fact-tank/2015/08/10/5-facts-about-americas-students/

Kettler, R. J. (2012). Testing accommodations: Theory and research to inform practice. *International Journal of Disability, Development, and Education, 59*(1), 53–66.

Kewal-Ramani, A., Gilbertson, L., Fox, M., & Provasnik, S. (2007). *Status and trends in the education of racial and ethnic minorities* (NCES 2007-039). Washington, DC: National Center for Education Statistics.

Keyes, M. W., & Owens-Johnson, L. (2003). Developing person-centered IEPs. *Intervention in School and Clinic, 38*(3), 145–152.

Keyser-Marcus, L., Briel, L., Sherron-Targett, P., Yasuda, S., Johnson, S., & Wehman, P. (2002). Enhancing the schooling of students with traumatic brain injury. *Teaching Exceptional Children, 34*, 62–67.

Kidd, J. K., Pasnak, R., Gadzichowski, K. M., Gallington, D. A., McKnight, P., Boyer, C. E., & Carlson, A. (2014). Instructing first-grade children on patterning improves reading and mathematics. *Early Education and Development, 25*(1), 134–151.

Kim, A., Vaughn, S., Wanzek, J., & Wei, S. (2004). Graphic organizers and their effects on the reading comprehension of students with LD: A synthesis of research. *Journal of Learning Disabilities, 37*(2), 105–118.

Kim, S. H. (2015). Preparing English learners for effective peer review in the writers' workshop. *The Reading Teacher, 69*(8), 599–603.

Kim, Y. (2010). Personal safety programs for children with intellectual disabilities. *Education & Training in Autism & Developmental Disabilities, 45*(2), 312–319.

Kim, Y. K, Hutchison, L. A., & Winsler, A. (2015). Bilingual education in the United States: An historical overview and examination of two-way immersion. *Educational Review, 62*(2), 236–252.

King, K. A., Artiles, A. J., & Kozleski, E. B. (2011, June). Professional learning for culturally responsive teaching. Retrieved from http://www.nccrest.org

King-Sears, M. E., Swanson, C., & Mainzer, L. (2011). Technology and literacy for adolescents with disabilities. *Journal of Adolescent & Adult Literacy, 54*(8), 569–578.

King-Sears, M., Brawand, A., Jenkins, M., & Preston-Smith, S. (2014). Co-teaching perspectives from secondary science co-teachers and their students with disabilities. *Journal of Science Teacher Education, 35*(6), 651–680.

Kirstein, I., & Bernstein, C. (1981). *Oakland schools picture dictionary*. Pontiac, MI: Oakland Schools Communication Enhancement Center.

Kitchel, J. E. (2004). Large print: Guidelines for optimal readability and APHont™, a font for low vision. Retrieved from http://www.aph.org/edresearch/lpguide.htm

Kitchel, J. E. (2012). *APH guidelines for print document design*. Louisville, KY: American Printing House for the Blind. Retrieved from http://www.aph.org/edresearch/lpguide.htm

Klauda, S. L., & Guthrie, J. T. (2015). Comparing relations of motivation, engagement, and achievement among struggling and advanced adolescent readers. *Reading and writing, 28*(2), 239–269.

Kleinert, H. L., Jones, M. M., Sheppart-Jones, K., Harp, B., & Harrison, E. M. (2012). Students with intellectual disabilities going to college? Absolutely! *Teaching Exceptional Children, 44*(5), 26–35.

Kleinert, H. L., Jones, M. M., Jones, K. S., Harp, B., & Harrison, E. M. (2012). Students with intellectual disabilities going to college? Absolutely! *Teaching Exceptional Children, 44*(5), 26–35.

Kleinert, H. L., Miracle, S. A., & Sheppard-Jones, K. (2007). Including students with moderate and severe disabilities in extracurricular and community activities. *Teaching Exceptional Children, 39*, 33–38.

Kleinert, J. O., Harrison, E. M., Fisher, T. L., & Kleinert, H. L. (2010). "I can" and "I did"—self-advocacy for young students with developmental disabilities. *Teaching Exceptional Children, 43*(2), 16–26.

Klein-Ezell, C. E., LaRusso, R., & Ezell, D. (2008). Alternate assessment for students with developmental disabilities. In H. P. Parette & G. R. Peterson-Karlan (Eds.), *Research-based practices in developmental disabilities* (2nd ed., pp. 415–430). Austin, TX: PRO-ED.

Klingner, J. K. (2003). Introduction to Right #5. In P. A. Mason & J. S. Schumm (Eds.), *Promising practices for urban reading instruction* (pp. 222–228). Newark, DE: International Reading Association.

Klingner, J. K., & Edwards, P. (2006a). Cultural considerations with response-to-intervention models. *Reading Research Quarterly, 41*, 108–117.

Klingner, J. K., & Edwards, P. A. (2006b). RTI (response to intervention): Rethinking special education for students with reading difficulties (yet again). *Reading Research Quarterly, 41*, 108–117.

Klingner, J. K., & Solano-Flores, G. (2007). Cultural responsiveness in response-to-intervention models. In *Accommodating students with disabilities: What works?* Educational Testing Service.

Klingner, J. K., & Vaughn, S. (1998). Using collaborative strategic reading. *Teaching Exceptional Children, 30*(6), 32–37.

Klingner, J. K., & Vaughn, S. (1999). Promoting reading comprehension, content learning, and English acquisition through collaborative strategic reading. *The Reading Teacher, 52*(7), 738–747.

Klingner, J. K., & Vaughn, S. (2000). The helping behaviors of fifth-graders while using collaborative strategic reading during ESL content classes. *TESOL Quarterly, 34*(1), 69–98.

Klingner, J. K., & Vaughn, S. (2004). Strategies for struggling second language readers. In T. L. Jetton & J. A. Dole (Eds.), *Adolescent literacy research and practice* (pp. 183–209). New York: Guilford.

Klingner, J. K., Barletta, L. M., & Hoover, J. J. (2008). Response to intervention models and language learners. In J. K. Klingner, J. J. Hoover, & L. M. Baca (Eds.), *Why do English language learners struggle with reading?* (pp. 37–56). Thousand Oaks, CA: Corwin.

Klingner, J. K., Blanchett, W. J., & Harry, B. (2007). Race, culture, and developmental disabilities. In S. L. Odom, R. H. Horner, M. E. Snell, & J. Blacher (Eds.), *Handbook of developmental disabilities* (pp. 55–75). New York: Guilford Press.

Klingner, J. K., Vaughn, S., & Boardman, A. (2007). *Teaching reading comprehension to students with learning difficulties*. New York: Guilford Press.

Klingner, J. K., Vaughn, S., & Boardman, A. (2015). *Teaching reading comprehension to sudents with learning difficulties (What works for special-needs learners)* (2nd ed.). New York: Guilford.

Klingner, J. K., Vaughn, S., & Schumm, J. S. (1998). Collaborative strategic reading during social studies in heterogeneous fourth-grade classrooms. *Elementary School Journal, 99*, 3–22.

Klingner, J. K., Vaughn, S., Arguelles, M. E., Hughes, M. T., & Leftwich, S. A. (2004). Collaborative strategic reading: Real-world lessons from classroom teachers. *Remedial and Special Education, 25*(5), 291–302.

Klingner, J. K., Vaughn, S., Hughes, M. T., Schumm, J. S., & Elbaum, B. (1998). Outcomes for students with and without learning disabilities. *Learning Disabilities Research and Practice, 13*(3), 153–161.

Klingner, J., & Eppollito, A. (2014). *English language learners: Differentiating between language acquisition and learning disabilities*. Alexandria, VA: Council for Exceptional Children.

Klingner, J., Boele, A., Linan-Thompson, S., & Rodriguez, D. (2014). *Essential components of special education for English language learners with learning disabilities*. Arlington, VA: Council for Exceptional Children.

Kloo, A., & Zigmond, N. (2008). Co-teaching revisited: Redrawing the blueprint. *Preventing School Failure, 52*(2), 12–20.

Klotz, M. B., & Canter, A. (2007). *Response to intervention (RTI): A primer for parents*. Washington, DC: National Association of School Psychologists.

Knight, V., Browder, D., Agnello, B., & Lee, A. (2010). Academic instruction for students with severe disabilities. *Focus on Exceptional Children, 42*(7), 1–14.

Knight, V., McKissick, B. & Saunders, A. (2013). A review of technology-based interventions to teach academic skills to students with autism spectrum disorder. *Journal of Autism & Developmental Disorders, 43*(11), 2628–2648. doi:10.1007/s10803-013-1814-y

Knight-McKenna, M. (2008). Syllable types: A strategy for reading multisyllabic words. *Teaching Exceptional Children, 40*(3), 18–24.

Koegel, L. K., Matos-Fredeen, R., Lang, R., & Koegel, R. (2012). Interventions for children with autism spectrum disorders in inclusive school settings. *Cognitive and Behavioral Practice, 18*(3), 421–588.

Koellner, K., Colsman, M., & Risley, R. (2014). Multidimensional assessment: Guiding Response to Intervention in mathematics. *Teaching Exceptional Children, 47*(2), 103–111.

Koessler, M., & Derocquigny, J. (1928). *Les faux amis ou les trashions du vocabulaire Anglais.* Paris: Librairie Vuibert.

Koga, N., & Hall, T. (2004). *Curriculum modification.* Wakefield, MA: National Center on Accessing the General Curriculum. Retrieved from http://www.cast.org/publications/ncac/ncac_curriculummod.html

Kohler-Evans, P. A. (2006). Co-teaching: How to make this marriage work in front of the kids. *Education, 127*(2), 260–264.

Kohn, A. (2006). *The homework myth: Why our kids get too much of a bad thing.* Cambridge, MA: DaCapo Press.

Kohn, A. (2007). Digging themselves in deeper: More misleading claims about the value of homework. *Phi Delta Kappan, 88*(7), 514–517.

Konopasek, D., & Forness, S. R. (2004). Psychopharmacology in the treatment of emotional and behavioral disorders. In R. B. Rutherford, M. M. Quinn, & S. R. Mathur (Eds.), *Handbook of research in emotional and behavioral disorders* (pp. 352–368). New York: Guilford Press.

Konrad, M., Joseph, L. M., & Itoi, M. (2011). Using guided notes to enhance instruction for all students. *Intervention in School and Clinic, 46*(3), 131–140.

Kontovourki, S., & Campis, C. (2011). Meaningful practice: Test prep in a third-grade public school classroom. *The Reading Teacher, 64*(4), 236–245.

Kovacs, M., Obrosky, D. S., & Sherrill, J. (2003). Developmental changes in the phenomenology of depression in girls compared to boys from childhood onward. *Journal of Affective Disorders, 74*(1), 33–48.

Kovaleski, J. F., & VanDerHeyden, A. M. (2013). *RTI approach to evaluating learning disabilities.* Guilford Publications.

Kramer, J. M. (2015). Identifying and evaluating the therapeutic strategies used during a manualized self-advocacy intervention for transition-age youth. *OTJR: Occupation, Participation and Health, 35*(1), 23–33.

Kramer, L., McCabe, P., & Sinatra, R. (2012). The effect of read alouds of expository text on first graders listening comprehension and book choice. *Literacy Research and Instruction, 51*(2), 165–178.

Krashen, S. (1985). *The input hypothesis: Issues and implications.* London: Longman.

Krashen, S. (1989). We acquire vocabulary and spelling by reading: Additional evidence for input hypothesis. *Modern Language Journal, 73*, 440–464.

Krashen, S. (2002, Dec 11). Reading improves students' spelling. *Education Week.* Retrieved from http://www.edweek.org/ew/articles/2002/12/11/15letter.h22.htm.

Krawec, J., Huang, J., Montague, M., Kressler, B., & de Alba, A. (2013). The effect of cognitive strategy instruction on knowledge of math problem-solving processes of middle school students with learning disabilities. *Learning Disability Quarterly*,2(36), 80–92.

Krawec, J., Huang, J., Montague, M., Kressler, B., & de Alba, A. M. (2012). The effects of cognitive strategy instruction on knowledge of math problem-solving processes of middle school students with learning disabilities. *Learning Disabilities Quarterly, 36*(2), 80–92.

Kress, J. E., & Fry, E. B. (2015). *The reading teacher's book of lists* (6th ed.). Hoboken, NJ: Wiley.

Kretlow, A. G., Lo, Y., White, R. B., & Jordan, L. (2008). Teaching test-taking strategies to improve the academic achievement of students with mild mental disabilities. *Education and Training in Developmental Disabilities, 43*, 397–408.

Krogstad, J. M. (2015). *5 facts about Latinos and education.* Retrieved from http://www.pewresearch.org/fact-tank/2015/05/26/5-facts-about-latinos-and-education/

Krogstad, J. M., Stepler, R., & Lopez, M. H. (2015). *English proficiency on the rise among Latinos.* Retrieved from http://www.pewhispanic.org/2015/05/12/english-proficiency-on-the-rise-among-latinos/

Kroll, J. F. (2009). The consequences of bilingualism for the mind and the brain. *Psychological Science in the Public Interest, 10*(3), i–ii.

Kubler-Ross, E. (1969). *On death and dying.* New York: Macmillan.

Kucan, L. (2012). What is most important to know about vocabulary? *The Reading Teacher, 65*(6), 360–366.

Kundi, G. M., & Nawaz, A. (2010). From objectivism to social constructivism: The impacts of information and communication technologies (ICTs) on higher education. *Journal of Science and Technology Education Research, 1*(2), 30–36.

Labbo, L. D. (2004). Author's computer chair. *The Reading Teacher, 57*, 688–691.

LaBerge, D., & Samuels, S. J. (1974). Toward a theory of automatic information processing in reading. *Cognitive Psychology, 6*, 293–323.

Labov, W., Cohen, P., Robins, C., & Lewis, J. (1968). *A study of the non-standard English of Negro and Puerto Rican speakers in New York City* (Report on Cooperative Research Project 3288). New York: Columbia University.

Ladson-Billings, G. (2006). From the achievement gap to the education debt: Understanding achievement in U.S. Schools. *Educational Researcher, 35*, 3–12.

Ladson-Billings, G. (2007). Pushing past the achievement gap: An essay on the language of deficit. *The Journal of Negro Education, 76*, 316–323.

Ladson-Billings, G. (2009). *The dreamkeepers: Successful teachers of African-American children.* John Wiley & Sons, San Francisco.

LaGreca, A. M., & Vaughn, S. (1992). Social functioning of individuals with learning disabilities. *School Psychology Review, 21*, 423–427.

Lai, S. A., & Berkeley, S. (2012). High-stakes test accommodations research and practice. *Learning Disability Quarterly, 35*(3), 158–169.

Laird, J., Cataldi, E. F., Kewal-Ramani, A., & Chapman, C. (2008). Dropout and completion rates in the United States: 2006 (NCES 2008-053). Retrieved from http://nces.ed.gov/pubsearch/pubsinfo.asp?pubid=2008053

Lambert, N., Nihira, K., & Leland, H. (1993). *AAMR Adaptive Behavior Scale—School: Examiner's manual* (2nd ed.). Austin, TX: PRO-ED.

Landers, A., Schlaug, G., & Wan, C. Y. (2013). A review of methods for facilitating speech in nonverbal children with ASD. In D. Riva, S. Bulgheroni, & M. Zappella (Eds.), *Neurobiology, diagnosis and treatment in autism: An update* (pp. 203–216). Montrouge, France: John Libbey Eurotext.

Landers, E., Alter, P., & Servilio, K. (2008). Students challenging behavior and teachers' job satisfaction. *Beyond Behavior*, 26–33.

Lane, H., & Pullen, P. C. (2015). Blending wheels. *Teaching Exceptional Children, 48*(2), 86–92.

Lane, K. L., Carter, E. W., & Sisco, L. (2012). Paraprofesional involvement in self-determination instruction for students with high-incidence disabilities. *Exceptional Children, 78*(2), 237–251.

Lane, K. L., Wehby, J., Menzies, H. M., Doukas, G. L., Munton, S. M., & Gregg, R. M. (2003). Social skills instruction for students at risk for antisocial behavior: The effects of small-group instruction. *Behavioral Disorders, 28*, 229–248.

Lang, R., & Page, S. (2011). Benefits of teacher collaboration across varying stages of the research process. *Intervention in School and Clinic, 46*, 230–234.

Lang, R., Machalicek, W., Rispoli, M. J., & Regester, A. (2009). Training parents to implement communication interventions for children with autism spectrum disorders: A systematic review of training procedures. *Evidenced Based Communication Assessment and Intervention, 3*, 174–190.

Lang, R., O'Reilly, M., Lancioni, G., Rispoli, M., Machalicek, W., Chan, J. M., . . . & Franco, J. H. (2009). Discrepancy in functional analysis results across two applied settings: Implications for intervention design. *Journal of Applied Behavior Analysis, 42*, 393–398.

Lang, R., O'Reilly, M., Machalicek, W., Lancioni, G., Rispoli, M., & Chan, J. M. (2008). A preliminary comparison of functional analysis results when conducted in contrived versus naturalistic settings. *Journal of Applied Behavior Analysis, 41*, 135–139.

Lang, R., O'Reilly, M., Sigafoos, J., Machalicek, W., Rispoli, M., Lancioni, G., Aguilar, J., & Fragale, C. (2010). The effects of an abolishing operation intervention component on play skills, challenging behavior, and stereotypy. *Behavior Modification, 34*, 267–289.

Lang, R., Regester, A., Lauderdale, S., Ashbaugh, K., & Haring, A. (2010). Treatment of anxiety in autism spectrum disorders using cognitive behavior therapy: A systematic review. *Developmental Neurorehabilitation, 13*, 53–63.

Lang, R., Sigafoos, J., Lancioni, G., Didden, R., & Rispoli, M. J. (2010). Influence of assessment setting on the results of functional analyses of problem behavior. *Journal of Applied Behavior Analysis, 43*, 565–568.

Langlois, J. A., Rutland-Brown, W., & Thomas, K. E. (2006). *Traumatic brain injury in the United States: Emergency department visits, hospitalizations, and deaths.* Atlanta: Centers for Disease Control and Prevention, National Center for Injury Prevention and Control.

Larrivee, B. (1992). *Strategies for effective classroom management.* Boston: Allyn & Bacon.

Larrivee, B. (2005). *Authentic classroom management: Creating a learning community and building reflective practice* (2nd ed.). Boston: Allyn & Bacon.

Larson, C. N., & Slaughter, H. (1984). The use of manipulatives and games in selected elementary school classrooms, from an ethnographic study. In A. E. Uprichard & J. V. Perez (Eds.), *Focus on learning problems in mathematics* (pp. 31–49). Framingham, MA: Center for Teaching/Learning of Mathematics.

Larson, N. (2004). *Teacher reference materials: Saxon Math 2: Test preparation and practice for ISTEP.* Norman, OK: Saxon.

Lash, M. H. (2000). *Resource guide: Children, adolescents and young adults with brain injuries.* Wake Forest, NC: L & A Publishing/Training.

Lassonde, C., & Richards, J. C. (2013). Best practices in teaching planning for writing. In S. Graham, C. A. MacArthur, & J. Fitzgerald (Eds.). *Best practices in writing instruction* (2nd ed.) (pp. 193–214). New York: Guilford.

Layton, C. A., & Lock, R. H. (2007). 20 ways to … use authentic assessment techniques to fulfill the promise of No Child Left Behind. *Intervention in School and Clinic, 42*, 169–173.

Lederer, J. M. (2000). Reciprocal teaching of social studies in inclusive elementary classrooms. *Journal of Learning Disabilities, 33*(1), 91–106.

Lee, D. L., & Axelrod, S. (2005). *Behavior modification: Basic principles* (3rd ed.). Austin, TX: PRO-ED.

Lee, S., Soukup, J. H., Little, T. D., & Wehmeyer, M. L. (2009). Student and teacher variables contributing to access to the general education curriculum for students with intellectual and developmental disabilities. *Journal of Special Education, 43*(1), 29–44.

Lee, S.-H., Palmer, S. B., Wehmeyer, M. L. (2009). Goal setting and self-monitoring for students with disabilities: Practical tips and ideas for teachers. *Intervention in School and Clinic, 44*(3), 139–145.

Lee, S.-H., Soukup, J. H., Little, T. D., & Wehmeyer, M. L. (2008). Student and teacher variables contributing to access to the general education curriculum for students with intellectual and developmental disabilities. *Journal of Special Education, 43*, 29–44.

Leff, S., & Leff, R. (1978). *Talking pictures.* Milwaukee, WI: Crestwood Company.

Lehman, A. F., Kreyenbuhl, J., Buchanan, R. W., Dickerson, F. B., Dixon, L. A., & Goldberg, R. E. A. (2004). The Schitzophrenia Patient Outcomes Research Team (PORT). Updated treatment recommendations 2003. *Schizophrenia Bulletin, 30*, 193–217.

Leigh, J., & Johnson, A. (2004). Giving presentations the EVL way. Retrieved from http://www.evl.uic.edu/aej/PresentinginEVL

Lembke, E. S., & Strichter, J. P. (2006). Utilizing a system of screening and progress monitoring within a three-tiered model of instruction: Implications for students with emotional/behavioral disorders. *Beyond Behavior*, 3–9.

Lembke, E. S., Hampton, D., & Beyers, S. J. (2012). Response to intervention in mathematics: Critical elements. *Psychology in the Schools, 49*(3), 257–272.

LeMoine, N. R. (2001). Language variation and literacy acquisition in African American students. In J. L. Harris, A. G. Kamhi, & K. E. Pollock (Eds.), *Literacy in African American communities* (pp. 169–194). Mahwah, NJ: Erlbaum.

Lenski, S. (2011) What RTI means for content area teachers. *Journal of Adolescent and Adult Literacy, 55*(4) 278–282.

Lenz, B. K., & Deshler, D. D. (2004). *Teaching content to all: Evidence-based inclusive practices in middle and secondary schools.* Boston: Allyn & Bacon.

Lenz, B. K., Deshler, D. D., & Kissam, B. R. (2003). *Teaching content to all: Evidence-based inclusive practices in middle and secondary schools.* Upper Saddle River, NJ: Pearson Education.

Lenz, B. K., Schumaker, J. B., Deshler, D. D., & Beals, V. L. (1984). *The word identification strategy* (Learning Strategies Curriculum). Lawrence, KS: University of Kansas.

Lequia, J., Machalicek, W., & Rispoli, M. J. (2012). Effects of activity schedules on challenging behavior exhibited in children with autism spectrum disorders: A systematic review. *Research in Autism Spectrum Disorders, 6*(1), 480–492. Retrieved from http://dx.doi.org/10.1016/j.rasd.2011.07.008

Lerman, J. (2006). *101 best web sites for teachers: Tools and professional development.* Washington, DC: International Society for Technology in Education.

Lerner, J. (2006). *Learning disabilities and related disorders: Characteristics and teaching strategies* (10th ed). Boston: Houghton Mifflin.

Lerner, J. W., & Johns, B. (2015). *Learning disabilities and related disabilities: Strategies for success* (13th ed.). Independence, KY: Cengage Learning.

Lerner, J. W., Lowenthal, B., & Lerner S. R. (1995). *Attention deficit disorders: Assessment and teaching.* Pacific Grove, CA: Brooks/Cole.

Lesaux, N. K., Kieffer, M. J., Faller, S. E., & Kelley, J. G. (2010). The effectiveness and ease of implementation of an academic vocabulary intervention for linguistically diverse students in urban middle schools. *Reading Research Quarterly, 45*(2), 196–228.

Lesaux, N. K., Kieffer, M. J., Kelley, J. G., & Harris, J. R. (2014). Effects of academic vocabulary instruction for linguistically diverse adolescents evidence from a randomized field trial. *American Educational Research Journal*, 0002831214532165.

Lessow-Hurley, J. (2009). *The foundations of dual language instruction* (5th ed.). Upper Saddle River: Pearson.

Leu, D. J., & Kinzer, C. K. (2017). *Phonics, phonemic awareness, and word analysis: An interactive tool* (10th ed.). Boston: Pearson.

Leung, K. C. (2015). Preliminary empirical model of crucial determinants of best practice for peer tutoring on academic achievement. *Journal of Educational Psychology, 107*(2), 558–579.

Levendoski, L. S., & Cartledge, G. (2000). Self-monitoring for elementary school children with serious emotional disturbances: Classroom applications for increased academic responding. *Behavioral Disorders, 25*, 211–234.

Lewis, R. B. (1993). *Special education technology: Classroom applications.* Pacific Grove, CA: Brooks/Cole.

Lewis, T. J., Lewis-Palmer, T., Newcomer, L., & Stichter, J. (2004). Applied behavior analysis and the education and treatment of students with emotional and behavioral disorders. In R. B. Rutherford, M. M. Quinn, & S. R. Mathur (Eds.), *Handbook of research in emotional and behavioral disorders* (pp. 523–545). New York: Guilford Press.

Liederman, J., Kantrowitz, L., & Flannery, K. (2005). Male vulnerability to reading disability is not likely to be a myth: A call for new data. *Journal of Learning Disabilities, 38*(2), 109–129.

Linan-Thompson, S. (2007). *Research-based methods of reading instruction for English language learners.* Alexandria, VA: ASCD.

Linan-Thompson, S., & Vaughn, S. (2007). *Research-based methods of reading instruction for English language learners: Grades K–4.* Alexandria, VA: Association for Supervision and Curriculum Development.

Linan-Thompson, S., Vaughn, S., Hickman-Davis, P., & Kouzekanani, K. (2003). Effectiveness of supplemental reading instruction for second-grade English language learners with reading difficulties. *The Elementary School Journal, 103*, 221–238.

Lindamood, P. A., & Lindamood, P. (1998). *The Lindamood Phoneme Sequencing program for reading, spelling, and speech: The LiPS program.* Austin, TX: PRO-ED.

Lindamood, P., & Lindamood, P. (2011). *Lindamood Phoneme Sequencing–LiPs®* (4th ed.). Austin, TX: PRO-ED.

Lipson, M. Y., Chomsky-Higgins, P., & Kanfer, J. (2011). Diagnosis: The missing ingredient in RTI assessment. *The Reading Teacher, 75*(3), 204–208.

Lipson, M. Y., Mosenthal, J. H., Mekkelsen, J., & Russ, B. (2004). Building knowledge and fashioning success one school at a time. *The Reading Teacher, 57*(6), 534–542.

Little, M. A., Lane, K. L., Harris, K. R., Graham, S., Story, M., & Sandmel, K. (2010). Self-regulated strategies development for persuasive writing in tandem with schoolwide positive behavioral support: Effects for second-grade students with behavioral and writing difficulties. *Behavioral Disorders*, 157–179.

Loeber, R., Wung, P., Keenan, K., Giroux, B., Stouthamer-Loeber, M., Van Kammen, W., & Maughan, B. (1993). Developmental pathways in disruptive child behavior. *Development and Psychopathology, 51*(1/2), 103–134.

Loeffler, K. A. (2005). No more Friday spelling tests? An alternative spelling assessment for students with learning disabilities. *Teaching Exceptional Children, 37*(4), 24–27.

Long, C. (2012, January 29). States struggling with Common Core transitions. *NEA Today.* Retrieved from http://neatoday.org/2012/01/29/states-struggling-with-common-core-transition/

Los Angeles Times. (June, 4, 2014). Is bilingual education worth bringing back? Retrieved from http://www.latimes.com/opinion/editorials/la-ed-bilingual-education-proposition-227-repeal-20140605-story.html

Lucangeli, D., Coi, G., & Bosco, P. (1997). Metacognitive awareness in good and poor math problem solvers. *Learning Disabilities Research and Practice, 12*(4), 209–212.

Lucas, T., Henze, R., & Donato, R. (1990). Promoting the success for Latino language minority students: An exploratory study of six high schools. *Harvard Educational Review, 60*, 315–334.

Luckasson, R., & Schalock, R. L. (2012). Human function, supports, assistive technology, and evidence-based practices in the field of intellectual disability. *Journal of Special Education Technology, 27*(2), 3–10.

Luckasson, R., Borthwick-Duffy, S., Buntinx, W. H. E., Coulter, D. L., Craig, E. M., Reeve, A., Schalock, R. L., Snell, M., Spitalnik, D. M., & Spreat, S. (2002). *Mental retardation: Definition, classification, and systems of support* (10th ed.). Washington, DC: American Association for Mental Retardation.

Luckner, J., Bowen, S., & Carter, K. (2001). Visual teaching strategies for students who are deaf or hard of hearing. *Teaching Exceptional Children, 33*(3), 38–44.

Lucyshyn, J. M., Dunlap, G., & Albin, R. W. (2002). Families and positive behavior support: Addressing problem behavior in family contexts. *Adolescence, 37*(148), 863.

Lucyshyn, J. M., Horner, R. H., Dunlap, G., Albin, R. W., & Ben, K. R. (2002). Positive behavior support with families. In J. M. Lucyshyn, G. Dunlap, & R. W. Albin (Eds.), *Families and positive behavior support: Addressing problem behavior in family contexts* (pp. 3–43). Baltimore, MD: Paul H. Brookes.

Lusthaus, E., & Forest, M. (1987). The kaleidoscope: A challenge to the cascade. In M. Forest (Ed.), *More education integration* (pp. 1–17). Downsview, Ontario: G. Allan Roeher Institute.

Lydon, S., Healy, O., O'Reilly, M. F., & Lang, R. (2012). Variations in functional analysis methodology: A systematic review. *Journal of Physical and Developmental Disability.*

Lyle, M. L., & Simplican, S. C. (2015). Elite repudiation of the r-word and public opinion about intellectual disability. *Intellectual and Developmental Disabilities, 53*(3), 211–227.

Lynch, A., Theodore, L. A., Bray, M. A., & Kehle, T. J. (2009). A comparison of group-oriented contingencies and randomized reinforces to improve homework completion and accuracy for students with disabilities. *School Psychology Review, 38*(3), 307–324.

Lynch, E. W., & Hanson, M. J. (1992). *Developing cross-cultural competence: A guide for working with young children and their families.* Baltimore, MD: Paul H. Brookes.

Lynne, B. (2007). Technology for hearing impaired. Retrieved from http://www.teachingtechnology.suite101.com/article.dfm/technology_for_hearing_impaired

Lytle, R. (2011, August 10). Student-teacher social media restrictions get mixed reactions. Retrieved from http://education.usnews.rankingsandreviews.com/education/high-schools/articles

Maag, J. W. (2006). Social skills training for students with emotional and behavioral disorders: A review of reviews. *Behavioral Disorders, 32*, 5–17.

MacArthur, C. A., Graham, S., & Fitzgerald, J. (Eds.). (2008). *Handbook of writing research.* New York: Guilford.

MacGinitie, W. H., MacGinitie, R. K., Maria, K., Dreyer, L. G., & Hughes, K. E. (2006). *Gates-MacGinitie Reading Tests.* Riverside, CA: Riverside.

Machalicek, W., Shogren, K., Lang, R., Rispoli, M., O'Reilly, M., & Franco, J. (2009). Increasing play and decreasing the challenging behavior of children with autism during recess with activity schedules and task correspondence training. *Research in Autism Spectrum Disorders, 3*, 547–555.

Mack, K. (2004). Explanations for conduct disorder. *Child & Youth Care Forum, 33*(2), 95–112.

Maggin, D. M., Zurheide, J., Pickett, K. C., & Baillie, S. J. (2015). A systematic evidence review of the Check-In/Check-Out Program for reducing student challenging behaviors. *Journal of Positive Behavior Interventions*, 1098300715573630.

Magiera, K., & Zigmond, N. (2005). Co-teaching in middle school classrooms under routine conditions: Does the instructional experience differ for students with disabilities in co-taught and solo-taught classes? *Learning Disabilities Research & Practice, 20*(2), 79–85.

Magiera, K., Smith, C., Zigmond, N., & Gebauer, K. (2005). Benefits of co-teaching in secondary mathematics classes. *Teaching Exceptional Children, 37*(3), 20–24.

Mahapatra, A. K., Kumar, R. & Kamal R. (2012). *Textbook of traumatic brain injury.* New Delhi, India: Jaypee Brothers Medical Publishers.

Maheady, L., Harper, G. F., & Sacca, M. K. (1988). Peer-mediated instruction: A promising approach to meeting the needs of learning disabled adolescents. *Learning Disability Quarterly, 11*, 108–113.

Maker, C. J., & Schiever, S. W. (2010). *Curriculum development and teaching strategies for gifted learners* (3rd ed.). Austin, TX: PRO-ED.

Mallette, M. H., Henk, W. A., Waggoner, J. E., & Delaney, C. J. (2005). What matters most? A survey of accomplished middle-level educators' beliefs and values about literacy. *Action in Teacher Education, 27*, 33–42.

Maloy, R. W., Verock-O'Loughlin, R., & Edwards, S. A. (2014). *Transforming learning with new technologies.* Boston: Pearson.

Manning, S., Stanford, B. K., & Ruvek, S. (2010). Valuing the advanced learner: Differentiating up. *The Clearing House, 83*, 145–149.

Manyak, P. C. (2008). Phonemes in use: Multiple activities for a critical process. *The Reading Teacher, 61*(8), 659–662.

Manyak, P. C., Von Gunten, H., Autenrieth, D., Gillis, C., Mastre-O'Farrell, J., Irvine-McDermott, E., Baumann, J. F., & Blachowicz, C. L. A. (2014). Four practical principles for enhancing vocabulary instruction, *The Reading Teacher, 68*(1), 13–23.

March of Dimes. (2006). What's inside? Retrieved from http://www.marchofdimes.com/14332_1169.asp

March of Dimes. (2010). *Common birth defects.* Retrieved from http://www.marchofdimes.com/baby/birthdefects_common.html

March, J. K., & Peters, K. H. (2015). Telling the truth about the Common Core. *Kappan, 96*(8), 63–65.

Marchel, M. A., Fischer, T. A., & Clark, D. M. (2015). *Assistive technology for children and youth with disabilities.* Boston: Pearson.

Margolis, H. (2005). Resolving struggling learners' homework difficulties: Working with elementary school learners and parents. *Preventing School Failure, 50*(1), 5–12.

Marino, M. T., Marino, E. C., & Shaw, S. F. (2006). Making informed assistive technology decisions for students with high incidence disabilities. *Teaching Exceptional Children, 38*, 18–25.

Marks, S. U. (2008). Self-determination for students with intellectual disabilities and why I want educators to know what it means. *Phi Delta Kappan, 90*(1), 55–58.

Marotz, L. (2015). *Health, safety, and nutrition for the young child* (9th ed.). Stamford, CT: Cengage Learning.

Marsh, L. G., & Cooke, N. L. (1996). The effects of using manipulatives in teaching math problem solving to students with learning disabilities. *Learning Disabilities Research and Practice, 11* (1), 58–65.

Marston, D. (1996). A comparison of inclusion only, pull-out only, and combined service models for students with mild disabilities. *The Journal of Special Education, 30*(2), 121–132.

Marston, D., Muyskens, P., Lau, M., & Canter, H. (2003). Problem solving model for decision-making with high-incidence disabilities: The Minneapolis experience. *Learning Disabilities Research and Practice, 18*(3), 187–200.

Martin, J. E., Marshall, L., & Sale, P. (2004). A 3-year study of middle, junior high, and high school IEP meetings. *Exceptional Children, 70*(3), 285–297.

Martinez, R., & Young, A. (2011). RtI: How is it practiced and perceived? *International Journal of Special Education, 26*(1), 44–52.

Marzano, R. J. (2009). *Formative assessment and standards-based grading.* Bloomington, IN: Solution Tree.

Marzano, R. J. (2011). Objectives that students understand. *Educational Leadership, 68*(8), 86–87.

Marzano, R. J. (2012). *Developing expert teachers.* Bloomington, IN: Solution Tree Press.

Marzano, R. J., & Haystead, M. W. (2008). *Making standards useful in the classroom.* Alexandria, VA: Association for Supervision and Curriculum Development.

Marzano, R. J., & Marzano, J. S. (2009). The key to classroom management (pp. 160–167). In *Kaleidoscope: Contemporary and classic readings in education.* Belmont, CA: Wadsworth.

Marzano, R. J., & Pickering, D. J. (2007). The case for and against homework. *Educational Leadership, 64*(6), 74–79.

Mason, C., Field, S., & Sawilowsky, S. (2004). Implementation of self-determination activities and student participation in IEPs. *Exceptional Children, 70*(4), 441–451.

Mason, H., & McCall, S. (Eds.). (2013). *Visual impairment: Access to education for children and young people.* New York: Routledge.

Mason, L. H. (2009, Summer). Effective instruction for written expression. *Perspectives on Language and Literacy*, 21–24.

Mason, L. H., & Graham, S. (2008). Writing instruction for adolescents with learning disabilities: Programs of intervention research. *Learning Disabilities Research & Practice, 23*(2), 103–112.

Mason, L. H., Harris, K. R., & Graham, S. (2011). Self-regulated strategy development for students with writing difficulties. *Theory into Practice, 50*(1), 20–27.

Mason, L. H., Kubina, R. M., & Taft, R. J. (2011). Developing quick writing skills of middle school students with disabilities. *The Journal of Special Education, 44*(4), 205–220.

Mason, L. H., Kubina, R. M., Valasa, J. L., & Cramer, A. M. (2010). Evaluating effective writing instruction for adolescent students in an emotional and behavior support setting. *Behavioral Disorders, 35*(2), 140–156.

Mastropieri, M. A., & Scruggs, T. E. (1997). Best practices in promoting reading comprehension in students with learning disabilities: 1976–1996. *Remedial and Special Education, 18,* 197–213.

Mastropieri, M. A., & Scruggs, T. E. (2005). Feasibility and consequences of response to intervention: Examination of the issues and scientific evidence as a model for identification of individuals with learning disabilities. *Journal of Learning Disabilities, 38,* 525–531.

Mastropieri, M. A., Leinart, A., & Scruggs, T. E. (1999). Strategies to increase reading fluency. *Intervention in School and Clinic, 34*(5), 278–283.

Mastropieri, M. A., Scruggs, T. E., Graetz, J., Norland, J., Gardizi, W., & McDuffie, K. (2005). Case studies in co-teaching in the content areas: Successes, failures, and challenges. *Intervention in School and Clinic, 40*(5), 260–270.

Mathes, P. G., Fuchs, D., Roberts, P. H., & Fuchs, L. S. (1998). Preparing students with special needs for reintegration: Curriculum-based measurement's impact on transenvironmental programming. *Journal of Learning Disabilities 31,* 615–624.

Matson, J. L., & Cervantes, P. E. (2013). Comorbidity among persons with intellectual disabilities. *Research in Autism Spectrum Disorders, 7,* 1318–1322.

Matson, J. L. (2007). Current status of differential diagnosis for children with autism spectrum disorders. *Research in Developmental Disabilities, 28,* 109–118.

Matson, J. L., & Boisjoli, J. A. (2009). The token economy for children with intellectual disability and/or autism: A review. *Research in Developmental Disabilities, 30,* 240–248.

Matson, J. L., Belva, B. C., Horovitz, M., Kozlowski, A. M., & Bamburg, J. W. (2012). Comparing symptoms of autism spectrum disorders in a developmentally disabled adult population using the current *DSM-IV-TR* diagnostic criteria and the proposed *DSM-5* diagnostic criteria. *Journal of Developmental and Physical Disabilities, 24*(4), 403–414. Retrieved from http://dx.doi.org/10.1007/s10882-012-9278-0

Mattingly, J. C., & Bott, D. A. (1990). Teaching multiplication facts to students with learning problems. *Exceptional Children, 56*(5), 438–449.

Mattison, R. E. (2004). Psychiatric and psychological assessment of emotional and behavioral disorders during school mental health consultation. In R. B. Rutherford, M. M. Quinn, & S. R. Mathur (Eds.), *Handbook of research in emotional and behavioral disorders* (pp. 163–180). New York: Guilford Press.

Matus, R. (2009). Bright students still get bored. Retrieved from http://www.tampabay.com/news/education/k12/article970309.sec

Mayes, S. D., & Calhoun, S. L. (2006). Frequency of reading, math, and writing disabilities in children with clinical disorders. *Learning and Individual Differences, 16,* 145–157.

Mazotti, V. L., & Rowe, D. A. (2015). Meeting the transition needs of students with disabilities in the 21st century. *Teaching Exceptional Children,6*(47), 298–300.

McCaleb, J., & White, J. (1980). Critical dimensions in evaluating teacher clarity. *Journal of Classroom Interaction, 15,* 27–30.

McCormick, S., & Zutell, J. (2011). *Instructing students who have literacy problems* (6th ed.). Upper Saddle River, NJ: Pearson.

McCoy, J. D., & Ketterlin-Geller, L. R. (2004). Rethinking instructional delivery for diverse student populations: Serving all learners with concept-based instruction. *Intervention in School and Clinic, 40,* 88–95.

McDougall, D. (1998). Research on self-management techniques used by students with disabilities in general education settings: A descriptive review. *Remedial and Special Education, 19,* 310–320.

McEvoy, A., & Welker, R. (2000). Antisocial behavior, academic behavior, and school climate: A critical review. *Journal of Emotional and Behavioral Disorders, 8,* 130–140.

McGee, C. D. (2012). Developmentally appropriate practice and gifted students: What should it mean? *Parenting for High Potential, 2*(2), 26–28.

McIntosh, K., & MacKay, L. D. (2008). Enhancing generalization of social skills: Making social skills curricula effective after the lesson. *Beyond Behavior,* 18–25.

McIntosh, R., Vaughn, S., Schumm, J. S., Haager, D., & Lee, O. (1993). Observations of students with learning disabilities in general education classrooms. *Exceptional Children, 60,* 249–261.

McKenna, J. W., Shin, M., & Ciullo, S. (2015). Evaluating reading and mathematics instruction for students with learning disabilities: A synthesis of observation research. *Learning Disabilities Quarterly, 38*(4), 195–207.

McKeown, M. G., & Curtis, M. E. (2014). *The nature of vocabulary acquisition.* New York: Psychology Press.

McKinley, N., & Larson, V. (1991, November). *Seventh, eighth, and ninth graders' conversations in two experimental conditions.* Paper presented at the annual convention of the American Speech-Language-Hearing Association, Atlanta, GA.

McKinnon, D. H., McLeod, S., & Reilly, S. (2007). The prevalence of stuttering, voice, and speech-sound disorders in primary school students in Australia. *Language, Speech, and Hearing Services in Schools, 38,* 5–15.

McLaughlin, M. J. (2012, September/October). Access to the Common Core for all: Six principles for principals to consider in implementing CCSS for students with disabilities. *Principal*, pp. 22–26. Retrieved from: http://www.udlcenter.org/sites/udlcenter.org/files/McLaughlin_2012.pdf

McLaughlin, S. (1998). *Introduction to language development.* San Diego, CA: Singular Publishing Group.

McLoughlin, J. A., & Lewis, R. B. (2005). *Assessing students with special needs* (6th ed.). Upper Saddle River, NJ: Merrill/Pearson.

McLoughlin, J. A., & Lewis, R. B. (2008). *Assessing students with special needs* (7th ed.). Boston: Pearson.

McMaster, K., Shu-Hsuan, K., Insoon, H., & Cao, M. (2008). Peer-assisted learning strategies: A "Tier 1" approach to promoting English learners' response to intervention. *Exceptional Children, 74*(2), 194–214.

McMillan, J. H., & Hearn, J. (2008). Student self-assessment: The key to stronger student motivation and higher achievement. *Educational Horizons, 87,* 40–49.

McNamara, J. K., & Wong, B. (2003). Memory for everyday information in students with learning disabilities. *Journal of Learning Disabilities, 36* (5), 394–406.

McTighe, J., & Lyman, F. T., Jr. (1988). Cueing thinking in the classroom: The promise of theory-embedded tools. *Educational Leadership, 45*(7), 18–24.

Mechling, L. C. (2008). Thirty year review of safety skill instruction for persons with intellectual disabilities. *Education and Training in Developmental Disabilities, 43,* 311–323.

Meichenbaum, D., & Biemiller, A. (1998). *Nurturing independent learners: Helping students take charge of their learning.* Newton, MA: Brookline Books.

Melby-Lervåg, M., Lyster, S. A. H., & Hulme, C. (2012). Phonological skills and their role in learning to read: A meta-analytic review. *Psychological bulletin, 138*(2), 322–352.

Menken, K. (2013). Restrictive language education policies and emergent bilingual youth: A perfect storm with imperfect outcomes. *Theory into Practice, 52,* 160–168.

Menzies, H. M., Lane, K. L., & Lee, J. M. (2009). Self-monitoring strategies for use in the classroom: A promising practice to support productive behavior for students with emotional or behavioral disorders. *Beyond Behavior, 18,* 27–35.

Mercer, C. D., & Miller, S. P. (1992). Teaching students with learning problems in math to acquire, understand, and apply basic math facts. *Remedial and Special Education, 13*(3), 19–35, 61.

Merkley, D., Schmidt, D., Dirksen, C., & Fuhler. (2006). Enhancing parent teacher communication using technology: A reading improvement clinic example. *Contemporary Issues in Technology and Teacher Education, 6*(1). Retrieved from http://www.citejournal.org/vol6/iss1/languagearts/article1.cfm

Merrell, K. W., Gueldner, B. A., Ross, S. W., & Isava, D. M. (2008). How effective are school bullying intervention programs? A meta-analysis of intervention research. *School Psychology Quarterly, 23*(1), 26–42.

MetLife. (2007). The MetLife survey of American teacher: The homework experience. Retrieved from http://www.ced.org/docs/report/report_metlife2008.pdf

Meyer, L. H., Bevan-Brown, J., Harry, B., & Sapon-Shevin, M. (2005). School inclusion and multicultural issues in special education. In J. A. Banks & C. A. M. Banks (Eds.), *Multicultural education: Issues and perspectives* (5th ed., pp. 350–378). Hoboken, NJ: Wiley.

Meyer, M. S., & Felton, R. H. (1999). Repeated reading to enhance fluency: Old approaches and new direction. *Annals of Dyslexia, 49,* 283–306.

Michelson, L., Sugai, D. P., Wood, R. P., & Kazdin, A. E. (2013). *Social skills assessment and training with children: An empirically based handbook.* New York: Springer Science & Business Media.

Miles, P., Bruns, E. J., Osher, T. W., Walker, J. S., & National Wraparound Initiative Advisory Group. (2006). *The wraparound process user's guide: A handbook for families.* Portland, OR: National Wraparound Initiative, Research and Training Center on Family Support and Children's Mental Health, Portland State University.

Miller, M. C., Cooke, N. L., Test, D. W., & White, R. (2003). Effects of friendship circles on the social interactions of elementary age students with mild disabilities. *Journal of Behavioral Education, 12,* 167–184.

Miller, S. P., Stringfellow, J. L., Kaffar, B. J., Ferreira, D., & Mancl, D. B. (2011). Developing computation competence among students who struggle with mathematics. *Teaching Exceptional Children, 44*(2), 38–46.

Miller, S. P., Stringfellow, J. L., Kaffar, B. J., Ferreira, D., & Mancl, D. B. (2011). Developing computation competence among students who struggle with mathematics. *Teaching Exceptional Children, 44*(2), 38–46.

Miyasaka, J. R. (2002, April). A framework for evaluating the validity of test preparation practices. Paper presented at the annual meeting of the American Educational Research Association, New Orleans, LA.

Moats, L. C. (2000). *Speech to print: Language essentials for teachers.* Baltimore: Paul H. Brookes.

Moats, L. C. (2009). *The speech sounds of English: Phonetics, phonology, and phoneme awareness.* Longmont, CO: Sopris West Educational Services.

Moats, L. C. (2010). *Speech to Print: Language Essentials for Teachers* (2nd ed.). Baltimore, MD: Paul H. Brookes.

Mobbs, F., Reed, V. A., & McAllister, I. (1993, May). Rankings of the relative importance of selected communication skills in adolescent peer interactions. Paper presented at the annual conference of the Australian Association of Speech and Hearing, Darwin, Australia.

Moeller, M. P. (2000). Early intervention and language development in children who are deaf and hard of hearing. *Pediatrics, 106*(2), 43–62.

Moeschler, J. B., Shevell, M., Saul, R. A., Chen, E., Freedenberg, D. L., Hamid, R., & Tarini, B. A. (2014). Comprehensive evaluation of the child with intellectual disability or global developmental delays. *Pediatrics, 134*(3), e903–e918.

Mokhtari, K., Rosemary, C. A., & Edwards, P. A. (2008). Making instructional decisions based on data: what, how, and why. *The Reading Teacher, 61*(4), 354–359.

Moll, L. C. (2010). Mobilizing culture, language, and educational practices: Fulfilling the promise of Mendez & Brown. *Educational Researcher, 39*(6), 451–460.

Moll, L. C. (Jul–Sep 2015). Tapping into the "hidden" home and community resources of students. *Kappa Delta Pi Record, 51*(3), 114–117.

Montague, M. (1992). The effects of cognitive and metacognitive strategy instruction on the mathematical problem solving of middle school students with learning disabilities. *Journal of Learning Disabilities, 25,* 230–248.

Montague, M. (2008). Self-regulation strategies to improve mathematical problem solving for students with learning disabilities. *Learning Disability Quarterly, 31,* 37–44.

Montague, M., & Graves, A. (1993). Improving students' story writing. *Teaching Exceptional Children, 25,* 36–37.

Montague, M., & Jitendra, A. K. (2006). *Teaching mathematics to middle school students with learning disabilities: What works for special needs learners?* New York: Guilford.

Montague, M., & van Garderen, D. (2003). A cross-sectional study of mathematics achievement, estimation skills, and academic self-perception in students of varying ability. *Journal of Learning Disabilities, 36,* 437–447.

Montague, M., Enders, C., & Castro, M. (2005). Academic and behavioral outcomes for students with emotional and behavioral disorders. *Behavior Disorders, 31,* 18–32.

Montague, M., Enders, C., & Dietz, S. (2011). Effects of cognitive strategy instruction on math problem solving of middle school students with learning disabilities. *Learning Disabilities Quarterly, 34*(4) 262–272.

Montague, M., Penfield, R. D., Enders, C., & Huang, J. (2010). Curriculum-based measurement of math problem solving: A methodology and rationale for establishing equivalence of scores. *Journal of School Psychology, 48*(1), 39–52.

Montgomery, W. (2001). Creating culturally responsive, inclusive classrooms. *Teaching Exceptional Children,* 4–9.

Mora-Harder, M. (2009). English reading/language arts instruction in first-grade classrooms serving English language learners: A cross-analysis of instructional practices and student engagement. Unpublished doctoral dissertation, University of Miami, Coral Gables, FL.

Moran, S., Kornhaber, M., & Gardner, H. (2006). Orchestrating multiple intelligences. *Educational Leadership, 64,* 22–27.

Morphy, P., & Graham, S. (2012). Word processing programs and weaker writers/readers: A meta-analysis of research findings. *Reading & Writing, 25,* 641–678.

Mraz, M., Rasinski, T., & Padak, N. D. (2008). *Evidence-based instruction in reading: A professional development guide to phonemic awareness.* Boston: Pearson.

Mueller, T. G. (2009). IEP facilitation. *Teaching Exceptional Children, 41*(3), 60–67.

Mulcahy-Ernt, P. I., & Caverly, D. C. (2009). Strategic study-reading. In R. F. Flippo & D. C. Caverly (Eds.), *Handbook of college reading and study strategy research* (2nd ed., pp. 177–198). New York: Routledge.

Munk, D. D., & Van Laarhoven, T. (2008). Grouping arrangements and delivery of instruction for students with developmental disabilities. In H. P. Parette & G. R. Peterson-Karlan (Eds.), *Research-based practices in developmental disabilities* (2nd ed., pp. 269–290). Austin, TX: PRO-ED.

Munoz, M. A., & Guskey, T. R. (2015). Standards-based grading and reporting will improve education. *Kappan, 96*(7), 64–68.

Murawski, W. W. (2009). *Collaborative teaching in secondary schools: Making the co-teaching marriage work.* Thousand Oaks, CA: Corwin Press.

Murawski, W. W. (2012). 10 tips for using co-planning time more efficiently. *Teaching Exceptional Children, 44*(4), 8–15.

Murawski, W. W., & Dieker, L. A. (2008). 50 ways to keep your co-teacher. *Teaching Exceptional Children 40*(4), 40–48.

Murawski, W. W., & Hughes, C. E. (2009). Response to intervention, collaboration, and co-teaching: A logical combination for successful systemic change. *Prevention in School and Clinic, 53*(4), 267–277.

Murawski, W. W., & Lochner, W. W. (2011). Observing co-teaching: What to ask for, look for, and listen for. *Intervention in School and Clinic, 46*(3), 174–183.

Murawski, W. W., & Swanson, H. L. (2001). A meta-analysis of co-teaching research. *Remedial and Special Education, 22,* 258–267.

Murdick, N. L., Gartin, B. C., & Fowler, G. A. (2014). *Special education law* (3rd ed.). Boston: Pearson.

Murray, M. M., & Curran, E. M. (2008). Learning together with parents of children with disabilities: Bringing parent-professional partnership education to a new level. *Teacher Education and Special Education, 31*(1), 59–63.

Muscular Dystrophy Association. (2009). Diseases. Retrieved from http://www.mda.org/disease/

Myers, A., & Eisenman, L. (2005). Student-led IEPs: Take the first step. *Teaching Exceptional Children, 37*(4), 52–58.

Nagro, S. A. (2015). PROSE checklist: Strategies for improving school-to-home written communication. *Teaching Exceptional Children, 47*(5), 256–263.

Nagy, W., & Townsend, D. (2012). Words as tools: Learning academic vocabulary as language acquisition. *Reading Research Quarterly, 47*(1), 91–108.

Nahmias, M. (1995). *Project ADEPT.* Tucson, AZ: University of Arizona, Department of Special Education and Rehabilitation.

Narkon, D. E., Wells, J. C., & Segal, L. S. (2011). E-word wall. *Teaching Exceptional Children, 43*(4), 38–45.

National Association for Gifted Children. (2005). National Association for Gifted Children: Position paper: Differentiation of curriculum and instruction. Retrieved from http://www.nagc.org

National Association of School Psychologists. (2001). Save a friend: Tips for teens to prevent suicide. Retrieved from http://www.nasponline.org/resources/crisis_safety/savefriend_general.aspx

National Association of School Psychologists. (2006). New roles in response to intervention: Creating success for schools and children. Retrieved from http://www.nasponline.org/advocacy/New%20Roles%20in%20RTI.pdf

National Center for Children in Poverty. (2008). Child poverty. Retrieved from http://www.nccp.org/topics/childpoverty

National Center for Children in Poverty. (2015).

National Center for Education Statistics, IES. (2010, July). The condition of education 2010 (NCES 2010–028), Indicator 5.

National Center for Education Statistics, IES. (2010, June). Status and trends in the education of racial and ethnic minorities, 2010. (NCES 2010-015), Indicator 8.1.

National Center for Education Statistics, IES. (2011, May). The condition of education 2011. Table A-6-1.

National Center for Education Statistics, Institute of Education Sciences, U.S. Department of Education. Washington, DC.

National Center for Education Statistics. (2010). Number and percentage of children and youth age 3–21 served under the Individuals with Disabilities Education Act (IDEA). (Table A-9-1). Retrieved from: http://nces.ed.gov/programs/coe/tables/table-cwd-1.asp

National Center for Educational Statistics, IES. (2009). IES stands for Institute for Education Sciences. *Fast facts.* Retrieved from http://nces.ed.gov/fastfacts/display.asp?id=59

National Center for Educational Statistics. (2009). Fast facts. Retrieved from http://nces.ed.gov/fastfacts/display.asp?id=64

National Center for Educational Statistics. (2015). Fast facts. Retrieved from http://nces.ed.gov/fastfacts/display.asp?id=59

National Center for Hearing Assessment & Management. (2009). Retrieved from http://www.infanthearing.org/screening/index.html

National Center for Hearing Assessment and Management. (2011). State EHDI/UNHS mandates: Summary table. Retrieved from http://www.infanthearing.org/legislative/summary/index.html

National Center on Accessible Instructional Materials. (2011). Disability-specific resources. Retrieved from http://aim.cast.org/learn/disabilityspecific

National Center on Educational Outcomes. (2012). Alternate assessments for students with disabilities. Retrieved from http://www.cehd.umn.edu/NCEO/TopicAreas/AlternateAssessments/altAssessTopic.htm

National Center on Secondary Education and Transition (NCSET). (2004). Post-secondary supports. Retrieved from http://ncest.org/topics/preparing

National Council of Teachers of English. (2011). Beliefs about the teaching of writing. Retrieved from http://www.ncte.org/

National Council of Teachers of Mathematics. (1989). *Curriculum and evaluation standards for school mathematics* (Report No. SE–050–418). Reston, VA: Author. (ERIC Document Reproduction Service No. ED 304 338)

National Council of Teachers of Mathematics. (2000). Retrieved from http://www.nctm.org

National Council of Teachers of Mathematics. (2006). *Curriculum focal points for prekindergarten through grade 8 mathematics: A quest for coherence.* Reston, VA: National Council of Teachers of Mathematics.

National Council of Teachers of Mathematics. (2009). *Focus in high school mathematics: Reasoning and sense making.* Reston, VA: Author.

National Council of Teachers of Mathematics. (2010). *Making it happen: A guide to interpreting and implementing the Common Core State Standards for mathematics.* Reston, VA: Author.

National Council of Teachers of Mathematics. (2014). *Principles to actions: Ensuring mathematics success for all.* Reston, VA: Author.

National Council on Educational Outcomes. (2012). Accommodations for students with disabilities. Retrieved from http://www.cehd.umn.edu/NCEO/TopicAreas/Accommodations/Accomtopic.htm

National Dissemination Center for Children with Disabilities. (2006). Traumatic brain injury. Retrieved from http://www.old.nichcy.or/pubs/factshe/fsl8txt.htm

National Down Syndrome Society. (2009). Myths and truths. Retrieved from http://www.ndss.org/index.php?view=article&catid=35%3Aabout-down-syndrome&id

National Down Syndrome Society. (2012). Myths and truths. Retrieved from http://www.ndss.org/en/About-Down-Syndrome/Myths-and-Truths/

National Down Syndrome Society. (2015). Down syndrome facts. Retrieved from http://www.ndss.org/down-Syndrome/Down-Syndrome-Facts/

National Early Literacy Panel. (2008). *Developing early literacy: Report of the National Early Literacy Panel.* Washington, DC: National Institute for Literacy.

National Education Association. (2011). Here come the Common Core Standards. Retrieved from http://neatoday.org/2011/05/17/here-come-the-common-core-standards/

National Education Association. (2015). *Understanding the gaps: Who are we leaving behind – and how far?* Retrieved from https://www.nea.org/assets/docs/18021-Closing_Achve_Gap_backgrndr_7-FINAL.pdf

National Education Association. (2016). ESSA implementation beings. Retrieved from http://www.nea.org/home/65276.htm

National Federation for the Blind. (2011). Technology resource list. Retrieved from http://www.nfb.org/technology-resource-list

National Federation of the Blind. (2009). Technology resource list. Retrieved from http://www.nfb.org/nfb/Technology_Resource_List1.asp

National Fragile X Foundation. (2009). What is fragile X? Retrieved from http://www.fragilex.org/html/what.htm

National Fragile X Foundation. (2012). Prevalence of fragile X syndrome. Retrieved from http://www.fragilex.org/?s=prevalence

National Fragile X Foundation. (2012). Prevalence. Retrieved from https://fragilex.org/fragile-s-associated-disorders/prevalence/print/

National Governors Association Center for Best Practices and Council of Chief State School Officers. (2010). *Common Core State Standards for English language arts and literacy in history/social studies, science, and technical subjects: Appendix A: Research supporting key elements of the standards and glossary of key terms.* Washington, DC: Authors. Retrieved from http://www.corestandards.org/assets/Appendix

National Health Information Center. (2004). Retrieved from http://www.health.gov/nhic

National Institute of Mental Health (HIMH). (2008). *Attention deficit hyperactivity disorder*. Bethesda, MD: Author.

National Institute of Mental Health. (2009a). Anxiety disorders. Retrieved from http://www.nimh.nih.gov/health/topics/anxiety-disorders/index/shtml

National Institute of Mental Health. (2009b). Bipolar disorder in children and teens. Retrieved from http://www.imh.nih.gov/health/publications/bipolar-disorder-in-children-and-teens-easy-to-read/

National Institute of Mental Health. (2009c). Schizophrenia. Retrieved from http://www.nimh.nih.gov/health/topics/schizophrenia/index.shtml

National Institute of Mental Health. (2015). Attention deficit hyperactivity disorder. Retrieved from: http://www.nimh.nih.gov/health/topics/attention-deficit-hyperactivity-disorder-adhd/index.shtml

National Institute on Deafness and Other Communication Disorders. (2014). *Stuttering*. Retrieved from http://www.nidcd.nih.gov/health/voice/pages/stutter.aspx

National Institute on Deafness and Other Communication Disorders. (2015). *Specific language impairment*. Retrieved from http:/www.nidcd.hig.gov/health/voice/pages/specific-language-impairment.aspx

National Institutes of Health and Human Development. (2009). Fragile X syndrome. Retrieved from http://www.nichd.nih.gov/health/topics/fragile_x_syndrome.cfm?renderforprint=1

National Institutes of Health. (2001). *Rett syndrome—Autism research at the NICHD* (01-4960). Washington, DC: U.S. Government Printing Office.

National Joint Committee on Learning Disabilities (2011, January 1). Comprehensive assessment and evaluation of students with learning disabilities: A paper prepared by the national joint committee on learning disabilities. *The Free Library*. Retrieved from http://www.thefreelibrary.com/Comprehensive assessment and evaluation of students with learning ... -a0251534699

National Joint Committee on Learning Disabilities (NJCLD). (2004). State and district-wide assessments and students with learning disabilities: A guide for states and school districts. *Learning Disability Quarterly, 27*, 67–71.

National Middle School Association. (2006). Highly qualified: A balanced approach. Retrieved from http://www.nmsa.org/portals/o/pdf/about/position_statements/EdWeek.pdf

National Organization on Fetal Alcohol Syndrome. (2009). FAQs. Retrieved from http://www.nofas.org/faqs.aspx?id=9

National Organization on Fetal Alcohol Syndrome. (2012). FAQs. Retrieved from http://www.nofas.org/faqs.aspx?id=19 (NOFAS)

National Organization on Fetal Alcohol Syndrome. (2014). What is the prevalence of fetal alcohol spectrum disorders in the United States? Retrieved from http://nofas.org/faqs/what-is-the-prevalence-of-fetal-alcohol-spectrum-disorders-in-the-united-states.html

National Reading Panel. (2000). *Teaching children to read: An evidence-based assessment of the scientific research literature on reading and its implications for reading instruction*. Bethesda, MD: National Institutes of Health, National Institute of Child Health and Human Development.

National Research Council. (2001). *Educating children with autism*. Washington, DC: National Academies Press.

Navarrete. L. (2013). English language learners: The impact of language and socio-cultural factors on learning. Retrieved from: http://www.council-for-learning-disabilities.org/wp-content/uploads/2013/11/CLD-Infosheet-Diversity-2013.pdf

Neale, M. H., & Test, D. W. (2010). Effects of the "I Can Use Effort" strategy on quality of student verbal contributions and individualized education program participation with third- and fourth-grade students with disabilities. *Remedial and Special Education, 33*(3), 184–194.

Neef, N. A., McCord, B. E., & Ferreri, S. J. (2006). Effects of guided notes versus completed notes during lectures on college students' quiz performance. *Journal of Applied Behavior Analysis, 39*, 123–130.

Nelson, J. R., Stage, S., Duppong-Hurley, K., Synhorst, L., & Epstein, M. (2007). Risk factors predictive of the problem behavior of children at risk for emotional and behavioral disorders. *Exceptional Children, 73*, 367–379.

Nese, J. F., Park, B. J., Alonzo, J., & Tindal, G. (2011). Applied curriculum-based measurement as a predictor of high-stakes assessment: Implications for researchers and teachers. *Elementary School Journal, 111*(4), 608–624.

Ness, M. K. (2008). Supporting secondary readers: When teachers provide the "what," not the "how." *American Secondary Education, 37*, 80–95.

Neubert, D. A. (2003). The role of assessment in the transition to adult life process for students with disabilities. *Exceptionality, 11*(2), 63–76.

Nevin, A. I., Villa, R. A., & Thousand, J. S. (2009). *A guide to co-teaching with paraeducators: Practical tips for K–12 educators*. Corwin.

Newman, R. S. (1990). Children's help-seeking in the classroom: The role of motivational factors and attitudes. *Journal of Educational Psychology, 82*(1), 71–80.

Newman, R. S., & Goldin, L. (1990). Children's reluctance to seek help with schoolwork. *Journal of Educational Psychology, 82*(1), 92–100.

Newton, K. J., Willard, C., & Teufel, C. (2014). An examination of the ways that students with learning disabilities solve fraction computation problems. *The Elementary School Journal,115*(1), 1–21.

Nierengarten, G. (2013). Supporting co-teaching teams in high schools: Twenty research-based practices. *American Secondary Education, 42*(1), 73–83.

Nieto, S. (1992). *Affirming diversity: The sociopolitical context of multicultural education*. New York: Longman.

Nieto, S. (1994). Lessons from students on creating a chance to dream. *Harvard Educational Review, 64*, 392–426.

Nilsson, N. (2008). A critical analysis of eight informal reading inventories. *The Reading Teacher, 61*(7), 526–536.

Nippold, M. A., (1998). *Later language development: The school age and adolescent years*. (2nd ed.). Austin, TX: PRO-ED.

No Child Left Behind Act of 2001. Pub. L. No. 107-110, 115 Stat. 1425. (2001).

Nordness, P. D. (2005). A comparison of school-based and community-based adherence to wraparound during family planning meetings. *Education and Treatment of Children, 28*, 308–320.

Nunley, K. F. (2006). *Differentiating the high school classroom: Solution strategies for 18 common obstacles*. Thousand Oaks, CA: Corwin Press.

O'Bryon, E. C., & Rogers, M. R. (2010). Bilingual school psychologists' assessment practices with English language learners. *Psychology in Schools, 47*, 1018–1034.

O'Connor, R. (2000). Increasing the intensity of intervention in kindergarten and first grade. *Learning Disabilities Research and Practice, 15*, 43–54.

O'Connor, R. E. (2011). Phoneme awareness and the alphabetic principle. In R. O'Connor & P. Vadasy (Eds.), *Handbook of reading interventions* (pp. 9–26). New York, NY: Guilford Press.

O'Donnell, J., & Kirkner, S. L. (2014). The impact of a collaborative family involvement program on Latino families and children's educational performance. *School Community Journal, 24*(1), 211–234.

O'Kelley Wingage, K., Rutledge, V. C., & Johnston, L. (2014). Choosing the right word walls for your classroom. *Young Children, 69*(1), 52–57.

O'Neill, R. E., Horner, R. H., Albin, R. W., Storey, K., & Sprague, J. R. (1997). *Functional assessment and program development for problem behavior: A practical handbook*. Sycamore, IL: Sycamore Publishing.

O'Reilly, M. F., & Glynn, D. (1995). Using a process social skills training approach with adolescents with mild intellectual disabilities in a high school setting. *Education and Training in Mental Retardation and Developmental Disabilities, 30*, 187–198.

O'Reilly, M. F., Lancioni, G., & Kierans, I. (2000). Teaching leisure social skills to adults with moderate mental retardation: An analysis of acquisition, generalization, and maintenance. *Education and Training in Mental Retardation and Developmental Disabilities, 35*, 250–258.

O'Reilly, M. F., Lancioni, G., Sigafoos, J., O'Donoghue, D., Lacey, C., & Edrisinha, S. (2004). Teaching social skills to adults with intellectual disabilities: A comparison of external control and problem-solving interventions. *Research in Developmental Disabilities, 25*, 399–412.

O'Reilly, M. F., McNally, D., Sigafoos, J., Lancioni, G. E., Green, V., Edrisinha, C., ... Didden, R. (2008). Examination of a social problem-solving intervention to treat selective mutism. *Behavior Modification, 32*(2), 182–195.

O'Reilly, M., Sigafoos, J., Lancioni, G., Edrishina, C., & Andrews, A. (2005). An examination of the effects of a classroom activity schedule on levels of self-injury and engagement for a child with severe autism. *Journal of Autism and Developmental Disorders, 35*, 305–311.

O'Shea, D. J., & O'Shea, L. J. (2001). Why learn about students' families? In D. J. O'Shea, L. J. O'Shea, R. Algozzine, & D. J. Hammitte (Eds.), *Families and teachers of individuals with disabilities: Collaborative orientations and responsive practices* (pp. 5–24). Boston: Allyn & Bacon.

O'Shea, D. J., O'Shea, L. J., Algozzine, R., & Hammitte, D. J. (2001). *Families and teachers of individuals with disabilities: Collaborative orientations and responsive practices*. Boston: Allyn and Bacon.

Oczkus, L. (2009). *Interactive think aloud lessons: 25 surefire ways to engage students and improve comprehension*. Newark, DE: International Reading Association.

Odom, S. L., Horner, M. E., Snell, M. E., & Blacher, J. (2007). The construct of developmental disabilities. In S. L. Odom, R. H. Horner, M. E. Snell, & J. Blacher (Eds.), *Handbook of developmental disabilities* (pp. 3–14). New York: Guilford Press.

Offit, P. A. (2008). *Autism's false prophets: Bad science, risky medicine, and the search for a cure*. New York: Columbia University Press.

Ogbu, J. U. (1978). *Minority education and caste: The American system in cross-cultural perspective*. New York: Academic Press.

Ogbu, J. U. (1990). Minority education in comparative perspective. *Journal of Negro Education, 59*, 45–57.

Ogbu, J. U. (1992). Understanding cultural diversity and learning. *Educational Researcher, 21*(8), 5–14 + 24.

Ogbu, J. U. (2008). *Minority status, oppositional culture, and schooling*. New York: Routledge.

Ogle, D. (1986). KWL: A teaching model that develops active reading of expository text. *The Reading Teacher, 39*, 564–570.

Ogle, D. (1989). Implementing strategic teaching. *Educational Leadership, 46*(4), 47–48, 57–60.

Oliver, R. M., & Reschly, D. J. (2007). *Effective classroom management: Teacher preparation and professional development*. Washington, DC: National Comprehensive Center for Teacher Quality.

Orelove, F. P., Sobsey, D., & Silberman, R. K. (2004). *Educating children with multiple disabilities: A collaborative approach* (4th ed.). Baltimore, MD: Paul H. Brookes.

Orosco, M. J. (2014). Word problem strategy for Latino English language learners at risk for math disabilities. *Learning Disability Quarterly, 37*(1), 45–53.

Osborne, A. G., & DiMattia, P. (1994). The IDEA's least restrictive environment mandate: Legal implications. *Exceptional Children, 61*, 6–14.

OSEP Technical Assistance Center on Positive Behavioral Interventions and Supports. (2009). Reducing behavior problems in the elementary school. Retrieved from http://www.pbis.org/

Otero, T. L., Schatz, R. B., Merrill, A. C., & Bellini, S. (2015). Social skills training for youth with autism spectrum disorders: A follow-up. *Child and Adolescent Psychiatric Clinics of North America, 24*(1), 99–115. Retrieved from http://dx.doi.org/10.1016/j.chc.2014.09.002

Ovando, C. J, & Combs, M. C. (2012). *Bilingual and ESL classrooms: Teaching in multicultural contexts* (5th ed.). Boston: McGraw-Hill.

Ovando, C. J., & Collier, V. P. (1998). *Bilingual and ESL classrooms: Teaching in multicultural contexts* (2nd ed.). Boston: McGraw-Hill.

Ovando, C. J., Collier, V. P., & Combs, M. C. (2006). *Bilingual and ESL classrooms: Teaching in multicultural contexts* (4th ed.). Boston: McGraw-Hill.

Owens, E. B., Cardoos, S. L., & Hinshaw, S. P. (2015). Developmental progression and gender differences among individuals with ADHD. In R. A. Barkley (Ed.), *Attention-deficit hyperactivity disorder: A handbook for diagnosis and treatment* (4th ed., pp. 223–255). New York: Guilford.

Owens, R. E. (2010). *Language disorders: A functional approach to assessment and intervention* (5th ed.). Boston: Pearson/Allyn & Bacon.

Owens, R. E., Farinella, K. A., & Metz, D. E. (2015). *Introduction to communication disorders: A lifespan evidence-based approach* (5th ed.). Boston: Pearson.

Owens, R. E., Jr. (2008). *Language development: An introduction* (7th ed.). Boston: Allyn & Bacon.

Owens, R. E., Jr. (2016). *Language development: An introduction* (9th ed.). Boston: Pearson.

Pacheco, M. B., & Goodwin, A. P. (2013). Putting two and two together: Middle school students' morphological problem-solving strategies for unknown words. *Journal of Adolescent and Adult Literacy, 56*(7), 541–553.

Padden, C. A., & Humphries, T. L. (2006). *Inside deaf culture*. Cambridge, MA: Harvard University Press.

Palincsar, A. S. (1986). The role of dialogue in providing scaffolded instruction. *Educational Psychologist, 21*(1/2), 73–98.

Palinscsar, A. S., & Brown, A. L. (1984). The reciprocal teaching of comprehension-fostering and comprehension-monitoring activities. *Cognition and Instruction, 1*, 117–175.

Palumbo, A., Kramer-Vida, L., & Hunt, C. V. (2015). Teaching vocabulary and morphology in intermediate grades. *Preventing School Failure: Alternative Education for Children and Youth, 59*(2), 109–115.

Papay, C., & Griffin, M. (2015). Developing inclusive college opportunities for students with intellectual and developmental disabilities. *Research and Practice for Persons with Severe Disabilities, 38*(2), 110–116.

Papazoglou, A., Jacobson, L. A., McCabe, M., Kaufmann, W., & Zabel, T. A. (2014). To ID or not to ID? Changes in classification rates of intellectual disability using *DSM-5*. *Intellectual and Developmental Disabilities, 52*(3), 165–174.

Pardini, P. (2002). The history of special education. *Rethinking Schools Online, 16*(3), 1.

Parette, H. P., Hourcade, J., & Blum, C. (2011). Using animation in Microsoft PowerPoint to enhance engagement and learning in young learners with developmental delay. *Teaching Exceptional Children, 43*(4), 58–67.

Park, H. S., & Gaylord-Ross, R. (1989). A problem- solving approach to social skills training in employment settings with mentally retarded youth. *Journal of Applied Behavior Analysis, 22*(4), 373–380.

Park, J., Turnbull, P., & Turnbull, H. R. (2002). Impacts of poverty on quality of life in families of children with disabilities. *Exceptional Children, 68*, 151–170.

Parrish, P. R., & Stodden, R. A. (2009). Aligning assessment and instruction with state standards for children with significant disabilities. *Teaching Exceptional Children, 41*, 46–56.

Pastor, P. N., & Reuben, C. A. (2008). Diagnosed attention deficit hyperactivity disorder and learning disabilities: United States 2004–2006. *Vital Health Statistics* (10), 1–14.

Patall, E. A., Cooper, H., & Robinson, J. C. (2008). Parent involvement in homework: A research synthesis. *Review of Educational Research, 78*(4), 1039–1101.

Patterson, D. S., Jolivette, K., & Crosby, S. (2006). Social skills training for students who demonstrate poor self-control. *Beyond Behavior, 15*, 23–27.

Pauk, W. (1989). *How to study in college* (4th ed.). Boston: Houghton Mifflin.

Payne, K. T., & Taylor, O. L. (1998). Communication differences and disorders. In G. H. Shames, E. H. Wiig, & W. A. Secord (Eds.), *Human communication disorders: An introduction* (5th ed., pp. 118–154). Boston: Allyn & Bacon.

PCI Education. (2008). *SpellRead©*. San Antonio, TX: Author.

Peal, E., & Lambert, W. (1962). The relation of bilingualism to intelligence. *Psychological Monographs, 7*(546), 1–12.

Pearson, P. D., & Johnson, D. D. (1978). *Teaching reading comprehension*. New York: Holt, Rinehart & Winston.

Pearson, P. D., Hiebert, E. H., & Kamil, M. L. (2007). Theory and research into practice. Vocabulary assessment: What we know and need to learn. *Reading Research Quarterly, 42*(2), 282–296.

Pearson, P. D., Hiebert, E. H., & Kamil, M. L. (2007). Vocabulary assessment: What we know and what we need to learn. *Reading Research Quarterly, 42*(2) 282–296.

Peberdy, D., & Hammersley, J. (2009). *Brilliant meetings: What to know, say, and do to have fewer, better, meetings*. Upper Saddle River, NJ: Prentice Hall.

Pecyna-Rhyner, P., Lehr, D., & Pudlas, K. (1990). An analysis of teacher responsiveness to communicative initiations of children with handicaps. *Language, Speech, and Hearing Services in Schools, 21*, 91–97.

Pedulla, J. J., Abrams, L. M., Madaus, G. F., Russell, M. K., Ramos, M. A., & Miao, J. (2003). *Perceived effects of state-mandated testing programs on teaching and learning: Findings from a national survey of teachers*. Boston: National Board on Educational Testing and Public Policy, Boston College.

Peng, P., & Fuchs, D. (2014). A meta-analysis of working memory deficits in children with learning difficulties: Is there a difference between verbal domain and numerical domain? *Journal of Learning Disabilities*, 0022219414521667.

Peregoy, S. F., & Boyle, O. F. (2005). *Reading, writing, and learning in ESL: A resource book for K–12 teachers* (4th ed.). Boston: Allyn & Bacon.

Peregoy, S. F., & Boyle, O. F. (2013). *Reading, writing, and learning in ESL: A resource book for K–12 teachers* (6th ed.). Boston: Pearson.

Pereira, N., & de Oliveira, L. C. (2015). Meeting the linguistic needs of high-potential English language learners: What teachers need to know. *Teaching Exceptional Children, 47*(4), 208–215.

Perry, Y. D. (2012). *Practitioner perceptions of their implementation of response to intervention (RtI)* (Order No. 3511789). Available from Dissertations & Theses @ University of Miami. (1023124881). Retrieved from http://search.proquest.com/docview/1023124881?accountid=14585.

Perry, Y., & Schumm, J. S. (in progress). Practitioner perceptions of the implementation of components of response to intervention.

Peterson, P. E., & Hess, F. M. (2008). Few states set world-class standards. *Education Next, 8*, 70–73.

Peterson, S. K., Mercer, C. D., & O'Shea, L. (1988). Teaching learning disabled students place value using the concrete to abstract sequence. *Learning Disabilities Research, 4*, 52–56.

Petrilli, M. J. (2011). All together now? Educating high and low achievers in the same classroom. *Education Next, 11*(1), 48–55.

Peverly, S. T., Garner, J. K., & Vekaria, P. C. (2014). Both handwriting speed and selective attention are important to lecture note-taking. *Reading and Writing, 27*, 1–30.

Pfannensteil, K. H., Bryant, D., Bryant, B., & Porterfield, J. (2015). Teaching word problems to primary-level struggling students. *Intervention in School & Clinic, 5*(50), 291–296.

Phillips, V., & Wong, C. (2012). Teaching to the Common Core by design, not accident. *Phi Delta Kappan, 93*(7), 31–38.

Pickett, A. L. (2008). Roles and responsibilities of paraeducators working with learners with developmental disabilities: Translating research into practice. In H. P. Parette & G. R. Peterson-Karlan (Eds.), *Research-based practices in developmental disabilities* (2nd ed., pp. 501–520). Austin, TX: PRO-ED.

Pierangelo, R., & Giuliani, G. (2007). *The educator's diagnostic manual of disabilities and disorders*. San Francisco, CA: Wiley.

Pierce, C. D., Reid, R., & Epstein, M. H. (2004). Teacher-mediated interventions for children with EBD and their academic outcomes. *Remedial and Special Education, 25*(3), 175–188.

Pimperton, H., & Kennedy, C. R. (2012). The impact of early identification of permanent childhood hearing impairment on speech and language outcomes. *Archives of Disease in Childhood*, archdischild-2011.

Pliszka, S. R. (2015). Comorbid psychiatric disorders in children with ADHD. In R. A. Barkley (Ed.), *Attention-deficit hyperactivity disorder: A handbook for diagnosis and treatment* (4th ed., pp. 140–168). New York: Guilford.

Plotner, A. J., & Marshall, K. J. (2015). Postsecondary education programs for students with an intellectual disability: Facilitators and barriers to implementation. *Intellectual and Developmental Disabilities, 53*(1), 58–69.

Plumley, K. (2008). Assistive listening devices in the classroom. Retrieved from http://www.deaf-students.suite101.com/article.cfm/assistive_listening_devices_in_the_classroom

Pocock, A., Lambros, S., Karvonen, M., Test, D. W., Algozzine, B., Wood, W., & Martin, J. E. (2002). Successful strategies for promoting self-advocacy among students with LD: The LEAD group. *Intervention in School and Clinic, 37*, 209–216.

Polloway, E. A., Lubin, J., Smith, J. D., & Patton, J. R. (2010). Mild intellectual disabilities: Legacies and trends in concepts and educational practices. *Education and Training in Autism and Developmental Disabilities, 45*(1) 54–68.

Polsgrove, L., & Smith, S. W. (2004). Informed practice in teaching self-control to children with emotional and behavioral disorders. In R. B. Rutherford, M. M. Quinn, & S. R. Mathur (Eds.), *Handbook of research in emotional and behavioral disorders* (pp. 399–425). New York: Guilford Press.

Popham, W. J. (2009). Assessment literacy for teachers: Faddish or fundamental? *Theory into Practice, 48*(1), 4–11.

Popham, W. J. (2011). Assessment literacy overlooked: A teacher educator's confession. *The Teacher Educator, 46*, 265–273.

Popham, W. J. (2014). *Classroom assessment: What teachers need to know* (7th ed.). Boston: Pearson.

Porter, A., McMaken, J., Hwang, J., & Yang, R. (2011). Common Core Standards: The new U.S. intended curriculum. *Educational Researcher, 40*(3), 103–116.

Portway, S., & Johnson, B. (2005). Do you know I have Asperger's syndrome? Risks of a non-obvious disability. *Health, Risk, and Society, 7*, 73–83.

Powell, S. R., & Stecker, P. M. (2014). Using data-based individualization to intensify mathematics intervention for students with disabilities. *Teaching Exceptional Children, 46*(4), 31–37.

Prater, M. A., & Dyches, T. T. (2008). Books that portray characters with disabilities: A topic 25 list for children and young adults. *Teaching Exceptional Children, 40*, 32–38.

Presley, I., & D'Andrea, M. (2009). *Assistive technology for students who are blind or visually impaired: A guide to assessment*. New York: American Federation for the Blind Press.

Pressley, M., & Harris, K. R. (2006). Cognitive strategies instruction: From basic research to classroom instruction. In P. A. Alexander & P. Winne (Eds.), *Handbook of educational psychology* (2nd ed., pp. 265–286). New York: Macmillan.

Pressley, M., & McCormick, C. (1995). *Advanced educational psychology for educators, researchers, and policymakers*. New York, NY: HarperCollins.

Pressman, R. M., Sugarman, D. B., Nemon, M. L., Desjarlais, J., Owens, J. A., & Schettini-Evans, A. (2015). Homework and family stress: With consideration of parents' self confidence, educational level, and cultural background. *The American Journal of Family Therapy, 43*(4), 297–313.

Prevatte, L. (2007). *Middle school literacy centers: Connecting struggling readers to literature*. Gainesville, FL: Maupin House Publishing.

Protacio, M. S., & Edwards, P. A. (2015). Restructuring sharing time for English learners and their parents. *The Reading Teacher, 69*(60), 413–421.

Protheroe, N. (2009). Good homework policy=good teaching. *Principal, 89*(1), 42–25.

PubMed. (2010, May). Retrieved from http://www.ncbi.nim.nih.gov/pubmedhealth

Pugach, M. C., & Johnson, L. J. (1995). *Collaborative practitioners, collaborative schools*. Denver, CO: Love.

Pugach, M. C., & Johnson, L. J. (2002). *Collaborative practitioners, collaborative schools* (2nd ed.). Denver, CO: Love.

Quay, H. C., & Hogan, A. E. (Eds.). (2013). *Handbook of disruptive behavior disorders*. New York: Springer Science & Business Media.

Quay, H. C., & Werry, J. S. (1986). *Psychopathological disorders of childhood*. New York: Wiley.

Quinlan, T. (2004). Speech recognition technology and students with writing difficulties: Improving fluency. *Journal of Educational Psychology, 96*, 337–346.

Quinn, M. M., Rutherford, R. R., Leone, P. E., Osher, D. M., & Poirier, J. M. (2005). Youth with disabilities in juvenile corrections: A national survey. *Exceptional Children, 71*(3), 339–345.

Radencich, M. C., Beers, P. C., & Schumm, J. S. (1993). *A handbook for the K–12 reading resource specialist*. Boston, MA: Allyn & Bacon

Rafferty, L. A. (2007). "They just won't listen to me": A teacher's guide to positive behavioral interventions. *Childhood Education, 84*, 102–105.

Rakow, S. (2012). Helping gifted students SOAR. *Educational Leadership, 69*(5), 34–40.

Ralabate, P. K. (2011). Universal design for learning: Meeting the needs of all students. *The ASHA Leader, 16*, 14–17.

Ralabate, P. K., Currie-Rubin, R., Boucher, A., & Bartecchi, J. (2014). Collaborative planning using universal design for learning. *Perspectives on School-Based Issues, 15*, 26–31.

Ramani, G. B., & Eason, S. H. (2015). Learning early math through play and games. *Kappan Magazine, 96*(8), 27–32.

Ramdoss, S., Lang, R., Mulloy, A., Franco, J., O'Reilly, M., Didden, R., & Lancioni, G. (2011). Use of computer-based intervention to improve communication in individuals with autism spectrum disorders: A systematic review. *Journal of Behavioral Education, 20*, 55–76.

RAND Reading Study Group. (2002). *Reading for understanding: Toward an R&D program in reading comprehension.* Washington, DC: RAND.

Rao, K., Hitchcock, C. H., Boisvert, P. C., Kilpatrick. E., & Corbiell, C. (2012). Do it yourself: Video self-modeling made easy. *Teaching Exceptional Children, 45*(1), 1.

Raphael, T. E. (1982). Question-answering strategies for children. *The Reading Teacher, 36*, 188.

Raphael, T. E. (1984). Teaching learners about sources of information for answering comprehension questions. *Journal of Reading, 27*, 303–311.

Raphael, T. E. (1986). Teaching question–answer relationships revisited. *The Reading Teacher, 39*(6), 516–523.

Raphael, T. E., Highfield, K., & Au, K. H. (2012). *QAR now: Question answer relationships.* New York: Scholastic.

Rasinski, T. V. (2010). *The fluent reader: Oral and silent reading strategies for building fluency, word recognition, and comprehension* (2nd ed.). New York: Scholastic.

Rasinski, T. V., & Nageldinger, J. K. (2015). *The fluency factor: Authentic instruction and assessment for reading success in the Common Core classroom.* New York: Teachers College Press.

Rasinski, T., Tildirim, K., & Nageldinger, J. (2011). Building fluency through the phrased text lesson. *The Reading Teacher, 65*(4), 252–255.

Raskind, M. H., Goldberg, R. J., Higgins, E. L., & Herman, K. L. (1999). Patterns of change and predictors of success in individuals with learning disabilities: Results from a twenty-year longitudinal study. *Learning Disabilities Research and Practice, 14*(1), 35–49.

Rathvon, N. (2004). *Early reading assessment: A practitioner's handbook.* New York: Guilford Press.

Ravitch, D. (1995). *National standards in American education: A citizen's guide.* Washington, DC: Brookings Institution.

Raygor, A. L. (1977). The Raygor readability estimate: A quick and easy way to determine difficulty. In P. D. Pearson (Ed.), *Reading: Theory, research and practice: Twenty-sixth yearbook of the National Reading Conference* (pp. 259–263). Clemson, SC: National Reading Conference.

Raymond, E. B. (2012). *Learners with mild disabilities: A characteristics approach.* (4th ed.). Boston: Pearson.

Rayner, G. (2005). Meeting the educational needs of the student with Asperger syndrome through assessment, advocacy, and accommodations. In K. P. Stoddart (Ed.), *Children, youth and adults with Asperger syndrome: Integrating multiple perspectives* (pp. 184–196). London: Jessica Kingsley.

Rea, P. (2005). 20 ways to engage your administrator in your collaboration initiative. *Intervention in School and Clinic, 40*, 312–316.

Read, S., Landon-Hays, M., & Martin-Rivas, A. (2014). Gradually releasing responsibility to students writing persuasive text. *The Reading Teacher, 67*(6), 469–477.

Reddy, L. A., Newman, E., De Thomas, C. A., & Chun, V. (2009). Effectiveness of school-based prevention and intervention programs for children and adolescents with emotional disturbance: A meta-analysis. *Journal of School Psychology, 47*(2), 77–99.

Reed, F. D., Hirst, J. M., &, Hyman, S. R. (2012). Assessment and treatment of stereotypic behavior in children with autism and other developmental disabilities: A thirty year review. *Research in Autism Spectrum Disorders, 6*, 422–430.

Reichow, B., & Volkmar, F. R. (2010). Social skills interventions for individuals with autism: Evaluation for evidence-based practices within a best evidence synthesis framework. *Journal of Autism and Developmental Disorders, 40*(2), 149–166.

Reid, R., Lienemann, T. O., & Hagaman, J. L. (2013). *Strategy instruction for students with learning disabilities.* New York: Guilford Publications.

Reinke, W. M., Herman, K. C., & Stormont, M. (2013). Classroom-level positive behavior supports in schools implementing SW-PBIS identifying areas for enhancement. *Journal of Positive Behavior Interventions, 15*(1), 39–50.

Reis, S. M., & Renzulli, J. S. (2005). *Curriculum compacting: An easy start to differentiating instruction.* Waco, TX: Prufrock Press.

Reis, S. M., & Renzulli, J. S. (2009). Myth 1: The gifted constitute one single homogeneous group and giftedness is a way of being that stays in the person over time and experiences. *Gifted Child Quarterly, 53*(4), 233–235.

Renzulli, J. S. (2012). Reexamining the role of gifted education and talent development for the 21st century: A four-part theoretical approach. *Gifted Child Quarterly, 56*(3), 150–159.

Resnick, L., & Zurawsky, C. (2005). Standards-based reform and accountability: Getting back on course. *American Educator,* 1–13.

Reuda, R., & Genzuk, M. (2007). Sociocultural scaffolding as a means toward academic self-regulation: Paraeducators as cultural brokers. *Focus on Exceptional Children, 40*(3), 1–6.

Reutzel, D. R., & Clark, S. (2011). Organizing literacy classrooms for effective instruction: A survival guide. *The Reading Teacher, 66*(2), 96–109.

Reutzel, D. R., & Cooter, R. B. (2011). *Strategies for reading assessment and instruction.* Upper Saddle River, NJ: Pearson.

Reutzel, D. R., & Hollingsworth, P. M. (1993). Effects of fluency training on second graders' reading comprehension. *Journal of Educational Research, 86*, 325–331.

Reyes, E. I., & Bos, C. S. (1998). Interactive semantic mapping and charting: Enhancing content-area learning for language-minority students. In R. M. Gersten & R. T. Jimenez (Eds.), *Promoting learning for culturally and linguistically diverse students* (pp. 133–150). Belmont, CA: Wadsworth.

Reyes, I., Kenner, C., Moll, L. C., & Orellana, M. F. (2012). Biliteracy among children and youths. *Reading Research Quarterly, 47*(3), 307–327.

Richardson, J. (2005). Transform your group into a team. *Tools for Schools: For a Dynamic Community of Learners and Leaders, 9*(2), 1–8

Richler, J., Bishop, S. L., Kleinke, J. R., & Lord, C. (2007). Restricted and repetitive behaviors in young children with autism spectrum disorders. *Journal of Autism and Developmental Disorders, 37*(1), 73–85. Retrieved from http://dx.doi.org/10.1007/s10803-006-0332-6

Riddle M. A., Yershova, K., Lazzaretto, D., Paykina, N., Yenokyan, G., Greenhill, L., Abikoff, H., Vitiello, B., Wigal, T., McCracken, J. T., Kollins, S. H., Murray, D. W., Wigal, S., Kastelic, E., McGough, J. J., dosReis, S., Bauzó-Rosario, A., Stehli, A., & Posner, K. (2013). The Preschool ADHD Treatment Study (PATS) 6-year follow-up. *Journal of the American Academy of Child and Adolescent Psychiatry, 3*(52), 264–278.

Rieger, A., & McGrail, E. (2015). Exploring children's literature with authentic representations of disability. *Kappa Delta Pi Record, 51*(1), 18–23.

Rinaldi, C., & Samson, J. (2008). English language learners and response to intervention: Referral considerations. *Teaching Exceptional Children, 40*, 6–14.

Risko, V. J., & Walker-Dalhouse, D. (2009). Parents and teachers: Talking with or past one another or not talking at all? *The Reading Teacher, 62*(5), 442–444

Rispoli, M., Franco, J., Van der Meer, L., Lang, R., & Camargo, S. (2010). The use of speech generating devices in communication interventions for individuals with developmental disabilities: A review of the literature. *Developmental Neurorehabilitation, 13*, 276–293.

Rispoli, M., Neely, L., Lang, R., & Ganz, J. (2011). Training paraprofessionals to implement interventions for people autism spectrum disorders: A systematic review. *Developmental Neurorehabilitation, 14*, 378–388.

Rispoli, M., O'Reilly, M. F., Sigafoos, J., Lang, R., Kang, S., Lancioni, G., & Parker, R. (2011). The effects of presession satiation on challenging behavior and academic engagement for children with autism during classroom instruction. *Education and Training in Autism and Developmental Disabilities, 46*, 607–618.

Rittle-Johnson, B., Fyfe, E. R., Loehr, A. M., & Miller, M. R. (2015). Beyond numeracy in preschool: Adding patterns to the equation. *Early Childhood Research Quarterly, 31*, 101–112.

Rivera, D., & Deutsch-Smith, D. (1988). Using a demonstration strategy to teach midschool students with learning disabilities to compute long division. *Journal of Learning Disabilities, 21*, 71–81.

Roach, A. T., Kurz, A., & Elliott, S. N. (2015). Facilitating opportunity to learn for students with disabilities with instructional feedback data. *Preventing School Failure: Alternative Education for Children and Youth*, (ahead-of-print), 1–11.

Roberts, W., Milich, R., & Barkley, R. A. (2015). Primary symptoms, diagnostic criteria, subtyping, and prevalence of ADHD. In R. A. Barkley (Ed.), *Attention-deficit hyperactivity disorder: A handbook for diagnosis and treatment* (4th ed., pp. 51–80). New York: Guilford.

Robinson, F. P. (1941). *Effective study.* New York: Harper & Row.

Robinson, N., Zigler, E., & Gallagher, J. (2000). Two tails of the normal curve: Similarities and differences in the study of mental retardation and giftedness. *American Psychologist, 55*, 1413–1424.

Roblyer, M. D. (2016). *Integrating educational technology into teaching* (7th ed.). Boston: Pearson.

Rock, M. L. (2005). Use of strategic self-monitoring to enhance academic engagement, productivity, and accuracy of students with and without exceptionalities. *Journal of Positive Behavior Interventions, 7*(1), 3–17.

Rodger, E. B. (2011). Parents as partners: Tips for involving parents in your classroom. *Child Education, 87*(5), 7–8.

Roeber, E. (2002). *Setting standards on alternate assessments* (Synthesis Report 42). Minneapolis: University of Minneapolis, National Center on Educational Outcomes. Retrieved from http://education.umn.edu/NCEO/OnlinePubs/Synthesis42.html

Roid, G. (2003). *Stanford-Binet Intelligence Scales* (5th ed.). Itasca, IL: Riverside.

Roisen, N. J., Blondis, T. A., Irwin, M., & Stein, M. (1994). Adaptive functioning in children with attention-deficit hyperactivity disorder. *Archives of Pediatric and Adolescent Medicine, 148*, 1037–1088.

Rolstad, K., Mahoney, K., & Glass, G. V. (2005). The big picture: A Meta-analysis of program effectiveness research on English language learners. *Educational Policy, 19*(4), 572–594.

Ronan, K. R., & Kazantzis, N. (2006). The use of between-session (homework) activities in psychotherapy: Conclusions from the Journal of Psychotherapy. *Journal of Psychotherapy Integration, 16*(2), 254–259.

Ronksley-Pavia, M. (2015). A model of twice-exceptionality explaining and defining the apparent paradoxical combination of disability and giftedness in childhood. *Journal for the Education of the Gifted*, 0162353215592499.

Rose, D. H., & Gravel, J. W. (2010). Universal design for learning. In P. Peterson, E. Baker, & B. McGraw (Eds.), *International encyclopedia of education* (pp. 119–124). Oxford: Elsevier.

Rose, D. H., & Meyer, A. (2002). *Teaching every student in the digital age: Universal design for learning.* Alexandria, VA: ASCD Publications.

Rose, M. C. (2005). Handle with care: The difficult parent–teacher conference. Retrieved from http://teacher.scholastic.com/products/instructor/handlewithcare.htm

Rosel, J., Caballer, A., Jara, P., & Oliver, J. C. (2005). Verbalism in the narrative language of children who are blind and sighted. *Journal of Visual Impairment and Blindness, 99*, 413–425.

Rosenberg, M. S., Wilson, R., Maheady, L., & Sindelar, P. T. (1997). *Educating students with behavior disorders* (2nd ed.). Boston: Allyn & Bacon.

Rosenshine, B., & Meister, C. (1994). Reciprocal teaching: A review of the research. *Review of Educational Research, 64*, 479–530.

Roth, K., & Dabrowski, J. (2014). Extending interactive writing into grades 2–5. *The Reading Teacher, 68*(1), 33–44.

Roth, R. M., & Saykin, A. J., (2004). Executive dysfunction in attention-deficit/hyperactivity disorder: Cognitive and neuroimaging findings. *Psychiatric Clinics of North America, 27*(1), 83–96.

Rourke, B. P. (1993). Arithmetic disabilities, specific and otherwise: A neuropsychological perspective. *Journal of Learning Disabilities, 26*(4), 214–226.

Rowe, M. B. (1986). Wait time: Slowing down may be a way of speeding up! *Journal of Teacher Education, 37*(1), 43–50.

Rubia, K., Oosterlaan, J., Sergeant, J. A., Brandeis, D., & van Leeuwen, T. (1998). Attention deficit/hyperactivity disorder—From brain dysfunctions to behavior. *Behavioral Brain Research, 94*, 1–10.

Ruhl, K. L., Hughes, C. A., & Gajar, A. H. (1990). Efficacy of the pause procedure for enhancing learning disabled and nondisabled college students' long- and short-term recall of facts presented through lecture. *Learning Disabilities Quarterly, 13*(1), 55–64.

Ruiz, N. T., Garcia, E., & Figueroa, R. A. (1996). *The OLE curriculum guide: Creating optimal learning environments for students from diverse backgrounds in special and general education.* Sacramento, CA: California Department of Education, Specialized Programs Branch.

Rummel, N., Levin, J. R., & Woodward, M. M. (2003). Do pictorial mnemonic text-learning aids give students something worth writing about? *Journal of Educational Psychology, 95,* 327–334.

Rutter, M. (2005). Aetiology of autism: Findings and questions. *Journal of Intellectual Disability Research, 49,* 231–238.

Ryan, A. L., Halsey, H. N., & Matthews, W. J. (2003). Using functional assessment to promote desirable student behavior in schools. *Teaching Exceptional Children, 35*(5), 8–15.

Ryan, J. B., Pierce, C. D., & Mooney, P. (2008). Evidence-based teaching strategies for students with EBD. *Beyond Behavior,* 22–29.

Saaty, T. L., & Peniwati, K. (2013). *Group decision making: drawing out and reconciling differences.* Pittsburgh, PA: RWS Publications.

Sabbatino, E. (2004). Students with learning disabilities construct meaning through graphic organizers: Strategies for achievement in inclusive classrooms. *Learning Disabilities: A Multidisciplinary Journal, 13*(2), 69–73.

Sacks, G., & Kern, L. (2008). A comparison of quality of life variables for students with emotional and behavioral disorders and students without disabilities. *Journal of Behavioral Education, 17,* 111–127.

Sacks, S. Z., & Wolffe, K. E. (2006). *Teaching social skills to students with visual impairments: From theory to practice.* New York: American Federation for the Blind Press.

Sacks, S. Z., Lueck, A. H., Corn, A. L., & Erin, J. N. (2011). *Supporting the social and emotional needs of students with low vision to promote academic and social success.* Position paper of the Division on Visual Impairments, Council for Exceptional Children. Arlington, VA: Council for Exceptional Children.

Saddler, B. (2004). 20 ways to improve writing ability. *Intervention in School and Clinic, 39,* 310–314.

Salend, S. J. (1994). *Effective mainstreaming: Creative inclusive classrooms* (2nd ed.). New York: Macmillan.

Salend, S. J. (2004). Fostering inclusive values in children: What families can do. *Teaching Exceptional Children, 37,* 64–69.

Salend, S. J. (2008). Determining appropriate testing accommodations. *Teaching Exceptional Children, 40*(4), 4–22.

Salend, S. J. (2011a). Addressing test anxiety. *Teaching Exceptional Children, 44*(2), 58–58.

Salend, S J. (2011b). Creating student-friendly tests. *Educational Leadership, 69*(3), 52–58.

Salend, S. J. (2016). *Creating inclusive classrooms: Effective, differentiated, and reflective practices* (8th ed.). Boston: Pearson.

Salend, S. J., & Duhaney, L. M. (2002). What do families have to say about inclusion?: How to pay attention and get results. *Teaching Exceptional Children, 35*(1), 62–66.

Salend, S. J., & Duhaney, L. M. (2004). Understanding and addressing the disproportionate representation of students of color in special education. *Intervention in School and Clinic, 40,* 213–221.

Salend, S. J., Duhaney, D., Anderson, D. J., & Gottschalk, C. (2004). Using the Internet to improve homework communication and completion. *Teaching Exceptional Children, 36,* 64–73.

Salend, S. J., Duhaney, L. M., & Montgomery, W. (2002). A comprehensive approach to identifying and addressing issues of disproportionate representation. *Remedial and Special Education, 23,* 289–299.

Salend, S. J., Elhoweris, H., & Van Garderen, D. (2003). Educational interventions for students with ADD. *Intervention in School and Clinic, 38*(5), 280–289.

Salend, S., & Duhaney, L. M. (2007). Inclusion: Yesterday, today, and tomorrow. In McLeskey, J. (Ed.), *Reflections on inclusion: Classic articles that shaped our thinking* (pp. 125–159). Arlington, VA: CEC.

Salvia, J., Ysseldyke, J. E., & Bolt, S. (2013). *Assessment in special and inclusive education* (12th ed.). Belmont, CA: Cengage Learning.

Samuels, C. (2015). What we (don't) know about English-learners and special education. Retrieved from: http://blogs.edweek.org/edweek/speced/2015/07/ELL_and_special_education.html

Samuels, C. A. (2007). Minorities in special education studied by U.S. panel. *Education Week, 27,* 18.

Samuels, C. A. (2011). Special educators look to align IEPs to Common Core Standards. *Education Week, 30*(15), 8–9.

Sandomierski, T., Kincaid, D., & Algozzine, B. (2009). Response to intervention and positive behavior support: Brothers from different mothers or different misters? *PBIS Newsletter, 4,* 1–11.

Sands, D. J., Kozleski, E. B., & French, N. K. (2000). *Inclusive education in the 21st century.* Belmont, CA: Wadsworth.

Santa, C. (1988). *Content reading including secondary systems.* Dubuque, IA: Kendall Hunt.

Santa, C. M., Havens, L. T., & Valdes, B. J. (2004). *Project CRISS: Creating independence through student-owned strategies* (3rd ed.). Dubuque, IA: Kendall Hunt.

Santangelo, T. (2009). Collaborative problem solving effectively implemented, but not sustained: A case for aligning the sun, the moon, and the stars. *Exceptional Children, 75,* 185–209.

Satsangi, R., & Bouck, E. C. (2015). Using virtual manipulative instruction to teach the concepts of area and perimeter to secondary students with learning disabilities. *Learning Disabilities Quarterly, 38*(3), 174–186.

Sattler, J. M. (1988). *Assessment of children* (3rd ed.). San Diego: Jerome Sattler.

Saunders, A. F., Bethune, K. S., Spooner, F., & Browder, D. (2013). Solving the Common Core equation: Teaching mathematics CCSS to students with moderate and severe disabilities. *Teaching Exceptional Children, 45*(3), 24–33.

Saunders, A. F., Spooner, F., Browder, D., Wakeman, S., & Lee, A. (2013). Teaching the Common Core in English language arts to students with severe disabilities. *Teaching Exceptional Children, 46*(2) 22–33.

Saxon, J. (2003). *Algebra* (3rd ed.). Norman: OK: Saxon.

Scammacca, N., Roberts, G., Vaughn, S., Edmonds, M., Wexler, J., Reutebuch, C. K., & Torgesen, J. (2007). *Interventions for adolescent struggling readers: A meta-analysis with implications for practice.* Portsmouth, NH: RMC Research Corporation, Center on Instruction.

Schaler, J. A. (2006). *Howard Gardner under fire: The rebel psychologist faces his critics.* Open Court.

Schalock, R. L., Luckasson, R. A., & Shogren, K. A. (2007). The renaming of mental retardation: Understanding the change to the term *intellectual disability. Intellectual and Developmental Disabilities, 45,* 116–124.

Schaps, E. (2003). Creating a school community. *Education Leadership 60,* 31–33.

Schatschneider, C., Fletcher, J. M., Francis, D. J., Carlson, C. D., & Foorman, B. R. (2004). Kindergarten predictions of reading skills: A longitudinal comparative analysis. *Journal of Educational Psychology, 96*(2), 265–282.

Scheuerman, B. K., & Hall, J. A. (2012). *Positive behavior supports for the classroom.* Boston, MA: Pearson.

Schlagal, B. (2013). Best practices in spelling and handwriting. In S. Graham, C. A. MacArthur, & J. Fitzgerald (Eds.). *Best practices in writing instruction* (2nd ed.) (pp. 257–283). New York: Guilford.

Schmidt, P. R. (1999). KWLQ: Inquiry and literacy learning in science. *The Reading Teacher, 52*(7), 789–792.

Schmoker, M., & Marzano, R. J. (1999). Realizing the promise of standards-based education. *Educational Leadership, 56,* 17–21.

Schoenfeld, N. A., & Janney, D. M. (2008). Identification and treatment of anxiety in students with emotional or behavioral disorders: A review of the literature. *Education and Treatment of Children, 31,* 583–610.

Schulte, A. C., & Stevens, J. J. (2015). Once, sometimes, or always in special education: Mathematics growth and achievement gaps. *Exceptional Children, 81*(3), 370–387.

Schumm, J. S. (2001). *School power: Study skill strategies for succeeding in school.* Minneapolis, MN: Free Spirit.

Schumm, J. S. (2006). Putting it all together in classroom and resource settings: Organizational frameworks for differentiated instruction. In J. S. Schumm (Ed.), *Reading assessment and instruction for all learners* (pp. 460–492). New York: Guilford Press.

Schumm, J. S. (Ed.) (2006). *Reading assessment and instruction for all learners: A comprehensive guide for classroom and resource settings.* New York: Guilford.

Schumm, J. S., & Arguelles, M. E. (2006). No two learners learn alike: The importance of assessment and differentiated instruction. In J. S. Schumm (Ed.). *Reading assessment and instruction for all learners* (pp. 27–58). New York: Guilford Press.

Schumm, J. S., & Avalos, M. A. (2009). Responsible differentiated instruction for the adolescent learner: Promises, pitfalls, and possibilities. In K. D. Wood & W. E. Blanton (Eds.), *Literacy instruction for adolescents: Research-based practices* (pp. 144–169). New York: Guilford Press.

Schumm, J. S., & Mangrum, C. T. (1991). FLIP: A framework for content area reading. *Journal of Reading, 35*(2), 120–124.

Schumm, J. S., & Post, S. A. (1997). *Executive learning: Successful strategies for college reading and studying.* Upper Saddle River, NJ: Prentice Hall.

Schumm, J. S., & Radencich, M. (1992). *School power: Strategies for succeeding in school.* Minneapolis, MN: Free Spirit Publishing.

Schumm, J. S., Radencich, M. C., & Espeland, P. (1992). *School power: Strategies for succeeding in school.* Minneapolis, MN: Free Spirit Pub.

Schumm, J. S., & Strickler, K. (1991). Guidelines for adapting content area textbooks: Keeping teachers and students content. *Intervention in School and Clinic, 27*(2), 79–84.

Schumm, J. S., & Vaughn, S. (1991). Making adaptations for mainstreamed students: General classroom teachers' perspectives. *Remedial and Special Education, 12*(4), 18–27.

Schumm, J. S., & Vaughn, S. (1992). Planning for mainstreamed special education students: Perceptions of general classroom teachers. *Exceptionality, 3,* 81–98.

Schumm, J. S., Adelman, A., & McLeod, T. (2012). Facing the challenges of accountability and standards-based instruction: What do highly successful teachers recommend to preservice teachers? Unpublished resource.

Schumm, J. S., Hughes, M. T., & Arguelles, M. E. (2001). Co-teaching: It takes more than ESP. In V. J. Risko & K. Bromley (Eds.), *Collaboration for diverse learners* (pp. 52–69). Newark, DE: International Reading Association.

Schumm, J. S., Moody, S. W., & Vaughn, S. R. (2000). Grouping for reading instruction: Does one size fit all? *Journal of Learning Disabilities, 33*(5), 477–488.

Schumm, J. S., Vaughn, S., & Harris, J. (1997). Pyramid power for collaborative planning. *Teaching Exceptional Children, 29*(6), 62–66.

Schumm, J. S., Vaughn, S., & Leavell, A. G. (1994). Planning pyramid: A framework for planning for diverse student needs during content area instruction. *The Reading Teacher, 47*(8), 608–615.

Schumm, J. S., Vaughn, S., & Saumell, L. (1992). What teachers do when the textbook is tough: Students speak out. *Journal of Reading Behavior, 24*(4), 481–503.

Schumm, J. S., Vaughn, S., Haager, D., McDowell, D., Rothlein, L., & Saumell, L. (1995). General education teacher planning: What can students with learning disabilities expect? *Exceptional Children, 61*(4), 335–352.

Schur, L. A. (2003). Barriers or opportunities? The causes of contingent and part-time work among people with disabilities. *Industrial Relations, 42*(4), 589–622.

Schuster, J. W., Stevens, K. B., & Doak, P. K. (1990). Using constant time delay to teach word definitions. *Journal of Special Education, 24,* 306–318.

Schwartz, A. A., Jacobson, J. W., & Holburn, S. C. (2000). Defining person centeredness: Results of two consensus methods. *Journal of Education and Training in Mental Retardation and Developmental Disabilities, 35*(3), 235–249.

Scott, B. J., & Vitale, M. R. (2003). Teaching the writing process to students with LD. *Intervention in School and Clinic, 38,* 220–224.

Scott, B. J., Alter, P. J., Rosenberg, M., & Borgmeier, C. (2010). Decision-making in secondary and tertiary interventions of school-wide systems of positive behavior support. *Education and Treatment of Children, 33*(4), 513–535.

Scott, T. M., Park, K. L., Swain-Bradway, J., & Landers, E. (2007). Positive behavior support in the classroom: Facilitating behaviorally inclusive learning environments. *International Journal of Behavioral Consultation and Therapy, 3,* 223–235.

Scruggs, T. E., Mastropieri, M. A., & McDuffie, K. A. (2007). Co-teaching in inclusive classrooms: A metasynthesis of qualitative research. *Exceptional Children, 47,* 392–416.

Scruggs, T. E., Mastropieri, M. A., & Okolo, C. H. (2008). Science and social studies for students with disabilities. *Focus on Exceptional Children, 41,* 1–24.

Sealey-Ruiz, Y. (2005). Spoken soul: The language of Black imagination and reality. *The Education Forum, 70,* 37–46.

Seals, L. M., Pollard-Durodola, S. D., Foorman, B. R., & Bradley, A. M. (2007). *Vocabulary power.* Baltimore, MD: Paul H. Brookes.

Searfoss, L. W., & Readence, J. E. (1989). *Helping children learn to read* (2nd ed.). Upper Saddle River, NJ: Prentice Hall.

Seltzer, M. M., Greenburg, J. S., Floyd, F. J., Pettee, Y., & Hong, J. (2001). Life course impacts of parenting a child with disability. *American Journal on Mental Retardation, 106,* 265–286.

Senokossoff, G. W., & Stoddard, K. (2009). Swimming in deep water: Childhood bipolar disorder. *Preventing School Failure, 53,* 89–93.

Seuss, Dr. (1974). *There's a wocket in my pocket.* New York: Random House.

Sexson, S. B., & Madan-Swain, A. (1993). School reentry for the child with chronic illness. *Journal of Learning Disabilities, 26,* 115–125.

Seymour, P. H. K. (2006). Framework for beginning reading in different orthographies. In R. Maltesha Joshi & P. G. Aaron (Eds.), *Handbook of orthography and literacy.* Mahwah, NJ: Erlbaum.

Shaftel, J., Pass, L., & Schnabel, S. (2005, January/February). Math games for adolescents. *Teaching Exceptional Children,* 25–28.

Shalaway, L. (2005). Planning for parent conferences. Retrieved from http://teacher.scholastic.com/products/instructor/planning_parent_conf.htm

Shanahan, C., & Shanahan, T. (2014a). Does disciplinary literacy have a place in elementary school? *The Reading Teacher,* 67(8), 636–639.

Shanahan, C., & Shanahan, T. (2014b). The implications of disciplinary literacy. *Journal of Adolescent and Adult Literacy,* 57(8), 628–631.

Shanahan, T. (2012). What is close reading? Retrieved from http://www.shanahanonliteracy.com/2012/06/what-is-close-readinghtml

Shanahan, T. (2013). Letting the text take center stage: How the common core state standards will transform English language arts instruction. *American Educator,* 37(3), 4–12.

Shanahan, T. (2014a). Handwriting in the time of Common Core. Retrieved from http://www.readingrockets.org/blogs/shanahan-on-literacy/handwriting-time-common-core

Shanahan, T. (2014b). How and how not to prepare students for the new tests. *The Reading Teacher,* 68(3), 194–188.

Shanahan, T. (2015). What teachers should know about Common Core. *The Reading Teacher,* 68(8), 583–588.

Shanahan, T., & Lonigan, C. (2012). *Early childhood literacy: The National Early Literacy Panel and beyond.* Baltimore, MD: Brookes.

Shanahan, T., & Shanahan, C. (2008). Teaching disciplinary literacy to adolescents: Rethinking content-area literacy. *Harvard Educational Review,* 78(1), 40–59.

Shaughnessy, J. M. (2013). Mathematics in a STEM context. *Mathematics Teaching in the Middle School,* 18(6), 324.

Shaywitz, S. (2003). *Overcoming dyslexia: A new and complete science-based program for reading problems as any level.* New York: Alfred A. Knopf.

Shaywitz, S., Morris, R., & Shaywitz, B. A. (2008). The education of dyslexic children from childhood to young adulthood. *Annual Review of Psychology, 69,* 451–475.

Sheppard, L., & Unsworth. (2011). Developing skills in everyday activities and self-determination in adolescents with intellectual and developmental disabilities. *Remedial and Special Education,* 32(5), 393–405.

Sheridan, S. M. (2009). Homework interventions for children with attention and learning problems: Where is the "home" in "homework"? *School Psychology Review,* 38(3), 334–337.

Sherman, C. K., & De La Paz, S. (2015). FIX: A strategic approach to writing and revision for students with learning disabilities. *Teaching Exceptional Children,* 48(2), 93–101.

Shin, M., & Bryant, D. P. (2015). A synthesis of mathematical and cognitive performances of students with mathematics learning disabilities. *Journal of Learning Disabilities,* 48(1), 96–112.

Shin, N., Sutherland, L. M., Norris, C. A., & Soloway, E. (2012). Effects of game technology on elementary student learning in mathematics. *British Journal of Educational Technology,* 43(4), 540–560.

Shippen, M. E., Simpson, R. G., & Crites, S. A. (2003). A practical guide to functional behavioral assessment. *Teaching Exceptional Children,* 35(5), 36–44.

Shogren, K. A., & Broussard, R. (2011). Exploring the perceptions of self-determination of individuals with intellectual disability. *Intellectual and Developmental Disabilities,* 49(2), 86–102.

Shogren, K. A., Wehmeyer, M. L., Palmer, S. B., Rifenbark, G. G., & Little, T. D. (2013). Relationships between self-determination and postschool outcomes for youth with disabilities. *The Journal of Special Education,* 0022466913489733.

Shulkind, S. B. (2008). New conversations: Student-led conferences. *Principal,* 9(1), 54–58.

Sigafoos, J., Arthur, M., & O'Reilly, M. F. (2003). *Challenging behavior and developmental disability.* London: Whurr Publishers. (Distributed in the United States by Brookes.)

Sigafoos, J., Green, V., Schlosser, R., O'Reilly, M. F., Lancioni, G. E., Rispoli, M., & Lang, R. (2009). Communication intervention in Rett syndrome. *Research in Autism Spectrum Disorders,* 3(2), 304–318.

Sileo, J. M. (2011). Co-teaching: Getting to know your partner. *Teaching Exceptional Children,* 43(5), 32–38.

Simmonds, E. P. (1992). The effects of teacher training and implementation of two methods for improving the comprehension of students with learning disabilities. *Learning Disabilities Research & Practice,* 7(4), 194–198.

Simmons, D., & Vaughn, S. (2008). [Comprehension strategies in social studies]. Unpublished data.

Simmons, D., Hairrell, A., Edmonds, M. S., & Vaughn, S. (2008). *Teacher quality research—Reading/writing.* Washington, DC: Institute of Education Sciences.

Simon, V., Czobor, P., Bálint, S., Mészáros, A., & Bitter, I. (2009). Prevalence and correlates of adult attention-deficit hyperactivity disorder: Meta-analysis. *British Journal of Psychiatry, 194,* 204–211.

Simonsen, B., Fairbanks, S., Briesch, A., Myers, D., & Sugai, G. (2008). Evidence-based practices in classroom management: Considerations for research to practice. *Education and Treatment of Children,* 31(3), 351–380.

Simonsen, B., Sugai, G., & Negron, M. (2008). Schoolwide positive behavior supports: Primary systems and practices. *Teaching Exceptional Children, 40,* 32–40.

Simpson, R. L. (1988). Needs of parents and families whose children have learning and behavior problems. *Behavioral Disorders, 14,* 40–47.

Singer, H. (1986). Friendly texts: Description and criteria. In E. K. Dishner, T. W. Bean, J. E. Readence, & D. W. Moore (Eds.), *Reading in the content areas: Improving classroom instruction* (2nd ed., pp. 112–128). Dubuque, IA: Kendall Hunt.

Skiba, R. J., Simmons, A. B., Ritter, S., Gibb, A. C., Rausch, M. K., Cuadrado, J., & Chung, C. (2008). Achieving equity in special education: History, status, and current challenges. *Exceptional Children, 74,* 264–288.

Skoulos, V., & Shicktryon, G. (2007). Social skills of adolescents in special education who display symptoms of oppositional defiant disorder. *American Secondary Education, 35,* 103–115.

Skutnabb-Kangas, T. (1981, February). Linguistic genocide and bilingual education. Paper presented at the California Association for Bilingual Education, Anaheim, California.

Slavin, R. E. (1991). Synthesis of research on cooperative learning. *Educational Leadership,* 48(5), 71–82.

Slavin, R. E. (1995). *Cooperative learning: Theory, research and practice* (2nd ed). Boston: Allyn & Bacon.

Slavin, R. E. (2011). Cooperative learning. In Vibeke Grøver Aukrust (Ed.), *Learning and cognition in education* (pp. 160–166). Boston, MA: Elsevier Academic Press.

Slavin, R. E. (2015). Cooperative learning in elementary schools. *Education 3-13,* 43(1), 5–14.

Slavin, R. E., & Cheung, A. (2005). A synthesis of research on language of reading instruction for English language learners. *Review of Educational Research, 75,* 247–284.

Slavin, R. E., Madden, N. A., & Leavey, M. (1984). Effects of team-assisted individualization on the mathematics achievement of academically handicapped and nonhandicapped students. *Journal of Educational Psychology,* 76(5), 813–819.

Smith, B. H., & Shapiro, C. J. (2015). Combined treatments for ADHD. In R. A. Barkley (Ed.), *Attention-deficit hyperactivity disorder: A handbook for diagnosis and treatment* (4th ed., pp. 686–704). New York: Guilford.

Smith, C. R. (1998). From gibberish to phonemic awareness: Effective decoding instruction. *Teaching Exceptional Children,* 30(6), 20–25.

Smith, J. O., & Lovitt, T. C. (1982). *Computational arithmetic program.* Austin, TX: PRO-ED.

Smith, T. E. C. (2008). Developmental disabilities: Definition, description, and directions. In H. P. Parette & G. R. Peterson-Karlan (Eds.), *Research-based practices in developmental disabilities* (2nd ed., pp. 59–74). Austin, TX: PRO-ED.

Smith, T. W., & Lambie, G. W. (2005, January). Teachers' responsibilities when adolescent abuse and neglect are suspected. *Middle School Journal,* 36(3), 33–40.

Snell, M. E., & Luckasson, R. (2009). Characteristics and needs of people with intellectual disability who have higher IQs. (2009). *Intellectual and Developmental Disabilities,* 47(3), 220–233.

Snow, C. E., Burns, M. S., & Griffin, P. (Eds.). (1998). *Preventing reading difficulties in young children.* Washington, DC: National Academies Press.

Snow, C. E., Porche, M. V., Tabors, P. O., & Harris, S. R. (2007). *Is literacy enough?* Baltimore, MD: Paul H. Brookes.

Snow, C., & O'Connor, C. (2013). *Close reading and far-reaching classroom discussion: Fostering a vital connection.* Newark, DE: International Reading Association.

Snowling, M. J., & Hulme, C. (2012). Annual research review: The nature and classification of reading disorders—a commentary on proposals for DSM-S. *Journal of Child Psychology and Psychiatry,* 53(5), 593–607.

Snyder, T. D., and Dillow, S. A. (2015). *Digest of education statistics 2013* (NCES 2015-011).

Sobsey, D., & Wolf-Schein, E. G. (1996). Sensory impairments. In F. P. Orelove & D. Sobsey (Eds.), *Educating children with multiple disabilities: A transdisciplinary approach* (3rd ed.). Baltimore, MD: Paul H. Brookes

Solis, M., Cuillo, S., Vaughn, S., Pyle, N., Hassaram, B., & Leroux, A. (2011). Reading comprehension interventions for middle school students with learning disabilities: A synthesis of 30 years of research. *Journal of Learning Disabilities.* Advance online publication. doi: 10.1177/0022219411402691

Solis, M., Miciak, J., Vaughn, S., Fletcher, J. M. (2014). Why intensive interventions matter: Longitudinal studies of adolescents with reading disabilities and poor reading comprehension. *Learning Disability Quarterly* 37(4), 218–229. doi:10.1177/0731948714528806

Solis, M., Vaughn, S., Swanson, E., & McCulley, L. (2012). Collaborative models of instruction: The empirical foundations of inclusion and co-teaching. *Psychology in the Schools,* 49(3), 498–510.

Soller, J. (2003). Re-occurring questions about giftedness and the connections to myths and realities. *Gifted and Talented, 7,* 42–48.

Sorrentino, J. (July 29, 2013). The homework debate. Retrieved on May 21, 2015 from http://www.education.com/magazine/article/The_Homework_Debate/.

Soukup, J. H., Wehmeyer, M. L., Bashinski, S. M., & Bovaird, J. (2007). Classroom variables and access to the general education curriculum of students with intellectual and developmental disabilities. *Exceptional Children, 74,* 101–120.

Southerland, L. (2011). *The effects of using interactive word walls to teach vocabulary to middle school students* (Doctoral dissertation). Retrieved from ProQuest Dissertations & Theses Global. (UMI No. 3492703)

Sparks, R. L., Javorsky, J., & Philips, L. (2004). College students classified with ADHD and the foreign language requirement. *Journal of Learning Disabilities,* 37(2), 169–180.

Sparks, S. (2008). Culturally and linguistically diverse learners with developmental disabilities. In H. P. Parette & G. R. Peterson-Karlan (Eds.), *Research-based practices in developmental disabilities* (2nd ed., pp. 125–141). Austin, TX: PRO-ED.

Sparks, S. D. (2015). Research on quality of conversation holds deeper clues into word gap. *Education Week,* 34(28), 1–11.

Sparrow, S. S., Balla, D. A., & Cicchetti, D. V. (2005). *Vineland Adaptive Behavior Scales* (2nd ed.) (*Vineland-II*). Upper Saddle River, NJ: Pearson Assessments.

Spear-Swerling, L. (2006). The importance of teaching handwriting. Retrieved from http://www.ldonline.org/spearswerling/10521

Spear-Swerling, L. (2015). *The power of RTI and reading profiles.* Baltimore: Paul H. Brookes.

Spear-Swerling, L. (2015). *The power of RTI and reading profiles.* Baltimore: Paul H. Brookes.

Spencer, M., Wagner, R. K., Schatschneider, C., Quinn, J. M., Lopez, D., & Petscher, Y. (2014). Incorporating RTI in a hybrid model of reading disability. *Learning Disability Quarterly*, 0731948714530967.

Spencer, M., Wagner, R. K., Schatschneider, C., Quinn, J. M., Lopez, D., & Petscher, Y. (2014). Incorporating RTI in a hybrid model of reading disability. *Learning Disability Quarterly*, 0731948714530967.

Spielberger, C. D. (Ed.). (2013). *Anxiety: Current trends in theory and research.* Philadelphia, PA: Elsevier.

Spies, T. G., & Dema, A. A. (2014). Beyond word meaning: Vocabulary instruction for students with exceptional language needs. *Intervention in School and Clinic, 49*(5), 271–280.

Spina Bifida Foundation. (2009). *FAQ about spina bifida.* Retrieved from http://www.spinabifidaassociation.org/site/LiKWL7PLLrF/b.2642327/k.5899/FAQ_About_Spina_Bifida.htm

Spooner, F., Ahlgrim-Delzell, L., Kemp-Inman, A., & Wood, L. A. (2014). Using an iPad2® with systematic instruction to teach shared stories for elementary-aged students with autism. *Research and Practice for Persons with Severe Disabilities, 39*(1), 30–46. Retrieved from http://dx.doi.org/10.1177/1540796914534631

Squires, K. E., Gillam, S. L., & Reutzel, D. R. (2013). Characteristics of children who struggle with reading: Teachers and speech-language pathologists collaborate to support young learners. *Early Childhood Education Journal, 41*, 401–411.

Stach, B. (1998). *Clinical audiology: An introduction.* San Diego, CA: Singular Publications.

Stahl, G. K., Mazhevski, M. L., Voigt, A., & Jonsen, K. (2009). Unraveling the effects of cultural diversity in teams: A meta-analysis of research on multicultural work groups. *Journal of International Business*, 28–36.

Stahl, S. (2004). *The promise of accessible textbooks: Increased achievement for all students.* Wakefield, MA: National Center on Accessing the General Curriculum. Retrieved from http://www.cast.org/publications/ncac/ncac_accessible.html

Stahl, S. A. (1983). Differential word knowledge and reading comprehension. *Journal of Reading Behavior, 15*(4), 33–50.

Stahl, S. A. (2003). How words are learned incrementally over multiple exposures. *American Educator, 27*(1), 18–19.

Stainback, S., & Stainback, W. (1992). *Curriculum consideration in inclusive classrooms: Facilitating learning for all students.* Baltimore, MD: Paul H. Brookes.

Stanford, P. (2003). Multiple intelligence for every classroom. *Intervention in School and Clinic, 39*, 80–85.

Stanovich, K. E. (1986). Cognitive processes and the reading problems of learning-disabled children: Evaluating the assumption of specificity. In J. K. Torgesen & B. Y. L. Wong (Eds.), *Psychological and educational perspectives on learning disabilities* (pp. 87–131). Orlando, FL: Academic Press.

Stanovich, K. E. (1992). Speculations on the causes and consequences of individual differences in early reading acquisition. In P. B. Gough, L. D. Ehri, & R. Treiman (Eds.), *Reading acquisition* (pp. 307–342). Mahwah, NJ: Erlbaum.

State of Florida. (2009). Access points for students with significant cognitive disabilities. Retrieved from http://www.floridastandards.org/page24.aspx

Stead, T. (2014). Nurturing the inquiring mind through the nonfiction read-aloud. *The Reading Teacher, 67*(7), 488–495.

Stecker, P. M., & Fuchs, L. S. (2000). Effecting superior achievement using curriculum-based measures: The importance of individualized progress monitoring. *Learning Disabilities Research and Practice, 15*, 128–134.

Steele, M. M., & Steele, J. W. (2003). Teaching algebra to students with learning disabilities. *Mathematics Teacher, 96*(9), 622–624.

Steinman, B. A., LeJeune, B. J., & Kimbrough, B. T. (2006). Developmental stages of reading processes in children who are blind and sighted. *Journal of Visual Impairment and Blindness, 100*, 36–46.

Stenhoff, D. M., & Lignugaris/Kraft, B. (2007). A review of the effects of peer tutoring on students with mild disabilities in secondary settings. *Exceptional Children, 74*, 8–30.

Stephens, K. R., & Karnes, F. A. (2000, Winter). State definitions for the gifted and talented revisited. *Exceptional Children, 66*(2), 219–238.

Stetson, R., Stetson, E., & Anderson, K. A. (2007). Differentiated instruction, from teachers' experiences. *The School Administrator, 64*(8), 28.

Stevens, K. B., & Schuster, J. W. (1987). Effects of a constant time delay procedure on the written spelling performance of a learning disabled student. *Learning Disability Quarterly, 10*, 9–16.

Stevens, K. B., & Schuster, J. W. (1988). Time delay: Systematic instruction for academic tasks. *Remedial and Special Education, 9*(5), 16–21.

Stevens, S. (2001). A teacher looks at the elementary child with ADHD. In B. P. Guyer (Ed.), *ADHD: Achieving success in school and in life* (pp. 67–80). Boston: Allyn & Bacon.

Stewart, M. A. (2013). Giving voice to Valeria's story: Support, value, and agency for immigrant adolescents. *Journal of Adolescent and Adult Literacy, 57*(1), 42–50.

Still, G. F. (1902). Some abnormal psychical conditions in children. *Lancet, 1*, 1008–1012, 1077–1082, 1163–1168.

Stockall, N. S. (2014). When an aide really becomes an aid: Providing professional development for special education paraprofessionals. *Teaching Exceptional Children, 46*(6), 197–205.

Stoneman, Z. (2007). Disabilities research methodology: Current issues and future challenges. In S. L. Odom, R. H. Horner, M. E. Snell, & J. Blacher (Eds.), *Handbook of developmental disabilities* (pp. 35–54). New York: Guilford Press.

Strichart, S. S., & Mangrum, C. T. (2010). *Study skills for learning disabled and struggling students: Grades 6–12* (4th ed.). Boston: Allyn & Bacon.

Strichart, S. S., & Mangrum, C. T., II. (1993). *Teaching study strategies to students with learning disabilities.* Boston, MA: Allyn & Bacon.

Strickland, D. S., Galda, L., & Cullinan, B. E. (2004). *Language arts: Learning and teaching.* Belmont, CA: Thomson/Wadsworth.

Stronge, J. H., Ward, T. J., & Grant, L. W. (2011). What makes good teachers good? A cross-case analysis of the connection between teacher effectiveness and student achievement. *Journal of Teacher Education, 62*(4), 339–355.

Stuart, M. (1999). Getting ready for reading: Early phoneme awareness and phonics training improves reading and spelling in inner-city second language learners. *British Journal of Educational Psychology, 69*(4), 587–605.

Stuebing, K. K., Fletcher, J. M., Branum-Martin, L., & Francis, D. J. (2012). Evaluation of the technical adequacy of three methods for identifying specific learning disabilities based on cognitive discrepancies. *School Psychology Review, 41*(1), 3.

Stuebing, K. K., Fletcher, J. M., LeDoux, J. M., Lyon, G. R., Shaywitz, S. E., & Shaywitz, B. A. (2002). Validity of IQ-discrepancy classifications of reading disabilities: A meta-analysis. *American Educational Research Journal, 39*, 469–518.

Sugai, G., Horner, R., & Gresham, F. (2002). Interpreting outcomes of social skills training for students with high-incidence disabilities. *Exceptional Children, 67*(3), 331.

Sugai, G., Simonsen, B., Bradshaw, C., Horner, R., & Lewis, T. J. (2014). Delivering high quality school-wide positive behavior support in inclusive schools. In *Handbook of Effective Inclusive Schools: Research and Practice*, 306–321.

Sullivan, A. L. (2011). Disproportionality in special education identification and placement of English language learners. *Exceptional Children, 77*(3), 317–334.

Sullivan, A. L., & Bal, A. (2013). Disproportionality in special education: Effects of individual and school variables on disability risk. *Exceptional Children, 79*(4), 475–494.

Suritsky, S. K., & Hughes, C. A. (1996). Notetaking strategy instruction. In D. D. Deshler, E. S. Ellis, & B. K. Lenz (Eds.), *Teaching adolescents with learning disabilities* (2nd ed., pp. 267–312). Denver, CO: Love.

Sumner, E., Connelly, V., & Barnett, A. L. (2012). Children with dyslexia are slow writers because they pause more often and not because they are slow at handwriting execution. *Reading and Writing, 26*, 991–1008.

Suskind, D. (2012). What students would do if they did not do their homework. *Kappan, 94*(1), 52–55.

Sutton, S. (2009). School solutions for cyberbullying. *Principal Leadership, 9*, 38–40, 42.

Swain, M. (1986). Communicative competence: Some roles of comprehensible input & comprehensible output in its development. In J. Cummins & M. Swain (Eds.), *Bilingualism in education.* New York: Longman.

Swain, R., Lane, J. D., & Gast, D. L. (2015). Comparison of constant time delay and simultaneous prompting procedures: Teaching functional sight words to students with intellectual disabilities and autism spectrum disorder. *Journal of Behavioral Education, 24*, 210–229.

Swanson, E., Edmonds, M. S., Hairrell, A., Vaughn, S., & Simmons, D. (2011). Applying a cohesive set of comprehension strategies to content-area instruction. *Intervention in School and Clinic, 46*(5), 266–272.

Swanson, H. L. (2009). Working memory, short-term memory, and reading disabilities: A selective meta-analysis of the literature. *Journal of Learning Disabilities, 42*(3), 260–287.

Swanson, H. L., & Deshler, D. (2003). Instructing adolescents with learning disabilities: Converting a meta-analysis to practice. *Journal of Learning Disabilities, 36*(2), 124–135.

Swanson, H. L., Hoskyn, M., & Lee, C. (1999). *Interventions for students with learning disabilities: A meta-analysis of treatment outcomes.* New York: Guilford Press.

Swanson, J., Baler, R. D., & Volkow, N. D. (2011). Understanding the effects of stimulant medications on cognition in individuals with attention-deficit hyperactivity disorder: A decade of progress. *Neuropsychopharmacology Reviews, 36*, 207–226.

Sweigart, C. A., & Landrum, T. J. (2015). The impact of number of adults on instruction: Implications for co-teaching. *Preventing School Failure, 59*(1), 22–29.

Switsky, H. N. (2006). The importance of cognitive-motivational variables in understanding the outcome performance of persons with mental retardation: A personal view from the early twenty-first century. *International Review of Research in Mental Retardation, 31*, 1–29.

Szabo, S. (2006). KWHHL: A student-driven evolution of the KWL. *American Secondary Education, 34*(3), 57–67.

Szatmari, P., Bryson, S. E., Streiner, D. L., Wilson, F., Archer, L., & Ryerse, C. (2014). Two-year outcome of preschool children with autism or Asperger's syndrome. *American Journal of Psychiatry, 157*(12), 1980–1987. Retrieved from http://dx.doi.org/10.1176/appi.ajp.157.12.1980

Sze, S., & Valentin, S. (2007). Self-concept and children with disabilities. *Education, 27*, 552–557.

Tacket, K. (2009). Response to intervention: Case studies. Doctoral dissertation, University of Texas, Austin.

Taft, R. J., & Mason, L. H. (20111). Examining effects of writing interventions: Highlighting results for students with primary disabilities other than learning disabilities. *Remedial and Special Education, 32*(5), 359–370.

Tager-Flusberg, H., & Kasari, C. (2013). Minimally verbal school-aged children with autism spectrum disorder: The neglected end of the spectrum. *Autism Research, 6*(6), 468–478. Retrieved from http://dx.doi.org/10.1002/aur.1329

Tambyraja, S. R., Farquharson, K., Logan, J. A. R., & Justice, L. M. (2015). Decoding skills in children with language impairment: Contributions of phonological processing and classroom experiences. *American Journal of Speech-Language Pathology, 24*, 177–188.

TASH. (2000). TASH resolution on the people for whom TASH advocates. Retrieved from http://www.tash.org/resolutions/res02advocate.htm

Taylor, B. M., & Duke, N. K. (2011). *Catching readers, grade K: Day-by-day, small-group reading interventions.* Portsmouth, NH: Heinemann.

Taylor, B. (2008). Tier 1: Effective classroom reading instruction in the elementary grades. In D. Fuchs, L. S. Fuchs, & S. Vaughn (Eds.), *Response to intervention: A framework for reading educators* (pp. 5–25). Newark, DE: International Reading Association.

Taylor, B., Harris, L. A., & Pearson, P. D. (1988). *Reading difficulties: Instruction and assessment.* New York: Random House.

Taylor, C. (2013). Letting go: Parents sending students with intellectual disabilities to college. *Exceptional Parent, 43*(3), 17–19.

Templeton, S., Bear, D. R., Invernizzi, M. R., Johnston, F., Flanigan, K., Townsend, D. R., . . . & Hayes, L. (2015). *Vocabulary their way: Word study with middle and secondary students.* Boston, MA: Pearson.

Test, D. W., Fowler, C. H., Wood, W. M., Brewer, D. M., & Eddy, S. (2005). A conceptual framework of self-advocacy for students with disabilities. *Remedial and Special Education, 26*(1), 43–54.

Test, D. W., Mason, C., Konrad, M., Neale, M., & Wood, W. M. (2004). Student involvement in individual education program meetings. *Exceptional Children, 70*(4), 391–412.

Tharp, R. G., Estrada, P., Dalton, S. S., & Yamaguchi, L. (1999). *Teaching transformed: Achieving excellence, fairness, inclusion, and harmony.* Boulder, CO: Westview Press.

Tharpe, A. M., Ashmead, D., Sladen, D. P., Ryan, H. A., Rothpletz, A. M. (2008). Visual attention and hearing loss: Past and current perspectives. *Journal of the American Academy of Audiology, 19,* 741–747.

The Association for Persons with Severe Handicaps (TASH). (2000). TASH resolution on the people for whom TASH advocates. Retrieved from http://www.tash.org/IRR/resolutions/res02advocate.htm

The National Education Association of the United States. (2005). *The NEA handbook for paraeducators.* Washington, DC: Author.

The National Joint Committee on Learning Disabilities. (2011). Comprehensive assessment and evaluation of students with learning disabilities. *Learning Disability Quarterly, 34*(1), 3–16.

The White House. (2015). Fact sheet: Congress acts to fix No Child Left Behind. Retrieved from: https://www.whitehouse.gov/the-press-office/2015/12/03/fact-sheet-congress-acts-fix-no-child-left-behind

Thomas, C. C., Correa, V. I., & Morsink, C. V. (2001). *Interactive teaming: Consultation and collaboration in special programs* (3rd ed.). Upper Saddle River, NJ: Merrill/Pearson.

Thomas, W. P., & Collier, V. P. (1997). Two languages are better than one. *Educational Leadership, 55*(4), 23–26.

Thompson, B. C., Mazer, J. P., & Grady, E. F. (2015). The changing nature of parent–teacher communication: Mode selection in the smartphone era. *Communication Education, 64*(2), 187–207.

Thompson, J. R., & Wehmeyer, M. L. (2008). Historical and legal issues in developmental disabilities. In H. P. Parette & G. R. Peterson-Karlan (Eds.), *Research-based practices in developmental disabilities* (2nd ed., pp. 13–42). Austin, TX: PRO-ED.

Thompson, J., Bryant, B. R., Campbell, E. M., Craig, E. M., Hughes, C., Rotholz, D. A., Schalock, R. L., & Whemeyer, M. L. (2004). *Supports Intensity Scale manual.* Washington, DC: American Association for Mental Retardation.

Thompson, T., & Sproule, S. (2005). Calculators for students with special needs. *Teaching Children Mathematics, 11*(7), 391–395.

Thornberry, T. P., Huizinga, D., & Loeber, R. (2004). The causes and correlates studies: Findings and policy implications. *Juvenile Justice, 10*(1), 3–19.

Thornton, C. A., & Toohey, M. A. (1985). Basic math facts: Guidelines for teaching and learning. *Learning Disabilities Focus, 1,* 44–57.

Thornton, C. A., Tucker, B. F., Dossey, J. A., & Brazik, E. F. (1983). *Teaching mathematics to children with special needs.* Menlo Park, CA: Addison-Wesley.

Thousand, J., Rosenberg, R., Bishop, K., & Villa, R. (1997). The evolution of secondary inclusion. *Remedial and Special Education, 18*(5), 270–284.

Thurlow, M. L., & Kopriva, R. J. (2015). Advancing accessibility and accommodations in content assessments for students with disabilities and English learners. *Review of Research in Education, 39*(1), 331–369.

Thurlow, M. L., Elliott, J. L., & Ysseldyke, J. E. (2002). *Testing students with disabilities: Practical strategies for complying with district and state requirements.* Thousand Oaks, CA: Corwin Press.

Tiedt, P. L., & Tiedt, I. M. (2006). *Multicultural teaching: A handbook of activities, information, and resources* (7th ed.). Boston: Allyn & Bacon.

Tiedt, P. L., & Tiedt, I. M. (2010). *Multicultural teaching: A handbook of activities, information, and resources* (8th ed.). Boston: Pearson.

Tilly, W. D. III, Reschly, D. J., & Grimes, J. (1999). Disability determination in problem solving systems: Conceptual foundations and critical components. In D. J. Reschly, W. D. Tilly, & J. P. Grimes (Eds.), *Special education in transition: Functional assessment and noncategorical programming* (pp. 221–251). Longman, CO: Sopris West.

Todd, A. W., Horner, R. H., & Sugai, G. (2000). Self-monitoring and self-recruited praise: Effects on problem behavior, academic engagement, and work completion in a typical classroom. *Journal of Positive Behavioral Interventions, 1,* 66–76.

Togerson, C. W., Miner, C. A., & Shen, H. (2004). Developing student competence in self-directed IEPs. *Intervention in School & Clinic, 39*(3), 162–167.

Tomlinson, C. A. (2001). *How to differentiate instruction in mixed-ability classrooms* (2nd ed.). Alexandria, VA: Association for Supervision and Curriculum Development.

Tomlinson, C. A. (2003). *Fulfilling the promise of the differentiated classroom: Strategies and tools for responsive teaching.* Alexandria, VA: Association for Supervision and Curriculum Development.

Tomlinson, C. A. (2005). Grading and differentiation: Paradox or good practice? *Theory Into Practice, 44*(2), 262–269.

Tomlinson, C. A. (2008). The goals of differentiation. *Educational Leadership, 66*(3), 26–30.

Tomlinson, C. A. (2012). Differentiated instruction. In C. M. Callahan & H. L. Hertber-Davis (Eds.). *Fundamentals of gifted education: Considering multiple perspectives* (pp. 287–289). New York: Routledge.

Tomlinson, C. A. (2012). What is differentiated instruction? Retrieved from http://www.readingrockets.org/article/263/

Tomlinson, C. A. (2014). *Differentiated classroom: Responding to the needs of all learners.* Ascd.

Tomlinson, C. A. (2014). *The differentiated classroom: Responding to the needs of all learners.* Ascd.

Tomlinson, C. A., & Imbeau, M. B. (2010). Leading and managing a differentiated classroom. Alexandria, VA: ASCD.

Tomlinson, C. A., Kaplan, S. N., Renzulli, J. S., Purcell, J. H., Leppien, J. H., & Burns, D. E. (2001). *The parallel curriculum.* Thousand Oaks, CA: Corwin Press.

Tompkins, G. E. (2012). *Teaching writing: Balancing process and product.* Boston: Pearson.

Tompkins, G. E. (2014). *Literacy for the 21st century: A balanced approach* (6th ed.). Boston: Pearson.

Toppel, K. (2015). Enhancing core reading programs with culturally responsive practices. *The Reading Teacher, 68*(7), 552–559.

Torgerson, C. W., Miner, C. A., & Shen, H. (2004). Developing student competence in self-directed IEPs. *Intervention and School and Clinic, 39*(3), 162–167.

Torgesen, J. K. (1999). Assessment and instruction for phonemic awareness and word recognition skills. In H. W. Catts & A. G. Kamhi (Eds.), *Language and reading disabilities* (pp. 128–153). Boston: Allyn & Bacon.

Torgesen, J. K., & Burgess, S. R. (1998). Consistency of reading-related phonological processes throughout early childhood: Evidence from longitudinal, correlational and instructional studies. In J. Methsala & L. Ehri (Eds.), *Word recognition in beginning literacy* (pp. 161–188). Mahwah, NJ: Erlbaum.

Torgesen, J. K., Wagner, R. K., & Rashotte, C. A. (1994). Longitudinal studies of phonological processing and reading. *Journal of Learning Disabilities, 27,* 276–286.

Touchette, P. E., MacDonald, R. F., & Langer, S. N. (1985). A scatter plot for identifying stimulus control of problem behavior. *Journal of Applied Behavior Analysis, 18*(4), 343–351.

Towles-Reeves, E., Kleinert, H., & Muhomba, M. (2009). Alternate assessment: Have we learned anything new? *Exceptional Children, 75,* 233–252.

Townsend, B. L. (2000). The disproportionate discipline of African American learners: Reducing school suspensions and expulsions. *Exceptional Children, 66*(3), 381–391.

TPRI. (2010). *The Texas Education Agency and the University of Texas System.* Baltimore: Brooks.

Trelease, J. (1995). *The new read-aloud handbook* (4th ed.). New York: Penguin.

Trinter, C, P., Brighton, C. M., & Moon, T. R. (2015). Designing differentiated mathematics games: Discarding the one-size-fits-all approach to educational game play. *Gifted Child Today,* 88–94.

Troia, G. A., & Olinghouse, N. G. (2013). The Common Core State Standards and evidence-based educational practices: The case for writing. *School Psychology Review, 42*(3), 343–357.

Trower, P., & Hollin, C. R. (Eds.). (2013). *Handbook of social skills training: Clinical applications and new directions.* Philadelphia, PA: Elsevier.

Trujillo, T., & Howe, K. R. (2015). Weighing the effects of federal educational policy on democracy: Reframing the discourse on high-stakes accountability. *Teachers College Record, 117*(6), 1–6.

Ttofi, M. M., & Farrington, D. P. (2011). Effectiveness of school-based programs to reduce bullying. *Journal of Experimental Criminology, 7*(1), 27–56.

Turnbull, A. P., & Turnbull, H. R. (2001). Building reliable alliances. In A. P. Turnbull & H. R. Turnbull (Eds.), *Families, professionals, and exceptionality: Collaborating for empowerment* (4th ed.). Upper Saddle River, NJ: Merrill/Pearson.

Turnbull, A. P., Turnbull, H. R., Erwin, E. J., & Soodak, L. C. (2007). *Families, professionals, and exceptionality: Positive outcomes through partnership and trust* (5th ed.). Upper Saddle River, NJ: Merrill/Pearson.

Turnbull, A. P., Turnbull, H. R., Erwin, E. J., Soodak, L. C., & Shogren, K. A. (2010). *Families, professionals, and exceptionality: Positive outcomes through partnership and trust* (6th ed). Upper Saddle River, NJ: Prentice-Hall.

Turnbull, A., & Turnbull, H. R. (2001). *Families, professionals, and exceptionality: Collaborating for empowerment* (4th ed.). Upper Saddle River, NJ: Merrill/Pearson.

Turnbull, A., Turnbull, R., & Wehmeyer, M. L. (2010). *Collaborating for exceptional populations.* Upper Saddle River, NJ: Merrill/Pearson.

Turnbull, A., Turnbull, R., Erwin, E. J., Soodak L.C., & Shogren, K. A. (2015). *Families, professionals, and exceptionality: Positive outcomes through partnerships and trust* (7th ed.). Boston: Pearson.

Turnbull, A., Turnbull, R., Soodak L.C., Erwin, E. J., & Shogren, K. A. (2011). *Families, professionals, and exceptionality: Positive outcomes through partnerships and trust* (6th ed.). Boston: Pearson.

Turnbull, H. R., Stowe, M., & Huerta, N. (2008). *The Individuals with Disabilities Education Act in 2004.* Upper Saddle River, NJ: Merrill/Pearson.

U.S. Census Bureau. (2008). An older and more diverse nation by midcentury. Retrieved from http://www.census.gov/newsroom/releases/archives/population/cb08-123.html

U.S. Department of Education, National Center for Education Statistics (2015). *Digest of Education Statistics,* 2013 (NCES 2015-011), Table 204.30.

U.S. Department of Education. (2008). Teaching children with attention deficit hyperactivity disorder: Instructional strategies and practices. Retrieved from: http://www2.ed.gov/rschstat/research/pubs/adhd/adhd-teaching_pg3.html#skipnav2

U.S. Department of Education. (2002a). *A new era: Revitalizing special education for children and their families.* Jessup, MD: Author.

U.S. Department of Education. (2002b). Retrieved from http://www.ed.gov

U.S. Department of Education. (2004). *No Child Left Behind: A toolkit for teachers.* Jessup, MD: Author.

U.S. Department of Education. (2005). To assure the free appropriate public education of all Americans: Twenty-seventh annual report to Congress on the implementation of the Individuals with Disabilities Education Act. Retrieved from http://www.ed.gov/about/reports/annual/osep/2005/index.html

U.S. Department of Education. (2007a). *27th annual (2005) report to Congress on the implementation of the Individuals with Disabilities Education Act* (No. ED01CO0082/0008). Washington, DC: Author.

U.S. Department of Education. (2007b). *Individuals with Disabilities Education Act (IDEA) data* (Table 1-3). Washington, DC: Author. [Available online: https://www.ideadata.org/PartBReport.asp]

U.S. Department of Education. (2008a). *Foundations for success: The final report of the National Mathematics Advisory Panel.* Jessup, MD: Author.

U.S. Department of Education. (2008b). *Twenty-seventh annual report to Congress on the implementation of the Individuals with Disabilities Education Act, 2006.* Washington, DC: U.S. Department of Education, Office of Special Education and Rehabilitative Services, Office of Special Education Programs.

U.S. Department of Education. (2009). *Twenty-eighth annual report to Congress on the implementation of the Individuals with Disabilities Education Act, 2006.* Washington, DC: U.S. Department of Education, Office of Special Education and Rehabilitative Services, Office of Special Education Programs.

U.S. Department of Education. (2010, November). *Thirty-five years of progress in educating children with disabilities through IDEA.* Office of Special Education. Washington, DC: Author.

U.S. Department of Education. (2014). *Science, technology, engineering and math: Education for global leadership.* Retrieved from: http://www.ed.gov/stem.

U.S. Department of Education. (2015). Developing programs for English language learners. Retrieved from http://www2.ed.gov/about/offices/list/ocr/ell/glossary.html

U.S. Department of Education. (n.d.). Building the legacy: IDEA 2004. Retrieved from http://idea.ed.gov

U.S. Department of Health and Human Services. (2009). Mood disorders. Retrieved from http://mentalhealth.samhsa.gov/publications/allpubs/KEN98-0049/

U.S. Social Security Administration. (2015). If you're blind or have low vision—How we can help (SSA Publication No. 05-10052, ICN 462554).

Uberti, H. A., Scruggs, T. E., & Mastropieri, M. A. (2003). Keywords make a difference: Mnemonic instruction in inclusive classrooms. *Teaching Exceptional Children, 35,* 56–61.

United Cerebral Palsy. (2009). Cerebral palsy fact sheet. Retrieved from http://www.ucp.org/ucp_general-doc.cfm/1/9/37/37-37/447

United Cerebral Palsy. (2011). *Cerebral palsy fact sheet.* Retrieved from http://www.ucp.org/uploads/media_items/cerebral-palsy-fact-sheet.original.pdf

United Nations Programme on HIV/AIDS (2010). Global report: UNAIDS report on global AIDS epidemic. Retrieved from http://www.unaids.org/globalreport/documents/20101123_GlobalReport_full_en.pdf

United States Census Bureau. (2012). U. S. Census Bureau projections show a slower growing, older, more diverse nation a half century from now. Retrieved from http://www.census.gov/newsroom/releases/archives/population/cb12-243.html

United States Census Bureau. (2015a). Language spoken at home and difficulty speaking English. Retrieved from http://www.childstats.gov/americaschildren/tables/fam5.asp?popup=true

United States Census Bureau. (2015b). Quick Facts from the U.S. Census Bureau. Retrieved from http://quickfacts.census.gov/qfd/states/00000.html

United States Department of Education, National Center for Education Statistics. (2014). The Nation's Report Card Mathematics and Reading 2013: Trend in fourth- and eight-grade NAEP mathematics and reading achievement-level results, by race/ethnicity (1990–2013). Institute of Education Sciences. Retrieved from http://www.nationsreportcard.gov/reading_math_2013/#/student-groups

United States Department of Education, National Center for Education Statistics. (2015a). Racial/ethnic enrollment in public schools. Retrieved from http://nces.ed.gov/programs/coe/indicator_cge.asp

United States Department of Education, National Center for Education Statistics. (2015b). *The Condition of Education 2015* (NCES 2015-144), Status Dropout Rates. Retrieved from http://nces.ed.gov/programs/coe/indicator_coj.asp

Vaca, J., Lapp, D., & Fisher, D. (2011). Designing and assessing productive group work in secondary schools. *Journal of Adolescent & Adult Literacy, 54*(5), 372–375.

Vacca, R. T., & Vacca, J. L. (2005). *Content area reading: Literacy and learning across the curriculum.* Boston: Allyn & Bacon.

Vacca, R. T., & Vacca, J. L. (2008). *Content area reading: Literacy and learning across the curriculum* (9th ed.). Boston: Allyn & Bacon.

Vacca, R. T., Vacca, J. L., & Mraz, M. E. (2011). *Content area reading: Literacy and learning across the curriculum* (10th ed.). Boston: Allyn & Bacon.

Valencia, S. W., Wixson, K. K., & Pearson, P. D. (2014). Putting text complexity in context: Refocusing on comprehension of complex text. *The Elementary School Journal, 115*(2), 270–289.

van Belle, J., Marks, S., Martin, R., & Chun, M. (2006). Voicing one's dreams: High school students with developmental disabilities learn about self-advocacy. *Teaching Exceptional Children, 38,* 40–46.

Van de Walle, J. A., Karp, K. S., & Bay-Williams, J. M. (2010). *Elementary and middle school mathematics: Teaching developmentally* (7th ed.). Boston: Allyn & Bacon.

Van de Walle, J. A., Karp, K. S., & Bay-Williams, J. M. (2016). *Elementary and middle school mathematics: Teaching developmentally* (9th ed.). Boston: Pearson.

Van der Lee, J. H., Mokkink, L. B., Grootenhuis, M. A., Heymans, H. S., & Offringa, M. (2007). Definitions and measurement of chronic health conditions in childhood. *Journal of the American Medical Association, 297,* 2741–2751.

Van Gardenen, D., Stormont, M., & Goel, N. (2012). Collaboration between general and special educators and student outcomes: A need for more research. *Psychology in the Schools, 49*(3), 483–497.

Van Kleek, A. (1995). Emphasizing form and meaning repeatedly in prereading and early reading instruction. *Topics in Language Disorders, 16,* 27–49.

Van Loon, J., Claes, C., Vandevelde, S., Van Hove, G., & Schalock, R. L. (2012). Assessing individual support needs to enhance personal outcomes. *Exceptionality, 18,* 193–202.

Van Reusen, A. K., & Bos, C. S. (1990). I PLAN: Helping students communicate in planning conference. *Teaching Exceptional Children, 22*(4), 30–32.

Van Reusen, A. K., & Bos, C. S. (1992). *Use of the goal-regulation strategy to improve the goal attainment of students with learning disabilities* (Final Report). Tucson, AZ: University of Arizona.

Van Reusen, A. K., & Bos, C. S. (1994). Facilitating student participation in individualized education programs through motivation strategy instruction. *Exceptional Children, 60*(5), 466–475.

Van Reusen, A. K., Bos, C. S., Schumaker, J. B., & Deshler, D. D. (1994). *The self-advocacy strategy for education and transition planning.* Lawrence, KS: Edge Enterprises.

Van Tassel-Baska, J., & Brown, E. F. (2007). Toward best practice: An analysis of the efficacy of curriculum models in gifted education. *Gifted Education Quarterly, 51,* 342–358.

Van Tassel-Baska, J., & Wood, S. (2010). The integrated curriculum model (ICM). *Learning and Individual Differences, 20*(4), 345–357.

Van Tassel-Baska, J., Quek, C., & Feng, A. X. (2007). The development and use of a structured teacher observation scale to assess differentiated best practice. *Roeper Review, 29,* 84–92.

Vanderbilt, A. A. (2005). Designed for teachers: How to implement self-monitoring in the classroom. *Beyond Behavior, 15,* 21–24.

Vandercook, T., York, J., & Forest, M. (1989). The McGill action planning system (MAPS): A strategy for building the vision. *Journal for the Association for Persons with Severe Handicaps, 14,* 205–215.

VanDerHeyden, A. M. (2009). Analysis of Universal academic data to plan, implement, and evaluate schoolwide improvement. In G. G. Peacock, R. A. Ervin, E. J. Daly III, & K. W. Merrell (Eds.), *Practical handbook of school psychology: Effective practices for the 21st century* (pp. 33–47). New York: The Guilford Press.

VanDerHeyden, A. M. RTI and math instruction. Retrieved from http://www.rtinetwork.org/learn/why/rtiandmath?tmpl=component&print=1

Vannest, K. J., Temple-Harvey, K. K., & Mason, B. A. (2009). Adequate yearly progress for students with emotional and behavioral disorders through research-based practices. *Preventing School Failure, 53,* 73–83.

VanTassel-Baska, J. (2013). Curriculum issues: Curriculum, instruction, and assessment for the gifted: A problem-based learning. *Gifted Child Today, 36*(1), 71–75.

VanTassel-Baska, J. (2015). Arguments for and against the Common Core State Standards. *Gifted Child Today, 38*(1), 60–62.

VanTassel-Baska, J., & Johnson, S. K. (2016). From the classroom: Implementing the Common Core in English language arts and mathematics. *Gifted Child Today, 39*(1), 51–62.

Varghese, M. M., & Stritikus, T. (2013). Language diversity and schooling. In J. A. Banks, & C. A. M. Banks (Eds.), *Multicultural education: Issues and perspectives* (8th ed.), pp. 219–239. Hoboken, NJ: Wiley.

Vatterott, C. (2010). Five hallmarks of good homework. *Educational Leadership, 68*(1), 10–15.

Vatterott, C. (2011). Making homework central to learning. *Educational Leadership, 69*(3), 60–64.

Vaughn, B. J., & Horner, R. H. (1997). Identifying instructional tasks that occasion problem behaviors and assessing the effects of student versus teacher choice among these tasks. *Journal of Applied Behavior Analysis, 30,* 299–312.

Vaughn, S., & Bos, C. (2015). Strategies for teaching students with learning and behavior problems (9th ed.). Boston, MA: Pearson.

Vaughn, S., & Bos, C. (2015). *Strategies for teaching students with learning and behavior problems* (9th ed.). Boston, MA: Pearson.

Vaughn, S., & Bos, C. S. (2012). *Strategies for teaching students with learning and behavior problems* (8th ed.). Upper Saddle River, NJ: Pearson.

Vaughn, S., & Bos, C. S. (2015). *Strategies for teaching students with learning and behavior problems* (9th ed.). Boston, MA: Allyn & Bacon.

Vaughn, S., & Fletcher, J. M. (2012). Response to intervention with secondary school students with reading difficulties. *Journal of Learning Disabilities, 45*(3), 244–256.

Vaughn, S., & Fuchs, L. S. (2003). Redefining learning disabilities as inadequate response to treatment: The promise and potential problems. *Learning Disabilities Research and Practice, 18*(3), 137–146.

Vaughn, S., & Gersten, R. (1998). Productive teaching of English language learners: What we know and still need to know. In R. M. Gersten & R. T. Jimenez (Eds.), *Promoting learning for culturally and linguistically diverse students* (pp. 230–238). Belmont, CA: Wadsworth.

Vaughn, S., & Klingner, J. K. (2007). Response to intervention (RTI): A new era in identifying students with learning disabilities. In D. Haager, J. Klingner, & S. Vaughn (Eds.), *Validated reading practices for three tiers of intervention* (pp. 3–9). Baltimore, MD: Paul H. Brookes.

Vaughn, S., & Schumm, J. S. (1994). Middle school teachers' planning for students with learning disabilities. *Remedial and Special Education, 15*(3), 152–161.

Vaughn, S., & Schumm, J. S. (1995). Responsible inclusion for students with learning disabilities. *Journal of Learning Disabilities, 28*(5), 264–270, 290.

Vaughn, S., Cirino, P. T., Linan-Thompson, S., Mathes, P. G., & Carlson, C. D., Cardenas-Hagan, E., et al. (2006). Effectiveness of a Spanish intervention and an English intervention for English language learners at risk for reading problems. *American Educational Research Journal, 43*(3), 449–487.

Vaughn, S., Elbaum, B., & Boardman, A. G. (2001). The social functioning of students with learning disabilities: Implications for inclusion. *Exceptionality, 9,* 47–65.

Vaughn, S., Gersten, R., & Chard, D. J. (2000). The underlying message in LD intervention research: Findings from research syntheses. *Exceptional Children, 67*(1), 99–114.

Vaughn, S., Klingner, J. K. (1999). Teaching reading comprehension through collaborative strategic reading. *Intervention in School and Clinic, 34*(5), 284–292.

Vaughn, S., Klingner, J. K., & Bryant, D. P. (2001). Collaborative strategic reading as a means to enhance peer-mediated instruction for reading comprehension and content area learning. *Remedial and Special Education, 22,* 24–38.

Vaughn, S., Klingner, J. K., Swanson, E. A., Boardman, A. C., Roberts, G., Mohammed, S. S., & Stillman-Spisak, S. J. (2011). Efficacy of collaborative strategic reading with middle school students. *American Educational Research Journal, 48*(4), 938–964.

Vaughn, S., Linan-Thompson, S., Pollard-Durodola, S. D., Mathes, P. G., & Cardenas-Hagan, E. (2006). Effective interventions for English language learners (Spanish-English) at risk for reading difficulties. In D. K. Dickinson & S. B. Neuman (Eds.), *Handbook of early literacy research* (Vol. 2, pp. 185–197). New York: Guilford Press.

Vaughn, S., Martinez, L. R., Linan-Thompson, S., Reutebuch, C., K., Carlson, C. D., & Francis, D. J. (2009). Enhancing social studies vocabulary and comprehension for seventh-grade English language learners: Findings from two experimental studies. *Journal of Research on Educational Effectiveness, 2*(4), 297–324.

Vaughn, S., Mathes, P. G., Linan-Thompson, S., & Francis, D. J. (2005). Teaching English language learners at risk for reading disabilities to read: Putting research into practice. *Learning Disabilities Research & Practice, 20*(1), 58–67.

Vaughn, S., Mathes, P. G., Linan-Thompson, S., Cirino, P. T., Carlson, C. D., Pollard-Durodola, S. D., & Francis, D. (2006). Effectiveness of an English intervention for first-grade English language learners at-risk for reading problems. *Elementary School Journal, 107*(2), 153–180.

Vaughn, S., Schumm, J. S., & Arguelles, M. E. (1997). The ABCDEs of co-teaching. *Teaching Exceptional Children, 30,* 4–10.

Vaughn, S., Swanson, E. A., Roberts, G., Wanzek, J., Stillman-Spisak, S. J., Solis, M., & Simmons, D. (2013).

Improving reading comprehension and social studies knowledge in middle school. *Reading Research Quarterly, 48*(1), 77–93.

Vaughn, S., Zumeta, R., Wanzek, J., Cook, B., & Klingner, J. K. (2014). Intensive interventions for students with learning disabilities in the RTI era: Position statement of the Division for Learning Disabilities Council for Exceptional Children. *Learning Disabilities Research & Practice, 29*(3), 90–92.

Vellutino, F. R., Scanlon, D. M., Sipay, E. R., Small, S. G., Pratt, A., Chen, R., & Denckla, M. B. (1996). Cognitive profiles of difficult-to-remediate and readily remediated poor readers: Early intervention as a vehicle for distinguishing between cognitive and experiential deficits as basic causes of specific reading disability. *Journal of Educational Psychology, 88,* 601–638.

Vellutino, F. R., Scanlon, D. M., Small, S. G., Fanuele, D. P., & Sweeney, J. (2007). Preventing early reading difficulties through kindergarten and first grade intervention: A variant of the three-tier model. In D. Haager, J. Klingner, & S. Vaughn (Eds.), *Validated reading practices for three tiers of intervention.* Baltimore, MD: Paul H. Brookes.

Venn, J. J. (2013). *Assessing students with special needs* (5th ed.). Boston: Pearson.

Verhoeven, L. (2011). Reading instruction for English language learners. In M. L. Kamil, P. D. Pearson, E. B. Moje, & P. P. Afflerbach (Eds.), *Handbook of reading research, Vol. IV* (pp. 661–683).

Verschuur, R., Didden, R., Van der Meer, L., Achmadi, D., Kagohara, D., Green, V., Lang, R., & Lancioni, G. (2011). Investigating the validity of a structured interview protocol for assessing the preferences of children with autism spectrum disorders. *Developmental Neurorehabilitation, 14,* 366–371.

Viadero, D. (2007). Study: Low, high fliers gain less under NCLB. *Education Week, 44,* 7.

Villa, R. A., Thousand, J. A., & Nevin, A. I. (2008). *A guide to co-teaching; Practical tips for facilitating student learning.* Thousand Oaks, CA: Corwin Press.

Vintinner, J. P., Harmon, J., Wood, K., & Stover, K. (2015). Inquiry into the efficacy of interactive word walls with older adolescent learners. *High School Journal, 98*(3), 250–261.

Volkmar, F. R., & McPartland, J. C. (2014). From Kanner to *DSM-5*: Autism as an evolving diagnostic concept. *Annual Review of Clinical Psychology, 10,* 193–212. Retrieved from http://dx.doi.org/10.1146/annurev-clinpsy-032813-153710

Volkmar, F. R., Klin, A., Paul, R., & Cohen, D. J. (Eds.). (2005). *Handbook of autism and pervasive developmental disorders.* Hoboken, NJ: Wiley.

Voorhees, S. (2011). Why the dog eats Nikki's homework: Making informed assignment decisions. *Reading Teacher, 64*(5), 363–367.

Voyager Expanded Learning. (2008). *V-Math: 3–8 Math Intervention.* Dallas, TX: Author.

Voyager Sopris Learning. (2009). Vmath Third Edition. Dallas, TX: Author.

Vygotsky, L. S. (1978). *Mind in society: The development of higher psychological processes.* Cambridge, MA: MIT Press.

Wagner, E. (2004). Development and implementation of a curriculum to develop social competence for students with visual impairments in Germany. *Journal of Visual Impairment and Blindness, 98,* 703–709.

Wagner, M. O., Haibach, P. S., Pierce, T., & Lieberman, L. J. (2013, March). The impact of visual impairment on gross motor skill performance. *Research Quarterly for Exercise and Sport,* 84, A93

Wagner, M., Kutash, K., Duchnowski, A. J., Epstein, M. H., & Sumi, W. C. (2005). The children and youth we serve: A national picture of the characteristics of students with emotional disturbances receiving special education. *Journal of Emotional and Behavioral Disorders, 13,* 79–96.

Wagner, R., Torgesen, J., Rashotte, C., & Pearson, N. (2012). *Comprehensive test of phonological processing* (2nd ed.). Austin, TX: Pro-Ed.

Wagner, R. K., Francis, D. J., & Morris, R. D. (2005). Identifying English language learners with learning disabilities: Key challenges and possible approaches. *Learning Disabilities Research & Practice, 20,* 6–15.

Wagner, R. K., Torgesen, J. K., & Rashotte, C. A. (1999). *Comprehensive test of phonological processing.* Austin, TX: PRO-ED.

Wakeman, S., Karvonnen, M., & Ahumada, A. (2013). Changing instruction to increase achievement for students with moderate to severe intellectual disabilities. (2013). *Teaching Exceptional Children, 46*(2), 6–13.

Waldron, N. L., & McLeskey, J. (1998). The effects of an inclusive school program on students with mild and severe learning disabilities. *Exceptional Children, 64,* 395–405.

Walker, H. M., & Severson, H. H. (1992). *Systematic screening for behavior disorders* (2nd ed.). Longmont, CO: Sopris West.

Walker, H. M., Ramsey, E., & Gresham, F. M. (2004). *Antisocial behavior in school: Evidence-based practices* (2nd ed.). Florence, KY: Cengage Learning.

Walker, H. M., Seeley, J. R., Small, J., Severson, H. H., Graham, B. A., Feil, E. G., … Forness, S. R. (2009). A randomized controlled trial of the First Step to Success Early Intervention: Demonstration of program efficacy outcomes in a diverse, urban school district. *Journal of Emotional and Behavioral Disorders, 17*(4), 197–212.

Walker, H. M., Severson, H. H., & Feil, E. G. (2010). *Systematic Screening for Behavior Disorders (SSBD).* Frederick, CO: Sopris West.

Wallach, G. P., & Miller, L. (1988). *Language intervention and academic success.* San Diego, CA: College Hill.

Wallerstein, J. S., Lewis, J. M., & Blakeslee, S. (2000). *The unexpected legacy of divorce.* New York: Hyperion.

Walpole, S., & McKenna, M. C. (2006). The role of informal reading inventories in assessing work recognition. *The Reading Teacher, 59*(6), 592–594.

Walsh, J. M., & Jones, B. (2004). New models of cooperative teaching. *Teaching Exceptional Children, 36,* 14–20.

Walsh, K. M., & Matthews, B. P. (2010). Maltreated children in the early years: International perspectives on the teacher's role. In V. Green & S. Cherrington (Eds.), *Delving into diversity: An international exploration of issues of diversity in education* (pp. 195–207). Wellington, New Zealand: Nova Science Publishers.

Wang, S. Y., Parrila, R., & Cui, Y. (2013). Meta-analysis of social skills interventions of single-case research for individuals with autism spectrum disorders: Results from three-level HLM. *Journal of Autism and Developmental Disorders, 43*(7), 1701–1716. Retrieved from http://dx.doi.org/10.1007/s10803-012-1726-2

Wanzek, J., & Vaughn, S. (2007). Research-based implications from extensive early reading interventions. *School Psychology Review, 36*(4), 541–561.

Wanzek, J., & Vaughn, S. (2008). Response to varying amounts of time in reading intervention for students with low response to intervention. *Journal of Learning Disabilities, 41*(2), 126–142.

Wanzek, J., Vaughn, S., Wexler, J., Swanson, E. A., Edmonds, M., & Kim, A.-H. (2006). A synthesis of spelling and reading interventions and their effects on the spelling outcomes of students with LD. *Journal of Learning Disabilities, 39*(6), 528–543.

Warger, C. (2011). Five homework strategies for teaching students. Retrieved from http://www.readingrockets.org/article/202/

Wasburn-Moses, L. (2003). What every special educator should know about high-stakes testing. *Teaching Exceptional Children, 35,* 12–15.

Washington, DC: National Center for Education Evaluation and Regional Assistance, Institute of Education Sciences, U.S. Department of Education. Retrieved from http://ies.ed.gov/ncee/wwc/publications/practiceguides

Watkins, P. J., & Stevens, D. W. (2013). The Goldilocks dilemma: Homework policy creating a culture when simply good is just not good enough. *The Clearing House, 86,* 80–85.

Watson, G. D., & Bellon-Harn, M. L. (2013). Speech-language pathologist and general educator collaboration: A model of Tier 2 service delivery. *Intervention in School and Clinic, 49*(4), 237–243.

Watson, S. M. R., & Gable, R. A. (2012). Unravelling the complex nature of mathematics learning disability: Implications for research and practice. *Learning Disability Quarterly, 36*(3), 178–187.

Wehman, P. (2002). A new era: Revitalizing special education for children and their families. *Focus on Autism and Other Developmental Disabilities, 17,* 194–197.

Wehmeier, P. M., Schacht, A., & Barkley, R. A. (2010). Social and emotional impairment in children and adolescents with ADHD and the impact on quality of life. *Journal of Adolescent Health, 46*(3), 209–217.

Wehmeyer, M. L. (2007). *Promoting self-determination in students with developmental disabilities.* New York: Guilford Press.

Wehmeyer, M. L. (2015). Framing the future self-determination. *Remedial and Special Education, 36*(1), 20–23.

Wehmeyer, M. L., & Schwartz, M. (1997). Self-determination and positive adult outcomes: A follow-up study of youth with mental retardation and learning disabilities. *Exceptional Children, 63,* 245–255.

Wehmeyer, M. L., Buntinx, W. H. E., Lachapelle, Y., Luckasson, R. A., Schalock, R., L., & Verdugo, M. A. (2008). The intellectual disability construct and its relation to human functioning. *Intellectual and Developmental Disabilities, 46,* 311–318.

Wehmeyer, M. L., Lattin, D. L., Lapp-Rincker, G., & Agran, M. (2003). Access to the general curriculum of middle school students with mental retardation. *Remedial and Special Education, 24,* 262–272.

Wehmeyer, M. L., Martin, J. E., & Sands, D. J. (2008). Self-determination and students with developmental disabilities. In H. P. Parette & G. R. Peterson-Karlan (Eds.), *Research-based practices in developmental disabilities* (2nd ed., pp. 99–122). Austin, TX: PRO-ED.

Wehmeyer, M. L., Sands, D. J., Knowlton, E., & Kozleski, E. B. (2002). *Teaching students with mental retardation: Providing access to the general curriculum.* Baltimore, MD: Paul H. Brookes.

Weiner, D. (2005). *One state's story: Access and alignment to the GRADE-LEVEL content for students with significant cognitive disabilities* (Synthesis Report 57). Minneapolis: University of Minnesota, National Center on Educational Outcomes. Retrieved from http://education.umn.edu/NCEO/OnlinePubs/Synthesis57.html

Weintraub, N., & Graham, S. (1998). Writing legibly and quickly: A study of children's ability to adjust their handwriting to meet common classroom demands. *Learning Disabilities Research and Practice, 13,* 146–152.

Weiss, M. P., & Lloyd, J. (2003). Conditions for co-teaching: Lessons from a case study. *Teacher Education and Special Education, 26*(1), 27–41.

Welch, M. (1992). The P.L.E.A.S.E. strategy: A metacognitive learning strategy for improving the paragraph writing of students with mild learning disabilities. *Learning Disability Quarterly, 15,* 119–128.

Welch, M., & Link, D. P. (1989). *Write, P.L.E.A.S.E.: A strategy for efficient learning and functioning in written expression* [video cassette]. Salt Lake City, UT: University of Utah, Department of Special Education, Educational Tele-Communications.

Wells, J. C, & Sheehey, P. H. (2012). Person-centered planning: Strategies to encourage participation and facilitate communication. *Teaching Exceptional Children, 44*(3), 32–39.

Welsh, M. E., Eastwood, M., & D'Agostino, J. V. (2014). Conceptualizing teaching to the test under standards-based reform. *Applied Measurement in Education, 27*(2), 98–114.

Wentzek, K. R., & Brophy, J. E. (2014). *Motivating students to learn.* New York: Routledge.

Westling, D. L., & Fox, L. (2009). *Teaching students with severe disabilities* (4th ed.). Upper Saddle River, NJ: Merrill/Pearson.

Westling, D. L., Fox, L., & Carter, E. W. (2015). *Teaching students with severe disabilities* (5th ed.). Boston: Pearson.

Wexler, J., Edmonds, M. S., & Vaughn, S. (2008). Teaching older readers with reading difficulties. In R. J. Morris & N. Mather (Eds.), *Evidence-based interventions for students with learning and behavioral challenges* (pp. 193–214). New York: Routledge.

Wexler, J., Vaughn, S., Edmonds, M., & Reutebuch, C. K. (2008). A synthesis of fluency interventions for secondary struggling readers. *Reading and Writing: An Interdisciplinary Journal, 21*(4), 317–347.

Wexler, J., Vaughn, S., Roberts, G., & Denton, C. A. (2010). The efficacy of repeated reading and wide reading practice for high school students with severe reading disabilities. *Learning Disabilities Research & Practice, 25*(1), 2–10.

What Works Clearing House. (2007a, July 9). Intervention classwide peer tutoring. Retrieved from http://ies.ed.gov/ncee/wwc/pdf/wwc_cwpt

What Works Clearing House. (2007b, July 16). Intervention peer-assisted learning strategies. Retrieved from http://ies.ed.gov/ncee/wwc/pdf/wwc.pals

What Works Clearinghouse. (2012a, January). Adolescent Literacy intervention report: Peer-Assisted Learning Strategies. Retrieved from http://whatworks.ed.gov.

What Works Clearinghouse. (2012b, June). Students with Learning Disabilities intervention report: Peer-Assisted Learning Strategies. Retrieved from http://whatworks.ed.gov.

Wheatley, J. P. (2005). *Strategic spelling: Moving beyond word memorization in the middle grades.* Newark, DE: International Reading Association.

Whittaker, C. R., Salend, S. J., & Duhaney, D. (2001). Creating instructional rubrics for inclusive classrooms. *Teaching Exceptional Children, 34,* 8–13.

Wiederholt, J. L., & Bryant, B. R. (2012). *Gray Oral Reading Test* (5th ed.). San Antonio: Pearson.

Wiig, E. H., & Semel, E. (1984). *Language assessment and intervention for the learning disabled* (2nd ed.). Columbus, OH: Merrill.

Willcutt, E. G., Betjemann, R. S., McGrath, L. M., Chhabildas, N. A., Olson, R. K., De Fries, J. C., & Pennington, B. F. (2010). Etiology and neuropsychology of comorbidity between RD and ADHD: The case for multiple-deficit models. *Cortex, 46*(10) 1345–1361.

Williams, P. (2009). Exploring teachers' and black male students' perceptions of intelligence. Unpublished doctoral dissertation, University of Miami, Coral Gables, FL.

Willis, J. (2008). *Teaching the brain to read: Strategies for improving fluency, vocabulary, and comprehension.* Alexandria, VA: ASCD.

Wilson, B. (2004). *Wilson Reading System®.* Austin, TX: PRO-ED.

Wilson, B. A. (1996). *Wilson Reading System.* Millbury, MA: Wilson Language Training Corporation.

Wilson, G. (2008). Be an active co-teacher. *Intervention in School and Clinic, 43*(4), 240–243.

Wilson, J. A., Faggella-Luby, M., & Wei, Y. (2013). Planning for adolescent Tier 3 reading instruction. *Teaching Exceptional Children, 46*(1), 26–34.

Wilson, W. J., Marinac, J., Pitty, J., & Burrows, C. (2011). The use of sound-field amplification devices in different types of classrooms. *Language, Speech, and Hearing Services in Schools, 42,* 395–407.

Winebrenner, S. (1992). *Teaching gifted kids in the regular classroom.* Minneapolis, MN: Free Spirit.

Winebrenner, S., & Espeland, P. (2000). *Teaching gifted kids in the regular classroom.* Minneapolis, MN: Free Spirit Publishing.

Winer, R. A., Qin, X., Harrington, T., Moorman, J., & Zahran, H. (2012). Asthma incidence among children and adults: Findings from the behavioral risk factor surveillance system asthma call-back survey—United States, 2006–2008. *Journal of Asthma, 49*(1), 16–22.

Wing, L., Gould, J., & Gillberg, C. (2011). Autism spectrum disorders in the DSM-V: Better or worse than the DSM-IV? *Research in Developmental Disabilities, 32,* 768–773.

Wiseman, A. (2011). Interactive read alouds: Teachers and students constructing knowledge and listening together. *Early Childhood Education Journal, 38*(6), 431–438.

Wixson, K. K., & Lipson, M. Y. (2012). Relations between the CCSS and RTI in literacy and language. *The Reading Teacher, 6,* 387–391.

Wixson, K. K., & Valencia, S. W. (2011). Assessment in RTI: What teachers and specialists need to know. *The Reading Teacher, 64*(6), 466–496.

Wolery, M. (1989). Transitions in early childhood special education: Issues and procedures. *Focus on Exceptional Children, 22,* 1–16.

Wolery, M., Cybriwsky, C. A., Gast, D. L., & Boyle-Gast, K. (1991). Use of constant time delay and attentional responses with adolescents. *Exceptional Children, 57,* 462–474.

Wolf, M. K., Herman, J. L., & Dietel, R. (2010, Spring). Improving the validity of English language learner assessment systems. CRESST. Retrieved from http://www.cresst.org.

Wolfe, P. S., & Hall, T. E. (2003). Making inclusion a reality for students with severe disabilities. *Teaching Exceptional Children, 35,* 56–61.

Wolfelt, A. D. (2002). Children's grief. In S. E. Brock, P. J. Lazarus, & S. R. Jimerson (Eds.), *Best practices in school crisis prevention and intervention* (pp. 653–671). Bethesda, MD: National Association of School Psychologists.

Wolter, J. A., & Pike, K. (2015). Dynamic assessment of morphological awareness and third-grade literacy success. *Language, Speech, and Hearing Services in Schools, 46,* 112–126.

Wong, B. Y. L., Butler, D. L., Ficzere, S. A., & Kuperis, S. (1997). Teaching adolescents with learning disabilities and low achievers to plan, write, and revise compare-and-contrast essays. *Learning Disabilities Research & Practice, 12*(1), 2–15.

Wong, Y. L., Graham, L., Hoskyn, M., & Berman, J. (2008). *The ABCs of learning disabilities* (2nd ed.). Burlington, MA: Academic Press.

Wood, C. L., Mustian, A. L., & Cooke, N. L. (2012). Comparing whole-word and morphograph instruction during computer-assisted peer tutoring on students' acquisition and generalization of vocabulary. *Remedial and Special Education, 33*(1), 39–47.

Wood, J. W., & Wooley, J. A. (1986). Adapting textbooks. *The Clearing House, 59,* 332–335.

Wood, K. D., & Blanton, W. E. (2009). *Literacy instruction for adolescents: Research-based practices.* New York: Guilford.

Wood, K. D., Lapp, D., Flood, J., & Taylor, D. B. (2008). *Guiding readers through text: Strategy guides for new times* (2nd ed.). Newark, DE: International Reading Association.

Wood, W. M., Karvonen, M., Test, D. W., Browder, D., & Algozzine, B. (2004). Promoting student self-determination skills in IEP planning. *Teaching Exceptional Children, 36*(3), 8–16.

Woodruff, S., Schumaker, J. B., & Deshler, D. D. (2002). *The effects of an intensive reading intervention on the decoding skills of high school students with reading deficits.* Lawrence: University of Kansas Institute for Academic Access.

Worden, J. W. (1996). *Children and grief.* New York: Guilford Press.

Worden, J. W. (2001). *Children and grief: When a parent dies.* New York: Guilford Press.

World Health Organization (2013). HIV and adolescents: guidance for HIV testing and counselling and care for adolescents living with HIV: Recommendations for a public health approach and considerations for policy-makers and managers. (WHO Publication No. WC 503.1) Retrieved from http://apps.who.int/iris/bitstream/10665/94334/1/9789241506168_eng.pdf

Wormeli, R. (2006a). *Fair isn't always equal: Assessing & grading in the differentiated classroom.* Portland, ME: Stenhouse.

Wormeli, R. (2006b). Differentiating for tweens. *Educational Leadership, 63*(7), 14–19.

Wright, C., & Bigge, J. L. (1991). Avenues to physical participation. In J. L. Bigge (Ed.), *Teaching individuals with multiple and physical disabilities* (3rd ed., pp. 132– 174). Upper Saddle River, NJ: Merrill/Prentice Hall.

Wu, P., Hoven, C. W., Liu, X., Fuller, C. J., Fan, B., Musa, G., Wicks, J., … Cook, J. A. (2008). The relationship between depressive symptom levels and subsequent increases in substance use among youth with severe emotional disturbance. *Journal of Studies on Alcohol and Drugs, 69*(4), 520–527.

Wylie, R. E., & Durrell, D. D. (1970). Teaching vowels through phonograms. *Elementary English, 47,* 787–791.

Wysocki, K., & Jenkins, J. R. (1987). Deriving word meanings through morphological generalization. *Reading Research Quarterly, 22,* 66–81.

Yagi, N., & Kleinberg, J. (2011). Boundary work: An interpretive ethnographic perspective on negotiating and leveraging cross-cultural identity. *Journal of International Business Studies, 42*(5), 629–653.

Yang, T., Gathercole, S. E., & Allen, R. J. (2014). Benefit of enactment over oral repetition of verbal instruction does not require additional working memory during encoding. *Psychonomic Bulletin & Review, 21*(1), 186–192.

Yates, P., Cuthrell, K., & Rose, M. (2011). Out of the room and into the hall: Making content word walls work. *The Clearing House, 84*(1), 31–36.

Yell, M. L. (1998). *The law and special education.* Upper Saddle River, NJ: Merrill.

Yell, M. L. (2005). *The law and special education: Includes the IDEA Improvement Act* (2nd ed.). Boston: Pearson.

Yell, M. L. (2016). *The law and special education* (4th ed.). Boston: Pearson.

Yeo, S., Kim, D., Branum-Martin, L., Wayman, M. M., & Espin, C. A. (2012). Assessing the reliability of curriculum-based measurement: An application of latent growth modeling. *Journal of School Psychology, 50*(2), 275–292.

Yopp, H. K. (1995). A test for assessing phonemic awareness in young children. *The Reading Teacher, 49,* 20–29.

Yopp, H., & Yopp, R. H. (2010). *Purposeful play for early childhood phonological awareness.* Huntington Beach, CA: Shell Education.

Young, C. Y, Austin, S. M., & Growe, R. (2013). Defining parental involvement: Perception of school administrators. *Education, 133*(3), 291–297.

Young, C., Mohr, K. A. J., & Rasinski, T. Reading together: A successful reading fluency intervention. *Literacy Research and Instruction, 54*(1), 67–81.

Young, S. E., Friedman, N. P., Miyake, A., Willcutt, E. G., Corley, R. P., Haberstick, B. C., & Hewitt, J. K. (2009). Behavioral disinhibition: Liability for externalizing spectrum disorders and its genetic and environmental relation to response inhibition across adolescence. *Journal of Abnormal Psychology, 118*(1), 117–130.

Ysseldyke, J., Nelson, R. J., Christenson, S., Johnson, D. R., Dennison, A., Triezenberg, H., & Hawes, M. (2004). What we know and need to know about the consequences of high-stakes testing for students with disabilities. *Exceptional Children, 71*(1), 75–95.

Zaragoza, N. (1987). Process writing for high-risk and learning disabled students. *Reading Research and Instruction, 26*(4), 290–301.

Zaragoza, N., & Vaughn, S. (1992). The effects of process instruction on three second-grade students with different achievement profiles. *Learning Disabilities Research and Practice, 7*(4), 184–193.

Zebehazy, K. T., & Smith, T. J. (2011). An examination of characteristics related to the social skills of youths with visual impairments. *Journal of Visual Impairment & Blindness, 105*(2), 84–95.

Zeitlin, V. M., & Curcic, S. (2014). Parental voices on individualized education programs: "Oh, IEP meeting tomorrow? Rum tonight!" *Disability & Society, 29*(3), 373–387.

Zentall, S. S. (2006). *ADHD and education: Foundations, characteristics, methods, and collaboration.* Upper Saddle River, NJ: Merrill/Pearson.

Zentall, S. S., & Smith, Y. N. (1993). Mathematical performance and behavior of children with hyperactivity, with and without coexisting aggression. *Behavior Research and Therapy, 31*(7), 701–710.

Zhang, D., Katsiyannis, A., Ju, S., & Roberts, E. (2014). Minority representation in special education: 5-year trends. *Journal of Child and Family Studies, 23,* 118–127.

Zhang, Z., & Schumm, J. S. (2000). Exploring effects of the keyword method on limited English proficient students' vocabulary recall and comprehension. *Reading Research and Instruction, 39,* 202–221.

Zheng, X., Flynn, L. J., & Swanson, H. L. (2012). Experimental intervention studies on word problem solving and math disabilities: A selective analysis of the literature. *Learning Disability Quarterly, 36*(2), 97–111.

Ziegler, A., & Heller, K. A. (2000). Attribution retraining with gifted girls. *Roeper Review, 23,* 217–248.

Ziegler, J. C., Pech-Georgel, C., George, F., Alario, F. X., & Lorenzi, C. (2005). Deficits in speech perception predict language learning impairment. *Proceedings of the National Academy of Sciences of the United States of America, 102*(39), 14110–14115.

Zigmond, N. (2001). Special education at a crossroads. *Preventing School Failure, 45,* 70–74.

Zigmond, N. (2003). Where should students with disabilities receive special education services? Is one place better than another? *The Journal of Special Education, 37*(3), 193–199.

Zigmond, N., Jenkins, J., Fuchs, L. S., Deno, S., Fuchs, D., Baker, J., & Couthino, M. (1995). Special education in restructured schools: Findings from three multi-year studies. *Phi Delta Kappan, 76,* 531–540.

Zigmond, N., Kloo, A., & Volonino, V. (2009). What, where, and how? Special education in the climate of full inclusion. *Exceptionality, 17*(4), 189–204.

Zipprich, M. (1995). Teaching web-making as a guided planning tool to improve student narrative writing. *Remedial and Special Education, 16*(1), 3–15, 52.

Zirkel, P. A. (2011). State laws and guidance for RTI. *Communique, 39* (7), 30–32.

Zwiers, J. (2008). Academic classroom discussions. In J. Zwiers (Ed.), *Building academic language.* San Francisco/Newark, DE: Jossey-Bass.

Name Index

T

U

V

Subject Index

D

Z